Principles
of Psychology

Richard H. Price
University of Michigan, Ann Arbor

Mitchell Glickstein
Brown University

David L. Horton
University of Maryland

Ronald H. Bailey

Holt, Rinehart and Winston
New York   Chicago   San Francisco   Philadelphia
Montreal   Toronto   London   Sydney   Tokyo
Mexico City   Rio de Janeiro   Madrid

Editor   Dan Loch
Development Editor   Lauren S. Bahr
Senior Project Editor   Arlene Katz
Production Manager   Pat Sarcuni
Art Director   Lou Scardino
Administrative Editor   Jeanette Ninas Johnson
Cover Designer   Skip Sorvino
Interior Designer   Caliber Design Planning
Photo Researcher   Betsy Wyckoff

Library of Congress Cataloging in Publication Data

Main entry under title:

Principles of psychology.

    Bibliography: p. 587
    Includes index.
    1. Psychology.   I. Price, Richard H. [DNLM: 1. Psy-
    chology.   BF 121 P957]
BF121.P7   150   82-907
                                      AACR2

ISBN: 0-03-048411-1

CBS COLLEGE PUBLISHING
Holt, Rinehart and Winston
The Dryden Press
Saunders College Publishing

Contents

5 *Consciousness* 127

Julian M. Davidson

Preface

Of the more than 150 introductory psychology textbooks now in print, most choose to be either "scholarly" but dull, or superficial but "lively." PRINCIPLES OF PSYCHOLOGY grew out of the authors' conviction that an academically rigorous textbook in general psychology can be both stimulating and scientifically sophisticated—appropriate even for students majoring in the discipline. Certainly the science of psychology itself is alive and well and intrinsically interesting. Its principles, its methods, and, above all, its focus on mental processes and behavior are endless sources of fascination for the layperson and specialist alike. We felt there is no need to pump life artificially into the study of psychology by resorting to gimmicks or gross oversimplification. Our challenge was to present this vibrant science as it really is.

Four Goals

We were guided by four goals in the preparation of PRINCIPLES OF PSYCHOLOGY: emphasis on research, comprehensive content, rigorous scholarship, and lucid, interesting prose.

Emphasis on research Psychology is a method of inquiry as well as a body of knowledge. In addition to describing what we know about behavior and mental processes, we want to explain precisely how we know it. For example, one of the most exciting new areas of psychological research focuses on the chemistry of the brain. Our aim is to describe not only the newest findings about the ways in which these chemicals influence behavior but also to tell the fascinating story of how they were discovered in the first place. Such stories, interesting in their own right, demonstrate the everyday processes of psychological research. By understanding these processes, students are more likely to retain important information and to achieve an insight into psychology as a dynamic science rather than as a static body of knowledge.

Comprehensive content Our first goal is to provide as thorough a text as possible, a book with both breadth and depth, within the constraints of the introductory course. This means a sophisticated, straightforward text appropriate for psychology majors and comprehensive enough even for a two-semester course. The entire, wide range of topics traditional in the mainstream course is treated in depth in this text. In addition, PRINCIPLES presents in unusual detail several areas of investigation that reflect the widening scope of psychological research. An entire chapter, for example, is devoted to sexual behavior. This chapter gives special emphasis to recent findings about sex-role differentiation and development. PRINCIPLES also pays particular attention to the rapid growth of psychobiological research in the past two decades. While Chapter 2 describes the basic structures and functions of the nervous system, including the substrates of behavior at the cellular level, other chapters—for example, Sensation, Perception, Consciousness, and Abnormal Behavior—expand the discussion of the role of the brain.

Rigorous scholarship Extraordinary effort is given to the meticulous documentation of research and findings in all areas of psychology. The hundreds of references cited in PRINCIPLES reflect the authors' concern for classic early experiments and studies as well as for the most significant examples of recent research. The earliest of the references date to the beginning of the nineteenth century; the most recent were still in press when PRINCIPLES was published.

Lucid and interesting prose Without sacrificing depth or accuracy, we seek to present psychology in prose that is unusually clear, interesting, and lucid. The concepts and methods of psychology are often complex, and PRINCIPLES does not pretend that they are easily grasped. Yet the most rigorous of experiments and studies typically possess an essence of elegant simplicity. PRINCIPLES illustrates such work not only with relevant examples taken from everyday life, but also with stories drawn from the human framework in which research is carried on. Chapter 1, for example, presents profiles of six leading contemporary psychologists: Jean Piaget, B. F. Skinner, Carl Rogers, Albert Bandura, Roger Sperry, and Stanley Schachter. These profiles describe in detail how each person came to psychological research, the methods of investigation, and the principal findings.

Format

The goals that have guided the content of PRINCIPLES also have shaped its straightforward format. Each chapter begins with a brief outline of the main topics to be covered and ends with a concisely detailed summary. Each chapter (except Chapter 1) also contains two special features set off from the main text.

One feature, labeled "Research," makes explicit the methodology of psychology and provides an up-close look at how psychologists work. It takes the reader step-by-step through an important experiment or study, from the original hypothesis and how it was formulated to the results and the implications of the findings. Discussion centers on studies and experiments related to or expanding on chapter topics. For example, the Research feature in Chapter 5 (Consciousness) discusses a surprising, recent study of "The Near-Death Experience." Chapter 13 (Intelligence) recalls in careful detail "A Classic Study of Environmental Influence." Chapter 16 (Social Influence) takes the reader to the race track for a novel experiment on "Dissonance and the $2 Bettor."

The second feature, "Focus," highlights a topic of special interest intended to supplement or amplify material in the main text. The Focus may be on an important new finding as in Chapter 2 (The Nervous System)—"The Brain's Own Opiates"; an intriguing sidelight from animal research as in Chapter 4 (Sensation)—"Senses We Do Not Have"; a controversial social issue as in Chapter 10 (Motivation and Emotion)—"The Effects of TV Violence"; or an unconventional approach to treatment as in Chapter 15 (Behavior Change)—"Therapy Through Folk Healing."

The Authors

PRINCIPLES, from its inception more than three years ago, has been a collaborative effort. Such is the breadth of modern psychology that no single author can hope to encompass all of its variety with the accuracy and authority born of sound scholarship and firsthand research. The principal authors represent a wide range of authority and expertise: Richard H. Price of the University of Michigan (personality, intelligence, abnormal psychology, behavior change); Mitchell Glickstein of Brown University (physiological psychology, sensation and perception); and David L. Horton of the University of Maryland (learning, memory and cognition, language, statistics).

To ensure comprehensive coverage, we asked four other psychologists to contribute to PRINCIPLES: Steven J. Sherman and Russell M. Fazio, both of Indiana University (social psychology, motivation and emotion); Julian M. Davidson of Stanford University (consciousness, sexual behavior); and Joseph Glick of the City University of New York (developmental psychology).

The role assigned to the fourth of the principal authors, Ronald H. Bailey, a professional writer, was an unusual one. His task was not to popularize or somehow make "palatable" the written drafts provided by his colleagues; rather, it was to ensure stylistic consistency and clarity and to make certain that the final text captured the built-in fascination of psychology as a science.

Ancillary Materials

The needs of today's instructors and students demand not only a text with a solid base in scientific research but also a full and broad array of ancillary materials to make teaching and learning more effective.

To begin with, the entire teaching/learning package was constructed and coordinated by one author, George Hampton of the University of Houston, who also intensively reviewed and intimately knew the text, rather than by separate and geographically scattered authors. He organized the Instructor's Manual, Student Study Guide, and Test Bank around learning objectives in order to provide these items with an overall, coherent instructional design.

All instructor resources—Instructor's Manual, Test Bank, Transparency Masters, and Transparency Masters Resource Guide—come to you in a convenient three-ring binder.

The Instructor's Manual is an especially useful tool for first-time instructors and teaching assistants. It includes all the "how tos"; how to use the manual, how to design and teach a course, how to prepare a lecture and syllabus, how to guide students, and how to construct effective student tests. The chapter-by-chapter resources include: teaching objectives, lists of package resources and film suggestions, chapter outlines, key terms, lectures (short narratives offering several potential topics for a lecture on a given chapter), ideas for credit with honors, and class discussions, demonstrations, experiments, and projects.

The telephone-directory sized Test Bank will save you valuable preparation time. It consists of over 2,000 multiple-choice items on detachable cards so that instructors can develop individual test-item files. Each item is preceded by a block of codes that give the learning objective being tested, text page reference, minor subject area, tell whether the item tests knowledge or applications reserve space for item analysis scores, and provide the six-digit code needed for item selection by users of the Computerized Test Bank. An introduction to the Test Bank tells instructors how to prepare their own multiple-choice items and how to compile item analysis scores.

The Transparency Masters include 80 illustrations that demonstrate and reinforce text material. The Transparency Masters Resource Guide gives instructors a prose narrative background and ''script'' for the transparency masters.

The package also features a Computerized Test Bank, a Student Study Guide, and an Introductory Slide Program with Resource Guide. The comprehensive Student Study Guide offers study tips and techniques, a section on careers in psychology, learning objectives (the same ones found in the Instructor's Manual), chapter outlines, key terms, step-by-step chapter reviews (consisting of prose-like paragraphs with blanks at key points), diagrams from the text, exercises, and multiple-choice items (two 20-item multiple-choice self-tests with answers).

The Computerized Test Bank combines the 2,000 printed test items with our random access program. Finally, the Introductory Psychology Slide Program of 150 color slides uses vivid photographs, charts, graphs, cartoons, figures, and tables to illustrate key concepts and topics. The Resource Guide presents actual lecture notes for each slide. Both the Computerized Test Bank and the Slide Program are given free, one each per school, upon bookstore purchase of 100 or more copies of the textbook.

No such modern aids to learning and teaching were available in 1890 when Henry Holt and Company published its first comprehensive survey of what was then an infant science. The title was PRINCIPLES OF PSYCHOLOGY; the author was William James. Nine decades later its contribution to psychology is still acknowledged. Now, in adopting the same title for our text with the same publisher nearly a century later, we hope our serious commitment to psychology will help affirm and expand the proud tradition launched by this American pioneer of psychological study.

Acknowledgments

The writing and preparation of this textbook required the effort and support of many individuals. Our appreciation is extended to those psychologists who reviewed the manuscript in its several drafts and who contributed to its improvement, coherence, and overall refinement. They are:

Charles K. Allen *University of Montana*
Arline L. Bronzaft *Herbert H. Lehman College*

Louis Buffardi *George Mason University*
John Clark *Macomb County Community College*

Charles Clifton *University of Massachusetts, Amherst*

Richard Cokler *University of the District of Columbia*

Sharon Cool *Indiana University East*

William Curry *Wesleyan College*

Frank Dane *State University of New York*

Barbara Anne Dosher *Columbia University*

Gene Elliott *Glassboro State College*

Gabriel P. Frommer *Indiana University*

Ronald Gandelman *Rutgers University—Busch Campus*

Gary Greenburg *Wichita State University*

Leonard W. Hamilton *Rutgers University*

George Hampton *University of Houston, Downtown Campus*

Julie Jubala *Point Park College*

Alan Kamil *University of Massachusetts, Amherst*

Theodore Maiser *Muhlenberg College*

Jerry W. O'Dell *Eastern Michigan University*

James N. Olson *University of Texas of the Permian Basin*

Joseph Palladino *St. Francis College*

Kenneth Pfeiffer *University of California, Los Angeles*

David Pomeranz *State University of New York*

Donald Reutener *Smith College*

Christopher Rhoades *Milbert College*

Don Scarborough *Brooklyn College*

David Schneider *University of Texas, San Antonio*

Richard Schuberth *Rice University*

Thomas Scott *University of Delaware*

Richard Straub *University of Michigan*

Joel West *Northern Michigan University*

Allen Wolach *Lewis College of Sciences & Letters*

We wish to single out for special thanks Rob Fry, for preparation of the glossary, Al Kamil of the University of Massachusetts at Amherst for his contributions to Chapters 6 and 10, and Alice Greenwald for her early content analysis in comparison to the major competing texts.

And we wish to thank our friends, the competent and supportive people at Holt, Rinehart and Winston, whose aid and resourcefulness literally pulled us along and through the whole project. They are Dan Loch, Acquiring Editor, who organized and oversaw the entire endeavor; Lauren S. Bahr, Senior Development Editor, who tirelessly and efficiently performed the day-to-day close inspection of the manuscript that resulted in the eventual polished and complete text; Arlene Katz, Senior Project Editor, who kept the many parts of the text moving crisply into production once the manuscript was complete; Pat Sarcuni, Production Manager, who shepherded the manuscript through composition, printing, and binding and ensured the high production quality of the published text you now hold; and Lou Scardino, Art Director, who so creatively supervised the design of the cover, interior layout, and visuals of the text in keeping with our goals for its look and feel. The dedication of these friends, their patience, tolerance, enthusiasm, and encouragement, made this book possible.

Richard H. Price
University of Michigan, Ann Arbor

David L. Horton
University of Maryland

Mitchell Glickstein
Brown University

Ronald H. Bailey
Meredith, New York

Principles of Psychology

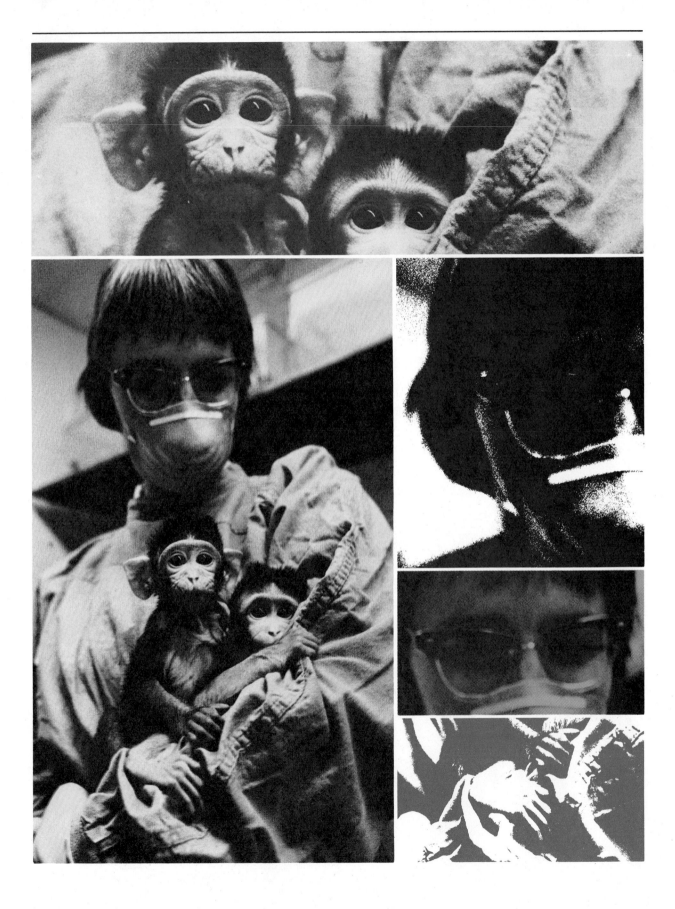

Part One

Psychology: The Science and the Scientists

Chapter 1
The Science and the Scientists

odern novelists often describe in minute detail practically everything the protagonist thinks, feels, and does during a single day. If you were to attempt such a narrative of 24 hours in your own life, the result might be as long as a novel such as James Joyce's *Ulysses*. As a matter of fact, themes woven through your narrative would resemble the chapter headings in our table of contents.

For example, your every breath and heartbeat are controlled by the nervous system (Chapter 2).

What you see and hear would be discussed under the titles of sensation and perception (Chapters 3 and 4). Your dreams and daydreams would be described as states of consciousness (Chapter 5). Your classroom performance would reflect processes of learning (Chapter 7) and memory (Chapter 8), along with motivation (Chapter 10) and intelligence (Chapter 13). Your relationships with others would represent social influence (Chapter 16) and social interaction (Chapter 17).

TABLE 1.1 Specializations within psychology

SUBAREA OR BRANCH	PERCENT OF PSYCHOLOGISTS	MAJOR FOCUS/INTERESTS
Clinical Psychology	29	Study both the causes and treatment of behavioral problems. Often, conduct therapy and give psychological tests.
Counseling Psychology	10	Assist individuals in dealing with a wide range of personal problems (for example, personal adjustment, interpersonal relations, career plans).
School Psychology	9	Perform such activities as testing, guidance, and counseling, primarily with students.
Educational Psychology	10	Help design curricula and develop new methods of instruction. Also deal with special problems such as learning disabilities, the effects of school desegregation, and so on.
Psychometrics	3	Specialize in the administration and interpretation of various psychological tests.
Industrial Psychology	8	Focus on various aspects of behavior in employment settings (for example, work attitudes, work motivation, leadership). Often, perform such tasks as designing effective methods of personnel selection, and improving workers' morale.
Consumer Psychology	1	Focus on consumer behavior—especially factors influencing consumer decisions (for example, advertising, brand loyalty).
Social Psychology	5	Study all aspects of social behavior—everything from love and attraction to aggression and violence.
Developmental Psychology	4	Examine changes in physical state, cognitive abilities, and social behavior across the entire span of life.
Experimental Psychology	7	Study basic psychological processes such as perception, learning, motivation, and cognition. (Experimental psychology is often viewed as providing the basic foundation for other branches of psychology.)
Physiological Psychology	2	Examine biological and physiological bases of behavior.
Comparative Psychology	1	Study various forms of behavior (for example, sexual, parental) across different species.
Environmental Psychology	1	Study effects of the physical environment (for example, heat, noise, crowding) upon behavior, feelings, and health.
Other (Community Psychology, Psychopharmacology, Humanistic Psychology, etc.)	10	Varied activities, depending upon subarea.

Source: Robert A. Baron, Donn Byrne, and Barry H. Kantowitz, *Psychology: Understanding Behavior* (2nd ed.), (New York: Holt, Rinehart and Winston, 1980), pp. 19-20.

All of this and more—24 hours in your life, all of the years in all of our lives—is the province of psychology and the scope of this textbook. Psychology is the study of behavior of organisms. It embraces a dozen or more areas of specialization as shown in Table 1.1. What holds together the complex pluralism of psychology is the effort of psychologists to understand, predict, and control behavior.

This book reflects our conviction that psychology can be most fruitfully studied in terms of processes rather than as an established and static body of truth. There are few immutable laws of behavior; theories and knowledge change in all sciences. Thus, where possible, our approach will be to focus on psychology as a method of inquiry, a way of thinking about problems and approaching them through observation and experiment. In addition to describing what we know about behavior and mental processes, we will explain how we know it. By understanding psychology as a process, you will be better able to achieve insights into this science of behavior.

It has been said that all scientific research begins with a question—usually a why or a how. In this chapter, we will attempt to answer three questions: Who are psychologists? What are their theoretical approaches or points of view? What are the methods they use to study behavior?

Profiles in Psychology

There are an estimated 65,000 psychologists in the world, and about two thirds of them live in the United States. The American Psychological Association, which was founded in 1892 with 31 charter members, now has a membership of 52,000. In addition, thousands of professionals in other fields, such as the physical and natural sciences and in medicine, contribute directly or indirectly to the study of psychology. For example, the United States has approximately 29,000 psychiatrists—medical doctors who specialize in the treatment of mental illness or deal with the problems of adjustment.

In this section we will look briefly at the lives and work of six psychologists who represent psychology's broad scope of theoretical research and of practical application. With the exception of Jean Piaget, the eminent Swiss researcher who died recently, all live and work in the United States. Each has made a noteworthy contribution to our understanding of behavior. Their profiles provide a capsule preview of important themes—theoretical perspectives, methodology, and significant findings— that will be developed more fully in this and subsequent chapters.

Jean Piaget: How Children Think

When Jean Piaget died in 1980, at age 84, he had established a formidable reputation as the most influential theorist in the history of developmental psychology. Developmental psychologists study the factors that shape changes in behavior from infancy through adulthood. For nearly six decades, Piaget investigated how children think, illuminating the ways in which their thoughts differ from adult reasoning and showing the progressive stages in the process of mental growth.

Piaget himself was something of a prodigy. At age 10 he published his first scientific paper on mollusks (marine invertebrates such as oysters). Later he was offered a curatorship in a museum in Geneva but had to turn it down because he was still in high school. By age 22 he had his doctorate in

Jean Piaget

biology but was switching his intended field of research from mollusks to children. While studying at the Sorbonne in Paris, he worked with children in the laboratory of Theophile Simon, the codeveloper of early intelligence tests, and there Piaget evolved some of the methods that would characterize his later research. He returned to Geneva to teach and to seek among children a sort of "embryology" of intelligence—an understanding of how thinking grows and develops.

Piaget's research methods differed from those of most psychologists. He watched and listened to children, including his own two young daughters. He played with children, getting down on his knees to shoot marbles, or got involved in other games, sharing the child's view of the world. He constantly asked children questions and, by asking more questions, attempted to understand the thought processes behind their answers. He also devised simple experiments but had little use for the scientific controls or statistical measurements that characterize much of modern psychology.

From his observations, Piaget distilled a whole new perspective on cognitive development, the ways in which children learn to think (Piaget, 1926/1959). Children do not think like miniature adults, as many people believe. He demonstrated, for example, that infants do not possess a characteristic that psychologists call object permanency—if an object is no longer in sight, infants act as if it no longer exists (Piaget, 1963/1974). Similarly, not until about age seven do children develop the notion of conservation of quantities—comprehension that the quantity of a liquid, for example, does not change when it is poured into differently shaped vessels.

Piaget formulated his findings into a theory that intellectual development proceeds in an orderly schedule of four stages. According to Piaget, this sequence is universal and invariable, the result of genetic programming and of the child's interaction with the environment. The four stages range from the infant's exploration of simple physical objects to the adolescent's development of abstract reasoning (Piaget, 1962).

Piaget's work, set forth in more than 60 books, has had important implications for the education of children. His theory of the four stages of mental growth suggests limitations: learning must be geared to what a child can comprehend at a given age. On the other hand, his emphasis on the child as an active problem solver who is constantly acting upon the environment suggests new possiblilities; for example, it has helped popularize the so-called discovery method of education whereby children learn by doing. Perhaps most important, Piaget demonstrated that practically all children will inevitably develop intellectually and learn—sometimes in spite of the educational system available to them.

B. F. Skinner: Of Pigeons and Men

B. F. Skinner is probably America's best-known psychologist. His name has become synonymous with an approach to learning—in animals and in humans—that is formally called operant conditioning. The essence of Skinner's approach, which has long been a dominant force in American psychology, is the assertion that behavior is shaped not from within the organism but from without—by reinforcements (Skinner, 1938).

Growing up early in this century in Susquehanna, Pennsylvania, Skinner was intrigued by animal behavior, mechanical gadgetry, and writing—three interests that would mark his career. At Hamilton College he majored in English but was fascinated by the writings of John B. Watson, the founder of the

B. F. Skinner

behaviorist movement, which held that the environment alone determined behavior. After two years during which Skinner later said he "failed as a writer," he entered the doctoral program in psychology at Harvard University.

At the University of Minnesota, Indiana University, and finally back at Harvard, Skinner conducted his famous laboratory experiments in learning through operant conditioning (operant because the organism operates upon the environment). In these experiments, Skinner demonstrated how pigeons and rats could be conditioned by systematic rewards. The animals were placed in a special apparatus Skinner had designed. Now known as the Skinner box, or operant chamber, it was a sound-proof enclosure with a food dispenser that a rat could operate by pressing a lever and a pigeon could operate by pecking a key. Food was used to reward the animals, at first for lever pressing or key pecking and later for more complex actions (Skinner, 1956).

By rewarding parts of a desired behavioral sequence, Skinner was able to condition his animals to perform seemingly extraordinary feats. He taught pigeons to play a kind of Ping-Pong and to dance with each other, and during World War II he even worked out a scheme to guide missiles by the pecking of pigeons (Edson, 1975). Although the plan was not put to use, Skinner convincingly demonstrated that he could indeed train pigeons to guide missiles. Here is how Skinner explained the way in which he conditioned pigeons to walk in figure eights:

> I watch a hungry pigeon carefully. When he makes a slight clockwise turn, he's instantly rewarded for it. After he eats, he immediately tries it again. Then I wait for more of a turn and reinforce again. Within two or more minutes, I can get any pigeon to make a full circle. Next I reinforce only when he moves in the other direction. Then I wait until he does both, and reinforce him again and again unti it becomes a kind of drill. Within 10 to 15 minutes, the pigeon will be doing a perfect figure eight (*Time*, 1971).

From his work with animals Skinner concluded that all behavior could be explained in terms of the contingencies of reinforcement—when and how the subject is rewarded for what action. This perspective has had enormous influence on the study of psychology and on learning theory in particular. It has also resulted in widespread practical applications. These include teaching machines, which provide immediate reinforcement during learning, and programs of behavior modification in which systematic rewards are aimed at changing the behavior, for example, of prison inmates and mental patients (Skinner, 1953).

Skinner has reached a wide audience with his ideas about controlling behavior in two popular and highly controversial books. *Walden Two*, published in 1948, is a fictional account of a utopian community based on the benevolent control of people through the principles of operant conditioning. In his nonfiction version of behavioral control, *Beyond Freedom and Dignity*, published in 1971, Skinner argues that none of us has real freedom of choice. Because we are already being shaped by external influences that tend to be haphazard, Skinner says, we should utilize the principles of systematic behavioral control in order to attain the good of all, thereby creating a world free of war, pollution, and other threats to survival.

Carl Rogers: The Humanistic Approach

The approach to behavior advocated by Carl Rogers differs sharply from that of his frequent and friendly antagonist, Skinner. Whereas Skinner is an experimental psychologist, deriving his ideas originally from carefully controlled laboratory studies, Rogers represents an area of research and practice in which intuition often plays a decisive role. Rogers is a clinical psychologist whose theories have greatly influenced the study of personality and the treatment of emotional disturbances.

Rogers' own career has been marked by the processes of change and growth that characterize his views of the human organism. He grew up in an intensely religious family, spending his adolescent years on the Illinois farm that his father, a successful building contractor, operated as an experiment in scientific agriculture. Young Rogers enrolled at the University of Wisconsin in 1919, intending to major in agriculture. He soon switched to a pre-ministry curriculum and, after graduation, attended Union Theological Seminary. Rogers later wrote that many of the students, himself included, "thought their way right out of religious work" (Rogers, 1961). Rogers already had taken several psychology courses at nearby Columbia University, and he transferred there, completing a doctorate in clinical psychology.

During the 1930s, Rogers worked with delinquent

and deprived children for a community agency in Rochester, New York. Guided by the principle that "man's ultimate reliance is upon his own experience," he chafed under the prevailing tenets of clinical treatment, especially the Freudian emphasis on the therapist as an interpreter of the patient's problems. Increasingly, he relied on the client to determine the direction therapy would take. His work led him to formulate a new approach to clinical treatment.

Rogers' approach, nondirective or client-centered therapy, was set forth in 1942 in his book *Counseling and Psychotherapy*. This approach—as refined in research and teaching at Ohio State University, the University of Chicago, and the University of Wisconsin—was a marked departure from orthodox views and made Rogers the subject of considerable controversy. In client-centered therapy, no formal guidance is provided the client. The therapist attempts to empathize with clients and to help them clarify their own feelings. The task of the therapist is to facilitate an inner force for growth—what Rogers calls the "self-directed process of becoming"—but not to try to shape it.

In the 1960s, Rogers became interested in a phenomenon that he had first experimented with 15 years earlier at the University of Chicago—the group encounter. He helped popularize this method through books, television, and even a documentary movie, which won an Academy Award. This deviation from the mainstream of psychology brought further criticism that Rogers' humanistic approach was unscientific. Even his critics, however, concede that Rogers' ideas and his personal example have helped extend the scope of clinical psychology and fostered an expansion of counseling services.

Albert Bandura: Learning By Example

The research and theoretical concepts of Albert Bandura reflect the increasing trend among contemporary psychologists to cut across traditional boundaries of specialization. Bandura was trained in clinical psychology but is best known for his systematic investigation of a form of learning that had somehow escaped experimental scrutiny—the process variously known as observational learning, or modeling. This process, through which learning takes place by observing and imitating the actions of models, has been shown by Bandura and his colleagues at Stanford University to be highly im-

Carl Rogers

Albert Bandura

portant in shaping behavior of many kinds, including aggression against others (Bandura, 1971).

The son of wheat farmers in the tiny town of Mundare, Alberta, Canada, Bandura attended a high school that had only two teachers. The school's 20 students largely educated themselves, Bandura recalls, and virtually every graduate went on to a successful professional career. After graduation from the University of British Columbia, he earned a doctorate in clinical psychology at the University of Iowa.

At first Bandura conducted field studies of families of juvenile delinquents. These studies suggested to him that the parents in such families often served as models of aggression and that their children simply learned by example. This led to his hypothesis that children can acquire aggressive behaviors by observing an aggressive adult model. Beginning in the late 1950s, Bandura put this idea to the test in a series of now-classic experiments in which children were exposed to adult models who behaved aggressively. As predicted by Bandura's hypothesis, children who had watched aggressive models tended to be much more aggressive than those who had not. From the models, they had learned distinctly new ways of being aggressive. Later experiments by Bandura and his colleagues demonstrated that this learning process can occur whether aggressive models were actually present, or merely shown in a film or on a television screen (Bandura, 1963, 1976).

Bandura's demonstration of how children learn by example has obvious implications concerning the portrayal of violence on television. It also lies at the heart of his social learning theory, which attempts to account for the development of personality and of abnormal behavior. Because Bandura is interested in "translating theory and principles into practice," he has devoted considerable time to developing practical applications such as the use of observational modeling to cure phobic fears. By imitating the responses of a model, children have lost much of their fear of dogs; adults with an intense fear of snakes have even learned to fondle them (Bandura, Blanchard, and Ritter, 1969).

Bandura has gone on to suggest that it should be no more difficult to build in safeguards against acts of violence than it now is to aid snake phobics. He is interested in personality change. "You can't change behavior without changing the causes, the determining conditions. After all, behavior doesn't just lie there (Kiester and Gudhea, 1974)."

Roger Sperry: How the Brain Is "Wired"

Roger Sperry has spent more than four decades studying the relationships between behavior and the intricate and interconnecting patterns that link the brain's nerve cells. In the early 1940s, he provided new insights into how the interconnections developed; a decade later he began a series of important experiments that illuminated the differing functions of the brain's two hemispheres (Sperry, 1961).

Sperry, a native of Hartford, Connecticut, majored in English at Oberlin College. Influenced by his undergraduate courses in psychology, he went on to take a master's degree in psychology at Oberlin and then a doctorate in zoology at the University of Chicago. At Chicago, he came under the influence of a distinguished brain researcher, Paul Weiss, and began the study of how vision is organized in amphibians such as the newt and frog.

Amphibians were the appropriate animals for his experiments because, unlike mammals, their nerve cells regenerate, or grow back, after injury.

Roger Sperry

Sperry's method was a typical one in physiological psychology—manipulate nerve tissue and then observe the behavioral effects of this intervention. The focus of his experiments was the optic nerve, a bundle of many thousands of individual nerve cell fibers that connect the eye and the brain. In one experiment, Sperry severed the optic nerve and then waited for it to regenerate; the nerve grew back in its original position, restoring normal sight. Then, he cut the optic nerve and placed an obstacle in its path; the nerve grew back in the same position even though it had to twist and turn to avoid the obstacle. Finally, he cut the optic nerve and removed the eye from the socket of the animal, rotated it 180 degrees and then replaced it; once again the nerve grew back in its original position, although the animal now saw in reverse (Sperry, 1968). These experiments demonstrated that little is left to chance or experience in the organization and development of the brain's wiring patterns; these patterns appear to be laid down with fine precision by heredity.

In the early 1950s, first at the University of Chicago and then at the California Institute of Technology, Sperry conducted his famed "split-brain" experiments and made his second major set of findings (Sperry, 1968). The purpose was to investigate the function of the corpus callosum, a band of nerve fibers that connects the two hemispheres of the brain. In the beginning, Sperry and his colleagues worked with experimental animals, severing the corpus callosum and rearranging the fibers of the optic nerve so that the visual input from one eye could be isolated in one hemisphere. Later, they studied human subjects who, in order to prevent severe epileptic seizures from being transmitted from one hemisphere to the other, had undergone surgery to sever the corpus callosum.

Through experiments Sperry found that each of the hemispheres is highly specialized for the processing of information. In most of us, the left hemisphere is the principal seat of language and mathematical skills and of logical reasoning; the right hemisphere, by contrast, seems to be superior at such tasks as spatial perception. Furthermore, Sperry discovered that each hemisphere can work independently and has separate consciousness and emotions. Sperry's split-brain work triggered a surge of research into hemispheric specialization and focused interest on that most tantalizing mystery of neuropsychology—how the physiology of the brain generates consciousness.

Stanley Schachter: People Need People

The interaction of people, and how that interaction affects attitudes and behavior, is the province of social psychologists. In order to conduct laboratory experiments, researchers in this field must possess something of the imagination and flair of film directors. They must create in the laboratory the illusion of a real-life situation while sometimes concealing from the "actors," or subjects, the true purpose of the experiment. In some cases, knowledge of the experiment's real aim would prejudice the subject's behavior and risk the loss of spontaneity. At the same time, experimenters must be aware of the ethical risks of deception and consider the welfare of their subjects first and above all. The potential risk to subjects must always be weighed against the potential gain in scientific knowledge.

An eminent social psychologist often cited for his ingenuity in designing and staging experiments is Stanley Schachter of Columbia University. Schachter is a native of New York City who studied at Yale University and M.I.T. and received his doctorate from the University of Michigan in 1950. His explorations of the effects of social context have

Stanley Schachter

ranged from the experience of deviance in a group to eating behavior and obesity.

To understand better how Schachter approaches a problem in social psychology, let us look at his study of the circumstances under which people affiliate, or seek out one another (Schachter, 1959). Schachter began with a question: What factors increase or decrease the tendency of people to seek out others? One possible clue, Schachter decided, might be provided by what happens to people who are deprived of the chance to affiliate—shipwrecked sailors, for example, or volunteers in isolation experiments. Schachter read a number of case histories of such people and noted that, in practically all instances of long-term isolation, there were reports of feelings of fear and anxiety. This suggested to Schachter a close link between fear and affiliation: if isolation results in fear, perhaps affiliation reduces fear. By this reasoning, Schachter arrived at a specific hypothesis: persons with high fear will tend to affiliate more than those with low fear.

To test this hypothesis, Schachter designed an experiment in which he could manipulate the degree of fear experienced by his subjects and then measure their consequent tendency to affiliate. Subjects were told that the purpose of the experiment was to test the effects of electric shock. So that some of these subjects would be more afraid than others, two different descriptions of shock were given. Subjects in the high-fear condition were told that the shocks would be quite painful. Subjects in the low-fear condition were told that the shocks would cause nothing more than a tickle or a tingle.

Once those two different degrees of fear were aroused, of course, there had to be a way of measuring the subsequent tendency to affiliate. Schachter's solution was to announce a 10-minute delay in the experiment while the shock equipment was being prepared. Subjects were given a choice of how they would spend this delay: alone in a comfortable room, or with the other subjects in the experiment in a classroom. Subjects were asked not only their preference, but also how strongly they felt about it. These preferences and their intensity served as the measure of the subject's desire to affiliate.

Schachter's hypothesis was verified by the results of his experiment. Subjects with high fear were almost twice as likely to seek the company of others than were subjects with low fear. Using this same basic experimental design, Schachter and his colleagues then went on to test the effects of other factors on the tendency of people to like and want to be with people. Schachter has made important contributions to social psychology by devising ways to measure difficult-to-measure emotions and feelings and the actions that result from them.

Approaches in Psychology

These profiles of six psychologists make clear that there are several different approaches to the study of behavior and psychological processes. Each of these approaches looks at behavior from a different point of view, fixing attention on one particular aspect. Sperry, for example, focuses on the biological bases of behavior, the ways in which the chemistry and physiology of the brain underlie our thoughts and actions. Piaget's approach was essentially cognitive, seeking to understand the development of reasoning processes. Skinner's emphasis is behavioral, concerned with overt responses to stimuli in the environment. Rogers' approach is usually called humanistic because its primary concern is the potential for human growth. In addition, we will examine a fifth approach in psychology: the psychodynamic perspective first formulated by Sigmund Freud, which gives great significance to unconscious mental factors in the determination of behavior.

Historical Roots

Before we describe these five contemporary approaches in more detail, let us look briefly at the roots of psychology, tracing some of the themes that persist in contemporary research. Although people have always attempted to understand behavior and the workings of the brain, the study of psychology as a distinct science is scarcely more than a century old. Most historians date the founding of scientific psychology to 1879, the year when Wilhelm Wundt established his psychology laboratory at the University of Leipzig in Germany.

The new discipline represented a convergence of two streams in philosophy and science. One was the tradition of empiricism with its emphasis on experience. *Empiricism*, proposed as a philosophy by John Locke in the seventeenth century, stressed experience of the world as the source of all knowledge. Because the world is communicated to people through the sensory organs, Wundt was interested in the relationship between the activation of the sense organs by physical events and the resulting psychological experiences.

The other tradition was the science of physiology, which in nineteenth-century Europe was responsible for the first systematic explorations of the brain and nervous system. Wundt was himself a physiologist. The son of a Lutheran minister, and an indefatigable but irascible man (his name in an old German spelling means "sore" or "wounded"), Wundt wanted to study the contents of the mind. His experimental methods may seem naive now, but at least they were systematic. For example, Wundt and his colleagues attempted to analyze all of the conscious experiences that occurred while they were listening to the beat of a metronome.

In launching the new science, Wundt also founded the first school of psychological thought, which was later called *structuralism*. Through identification of the basic elements of mental experience—he considered them to be sensations, images, and feelings—Wundt and his followers sought to understand the structure of the mind.

During the next four decades, at least four other

Wilhelm Wundt

distinct schools of psychology arose to oppose structuralism. Each school had its own particular theoretical approach, methodology, and area of interests: *functionalism* was concerned with the use of the mind rather than its contents; *behaviorism* rejected the study of the mind and focused on behavior; *Gestalt psychology* emphasized the wholeness and organization of mental experience; and the *psychodynamic* approach of Sigmund Freud looked beyond conscious awareness to unconscious desires and impulses.

Bitter rivalries often marked the differences among the five schools. Today many of these differences are largely of historical interest. But as we consider five contemporary approaches, we will see ways in which the earlier contending schools have influenced modern thought. Indeed, two of the schools—behaviorism and psychoanalysis—have survived with their theoretical perspectives and rivalries virtually intact.

The Behavioral Approach

Concerned chiefly with stimuli—events in the environment—and the resulting behavioral responses, the behavioral approach is sometimes called S-R psychology (for stimulus-response). Behavior is viewed as a series of learned responses. In effect, psychological experience is conceptualized as events occurring in a "black box" and disregarded. What goes on inside the black box cannot be objectively observed or measured, it is argued—only what goes in (the environmental stimuli) and what comes out (the behavioral response) can be observed and measured.

Behaviorism has dominated American psychology for most of the seven decades since it was formulated by John B. Watson of Johns Hopkins University in 1913. Watson was greatly influenced by the work of the Russian Ivan Pavlov, who had conditioned dogs to salivate at the sound of a bell. Behavior, Watson said, was a succession of conditioned responses to environmental stimuli. Such stimuli are objectively observable and measurable, Watson pointed out, unlike subjective mental processes. He defined the new goal of psychology as "the prediction and control of behavior" (Watson, 1913).

In 1924 in his book *Behaviorism*, Watson, a skillful and enthusiastic propagandist who later became a successful advertising executive, wrote as if that goal were already within reach: "Give me a dozen healthy infants, well formed, and my own specified world to bring them up in, and I'll guarantee to take anyone at random and train him to become any type of specialist I might select—doctor, lawyer, artist, merchant-chief, and yes, even beggarman and thief, regardless of his talents, penchants, tendencies, abilities, vocations, and race of his ancestors."

Watson's strident behaviorism has been qualified by a number of later researchers, principally Edward Tolman, Clark Hull, and Skinner. Tolman and Hull made behaviorism less simplistic. Specifically, Tolman demonstrated how a behavioral model could be developed to handle cognitive constructs—what goes on in the black box (Tolman, 1932, 1938, 1948). Hull showed how theoretical constructs could be quantified. Hull's theoretical efforts remain the most ambitious attempt to explain all behavior—animal and human—with a single model (Hull, 1943, 1951, 1952). Skinner's research is more oriented to empirical data. He does not use a theoretical "superstructure" to dictate the experimental manipulations (changes in the environment) that he imposes on his subjects.

As we saw in our earlier profile, Skinner developed operant conditioning with its precise methods

John B. Watson

for measuring the role of reward and punishment in shaping the responses to stimuli. Skinner, in turn, has influenced the work of many psychologists who do not adhere to a strict behavioral viewpoint, thus affecting the approach of many social psychologists, personality theorists, and clinical psychologists.

The Cognitive Approach

The cognitive approach stresses the importance of what intervenes between stimulus and response— the psychological processes themselves. In this view, behavior is the outward manifestation of internal psychological processes. As we have seen, psychology as a science began with Wundt's attempt to analyze mental processes, which also was the focus of the functionalist and Gestalt schools. The best known of the early American psychologists, William James, brother of novelist Henry James, was particularly concerned with the study of consciousness. To James, the mind was a continuous, ongoing "stream of consciousness" that could not be analyzed into elementary building blocks. His method, like Wundt's, was simple introspection—looking inward to examine one's own mental and emotional states.

In recent years, after decades of dominance by the behavioral tradition, American psychology has begun looking inward again at such cognitive functions as perception, thinking, memory, and consciousness. One impetus for this renewed interest has been the popular concern with altered states of consciousness, particularly those states associated with psychoactive drugs such as marijuana and LSD.

More relevant to cognitive theorists is the information-processing model provided by the modern computer. Many cognitive theorists view psychological processes as a kind of information processing, which receives inputs from stimuli, retrieves stored-up memories, makes comparisons and decisions to solve problems, and produces outputs in the form of behavioral responses.

This rather abstract information-processing concept becomes more concrete if we look at perception. When we see an old friend, we are not passive receivers of an image from the physical world. The stimulus, or input, in fact, consists of nothing more than pinpoints of light. Our brains actively process these pinpoints of light and transform them into an image. The image is recognizable as an old friend because of stored memories. Retrieval from storage occurs here, along with some sort of comparison process. There is further processing and decision making that lead to the response: we say "hello" to our old friend.

The boundary between the cognitive and behavioral perspectives is often not clearly delineated. One example is the social learning theory of Bandura. As we saw, Bandura's classic early experiments in observational learning were essentially behavioral in their focus on stimulus (model acting aggressively) and response (children acting aggressively). But Bandura's subsequent work has emphasized what behaviorists sometimes call intervening variables—the cognitive processes that occur between stimulus and response.

The Psychodynamic Approach

The psychodynamic approach suggests that human behavior is the result of a complex interplay of psychological processes, both conscious and unconscious. This approach frequently has been ap-

Sigmund Freud

plied in the treatment of people who are experiencing emotional distress. In turn, it has derived its principal theoretical underpinnings from the observation of such people during treatment and from their case histories.

The originator of the psychodynamic approach was Sigmund Freud, a Viennese physician. In the late 1880s, Freud was treating patients who suffered from hysteria, a disorder in which people displayed physical symptoms, such as temporary paralysis, that had no apparent physiological basis. Freud and his colleague Josef Breuer used hypnosis as a means of trying to retrieve lost memories and experiences from their patients (Breuer and Freud, 1895/1966; Freud, 1905/1953). To Freud's surprise, the patients revealed past experiences and early traumas that appeared to be symbolically related to their symptoms of paralysis. From these early observations and later analyses of dream content, Freud developed the idea that much of the psychological life of the individual was unconscious—inaccessible to the individual by ordinary means. The concept of the unconscious and the idea that each of us experiences conflicting inner motives and drives that we must reconcile are two of the cornerstones of Freud's theory of the development of abnormal behavior and its treatment.

Aside from his discovery of the unconscious, Freud is probably best known for his psychosexual theory of human development. He believed that everyone is born with an innate sexual instinct that influences a fairly regular sequence of psychological and sexual (psychosexual) development in children. Freud saw people's character as developing out of the ways in which their psychosexual development was handled. These concepts have influenced the modern study of personality and, in particular, the treatment of the emotionally disturbed.

Although Freudian psychoanalysis launched the psychodynamic movement, the two terms are not synonymous. The psychodynamic perspective also embraces the theories of disciples who later broke with Freud, most prominently the Swiss psychologist Carl Jung. Differing with Freud on the importance of sexual motives (Jung thought them less significant), Jung established his own movement called analytical psychology, which draws heavily on the insights of myth, literature, and art (Jung, 1954-1979). Other followers of Freud such as Erich Fromm and Karen Horney (sometimes called neo-Freudians) modified psychoanalytic theory to take into account the role of social and cultural factors.

The psychodynamic approach has been used not only in understanding abnormal behavior but also by historians, biographers, and literary critics as a conceptual tool for understanding the formative experiences of historical figures. The writing of psychohistory—as practiced, for example, by Erik Erikson in his biography, *Ghandi's Truth* (1969)—has stimulated a major intellectual movement in this direction.

In addition, psychodynamically oriented hypotheses have stimulated modern psychological research on sleep and dreaming. For example, sleep researchers have discovered that it is possible to determine when a person is dreaming by observing rapid eye movements. This has enabled researchers to deprive people of their dream activity and to measure the resulting effects on personal adjustment. Thus, the dynamic approach continues to offer insights into a wide variety of fields including development, personality, abnormal psychology, and the study of consciousness.

The Humanistic Approach

Of all the viewpoints in psychology, the humanistic approach is at once the newest and the most difficult to encapsulate. In large part, it represents a reaction against what is perceived as the deterministic emphasis of the other approaches: of human beings as simple stimulus-response machines, supercomputers, or helpless creatures of unconscious forces. It opposes the reduction of behavior to mechanistic processes and affirms the unique wholeness of each human being. In this view, the keys to understanding the nature of the mind is subjective experience—the individual's own perception and interpretation of external events and personal goals.

The humanistic stress on the wholeness of human experience stems in some measure from the earlier school of Gestalt theorists who insisted that the psychological experience is greater than the sum of its parts. A more important influence, however, has been exerted by the philosophy of existentialism as manifested in the writings of the Danish theologian Hans Kierkegaard and the French author Jean-Paul Sartre.

The leading contemporary force in humanistic psychology is Rogers. As we noted earlier, Rogers' client-centered, nondirective therapy has helped shape the course of clinical psychology and of counseling. Other humanistic theorists have included the existential psychologists Rollo May and

Abraham Maslow, who developed the concept of self-actualization to describe what Rogers calls the highest human motivation—the need to fulfill one's individual potential.

The methods of the humanistic approach are highly intuitive; some psychologists would call them unscientific and unsystematic. Perhaps the greatest impact has been felt outside the formal discipline of psychology. In the so-called human potential movement, the approach's antimaterialism, essential optimism, and refusal to impose theoretical preconceptions have appealed to millions of people in search of self-fulfillment.

The Biological Approach

The roots of the biological approach can be traced to the surge of physiological research that occurred in the second half of the nineteenth century. It was during this period that physiologists were first able to localize, in particular areas of the brain, structures that mediate behavior, such as speech and voluntary movement. In the late 1860s, for example, two Prussian physicians, Edward Hitzig and Gustav Fritsch, inserted wires into the cortical surface of a dog's brain and found that passing electric current through the wires caused the animal's limbs to move. Thus they discovered the motor cortex, which plays a major role in voluntary movement in both animals and humans. In subsequent experiments involving electrical stimulation of the brain, physiological psychologists have found areas that elicit a variety of emotion and feelings, including pleasure and pain.

Today, researchers are able to investigate the neural basis of perception and other processes by recording the naturally occurring electrical activity in single cells of the brain. Other research has begun exploring the neural processes of various levels of consciousness such as sleep, dreams, and drug states. We noted earlier the investigation by Sperry of epileptic patients who had undergone surgery that severed the major connection between the two hemispheres of the brain. His work, by demonstrating that the two hemispheres appeared to have distinctly different functions, provides new clues to the biological basis of consciousness.

In recent years, the chemistry of the brain has become a significant area of research (see Focus). The study of neural chemistry is turning up clues

15

to the biological correlates of pain, anxiety, depression, and schizophrenia. Psychoactive drugs, such as the major tranquilizers, which helped spur research into the chemistry of behavior, have proved helpful in alleviating the symptoms of mental illness.

In addition, the biological approach investigates possible genetic bases of behavior—inborn predispositions toward a given level of intelligence, for example, or the genetic basis of schizophrenia. Nonetheless, biological researchers aim basically at supplementing, rather than supplanting, the other perspectives in psychology. For example, the new biological hypothesis that schizophrenia is associated with an excess of a chemical neurotransmitter called dopamine does not necessarily rule out environmental determinants. It is quite possible that neural chemistry is somehow affected by the early childhood traumas stressed by the psychodynamic perspective, or by the learning experiences emphasized by the behavioral point of view.

Methods in Psychology

Like all scientists, psychologists are stalkers of facts. But as Sir Peter Medawar, the British Nobel laureate in biology, has pointed out in his book, *Advice to a Young Scientist*, the scientist is less a hunter of facts than a "seeker after truth." Scientists look for the relationships among facts and try to conceive possible links between cause and effect. "Every discovery," writes Medawar, "every enlargement of the understanding begins as an imaginative preconception of what the truth might be" (Medawar, 1979).

The beginning point for the psychologist then is "an imaginative preconception of what the truth might be"—in short, the *hypothesis*, or testable educated guess. The hypothesis may be derived from a larger psychological framework, such as Freud's theory of psychosexual development, or it may stem from a particular interest of the psychologist, as in Schachter's educated supposition that fear increases the tendency of people to seek the company of others. In other instances the hypothesis may deal less with very specific questions than with a broad area of inquiry, as in Piaget's approach to the stages of cognitive development in children.

The particular characteristics of a phenomenon with which the researcher is concerned are called variables; they can take on different, or variable,

values. The researcher seeks evidence of a relationship between two or more variables. As an example, if we wanted to study the influence of one variable, reading habits, on another variable, language development, we could compare two groups of children: a group of eight-year-olds who read a great deal and a group of eight-year-olds who read considerably less. We could then measure the size of the vocabularies of the children in each group. Differences in vocabulary size may depend, at least in part, on differences in exposure to printed language. Of course, reading habits are only one possible influence on language development. The verbal behavior of parents, language exposure in school, and even television may have influence on vocabulary size as well. Ultimately, an investigator may come to see reading behavior as only one aspect of a broader concept, such as language environment, that may affect language development.

Our hypothesis, then, would have been that there is a relationship between reading habits and vocabulary size. The hypothesis states an inferred relationship between variables. A *theory* is simply a systematic explanation that consists of a group of unified hypotheses. In the case of our example, the theory might involve the relationship between language environments and language development.

In formulating and testing hypotheses about behavior, the psychologist can utilize a number of different research methods. These methods can be classified into two basic categories: the correlational approach and the experimental approach.

Correlational Research

Correlational research techniques analyze relationships between variables through observing people or animals, asking people questions, or gathering data from existing documentary sources such as books and previous studies. Psychologists sometimes use a statistical measurement called the coefficient of correlation to measure the degree of relationship (see Appendix). A positive correlation exists if high scores on one set of variables tend to go with high scores on the other set of variables or when low scores on two sets of variables tend to go together. For example, a strong positive correlation has been found between scores on the Scholastic Achievement Test (SAT) given to college-bound high school students and their academic performance in college. People with high SAT scores generally perform well in college. A perfect positive correlation is designated as plus 1.00. If there is no relationship at all between the two variables, the correlation is said to be .00. If, on the other hand, there is an inverse relationship—that is, when high scores from one set of variables go with low scores from the other set or vice versa—the correlation is described as negative. A perfect negative correlation is minus 1.00.

Observation All of us are observers of behavior and of our own inner processes. We are constantly making mental notes about these observations and inferring hypotheses from them. For example, one variable in a fellow student's behavior may be a tendency to do extremely well on classroom examinations. We ask ourselves why and look for a possible cause for this effect. If we observe the student spending a lot of time studying, we may conclude that there is a direct relationship between that student's grades and the time spent studying. If, on the other hand, we see that student often at parties and other campus events, we may assume that the other variable resides not in amount of effort but in another condition: the student is highly intelligent, perhaps, or simply very gifted at taking tests.

Psychologists use the *observational method* but in a much more systematic way than lay people. For one thing, they attempt to maintain an objective attitude, putting aside personal biases and preconceptions. They also attempt to observe with precision, attending closely to the events before them and resisting the temptation to be diverted from the data by premature speculation about cause and effect.

Psychological observation may be as informal as merely being in a setting and making mental notes. The psychologist may even be a participant, as when Piaget got down on his knees and played marbles with the groups of Swiss children he was studying. More often, the investigator remains inconspicuous and records observations in an orderly manner, perhaps with the help of rating scales that permit statistical measurement of the behavior in question. Psychologists who study perception sometimes use introspection, or self-observation.

Highly formal observations typically take place in the psychologist's laboratory. For example, a developmental psychologist studying spontaneous aggression in young children might be stationed behind a one-way mirror that permits the researcher to see without being seen. Laboratories may also be equipped with videotaping equipment to record events or with elaborate electronic devices to monitor physiological changes in the subjects

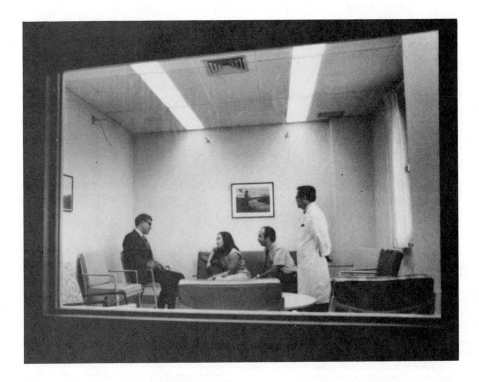

Observation is an important tool in psychological research. One approach involves the use of one-way mirrors, by which the observer can watch and listen to subjects without being seen.

being observed. Thus, observation can range from the most naturalistic of situations—standing on a street corner and closely watching the behavior of motorists at a stoplight—to laboratory situations in which sophisticated equipment and recording devices may be used.

Asking People Psychologists can observe behavior and their own mental processes, but they can also ask others. This method comprises a formidable array of correlational research methods: tests, interviews, questionnaires, and surveys.

1. *Tests.* Testing is such an important part of modern psychology that it comprises a special branch of study called *psychometrics.* Psychologists have devised tests to measure all kinds of abilities, interests, attitudes, traits, and behavioral tendencies. These measurements are often helpful in detecting the differences among individuals. The most familiar of such measurements is the general intelligence quotient, or IQ, test. In the diagnosis and treatment of clients in clinical psychology, tests may also be especially useful. One well-known test in clinical psychology is the Rorschach technique,

which requires an individual to describe what he or she sees in an ambiguous series of inkblots. From these descriptions, the clinician then attempts to draw inferences about clients' needs and impulses.

2. *Interviews.* The most direct technique for asking people is the interview, which allows a human, give-and-take interaction between psychologist and subject. Some interviews, especially those with clients in clinical psychology, are structured along a predetermined course. Other interviews are less formal, allowing the psychologist to pursue insights as they develop.

3. *Questionnaires.* The questionnaire can provide valuable data for the researcher. This is particularly true in *longitudinal studies* that investigate behavior of the same subjects over a lengthy period of time. One of the most notable longitudinal studies in psychology is the investigation of a group of intellectually gifted children that was begun in California in 1921 by Louis Terman. Questionnaires mailed to these subjects periodically have enabled several generations of researchers at Stanford University to keep abreast of the subjects' career achievements and personal lives.

One well-known tool in clinical psychology is the Rorschach test, which requires subjects to identify what they see in an ambiguous series of inkblots. The clinician analyzes the responses in order to draw inferences about the clients' needs and impulses.

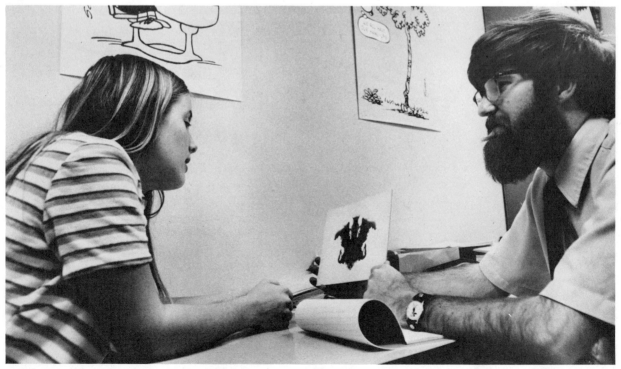

4. *Surveys.* The advantage of the *survey* is that the opinions, attitudes, and experiences of large numbers of people can be assessed. The survey may be in the form of a brief written questionnaire or of an interview conducted by a carefully trained person. As in the questionnaire, the queries must be constructed in such a way as to avoid creating a bias in the answers. The respondents must be chosen so as to be representative of the population being sampled. Political polls are a familiar example of the survey method. The classic example of the political poll that went awry because of an imbalance in the sample was the survey conducted by *Literary Digest*, a national magazine, during the 1936 presidential election campaign. The Republican candidate, Alfred Landon, won the poll hands down. Only after Franklin Roosevelt swept the election, winning every state except Maine and Vermont, did the basic flaw of the magazine's survey become apparent. The survey was conducted by telephone. In those days only citizens with substantial income could afford a telephone and, as

Taking a survey enables researchers to assess the opinions, attitudes, and experiences of large numbers of people.

many other surveys have shown, upper-income people tend to vote Republican (Link, 1980).

When psychologists use the research method of asking people, they frequently draw on a sample of a population. A *population* is an entire group—for example, the population of California is made up of all the people living in that state. In statistical research a population might be made up of all the residents of California under age 20 who suffer from epilepsy. A population could be all the verbs in English or all the temperatures recorded in Chicago in a given year.

Typically, researchers cannot query an entire population, so they choose a *random* (unbiased) *sample* of the population in question. Results from a study of a sample are projected to be representative—within the boundaries of sampling errors—of the population as a whole. Schachter was able to identify fear as an emotion that heightened the need for affiliation by studying a relatively small group of people. He then postulated that the sample was generally representative of the total population.

Case Histories A familiar technique in clinical psychology is the compilation of the *case history*, which is a kind of psychological biography of the client. The history may combine several of the correlational techniques we have described—observation, tests, interviews, questionnaires, and surveys. In addition, the researcher may seek data by examining diaries, books, and other documents.

Clinicians who compile such histories are in the position of detectives seeking clues to the solution of a case. They look for variables that seem to have a correlation with the behavior that is troubling the client. For the Fruedian analyst, these clues are likely to reside in the early experiences of the client. The most famous case history in all of psychology was written by Freud himself (Breuer and Freud, 1895/1966; Freud, 1905/1953). It was a biography of his first patient, "Anna O," whose symptoms of paralysis, Freud inferred, were associated with impulses previously out of her conscious awareness. This hypothesis was instrumental in Freud's formulation of psychoanalytic theory.

The case history also is valuable in other approaches to personality and abnormal behavior. The humanistic theorist Rogers relied on a combination of observations, tests, interviews, and case histories in developing his method of client-centered therapy and in verifying its efficacy.

Archival Studies   A research method closely related to the clinical case history is the *archival study*. Instead of focusing on one person, the archival study typically atempts to find historical data that shed light on a particular kind of behavior. For example, in testing the hypothesis that frustration leads to aggression, William Hovland and Robert Sears studied archival records describing the price of cotton and the number of lynchings in the American South during the period 1882–1930. They reasoned that low cotton prices—an indicator of a depressed agricultural economy—would cause frustration and, hence, aggression. And, in fact, they found a significant negative correlation: as cotton prices went down during that period, the number of lynchings increased (Hovland and Sears, 1940).

Of course, other factors may have influenced the number of lynchings—race relations, migration patterns, even economic factors other than cotton prices. This is called a confounding effect: two variables may be correlated with each other because of the effect a third variable has on both of them. As we shall see in the next section, experiments are designed to reduce, as far as possible, the effects of such third or confounding variables.

Experimental Research

The experimental method differs from correlational techniques in an essential way that can be summed up in one word—control. Experiments allow the researcher to control the variables under study systematically in order to arrive at a clear conclusion of cause and effect. Earlier, in describing the work of Schachter, we noted that he established a hypothesis—affiliation with others reduces fear—by reading case histories of people who were alone for long periods of time. Although this method provided Schachter with an interesting hypothesis, it could not furnish the means to test his hunch scientifically.

Schachter had to turn to the experimental method to gain control over the variables. The simplest experimental research involves only two variables. One is the *independent variable*, the condition manipulated by the experimenter: it is independent because the experimenter controls and manipulates it. In Schachter's affiliation experiment, the independent variable was fear: by employing the ruse of a shock machine, he created high fear in some subjects and low fear in others. The other variable is the response being measured: it is called the *dependent variable* because, under the hypothesis being tested, its value is presumed to be dependent upon the independent variable. Schachter's dependent variable was affiliation: he hypothesized that an increase in the independent variable, fear, would result in an increase in the dependent variable, affiliation, which it did. In short, Schachter was able to establish a cause, fear, and an effect, affilia-

Psychologists often use animals in experimental research.

tion. Other, more complex experiments may involve several independent and dependent variables. Such experiments require the use of sophisticated methods of statistical analysis.

Schachter's particular experiment involved people, but many involve animals. In B. F. Skinner's work with pigeons, the independent variable was reinforcement—a fixed amount of access time to food delivered to the bird on a certain schedule—and the dependent variable was the rate at which the animal learned to perform a given task such as pecking a key.

Comparative psychologists study animals because they are often interested in the evolution of behavior. For psychologists whose primary interest is human behavior, animals have several advantages in experimental research. Animal behavior is usually less complex and thus easier to observe and measure. Moreover, animals can be manipulated in ways that would be either impractical or unethical in the case of humans. With rats, for example, the researcher can control practically every variable over the animal's entire life leading up to the experiment. Diet, climate, exposure to other rats, even heredity—all can be manipulated. And because the rat's life span is relatively short, the effects of genetic or environmental influences can be investigated by one researcher over several generations.

Without animals, experimental research in neuropsychology would be virtually impossible. While taking care not to cause unnecessary pain, researchers physically manipulate the brain of a laboratory animal in ways that would be unthinkable in human subjects—cutting nerve tissue, stimulating it electrically, altering it chemically, probing it with microelectrodes, and then often sacrificing the animal for postmortem studies.

How much of the data gleaned from animal experiments can be generalized to human behavior and psychological processes is a continuing issue in psychology. This issue can be assessed only on a case-by-case basis. In the case of neuropsychology, most findings can reasonably be generalized to humans because, at the basic level of the nerve cell, the physiology and chemistry of the brain of lower animals and humans are very similar. Few psychologists doubt that the principles of operant conditioning formulated by Skinner from his experiments with rats have at least some limited application to human beings. On the other hand, the frenzied responses of rats to intense overcrowding in laboratory experiments may have little to tell us about how humans, with their enormous ability to adapt to the environment, respond to the high population density of big cities like New York and Tokyo.

Experimental Safeguards How can psychologists be reasonably certain that their experiments keep constant all factors except the variables they want to manipulate? The experimental method provides a number of possible safeguards; among them are the control group, random assignment, the "blind" techniques, and replication.

1. *The control group.* When Bandura exposed a group of young children to an aggressive model and then measured their responses, he needed to ensure that the results could be traced to the variable of the model's behavior and not to some other factor. Consequently, he used a *control group* of youngsters who underwent the same experimental procedure, except that the model they saw did not exhibit aggressive behavior. This control group provided a baseline against which to compare the experimental group.

Actually, Bandura employed two control groups. In addition to the two conditions we have recalled—aggressive model and nonaggressive model—there was a third condition in which a group of children was not exposed to any model. In Bandura's experiment, it was conceivable that exposure to any model—aggressive or not—might somehow cause the children to respond aggressively. By setting up a condition in which the children received no exposure to any model, Bandura thus had a second baseline against which to measure the behavior of subjects in the group who were exposed to the nonaggressive model.

2. *Random assignment.* There is the possibility that subjects in an experiment already possess the behavioral tendency that is being measured. A number of children in Bandura's experimental group might have been aggressive to begin with; Schachter's subjects in the high-fear condition may have sought out the company of others simply because they happened to be more gregarious than those in the low-fear condition; laboratory rats, through heredity or previous learning, may already have been skillful at running a maze. To prevent such other variables from influencing results, psychologists may first try to match the subjects in the various experimental conditions by sex, age, or

21

other characteristics that might influence the results: Schachter used only college-age males to eliminate possible variables associated with age or sex. Then to reduce the biasing effects of any other confounding variables, the researcher assigns the subjects to the various experimental conditions by methods of chance—a flip of the coin or random number tables, for example. Thus *random assignment* serves to neutralize the variables that are not being manipulated in the experiment.

3. *"Blind" techniques.* Researchers are human. They often have a vested interest in finding certain results in an experiment: they may want to find evidence for a pet theory. Even when researchers strive to avoid showing bias, they may nonetheless communicate subtle cues to the subjects. Simple tone of voice may suggest to subjects the expectations of the experimenters. And in order to please the experimenters—or to confound them—the subjects may alter their behavior accordingly, thus influencing the results.

Even rats may respond to the experimenter's expectations. It has been shown that when the experimenters think rats are bright, they learn faster than when the experimenters think they are dull. The most likely explanation is that the experimenters who harbor higher expectations for the "smart" rats tend to handle them in different ways than they handle dull rats.

To prevent this sort of influence, a technique can be used so that the experimenter carrying out the research is kept ignorant, or "blind," about the nature of each experimental condition or group. In human drug experiments, a *double-blind technique* is often used; neither the person administering the drug nor the patients know which group is getting the drug and which is getting an inert substance or placebo.

4. *Replication.* The ultimate safeguard in the experimental method is the ability of other researchers to duplicate the results. If any researcher can perform the experiment in the same manner and ob-

FOCUS: Candace Pert—A Young Woman on the Frontiers of Research

Many psychologists labor in the laboratory for decades before diligence, creative insight, and, perhaps, a measure of luck combine to provide an important contribution to the study of behavior. Others make their mark very early. A notable case of the latter is Candace Pert, a researcher who, while still in her twenties, helped pave the way for the remarkable discovery that the brain secretes its own painkillers.

Pert arrived at the frontiers of scientific research in a roundabout manner. She was working as a typist for a psychology professor at Hofstra University when she met her future husband, Agu Pert, a graduate student in brain research. At his urging she majored in biology at Bryn Mawr College and then began graduate work in 1970 at Johns Hopkins University, although already the mother of the first of two children.

Pert decided to specialize in the chemistry of behavior, a relatively new discipline in the branch of psychology known as physiological psychology, or neuropsychology. This fast-growing field of research now embraces several subareas, including neurophysiology, neuroanatomy, neurochemistry, and neuropharmocology. The goal is to understand the precise relationships between specific behaviors and psychological processes and the physical functioning of the brain and nervous system.

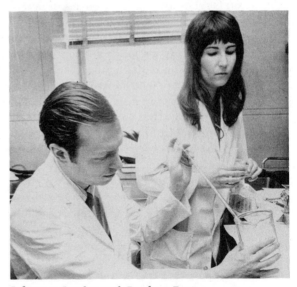

Solomon Snyder and Candace Pert

The study of the chemistry of behavior has produced some of the most exciting scientific discoveries of the past two decades. The principal focus is approximately 20 chemicals that are crucial to the process by which electrical impulses are propagated in the nerve cells of the brain. Several of these

tain the same results, the experiment is said to be replicable. This process helps rule out any flaws in experimental design, bias on the part of the researcher, mistakes in recording the results, and even the possibility of fraud. If an experiment can be repeated successfully, the reliability of the results is established beyond reasonable doubt. Failure to achieve reliable replication is one of the key reasons why research into paranormal phenomena, such as extrasensory perception, is disregarded by many psychologists.

Comparing the Correlational and Experimental Methods

Most psychologists consider the experiment the most powerful tool in exploring behavior. Its great advantage is in the control that enables researchers to establish reliable linkage between cause and effect. The correlational approach, by definition, allows the researcher only to find relationships between variables. If variable *A* increases when variable *B* increases, there is a positive correlation, but is there cause and effect and, if so, which is cause and which is effect?

This essential contrast between the experimental and the correlational methods is dramatically illustrated in studies of the effect of television violence on children's behavior. The Bandura experiments in observational learning show cause and effect: young subjects exposed to a film depicting an aggressive model, are more aggressive afterward than children exposed to a film of a nonaggressive model. Because the children were randomly assigned to the experimental and control groups, any already existing differences in character traits related to aggression presumably were controlled in examining group differences. By contrast, field studies that find—through tests, interviews, and questionnaires—a correlation between watching violence

---

chemicals, which are called neurotransmitters, have been implicated in mental disorders such as schizophrenia and depression.

For her doctoral dissertation at Johns Hopkins, Pert investigated the effects of morphine on the chemical neurotransmitters (Pert and Snyder, 1973; Snyder, 1977). It was suspected that morphine and other opiates exerted their psychological effects—a feeling of euphoria and the easing of pain—by interfering with the normal functioning of neurotransmitters. One possibility was that the opiates actually simulated the action of the neurotransmitters by occupying the receptor sites on the surface of nerve cells where neurotransmitters normally bind to the cells, something in the manner of a key fitting into a lock.

Working with Solomon Snyder, a noted neuropharmacologist, Pert set out to locate the actual receptor sites that morphine was thought to occupy. Pert and Snyder made use of a recently devised experimental technique called radioactive labeling. They injected into experimental animals morphine that contained a radioactive substance. The morphine with its radioactive "label" was taken up by the nerve tissue in the animal's brain. Then, at postmortem, the tissue was viewed with a device that reveals radioactivity.

The morphine concentrated on nerve cell receptors in two different areas of the brain. One area is involved in the regulation of mood; the other is involved in sensations of chronic pain. Pert and Snyder called these nerve cell sites "opiate receptors" and concluded it was here that morphine bound to the nerve cells, presumably acting as an artificial neurotransmitter.

The discovery of the opiate receptors set the stage for highly important research by other neuroscientists. Why does the brain contain specialized receptors for opiates? One possible answer is that the brain must have its own, naturally occurring painkillers. And, in fact, researchers soon discovered several such endogenous chemical compounds, which are called endorphins—from the Greek for "the morphine within." What began as a doctoral dissertation by Pert has launched several promising lines of research, including attempts by other scientists to synthesize a nonaddictive painkiller.

Pert, still not yet 40, is continuing her investigation of the brain's receptor sites as a researcher at the National Institute of Mental Health. Her work there includes the "mapping" of the sites where molecules of drugs, such as tranquilizers and marijuana, are believed to bind to particular receptors—work she hopes may lead eventually to better ways of treating mental illness.

on television and behaving aggressively must contend with a basic uncertainty: Which is cause and which is effect? Perhaps children who watch television violence tend to be more aggressive in the first place. In such a case, the presumed effect—aggressive behavior—would actually be the cause; the presumed cause—watching television violence—would actually be the effect.

Why then bother with the correlational techques? First, they provide a much more efficient means of gathering a great deal of data on a number of variables in a relatively short time. Second, they enable psychologists to study problems where the experimental method is not applicable because of ethical or practical considerations. Third, people studied by the correlational method often are more representative of a large sample of the population than are subjects in experiments. It has been said that much of experimental psychology has been built on the laboratory rat and the college sophomore: both are frequently used in experiments simply because they are readily available for study. Finally, correlational techniques typically study behavior in real-life situations, whereas experiments, despite the efforts of researchers to create the illusion of reality, risk being artificial. Even when subjects are successfully deceived about the true purpose of an experiment in social psychology, for example, they know they are being studied and thus are less likely to act naturally or spontaneously.

In summary, both methods of research have their advantages and disadvantages. Both are necessary in psychological research, and throughout this book we will draw upon the findings of both methods. Which method is preferable depends largely upon the problems being studied and the aims of the researcher. Ideally, the two methods complement each other: the correlational method is a rich source of ideas that can then be put to the test in experiments. In the final analysis, the experiment is only a technique; how well it serves the study of psychology depends on the quality of ideas being tested.

SUMMARY

1. Psychology is the study of behavior of organisms. Psychology is not one science but many, all examining behavior in different ways. Psychology is best seen in terms of processes rather than as an established and static body of knowledge. This text focuses on psychology as a method of inquiry about behavior—a way of thinking about problems and approaching them through observation and experiment.

2. Developmental psychologists study the factors that shape changes in behavior from infancy through adulthood. Jean Piaget showed that the thought processes of children differ from those of adults. Using observational techniques, Piaget distilled a new theory of cognitive development, a universal and relatively stable schedule of four stages. Piaget demonstrated that practically all children will inevitably develop intellectually and learn.

3. B. F. Skinner's name is nearly synonymous with the methods of operant conditioning, which emphasize the theory that behavior is shaped not from within the organism but from without—by reinforcement. By rewarding parts of a desired behavioral sequence, Skinner conditioned pigeons and rats to perform extraordinary feats. From his work with animals, Skinner concluded that behavior could be explained in terms of the contingencies of reinforcement. Skinner's methods have had a strong influence on the study of behavior.

4. Carl Rogers is a clinical psychologist whose theories have greatly influenced the study of personality and the treatment of emotional disturbances. Rogers' work with deprived and delinquent children during the 1930s led to his formulation of nondirective, or client-centered therapy. In client-centered therapy, no formal guidance is provided the client: the task of the therapist is to facilitate an inner force for growth—what Rogers calls the "self-directed process of becoming."

5. Though trained as a clinical psychologist, Albert Bandura is best known for his work in observational learning, or modeling—the processes through which organisms learn by observing and copying the behavior of models. Bandura is interested in "translating theory and principles into practice" and has devoted time to developing practical applications, such as the use of observational modeling to cure phobic fears.

6. Roger Sperry has made many contributions to the understanding of the neural workings of the brain, but two of his discoveries are especially important. First, he demonstrated that nerves are not functionally interchangeable as had been thought. His experiments with amphibians showed that the neural interconnections for vision are genetically preprogrammed. Sperry's second major contribution came from his split-brain studies, which

showed that each of the hemispheres is highly specialized for the processing of information, can work independently, and has distinctly different consciousness and emotions associated with each.

7. Social psychologist Stanley Schachter brought exceptional experimental ingenuity to bear in his explorations. His work on affiliation and on the circumstances under which people tend to seek out others has been important to our understanding of the nature of group support. Working in areas where experimental control is difficult to design, Schachter has overcome those difficulties and obtained evidence for his hypotheses.

8. The discipline of psychology is scarcely a century old, dating from Wilhelm Wundt's establishment of his laboratory at the University of Leipzig in 1879. Psychology represented a convergence of the tradition of empiricism with its emphasis on experience and the burgeoning science of physiology. Wundt's school of thought, later called structuralism, sought to identify the basic elements of psychological experience in order to understand the structure of the mind. The next 40 years saw the growth of other theories and schools of psychological thought. Functionalism was concerned with the use of the mind rather than its contents; behaviorism rejected the study of the mind and focused on behavior; Gestalt psychology emphasized the wholeness and organizations of mental experience; the psychoanalysis of Sigmund Freud looked beyond conscious awareness to unconscious desires and impulses. Today, we group the study of behavior into five broad approaches.

9. The behavioral approach is concerned chiefly with stimuli—events in the environment—and the resulting behavioral responses. Behaviorism, which was formulated by John B. Watson, sees psychological processes as a "black box." What goes on inside the black box cannot be objectively observed or measured—only what goes in (the environmental stimuli) and what comes out (the behavioral response). Behaviorism was modified by later researchers—principally B. F. Skinner, who developed the precise methods and measurements of operant conditioning.

10. The cognitive approach stresses the importance of what intervenes between stimulus and response—the psychological experience. Behavior is viewed as the outward manifestation of internal psychological processes. The cognitive approach is particularly applicable to such functions as the learning process, perception, thinking, memory, and consciousness. Many cognitive theorists see the individual as a kind of computer, an information processor that receives inputs from stimuli, retrieves stored-up memories, makes comparisons and decisions to solve problems, and produces outputs in the form of behavioral responses.

11. The psychodynamic approach, based on the work of Sigmund Freud, sees human behavior as the result of a complex interplay of psychological processes, both conscious and unconscious. Emphasis on unconscious processes concerns many experimental psychologists because of the difficulties in scientifically observing and measuring it. Nonetheless, the psychodynamic approach remains a strong influence on research attempting to understand personality, sexual behavior, and emotional disturbance.

12. The humanistic approach opposes the reduction of behavior to mechanistic processes. The humanistic approach stresses subjective factors—the individual's own perception, interpretation of external events, and personal goals—and, in particular, the wholeness of human experience as keys to understanding the nature of human behavior. The methods of the humanistic approach are highly intuitive and have been criticized by some psychologists as unscientific.

13. The biological approach focuses on the physiological and chemical bases of behavior, relating those behaviors to the workings of the brain and nervous system. In addition, the biological approach investigates the possible genetic bases of behavior—inborn predispositions toward a given level of intelligence, for example.

14. Psychologists utilize two basic methods of formulating and testing hypotheses about behavior: correlational research and experiments. In both methods, researchers seek evidence of a relationship between two or more variables. When they are not able to control the independent variables under study, investigators use correlation to study how one variable changes as the other changes. Among the techniques used in correlational studies are observation, asking people (tests, interviews, questionnaires, and surveys), case histories, and archival studies.

In experimental research the variables can be

systematically controlled in order to arrive at a conclusion of cause and effect. All variables, except the one being studied, are controlled, and the independent and dependent variables are precisely measured. The experimenter manipulates the independent variable while the dependent variable is affected by the changing independent variable.

15. Animals are widely used as subjects in psychologists' experiments. Some animal experimentation is done to study the evolution of behavior. Other researchers seek to translate their findings from animal research into application to human behavior. Animal research offers the advantages of studying behaviors that are less complex than those of humans and thus are easier to observe and measure; moreover, practical and ethical considerations dictate the use of animals in some experiments.

The experimental method offers researchers a number of safeguards for ensuring that all variables except those they want to manipulate are kept constant—control groups, random assignment, "blind" techniques, and most important, replication.

16. The experiment is the psychologist's most important tool in exploring behavior. Its great advantage is in the control that enables researchers to establish a reliable linkage between cause and effect. The correlational approach, by definition, allows the researcher only to find relaionships between variables. Ideally, the two methods complement each other; the correlational method is a rich source of ideas that can be put to test in more highly controlled experiments.

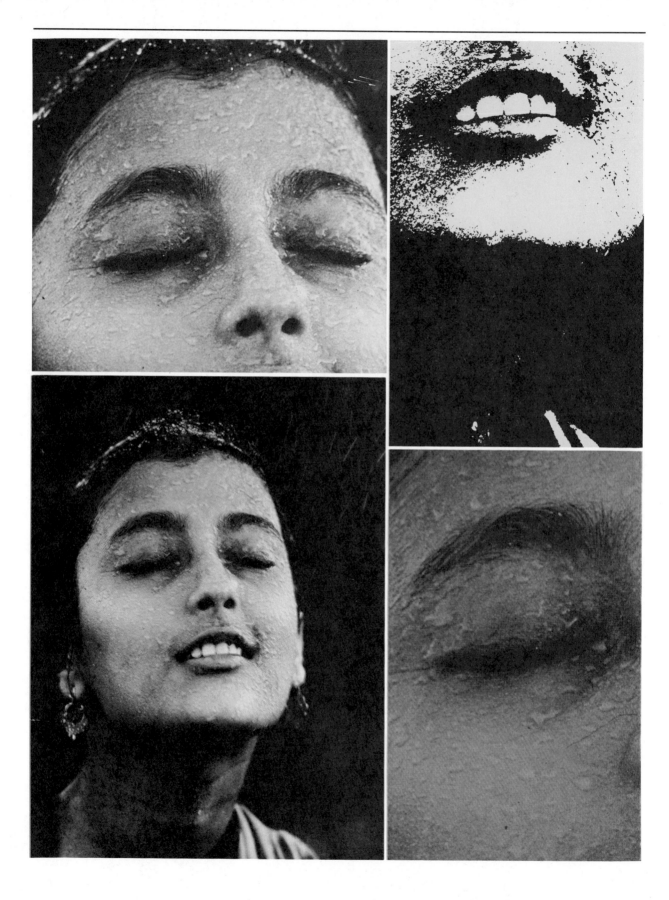

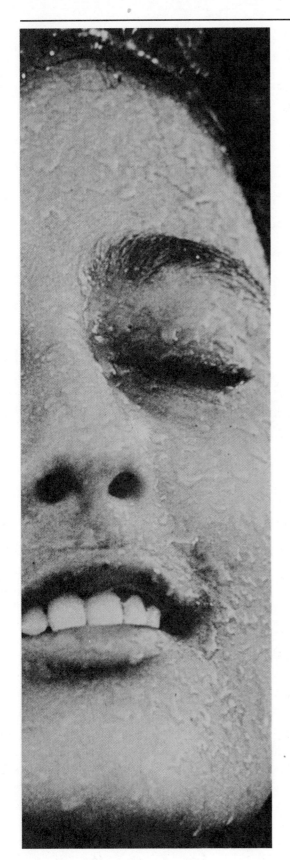

Part Two
Perception and Consciousness

Chapter 2

The Nervous System

On April 11, 1861, a patient in an insane asylum near Paris was taken to see Paul Broca, an eminent French surgeon who specialized in disorders of the nervous system. Although the patient's immediate problem was a severe infection in his right leg, Broca was more interested in a problem of longer standing. The patient could not or would not talk, but there was apparently nothing wrong with his vocal cords. Because the authorities reasoned that no sane man would consciously choose silence, the patient's failure to talk had kept him in the asylum for 21 years. They called him "Tan"; except for an occasional swear word, that syllable was his only utterance.

Broca could not alleviate his patient's infection or speech problem, and six days later Tan died. At the autopsy, he examined Tan's brain. On its surface, in the front part of the left side near the temple, he found a lesion—that is, a mass of scar tissue—that apparently had resulted from disease or an old injury. Broca concluded that the site of the lesion was the area of the brain that controls speech.

Paul Broca, a French surgeon, specialized in disorders of the nervous system.

About two decades later, in the early 1880s, a little-known Spanish anatomist named Santiago Ramon y Cajal began studying human behavior at a radically different level. Cajal had become obsessed with the new science of histology, the study of organic tissue under a microscope. In fact, he was so enthralled with histology that he once spent 20 hours at the microscope watching a white blood cell escape from a capillary.

Working with nerve tissue taken from the brain and spinal cord of birds and other small animals, Cajal (1909–1911) painstakingly pieced together the first coherent picture of behavior at its most basic physiological level. The nervous system, he concluded, is a complex communications network of tiny self-contained cells, or neurons.

In Cajal's day very little was known about how nerve cells work, although it was already clear that the basic mechanism of a nerve cell's action is electrical. It is now clear that conduction in the nervous system is accomplished by electrical changes across the outer membrane of nerve cells. Cajal's most important contribution was to recognize that the nervous system, like the rest of the body, is made up of a complex set of individual cells. Successive nerve cells along a sensory pathway, for example, are not fused. In most . cases, as we shall see, the actual transmission from one nerve cell to the next is brought about by the release of a tiny amount of a specific chemical substance.

The discoveries of these two men, the Frenchman Broca and the Spaniard Cajal, illustrate two of the foundations of physiological psychology. Drawing on knowledge from a variety of disciplines, including medicine, anatomy, histology, physiology, and chemistry, physiological psychologists seek the answers to fundamental questions about the relationship between the brain and behavior. Like Broca, they ask: Where are the control centers for behavior? Like Cajal they ask: How are the nerve circuits that control behavior organized at a microscopic level? A third, and related, question is: How is behavior related to the functioning of individual nerve cells?

Consider these questions as you read the words on this page. Even though you are sitting quietly, specific nerve cells in your head and body are bustling with electrical and chemical activity. Some guide your eyes along printed lines. Others register the shapes of the letters and, matching these forms against memory, render them into words. Still others monitor the actions of your heart and lungs, indicate the feel of your hands upon the book, and perhaps even order one hand to your mouth to stifle a yawn.

The most complex circuits of all make you conscious of the fact that you are reading about all of this unseen, unfelt activity in the nervous system. They enable you to ask mentally the questions that confront physiological psychologists, and to understand, along with them, the basic what, where, and how of the nervous system.

Structures and Functions of the Nervous System

The *nervous system*, of which the brain is the principal part, refers to all of the nerve cells in the body and to all their supporting cells and is one of the body's main communications networks. The nervous system consists of two major subdivisions: the central nervous system and the peripheral nervous system. The central nervous system includes the nerve cells and fibers within the brain and spinal cord.

Santiago Ramon y Cajal first demonstrated that the nervous system is a coherent network of neurons.

Organs and muscles in the periphery are connected to the central nervous system by the peripheral nervous system, which is made of groups of nerve cells called *ganglia* and fiber tracts that lie outside of the central nervous system. The peripheral nervous system carries information from the senses, muscles, and organs of the body to the central nervous system. Nerve fibers in both systems serve to conduct nerve impulses along great distances in the body, within the brain and spinal cord, and from the brain and spinal cord to and from sense organs and muscles in the body.

The central and peripheral nervous systems are, of course, interrelated. The so-called peripheral nerves, for example, are made up of large bundles of nerve fibers, many of which have cell bodies that are actually located in the spinal cord. The peripheral nerves connect the brain and spinal cord with *effectors*, or muscles and glands, and with *receptors*, in the skin and deep structures of the body. A similar set of motor and sensory nerves called *cranial nerves* serve the muscles and sense organs in the head.

The Central Nervous System

The *central nervous system* regulates and controls the activity of the entire body. The brain and spinal cord, which together make up the central nervous system, are clearly the best protected parts of the body (see Figure 2.1). Both are encased in bone. But bone is only the beginning of the protection afforded the brain and spinal cord. Imagine the head from the outside inward. After removing layers of scalp, we come to the skull. If we continue our dissection with appropriate bone-cutting tools and cut through the skull, we come to a heavy, skinlike membrane, or *meninges*. The first membrane we encounter, which is heavy and leathery, and surrounds the entire brain and spinal cord, is called the *dura mater*, or hard mother. It is the outermost of the three meninges that surround the central nervous system. The innermost is a delicate membrane called the *pia mater*, the tender mother. Between the pia, the innermost covering, and the dura, the outermost is the third of the meninges, the *arachnoid*.

In the thin layer of space between the arachnoid and the pia mater is yet another protective element, *cerebrospinal fluid*. This fluid supplements the

FIGURE 2.1 Outer layers of brain and spinal cord.

Skull **Skin** **Pia mater**

Dura mater

Brain

Corpus callosum

Arachnoid

Lateral ventricle

Fourth ventricle

Third ventricle

Spinal cord

brain's arterial circulatory system by supplying nutrients and removing waste matter. It also serves as a buoyant shock absorber, not only further cushioning the brain from the impact of blows to the head but also protecting it from the pull of gravity. Brain tissue is so soft that, if the brain were placed unsupported on a hard surface such as a table, gravity alone would distort it.

Continuing our imaginary dissection, we remove the dura and the arachnoid from the surface of the brain. The pia, which clings to the brain tissue, would be harder to remove. But the pia is so thin that it presents no problem in allowing us to see the true shape of the brain and spinal cord. If the spinal cord were completely exposed, it would be seen as a long cylinder (in humans about as thick as a thumb and about 18 inches long) connecting directly to the brain.

Suppose we cut across the spinal cord at some level (see Figure 2.2). We would see a butterfly-shaped gray mass made up of nerve cell bodies surrounded by white nerve fibers which together are called the *funiculi*. Among these fibers are af-

ferent tracts that carry sensations of warmth, cold, touch, pain, and body awareness from the receptors, or sense organs, to the spinal cord, and up to the brain. Others are *efferent tracts* that carry messages from the brain, down the spinal cord to the

FIGURE 2.2 Cross section of spinal cord showing spinal tracts and afferent and efferent nerve fibers. The nerve fibers surrounding the butterfly-shaped mass make up the funiculi.

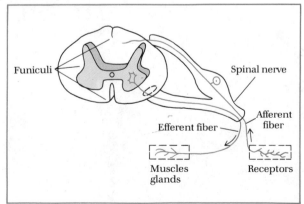

Funiculi

Spinal nerve

Efferent fiber

Afferent fiber

Muscles glands

Receptors

effectors, or muscles and glands. By severing the spinal cord we would cut off communication to and from the brain, thus depriving the brain of all information from the areas served by these sensory fibers and of all voluntary movement in the muscles served by these motor fibers. A few reflexes, or automatic movements would remain. For example, a leg might still be withdrawn if a noxious stimulus were applied to the toe, but the person would not feel pain.

The Peripheral Nervous System

The *peripheral nervous system* transmits information back and forth between the various organs in the body and the central nervous system. It comprises the *somatic nervous system*—peripheral nerves that control movement and receive sensory information—and the *autonomic nervous system*—neural networks that control the functioning of the internal organs such as the arteries, heart, stomach, and sweat glands (*viscera*). The autonomic nervous system, in turn, has two parts: the *sympathetic nervous system* and the *parasympathetic nervous system* (see Figure 2.3). These two systems tend to have opposite effects on the organs that they control and from which they receive information. For example, the parasympathetic system decreases the heartbeat, while the sympathetic system speeds it up—a function the occurs during emotional arousal. Generally speaking, the sympathetic system mobilizes resources for emergencies; the parasympathetic system, by contrast, tends to conserve bodily resources.

Structures and Functions of the Brain

All of our behaviors—from kicking a ball to solving an equation, from flying a kite to composing a song, from firing a gun to picking up a wounded bird—are made possible and controlled by the elegant and complex processes that take place in our brains. It would seem logical that the brain would have to be much larger than it is to encompass and perform all its myriad tasks. But the brain is a marvel of miniaturization.

All human brains look very much alike but show some variation in size. Popular lore would have it that the bigger the brain the more intelligent the creature. However, there appears to be no relationship between size and function in the human brain, except in extremely rare cases where the brain never attains full growth.

Without any appreciable advancements to the neural sciences, the brains of a number of notable historical figures—among them Lenin and Napoleon—have been weighed and measured with great interest after their deaths. On the average, the human brain weighs about 1,500 grams. The brain of the Russian novelist Ivan Turgenev weighed more than 2,000 grams, but that of another gifted writer, the American poet Walt Whitman, weighed only 1,282 grams. Such variations appear to be related in part to body weight. The average weight of a woman's brain, for example, is about 10 percent less than that of a man—approximately the same difference as in average body weight. The largest brain, in fact, belongs to the whale. Its brain weighs 6,000 grams, four times the human average, but then whales often tip the scales at 50 tons.

Although brain size does not have important influence on our behavior, just where in the brain certain processes take place is quite important to our movements and thoughts and perceptions. Broca's discovery of the speech area furnished the first anatomical proof of a theory that he had developed early in the nineteenth century. This theory, known as *localization*, held that many aspects of behavior could be traced to specific regions of the brain.

Localization marked a great step forward in the orderly study of the biological basis of behavior. In ancient times most observers were unable even to link behavior to the brain and nervous system. The early Egyptians thought the heart and liver were the seats of human emotions. The Greek philosopher Aristotle was certain the brain could not be the source of feelings because he observed—correctly—that nerve tissue itself is insensitive to pain.

But in about 400 B.C. a fellow Greek, Hippocrates, the father of medicine, was able to draw the correct conclusions. After observing the behavior of patients who had suffered head injuries, Hippocrates wrote: "Man ought to know that from the brain and from the brain only arise our pleasures, joys, laughter, and just as well our sorrows, pains, griefs and tears."

The functions of many parts of the brain have been learned by a variety of methods. One method, as we have seen in the work of Broca, is to observe behavioral symptoms in humans and then to examine their nervous systems at autopsy. Another

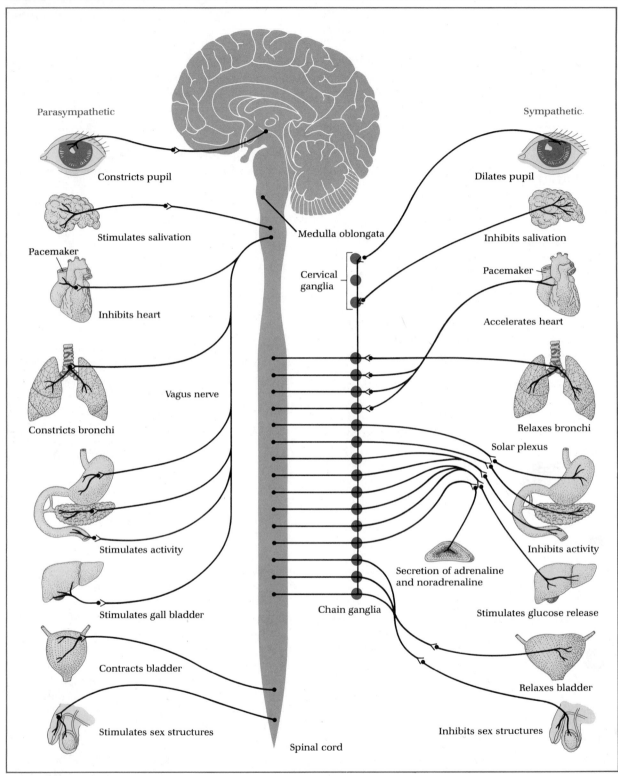

Parasympathetic

Constricts pupil

Stimulates salivation

Pacemaker

Inhibits heart

Vagus nerve

Constricts bronchi

Stimulates activity

Stimulates gall bladder

Contracts bladder

Stimulates sex structures

Medulla oblongata

Cervical ganglia

Chain ganglia

Spinal cord

Sympathetic

Dilates pupil

Inhibits salivation

Pacemaker

Accelerates heart

Relaxes bronchi

Solar plexus

Inhibits activity

Secretion of adrenaline and noradrenaline

Stimulates glucose release

Relaxes bladder

Inhibits sex structures

FIGURE 2.3 Schematic layout of the autonomic nervous system showing both the sympathetic and parasympathetic systems and the structures they control.

method is to create lesions surgically in experimental animals and then observe the resulting behavior. Newer methods involve the stimulation of a test animal's brain by electrical or chemical means. Electrical activity from the individual nerve cells is recorded by means of ultrafine (no thicker than one thousandth of a millimeter) microelectrodes— very fine wires or fluid-filled glass tubes that record the electrical activity of individual nerve cells.

As the early anatomists explored the brain and the rest of the nervous system, however, they had little clear knowledge of the functions of the various structures. Typically they named the structures in terms of their appearance. Hence, much of the terminology used today to describe parts of the nervous system derives from Greek and Latin roots and bears no relationship to function. One structure in the brain, for example, which we now know is related to emotional control, appeared to be shaped like an almond; thus, it was named amygdala— Greek for almond. Similarly, the hippocampus, a structure involved in learning and memory, got its name from the Latin for seahorse, which—at least in the anatomist's fancy—it resembled.

The Brain Stem

At the base of the skull, rising stalklike from the spinal cord into the skull, is the *brain stem* (see Figure 2.4). From an evolutionary standpoint it is the oldest part of the brain. The lowest part of the brain stem is the *medulla*. Just above the medulla at the base of the brain is an arching band of nerve fibers, which marks the region known as the *pons*. The pons and the medulla control such largely automatic functions as heart rate and respiration. A broken neck may bring on death by suffocation if it severs nerve connections between the brain stem and the muscles that control chest expansion.

The Midbrain

The *midbrain*, which forms the top of the brain stem (see Figure 2.4), contains a large number of nerve fibers that connect structures above and below it. Attached to the base of the brain just in front of the brain stem is another small gland called the *pituitary*. Attached to the top of the brain stem is a small gland called the *pineal*. Though not composed of nerve cells, both serve as regulators of body chemistry and thus influence behavior so markedly that they are considered to be functional parts of the brain. The pituitary secretes hormones that influence a wide range of functions, from body growth to human reproduction. The pineal gland was thought by the seventeenth-century philosopher René Descartes to be "the seat of the soul." In some

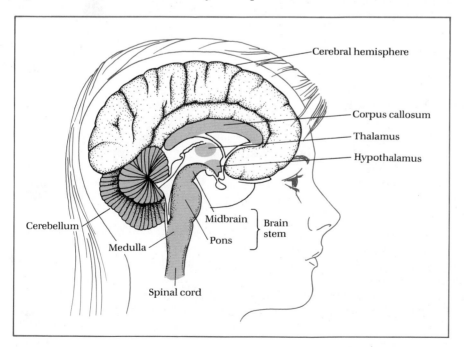

Cerebral hemisphere
Corpus callosum
Thalamus
Hypothalamus
Cerebellum
Medulla
Midbrain
Pons
Brain stem
Spinal cord

FIGURE 2.4 Basic structure of the human brain. In this drawing the brain has been split in two vertically, and the view is of the inner surface of one of the two halves, showing the positions of the spinal cord, brain stem, medulla, pons, midbrain, cerebellum, cerebral hemisphere, corpus callosum, thalamus and hypothalamus.

amphibians, such as the frog, its light-sensitive cells function as a kind of third eye. In humans, recent research suggests, the pineal serves as a built-in timekeeper for the menstrual cycle and manufactures hormones involved in the development of sexual organs.

The interior of the midbrain is made up of a structure called the *reticular formation*, which plays an important role in our state of arousal or awareness. If an animal's reticular formation is massively damaged, it will fall into a coma. The reticular formation also may influence our ability to focus attention by acting as a type of filter permitting some messages from the sense receptors to pass on to conscious awareness while blocking or toning down other messages.

The Cerebellum

Attached to the rear of the brain at the level of the pons is the *cerebellum*, a large structure about the size of a peach (see Figure 2.4). The cerebellum is densely fissured and consists of two distinct hemispheres separated by a central, unpaired region, called the *vermis*. It is now known that the cerebellum helps to maintain the body's equilibrium and to coordinate muscles during fine movements such as threading a needle. Its physical prominence made the cerebellum the subject of much erroneous speculation among early investigators, one of whom, noting that it was especially large in bulls and stallions, concluded that the cerebellum must be a sex center.

The Cerebrum

The brain stem and its associated structures are practically hidden by the two massive connected bodies that arch above and around them, the *cerebral hemispheres* (see Figure 2.4). Taken together, these hemispheres form the *cerebrum*, which is the center of higher thought and perceptual processes. Several bands of nerve fibers, or *commissures*, join the two hemispheres of the cerebrum across the middle. The largest of these is the *corpus callosum* (Latin for hard body), which is about 3½ inches long and ¼ inch thick and contains an estimated 200 million nerve fibers (see Figure 2.4). It is the relative size of the cerebrum—about four fifths of the brain's volume and weight—and especially its wrinkled gray surface, or cerebral cortex, that distinguishes the human brain most from that of other organisms.

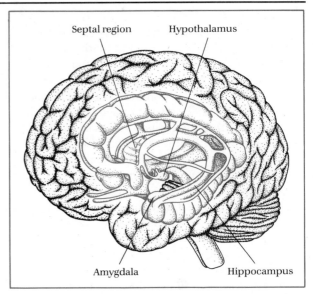

FIGURE 2.5 View of the interior of the brain through the right hemisphere showing the structures of the limbic system, including the amygdala, hippocampus, and septal region.

Deep within the cerebrum, clustered around the top of the brain stem, are a number of complex structures: the *thalamus* (see Figure 2.4), a kind of relay station through which nerve fibers carry all the sensory impressions except smell, which has its own private connection to the higher centers of the brain; the *hypothalamus* (see Figure 2.4), which governs the autonomic nervous system and the pituitary gland, and hence is involved in the regulation of body temperature, appetite, thirst, and sexual activities; and the *limbic system* (see Figure 2.5), a ringlike collection of various centers including the almond-shaped *amygdala*, the seahorse-shaped *hippocampus*, and the *septal region*. Together the hypothalamus and the limbic system are involved in intense emotions, such as anger, fear, and even pleasure. These structures and their apparent functions will be described in detail in Chapter 10.

The Cerebral Cortex

The brain is very roughly spherical. Viewed from the top, it is pink and gray and wrinkled like a walnut. This wrinkled, or fissured, surface, which covers much of the brain's exterior, is the *cerebral cortex* (see Figure 2.6). Its grayish color has given rise to the popular expression for people of high intelligence—they have "lots of gray matter." In the brain and the rest of the nervous system, gray matter is made up of masses of nerve cells. The uniqueness of the human brain resides principally in the convoluted folds of the cerebral cortex. These folds or grooves are known as *fissures*. In this crumpled covering, the gray matter of nerve cells is about 2 to 3 millimeters deep and is arranged in a series of parallel layers, each of which tends to have nerve cells of different sizes and shapes. Fish and amphibians have no cortex, and in reptiles and birds it is less well developed than it is in mammals. Some mammals like the rat have cortex, but it is relatively smooth. Human cortex, by contrast, folds in upon itself so much that it triples the surface area that can fit inside the skull. Stretched out flat, it would constitute a sheet of gray matter 3 feet long and 2 feet wide. The convolutions make it possible for as many as 100 million nerve cells to be packed into a single cubic inch of cortex.

The deep fissures between the folds create a series of landmarks that serve as convenient reference points on the cortical terrain. Two of them serve as major landmarks and appear on the surface of each half, or hemisphere, of the brain. Both are named for early anatomists: the *central fissure*, also called the *fissure of Rolando*, which cuts later-

ally across the surface, and the *lateral fissure* or *fissure of Sylvius*, which emerges from the bottom of the hemisphere and curves upward and back along the side. These fissures demarcate each hemisphere into distinct regions, or *lobes*. Each lobe has functions that will help us associate the name and region with particular phenomena of everyday behavior such as speech, movement, and sight. The lobes, which take their respective names from prominent nearby bones in the skull, and some of their functions are as follows:

Occipital lobe, at the back of the head, contains the visual cortex, which processes the sensations of light originating in the eyes.

Parietal lobe, at the top of the head, monitors such sensations as pressure on the skin, heat and cold, and awareness of the location of the body's limbs.

Temporal lobe, next to the temple, has areas concerned with hearing, visual recognition, and the understanding of language.

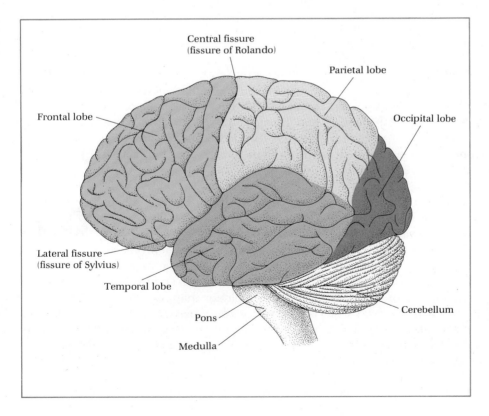

FIGURE 2.6
The cerebral cortex.

Frontal lobe, behind the forehead, contains the motor cortex, which helps control voluntary movements. Near the motor cortex is the area, discovered by Broca, which helps control speech.

Mapping the Cortex The first major attempt at mapping or localizing precise functions in the cerebral cortex was carried out in about 1800 by a Viennese physician, Franz Joseph Gall (Gall and Spurzheim, 1810–1819). Gall was an early champion of localization but his methods and conclusions were all wrong.

Gall was intrigued by the bumps he observed on the heads of his patients and others. These bumps, he theorized, were caused by the mental exercise of certain centers in the cortex that Gall thought bulged like overused muscles. From his everyday observations he pinpointed 24 different areas and related them to behavioral traits. For example, he put the capacity for speech in the very front of the brain because he had observed that the eyes of prominent public speakers seemed to bulge there. He even claimed to have pinpointed a "destructiveness center" just behind the ear of a medical student who was "so fond of torturing animals," Gall observed, "that he later became a surgeon."

Gall and his followers expanded his erroneous version of localization into the pseudoscience known as *phrenology* (see Figure 2.7). Phrenology became a craze in both Europe and the United States, attracting thousands of adherents, including Karl Marx. These followers flocked to their nearest phrenologist to have their skull bumps read so they could better understand their own character and mental abilities.

Gall's notion, for all its wrongheadedness, helped further the theory of localization. As we have seen, Broca's discovery of Tan's speech area in 1861 gave the idea of localization a scientific foundation. Broca's method of mapping the cortex—postmortem examination coupled with observation of the patient's previous behavior— tended to be slow and cumbersome, however.

A much more direct method was inaugurated a few years later by two German physicians, Gustav Fritsch and Eduard Hitzig. Fritsch had served in the Prussian War and, while treating wounded soldiers, had noted that the muscles of the men sometimes twitched if he accidentally brushed against head injuries where the brain was laid bare. He had even experimented by applying a weak

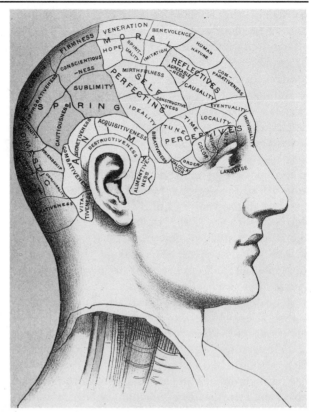

FIGURE 2.7 Chart used in the pseudoscience of phrenology, which expanded the concept of localization of mental activity.

electric current to the exposed brain of several of his patients, a stimulation that produced movement. In 1870, back home in Berlin after the war, he and Hitzig contrived an epic experiment, which, because they lacked laboratory space, was carried out on Frau Hitzig's dressing table. They cut open the skull of a dog and placed the tips of electric wires on its brain. Current at one point of the cortex moved the dog's legs. At another point, it twitched the muscles of the dog's head. Fritsch and Hitzig had found in the frontal lobe an area that controls voluntary movement, the motor cortex.

From this bizarre beginning on Frau Hitzig's dressing table, electrical stimulation became one of the prime tools for mapping the functions of the cortex. Since most nerve tissue is insensitive to pain, it is possible to perform stimulation experiments on humans during the course of brain surgery with the patient awake and alert. When the electrode is placed on the cortex of the occipital lobe at the back of the head, the patient reports seeing flashing lights and other visual phenomena. Stimulation in the sensory area of the parietal lobe brings reports of an odd prickly feeling in the skin. In the auditory area of the temporal lobe, it produces bursts of unintelligible sounds.

Among the most precise cortical maps are those describing the motor cortex, the region where Fritsch and Hitzig conducted the first experiment in electrical stimulation. Patients whose motor cortex is stimulated during surgery will move an arm or a hand or a leg without seeming to will the movement. They invariably report a feeling that the movement is completely automatic. For example, a patient does not choose to move an arm: it just moves.

The Motor Cortex The organization of the *motor cortex* is of particular interest. Here, stretched around the curving surface of cortex, is in effect an upside-down map of the entire body's topography, from toes and ankle to tongue and throat. Neighboring points of cortex represent neighboring regions of the body so faithfully, in fact, that a *homunculus,* or little man, can be drawn. This homunculus illustrates the proportion of cortex devoted to control of the various muscles in the body.

As Figure 2.8 shows, the little man is amusingly

FIGURE 2.8 The motor homunculus, showing the proportion of cortex devoted to control of the body's various muscle groups.

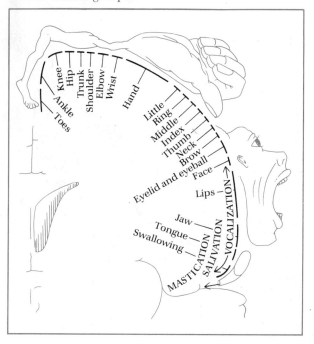

distorted, revealing the disproportionate amounts of cortex necessary for control of different muscle groups. These distortions demonstrate two important traits that help distinguish humans from their fellow animals. The little man has enormous hands, reflecting the large area of cortex necessary to control intricate manual tasks such as handwriting. And he has a big mouth, reflecting the large area necessary for controlling the tongue, throat, and lips in speech.

If we were to depict the organization of the motor cortex in other mammals, the resulting image similarly would reveal something of those animals' special behavioral traits. A drawing of a raccoon, for example, would show a large area of cortex devoted to its fingers, with which it carefully feels objects.

The Silent (Association) Areas The mapping of localized functions in the cerebral cortex is far from complete. There are less well-understood regions, which are sometimes called *silent areas* because electrical stimulation there fails to elicit either movement or sensation. They also are called *association areas* because they are presumed to integrate or associate information arriving at the precisely mapped cortical centers for sensation and movement. If so, centers for the so-called mental processes such as learning, memory, and thought presumably would be here. But large portions of association cortex can be lost to injury, disease, or the surgeon's scalpel without clearly defined effects on behavior. Much of the current research in the neurosciences is directed toward learning the functions of these uncharted areas.

The Connecting Pathways

Our discussion of structures and functions of the brain should not be taken to suggest that the nervous system consists of discrete and independent units. Rather, these anatomical parts are complexly interdependent, intricately linked by tracts or bundles of nerve fibers. Most voluntary movement, for example, depends upon the close coordination not only of the motor cortex but also of the cerebellum and other structures deep within the brain.

Nerve fibers and their connections are usually so intertwined that they can be sorted out and identified only with the aid of specialized staining methods and microscopic study. In some instances, however, large fiber tracts may stand out distinctly and can be followed by simple dissection for considerable distances. By tracing these connecting pathways with the naked eye, we can often deduce a great deal about the functions of a given part of the brain.

For example, we can see at the back of the eye a large fiber tract that proceeds toward the brain. After entering the brain, it is called the optic tract (see Figure 2.9). Physiological study shows that each of the fibers of the optic tract—about a million in monkeys and humans and 100,000 in cats—carries visual information. If we follow the course of the optic tract, we can see that it goes to, among other structures, a subdivision of the thalamus called the *lateral geniculate body.* All of the cells in the geniculate are involved in the transmission, or regulation of transmission, of visual information from the eye to the cerebral cortex.

Similar fiber systems originate in other sensory structures and project upward in the brain, connecting at one or more relay stations along the way. Most wind up in the cerebral cortex, where they end in separate and identifiable areas. Thus in the human visual system the fibers of cells in the lateral geniculate body project to a fissure in the occipital lobe at the back end of the cortex, the *calcarine fissure.*

Just as there are many sensory pathways from peripheral structures to the cortex, there are also motor pathways. These, however, originate in the brain and descend to connect to the nerve cells that control muscles. One of the major motor systems, the *pyramidal tract,* projects from the cerebral cortex all the way down to the spinal cord. In humans and the higher primates some pyramidal tract fibers end directly on spinal motor nerve cells. These cells in turn send fibers via spinal nerves to connect directly to muscles.

Symmetry of the Brain

One of the most striking characteristics of brain anatomy has been only touched on so far in our discussion of structures. Like most parts of the body, these structures either come in pairs, or are arranged symmetrically. Just as we have two lungs, two arms, and two legs, we have two cerebellar hemispheres, each the mirror image of the other.

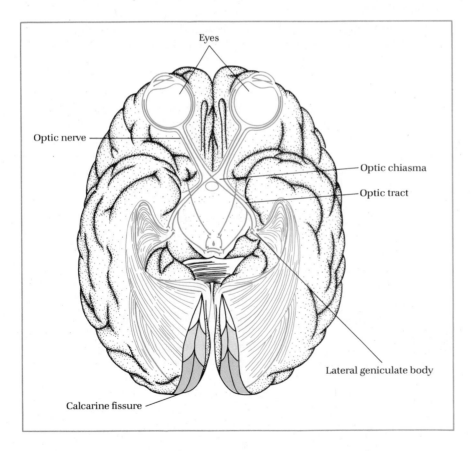

FIGURE 2.9 Visual pathways from the optic nerve that form the optic tract upon entering the brain, where it proceeds to the lateral geniculate body, fibers from which proceed to the calcarine fissure in the occipital lobe at the back of the cortex.

Eyes

Optic nerve

Optic chiasma

Optic tract

Lateral geniculate body

Calcarine fissure

Even single structures, such as those in the brain stem, are divided in halves, and each half mirrors the other. This arrangement by which structures are paired or divided into similar halves is called *bilateral symmetry.*

Not only the brain but also most of the nervous system is bilaterally symmetrical. The brain and nervous system can be visualized as split vertically down the middle. Some nerve fiber tracts cross over to the opposite side within the spinal cord and some cross within the brain itself. The effect of this crossover is that each side of the brain presides over the opposite side of the body. Thus, movement of the right hand is controlled largely by the left side of the brain. Similarly, a pain in the left leg is represented in the right side of the brain.

A dramatic illustration of this crossover is found in the neurological disorder called *parietal lobe syndrome.* One area of the parietal lobe monitors skin sensations and body awareness. Parietal lobe syndrome affects half of this area. If it occurs in the right hemisphere, the patient loses awareness of the left side of the body and may completely neglect it. Often, the patient appears to be two people, with the right side of the body well-groomed, the left side unkempt.

Cerebral Dominance Though the cerebral hemispheres appear to be anatomical twins, they are not identical in function. Each hemisphere has uniquely developed capabilities in carrying out certain tasks. The most evident instance of this specialization is the universal tendency of human beings to favor one hand over the other for tasks, such as writing or throwing a ball, that require finely tuned coordination. Most of us (an estimated 90 percent) are right-handed, meaning that highly developed control is exerted by the left hemisphere. For right-handedness, then, the left hemisphere is said to be dominant. The specialization of one or the other hemisphere is known as *cerebral dominance.*

A less obvious but even more pronounced instance of cerebral dominance is the fact that, in practically all human brains, the capacity for speech and language also resides on the surface of a single hemisphere. In 97 out of 100 persons, it is the left hemisphere. For this reason, a stroke that paralyzes the right side of the body (controlled by the left hemisphere) often also impairs the victim's language abilities.

During a stroke, blockage in the blood vessels serving the brain may cut off the oxygen supply to any of several language centers on the surface of the left hemisphere, killing millions of nerve cells. The result is *aphasia,* a term used for the impairment of the ability to speak, write, or understand language.

As a result of success in mapping much of the cortex, the symptoms of stroke-related language difficulty, or aphasia, often suggest the precise site of damage (see Figure 2.10). In one type of aphasia, for example, the patient speaks with great difficulty in an abbreviated style that omits the endings of verbs and nouns. These symptoms suggest that the damage is to Broca's area in the frontal lobe near the motor cortex. In a second type of asphasia, articulation seems normal, but the patient's speech lacks content and is likely to contain roundabout substitutes for a simple word—for example, "What you use to cut with" instead of "knife." These symptoms usually indicate damage to Wernicke's area. In a third type of aphasia, the patient loses understanding of speech. This loss implies damage to an area in the temporal lobe near the region concerned with hearing. Inability to comprehend written language implicates an area farther back in the cortex, a region with direct connections to the visual cortex in the occipital lobe.

The dominant hemisphere also contains other regions, less precisely mapped, that appear to be

FIGURE 2.10 Approximate locations of the "speech" areas in the human brain. Damage to Broca's area causes prolonged aphasia, but recovery usually occurs, while damage to Wernicke's area causes devastating and permanent aphasia.

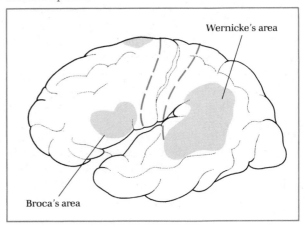

involved in language. The simple act of handwriting, for example, may engage many portions of the cortical surface, including areas in the frontal lobe that, some researchers suggest, are essential to purposeful action. A woman with frontal-lobe damage wrote the following letter to a Russian neurosurgeon, repeating the same words page after page: "Dear Professor, I want to tell you that I want to tell you that I want to tell you. . . ."

In many cases of aphasia, the brain demonstrates a remarkable adaptability. If the damage to a relevant area is slight, the language capability may be restored after a short time. If the area is destroyed, however, it cannot recover, because, unlike other cells, nerve cells cannot replace themselves. But the brain possesses built-in backup mechanisms that often take over when things go wrong. This duplication of functions, or *redundancy*, is especially evident in young children. During the first years of life, both hemispheres apparently have an independent capacity for language. A young child can lose the entire left hemisphere and still regain speech through the right hemisphere. By approximately age 10, however, the opposite hemisphere no longer seems able to assume control of language functions.

The localization of cerebral dominance for handedness and language predominately in the left hemisphere raises obvious questions: what of the right hemisphere? Does it possess its own special behavioral capabilities? For many years these questions went unanswered, indeed largely unasked. Scientists labeled the left hemisphere the *major hemisphere* and relegated the right hemisphere to a limited role as the *minor hemisphere*.

Nonetheless, the early medical literature offered an occasional tantalizing hint of the right hemisphere's special abilities. One such ability appears to relate to music. In 1745 a physician wrote of a stroke victim whose symptoms, we now know, indicated damage to the language centers of the left hemisphere (Bogen, 1969). The patient's spoken utterances were limited to the word "yes." However, the physician noted, "He can sing certain hymns, which he had learned before he became ill, as clearly and distinctly as any healthy person."

The Split Brain These early hints about the right hemisphere went largely unexplored until the early 1950s when the American psychologist Roger Sperry (1961) and his associates began the remarkable series of experiments known as the "split-brain" studies. These studies, which would yield extraordinary new insights into the roles played by both hemispheres, began on a somewhat different track. Sperry wanted to investigate the route by which visual learning is transferred from one hemisphere to the other.

Sperry put the problem to one of his graduate students, Ronald Myers, suggesting he work with cats. Myers' first step was to eliminate one means by which visual information was known to reach both hemispheres. Recall that in mammals such as cats, visual information from each eye is normally transmitted directly to both hemispheres via the optic tract. For his experiment, however, Myers (1955) changed this. He divided the optic chiasma— the optic nerve fibers that cross the midline— leaving intact only those fibers that connected the right eye to the right side of the brain and the left eye to the left side of the brain. Thus, what the cat saw in its left eye would be transmitted only to the left hemisphere; what it saw in its right eye would be received only in the right hemisphere.

Myers then covered one of the cat's eyes with a leather mask and, using food as a reward, taught the animal a simple task in visual learning: to discriminate between a circle and a square. Next, Myers reversed the mask and covered the eye that had been trained. Because of Myers' surgical interruption of the optic tract, we might expect the untrained eye to show no recognition or memory of the circle-square task. But, in fact, the cat had no problem with it. Information from the trained eye had reached not only its corresponding cerebral hemisphere but also had somehow "leaked" to the other hemisphere as well. This transfer of information, Myers and Sperry suspected, might have occurred through the corpus callosum, the most prominent of the several commissures that connect the two hemispheres.

To test this possibility, Myers (1956) proceeded with new surgery on his experimental cats. He repeated his surgical procedure on the optic chiasma and also completely severed the corpus callosum between the two cerebral hemispheres. This time the results of the visual learning test were far different. When the untrained eye was exposed to the circle and square, the cat acted as if it had never seen the problem before. Indeed, it was as if the cat's two hemispheres were now two separate brains: one brain had learned the task; the other was completely ignorant of it. In subsequent experiments, split-brain cats were taught to make opposite choices with each eye—the square with one, the circle with the other. The cats learned to obey these conflicting instructions without the slightest evidence of confusion, confirming that their newly bisected hemispheres were functioning as independent units.

Though these experiments were fascinating, they had limited significance in terms of cerebral specialization. In cats and other mammals tested, both hemispheres are functionally equal; unlike human beings, these animals show no cerebral specialization. Humans, with their left hemispheric dominance for language and handedness, could be expected to exhibit far more interesting results if their brains could be safely split.

In fact, people did exist whose corpus callosum had been split in a surgical attempt to alleviate severe epilepsy. This neurological disorder is marked by seizures during which the victim suffers convulsions and sometimes falls on the ground. During a seizure, nerve signals in one cerebral hemisphere go awry in a way that is still not fully understood, often generating a mirror image of the aberrant nerve activity in the opposite hemisphere. Many cases of epilepsy can be controlled by drugs. However, some neurosurgeons tried the radical practice of cutting the corpus callosum in hopes that such surgery might prevent the spread of a seizure from one hemisphere to the other. In some cases the surgery was helpful; it almost totally eliminated the worst seizures and produced no noticeable changes in temperament, personality, or general behavior.

When Roger Sperry began studying patients whose brains had been split, he was struck by their apparent normality. One of the subjects he interviewed was a 48-year-old veteran of World War II whose seizures had begun after bomb fragments penetrated his brain. Sperry (1968) later wrote of this man whose cerebrum had been bisected: "In casual conversation over a cup of coffee and a cigaret, one would hardly suspect that there was anything at all unusual about him."

To examine more closely the behavioral effects of the split brain in these human subjects, Sperry and his graduate student Michael Gazzaniga (1967), had to devise a series of special tests. The aim of the tests was to restrict sensory information so that it would reach only one hemisphere or the other of the subject's bisected brain.

This could be done in the case of vision because of the way in which the eyes connect to the brain. If we stare straight ahead at an imaginary vertical line on the wall, everything to the right of that line is transmitted to the brain's left hemisphere; everything to the left goes to the right hemisphere. In one test, split-brain subjects had no trouble reporting a light's presence when it was flashed onto the right of a screen in front of them. Information about the light was transmitted to the left hemisphere, which contains the speech center. But when the light was flashed onto the left part of the screen, the subjects denied having seen it. The information had reached only the right hemisphere, which lacks speech, and the subjects had to remain mute. There was no question that the right hemisphere had perceived the light: when the subjects were asked to show where the image had been flashed on the screen, they quickly pointed with their right-hemisphere-controlled left hands, to the correct place.

In the case of touch, the problem of restricting information to one hemisphere was easily solved. For example, the subject would be told to grasp an object with the left hand. The object—for example, a pencil or spoon—was hidden from view behind a partition so that the only information about its nature reaching the brain came from the left hand (see Figure 2.11). This information was transmitted to the right hemisphere, because, as we noted earlier, the sensory nerves cross over to the opposite side en route to the brain. Because no information about the object had reached the left hemisphere, subjects could not name or describe the objects placed in their left hands. Instead, they would simply guess, calling a pencil, for example, a can opener. The "talking" left hemisphere—and the right hand— did not know what the left hand was doing.

Some results of these special tests are easily predictable based on our knowledge of the left hemisphere's dominance for language. However, tests demonstrated that the right hemisphere had unexpected abilities of its own. By manipulating objects with the left hand, it could add up to 10. And it even demonstrated an elementary capacity to reason. On one test, a picture of a spoon was flashed onto the left of the screen so it could be "seen" only by the right hemisphere. Subjects could not name the spoon, of course, because the image was not available to the left hemisphere. But they were orally instructed to select with their left hands the matching item from an assortment of hidden

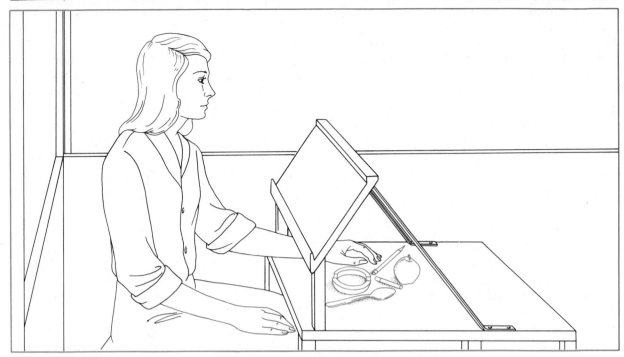

FIGURE 2.11 In split-brain experiments using touch, a subject could not identify an object hidden behind a screen by grasping it with the left hand because no information about the object reached the left hemisphere.

objects. The left hand—and right hemisphere—came up with the spoon (see Figure 2.12).

At certain tasks, the right hemisphere actually turned out to be superior to its counterpart on the left. It was better at recognizing faces and, through its control of the left hand, it was better at copying drawings and at arranging blocks to match a pictured design.

From the split-brain experiments a fascinating new picture of cerebral specialization has emerged, a picture later confirmed and extended by research using new techniques on normal subjects in which the corpus callosum is intact (Rizzollatti, Umilta, and Berlucchi, 1971). The left hemisphere appears to be verbal, analytic, and gifted in the step-by-step logic necessary for understanding science and mathematics. The right hemisphere appears to be intuitive, nonverbal, superior at spatial perception, and more attuned to art and music, where it seems able to perceive patterns as a whole.

The differences are so great that Sperry (1968) was led to hypothesize that all of us have, in effect, two brains, each with a will of its own. These two brains, connected by the corpus callosum, normally cooperate. But in the instance of the split-brain subjects, Sperry has observed, the two brains sometimes seemed to belong to "two different selves." The potential for conflict between the two hemispheres was dramatically illustrated in the behavior of one of the split-brain subjects (Gazzaniga, 1970). His two hands, directed by two separated hemispheres, had a tendency to be quarrelsome. He would sometimes attempt to pull his pants up with one hand while pulling them down with the other. In experiments involving the manipulation of blocks, his hands would similarly battle for control of the task. And on one occasion, he grabbed his wife with his left hand and shook her violently until his right hand came to her aid.

Such observations have spurred much speculation and sparked many new investigations into the relationship between cerebral specialization and the brain's highest function, consciousness itself. These issues will be described in Chapter 5.

So far, we have considered the nervous system only in terms of the control centers of behavior. We have surveyed the where of the structures of the nervous system and attempted to localize the control of the various forms of behavior. Now we must look at how the nervous system works at the most basic level.

Structures and Functions of the Neuron

The basic mechanisms of behavior can be viewed in three stages. First is the nerve cell, or neuron, the fundamental unit of all the structures of the nervous system. Second is the generation and propagation of electrical impulses within the individual neuron. Third is the transmission of those impulses between neurons. Considered together, these three stages will demonstrate the basic means by which all behavior—our every thought, feeling, sensation, action—is governed by the nervous system.

The Neuron

One of the fundamental insights in all biology was the recognition by the German scientist Theodor Schwann in 1838 that all living tissue is made up of cells. These are individual elements, typically microscopic in size, each of which usually contains its own nucleus and a surrounding membrane. The fundamental principle of neuroanatomy, called the *neuron doctrine*, which was first enunciated most

clearly in its modern form by Cajal in the 1880s, is simply an extension of Schwann's insight. The neuron doctrine is the realization that the nervous system also is made up of cells called *neurons*, and that they interact with one another.

There are billions of neurons in the central nervous system of a human being, perhaps as many as 100 billion. Practically all of these neurons are present at birth and, unlike other cells, they do not multiply. Nor can a neuron be regenerated once it dies. Because of redundancy in the nervous system, a human may lost millions of neurons during his or her lifetime without apparent effects on behavior.

Neurons come in assorted sizes and shapes. Most of them are tiny—a cubic inch of brain matter contains up to 100 million neurons. They can resemble stars, pyramids, uprooted trees, or even strangely shaped balloons on a long string. But all neurons share certain essential properties. Hence, if we comprehend the structure of a single neuron, we will have a basis for understanding all nerve cells.

Let us look at a neuron under the light microscope. This neuron belongs to nerve tissue taken from the front portion of the spinal cord. The tissue was fixed with formalin or alcohol to preserve its

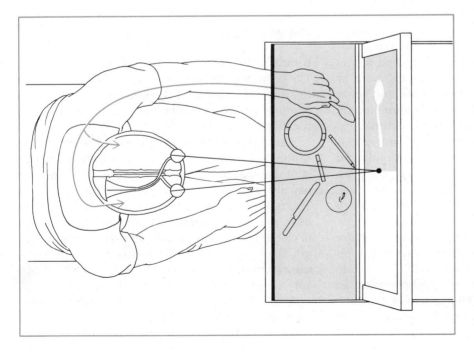

FIGURE 2.12 Visual-tactile association performed by a split-brain patient. A picture of a spoon is flashed to the right hemisphere and retrieved with the left hand from behind a screen. The touch information from the left hand projects to the right hemisphere to enable the patient to select the correct item.

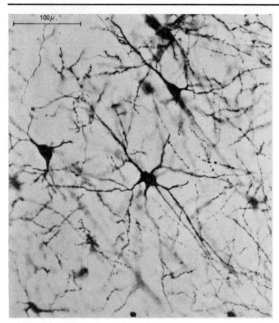

A stellate neuron with its axon, which can be seen as a fine process running from the neuron to the righthand bottom corner of the photograph.

structural features, then hardened by freezing or embedded in a solid material like wax. The tissue was then sliced into transparent sections with a guillotinelike instrument called a microtome. Finally, it was treated with one of a variety of stains, chemical agents that enable the viewer to distinguish particular features in the densely packed section of nerve cells. In this instance, the method was one favored by Cajal, the Golgi stain, a solution of silvery salts that affect only a few of the neurons, so that they stand out clearly under the microscope.

The view we see under the microscope shows the neuron's three essential parts: the cell body or *soma*, which uses oxygen and glucose and other material from the blood to manufacture protein and other materials necessary for the neuron's survival and functioning; a network of projections called *dendrites* that jut out from the cell body and receive messages from adjacent neurons; and from the other side of the body, a single long appendage known as the *axon*, which transmits messages to other neurons or to muscles and glands.

In appearance, the dendrites and axons differ in several important characteristics. Neurons typically have many dendrites but only one axon. Dendrites often branch and rebranch, forming an elegant treelike expansion. The pattern of dendritic branching varies widely among cell types and, indeed, it is usually either the pattern of dendritic branching or the shape of the cell body itself that gives classes of neurons their names. For example, two principal types of nerve cells in the cerebral cortex are the *stellate cell*, so named because the radial pattern of its dendrite branches gives it a starlike appearance, and the *pyramidal cell*, which takes its name from the pyramidal shape of its cell body.

Another significant difference between dendrites and axons is their surface texture. Whereas axons are typically smooth, dendrites are often covered with spines or thorns. These dendritic spines serve as specialized receptor surfaces for receiving information from incoming axons.

Dendrites are short, extending at most a millimeter or two. The axon, by contrast, may extend for a relatively great distance. In a tall person, the axon extending from a spinal cord neuron that controls a muscle in the foot may be more than 3 feet in length. Many axons are grouped together in bundles called *nerves*. Nerves are often thick enough to be seen by the unaided eye.

The axon originates on the nerve cell body in a gentle swelling known as the *axon hillock*. Sometimes an axon extends to its target, such as a muscle or another neuron, and ends there without branching. More commonly, it branches near the end into a number of fine *preterminal fibers* before making contact with the target neuron or muscle. A single axon may make several contacts with another neuron via that neuron's cell body or one of its dendrites. (See Figure 2.13 for a schematic diagram of a neuron.)

Electrical Activity in the Neuron

The portrait of the neuron painted above is essential to an understanding of the second element in our study of the basic mechanisms of behavior—electrical activity in the neuron.

The nervous system's basic means of communication is the *nerve impulse*, an electrically measured stimulus that travels down the axon of the neuron, usually in a direction away from the cell body. Though the nerve impulse is measured electrically, its nature differs markedly from a familiar example of electricity such as household current. It is slower, much less powerful, and depends on certain chemical characteristics of the neuron and the fluid that surrounds the neuron.

Much of what is known about the propagation of the nerve impulse along the axon derives from the research of two English neurophysiologists, Alan

FIGURE 2.13 Drawing of a typical neuron of a vertebrate animal. The neuron can carry nerve impulses for a considerable distance. The nerve impulses originate near the cell body and are propagated along the axon, which is folded here for diagrammatic purposes but would be a centimeter long at actual size. The axon's preterminal fibers form synapses with as many as 1,000 other neurons through the dendrites.

Hodgkin and Andrew Huxley (1952). Beginning in the late 1930s, Hodgkin and Huxley analyzed electrical activity in single axons taken from giant sea squids. These axons are sufficiently large so that electrodes can be inserted into them in order to study the nerve impulse. Indeed, a single squid axon is so thick that the scientist who at first discovered it mistook it for an artery.

In order to understand how the nerve impulse is transmitted down the axon, let us begin by imagining an experiment not unlike those conducted by Hodgkin and Huxley. Our hypothetical neuron, like all living cells, is surrounded by a thin membrane which encases the neuron's dendrites, cell body, and axon. There are charged molecules in fluid inside and surrounding the neuron.

Our testing apparatus consists of two fine-tipped electrodes connected to a voltmeter (see Figure 2.14). The device registers the voltage between two points. If we insert one electrode through the membrane of the neuron's axon and place the second electrode in the fluid that surrounds the neuron, a dramatic change will occur on the voltmeter. It will show an electric potential difference—or voltage—between the inside and outside of the axon. This difference is known as the *resting potential.* The inside and outside of the axon are electrically charged like the poles of a battery, with the inside of the cell negative and the outside positive. Hence, the axon is said to be polarized.

Polarization of the axon is caused by a slightly uneven distribution of electrically charged molecules, or *ions*, across the membrane. Ordinarily, ions would migrate in or out until an even distribution change across the membrane was achieved.

FIGURE 2.14 Experimental arrangement for recording axon resting potential. One electrode is inserted through the neuron's axon, and the second electrode is placed in the salt solution surrounding the neuron. The voltmeter measures the resting potential.

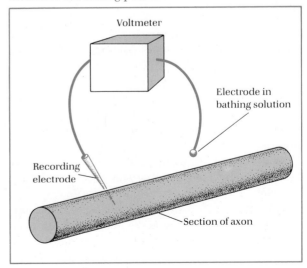

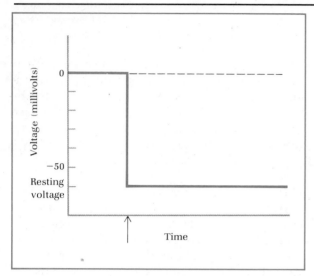

FIGURE 2.15 Resting potential across membrane of neuron. The electrode entered the axon at the time indicated by the arrow and recorded a negative charge.

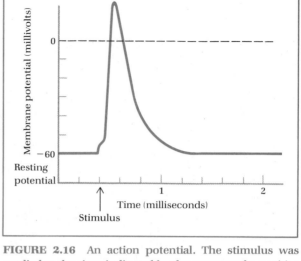

FIGURE 2.16 An action potential. The stimulus was applied at the time indicated by the arrow and a positive charge or action potential was recorded.

But when the neuron is at rest, the membrane does not permit all ions to pass through freely. For example, although the membrane does permit some sodium ions to leak into the axon from the outside, sodium is continuously pumped back out by the membrane. As a final result of the pumping of sodium ions, the inside of the axon acquires a negative charge (see Figure 2.15).

The resting potential can change quickly if the neuron is stimulated by an outside electrical force. Suddenly, the membrane becomes permeable to sodium ions, which pour into the axon, depolarizing it—changing the inside potential to positive, relative to the outside.

This sudden change can be recorded as a sudden change of voltage across the axon membrane called the *action potential* (see Figure 2.16). This occurs in a very short section of the membrane, perhaps only a few centimeters long, and it lasts a very short time—less than a millisecond (1/1,000 second). The action potential is so quick because the permeability of the axon membrane undergoes another sudden change: it stops letting in sodium ions and starts letting out potassium ions. The result is that the axon returns to its original state, that of polarization or the resting potential.

Nonetheless, the action potential has lasted long enough to affect the adjacent section of the axon membrane. It depolarizes that next patch of membrane, triggering the same sequence of changes in

permeability to the sodium and potassium ions. Hence the inside of the membrane at that point also swings briefly from negative to positive. This process of repeated action potentials begins at the axon hillock and proceeds down the length of the axon in a manner analogous to the burning of a firecracker fuse: Each patch sets off the patch next to it. Altogether, the nerve impulse at each point on the axon takes about a millisecond for completion. Then that portion of the axon is ready to begin the entire process again (see Figure 2.17).

We have not yet described how the electrical excitation of the axon actually begins in the neuron. This excitation is usually received at the neuron's dendrites. How does this excitation travel from the dendrite, through the cell body, to the beginning of the axon? The excitation depolarizes the dendrite membrane, but it usually does not spread by means of an action potential, as in the axon. Instead, it travels to the axon in a passive manner, like a ripple spreading in a pond.

It is important to note that the excitation reaching the axon hillock must be of sufficient intensity if the action potential is to be triggered there. If the excitation falls below the necessary *threshold*, no action potential will occur. By the same token, once the action potential is triggered, it does not vary much in intensity or speed along the axon no matter how strong the original excitation. In other words, the neuron either fires or it does not. When

50

it does fire, the action potential is always the same. This phenomenon is called the *all-or-none law* of nerve conduction. We will see the important implications of this law in Chapter 3 when we consider the coding of sensory messages in the nervous system. The pressure of a finger on one's skin, for example, is coded by how many neurons fire and how fast they fire. It is not controlled by the intensity of the firing, which does not change.

The speed of the nerve impulse depends, in part, on the thickness of the axon; the thicker the axon,

FIGURE 2.17 Arrows indicate the direction in which the repeated action potentials are propagated along the length of the axon. At the front of the impulse, sodium ions rush into the axon making the inside briefly positive relative to the outside. Potassium ions then rush out of the axon, restoring the resting potential. At the site of the action potential the cell membrane is depolarized, which triggers the same sequence of changes in the flow of sodium and potassium ions.

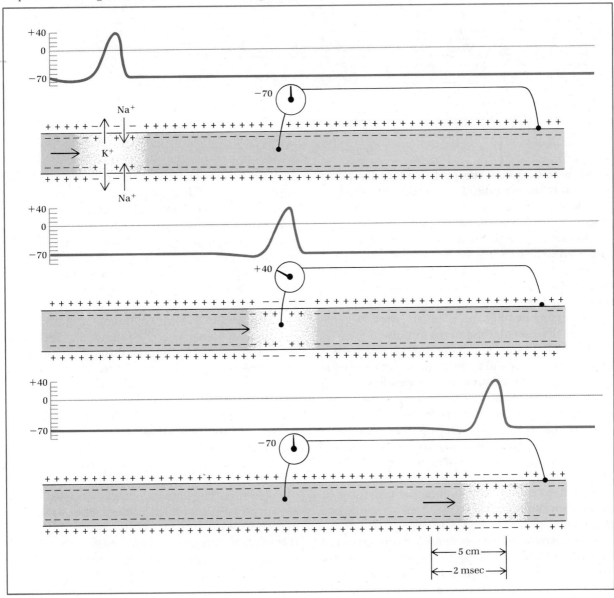

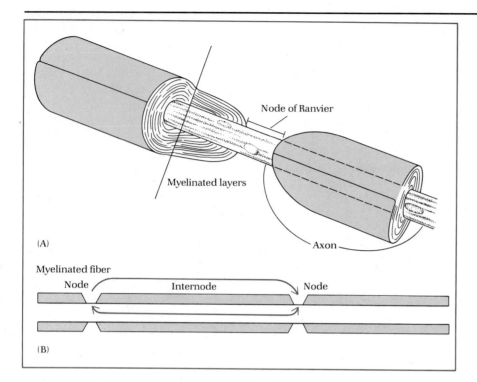

FIGURE 2.18 (a) View of myelin. The lengthwise view of a node of Ranvier shows the layers of myelin wound around the axon. (b) Saltatory conduction moves the nerve impulse very quickly along a myelinated fiber from one node of Ranvier to the next.

Node of Ranvier

Myelinated layers

(A)

Axon

Myelinated fiber

Node

Internode

Node

(B)

the faster the impulse. One probable function of the giant squid axons studies by Hodgkin and Huxley is to enable the creature to transmit fast nerve impulses. These impulses coordinate a system of jet propulsions used to escape predators. But such oversized axons cannot be accommodated in the anatomy of most creatures, including human beings. For example, human vision would require optic nerves more than an inch in diameter (and a much larger head) if axon diameter were the sole factor in the speed of the nerve impulse.

Most of the axons in the peripheral nervous system of vertebrates and many in the central nervous system have a special provision for greatly speeding up the nerve impulse. They are encased in a sheath of a fatty white substance, *myelin*, which serves to insulate the axon, preventing the free passage of sodium and potassium ions from taking place across each adjacent patch of membrane during an action potential.

How then can the action potential take place at all in a myelinated axon? If we look at the axons and its sheath under the light microscope, we can see that myelin is not continuous but is interrupted by gaps at intervals of about a millimeter or so. These gaps where the axon is left bare of myelin are the *nodes of Ranvier*, named after the nineteenth-

century French anatomist, Louis Antoine Ranvier (1871), who first described them. In a myelinated axon, an action potential can occur only at these bare nodes. Consequently, the nerve impulse leaps from node to node instead of being slowed by the laborious process of repeating action potentials across each patch of membrane. Such transmission of the nerve impulse along myelinated axons is termed *saltatory conduction*.

The speed of saltatory conduction in the fastest mammalian nerve fibers is about 225 miles per hour, approximately 20 times faster than the speed of the nerve impulse in an unmyelinated axon of the same diameter (see Figure 2.18). Thanks to saltatory conduction, for example, it takes only about 1/50 second for the nerve impulse to travel from toe to brain in the myelinated neuron that signals a touch on the big toe.

The importance of myelin to normal function becomes dramatically evident in the disease multiple sclerosis. The disease attacks the soft myelin sheath and replaces it with a hard fibrous tissue. As a consequence, timing of the nerve impulse is thrown off. Because motor pathways function poorly without precise timing, control of movement is impaired. If the disease affects nerve cells controlling respiration, it can lead to death by suffocation. Saltatory conduction probably also explains the delayed development of such motor skills as crawling and walking in human infants: the myelin sheath of many motor tracts is not fully developed until about a year after birth.

The production of myelin is one of the principal functions of a group of supportive cells found throughout the brain and nervous system. In the peripheral nervous system, they are known as *Schwann cells*, honoring Theodor Schwann (1839), the biologist who first described them. In the central nervous system, they are called *neuroglia*, or simply *glia*, from the Greek word for glue. There are so many glial cells in the brain (they outnumber neurons) that they appear to seal up the spaces between the neurons, literally sticking them together. Schwann cells and glia create the myelin sheath by fastening onto the bare axon and wrapping around it again and again.

Other functions of the supportive cells are less well-known. In the brain and spinal cord, the glial cells probably are important in nourishing the neurons and in directing their pattern of growth. One function, however, becomes graphically evident when an injury occurs in the brain. Glia proliferate rapidly in the affected region and serve as *phagocytes*, cells that eat up the debris left by the damage. Under the microscope, these cells can be seen engorged with bits of the ingested material.

Transmission of Impulses Between Neurons

Our picture of a single neuron in action has been relatively simple. A neuron becomes excited by an external stimulus, produces an action potential that is generated again and again as it passes down the axon as the nerve impulse. The voltage change of the nerve impulse is always the same in a given cell: only the frequency of firing changes. But changes in frequency are limited; during and just after each firing, the neuron is inexcitable. There is a small *refractory period* before it can fire again.

How then does the nervous system derive its unmatched complexity as a communications network? The answer lies in the remarkable manner in which nerve cells make contact with one another. Typically, such contact is made between the axon of one neuron and the cell body or dendrite of another neuron.

The Synapse The contact between the axon of one neuron and the cell body or dendrite of another

neuron is called a *synapse*. The existence of the synapse and its nature have been the subject of two of the most fascinating and bitter controversies in the history of the neural sciences. To understand both the structure of the synapse and the debates that raged around it, let us consider the neural theory that prevailed until the late nineteenth century.

In those days most scientists believed that nerve cells were physically connected to one another. Under a light microscope, sections of nerve tissue looked like a trellis network, a net or reticulum, of neurons in which axons were literally fused to dendrites or cell bodies in a continuous web. This point of view was known as the *reticular theory*. Its leading proponent was the Italian physician and anatomist Camillo Golgi (1883), who invented the staining method that bears his name.

Ironically, it was the Golgi stain that enabled Cajal to support a conflicting theory about the connections between nerve cells. Using the Golgi stain, Cajal (1909–1911) put forward evidence for the radical new theory, the neuron doctrine, that we described at the start of this chapter. The nervous system, he said, is composed of cells that make contact with one another but do not actually fuse. Cajal illustrated his theory with elegant drawings so accurate that they are still used in neuroanatomy textbooks today.

The debate between the old reticular theory and Cajal's neuron doctrine was a bitter one. Cajal could only infer the nature of the contacts between nerve cells, that is, the synapses: their structure was far too small to be seen under the light microscope. Since Cajal could not prove the existence of synapses, his old foe Golgi clung to the reticular theory. In 1906 the two men shared the Nobel Prize in medicine, but the bitterness did not abate. Cajal in his autobiography (1937) viewed Golgi's Nobel acceptance speech as an attempt to revive the reticular theory. It is said that, although they had nearby rooms in a Stockholm hotel, the two scientists passed without speaking.

Nearly half a century later, the powerful electron microscope vindicated Cajal's brilliant insight and revealed the true nature of the synapse. Under this new microscope, which can magnify up to 500,000 times, it is clear that nerve cells do not fuse; they are separated by a narrow cleft of about one millionth of an inch—a space 1,000 times smaller than the finest hair. The synapse is actually a gap.

The second great debate about the synapse concerned the nature of the activity that occurs there. If the synapse is indeed a gap, scientists asked, how does the nerve impulse from the axon of one neuron cross it to excite the adjacent neuron? In their answers, scientists tended to divide into two opposing schools: the "spark" group versus the "soup" camp (Eccles, 1964). The "spark" theorists believed that synapses worked by direct electrical coupling across the synaptic cleft in the manner of a spark crossing the cap in a spark plug. The "soup" theorists believed that the transmission of the nerve impulse across the synaptic cleft was effected by means of a chemical. We know now that both schools were right, although the "soup" theorists were closer to the truth. The great majority of synapses in the vertebrate nervous system are chemical, but there are also demonstrable examples of electrical synapses. In these rare cases in which the presence of electrical synapses has been proven, the synaptic cleft between nerve cells is much narrower than in chemical synapses. Such electri-

cal synapses are seen in certain giant neurons in the brain stem of a fish, for example.

With the insight provided by the electron microscope, let us construct a simplified picture of a typical chemical synapse (see Figure 2.19). We see an axon, which is called the *presynaptic element*, and a dendrite, or *postsynaptic element*. The membranes of these two elements are separated by the very thin *synaptic cleft*. On the presynaptic side, the tip of the axon is swollen into a knob. Inside this knob is an assemblage of tiny spheres called *synaptic vesicles*. These vesicles, each surrounded by a membrane, very likely contain an all-important chemical called a *neurotransmitter*.

Now, let us imagine the nerve impulse traveling down the length of the axon. When the nerve impulse reaches the tip of the axon, it triggers a series of events whereby the synaptic vesicles inside the axon become mobilized. They fuse with the axon's membrane and then release their tiny quantities of neurotransmitter into the synaptic cleft. Then, it is believed, the neurotransmitter diffuses across the cleft. When the neurotransmitter reaches the other side of the cleft, the postsynaptic dendrite, it binds

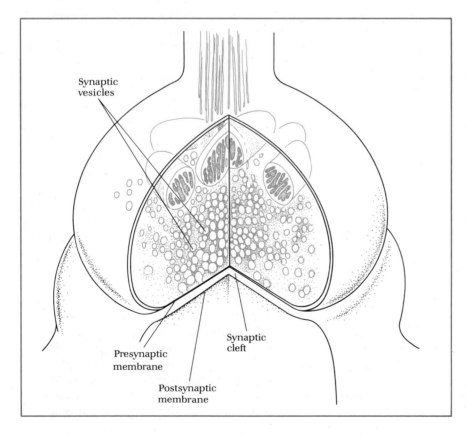

Synaptic vesicles

Presynaptic membrane

Synaptic cleft

Postsynaptic membrane

FIGURE 2.19 Simplified diagram of a synapse, the relay point where information is conveyed by chemical transmitters from neuron to neuron. A synapse consists of two parts: the knoblike tip of a presynaptic element (axon) and the receptor region of the postsynaptic element (dendrite). Chemical neurotransmitters, stored in the synaptic vesicles, are released into the synaptic cleft and depolarize the membrane of the postsynaptic neuron, which fires if the depolarization is great enough.

with special *receptor sites* on the dendrite membrane. The effect of this binding is to depolarize the membrane of the postsynaptic neurons. If the depolarization is great enough, it triggers a nerve impulse in the neuron's axon. Thus, by means of a neurotransmitter, electrical activity in one neuron is communicated to the next nerve cell in the pathway.

Neurotransmitters   The first direct evidence of neurotransmitters was discovered in the nervous system during a classic experiment carried out in 1921 by an Austrian physiologist named Otto Loewi. It has been said that the idea for the experiment came to Loewi one night during a dream. He woke up, scribbled notes for the experiment, and went back to sleep. The next morning Loewi could not decipher his own handwriting. That night, however, the same dream returned to Loewi and, when he woke up, he rushed to his basement to begin the experiment.

The experiment involved a simple preparation using the hearts from two frogs and a bundle of nerve fibers called the vagus nerve. The vagus nerve includes a group of long motor axons whose cell bodies are in the brain; these axons make contact with cells in the heart and other visceral organs. Interestingly, the heart does not require this innervation in order to function: it has its own built-in conduction system that is capable of maintaining heartbeat without input from the brain. As Loewi knew, the vagus nerve is part of the parasympathetic nervous system, and one of its functions is to slow down heartbeat. The question Loewi asked was how it did this.

Loewi placed a frog heart and its attached vagus nerve in a saline solution to keep it beating. He then stimulated the vagus nerve electrically. As he expected, the heart rate slowed down. During stimulation, Loewi collected the saline solution surrounding the heart. He found that this fluid alone, when injected into the heart, had the same effect as stimulation: it slowed down the heart. By contrast, if the saline solution was collected when the nerve had not been stimulated, it failed to slow down the heart.

Obviously, stimulation of the vagus nerve had released a substance that, when injected back into the heart, could slow it down. Loewi correctly suspected this substance was a chemical called acetylcholine, but since he could not be certain, he gave it the neutral name Vagusstoff.

Later research in the 1930s by the English biologist Henry Dale (1938) confirmed that Vagusstoff was indeed acetylcholine. Dale's work focused on the synapselike cleft between axons and voluntary muscles in the tongue of a cat and in the legs of various animals. Dale proved that acetylcholine serves as the neurotransmitter in these nerves also. The difficulty of his search for the substance at the axon endings is illustrated by his finding that a single nerve impulse in a neuron triggers the release of a very small amount of acetylcholine—only 10^{-16} gram.

Loewi (1935) had also identified a second neurotransmitter. When he stimulated a frog's sympathetic nerves, which speed up heartbeat, tiny amounts of a different transmitter, later identified as noradrenalin, were released by axon endings. Chemically, noradrenalin is a close relative of the hormone adrenalin, which is secreted by the body's adrenal gland and also has the effect of speeding up heartbeat.

The existence of neurotransmitters helps explain the effects of many drugs on the nervous system. One example is the paralysis caused by curare, the poison once applied by South American Indians to their arrow tips. Curare, it is now clear, blocks the action of acetylcholine in the synapse and thus prevents transmission of the nerve impulse. Nerve gases developed for warfare work in a different, but no less insidious, manner. Ordinarily, acetylcholine does not accumulate after crossing into the postsynaptic neuron: it is destroyed by chemical catalysts known as enzymes. In the case of acetylcholine the enzyme is called cholinesterase (Ach). But nerve gases interfere with Ach, and the resulting accumulation of neurotransmitter triggers repeated and uncontrolled firing of nerve impulses to the victim's muscles, heart, and lungs. Similarly, as we will see in Chapters 5 and 15, mood-altering drugs such as marijuana, LSD, antidepressants, and tranquilizers are capable of changing our behavior because they interfere with the synthesis, storage, release, or reuptake of neurotransmitters.

Many serious disorders of the nervous system or motor system appear to be related to the presence of too much or too little of a particular neurotransmitter. The classic instance of a deficit in neurotransmitter production is the disorder known as Parkinson's disease, which is characterized by the progressive loss of control over simple movements. Even at rest, patients with this disease exhibit uncontrollable tremors and masklike facial expressions.

For years, physicians examined during autopsy the brains of Parkinson's victims without finding definite focal damage that could account for the disease. Then, in 1959, an important clue to Parkinson's was discovered by a Swedish pharmacologist, Arvid Carlsson. He was testing the tranquilizer

RESEARCH: Studying Behavior at the Cellular Level

A fundamental aim of neurobiological research is to find precise relationships between human behavior and the activities that occur at the basic level of nerve cells. How do microscopic circuits of nerve cells, propagating minute bursts of electrical activity, enable us to walk, see, think, learn, and remember? Because simple ethics preclude tampering with the human nervous system, the search for answers typically focuses on the brains of other mammals. Cats, monkeys, and rats are among the favorite experimental animals in the research laboratories.

One problem with all of these animals is the enormous complexity of their nervous systems. Even a rat contains billions of nerve cells making trillions of connections with one another and tangled together in labryrinthine complexity. For this reason, many researchers concerned with the neural basis of behavior choose to study simple invertebrates. These creatures, such as the crayfish, insects, and snails, may have as few as 10,000 neurons. Their nerve cells are grouped in clusters called ganglia, consisting of about 500 to 2,000 cells. The ganglia are capable of fairly complex behavioral responses, and the fact that there are relatively few nerve cells makes it possible to relate the function of individual neurons directly to a particular behavior.

For nearly two decades, Eric Kandel and his associates (1970, 1976, and 1979) have been investigating the neural mechanisms of aplysia, a giant marine snail that grows to about a foot in length. In particular, they have studied the neural activities underlying the creature's gill-withdrawal response. Touching the animal in a particular place causes its gill to withdraw into a cavity for self-protection, much as the human hand pulls back reflexively from a potentially damaging stimulus such as a hot stove.

To study the neurons responsible for this reflex, Kandel made a small slit in the living animal and lifted out the abdominal ganglion, which consists of about 1,800 nerve cells, some of them nearly a millimeter in diameter. By inserting microelectrodes into various cells and firing them one at a time, he was able to identify five motor neurons that produce movements of the withdrawal reflex (see the accompanying figure).

Next, Kandel stimulated the surface of the animal's body with light brush strokes and recorded the resulting cellular electrical activity through microelectrodes. By this means, he was able to map the sensory neurons that activate the motor neurons and thus set in motion the gill-withdrawal response. All of these cells, Kandel found, are identifiable; that is, the same cells occur at the same place in every aplysia and make the same synaptic connections with one another. They also utilize the same neurotransmitters—chemicals that transmit the nerve impulse across the synaptic gap between neurons—as do cells in the human nervous system.

Now that he had a "wiring diagram" of the simple nerve circuits involved, Kandel went on to study the neural mechanisms underlying the elementary form of learning known as habituation. Habituation is the gradual decrease in behavioral response to a repeated stimulus. In effect, it is learning to ignore stimuli that have lost their novelty. Habituation occurs in aplysia when the area near the gill is touched repeatedly; after awhile, the novelty ceases and the withdrawal reflex gradually diminishes.

Kandel found that the electrical activity of the neurons paralleled behavior. Repeated stimulation of the sensory neuron caused a reduction in the electrical activity of the motor neuron. This led him to focus on the synaptic connection between the two nerve cells. He found that repeated stimulation of the sensory neuron apparently resulted in a decrease in the amount of chemical neurotransmitter released by that nerve cell into the synaptic gap. Because the transmitter triggers the firing of the nerve impulse in the neighboring motor neuron, this reduction in the amount of the transmitter would explain the habituation of the gill-withdrawal response.

In short, this rudimentary form of learning appears to result from a change in the functional effectiveness of the synaptic connection. The leap from this finding to complex learning in the brain of a human being is obviously an enormous one. But Kandel has shown that elementary aspects of mental processes can be found in just a few neurons. This is an important beginning, a significant step forward in understanding the links between behavior and activity at the cellular level.

chlorpromazine on rats and noted that the drug produced tremors closely resembling those of Parkinson's. Since the drug was known to block the action of a neurotransmitter called dopamine, Carlsson's finding suggested that the tremors might be related to a lack of dopamine. This suggestion was substantiated by autopsies performed on human victims that showed virtually no dopamine.

All of this indicated that patients might be helped if normal dopamine levels in the brain could somehow be restored. Dopamine cannot be administered directly because it does not pass freely from blood vessels into the brain. However, a researcher at Long Island's Brookhaven National Laboratory, George C. Cotzias (Cotzias, Papasilou, and Gellene, 1969), found a way around the impasse. He gave patients a drug called L-Dopa, a chemical that the brain then converts into dopamine.

The dramatic success of this combination of basic research and clinical application has been a model for further research into the mechanisms of other diseases caused by irregularities in the production or use of neurotransmitters. In fact, the dopamine story has yielded tantalizing clues about the possible physiological basis of schizophrenia, which will be discussed in Chapter 14.

In all, a dozen or more different neurotransmitters have been identified in the human nervous system. Not all of these serve to excite the postsynaptic neuron by triggering a nerve impulse. If they did, a kind of electrical storm, like a seizure of epilepsy, would constantly beset the nervous system. Some neurotransmitters serve to inhibit the firing of the nerve impulse: instead of depolarizing the membrane of the postsynaptic membrane, they hyperpolarize it, increasing the voltage outside the membrane. *Hyperpolarization* lessens the likelihood that a nerve impulse will be set off.

Several neurotransmitters are known to be both *excitatory* and *inhibitory*. Acetylcholine, for example, excites the voluntary muscles, but as we have seen in Loewi's experiment, it inhibits cells in the heart. This apparent contradiction probably results from subtle differences in the nature of the receptor sites, those areas on the postsynaptic neuron where the neurotransmitter chemically binds with the nerve cell's membrane. Receptor sites seem to recognize chemically their own particular neurotransmitter, although they can be fooled by certain drugs. In fact, recent investigations of morphine's relationship to receptor sites led to the discovery that the brain produces its own opiate-like painkillers, which apparently function as neurotransmitters (see Focus).

The fact that the neurotransmitters may be excitatory or inhibitory complicates our picture of communication within the nervous system. So, indeed, does the fact that a given neuron may make synaptic contact with many other neurons. It is estimated, for example, that some neurons in the cerebral cortex have as many as 60,000 synapses. In such cells, several different neurotransmitters may be conveying conflicting information across the synapses. Some of these messages are excitatory; they say fire. Others are inhibitory; they say do not fire. The net sum of these messages determines whether or not the neuron will fire. If this sum equals or exceeds the neuron's threshold for depolarization, it will fire a nerve impulse.

A "Wiring Diagram"

We now have seen how the nervous system works at the most basic level. Individual neurons generate nerve impulses. Then, by making functional connections at the synapse through the release of neurotransmitters, they form pathways or circuits that transmit the nerve impulse. Such circuits of neurons comprise the various structures of the nervous system and also serve to connect the structures. The motor cortex, for example, is connected to the cerebellum and other nuclei deep in the brain and thence is linked to clusters of nerve cell bodies in the spinal cord, and finally to the muscles of the arm or leg. Thus even the simplest of these circuits, involving perhaps only a few neurons, intersect with many other circuits in complex grids that resemble the intricacy of a spider's web, multiplied a millionfold. The act of jumping out of the way of an oncoming car may require the action of numerous interconnecting grids that may involve millions of neurons—circuitry concerned with seeing, hearing, feeling, memory, and, of course, movement.

The continuing challenge of the neurosciences is to map what might be called a "wiring diagram" of the nervous system, tracing the circuits neuron by neuron and relating them to behavior. This enormous task has been facilitated in recent years by the development of sensitive new laboratory techniques. One method, for example, enables scientists to record the firing of the nerve impulse in a single neuron in an animal's brain. Other methods involve the injection into live animals of radioactive substances that are taken up selectively by nerve cells. When these sections of nerve tissues are mounted on slides and coated with photographic emulsion, the radioactive substance exposes the emulsion, revealing the appropriate circuits of nerve cells.

Let us conclude our discussion of the what, where, and how of the nervous system by sketching a very rudimentary sort of wiring diagram and relating it to simple behavior. The simplest forms of behavior controlled by the nervous system are the automatic reflexes. These reflexes can occur automatically without intervention by the brain; in fact,

when Charles Sherrington (1906) made his intensive study of reflexes in the early part of this century, he worked with animals that were decerebrate; that is, the cerebrum had been surgically removed. Among the reflexes studied by Sherrington was the flexion reflex, the neural action by which a hand automatically draws back from a hot stove. Sherrington even investigated the so-called scratch reflex by devising a kind of artificial flea. He inserted a pin into the skin of a dog; when a slight electric current passed through the pin, it stimulated the nerve endings so that the dog automatically lifted its leg and began to scratch.

The simplest of these automatic actions studied by Sherrington was the stretch reflex. Sherrington

---

FOCUS: The Brain's Own Opiates

Perhaps the most remarkable discovery about the nervous system in the past decade is that it produces its own painkillers. These chemical substances are called endorphins—a contraction of two Greek words meaning "the morphine within"—because they appear to inhibit the perception of pain much in the same manner as morphine and other opiates.

The story behind this fascinating discovery begins with an understanding of how neurotransmitters function in the narrow synaptic cleft between nerve cells. When a neurotransmitter is released by the axon of one neuron, it crosses the synapse and then excites or inhibits the firing of the nerve impulse in the adjacent, or postsynaptic, neuron. The transmitter's effect on the postsynaptic neuron is assumed to occur at specific regions in the cell membrane known as receptor sites. These receptors appear to interact selectively with a given transmitter, binding with it chemically. Certain drugs can simulate the effect of a transmitter by similarly binding with its particular receptors.

In 1973, two neuropharmacologists at Johns Hopkins University, Candace Pert and Solomon Snyder, set out to determine whether morphine worked in this way. Morphine containing a radioactive substance was injected into experimental animals. If specific receptor sites existed for morphine and other opiates, they would thus become tagged with radioactive "labels." That is precisely what happened, and Pert and Snyder were able to map the location within the brain of the opiate receptors. The highest concentrations were in two different pathways of the central nervous system. One was deep

The ability of this holy man to withstand the pain of lying on a bed of nails may be related to the action of endorphins in the brain.

in the brain in the limbic system, which is involved in the regulation of mood. The other ascends from the spinal cord along the midline of the brain, and is a pathway long believed to convey sensations of chronic pain. Localization of the opiate receptors in these two pathways coincides neatly with the behavioral effects of morphine: the euphoric change in mood and the alleviation of severe pain.

These findings were fascinating, but the questions were even more intriguing. Why do opiate receptors exist in all vertebrates studied, including the hagfish, which evolved some 350 million years ago? Would evolution have provided us with special receptors that modify mood and alleviate pain just in case we might discover the healing effects of poppy's juice?

showed that when a muscle is stretched it will contract forcefully. A familiar example of the stretch reflex is the knee jerk, which physicians often test to determine whether there is damage to the spinal cord. The physician uses a rubber hammer to tap the knee just below the kneecap. Tapping the knee stretches the muscles of the upper thigh. The response in the healthy nervous system is powerful: the leg jerks up instantly, on its own. The stretch reflex enables muscles to adjust immediately to sudden changes in load. When an actor in a television Western leaps onto the back of a horse, it is the stretch reflex that keeps the poor animal from collapsing.

For our purposes here, the stretch reflex is sig-

nificant because it reveals, in miniature, the fundamental mechanisms of the nervous system. In essence, the knee jerk can be understood in terms of only two nerve cells—a sensory neuron and a motor neuron—connected by a single synapse. These two neurons form the circuit. It is a simple loop beginning at the quadriceps muscle on the top of the thigh, traveling up to the base of the spinal cord, and then circling back to the original muscle.

Now, with this wiring diagram, we can follow the neural basis of the knee jerk (see Figure 2.20). The tap of the rubber hammer stretches the muscle

---

One obvious possibility was that the receptors existed to serve some morphinelike substance, probably a neurotransmitter, that occurred naturally in the brain. Soon afterward, a group of investigators in Scotland (Hughes, Smith, Kosterlitz, Fothergill, Morgan, and Morris, 1975), succeeded in isolating two morphinelike substances from the brain of the pig. It was found that these two substances bind selectively to the opiate receptor sites mapped at Johns Hopkins. Meanwhile, other morphinelike chemicals had been found in the pituitary gland of various mammals, including camels (Li and Chung, 1976).

The biological function of these latter substances is still something of a mystery because hormones secreted by the pituitary gland apparently do not function directly in the central nervous system. Nonetheless, all the endorphins seem closely related to opiates in a number of ways. They are similar in chemical structure, they bind to opiate receptor sites, they modify response to chronic pain, and they exert a pronounced effect on mood. Evidence suggests that the two endorphins found in the brain are neurotransmitters that serve to inhibit or excite transmission of the nerve impulse. For one thing, they are highly concentrated in nerve endings—the tip of the axon where neurotransmitters normally accumulate.

Discovery of the endorphins has stimulated a number of new suggestions about the physiological mechanisms of behavior (Wei and Loh, 1976). Some researchers now think that certain psychiatric disorders may result from an abnormality in the brain's

level of endorphins. It also has been suggested that endorphins might somehow account for certain unusual reactions to pain that long have intrigued psychologists. Among these are the familiar instances of badly wounded soldiers who seem indifferent to pain during the heat of the battle and of religious holy men who walk on searing coals without complaint.

The endorphins also suggest a neurological basis for human addiction to opiates such as morphine and heroin. Perhaps the presence of morphine at the opiate receptors signals neurons to stop releasing their own "opiates," the endorphins. To make up for this lack, more and more of the morphine would have to be taken just to maintain a constant state at the opiate receptors. Then, if morphine is withdrawn, the receptors would lack both the drug and the endorphins and would signal the body to exhibit such symptoms of drug withdrawal such as shaking and diarrhea.

Although the discovery of endorphins initially raised hopes for the synthesis of a chemically similar painkiller that would be nonaddictive, the history of analgesics is not encouraging. When heroin was first synthesized in the late nineteenth century, it was hailed as a nonaddictive substitute for morphine. And the results of early tests of various endorphins similarly give little cause for hope. Experimental rats were injected with repeated dosages of endorphins. After the injections were stopped, the rats suffered all the physical withdrawal symptoms of human drug addicts.

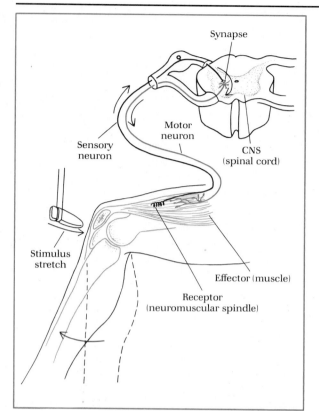

FIGURE 2.20 Wiring diagram of the stretch reflex. The tap of the hammer stretches the muscle, which, in turn, stretches the neuromuscular spindle. This stimulation excites the sensory neuron, which sets off a nerve impulse in the motor neuron causing the muscle to contract and the leg to jerk up.

slightly. This, in turn stretches a fiber from the sensory neuron that is wrapped like a tentacle around a specialized muscle cell, called the muscle spindle. The stimulation excites the sensory neuron, setting off the interchange of sodium and potassium ions across the cell membrane and triggering the nerve impulse in the axon. The axon tip releases neurotransmitter into the synapse separating it from the dendrite of the motor neuron. The neurotransmitter sets off the nerve impulse in the motor neuron. The axon of the motor neuron releases its neurotransmitter, acetylcholine, into the gap between neuron and muscle. This same process, occurring simultaneously in perhaps hundreds of simple two-neuron loops, causes the muscle to contract and the leg to jerk up.

From this simple beginning, we will turn in later chapters to explorations of the circuitry that control far more complex functions of the nervous system such as seeing, feeling, and remembering.

SUMMARY

1. The nervous system consists of two major subdivisions: the central nervous system and the peripheral nervous system. The spinal cord and the brain make up the central nervous system, and the peripheral nervous system is made up of groups of nerves cells called ganglia, and nerve fibers that lie outside of the central nervous system. Nerve fibers in both systems are called axons—long processes of nerve cells that conduct nerve impulses. The central and peripheral nervous systems are complexly interrelated.

2. The central nervous system regulates and controls the entire body. The brain and spinal cord are highly protected, by bone and by three membranes, or meninges: the dura mater, the arachnoid, and the pia mater. Among the fibers that make up the spinal cord are afferent nerves that carry sensations from the sense organs, or receptors, to the brain. Efferent nerves or effectors, carry messages from the brain, down the spinal cord, to the muscles and glands.

3. The peripheral nervous system transmits information between the various body organs and the central nervous system and is made up of the somatic and autonomic nervous systems. The autonomic nervous system is made up of, in turn, the sympathetic and parasympathetic nervous systems.

4. The brain stem is composed of nerve cells and fibers. The lowest part of the brain stem is the medulla, and just above it is the pons. These centers control automatic functions such as heart rate and respiration. The midbrain is situated at the top of the brain stem. Just above the midbrain are the pineal and pituitary glands which, although not composed of nerve cells, regulate body chemistry, influence behavior, and are considered functional parts of the brain. Attached to the rear of the brain at the level of the pons is the cerebellum, which helps to maintain body equilibrium and to coordinate fine movements.

5. Two cerebral hemispheres form the cerebrum, whose wrinkled, gray surface, the cerebral cortex, and its associated fiber system, makes up about four fifths of the brain's volume and weight. Within the cerebrum are the thalamus, a relay station for sensory impressions; the hypothalamus, governor of the autonomic nervous system and regulator of body temperature, appetite, thirsts, and sexual activities; and the limbic system which, along with

the hypothalamus, is involved in intense emotions such as anger, fear, and pleasure.

6. Each hemisphere of the cerebral cortex is demarcated by fissures into four distinct regions, or lobes: (1) the occipital lobe, which processes the sensation of vision, (2) the parietal lobe, which monitors skin sensations and location of the body's limbs; (3) the temporal lobe, which is concerned with hearing and the understanding of language; and (4) the frontal lobe, which receives the sensations of smell and contains the motor cortex.

7. The motor cortex, stretched around the curving surface of the cerebral cortex, controls movements. The association areas make up the rest, and the bulk, of the cortex.

8. Not only the brain but also most of the nervous system is bilaterally symmetrical. Because of the crossover of nerve fiber tracts within the spinal cord and brain, each side of the brain controls the opposite side of the body: movement of the left hand is largely controlled by the right hemisphere of the brain. The specialization of one or the other hemisphere (as evidenced in handedness) is known as cerebral dominance. The left, or major, hemisphere appears to control verbal, analytic, and mathematical skills; the right, or minor, hemisphere, appears to control intuitive, nonverbal, and spatial perception skills. The two cerebral hemispheres are connected by a band of nerve fibers, the corpus callosum.

9. The principal functional units of the nervous system, numbering in billions, are neurons, and they interact by contacting one another. Most neurons have three essential parts. The cell body, or soma, a network of projections called dendrites, and the appendage known as the axon. Typically, the axon of one neuron makes contacts with another neuron via that neuron's cell body or one of its dendrites.

10. The nervous system's basic means of communication is the nerve impulse or action potential, an electrical wave that travels down the axon of the neuron away from the cell body. The action potential involves the successive passage of charged sodium and potassium ions through the axon's membrane. Insulation provided by the myelin sheath surrounding some axons speeds up the nerve impulse.

11. Neurons do not actually fuse. Neurotransmitters, chemical intermediaries, activate neurons across a very narrow gap, the synapse. The neurotransmitter diffuses across the synaptic cleft and binds with receptor sites on the dendrite membrane of the next neuron. This binding depolarizes the membrane and triggers a nerve impulse in the neuron's axon. Thus, by means of a neurotransmitter, electrical activity in one neuron is communicated to the next nerve cell in the pathway.

12. A dozen or more different neurotransmitters have been identified in the human nervous system. Some are excitatory, and trigger the nerve impulse; some are inhibitory, and retard the nerve impulse; several neurotransmitters are known to be both excitatory and inhibitory.

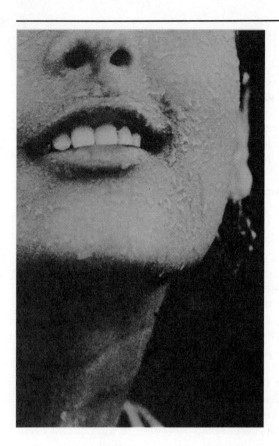

Chapter 3
Sensation

The wages were good, and the work was easy. The student volunteers at McGill University had only to lie around for a few days in an isolation chamber (Bexton, Heron, and Scott, 1954). The volunteers lay on a cot wearing translucent goggles over their eyes to filter out most of the light, with steady and unvarying hum from fans and an air conditioner in the room, heavy gloves on their hands, and cardboard mailing tubes on their arms. The experiment aimed to see what happens when we are largely deprived of sensations: the vision, hearing, and touch that ordinarily enrich our lives.

This sensory deprivation proved so difficult for the subjects that a few quit before the first day was over. The students who stayed on underwent stressful, even frightening experiences. They had difficulty with motor coordination, could not solve simple problems, and found it almost impossible to concentrate. Many experienced visual and auditory hallucinations. One saw a parade of marching squirrels; another heard a church choir.

Most of us have tried to imagine at one time or another what it would be like to be blind or deaf. But these volunteers and others in subsequent experiments learned what it is like to have their main windows to the world closed. They could not see or hear or touch, and without these essential sensations they temporarily lost some emotional balance and mental equilibrium.

In this chapter we will examine the sensory mechanisms through which we keep in touch with the world and our body's place in it. These mechanisms include seeing, hearing, the chemical senses (smell and taste), the skin senses (touch, temperature, and pain), and the sense of position and movement. For our purposes here, *sensation* is the process by which we receive and code a stimulus such as a spot of light or a musical tone. Perception, on the other hand, which will be discussed in Chapter 4, is the process by which we recognize a pattern such as the familiar face of a friend.

Characteristics of the Senses

All of the senses, no matter how diverse, share certain characteristics. These characteristics hold true even for the senses peculiar to some animals, which receive information about their world in fascinating and sometimes bizarre ways (see Focus).

All sensation can be described in three stages: stimulation, detection, and neural coding. To begin with, there must be some form of physical or chemical energy such as light or odor to stimulate the sensory mechanisms. Specialized organs such as the eye or nose receive or detect that energy. Finally, a means of converting the energy into a code understood by the central nervous system must exist.

Stimulation

The type of stimulus to which a sense organ normally responds is called the *adequate stimulus*. The adequate stimulus for the eye is the range of electromagnetic radiation that we call light. Why do we see light and not hear it? One of the fundamental principles of sensory coding was formulated by Johannes Müller during the nineteenth century (Müller, 1838/1948). His *law of specific nerve energies*, in its modern interpretation, simply states that only one kind of sensation is transmitted over a given nerve fiber. Axons in the optic nerve, for example, carry spike potentials to the visual centers of the brain, which, in turn, interpret the signals as visual information. This is not to imply, however, that only light can serve as the stimulus for visual information. A punch in the eye will indeed make the victim "see stars." You can experience a less painful demonstration if you poke gently at the corner of your eyes with a fingertip. Two sensations occur. You feel the sense of touch as a result of the pressure on the skin around the eye. You may also perceive a hazy blob of light because the pressure also activates the visual mechanisms. The important point is that even though visual fibers may be activated by a stimulus other than light, the brain perceives that activation as caused by light. Müller's reasoning led to the assumption of a direct link between the peripheral sensory organs and specific cortical neurons.

Detection

The remarkable structures that detect the physical and chemical stimuli are called receptors. Receptors come in various forms. They are either modified nerve endings or specialized nonneural cells that contact a nerve ending. Good examples of the nonneural type are the light-sensitive receptors of the eye. Although not actually neurons, these photoreceptors have special properties that enable them to respond electrically to changes in light intensity. In other cases, just as the skin responds to touch, temperature, and pain, the receptors may be elaborate connective tissue structures that encase the endings of nerve fibers, or they may be the free endings of the nerve fibers themselves.

Neural Coding

In addition to detecting the stimulus, receptors have a second key function: they convert, or transduce, that physical energy into the nervous system's language—electric signals or codes. This process resembles the generation of nerve impulses described in detail in Chapter 2. To review, the stimulus causes a change in the ionic permeability of the receptor's membrane. In most cases the stimulus depolarizes the receptor. The depolarization in response to a stimulus is called a *generator potential*. The generator potential is usually continuously variable over a range of values: the more intense the stimulus, the bigger the generator potential. If the generator potential reaches and maintains a certain threshold of intensity, it in turn creates a series of nerve impulses, or action potentials, that travel down the fiber of the sensory neuron. At the junction between the sensory neuron and the next cell in the pathway, the nerve impulse causes the release of a chemical, the neurotransmitter. This action across the synapse serves either to excite or inhibit the next neuron. By successive connections across one or more synapses, sensory information is brought from the periphery into the brain and within the brain to the cerebral cortex. In some cases the same cell does two jobs; it detects the sensory stimulus and codes it into a train of action potentials. In other cases the receptor cell does not fire action potentials but can produce them in subsequent cells to which it is connected. The rods and cones of the eye, for example, do not fire action potentials, nor do the next cells within the eye, the bipolar cells. But eventually all sensory information that reaches the brain must do so by a train of action potentials. In the eye it is the third cell in the pathway, the retinal ganglion cell, that fires action potentials.

Receptors vary in their response to the sensory stimulus. Some will maintain their generator potential and keep firing impulses as long as the stimulus is present. They are known as *sustained receptors.* Others, known as *transient receptors*, fire when the stimulus is first applied but quickly return to their normal state, the resting potential, even if the stimulus is maintained.

How does the firing of the receptor code the intensity of the stimulus? How can this process convey the apparent loudness of a noise? As we saw in Chapter 2, it cannot mirror the stimulus intensity by the size, or amplitude, of its action potential. Under the all-or-none law of nerve-impulse propagation, the voltage change of the action potential is always the same; only the frequency of the firing varies. Nerve cells in the sensory pathways thus usually represent the intensity of the stimulus only by firing more frequently.

Psychophysics

The branch of psychology concerned with the measurement of relationships between the physical attributes of stimuli and the resulting sensations is called *psychophysics.* Psychophysicists were interested in studying how the physical characteristics of a stimulus, such as its intensity, would affect a person's sensory impression, or judgment, of that aspect of the stimulus. For example, they would be interested in finding out how a person's impression of the brightness of a light would change when a 100-watt bulb was replaced with a 200-watt bulb.

Sensory Thresholds

Sensory thresholds are the levels at which a stimulus or changes in a stimulus can be detected. They are a major concern of psychophysicists. How much sugar (amount of stimulus) must be put into a glass of water before we can first taste its sweetness? How much more intense must the second of two tones (change in stimulus) be before it sounds louder than the first?

Absolute Thresholds The minimal level of intensity at which we can perceive a sensation is the *absolute threshold.* Suppose an experimenter sets the intensity of a tone well below the level at which you can hear it. The intensity is gradually raised until you say, "I hear it." The tone is then set well above that particular level and then decreased gradually until you say, "I don't hear it." In both cases, that point of transition between hearing and not hearing is your absolute threshold for sound intensity.

Table 3.1 shows approximate absolute thresholds for several different senses. As you can see, the human senses are, appropriately enough, remarkably sensitive. For example, with normal vision on a dark clear night, you can probably spot a candle flame 30 miles away. It is important to note, however, that the figures listed are only approximate. Absolute thresholds may not be precisely the same from individual to individual and even may vary slightly for the same observer on different occasions.

Most surprising is the fact that at extremely low levels of intensity the stimulus itself may vary and that such variability can affect threshold measurements. An example is the stimulus for vision—light. Light can be thought as tiny particles of energy, called *quanta.* We might assume that the same light source, say a light bulb, would emit the same number of quanta per second whenever it is switched on. But there is an inherent variability in the number of quanta given off by a light source. Normally this variance is very small when compared to the total number of quanta. But at very low levels of light intensity, this variance in the number of quanta that are emitted in a given time adds variability to any measurement of the absolute threshold. The human eye is so sensitive that at the threshold for vision much of the apparent variability in threshold is really due to this inherent variability in the number of quanta emitted by the light.

Although most psychophysical experiments are carried out with human subjects, the same sorts of procedures are applied to animals. For example, Donald Blough (1956) set out to determine the ab-

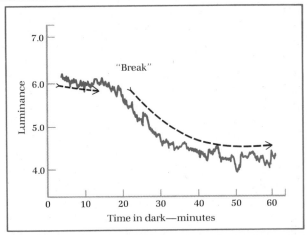

FIGURE 3.1 Sample dark-adaptation curve from one pigeon in a single hour obtained in a series of experiments by Blough. The curve can be separated into two continuous segments joined at a rather sharp "break." The run began with the stimulus at a superthreshold luminance (not shown), and the responses in the first three minutes were all to Key A, which served only to reduce the luminance to threshold.

solute threshold at which pigeons perceive light. He trained pigeons to peck a key for food reward in a box containing two keys. The animal pecked at Key A when the light was on and Key B when the light was off. The electronic circuit was arranged so that Key A not only recorded the fact of pecking but also lowered the intensity of the light. Key B recorded the pecking and increased the illumination. Figure 3.1 shows a representative curve traced by Blough's pigeons, illustrating changes in the sensitivity of their visual system when tested in a dark chamber. With a similar procedure, other researchers have measured the absolute thresholds for hearing, touch, and pain as well as vision in a large number of animals.

Difference Thresholds The absolute threshold describes only the minimal level of intensity at which we can perceive a sensation. But we also have the ability to discriminate between two stimuli of different intensities. The smallest difference between two stimuli that can be discriminated reliably is the *difference threshold.* The nineteenth-century German physiologist Ernst Weber (1978) pioneered the scientific study of difference thresholds in experiments based on lifting small weights. If a subject could discriminate between a 51-ounce weight and a 50-ounce weight, the difference threshold was 1 ounce.

TABLE 3.1 Absolute Thresholds for Several Different Senses

APPROXIMATE ABSOLUTE THRESHOLDS

Sensory Modality	Threshold
Vision	A candle flame at 30 miles on a dark, clear night
Hearing	The tick of a watch at 20 feet in a quiet roon
Taste	One ounce of quinine sulfate in 250 gallons of water
Smell	One drop of perfume diffused throughout a six-room house
Touch	Wing of a bee falling on the cheek from a distance of 1 centimeter

The 1 ounce was the *just noticeable difference,* or *jnd*. Weber found that over a surprisingly wide range, the difference threshold, or jnd, tended to be a constant ratio to the intensity of the stimulus. Thus, if it takes another ounce for a subject to tell the difference between 50 ounces and the next heavier weight, we would have to add 2 ounces for the subject to tell 100 ounces from 102, the next weight that could be felt to be heavier. *Weber's law* can be expressed as a formula: $\Delta I/I = K$, where ΔI stands for the change in intensity, I is the intensity of the reference stimulus, and K is a constant. In the example given if $I = 50$ ounces, $\Delta I = 1$ ounce; hence $\Delta I/I = 1/50$. The law says that this ratio will be constant no matter what value of I we choose. Weber's law works reasonably well for a number of senses and over a wide range of intensities, although it is usually inaccurate for stimuli with intensities that are either very small or very large.

Psychophysical Scales

Weber's work helped lead to a proposed solution to a problem that had troubled nineteenth-century researchers: how to measure precisely the relationship between the intensity of a stimulus and the intensity of the resulting sensation. This problem arose because it was clear there was not a one-to-one relationship between stimulus intensity and sensation magnitude. Doubling the physical intensity of a sound, for example, does not mean that we will perceive it as twice as loud.

Researchers needed a general principle for formulating scales that would relate stimulus intensity to its psychological magnitude, that is, how strongly we perceive the intensity of the stimulus. The clues for such a scale were found in Weber's law. Suppose that all difference thresholds, or jnds, were of roughly equal psychological magnitudes. For example, in the discrimination of weight differences, suppose that 1 ounce added an equal amount of "heaviness" to a 50-ounce weight as 2 ounces added to a 100-ounce weight. One added ounce would be equal in psychological magnitude to 2 added ounces depending on how much we were adding it to. We could construct a scale in which equal increments of psychological magnitude were based on the jnd at each stimulus value. Reasoning this way from Weber's law, the German physicist and philosopher Gustav Fechner derived in 1860 just such a scale. His solution climaxed a decade of Herculean effort by Fechner who, by his own account, made no fewer than 24,576 separate judg-

ments of difference thresholds using various small weights. Fechner also conducted numerous experiments investigating the just noticeable differences between varying stimulus intensities of both light and sound.

Fechner's law states that the relationship between stimulus intensity and the strength of sensation is a logarithmic one in which a constant ratio of stimulus produces a constant difference in sensation. This logarithmic relationship between stimulus intensity and sensation is a logical consequence of treating just noticeable differences as psychological equivalent units.

By using more direct methods of estimating the relationship between stimulus intensity and the magnitude of sensation, S. S. Stevens has shown that Fechner's law is not as generally applicable as it once was thought to be. Stevens presented subjects with a series of stimuli to which they had to assign numbers proportional to the corresponding subjective impressions of sensations (Stevens, 1957). For example, he would present subjects with a stimulus of a certain light intensity and tell them it had a brightness of 10. Then he would present another light intensity and ask them to assign it a number indicating its brightness relative to the first light. If subjects believed the second light was twice as bright as the first, they would assign it the number 20; if they thought it was half as bright as the first, they would assign it the number 5. Using this method, Stevens found that increases in light intensity produce progressively smaller changes in perceived brightness—the same general conclusion that Fechner drew. However, he also found that this relationship is not true for all types of stimuli. Doubling of an electric shock, for example, results in considerably more than a mere doubling in the reported sensation. As a result of numerous studies with different senses, Stevens concluded that the relationship between stimulus intensity and magnitude of sensation differs for each sense but remains constant over a wide range of stimulus intensities for a single sensory system. He summarized his findings in what is known as *Stevens' Power Law*, which states that the magnitude of a sensation is equal to the physical magnitude of the stimulus producing the sensation raised to a certain power, which varies depending on the sensation that is being measured (Stevens, 1961).

Although Stevens' law appears to be more accurate than Fechner's, many of Fechner's lasting contributions to psychophysics, a term that he coined, cannot be underestimated. He showed that psychological processes could be measured and, in doing so, gave the study of sensation its first tools. In addition his law also indicated a compression in perceptual capabilities as stimulus intensity increases. This compression reflects the fact that the nervous system can effectively code and discriminate a very wide range of stimulus intensities.

Signal Detection Theory

As we noted earlier, the measurement of absolute and difference thresholds is subject to human variability. Suppose you are the subject of a psychophysical experiment. You sit in a quiet room with a pair of earphones on. Every so often, a warning light flashes in front of you after which a tone may or may not be presented to you through the earphones. If you hear a tone, you say, "yes"; if not, you say, "no."

When the tone is very weak and close to your absolute threshold for sound, factors other than its intensity may affect your performance. Your expectations, your fatigue, your desire to please the experimenter, and your personal caution all may cause you to miss the tone or even to report hearing a tone when there is none. The researcher's instructions can also affect your responses. If you are told to report a tone even when you are uncertain (lenient criteria), you will tend to report more tones. On the other hand, if you are told not to report a tone when you are uncertain (strict criteria), you will tend to report fewer tones. In addition, background noise and stimulation from within, such as the throbbing of the pulse, can also interfere with your responses.

To separate out these factors and obtain a clear picture of how well a given stimulus can be detected, psychophysicists often have used a method called *signal detection theory* (Green and Swets, 1966). On a large number of trials in which the stimulus is presented at different intensities, the experimenter calculates the number of "hits" (the stimulus is present and the subject correctly identifies it) and "false alarms" (the stimulus is not present but the subject erroneously says it is). The percentages of "hits" versus "false alarms" are then plotted on a graph. The resulting plot is called a *ROC curve*—for *receiver operating characteristic* (see Figure 3.2). Giving subjects strict criteria might

shift their performance from the top part to the bottom part of the curve labeled d′ = 1. In contrast, a slight increase in stimulus intensity alone might shift performance from the point where 0.9 hits intersects with 0.6 false alarms on curve d′ = 1 to the point where 0.9 hits intersects with 0.3 false alarms on curve d′ = 2, which represents the stimulus of greater intensity. The higher the value of d′, the closer subjects can come to perfect discrimination (where the proportion of hits equals 1 and the proportion of false alarms equals 0). Thus d′ is a measure of the subjects' sensitivity that is independent of the researcher's instructions.

Signal detection theory was developed by scientists studying detectability of signals on a radar screen but has proved useful in many other contexts. It provides a handy way of analyzing the detectability of a sensory stimulus and the reliability of a human observer in a great number of detection tasks.

Whatever senses are measured and however they are measured, all follow a common path from stimulation, to detection, to neural coding. In the next section we shall examine in some detail just how the specific senses—sight, hearing, smell and taste, skin sensations, and movement and position—follow this three-stage pattern.

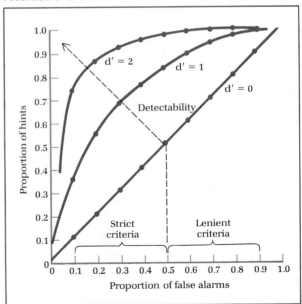

FIGURE 3.2 Signal detection theory is demonstrated in this ROC (receiver operating characteristic) curve. The number of "hits" and number of "false alarms" are recorded over numerous trials at different intensities.

Vision

We begin our study of the specific senses with vision for two reasons. First, much of our knowledge about the world around us comes to the brain via the eyes. Second, because of its obvious importance, researchers have devoted more effort to studying the mechanisms of vision than any other sensation. As a result, our understanding of how we see, although far from complete, exceeds our knowledge of any other sense.

Visual Stimulation: The Nature of Light

The stimulus for vision is light, a type of electromagnetic energy. Such energy can be thought of as traveling in waves. Wavelengths vary enormously, and the relative lengths of the waves determine the place in the spectrum of a given type of electromagnetic energy (see Figure 3.3 and Plate 1). At one end of the *electromagnetic spectrum* (the entire range of wavelengths or frequencies of electromagnetic radiation) are radio waves that may be many miles in length. At the other end are the shortest cosmic rays (gamma rays), which measure about 10 trillionths of an inch. Neither are visible to the eye.

Somewhere in between radio waves and cosmic rays is the narrow range of the electromagnetic spectrum that we can see: the *visible spectrum.* The wavelengths of light are measured in units called *nanometers.* A nanometer is one billionth of a meter. The visible spectrum ranges from wavelengths measuring about 400 nanometers to those of about 700 nanometers. In other words, that range

of electromagnetic energy activates the light-sensitive receptors of the human eye (see Research: "How Much Light Do We Need for Seeing?").

Structure of the Eye

If an animal such as a white rat is killed and its eye removed, an interesting observation can be made. We can hold its eye up to a brightly lit scene and, at the back of the eye, a tiny image of the scene appears. The image is reversed: it is upside down and backwards. Precisely the same sort of reversed image is formed at the back of the human eye by our own vision. How is the image formed at the back of the eye? How is it converted into signals that can be interpreted by the nervous system? How are those signals conveyed to the brain and to what part?

To understand the answers to those questions, let us consider in detail the structure of the eye and how it responds to light (see Plate 4). For simplicity's sake, we can liken the structure of the eye to the workings of an ordinary camera. As Figure 3.4 shows, light passes through the *cornea*, a transparent tissue, and through the hole formed by a structure called the *iris.* The iris changes shape to make the hole, called the *pupil*, larger and smaller. Like the aperture setting of a camera, the pupil regulates the amount of light by constricting (getting smaller) and dilating (getting larger). The light entering the eye is focused by the cornea and the *lens*—suspended by ligaments within the eye—

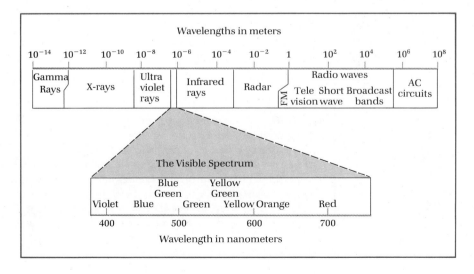

FIGURE 3.3 The total electromagnetic spectrum. The portion of the spectrum that is normally visible to the human eye, which occupies a rather narrow band of wavelengths, has been enlarged in the lower portion of the diagram.

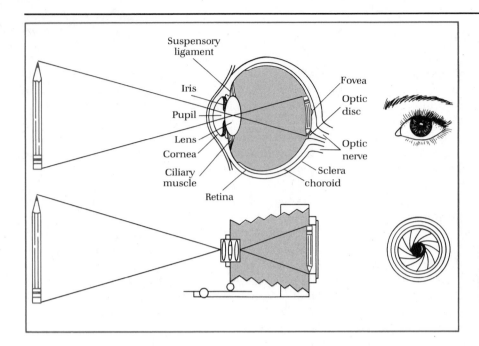

working together. Muscles within the eye can change the shape, or curvature, of the lens and hence the focus as objects approach or recede. This process is called *accommodation* (see Figure 3.5). As we view objects at close distances the lens becomes fatter; as we view distant objects it flattens. Finally, as in a camera, the light is focused onto a light-sensitive surface—the *retina.*

The eye does not really look like nor operate as simply as a camera, of course. As Figure 3.6 shows, it is basically a sphere that bulges a bit at the front. The bulge is filled with a watery fluid, *aqueous*

humor, and most of the interior of the sphere is filled with a transparent jellylike substance, *vitreous humor*. These substances help maintain the shape of the eye, which is critical to precise vision. In fact, most defects in vision result from abnormalities in the shape of the eyeball. If the eye is too long, the cornea and lens focus images slightly in front of the retina and distant objects appear fuzzy. This is nearsightedness. If the eyeball is too short, images are focused behind the retina and nearby objects are blurred. This is farsightedness.

The sphere is made up of three layers of tissue. The outermost layer, or white of the eye, is the *sclera*—from the Greek for "hard." The sclera is the major structural element of the eye, providing its firm outer framework. At the front, the sclera is modified to form the transparent cornea, through which we can see the colored iris with its pupil in the middle. The middle layer, the *choroid*, is a

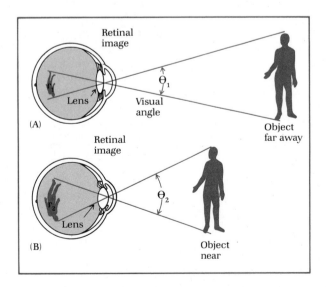

FIGURE 3.5 Two examples of optic arrays from objects, along with their retinal images. Only lines from the extremities of the objects are shown. In (A) the object is far away, so the visual angle is small and a correspondingly small image is projected on the retina. In (B) the object is closer, so there is a larger visual angle and a larger retinal image. To provide a sharp focus on the retina the lens has to change its curvature—a process called accommodation—so that it becomes thicker for close objects and thinner for distant ones.

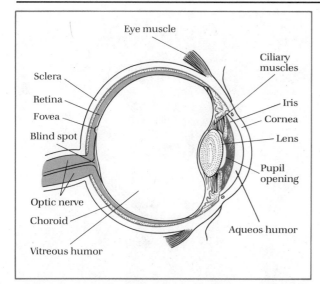

FIGURE 3.6 The eye is a complicated structure with many parts. Its purpose is to present an optical image of the world to the retina, where that image is transformed into nerve impulses.

dark-pigmented lining, rich in blood vessels, that serves to keep out all light except for that which enters through the pupil. The innermost layer contains the retina—the structure where light is converted into electric signals and transmitted to the brain.

The Retina The word *retina* derives from the Latin for "net" and, indeed, it is a net of millions of cells that, in connections and in function, resembles the neurons of the brain. The cells of the retina are clumped into three distinct layers (see Figure 3.7). One layer consists of the *rods* and *cones*, the light-sensitive receptor cells that receive and detect the electromagnetic energy, light, and convert it into neural signals. The second layer is the *inner nuclear layer*, consisting of *horizontal cells*, the *bipolar cells*,

and *amacrine cells*. These cells of the inner nuclear layer organize the information that comes from the rods and cones and transmit it to the third layer, the *ganglion cells*. Fibers projecting from the ganglion cells bundle together to form the optic nerve, which carries the electrical signals to the brain.

As we look at a microscopic view of the retina, there appears to be a paradox in the arrangement

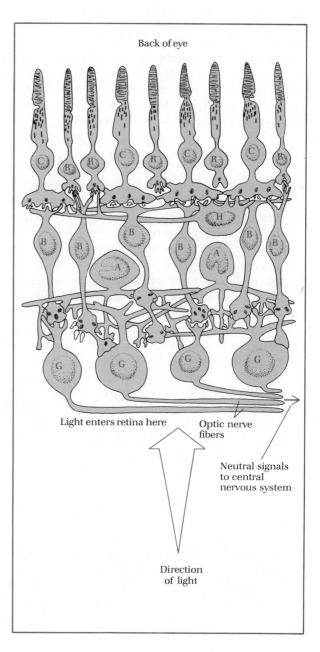

FIGURE 3.7 Light entering the retina first filters through three layers of cells. It first passes through the rods (R) and cones (C) where it is converted into neural signals. These neural signals then pass through the inner nuclear layer consisting of horizontal cells (H), bipolar cells (B), and amacrine cells (A), which organizes the information and transmits it to the third layer of ganglion cells (G). Fibers projecting from the ganglion cells bundle together to form the optic nerve, which carries the signals to the brain.

of the three layers of cells. The rods and cones, which are the receptors, are farthest from the light, and their tips, which contain photosensitive chemicals, face away from the light. In order to reach them, the light has to penetrate a network of blood vessels, the ganglion cell layer, and the inner nuclear layer. This strange arrangement makes sense, however. All of the layers except for the blood vessels are transparent and hence present no obstacle to the passage of light. And, as we shall see later, the eye has an ingenious mechanism that renders the blood vessels invisible. Moreover, the positioning of the rods and cones permits their tips to come into intimate contact with the *pigment epithelium*, a single cell lining between the rods and cones and the choroid, the middle layer of structures surrounding the eyeball. The pigment epithelium has three important functions: it absorbs stray light, it serves as a metabolic channel for nourishment of the receptors and, as has recently been discovered, it plays a role in the continuous renewal of the light-sensitive outer segments of the rods.

Rods and Cones Rods and cones are light receptors, but there are several important differences between them. The rods are slender and roughly cylindrical; each eye contains about 100 million rods. The cones vary in their width. Those in the periphery of the retina are plump and have a cone-shaped tip; those in the very center of the retina are as slender as rods. Each eye has some 6 million cones. Both rods and cones contain photosensitive chemicals, or pigments, that absorb light. When they absorb light, a chemical change occurs in the structure of the pigment molecule. This chemical change, in ways that are not yet completely understood, changes the voltage across the receptor membrane, and this generator potential is relayed to cells in the inner nuclear layer. Visual receptor cells of vertebrates are unlike most other sensory receptors in that they are hyperpolarized by light. Most of the receptor cells are depolarized by their adequate stimulus.

Rods and cones differ not only in shape and number but, most dramatically, in function. We can gain important clues to the differing functions of rods and cones in the human eye if we look first at the retina of two very different animals. For example, the retina of the hedgehog contains rods but very few cones. The hedgehog is a nocturnal animal, one that is active almost exclusively at night. By contrast, the retina of the tree shrew has only

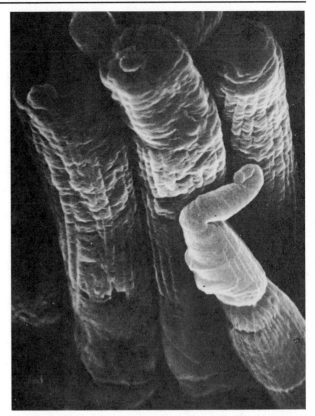

The human eye has some 100 million rods, which are slender and roughly cylindrical; also present are about 6 million cones, which vary in width. The rods function principally in dim illumination, whereas the cones work principally in bright illumination.

cone receptors. The tree shrew sleeps during the night and is active by day.

Similarly, in humans, the rods function principally in dim illumination such as at dusk and at night. With the rods, we see no true colors, only black, white, and shades of gray. With the cones, which function principally in bright illumination, we see black, white, and colors such as red, green, and blue. You can see for yourself the level of light at which the rods function best and at which the cones cease to operate. As the light fades at night, the world gradually loses its color: the rods have taken over.

The pigment that absorbs light in rods is called *rhodopsin* from two words meaning rose-colored and in the eye. One of the important components of rhodopsin is vitamin A. This helps explain the old folk wisdom that eating carrots and other sources of vitamin A improves the ability to see at night. Although there is no evidence that such remedies actually enhance normal night vision, a deficiency of vitamin A can produce night blindness by not allowing the production of enough rhodopsin.

The rods are distributed relatively uniformly throughout the retina. The cones are thinly distributed in the periphery and become much more densely packed toward the center of the retina. In fact, in the very center of the retina, an area of less than one square millimeter called the *fovea*, there are only cones, no rods. Because of this tight packing of receptors, our daylight vision is most acute in the fovea. When we fix a small object with a direct gaze, an image of that object is formed on the fovea. In bright light the densely packed cones of the fovea function to provide maximal visual sharpness, or *acuity*. By the same token, as the light dims, the foveal cones decrease in efficiency to the level where we can no longer make out that object. Indeed, in very dim light and in darkness we are blind in the fovea. If you look at a dim star at night you can make it disappear by looking directly at it, thus calling the fovea into play. When you look away it reappears; the image now is projected onto a region of the retina that contains rods. The rods and cones of the retina translate bright and dim stimuli into messages that are later carried by the ganglion cells to the brain.

Dark and Light Adaptation

The dual workings of the rods and cones of the retina allow our eyes to adapt to changing conditions of light and dark. Some time is required for this adaptation to take place. When we enter a darkened theater, a short period of adaptation is required before we can find our way down an aisle and to a seat.

Adaptation to darkness occurs in two stages. When we enter a dark room the cones adapt first, reaching a stable level of vision in less than 10 minutes. While increased sensitivity of the rods takes nearly an hour for completion, when fully dark-adapted, the eyes are around 1,000 times more sensitive then they were after the cone system adaptation.

The reverse process of adaptation to light—leaving a dark theater and entering a brightly lighted space, for example—is much faster. We may squint briefly, but the adaptation of cones and rods to light occurs quickly.

Dark adaptation within the rods is due in part to the resynthesis of rhodopsin. During normal daylight vision, rhodopsin in the rods is broken down into a protein (opsin) and a yellow pigment (retinene). In darkness the protein and pigment recombine into rhodopsin, which sensitizes the rods to low light.

Color Vision

Seeing in color is so much a part of our visual world that we seldom give it any thought. Yet, in dim illumination, when the retinal cones are not operating, color is lost. At night, it is as if the television screen we have been watching all day in full color fades and becomes old-fashioned black and white.

The scientific understanding of color vision began in 1671 with a simple experiment by Isaac Newton, the great English physicist. Newton darkened his room by closing the shutters; he then cut a small hole in one of the shutters. A thin shaft of sunlight came through this small hole. Newton placed a prism in the path of the light. On the opposite wall the prism produced a long rectangular patch of light made up of a series of rainbowlike colors. On one side of this rectangle, the light was red; next to it was orange, then yellow, green, and blue, to violet at the opposite end of the rectangle (see Figure 3.8).

Thanks to the understanding pioneered by Newton, we know that light that appears white is made up of many *wavelengths*; a prism bends light rays in inverse proportion to their respective wavelengths—the shortest wavelength light is bent the

FIGURE 3.8 When white light is shined through a prism, it is split into rays of different wavelengths, visible as different colors.

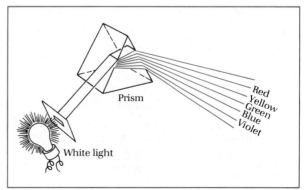

most, the longest wavelength light is bent the least. Different wavelengths of light are seen as different colors. Once a particular wavelength is isolated from white light, it maintains its characteristic color over a certain range of intensities. Newton, further and correctly, interpreted the colors of natural objects, such as green grass, brown soil, and so on, on the basis of their ability to absorb some of the rays of light and reflect others. Green grass is green because it absorbs the short and long wavelength rays and reflects light in the middle portion of the spectrum that is seen as green.

How do we see the great number of colors that we can distinguish? One suggestion was that the eye might contain receptors that are selectively tuned to different wavelengths of light. The problem with this view was that the human eye makes subtle color distinctions: the average person probably can distinguish a thousand or more different colors. If every hue had its own special receptor, a thousand colors would require 1,000 different receptors at each point on the retina.

Early in the nineteenth century, the English physicist Thomas Young (1802) suggested an ingenious solution to this problem. He speculated that there are only three types of broadly tuned receptors. Each of these, he suggested, is maximally sensitive to a given wavelength. These receptors would also respond, but less vigorously, to light whose wavelength was longer or shorter. Any three wavelengths thus might be sufficient to produce any color, provided they activated the three types of cones in correct proportion.

Color Mixing   Color mixing has proved to be an important source of data about the nature of human color vision. Color can be mixed in several ways. Imagine that you had two slide projectors, both projecting onto the same screen. Instead of the usual 35mm slides, you have a set of colored filters. You can mix the color on the screen as you choose. If you have three projectors, you can mix three colors. Another simple way to make a color mixture would be by spinning a disk with several colors on it. The disk is now spun fast enough to fuse the colors. Suppose you paste different colored triangles on a circle of cardboard. Like pie cuts, you make a wedge of yellow, a wedge of green, and a wedge of white. You could mix colors together by spinning the circle so fast that the eye cannot see the individual portions of the pie.

The spinning-disk method was adapted in the nineteenth century by James Clerk Maxwell (1855) for studying effects of mixtures of colors. Maxwell and others found that by appropriate mixtures of any three colors we can duplicate the appearance of any other color. Another giant of nineteenth-century science, Hermann von Helmholtz (1924), summarized his own view of the nature of color vision with a diagram. Figure 3.9 shows Helmholtz's colored circle. "If we think of the colors as plotted on a color chart by the method sketched above," he wrote, "it is evident from the rules given for the construction that all colors that are to be made by mixing three colors must be contained within the triangle whose vertices are the places in the chart where the three fundamental colors are." Helmholtz then went on to show that a simple triangular representation of the colors was insufficient and finally concluded that, "the boundary of the color chart must be a curved line which differs considerably from the perimeter of the triangle." Helmholtz's diagram allowed the color of any mixture of wavelengths to be predicted.

Helmholtz clarified another problem that confused most people, even Newton: as we see in Plate 2, a mixture of yellow and blue lights does *not* produce green as we would think. Rather, it produces a pale gray. The confusion comes from the difference between a mixture of different lights and a

FIGURE 3.9 In Helmholtz's colored circle the positions of the colors are indicated by the initial letters of their names—that is, indigo blue (I), blue (B), yellow (Y), violet (V), red (R), and green (G). All the colors that can be made by mixing red, blue, and yellow are comprised within the triangle RBY. The triangle VRG includes the colors obtained by mixing violet, red, and green.

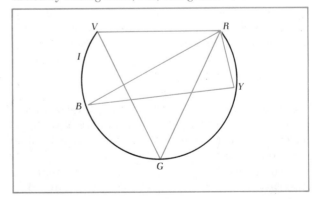

mixture of different pigments. A mixture of light of different wavelengths is called an *additive mixture*, that is, mixing two or more wavelengths will add up to a new color. On the other hand, a mixture of pigments—paints, for example—produces what is called a *subtractive mixture*. Pigments absorb and reflect light selectively: in effect, pigments subtract, or take away. They do not reflect all wavelengths falling on them. A leaf is green because its pigments absorb other wavelengths and reflect green. Lights add their wavelength to a mixture; pigments absorb or subtract some wavelengths and reflect remaining wavelengths to produce a given hue.

The early insights by Young, Maxwell, and Helmholtz proved remarkably accurate and useful for understanding color mixture. Although the three-color theory, or *trichromatic theory*, first proposed by Young remained highly controversial until recent years, we now know that the human eye does indeed have three different types of color-sensitive cones. Each of these three types of cones has a different pigment, just as the rods have their particular pigment, rhodopsin. One cone responds at peak sensitivity to the long wavelengths, another to the middle wavelengths, and a third to the short wavelengths.

Thanks to new developments in experimental techniques, it is now possible to measure the color sensitivity of cones very much as you might test a color filter. For example, by placing a color filter in a beam of light that is composed of a relatively equal mixture of all wavelengths, you can determine, using appropriate tests, how much of that light is absorbed at each wavelength. The same sort of test might be performed on a single human cone by employing a very narrow beam of light such as that provided by shining a light backwards through a microscope. How much light is absorbed by shining the light through the sensitive part of an individual cone would have to be tested first, and then measurements corrected for light absorption by other structures outside of the cone. Testing a large number of cones from the eye of a recently deceased person would reveal the results shown in Figure 3.10, which illustrates the spectral sensitivity for the three classes of color-catching cones.

As Young first suggested, the combinations in various degrees of the action of cones make up all of the color richness of our world. Precisely how these combinations are put together by the eye and brain is less clear. Some important clues have been discerned from a hypothesis set forth more than

a century ago by Ewald Hering (1878), who disagreed with Young's trichromatic, or three-receptor, theory. Hering focused on the appearance of colors instead of the receptor mechanisms. He argued that there are four basic colors, not three. These colors include yellow as well as red, green, and blue. He noted that certain pairs of these colors (blue versus yellow, and red versus green) seem to be opposite in a psychological sense: when combined, they cancel out each other (so that they appear gray). These are called *opposing colors*.

Although Hering's notion about the initial reception of colors by the cones was imprecise, the *opponent process* mechanism is in fact at work in cells farther along in the retina and the visual pathways (Svaetichin and MacNichol, 1958; DeValois, Smith, Karoly, and Kitai, 1958). These cells appear to code opposing colors by increasing or decreasing their rate of firing. A cell might be excited by long wavelengths of light in the red, for

FIGURE 3.10 Idealized spectral sensitivities of the three classes of color-catching cones. Curve A illustrates cones most sensitive to red, curve B illustrates cones most sensitive to green, and curve C illustrates cones most sensitive to blue.

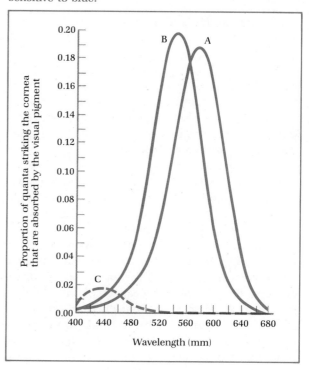

example, but inhibited by shorter wavelengths in the green. Another cell might show just the opposite responses. Recordings from microelectrodes have found an opponent process is already at work in the retinal ganglion cells where information is coded before transmission to the brain and in cells of the lateral geniculate body of the thalamus, the visual system's first way station in the brain itself (Wagner, MacNichol, and Wolbarsht, 1960).

The occurrence of colored afterimages also supports the opponent process theory. If you stare at a red patch and then look at a neutral gray or white surface, you are likely to see a gray spot tinged with green (see Plate 3). This is a *negative afterimage* because red is the complementary hue of green. The stimulus persists (briefly), but in a reversed state; chromatic and black-and-white effects are reversed. A less frequently encountered phenomenon is a *positive afterimage* in which the perception of the stimulus persists in its original chromatic or black-and-white configuration. Positive afterimages occur most often after dark-adapted eyes have received a brief but intense stimulation.

The further processing of color information in the brain is still something of a mystery. New discoveries, however, suggest the existence of specific centers in the cortex, which receives its inputs from the visual cortex, whose cells are specially tuned to the analysis of color.

The Psychological Nature of Color Newton's experiment with the shaft of light and the prism indicated that the perception of color depends on the wavelength of light. In psychological terms colors have three subjective, but measurable, attributes: hue, brightness, and saturation.

Hue is what we normally refer to as color itself—red, green, blue, yellow (the psychologically pure colors), or mixtures of them; gray, black, and white have no hue at all. We perceive a new color with a different hue when lights of two or more wavelengths are combined (see Plate 5). Most often, light reaching our eyes' cones is a mixture of wavelengths; the dominant wavelength determines the hue we experience. Wavelengths themselves are unaffected by mixture; the colors we experience are psychological products of the excitation of our receptors. *Brightness* is an aspect of the physical intensity of the color (see Plate 6). *Saturation* refers to a hue's vividness, richness, and purity. Deep, ruby-red is a highly saturated color, whereas pale pink is a desaturated color; saturation is an indica-

tion of the physical purity of a hue's wavelength. If a mixture of other wavelengths is added to the psychologically pure hues, the color is desaturated and may be altered to a different hue.

The *color spindle,* or solid (see Plates 7 and 8) visually represents the relationship among hue, brightness, and saturation. Hue is shown along the conical perimeter of the sphere. The horizontal dimension depicts brightness, and the vertical axis represents saturation, from black at the base to white at the top.

Remember that color is sensed, received, and coded, and then in turn perceived by the color-sensitive cones of our eyes and by our brains. The wavelengths of mixed lights do not physically combine or change; the combinations take place in the retina of our eyes and in our brains. All of us, however, do not sense and perceive all colors.

Color Blindness Because normal color vision is trichromatic—that is, it requires three different types of color-sensitive cones—we now can better understand some of the common problems in seeing color. Roughly 6 to 8 percent of the men in the world, and less than 1 percent of the women, suffer from some form of a hereditary visual disability, commonly called *color blindness* (see Plates 9 and 10). The vast majority are not truly color-blind; rather, they differ in various degrees from the normal in their mechanisms of color vision.

In some instances of color blindness, the retina has only two types of cones instead of three. If the red-sensitive long-wavelength cones are missing, the condition is called *protanopia.* If the green-catching middle-wavelength cones are absent, the condition is called *deuteranopia.* (There is a condition in which the short-wavelength, blue-sensitive cone is missing, but that is very rare.) An even more common condition is one in which the pigment in the middle or long-wavelength cones is present but has a different maximal sensitivity from the pigment of the cones in the normal eye. People with this condition are called *anomalous trichomats* because they still require the three wavelengths to match the spectrum.

A few people called *monochromats* suffer from an extreme and rare form of true color blindness. One type of monochromat may have very few cones: such people have only about 5 percent or less of the normal number of cones. They tend to have very poor visual acuity and to be overly sensitive to even moderate levels of light, much as the person with normal vision finds daylight uncomfortable when emerging from a dark movie theater.

Neural Coding of Light

Let us now look at the retina as an extension of the central nervous system and consider how light is coded and what sorts of information are transmitted from the eye to the brain. To do this, we need to analyze individual cells within the retina. A concept crucial to such an exploration is that of a cell's *receptive field*. A receptive field is simply that region of the visual world that acts on a given cell. In the simplest case, light might increase the firing of a visual cell, but light can also inhibit the cell. For example, suppose that a cell were firing at some steady rate in the dark. Light imaged on a part of the retina might activate the cell thus speeding it up or inhibiting it, thereby slowing its firing rate. The receptive field is the region of the visual field that can affect a given cell's response—either to excite or inhibit it.

Lateral Inhibition Much of the research in the neural activity of vision stems from work that began during the early 1930s (Hartline and Graham, 1932). H. K. Hartline recorded nerve impulses in the eye of the horseshoe crab. This creature has a compound eye composed of many small units called ommatidia, or "little eyes." Each ommatidium contains a dozen cells, which are clustered in segments around a single nerve fiber that projects to the brain.

Hartline beamed a light at a single ommatidium and then recorded nerve impulses from the individual nerve fibers that came from that ommatidium. He found that, as might be expected, these fibers fired faster when the intensity of the light was increased. The relationship was a relatively simple one, in which the frequency of firing was roughly proportional to the logarithm of the magnitude of the stimulus, a relationship that is reminiscent of Fechner's law.

Subsequent experiments on the horseshoe crab, however, brought a more surprising finding. When Hartline illuminated one ommatidium and then a neighboring one, an interesting thing happened: the frequency of firing in the original receptor unit decreased. The firing of nerve impulses in the second receptor served as a brake, or inhibitor, on its neighboring receptor.

This phenomenon is known as *lateral inhibition*. Although the compound eye of the horseshoe crab differs markedly from the eye of the human, a similar sort of physiological mechanism seems to be present. The idea of lateral inhibition has profound implications for the understanding of human vision. In the human retina a similar mechanism is produced by the cells of the inner nuclear layer, the structure containing the cells that connect the receptors, the rods and cones, with the ganglion cells. The net effect is to enhance the contrasts between different levels of illumination. In other words, lateral inhibition tends to emphasize contours or edges in what we see, and to ignore a steady level of illumination.

A process of this sort is at work, for example, in the so-called *Mach bands* shown in Figure 3.11. Notice that the white band appears whiter or brighter at the edge where it joins the gray band. Similarly, the black band looks blacker at the edge with the gray. In fact, the entire white band is of equal light intensity, as is the entire black band. Because of lateral inhibition, the contrast at the edges is enhanced, although the light intensity is unchanged. This illusion was observed some 100 years ago by the Austrian physicist Ernst Mach (Ratliff, 1965), who even then suspected that some sort of inhibitory effect in the retina might be responsible for it.

Stabilized Images Lateral inhibition provides striking evidence of the retina's sensitivity to changes or difference in the amount of light falling on different parts of it. Temporal changes also have profound implications for vision. In ordinary circumstances, images are never stabilized on the retina. Even when we try to keep our eyes still by staring at a fixed point, they are making tiny spontaneous movements, like small pendulum swings, at the rate of up to 70 per second and slower drifts and flicks. These movements mean that light from the fixed scene keeps falling on different receptors in the retina (Ratliff and Riggs, 1950).

In the early 1950s Lorrin Riggs and his collaborators at Brown University (Riggs, Ratliff, Cornsweet, and Cornsweet, 1953) and Robert Ditchburn (1973) at Reading University in England discovered that if the eye did not move, the resulting stabilized image would quickly fade and disappear. This can be demonstrated in the laboratory using a special device that stabilizes an image on the retina (see

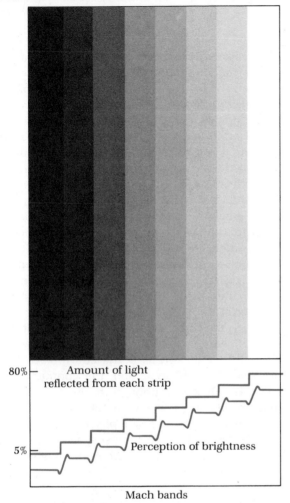

80%

Amount of light
reflected from each strip

5%

Perception of brightness

Mach bands

FIGURE 3.11 The phenomenon of lateral inhibition is illustrated by these Mach bands. Although each band is of uniform intensity throughout, the white band, for example, appears whiter or brighter at the edge where it joins the gray band. Similarly, the black band looks blacker at the edge where it meets the gray band.

Figure 3.12). A contact lens with a mirror on it is placed over the subject's eye. Targets can be reflected by the mirror onto a screen so that every time the eye makes one of its movements, the image on the screen moves with it. The image is thus stabilized on the retina of the eye wearing the contact lens.

When a stimulus is first turned on, the eye sees the image sharply and clearly. But within a few seconds, the image fades and soon disappears. This stabilized image falls constantly upon the same receptors. After a few seconds, information about that image no longer is transmitted to the brain.

The concept of *stabilized images* explains a

visual phenomenon of which we are not ordinarily aware. Recall from our description of the retina's structure that light entering the eye has to pass through an intricate network of blood vessels before it reaches the rods and cones. Why don't we see the shadows of all those blood vessels? The answer is that they are stabilized on the retina. Because these shadows fall constantly on the same sets of rods and cones, we do not see them.

You can make the shadows appear, however, with a simple demonstration. Take a slender flashlight, a penlight, switch it on, and place it firmly on the corner of your eye. Then jiggle the penlight. The eccentric source of light and the jiggling motion moves the shadows of the blood vessels sufficiently so that they now fall on a different from normal set

FIGURE 3.12 Apparatus for producing a stabilized retinal image. The image of a target is projected onto a contact lens with a mirror on it, which is placed over the subject's eye. The mirror reflects the image onto the screen S. The image from S reaches the subject's eye through the path indicated by the dotted line, reflected at points M_2, M_3, M_4, and M_5. Whenever the eye moves through a given angle, the mirror on the contact lens also moves, which in turn causes the image on the screen to move. Thus, the image that reaches the retina remains fixed in location despite normal eye movements.

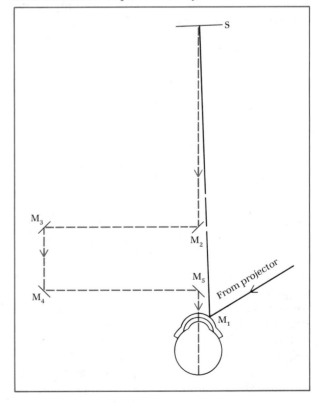

of rods and cones. These new receptors respond to the shadow of the blood vessels and begin signaling information to the brain. You will see a beautiful pattern of treelike forms—the shadows of the blood vessels you had never seen before.

Center-Surround Organization of Visual Receptive Fields   So far, we have considered the neural responses that apparently occur in two layers of the retinal structure: the rods and cones and in the inner nuclear layer. The rods and cones make synaptic connections with the bipolar and horizontal cells of the inner nuclear layer. By way of bipolar and amacrine cells in the inner nuclear layer, information reaches the last way-station within the retina, that is, the ganglion cells. In humans the neural pathways converge like a funnel into the ganglion cells. Whereas there are something like 125 million receptor cells—rods and cones—in each eye, there are only about a million ganglion cells. One ganglion cell may have connections, via the inner nuclear layer, from over 100 rods. On the other hand, certain ganglion cells may have connections with only a small number of foveal cones where daylight vision is most acute.

Because of their receptive field organization ganglion cells also function as detectors of contrasts or differences in light intensity over a minute portion of the visual field.

Typically, a number of cones send their visual information to a single ganglion cell. Such a ganglion cell has a larger receptive field than a cone and responds to a larger area of illumination. The receptive field of ganglion cells can be thought of as a small circle, which is organized concentrically. The ganglion cell compares how much light there is at the center of that circle—the illumination as reported by the cones in that circle—with that of the area surrounding the circle. This sort of concentric organization is called *center-surround*.

The center-surround organization was first described and investigated in detail by the physiologist Stephen Kuffler (1953). Working with cats, Kuffler placed tiny electrodes near single ganglion cells to monitor the firing of nerve impulses. He then focused tiny moveable spots of light on the cats' retina.

His first important observation was that a ganglion cell is never quiet; even in complete darkness it fires spontaneously. Light in the receptive field of a particular ganglion cell might thus have two possible effects: it could increase the neural firing rate

or it could suppress it. In fact, Kuffler found that the effect on the ganglion cell depended on which part of the receptive field was stimulated by light. For example, some ganglion cells increased their firing rate when the light fell on receptors in the center of the receptive field. These same cells decreased their firing rate when the light fell in the peripheral area surrounding the center of the receptive field. Such cells have been called *center-on*.

There are a roughly equal number of ganglion cells that responded in precisely the opposite manner. Light in the center of the receptive field decreased the firing rate; light in the surrounding area increased it. These cells are called *center-off*.

Kuffler's discovery of the center-surround organization of ganglion cells has at least two important implications. It suggests that one function of the ganglion cells is to analyze whether there are discontinuities in the amounts of light striking each small portion of the retina. Equally important from the standpoint of technique, it has established a way of exploring how cells in the brain itself code visual information.

The Brain and Vision

The ganglion cells send some one million nerve fibers from each eye directly to the brain. These fibers are bundled together in the two optic nerves, each of which exits from the eye near the fovea. Because there are no rods or cones at this point, a blind spot is created in the visual field of each eye. You can locate your own blind spot with a simple experiment. Close one eye, stare at the wall, and move a pencil slowly out of the field of vision. The pencil tip briefly disappears at the blind spot.

Ordinarily the brain fills in this blind spot with whatever image immediately surrounds it, but the reason why is a mystery. Some people, however, can literally see the mechanism in action. They suffer from large blind spots called *scotomas*, which sometimes appear during severe migraine headaches. The psychologist Karl Lashley used to describe the scotomas that appeared during his migraine attacks. He recalled one scotoma so big that it briefly beheaded a colleague who happened to be standing in front of Lashley. Lashley's brain quickly filled in the gap but with the wrong image—vertical stripes from the background wallpaper instead of the man's head (Gore, 1971).

The bundled fibers of the two optic nerves, before reaching the brain, meet and partially cross over at the *optic chiasma*. Here roughly half of the fibers from each eye stay uncrossed, while half cross over and project to the opposite side of the brain. The result of this arrangement is that each side of the brain receives information from both eyes: the retina on the right side of both eyes projects to the right half of the brain; the retina on the left side of both eyes projects to the left side of brain. Because of the optical inversion by the eye, information from the left half of each visual field is thus sent to the right side of the brain, and information from the right half of each visual field is sent to the left side of the brain.

The early anatomists could easily trace the path of the optic nerves by dissecting the brains of recently deceased people and animals. They could see the optic fibers enter the brain at the thalamus. Only in the last century, however, did it become clear precisely where in the brain the visual fibers project after they emerge from the thalamus.

The actual site of the visual cortex was the subject of much controversy among neural scientists. In 1876, for example, the eminent English physician and scientist David Ferrier incorrectly identified the parietal lobe as the site of the visual cortex. Ferrier came to this erroneous conclusion through an interesting experiment. He removed the parietal lobe from both hemispheres of a monkey and observed that the animal no longer seemed to respond to visual stimulation. One of Ferrier's observations was that a monkey, who was very fond of tea, no longer reached out for the teacup when it was offered. When the cup was placed in its hands, however, the monkey would eagerly drink it. Thus,

Ferrier argued that the monkey still liked tea but could no longer see the cup. What probably happened was that Ferrier destroyed those regions of the cerebral cortex that are a way-station between the visual and the motor cortex. The monkeys were probably not blind but unable to guide their movements under visual control.

In fact, it is in the occipital lobe that the visual cortex resides. This was established by the turn of the century on the basis of experiments with monkeys and later confirmed on the basis of reports of partial blindness—scotomas—in patients whose brains were damaged in the occipital lobe. Later, during World War I, cases of combat gunshot wounds enabled researchers to map accurately the organization of visual fields in the cortex. Dramatic confirmation came when the German brain surgeon, Ottfried Foerster (1929), was called on to treat a patient with recurrent epileptic fits stemming from a wartime brain injury. Foerster surgically removed the damaged area, which was under a local anesthetic. While the brain was still exposed, he electrically stimulated the region of the occipital lobe thought to be the visual cortex. (Remember that the brain itself is insensitive to pain because it lacks the nerve endings that signal this particular sensation.) When this region was stimulated electrically at various points, the patient reported seeing small spots of light. The location of these spots of light was consistent with the maps that had been constructed earlier on the basis of scotomas that followed gunshot wounds. Thus, the location of the visual cortex and the map of the visual fields was confirmed.

In recent years, researchers have begun recording electrical activity from single cells within the

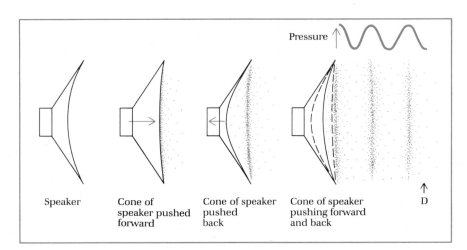

Pressure

Speaker

Cone of speaker pushed forward

Cone of speaker pushed back

Cone of speaker pushing forward and back

D

FIGURE 3.13 Representation of the concept of pressure and rarefaction in a loudspeaker. The dots represent the air molecules that transmit a tone. As the speaker moves forward, molecules are compressed, and as it returns to its original position the density of the molecules decreases. An observer at point D would experience a sequence of rarefaction and pressure that would result in sound.

visual cortex of experimental animals, much as Kuffler did in the ganglion cells of the retina of cats. This work has yielded fascinating clues about how the brain recognizes the patterns of light that fall upon the retina. We will discuss these single-cell responses when we take up visual perception in the next chapter.

Audition

Philosophers and physicists used to debate endlessly the answer to the old question: "If a tree falls in the forest and no one is around to hear it, will there be a sound?" The philosophers, insisting that sound is a sensory experience perceived by the listener, said no. The physicists, pointing out that sound is a movement of molecules caused by a vibrating body in a medium such as air or water, said yes.

The modern psychologist avoids the debate by saying that both the philosophers and the physicists were partially right. *Audition*, or the act of hearing, requires both rhythmical variations in the pressure of a medium near us *and* the reception of those variations by the ear, which in turn codes and transmits the information to the brain.

Auditory Stimulation: The Nature of Sound

Vision begins with light, a kind of electromagnetic energy. Sound begins with a mechanical disturbance; that is, vibrations create waves in a medium such as air or water. These waves resemble the ripples of water that radiate outward when you throw a stone into a pond. To understand this process more precisely, look at the musical tone represented in Figure 3.13. The dots are a highly schematic representation of the air molecules that transmit the tone. If air is pushed forward rapidly by a loudspeaker whose cone moves in the direction shown by the arrow, the air momentarily compresses just in front of the speaker (see Figure 3.13). If the speaker is returned to its original position with the same speed as it had moved earlier, it will leave a small region of rarefaction, or thinner air, adjacent to the loudspeaker. The molecules in this thinner air will be less densely distributed than is normal.

Suppose now that the loudspeaker cone moves back and forth continuously. The sequence of pressure and rarefaction will be transmitted through the air near the speaker. If the speaker continues to vibrate, there will be an orderly sequence of pressure and rarefaction in the surrounding air.

At room temperature sound waves travel in air at about 700 miles per hour, roughly 1,100 feet per second. It is important to remember that individual molecules of air do not move at this speed; it is the sequence of pressure and rarefaction involving millions of molecules that is moving at 1,100 feet per second.

Characteristics of Sound Waves Sound waves have three physical important characteristics: frequency, amplitude, and phase (see Figure 3.14). *Frequency* is the measurement of how many waves occur each second. The musical note A above middle C—the standard to which American instruments are tuned—consists of a frequency of 440 waves per second. During 1 second, there would be 440 complete cycles of pressure and rarefaction in the air around the tuning fork or instrument sounding the note. Researchers honor the nineteenth-century German physicist Heinrich Hertz, who did the first definitive studies of energy waves, by utilizing the unit *hertz* (abbreviated Hz) to de-

FIGURE 3.14 Schematic diagram showing the differences between the amplitude, frequency, and phase of a sound wave. (A) Two waves with the same phase and frequency but different amplitudes. (B) Two waves with the same phase and amplitude but different frequencies. (C) Two waves with the same amplitude and frequency but different phases.

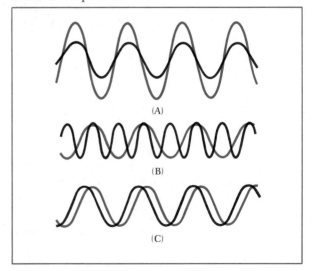

note 1 cycle per second. Hence our musical note A above middle C would have a frequency of 440 Hz.

Whereas the frequency of a sound wave determines *pitch* (that is, apparent highness or lowness of a note), the intensity or loudness is determined by the *amplitude*. The higher the peak of the sound wave, the greater its amplitude, and the louder it usually sounds. Amplitude and frequency are not quite enough to characterize sound waves, however. A third important characteristic is *phase*, which relates to the precise timing of a sound wave. Consider the pairs of waves shown in Figure 3.14. In pair 6, the waves have the same amplitude and frequency, but they are out of step with each other. They have a different phase. The peak of one wave occurs before the peak of the other wave. If two sound waves are completely "out of phase," the instant of compression in one coincides precisely with the instant of rarefaction in the other. In such a case, they would tend to cancel each other and would be perceived by the ear as silence.

Pitch and loudness are psychological characteristics of sound that are related to the physical dimensions of frequency, amplitude, and phase. A third psychological quality of sound is *timbre*, which is a measure of a sound's purity. Most instruments produce sounds that are mixtures of frequencies. The complex mixture of sound waves produces an instrument's unique timbre.

Additional psychological characteristics of sound are *consonance* and *dissonance*. When two tones are sounded together, we usually sense and perceive consonant pairs as pleasant and dissonant pairs as unpleasant. Custom and culture play a role in our perception of combined tones as consonant or dissonant. During the first part of the twentieth century, the works of Igor Stravinsky were considered to be highly dissonant; today the composer's *Firebird Suite* is a popular staple of the orchestral repertoire. A physical explanation of consonance or dissonance lies in frequency difference. Dissonance occurs when two tones sounded together produce a third tone, based on the difference in their frequencies, that does not harmonize with the fundamental tones sounded and thus produces a "roughness" in the sound. When the frequences of the two tones are sufficiently different to be heard as distinct sounds, the pair is perceived as consonant.

To measure the relative intensity of sound, scientists have worked out a unit called the *decibel—deci* from the Latin for one-tenth and *bel* after

Alexander Graham Bell, the inventor of the telephone. Decibels refer to the ratios between the physical energy in a sound and a standard sound (see Figure 3.15). On the decibel scale, the usual zero is near the absolute threshold for hearing a tone of 1,000 Hz—roughly the faintest sound audible to the average ear. Ordinary conversation usually measures between 60 and 80 decibels. Sounds about 140 decibels above threshold at 1,000 Hz feel uncomfortable to the human ear, and more intense sounds produce structural damage. Note that the decibel scale is a logarithmic scale: 30 decibels has 10 times the physical intensity of 20 decibels. In terms of frequency, the limits of human hearing range from about 20 Hz to 20,000 Hz. We do not hear equally well at each frequency, however. Humans hear best in a range of 1,000 to 4,000 Hz. The notes on a piano coincide roughly with this scale, ranging from 27 to 4,200 Hz.

Among different animals, there are great variations in auditory capacity. Cats, for example, can

FIGURE 3.15 The decibel (dB) scale indicates intensities of various common sounds.

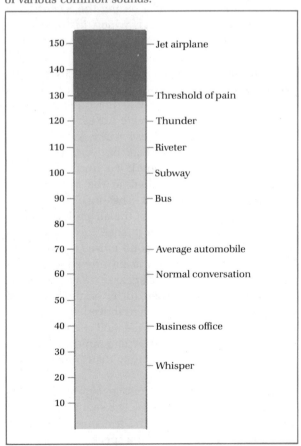

hear tones of 40,000 Hz—at least twice as high as the upper limit of human hearing. Dog-calling whistles emit frequencies up to 25,000 Hz, sufficiently above the human range so that we cannot hear them. One of the highest auditory capacity ranges belongs to some species of bats. These bats emit tones of up to 100,000 Hz or more and, by hearing and following the echoes of their own high-pitched squeaks, hunt prey, and navigate around objects in the dark. Like the bat, most animals do not make sounds that exceed their range of hearing frequencies. One exception is the grasshopper, which creates a "song" (by rubbing its legs against its own rough abdomen) of up to 100,000 Hz—too high to be picked up by the creature's primitive auditory system.

The auditory capacities of many different animals can be established easily in the laboratory. One very useful method has been developed by William Stebbins and his colleagues and used for assessment of damage to the ear (Stebbins, Miller, Johnsson, and Hawkins, 1969). For example, monkeys are trained to press a key, which turns on a loud tone. When the tone is on, the monkey is rewarded with a bit of food if it presses a second key. The monkey is taught that it can turn on a tone by pressing the first key. When the tone is on, and only when it is on, the monkey is rewarded with food for pressing the second key. Thus, switching to the second key tells the researcher that the monkey hears the tone. Since the monkey has audi-

tory capacities similar to humans (although its upper range is about twice as high), such experiments can help analyze sounds that are potentially damaging to the human ear. For example, hearing thesholds can be measured before and after the animal is subjected to an intense sound.

Structure of the Ear

The function of the ear is to detect sound waves and transform them into electrical impulses, the language of the nervous system. The manner in which the various parts of the ear achieve this is through a system of membranes, mechanical levers, and hydraulic fluids (see Figure 3.16).

Sound waves are funneled by the outer portion of the ear into its visible opening, the *auditory canal.* This hollow tube concentrates the sound waves and carries them to the *eardrum*, a taut membrane that vibrates rhythmically with the cyclical waves of pressure and rarefaction.

On the inner side of the eardrum is the *middle ear*, which contains three tiny bones, or *ossicles.* These ossicles are connected in linear fashion to the eardrum: attached to the eardrum is the *malleus* or hammer, which it resembles; then comes the *incus* (anvil) and the *stapes* (stirrup). The stapes, the last bone in the ossicular chain and about half the size of a grain of rice, couples directly with the

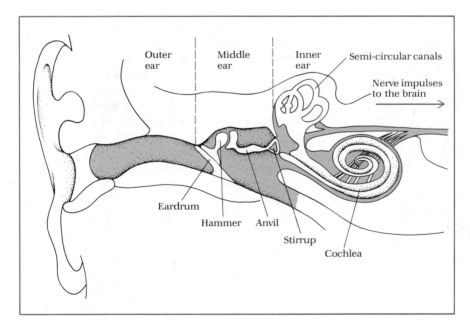

FIGURE 3.16 The structure of the human ear. Sound waves are funneled by the external portion of the ear through the auditory canal to the eardrum, which vibrates with the cyclical waves of pressure and rarefaction. The three little bones of the middle ear (hammer, anvil, and stirrup) together gear down the vibrations of the eardrum, multiplying their power severalfold. These vibrations are then transmitted to the cochlea in the inner ear, which converts the mechanical energy to electrical energy that is then carried to the brain.

83

oval window, a membrane that separates the middle ear from the *inner ear*.

The linkage of the three little bones of the middle ear acts as levers. It "gears down" the vibrations of the eardrum, multiplying their power severalfold. Moreover, the smallness of the oval window (about 1/25 the area of the eardrum) serves to further concentrate and thus amplify the forces reaching the inner ear. By the time a sound wave has set up vibrations in the oval window, the force may have been amplified up to 180 times that of the sound entering the outer ear.

The oval window is the gateway to the inner ear and to its principal structure, the *cochlea* (see Figure 3.17). No bigger than the tip of a little finger, the cochlea, as its Latin name suggests, looks like a snail shell. It is essentially a long, rolled-up bony tube filled with fluids. Inside the cochlea, running its coiled-up length, is the *cochlear partition*. On the bottom side of the cochlear partition is the *basilar membrane*. Attached to the basilar membrane is the command post of hearing, the *organ of Corti*. This structure is a gelatinous mass about an inch and a half long, consisting of thousands of

receptor cells from which project fine, hairlike fibers.

The mechanical vibrations of the oval window reach the hair cells of the organ of Corti by displacing the fluids adjacent to the cochlear partition, causing the basilar membrane to vibrate. The vibrations of the basilar membrane cause the hairs to bend. Finally, the bending of the hairs converts mechanical energy to electrical energy; that is, the bending motion creates a generator potential. If this potential is great enough, it triggers a nerve impulse, which is transmitted to the connecting fibers of the auditory nerve in the inner ear. Via the auditory nerve, the electrical impulses concerned with hearing travel to the brain.

Neural Coding of Sound

Scientists generally assume that the amplitude of a sound wave is coded by the number of nerve fibers that are activated. There are about 30,000 such fibers projecting from the inner ear, a sufficient number to code the loudest of sounds. How the frequency of a sound wave is coded, however, was long the subject of dispute. Two theories of how the ear codes pitch were postulated.

The first of these, the *place theory*, was set forth in the nineteeth century by that versatile scientist, Hermann von Helmholtz (1875). Helmholtz suggested that the pitch we hear depends on the place on the basilar membrane that is stimulated by the sound waves.

Later, an alternative hypothesis of pitch discrimination, the *frequency theory*, was put forward. Known also as the telephone theory, it postulated that the coding process was much like that of a microphone. According to this theory, the pitch we hear is determined by the frequency of the firing of nerve impulses in the auditory nerve fibers. Each nerve impulse in one fiber was said to coincide with 1 Hz, or one complete cycle of pressure and rarefaction. Thus, a tone of 500 Hz would cause a single nerve fiber to fire 500 times in a second. A major problem with the frequency theory was the built-in limitation on firing of a nerve fiber. A nerve fiber can fire at less than 1,000 times per second—not nearly enough to account for the human hearing range of up to 20,000 Hz (not to speak of the bat's range of more than 100,000 Hz).

Much of the place versus frequency debate was resolved by the work of the Hungarian engineer and physiologist Georg von Békésy (1960), for which he was awarded the Nobel Prize in 1961. Using

FIGURE 3.17 The gateway to the inner ear is the oval window, which opens to the cochlea, a long, rolled-up bony tube filled with fluids. On the bottom side of the cochlear partition, which divides the cochlea along its length, is the basilar membrane, to which is attached the organ of Corti that consists of thousands of receptor cells from which project hairlike fibers. Sound vibrations cause these hair cells to bend, thereby creating an electric potential. Through the auditory nerve the electrical impulses associated with hearing travel to the brain.

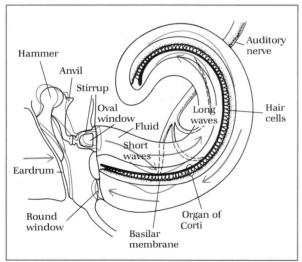

guinea pigs as his experimental animals, von Békésy watched through a microscope as the oval window was stimulated by tones of varying frequencies. He found that, in accordance with the place theory, as the frequency of sound varied, there was a different place in the basilar membrane that was maximally vibrated (see Figure 3.18). For high frequencies the vibration was greatest at the end of the basilar membrane nearest the oval window. But the fact that low tones activated the entire basilar membrane suggests that the frequency theory may also have some validity. For low frequencies the coding may indeed depend upon the number of firings by an individual nerve fiber.

In the brain itself there is also evidence that many of the cells in the successive relays in the brain that are concerned with hearing, from the medulla to the auditory cortex in the temporal lobe, respond selectively to various frequencies. Generally speaking, these auditory structures are organized *tonotopically;* that is, neighboring cells respond best to similar frequencies, and these frequencies change progressively from one place to another.

The Brain and Audition: Binaural Hearing

We are *binaural;* that is, we have two ears instead of one. The second ear might seem redundant because both ears send nerve connections to both the left and right sides of the brain. Loss of hearing in one ear does not substantially affect our ability to discriminate pitch and loudness. One reason for binaural hearing was offered more than 2,000 years ago by the Greek philosopher Zeno. "Nature," he said, "has given man one tongue, but two ears, that we might hear twice as much as we speak."

Zeno's wishful thinking notwithstanding, our two-eared system functions mainly to locate the precise direction from which a sound originates. To test the effectiveness of binaural hearing as a sound locator, try this demonstration. Blindfold a friend. Then move quietly around that person, stop, and suddenly snap your fingers. The friend will be able to point quite precisely in the direction the sound came from.

How does the friend know where the sound came from? Two different cues are responsible for direction finding. One is the relative intensities of the sound wave as it successfully reaches each of the two ears. This cue works better for higher-frequency sound waves. The wavelengths of higher-frequency sounds are shorter than the diameter of

the head. The head acts as a barrier to such waves and thus casts a kind of sonic shadow on the side of the head farthest from the origin of the sound. As a result, tones are detectably louder on the near side of the head than on the far side. Difference in intensity works less efficiently for lower-frequency sounds, however, because lower-frequency sounds have longer wavelengths. These wavelengths can bend around the head, thus reducing detectable differences in intensity.

A second cue, namely, difference in phase or time of arrival, governs the location of lower-frequency sounds. As we noted earlier, sound travels rather slowly, about 1,100 feet per second, or slightly more than 1 foot in a millisecond. If a person's ears are 6 inches apart, a sound originating at 90° from the right ear would arrive at the left ear about half a millisecond later than at the right ear. This means each ear would receive a different phase of the wavelength. The sounds in the ears, in other words, would be slightly out of phase with each other.

In your experiment on sound direction you might note that people sometimes make 180° errors in pointing to the source of a sound because both

FIGURE 3.18 The location on the basilar membrane that receives the maximum stimulation depends on the frequency of the sound. Note that at high frequencies the vibration is greatest at the end of the basilar membrane closest to the oval window.

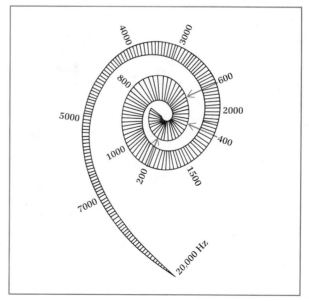

intensity and phase differences are lost when the sound source is directly in front of, or behind, the head.

How does the brain resolve small differences in time or intensity detected by the two ears? A structure in the brain stem probably serves as a major relay station for auditory signals en route to the cortex. Cells in this structure have dendrites projecting in two directions. On one side they receive connections from auditory fibers activated by the left ear; on the other side they receive connections from auditory fibers activated through the right ear. Thus these cells are in an excellent position to serve as a comparison mechanism for intensity and time differences in the two ears. Two other pieces of evidence support the belief that these cells play a crucial role in binaural sound location. Damage to these cells in experimental animals results in a loss of direction finding without apparent harm to the ability to discriminate pitch or intensity. Moreover, these cells fire only when there are differences of time or intensity in the sounds reaching the two ears.

Interestingly, the basic scientific research that led to our understanding of binaural sound location has yielded an electronic bonus: stereophonic sound reproduction. Stereo recordings that are made with two microphones set some distance apart detect the same differences in sound as the ears, and, when played back over two speakers, simulate our normal hearing in depth.

Deafness

There are two major types of deafness, or hearing loss: conduction deafness and nerve deafness. Conduction deafness results from deficiencies in the conduction mechanism of the auditory system, particularly the ear canal, the tympanic membrane, or the ossicles. Nerve deafness results from deficiencies or damage to the auditory nerves, the basilar membrane, or other closely linked neural connections in the cochlea. Some malfunctions in parts of the conduction mechanism, such as impairment of the ability of the ossicles to conduct sound vibrations, can be alleviated by the use of a hearing aid, which amplifies the sound stimulus so that it will still travel through the normal channels. When the neural mechanisms of hearing are destroyed, a hearing aid will not help: no hearing aid can force a nonexistent nerve cell to fire.

The causes of deafness vary. It may result from chronic infection of the middle ear, the overall effect of aging, and prolonged exposure to intensive acoustic stimulation including excessive exposure to rock bands (Lipscomb, 1969).

The Chemical Senses

As we have seen, many of our important sensory organs respond to physical stimuli in the world around us: the eye responds to light; the ear responds to sound. Smell and taste, however, are chemical senses. Smell is a response to certain chemicals in the air we breathe; taste is a response to chemicals in the foods and liquids we ingest. The senses of taste and smell are quite interrelated in our sensing of food. Flavor is a combination, largely, of smell and taste. Aside from the sensations encountered in eating, the two chemical senses are usually quite different in humans. They are not as distinct in some animals, however. Certain species of fish, for example, possess tastelike chemical sensors on the surface of their bodies. These taste receptors serve a function similar to the mammalian sense of smell, detecting odorants that are dissolved in the water.

Smell

Our sense of smell literally helps make life more pungent, but it is not essential. People who are deprived of this sense can get along quite well in the world. A clue to its importance in evolution can

FIGURE 3.19 Olfactory structures in the nasal cavity. Receptors high in the nasal cavity carry the sensation of smell directly to the two olfactory bulbs, which are joined to the olfactory cortex of the brain.

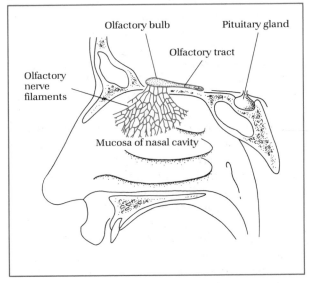

be found, however, in the anatomy of neural connections for smell. Of all the senses, olfaction has the most direct route to the brain. Receptors high in each nasal cavity carrying this sensation travel directly to the two *olfactory bulbs*, which lie just below the frontal lobes of the brain. The olfactory bulbs are joined to the olfactory cortex of the brain. No other synaptic connections need be made along the path of smell (see Figure 3.19).

Smell plays surprisingly diverse roles in different animals. When a recently mated mouse, for example, smells the urine of a male mouse other than her mate, her pregnancy is usually blocked (Bruce, 1959; Whitten, Bronson, and Greenstein, 1968). In certain animals, olfaction also is involved in a form of chemical communication. One process by which this occurs involves certain chemical substances called *pheromones*, which are secreted by specialized glands of the skin or through the urine (see Chapter 11). One indication of a pheromonal-type mechanism operating on the human level was reported in a study on women (all dormitory residents of a women's college) that indicates that the menstrual cycles of close friends and roommates fall into synchrony (McClintock, 1971). According to the study, the critical factor was that the women interacted and remained in close proximity to one another.

Odor is detected through receptor cells embedded in a small mucus-covered surface on the roof of each of our two nasal passages. Although for humans each of these areas is only about the size of a postage stamp, together they contain about 5 million receptor cells. Some species of dogs have 200 million or more receptor cells and a proportionately larger area of the brain devoted to smell. Dogs are so sensitive to certain odors that United States Customs officials have used them to sniff out contraband drugs such as marijuana.

From the receptor cells, hairlike filaments (cilia) project into the mucous area (see Figure 3.20). These filaments make contact with the molecules in odorants (the stimulants), and this process triggers a train of nerve impulses to the brain. Although the contact between odorant molecules and the nose's receptors is clearly chemical, the precise neural mechanism of it is still a puzzle. Some 2,000 years ago, the poet Lucretius guessed that tiny odorant molecules somehow entered tiny pores in what he called the "palate." One modern theory of olfaction holds that Lucretius was essentially right. This theory suggests that the geometry of a particular odorant molecule fits into certain sites on the filaments extending from the receptor cell in a way analogous to a key fitting into a lock (Amoore, 1970). Recent findings, however, indicate that in certain molecules changes that do not alter size or shape appreciably have a profound impact on smell quality, which brings into question the accuracy of the lock-and-key theory (Schiffman, 1974).

How do we distinguish one odor from another? Many researchers assume that olfactory receptors respond selectively to certain classes of odors. A number of attempts have been made to classify odors in a system that might correspond to selectively sensitive receptors. One early attempt at a classification scheme was suggested by Hans Henning (1916). He postulated a smell prism consisting of six corners labeled putrid, ethereal, resinous, spicy, fragrant, and burnt. All smells, he suggested, are combinations of these six elementary odors, just as all colors result from mixtures of light

Some species of dogs are so highly sensitive to certain odors that they can be trained to detect contraband drugs such as marijuana.

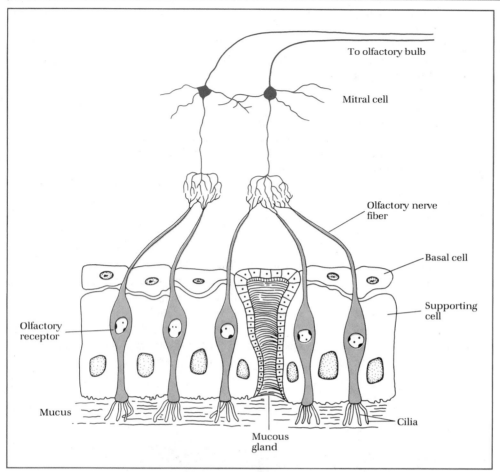

FIGURE 3.20 Schematic representation of olfactory receptor cells from which hairlike filaments (cilia) project into the mucous area. When these filaments make contact with the molecules in olfactory stimulants, a train of nerve impulses is triggered to the brain.

of different wavelengths. More recently, researchers have attempted to classify odorous molecules on the basis of their chemical similarities. None of these classification schemes is universally accepted.

One promising line of current research seeks out human subjects who cannot smell certain substances (Amoore, 1971). For example, some people lack the ability to smell sweat. By analyzing the spectrum of smells that are not perceived or are perceived differently, it might be possible to characterize receptors that are sensitive to a particular class of odors.

Taste

The mechanisms of taste are somewhat better understood than those of smell. The primary sensory receptors that detect taste are contained in the

taste buds, which are located on dark red spots known as *papillae*. There are an estimated 9,000 taste buds in the human tongue and soft palate; limited quantities are also found on the hard palate, pharynx, larynx, and other parts of the oral cavity. Each taste bud contains a variable number of receptor cells. A bundle of nerve fibers from these cells connect each taste bud to the cortex via relay nuclei in the medulla and thalamus. The nature of the contact between the stimulants of flavor molecules and these receptor cells has not been clearly established, although, as in smell, it is believed that a lock-and-key mechanism may trigger the nerve impulse.

Researchers usually classify taste into four basic qualities: sweet, salty, sour, and bitter. Evidence for these four distinct taste qualities is suggested by the specific action of certain chemicals. For example, the leaf of the plant, *Gymnema sylvestre*, contains a substance that temporarily abolishes sweet taste. If you rinse your mouth in a weak solution made from this plant and then eat sugar, the sugar will be tasteless for about an hour. The other tastes—salty, bitter, and sour—are not affected.

Another plant, *synsepalum dulcificum*, has a totally different effect. Grown in Africa and known as "miracle fruit," it complicates taste in a remarkable way. After it is chewed, sour substances taste both sweet and sour. A lemon, for example, tastes like sweetened lemonade. "Miracle fruit" apparently alters sweetness receptors in such a way that they can be temporarily activated by sour substances as well as remaining normally sensitive to sweet ones.

Additional evidence for the existence of four separate taste qualities comes from regional differences in the sensitivity of the tongue (see Figure 3.21). The back of the tongue is most sensitive to bitter substances. The tip of the tongue is most sensitive to sweet taste. Salty taste, however, seems uniformly distributed over the tongue.

Despite the apparent existence of these four distinct taste qualities, clear physiological evidence that the receptors are so neatly parceled out has yet to be established. Laboratory experiments in which neural activity is recorded from receptors have so far failed to show a precise relationship between a single receptor and a given taste.

FIGURE 3.21 Location of four separate taste qualities on the tongue.

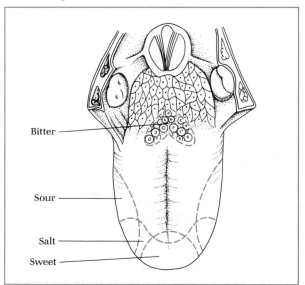

Somesthesis

Sensations arising from the skin are known collectively as *somesthesis*, Greek for "body knowledge." Researchers have identified four distinct skin sensations: touch, warmth, cold, and pain. Other sensations, such as tickle or itch, represent variations on these basic types.

Areas of the skin that are stimulated by touch, temperature, and pain are distributed all over the surface of the body and have been mapped in minute detail in the laboratory. You can map "cold spots" on the back of your own hand with a simple experiment. Probe gently with the point of a pencil until you feel the sensation of cold. Although the receptors here ordinarily respond to cold temperatures, they can also be activated by touch.

The existence of such spots uniquely sensitive to the four basic sensations at first led researchers to a logical hypothesis: perhaps there are structurally distinct types of skin receptors that detect only a given sensation. Indeed, several kinds of receptors are found in the skin. Some are free nerve endings—the branching fibers of sensory neurons. Other receptors are specialized structures of various sizes and shapes that encapsulate the endings of nerve fibers.

In early attempts to correlate the types of receptors with specific skin sensations, researchers conducted heroic experiments whose subjects were usually the researchers themselves. The subjects were tested first for the distribution of sensation spots on a small section of skin. These spots were marked and then the patch of skin was removed surgically (Wollard, 1935). When sections of the skin were studied under the microscope, however, there was seldom a perfect correlation between specific touch spots and receptor type. Nevertheless, it is likely that nerves are specialized for one or another class of skin sensation. Certain free nerve endings in the skin are almost certainly associated with pain sensations. Other nerve fibers coil around the base of hair follicles and respond to the slight bending of the hairs and hence are sensitive signals that the region has touched something.

The neural mechanisms by which the central nervous system locates skin sensations on a particular part of the body are much better understood. Generally speaking, sensory fibers leading from the

89

Researchers who study sensation must necessarily bridge two quite different realms of science—psychology and physics. This was recognized by Gustav Theodor Fechner, the nineteenth-century German pioneer in the study of sensation, when he founded the branch of psychology that he called psychophysics. The central concern of psychophysics is the measurement of the relationships between the physical attributes of a stimulus such as light or sound and the sensations that it produces.

From the beginning, psychophysicists attempted to measure what they labeled the absolute threshold—the minimum amount of physical energy that can be detected by our sensory apparatus. The absolute threshold of vision was of particular interest: How much light is necessary before we can see? At least a dozen attempts were made to answer this question over a period of half a century. The failings in these studies typically were ones of methodology. It was not until the early 1940s that a team of investigators at Columbia University were able to answer the question, and then only by means of their painstaking approach to the problem (Hecht, Shalaer, and Pirenne, 1942).

Because this work by Selig Hecht and his colleagues is still considered a classic in psychophysical research, let us examine the highlights of their approach. The subject was placed in a dark room in a dark cabinet with his head immobilized. Through a complex optical arrangement, a light of brief duration was flashed onto one part of his eye. The subject controlled when the light was flashed, but the experimenters controlled the intensity of the light, systematically varying its amount, which is measured in quanta.

The conditions of the experiment were arranged so as to yield the maximum possible sensitivity of the subject's retina. For example, the part of the retina exposed to the light was in a portion of the retina where the concentration of light-sensitive receptors called rods are much greater than in the center. Moreover, the subject was required to sit in the dark for at least 30 minutes before testing because the process of dark adaptation heightens the sensitivity of the rods. In addition, the wavelength of light used in the experiment—510 nanometers—was selected because the rods are most sensitive to this particular wavelength.

Seven subjects were tested in the experiment, four of them at sessions extending over 18 months. Each of a series of light intensities was presented to each subject many times, and the frequency of the subject's report of seeing the light was determined for each intensity. The subject had to report seeing a given intensity of light at least 60 percent of the time in order for it to be considered as his absolute threshold. Hecht found that, among these subjects, the minimum amount of light necessary for seeing ranged from 54 quanta to 148 quanta.

These results, however, were only the experiment's raw material, which had to be further processed. They represented the amount of light measured at the cornea. To calculate the light actually reaching the rods in the retina, Hecht had to make adjustments. He had to correct for the considerable amount of light that was lost in at least three ways: reflection from the cornea, absorption by other parts of the eye en route to the retina, and transmission through the retina without actually affecting the light-sensitive chemicals in the rods.

After these corrections, Hecht found that a range of only 5 to 14 quanta was necessary to activate the visual systems of his subjects. Statistical probability dictated that none of the rods affected by the light absorbed more than 1 quantum of light. Therefore, for human beings to see, he concluded, it is necessary for only 1 quantum of light to be absorbed by 5 to 14 rods. Further statistical analysis reduced this minimum to 5 to 8 rods.

Hecht also studied the variability in the performance of each subject's performance—why an individual's absolute threshold might be 5 quanta on one occasion, for example, and 6 on another. It previously had been assumed that such fluctuations depended upon the subject's psychological or biological variability from test to test. Hecht was able to show that these fluctuations were actually related to the inherent nature of light itself. The amount of quanta emitted by any light source is never constant but varies slightly.

skin travel in bundles that may contain fibers that respond to one or more class of sensation. The thickest nerve fibers arise from specialized receptors in the muscles and joints. A middle-thickness myelinated fiber carries touch sensation. The finest fibers, some of which are unmyelinated, carry only sensations of pain and temperature and travel at relatively slow speeds. Sensory cell bodies are situated just outside the spinal cord in a group of cells called the *dorsal root ganglia*. From here, the sensory pathways ascend by way of one or more relay to the thalamus deep in the brain and then to the cortex of the parietal lobe at the top. These pathways cross over en route to the brain or within it so that skin sensations from the right side of the body register in the left part of the parietal lobe and vice versa.

The portion of the parietal lobe devoted to skin sensations is sometimes called the *somatic sensory cortex.* Like the areas of cortex devoted to motor control (see Chapter 2) it is mapped somatotopically. Adjacent points on the cortex represent neighboring points on the surface of the body in such a way that a homunculus, or "little man," can be drawn. As in the case of the motor cortex, this little man (see Figure 3.22) depicts the disproportionate distribution of skin sensitivity. The skin of the back, for example, while occupying a vast expanse, is represented in a very modest region of the cortex. At the same time, large areas of cortex are devoted to inputs from our sensitive fingertips.

This disproportionate representation of sensation takes fascinating forms in various animal species. Whereas humans and monkeys have sensitive fingers, rats and mice possess enormously sensitive whiskers that are represented disproportionately in their cortexes. Thus equipped, the mouse can feel its way, literally whisker by whisker,

FIGURE 3.22 Homunculus, or "little man," depicting the disproportionate distribution of skin sensitivity in the somatic sensory cortex.

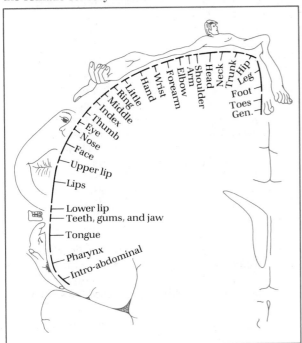

Senses of Position and Movement

The senses of position and movement are often regarded as the least important because we seldom are consciously aware that they even exist. Without these senses, however, each of us would be reduced to a helpless, writhing mass, unable to move and unable to stand upright against the force of gravity. Thanks to them, we constantly are aware of the position of our bodies in space, know when we move a limb, and know when we are standing up or lying down.

These least-appreciated of the senses can be classified into two broad categories. One category involves the vestibular system, which deals with the movement and position of the head. The other is our sense of the body and its parts, which is detected principally through receptor cells in muscles, tendons, and joints. It is sometimes called *kinesthesis.*

Kinesthesis

To test the sense of position that we usually take for granted, try this experiment. Ask a friend to close her or his eyes and extend an arm to the side with the index finger pointing down. Next, lift the arm so that it points to a definite spot on the wall. Now ask the subject to drop the arm to the side and then try to reposition it precisely in the same place it was before. You will find that people can do this with a great deal of accuracy, often within an inch or two of the original target.

This accuracy is made possible by sensations from two different types of receptors. One type is found in the joints. Nerve impulses signaling the position of the limbs from these receptors are transmitted to the brain. The sensory role of a second type of receptor, *muscle spindles*, has been discovered more recently. Muscle spindles, which are specialized organs located within voluntary muscles, have sensory nerve endings that signal to the spinal cord and the brain when a muscle is stretched. As we saw in Chapter 2, it long has been known that muscle spindles are involved in the regulation of the length of the muscle in stretch reflexes such as the knee jerk. Recent evidence indicates that muscle spindles also contribute to our sense of position and movement (Goodwin, McCloskey, and Mathews, 1972). During laboratory experiments, if a subject's limb is held in one position while muscle spindles are activated by vibrating the muscle, the subject experiences a feeling that the limb is actually being moved.

Vestibular System

The inner ear contains, in addition to the organ for hearing, two sets of structures vital to our balance and posture (see Figure 3.23). One set, which helps control posture, consists of two saclike organs, the *utricle* and the *saccule*. Inside the utricle and the saccule are sensory hairs. Attached to these hairs, and embedded in a gelatinous mass, are crystals. If the head is tipped away from the upright position, these crystals serve as weights. They deflect the sensory hairs and trigger nerve impulses that signal the change in posture.

A second set of structures, the three *semicircular canals*, serve to detect changes in the angular movement of the head. When the head moves, fluid in the canals is pressed against a series of hair cells. The bending of the hair sets off electrical impulses in nearby nerve fibers. Because the three canals are arranged at right angles to one another, they can detect movement in any direction.

As in the instance of the body's position detectors, we are unaware of the vestibular system until things go wrong. A disorder of the inner ear known as Ménière's syndrome affects the vestibular system and causes dizziness and feelings of disorientation. In extreme cases, the patient may not be able to remain upright.

A more familiar disruption of the vestibular system is motion sickness. The motion of a ship, for example, stimulates the vestibular system in a way that is quite different from its normal functioning in head-rotation. It cannot simply be activation of the vestibular system that produces motion sickness, because it is constantly activated by normal head movement. Rather, it must be the particular pattern

FOCUS: Senses We Do Not Have

Although evolution has endowed humans with an ingenious and highly useful array of sensory organs, the rest of the animal world has not been neglected. Most mammals, of course, are equipped with sight, hearing, and the other senses for perceiving the world. In other animals, however, special senses have evolved that serve unique functions that humans altogether lack.

The Electric Sense   Certain species of fish, such as the electric eel, produce a discharge that stuns or kills their prey. But several other species possess a subtler form of electrical organ that helps guide their locomotion and detects objects in space. One such species, the elephant nose fish of Africa, can be purchased in many pet stores.

Perhaps the most extensively studied species with the "electric sense" is the African knife fish. An organ in the tail of the knife fish generates a high-frequency alternating current. This current creates around the fish's body an electric field, which is distorted when objects enter it. These distortions are sensed by detectors lining the surface of the fish's body. Curiously, whereas human sensory organs send their information to the cerebral cortex of the brain, responses from the electric sense of the knife fish go to the cerebellum, a neural structure normally involved in movement.

Thermoreception   Boa constrictors and pit vipers such as the rattlesnake, though gifted with sight, also use a remarkable sensitivity to heat in detecting their prey. The sensory capability was discovered by Gaylord Noble and A. Schmidt (1937) in a fascinating series of experiments. They blindfolded snakes and presented them with a pair of light bulbs. Neither of the light bulbs was illuminated, but one had just been switched off and hence was slightly warmer than the other. The snakes struck repeatedly at the warm bulb. In boa constrictors the heat sensors, or thermoreceptors, are lined up in a row that runs roughly parallel to the animal's lips. In rattlesnakes the thermoreceptors can be found on each side of the head, between the eye and nostril, in the small pit that gives the family its name, pit viper.

In 1952, Theodore Bullock and R. B. Cowles recorded electrical activity in the nerve endings that connect to the rattlesnake's pit organ. They found that minute amounts of heat were enough to speed up markedly the firing of nerve impulses. The thermoreceptors are so sensitive that they can distinguish a human hand from its surroundings at a distance of more than a foot.

The Power of Smell   In some animals the olfactory sense, which is relatively unimportant in the human, serves as a powerful regulator of behavior. For example, in two widely disparate species, the salmon and the silkworm moth, smell plays a significant role in sexual reproduction. Salmon are born in fresh-

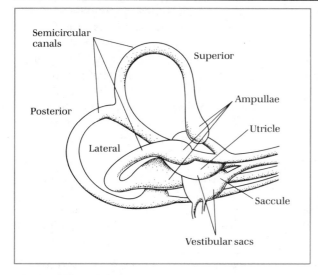

Semicircular canals
Superior
Ampullae
Posterior
Utricle
Lateral
Saccule
Vestibular sacs

FIGURE 3.23 The vestibular system, located in the inner ear, is vital to balance and posture. The utricle and saccule help control posture. The three semicircular canals, which are arranged at right angles to each other, can detect movement in any direction and hence serve to control balance.

of activation produced by moderately high waves or by bends in the road.

The vestibular system also has reflexive nerve connections with the muscles of the eye. This is evident if you rock back and forth in a rocking chair. The angular movement of the head induces activity in the semicircular canals. This activity, in turn, signals the eyes to move in a direction opposite to the chair rotation. The net effect of this so-called *vestibuloocular reflex* is to hold the visual world steady even when the head is moving. Try reading this page while moving your head rapidly

water rivers and streams and then migrate to the sea in the first year of life. But in the fourth year they return to spawn in the freshwater place where they were first hatched. The salmon's extraordinary homing ability stems from its olfactory organ. On the early outward journey, the salmon codes the turns and junctions of the water's branches and tributaries by recording their distinctive odors; returning to its birthplace, the salmon "reads" this well-remembered smell map to navigate its way home.

Among silkworm moths, smell is the cue for mating. The female releases a chemical odorant called a pheromone—the biologists's term for any chemical

In hunting small flying insects at night, bats rely on echolocation, a sensory system resembling sonar.

that triggers innate behavior patterns in a member of the same species. The male moth's olfactory organ, which is located in its antennae, can detect the pheromone from many miles away. Humans use the same chemical as the female odorant to attract males of certain insect species and then destroy them.

Echolocation Bats see better than legend would have it, but vision provides the night-flying bat with only crude recognition of the terrain during flight. To hunt small flying insects at night, bats rely on a sensory system called echolocation, a kind of sonar. They give off very high-frequency sounds—much higher than the human threshold for hearing—and then locate insects and other objects by listening as the sounds bounce off them (Griffin, 1958).

Interestingly, the bat's high-frequency cry can also be detected by one of its favorite prey, a night-flying moth. This moth has two simple and primitive ears on either side of the center portion of its body. Each ear has only two auditory fibers; these two fibers have different auditory thresholds. When the more sensitive of these two fibers detects bat cries at a distance, the moth responds by flying in the opposite direction. Higher intensity cries, indicating the bat is nearby, activate the other auditory nerve fiber. The moth thereupon takes dramatic evasive action, diving toward the ground or zooming away on a zigzag course.

back and forth or from side to side. Because of the vestibuloocular reflex, you can still read the page. If you move the book at the same rate instead of your head, however, the text will blur.

Sometimes it may be useful to override this reflex. Say you want to read while being rocked back and forth in the rocking chair. The reflex, by pushing your eyes in the opposite direction of the chair's rotation, would make reading impossible. But if you consciously choose to hold your eyes still, you can overcome the reflex. This ability, it has recently been suggested, may stem from nerve connections through the cerebellum, the so-called little brain (see Chapter 2) that plays an important role in voluntary movement.

As we noted at the beginning of the chapter, all the senses go through a three-stage process in delivering their varying messages to the brain where necessary control, direction, and reaction take place. A stimulus (salt on the tongue or a sound wave entering the ear) must enter or touch the body; detectors (taste buds or eardrums) must sense and react to the stimulators; finally, those reactions of the receptors must be translated into nerve impulses that tell the brain what is happening. All those stimulant-receiving detectors and receptors and their corresponding neural networks are appendages and servants to the marvelous brain, which, finally, perceives all sensations, both physically and psychologically. That complex perception is the subject of the following chapter.

SUMMARY

1. Sensation is the process by which we receive and code a stimulus such as a pattern of light or darkness, a sound wave, or a smell or taste. The sensory mechanisms include seeing, hearing, the chemical senses (taste and smell), the skin senses (touch, temperature, and pain), and the sense of position and movement. All human and animal senses can be described in three stages: (1) stimulation—some form of physical or chemical energy must stimulate the sensory mechanisms; (2) detection—receptors, either modified nerve endings or nonneural cells that contact a nerve ending, detect, or receive, stimuli; and receptors function as converters, or transducers of physical and chemical energy; and (3) neural coding—the electrical change in the receptor is converted into the nervous system's language, a train of nerve impulses.

2. Psychophysics measures the relationships between the physical attributes of stimuli and resulting sensations. Sensory thresholds are the levels at which a stimulus or changes in a stimulus can be detected. The absolute threshold is the minimal level of intensity at which we can perceive a sensation A difference threshold is the smallest difference between two stimuli that can be reliably discriminated. The just noticeable difference, or jnd, is that point at which discrimination is possible.

3. There is not a one-to-one relationship between the physical intensity of a stimulus and its sensation magnitude. In Fechner's law, sensation increases geometrically: the logarithm of the stimulus intensity, rather than its absolute value, determines its psychological magnitude.

4. Signal detection theory uses an orderly way of analyzing the detectability of stimuli. Stimulus detectability can be represented on graphs called ROC curves (receiver-operating characteristics).

5. Much of our knowledge about the world around us comes to the brain via the eyes, and a great deal of research has been devoted to the mechanisms of vision. The stimulus for vision is light, a kind of electromagnetic energy that travels in varying wavelengths. The wavelength of light is measured in nanometers (billionths of a meter); the visible spectrum for humans ranges from about 400 to 700 nanometers.

6. In the eye, light passes through the cornea, a transparent tissue, and then through the pupil. The light is focused by the cornea and the lens onto a light-sensitive surface, the retina. The retina is made up of millions of cells that, in connection and function, resemble the neurons of the brain. The cells of the retina are arranged in three distinct layers: (1) rods and cones, which receive and detect the electromagnetic energy of light; (2) the inner nuclear layer organizes the information from the rods and cones and transmits it to the ganglion; (3) fibers projecting from the ganglion cells bundle together to form the optic nerve, which carries the electric neural signals to the brain.

7. The human eye has about 100 million rods and 6 million cones. The rods function primarily in dim illumination; when the rods alone are working we can see only black, white, and shades of gray. With the cones, which function primarily in bright light, we see chromatic colors such as red, green, and blue as well as shades of gray. Rods are distributed relatively uniformly throughout the retina; cones

are thinly distributed in the periphery and are more densely packed in the center of the retina. In the very center of the retina, in an area of about 1 square millimeter called the fovea, there are cones but no rods.

8. Our eyes adapt to darkness in two stages. The cones reach a stable level of vision in less than 10 minutes; full sensitivity of the rods requires around 30 minutes or more. Reverse adaptation to light occurs much more rapidly.

9. We see different wavelengths of light as different colors. The average person can distinguish a thousand or more different colors. The human eye has three types of color-sensitive cones, each with different pigments, just as rods have their own pigment, rhodopsin. The three types of cones respond at peak sensitivity to long, middle, and short wavelengths. The processing of color information in the brain is still something of a mystery, but recent research suggests the existence of centers in the cortex whose cells are specially tuned to the analysis of color.

10. Perception of color depends on the wavelength of light. In addition, the colors we perceive have three psychological attributes: hue, brightness, and saturation. When lights of two or more wavelengths are combined, we see a new color. A mixture of wavelengths is an additive mixture; conversely, a mixture of pigments is a subtractive mixture. Each hue has a complementary one that lies directly opposite it on the color circle.

11. A negative afterimage is the persistence of a stimulus in a reversed state of chromatic and black-and-white effects. Less frequently occurring is a positive afterimage in which the stimulus persists in its original chromatic state.

12. The usual so-called color blindness is not really a true blindness to colors. Such color blindness is caused in some cases by retinas that have only two types of cones instead of three. In other cases the pigment in the red and green cones is present but has a different maximal sensitivity from normal pigment. A few people, monochromats, have very few cones at all, and poor general vision as well as complete color blindness.

13. Each cell of the retina has a receptive field, which is the region of the visual field that affects a given cell's response to light—either to excite it or inhibit it. Lateral inhibition is a process whereby cells inhibit neighboring cells, thus enhancing the contrasts between different levels of illumination and emphasizing the contours or edges of what we see. The rods and cones make synaptic connections with cells in the inner nuclear layer and send information by way of these cells to the ganglion cells, which transmit visual information to the brain.

14. Ganglion cells send about a million nerve fibers from each eye directly to the brain. These fibers are bundled together into two optic nerves, which meet and partially cross over at the optic chiasma before reaching the brain. In this way, each of the brain's hemispheres receives information from each eye. The optic nerves enter the brain at the level of the thalamus and proceed to the visual cortex, which is located in the occipital lobe.

15. Audition, or the act of hearing, requires both rhythmical variations in the pressure of a medium near us and the reception of those variations by the ear, which in turn codes and transmits information to the brain. Sound waves travel through air to our ears in a sequence of pressure and rarefaction.

16. Sound waves have three important characteristics: frequency, amplitude, and phase. Frequency is the measurement (in hertz units) of how many waves occur each second. It is frequency that principally determines the pitch of a sound; intensity, or loudness is largely determined by amplitude. The phase of a sound wave determines whether or not the wave is in synchronous frequency and amplitude with another wave.

17. The function of the ear is to detect sound waves and transform them into electrical impulses. Sound waves enter the ear through the auditory canal and travel to the eardrum, which is next to the middle ear. The ossicles (malleus, incus, and stapes) of the middle ear transmit the sound waves next to the oval window, which is the gateway to the inner ear and its principal structure, the cochlea. Inside the cochlea is the cochlear partition; on the bottom side of the cochlear partition is the basilar membrane. Located on the basilar membrane is the organ of Corti, which contains sensitive hair cells, the receptors of the inner ear. Vibrations of the basilar membrane cause the hairs to bend, converting mechanical energy to electrical energy, which triggers a nerve impulse to the auditory nerve; the electrical impulses concerned with hearing travel to the brain.

18. Smell and taste are chemical senses. Of all the senses, smell, or olfaction, has the most direct route to the brain. Receptors high in each nasal cavity carry smell directly to the two olfactory bulbs, which lie in the frontal lobes of the brain and are joined to the olfactory cortex.

19. The primary taste organs are the papillae, dark red spots on the tongue. There are some 9,000 taste buds in the human tongue and each bud contains several receptor cells. The nature of the contact between these receptor cells and the stimulants of flavor molecules has not been clearly established. Taste has been classified into four basic qualities: sweet, sour, salty, and bitter.

20. Skin sensations—touch, warmth, cold, and pain—are known collectively as somesthesis. Some skin receptors are free nerve endings, the branching fibers of sensory neurons; others are specialized structures that encapsulate nerve fibers. Generally speaking, sensory fibers leading from the skin travel in bundles that are segregated for each different sensation. Some large fibers are coated with myelin, which speeds up the transmission of the nerve impulse. Other, finer fibers, some unmyelinated, carry only sensations of pain or temperature. Sensory cell bodies lie in a small group of neurons just outside the spinal cord called the dorsal root ganglion. One branch of the sensory fibers ascends by relays to the thalamus deep in the brain and then to the cortex of the parietal lobe. The sensory pathways cross en route to the brain so that skin sensations from the right side of the body register in the left part of the parietal lobe, and vice versa.

21. The senses of position and movement are extremely important even though we are seldom conscious of them. One category of these senses is detected principally through receptor cells in muscles, tendons, and joints and is called kinesthesis. Kinesthesis encompasses the senses by which we discriminate body movement and position. The other category involves the vestibular system, which deals with the movement and position of the head and is important to equilibrium.

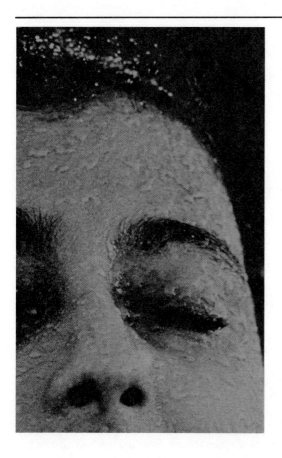

Chapter 4
Perception

The late American brain researcher Karl Lashley liked to tell his friends stories about his migraine headaches. These headaches often were preceded or accompanied by large *scotomas*, or blind spots, in his field of vision. On one occasion, Lashley recalled, the scotoma was so large that it momentarily beheaded a colleague who happened to be standing in front of him. But Lashley's perceptual mechanisms instantly filled in the gap with vertical stripes from the wallpaper in the background. Lashley also remembered vividly the time on a Florida road when a pursuing patrol car disappeared in his scotoma, which was then filled in by patterns from the surrounding landscape (Gore, 1971).

Lashley's experiences help us make an important distinction between the senses, which we discussed in the preceding chapter, and the process of perception. By receiving and coding stimuli around us, such as light and sound waves, the senses provide the raw materials for perception. But *perception* is a far more creative process: it is the transformation of the evidence of our senses into mental representations (see Plate 13). Facts, or data, are fed into computers, but they mean nothing until the machine has processed the coded information and arranged it in a meaningful way. In a similar way our senses feed information to our brains. It is only after the brain has processed stimuli from the senses that we perceive. Through perception, a mosaic of light and darkness is transformed and interpreted as the beauty of an autumn sunset; pressure waves in the air become a Bach fugue; signals from touch receptors in our skin are felt as the caress of a lover.

In his book *Eye and Brain* (1977), the English psychologist Richard Gregory calls perception "a dynamic searching for the best interpretation of the available data." Such interpretations are made in the light of expectations, existing or preconceived notions that may be quite independent of incoming sensory data. Some of these expectations are based on cues that seem to be built into our perceptual apparatus—for example, the way linear perspective helps us determine depth. Such cues are dramatically illustrated in those fascinating puzzles known as visual illusions, which can mislead us to incorrect interpretations of the sensory data (see Figure 4.1). Other expectations depend on psychological concepts and processes discussed elsewhere in this

FIGURE 4.1 Visual illusions. (A) The center circles in both patterns are equal in diameter but appear unequal. (B) The heavy form in the lefthand figure is a perfect circle and the heavy form in the righthand figure is a perfect square, although they appear to be distorted by the background pattern. (C) The three cylinders are the same size but appear to be different sizes. (D) The two lines are equal but appear unequal.

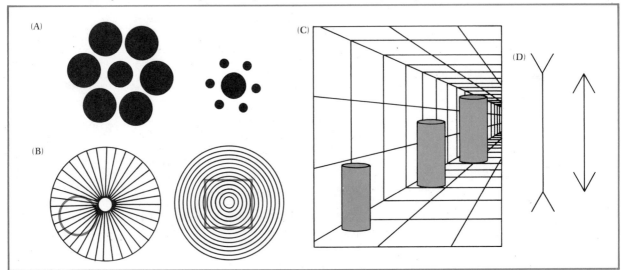

text: learning and memory (we know it's a Bach fugue because we have heard it before); emotion and mood (which can determine whether stimulation of the pressure receptors in the skin is interpreted as a loving caress or an irritant). Even individual personality can influence perception: witness the varying ways in which people interpret the chaotic forms that comprise the Rorschach inkblot test (see Chapter 12).

In this chapter we will focus principally on visual perception, the dominant means by which we build up mental representations of the world. A majority of the external stimuli to which we respond is visual. Vision is the "dominant" sense: if we receive conflicting information from our visual apparatus and a different sensory modality—touch, for example—we will usually respond to the visual appearance.

We will begin with an introduction to visual perception, then go on to discuss the mechanisms of form vision and the perception of depth and motion. Next, we will consider several issues relating to the roles of heredity and learning in the development of visual perception. Following that is a brief discussion of auditory perception, a subject no less fascinating than vision but one about which far less is known. Finally, we will examine some of the biological and cognitive bases of time perception.

Visual Perception: An Introduction

From childhood, we have looked out at the world and recognized familiar objects and faces. Small children can go through a large and elaborate picture book and correctly identify all of the objects in it. We walk to school or work in the morning and guide our footsteps over the pavement without thinking about it. We watch a tennis ball coming across the net and organize all of our movements to meet it with the racket. Visual perception is so natural, so much a part of our everyday life, that it is difficult to think about it analytically. It seems evident to us that things look as they do because they are there.

Yet vision requires an enormous amount of active registration, analysis, sorting, filtering, and comparing by our perceptual mechanisms—first in the eye itself, but chiefly at centers within the brain. For example, although we are not aware of it, all of us have a blind spot in each eye, a smaller version of the scotoma that occurred in Karl Lashley's

migraine attacks (see Chapter 3). Ordinarily we are unaware of this small hole in our vision because the perceptual mechanisms of the brain fill it up with the surrounding patterns.

We will look first at three characteristics of visual perception that long have intrigued researchers—perceptual adaptation, visual capture, and perceptual constancy.

Perceptual Adaptation

For more than a century, a favorite experimental tool of researchers who study visual perception has been goggles that distort what is seen. In his treatise on physiological optics, the nineteenth-century researcher Hermann von Helmholtz (1962) suggested the following experiment:

> Take two glass prisms with refracting angles of about 16° or 18° and place them in a spectacle frame, with their edges both turned toward the left. As seen through these glasses, the objects in the field of view will all apparently be shifted to the left of their real position. At first, without bringing the hand into the field, look closely at some definite object within reach, and then close the eyes, and try to touch the object with the forefinger. The usual result will be to miss it by thrusting the hand too far to the left. But, after trying for some little while, or more quickly still, by inserting the hand in the field, and under the guidance of the eye, touching the objects with it for an instant, then on trying the above experiment again, we shall discover that now we do not miss the objects, but feel for them correctly. It is the same way when new objects are substituted for those with which we have become familiar. Having learned how to do this, suppose now we take off the prisms and remove the hand from the field of view, and then after gazing steadily at some object, close our eyes, and try to take hold of it. We find then that the hand will miss the object by being thrust too far to the right; until after several failures, our judgment of the direction of the eyes is rectified again.

This simple effect of a prism on visual reaching is easy to replicate. When you first put a prism in front of your eye and reach for an object, you miss the object by about the same degree that the prism displaces the visual world. After a few tries with the prism in place, your reach becomes accurate again. When the prism is taken away, you misreach in the opposite direction.

The ability to compensate for an artificially displaced visual field is called *perceptual adaptation.* Perceptual adaptation is a form of learning or re-learning. In the first few days after beginning to wear corrective contact lenses, one's entire visual apparatus has to adjust to a changed sensing of stimuli. The perceptual apparatus is altered or adapted. We might assume that this perceptual adaptation takes place in the mechanisms that control visual direction. However, Charles Harris (1965) found that subjects who adapt to a prism and then are asked to point in the direction of a sound source do not point accurately. If perceptual adaptation involved only vision, such an error should not occur.

Moreover, when Harris's subjects were adapted to the prism with their right arm and could successfully point to the target, they showed no sign of such adaptation with the left arm. When they were asked to point at the target while looking through the prism, they missed. This finding further supports the argument against a simple visual mechanism of prism adaptation. Harris concluded that the adaptation actually occurred because of a recalibration in the felt position of the arm—that is, the kinesthetic sense by which we determine position and movement in various parts of the body.

In summary, although perceptual adaptation may be induced visually, its principal effect may be on other senses.

Visual Capture

The findings on prism adaptation suggest another important characteristic of visual perception. When visual perception and another sense come into conflict, vision tends to win. In the Harris experiment, seeing was indeed believing. What the subjects saw was more convincing than what they felt in their arms. Vision, for humans, seems to be the dominant sense.

This tendency of vision to dominate the other senses has been called *visual capture.* Experiments have shown that if we view a square through a distorting lens that makes the square appear as a rectangle and feel the square object at the same time, we will still perceive the object as a rectangle. (Rock and Victor, 1964). Vision dominates touch in this example of visual capture (see Figure 4.2). Another instance of visual capture was dramatically demonstrated half a century ago by James J. Gibson (1933), who had his subject wear prism spectacles that created the illusion that everything was curved. Then he presented her with a rulerlike straightedge. As expected, the subject saw the straightedge as a curved rather than a straight object. When she ran

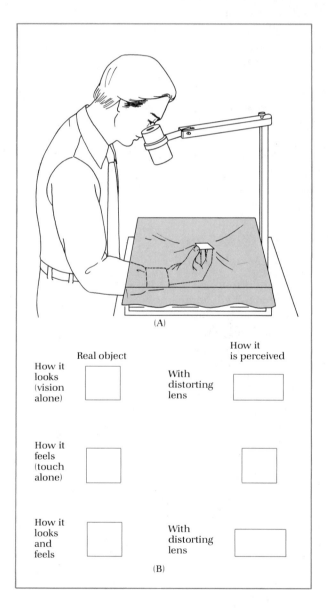

(A)

	Real object		How it is perceived
How it looks (vision alone)	☐	With distorting lens	☐
How it feels (touch alone)	☐		☐
How it looks and feels	☐	With distorting lens	☐

(B)

FIGURE 4.2 The experimental arrangement used to demonstrate visual capture includes a distorting lens and a cloth to cover the subject's hand to prevent him from detecting the distortion. The object being grasped is a small plastic square. As the schematic drawings of the results indicate, if the square is viewed through a distorting lens, it is perceived as a rectangle; if it is felt without being seen, it is perceived as a square; if it is viewed with a distorting lens and felt at the same time, it is perceived as a rectangle.

her hand along the edge of the object while looking at it through the prism spectacles, an additional illusion was created. Not only did the straightedge look curved, it also felt curved. The subject's visual perception mechanisms had dominated her sense of touch; that is, her sense of touch had been visually captured.

What happens when hearing comes into conflict with vision? The illusion created by ventriloquists depends on visual capture. Ventriloquists do not actually throw their voices. They merely assume that our vision, fixed upon the moving lips of the dummy, will win out over our hearing, which if not for visual capture, would perceive that the sound was in fact coming from the ventriloquist. The discrepancy between visual and auditory information is thus resolved in favor of vision.

Perceptual Constancy

Another highly important characteristic of visual perception is the stability, or *perceptual constancy*, of the shape, size, brightness, and color of objects in our visual fields. We recognize the same objects at a variety of angles, at various distances, and even under sharply differing kinds of light. We perceive a piece of coal as black whether it is in shade or bright sunlight. We perceive people to be the same size whether they are 5 or 15 meters away. We perceive a door as a rectangle whether it is closed or half open. Although the sensory stimuli imaged on the retina change with shape, size, and brightness, we recognize the objects as stable, and our perception of them tends to remain the same. The mechanisms of constancy produce adaptive perception: we perceive objects as having relatively permanent physical properties in spite of variation in physical stimulus.

Shape Probably the easiest kind of perceptual constancy to demonstrate is *shape constancy.* Hold up a coin in front of your eyes and rotate it. As you rotate the coin, the image of it on your retina becomes an ellipse that grows smaller and smaller, then it becomes a line, and finally an ellipse again (see Figure 4.3). Nonetheless, at each orientation, it is still perceived as a circular coin. Similarly, a square rotated in front of your eyes becomes a distorted trapezoid on your retina; yet if you are aware that the figure is being rotated, you still perceive it as a square. A door or window casts a rectangular image only when viewed from a certain point; however, both appear rectangular from whatever point we view them. Thus, objects maintain their apparent constancy of shape despite rotation or differences in the point from which we view them.

Size Look at someone standing near you and then compare that perception with your perception of someone standing across the street. They look about the same size to you even though the actual size of the respective images on your retina may differ by a factor of 10 to 1 or more. Perceived size does not regularly follow retinal size. As we will discuss in detail later in this chapter, we interpret the size of objects in terms of their distance from us; we interpret relative size appropriate to the distance. This tendency for the perceptual apparatus to take into account the distance of an object in judging its size is called *size constancy*. It also further illustrates the adapative nature of perceptual constancy.

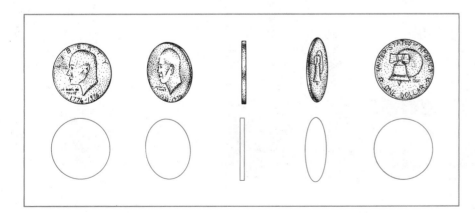

FIGURE 4.3 Demonstration of shape constancy. As a coin is rotated, its image becomes an ellipse that grows narrower and narrower until it becomes a thin rectangle, an ellipse again, and then a circle. At each orientation, however, it is still perceived as a circular coin.

The concept of size constancy provides a reasonable explanation for why we are fooled by certain visual illusions. In the *Ponzo illusion*, for example, two lines of equal length are drawn between two converging lines (see Figure 4.4). Although drawing is two-dimensional, the converging lines appear to add the third dimension of depth or distance. As the converging lines come closer together like railroad tracks receding in the distance, we interpret them as parallel lines that are becoming more and more distant. Thus, the top line in the Ponzo illusion appears to be farther away. Because the line appears to be more distant, the principle of size constancy is called into play; our perceptual system assumes that the top line would look shorter than the bottom line if they were of the same length. Because it is the same length, the distance cue makes it actually appear to be longer.

The famous ventriloquist Edgar Bergen converses with his dummy Charlie McCarthy. The voice appears to be coming from the dummy because the discrepancy between visual and auditory information is resolved in favor of vision.

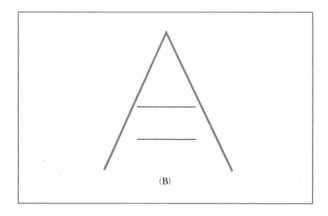

(B)

FIGURE 4.4 The Ponzo illusion, demonstrated in a photograph (A) and a sketch (B). The converging lines add a dimension of depth, and hence the distance cue makes the top (or "more distant") line appear larger than the bottom line even though they are actually the same length.

(A)

Brightness   A lump of coal in sunlight reflects a larger amount of light than does a white paper in a dimly lit room. Yet the coal still looks black in the sunlight, and the white paper still looks white in the dimly lit room. This tendency of our perception of an object's brightness to remain stable over a wide range of illumination is called *brightness constancy*.

To understand brightness constancy, we need to review the process by which we perceive whether an object is white or black. We know that white surfaces reflect more light than do black surfaces. However, perception of brightness does not depend on the absolute amount of light reflected from an object but on the relative amount. T. K. Gelb (1929) demonstrated this principle in a classic experiment. Gelb positioned a spinning disk of black paper in a doorway so that when he projected a light on it, the illumination would fall only on the disk. The result was that the black disk actually looked white. However, when Gelb placed a bit of white paper in front of it, the disk appeared to turn black. In the absence of an external clue such as the bit of white paper, the brightly lit disk gave off more light than anything in its surroundings and hence was perceived as white. The presence of the white paper changed this perception because the white paper reflected much more light than the black disk. Thus, the relative amount of light—not the absolute amount—determines our perception of brightness (see Chapter 3).

A phenomenon based on similar principles of brightness perception is shown in Figure 4.5. Suppose we draw a disk of neutral gray. The apparent brightness or darkness of the gray disk is influenced powerfully by what surrounds the disk. If we surround the disk with a black band, the gray of the central disk appears quite light. If we surround the disk with a white band, it appears much darker.

FIGURE 4.5   The apparent brightness or darkness of a gray disk is influenced by what surrounds the disk. If the disk is surrounded by a white band, it appears much darker than an identical disk surrounded by a black band.

Again our perception is influenced by the relative amount of light (Cornsweet, 1970).

Animal vision operates in a similar manner. In one of the best experiments in modern animal psychophysics, Donald Blough (1961) showed that pigeons are influenced powerfully by the lightness of the surround in their judgment of the brightness of a center target. Even pigeons take background illumination into account and thus show brightness constancy.

Color   We perceive the colors of an object as a constant if we are able to see the object's surroundings. The color of a lemon viewed through a tube so that only the lemon is visible may or may not be perceived as yellow depending on the wavelength of the light rays striking it. If, however, we can see the lemon on a table or in a bowl of other fruit, we will see a yellow lemon because we have background clues as color referents. *Color constancy* is analogous to brightness constancy in that the light falling on an object and its surroundings determine the hue we perceive.

Perception of Shape and Form

When we look at the world around us, we break it down into meaningful units of shape and form without thinking. How do we perceive form? How are the stimuli of light imaged on the retina transformed into the pattern that we recognize as the familiar face of our grandmother? There are many ways to approach the study of form perception. We will consider first early psychological studies by the Gestalt theorists and then describe in detail the more recent attempts to understand the neural basis of form perception.

Figure-Ground Differentiation

The Danish psychologist, Edgar Rubin, in 1915 presented evidence that parts of any differentiated visual field will stand out from other parts. That part appearing as a distinct, delineated shape is the figure; the remainder is the ground. Shape and form tend to stand out against a background. This is called the *figure-ground relationship*. There are

103

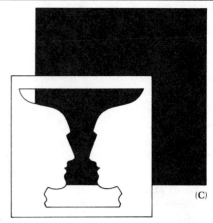

(A)　　　　　　　　　　　　(B)　　　　　　　　　　　　(C)

FIGURE 4.6 The Rubin vase is often used to illustrate the distinction between figure and ground. In (A) the figure-ground relationship is ambiguous. If the lines are perceived as marking the edges of the shaded space in the center, then the shaded space is the figure, the white space is the ground, and we see a vase; if the lines are perceived as marking the right and left edges of the white space, then the white space is the figure, the shaded space is the ground, and we see two facing profiles. In (B) the ambiguity is reduced to accent the vase, and in (C) the profiles are accented.

instances in which the relationship between figure and ground is ambiguous. For example, in the classic visual illusion shown in Figure 4.6, figure and ground keep changing; the white goblet against the dark background is clearly the figure until we perceive the two faces against the white background. Ambiguous relationships between figure and ground are frequently encountered in the natural world in the form of protective camouflage (see Plate 12).

An early contribution to our thinking about form vision came from the group who called themselves *Gestalt* psychologists, from the German word for shape or form. This group, working mainly at the University of Berlin during the 1920s, studied several important phenomena in the organization of perception. Through a combination of description, intuition, and experimentation, the Gestalt psychologists attempted to formulate underlying principles by which we organize the visual field into figure and ground. These principles include the following:

Closure The perceptual tendency to fill in gaps in an otherwise continuous pattern is known as *closure* (see Figure 4.7).

Continuity A principle closely related to closure is *continuity.* We perceive elements in interesting patterns as being grouped together (see Figure 4.8). When continuity prevails it is as though a pattern were generated that creates a sense of smooth movement, which takes precedence over any of the separate elements that make up the actual pattern.

Proximity Elements that are physically close to one another look as if they go together. For example, when we see an array of dots like the following;

. . . .
. . . .
. . . .

we see it as three horizontal rows of dots. But if we see

. . . .
. . . .
. . . .

we interpret it as eight short columns of dots. *Proximity* organizes the total pattern into meaningful subunits (see Plate 13).

FIGURE 4.7 Because of closure, the tendency to fill in gaps, we perceive the sketch at the left as a circle and the sketch at the right as a horse and rider.

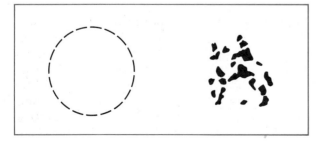

FIGURE 4.8 Because of continuity, the square element in this illustration is perceived as belonging to the wave-shaped pattern, while the dot to the right is perceptually isolated.

Similarity We perceive similar elements (if proximity is equal) as being grouped together. *Similarity* organizes the elements as part of a meaningful pattern.

Some of the Gestalt principles are very similar to ideas suggested by contemporary scientists interested in the computer analysis of visual scenes. In this sense, Gestalt psychologists were pioneers in a new and important way of studying perception. But when the Gestalt theorists attempted to infer what might be happening in the brain itself during form perception, they did not have enough information. Gestalt theorists speculated that what we see is generated on the surface of the brain in electrical patterns that correlate point by point with the shapes imaged on the retina. Such speculation occurred because at that time the major tool for the study of the physiological processes in form perception was not yet available. It is this tool—the recording of responses of individual cells in the visual pathways—that has given the first insights into how form is processed in the brain.

Feature Detectors

How is the stimulus of light processed and transformed by the nervous system into recognizable forms? Although the answer to that complex question is still far from clear, research over the past few decades has supplied some tantalizing clues. The aim of such research is to establish systematically the response properties of individual cells at the various way stations that comprise the visual pathways. To do this, a microelectrode is placed near a given cell in the eye or brain of a research animal, and the electrical responses there are measured when various stimuli are presented to the eye.

As we saw in the preceding chapter, such experiments have shown that cells at the early stages in the visual pathways have relatively simple spatial response properties. For example, at the very first stage the rods and cones of the retina are activated in response to the absolute amount of light that falls upon them. Farther along in the retina, the ganglion cells respond to a very specific distribution of light and shade or to changes in illumination in their receptive field. The individual retina cells react only to tiny regions of light and dark; they are, in effect, indifferent to the overall shapes on the retina.

These discoveries, although important to our understanding of the physiological basis of vision, tell us little about how the perception of form takes place at the cellular level. For clues to that process we must look farther back in the visual pathways, at the brain itself.

The visual cortex of the brain is mapped in a point-to-point relationship with the retina. The fact that an image is formed on the retina means that neighboring rods and cones in the retina sense adjacent areas in the visual field; so too do neighboring nerve cells in the cortex respond to inputs from adjacent areas in the visual field. But in the cortex this relationship of neighboring points is characterized by distortions in shape and size. A square in the visual field does not activate a corresponding square of neurons in the cortex.

The work of David Hubel and Torsten Wiesel (1962) has made clear that the visual cortex contains nerve cells that respond to specific features of shape or orientation in their receptive fields. These cells have been called *feature detectors*. The features they appear to detect are linear in nature—for example, lines, bars, and edges at a particular orientation. Such feature detectors are doubtless the building blocks of perception.

Working first with cats and then with monkeys, Hubel and Wiesel placed microelectrodes near individual cells of the visual cortex and recorded the cellular activity that occurred when simple shapes were projected onto a screen in front of the animal. Hubel and Wiesel have described three different types of cells found in the visual cortex that show increasing complexity in their response properties.

Simple cells respond best to a linear shape or edge at a particular orientation and place in their receptive field—for example, a vertical line.

Complex cells resemble simple cells in their sensitivity to a line or edge at a given orientation, but unlike simple cells, certain complex cells also respond to an edge or line at any place in their receptive field. For example, as long as the orientation is correct, the cell will respond to a black-white edge anywhere within its receptive field if the black and white are arranged in a specific way:

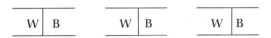

Note that in this case the white region is positioned to the left; the black to the right. Thus, a complex cell with this receptive field would fire whenever a black edge of this orientation was placed anywhere within its receptive field.

Hypercomplex cells, as their name implies, have even more complex and selective response properties. One class of hypercomplex cell responds to a line anywhere in the visual field, but only if the edge has a specific length as well as orientation.

The relationships among these three classes of cells is still not entirely clear. Hubel and Weisel suggested a serieslike schema whereby complex cells receive their input from many simple cells, and hypercomplex cells in turn are activated by several complex cells. But the fact that complex cells may be activated at the same time or even before simple cells suggests that simple cells do not necessarily provide the functional inputs to complex cells.

Pattern Recognition

Feature detectors probably represent a relatively early step in recognizing patterns such as letters of the alphabet or specific shapes. Somehow and somewhere in the brain there must be a further synthesis of the simple information extracted by the feature detectors. Some neural mechanism for comparison that matches a given pattern with our stored memory of what it looks like must exist. Although feature detectors may prove to be the building blocks of perception, it is unlikely that the further processing necessary for pattern recognition actually takes place in the first way station for vision—the primary visual cortex. For one thing, the nerve cells there are highly localized in their responses; they fire only when an appropriate target is placed in just the right region of the visual field. Our perception of forms is inconsistent with such a strict preservation of a point-to-point map of the visual fields. For example, we can recognize the letter E independently of the precise region of the visual fields in which we see it or its size. It is the pattern of activation to which we respond, not its precise position or size.

In humans and monkeys, the visual cortex makes connections with other cortical areas and with several targets deep in the brain. There is excellent evidence that a part of the temporal lobe is heavily involved in pattern recognition. During the 1950s, Kao Liang Chow (1951), and Mortimer Mishkin and Karl Pribram (1954) established that lesions in the inferior temporal cortex of monkeys greatly impair the animal's ability to learn form discrimination. The resulting deficit was even greater than that produced by lesions of an equal size in the visual cortex itself.

Is There a Grandmother Cell? A possible relationship between nerve cells and pattern recognition has led to speculation that in some cases the firing of a specific cell might be the neural equivalent of a specific perception. Brain scientists have given a colorful shorthand name to such a supposed processing mechanism: they refer to it as the *grandmother cell*. The idea is that either in the temporal cortex or somewhere else in the brain there might be a cell that is able to recognize all the features that add up to the pattern that constitutes your grandmother. If you see someone who looks something like your grandmother, the cell will fire but not at optimal frequency. It fires best only when it recognizes your grandmother.

The notion of a grandmother cell is only speculation, of course, and few neural scientists believe that the activity of any one cell is the key to understanding pattern recognition.

One obvious problem with the idea of a grandmother cell is that we would have to have a master cell for recognizing each of the people, objects, and patterns we know—a number so large that even the brain probably could not accommodate them. But there is some evidence that a process like a grandmother cell may be involved in some instances of visual recognition. Charles Gross and his colleagues found cells in the inferotemporal cortex of a monkey with highly specific trigger features. One of these was activated briskly by the image of a monkey's hand (Gross, Rocha-Miranda, and Bender, 1972).

Ensemble Coding An alternative view of pattern recognition is that it involves a group of nerve cells firing in some definite pattern. According to this view, each perception must be represented by some kind of *ensemble code*—that is, the firing of various combinations of the same set of nerve cells that should signify different perceptions.

How ensemble coding might work is harder to grasp intuitively than the grandmother cell concept. It may be useful to think of your memory cells as having a "feature list." Such a list for your grandmother might include the angle of her eyebrows, the width of her nose and mouth, her browline, and so forth. When you see a woman of your grandmother's age and size (or anyone, for that matter), the feature detectors are activated and messages are sent to the memory cells. Your brain would compare the face you now see with the list associated in your memory cells with your grandmother. If the list matches, then it is, indeed, your grandmother.

Perception of Depth

One of the most prosaic and yet profound statements about visual perception is that we live in a three-dimensional world. Although the retina is essentially a flat, two-dimensional surface, we perceive depth and distance: our visual landscape unfolds in an orderly manner with some objects appearing to be near us and others farther in the distance.

What are the visual cues that enable us to perceive depth? Some of these cues require the use of only one eye and are thus *monocular*. Other cues are *binocular*, requiring the use of both eyes.

Monocular Cues

An interesting way to identify the monocular cues for perceiving depth is to consider the techniques painters use to portray the three-dimensional world on a two-dimensional canvas.

Perspective   Artists typically discuss the problem of representing three-dimensional space in terms of perspective—that is, cues that are important to our perception of depth. Although perspective is so widely used in painting that we take it for granted, the idea is a comparatively recent one. One technique for portraying depth on a canvas is *linear perspective*. Parallel lines are drawn so that they seem to converge on a distant spot known as the vanishing point. Distant objects are drawn much smaller than nearby objects (see Figure 4.9).

We experience linear perspective often in everyday perception. Imagine, for example, a row of equally spaced telephone poles along the roadside. As you look down the road, the edges of the road appear to converge, the telephone poles get progressively smaller, and the apparent distance between the equally spaced poles seems to lessen as the distance increases (see Figure 4.10).

Another instance of linear perspective, with its apparent convergence of parallel lines as they recede, can be experienced when we look up at a tall building. The two sides of the building seem to

FIGURE 4.9   In this Italian painting by Bellini, depth is achieved through use of the technique of linear perspective. The buildings on both sides of the canvas are drawn so that they appear as if they are on parallel lines that would converge at some distant point. Also, distant objects are drawn much smaller than nearby ones.

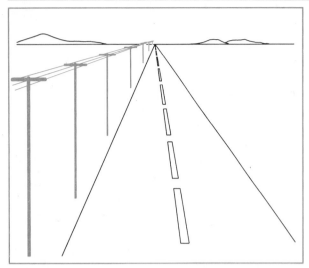

FIGURE 4.10 As you look at these rows of equally spaced telephone poles along the side of a road, the edges of the road appear to converge, the poles get progressively smaller, and the distance between poles seems to decrease.

converge toward the top, giving the impression that the building is tapered (see Figure 4.11). To counteract this impression, some architects actually have designed buildings that are wider at the top than at the bottom. A notable example is the Bell Tower in the Cathedral of Florence (see Figure 4.12). The increase in width at the top helps compensate for the effects of linear perspective. As a result, the building looks more uniformly rectangular than would a building whose sides were truly parallel.

In addition to linear perspective, painters use *aerial perspective* as another cue to depth perception. Light reflected from a distant object is partially scattered or absorbed by small particles in the atmosphere before it reaches our eyes. The longer the distance, the more the light is affected by the atmosphere. Light reflected from distant mountains may travel many miles before reaching our eyes; hence, the outline of the mountains appears blurred and fuzzy and bluish color. Painters use aerial perspective to achieve the impression of great distance (see Figure 4.13).

FIGURE 4.11 When we look up at a tall building that is actually rectangular, such as New York City's World Trade Center, the sides appear to converge at the top, and the building appears to be tapered.

FIGURE 4.12 The Bell Tower of the Cathedral of Florence was designed to be wider at the top than at the bottom to compensate for the tapering effect shown in Figure 4.11.

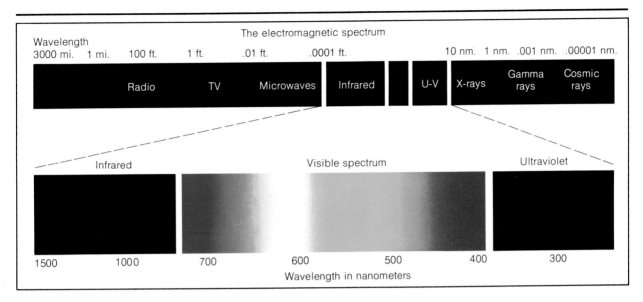

PLATE 1 THE ELECTROMAGNETIC SPECTRUM
At the top is shown the full spectrum of electromagnetic radiation. The human eye can only see the narrow band extending from 400 to 700 nanometers, which is shown enlarged in the bottom portion of the figure.

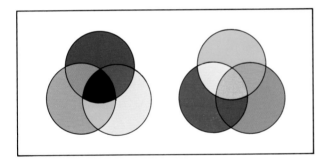

PLATE 2 COLOR MIXTURES
Additive mixtures (left) are mixtures of light of two or more wavelengths that will add up to a new color. Subtractive mixtures (right) are mixtures of pigments that absorb or subtract certain wavelengths and reflect the remaining wavelengths.

PLATE 3 OPPOSING COLORS
Stare at the red square for about 30 seconds. Then look at a white wall or sheet of paper. You will see a negative afterimage in green, the opposing color of red. Now look at the gray square in the green frame. The gray patch takes on a reddish cast when seen against the green background, demonstrating the same kind of opposite color pairing that shows up in the afterimage of the red square.

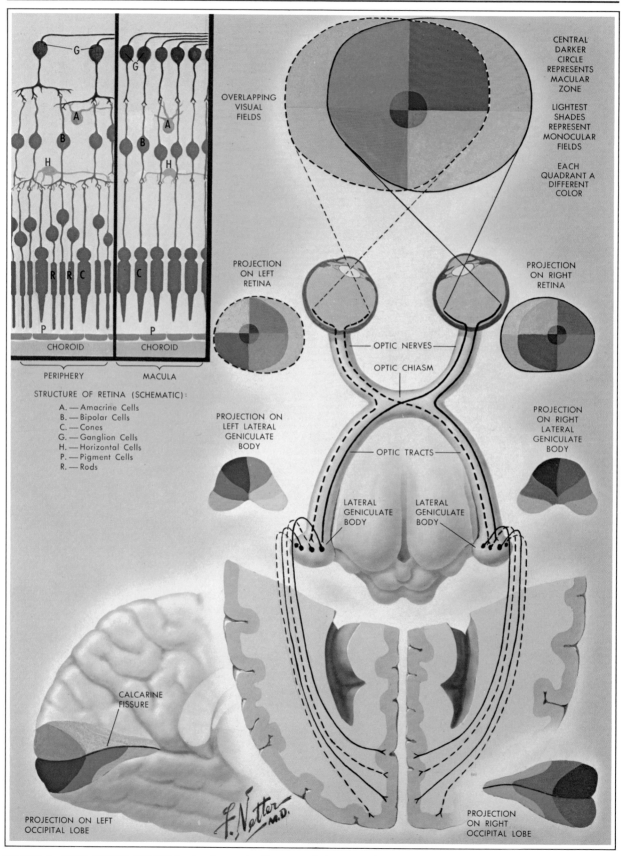

CENTRAL DARKER CIRCLE REPRESENTS MACULAR ZONE

LIGHTEST SHADES REPRESENT MONOCULAR FIELDS

EACH QUADRANT A DIFFERENT COLOR

OVERLAPPING VISUAL FIELDS

PROJECTION ON LEFT RETINA

PROJECTION ON RIGHT RETINA

OPTIC NERVES

OPTIC CHIASM

PROJECTION ON LEFT LATERAL GENICULATE BODY

PROJECTION ON RIGHT LATERAL GENICULATE BODY

OPTIC TRACTS

LATERAL GENICULATE BODY

LATERAL GENICULATE BODY

G

A

B

H

R R C

C

P

CHOROID

A

B

H

C

P

CHOROID

PERIPHERY

MACULA

STRUCTURE OF RETINA (SCHEMATIC):

A. — Amacrine Cells
B. — Bipolar Cells
C. — Cones
G. — Ganglion Cells
H. — Horizontal Cells
P. — Pigment Cells
R. — Rods

CALCARINE FISSURE

F. Netter M.D.

PROJECTION ON LEFT OCCIPITAL LOBE

PROJECTION ON RIGHT OCCIPITAL LOBE

PLATE 4   THE OPTIC SYSTEM   A schematic diagram of the complex structures of the optic system.

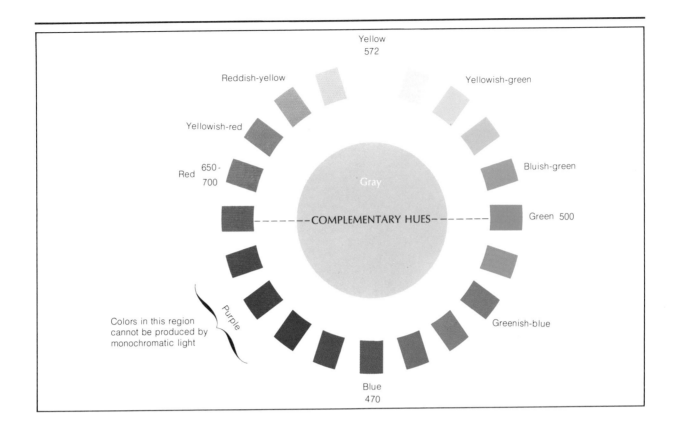

PLATE 5   HUE

The color circle illustrates the concept of hue. The color names and their corresponding wavelengths (in nanometers) are given along the outside of the circle. Complementary hues are those colors opposite each other in the circle (such as reddish-yellow and greenish-blue); they will result in gray when mixed. The mixing of any two wavelengths that are not opposite each other will result in an intermediate hue. For example, equal amounts of reddish-yellow and green yield yellow. Some hues, such as purple (a mixture of yellowish-red and blue) cannot be produced by a single wavelength.

PLATE 6   BRIGHTNESS AND SATURATION

Brightness ranges from black to white are shown on the vertical scale. Saturation range from a hue approaching gray to a "pure" red is shown on the horizontal scale. (Steps are numbered according to a standard system known as the Munsell system of notation.)

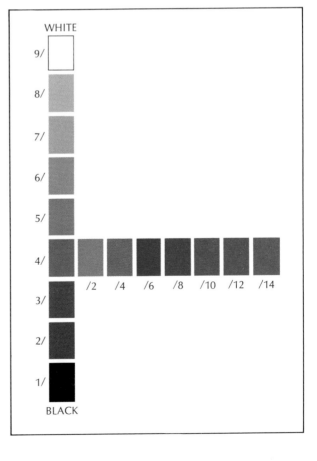

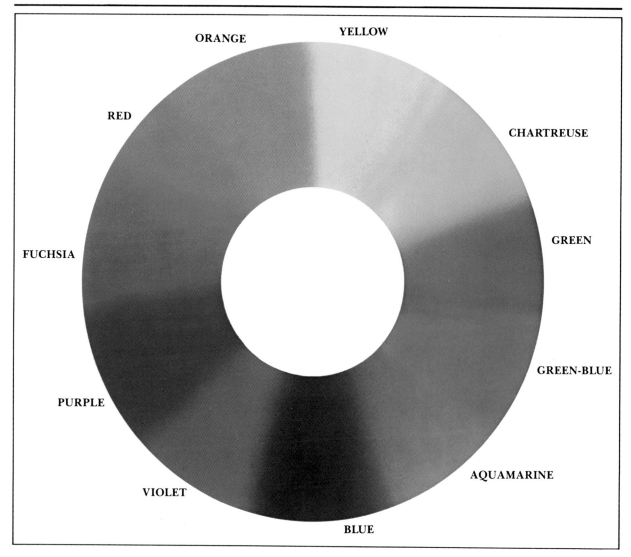

PLATE 7 CIRCLE OF PIGMENTS

When people are given an assortment of patches of pigments of various colors to organize, most order them in the same way. For example, orange and red are treated as similar and placed next to each other; yellow is treated as similar to orange, so it is placed next to orange. By continuing these comparisons, green will be placed between yellow and blue, blue will be placed between green and purple, and purple will be placed between blue and red. This procedure generates the circle of pigments.

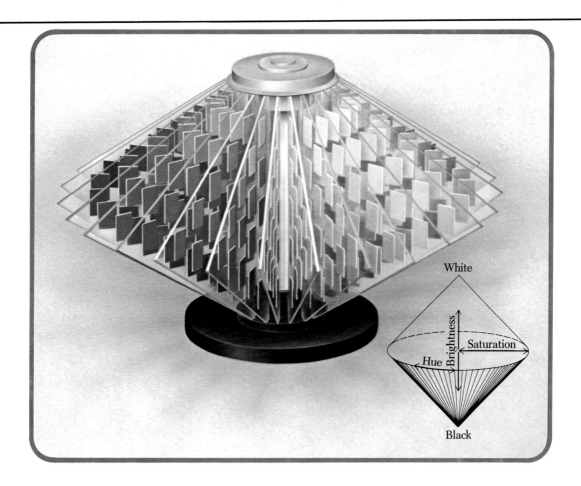

White

Brightness

Saturation

Hue

Black

PLATE 8   THE COLOR SPINDLE

The circle of pigments shown in Plate 7 does not account for many colors; where, for example, do pink, brown, royal blue, and pale yellow fit? Although pink is related to red, it differs from the red pigment because it is less intense. Brown does not resemble any of the other colors, nor does it appear to be a mixture of any of the colors. Royal blue is like blue but more intense. Pale yellow is like pure yellow, except that it looks less pure—as if a lot of white pigment had been mixed with the yellow. These colors can be represented along with those forming the circle of pigments by using two more dimensions. When all the hues at the rim of the circle represent the same amount of brightness, then the radius from the perimeter in toward the center can be used to represent decreasing amounts of saturation. The very center is that degree of grayness in which there is not even a hint of hue. The degree of brightness is represented by different color circles stacked on top of one another. The three dimensions form the color spindle, which represents the relationships among hue, saturation, and brightness. A complete color spindle would contain 350,000 patches of discriminable colors.

PLATE 9   COLOR BLINDNESS

These two illustrations are from a series of color-blindness tests. In the top illustration, people with normal vision see a number 6, while those with red-green color blindness do not. In the bottom illustration, people with normal vision see a number 12, while those with red-green color blindness may see one number or none. These reproductions of color recognition tests cannot be used for actual testing: they are only representative examples of the total of 15 charts necessary for a complete color recognition examination.

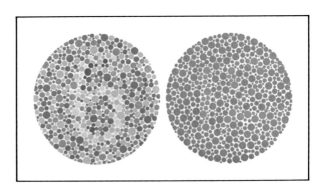

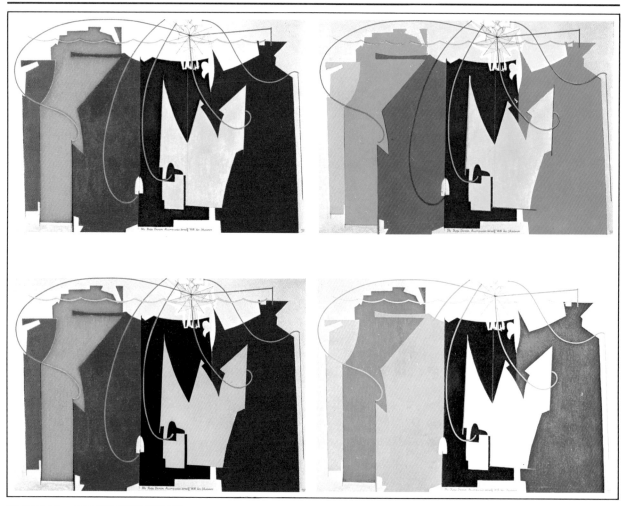

PLATE 10   COLOR BLINDNESS

The painting in the upper left panel appears as it would to a person with normal color vision. For people with red-green color blindness, the same picture would be seen as shown in the upper right panel. The lower left panel shows how the picture would be seen by people with yellow-blue color blindness, and the lower right panel shows how it would appear to people with total color blindness.

PLATE 11   RORSCHACH INKBLOT

This water color is similar to the colorful inkblots used in the Rorschach test. A psychologist can gather information about an individual's personality by asking that person to report what he or she sees in the inkblots.

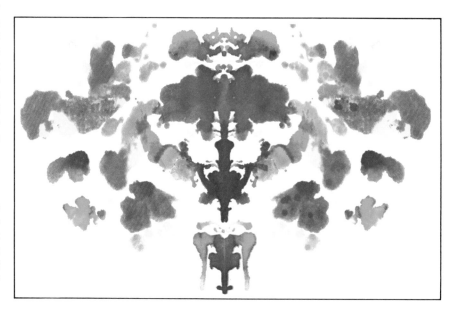

PLATE 12   CAMOUFLAGE
Ambiguous relationships between figure and ground often serve creatures in the natural world as protective camouflage. The coloration and striping of many animals enables them to blend with their background, so they remain concealed from potential prey or predators. The coloration of the mantid, for example, forms a pattern that does not coincide with the contours of the insect's body and thus aids in concealing its presence in foliage.

PLATE 13   POINTILLISM
The painter Georges Seurat used the technique known as pointillism to create *Port-en-Bessin, Entrance to the Harbor.* Your perceptual abilities allow you to look at this painting, which is really a series of points or dots, and see a complete scene.

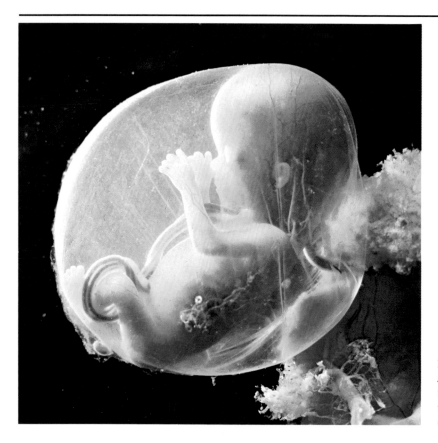

PLATE 14   THE HUMAN FETUS
At three months of age, the human fetus is about three inches (7.6 centimeters) long and weighs about 1 ounce (28 grams).

PLATE 15   THE HUMAN FETUS
The size of a three-month-old human fetus relative to an adult human hand.

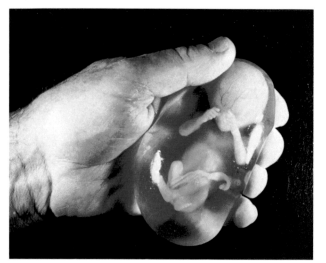

Overlap Perhaps the simplest monocular cue is *overlap*, or *interposition*. If, in a painting or in our view of a scene, a park bench partially obscures the grass behind it, we know that the bench is nearer to us than is the grass. In a drawing of two circles, if one overlaps the other, the fully exposed one is perceived as nearer (see Figure 4.14).

Relative Size Another monocular cue to depth is the *relative size* of objects. If we look at a large crowd, the people closest to us look bigger than the ones farther away. Because we assume that people do not vary all that much in size, we interpret the smaller-appearing person as being more distant. The American psychologist Adelbert Ames, who was formerly a painter, has made clever use of this effect in several illusions (Ittelson, 1952). One of the most celebrated is the Ames Room (see Figure 4.15), which is viewed from an observation station in the front wall. The two adjacent walls are parallel but the far wall is highly distorted. It angles away from the observer and, as this far wall recedes, the height increases. When no one is in the room, it looks normal. But when people of equal height are placed along the far wall, they appear grotesquely different in size. Because we see the far wall as rectangular, the person who nearly reaches the ceiling looks huge compared to the person who reaches only about halfway up.

Texture The American psychologist James Gibson (1950) has called attention to the importance of another cue in determining depth—that of *texture.* Texture is a form of microstructure characteristic of most surfaces and is generally seen as a grain. If we look down at a textured surface such as a rock-strewn beach, the appearance of the texture varies with distance. As the distance increases, the texture, or grain, appears to change gradually from coarse to fine (see Figure 4.16).

Motion Parallax A final monocular cue for depth perception, *motion parallax*, involves movement by

FIGURE 4.13 The use of aerial perspective permitted the artist to achieve the impression of great distance in this painting. The outline of the mountains is blurred to indicate what happens to light reflected from distant objects, which is partially scattered and absorbed before it reaches the viewer's eyes.

FIGURE 4.14 In this picture, we perceive the people sitting on the park bench as being closer to us than the grass and buildings because of overlap. The bench partially obscures the grass behind it, and the little girl partially blocks out the house, indicating that the grass and buildings are further away than the people and the bench.

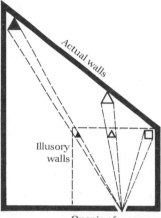

▲ Actual place and size of "smallest" man

▲ Illusory place and size of "smallest" man

△ Actual place and size of "medium" man

△ Illusory place and size of "medium" man

□ "Largest" man

Actual walls

Illusory walls

Opening for one eye

FIGURE 4.15 (A) A diagram of the Ames "distorted room," as seen from the top. (B) The Ames Room as seen from the front. The man on the left is actually the same height as the other two men.

the perceiver. Motion parallax is the difference in the apparent rate of movement of objects at different distances. For example, when you take a walk in the country, nearby objects such as fence posts and trees appear to change their position in step with your movements, while distant objects such as a mountain on the horizon seem to stay fixed in place. This difference in the apparent rate of movement helps us perceive relative depth. Motion parallax depends on the position of the observer. When the head moves, close elements (the fence posts) in the visual field appear to move faster than far objects (the mountains). The relative amount of apparent movement is less for far-away objects.

Binocular Cues

Although some monocular cues serve the painter and other perceivers quite well, even Leonardo da Vinci, who first formulated clearly the laws of linear perspective, recognized that a painting can never produce an impression of depth as compelling as that in the original scene. A major reason is that a painting, unlike our perceptions, lacks the advantages inherent in binocular vision. We can see and perceive with each eye singly, but the images from each eye are also combined in the brain. We become aware of this mechanism of binocular fusion only when something goes wrong with it. For example, if the coordination of the position of the two eyes does not work properly, we can have double vision or suppression of the image from one of the two eyes. When coordination works normally, the brain gives us single vision from each of two eyes and also extracts major cues for depth perception.

Convergence   One cue from binocular vision is the angle formed by the *convergence* of our two eyes as they pivot inward to focus on a single object. The function of convergence is to regulate the pattern of stimulation on each eye so as to avoid double images, which arise because the two eyes view the world from different positions on the head. Ordinarily, we are not consciously aware of these double images, but they can be illustrated by a simple demonstration (Woodworth, 1938). Hold a pencil vertically at a reading distance between your eyes,

FIGURE 4.16   Texture can be used as a cue for determining depth. As we look down a rock-strewn beach, the texture of the rocks appears to vary with distance. As the distance increases, the texture gradually appears to change from coarse to fine.

and fixate on a conspicuous and somewhat isolated object at the far end of the room. You will see a double image of the pencil. In order to yield a single image, the input from the two eyes must converge.

Convergence occurs only when objects are nearby—that is, less than about 3 meters away (Gogel, 1977). At these nearby distances, the eyes can serve as a rangefinder, signaling distance to the brain by recording the angle of convergence, which then indicates the relative depth. Because single vision for objects at different distances requires different degrees of inward pivoting of the eyes, kinesthetic feedback from the extraocular muscles, which control the movement of the eyeballs, might also provide cues to the depth and distance of a nearby object. At greater distances the visual axes of the two eyes are parallel, and hence there is no convergence. A major limitation of convergence is that the depth of only a single object can be gauged at any one time. In addition, the role of convergence as a primary source of depth or distance information has been difficult to assess, and its importance as a spatial cue is not agreed on (Ogle, 1962; Gregory, 1973).

Stereoscopic Vision The existence of two separate eyes provides an even more important cue for depth than convergence. Because our eyes are about 6.3 centimeters apart, each one has a slightly different point of view and thus records an image that is slightly different from that of the other eye. This slight disparity results in the perception of depth through *stereoscopic vision.*

The first clear account of the role of disparity was given in 1838 in a classic paper published by Charles Wheatstone, the English physicist. Wheatstone began by wondering whether a painting could ever represent a scene so perfectly that we could not tell it from reality. For the representation of distant scenes or objects his answer was affirmative: it should be possible for a painting to "render such perfect resemblances of the objects they are intended to represent, as to be mistaken for them." Then Wheatstone went on to point out how the accurate rendering of nearby scenes or objects was complicated by the problem of *disparity.* Each eye sees a subtly different aspect of the same nearby object. If, for example, you cover your right eye and look at a nearby object and then repeat the process with the other eye, it is clear that each eye sees a somewhat different view.

To test the effects of disparity, Wheatstone constructed a simple device using a pair of right-angle mirrors that simulated the effects of binocular perception. He drew a picture of two flagpoles at different distances as seen by his left eye only; then he drew the same scene as viewed by his right eye only. When Wheatstone viewed this pair of two-dimensional drawings on his new device, he saw in three dimensions. A powerful impression of depth was created—a stereoscopic view similar to that which occurs when the disparate views from each eye are fused in the brain.

Wheatstone had discovered stereoscopic vision and, in the process, had invented the stereoscope (see Figure 4.17). This instrument, perfected by Wheatstone and others, became a popular form of home entertainment toward the end of the nineteenth century, a way of looking at photographs of the Grand Canyon and other scenic wonders in three dimensions. The photographs for the device were sold in stereo pairs—that is, two pictures made by a pair of cameras separated by the same distance that separates our two eyes.

A modern tool for the study of the mechanism of stereoscopic vision is a device called the *random dot stereogram*, which was invented by Bela Julesz (1971) of the Bell Telephone Laboratories. The stereogram consists of a pair of patterns of computer-generated randomly positioned dots (see Figure 4.18). The stereograms, in fact, are identical except

FIGURE 4.17 The adjustable stereoscope provided an early method of looking at photographs in three dimensions through the use of two pictures separated by the same distance that separates our two eyes.

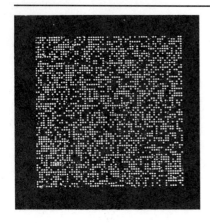

FIGURE 4.18 When the two random dot stereograms shown here are viewed one at a time, they are identical except the dots in the one on the right are moved slightly to the right. However, if they are viewed together in a stereoscope, a center square is seen floating above the background in vivid depth.

that, in one of them, one group of dots in the center has been moved slightly to one side or the other. The group that has been moved forms a recognizable shape such as a square. If these stereograms are viewed one at a time, the square shape is not apparent. But in the stereoscope, the pair of them create a powerful illusion of depth. The square seems to float in space above a background of random dots. The disparity between the two squares has been converted to depth.

Just where in the brain that fusing of stereoscopic images takes places is not entirely clear. Fusion of stereoscopic images most likely takes place in the brain at a level beyond the primary visual cortex.

The Pulfrich Effect   The role of disparity as a cue for depth perception is illustrated in a curious illusion known as the *Pulfrich effect*. Named after its discoverer, who was blind in one eye, it is all the more striking because the effect cannot be seen without two functional eyes. To see the Pulfrich effect, try the following experiment:

Tie a weight onto a string and allow the weight to swing back and forth in front of you. The weight should move like a pendulum without coming toward or away from you. As you watch the weight swinging back and forth with both eyes, place a filter over one eye so that the amount of light reaching that eye is less than the amount reaching the other. A neutral gray filter, a photographic negative, one lens of a pair of sunglasses, or even a piece of colored cellophane will work. When you look at the weight moving back and forth with the filter in front of one eye, you will notice an interesting effect. The weight now appears to move in an elliptical orbit, coming closer at one end of its pendulum swing

and then moving away from you on the other end. If you now shift the filter to the other eye, the direction of the ellipse is reversed (see Figure 4.19).

In order to understand the Pulfrich effect, we need to remember that a slight disparity in the position of an object on the two retinas can serve as a cue for depth. We also need to know that weak stimuli take a longer time to be processed by the eye and the brain than strong stimuli: because the less illuminated scene may require a longer period of time to cause a threshold potential to be reached, the retina of the eye viewing such a scene would take a longer period of time to get its messages going to the brain than the retina of the eye viewing a more brightly illuminated scene (Enright, 1970; Gregory, 1973). If less light enters the right eye than the left, the image from the right eye is received by the brain a bit more slowly than the image from the left eye. Because the pendulum is moving, the right eye sees it slightly behind the place where the left eye sees it. A small disparity is thus created in your perception of the location of the pendulum. This disparity is interpreted by the brain as a depth cue. The weight appears to move first toward you and then away from you. You can produce this same effect on your own television screen. If you put a filter in front of one eye, the screen will appear to have depth when there is movement across the screen.

Perception of Motion

Our visual world is seldom still. We are moving most of the time, and many of the objects around us are in constant motion. How do we tell whether something is moving or standing still?

Real Motion

An object must reach a certain speed before we can detect that it is moving. This threshold for motion perception varies, however, with circumstances such as the background. Against a uniform background, a small spot will appear to be moving only if it moves at least a third of a degree per second. Put another way, you will be able to see the spot only it if takes six seconds or more to move across the width of your thumb held at arm's length. Most normal perception of movement demands a frame of reference in order to sense that movement is taking place. It is possible however, to perceive motion without movement actually taking place.

Apparent Motion

If frames of reference are absent or distorted, objects do not have to move at all and can still be perceived as moving.

FIGURE 4.19 The Pulfrich pendulum effect occurs when a pendulum swinging in a straight arc in a plane perpendicular to the line of sight is viewed with a filter over one eye, it appears to swing in an ellipse. This is due to the fact that the signals from the eye covered by the filter are delayed, causing an apparent displacement of the pendulum bob away from the viewer when it moves from the filtered to the unfiltered side of the visual field and a displacement toward the viewer when the pendulum bob moves in the opposite direction.

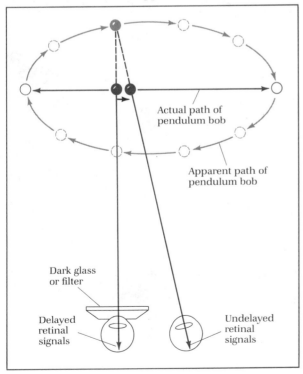

Actual path of pendulum bob

Apparent path of pendulum bob

Dark glass or filter

Delayed retinal signals

Undelayed retinal signals

The Phi Phenomenon Consider the following motion experiment. A few feet in front of you are two lights, *A* and *B*, separated by a short distance. These lights are alternately illuminated, each for a brief time. What you perceive will depend upon the length of the interval between the illumination of the two lights. If the interval between the illumination of *A* and *B* is less than 1/50 second, both appear to light up at the same time. If the interval is longer than 1/5 second, you will perceive what has in fact happened, *A* lights, and then *B* lights. If the interval is about 1/20 second, however, an illusion of movement is created. The light appears to move across the space from *A* to *B*.

This illusion of apparent movement is known as the *phi phenomenon* (Wertheimer, 1912). It is the basis for one of the most instructive and entertaining illusions of our time: motion pictures. Movies are a series of still pictures that are projected at a speed (24 frames per second for commercial films) that approximates the 1/20-second interval in the phi phenomenon. Commercial films give a total illusion of movement; whatever perceptual mechanism is responsible for the phi phenomenon neatly fills in the gaps between the frames. If you have ever made films with a home movie camera at very slow speeds—say about eight frames per second—you have noticed that the movement appears to be unnatural and jerky. This is because the film, at eight frames per second, is so slow that it is on the threshold of being perceived as a succession of still pictures rather than as motion pictures.

The Autokinetic Effect Another instance of apparent motion is the *autokinetic effect*, so named because it creates an illusion of spontaneous (auto) motion (kinetic). If you gaze at a small spot of light in a totally darkened room, the spot appears to move erratically, oscillating back and forth or even swooping off in one direction. The autokinetic effect is so powerful that, in the earlier days of flying, navigational beacons and other steady light sources at night caused pilots considerable confusion.

What creates the autokinetic effect is not entirely clear. Our own eye movements probably provide at least part of the explanation (Matin and MacKinnon, 1964). But eye movements cannot be the entire explanation because the illusion abruptly disappears when the background is even faintly illuminated (Levy, 1972).

Corollary Discharge   You can create the perception of apparent motion by placing your finger at the corner of your eye and then gently tapping it. As you can see, the world appears to jump back and forth. If you stop to think about it, this is remarkable: we are constantly moving our heads or eyes, but our movement does not make the scenes in front of us jump back and forth.

Researchers believe the reason for this lack of perceived motion lies in a hypothetical neural event they have labeled the *corollary discharge* (von Holst and Mittelstadt, 1950; von Holst, 1954). When the brain gives the command for the eyes to move, a

RESEARCH: Perceiving Motion in Depth

- The baseball zooms toward home plate at nearly 90 mph; the bat lashes out, catches the ball squarely and sends it over the left-field wall.
- The jet aircraft hurtled toward the ground; the pilot's precise touch on the controls eases the plane to a landing so gentle the passengers scarcely know they have touched ground.

Both of these highly skilled performances depend upon acute perception of the position and direction of the motion of objects in three-dimensional space. What is so remarkable is that such judgments are made by the brain on the basis of visual information that would seem to be woefully unsuited to the task: the flat two-dimensional images formed on the retina of each eye.

How can these two-dimensional retinal images provide the information necessary for the brain to make judgments about motion in three-dimensional space? Psychologists have identified several types of informational cues contained in the retinal images. They call these cues stimulus correlates of motion. The pilot, in order to achieve a safe landing, must make visual judgment of his own motion relative to a stationary world. A stimulus correlate in this instance is the flow pattern he sees as the plane approaches the ground—the manner in which objects in his visual field appear to flow radially away from the landing point. The baseball batter, on the other hand, depends upon other stimulus correlates of motion, including the changing size of the ball, which appears to grow larger as it comes closer.

A group of researchers at Dalhousie University in Canada, David Regan, Kenneth Beverley, and Max Cynader (1979), have investigated the ways in which the stimulus correlates of motion are perceived and interpreted. Their theoretical approach derives from a widely held view that the information on the retinal image is broken down into a number of abstract features that are processed separately by different channels in the visual pathways of the brain. For example, color-processing channels detect wavelength differences in the retinal image. Other channels appear to process form or shape. This view is based in part on direct physiological evidence showing that certain nerve cells respond selectively to various stimulus features.

Regan and his colleagues postulate the existence of two distinct channels that process information concerning motion in depth. One of these channels appears to be involved in two stimulus correlates, changing size and flow pattern, both of which are monocular— that is, available to one eye. The other channel is related to the processing of stereoscopic information requiring the use of both eyes.

Their channel hypothesis has been developed and tested using modern electronic equipment that can generate on the screen of a cathode ray tube various examples of stimulus correlates. For example, in one experiment, the researchers exposed human subjects to electronically simulated flow patterns like those seen by a pilot landing an airplane. They also exposed the subjects to a square pattern that appeared to change in size, giving the illusion of moving toward or away from this observer. Regan and his associates found the exposure to flow patterns for ten minutes made it more difficult for the subjects to see apparent changes in the size of the test square. This finding suggests that both of these stimulus correlates of motion—flow pattern and changing size—are processed by the same channel in the brain.

A separate channel investigated by Regan and his associates appears to respond only to binocular cues—information from both of the eyes. One possibility is that the brain uses the same stereoscopic mechanisms that enable us to perceive position in depth. If so, however, the brain of the baseball batter would have to create, in effect, a sequence of snapshots of the successive positions of the ball as it whizzed toward him. This would appear to be too sluggish a process to make possible the batter's split-second judgments of the ball's speed and direction of motion.

Regan and his associates postulate instead a stereoscopic channel responsive to the relative velo-

second signal is also sent as a corollary of that command. The second signal, or corollary discharge, travels to some way station on the visual pathways within the brain and, in effect, tells the perceptual mechanisms to compensate for the fact that the image on the retina will be moving. Thus, when our eyes move, we perceive no motion. By this reasoning we can understand why the world appears to jump back and forth when we jiggle the eye with a finger. There is no corollary discharge to register the intention to move the eye and prepare the brain to compensate; hence movement on the retina is perceived as real motion.

Relative velocities of the left and right retinal images of an object provide a cue to the object's direction of motion in depth. For example, if the left and right images of the object are moving in the same direction (A, B, H, I), the object will pass wide of the observer's hand, whereas if only one image is moving (C, G), the object will hit the observer directly in one eye. If the images are moving in opposite directions at the same speed (E), the object will hit the observer directly between the eyes. In addition, if the left image is moving slower than the right one (D), the object will pass closer to the left eye than to the right eye, and if the right image is moving more slowly (F), the object will pass closer to the right eye than to the left eye.

cities of the left and right retinal images of the moving object. The accompanying figure illustrates how this might work. When the left and right retinal images of the object move in the same direction (A, B, H, I), the object being observed will pass wide of the observer's head. But when these images move in opposite directions at the same speed (E), the object will hit him directly between the eyes. Moreover, if the left eye's image moves more slowly than the right eye's image, the object will pass closer to the left eye than to the right eye, and vice versa.

The postulated channel for the detection of the direction of motion in depth appears to be different from the mechanisms that detect the position of objects in depth. By recording the electrical activity in single nerve cells in the visual cortex of cats, the researchers found cells that responded to the direction of motion in depth but not to simple position in depth. Interestingly, some neurons fired strongest in response to trajectories directed straight at the animal's head.

Which of the channels—changing size and flow pattern or stereoscopic motion—provides the more effective means of perceiving motion in depth? The researchers found that this depended in part on the object's velocity and the duration of the observer's sight of the object. The changing-size channel appeared to be more effective for a slowly moving object glimpsed for only 0.2 second. The stereoscopic motion channel was more effective for a rapidly moving object seen for about a second. In addition, the researchers found that relative effectiveness varied with the individual. In some people, for example, the stereoscopic channel appears to play little role in perception of motion in depth.

This finding may help explain the results of a heroic experiment in which pilots landing jet aircraft were suddenly deprived of the vision of one eye. There was surprisingly little loss in landing performance, suggesting that these pilots may rely primarily on the monocular channel—changing size and flow pattern—rather than the stereoscopic mechanism.

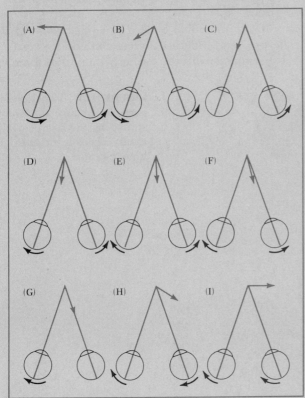

Let us imagine an interesting variation of this process involving the corollary discharge. Suppose you were to command your eyes to move but, for some reason, they failed to do so. The corollary discharge would be given in the brain, setting up the expectation of an eye movement, but there would be no motion across the retina. This very scenario was undertaken recently in an experiment carried out by a vision researcher who served as his own subject (Stevens, Emerson, Gerstein, Kallos, Neufeld, Nichols, and Rosenquist, 1976). To prevent his eyes from moving on command, he had himself paralyzed by an injection of a drug. (Because this drug also abolished normal respiratory movement of the chest, he had to be artificially respirated.) When the researcher attempted to move his eyes, they were paralyzed, and would not move. But in the process of his willing the eyes to move, the corollary discharge presumably was given in the brain.

In this experiment it was found that when the eyes were partitially paralyzed, the visual world indeed appeared to jump if the subject attempted to move the eyes. But when the paralysis was complete, no apparent movement was seen. It seems possible that the jumping of the visual world when the eyes were partially paralyzed may have been an illusion caused by the corollary discharge. But it is not at all clear why no movement was perceived when the eyes were totally paralyzed.

Development of Visual Perception

Several central questions in the study of perception concern its development. How much of human perception is innate? How much must be learned? Are the mechanisms for such perceptions as form, depth, and motion present in infancy or are learning and experience necessary for their operation? There are no simple answers to these questions but, as we will see, evidence has been accumulated in support of both innate and learned factors: some mechanism of perception appear to be innate, while early experience plays a critical role in the normal development of other functions.

We know, for example, that blind people whose vision has been restored have a great deal of trouble learning to interpret what they see. When cataract surgery was first introduced, adults who had been functionally blind all of their lives experienced normal retinal images for the first time. Some of these adults were never able to develop normal vision. For example, if they could discriminate a given triangle from a circle, they could not discriminate the two objects when the triangle was rotated several degrees. Such evidence suggests that there are periods early in life that are critical for learning various aspects of visual perception.

In an influential book, *The Organization of Behavior*, D. O. Hebb (1949) concluded as a result of experiments with the formerly blind that there are

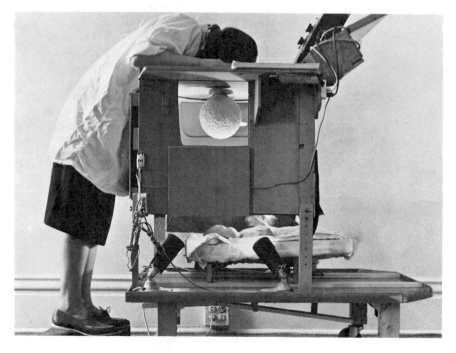

FIGURE 4.20 Visual preference in infants is demonstrated by the use of equipment originally designed by Robert Fantz.

two categories of visual skills: *unity* and *identity*. Hebb used the term *unity* to describe the ability to detect the presence of an object—that is, to separate an object from its background. Identity goes further and requires the ability to distinguish classes of objects—for example, a triangle from a circle. Hebb concluded that unity is innate, while identity requires learning or experience. The acquisition of the perceptual skills of identity in infants is similar to the process the resighted people went through. But in such cases, it often is hard to distinguish a lack of identity skills from simple lack of experience with vision. Therefore, let us look at some of the experiments that have helped us to understand the role of experience in vision.

Visual Perception in Infants

If newborn infants demonstrate the ability to perceive form, depth, and motion, then clearly these abilities are innate. But before perceptual ability in infants can be studied, a formidable hurdle must be overcome. The testing of visual functions in humans typically requires verbal responses, and infants cannot talk.

Robert Fantz (1961) invented a simple but highly effective method for determining what visual stimulus an infant prefers (see Figure 4.20). The baby is placed in a crib and then a pair of targets are placed on the ceiling above the baby—one to the left, the other to the right. The researcher watches from a chamber behind the targets to see if the baby turns its eyes or head to look at one of the two targets. As a safeguard against simple position preference on the part of the baby, the left-right position of the two targets is changed from time to time. The situation also is varied so that the researcher does not know which target is on the left and which is on the right; the researcher sees only the infant's face. Time spent staring at each stimulus is the measure for degree of preference.

Fantz's apparatus has given psychologists reliable methods for studying such aspects of visual learning as visual acuity and face preference.

Visual Acuity The Fantz preferential looking method can be used to study several aspects of perception. For example, it can be employed to test a child's *visual acuity*—the ability to resolve fine detail. Through this method, it has been determined that young infants will look at a striped target in preference to a gray card. When the stripes are very narrow, however, they are beyond visual acuity of the infant; the child cannot distinguish them from a neutral gray. By presenting targets of varying stripe widths and noting the child's preference, researchers can calculate a rough measure of the child's visual acuity. With this method, several researchers, including Janette Atkinson and Oliver and Fleur Braddick (1974) and Davida Teller (Teller, Morse, Borton, and Regal, 1974), have found that newborn infants have only about one-tenth of the visual acuity of adults. Visual acuity improves gradually in the first few months of life and is essentially normal by one year of age.

Face Preference One of the most fascinating findings achieved through the Fantz method was that very young infants display a marked preference for the human face. Fantz presented the infants with a sketch of a face on one target and, as the other target, either a figure with facial features drawn in a scrambled pattern or two solid patches of color separated by a straight line (see Figure 4.21). Even infants as young as four days showed a preference for looking at the sketch of a real face. This tendency is probably based on a preference for certain visual components that comprise a human face such as curved rather than straight contours (Fantz, 1970). This finding suggests that there is an innate predisposition to look at facelike forms that requires no learning.

Directional Vision One of the simplest of visual functions is *directional vision*, the ability to determine accurately the direction of a stimulus. If someone holds a light above or below your eyes or to the left or to the right, you can describe its location and point to it accurately. Is this ability innate or learned?

FIGURE 4.21 Infants using Fantz's apparatus looked at the simple face longer than they looked at the design with scrambled facial features.

At the turn of the twentieth century, a German physician named Walter Schlodtmann set out to answer that question in a classically simple experiment (1902). Scholdtmann went to a home for blind children in Germany. He sought children who had been blind from birth and thus never had experienced normal patterned light but who had at least one eye with a retina that was functional. He found three such children, aged 11, 14, and 18, and tested them for directional vision. His three subjects were totally incapable of pointing to the direction of a window in daylight or a lamp in darkness; when a bright beam of light was shone at their faces, they were aware of the light but could not localize its position.

Then Schlodtmann made use of a simple technique that you can try on yourself. If you gently push at the outer corner of your eye with a pencil eraser, you will see a diffuse flash of grayish light. (Because the optics of the eye are inverted, pressure on the lower point of the eye produces light at the top of the visual field.) The flash of light is called a *phosphene*, and it occurs because the pressure activates cells in the retina.

Schlodtmann tested the three blind children for the presence of pressure phosphenes by gently pushing with a blunt probe on the corner of the eye. He asked each child to point to where the sensation of light seemed to come from. In all three cases, the children were able accurately to localize the phosphenes; they reported that the apparent light source was a direction opposite to that from which the retina had been stimulated. Thus, through this novel method, the children demonstrated evidence of directional vision.

Because these children had never experienced patterned light, Schlodtmann concluded that directional vision must be an innate capacity genetically wired into our perceptual apparatus.

Perception of Depth: The Visual Cliff Among the most ingenious experiments in the study of perceptual development are those conducted by Eleanor J. Gibson and her collaborator Richard Walk (1960). The aim of these experiments was to study depth perception in infants. They grew out of some thoughts Gibson had one day while enjoying a picnic on the rim of the Grand Canyon. Peering over the rim, she wondered whether a young baby could perceive the perilous depths and avoid crawling off.

Back in the laboratory, she and Walk designed a kind of miniature Grand Canyon, which they called the *visual cliff* (see Figure 4.22). A board is placed in the middle of a large sheet of heavy transparent glass. At one side of the board is a covering of checkerboard material that is mounted practically flush with the underside of the glass. At the other side of the board the same material is placed at a depth of a foot or more below the glass. To an adult standing on the center board, this latter side has the appearance of a small cliff.

When infants of six months and older were placed on the center board, they rarely ventured onto the cliff side of the board, even when the mother coaxed them with rattles. It was not a question of leaving the board; three fourths of the children who were tested crawled off the board but nearly always toward the "shallow" side.

Which of the possible depth cues—monocular or binocular—enable young beings to perceive the visual cliff? In a number of visual cliff experiments in which binocular cues were eliminated and textural cues were neuturalized, both human infants and animals, permanently and temporarily monocular, behaved as did binocular subjects even when using only one eye: they avoided the "deep" side of the cliff. From these experiments, Gibson and Walk concluded that motion parallax is an adequate cue for depth perception.

Because six-month-olds already have considerable visual experience, these experiments do not necessarily establish that depth perception is innate. However, experiments with very young animals—chicks, goats, and kittens—on the visual cliff substantially bolster the argument that these depth perception mechanisms are inborn. For example, newly hatched chicks never hopped off the board onto the deep side of the cliff. A one-day-old goat, when placed on the deep side, extended its forelegs in a defensive posture and, when it saw the shallow side, leaped onto it. Young kittens avoided the cliff side even when they had been raised in the dark and thus lacked any visual experience. In short, several different animals, and probably people, appear to possess innate mechanisms that enable them to discriminate depth.

Learning and Visual Perception

The evidence presented thus far does little to support contentions that the perceptual world of the infant is, as William James described it nearly a century ago, "a blooming, buzzing confusion." To the contrary, we have seen aspects of a remarkable orderliness in the development of perception. Directional vision, depth perception, even an apparent preference for the human face, all seem present from birth.

That is only part of the picture, however. Other aspects of perception seem to develop only with learning and experience. Indeed, normal development of these perceptual mechanisms appears to depend upon certain experiences occurring at critical periods early in infancy. If certain animals, and presumably humans, are deprived of stimulation by patterned light in infancy, they suffer deficiencies in form perception. Austin Herbert Riesen (1950) raised chimpanzees either in darkness or wearing translucent goggles that permitted some light to enter but not enough to allow perception of shapes or patterns. These animals later were unable to discriminate accurately among various geometric shapes, a finding that suggests that the experience of patterned light during an early period is critical for the development of form perception.

Feature Detectors Another dramatic instance of the brain's *plasticity*— that is, its capacity for modification through experience—has been demonstrated in experiments showing changes in the response properties of cells in the visual cortex. These cells are the feature detectors, described earlier, that respond to small targets presented at various orientations in the visual field.

Helmut Hirsch and Nico Spinelli (1970) raised kittens with goggles that presented one eye with only vertical stripes and the other with only horizontal stripes. The kittens later were tested by placing microelectrodes near individual cells of the visual cortex. Cells activated from the eye that had been exposed to vertical stripes responded mostly or only to vertical bars; similarly those activated from the eye exposed to horizontal stripes responded mostly or only to horizontal bars.

These experiments suggested that the response properties of the feature detectors are shaped by interaction with the environment. Kittens, and presumably humans, deprived of the experience of vertical or horizontal stripes during a critical period (apparently the first four months of life in kittens) fail to develop fully normal perception of form.

Binocular Vision There is also an early period that is critical for development of binocular vision. This has been established in recent animal experiments that permit normal vision experience for each eye but not for simultaneous use of the two eyes. Researchers have found that if one of the extraocular muscles of a kitten is cut so as to produce a misalignment of the eyes, subsequent testing shows a marked reduction in the number of cortical cells that can be activated from either eye

FIGURE 4.22 The "visual cliff," actually a solid glass surface, reveals a checked material that cascades to the floor. When infants of six months and older were placed on the center board, they seldom ventured onto the "cliff" side, even when coaxed.

119

(Hubel and Wiesel, 1965). Cells in the visual cortex of the brain can be activated by one eye or the other but rarely by both.

A similar deficit has been demonstrated in animal experiments in which binocular fusion of the images from both eyes is prevented optically (Van Sluyters and Levitt, 1980). For example, a prism fixed over one eye prevents the placement of that eye in ways that normally would allow fusion of the images in the two eyes. Such animals are analogous to children who are born with an eye that deviates in direction, a condition called *strabismus* or "crossed eyes." Although surgery can correct the extraocular muscle imbalance, these children may fail to develop normal binocular vision. In order to perceive depth, they must depend solely upon monocular cues (such as motion parallax) available to each of the eyes.

The critical period for the development of binocular vision in cats seems to occur during the first few months of life. During that period normal binocular connections are made from eye to brain. In normal circumstances, when the eyes are correctly aligned, an orderly and roughly equal division of inputs from each eye make connection to the cortex. But without binocular experience, the fibers representing one eye or the other lose out. Normal binocular vision fails to develop.

Adaptability of Visual Perception The role of learning in modifying the visual perception mechanisms is not limited to critical periods early in development. That plasticity is possible even in adults has been shown in experiments involving the *vestibuloocular reflex.* This reflex, as we saw in Chapter 3, originates in the three semicircular canals of the inner ear, which are vital to our sense of position, and serves the important function of stabilizing our body and eyes in space.

The usefulness of the vestibuloocular reflex is illustrated in the following example. If you move this page of text back and forth rapidly while keeping your head still, you will not be able to read the words. If, however, you move your head back and forth rapidly instead of the book, you are able to read the text due to the vestibuloocular reflex. The semicircular canals in the inner ear register the position of your head as it moves and automatically signal the muscles controlling the position of your eyes. This signal causes the eyes to move an equivalent distance in the opposite direction. As a result, your eyes stay lined up on the text even though your head is moving.

Now let us suppose you are wearing an optical device that distorts the visual world—say, a pair of spectacles that shrinks the size of everything you see by half. Thus, if you were to move your eyes or head 6 degrees, the world would appear to move only 3 degrees. The vestibuloocular reflex would overcompensate. For a move of the head 6 degrees to the right, the reflex would move the eyes 6 degrees to the left—twice as much compensation as would be needed to stabilize the visual world, which has moved only 3 degrees. Hence, the eyes would overshoot the target.

What happens if you wear these spectacles for several days? Fred Miles and his collaborators found in monkeys that the strength of the vestibuloocular reflex decreased steadily from day to day until it adjusted to the new magnification of the visual world. Similarly, when monkeys wore lenses that magnified the visual world, the reflex at first underestimated the amount of correction needed and then increased after a few days to adapt to the new magnification (Miles and Eighmy, 1980).

Studies with human subjects indicate that the vestibuloocular reflex can adapt to even more severe rearrangements of the visual world. G. Melvill Jones and his associates wore special prisms that reversed the world (Gonshor and Melvill Jones, 1976). They wore these for 2 to 27 days and tested the reflex periodically. As could be expected, at first the reflex went in a direction that was maladaptive for perception through reversing prisms. Because the prisms reversed the world, the subjects had to turn their heads to the right to look at things that were actually to their left. The vestibuloocular reflex, as usual, attempted to compensate for the rightward movement of the head by moving the eyes to the left. Ordinarily, this would stabilize the eyes in space. Because of the reversing prisms, however, the apparent movement of the world on the retina increased. Jones and his colleagues found that, over time, the vestibuloocular reflex and the disconcerting perception of motion slowly weakened. In fact, after a week or so, the direction of the reflex actually changed. Now a movement of the head to the right would cause a weak tendency for the eyes to move to the right. Because the visual world was reversed this is a proper adaptation.

Precisely how this remarkable adaptation takes place in the brain is not yet clear. But its occurrence in a system formerly thought to be "hard-wired"—

that is, immutably fixed at birth—points to the possibility that other instances of perceptual plasticity may occur not only in infancy but also over the entire life span.

Auditory Perception

Most of what we know about perception is really about one type of perception—visual. Our perception of sound is less clearly understood. If you look at a picture on the wall, your perceptual mechanisms instantly provide a great deal of information without taking much time to analyze it. By contrast, even the simplest auditory perceptions—such as hearing a friend say your name or recognizing a short melody on the harmonica—require the analysis of sequential sensory information.

Neural Processing of Sound

As we saw in Chapter 3, the auditory structures in the inner ear and the pathways leading into the brain are characterized by tonotopic organization. Neighboring cells of the cochlear nucleus are most sensitive to similar frequencies, and there is an orderly shift from low to high tones at different positions. This tonotopic organization appears to be preserved in the pathways leading to the auditory cortex of the brain. At these higher stations, however, the properties of auditory cells are far more complex and far more difficult to discern. Let us look at research concerning two different aspects of the neural processing of sound.

The Role of the Cortex Although it is assumed that hearing depends on processing within the auditory cortex, there are surprisingly little data on the precise cortical functions. Cortical injuries often lead to profound disorders of language but seldom to deafness.

One likely role of the auditory cortex has been suggested by the experiment of Irving Diamond and William D. Neff (1957). Cats were trained to respond differently to tones of two different frequencies and to distinguish between two simple melodic patterns of three notes. Then the auditory cortex on both sides of each cat's brain was removed surgically. Diamond and Neff found that the cats were able to relearn the frequency discrimination task, but the ability to detect patterns of notes was permanently lost. From this result it seems that the auditory cortex is critical for perceiving or learning sequences of tones, but that simple aspects of

hearing can be handled by subcortical auditory structures.

Directional Hearing We perceive not only the presence of a sound but also the direction from which it comes. This ability depends upon neural processing of differences in intensity, in time of arrival, or in phase of the sound that are registered at the two ears. At high frequencies the intensity of the sound at the two ears differs because the head acts as a kind of "sound shadow." At low frequencies, where the head shadows the sound much less, the cue for direction is either the disparity in time of arrival of the sound at the two ears or the phase difference between otherwise identical sounds in the two ears.

Recent work by Eric Knudsen and Masakazu Konishi (1978) suggests that some animals have a brain structure that is specially organized for representing directional sound. In the midbrain of the owl, Knudsen and Konishi found nerve cells that appear to form a kind of sound map of the auditory world with neighboring points in this structure responding to neighboring regions in the auditory space.

Two phenomena of auditory perception—auditory masking and selective attention—are of special interest. They help explain why we sometimes hear a pattern of sounds and at other times fail to do so.

Auditory Masking

If you are trying to listen to music and a fire engine happens to race by your window, you may fail to hear the music. This is an instance of *auditory masking*. Auditory masking is not simply a matter of one sound's drowning out another because of its intensity. It occurs most strongly for tones whose frequencies are close to the one you are attempting to listen to. Tones that are more distant in frequency fail to mask. For any given frequency, there appears to be a critical band of nearby frequencies capable of masking it.

It has been suggested that the concept of critical bands may help account for our perception of consonance and dissonance in music. For example, some musical intervals might sound dissonant because they lie within the critical band in which one tone masks the other; a major third may sound

consonant because it is outside the critical
r auditory masking.

Selective Attention

What we hear often depends upon what we pay
attention to. Suppose, for example, you are at a
party in a large crowded room, and a dozen or
more people are talking. At first, all you hear is a
low, buzzing noise. Now a friend with whom you
want to talk begins to speak. Despite all of the other
noises, you can hear and understand what your
friend is saying. This ability to track someone's
voice in a crowded noisy room has been called the
cocktail party effect.

Psychologists study selective attention in a laboratory situation that simulates the cocktail party

---

FOCUS: The Study of ESP

In the late 1920s, a young Duke University researcher, Joseph Banks Rhine, set out to study a
phenomenon beside which even the mysteries of
normal sensory perception seemed quite pale. Rhine
wanted to investigate evidence of what he called extrasensory perception (ESP)—perception that is said
to occur independently of the known senses. Reports of people capable of "mind reading" and pos-
sessing other paranormal abilities have persisted
throughout history, but Rhine pioneered in the attempt to study such matters in the laboratory using
the scientific method.

Rhine's basic method was simple. He recruited
Duke students and faculty members as his subjects
and asked them to guess the symbols contained in a
special deck of cards. The deck consisted of 25 Zener
cards, each imprinted with one of five symbols—star,
circle, square, cross, or wavy parallel lines as in the
figure shown here. In the test for telepathy (mind-to-
mind communication), the subject attempted to
perceive the identity of the card, which was known
only to the experimenter. In the test for clairvoyance
(direct extrasensory perception of an object or
event), the subject sought to identify the card, which
was not known to the experimenter. And in the test
for precognition (perception of the future), the subject tried to predict accurately the order the cards
would take after they had been shuffled.

The five symbols that appear on the Zener cards most
commonly used in ESP research. Each card has a
distinctive pattern.

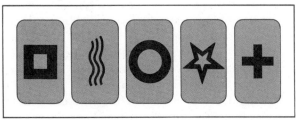

To these areas of ESP investigation, Rhine later
added experiments for psychokinesis—that is, influence over external matter through the force of mind.
In the psychokinesis experiments, subjects were
asked to attempt mental influence over the outcome
of rolling dice. ESP and psychokinesis, taken together, are now sometimes referred to as psi—from
the twenty-third letter of the Greek alphabet. People
who study psi and other paranormal phenomena
such as psychic healing and out-of-body experiences
are called parapsychologists—literally "beyond psychologists."

In assessing the results of their experiments,
Rhine and other psi researchers relied on statistical
measures widely used in psychology and other experimental sciences. Because the Zener deck contains 5 suits of 5 cards each, a subject can be expected by mere chance to score, on the average, 5
correct guesses in a run through the 25-card deck.
The laws of probability indicate when the results are
significantly above chance—for example, 9 hits in a
25-card run—and hence suggest the operation of
something other than chance.

In 1935 Rhine published the results of his early
experiments in clairvoyance and telepathy. He reported that a number of subjects had scored significantly above chance, including one who, in long-distance telepathy tests, had achieved odds against
chance of an astronomical number consisting of 10
followed by 22 zeros against 1. Since that first monograph, positive results of thousands of experiments
in ESP and psychokinesis have been published. The
Zener cards and dice have been supplanted by
automated equipment such as the random number
generator, which presents experimental targets on
the basis of the unpredictable decay of radioactive
nuclei.

In addition to establishing to their own satisfaction that ESP and psychokinesis exist, parapsychologists have described a number of characteristics of
the various psi phenomenon. One is the decline effect (the tendency of subjects to score significantly

setting. In a dichotic listening experiment, the subject wears earphones and is presented with two separate spoken tape-recorded messages, one to each ear. The subject is asked to attend to one of the messages. Typically, subjects have no difficulty following the attended message; they can even repeat the words as they listen despite the fact that a second message is droning on in the other ear. But subjects understand virtually nothing of the second message; they are typically unaware of it even if the voice suddenly switches from English to another language such as German.

This research suggests that people usually cannot listen to more than one conversation at once. It is as if somewhere in the central nervous system a selective filter tunes in the message we are paying attention to and tunes out all other auditory stimuli.

---

higher early in the experiment), an effect attributed to fluctuations in mood and interest. Another is the sheep-goat effect—the tendency for subjects who believe in ESP to go along wth the experiments like sheep and achieve higher scores than the goats, who are skeptical and balk at demonstrating ESP.

Despite a large accumulation of experimental data in support of ESP and despite widespread popular interest, most psychologists and other scientists remain skeptical. (In a recent survey of scientists, only 9 percent accepted ESP as "established fact," although 45 percent described it as "a likely possibility.") Parapsychologists have largely been excluded from the mainstream of science, and their findings have been ignored by the leading journals. Not until 1969 was the Parapsychological Association accepted for membership by the prestigious American Association for the Advancement of Science. Only a handful of American universities have funded psi research or given faculty status to parapsychologists. Even Duke University, where ESP research began, withdrew its support after J. B. Rhine's retirement in 1965.

Why does science continue to shun the study of ESP? One reason is that mind reading and clairvoyance smack of the occult, of supernatural phenomena that science, by definition, seeks to reduce to the known, to natural laws; ESP, by definition, depends upon the unknown. In fact, ESP is assumed to have properties that are inconsistent with our knowledge of energy. For example, ESP researchers assert that it does not obey the inverse-square law: they say that ESP does not typically improve when a subject moves closer to a purported transmission source.

Another reason for skepticism focuses on methodology of ESP research. It is difficult to develop appropriate control groups for experiments because researchers do not know what to control. The case has been well summarized by a leading critic, the British psychologist C. E. M. Hansel, in his book *ESP and Parapsychology* (1979). Hansel suggests that because negative data from ESP experiments are seldom reported, overall statistical results are biased. He also suggests that slipshod experimental controls and sensory cues can account for many of the positive results: for example, the Zener cards used in Rhine's early work had a flaw that permitted them to be read from the back under certain kinds of illumination. When controls are tightened up, Hansel says, positive results typically decline.

Hansel also points to the difficulty in replicating ESP experiments. Disinterested researchers often have been unable to replicate the results of others and, indeed, even Rhine and other ESP enthusiasts often could not replicate their own results. In experimental science, successful replication is essential in order to rule out the possibility of error or fraud. This latter possibility, fraud or its suspicion, long has haunted parapsychology. Although no branch of science is immune from unethical researchers who tamper with evidence or fabricate data, parapsychology is particularly vulnerable because of its admitted difficulty in reliably replicating experimental results. Although Rhine himself was virtually above suspicion, one of his trusted associates was caught tampering with the automated apparatus in order to produce positive results in a psychokinesis experiment. (Other parapsychologists brought the fraud to light.)

Beyond the issues of methodology and possible fraud, however, there remains a further barrier to acceptance of psi studies by the mainstream of science. Parapsychologsts have failed to develop plausible theories to account for phenomena that seem so implausible and so incompatible with our current knowledge of both physics and perception. Without such theories, the study of ESP is likely to remain, as one critic has described its current status, "a no-man's-land between the lunatic fringe on the one hand and the academically unorthodox on the other."

Certain messages can break through this hypothetical filter, however, causing us to switch channels. Dichotic listening experiments have established what cocktail party guests long have known: a subject fully occupied listening to a message in one ear will suddenly hear what's happening in the other ear if the words carry an unusual significance (such as the subject's own name).

Perception of Time

Because time is such an important aspect of all our lives, the perception of time is an area that has piqued the interest of psychologists. The perception of time as a subjective experience involves no obvious sensory organs or any observable cues. Unlike visual and auditory perception, the perception of time does not involve any physical stimuli.

Psychologists are primarily interested in the duration of time of which one is aware as opposed to physicists' measurement of time. Perceived time has been termed *protensity* (Woodrow, 1951) to differentiate it from physical duration.

Biological Basis of Time Perception

Some studies have shown that biological functions affect our perception of relatively brief time intervals. Increases in body temperature cause us to perceive time as passing more quickly than reality; decreases in body temperature have the opposite effect: that is, time seems to pass more slowly than

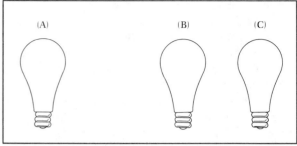

FIGURE 4.23 According to the kappa-effect, perception is influenced by the manipulation of distance. The three lights, (A), (B), and (C), are spaced at unequal intervals: the distance between lights (A) and (B) is greater than between (B) and (C). When all three are flashed on at equal temporal intervals, time between the flashing of lights (A) and (B) will be perceived as longer than the time between the flashing of lights (B) and (C).

it actually does (Baddeley, 1966; Hoagland, 1933, 1935).

Drugs definitely have an effect on protensity. In general, drugs, such as amphetamines, that accelerate body functions lead to an overestimation of time; drugs that slow down these functions lead to an underestimation of time (Fraisse, 1963). Psychedelic drugs generally produce a dramatic lengthening of time perception (Fisher, 1967). Whether psychedelics produce this altered perception by influencing the biological clock or by speeding up body processes is not yet clear.

The term *cocktail party effect,* has been given to the ability to track individual voices in a crowded, noisy room.

Cognition and Time Perception

Psychedelics may lead to overestimation of time duration because of cognitive processes: that is, because of increased mental activity and more information being received by the brain, time is perceived of as having longer duration (Ornstein, 1969). In fact, this premise holds that the amounts of information registered during a given time period, irrespective of drugs, affects perceived time.

Our perception of time seems to be influenced by both simple biological and more complex cognitive processes. At the current state of knowledge, it seems safest to say that physiological processes are most useful in explaining the perception of short intervals, whereas cognitive processes seem to hold the key to time perception of longer intervals (Schiffman, 1976).

Time and Space Perception

Our perception of experienced time and space can be interrelated in what is called the *kappa-effect;* that is, perception is influenced by the manipulation of distance. If three light bulbs are spaced at unequal intervals but flashed on at equal temporal intervals (see Figure 4.23), the time between the two lights farthest apart will be perceived (incorrectly) as being longer (Cohen, Hansel, and Sylvester, 1954).

Conversely, in the *tau-effect,* spatial perception is influenced by time. Three equidistant spots on the forearm are stimulated (see Figure 4.24). If the time interval between stimulation of points 1 and 2 is greater than that between 1 and 3, the distance between points 1 and 2 will be perceived (incorrectly) as being longer than that between points 1 and 3 (Helson and King, 1931).

It is important to recall the difference between perception and sensing. Our sensory organs receive and code stimuli, but it is in the brain that perception—the transformation of the evidence of our senses—takes place. Research in the coming decades should tell us a great deal more about the processes of perception and just where in the brain those processes take place.

SUMMARY

1. Our senses receive and code stimuli such as sound and light waves. Perception is the transformation of the evidence of our senses into mental representations. Perceptions are interpretations made in the light of existing or preconceived notions that may be independent of incoming sensory data. Vision requires an enormous amount of registration, analysis, sorting, filtering, and comparing by our perceptual mechanisms—first in the eye itself but chiefly at centers within the brain.

2. A basic understanding of perceptual adaptation, visual capture, and perceptual constancy helps in understanding how we perceive ourselves and the world around us. Perceptual adaptation is the ability to compensate for an artificially displaced visual field. Visual capture refers to the tendency of vision to dominate input from the other senses. Perceptual constancy is the stability of the shape, size, brightness, and color of subjects in our visual fields; we recognize the same objects at a variety of angles, at various distances, and under different kinds of light.

3. Objects maintain their apparent constancy of shape despite differences in the point from which we view them. Size constancy is the tendency of the perceptual apparatus to take into acccount the dis-

FIGURE 4.24 According to the tau-effect; spatial perception is influenced by time. If the three equidistant points, *A*, *B*, and *C*, on the forearm are stimulated at different times, the points will be perceived as being different distances apart. If the interval of time between stimulating points (A) and (B) is greater than that between (A) and (C), then the distance between (A) and (B) will be perceived as greater than that between (A) and (C).

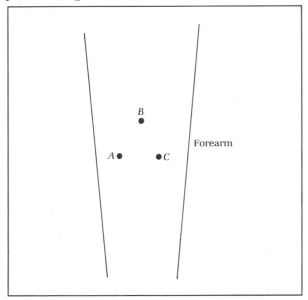

tance of an object in judging its size. Brightness constancy refers to the tendency of our perceptions of an object's brightness to remain stable over a wide range of illumination. Objects have color constancy if we are able to see the object's surroundings—that is, if we have references for perceiving an object's hue.

4. The shape and form of an object tend to stand out against a background. In a differentiated visual field, that part appearing as a distinct, delineated shape is the figure; the remainder is the ground. This is called the figure-ground differentiation. Among the perceptions by which we organize a visual field into figure and ground are closure, continuity, similarity, and proximity.

5. The stimulus of light is processed and transformed into recognizable forms by both the receptors in our eyes and by the nerve cells of the visual cortex. These latter cells have been called feature detectors. Feature detectors—simple, complex, and hypercomplex—appear to detect features that are linear in nature. It is postulated that some neural mechanism in the brain compares complex features with a stored memory of patterns. Visual synthesis likely takes place in a part of the temporal lobe.

6. We perceive depth through monocular cues that require the use of only one eye and through binocular cues that require the use of both eyes. Among the monocular cues for depth perception are perspective, overlap, relative size, texture, and motion parallax. Binocular cues include convergence and stereoscopic vision.

7. Perception of slow motion normally demands a frame of reference in order to sense that motion is taking place; however, it is possible to perceive motion without movement actually taking place. The phi phenomenon, autokinetic effect, and corollary discharge are examples of apparent motion.

8. Some mechanisms of perception appear to be innate while early experience plays a critical role in the normal development of other functions. Visual acuity, a perference for faces, and directional vision all seem to be present at birth. It seems likely that some depth perception mechanisms are inborn.

9. Some aspects of perception do not seem to be innate; they develop only with learning and experience. The brain's plasticity—its capacity for modification through experience—has been demonstrated in experiments showing changes in the response properties of the feature detectors in the visual cortex. In cats, normal binocular vision seems to develop during the first few months of life. Experiments have shown that even adults can adapt seemingly hard-wired mechanisms, such as the vestibuloocular reflex, which is vital to the sense of position and for stabilizing the body and the eyes. Other instances of perceptual plasticity may occur over the entire life span.

10. Auditory perception requires the analysis of sequential sensory information. Animal research indicates that neural processing in the auditory cortex is necessary for perceiving sequences of tones; however, simple aspects of hearing can be handled by subcortical auditory structures. Directional hearing depends upon neural processing of differences in intensity, in time of arrival, or in phase of sound that are registered at the two ears.

11. Auditory masking, the blocking of one of two sounds, occurs most frequently when the frequencies of the conflicting sounds are close. Auditory and visual perception are selective; we are able to choose between conflicting stimuli by a process of selective attention.

12. Perceived time may differ from its actual physical duration. Some biological functions, body temperature, for example, and some drugs have definite effects on our perception of time. Some cognitive processes may also affect perceived time.

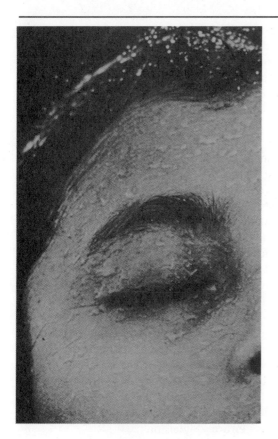

Chapter 5
Consciousness

"... Our normal waking consciousness, rational consciousness as we call it, is but one special type of consciousness, whilst all about it, parted from it by the filmiest of screens, there lie potential forms of consciousness entirely different. We may go through life without suspecting their existence; but apply the requisite stimulus, and at a touch they are there in all their completeness.... No account of the universe in its totality can be final which leaves these other forms of consciousness quite disregarded ... they forbid a premature closing of our accounts with reality."

These words, which sound so contemporary, were written more than 80 years ago by the American psychologist William James and published in 1900 in his *The Varieties of Religious Experience.* James was describing his own introspective experi-

American psychologist William James reported his own introspective experiences in connection with experiments with nitrous oxide.

ences after experimenting with nitrous oxide, the so-called laughing gas then used by dentists and surgeons as an anesthetic. In those days the study of consciousness was a principal focus of the new science of psychology. But the study of what goes on in people's minds soon proved to be too subjective for most practitioners of psychology; it was difficult to measure and verify. Psychology was a latecomer to the family of scientific disciplines and, after the turn of the century, psychologists increasingly sought to emulate the apparent methodological purity of physics and chemistry by emphasizing quantitative, objective measurements of behavior. Through much of this century, subjects such as sleep and dreams, hypnosis, meditations, and drug-induced states were relegated to abnormal psychology or simply regarded as irrelevant to science.

Only in recent years has the study of consciousness begun to reenter the mainstream of psychology. The resurgence of interest stems partly from the growth of cognitive psychology, but it also results from the groundswell that has arisen in the general culture, beginning largely with the youth of the 1960s who turned inward in search of what James described as those "potential forms of consciousness entirely different."

Normal Versus Altered States of Consciousness

Psychologists describe the Jamesian "forms of consciousness" as *states of consciousness.* These states may be seen as sets of structural conditions that are distinct from the actual content of consciousness. Structure denotes the major features that influence the ways in which we experience ourselves or the world; content is the experience itself. For example, imagine that a soldier on night guard duty at the front line hears a rustle in the bushes outside the camp. His state of consciousness—in this case, high vigilance—determines the content of his consciousness; he responds very differently than he would on hearing the same sound while sunbathing at the same spot in peacetime. His state of consciousness greatly influences his consciousness in two different domains—the cognitive (how he solves problems) and the affective (how he responds emotionally).

Another common distinction differentiates normal states from *altered states of consciousness (ASC).* The soldier's high vigilance might be described as a *normal waking state of consciousness;* that is, maintaining maximum alertness to the external environment is necessary for survival. By contrast, altered states are variously typified by such characteristics as lack of self-awareness, hallucination, altered time perception, and loss of contact with present reality.

The distinction between normal and altered states of consciousness implies that altered states are abnormal. It suggests that the alert, rational mode of experiencing the world is normal while all other states of consciousness are abnormal. In fact, some aspects of altered states are frequently present in the normal waking consciousness of quite normal people. Ronald Shor (1960) found in a group of college students that hallucinations (perceptions of scenes that do not exist) and other phenomena similar to those thought to be characteristic of altered states of consciousness, were rather common in ordinary life. In a recent study, Kenneth Pope and Jerome Singer (1980) asked subjects to report ongoing mental experiences while the subjects were "sitting and doing nothing." The results contrasted sharply with the picture of purposeful mental activities such as reacting to the present environment, solving problems, making plans, and generally thinking rationally, all of which are typically associated with normal waking consciousness. Most of the content of consciousness, it was found, consisted of a kaleidoscope of chaotic imagery, including fantasy, the reliving of past experiences, and the like. Indeed, excerpts from the subjects' reports resembled fiction's stream-of-consciousness technique.

"Water and scotch," reported one subject, "scotch with water, with ice, with uh soda, with soda on the side, uh wine, beer, uh vomit, nausea, headaches, uhm aspirin. No-doz, Tums, uh Tums, little metal cases with railroad pictures on them and uh the trains into clouds of smoke and dust and the paintings in the Fogg museum and fog also, and hum California and uhm California and uhm P. G. Wodehouse in Jeeves and Little Orphan Annie" (Pope and Singer, 1980).

The occurrence of such phenomena in normal people leading normal lives has led to the suggestion that the terminology be changed. It has been suggested that instead of referring to altered states and normal waking consciousness, we should use the term *alternate states* to cover all forms of consciousness. This change has not yet been generally adopted.

By any name, altered states are difficult to define, and there is, as yet, not general agreement on what constitutes an altered state. In this chapter we will consider two major and distinct altered states, sleeping and dreaming, which can be defined both in terms of subjective experience and physiological measurement, along with four other areas of vital interest to the study of consciousness: biofeedback, meditation, hypnosis, and drug-induced states. Finally, we shall see that human consciousness is enriched by a great variety of unusual, or anomalous phenomena that resemble certain aspects of altered states.

Neural Approaches to Consciousness

The study of altered states of consciousness is of particular interest to neuroscientists. Altered states provide important models for investigating the complex and elusive relationships between mind and brain—the so-called mind-body problem, which has baffled philosophers and scientists for many centuries.

The Mind-Body Problem

The *mind-body problem* (or the mind-brain problem) is the difficult question of how the mind affects the behavior of the body and how the body affects the behavior of the mind. René Descartes, the French philosopher, believed that the mind and body are closely related and interact with each other (Descartes, 1862/1911). Three centuries later, Descartes' statement is just about as accurate a one as can be made.

Scientists prefer to study what can be measured, and the chemical and electrical workings of the brain can be, more and more, precisely observed. The workings of the mind—the individual consciousness and personality that we each possess—still cannot be tracked in as accurate a fashion as researchers would want.

In Chapter 2 the findings of Paul Broca and of Gustav Fritsch and Eduard Hitzig were described. Broca located the speech center in the left half of a patient's brain. Fritsch and Hitzig made some of the first findings about the effect of electricity on brain functions. In the years that followed (roughly the

129

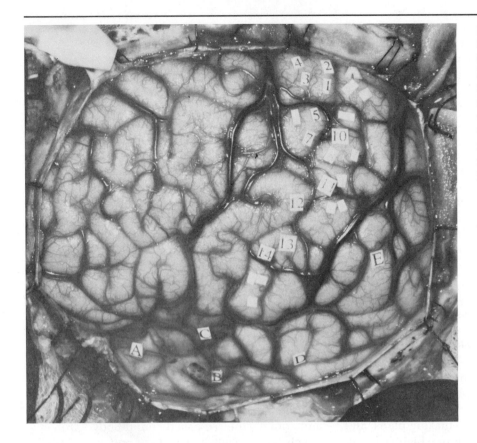

During an operation at the Montreal Neurological Institute, the right side of a living human brain is exposed. The numbers indicate the points on the surface of the brain where electrical stimulation was adminstered and the effects on the patient, who remained conscious during the procedure, were observed.

end of the nineteenth century onward), scientists were torn between the view that either specific brain sites for each and every behavior existed or that the entire brain functioned in an equivalent and complex way to cause behavior. The truth lies somewhere between these two views.

Because it is not conceivable to most of us how mental events could be reduced to the physical-chemical processes with which scientists deal, science cannot lay claim to being able to "solve" the mind-body problem. What can be done is to look for correlations between subjective experience and physiological variables and then attempt, as far as possible, to unravel the tangled skein of cause and effect. In this pragmatic fashion we may learn to understand more and more of the ways in which mind and body influence each other, an attainable goal of immense practical importance in relation to psychosomatic (the combination of psychological and physical) health.

A key tenet of the neural sciences is that all conscious experiences depend upon activity in the brain, in particular, in the cerebral cortex. It is in the cortex, with its many folded convolutions multiplying the available surface area of the brain, that the human nervous system reaches its highest level of development. Here too, in the cortex, electrical stimulation of the temporal lobe can evoke conscious experiences. Wilder Penfield was able to stimulate long-forgotten memories in the exposed brains of neurosurgical patients who relived events out of the past while on the operating table (Penfield and Roberts, 1959).

Neurophysiology

For evidence of the biological events that underlie conscious experience, we must look to the two major scientific disciplines involved in the study of the brain, neurochemistry and neurophysiology. Later in this chapter, in the discussion of drug-induced states of consciousness, we will describe some of the most recent findings about the brain's chemistry. Here, however, let us focus on neurophysiology.

Localization

The methods of neurophysiology have demonstrated a great deal about the control of specific behavioral functions by specific areas of the brain. One area of the cortex, for example, controls voluntary movement; another mediates vision, and so on (see Chapter 2). Such findings represent the localization of psychobiological functions in the cortex.

Localization is complicated, however, by the brain's *plasticity*—that is, its capacity to compensate for damage to a given neural area. How this occurs is not yet understood. Even speech, one of the earliest functions neurophysiologists were able to localize, does not always disappear permanently after a stroke or injury damages the relevant brain areas. President Eisenhower, for example, suffered a stroke while in office and showed considerable aphasia, or speech difficulty, but later recovered his powers of speech.

Consciousness has not been localized in any specific area of the cerebral cortex. It seems likely that the neural basis of consciousness is widely distributed, perhaps involving virtually the entire brain. Indeed, regions of the brain far removed from the cortex, such as the reticular formation, play a vital role in consciousness. This neural system receives information from the various sensory modalities; through its activity noise or touch can waken a sleeper. Destruction of the reticular formation of a cat can result in permanent coma. But when this system is destroyed in multiple stages, with a few days intervening between each stage, an astonishing demonstration of plasticity occurs: the brain somehow reorganizes itself, takes over for the destroyed areas, and maintains the waking state. In the same way, the human brain, with its 10 billion neurons, appears capable of molding itself to the needs of human consciousness, overcoming trauma by recruiting other cells to take on new functions.

Electroencephalographs: Recording Brain Waves

An instrument that has been widely used in the study of consciousness is the *electroencephalograph*, or *EEG*, which records gross electrical activity in the brain. The EEG was invented by a German psychiatrist, Hans Berger, who had long been intrigued by the relationship between mental events and the electrical activity of the brain. Berger succeeded in obtaining his first electroencephalogram in 1929 by pasting metal disks on the scalp of his teenage son, Klaus, and connecting them to a simple recorder.

The wavy patterns, or *brain waves*, that Berger recorded represent fluctuations or oscillations in voltage, which in turn reflect the sum of many nerve cells firing in the cerebral cortex. Berger

delineated two different EEG patterns. When his subject was awake but relaxed, with eyes closed or not attending to external stimuli, Berger recorded a relatively slow synchronous rhythm (neurons firing in an orderly pattern) with a frequency of about 10 waves per second. He called these *alpha waves*. When the subject was more alert, mentally active, and attending to external stimuli, Berger recorded more rapid waves of smaller amplitude (height) and less synchrony, which he called *beta waves*.

The modern EEG machine greatly amplifies the weak signals and graphs them on a strip of paper or on the display of a monitor (see Figure 5.1). In addition to its use in the study of consciousness, the EEG has been used clinically in the diagnosis of epilepsy, brain tumors, and injuries to the brain.

Operation of an electroencephalograph, or EEG, which records gross electrical activity of the brain and has been widely used in consciousness studies. Here the weak electrical signals are amplified and graphed on a strip of paper at Mandala Center, Winston-Salem, North Carolina.

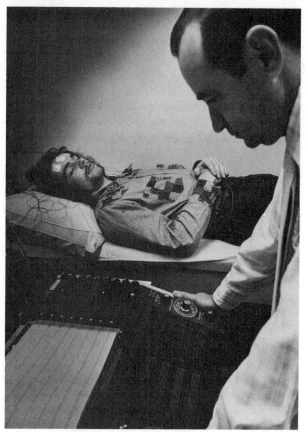

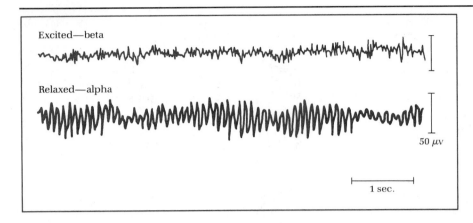

FIGURE 5.1 The contrast between alpha waves (relaxed subject) and beta waves (mentally alert subject) can be seen on this typical EEG.

Excited—beta

Relaxed—alpha

50 μv

1 sec.

The Split Brain

Of all the findings in the recent mushrooming of neuroscientific research, the most influential in developing new concepts of consciousness derives from Roger Sperry's research on the split brain (Sperry, 1974). This work is discussed in detail in Chapter 2. Here it will suffice to recall that Sperry studied men and women whose corpus collosum (the principal connection between the two cerebral hemispheres) had been surgically cut to alleviate severe epilepsy. Before Sperry's work, the left hemisphere in most people was known to be dominant for language, but the right hemisphere was thought to have little importance. After Sperry's studies and the body of research inspired by his work, we now know that both hemispheres have vital functions but that they are specialized for different modes of information processing. The left hemisphere dominates in situations where linear, or sequential, processing of information is required (speech, for example); the right dominates in situations that require the simultaneous processing of information, as in problems involving the relationships between different elements (spatial perception, for example).

These findings are of enormous importance to the understanding of the brain, of course, and their implications for the study of consciousness are startling. They imply that each of us has two quite different minds coexisting in one body, each with its "own private sensations . . . thoughts and ideas . . . memories and learning experiences" (Sperry, 1974). Often during the Sperry experiments, two different hemispheres seemed to demonstrate different and even conflicting levels of consciousness. Consider the split-level responses of one of Sperry's female patients. She was seated at a special instru-

ment on which a series of ordinary images could be flashed at random to parts of one eye or the other in such a way that the information about the image reached only the opposite hemisphere. When a picture of a nude was unexpectedly flashed onto the right part of a screen, she laughed and had no trouble identifying the image because it was available to her verbal left hemisphere. But when the same picture was shown to her left visual field, and thus was registered in her mute right hemisphere, she denied seeing anything. But the right hemisphere, although it could not verbalize the image, could respond to it emotionally because she could not help chuckling. When the subject was asked what was wrong, her left hemisphere could only convey a vague feeling of embarrassed amusement: "I don't know . . . nothing . . . oh—that funny machine." In fact, much split-brain research indicates that the two hemispheres may participate in different kinds of conscious experiences; this could be the basis for much of our ambivalence and the internal conflicts that often generate psychiatric problems (Galin, 1976).

Since Sperry's split-brain experiments, a variety of methods have been developed to investigate hemispheric functions in normal subjects. One method used in neurosurgery is to inject an anesthetic into the main artery serving one hemisphere. In effect, this puts that hemisphere to sleep while leaving the other alert and awake. Another method is to record an EEG separately from the two sides of the head while the subject is engaged in different tasks. It has been found, for example, that there is a greater incidence of slow, synchronous alpha rhythm on the right side when the subject is reading or speaking. Because alpha is regarded as a manifestation of relaxation and less neural activity, this suggests the greater involvement of the left hemisphere in verbal tasks. By the same token, there is more alpha—and hence less neural—activity on the left side during spatial tasks such as pattern recognition by touching objects (Ornstein, 1972).

Researchers have implicated the right hemisphere—the side of the brain once thought to be "silent"—in a remarkable array of functions. Among the functions that investigators suspect to be largely related to the right brain are musical and artistic appreciation, visual imagery, fantasy, and emotional experiences. There is also evidence that the right brain is highly involved with hypnotic and other altered states of consciousness and even with the unconscious mind in general.

Research on hemispheric specialization has generated a great deal of excitement among people far removed from the neurosciences—educators, philosophers, artists, and lay people. With this growing interest some tendencies to take preliminary research findings and even wild speculation for established fact have appeared. Individuals, professions, behaviors, and cognitions have been assigned as right or left brain in cavalier fashion. Among the really difficult questions raised by split-brain research are the following:

- How can two quite different brains (or minds) coexist in one person?
- How are the different, sometimes conflicting, messages from the two hemispheres integrated?
- How does one hemisphere dominate the other?
- Is hemispheric differentiation the neural basis of our confusion and ambivalence?
- How and why did this strange dichotomy evolve in the human brain?

The possible evolutionary benefit and the cost of such an arrangement has been described by David Galin (1976): "The evolutionary advantage of having two different minds is obvious; possession of two independent problem solving organs increases mightily the likelihood of a creative solution to a novel problem. At the same time there is an enormous increase in the likelihood of internal conflict. And so we have man, the most innovative of species and at the same time the most at odds with himself." In considering the possibilities and problems of the split brain, however, it is important to emphasize that in normal circumstances and regardless of whether one hemisphere is more active at a given time, both function together in an integrated fashion.

State-Dependent Learning

An important question for neural scientists and other students of consciousness concerns the possible continuity of physiological and psychological functions in altered states. Are random or altered states episodic events that are without relationship to the patterns of rational thought?

Evidence to the contrary comes from a phenomenon known as *state-dependent learning,* which has been demonstrated in experimental animals. One of the pioneers in this research, D. A. Overton (1974), taught rats to turn right in a T-maze while under the influence of a drug. Later, when the drug had worn off, the rats could not perform this task: it was as if they had never learned it. But when Overton administered the same drug again, the rats "remembered" their earlier lesson. What was learned in the drug state apparently was simply unavailable to the rats in their normal conditions: availability of the learning depended upon a return to the drug state; it was state-dependent learning.

There are several human parallels to state-dependent learning. One such parallel is evident in studies where subjects under hypnosis were able to recall, for the first time, experiences that had occurred while under anesthesia; they could remember, for example, hearing the doctors discussing their case (Levinson, 1967). Even closer parallels to state-dependent learning are the frequent reports of alcoholics who can recall events that occurred while they were intoxicated but only when they get drunk again. A classic example is depicted in Charlie Chaplin's film *City Lights:* the hero saves a drunk millionaire from attempting suicide. Each time the millionaire is drunk again and sees Charlie, he is lavish with his friendship, but the next morning when sober, he forgets the whole incident and has Charlie thrown out of his house.

A phenomenon similar to state-dependent learning also has been observed in studies of radical mood fluctuations. Herbert Weingartner and his associates (Weingartner, Miller, and Murphy, 1979), studied manic depressives who swung rapidly between mania and depression. He found that they could recall information more easily during recurrence of the state during which they first acquired it—whether mania or depression. This finding has been reproduced in normal volunteers who underwent cyclical mood swings after being deprived of sleep (Reus, Weingartner, and Post, 1979).

These findings suggest that certain learned psychological reactions may be related to a given physiological state and that these reactions become available when the brain enters this state.

Sleep and Dreams

Among the general public, the very phrase "altered states of consciousness" often conjures up images of mystical trances or drug-induced euphoria. In fact, the most common and familiar of the altered states is experienced by all of us each day. Typically, we spend seven or eight hours a day in a state in which we are incapable of experiencing the environment or relating to people—sleep. And often during this period of sleep, perhaps four or fives times a night, we experience yet another altered state—up to half an hour of fantasy and hallucination that seem achingly real and yet inexpressibly different from waking consciousness.

Because of its universality, sleep, with or without dreams, fascinates students of biology and psychology. Furthermore, it provides a rich model for investigating the interaction of body and mind. We will look first at the structure of sleep, a subject about which investigators have learned a great deal in the past two decades or so, and then we will examine the far more difficult questions of why we sleep and why we dream.

Our Biological Clock: The Circadian Rhythm

Our daily round of sleep and waking is governed by a biological cycle known as a *circadian rhythm*—from the Latin for "about one day." Internal timekeeping mechanisms, often called the *biological clock*, control the circadian rhythm, of which there are many examples in human and animal physiology. Human body temperature, for example, typically fluctuates in a daily cycle, peaking in the second half of the day. Travelers become uncomfortably aware of the biological clock when they pass through different time zones and feel the internal effects of "jet lag," the discomfort resulting from having to reset daily rhythms.

The biological clock is set for roughly 24 hours. Ordinarily, the clock is reset by the environmental

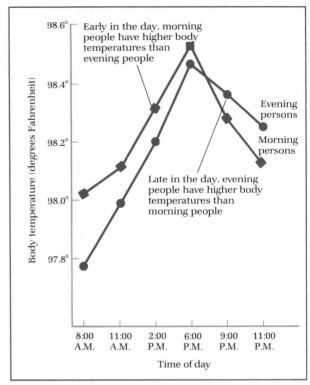

Individual differences in one circadian rhythm. As shown, morning people tend to have higher body temperatures early in the day than do evening people. After about 8 P.M., however, this difference is reversed.

cues of light and dark. But the clock reverts to its built-in circadian rhythm when we are removed from the environmental cues. Volunteers who have lived experimentally in caves and mines typically maintain a circadian cycle of sleep and waking of between 23 and 25 hours.

Until 1972 the precise location of the internal timekeeper in humans had eluded neuroscientists. Then Irving Zucker and others pinpointed a specific area in the hypothalamus, the *suprachiasmatic nuclei*, located where the two optic nerves cross as they enter the brain. Experimental destruction of this area in rats and other animals wipes out the normal cycle of sleep and wakefulness along with other processes involving a circadian rhythm such as eating, drinking, and production of adrenal cortical hormones (Zucker, 1980).

The Structures of Sleep

The basic instrument for recording neural measurements during sleep is the electroencephalograph. For many years, sleep was assumed to be a single state. Investigators using the EEG were able to differentiate four sequential stages of this single state (see Figure 5.2):

1. The alpha waves that characterize the EEG as we close our eyes and relax show a decrease and slower *theta waves* of 4 to 6 cycles per second appear, along with slow rolling eye movements. This drowsy interval between waking and sleep-

ing is known as the *hypnagogic state.* During this brief period short, hallucinatory, dreamlike experiences appear that resemble vivid still photographs. These experiences are often forgotten, but it has been hypothesized that the imagery in them is conducive to creativity, potentially leading to solutions to scientific or artistic problems.

FIGURE 5.2 (A) In the first of normal sleep's four stages, small, fast brain waves appear on EEG record (below sleeper).

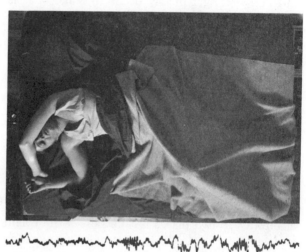

(B) In the second stage, brain waves show short bursts of activity (resembling spindles) as light sleep begins to deepen.

(C) In the third stage, larger, slower brain waves appear as the half-hour descent to deep sleep continues.

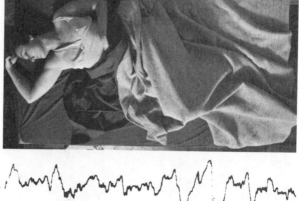

(D) In the fourth stage, the large delta waves of deep sleep increase in number.

2. *Sleep spindles*, short periods of ryhthmical responses, with a frequency of 13 to 15 cycles per second, appear as light sleep begins to deepen.
3. Large slow *delta waves* of 1 to 4 cycles per second show up on the EEG as the descent into deep sleep continues.
4. The delta waves of deep sleep increase in number.

These four stages comprise the state sometimes called "quiet sleep," a not quite accurate description because snoring, sleep-talking, sleepwalking, and bed-wetting typically occur in Stage 4. It is quiet, however, when compared with another stage of sleep, a stage so different from quiet sleep that it constitutes a distinct state of consciousness. This separate state was discovered in 1953 by the University of Chicago sleep researcher Nathaniel Kleitman and one of his students, Eugene Aserinsky (Aserinsky and Kleitman, 1953). Like many important discoveries, it was triggered by a kind of "chance" observation. Aserinsky and Kleitman noticed that as infants went to sleep their eyes moved rapidly though the rest of the body was still. To study these eye movements in adults without disturbing the sleeper, the researchers attached electrodes to two places on the skin of the eyelid and wired the electrodes to their recording machine in the next room. When the sleeper's eyes moved, the machine recorded a potential difference that reflected a voltage developing between the cornea and retina.

These bouts of rapid eye movements began after their subjects had passed through the four stages of quiet sleep, about 70 or 80 minutes after the onset of slumber. When the sleepers were awakened during these rapid eye movements, they almost invariably reported they had been dreaming. This new state of sleep has come to be known as *rapid-eye-movement (REM) sleep*. It also has been termed paradoxical sleep, because, while the EEG shows that the brain is in a state of high "wakefulness" or activity, the subject is hardest to awaken during this stage (see Figure 5.3). (Interestingly, a quiet sound is more effective in arousing subjects during both REM and non-REM sleep if it has a personal significance, such as the sleeper's name.) As Figure 5.4 shows, we typically go through several periods of REM sleep in a cycle. Toward the end of the cycle, the REM periods are separated by increasingly more wakeful states.

REM Sleep and Dreams

Researchers now assume that REM sleep is virtually always accompanied by dreams. In recent studies, subjects reported dreams about 85 percent of the time when they were awakened during REM sleep; it is quite possible that the remaining 15 percent can be accounted for by simple failure to recall dreaming. Something like dreaming also occurs during non-REM sleep. Subjects awakened then frequently report mental activity (words and phrases, for example), but the activity is more thoughtlike—more conceptual and plausible and less visual—than actual dream content, which more closely resembles hallucinations.

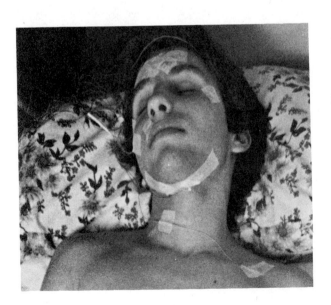

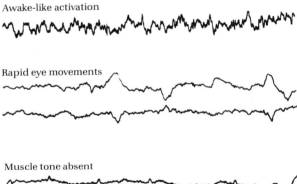

Awake-like activation

Rapid eye movements

Muscle tone absent

FIGURE 5.3 In REM sleep, when dreams take place, a volunteer shows brain waves similar to waking state (top row), intense rapid eye movement (middle), and virtually no activity of chin muscles (bottom).

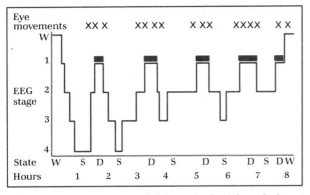

FIGURE 5.4 A young adult's typical night of sleep, showing wakeful (W), sleeping (S), and dreaming (D) states. The heavy lines indicate dreaming sleep accompanied by rapid eye movements.

Everyone dreams, it is now believed, whether or not the dreams are actually remembered. Dreaming follows a fairly regular cycle, beginning after completion of the four stages of non-REM sleep. A notable exception to this pattern occurs among people with *narcolepsy*, a disorder characterized by uncontrollable seizures of sleep during waking hours. Narcoleptics may fall asleep unpredictably—at the wheel of a car, during conversation, even while making love—and many of them bypass the other four stages of sleep and plunge directly into REM. Most people dream in cycles of about 90 minutes that recur about four to six times a night. Typically, the duration of REM periods increases through the night to a maximum of about an hour. Babies spend a higher percentage of their time in REM sleep, although there is no way of knowing when and what they dream.

In fact, all mammals that have been studied show REM sleep. Does this mean that these animals dream? Dog owners watching their pets twitch and paw during sleep have long suspected that their dogs do indeed dream. Because animals cannot tell us, there is no final answer to this old question. However, one piece of experimental evidence suggests that monkeys experience dreamlike visual images during REM sleep. C. J. Vaughan (1963) trained monkeys to press a lever every time pictures were flashed onto a screen. When the monkeys went to sleep and no pictures were being shown, they pressed the lever—but only during periods of REM.

Dreaming and Waking What does research in REM sleep tell us about relationships between the dream state and normal waking consciousness? Some findings support Sigmund Freud's contention that we integrate the residues of the activities of the previous day into the dream. However, they also contradict his assertion that it is always necessary to look beyond the manifest, or surface, content of dreams and focus on the latent, or hidden, meaning.

In fact, studies of children and adults, including cross-cultural investigations, show a very clear continuity between the manifest content of dreams and the concerns of an individual's waking life. We tend to take to bed with us our waking interests and worries. For example, a man with an unusually intense daytime preoccupation with the American sport of football reported that 36 percent of his remembered dreams were about football (Hall and Van de Castle, 1966).

Studies indicate that dreams even reflect the differences in social relations between men and

A dog displaying all the symptoms of narcolepsy first barks, then nods, and quickly falls asleep.

women of different cultures. For example, a recent study of Americans has shown that women's dreams have more characters, friendly interactions, emotion, indoor settings, and themes of home and family than do men's dreams. Men's dreams, meanwhile, manifest more frequent aggression, striving for achievement, castration anxiety, and overt hostility (Hall and Van de Castle, 1966). These elements of dream content seem to reflect traditional sex roles in our society. Future studies may reveal different dream contents for women and men as changing sex roles evolve.

Other links between the dreaming and waking states have been demonstrated (Dement and Wolpert, 1958). Investigators sprayed cold water on a sleeping subject shortly after REM sleep had begun. When they woke up the subject he reported the following dream: "I was walking behind a leading lady when she suddenly collapsed and water was dripping on her. I ran over to her and water was dripping on my back and head. The roof was leaking" (Dement, 1972). Thus, in addition to including residues from the previous day as Freud suggested, dreams can also incorporate events occurring in the environment at the time the dream is taking place.

The same experiment helped demonstrate another link to waking consciousness: dreams occur in real time—not, as it was once thought, compressed into a few moments. The subject was awakened a measured time after the water spray and, after reporting the dream, was asked to repeat it in pantomine. The amount of time it took for the water to awaken the subject in the pantomine was close to the actual time it took the water spray application to awaken the subject during the experiment.

Perhaps the most dramatic illustration of a link between dreams and waking is that the two states actually appear to overlap. Researchers have reported a 90-minute cycle of minimal REM's during a 10 hour waking period, which appeared to coincide with daydreaming (Kripke and Sonnenschein, 1973). In a study of cognitive activity during relaxed wakefulness, subjects lay alone in a room and were periodically interrupted to be asked about their mental activity (Foulkes and Fleischer, 1975). About one fourth of the reports involved internal sensory imagery; of these reports, 44 percent were regarded by the subjects as either hallucinatory (had been accepted by the subjects as unreal during the experience) or considered bizarre or distorted.

Physiology of Dreaming   One important line of research growing out of the discovery of REM sleep is the attempt to relate physiological events to dreaming. Two classes of physiological events have been found during REM sleep.

Phasic (abrupt) *events* include the rapid eye movements and increases in various phenomena controlled by the autonomic nervous system such as pulse, respiration, and blood pressure.

Tonic (longer-lasting) *events* include penile erection in men and probably increased blood supply to the vagina in women and a decrease in muscle activity in both men and women.

How do these physiological events relate to the content of dreaming? It has been suggested that the rapid eye movements may represent a scanning of the dream image by the sleeper. William Dement (1972) reported an instance where side-to-side eye movement seemed to reflect a dream about watching a ping-pong game, but this rare observation does not exemplify any generally accepted principle. Similarly, penile erection might seem to suggest dream content of a sexual nature. However, studies indicate that only a small percentage (about 12 percent) of dreams manifest sexual content while male erection almost inevitably accompanies any REM sleep (Fisher, Gross, and Zuch, 1965). In fact, penile erections persist into non-REM sleep when laboratory subjects are deprived of REM sleep by awakening them whenever REM begins.

Investigators have attempted without success to link dream content to other signs of arousal during REM such as increases in heartbeat and respiration. These events, like penile erection, occur irrespective of the emotional content of the dream.

Why Sleep? Why Dream?   Why do we sleep and why do we dream? What is the biological value of sleep and dreams? We do know that sleep is necessary at least for survival. In the laboratory, sleep-deprived animals will eventually die; in medieval times, historians recorded instances where people were executed by being deprived of sleep. But why is it necessary?

Studies on experimental sleep deprivation have shown dramatic short-run effects but nothing lasting. In 1959 Peter Tripp, a New York disc jockey, stayed awake for 201 hours in a booth in Times Square to raise money for charity. Throughout his eight-day marathon he was studied by a highly qualified group of psychological and medical personnel. On his third day he began to see cobwebs in his shoes and rabbits in his booth, and he began to suffer memory impairment. Halfway through his ordeal, he found it unbearable to attempt psychological tests requiring attention or even minimum mental agility. By 110 hours he showed signs of delirium and was still hallucinating. At 120 hours he showed signs of paranoia: he imagined that flames were spurting out of a drawer and that these had been set deliberately in order to test him. Yet at 150 hours (almost a week without sleep), although he was so disoriented that he was not sure where or who he was, he was able to summon up his energies for his evening broadcast from 5 to 8 P.M. He functioned as an effective disc jockey, but his brain waves showed deep sleep rhythms while he was in fact behaviorally awake.

On the last day of Tripp's marathon, a distinguished neurologist came to examine him. He was carrying an umbrella and wore rather old-fashioned clothes. Tripp imagined that he was an undertaker and jumped off the examining table in an attempt to escape from this apparent conspiracy of his doctors. Yet he managed to complete the day and get through his last broadcast. After a final hour of tests, he fell asleep for 13 hours, to awake totally restored except for a slight depression that bothered him somewhat for three months thereafter (Luce and Segal, 1966).

In addition to such naturalistic studies, there have been a number of laboratory experiments in which subjects were deprived of only REM sleep. This was accomplished by waking them every time the rapid eye movements began. Studies of both humans and animals show an apparent tendency for subjects to experience extra amounts of REM sleep after deprivation as if to catch up (Dement, 1960). However, in contrast to earlier data suggesting that REM deprivation produced impulsiveness and other temporary behavioral changes in humans, there is no acceptably clear-cut evidence of specific emotional or physiological effects.

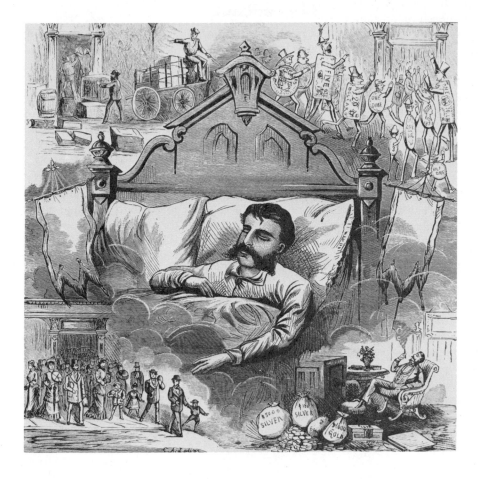

An artist's rendering of what composes dreams.

A number of theories about why we need to sleep and dream have been advanced. Freud, for example, said dreams were the "guardian of sleep," giving vent to thoughts and images that otherwise would awaken the sleeper, but this notion has found little support in laboratory studies. Most current theories of sleep and dreams emphasize a restorative role for physiological or psychological functioning. Ernest Hartmann (1973) proposed that quiet sleep may enable the body to recuperate from physical fatigue caused by muscular exercise, and dreaming enables the brain to recuperate from mental fatigue caused by intellectual effort and stressful emotional experiences. Or, as Shakespeare put it more poetically long before the discovery of REM, sleep is "the chief nourisher of life's feast" and "knits up the ravelled sleave of care."

Uses of the Dream

Long before the discovery of REM sleep, of course, dreams were the subject of mystery, fascination, and speculation. In biblical days dreams were considered prophetic. In more recent times they have provided the inspiration for literature and even scientific discovery. The idea for Samuel Taylor Coleridge's poem "Kubla Khan" came to him in a dream. The German chemist Friedrich Kekulé deciphered the ringlike molecular structure of benzene after a dream in which a snake devoured its own tail. Even stranger perhaps, in view of the brain's role in REM sleep, the chemical nature of nerve impulses was demonstrated by Otto Loewi in an experiment that was dream-inspired.

Freud (1900) called dreams the "royal road to the unconscious." His formulation of psychoanalysis at the beginning of this century made use of dream content to reveal urges and problems of which the patient was not conscious (see Chapters 12 and 15). To Freud dreams were often a form of wish fulfillment or manifestations of a primitive, irrational, childlike type of thinking that he called *primary process*. His disciple, Carl Jung, who later broke with Freud, also used dreams in his therapy, analytical psychology, but he took a more positive view. He believed dreams were symbolic messages from neglected parts of the dreamer's psyche that could help point the way to individual development. Moreover, to Jung, dreams expressed not only unconscious themes of an individual's life but also the grand themes of human existence—ideas and images that were inherited by all mankind and resided in what Jung called the *collective unconscious* (1936).

The use of dreams in psychotherapy to fish material out of the unconscious mind, as it were, is now common in the Western world (see Chapter 15). But they are or were nowhere more important to daily life than among the Senoi, an aboriginal tribe of Malaysia. An unusual anthropological study by the late Kilton Stewart described the ways in which the Senoi made use of dreams to solve everyday problems and improve human relations. Stewart reported that families would conduct regular "dream clinics" each morning. Parents would discuss the night's dreams with their children and, if an interpersonal problem manifested itself in a dream, efforts would be made during the day to placate any offended individuals by giving them presents. This therapeutic use of dreaming was believed to be an important factor in the life of the Senoi, contributing perhaps to a peaceful social order in which violent crime reportedly was extremely rare (Stewart, 1969).

Biofeedback

A potentially important area of research grew quite incidentally out of the pioneering sleep studies at the University of Chicago during the 1950s. Joseph Kamiya noted that volunteers in the sleep laboratory seemed able to guess when their brain waves, as recorded by the EEG, were registering the slow, relaxed alpha rhythm (Kamiya, 1969). He put subjects in a darkened, soundproof room, hooked them up to the EEG machine, which sounded a pleasant musical tone every time they produced alpha waves. With the tone providing the feedback, many volunteers soon learned to produce alpha waves at will, although they were never quite sure how they did it. Kamiya's work helped launch a new area of research and clinical application known as biological feedback, or *biofeedback*. In biofeedback training, the subject is given information, or feedback, on physiological processes that do not ordinarily reach awareness such as brain waves and blood pressure, so that the subject can consciously attempt to control them.

Brain-Wave Control

The subjects in Kamiya's experiments reported that increasing the alpha rhythm seemed to be accompanied by a serene state of consciousness not unlike that reported in the literature on meditation.

Biofeedback through brain-wave control.

ceral activities as heart rate, blood pressure, and even skin temperature. These functions are controlled by so-called smooth or involuntary muscles, which in turn are regulated by the autonomic nervous system. Until recently, control of the autonomic nervous system was thought to be automatic and not subject to the kind of conscious control that we have over our voluntary, or skeletal, muscles.

Although Eastern yogis were said to be able to perform such feats as slowing their metabolic rate and making their hearts slow down or stop, these claims were usually dismissed for various reasons including the presumption that skeletal muscles were responsible. In the so-called Valsalva maneuver, for example, Indian yogis can use their skeletal muscles to give the appearance that their heart has stopped. The yogis take a deep breath, hold it in, close their windpipe, lock their chin

Biofeedback through visceral control as practiced by Eastern yogi.

These reports caught the public fancy and alpha control was touted, and even commercially exploited, as a means of attaining higher or mystical consciousness. The public interest was spurred by ingenious stunts such as the demonstration of a young boy operating his toy electric train by amplifying his alpha rhythm. Electrodes on his scalp picked up the brain waves and activated an electronic switching mechanism; the more alpha, the faster the train went (Brown, 1974).

Although alpha control undoubtedly contributes to relaxation, subsequent research has failed to establish a significant correlation between the alpha rhythm and a specific state of consciousness. In fact, high alpha conditions can coexist with the conscious experience of anxiety. Studies indicate that simply sitting quietly and closing one's eyes matches biofeedback training in increasing the alpha rhythm. Opening the eyes suppresses alpha; suppression of eye movements increases it (Miller, 1978).

Visceral Control
Another form of biofeedback research and training aims at achieving conscious control over such vis-

141

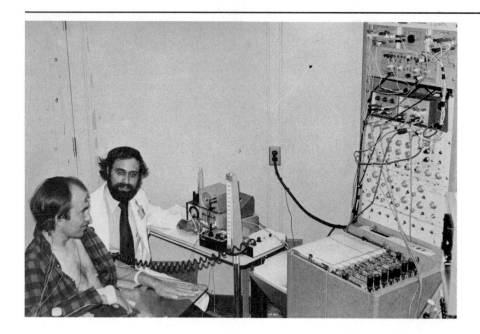

Patient with injured spinal cord being trained by Dr. Bernard Brucker to control his blood pressure using biofeedback techniques. Patients with high-level spinal cord injuries suffer from unregulated blood pressure and are thereby prevented from standing or even from sitting up in severe cases. Dr. Neal Miller and Dr. Brucker have worked on developing biofeedback techniques to train these patients to control their blood pressure, thus enabling them to sit erect and to stand with braces and crutches.

against their chest, and contract chest and abdominal muscles. This builds up pressure in the chest cavity, blocking blood return to the heart and preventing the heartbeat from being detected by a stethoscope, although the heart may actually be beating more rapidly.

During the 1960s Neal Miller tried to determine if it was possible to control autonomic activities consciously. One of the key experiments, conducted with his student Leo V. DiCara, tested whether rats could learn to change their heart rate and blood pressure through expanding and contracting their blood vessels (Miller, 1969). To rule out the possibility that the rats might "cheat" by using their skeletal muscles, they were given curare, a poison that paralyzes the skeletal muscles but not the nerves and smooth muscles of internal organs and blood vessels. (Surgeons learned this the hard way during the 1940s while experimenting with curare as an anesthetic: their patients had to suffer through the pain of the knife in silence because the skeletal muscles controlling speech were paralyzed.) Since chest muscles are necessary for breathing, the animals had to be artificially respirated. They were rewarded for achieving success in regulating their blood vessels or punished for not succeeding.

Miller and DiCara reported positive results: one rat, it was said, even learned to blush in one ear by dilating the blood vessels. Interestingly, Miller and others have had great difficulty in replicating the results of the experiments with curare, and their results are still the subject of debate. Nonetheless, the work gave a great impetus to biofeedback research. Later experiments appear to bear out Miller's hypothesis that conscious control of autonomic functions can be learned. Some humans have learned to control different responses simultaneously—for example, increasing blood pressure while decreasing heart rate, or vice versa—and this cannot be explained in terms of skeletal muscle effects. Recent work has shown that patients paralyzed by polio or muscular dystrophy can learn to increase their blood pressure.

While the mechanisms by which biofeedback works are still subject to dispute, there is little doubt that a primary role is played by cognitive factors. The first thing a subject does in trying to exercise control over visceral activities is to concentrate on the goal. One male subject raised his heart rate 30 beats a minute by imagining that he was running to catch a train.

Clinical Applications

Whatever the controversies surrounding brain wave control and visceral control, the techniques of biofeedback offer a great deal of promise for the treatment of psychosomatic disorders (psychologically induced diseases) by their focus on mind and body functioning together.

Biofeedback of skeletal muscle activity has been

used to train patients with neuromuscular disorders to alleviate tension headaches. Biofeedback also has been successful in helping patients control various visceral functions in addition to heart rate and blood pressure—for example, by increasing blood flow to the hands instead of the head by warming them in order to relieve migraine headaches. Epileptics have reduced the frequency of their seizures by learning to increase certain brain waves that are associated with muscle inactivity. Since the conditions treated with biofeedback are generally stress-related, it is relevant that biofeedback training is usually very relaxing.

Meditation and Peak Experiences

Whereas biofeedback represents a recent method for developing conscious control over bodily functions, a means for achieving the same or similar goals has existed for many centuries in the practice of *meditation*. Most forms of meditation, of course, aim even higher, seeking to alter consciousness and attain something like the state described by the nineteenth-century writer and social reformer Edward Carpenter:

> Of all the hard facts of science, I know of none more solid and fundamental than the fact that if

you inhibit thought (and persevere) you come at length to a region of consciousness below or behind thought . . . and a realization of an altogether vaster self than that to which we are accustomed. . . . It is to die in the ordinary sense, but in another sense, it is to wake up and find that the "I," one's real, most intimate self, pervades the universe and all other beings.

For many centuries, mystics in every major religion, particularly in the East, have reported such transcendental experiences. In recent years, however, meditation has become a subject of widespread secular interest in the West. To many people, it represents a way to transcend the self, a kind of spiritual "high" without drugs. To psychologists, it offers promise for the treatment of psychosomatic disorders and for a better understanding of the relationship between the mind and body.

Types of Meditation

From the psychological point of view there are two principal types of meditative practice: concentrative and mindfulness (Goleman, 1977; Ornstein, 1972).

Concentrative meditation seeks alteration of consciousness through detachment from the external environment and from the internal thought processes.

Concentrative Meditation In *concentrative meditation*, such as that practiced in the Hindu tradition, alteration of consciousness is sought through detachment from both external environment and internal thought processes. To avoid distraction, the individual concentrates on a single thought, image, sound, or movement. For example, the meditator may use a mandala, a fixed visual image on which all attention is focused, or a mantra, a word repeated silently to oneself. Moslem Sufi, "whirling dervishes," sometimes concentrate on continuous and prolonged body movement or, more commonly, the rhythm of their own labored breathing while whirling. For the successful practitioner, this concentration can result in a state of consciousness that Daniel Goleman (1977) summarizes as "loss of sense awareness, one pointed attention to the exclusion of all other thoughts, and sublimely rapturous feelings. . . . The concentrative path leads the meditator to merge with his meditation subject . . . and then to transcend it."

A variant of the concentrative type known as *transcendental meditation* (TM), is the meditative practice most familiar in the Western world.

In transcendental meditation (TM), novices sit with their eyes closed, resisting the intrusion of thoughts by the silent repetition of a specially chosen mantra.

Founded and led by Maharishi Mahesh Yogi, the TM organization is largely responsible for making the practice of meditation accessible to many Americans and others who know little of the mystical traditions of the East. TM is actually a simple technique, common to many schools of concentrative meditation. Novices are instructed to sit with their eyes closed, relaxed but with an upright spine, and to repeat silently a specially chosen mantra. Meditation takes place for about 20 minutes, twice a day, in a quiet environment. Meditators make no active attempt to control their mental experiences but try with a minimum of effort to keep their attention on the mantra, thereby indirectly resisting the intrusion of thoughts.

Devotees of TM have emphasized the physiological responses that occur in meditation, asserting that TM produces a unique psychophysiological state. This unique state, however, has not been scientifically described by practitioners. The TM organization has sponsored, directly and indirectly, programs of physiological research as well as work aimed at demonstrating the benefits of TM. These benefits, it is said, range from psychological well-being to changes in perception and diverse improvements in health (Davidson, 1976).

Mindfulness Meditation In *mindfulness meditation*, such as that practiced in the Zen tradition of *shikan taza*, the process is quite different. Instead of ignoring internal and external stimuli, the meditator deliberately directs attention to all such distractions—the chirping of a bird, for example, or the tenderness in a leg that comes from prolonged sitting, or simply random thoughts that pass through the mind. The object is to observe these impressions and thoughts with detachment, to receive them while striving not to react to them. A Zen master has described this as "noticing every person one sees on the street but not looking back with emotional curiosity." Paradoxically, while the process demands increasingly intense immersion in the present, the ultimate goal is to achieve a state of nirvana, a state that is the negation of self-awareness, the total absence of ordinary experience.

In both basic types of meditation, the usual normal relationship between an individual and the internal and external environments seems to be eliminated so that stimuli from neither exert control over thought processes or behavior. The internal dialogue—the mind's ongoing stream of con-

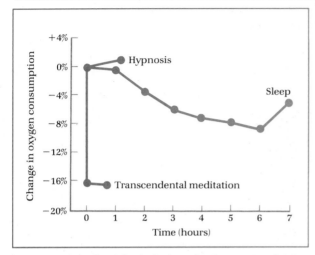

FIGURE 5.5 Physiological changes that occur during transcendental meditation are demonstrated by the dramatic drop in metabolic rate as reflected by the decrease in oxygen consumption.

sciousness—disappears and, with it, planning, problem solving, imagining, remembering, and daydreaming.

Physiological Responses

What physiological changes actually occur during meditation? Widely publicized studies on TM practitioners have reported a number of physiological responses (Davidson, 1976). These are decreases in the heart and respiration rates and in the consumption of oxygen and metabolic rate (see Figure 5.5). Electroencephalograph measurements show increases primarily in amount (of amplitude) of alpha waves, which are characteristic of relaxed wakefulness. Various changes in blood chemistry also are reported, including a decrease in blood lactate, a substance believed to be correlated with a high level of anxiety. Most of these responses are the opposite of those occurring during the stress that seems to be associated with many psychosomatic disorders such as high blood pressure (Benson, 1975).

The major question about these findings is whether the reported physiological responses are in any important way unique to meditation. It is possible, for example, that most of them simply denote a general state of relaxation, which can be induced by various nonmeditative techniques such as self-hypnosis or biofeedback training (Davidson, 1976).

Although physiological relaxation seems to be a characteristic of many forms of meditation, evidence of increased arousal has also been found. In studies of Zen adepts, yogis, and others, EEG responses that may be related to specific experiences in meditation have also been reported. These include increases in fast frequencies of the dominant beta rhythm (indicative of increased arousal) and also increased theta, both in connection with more profound meditative experiences. (Corby, Roth, Zarcone, and Kopell, 1978, Kasematsu and Hirai, 1966).

Appropriately, the Corby study presented evidence that increased physiological arousal (EEG beta as well as increased heart and respiration rates) may be related to those meditative disciplines that stress a more active struggle toward the achievement of higher states, or peak experiences.

Peak Experiences

Meditation is a potential means for achieving those mysterious states of consciousness that have been called *peak experiences* by Abraham Maslow (1971), a founder of the modern tradition of humanistic psychology (see Chapter 1). The practice of meditation, however, is not the only means, nor in itself necessarily sufficient, for producing peak experiences. Such states have been described by mystics and others in a vast literature deriving from all parts of the world and throughout recorded history. William James called them "mystical experiences"; Saint Paul spoke of "the peace that passeth understanding"; Quakers refer to the "inner light"; Zen Buddhists aspire to "satori" and yogis to "samadhi." These experiences have been induced not only by meditation but also by other conditions such as intense stress, creative efforts, or even (apparently) spontaneously.

What constitutes a peak experience is obviously highly subjective and may have nothing to do with intellectual profundity. Winston Churchill is said to have awakened once in the middle of the night with a sense of having discovered the secret of the universe. He wrote it down and then read his message the next morning in the hard light of normal waking consciousness: "The whole is pervaded by a strong smell of turpentine."

According to an extensive analysis of mystical literature, peak experiences share a number of

The publication in 1976 of the book *Life After Life* introduced a fascinating concept to the reading public, "the near-death experience." The author, Raymond Moody, Jr., who was trained in philosophy and medicine, reported on interviews he had conducted with a number of people who had experienced a close brush with death or who had been revived after apparent clinical death. These people told Moody that during this near-death state they had undergone an extraordinary series of phenomena, which he summed up in the following version of the "ideal" or "complete" experience:

A man is dying and, as he reaches the point of greatest physical distress, he hears himself pronounced dead by his doctor. He begins to hear an uncomfortable noise, a loud ringing or buzzing, and at the same time feels himself moving very rapidly through a long dark tunnel. After this, he suddenly finds himself outside of his own physical body . . . and he sees his own body from a distance, as though he is a spectator. . . . He glimpses the spirits of relatives and friends who have already died, and a loving, warm spirit of a kind he has never encountered before—a being of light—appears before him. This being asks him a question, nonverbally, to make him evaluate his life and helps him along by showing him a panoramic, instantaneous playback of the major events of his life. . . . He is overwhelmed by intense feelings of joy, love, and peace. Despite his attitude, though, he somehow reunites with his physical body and lives.

Although Moody's book understandably created a stir among the general public, selling more than 3 million copies in the United States alone, it was at first generally disregarded by psychologists. Moody's report was anecdotal in nature; it had not been published in a scientific journal; his data were not quantified in a scientific manner. (For example, he did not spell out how many people he had interviewed or how many of them did not report the near-death experience.)

Recently, however, a number of psychologists and medical scholars have begun systematic research into the near-death experience. Of particular interest is the study conducted by Kenneth Ring (1980). Ring studied 102 persons who had been resuscitated after showing signs of clinical death. Of these subjects, 49 percent reported experiences almost identical in some major respects to those described by Moody.

Separating these near-death experiences into subcategories, Ring stated that 60 percent reported a sense of peace and well-being, 37 percent had the out-of-body feeling, 53 percent "entered the darkness," 33 percent "saw the light" and 20 percent entered it, 25 percent reviewed their lives, and 33 percent said they had chosen, bargained, or willed themselves to return to life. Ring also investigated the impact on the individual's subsequent life: 37 percent of those who had a near-death experience reported an increased appreciation of life; 29 percent of those who did not have a near-death experience reported an increased appreciation of life.

Since this report, Ring has interviewed more than 100 additional subjects. He has found that the earlier rate of about 50 percent reporting near-death experiences holds true for the new sample. His studies appear to have been conducted in such a manner as to exclude such easy explanations as lying by the subject or self-delusion by subjects who had read Moody's book. Although it is very difficult to obtain truly random samples of people who have been near death, there is no longer any doubt that substantial numbers have undergone the near-death experience.

Thus, for the first time, science has taken seriously a profound experience that surely must have existed since time immemorial but that, until Moody's book, had been noted only in fragmentary references in popular literature. The near-death experience must be regarded as occurring during an altered state of consciousness. How and why this particular state happens is far from clear, although its frequency suggests to many psychologists that the human species may have a genetic predisposition to the near-death experience. In any event, so much interest finally has been aroused that a group of scientists have organized the Association for the Study of Near-Death Phenomena to foster further research into this remarkable occurrence.

characteristics (Stace, 1960). First and foremost is the experience of "unity" or "union," which can be expressed negatively as a loss of the sense of separateness of self from others and from the outside world. Six other characteristics were noted: a feeling of bliss; a sense of sacredness; ineffability or difficulty in describing the experience; enhanced sense of reality or meaning; transcendence of time and space; paradoxicality or reconciliation of propositions that seem contradictory in normal consciousness. For example, a mystic might claim to have died or to "have experienced an empty unity that at the same time contains all reality." Many of these categories were mentioned earlier by William James (1900).

Physiologically, little is known about peak experiences because they do not lend themselves to reproduction upon demand in the scientist's laboratory. As we will see later in this chapter, descriptions of mystical experiences often resemble the reports of subjects in drug-induced states. Arnold Mandell (1980) has proposed that the same series of complex chemical interactions in the brain may underlie all peak experiences from the meditative "high" to the drug-induced state.

Hypnosis

One of the least understood phenomena of consciousness is the hypnotic state. *Hypnosis* was first demonstrated in the late eighteenth century by a Vienna physician named Anton Mesmer. Mesmer was fascinated, as were many scientists then, by naturally occurring electrical phenomena such as magnetism. He used hypnosis to treat his patients for a variety of physical and mental ailments but could explain it only in terms of an "animal magnetism" that flowed from him to his patients (Mesmer and Bloch, 1980).

First known as mesmerism, hypnosis received its current name from the Greek for "sleep," because the hypnotic state was wrongly thought to represent a kind of psychological sleep. Freud was an early practitioner and experimented with hypnosis in treating patients with symptoms that lacked any physiological basis. The fact that some patients were able to recall long-forgotten childhood traumas under hypnosis helped lead Freud to hypothesize the existence of an unconscious, the bedrock on which he founded psychoanalysis.

Hypnotism is a relatively simple procedure, although folklore has endowed it with various properties of magical hocus-pocus. The hypnotist may use any of a number of methods, all aimed at relaxing the subject and narrowing normal consciousness. The subject may be instructed to focus attention on a shiny object, for example, or a thumbtack on the wall, while the hypnotist keeps repeating that the subject is getting relaxed and sleepy. Some subjects can even hypnotize themselves by listening to a tape recording of their own voice or of the amplified sounds of their own breathing.

Characteristics of the Hypnotic State
Under hypnosis, people sometimes report regressing to early childhood and remembering events that they had forgotten. They lift weights and per-

Demonstration of hypnosis, a state characterized by high suggestibility, easy access to mental imagery and imagination, decline of the conscious planning function, and the tendency to see and hear things that are not there.

form other feats of strength that they are not apparently capable of under ordinary circumstances. They respond to things that do not exist in their present environment. They sometimes report themselves to be psychologically deaf or blind or insensitive to pain. Teeth have been pulled or even legs amputated without the patient's having an apparent conscious awareness of pain.

A leading modern investigator of hypnosis, Ernest Hilgard, has delineated a number of characteristics of the hypnotic state (Hilgard, 1977), including the following:

- High suggestibility (responsiveness to hypnotic suggestions), which is often regarded as the defining condition of hypnosis but actually is only one of many characteristics. Studies indicate an increase in suggestibility after hypnotic induction.
- Easy access to mental imagery and imagination—an ability that is also highly correlated with susceptibility to hypnosis. People with vivid imaginations are frequently good subjects for hypnosis.
- Decline of the conscious planning function. Subjects wait for the hypnotist to suggest actions.
- Reduction in reality testing; that is, subjects tend to see and hear things that are not there. Under deep hypnosis, a subject might "eat" an imaginary pear.

Subjects who are particularly susceptible can be placed in deep hypnosis. The method is to induce hypnosis and then suggest that subjects deepen this state by themselves. In deep hypnosis, subjects may no longer respond to the suggestions of the hypnotist but experience, on their own, ego loss (lack of self-consciousness or awareness of self), feelings of timelessness and bliss, and other feelings removed from normal consciousness.

Alterations in consciousness can endure beyond the hypnotic state. This is achieved through *posthypnotic suggestion*. While still hypnotized, subjects are told that they will forget everything that occurred during hypnosis (*posthypnotic amnesia*) and then remember it all at some prearranged signal. The hypnotist may also suggest that, after hypnosis, the subject will be capable of performing unusual skills: a common example is automatic writing, the act of writing understandably without awareness of what is being written.

Despite the fact that hypnotism has been well documented in the laboratory, so many enigmas remain that some investigators have suggested that it does not constitute an altered state of consciousness at all (Barber, 1970). Not everyone is equally susceptible to hypnotism, and although it is not clear what factors lead to susceptibility, children and imaginative people tend to be more susceptible. Hypnosis can take place during various kinds of physiologic states. Although the usual situation is extreme relaxation, subjects can be hypnotized during strenuous activities such as bicycling. A final enigma is that all attempts to find distinguishing physiological characteristics of the hypnotic state have met with failure. Unlike sleep and dreams, for example, which are characterized by distinct EEG patterns, the brain waves present in the hypnotic state do not appear to differ from the rhythms of normal waking consciousness. The clear distinction between hypnosis and the physiologically well-defined states of sleep contrasts sharply with the common instruction of hypnotists to their subjects that they are falling asleep.

The "Hidden Observer"   A concept that can help explain the psychological processes occurring in hypnosis is *dissociation*. This concept describes a postulated process whereby certain mental processes split off from normal consciousness and function independently. It was first used in 1889 by the French psychologist and neurologist Pierre Janet, who employed hypnosis in treating mental disorders. An example of dissociation as described by Janet was the automatic writing performed by one of his patients, Lucie. Under posthypnotic suggestion, Lucie could write letters or solve mathematical problems on paper while chatting blithely along. She was unaware of what her hand was doing and she had no subsequent memory of the writing. The automatic writing was dissociated from her normal consciousness (Hilgard, 1977).

Hilgard (1977), using the dissociation concept, postulates a kind of divided awareness at work during hypnosis—two levels of consciousness each operating independently. One level is the consciousness that is apparent on the surface; the other is concealed and has been described by Hilgard as the "hidden observer."

The apparent presence of the *hidden observer* has been demonstrated in a number of Hilgard's experiments, especially those involving a painful stimulus during hypnosis. For example, subjects are told that they will feel no pain when they put their hand in a bucket of ice water. The subjects do as they are instructed and their surface consciousness reports no feeling of pain. If, however, the subjects are told to tell about their feelings through automatic writing, the hidden observer will report the pain.

Chemistry and Consciousness

With the exception of hypnosis, the alterations of consciousness we have discussed so far are for the most part self-induced. Sleep and dreams, for example, occur spontaneously; biofeedback and meditation are achieved basically through the individual's own efforts; and even hypnosis, as we have noted, can be self-induced. By contrast, the use of drugs represents a kind of external tinkering with the consciousness, a fact that may explain some of the controversy that surrounds the topic of drug use in our society.

The chemical approach to consciousness is both radically new and very old. It is new in the sense that the past three decades have witnessed a revolution in *psychoactive drugs*—chemical substances that affect mood, thought, and behavior. As we will see more fully in Chapters 14 and 15, the development of mood-influencing (psychoactive or psychotherapeutic) drugs for the treatment of schizophrenia, depression, and other disorders has exerted a powerful impact on our understanding of abnormal behavior. At the same time, the synthesis of psychedelic ("mind manifesting") drugs such as LSD and the widespread use of cannabis, or marijuana, have introduced millions of others to the effects of chemistry on consciousness. The latter group of drugs have been used primarily for recreational, rather than psychiatric, purposes.

From before the time of recorded history, people have experimented with drugs derived from herbal and other plants. The drug alcohol was used by the Egyptian and Indo-Aryan civilizations around 6400 B.C. and possibly as early as 9000 B.C. in the Indus Valley. Cannabis was also in use around 3000 B.C. in Indian and Chinese civilizations. It is believed that opium was used by Sumerians and Egyptians around 3500 to 4000 B.C. Records exist of the use by Indians of the New World of many plants containing psychedelic substances including mimosa, morning glory, *datura* (ginseng weed), peyote, various mushrooms including psilocybe, and coca (cocaine). In many tribal cultures, however, the use of psychoactive substances has seldom been accompanied by the problems of drug abuse that we associate with drug use in modern industrial societies. Later in this section we will examine some of the reasons.

Alcohol

Perhaps the most widely used, and abused, drug in modern Western societies is a depressant, alcohol. Alcohol, like other depressants, or downers, slows down neural activity as well as breathing and other physical activities. A small amount of alcohol acts as an intoxicant, presumably releasing "lower" brain mechanisms from inhibitory controls by the cortex. After a couple of drinks, however, most people become more lethargic, and deterioration in their locomotor skills and moods occurs.

Alcohol is not even regarded as a drug by most people, but a drug it is. Excessive consumption of alcohol can result in addiction and in both psychological and physical impairment. Some researchers consider *alcoholism*, or alcohol addiction, to be a disease; others classify it as a behavioral disorder. Some studies have even suggested the possibility of a genetic disposition to alcoholism (Cruz-Coke and Varela, 1966; McClearn, G. and Rodgers, D., 1959).

The amount of alcohol consumed and its effects are measured in percentages of blood alcohol concentration—that is, the proportion of alcohol per unit of blood. After two cocktails on an empty stomach, an average-sized person will have a blood alcohol concentration of around 0.06 percent and feel "high" and mildly intoxicated. When blood alcohol concentrations reach the order of 0.1 percent, reflexive behaviors are seriously affected; the person is "drunk." When concentrations reach the order of 0.15 percent the individual will appear obviously to be drunk.

Classification of Psychoactive Drugs

Table 5.1 shows the main drug groups that affect consciousness, classified as to general effects and chemistry. It should be noted that a drug may have very different effects depending on the dose used. For this reason and because drugs have multiple effects, their classification is somewhat arbitrary. The terms *stimulant* and *depressant* refer to stimulation or depression of the central nervous system in the present context. We will focus here on two categories: anesthetics and analgesics, and psychedelics.

149

TABLE 5.1 Major Classes of Psychoactive Drugs Based on General Biological or Behavioral Effects

DRUG CLASS	GROUP	TRADE OR COMMON NAME	EXAMPLE	EVIDENCE OF ADDICTION?
Anesthetics and analgesics	General anesthetics	"laughing gas"	nitrous oxide	no
			diethyl ether	no
			chloroform	no
	Local anesthetics	coca	cocaine	yes
		Novocaine	procaine	no
	Narcotic analgesics	morphine, heroin	opium derivatives	yes
Sedative-hypnotics	General		alcohol	yes
	Barbiturates	Luminal	phenobarbital	yes
	Bromides		potassium bromide	no
Stimulants	Analeptics	Metrazol	pentylenetetrazol	no
	Nicotinics		nicotine	yes
	Sympathomimetics	Benzedrine, speed	amphetamine	yes
	Xanthines		caffeine	yes
Psychedelics	*Cannabis sativa*	hemp, hashish	marijuana	no
	Ergot derivative	LSD, "acid"	lysergic acid diethylamide	no
	Lophophora williamsii	peyote buttons	mescaline	no
	Psilocybe mexicana		psilocybin	no

Source: Adapted from R. F. Thompson, *Introduction to Physiological Psychology* (New York: Harper & Row, 1975), pp. 170–171.

Anesthetics and Analgesics *Anesthetics* and *analgesics* are both drugs used to block pain. Anesthesia was introduced in the nineteenth century when Hollis Wells, a dentist in Hartford, Connecticut, began using nitrous oxide for pulling teeth. *General anesthesia,* or the loss of sensation with the loss of consciousness, was first used by William Morton who introduced ether for surgery. This was strongly opposed by the churches on the basis that people are meant to suffer. Apparently the most effective argument against this opposition was that God anesthetized Adam during the creation of Eve. General anesthetics may produce altered-state experiences during the induction of anesthesia and in awakening from it if the transitions to unconsciousness are not too rapid. Even *local anesthetics,* which produce *analgesia*—loss of pain without loss of consciousness when used at the site of the source of pain—may alter the conscious state when taken internally. The best-known example of this reaction comes from cocaine, which is also a stimulant, which produces a sense of well-being and is widely used today as a recreational drug. Freud was the first modern scholar to study cocaine's effectiveness as a local anesthetic and its behavioral effects.

In the process he became an enthusiast and addict.

The *narcotic analgesics,* such as the opium derivatives morphine and heroin, ease pain while inducing significant elevation of mood. Opium is believed to have been used in ancient Greek rituals during the classical period as well as in ancient Egypt and Sumeria. Its derivatives are among the most addictive drugs. *Addiction* has two main aspects, the first of which is psychological dependence, wherein the addict develops a need for the drug in order to maintain feelings of well-being. The second is physical dependence, in which withdrawal of the drug from an addict results in severe illness and in some cases even death. A less extreme phenomenon common to many addictive and nonaddictive drugs is *tolerance* or the need to increase the dose, following repeated use of the drug, in order to achieve the same effect previously experienced from a smaller dose.

Many things are still not understood about anesthetics and consciousness; people sometimes remember at a later point statements made by the surgeon while they were deeply anesthetized, but the reasons for this are not clear. Such memories can be recovered under hypnosis, a fact that can be most embarrassing to the surgeon.

Sedatives and Hypnotics   *Barbiturates* and other sedative-hypnotic drugs in large doses induce general anesthesia. In smaller doses, they are considered *sedatives* (minor depressants). Unlike local anesthetics and analgesics, sedatives suppress the sensation of pain but impair consciousness in the process; subjects get sleepy as they lose sensation.

Stimulants   The most commonly used stimulants are amphetamines and related drugs, known popularly as speed. These drugs increase locomotor activity in animals at doses well below those that produce convulsions. In humans they produce euphoria, but repeated or higher doses can cause tremors, restlessness, agitation, and even paranoid psychosis. They are used medically to counter sleepiness (for example in pregnant women) and also for weight reduction because they reduce appetite by action on the brain.

Smoking marijuana, a mild psychedelic, often gives users feelings of well-being or euphoria and enhancement of sensory pleasure.

Psychedelics

The most interesting of the drugs from the standpoint of altered consciousness are the *psychedelics*, a term that means "mind manifesting." They are also sometimes referred to as *hallucinogens.* This is a misnomer, because contrary to popular belief, psychedelics do not generally induce true hallucinations, which are perceptions of scenes that do not exist. Rather, psychedelics typically modify the normal perceptual environment by greatly intensifying the sensory intensity of characteristics such as color and texture.

Several psychedelics occur naturally. The minor (less effective) psychedelic, marijuana, derives from the hemp plant, *Cannabis sativa.* Mescaline is present in buttons of the peyote cactus and psilocybin is found in certain mushrooms. Other psychedelics are products of the laboratory. The most potent of the well-known psychedelics is LSD (lysergic acid diethylamide-25).

The known physiological effects of marijuana are not particularly dramatic: most characteristic are increased heart rate, increased pulse, and reddening of the eyes. The change in heart rate reaches its maximum about half an hour after ingestion of the drug, whose total time course is about three hours. This effect is the main basis for suggestions that the drug may be hazardous to people with heart problems. Other physiological effects are indicated by the fact that marijuana is finding medical applications in the treatment of glaucoma and the nausea induced by cancer chemotherapy.

The psychological effects of marijuana include decreased performance on simple intellectual and psychomotor tests, including some impairment of driving ability and decreased activity levels. Generally these effects are less intense for experienced users (Grinspoon, 1977). However, marijuana in some cases shows what seems to be a reversed tolerance—with naive users needing to take more of the drug to get "high" (Weil, 1973). From the point of view of the user, of course, the important effects are the mood changes: feelings of well-being or euphoria and enhancement of sensory pleasure. People on marijuana commonly have an urge to snack.

Although marijuana is physically nonaddictive, some users feel they need it regularly for the sense

151

of well-being it provides. More research into the effects of marijuana is still needed. However, it is not nearly as potentially dangerous as the major psychedelics, one of which is LSD.

Just one tenth of a milligram of LSD can induce an immense transformation of the conscious state. LSD, a slight chemical modification of compounds present in a certain fungus that attacks rye, is the product of both nature and the psychopharmacologist's laboratory. Its powerful effects on consciousness were discovered by the Swiss pharmacologist Albert Hofmann, who accidentally ingested a large dose of LSD in his laboratory one memorable May day in 1943. As Hofmann described it: ". . . there surged upon me an uninterrupted stream of fantastic images of extraordinary plasticity and vividness and accompanied by an intense, kaleidoscope-like play of colors" (Sankar, 1975).

Physiological effects of LSD include feelings of weakness, dizziness, and slight nausea early in the "trip" (Sankar, 1975). Pupillary dilation is an effect that is easily recognized (and therefore used by the police). A decreased threshold for arousal is usually seen along with increased sensory perception in all modalities. An increase in body temperature and blood sugar with a reduced urge for food intake is common. Thus the major observed physiological alterations reflect increased central sympathetic arousal, which clearly is insufficient to explain the profound psychological effects.

Psychological changes with LSD include alterations in body image, dreamy, detached feelings, time distortions, transformation of the visual environment often including apparent undulations, heightened suggestibility, and a variety of mood changes (Sankar, 1975). The effectiveness of the drug seems to depend upon personality; it is less effective in rigid, dogmatic, controlled people and more effective in esthetic, imaginative introverts.

Several explanations have been proposed for the psychological and physiological effects of LSD. For example, it has been speculated that time appears to pass more slowly because there is a higher density of intense conscious experiences. Some of the visual effects may be caused by pupil dilation, which increases the light reaching the retina. This results in decreased depth of focus, which maximizes spherical and chromatic aberrations and causes blurring and rainbow effects at the edges of the visual field (Barber, 1970).

It is interesting to note that between LSD, psilocybin, and mescaline there is *cross tolerance*; that is, development of tolerance to one of them by repeated use renders not only it, but also the others, less effective. However, there is no cross tolerance between these three drugs and marijuana. This indicates a substantial difference between the action of marijuana and of the major psychedelics.

More than any other class of drugs, the psychedelics have inspired debate and controversy in our society, and their possession and sale is illegal in the United States except for carefully prescribed medicinal or experimental purposes. (Prohibition of drugs is nothing new, of course; a number of societies have banned tobacco; among them Russia in the seventeenth century where the use of snuff was thought to have such ill effects on the breath that one penalty authorized slitting the nose of the offender.)

In an attempt to clarify myths and misconceptions, let us consider two important questions in the debate over psychedelics.

Are Psychedelics Dangerous? A variety of deleterious effects have been ascribed to marijuana. Early reports of brain damage and chromosome destruction have not survived the test of careful scientific research. In several studies, marijuana was shown to lower blood levels of the male sex hormone testosterone; it is not known if the change is sufficient to have ill effect (Kolodny, Masters, Kolodner, and Toro, 1974). A further danger of marijuana may be the "amotivational syndrome"—loss of motivation for work or studies. In fact, it is impossible so far to distinguish cause and effect; propensities to "amotivation" may themselves be the cause of heavy drug usage. For good or ill, marijuana is now being used by many millions of Americans. Further research on marijuana is needed; given the present state of knowledge, however, some investigators have concluded that, in normal usage, marijuana is a safer drug than either tobacco or alcohol, both of which are potentially lethal.

LSD, for all its potency and profundity of effect on consciousness, at present appears to be devoid of destructive effects on the body despite earlier unsubstantiated claims. The known dangers relate primarily to its psychological effects. Like marijuana, it is physically nonaddictive; unlike marijuana, it seldom seems to cause psychological dependence. Often a person will be deeply affected by an experience with LSD and yet never return to it.

The major known danger with LSD is the possibility of a "bad trip." Particularly when LSD is taken without appropriate supervision, the experience can be profoundly fearful with deleterious emotional effects outlasting the period of drug action. While there is no reliable evidence that LSD can induce a psychotic state in an individual with normal mental health, severely disturbed people should certainly avoid the drug, with the possible exception of its use in carefully supervised psychotherapy (Smart, 1967).

Any discussion of the possible dangers of psychedelic drugs must take into account the circumstances in which they are used. Many tribal groups have used psychedelic herbs for the purpose of seeking spiritual experiences including the Native

American Church, a North American Indian religion whose members are legally permitted to use peyote in their rituals. In such circumstances there seem to be no problems with abuse of the drugs. One reason, according to Andrew Weil (1973), who did the first modern laboratory research on the effects of marijuana, is that tribal societies use psychedelics in natural—and therefore less potent—form. Weil suggests that the variety of substances contained in the plants may somehow lessen overall deleterious effects.

Perhaps more important, the drugs are used in

A subjective report on the physiological and perceptual effects of LSD was obtained by means of a questionnaire containing 47 items. Six of these are presented here. Volunteers were questioned at one-hour intervals beginning half an hour after they took the drug. The curves show the percentage of the group giving positive answers at each time. The long-broken curves are for those given an inactive substance, the short-broken curves for those given 25 to 75 micrograms of LSD, and the solid curves for those given 100 to 225 micrograms of LSD.

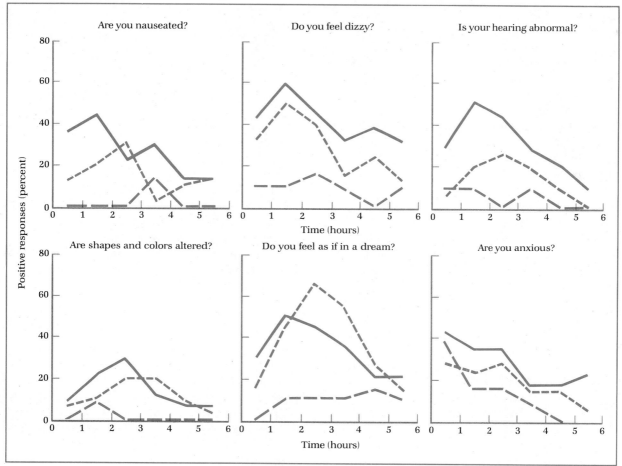

tribal societies in highly ritualized ways. Some are used only by medicine men or shamans for divination or diagnosing illness; others are used only in particular rites of passage where hallucinations are sought to arouse visions of the spirit realm. For instance, Zuni Indian rain priests take toloache (*datura*) before going out to commune with the bird kingdom to intercede for rain (Schultes, 1972). The rituals surrounding the preparation and ingestion of the herbs, along with the support of the group and the presence of religious leaders to provide guidance, appear to channel the effects of the drugs in desired directions. It is not merely coincidental that people in industrial societies whose use of alcohol is connected with ritual—drinking only with food, for example, or in the company of others—are much less likely to become abusers of this drug.

The ritual use of psychedelics exemplifies the well-documented fact that psychedelics do not necessarily impose specific experiences on the individual. Rather, the nature of the resulting alterations in the state of consciousness depends to a great degree on two psychological factors: *set* (the mental state of the individual before ingestion) and *setting* (external conditions). The importance of set and setting applies to the use of marijuana as well as to the more potent psychedelics such as LSD. Use of marijuana by an individual trying to counter depression often leads only to intensification of that depression. Finally it should be emphasized that research on marijuana and particularly on LSD has not been sufficient to regard them as "safe" drugs.

Do Psychedelics Produce Mystical Experiences?

This question is raised by the many similarities between psychedelic states and those states we have previously described as peak or mystical experiences. For one thing, it is often impossible to distinguish between first-person reports of the two experiences. Consider the following two accounts; one is a first-person description of experiences under the influence of LSD; the other is an account by R. M. Bucke of a spontaneous experience that he called "cosmic consciousness" and published in a book of that name in 1900.

Influence of LSD

Suddenly I burst into a vast, new, indescribably wonderful universe. Although I am writing this over a year later, the thrill of the surprise and amaze-

ment, the awesomeness of the revelation, the engulfment in an overwhelming feeling-wave of gratitude and blessed wonderment, are as fresh, and the memory of the experience is as vivid, as if it had happened five minutes ago. And yet to concoct anything by way of description that would even hint at the magnitude, the sense of ultimate reality . . . this seems such an impossible task. The knowledge which has infused and affected every aspect of my life came instantaneously and with such complete force of certainty that it was impossible, then or since, to doubt its validity.

"Cosmic Consciousness"

All at once, without warning of any kind, I found myself wrapped in a flame-colored cloud. For an instant I thought of fire . . . the next, I knew that the fire was within myself. Directly afterward there came upon me a sense of exultation, of immense joyousness accompanied or immediately followed by an intellectual illumination impossible to describe. Among other things, I did not merely come to believe, but I say that the universe is not composed of dead matter, but is, on the contrary, a living Presence; I became conscious in myself of eternal life. . . . I saw that all men are immortal: that the cosmic order is such that without any peradventure all things work together for the good of each and all; that the foundation principle of the world . . . is what we call love, and that the happiness of each and all is in the long run absolutely certain (Bucke, 1900).

Other apparent similarities can be found in the lasting beneficial effects on personality that have been reported in the aftermath of both states. These include enhancement of creativity (Harman, McKim, Mogar, Fadiman, and Stolaroff, 1966) and decreased anxiety, guilt, and repression; increased capacity to experience wide ranges of emotions; tolerance of ambiguity; and enhanced acceptance of self (Chwelos, Blewett, Smith, and Hoffer, 1959; Smart, 1967).

The writer Aldous Huxley believed that psychedelic and mystical experiences were essentially the same. His experiments with mescaline came against a background of scholarly involvement in Eastern religious thought. The issue was beclouded, however, by the antics of such drug prophets of the 1960s as Timothy Leary, the former psychologist who founded the League of Spiritual Discovery (LSD) and handed down the new commandments: "Tune in, turn on, and drop out." The publicity accorded Leary, along with the spread of irresponsible use of psychedelic drugs, helped create the climate in which psychedelics were essentially banned during the 1960s for scientific research on humans.

Before the drugs became generally unavailable for human research, an experiment conducted by Walter Pahnke (Pahnke and Richards, 1966) produced evidence of parallels between psychedelic and religious-mystical experiences. The circumstances of the experiment, which has been dubbed "the miracle of Marsh Chapel," were carefully arranged to make maximum use of both mental set and environmental setting. On Good Friday, 20 Protestant theological students were assembled in a room adjacent to the chapel where services were being conducted. The students were given either psilocybin or a placebo under a double-blind procedure. For the next 2½ hours, the Good Friday service next door was piped into the room.

Later, the experience and its aftermath were assessed through questionnaires, written reports, and interviews. These assessments were aimed particu-larly at eliciting information relating to the categories of mystical experience, which we discussed in the section on meditation and peak experiences. The subjects who took psilocybin scored significantly higher on Stace's categories (see Table 5.2). Moreover, they reported more lasting positive changes in attitude and/or behavior than did the subjects who took a placebo. Interestingly, one of the categories that showed the least difference between the psilocybin- and placebo-treated subjects was a sense of "sacredness." The control subjects had high scores on this item in part because they were affected by the carefully prepared religious environment. Although Pahnke did not assert that these subjects had true mystical experiences, the basic elements clearly were present.

One case against the equation of psychedelic states and mystical experiences presents some interesting arguments (Zaehner, 1972):

TABLE 5.2 Summary of Percentage Scores and Significance Levels Reached by the Experimental Versus the Control Group for Categories Measuring the Typology of Mystical Experience

CATEGORY	PERCENT OF MAXIMUM POSSIBLE SCORE FOR 10 Ss	
	EXPERIMENTAL	CONTROL
I. *Unity*	62	7
A. Internal	70	8
B. External	38	2
II. *Transcendence of time and space*	84	6
III. *Deeply felt positive mood*	57	23
A. Joy, blessedness, and peace	51	13
B. Love	57	33
IV. *Sacredness*	53	28
V. *Objectivity and reality*	63	18
VI. *Paradoxicality*	61	13
VII. *Alleged ineffability*	66	18
VIII. *Transiency*	79	8
IX. *Persisting positive changes in attitude and behavior*	51	8
A. Toward self	57	3
B. Toward others	40	20
C. Toward life	54	6
D. Toward the experience	57	31

Source: W. Pahnke, "The Contribution of the Psychology of Religion to the Therapeutic Use of Psychedelic Substances." In H. Abramoon (ed.), *The Use of Psychotherapy and Alcoholism* (Indianapolis: Bobbs-Merrill, 1967), pp. 629–652.

- Psychedelics heighten sensory experiences, whereas mystical experiences such as those induced by meditation are devoid of sensations.
- Psychedelic experiences are "involuntary" and dependent upon an outside stimulus, whereas individuals in the mystical state apparently can control their thoughts and feelings. R. H. Ward (1957) likens the psychedelic experience to "being on an express train at night, with no driver and no brakes."
- Psychedelic, as opposed to "true" mystical experiences, are devoid of the "Love of God."

One key point in the debate focuses on differences in personal effort. Drug taking is essentially a passive activity, whereas mystical experiences often come only after years of effort, study, and perhaps of suffering. This has been described as essentially the difference between climbing the Matterhorn and going up it in a cable car. The philosopher Huston Smith has pointed out that people some-

times report deep suffering in the psychedelic state. This suffering, he suggests, may be so intense that it telescopes into a few vivid hours of radically altered consciousness the troubles that are ordinarily experienced over many years.

Finally, it must be reemphasized that, regardless of any possible value of psychedelics, those contemplating their use cannot afford to disregard the potential health hazards of these very potent drugs, not to mention the legal consequences involved.

Drugs and the Brain

The study of how psychoactive drugs affect the brain is among the most intriguing and potentially rewarding areas in the neurosciences. This research focuses on neurotransmitters, the chemical substances that convey electric impulses across the synaptic gap between nerve cells in the brain (see Chapter 2).

Drugs can influence the action of neurotrans-

FOCUS: Anomalous Experiences

What we call "normal" waking consciousness can be marked by an extraordinary range of irregularities, or anomalies, that in many respects resemble the altered states described in this chapter. A familiar instance of these anomalous experiences—as Graham Reed (1972) has labeled them—is the *déjà vu* (already seen), the overpowering feeling of having been in a place or situation before though one has no conscious recollection of it. Less common is the converse, *jamais vu* (never seen), a sense that a scene, though consciously known to be familiar, suddenly seems completely strange.

Anomalous experiences often occur under conditions of high stimulation. Examples include the alterations of consciousness sometimes experienced during religious revival meetings, long-distance running, and orgasm. Other anomalous experiences involve extreme reduction of stimulation. Subjects deprived of most of their normal sensory input—by floating in a dark water tank for a long time, for example—sometimes have hallucinations not unlike those that mark mental disorders (Lilly, 1977). Although these experiences are at least as intense as the altered states described in this chapter, they may occur in the context of a person's normal regular activities such as going to church, jogging, or having sex.

Anomalous experiences often occur during high-stimulation situations such as long-distance running.

Something akin to a mystical experience has been reported by many people who suffered severe physical trauma or disease bringing them close to death. For example, people who have had an apparently fatal heart attack or received seemingly mortal injuries in an auto accident and are clinically dead

mitters in a number of ways. For example, they may increase or decrease the levels of certain neurotransmitters. Mood-affecting drugs such as antidepressants (used to treat severe psychological depression), and antipsychotics (used to treat the major psychoses) appear to work in this way (see Table 5.1). Antipsychotic drugs such as chlorpromazine have been used in the treatment of schizophrenia; antidepressants such as impramine are mood elevators. As we will see in Chapter 15, the effects of such drugs have provided the basis for new theories about the neurochemical underpinnings of abnormal behavior. The opiate, morphine, seems to mimic the role of a neurotransmitter by occupying its receptor sites on the postsynaptic nerve cell. This discovery led to the startling finding that the neurotransmitter(s) that ordinarily use those sites are endogenous painkillers—in effect, the brain's own opiates (see Chapter 2).

It is now clear that neurotransmitter action is a highly complex process and that psychoactive drugs can affect the process at practically any point (see Chapter 2). Thus, a drug might alter the process anywhere from synthesis of the neurotransmitter in the nerve cell body through subsequent steps, including the breakdown of excess transmitter by enzymes, the action of the transmitter in binding to receptor sites on the postsynaptic cell, and the reuptake of excess transmitter by the presynaptic neuron.

Various active drugs, including amphetamine and LSD, are known to interfere with the action of the neurotransmitter serotonin. Serotonin has a generally inhibitory effect on a variety of brain-behavioral functions, including sensory thresholds. The psychedelics (particularly LSD) are believed to decrease the level of serotonin, each drug achieving this in a different manner in the synaptic transmission process. In effect, they apparently inhibit the inhibitor, thereby likely removing the brake that serotonin ordinarily imposes on consciousness.

---

but "restored to life" by emergency medical care, have been able to describe afterward the sensation of having floated above the operating table, calmly observing doctors trying to resuscitate their body (Moody, 1976; Ring, 1980).

Even that familiar butt of campus jokes, the absentminded professor, can be considered guilty more of having an anomalous experience rather than a memory lapse. A passerby once encountered the mathematician Norbert Wiener in a corridor at M.I.T. After a brief conversation, Wiener asked the passerby in which direction he (Wiener) had been going when they met. The passerby told him, and Wiener smiled in relief. "Ah, good," he said, "That means I have already had my lunch." According to Reed (1972), absentmindedness stems not from a lack of attentiveness but, on the contrary, from an extreme degree of attentiveness to an internal conscious matter of more immediate concern than external things.

Here, as is usual in altered states of consciousness, ordinary self-awareness seems to disappear. This loss of self-awareness also appears to be important in the performance of highly skilled motor functions such as expert skiing or even of highly creative artistic endeavors such as music, painting, or writing. One is aware of the activity, superaware in fact, and yet unaware that one is aware. Self-consciousness is sacrificed or at least reduced; this seems to ensure a more intense involvement in the act— whether it be play, work, or creative thought.

This latter anomaly has been called the flow experience by psychologist Mihalyi Csikszentmihalyi (1975). In many ways, the flow experience resembles an altered state. Conscious thought disappears: "When I get hot in a game . . . like I said you don't think about it at all," said a high school basketball player. Perception of time undergoes change: "Time passes a hundred times faster," said a chess player. "A whole story can unfold in seconds, it seems." And the sense of control that is present in normal consciousness seems to vanish: "You yourself are in an ecstatic state to such a point that you almost don't exist," said an eminent composer: ". . . I have nothing to do with what is happening. I just sit there watching it in a state of awe and wonderment. And it just flows out by itself" (Csikszentmihalyi, 1975).

While arduous training is obviously essential to skilled activities and to creativity in science and the arts, it is becoming widely recognized that the flow experience may also be vital to success. Even athletic coaches are now experimenting with meditation and other relaxation techniques to help their teams "go with the flow."

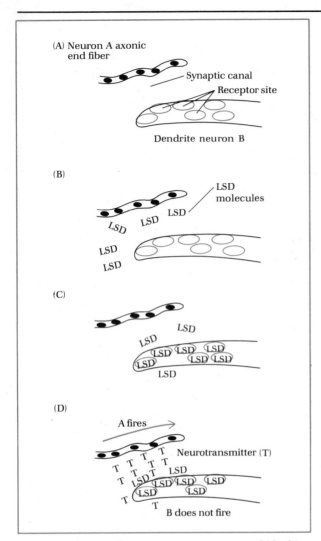

(A) Neuron A axonic end fiber

Synaptic canal

Receptor site

Dendrite neuron B

(B)

LSD molecules

(C)

(D)

A fires

Neurotransmitter (T)

B does not fire

Diagrams showing how LSD serves as a neural blocking agent that prevents a nerve cell from firing.

The study of consciousness, of the workings of the mind, and of the effects of drugs on the brain is likely in its infancy. Further research into neurotransmitter action may reveal exciting possibilities for curing psychosomatic illnesses and neurological impairments. Social attitudes toward both medical and recreational use of drugs may change drastically.

Perhaps most important, research into the causes and workings of altered states may lead to a much greater understanding of human consciousness in its normal, or unaltered, states. A great deal of our discussion has focused on altered states of consciousness, but most of us live in unaltered states most of the time. The expectation of learning more about normal consciousness is an exciting prospect.

SUMMARY

1. States of consciousness are sets of structural conditions that are distinct from the actual content of consciousness. Structure denotes the major features that influence the ways in which we experience ourselves or the world; content is the experience itself. The state of consciousness influences consciousness in two different domains: the cognitive (how we solve problems) and the affective (how we respond emotionally). Altered states of consciousness may be differentiated from normal states by such characteristics as lack of self-awareness, hallucination, altered time perception, and loss of contact with present reality. Altered states are not necessarily abnormal; some aspects of altered states are frequently present in normal waking consciousness.

2. The study of altered states may eventually lead to some insights into the mind-body problem— whether the body causes the mind to think or whether the mind causes the body (the brain) to act (think). A key tenet of neural science is that all conscious experiences depend upon activity in the brain—in particular, in the cerebral cortex where the human nervous system reaches its highest level of development.

3. The three major research methods of neurophysiology are (1) selective destruction of specific brain areas in animals and the study of brain damage in humans, (2) observation of the effects of electrical stimulation of the brain, and (3) recording the electrical activity of the brain. Localization of some specific psychobiological functions in the cortex is well established. Localization is complicated, however, by the brain's plasticity—that is, its capacity to compensate for damage to a given neural area of the cerebral cortex. It seems likely that the neural basis of consciousness is widely distributed, perhaps involving virtually the entire brain.

4. The electroencephalograph, or EEG, is an instrument that has been widely used in the study of consciousness and in clinical applications such as the diagnosis of epilepsy and brain tumors. The patterns produced by an EEG represent fluctuations, or oscillations, in voltage, which in turn represent the sum of many nerve cells firing in the cerebral cortex. Relatively slow, synchronous waves—alpha waves—generally indicate a subject who is relaxed, but awake. Smaller waves of less

amplitude and synchrony—beta waves—generally indicate a more alert and mentally active subject.

5. As a result of the research of Roger Sperry and others on the split brain, we now know that both hemispheres of the brain have vital functions but are specialized for different kinds of information processing. The left hemisphere dominates whenever linear, or sequential, information processing is required (speech, for example); the right dominates whenever simultaneous processing is required (spatial perception, for example). In normal circumstances, regardless of whether one hemisphere is more active than the other, both function together in an integrated fashion.

6. Research with both animals and humans indicates the existence of a phenomenon known as state-dependent learning: certain learned psychological reactions may be related to a given psychological state, and these reactions become available when the brain enters this state. Most research into state-dependent learning has been based on psychological reactions acquired in some kind of altered state of consciousness.

7. The most common forms of altered states are the sleeping and dreaming we all experience daily. Sleeping and waking alternate in a daily biological cycle known as a circadian rhythm. Internal time-keeping mechanisms, the biological clock, control this rhythm. Research has pinpointed a location of these internal mechanisms in a specific area of the hypothalamus, the suprachiasmatic nuclei.

8. By use of the EEG, researchers have identified four stages of sequentially occurring sleep depth; later study has disclosed a fifth stage known as rapid-eye-movement (REM) sleep, during which dreams commonly occur. After passing through the four stages of "quiet" sleep, sleepers normally enter a period of REM sleep. When awakened from REM sleep, subjects in experiments have typically reported that they were dreaming. Researchers now assume that REM sleep is virtually always accompanied by dreams. Dreaming follows a fairly regular cycle, beginning after completion of the four stages of non-REM sleep. Most people dream in cycles of about 90 minutes that recur four to six times a night. An exception to this pattern occurs among people with narcolepsy, a disorder characterized by uncontrollable seizures of sleep during waking hours.

9. Investigations show a clear continuity between the manifest content of dreams and the concerns of waking life; that is, we take our interests and worries to bed. Experiments have also demonstrated that dreams occur in real time—not, as it was once thought, compressed into a few moments.

10. Two classes of physiological events have been found during REM sleep: (1) phasic (abrupt) events include the rapid eye movements and increases in various phenomena controlled by the autonomic nervous system such as pulse, respiration, and blood pressure, and (2) tonic (longer-lasting) events include penile erection in men, a probable increase in the blood supply to the vagina in women, and a decrease in muscle activity in both sexes.

11. Sleep is necessary for survival; however, studies on experimental sleep deprivation have shown dramatic short-term effects but no lasting ones. Most current theories of sleep and dreams emphasize a restorative role for physiological and psychological functioning.

12. Psychoanalysts from Freud and Jung onward have used the content of patients' dreams in their therapies. The use of dreams in psychotherapy, to draw material from the unconscious mind, is now common in the Western world.

13. In biofeedback training, subjects are given information, or feedback, on physiological processes that do not ordinarily reach awareness, such as brain waves, so that the subjects can attempt to control them consciously. The ability to produce alpha waves undoubtedly contributes to relaxation, but research has failed to establish a significant correlation between the alpha rhythm and a specific state of consciousness. Biofeedback training has had some success in helping subjects to achieve conscious control over such visceral activities as heart rate, blood pressure, and even skin temperature (visceral control). The techniques of biofeedback training offer a great deal of promise for the treatment of psychosomatic disorders by their focus on mind and body functioning together.

14. While meditation to many people represents a way to transcend the self, to psychologists it offers promise for the treatment of psychosomatic disorders and for a better understanding of the relationships between mind and body. From the psychological point of view, there are two principal

159

types of meditative practice. In concentrative meditation, alteration of consciousness is sought through detachment from both the external environment and internal thought processes: to avoid distraction, the individual concentrates on a single thought, image, sound, or movement. In mindfulness meditation, conversely, meditators deliberately direct attention to all distractions. The goal is to achieve nirvana, the state that is the negation of self-awareness, by receiving sense impressions while striving not to react to them. In transcendental meditation (TM), a form of concentrative meditation, meditators seek altered consciousness by repeating a mantra, an individually assigned Hindu word. Widely publicized studies on TM practitioners have reported a number of measurable physiological responses; however, these responses may not be unique to meditation. The responses may denote a general state of relaxation.

15. Mysterious states of consciousness that have been called peak experiences have been reported by mystics and others throughout recorded history. Little is known physiologically about peak experiences, but descriptions of mystical experiences often resemble reports of subjects in drug-induced states.

16. Characteristics of the hypnotic state include high suggestibility, a decline of the conscious planning function, and a reduction in reality testing by those hypnotized. Alterations in consciousness can endure beyond the hypnotic state through posthypnotic suggestion. The hypnotic state is not characterized by any identified physiological responses.

17. The psychological processes occurring in hypnosis can be partially explained by a postulated process called dissociation, whereby certain mental processes split off from normal consciousness and function independently. Two levels of consciousness seem to be operating during hypnosis. One level is the consciousness that is apparent on the surface; the other is concealed and has been described as the hidden observer.

18. Altered states of consciousness may also be produced by drugs. The development of mood-influencing (psychoactive or psychotherapeutic) drugs has increased our understanding of abnormal behavior. Synthesis of psychedelic ("mind-manifesting") drugs, such as LSD, and the use of marijuana have introduced many people to the profound effects of chemistry on consciousness. The most widely used, and abused, mind-altering drug is alcohol.

19. Anesthetics produce a loss of sensation and, in large doses, a loss of consciousness; analgesics produce a loss of pain without loss of consciousness. Barbiturates in large doses induce general anesthesia; in smaller doses, they are considered sedatives (minor depressants). Sedatives suppress pain but impair consciousness. Narcotic analgesics, such as the opium derivatives morphine and heroin, ease pain while inducing significant elevation of mood. Addiction to drugs produces both psychological and physical dependence.

20. Psychedelics, sometimes erroneously referred to as hallucinogens, modify normal perceptions by intensifying sensory reactions to color and texture. The most common psychedelics, LSD and marijuana, both produce a number of readily identifiable physiological and psychological effects. The use of psychedelics has been, and continues to be, widely debated.

21. A great deal of recent research has been devoted to the effect of psychoactive drugs on the action of the brain's neurotransmitters. The effects of drugs on neurotransmitters have provided the basis for new theories about the underpinnings of abnormal behavior.

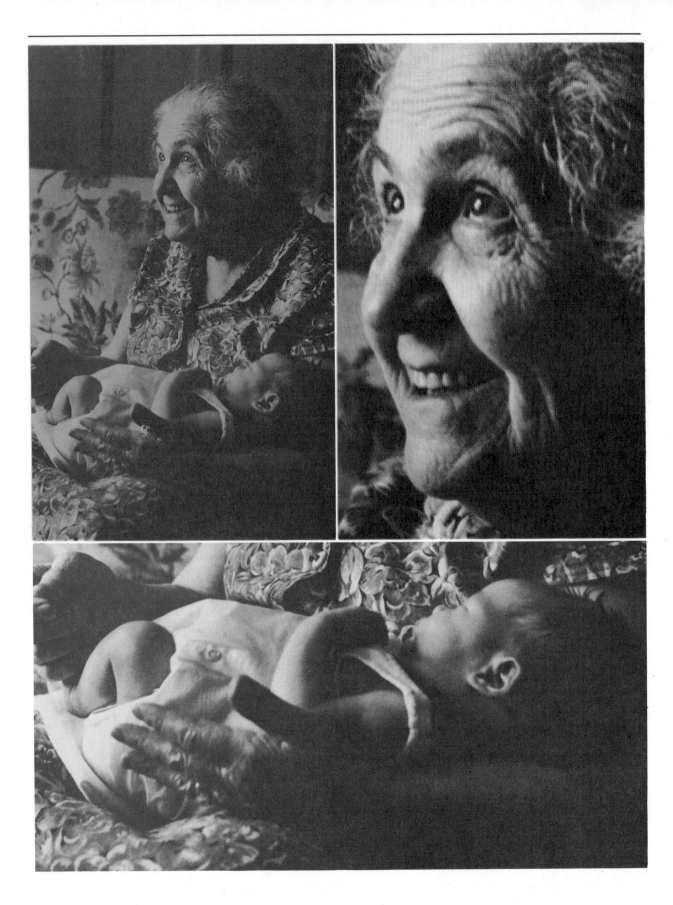

Part Three
Growth, Learning, and Language

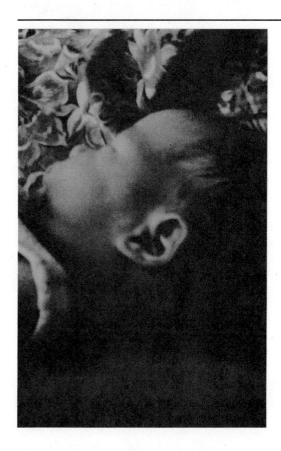

Chapter 6
Development

One of the most fascinating aspects of human behavior is its infinite variability: thought and action vary from individual to individual and from moment to moment even within the same individual. Perhaps most marked of all is the manner in which behavior changes over an individual's life span. Such changes are most prominent, of course, in the first two decades of life. As a rapidly maturing adult in your early twenties, you think and behave differently than you did as a child of eight or nine. And as an eight- or nine-year-old, you thought and behaved quite differently than you did as an infant.

In this chapter we will take up *development*, the branch of psychology concerned with the scientific study of changes that occur in individual growth, thinking, and learning, and social behavior over time. Within the broad field of psychology, developmental psychology operates as a growing subset of the discipline. How humans develop—from conception through old age—is a complex study and one that is frequently difficult to quantify. The study of development embraces all the areas of human life, from infancy through old age, and has profound implications for society. Its findings affect how parents raise their children, how schools educate the young, and how the elderly can be helped to lead more fruitful lives. The amount of research generated by developmental psychologists in recent years is so enormous, in fact, that this chapter must necessarily be highly selective, covering just a few topics.

Other chapters will discuss in detail development as it pertains to a number of specific subject areas: for example, language (Chapter 9), sexual development (Chapter 11), and personality (Chapter 12). In this chapter we will emphasize physical, social, cognitive, and moral development in turn. These divisions are arbitrary: all development affects development in other spheres. As we trace our arbitrary divisions in a generally chronological way, it is important to remember that different types of development are actually intertwined and interactive. Physical development affects cognitive growth, which, in turn, affects social development, moral development, and adaptation. As a framework we will first examine the relationship between genetics and environmental influences on human development.

Determinants of Development

All organisms have some behaviors to begin with. Accordingly, there must be some concept that accounts for the initial behaviors of organisms. Subsequent behaviors must also be accounted for.

The study of biological development uses concepts borrowed from the field of genetics. Organisms are structured in certain ways (a human child is a human child; a goose is a goose), and these structures relate to the genetic materials of the organisms' forebears. Although it is tempting to push the concept of genetic determination as far as possible to account for as much as possible of both the initial behaviors and the newly developed behaviors of organisms, it is also clear that genetically structured organisms live in environments. These environments are both intrauterine (influencing the organism before it is born), and extrauterine (ordinary life experiences). A major controversy exists in the field of development over the relative importance of each of these factors—genetics and environment; it is known as the *nature-nurture controversy*. The argument concerns which is more important, nature—factors based on the genetic endowment of the organism—or nurture—factors based on the previous experience of the organism.

The Nature-Nurture Controversy
When we call a behavior instinctive, we generally mean that the behavior is somehow genetically programmed in the structure of the nervous system of the organism. This implies that the behavior is independent of the previous experience of the animal. On the other hand, when we label a behavior as learned, we mean that the behavior is the result of some specific previous experience that resulted in the necessary learning. On the face of it, it seems that it should be possible to divide behaviors into two categories—those that are instinctive, or genetically determined and independent of previous experience, and those that are dependent on previous experience. Although this is a temptingly neat classification, it is not a particularly good one. Most current researchers in human development emphasize the interaction of genetic and environmental influences on behavior.

Take for example a specific instance of a behavior that has been considered instinctive: the egg-retrieving behavior of the greylag goose shown in Figure 6.1 (Lorenz and Tinbergen 1938/1957). When the goose spies an egg outside its nest, it approaches the egg and attempts to roll the egg backward toward the nest by placing its bill on the far side of the egg and shoveling it toward its body and through its legs. This behavior shows many of the characteristics that instinctive behaviors are supposed to show. The shoveling movement is highly stereotyped—occurring in the same way time after time by goose after goose. It also appears to be highly automatic: once the egg-rolling motion starts, it will continue through to completion, the point where the goose's beak is close to its tail, even if the egg rolls sideways off the bill. If a very large model of an egg is placed outside of the nest, the goose will try to retrieve it in the usual way, even though the model may be so large that the model will not fit between the goose's legs. However, although the egg-retrieving behavior of the greylag goose is highly stereotyped, it is almost impossible to determine whether it would develop in the same way in any and all environments. Thus, it would be logically impossible to say with certainty that the behavior is completely independent of previous experience, making it impossible to classify the behavior as either instinctive or environmental.

The nature-nurture controversy is not likely to be resolved in any simple way because all organisms have both genetic material and experience. In order to understand the elements of the argument, it is necessary to examine the modern view of genetics and then to blend that view with existing models of the relationship between genetic and environmental determinants.

Genetics

Some features of human development are, in effect, preprogrammed by the genetic blueprints laid down by heredity, which dictates normal individual characteristics such as hair color and bone structure.

Classical View of Genetics The laws of heredity were first proposed more than a century ago, by Gregor Mendel, an Austrian monk. Mendel's formulation of the laws of heredity stemmed from years of research in the monastery garden. He experimented with peas, crossbreeding different varieties. By breeding these plants selectively for characteristics such as height and color, he was able to work out mathematically the laws of probability under which these characteristics were passed on to the plants' progeny.

Since Mendel's pioneering work, genetic researchers have developed a much more precise model of the mechanisms of human heredity. Each of the reproductive cells—the male sperm and the female ovum, or egg—carries half of the genetic information normally present in a body cell. Each reproductive cell contains 23 *chromosomes*, microscopic rodlike units. Inside each chromosome are many *genes*, perhaps a thousand or more. The

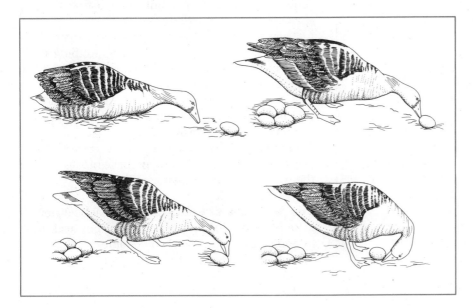

FIGURE 6.1 A classic example of an instinctive behavior pattern is demonstrated by the way a greylag goose rolls an egg back into its nest. The goose always rolls the egg back through its legs using its bill in the manner shown.

genes, in turn, contain the transmitter of the genetic code, the complex nucleic acid known as DNA, or deoxyribonucleic acid. At conception, the sperm and ovum merge, forming a single cell within which the chromosomes—half from each parent—form 23 pairs. This cell divides, and the subsequent process of cell division results in the embryo and, eventually, the human organism. Because of the astronomical number of possible gene combinations, practically every human being is genetically unique. The exceptions are identical twins, both of whom result from the same fertilized egg, or zygote (hence, they are monozygotic twins). Fraternal twins develop from two different zygotes (hence they are dizygotic twins) and are thus no more similar genetically than are ordinary siblings.

The sex of the progeny is determined in the 23rd pair of chromosomes in the fertilized egg. The cells of the female parent have a pair of X chromosomes

(XX); those of the male parent have an X chromosome and a Y chromosome (XY). The female's contribution to the fertilized egg can only be an X chromsome, but the male's may be either an X or a Y. Thus, it is the father's sperm that determines the sex of the offspring (see Figure 6.2).

Like the chromosomes, the genes themselves are also paired together. Genes controlling physical characteristics are classified as either dominant or recessive. Dominant genes control the development of a characteristic regardless of the nature of the genes with which they are paired. Recessive genes, by contrast, do not control development of a specific characteristic unless they are paired with similar recessive genes.

To see how this works in a simple case, take the example of eye color. If the gene for brown eyes is dominant, an offspring whose pair of genes specify both brown and blue eyes will have brown eyes. The gene for blue eyes is recessive; thus, a blue-eyed offspring can result only if the blue-eye gene is paired with another recessive blue-eye gene (see Figure 6.3). From these facts of comparative gene power, it is possible to compute the statistical probability of the offspring's eye color if the genetic makeup of the parents is known. If one parent has brown eyes that are determined by two brown-eye genes, then all offspring will have brown eyes. However, if the parent's brown eyes are due to a pairing of a dominant brown-eye gene and a recessive blue-eye gene and this parent pairs with a mate of similar genetic eye-color determination (dominant brown-eye gene and recessive blue-eye gene), there is a 25 percent chance that the offspring will have blue eyes.

This example raises an important distinction made by geneticists. *Genotype* refers to the genetic makeup of an individual; *phenotype* refers to the outward expression of that genetic makeup. Brown eyes are visibly the phenotype; the individual's genotype, on the other hand, might be composed of either of a pair of brown-eye genes or a pairing of a dominant brown-eye gene with a recessive blue-eye gene. Thus the phenotype brown eyes can be the result of either of two genotypes.

The New View of Genetics The classical view of genetics is one of simple control of physical traits by individual genes or chromosomes. Modern approaches—especially that of behavior genetics, which studies the relative influences of heredity and environment—has developed several impor-

FIGURE 6.2 Sex is determined by the chromosomes in the fertilized egg. The cells of the female parent have a pair of X chromosomes (XX), whereas those of the male parent have an X and a Y (XY) chromosome. Because the female can contribute only an X, but the male can contribute either an X or a Y chromosome, it is the sperm of the father that determines the sex of the child.

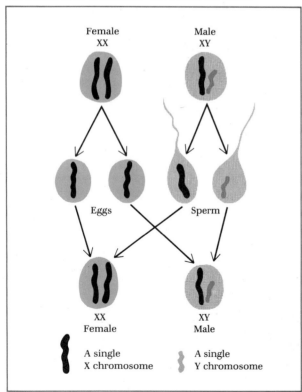

tant concepts that modify the traditional view of heredity as it applies to human development (McClearn, 1970).

A trait such as eye color is a relatively simple one; the classic view that it is directly controlled by a given pair of genes makes sense. However, most developing systems are not nearly as simple as eye color. What we call intelligence, for example, is a complex concept covering a number of different functional systems. A single intelligence test may cover a number of different types of performance, testing mathematical ability, knowledge of the world, and pattern discrimination. It is highly doubtful that a simple gene-trait model of the kind appropriate for eye color would apply to such complex systems as intelligence. Instead, the modern view regards the genetic contribution to complex systems as itself complex. Presumably, many different genes and gene combinations contribute to intelligence and other complex systems. Many important developing systems are thus thought to be *polygenetically determined*—related to the control of many genes rather than to the control of a single gene. It is interesting to note, for example, that while rats can be selectively bred for their ability to run laboratory mazes, the "maze-brightness" that results applies only to this particular task; when tested at other tasks, they fail to show marked superiority.

A second important modification of the classic view of heredity relates to the timing by which genetically determined features appear. Traits such as eye color are relatively well fixed early in development, but other systems take a much longer time to appear. Indeed, many developmental systems—motor coordination, for example, and language—are characterized by the gradual emergence of different behaviors at different ages. These behaviors seem to follow one another in a fixed sequence and occur at approximately the same ages for different individuals. To account for this fixedness of order and apparent universality of age of appearance, modern genetics assumes the existence of *pacing genes*. Such genes, in effect, set the pace for emerging systems of development.

Modern genetic theory has led to attempts to account for the relationship between genetically determined and paced factors and the interaction between the developing organism and its environment.

The Epigenetic Approach

One model for the relationship between genetics and environment is known as the *epigenetic landscape* (Waddington, 1957). The epigenetic landscape depicts the biological control of development

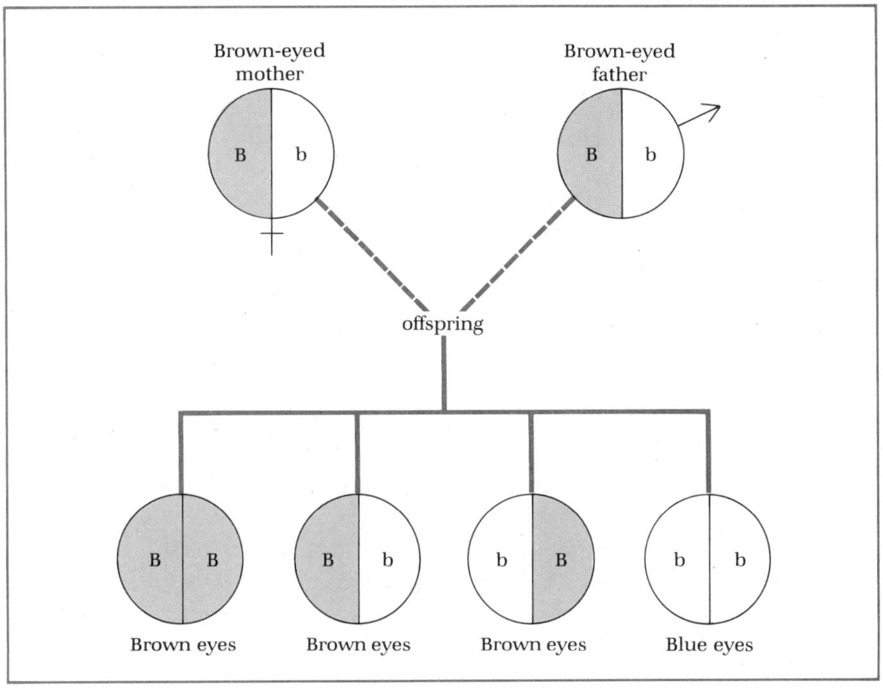

FIGURE 6.3 Because the gene for brown eyes (B) is dominant, whereas the gene for blue eyes (b) is recessive, the pairing of two brown-eyed parents who both carry the recessive blue-eyed gene will generally result in three-brown-eyed children for every blue-eyed child.

169

in terms of constraints of varying strengths (see Figure 6.4). The biological constraints are likened to pathways that control the direction of a ball rolling down an incline. The environmental constraints are likened to forces that can jostle the incline and threaten to jar the ball out of its pathway depending on the pathway's characteristics. If the pathway is shallow and broad, the environment might succeed in deflecting the ball. If it is deep and narrow, the pathway would tightly constrain the path of the ball even in the face of a great deal of environmental jostling.

For example, if you go for a walk in the woods in the spring, you will hear an incredible variety of bird songs. The males of many species sing distinct, recognizable songs. In fact, experienced bird-watchers can usually identify a number of species by their songs without seeing the birds. These songs are important to the birds, serving to attract mates and to warn off potential competitors. How do these birds come to sing their songs?

Song learning has been studied extensively in the white-crowned sparrow. The song of the males of this species consists of two parts, an introductory whistle followed by a trill. In any given location, all the males sing the same song, but in different areas the males sing different songs. These songs can be quite discrete, with a sharp demarcation between adjoining areas. For example, the birds on the east side of Grizzly Peak Boulevard in the Berkeley Hills of California sing one dialect, while those to the west sing another.

The different dialects could be due to genetic differences between the birds living in different areas, but this is not the case. If a young male white-crown is taken from its nest when just a few days old and is raised without hearing other birds' songs, his song will be abnormal, different from any normal white-crowned sparrow dialect. Some environmental event (or set of events), therefore, must be necessary for the appearance of normal song.

Peter Marler (1970) conducted a series of experiments that looked at the effects of hearing normal song at different ages. White-crowned sparrows were captured when young and exposed to several minutes of song each day at different ages. When birds under ten days of age were exposed to songs, there was little effect on their adult song. Such birds sang like isolates. When birds between 10 and 50 days old were exposed to a white-crowned dialect, their adult song closely resembled the dialect they had been exposed to. When birds

FIGURE 6.4 The epigenetic landscape depicts development in terms of both biological and environmental constraints of varying degrees. The biological constraints are depicted as pathways that control the direction of a ball rolling down an incline. The environmental constraints are likened to forces that can jar the ball out of its pathway. The pathway followed by the ball in this illustration, begins with an alternative: the ball can go either right or left. Along the path to the right there is another alternative: the ball can either follow the main path to the left or branch off to the right. The pathway followed by the ball corresponds to the actual developmental history of the organism.

between 50 and 100 days of age were exposed to a dialect, their adult song resembled to some degree, but not completely, the dialect they had heard. Finally, exposure to adult song after 100 days of age had no discernible effect: like the birds hearing song when under ten days old, these birds also sang like isolates. These results indicate that the critical event is the opportunity to hear adult song during a restricted period of time—roughly from 10 to 50 days of age. Thus, the song of the male white-crowned sparrow cannot be classified as either innate or environmental; neither factor can be excluded.

The relative importance of environmental and genetic influences on behavior varies in different cases. For instance, the role of experience in song learning varies among different species of birds. The young cowbird develops completely normal song even if while young it never hears normal cowbird song. This fits well with the life-style of the cowbird, a social parasite that lays its eggs in the nests of other species. Because the young cowbird is raised by foster parents, it does not hear cowbird song during the first few months of life.

The epigenetic landscape provides a way of visualizing the relationship between heredity and environment. Some developmental systems are like shallow pathways and relatively open to environmental influence. The young white-crowned sparrow is easily influenced by the song it hears. Other developmental systems are more like deep canals and less susceptible to environmental influence. The young cowbird will sing cowbird song as an adult no matter what song its foster father may sing. Such systems are described as highly *canalized:* in the genetic and environmental interaction, the genetic influence is relatively strong.

The Alloplastic View

The Darwinian view of the relationship between the organism and the environment stresses gradual evolutionary change produced by the environment through natural selection (discussed more fully in Chapter 10). However, the extensive ability of humans to alter their environment has given rise to another point of view known as the *alloplastic view,* which literally means "change outside of self." This approach stresses the ability of the organism to alter nature and thus affect canalization.

Many animal species behave in ways that alter their environment. Some plants exude chemicals into the soil that inhibit the growth of other species, beavers build lodges and dams, and so on. But the human species has developed the ability to alter nature more than any other animal, and the alloplastic view seems particularly appropriate as a perspective from which to look at human growth and development. A number of specific human characteristics contribute to our ability to change our environments. Although we are not unique in the possession of any one of these capabilities, we are unique in the extent to which we use them, especially in combination.

Tool Use Many animals use tools. Sea otters use rocks to break open sea urchins, Galapogos finches use sticks to pry insects out of holes, and chimpanzees use sticks to get termites out of their mounds (Alcock, 1972). But only among humans is the manufacture and use of tools a way of life. We live in houses made with tools surrounded by the products of an advanced technology that transform our environment. While other species may use tools on occasion, tool use is basic to the human lifestyle.

Sharing of Skills Adaptive skills are handed down from generation to generation through social and cultural interaction in many species. Song learning in white-crowned sparrows is one example. Many other instances have been observed, especially among the nonhuman primates. For example, some years ago on an island in south Japan an attempt was made to relieve famine among a group of macaque monkeys by giving them grains of wheat thrown on a sandy beach. The monkeys learned that the wheat could be separated from sand by throwing the mixture into the water: wheat floats, while sand sinks. In succeeding generations this behavior became widespread within the group, indicating cultural transmission (Sagan, 1977). The water-sifting of wheat spread most rapidly among younger animals, with many adults never acquiring the behavior. This suggests the importance of the early years of life in cultural transmission. Among humans the cultural sharing of skills is particularly strong: some mechanisms of cultural transmission exist in all human societies.

Language The complex and widespread sharing of skills among humans is made possible by the complex system of communication called language. The development of language appears to be highly canalized and built into our biology. Human language permits the sharing of information about things that need not be physically present and even about things that may not have physical reality. A richly elaborate linguistic system is found wherever human societies exist (Bruner, 1966).

Extended Childhood Humans spend a prolonged amount of time in childhood, dependent on adults for food and protection. Among animals in general, ecologists differentiate two basic strategies that govern reproductive patterns and the amount of time spent in dependent childhood. At one extreme some species produce many young but invest little time and effort in their care. In these species no dependence on parents exists, and relatively few of the young survive. At the other extreme are species in which parents have few offspring and invest great time and effort in each. In these species the young have a lengthy period of dependence on adults, and most of the young survive. Primates have a long period of dependence with consequent high levels of parental investment. This is most extreme in humans and makes overall sense in view of the importance of tool use, language, and cultural transmission. Young humans can live in protected, nurturing environments while acquiring the environment-altering skills typical of their species.

A Model of Development

The discussion of the role of heredity and environment can be summed up by posing a basic model of development that is framed in terms of the interactions between biological constraints, on the one hand, and environmental influences on the other. In a developing organism, a number of systems come into play by virtue of maturational changes that are genetically paced. These maturational changes are the organism's biological contribution to interaction with a caregiving environment. The interaction between organism and environment allows for environmental modification and lays the foundation for the next developing system to come into place. Succeeding development will be jointly influenced by the history of interactions with the environment and by genetically paced biological factors. Thus, biology and experience are constantly interacting. Some of the developing systems are highly canalized, which means the environment will exert less influence. In terms of the earlier discussion of alloplastic evolution, it might be expected, that the highly canalized systems would be those that serve to bond the organism to a caregiving environment. This would then allow for the development of flexible exploration of the environment by the child. In general, those systems would be canalized that allow for the development of adaptive flexibility.

It is important to keep in mind the relationship between genetically paced biological factors and the environment when considering the physical, cognitive, social, and moral development of human beings. Although everyone goes through developmental stages in the same sequence and the same general chronology, each individual does so at his or her own particular pace. Therefore, ages and stages are approximate and should be considered as such.

Physical Development

The study of physical development is primarily a biological one. *Physical development* is defined as the changes in an individual's physiological functioning over time reflecting the process known as physical maturation. Physical development begins before birth and continues throughout the nine-month period during which a child grows in the mother's womb (see Plates 14 and 15). It follows the rules of cephalocaudal (head to toe) and proximodistal (near to far). The upper parts of the body develop before the lower, and the central parts of the body, such as the heart and lungs, develop before the extremities.

Researchers have found that the human fetus does more than develop physically during the prenatal period. It reacts to touch and sound and is even thought to experience needs such as hunger and thirst. Therefore, the movements the fetus makes may be more than just random reflexes: the turning, kicking, and sucking actions that take place in the womb may be purposeful movements designed to make the fetus more comfortable (Carmichael, 1970).

After birth, physical changes are particularly dramatic during the first few years of life.

The Neonate

The newborn, or *neonate*, usually cries and breathes immediately, then is weighed, measured, and examined for abnormalities. The head may appear abnormally elongated because the bones may have been squeezed together during birth. There is no lasting damage because the skull bones do not fuse until several months after birth. Almost all hospitals now assess a neonate's physical condition at one and five minutes after birth by use of the Apgar scale. This scale notes the baby's reflexes, color, muscle tone, breathing, and heart rate (Apgar, 1953).

Babies are born with dozens of reflexes—some indicative of brain maturity and some necessary for life itself. In the first category, normal, full-term neonates have the following five reflexes:

1. Babinski reflex. Toes fan upward when the feet are stroked.
2. Stepping reflex. Legs move as if to walk when the feet touch a flat surface.
3. Swimming. Arms and legs stretch out when the baby is held horizontally, stomach downward.
4. Grasping reflex. Hands grip tightly when anything touches the palms.
5. Moro reflex. Arms are flung outward and then brought together over the chest when someone bangs the table on which the neonate is lying.

These reflexes, which disappear in the first months of life, are signs that the baby's body and brain are functioning normally.

In the second category, three sets of reflexes are critical for survival and become stronger with maturity:

1. The first set helps the neonate maintain constant body temperature and includes crying, shivering, and tucking the legs close to the body.
2. The second set helps ensure adequate nourishment and includes the sucking, rooting, swallowing, and crying reflexes.
3. The third set maintains an adequate oxygen supply. The most obvious reflex in this set is breathing.

The Brazelton Neonatal Behavior Assessment Scale is widely used to assess infants' responses to people and the maturation of the central nervous system. The scale measures 26 behaviors and 20 reflexes, automatic responses that involve only one part of the body. The effects of birth problems and anesthesia given to the mother can be measured by the Brazelton scale, which can also be used to predict possible future psychological difficulties for certain babies (Brazelton, 1974).

Childhood

A child's physical growth is astoundingly rapid. Between birth and age two, most children grow about 15 inches and gain about 20 pounds, nearly four times their birth weight. By age two, most males have reached half their adult height, and most females have passed the halfway mark by an inch or two. From ages two through six, children gain about 4½ pounds and grow almost 3 inches a year. Children grow more slowly in middle childhood than they did in infancy and early childhood or than they will in adolescence. The average child gains about 5 pounds and grows 2½ inches per year, growing proportionally slimmer.

Brain Growth   At birth, the brain already weighs about 25 percent of its adult weight. By age two, the brain is about 75 percent of its adult weight; the body weight at age two is only about 20 percent of its adult weight (Tanner, 1970). In the first months, those areas that control the senses and simple motor abilities—the primary motor areas of the cortex and the primary sensory areas of the cortex—grow most rapidly. The brain develops faster than any other part of the human body. By age five, a child's brain is at about 90 percent of its eventual weight, even though the average five-year-old's body weight is less than one-third of the average adult's (Tanner, 1970).

Development of Motor Abilities   Infants can lift their heads before they can sit up, and they can sit up before they can stand. In other words, the de-

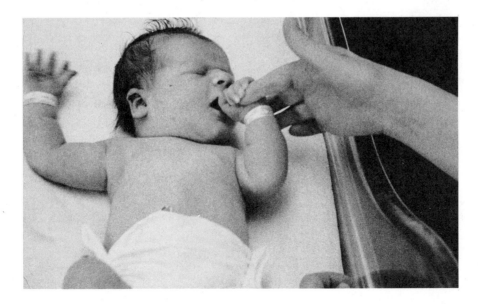

One of the five reflexes indicative of brain maturity in newborn babies is the grasping reflex, wherein the hand grips tightly when anything touches the palm.

173

velopment of motor skills is cephalocaudal and proximodistal (see Figure 6.5).

Most babies first learn to move from place to place by crawling, lying on their stomachs, and pulling themselves ahead with their arms. Creeping, which involves coordination of arms and legs, begins anywhere from 5 to 12 months after birth. Most babies take their first steps soon after age one and walk and run well by age two. After they begin to walk, babies are called toddlers, although, technically, children are infants until they begin to talk.

By six months, most babies can reach, grab, and hang onto a dangling object, but they have trouble letting go of the object. Usually in a month's time, they will have mastered this skill as well. As babies attempt to use their fingers to pick up objects, they progress through stages that end with the ability to use thumb and forefinger together between the ages of 9 and 14 months.

Infants develop major motor skills at different rates. Norms, or averages, vary from place to place and time to time. The average Swedish baby walks a month earlier than the average French baby (Hindley, Filliozat, Klakenberg, Nocolet-Meister, and Sand, 1966). The earliest walkers in the world seem to be from Central Uganda, where the average baby walks at ten months (Ainsworth, 1967). The interaction of inherited and environmental factors determines the age at which a particular child begins to evidence specific motor skills.

Growth Variation The two most significant causes of height differences are ethnic origin and nutrition (Meredith, 1978). Partly because of better nourishment and health care, urban, upper-class, and firstborn children are generally taller than rural, lower-class, and later-born children. Children of mothers who did not smoke during pregnancy tend to be taller (about a half inch) at age five than children of mothers who smoked during pregnancy. Ethnic differences in the height of Americans are primarily genetic: Afro-American children are tallest, followed by Caucasian Americans, and then Asian-Americans (Meredith, 1978). In some regions of the world, variations in height are caused by malnutrition. In North America, heredity, rather than diet, causes most variation in size (Eveleth and Tanner, 1976).

Gross motor skills, which involve large body movements such as running, improve dramatically

FIGURE 6.5 Typical "milestones" of infant motor development, from 1 month to 15 months.

Some Milestones of Infant Motor Development			
Behavior	Average age at which it is performed	Behavior	Average age at which it is preformed
Child can raise chin from ground	1 month 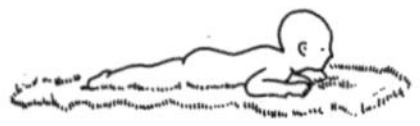	Child can crawl	10 months 
Child can sit with support	4 months 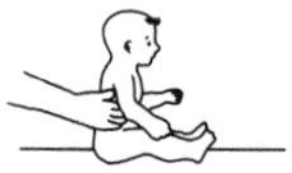	Child can walk when held by hand and led	11 months 
Child can sit alone	7 months 	Child can stand alone	14 months 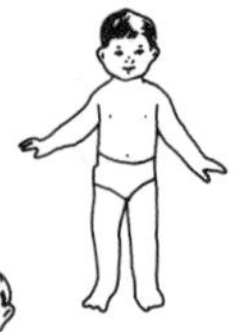
Child can stand by holding onto furniture	9 months 	Child can walk alone	15 months 
Please note that these are average figures. Most children will vary from them in some respect.			

between the ages of two and six. In fact, almost any gross motor skill that does not require much strength or judgment can be learned by most healthy five-year-olds.

Fine motor skills—painting a picture, for example—involve smaller body movements that are much harder for young children to master because they have not developed the muscular control or careful judgment needed to accompany delicate tasks. Their efforts are further complicated by their short, chubby fingers.

Children gain skill in controlling their bodies during middle childhood, in part because they grow more slowly. Children from 7 to 11 can perform almost any motor skill as long as it does not require much power or judgment. Males and females are about equal in physical abilities, except that males have greater forearm strength (Tanner, 1970), and girls have greater flexibility.

Adolescence: Ages 12 to 18

Puberty is that period of physical growth that ends childhood and brings the young person to adult size, shape, and sexual potential. The changes of puberty may be grouped into two categories: those that are generally related to the overall growth of the body and those that are specifically related to the development of sexual characteristics. The distinction between sexual growth and other physical growth is not precise, however. Sexual dimorphism—differences in the appearances of males and females—is present in every aspect of pubescent growth.

The Growth Spurt Although it is preceded by some hormonal changes and the initial enlargement of female breasts and male testes, the first readily observable sign of the onset of puberty is the beginning of a rapid period of physical growth—the *growth spurt*—which starts with a rapid weight gain toward the end of middle childhood. Soon after, a height spurt begins, redistributing some of the child's body fat and burning up the rest. During the 12 month period of their greatest growth, many females gain as much as 20 pounds and 3½ inches; many males gain up to 26 pounds and 4 inches (Tanner, 1971). About a year after the greatest height increase, the period of greatest muscle growth occurs.

The growth process does not occur in every part of the body simultaneously (Katchadourian, 1977). Growth in puberty, unlike that of earlier periods, is

distal-proximo (far to near). In most cases, adolescents' hands and feet lengthen before their arms and legs do, and the torso is the last part to grow. In addition, the lips, nose, and ears usually grow before the head itself reaches adult size and shape. Moreover, the two halves of the body do not always grow at the same rate—perhaps giving rise to the phrase "awkward adolescence." Once the growth starts, every part of the body reaches adult size and shape in about three years.

Sex Characteristics All the sex organs become much larger during adolescence. In females, the uterus begins to grow and the vaginal lining to thicken. In males, the testes begin to grow, and about a year later, the penis begins to lengthen and the scrotal sac enlarges and becomes pendulous.

Sex organs reach sufficient size and maturity to make reproduction possible toward the end of puberty. For females, the first menstrual period is the first indicator of fertility. For males, the comparable indicator of reproductive potential is ejaculation, the discharge of seminal fluid containing sperm.

Changes in many other parts of the body indicate that sexual maturation is occurring. By the end of puberty, the typical boy has considerably wider shoulders; the typical female has wider hips and relatively narrow shoulders. Other major body changes include breast development, the appearance of body hair, and the lowering of the voice.

The changes of puberty occur in predictable sequence and tempo. The entire process begins when hormones from the hypothalamus trigger hormones in the pituitary gland, which in turn triggers increased hormonal production by the gonads, or sex glands (see Chapters 2 and 11).

For females, the most important hormones produced by the sex glands are estrogen and progesterone, which produce—usually in this sequence—the beginning of breast development, first pubic hair, widening of hips, growth spurt, menarche, and completion of breast and pubic-hair growth. For males, the most important hormone is testosterone, which produces—usually in this sequence— growth of the testes, growth of the penis, first public hair, capacity for ejaculation, growth spurt, voice changes, beard development, and completion of pubic-hair growth.

While the sequence of pubertal events is similar for all young people, there is great variation in the age at which it starts. The young person's sex, genes, body type, and nourishment all play a role in this variation.

Adulthood: Ages 20 to 60

Females reach their full adult stature at an average age of 17.3 years; males do not reach full growth until an average age of 21.2 years (Roche and Davila, 1972). Today's 20-year-olds tend to be taller and to mature earlier than their parents because of improved standards of living and nutrition. Our higher standards of living allow fuller expression of genetic potential (Schmeck, 1976).

Muscular strength peaks for most people sometime between 5 to 30 years of age (Bromley, 1979). A gradual loss of strength occurs between ages 30 to 60—about 10 percent. Most body functions begin to decline during early adulthood, but the changes are so imperceptible that little effect is actually felt until after age 40. Motor skills and dexterity peak between 19 and 26; agility begins to lessen in the mid-thirties (Troll, 1975). The brain continues to grow during young adulthood; brain size and weight diminish thereafter (Bischoff, 1976).

Physical growth stops and aging begins well before age 40. These changes are quite gradual. Health in middle adulthood is generally good, but the trend is downward. Minor ailments begin to appear: muscles get sore, sleep is sometimes fitful, indigestion may occur after a rich and spicy meal.

Individual variations are wide as they are in every other life period: one 40-year-old female may be physically active, with a healthy lifestyle and youthful looks; another female of the same age may look older than average, be sedentary, and in much poorer health, generally, than her counterpart.

How people have lived for the preceding years of their lives "comes home to roost" during middle adulthood. Smoking-related illnesses, such as emphysema and cancer of the mouth, throat, and lungs, manifest themselves. Nonsmokers have only half the health problems of smokers (Turner and Helms, 1979). Obesity is a critical health problem. The probability of dying in middle age increases by 40 percent for those who are 30 percent or more overweight (Turner and Helms, 1979).

The median age for the occurrence of menopause in females is 49.5 (Olds, 1970). Some evidence for male, mid-life, biological changes—the male climacteric—exists. These include a decreased rate of testosterone production, decreased fertility, and an increase in impotency (Beard, 1975).

Late Adulthood: After 60

The choice of age 60 for a dividing line between middle and old age is arbitrary. Some people refer to early old age—ages 65–74—and advanced old age—from 75 on—the point at which physiological changes occur to a marked degree (Butler, 1975). Others distinguish between the "young-old," people who have already retired from work, and the "old-old," those who have diminished vigor and social involvement (Neugarten, 1975).

Senescence, that period during which people grow old, begins at different ages for different people. Declines in body functioning begin late for some people but early for others. This physical aging is the critical point for the beginning of late adulthood. The way a person acts and feels is a more satisfactory index of aging than chronological years. The surface signs of aging are obvious: the skin wrinkles, hair loses color, and weight gain is likely. Muscle strength diminishes, and the shoulders become stooped; a reduction in height goes along with the elderly person's posture (Kart, 1976).

Many people have the capacity to live more years than they do, but external events shorten the life span that has been genetically "programmed." A great deal remains to be learned about the workings of fixed genetic programs: evidence does, however, point strongly to genetic influences on the aging process.

Several theories have been proposed to explain the aging process. Genetic programming may determine an outside limit for life's length. Within this genetic program, wear and tear takes place. As cells grow older, they are less able to repair or replace damaged components and so they die. As the parts of a machine wear out, so do the organs of the body. Internal and external stresses seem to aggravate this process of wear and tear. Researchers are investigating the roles of DNA and enzymes, various chemical changes, and the weakening of the body's immune system in efforts to understand aging better (Rockstein and Sussman, 1979).

From conception to death, physical development and aging are complex processes that are continuous throughout the life span. Cognitive and social development and aging are equally complex processes but not as obviously continuous.

Cognitive Development

The alloplastic view of human development places great stress on the acquisition of flexible strategies of adaptation through the use of tools to alter the environment. Essential to tool-use is the concept of thinking, or cognition. The major theories about *cognitive development* attempt to explain the processes of intellectual growth and the stages at which they come into play.

Piaget: The Growth of Logic

The most comprehensive and influential theory of cognitive development was formulated by the eminent Swiss genetic epistemologist Jean Piaget, who died in 1980. Originally trained as a biologist, Piaget began his studies of child development in the 1920s. He worked first with his own son and two daughters and later investigated cognitive development in thousands of children. Although Piaget used a number of different methods of study, including clinical interviews and special manipulative tasks designed to test intellectual development, his principal method was systematic and acutely sensitive observation of children. From these studies came more than 150 articles and more than 30 books that attempt to formulate a coherent and detailed view of how cognition develops from infancy onward (Piaget, 1970).

Piaget's careful analysis showed that, contrary to previous assumptions, children do not think the same way as adults. Children think differently, and these differences are reflected in the growth of logic. As children develop, their thoughts go beyond a merely accurate reflection of the objective properties of the world in which they live. By applying the rules of logic, developing children learn to ascertain realities that are not directly perceivable. Much of science is based on things that cannot be seen: by inferring through indirect indications, scientists "know" submicroscopic phenomena, such as electrons, exist and that the earth orbits the sun even though appearances suggest just the opposite. For Piaget, this fact posed one of the fundamental questions concerning human thought in general and alloplastic evolution in particular: how do we get from the physically real world to a world whose reality is conceptual? In other words, how do we get from the actual to the theoretically possible?

Piaget attempted to account for the growth of logic in terms of a continual interplay between the individual's current understandings and the external reality that the individual encounters. Specifically, Piaget looked to the interaction of two cognitive processes that he called assimilation and accommodation. *Assimilation* is the process through which individuals take in and incorporate their environment in terms of their current understandings of the world. *Accommodation* is the process through which these understandings of the world are modified by new information from the environment.

Underlying these two processes are several important themes. The child encountering the world has a number of hypothetical internal structures or organizations that Piaget calls *schemes*. Children are constantly encountering the environment in terms of these internal schemes, attempting to assimilate it in the framework of what they already know. As they attempt to assimilate the world, children necessarily will encounter discrepancies between what a given scheme is prepared to deal with and the reality of the world. In the course of such discrepancies the assimilatory scheme will undergo a slight modification, or accommodation, to deal with the objective properties of the world. Each modification of an assimilatory scheme that results from some accommodating encounter with the world serves to elaborate and differentiate the schemes available for future encounters.

For example, a two-month-old infant's schemes, or organized capacities for acting on the world, are limited to little more than a few reflexes. One of these reflexes is sucking, which involves opening the lips in a certain manner and then sucking whenever the surfaces around the mouth are stimulated. This reflex pattern typically has a very stereotyped form, so that the mouth opens in the shape of an "O." The reflex is also rigidly organized so that opening the mouth is immediately followed by swallowing. Obviously, the reflex is very suitable for feeding, especially at the breast. But one of the first facts about babies—and about assimilation—is that infants continuously act on the world in any way they can. If they can only suck, they will attempt to suck everything in sight such as a blanket or finger. But the sucking reflex that we have described will be less suitable for a blanket or a finger: the shape of the object is different, and it will not deliver milk. At first, infants will attempt to suck on these objects in the same way that they have nursed. Soon, however, accommodation will occur: the shape formed by the mouth will change as will the relationship between mouthing and swallowing. In the future, the infant will have more than one way of encountering the world: the choice to suck with the "nipple mouth" or with the "blanket mouth" must be made. This simple and yet subtle change is, in Piaget's view, the beginning of the growth of logic.

For Piaget, the balancing of assimilation ("what you already know how to do") with accommodation ("how you have to change what you know to get something done here and now") defines the child's adaptation to the world. Through successive encounters with the world, the range of internal assimilatory schemes gradually increases so that more and more the world is understood and hence acted on in an adapted manner.

Each successful adapted encounter with the world is somehow an isolated event for children. Children seem to build a mental catalog of different features of the real world and of the appropriate responses to those features. This catalog alone is obviously not sufficient to account for the kind of knowledge we have about our world.

According to Piaget, however, an essential process occurs during the course of development. The various things that we learn about objects in our environment become organized with respect to one another. This organization is the most fundamental development in the progress toward logical thinking. From this concept of organization, Piaget was able to discern fundamental differences between the way children think at a given age and the way adults think. These differences relate less to the range of things that are known than to the organization of this knowledge. For example, infants who have learned that there are different kinds of suckables requiring different responses know these suckables through the separate schemes they have available. To adults, who know that a blanket has a particular shape and will feel a particular way, the blanket is a unitary object. But it is quite possible that to infants it is really several objects. The blanket that they suck on is known to the mouth scheme and need not relate to the blanket as seen by the visual scheme.

This phenomenon is rather like the story of the blind men and the elephant; each touches a different part of the elephant and fails to relate his perception to that experienced by the others. Thus, they each identify what they think the elephant is only in relation to the small section they have experienced. Because they fail to pool their knowledge, they are unable to identify the elephant as such. Only when children's various schemes for knowing are organized can they achieve an integrated view that unites an object's various properties.

Thus, the world as adults know it is in fact constructed out of the integration of various cognitive schemes. The knowledge of separate parts of the world are organized in respect to one another and from this process comes an organized view of the world.

Using the major themes of assimilation, accommodation, and the organization of knowing, Piaget traced the development of cognition through four major stages:

- Sensorimotor period—from birth through age 1.
- Preoperational period—from age 2 through about age 6.
- Period of concrete operations—from about age 7 through age 10.
- Formal operational period—from age 11 through age 16.

These stages are assumed to occur in a fixed sequence based on the interaction of biological maturation and experience and at approximately the same ages in all cultures (see Table 6.1).

Infancy and Toddlerhood

During the first two years, children explore the relationship between sensory processes and their own bodily movements. This period is marked by a gradual shift from newborns' rudimentary reflexes, which are at first only minimally modified by contact with the environment, to the development of planned action that involves mental representation—that is, visual pictures of the results of actions.

To account for the many changes that occur during the first two years, the *sensorimotor period* is subdivided into six separate stages.

Stage 1 In the first month, infants are largely a bundle of relatively isolated reflexes such as sucking. Although these reflexes are triggered by stimuli from the environment, such encounters cause little modification of the reflex. For instance, when an object is placed in an infant's hand, the infant will grasp it. The grasp may conform to the shape of the object, but on other occasions of grasping, there is no observed change—the initial grasp will be the same.

178

Stage 2 By about the second month, infants begin to show evidence of slight modification of reflex schemes as a result of experience. As was discussed earlier, the shape of the open mouth may be altered during the sucking reflex to fit a blanket or finger. Moreover, a highly significant pattern of activity now occurs that Piaget terms the circular reaction. Infants begin to repeat interesting activities. For example, infants whose sucking reflex has been modified to deal with a blanket instead of a breast will keep repeating this new scheme of action as if experimenting with it. For Piaget, the circular reaction is a general model of how new behaviors are acquired and perfected. Key to this concept is not just that children learn through repetition, but that children themselves generate the repetition as they attempt to explore their effective actions.

Piaget divides the circular reaction into three phases: primary, secondary, and tertiary. The primary circular reaction is characteristic of children in the second stage of sensorimotor development. In stage 2, the repetitions of behavior that define circular reactions are limited to the exercise of innate reflexes.

Stage 3 From the fourth to the eighth month, children become interested in the relationships between their own activities and the effects of those activities on the world. The repeated exploration of these relationships make up Piaget's secondary circular reaction. A characteristic secondary circular reaction has been termed "procedures to make interesting sights last." Suppose, for example, that an infant is lying in bed kicking its legs and looking at a mobile suspended above the bed. At that moment, a breeze moves the mobile. The infant, suddenly intrigued by the movement of the mobile, would engage in a circular reaction, kicking the legs and looking at the mobile for signs of movement. The infant might do this repeatedly, indicating its growing sense that its actions might somehow affect the world, although there is indeed no actual relationship between kicking and the mobile's movement. Such "procedures to make interesting sights last" thus demonstrate a new orientation of the infant's activities—that is, an awareness of the relationship between action and result. But these procedures also show the limitations of infants' abilities because they still do not have a notion of precisely how action and result are related.

Stage 4 From the eighth to the twelfth month, infants begin to show evidence of a rudimentary understanding of cause and effect. In stage 3, infants' achievements are limited to attempting to reproduce accidental effects that their actions

---

TABLE 6.1 **Piaget's Stages of Cognitive Development**

Piagetian Stage of Development	Approximate Age Range	Some Characteristics of this Stage
Sensorimotor Stage	Birth to about 18–24 months	Child knows world through motor activities and sensory impressions. Verbal symbols and even images not present. Child lacks understanding of *object permanence* (for instance, will not search for hidden objects).
Preoperational Stage	18–24 months to about 7 years	Child can use mental symbols (for instance, words) and shows some intuitive thought. However, both *serialization* (ability to order items along a dimension) and *conservation* are absent. Child is also *egocentric*—has difficulty in understanding that others may perceive the world differently.
Stage of Concrete Operations	7 years to about 11 or 12 years	Conservation and serialization are present. Child also understands *reversibility*. *Logical thought* appears, but only about objects which are present and observable.
Stage of Formal Operations	12 years and on	*Deductive reasoning* and *abstract thought* appear. Individual can take many different factors into account in making decisions, solving problems, and so on.

According to Piaget, cognitive development involves orderly movement through the stages described here. Please note that the age ranges shown are approximate. Many factors can influence the age at which a given child moves from one stage to another.

might be related to. In stage 4 infants' behaviors indicate that they are beginning to have some understanding of the relationship between means and ends. For example, they have discovered object permanence—that is, the fact that an object continues to exist even though it can no longer be seen. Thus they will remove a barrier to get at a ball or rattle that has been hidden behind the barrier. The independent schemes of action for solving such practical problems may already have existed but in isolation from one another. Now these independent schemes become organized with respect to one another. The coordination of these schemes produces the ability to solve a number of practical problems that require complex action sequences.

Stage 5 From approximately the twelfth to the eighteenth month, children display a new form of circular reaction that transcends the limitations of the previous stage. The tertiary circular reaction describes activities in which infants actively experiment with available action schemes. They discover, for example, that there is more than one way to knock down a tower of blocks: the thrust of their legs will work as well as the sweep of their arms. During this stage, infants explore the equivalences that can be established among various ways of accomplishing the same end. In contrast to the secondary reaction, where they attempt to repeat the same environmental effect by repeating a single means to that end, they now vary the way in which they try to alter the world. The means rather than the end seems to be their focus. This sort of activity moves infants closer to the model of tool-use that characterizes human adaptation. Infants' "tools," or action schemes, begin to develop flexible ranges of application; no longer are they limited to only one application. Nor are children now limited to the action schemes already in their repertoire; by experimenting with means, they discover in this stage new tools for acting on the environment.

Stage 6 From 18 months to 24 months, children show evidence of mental planning. Suppose, for example, that a child is presented with a problem such as obtaining a loaf of bread that is beyond reach. The child will use a stick to reach it, whereas prior to this stage the stick would not be used as a tool. This suggests that children's activities are beginning to incorporate mental representations of possible actions—that is, mental images of the different possibilities in a given situation. Using these representations, they can sort out the combinations of possible actions and select the action they will take. Now they are interested not only in the means but in the means to an end.

Thus cognitive development during the six stages of the sensorimotor period takes children from a bundle of simple reflexes to individuals capable of imagining possible actions and of planning intelligently.

Childhood

At the end of the second year, children enter a long period of transition that extends to their sixth or seventh year. With the acquisition of language, they begin to extend their adaptations from a reality that can be acted on to a reality that can be talked and thought about.

The Preoperational Period During the *preoperational period*, children begin to deal with the world symbolically: they begin to recognize that one thing can stand for another. This is evidenced in play, for example, where a cardboard box becomes a "house" and a group of dolls the "family" that lives there.

However, although preoperational children have become competent practical actors on their world, they have difficulty in organizing their thoughts about practical actions. They act on the world in a perfectly coherent way but are unable to present an equally coherent formulation of the action. For example, Piaget reported in *The Grasp of Consciousness* (1976) on studies in which children were asked to describe how they could crawl. Although the children could indeed crawl efficiently, their descriptions bore little relationship to what they actually did while crawling. Even while in the act of crawling, children would describe their actions in terms quite different from what they were doing with their arms and legs. Invariably, the children said crawling was accomplished by moving the left hand and left foot forward at the same time followed by the right hand and right foot. As anyone who has ever tried this can attest, it does not work: the hand and foot advanced at the same time have to be contralateral—that is left hand, right leg.

In addition to such problems as describing simple actions with language, preoperational children also have difficulties with information that can be encoded only in language. A three-year-old boy might not understand, for example, that he is his brother's brother or that, if he has two brothers, his family contains three brothers.

The lack of logical organization that characterizes thinking during this period can best be understood when contrasted with the next stage of cognitive development, the period of concrete operational thought.

The Concrete Operational Period   Between the ages of 7 and 11, children display a logical organization of thought that contrasts sharply with the previous period. Children in the *concrete operational period* reason logically—that is, they perform mental operations or mental actions that previously had to be carried out in actuality—although largely in terms of concrete objects.

A dramatic example of the new logical organization of thought is the acquisition of the concept of conservation, which says, in essence, that the amount of a substance is not changed when its shape is altered. One of the many forms of conservation that Piaget studied was the conservation of continuous quantities (see Figure 6.6). Piaget devised a simple test for children. The researcher takes two short stubby glasses of the same size and fills them equally with milk or lemonade. The child looks at the two glasses and agrees they contain the same amounts of liquid. Then the researcher transfers the liquid from one of the stubby glasses into a third glass that is taller and much thinner. Then the child is asked whether the short glass and the tall thin glass contain the same amount of liquid. Younger children, still in the preoperational stage, typically will assert that the tall thin glass has more liquid because it is taller. By contrast, children in the concrete operational period will correctly assert that both glasses contain the same amount. Nothing

has been added and nothing has been taken away, they might point out.

Note the crucial difference in the ways that preoperational and concrete operational children make their judgments of the amount of liquid in the glasses. Preoperational children base their judgments on appearances: the taller glass looks bigger. Concrete operational children base their judgments on the relationship between actions. This logical functioning reflects the developing organization of various schemes with respect to one another. Thought proceeds from what is known to what can be known by definite rules of implication. Using these rules of logic, concrete operational children override their perceptions of the appearances of things.

In terms of alloplastic evolution, children develop an important new basis for adapting during the concrete operational period. Thought becomes a powerful tool for restructuring reality and giving up the practice of judging things by the way they look in favor of judging things by the way in which they may be known to be in a system of logic.

Adolescence

Beginning in about the twelfth year, childrens' formulations of the world in terms of logical principles take a highly significant turn. In the concrete operational period the ability to reason logically was limited to concrete situations. Now in the fourth and final stage of cognitive development, the *formal operational period,* the ability to reason logically

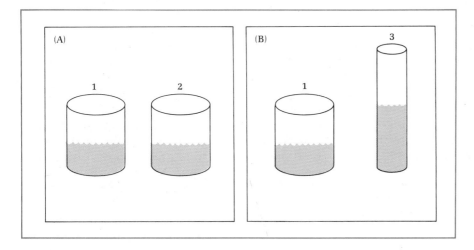

FIGURE 6.6 When a five-year-old child is shown two beakers of liquid, as shown in (A), and asked, "Which contains more, 1 or 2?" The child will say that they contain equal amounts. When the contents of 2 are poured into 3, a taller and thinner beaker as shown in (B), and the child is again asked, "Which contains more?" he or she will answer, "3." The child is said to be unable to conserve volume.

extends to more abstract matters. Childrens' intelligence is no longer limited to operating on things themselves but can reason in terms of hypotheses about reality. Hypothetical thinking—reasoning on the basis of a number of related "if such is true, then so and so must also be true" statements—is the hallmark of the most advanced logical thinking. In terms of alloplastic development, it lies at the heart of scientific research and discovery. More generally, it makes possible human formulations of moral, religious, and philosophical principles. Piaget's model only goes through adolescence in explaining intellectual development. Many other psychologists, however, have been interested in intellectual development beyond adolescence.

Adulthood

For many years, psychologists believed that general intellectual activity peaked in young adulthood and then declined. However, this theory was based on results of cross-sectional studies that compared test scores of different groups in different age groups. On the other hand, longitudinal studies, which test the same group of people periodically over years, show that general intelligence appears to increase until at least the fifties (Owens, 1966). Research (Lehman, 1953; Dennis, 1968) indicates that the peak of intellectual productivity occurs between ages 30 to 40 or even from ages 40 to 50.

There is no question that young adults do better on intelligence tests (particularly on tests that are timed or required speed) than middle-aged adults. Many of the factors that affect test performance—speed, motivation, health, sensory abilities, and so on—may be influenced by increasing age, resulting in lower test scores for older adults. Older adults, conversely, may bring wisdom and experience to problem solving that make them better able to cope than young adults. Although sensory abilities do decline from young adulthood onward, there is virtually no evidence that any physiological changes occur in the brain during middle adulthood (Welford and Birren, 1965).

It seems that flexibility in thinking, comprehension, and creativity actually improve during middle age, whereas short-term memory and certain sensory abilities wane (Baltes and Schaie, 1974).

Late Adulthood

Health is a primary factor in intellectual functioning in old age. Elderly people in good health show little or no loss of intellectual abilities; older people approaching death or fighting illness show a marked decline in intellectual functioning (Riegel and Riegel, 1972). A decrease in blood supply to the brain or extensive hardening of the arteries may also cause a change in thinking processes.

Speed of response is also a critical factor in judging the mental abilities of the aged. Response time is indeed slower in later life, and short-term memory does decline. Long-term memory, however, seems to remain constant, and although speed in mental responses declines, the elderly may be more accurate (Botwinick, 1967). As evidence points to more effective cognitive functioning in old age than was previously believed, our society may be wasting a resource—the potential contribution of a growing percentage of our population.

Other Theories

Piaget's account of cognitive development is essentially an individualistic theory of the growth of intelligence. Children, armed with their schemes of action, repeatedly act on the world and learn about the interrelationships of these actions. From the alloplastic perspective, his theory accounts for the developing logical basis of tool-use. However, the evolution of tool-use is not a matter of individual development alone: many of our technological interventions are matters of shared activity backed by cultural tradition. The significance of cultural influence in cognitive development has been emphasized by Jerome Bruner, L. S. Vygotsky, and John Flavell.

Bruner's Cultural Studies Bruner has studied the growth of logical intelligence in different cultures. His studies have attempted to show that Piaget's individualized model of development is subject to direct cultural influence (Bruner, Olver, and Greenfield, 1966). A study of children in West Africa showed that children eventually attain an understanding of the concept of conservation (changing the shape of a liquid or solid does not change the amount) whether or not they attended school (Greenfield, 1966). In another study, unschooled Wolof children in Senegal were tested for conservation of continuous quantity in the standard manner: they were presented with two short glasses containing equal amounts of liquid; then, after the liquid was transferred from one of the stubby glasses into a taller and thinner glass, they were asked whether the two glasses now contained the same amount of liquid. When the experimenter poured the liquid from one glass to another, the unschooled Wolof children said the amount had been changed—an indication they had not yet achieved the concept of conservation. It turned out, however, that the children's judgment stemmed from another cultural factor: they regarded the experimenter as a powerful, magical figure who was able to change the amount. When children did the pouring themselves, they arrived at the correct conservation judgment at an earlier age (Greenfield, 1966).

Although cultural influences, such as schooling, may not actually directly affect the growth of logical abilities, they may alter the subject's approach to the experimental task.

Vygotsky: The Importance of Others Another theorist vitally concerned with the impact of culture on cognitive development was the Russian psychologist L. S. Vygotsky. Although Vygotsky died in 1934, his work only recently has been translated into English, and it is exerting an important influence on current research. Many of Vygotsky's concepts have been elaborated on and subjected to experimental testing by the American psychologist John Flavell (1978).

Vygotsky's view stresses the importance of others in cognitive development (Vygotsky, 1978). Children on their own are limited in intellectual achievement: much of what they know comes through the medium of communication with self and others. Vygotsky focused on children's understanding of this limitation—their awareness that they need help to perform a task such as reaching a piece of candy with the use of a tool. In studying children's ability to perform such a task, for example, Vygotsky looked at the kinds of processes they used in arriving at solutions—speaking out loud or directing questions to the experimenter. Thus, to Vygotsky children's cognitive development is not completely independent but requires the help of others, particularly adults.

Social Development

Young human beings acquire the social skills and knowledge needed to function as members of their culture through the process of *socialization*. The emerging needs of the individual are expressed in interactions with a social environment—at first the parents, then an ever-widening context of people. The organization of the social environment may vary considerably from culture to culture, subcul-

ture to subculture. Some social organizations may allow for smooth transitions to occur from stage to stage; others might lead to an excessive crisis around a developing need.

Erikson's Theory of Psychosocial Development

Social development throughout life is a process of integration—of adapting inherited and learned traits to the social environment. A detailed view of social integration has been offered by Erik Erikson (1950) to account for social and emotional development over the entire life span. Erikson's view attempts to link in a closely knit fashion three key

As stressed by Vygotsky's studies, cognitive development in children is not completely independent but requires the help of others, especially adults.

elements—highly canalized elements of biological development, child-rearing practices, and the social-cultural context within which the first two elements occur. It is derived from the analysis of case histories of abnormal development, not from experimental psychology.

Erikson distinguished eight different stages in a lifelong process of what he calls *psychosocial development.* Biological factors, social context, development over the life span, and the continuity of stages all interrelate in the eight stages proposed by Erikson. As illustrated in Table 6.2, these stages range from the first year of life, through adolescence, and into the aging years. Each of these stages is characterized by new social situations and a central psychosocial crisis point that can have either a favorable or an unfavorable outcome. Successful resolution of each crisis depends essentially on the smoothness with which the developing individual satisfies needs particular to that stage and then is able to express that resolution in social life.

Interestingly, most of the studies that have looked for simple, linear relationships between early and late behavior have failed to find them (Sroufe and Waters, 1977; Waters, Wippman, and Sroufe, 1979). On the other hand, recent studies have been carried out from the perspective of the Erikson model, seeking behaviors that suggest mastery for a given age group and then testing to see whether they relate to behaviors that indicate mastery of a

TABLE 6.2 Erikson's Stages of Psychosocial Development

PSYCHOSOCIAL STAGE		TASK OR CRISIS	SOCIAL CONDITIONS	PSYCHOSOCIAL OUTCOME
Stage 1 (birth to 1 year)	Oral-sensory	Can I trust the world?	Support and provision of basic needs	Basic trust
			Lack of support and deprivation	Basic distrust
Stage 2 (2–3 years)	Muscular-anal	Can I control my own behavior?	Permissiveness and support	Autonomy
			Overprotection and lack of support	Shame and doubt
Stage 3 (4–5 years)	Locomotor-genital	Can I become independent of my parents by exploring my limits?	Encouragement to explore	Initiative
			Lack of opportunity to explore	Guilt
Stage 4 (6–11 years)	Latency	Can I master the necessary skills to adapt?	Adequate training and encouragement	Industry
			Poor training and lack of support	Inferiority
Stage 5 (12–18 years)	Puberty and adolescence	Who am I? What are my beliefs, feelings, and attitudes?	Internal stability and positive feedback	Personal identity
			Confusion of purpose and unclear feedback	Role confusion
Stage 6 (young adulthood)	Young adulthood	Can I give fully of myself to another?	Warmth and sharing	Intimacy
			Loneliness	Isolation
Stage 7 (adulthood)	Adulthood	What can I offer succeeding generations?	Purposefulness and productivity	Generativity
			Lack of growth and regression	Stagnation
Stage 8 (maturity)	Maturity	Have I found contentment and satisfaction through my life's work and play?	Unity and fulfillment	Integrity
			Disgust and dissatisfaction	Despair

Source: Adapted from E. H. Erikson, *Childhood and Society,* 2nd. rev. ed. (New York: W. W. Norton & Company, Inc., 1963).

different area at a different age. These studies have found quite strong relationships between age-typical behaviors, for example, between early attachment and later explorations.

Infancy and Toddlerhood

Infants' first social relationships are with the principal care giver, usually the mother. The special bond that forms between infant and care giver is known as *attachment*. Most information about this relationship comes from research that has been done with monkeys. It is necessary to use caution in generalizing the results of animal studies to humans, but many important experiments can be carried out only with animals for ethical or practical reasons.

The classic, pioneering research on attachment in monkeys was done by Harry and Margaret Harlow (1965). Their observations demonstrate the importance and potency of mother-infant attachment in the species they have studied, the rhesus monkeys. Infant rhesus monkeys show the strength of their attachment to the mother in many ways.

A number of indirect measures are used to study the strength of an infant's response to its mother. One such measure is the frequency of proximity-seeking behaviors such as looking at the mother, attempting to touch the mother, or approaching the mother. Another measure is the degree of separation protest, such as crying or huddling in a corner, when the mother is not present. Infant rhesus monkeys show both of these types of behaviors: they spend a great deal of time in contact with their mothers and become very agitated when separated from them.

The dynamics of this attachment and its functional significance were demonstrated by experiments in which young monkeys were raised with artificial mothers, called surrogates. These surrogate mothers were made with soft cloth bodies, and the infants became quite attached to them (see Figure 6.7). During the developmental stage that the Harlows called the comfort and attachment stage, infants stay in very close proximity to their mothers. In the case of infants with cloth surrogates, the infants often spent 17 hours a day in contact with the surrogates, even though food was obtained away from the surrogate mothers. The Harlows believe that during this stage the infant establishes a bond of trust, which is later used as a base for the development of broader social contacts and behaviors.

In the next developmental stage, which the Harlows called the stage of security, the infants appear to gain a sense of self-confidence from the presence of the mother. For example, in one study infants were introduced into an open field, a room containing many new objects. Sometimes the surrogate mothers were present; sometimes they were not. When the surrogates were absent, the infants appeared very distressed—vocalizing, crouching, huddling, and rarely exploring the room. When the surrogates were introduced, the infants' behavior was much different. They rushed to the "mother" and clutched it intensely; then they relaxed, and all signs of apprehension disappeared. The surrogate mothers became a base for exploration of the room and manipulation of the objects in it. The presence of the "mothers" seemed to impart a sense of security to the infants. Observation of real rhesus mothers and their infants indicates that the same type of behavior takes place: in a play situation infant monkeys use their mothers as a base of operations.

These observations show how the attachment between infant and mother serves a critical function

FIGURE 6.7 The importance of infant-mother attachments was demonstrated in studies by Harry and Margaret Harlow. Surrogate mothers, made with soft cloth bodies, were used in experiments with infant rhesus monkeys. The infants developed quite an attachment to the surrogate mothers, which appeared to provide a sense of security.

in promoting the interactions of the developing organism and its environment. With the mother present, the infant monkey interacts with, and presumably begins to learn how to manipulate, its environment. But the absence of the mother prevents such interaction. Infants raised without effective surrogate mothers failed to interact effectively with the environment. For example, infants raised with surrogate mothers made only of wire mesh failed to develop attachments to the surrogates, and when placed in the open field, these infants appeared terrorized whether or not the surrogate was present.

The mother-infant system in rhesus monkeys appears to supply not only protection for the relatively helpless infant but a secure base for the development of exploration of the environment and interaction with it. In the case of human beings, this base is provided not only by the relationship of infants to their primary caregivers but also by the family, which supplies both protection and a base for development of the ability to influence the environment.

Human development studies show an overall pattern similar to that of rhesus monkeys— a sys-tem that is particularly tuned to the development of interaction with the environment. Proximity-seeking behaviors and separation protest associated with the process of attachment are manifested very early in human infancy. For example, very young infants seem to be more attracted to human beings than to objects. According to one study, infants discriminate between social objects: infants as young as two weeks tend to look longer at the mother than at a stranger (Carpenter, 1975). Another study indicates that four-week-old infants display a tendency to move toward people rather than objects (Brazelton, Koslowski, and Main, 1974).

An ambitious field study of separation protest investigated the intensity and age of onset of separation protest in a sample of 60 Scottish infants (Schaffer and Emerson, 1964). Every four weeks for more than a year the researchers visited the infants' homes and asked their mothers to report the infants' behaviors in a variety of situations—for example, when the infant was left alone in a room with strangers or when left in a carriage outside a place of business. The results of this study are shown in Figure 6.8. The youngest infants—between 5 and 29 weeks—showed moderate amounts

Infants tend to feel more comfortable exploring the environment when they are in the presence of parents.

of separation protest when they were left alone not only by the mother but also by a large array of other individuals, even strangers. However, at about 29 weeks of age and beyond, indiscriminate protest declined and more intense protest to the departure of specific individuals—most often the mother—increased. These discriminate protests reached a peak at between 12 and 18 months of age. These results suggest that as development proceeds, attachment becomes specific—to mother, father, or other primary care giver.

Studies by John Bowlby (1960) indicate that if an infant's relationship with a caregiver is limited only to the provision of basic physical needs, an attachment relationship usually does not develop, and the social interaction that permits expression of emotion is missing. Some theorists relate the emergence of specific attachment to an important stage of cognitive development that occurs at about the same time—the onset of the belief in object permanence (Kagan, 1958).

Object Permanence   This idea of *object permanence* was first noted by Piaget, as we saw earlier in this chapter (see Figure 6.9). In the first few months of life, infants act as if an object ceases to exist when it disappears from view. For example, a young infant can be actively engaged in tracking an object and attempting to hold it, but if someone covers the object with a handkerchief so that it is no longer visible, the infant stops pursuing the object. The object has ceased to exist: as if it lacks permanence. The infant's failure to search for the missing object resembles the young infant's failure to protest when a social object—mother or other caregiver— disappears.

If the world of young infants is composed of appearances that come and go willy-nilly, then behaviors, such as separation protest cannot be expected. It may be necessary for infants first to develop a belief in object permanence before they can protest at the disappearance of social objects.

Canalization   An alternate view of the emergence of attachment is provided by an evolutionary perspective (Bowlby, 1969). As the research of the Harlows suggests, attachment behaviors make sense in

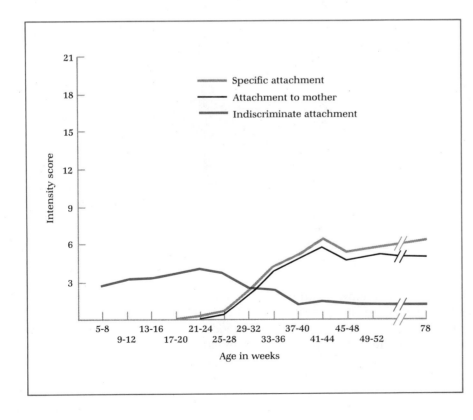

FIGURE 6.8   The results of the Shaffer and Emerson study suggest that attachment becomes specific as development proceeds.

(A)

(B)

FIGURE 6.9 The concept of object permanence was first noted by Piaget. (A) In the first few months of life an infant attends only to objects that are physically present. If the object is obscured, it ceases to exist in the infant's mind. (B) Older infants, however, will look for an object that has been covered or otherwise obscured.

terms of the survival of the infant and its development of skills in interacting with the environment. There is some evidence that both infants and caregivers come preequipped to establish this important bond—that is, genetic factors appear strongly to control the developmental path of behavior.

It is difficult to demonstrate genetic effects un-

equivocally in human infants because complete environmental control is impossible. Although the preference for social objects shown by infants as young as two to four weeks may be due to innate influences, environmental factors cannot be discounted because the infants studied did have experience with other humans. However, studies with animals, in which the environment is easier to control, seem to support the idea of genetic influence. In one important experiment, monkeys were raised in total social isolation, never seeing another monkey (Sackett, 1966). The monkeys were periodically exposed to various slides projected on the walls of their cages: in some cases the experimenter controlled the slides and recorded the monkeys' reactions to the pictures; in other cases, the monkeys themselves could turn on specific slides if they wanted to look at them by touching a brass lever. The slides used included pictures of other infants, of adult monkeys engaged in various behaviors, and control pictures that showed no monkeys but scenes of sunsets, trees, and a living room. Although they had no experience with other monkeys, the infants responded differentially to these slides. For example, they were likely to turn on pictures of other monkeys, particularly other infants. And they acted especially disturbed by, and did not often turn on, pictures of monkeys shown in threatening postures. Because these infants had never seen another monkey, their responses could not have been learned through social interaction. These results show that infants probably possess innate responses to certain characteristics of other members of their species.

Human studies suggest that adults may possess innate responses to several built-in signaling systems from infants. Physical features, such as the size of the eyes and the size and shape of the head, are recognized as "babyish" by adults who respond favorably to them. In a study of the responses of various groups of adults to pairs of pictures showing an adult and the young of various animal species, women—no matter what their age, marital status, or whether or not they were mothers—preferred the pictures of infants (Cann, 1953). Similar adult responsiveness to photographs showing infants has also been found by measuring the subjects' eye pupil dilation—an established measure of interest (Hess and Polt, 1960).

In addition to babyish features, infants display another characteristic that serves to strengthen the social bond with adults—smiling, which occurs so early in life and so universally that it is probably a highly canalized activity. Most newborn babies smile, and there is some evidence of fully developed smiles in prematurely born babies. Babies in all cultures smile, sometimes in the absence of any external stimulus; even blind babies smile. After the first month, smiling becomes more pronounced. It can clearly be elicited by anything that resembles a human face—even a schematic drawing or a cardboard mask. Thus, several months before attachment behaviors provide a clear indication of bonding, smiling provides a mechanism for establishing social interaction with human caregivers.

Further evidence of such early social mechanisms comes from videotaped social interchanges such as cooing and looking between mothers and infants as young as three months of age (Stern, 1974). These videotapes make clear that a "fine-tuned" relationship exists between mothers and young infants. Both mothers and infants adjust their behavior relative to one another, with mothers engaging in highly rhythmic interchanges with the infants. Infants, in turn, are able to reciprocate and often to pace the interaction.

Babyish features, smiling, "fine tuning"—all of these characteristics suggest that the infants are well equipped to attain and maintain social interactions with caregivers. Infants' physiognomy and behavior combine in a way that is satisfying to caregivers, who themselves seem specially attuned to infants' social signals.

Social Integration Although infants and caregivers may, as evidence suggests, come preequipped to be mutually responsive, there is nonetheless considerable variation in their degree of social inte-

Smiling in infants manifests itself very early in life and is generally considered to be a canalized activity. Smiling seems to provide a mechanism for establishing social interaction with care givers.

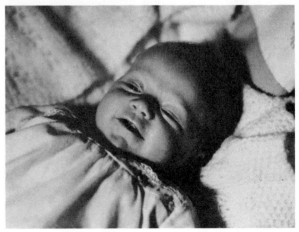

gration. Many intervening factors—biological or environmental—can disturb the mutually fine-tuned relationship between caregivers and infants. Some infants may be colicky and thus display patterns of distress that caregivers find difficult to ameliorate. This can result in frustration that might disrupt the caregivers' responsiveness. Similarly, environmental stresses, such as economic problems or having no adult social outlet, can intervene to divert caregivers' abilities to respond to children's social signals.

Variations in infant-caregiver relationships have been investigated by Mary Ainsworth and her colleagues (Ainsworth, Bell, and Stayton, 1971). These researchers make an important distinction between two types of mother-child interaction patterns—sensitive and insensitive. In this distinction, sensitivity relates to the caregiver's ability to be aware of the presence of social signals from the infant and the ability to interpret correctly the meaning of these signals; insensitivity implies a lack of such awareness and a tendency to force compliance with commands without regard for the particular situation or the particular state of the child. Ainsworth and her colleagues have found that the relative sensitivity of the caregiver's responsiveness affects the quality of attachment shown by the infant. Sensitive patterns of interaction, they suggest, lead to secure attachment, which is marked by the infant's greater tolerance for brief absences of the care giver. Insensitive patterns yield anxious attachment, a tendency by the infant to protest any separation from the caregiver.

These findings were bolstered by a more recent study that looked at face-to-face interactions between mothers and infants aged 6 to 15 weeks—a stage at which attachment behaviors are not yet evident (Blehar, Lieberman, and Ainsworth, 1977). The results showed considerable differences among the mother-infant pairs in the degree of mutuality of interaction patterns. These variations, in turn, were related to the security of attachment later measured when the infants were 12 months old.

Exploration Earlier in this chapter, it was suggested that an important function of secure attachments was to provide the infant with protection and a sense of security that allows for alloplastic explorations of the environment. This observation was based on research with monkeys, but there is also experimental evidence supporting this function of secure attachments in humans.

One study tested the effects of attachment on infant responsiveness to a strange environment (Rheingold and Eckerman, 1973). When 10-month-old infants were placed in a strange room without their mothers, they cried. However, when they were placed in a room with the mother and with a door leading to a strange room, the infants would often leave the mother to explore the strange room. The presence of the mother—and presumably the attachment to her—enabled these infants to explore a new environment without evident fear.

Elaboration of these findings on the relationship between attachment and exploration comes from the work of Ainsworth and her colleagues (Ainsworth, Bell, and Stayton, 1971). Their research demonstrated that the infant's exploratory activities depended on the strength of attachment, which in turn depended on the sensitivity of mutual interaction with the caregiver. Infants with secure attachments used the mother as a base from which to explore wider aspects of the environment; those with anxious attachments tended to orient toward the mother instead of the wider environment and were thus limited in their exploratory activities.

Successful adaptation to the environment, as shown by characteristics such as active exploration, is related to the smooth intercoordination of factors on both sides of the social equation—the meshing of the child's emerging needs and capacities with caregiving routines that are sensitive to the infant's own agenda. As the child's behaviors change with

Videotapes of mothers and infants have shown a fine-tuned relationship to exist between them. Mothers and infants adjust their behaviors relative to one another. The mothers engage in highly rhythmic interchanges with the infants, who are able to reciprocate and often even will pace the interaction themselves.

maturation, a number of crisis points crop up in the interactions between caregiver and child. The caregiver's recognition that the child is developing and changing, coupled with the infant's characteristics such as smiling that provide a reward for the caregiver, help to maintain a system that is both protective and liberating.

Childhood

Interaction with siblings and other children really begins in the preschool years. Children begin social play learning give-and-take and adaptation. Children with earlier secure attachments to care givers seem to be more successful at early social behaviors than do those children who had anxious attachments (Lieberman, 1977).

Peer groups assume an even more influential role in middle childhood because children spend more and more time away from home and in the company of friends. The peer group is important in the development of identity, attitudes, and values. Group influence is powerful, and a child's position in the group greatly influences self-concept.

Adolescence

There is no doubt that other young people are an important influence on adolescents today; they are the main source of information about sex (Dickinson, 1978) and the chief encouragers of drug use (Kandel, 1974). Adolescent subculture provides a buffer between the world of children and that of adults, allowing, for example, a social context for the development of mature friendships and sexual relationships. Sexual gratification is now aimed at developing satisfactory relationships with people outside the family and in finding a suitable partner.

Many adolescents identify strongly with their peer groups and their generation. In fact, teenagers identify with other teenagers more than with older people of their own race, religion, community, or sex (Sorenson, 1973). And they consider themselves more idealistic, less materialistic, healthier in their sexuality, and better able to understand friendship than are members of the older generation (Sorenson, 1973).

According to Erikson, the psychosocial crisis of adolescence is identity versus role confusion. Ideally, adolescents resolve this crisis by developing a sense of their own uniqueness and a concept of their relationship to the larger society, establishing a sexual, political, moral, and vocational identity in the process (Erikson, 1975).

Parents remain, however, vital influences on adolescents, especially when there is discussion and respect among family members. Adolescents whose parents are indifferent or overly strict tend to depend on peers for social support.

Adulthood

Friendships are very important during young adulthood. People make friends as couples as well as individuals. Couple friendships allow the partners to be involved with others, avoid isolation, and find extra stimulation (Leefeldt and Callenbach, 1979).

Middle-aged people tend to invest less time in developing friendships, especially new ones, because their energies are devoted to family, work, and building up security for retirement. When new friendships do develop, they evolve from similarities in life stage, such as age of children, duration of marriage, or occupational status, rather than chronological age (Troll, 1975). Robert Peck (1968) specified four psychological developments critical to successful adjustment during middle age: valuing wisdom versus valuing physical prowess, socializing versus sexualizing in human relationships, cathetic (emotional) flexibility versus cathetic impoverishment, and mental flexibility versus mental rigidity.

Children's interactions with siblings and other children generally begin in the preschool years. Children who enjoyed secure early attachments with care givers seem to have more success in social situations than do those who had anxious attachments.

Many teenagers identify with other teenagers more than with older people of their own race, religion, community, or sex. They consider themselves to be better adjusted to the outside world than are members of the older generation.

Late Adulthood

Erikson's model makes clear that development is an ongoing process, extending from the cradle to the grave. Each stage of the life cycle involves transitions and problems that may find help or hurt in the social environment. Just as at the beginning of the cycle the infant's oral needs may present a crisis in the first year, there is a potential crisis to be resolved at the other end of the developmental spectrum—namely, the transition from the adult world of work into the aging years of retirement.

Research data relevant to this transitional crisis of old age has been presented by Ellen Langer (Langer and Rodin, 1976), who studied nursing homes for the aged in Connecticut. Langer noted that, while the homes were well run and provided many benefits for the residents, much of the environment was controlled by the staff. In one nursing home she obtained agreement to stage an unusual

RESEARCH: Continuity of Adaptation in Early Childhood

The various theories of emotional development in childhood all share a common assumption. They assume that, throughout a child's advances in level and dramatic changes in behavioral repertoire, development is characterized by continuity in the quality of adaptation. Thus, it is assumed, psychological assessments at an early stage of development can predict the presence of later strengths and difficulties.

A research group including Alan Sroufe and Leah Matas has examined this assumption in the context of the concept known as attachment (Matas, Arend, and Sroufe, 1978). This special bond that forms between infant and care giver is manifested by the tendency of the infant to seek the proximity of his or her mother and to show distress when they are separated. Other investigators had shown differences in the quality of attachment that depended on the responsiveness of the care giver— typically the mother—to the baby's needs. Infants with secure attachments, it further had been demonstrated, tended to use the care giver as a base from which to explore and master wide aspects of their environment.

In order to test the notion of continuity of adaptation, Matas and her associates designed a short-term longitudinal study aimed at determining the link between quality of attachment at age 18 months and the quality of play and problem-solving behavior at age 2.

Their subjects were 25 male and 23 female white middle-class infants and their mothers. At 18 months, the infants were assessed for quality of attachment,

using the laboratory setting and method developed by Ainsworth (Ainsworth, Bell, and Stayton, 1971). The laboratory setting is the so-called strange situation, which involves a precise sequence of events. The mother leaves the child in the room with a group of toys and a stranger. She then returns to the room while the stranger leaves. The mother exits again, leaving the child alone for a few minutes. The stranger returns and, shortly thereafter, so does the mother. During this sequence of two separations and two reunions, the child's behavior is observed and recorded on videotape by the researchers through a one-way mirror.

Based upon these observations, the subjects were classified into three main groups:

• Securely attached (Group B): This group was active in seeking physical contact or interaction on reunion—contact that was effective in terminating distress and promoting a return to play activity.
• Avoidant (Group A): This group avoided the mother upon reunion, especially in the instance of the second reunion when the child's distress at separation presumably would have built up and been greater.
• Ambivalent (Group C): This group had difficulty becoming settled on reunion, sometimes trying to get away from the mother.

When the toddlers were 2 years old, they and their mothers returned to the laboratory for further observation. During a ten-minute free-play period, the chil-

experiment. Residents on one floor of the nursing home constituted her control group. As before, decisions resided principally with the staff: the staff chose the movies that were shown and even cared for the plants in the rooms. On another floor, where the physical condition of the patients approximately matched those of the control group, changes were instituted. The residents chose the movies that were shown and selected and cared for the plants.

Langer used several different measures to indicate what effect these changes might have on the patient's lives. One measure was the activity level of the residents. On this measure, the results of the experiments were quite striking. Residents on the choice-and-take-responsibility floor maintained a much higher activity level than those in the control group on the passively-cared-for floor. Even more remarkable, follow-up studies found that death

rates on the two floors proved to be markedly different. Over a two-year period, there were far fewer deaths on the choice-and-take-responsibility floor.

This study speaks directly to Erikson's model of developmental transitions over the life span. Providing residents with choice and responsibility smoothed the difficult transition from the previous stage of work—where those factors are essential characteristics—to retirement, a stage that threatens the old person's sense of identity.

Moral Development

An important aspect of growing up in any society is *moral development*—that is, the growth of the ability to distinguish between right and wrong. Life

---

dren were assessed for symbolic play that showed pretending and imagination—for example, placing a small wooden figure in a tractor seat and having the child "drive" around, or pretending to pour a cup of tea and offer it to the mother. Following free-play, the mother initiated a six-minute cleanup period, allowing observations of the child's reactions, such as anger or noncompliance, when a pleasant activity was interrupted.

Finally, the subjects were presented with a series of manual problem-solving tasks that involved the use of sticks, blocks, and levers and required the mother's help. The child's behavior during these tasks was monitored for such factors as frustration, instances of seeking help from the mother, and compliance with the mother's suggested way of solving the problem.

The key results are shown in the table below.

As the table indicates, in the measure of symbolic play during free play, securely attached infants engaged in more imaginative activity than did either avoidant or ambivalent infants. In the manual-task-solving situation, securely attached infants were more enthusiastic and complied with maternal requests more frequently than did the other subjects; they ignored the mother less and spent less time away from the task.

These and all other measures fell in the predicted direction. Infants assessed as securely attached at 18 months were found to be more enthusiastic, persistent, cooperative, and generally more effective than insecurely attached infants when tested at age two. By demonstrating a relationship between attachment and competence over a six-month period, the study provided evidence for continuity of adaptation.

Means and Standard Deviations for Dependent Variables

MEASURES	Sample $\bar{X}$	Sample SD	Group B $\bar{X}$	Group B SD	Group A $\bar{X}$	Group A SD	Group C $\bar{X}$	Group C SD
% comply	.28	.15	.36	.17	.22	.08	.20	.08
% comply or attempt comply	.45	.19	.57	.22	.39	.12	.40	.12
% ignoring	.36	.18	.26	.18	.44	.13	.46	.11
Enthusiasm rating (both tools)	7.96	2.95	9.22	2.63	6.08	2.92	7.70	2.36
Bouts of symbolic play	2.26	2.27	3.40	2.47	1.35	1.66	.12	1.38

within social groups requires adherence to common sets of rules and principles that transcend the mutual attractions and attachments of familial relationships and friendships. How do we come to tell right from wrong? The answer to this question has been pursued in substantially different ways by two research traditions in psychology. One tradition, established by learning theorists, focuses on the effects of parental socialization and disciplinary practices. The other tradition, espoused by Piaget and other cognitive theorists, stresses developmental differences in the child's ability to reason about moral matters.

Learning Approach

The learning tradition has placed great importance on reward and punishment as teaching mechanisms of morality. Although the precise effectiveness of reward versus punishment depends on a number of conditions, reward generally emerges as a better teacher of moral behavior. A new learning model emphasizes the role of moral explanation in early disciplinary encounters between parent and child (Hoffman, in press). According to this model, children's moral behavior is best enhanced when a moral explanation for the discipline is provided. For example, "Don't do that because it might hurt the other person" is more effective than a simple "don't do that."

Parents also influence the moral behavior of their children by serving as models. The tendency of children to imitate the behavior of others—especially of their parents—is legendary, and this effect has been repeatedly demonstrated in the

FOCUS: Children Raised in Isolation

The nature-nurture issue will probably never be resolved totally, at least in its application to the human species. One reason for this is that the critical experiment cannot be done with humans. Many studies have shown that early experience is critical to the development of normal behavior in animals. But one is left wondering what a human being raised in complete isolation from other humans would be like. Such experiments cannot and should not be done. But occasionally an accidental series of events arranges things so that we can get some idea of what the results of such an isolation experiment might be.

One example of such a natural experiment is the case known as the Wild Boy of Aveyron. Early in the morning of January 9, 1800, a boy who appeared to be about 11 or 12 years of age came out of the woods near a small French village and was captured. He was virtually naked, wearing only the tattered remains of a shirt. He could not speak and did not react to anything that was said to him. He was totally "unhousebroken," urinating and defecating whenever he felt like it. He refused to tolerate clothing and showed a great aversion to sleeping in a bed.

Eventually, the Wild Boy was sent to Paris, where he came under the care of a young doctor named Jean-Marc Gaspard Itard. Itard took a keen interest in the case and undertook a program of testing and training the Wild Boy that was to last for five years (Itard, 1932; Shattuck, 1980).

Itard began his work with several goals. First, he wanted to train Victor, the name by which the Wild Boy came to be called, to respond appropriately to other people. In this Itard was partly successful. For example, Victor became very attached to Itard and particularly to Madame Guerin, the housekeeper who cared for him. But his behavior with strangers was often erratic and unpredictable, and he apparently never learned to interact well with women, even after passing through puberty.

Second, Itard wanted to train Victor's senses, so that Victor would be more responsive to the world around him. When first captured, Victor seemed almost totally unaware of events in his surroundings. For example, he seemed never to focus his gaze on any single object, he paid no attention to sounds unless they were connected with eating, and he seemed completely insensitive to cold and heat. Itard tackled this problem successfully, using a number of different techniques that exposed Victor to new sensations and made these stimuli relevant. For example, Itard and Madame Guerin began giving Victor a daily warm bath, for two to three hours. Victor enjoyed these baths and first showed sensitivity to temperature in this setting. One day he was given a cold bath, and he refused to get in. He even took Itard's hand and placed it in the water to make his point.

Third, Itard wanted to train Victor to speak. In this, even after immense labor, he failed almost completely. Although he did manage to get Victor to respond appropriately to certain words and even to utter a few, Victor never really learned to speak. For example, although Victor would say *lait* (French for

observational learning experiments conducted by Albert Bandura and his colleagues. Children also are likely to pay more attention to, and emulate, what parents actually do in practice rather than what they preach should be done (Hetherington and Morris, 1978).

Cognitive Approach

The second major tradition in attempting to explain moral development, the cognitive approach, has been most vigorously espoused by Lawrence Kohlberg (1963). Kohlberg's model, like the theory of cognitive development constructed by Jean Piaget, distinguishes a series of sequential stages in the ontogeny of reasoning. Kohlberg began to think seriously about the problem of moral development after World War II when, as a seaman in the U.S. Merchant Marine, he helped Jewish immigrants break through the British blockade of Palestine. In that situation, Kohlberg was confronted by a moral dilemma: was he justified in breaking the law in order to attain what he considered a greater good?

Kohlberg's research method hinges upon the consideration of such moral dilemmas. He presented children with hypothetical dilemmas in which there is a clear conflict between obedience to social rules or laws and the needs of others. For example, if a man's wife is dying of cancer for want of an expensive drug that he cannot afford, would he be justified in stealing the drug? If a physician is confronted by a fatally ill patient who begs to be relieved of pain, should the physician consent to the patient's request to die?

---

milk), when given a glass of milk, he would never say *lait* to ask for a glass of milk.

Fourth, Itard attempted to train Victor to think clearly. Partial success was achieved, again after incredible effort.

Finally, after five years, Itard became discouraged. He concluded that although real progress had been made in several areas—training the senses, learning some simple written signs, developing the capability for friendship—Victor would never learn to hear speech normally or to talk himself and would never match ordinary children in intellectual progress. Itard abandoned his training program, and Victor lived out his life quietly in a house on a side street in Paris looked after by Madame Guerin.

A more recent case of a socially isolated child also has been extensively studied. Genie was admitted into Childrens Hospital of Los Angeles in November 1970. She was 13 years, 9 months old and an unsocialized, primitive human being, emotionally disturbed, unlearned, and without language. Evidently, from about the age of 20 months, Genie had been confined in a small, closed, and curtained room, tied to a potty chair. Her mother spent only a few minutes a day with her and fed her only cereal and baby food. Her father was intolerant of any noise, and there was no radio or TV in the house. Not only was Genie isolated and severely mistreated—her father physically punished her if she made any sound—she was exposed to virtually no acoustic stimuli.

In the months after she was admitted to the hospital, an extensive series of tests showed that Genie was biologically and genetically normal with no evidence of early brain damage. It appears that her retardation was principally due to the extreme isolation to which she was subjected with its attendant social, perceptual, and sensory deprivation.

Several researchers undertook an intensive testing and teaching experiment with Genie to see if she could acquire language (Fromkin, Krashen, Curtiss, Rigler, and Rigler, 1972/1973). At the heart of the investigation was a test of the hypothesis that a "critical period" for learning language exists for human beings—from about age two to puberty—and that language acquisition is impossible after this period (Lenneberg, 1967).

Genie's case seems to disprove part of E. H. Lenneberg's hypothesis because Genie has acquired some language—and after puberty. She has learned some basic grammatical patterns, but it does not seem likely that Genie will progress much further in her learning. Her deprivation was too severe, a fact that does support the existence of a critical period. At this point in research, the aptest statement would seem to be that a critical period for acquiring language does exist, but some first language learning can occur after puberty.

Because of the infrequency of cases such as Victor's and Genie's, evidence for the damaging effects of isolation on children is scanty. The small number of known incidences of isolation, however, are dramatic and informative.

Kohlberg asked such questions not only of American children but also of children in different countries. By analyzing their answers and, more importantly, the reasoning behind the answers, he delineated six stages in the development of moral reasoning. These six stages were grouped by Kohlberg on three major levels (see Table 6.3):

1. *Premoral level.* Children evaluate their behavior in terms of its consequences. Does a given action bring reward or punishment? In Stage One, the child justifies moral choice in the framework of avoiding punishment from powerful people. In Stage Two, rewards or the return of favors dominate the child's reasoning about moral choices. This often takes the form of a "tit for tat" notion of social relationships—"I'll lend you my blocks if you let me play with your wagon."

2. *Conventional level.* At the conventional level of morality, the child's choices invoke the concept of social rules and obligations. In Stage Three, the desire for approval from others, to be considered a "good boy" or "nice girl," is uppermost. In Stage Four, the child's concepts of duty and of established law and authority play the major role in justification of moral choice.

3. *Postconventional level.* Self-accepted moral principles that are arrived at by increasingly abstract reasoning characterize Kohlberg's third level of development. Obedience to a rule no longer depends upon the mere existence of the rule; the rule itself may be put into question and subjected to a developing self-standard of moral behavior. Thus, at this level, personal morality and conventional morality may come into conflict. In Stage Five, the child tends to resolve conflicts between individual and social morality in favor of social. Unlike Stage Four, in which the concepts of duty and law are predominant, the social choice is based on principle; the child may decide that the rules are unfair but that it is in the general interest of people to abide by them. In Stage Six, the child's inner compass rather than social rules dictates moral choice. The commandments of the individual conscience, based on universal principles such as the golden rule, take precedence.

According to Kohlberg, the progression through three levels of moral development does not simply reflect social teachings but also intellectual changes. Kohlberg asserts that the six stages occur in an orderly progression. As in Piaget's theory of cognitive development, each stage builds upon previous stages and is determined by the increasing intellectual capacities of the child.

Evidence for the logical ordering of these stages

Maintaining a high level of activity in the elderly seems to go hand in hand with physical and emotional well-being and thus helps to promote longevity.

TABLE 6.3   Kohlberg's Stages of Moral Development

LEVEL	STAGE
Level one	*Premoral*
Step 1	Punishment and obedience orientation. Obey rules to avoid punishment.
Step 2	Naive instrumental hedonism. Conform to obtain rewards, have favors returned.
Level two	*Conventional role conformity*
Step 3	Good boy/girl morality. Conform to avoid disapproval or dislike by others.
Step 4	Law and authority maintaining morality. Conform to avoid censure by authorities.
Level three	*Self-accepted moral principles*
Step 5	Morality of contract, individual rights, and democratically accepted law. Conform to maintain community welfare.
Step 6	Morality of individual principles of conscience. Conform to avoid self-condemnation.

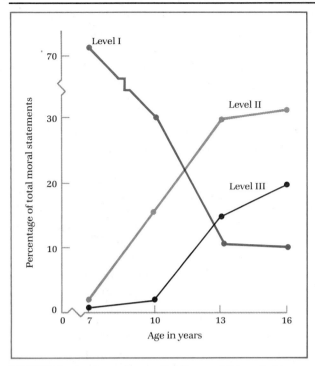

FIGURE 6.10 According to Kohlberg, children between 7 and 16 years old show decreasing amounts of premoral reasoning (Level I), dramatically increasing amounts of conventional morality (Level II), and slighty increasing amounts of postconventional morality (Level III).

comes from several studies. Kohlberg, himself, (1963) shows that children in the age range from 7 to 16 demonstrate decreasing amounts of premoral reasoning (Level 1), sharply increasing amounts of conventional morality (Level 2), and slightly increasing amounts of postconventional morality (Level 3). These changes are shown in Figure 6.10. In addition, instead of skipping stages, children tend to take moral reasoning a stage at a time (Turiel, 1966). When children were presented with models that reasoned either at one stage above, one stage below, or two stages above their own level, they showed maximum change to the model that reasoned on a stage above their own level.

Although Kohlberg does not attempt to predict a direct relationship between age and moral maturity, some general conclusions can be drawn from his work. Premoral reasoning (Level 1) occurs in children age 7 and younger. Conventional morality applies predominantly to ages 8 through 13. Many people never exceed this level. In Kohlberg's research, fewer than 10 percent of his subjects over 16 reached Stage 6—the point at which individual conscience provides the guide for moral decisions.

SUMMARY

1. Developmental psychology is concerned with the scientific study of changes that occur in individuals over time. For simplicity's sake, development, which continues over the life span, is traced through its physical, cognitive, and social aspects. However, these divisions are arbitrary: development in one sphere affects development in all the other spheres.

2. Although the controversy over causes of development—nature versus nurture or heredity versus environment—continues, most researchers emphasize the interaction between genetic and environmental influences. Heredity dictates normal individual characteristics such as eye color and bone structure through the genetic mechanisms of chromosomes and genes. Genotype refers to the genetic makeup of an individual; phenotype refers to the outward expression of that makeup. The modern view of genetics regards the development of complex systems, such as intelligence, as being polygenetically determined—related to the control of many genes. In addition, research with animals has modified the classic view of heredity regarding the timing in which genetically determined features appear. In physical maturation the process of change is apparently largely controlled by a special type of gene known as a pacing gene, which sets the pace for emerging systems of development. By virtue of maturational changes that are genetically paced, the organism interacts with its environment, laying the foundation for further interaction in the process of development.

3. Two theories advanced in recent years make headway in resolving the nature-nurture debate. The epigenetic landscape is a model that depicts the biological control of development in terms of constraints of varying strengths. These biological constraints are likened to pathways or canals that control the direction of a ball rolling down an incline. Forces (the environment) may jar the ball out of its pathway or canal if the groove is shallow. Similarly, some hereditary traits are seen as highly canalized and resistant to environmental influence; other traits are seen as less canalized and less resistant to environmental effect.

The alloplastic approach to the study of development emphasizes the ability of the organism to alter nature through tool use, sharing of skills, and extended childhood. This developmental approach has particular application to, but is not limited to, the study of human growth and behavior.

4. The study of physical development focuses on the biological growth of the organism from conception to death. Heredity sets the boundaries for physical development, but an impoverished environment can have adverse influence. Developmental processes cannot be skipped, but wide variation exists in the age at which humans go through these processes. Normal physical development is orderly, sequential, and maturational; all children crawl, stand, and walk in the same sequence and at roughly the same age.

5. Physical growth is fastest during infancy and early childhood, slows its pace during middle childhood, and speeds up again during adolescence. In adolescence, physical growth is accompanied by the emergence of sex characteristics. Most people reach peak physical development in their early twenties; thereafter, the physical development processes become those of aging.

6. Jean Piaget traced cognitive, or intellectual, growth through four major stages: (1) sensorimotor period—birth to age 2; (2) preoperational period—ages 2 to 6; (3) concrete operational period—ages 7 to 11; and (4) formal operational period—ages 11 to 16. Important events in these periods, respectively, are the discovery of object permanence, the use of symbols, the development of the concept of conservation, and the systematic testing of hypotheses.

7. Piaget's view of cognitive development is basically an individualistic theory of the growth of intelligence. As a result of studies of the growth of logical intelligence in different cultures, Jerome Bruner has attempted to show that Piaget's individualized model of development is subject to direct cultural influence. The work of L. S. Vygotsky and John Flavell indicates the importance of others in the cognitive developmental process.

8. Scores on IQ tests typically peak in early adulthood, taper off gradually, and decline in old age. IQ tests are not reliable indicators of adult competencies and wisdom, however. Factors such as reaction speed, motivation, and health tend to penalize adults on IQ tests. Recent research indicates that peak intellectual achievement may come as late as age 50 for some people. Many people are mentally active and alert well into old age.

9. Social development requires psychological adjustments throughout the life span. Erik Erikson proposed eight psychosocial crises that must be confronted by all people at various points in life. The crises range from trust versus mistrust in the first months of life to integrity versus despair as death approaches. The beginnings of social development can be observed in the very young through such processes as attachment, discovery of object permanence, social integration, and exploration.

Social interactions and peer groups are important throughout the life span. Interaction with siblings and other children begins in the preschool years and intensifies in middle childhood. Adolescents identify strongly with their peer groups, but parents remain strong influences on young people. In adulthood and in old age, social interaction is based strongly on similarity; friends are likely to be of the same sex, same marital status, same race, same socioeconomic class, and about the same age.

10. The development of morality—the ability to distinguish between right and wrong—is an important aspect of growing up in any society. Learning theorists explain the growth of moral understanding by focusing on the effects of parental socialization and disciplinary practices. Piaget and other cognitive theorists stress developmental differences in the child's ability to reason about moral questions.

Lawrence Kohlberg, using Piaget's work on moral reasoning as a base, proposed three levels (including six stages) of moral development. These range from obeying rules simply to avoid punishment to the morality of individual principles of conscience.

Chapter 7
The Varieties of Learning

A hungry cocker spaniel hears the rattle of dishes and begins to drool. A cat finds release from a cage by poking about until it finds the latch string. A pigeon pecks at a disk in return for a pellet of food. A student works through an algebra problem. An infant begins to recognize round things that bounce as belonging to a certain concept—ball.

Each of these situations describes a different example of one of the most important processes studied by psychologists—*learning*. As an area of psychological study, learning can be broadly described as a relatively permanent change of behavior that results from prior experience.

Because learning is such a vital aspect of both human and animal behavior, its underlying processes are of key importance in psychological thought. From birth until death there are continuous changes in behavior in most organisms from which learning can be observed or inferred. In humans, learning is most dramatic during the acquisition of basic skills in the preschool and school years. Children learn to read and to write; they acquire vast amounts of information; they learn ways of ordering that information mentally. Children begin amassing vocabularies that typically amount to more than 50,000 words over a lifetime. In addition to these cognitive skills, the continuous accumulation of social skills and attitudes characterizes interactions with others. Learning continues to be of central importance throughout our lives: adults must learn the skills required for a particular job, how to care for home and family, and how to adjust to their constantly changing world.

It is important to distinguish between learning and *performance:* learning is inferred from performance, but it is not the same as performance. Learning as opposed to performance cannot be observed directly. We usually have to be motivated to perform before learning will be manifest in performance. Also, certain aspects of performance are not the result of learning. These may include temporary changes in behavior such as those resulting from intoxication, illness, or fatigue as well as more permanent changes caused by injury or long-term exposure to drugs such as LSD. Other forms of behavior are innate and thus do not reflect learning. These include reflexes such as the automatic constriction of the pupil of the eye in response to an increase in illumination, tropisms, or responsive movements, such as the movements of a moth flying into a flame, and at least some aspects of partially instinctive activities such as the nest-building activities of birds.

The distinction between learning and performance can also be described in terms of capability and action: learning reflects what we are able to do, whereas performance pertains to what we actually do. The fact that a person is not dancing at a given moment does not imply that the person has not learned how to dance. An organism must be motivated before learning will be demonstrated by performance. If a dog is not motivated by hunger, it ignores the food dish even though it knows the location of the dish.

The use of the term *learning* is usually restricted not only to relatively permanent changes in behavior but also to continued demonstrations of knowledge and skill. A traditional part of most definitions of learning has been the role of experience. This is perfectly reasonable because much of what we learn requires considerable practice; that is, learning is often a gradual process. Changes in behavior that result from learning often would not occur without particular experiences, even though the specific contribution of experience may differ from one learning situation to another.

Because learning plays such a central role in most forms of behavior, its processes necessarily are discussed throughout this book. Memory, for example, is intimately related to learning and will be examined in Chapter 8. Other varieties of learning, such as the acquisition of language and those relating to social and abnormal behavior, will also be discussed in separate chapters. In this chapter we will focus on several aspects of learning. We will start with relatively simple situations in which learning occurs passively. Then we will focus on learning that takes place only if a subject actively responds to the environment. Finally we will examine the complex ways in which humans acquire conceptual knowledge of the world around them.

All varieties of learning—no matter how fundamental they may be—depend on complex interactions. These interactions involve a number of variables: the species of the learner, the particular setting or task, and what the organism brings to the situation in terms of prior experience and internal processes. Throughout this chapter we will see examples of species-specific learning, the influence of different tasks on learning, and the contribution of past experience on what is learned.

Imprinting

Even a basic type of learning such as *imprinting* serves as an illustration of innate factors and experience working together to produce behavior change (Lorenz, 1937). Imprinting is the process by which certain young animals learn to follow their mothers. Although it has been found in several species including dogs and sheep, imprinting is most pronounced in young birds—geese, for example—that are able to swim or walk immediately after birth. Imprinting typically occurs very soon after hatching, usually within a day or two, and it does not occur at all—or only very weakly— outside of this *critical period.* Eckhard Hess (1959) reports maximum sensitivity for ducklings within the first day and a peak at 13 – 16 hours of age (see Figure 7.1).

Ordinarily, the stimulus for imprinting is the movement of the young animal's mother. But the Austrian Konrad Lorenz (1937) and other *ethologists*—scientists who study animals in their natural environments—have shown that, in the absence of the mother, ducklings and chicks will imprint on practically any prominent moving ob-

FIGURE 7.1 Imprinting as a function of age at exposure to imprinting stimulus. In studies by Eckhard Hess, maximum sensitivity for ducklings was found to be about 13 to 16 hours after hatching.

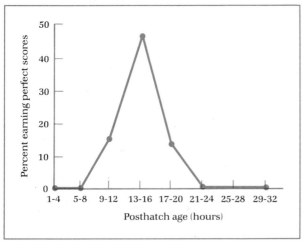

ject—a wooden decoy, a flashing light, even the experimenter. Once imprinting has occurred, the animal will thereafter follow the substitute stimulus in preference to its own mother. Under normal conditions, imprinting serves an important adaptive function by keeping the young chicks and ducklings close to their mothers.

The study of imprinting, together with other ethological studies involving phenomena such as nest building and courtship sequences, clearly points to the importance of innate factors in some varieties of learning. In imprinting, an innate behavior pattern is triggered by interaction with the critical period of time and a highly particular experience—the prominent moving stimulus. Only through the interaction of all three elements does this type of learning occur.

Imprinting requires that a behavior pattern be innate; most forms of learning, however, are not so clearly based on an inborn pattern. Most basic learning requires a learned association of stimuli such as a dog's learning to approach its food bowl before the bowl is placed on the floor. The two basic forms of association learning are classical conditioning and operant conditioning.

Classical Conditioning

Infants who have been fed every three hours since birth become restless and cry when fed an hour late. Adults become so depressed that they behave as though nothing they might do would "make things better." Teenagers may feel like throwing up whenever they smell whiskey. How might these rather diverse behaviors be explained? Psychologists believe that they are the result of *classical conditioning*, one of the most extensively investigated varieties of learning.

Classical conditioning is based on an organism's learning that two stimuli go together. It is primarily restricted to the association of some reflex behavior with a neutral stimulus. A reflex behavior is usually produced involuntarily by a specific stimulus: for example, blinking when a strong puff of air hits your eye or salivating at the sight of food if you are hungry. These and other reflex behaviors can be classically conditioned to some neutral stimulus. Classical conditioning does not explain the acquisition of complicated skills such as talking or writing.

The first student of classical conditioning was the eminent Russian physiologist Ivan Petrovich Pavlov, who performed what is probably the most famous series of experiments in the history of psychology. Pavlov's influence on the study of classical conditioning has been so great that many writers refer to this form of learning as *Pavlovian conditioning*.

Pavlov came upon classical conditioning by fortuitous accident just after the turn of the twentieth century. He was studying the digestive system in dogs and thereby successfully demonstrating the link between digestion and the nervous system. This work would win for Pavlov in 1904 the Nobel Prize; it was a chance discovery, however, that led to his lasting fame.

Pavlov's dogs, like all hungry animals, salivated when food was placed in their mouths. This, Pavlov knew, was an automatic *reflex;* it was built into the nervous system and required no prior learning. However, Pavlov noticed something he did not expect: the dogs would also salivate in response to stimuli merely associated with the food—the sight of the food dish, for example, or even the sound of the footsteps of the attendant who brought the food.

Although Pavlov was irritated at first because the premature salivation interfered with his experiments on digestion, the phenomenon intrigued him nonetheless. He reasoned that, unlike an automatic reflex, it constituted a form of learning that might involve higher centers in the brain's two cerebral hemispheres. For this reason, Pavlov referred to the salivation as "psychic secretions." Pavlov knew that the cerebral hemispheres were of unquestioned importance in humans; he also presumed that, in dogs, they also governed complex learning activities, such as guarding or hunting, that these animals had been taught for centuries. Thus, he began his epic experiments with dogs, hoping the study might lead to a means of measuring the brain's learning activity (Pavlov, 1927).

In contemporary applications, classical conditioning is often used to explain many physiological reactions, especially those related to emotional states. For example, irrational fears or phobias are thought to be the result of classical conditioning (Wolpe and Lazarus, 1969). Thus, fear of snakes may result not from any actual experience with snakes but from merely seeing a picture of a snake in some emotional context.

Acquisition: Stimulus and Response

The essence of Pavlov's classical conditioning experiments involves procedures that have since been repeated countless times in psychologists' laboratories. We will recreate Pavlov's experiments, beginning with the dog's natural response (salivation) to a particular stimulus (the presentation of food). Because the response is not learned, the salivation

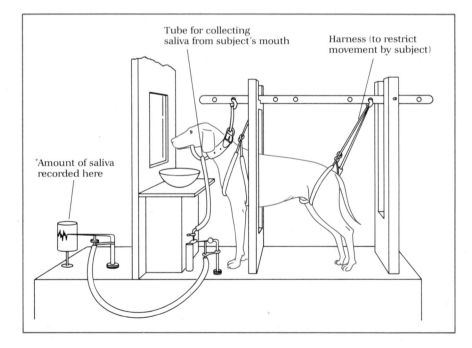

Tube for collecting saliva from subject's mouth

Harness (to restrict movement by subject)

Amount of saliva recorded here

FIGURE 7.2 Laboratory setup for conducting Pavlovian or classical conditioning experiments. After several repetitions in which a tone is sounded followed by the presentation of food, which causes a natural reflex—salivation—the dog will begin to salivate in increasing amounts at the sound of the tone even if food is no longer presented.

is termed the *unconditioned response* (UR), and the food is termed the *unconditioned stimulus* (US). We also need to select a neutral stimulus, such as a tone or bell, that does not ordinarily elicit the salivary response.

Now we are ready to replicate the experiment by surgically attaching a small capsule to an exposed part of the dog's salivary gland so that the amount of salivation can be measured. The hungry dog is then placed in a restraining harness in a soundproof laboratory where there will be no distractions (see Figure 7.2). The tone is sounded and, as might be predicted, the dog does not salivate. However, the dog does turn its head and shoulders toward the direction from which the tone is sounded, prick up its ears, and look attentive. This reaction to the tone is called an *orienting reflex*, which Pavlov sometimes called the "What-is-it? reflex." A number

FIGURE 7.3 Diagram of classical conditioning. The association between the food—unconditioned stimulus (US)—and salivation—unconditioned response (UR)—exists at the start of the experiment and does not have to be learned. The association between the tone—conditioned stimulus (CS)—and salivation—conditioned response (CR)—is learned. It arises through a pairing of the CS and US followed by the UR. The CR and UR resemble each other but may differ slightly.

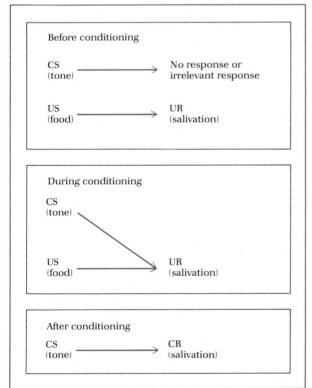

of investigators have noted that much of the orienting-reflex behavior that occurs after a CS is presented seems to function as preparation for the upcoming US (Zener, 1937; Wagner, Thomas, and Norton, 1967).

A short time after the tone is sounded the food is presented, and the dog does salivate. If we repeat this sequence of events several times, with the tone always preceding the food presentation, classical conditioning will result. The dog begins to salivate in increasing amounts at the sound of the tone even when the food is no longer presented. Learning has taken place, and we can describe the learning in the language used by investigators who employ classical conditioning techniques. The tone is now termed the *conditioned stimulus* (CS), and the salivary response to the tone alone is termed the *conditioned response* (CR). Usually the CR is very similar to the UR, but they are not identical. In salivary conditioning, for example, the UR is greater in volume and richer in digestive enzymes than the CR. What we have seen is the essence of classical conditioning: the dog has learned to associate a previously unrelated event, the sound of the tone, with salivation (see Figure 7.3).

Time Factors

One of the important factors in classical conditioning is the time interval between the two stimuli—the conditioned stimulus (tone) and the unconditioned stimulus (food). Time relationships define the types of classical conditioning. In *simultaneous conditioning*, the conditioned stimulus and the unconditioned stimulus are presented together at exactly the same time. This is not very effective. Conditioning is best when the conditioned stimulus precedes the unconditioned stimulus, although the time interval need not be large. In fact, an interval as short as 0.5 second, depending on the response being conditioned, often leads to very rapid conditioning. Classical conditioning also can be demonstrated with substantially longer intervals between the conditioned stimulus and the unconditioned stimulus. When the conditioned stimulus begins before the unconditioned stimulus and continues to the onset of the unconditioned stimulus, the resulting learning is termed *delayed conditioning*. This term is used because there is a delay between the presentation of the conditioned stimulus and

The Russian physiologist Ivan Petrovich Pavlov performed a series of experiments in classical conditioning that have become so well known that this form of learning is often called Pavlovian conditioning.

the appearance of the unconditioned stimulus. The offset of the conditioned stimulus either coincides with or follows the onset of the unconditioned stimulus. In another type, *trace conditioning*, the conditioned stimulus is presented briefly and then removed; then, after an interval, the unconditioned stimulus is presented. Trace conditioning is so named because some residue or "trace" of the conditioned stimulus is presumed still to be present when the unconditioned stimulus occurs. Generally, the shorter the interval between the conditioned stimulus and the unconditioned stimulus, the more effective the association will be (see Figure 7.4).

Essential Features and Measurement

Pavlov's relatively pure form of classical conditioning is a rather passive process for the learner. It requires no active participation by the subject; the response to be conditioned is an automatic reflex; presentation of the conditioned stimulus (tone) and unconditioned stimulus (food) are controlled by the experimenter. We can thus sum up the three essential features of classical conditioning:

1. A reflexive relationship exists between some stimulus (the US) and some response (the UR).
2. Prior to conditioning, there is some other stimulus, or potential conditioned stimulus (such as the tone), that does not elicit the unconditioned response but prepares the organism for the unconditioned stimulus to come.
3. Conditioning involves repeated pairings of the conditioned and unconditioned stimulus with the conditioned stimulus occurring a fixed interval before the unconditioned stimulus.

In classical conditioning there are two primary measures of the extent to which learning has occurred. One is the regularity with which the conditioned response occurs; the other is the intensity or magnitude of the conditioned response. These two variables are often plotted on a graph known as a learning curve, on which the vertical axis represents some measure of response strength and the horizontal axis represents learning trials (see lefthand graph in Figure 7.5). As you might expect, these measures often are closely related. As the salivary response occurred more regularly in Pavlov's dogs, for example, the number of drops of saliva also increased. An additional measure is the permanence of the conditioned response.

Extinction and Spontaneous Recovery

Pavlov found that, once a conditioned response has been well established, it can be weakened by continuously presenting the conditioned stimulus (the tone) without the unconditioned stimulus (food). He called this *extinction*, or weakening of the response (see Figure 7.5). Pavlov also found, however, that the conditioned response may not be completely extinguished even if it no longer occurs in one set of tests, or trials. If the animal is tested again a few days after extinction has been demonstrated, the conditioned stimulus again will often elicit the conditioned response although in weaker form. This phenomenon of partial recovery of the conditioned response following extinction has been called *spontaneous recovery*. The strength of a conditioned response is also demonstrated by the subject's response to similar, but not identical, stimuli.

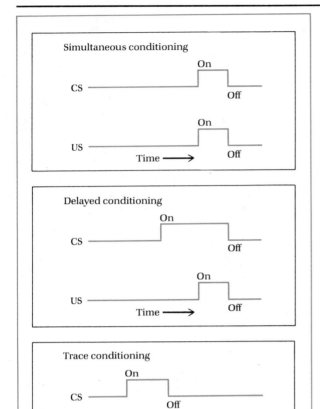

Generalization and Discrimination

The following experiment demonstrates a striking characteristic of classical conditioning. First, a dog is conditioned so that salivation occurs whenever a tone of a particular frequency or pitch is sounded. Interestingly, if that tone is changed to differing frequencies the dog will also produce the conditioned response, salivation. This phenomenon, in which similar stimuli evoke the conditioned response, is called *stimulus generalization.* As might be expected, however, generalization decreases as the stimuli become less similar to the original conditioned stimulus. In this experiment, for example, salivation would decrease as the tone sounded less

FIGURE 7.4 Time relationships define the types of classical conditioning. In simultaneous conditioning, the conditioned stimulus (CS) and the unconditioned stimulus (US) are presented together. In delayed conditioning, the conditioned stimulus (CS) precedes by at least several seconds the unconditioned stimulus (US), and then they continue to be present together. In trace conditioning, the conditioned stimulus (CS) is presented briefly and then removed, followed after a short interval by the unconditioned stimulus (US). Conditioning becomes progressively poorer in both delayed and trace conditioning as the CS-US interval increases.

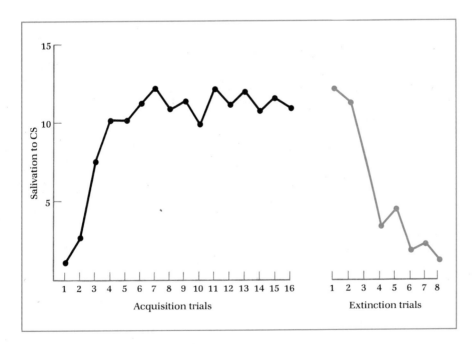

FIGURE 7.5 The graph on the left depicts the acquisition phase of a classical conditioning experiment. Drops of salivation in response to the conditioned stimulus are plotted on the vertical axis, and number of trials on the horizontal axis. After 16 acquisition trials the experimenter starts extinction, the results of which are presented in the graph on the right. The conditioned response decreases the more trials the conditioned stimulus is presented alone.

and less like the tone used to condition the dog (see Figure 7.6).

A classic but controversial study reported in 1920 by John B. Watson and Rosalie Rayner illustrates generalization of a conditioned response in humans. The chief investigator was Watson, an enthusiastic follower of Pavlov's work. Watson, who had hopes that Pavlovian conditioning techniques could be used to improve the quality of American education, was studying a particular conditioned response, fear or anxiety. In everyday life, certain irrational fears may be conditioned in humans—fear of snakes, for example. But Watson was the first to condition fear in a human in a laboratory.

His subject was Albert, an 11-month-old boy. Watson and his assistant, Rayner, placed Albert in a room with a gentle white rat. At first the boy petted the rat and showed no fear. Then, just as Albert was reaching for the animal, one of the experimenters stood behind the boy and made a loud noise by striking a steel bar with a hammer. Not surprisingly, the noise frightened Albert and he began to cry. The experimenters repeated this process several times, pairing the white rat and the loud noise, and Albert soon produced the conditioned response, fear, every time he saw the conditioned stimulus, the white rat (see Figure 7.7). Moreover, as we might expect from our experiment with the dog and tones of differing frequencies, Albert's fear of the white rat generalized to similar stimuli. When other white objects, such as a fur coat or a rabbit, were introduced into the room, they elicited the same fearful response. Albert's conditioned response seemed to generalize to any white, soft, and furry stimuli.

Other experiments have shown that stimulus generalization is not limited to stimuli related on one or more physical dimensions such as color or tone frequency. We can demonstrate this with a typical classical conditioning procedure that is based on a measure of emotional reaction known as the galvanic skin response (GSR). The galvanic skin response is a measure of changes in electrical conductivity in the palm of the hands. These changes result from the increase in sweat gland activity that typically accompanies an emotional response. The glavanic skin response is used as part of lie detector tests on the grounds that sweaty palms—and hence an emotional reaction to a particular question—might suggest guilt. In the psychologist's laboratory the galvanic skin response can be easily elicited by administering a mild shock

FIGURE 7.7 Depiction of John B. Watson's experiment in which he conditioned an infant, Albert, to fear a gentle white rat by striking a steel bar loudly each time the rat approached.

FIGURE 7.6 Stimulus generalization refers to the fact that similar stimuli will produce a conditioned response. Note, however, that the generalization decreases as the stimuli become less similar to the original conditioned stimulus (in this case a tone of 1000 Hz).

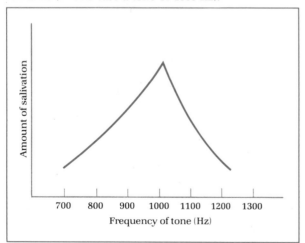

to a human subject's skin. The galvanic skin response can then be conditioned in the subject by pairing a flashing light with the shock. Let's say the light—the conditioned stimulus—is blue. After conditioning, a striking instance of generalization often occurs. The spoken word "blue" alone can cause the conditioned response, the galvanic skin response, to appear. This type of generalization, which is based on a meaningful relationship as opposed to a physical relationship between the conditioned stimulus (flashing blue light) and the test stimulus (spoken word "blue"), is called *semantic generalization* (Kimble, 1961).

Generalization, Pavlov noted, has obvious biological significance for an animal's survival. Natural stimuli that have survival value for an organism—for example, the sound of a predator—are not constant. Thus, generalization of stimuli enables an animal to flee even though the predator's sound may vary widely in pitch or loudness.

At the same time, extreme generalization—fleeing from any sound—would have little survival value for the animal. The animal obviously must make appropriate and relatively precise choices, or *discriminations*, among stimuli. Pavlov (1927) tested several procedures in his studies of discrimination. The first method involved repeated presentation of a single conditioned stimulus (tone) with the unconditioned stimulus (food). The dog failed to learn to discriminate one particular conditioned stimulus tone from other tones differing in frequency, even after a thousand pairings. The second procedure proved more effective. During the conditioning sessions Pavlov presented several tones differing in frequency. Only one of these, however, was followed by the unconditioned stimulus, food. With this procedure, which Pavlov called the *method of contrast*, precise and rapid discrimination among tones was produced.

Special Types of Conditioning

Classical conditioning can be investigated using variations on the basic stimulus-response pattern. Three such variations are higher-order conditioning, temporal conditioning, and taste aversion.

Higher-Order Conditioning Once the relationship between the conditioned stimulus and the unconditioned stimulus is strongly established, the conditioned stimulus can serve to condition other stimuli. Pavlov demonstrated this phenomenon, known as *higher-order conditioning*, by first condi-

tioning a dog to salivate at the sound of a bell and then training the dog to make a further association: the animal was presented with a light followed only by a bell (and not with the unconditioned stimulus of food). The animal began to salivate at the presence of the light alone (see Figure 7.8). The original

FIGURE 7.8 Diagram of higher-order conditioning of salivation from one conditioned stimulus to another. After traditional conditioning to a bell, another conditioned stimulus, a light, is introduced followed only by the bell (without the unconditioned stimulus of food). Eventually the light alone produces the conditioned response of salivation. The original conditioned stimulus (the bell) reinforced a new association in much the same way as the original unconditioned stimulus (food) had done.

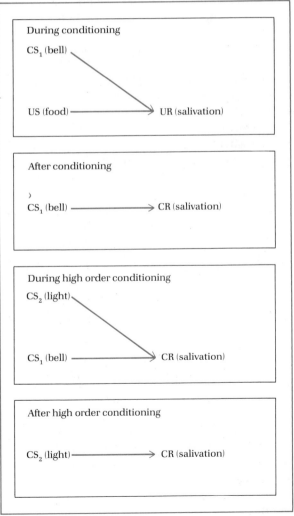

conditioned stimulus (the bell) functioned as the unconditioned stimulus for a new association in much the same way as had the original unconditioned stimulus (food).

Another example of higher-order conditioning can be found in a child's involuntary fear of fire. The child may have been accidentally burned or frightened by a parent's strong admonition about the danger of fire. Stimuli such as these can serve as unconditioned stimuli to bring about a conditioned response (fear of fire) in the child at the sight of fire alone.

Higher-order conditioning, unlike stimulus generalization, involves a new association with a new stimulus that may be quite different from the original conditioned stimulus. Higher-order conditioning, however, is fairly weak because the new unconditioned stimulus—for example, the light in Pavlov's experiment—is never paired with the original conditioned stimulus—food. The process of higher-order conditioning has been demonstrated only as far as third-order conditioning—using the light as the unconditioned stimulus for establishing yet another association. The process cannot go on indefinitely because the initial unconditioned stimulus on which the original association was based is no longer present, and the conditioned response to the earlier stimulus begins to extinguish. While the salivation response to the bell is established, salivation to the light extinguishes.

Temporal Conditioning A remarkable range of stimuli can serve as the conditioned stimulus—even the mere passage of time itself. Observations of such *temporal conditioning* in the dog were reported by Pavlov (1927). A dog was given food every 30 minutes. Then, after this pattern was well established, a feeding was omitted. Nonetheless, the dog salivated: it was as if the lapse of 30 minutes had acquired the properties of a conditioned stimulus.

As most parents can attest, temporal conditioning seems to occur quite regularly in hungry infants. Experimental evidence of this is reported by Donald Marquis (1941). In this study, one group of newborn infants was fed on a three-hour schedule for eight days and then was shifted to a four-hour schedule on the ninth day. Predictably, between the third and fourth hour on the ninth day, the general activity level of these infants was substantially higher than that of infants fed on a four-hour schedule since birth. It should be noted, however, that the infants may have eaten only enough to tide them

over for three hours and simply and naturally got hungry at the fourth hour. Caution is always necessary in interpreting the results of any experiment.

Taste Aversion Innate factors work together with conditioning factors in producing behavior changes. Suppose a rat is permitted access to a novel, sweet-tasting solution. Shortly after drinking, the animal is given an injection that will make it violently ill. When the animal is fully recovered, it is again permitted access to the same solution; this time, however, the rat avoids drinking it. In just one trial, the rat apparently has been conditioned to avoid drinking the solution even though the interval between the taste and illness is relatively long. In fact, rats can learn to avoid a flavor when the interval between taste and illness is as long as 12 hours (Revusky and Garcia, 1970).

Rapid learning of taste aversion is of considerable survival value to any species; what serves as the effective conditioned stimulus, however, may vary from one species to another. For example, quail made ill after drinking blue-colored sour water subsequently show a much stronger aversion to blue water than to sour water. In contrast, rats tested under the same conditions avoid sour water more than blue water (Wilcoxin, Dragoin, and Kral, 1971).

Taste aversion is also found in humans—as the following real-life story illustrates. The reader is cautioned not to repeat the procedure because it can be quite dangerous. The situation involved a teenage boy, call him Bill, who drank a fifth of Scotch whiskey in less than 30 minutes. Shortly thereafter, Bill passed out and remained unconscious for several hours. While unconscious he was violently ill and was still quite sick after regaining consciousness. For the next four to five years Bill experienced stomach contractions characteristic of retching whenever he smelled any kind of whiskey. However, this response did not generalize to beer and, perhaps unfortunately for Bill, the conditioned response to the smell of whiskey weakened in subsequent years and eventually disappeared.

Because the phenomenon of conditioned taste aversion shares many of the characteristics of classical conditioning—a conditioned stimulus (taste) followed by an unconditioned stimulus (gastrointestinal dysfunction)—we have included it as a special type of classical conditioning. However, because of the long time interval between the onset of the unconditioned response (illness) and the presentation of the conditioned stimulus plus other factors, many investigators believe that taste aversion is not classical conditioning at all but another type of learning altogether (McGowan, Hankins, and Garcia, 1972; Weisman, Hamilton, and Carlton, 1972). The debate is still going on.

Limitations of Classical Conditioning

Despite the widespread demonstrations of classical conditioning, it is important to keep in mind the limitations of this variety of learning. For the most part, the responses that have been classically conditioned are those largely controlled by the autonomic nervous sytem. In natural—as opposed to laboratory—settings, emotional reactions such as sweaty palms and increased heartbeat appear to be largely involuntary and hence can occur without conscious control.

Moreover, the conditioned response measured in most laboratory studies may be only one of several learned responses that occur. For example, responses characteristic of excitement, such as a speedup in heartbeat or respiration, may be elicited by the unconditioned stimulus—food—used to condition salivation. These responses may also be conditioned to appear at the presentation of a tone or other conditioned stimulus. A dramatic example of the multiple responses occurring in classical conditioning was reported from Pavlov's own laboratory. A dog, after it was released from the restraining harness, approached the harness, wagged its tail, and begged for food. This dog evidently had learned something during classical conditioning that was never part of the unconditioned response to food.

Although classical conditioning is a way of learning, it is a limited one. It is an unconscious, usually passive, process that does not involve an active acquisition of knowledge. For the kind of learning humans and animals need to cope with their environments, a different and more sophisticated process is needed. It can be called instrumental learning, operant conditioning, or, simply "trial and error."

Instrumental and Operant Conditioning

A gambler continues to play the slot machine even though it rarely pays off. A psychotic patient who has not spoken for 19 years begins to speak again. A circus seal balances a ball on its nose. These di-

verse behavior patterns result, according to many psychologists, from instrumental or operant conditioning. As distinct from a subject's role in classical conditioning, an individual "operates" on the immediate environment to achieve a goal and the response is "instrumental" in achieving the goal.

Instrumental Conditioning

In the 1890s, even before Pavlov had begun his investigations of classical conditioning, the American psychologist Edward L. Thorndike was studying another variety of learning. Pavlov was able to work with his dogs in a laboratory, but Thorndike, who was still a graduate student at Columbia University, had to improvise. He collected scores of stray cats from the streets and alleys of New York and took them to his quarters in a rooming house. There, using packing boxes, he constructed cages that he called "puzzle boxes." The puzzle confronting the cat was to find a way to open the box's latch. If the animal succeeded in pulling the string, it could escape and gain access to a bowl of food placed outside the box. Because the necessary response—pulling the string—was instrumental in obtaining the food, this variety of learning has been called *instrumental conditioning*.

Thorndike's vivid description of this form of learning was included in his doctoral dissertation:

> When put into the box the cat would show signs of discomfort and an impulse to escape from confinement (not a reaction to the sight of food, but only a blind attempt to escape). It tries to squeeze through any opening; it claws and bites at the bars and wire; it thrusts its paws out through any opening and claws at everything it reaches; it continues its efforts when it strikes anything loose and shaky; it may claw at things within the box. It does not pay very much attention to the food outside, but seems simply to strive instinctively to escape confinement.... Whether the impulse to struggle be due to an instinctive reaction to confinement or to an association, it is likely to succeed in letting the cat out of the box. The cat that is clawing all over the box in her impulsive struggle will probably claw the string or loop or button so as to open the door. (Thorndike, 1898)

In this quotation we see the basic elements of Thorndike's doctrine of learning by *trial and error*. The cat did not appear to solve the problem of escape in an orderly manner; rather, it responded almost at random until the correct response was made by chance. Thorndike did not deny insightful learning, especially in humans, but it was not assigned any special role in the learning process.

On subsequent trials, however, the cat took less and less time to find the latchstring and to escape successfully. Thorndike plotted the times required for escape on a graph: the first trial-and-error attempt might take nearly four minutes, but by the seventh trial the cat might succeed in only about 30 seconds (see Figure 7.9). As Thorndike described the process, "And gradually all the other nonsuccessful impulses will be stamped out and the particular impulse leading to the successful act will be stamped in by the resulting pleasure until, after many trials, the cat will, when put in the box, immediately claw the loop or button in a definite way."

The basic principle of learning by trial and error, according to Thorndike, was the *law of effect*. Rewards strengthened, or "stamped in," connections between stimuli and responses, whereas punishment "stamped out" such connections. Thorndike (1932) subsequently revised his position on punishment, concluding it had little or no effect on learning—an issue we will return to later in this chapter.

Operant Conditioning

During the late 1930s, research into instrumental conditioning took a new turn, and this form of learning took a new name. The Harvard psychologist B. F. Skinner (1938) called it *operant conditioning* because, in his pioneering experiments, the animal had to operate on the environment in order to produce a particular consequence such as obtaining food.

Skinner's early experiments in operant conditioning involved placing a rat in a chamber that has come to be known as a "Skinner box" (see Figure 7.10). The chamber was empty except for a food cup and small bar extending from one wall. The apparatus was designed so that the animal received a small pellet of food each time the bar was depressed. If the animal was deprived of food, it could be taught to press the bar to obtain the food pellets. When this happened, operant conditioning occurred. The learned behavior—bar pressing—was termed *operant behavior*.

Many investigators reserve the term *operant* for situations in which a subject is freely able to re-

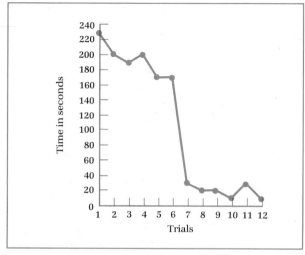

FIGURE 7.9 A plot of Edward L. Thorndike's experiment with a cat's attempt to escape from a puzzle box. The seventh trial shows a remarkable improvement in ability to solve the puzzle.

spond (Skinner's rat is free to press the bar at any time) and the term *instrumental* for situations in which the experimenter must initiate each trial that a subject experiences (Thorndike's cat could not start a new trial until it was again placed in the apparatus). Thus, Skinner's learning situation would be called operant learning and Thorndike's learning situation would be called instrumental learning.

Although the focus of the two researchers differed—Thorndike emphasized trial-and-error learning whereas Skinner emphasized the control of behavior—we can see the similarities in their experiments. In both instances the animals were required to play an active role—they had to perform an overt act to obtain reward—unlike the passive dogs in Pavlov's classical conditioning experiments. Moreover, the responses (escaping from Thorndike's cage, pressing the bar in the Skinner box) are instrumental or operant behaviors, unlike behaviors such as salivation, which require the presentation of specific stimuli. What is learned is *when* to perform the conditioned response.

One of the experimental advantages of Skinner's approach over Thorndike's is that the bar-pressing behavior can be brought under rather precise stimulus control. For example, a light can be placed above the bar and the animal rewarded for pressing the bar only when the light is turned on. Because this arrangement teaches the animal to discriminate by pressing only when the light is on, the light is called a *discriminative stimulus*. Discriminative stimuli set the occasion for responding.

Before beginning an operant conditioning experiment, the investigator must take into account the fact that the animal, say a rat, is apt to press the bar randomly even in the absence of reward. Therefore, it is necessary to establish a baseline or unstimulated norm of the rat's responses before the food is introduced. For example, the experimenter might count the number of times the rat presses the bar during a ten-minute interval in the absence of rewards. This number is termed the *operant level* of responding; it provides a baseline against which the extent of subsequent conditioning can be assessed.

The reward received during operant conditioning is known as reinforcement, which will be discussed in detail later in this chapter. Not surprisingly, the frequency of reinforcement—whether it occurs after every response, every other response, and so on—influences the rate of operant conditioning. The timing of the reinforcement is also important—at least in animals: the quicker the reward, the faster learning occurs. The significance of immediate reward to humans is more difficult to demonstrate. It no doubt plays a role in learning, but it is likely that knowing what one is being rewarded for is more important than the immediacy of the reward. Of course, immediate reward usually makes it clearer what the reward is for.

Similarities between Operant and Classical Conditioning

The procedures used to demonstrate these varieties of conditioning are quite different; nonetheless, many of the phenomena observed are the same. The learning curves of classical conditioning and operant conditioning are quite similar, as are the extinction curves. For example, an operant response can be extinguished by withholding reinforcement; the animal's response rate may then return to its preconditioning baseline, or operant level. A classically conditioned response often returns to previous levels. In addition, when an animal exposed to extinction training is returned to the operant chamber it may well show spontaneous recovery of the response without additional rewards. Spontaneous recovery also occurs in classical conditioning situations. Reexposure to the conditioned stimulus will produce the conditioned response. Relearning after extinction in both conditioning processes can be accomplished much more rapidly than the original learning.

As in classical conditioning, operant responses can be generalized to similar stimuli, meaning that discrimination training may be required to train an animal to respond to one stimulus but not to others. Although the notion of reward is more central in operant conditioning, it can be applied to classical conditioning as well. In the latter situation, presentation of the unconditioned stimulus can be seen as reinforcing the conditioned stimulus-conditioned response relationship. Thus, although the procedures used in operant and classical conditioning are quite different, many experimental manipulations have comparable effects in both situations. Further similarities will become apparent in subsequent sections of this chapter.

One main difference between the processes of classical conditioning and operant learning lies in the way that reinforcement is used and interpreted.

Reinforcement

The presentation of an unconditioned stimulus in contiguity (closeness) with the conditioned stimulus makes up the reinforcement aspect of classical conditioning. *Reinforcement* is often defined as the use of stimuli to increase the likelihood of re-

FIGURE 7.10 An experimental chamber, often called a "Skinner box," is used for many studies of operant conditioning. When the rat pushes the lever, a pellet of food automatically drops into the food tray.

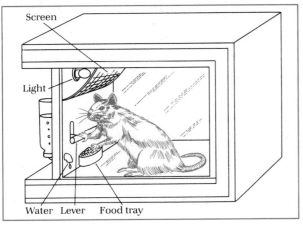

Screen

Light

Water   Lever   Food tray

sponses occurring before their presentation. There are, as we shall see, multiple types of reinforcers.

To begin with, there are two broad categories of reinforcement—primary and secondary. *Primary reinforcers* have usually been defined as those stimuli that meet biological needs of the organism—food when we are hungry, water when we are thirsty, and so on. However, the reinforcers that affect human behavior are more likely to be ones we have learned to value rather than those that satisfy our biological needs. These are termed *secondary reinforcers.*

Among the most effective secondary reinforcers in humans are money and praise. We value a secondary reinforcer such as money for many reasons,

FIGURE 7.11 Like human beings, chimpanzees can be trained to work for money (secondary reinforcement) that can be exchanged for food (primary reinforcement). The chimp shown here is about to put its money (a poker chip) into a "Chimp-O-Mat," which will dispense bananas or grapes. Chimps can be trained to work all day for poker chips if they have first learned that the poker chips can be used to obtain food.

but one reason is the obvious association with obtaining a primary reinforcer, food. This association is illustrated in laboratory experiments involving chimpanzees. In a now classic study, J. B. Wolfe (1936) taught chimpanzees the value of secondary reinforcers. Using a laboratory vending machine known as a Chimp-O-Mat, the chimps learn that by dropping tokens similar to poker chips into the machine, they will receive a food reward such as grapes (see Figure 7.11). Having learned this, the chimps can be conditioned to perform another task—pulling a lever—if they are given a secondary reinforcer—the tokens previously associated with getting food.

The effects of secondary reinforcers can be found in demonstrations of both classical and operant conditioning. Pavlov demonstrated that, once a dog had learned to salivate to a tone, the tone could then serve to condition salivation to a new conditioned stimulus such as a flashing light. In this instance of higher-order conditioning, the tone reinforced the relationship between the flashing light and salivation just as the food reinforced the original connection between tone and salivation.

Secondary reinforcement is readily demonstrated in operant conditioning. For example, suppose a rat learns to press a bar for food reward. Then suppose that, when the bar is depressed during training, the mechanism makes a noise when it releases the pellet of food. Now, because of the pairing of noise and food delivery, the noise itself will acquire the properties of a secondary reinforcer. That is, sounding the click following a response keeps the animal responding. This is easily shown during extinction by comparing resistance to extinction in animals that still hear the noise from the empty food mechanism with other animals who do not hear it because the mechanism has been disconnected.

Punishment and Negative Reinforcement

Now that we have described several types of learning involving the use of various types of reinforcement, it is appropriate to discuss reinforcement in more detail. First, let us make clear the often-misunderstood distinction between punishment and what psychologists call negative reinforcement. *Punishment* is pain or annoyance administered in an attempt to eliminate a particular behavior. *Negative reinforcement*, by contrast, results when a response leads to removal of an aversive stimulus called a negative reinforcer. In escape and avoidance (to be discussed later), the negative reinforcer is electric shock, and the dog learns to jump the partition in the shuttle box to escape from it or to avoid it. Escape from or avoidance of the shock thus serves the same purpose as would a "reward," or positive reinforcer: it increases the probability that the dog will perform the desired behavior. In this sense, escape from or avoidance of the shock is reinforcing.

Punishment, on the other hand, seems far less effective in learning situations. As we noted previously, that early advocate of punishment, Edward L. Thorndike, changed his views. He revised his original law of effect so that it excluded punishment as an influence on connections between stimuli and responses. This view was supported in subsequent research (Estes, 1944; Skinner, 1938), which appeared to indicate that, although punishment temporarily suppresses responding, it does not have long-lasting effects. In addition, it is clear that punishment often has unintended aversive consequences—such as creating hostility toward whoever administers it. In view of these facts, psychologists have generally emphasized reinforcing desirable behavior rather than punishing undesirable behavior.

It is true, of course, that punishment is effective in certain situations. For example, if punishment is used to suppress undesirable behavior while alternative behaviors are being reinforced, the outcome may be quite positive. It is also true that guidelines intended to make punishment more effective can be garnered from studies in the laboratory. These include the following: it should be as intense as possible; the delay between response and punishment should be as short as possible; punishment should be certain after each response; the punished response should not be rewarded in any way. These guidelines, however, are much easier to apply in the laboratory than in the everyday world.

Some of the problems associated with punishment are quickly evident if we consider a fairly typical example of adolescent misbehavior. A teenage boy begins drinking beer and whiskey. His parents strongly oppose his drinking and punish him in various ways if he is caught at it. Our guidelines for effective punishment would prescribe intensity, immediacy, certainty, and a complete absence of reinforcement. However, will the parents employ severe punishment and possibly incur the hostility of their son? How soon after drinking and how regularly following drinking can punishment

occur? Above all, how can the parents cope with the fact that the boy's drinking is reinforced by his peers, who consider it a sign of masculinity?

A major problem in assessing the effectiveness of both reinforcement and punishment is the difficulty in identifying which is which. One person's punishment may be another's reinforcement. To a child who feels neglected, for example, punishment by parents may seem welcome; their sudden attention serves as a reinforcement rather than a punishment and thus tends to reinforce misbehavior.

Schedules of Reinforcement

As we noted previously, much of the work in operant conditioning has focused on the control of behavior. An effective way to manipulate behavior is to manipulate the schedule under which reinforcement is provided. At first, an operant response is conditioned by reinforcing every occurrence of the response—a schedule known as *continuous reinforcement*. But after conditioning, the response can be maintained by a schedule of *partial reinforcement* under which it is only occasionally rewarded.

The concept of partial reinforcement is illustrated by the intermittent payoff of slot machines. Despite the low probability of payoff, people often continue playing for days on end.

In fact, very high rates of responding over long periods of time have been demonstrated under partial reinforcement. An unusual example of the power of partial reinforcement is the payoff of slot machines. Though a slot machine pays off only intermittently, people have been known to perform a peculiar operant response—pulling its lever—practically nonstop for days on end.

The effectiveness of partial reinforcement makes good sense from the standpoint of survival value. A predator stalking its prey is not always rewarded but, in order to survive, must keep at it.

Of the various forms of partial reinforcement that have been studied extensively, only a few basic schedules will concern us here.

Fixed Schedules Under a *fixed-ratio (FR) schedule* (see Figure 7.12), reinforcement is given only after a specific number of responses have been made. Fixed-ratio schedules produce very high and steady rates of responding. They resemble the piecework systems of payment used in some industries. Just as a rat may be rewarded only after 15 bar presses, a worker may get paid a certain amount for every 15 articles produced. However, if a rat experiences a long fixed ratio schedule, it takes a time out after each reinforcement—that is, it does not go back and press the bar immediately. But once the rat starts to press the bar again, it will do so at a high steady pace until the next reinforcement. This process occurs with human beings too.

FIGURE 7.12 Patterns of behavior that might typically occur under four simple schedules of reinforcement—fixed-ratio, fixed-interval, variable-ratio, and variable-interval. The steeper the lines, the higher the rate of responding.

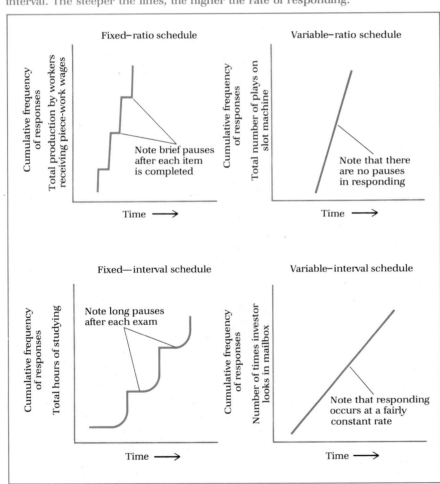

The failure of some people to show up for work on a Monday is analogous to the rat's pause, and once they get to work on Tuesday, they will work at a high steady pace the rest of the work week.

A different pattern of responding accompanies reinforcement schedules in which the reward depends on a lapse of time instead of the organism's behavior. In a *fixed-interval (FI) schedule,* (see Figure 7.12), reinforcement might follow the first response that occurs after one minute has elapsed since the last reinforced response. In this situation, the response rate drops to near zero following a reinforced response and then accelerates as the end of the next interval approaches.

Variable Schedules A *variable-ratio (VR) schedule* (see Figure 7.12) produces high and steady response rates. Although a variable-ratio schedule might require an overall average of 15 responses for reinforcement, the rate is varied so that, at one point, 5 unreinforced responses may precede a reinforced response while at another point 25 unreinforced responses may be required. If fixed-ratio and variable-ratio schedules of the same length are compared, the variable ratio schedule usually will produce higher and steadier (no pauses) rates of responding.

A *variable-interval (VI) schedule* (see Figure 7.12) is one in which the average interval might be one minute, although responses will be reinforced after time lapses of 5 seconds or 115 seconds. Interestingly, when a variable interval is employed, the response rate does not fluctuate as much as in the fixed-interval schedule because the organism cannot learn to anticipate when a particular interval will end. A variable-interval schedule produces the steadiest rate of responding of the four schedules discussed.

Variable-interval schedules function something like a prison supervisor who comes around occasionally to check on the guards on duty. Because the timing of appearances is not predictable, the guards are more likely to stay at their posts. If the supervisor arrived at fixed intervals, the guards might find a number of other things to do between appearances. In fact, research suggests that fixed-interval schedules may themselves encourage other behaviors that are quite excessive in nature. For example, rats were deprived of food but not water and were rewarded with food for bar pressing on a fixed-interval schedule. When water was freely available in the conditioning chamber the animals drank excessively, consuming nearly half of their body weight in water during a 3-hour session. This far exceeded the amount of water consumed in their home cage during an entire 24-hour period (Falk, 1971). Other examples of such schedule-induced excessive behaviors have been reported. That the excessive behavior is schedule-induced is indicated by the observation that water consumption returns to normal levels during extinction.

Reinforcement can be used to maintain behavior for long periods by first conditioning with continuous reinforcement and then switching to a partial reinforcement schedule. In this way it is no longer necessary to observe and reinforce each response; the desired behavior continues to occur without extinguishing.

Partial Reinforcement and Extinction
Acquisition training with partial reinforcement produces greater resistance to extinction than does continuous reinforcement. After training under partial reinforcement an animal will respond for a much longer period of time and respond more often in the absence of reward than after training under only continuous reinforcement. This phenomenon has been termed the *partial-reinforcement effect.*

This effect is partially explained by the similarity between extinction sessions and training sessions on a partial-reinforcement schedule. In partial-reinforcement training, animals experience periods of no reward that are comparable to the conditions during extinction sessions. While explanations of this sort have intuitive appeal, they are difficult to evaluate experimentally. For example, when animals are trained first on partial reinforcement and then on continuous reinforcement, they still show the partial-reinforcement effect during extinction when compared to animals trained only on continuous reinforcement (Jenkins, 1962; Theios, 1962). This effect holds even though the change in conditions between the end of training and extinction is the same for both groups of animals. The animals given initial training under partial reinforcement appeared to "remember" something about their initial experiences.

The possible importance of cognitive factors in explaining the partial-reinforcement effect is nicely illustrated in a study reported by Stewart Hulse

(1973). Hulse used a modified Skinner box in which the bar was automatically withdrawn after each response. This allowed separate trials in which a response could be either reinforced or not. At first, his rats were reinforced on a random 50 percent of the trials. Then they were shifted to a schedule in which every other response was reinforced. Finally, training was concluded under continuous reinforcement. The surprising result was that these animals extinguished even faster than animals trained only on continuous reinforcement. A possible explanation for this result is that the animals "noticed" that reinforcement was becoming increasingly predictable during training, changing from random, to single alternation, to continuous reinforcement. If this indeed was the case, the animals may have become increasingly attuned to the likelihood of reinforcement and more readily set to discriminate the beginning of extinction.

The learning brought about by conditioning and reinforcement goes far beyond the laboratory: practical goals and applications abound. A common use of reinforcement in learning can be found in behavior shaping.

Behavior Shaping

The training of novel behavior or sequences of actions—ones obviously not normally performed by the organism—is called *behavior shaping*. Behavior shaping typically is accomplished by breaking up the desired sequence of action into small steps and then reinforcing the animal as it approaches closer and closer to the proper response in each step. This method of *successive approximations* is evident in training household pets to do tricks. For example, a dog can be taught to retrieve the newspaper by successively reinforcing the animal with food for coming closer and closer to the paper, withholding reinforcement until the dog picks up the paper with its mouth, and finally reinforcing it for returning with the paper. At any given point in the sequence, the desired next step is reinforced and all others are extinguished.

The simple procedures involved in behavior shaping have been applied to teaching elaborate tricks and complex action sequences to thousands of animals. Porpoises have been taught to jump through hoops and circus seals to play musical instruments. A pig has learned to clean house, turn on a television set, and eat breakfast at a table. In fact, psychologists Keller Breland and Marian Breland have turned behavior shaping into a large business, Animal Behavioral Enterprises, and have trained thousands of animals of many species for television shows and tourist attractions around the world.

Techniques of behavior shaping are also applied in the human world: teaching machines, computer-assisted instruction, and other types of programmed learning use the method of successive approximations. A learning problem is broken down into steps. At each stage the student who makes the appropriate response by providing the correct answer receives immediate reinforcement—perhaps praise from the teaching machine. In addition, behavior shaping has been used as a therapeutic technique. Obesity, stuttering, and a variety of other problems have been treated successfully with such methods. In one notable instance a schizophrenic who had not spoken for 19 years was taught to speak again. Using chewing gum as the reward, the therapist reinforced a series of successive approximations by the patient—first, facing the therapist, then communicating through head gestures, and, finally, speaking (Isaacs, Thomas, and Goldiamond, 1960).

Successful behavior shaping is contingent on the effectiveness of the reinforcement. Birdseed would be effective in training pigeons to play Ping Pong; it would not be much help in training a dog to retrieve the newspaper. Even when the reinforcement is known to be effective for a particular organism, shaping may not be possible. Several interesting

Procedures involved in behavior shaping have been applied in teaching complicated tricks such as hoop jumping to porpoises.

cases of conditioning failures are reported by the animal trainers Breland and Breland (1961). One example involved their frustrating attempts to teach a raccoon to deposit coins in a piggy bank. The raccoon seemed to be a good candidate for the task. It normally conditions readily, has a good appetite, and possesses paws quite similar to the hands of primates. Using food for reinforcement, the Brelands had no difficulty in teaching the raccoon the first step in the sequence—picking up a coin. Then the troubles began. Once the coin was picked up, the raccoon behaved in a most miserly fashion, clutching and rubbing the coin before finally placing it in a metal box. And when the Brelands indicated that the raccoon was to drop two coins in the box prior to reinforcement, it became totally uncooperative, spending several minutes rubbing the coins together and dipping then in and out of the container. Making the raccoon hungrier only increased the "misbehavior."

The Brelands concluded that the raccoon was engaged in a natural response pattern known as "washing behavior," which is normally exhibited when the animal cleans shellfish for food. This instinctive behavior overrode the powerful inducement of food. Similarly, the inborn tendencies of pigs to root for food and of chickens to scratch for it sometimes foiled efforts to shape their behavior. When these reactions are activated in a given species, reinforcement no longer exerts its usual influence. The raccoon and other species cannot be trained to perform arbitrary actions when more basic instinctive reactions are aroused.

Superstitious Behavior

In conventional behavior shaping, as we have seen, delivery of the reinforcement is contingent on performance of the desired response. Another type of shaping has been identified in which a learned response results when there is no contingency between the response and reinforcement.

The setting for the experiment is one widely used in operant conditioning: a Skinner box with a food hopper and, on the wall, a small round disk that pigeons are taught to peck. Suppose a hungry but inexperienced pigeon is put in the box and provided with grain every 12 seconds no matter what the bird does. Under these conditions, Skinner (1948) reported that the pigeons tended to repeat whatever they happened to be doing when the reinforcement occurred—wing flapping, walking in circles, and so on. Because the responses were not

instrumental in obtaining food but coincidental with it, he referred to them as "superstitions."

The resemblance to superstitious behavior among humans seemed obvious. Athletes, especially, act out little rituals of superstition that they associate with past success. Basketball players wear the same socks game after game; baseball players stepping into the batter's box tug their caps, dig holes with their spikes, and go through other such rituals. This behavior has been reinforced in the past by coincidental success just as Skinner presumed the antics of his pigeons were reinforced by the coincidental arrival of food.

Although it is true that superstitious behavior in humans may sometimes result from such coincidental rewards, subsequent research has cast some doubt on Skinner's original interpretation of his pigeon's actions. Two other researchers, (Staddon and Simmelhag, 1971) repeated Skinner's experiment but ran their pigeons for many sessions. They noted that the birds eventually developed stereotyped responses after being fed; however, as the time for the next feeding approached, they were likely to engage in pecking responses directed at the food hopper. That is, as the time for feeding approached, the pigeons responded in a manner characteristic of the unconditioned response of eating even though the pecking response had nothing to do with the birds being fed.

Autoshaping

Now suppose the experiment described above is repeated, but this time the round disk is illuminated for a few seconds prior to the delivery of food. Under these conditions the pigeons rapidly learn to peck at the lighted disk. This phenomenon has been called *autoshaping* (automatic shaping). That is, the pecking response is automatically shaped by establishing a contingency between the lighted disk and reinforcement, even though the pecking response does not produce the reinforcement. In fact, simply pairing the illuminated disk with food delivery (the conditions for autoshaping) results in more rapid conditioning of the pecking response than is found with the more traditional method of behavior shaping through successive approximations.

The interesting aspect of these observations is that what initially appeared to be a demonstration of operant conditioning of "superstitious" behavior now seems to be a form of classical conditioning. Notice that the observations of J. E. R. Staddon and V. L. Simmelhag are strikingly similar to Pavlov's observation of temporal conditioning discussed earlier in this chapter. Just as Pavlov's dogs learned to salivate "on time," these pigeons learned to peck "on time."

Other experimental findings support the interpretation that autoshaping is a form of classical conditioning rather than an arbitrary response that just happened to be reinforced. An autoshaped response of pecking at an illuminated disk is different in form depending on whether the bird is hungry and food is provided or the bird is thirsty and water is provided. When autoshaped pecks are based on water, the pigeon appears to be trying to drink the disk. Autoshaped pecks based on food appear to be eating motions. If access to a sexually receptive mate follows illumination of the disk, the pigeons will "court" the disk: they coo at it just as they would a prospective mate. In each of these cases the autoshaped response is not at all arbitrary: the response is intimately related to the reward, even though it does not produce the reinforcement. Finally, it should be noted that the contingency between the lighted disk and reinforcement is critical if autoshaping is to occur. Thus, if food is provided when the disk is not illuminated as well as when it is, autoshaped pecking will not occur (Jenkins, 1973). It appears that for autoshaping to occur, the lighted disk must serve to signal a forthcoming reinforcement. Combinations of classical and instrumental conditioning are also found in other forms of learning such as escape and avoidance.

Escape and Avoidance Learning

Suppose a dog is placed in a shuttle box, a rectangular box with a low partition dividing the box into two sections. Let us further suppose that electric shock is delivered through the grid floor of the box and that the animal can escape shock by jumping over the partition to the other side of the box. Learning to jump the partition to escape shock is termed *escape learning*.

Now suppose a tone is sounded 10 seconds before each shock delivery so that the dog can avoid the shock by jumping the partition whenever the tone is heard. This type of learning is termed *avoidance learning*, and it involves a combination of classical and instrumental conditioning. A natural unconditioned response to shock is the emotional response of fear. During avoidance learning the fear response elicited by shock becomes conditioned to the tone. Once this stage of conditioning occurs, the fear response can serve as a stimulus for the instrumental avoidance response of jumping the partition to reach the "safe" side of the shuttle box. Thus the classically conditioned fear response to the tone serves as the stimulus for the instrumental avoidance response; reduction of fear following a jump reinforces the response of jumping (see Figure 7.13).

The procedures of avoidance learning have been used extensively in recent years to test an important new point of view about classical conditioning. This idea, initially developed by Robert Rescorla and Richard Solomon (1967), posits a much more cognitive interpretation of classical conditioning. Organisms learn to predict the occurrence of the unconditioned stimulus on the basis of the occurrence of the conditioned stimulus (the tone). The dog, for example, learns to predict that the conditioned stimulus (tone) signals the imminent presentation of the unconditioned stimulus (shock). This idea does not deny conditioning of a response such as fear but rather shifts the emphasis to the more cognitive notion of predictability of events.

FIGURE 7.13 An idealized graph to show the acquisition of active avoidance learning. Responses with latencies greater than 5 seconds are escape responses; those with latencies less than 5 seconds are avoidance responses.

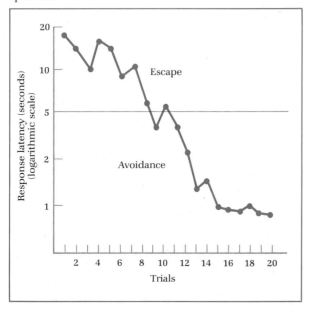

Tests of this idea involve training dogs in avoidance learning in the same manner that we described earlier. Then, after avoidance learning, the dogs are placed in situations where they receive unavoidable shocks. The shock always follows presentation of a high-frequency tone. Occasionally a lower-frequency tone is also presented, but it is never followed by shock. Now we return the dogs to the shuttle box. This time the two different tones are presented, but no shocks are administered.

What do you think the dogs would do under these conditions? In an experiment very similar to the one we have described, the animals jumped the shuttle box partition three times as often as their operant level, or baseline rate, when the high-frequency tone was presented. When the lower tone was presented, frequency of jumps dropped to near zero. When the tones were terminated, response rate gradually returned to the baseline level (Maier, Seligman, and Solomon, 1969).

These results support a highly cognitive interpretation of the predictive properties of the two stimuli. In effect, presentation of the high tone served as a "danger" signal; presentation of the lower tone served as a "safe" signal. The dogs apparently had learned that the lower tone was a reliable predictor of a time period safe from shocks.

The Predictability Hypothesis Other experiments have tested an important implication of the *predictability hypothesis*. This implication is that classical conditioning will not occur unless the conditioned stimulus serves as a reliable basis for predicting the occurrence of the unconditioned stimulus. An appropriate test would be to train three groups of animals in avoidance learning and then expose them to unavoidable shock. For the first group the shock is reliably signaled by a tone. For the second group the shock is always preceded by a tone but sometimes the tone is sounded without the shock follow-up. For the third group, the shock is sometimes preceded by a tone, but there are tones not followed by shock and shocks not preceded by a tone.

In which groups would you predict that fear conditioning actually occurs? According to our hypothesis, it should occur in the first group because the tone is a reliable predictor of shock. It should also occur in the second group because the shock never comes without being preceded by the tone warning signal, although some tone presentations are not followed by shock. But in the third group,

conditioning should not occur because th[an unreliable predictor of shock. These basic predictions have been confirmed in several experiments (Schwartz, 1978). Thus there is considerable support for the hypothesis that in classical conditioning the conditioned stimulus—in this case, the tone—must serve as a reliable basis for predicting the unconditioned stimulus—shock.

Learned Helplessness Avoidance learning depends upon the ability of the organism to control its environment. The dog learns that its response—leaping over the partition in the shuttle box—will avoid electric shock. Suppose, however, that inexperienced dogs are placed in a situation over which they have no control: they are subjected to a series of brief, intense shocks that cannot be avoided. This painful experience strongly affects their future capability for avoidance learning.

Investigators did, in fact, subject a group of dogs to unavoidable shock and then placed them in a shuttle box for avoidance training. The dogs now could avoid shock if they jumped over the partition within a specified period of time. Not many did. Only one-third of the dogs showed avoidance learning. By contrast, among a control group of dogs not previously exposed to unavoidable shock, 94 percent successfully demonstrated avoidance learning (Seligman, Maier, and Solomon, 1971).

For the dogs who were unable to learn the avoidance response after being exposed to unavoidable shocks, it was as if they had concluded that "nothing they do matters." The investigators termed this phenomenon *learned helplessness* (see Figure 7.14). In other experiments, learned helplessness occurred even when the dogs were given warning. For example, during both the unavoidable shock and the avoidance-learning situations, a tone preceded the shock. Inasmuch as the tone reliably predicted the shock, it should have served as a warning signal to the dogs; nonetheless, they seemed helpless to escape. The experimenters found that learned helplessness could be overcome if they actually pulled the dogs back and forth over the partition. After being given that helping hand, the dogs were able to learn avoidance (Seligman, Maier, and Geer, 1968).

It is significant that when dogs are given avoidance training before being subjected to unavoid-

219

able shocks, learned helplessness does not occur. This is another illustration of the powerful influence exerted by prior experience in determining what is learned in a given situation.

Learned helplessness has been demonstrated in humans as well as in a variety of animals and may have important implications for understanding several aspects of human behavior (Seligman, 1975). It has been suggested, for example, that learned helplessness may account for some cases of chronic failure in school: students who have failed often in the past may come to feel that nothing they do in school will enable them to avoid further failures. Moreover, as we will see in Chapter 14, the striking similarities between the behavior of the helpless dogs and that of some humans suggest new insights into one of the most common emotional disorders, depression. Depressed individuals often behave as if they think that "nothing they do matters."

The avoidance learning discussed in this section contains elements of both classical conditioning and operant conditioning. The tone (conditioned stimulus) prior to the electric shock (unconditioned stimulus) leads to the dogs' fear reaction (unconditioned response). The next step of jumping to the other, safe side of the box demonstrates the dogs' learning an instrumental response. The "reward" of avoiding the shock and consequently reducing fear

is the reinforcement, a subject to which we now return.

Factors Affecting Reinforcement

As with many other aspect of our lives, learning through reinforcement involves a complex interaction between the learner, the task or situation, and what the learner brings to the situation both in terms of species-specific characteristics and past experiences. Behavior that might at first seem bizarre often becomes perfectly logical if we understand the prior experiences of a person or animal.

A graphic illustration of this can be found in a report by James Barrett (1978), who worked in the laboratory using squirrel monkeys. These monkeys, on a five-minute, fixed-interval schedule of reinforcement, showed the same pattern of bar pressing whether the last event in each interval was "reward" (the presentation of food) or punishment (an intense electric shock). After each presentation of food or shock, the monkeys responded at a low rate that then increased steadily as the time for the next "reward" approached (see Figure 7.15).

At first glance these response patterns seem incomprehensible; it is as if the monkeys could not

FIGURE 7.15 Performance of squirrel monkeys under five-minute fixed-interval schedules of reinforcement. The first response after five minutes either produced a food pellet (top) or an electric shock (bottom). In both cases, patterns of responding were comparable regardless of the consequent event.

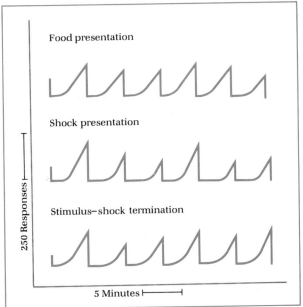

FIGURE 7.14 Results of an experiment in learned helplessness. The rapid rise in the solid line shows how quickly normal dogs learned how to cope with an electric shock delivered in a shuttle box, as explained in the text. The shaded line shows the very different behavior of animals that had acquired learned helplessness and, therefore, seemed incapable of learning how to do anything about the shock.

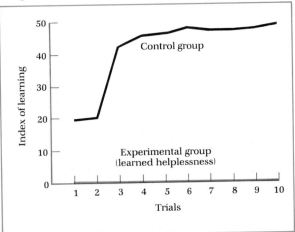

tell reward from punishment. But information about the monkeys' prior experiences makes their behavior more understandable. These animals had previously been trained to avoid shock by bar pressing. They had learned that pressing the bar would postpone the shock for 25 seconds and that not pressing the bar would lead to shocks every 5 seconds. Once we know this, the monkey's behavior on the fixed-interval schedule makes more sense. Having previously learned that bar pressing postpones shock, they continued to press the bar although this response no longer worked. Using human terms, we might say the monkeys concluded that even though shock was no longer totally avoidable by pressing the bar, at least the shock occurred only every so often. The monkeys could learn that bar pressing was no longer effective only if they were willing to endure the possibility of more frequent shocks.

Latent Learning

Latent learning refers to learning that occurs without any apparent reinforcement. *Apparent* is a key adjective because some psychologists have argued that no learning takes place without reinforcement; in their view, reinforcement is there but may not be readily observable (Hull, 1952). Evidence for latent learning was provided by a classic experiment (Tolman and Honzik, 1930) in which three groups of rats were run in a complex maze (see Figure 7.16). Group one was always reinforced with food in the goal box. Group two was never reinforced with the food. Group three was not reinforced until the beginning of the eleventh day. Until that point the performance of groups two and three was virtually identical: no special learning was evident. However, after the introduction of the food reinforcement, the third group quickly matched the performance of the first group. Evidently, the third group had learned a great deal about the maze without apparent reinforcement.

Although this experiment did not conclusively establish the existence of latent learning, it strongly suggested that learning can take place without reinforcement. It also showed that prior learning will not be manifested in performance without appropriate incentives.

As the preceding discussions indicate, the analysis of learning in terms of the phenomena of conditioning has been popular in psychology for a very long time. This analysis has proved to be quite successful in providing us with an understanding of a variety of learned behaviors. It has also provided the basis for a number of practical applications. Conditioning principles form the basis of a popular type of psychotherapy known as behavior modification (see Chapter 15). These same principles have provided a strong impetus for the development of systems for programmed instruction. As we have already seen, animal training techniques are almost exclusively based on principles established in the study of conditioning. Despite these successes, most psychologists believe that conditioning principles alone are not sufficient to explain many important aspects of learning.

Cognition and Learning

In various conditioning phenomena we have seen a number of instances in which cognitive factors—perception and knowledge—influence conditioning. These cognitive influences are most likely to arise in conditioning situations when memory structures established through prior experience determine the way new experiences are interpreted. Instances of these influences include the partial-reinforcement effect irregardless of whether learned helplessness develops, the importance of conditioned stimulus-unconditioned stimulus predictability in classical conditioning and latent learning. As you might expect, cognitive factors play a major role in situations having little to do with conditioning.

Insight Experiments

An early example of cognitive analysis can be seen in Wolfgang Köhler's work on *insight* in learning. Around 1913 he began a series of experiments with apes that demonstrated an important role for insight in problem-solving tasks. Köhler's basic argument with previous experiments such as Thorndike's was that they revealed only trial-and-error behavior because the tasks employed did not encourage insightful solutions. He argued that, with more appropriate tasks, insight in the form of novel (unpracticed) solutions would be quite common.

Köhler (1925) described the problem-solving behavior of apes in situations that were more or less natural for them. One famous example was that of the ape Sultan, who was unable to reach food with either of two short sticks but solved the problem by joining the sticks together. In another example the animal piled boxes on top of one another in order to reach food suspended from the ceiling (see Figure 7.17).

The ability of these apes to repeat these solutions without difficulty was taken as evidence that the original solution was not a random trial-and-error affair. This does not mean that such insightful solutions might not be facilitated by random behavior, but that the random behavior involves intelligent groping toward a solution and not a blind thrashing about, as Thorndike had implied (see Figure 7.18).

Insight during learning is a common phenomenon in humans, often associated with an "aha" experience. Such insightful solutions are not only readily repeated but also can be applied in new situations in which the solution is not specifically tied to the circumstances of initial learning. What is learned is a cognitive relationship between the re-

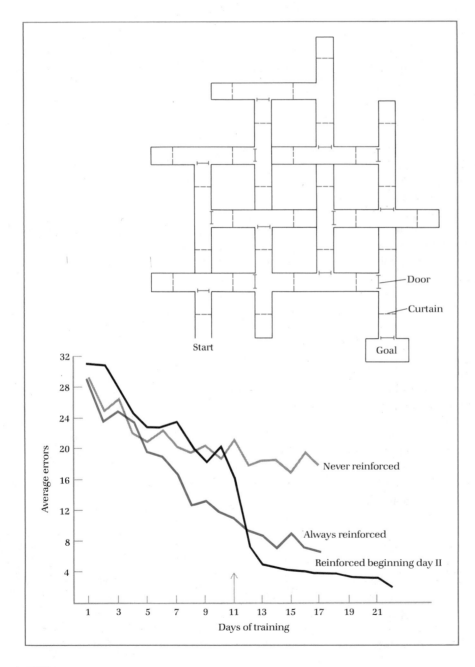

FIGURE 7.16 Latent learning in a complex maze. Three groups of rats were run through a maze similar to the one shown, containing both curtains and one-way doors. The number of errors made by each group is shown in the graph. Group I never got food at the goal box and after several days of training continued to make a considerable number of errors. Group II always got food at the goal box and made fewer and fewer errors progressively over several days of training. Group III, of primary interest, got no food at the goal box until the eleventh day (arrow), after which reinforcement was always present, and its performance quickly matched that of Group II.

sponses and the goal and not just a conditioned response.

Learning Abstract Concepts

A *concept* refers to the properties or relationships common to a class of objects or ideas. Concepts vary widely in terms of both concreteness and complexity. A triangle is a concept, a quite simple one; abstract ideas such as freedom and justice are concepts as well. Much of what we learn consists of concepts. When you finish reading this book, we hope you will have learned a large number of concepts. *Concept learning* is a way of ordering our experience and our perceptions of the world around us. Concepts enable us to grasp the important similarities between things while ignoring the irrelevant details.

FIGURE 7.17 Representation of one of Wolfgang Kohler's insight experiments, in which a chimpanzee stacked boxes on top of each other to reach food suspended from the ceiling.

Concepts are learned in a variety of ways. Many of the concepts we learn are directly taught to us by parents, friends, and teachers. Concepts also are learned through reading or by exposure to radio and television. In fact, almost every activity we engage in provides opportunities to learn new concepts or to modify previously learned concepts.

In the following chapter we will examine in some detail the nature of the memory structures that result from learning concepts, and the way these structures relate to one another. At this point in our discussion of cognitive aspects of learning, let us simply consider one experiment that deals with the learning of an abstract concept. There are two important things to note about this experiment. The first is that the concept that is learned is one the learners are never actually exposed to but one they learn nevertheless. The second is that the experiment is only one of many that show that such abstract concepts are learned, even though little is known as yet about the way they are learned.

The experiment to be considered did not involve the learning of a particular concept, such as a triangle or square, per se. Rather the experimenters, John Bransford and Jeffrey Franks (1971), presented a series of stimulus objects under the guise of an

FIGURE 7.18 Theoretical curves illustrating the relationship between speed of problem solving and degree of prior practice. According to trail-and-error theory, solution speed gradually increases with practice. According to insight theory, it increases on an all-or-none basis, independent of practice.

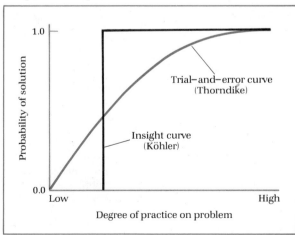

Two characteristics of words are often used as aids in learning and remembering information. One characteristic is acoustic—what the word sounds like. The other is imaginary—what visual representation the word conjures up in the mind. These aspects have been combined by two Stanford University psychologists, Richard C. Atkinson and Michael R. Raugh, to create a systematic method for learning the vocabulary of a foreign language. Known as the *keyword method*, it has been effectively applied in experiments using Russian and Spanish as the foreign languages.

The keyword method divides the learning of vocabulary into two stages. In the first stage, the subject hears the foreign word being pronounced and sees a translation of it along with an English keyword that sounds like the foreign word or some part of it. For example, the Russian word for building, *zdánie*, is pronounced somewhat like "zdawn-yeh," with emphasis on the first syllable. A logical keyword would be "dawn." In the second stage, the learner forms a mental image that links the keyword to the meaning of the foreign word. The image linking the keyword "dawn" with the meaning of *zdánie* might be a mental picture of the pink light of dawn being reflected in the windows of a tall building.

For their test of the keyword method in learning Russian vocabulary, Atkinson and Raugh (1975) employed 52 Stanford University undergraduates, 26 males and 26 females. All spoke English as their native language and none had previously studied Russian. The subjects were assigned to the experimental and control groups randomly except for the constraint that each group was to contain an equal number of males and females. The task for both groups was to learn 120 Russian words, which were presented in series of 40 words on each of three successive days. The experimental group used the keyword method; the control group was simply presented with the word and its meaning in English.

To ensure standardization, the entire experiment was conducted under computer control. A display scope gave subjects their instructions and, while the recorded Russian word was pronounced over their headphones, showed the English translation and—in the case of the experimental group only—the keyword. After being presented with the 120 Russian words over a three-day period, the subjects were given a comprehensive test. In addition, although they had not been forewarned about a subsequent test, the subjects were called back any time from 30 to 60 days later to take a randomized repeat of the comprehensive test.

The results indicated that the keyword method had proved highly effective. On the first comprehensive test, given after the three days of learning, the keyword subjects scored 72 percent correct; on the other hand, the control subjects scored only 46 percent correct. On the later test the keyword group also performed better, 43 percent correct compared to the control group's 28 percent correct.

A breakdown of the results from the first comprehensive test is presented in the table below. The table shows the probability of a correct response as a function of the day on which the word was studied, the sex of the subject and the group (keyword or control) to which he or she was assigned.

Interestingly, as the table indicates, females in both the keyword and control groups performed significantly better than their male counterparts. Although this implies female superiority in learning a foreign vocabulary, the authors point out that the subjects were volunteers and not a deliberately selected sample; thus, the results may have stemmed from a sampling error rather than from actual differences between males and females.

Study day	Keyword			Control		
	Male	Female	Mean	Male	Female	Mean
Day 1	.55	.73	.64	.27	.40	.33
Day 2	.63	.76	.70	.38	.47	.43
Day 3	.80	.82	.81	.60	.67	.63
Mean	.66	.77	.72	.42	.51	.46

Source, R. C. Atkinson and M. R. Raugh, "An Application of the Mnemonic Keyword Method to the Acquisition of a Russian Vocabulary," *Journal of Experimental Psychology: Human Learning and Memory*, 104 (1975): 130.

immediate memory experiment and subsequently used a recognition test as a basis for inferring what had been learned. Let us first consider the way in which stimulus materials were constructed.

The investigators began by selecting an arbitrary configuration consisting of four common shapes as a prototype. The prototype could be modified using a set of rules called transformation rules. One of the prototypes used, along with examples of the transformation rules, is shown in Figure 7.19. For example, applying the left-right reversal rule to the prototype results in the configuration shown just below the prototype.

The stimulus objects used in this experiment were configurations obtained by applying one or more transformations to the prototype. When two or more transformations were used, they were applied successively. For example, the prototype might first be modified using the left-right reversal rule. The resulting configuration could then be modified using the right-top-bottom reversal rule, and then the deletion rule could be applied. The resulting configuration, shown in Figure 7.19, is said to be three transformational steps away from the prototype. Configurations ranging from one to four transformations from the prototype were constructed for this experiment.

A subset of these configurations, but not including the prototype, was presented during the learning phase. Each stimulus object was presented for 5 seconds, followed by a short distractor task. The learners were then asked to reproduce the configuration they had just seen. This procedure was continued until each stimulus object had been presented twice.

In the recognition test a large number of configurations, including the prototype, were presented one at a time. The learners were asked to indicate whether or not each configuration had been presented during the learning phase and how confident they were of their answer. Other than the prototype, the configurations presented ranged from one to four transformations from the prototype. However, none of these configurations was actually presented during the learning phase.

The learners were most confident that they had seen the prototype before. Responses to the other configurations reflected the number of transformations applied to the prototype; that is, the configurations only one transformation away from the prototype were judged as next most likely to have been seen before. The further a configuration was from the prototype, the greater was the likelihood that it would be called a new one. However, the responses indicated that the learners thought that most of the configurations had been presented previously.

Franks and Bransford viewed their findings as indicating that what was learned was the prototype and the transformation rules rather than the specific configurations presented during the learning phase. Thus it appears that individuals are capable of abstracting a concept (the prototype) that was not presented as well as rules that were never presented formally. It should also be noted that these results cannot be explained on the basis of simple frequency with which the four shapes were presented.

Another study (Spear, 1972) further suggests that learning specific configurations is not necessary for abstraction of the prototype and rules to occur. Using essentially the same task as Franks and

FIGURE 7.19 Sample of visual forms used by John Bransford and Jeffrey Franks to demonstrate the learning of abstract concepts.

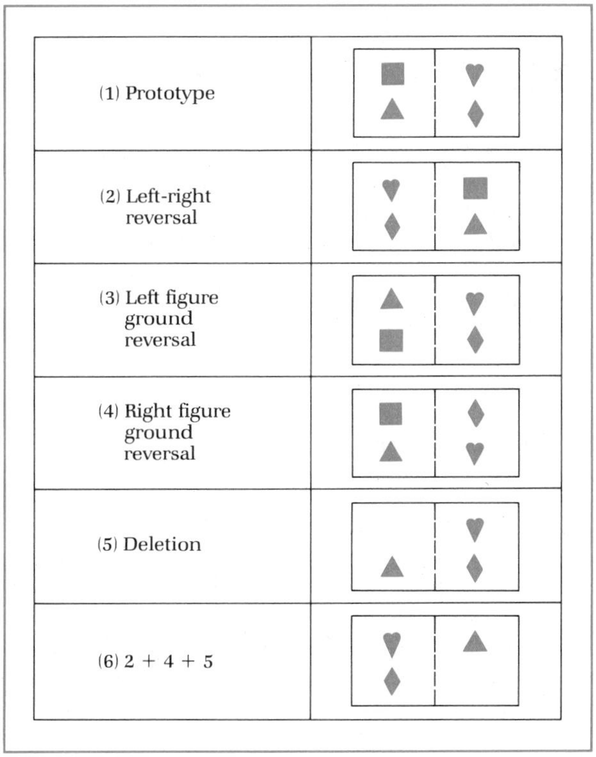

Bransford, N. E. Spear compared a group of severely brain-damaged people with a normal group. The recognition results for both groups were comparable to those noted above. However, she also evaluated performance in reproducing the stimulus configurations as they were presented during the learning phase. As expected, the normals were essentially perfect, but the brain-damaged people did very poorly. Thus, learning the configurations presented does not seem to be necessary for the abstraction of concepts involving prototypes to take place.

Motor Learning

Cognitive approaches to learning often place considerable emphasis on the establishment of, or modification of, cognitive structures during learning. In the case of motor learning the important cognitive structures are those referred to as motor programs. The existence of such programs is inferred from the nature of motor performance; however, before we consider motor programs further, let us first examine motor learning in more detail.

Many of the varieties of learning previously discussed in this chapter involve the body's motor

FOCUS: Observational Learning

The tendency of humans and many animals to learn by imitation is summed up by the adage, "Monkey see, monkey do." Particularly in the young, observational learning obviously is one of the most important varieties of learning. Children learn not only by imitating what they see but also by copying what they hear. The latter is evident whenever we listen with astonishment while a youngster, not old enough to understand the meaning, utters an explosive string of four-letter expletives.

Examples of observational learning among the young abound. By imitating the behavior of models (parents in particular), young children acquire much of their vocabulary, learn such motor tasks as tying their shoes, and attain many of the attitudes that characterize their social interactions with others. One explanation for the widespread importance of observational learning is its efficiency. Learners can often avoid the tedious trial-and-error procedures characteristic of instrumental conditioning: they can observe not only the behavior of the model but also whether or not the behavior is successful.

Perhaps the very fact that observational learning is so obvious helps explain why it has been relatively neglected by psychologists until recent years. Recent interest has been given increased impetus by controversies surrounding possible effects of mass media—especially television—on behavior. The most prominent of these controversies is the issue of whether or not exposure to violence on television can increase violent behavior on the part of children. Although this issue is not likely to be settled for some time, indirect evidence concerning the issue is available.

This indirect evidence stems from the work of Albert Bandura, pioneer in the study of observational learning. In the basic Bandura experiment,

groups of nursery school children were exposed to an adult model who behaved aggressively toward "Bobo," a 4-foot-high inflated plastic doll. In some experiments, the demonstration was live—that is, the model was present in the room with the children; in others, the demonstration was on film. After both live and filmed demonstrations the children tended to imitate the models' aggressive behavior. They copied specific acts of aggression such as lifting, throwing, and kicking the plastic doll; they even reported some of the same hostile comments used by the model—"Pow!" and "Sock him in the nose!" (Bandura, 1974; Bandura, Ross, and Ross, 1963). Interestingly, the filmed demonstrations resulted in greater observational learning than did the live demonstrations.

Variations on these experiments suggest some of the factors that may influence observational learning. For example, the status of the model proved to be important, a finding echoed by the fact that people tend to imitate the behavior of celebrities. Rewards also had a significant impact; in experiments where the model was rewarded for aggressive behavior, the resulting imitation was greater than when the model was punished.

To many psychologists, the Bandura findings have a double significance. Violence on television may increase the tendency of viewers to behave aggressively; it may also teach them a repertoire of particular forms of violent behavior. Recall that the children in the experiments not only were more aggressive after viewing the film but also imitated specific acts of the model. There also has been much speculation, though little data, that adults may learn new forms of violence by observing television and other media. In recent years, extensive media coverage of skyjackings, political assassinations, and other

system. Obviously, behavior such as bar pressing, key pecking, and leaping to avoid electric shock would be impossible without muscles and motor nerves. As we will use the term here, however, *motor learning* refers to a distinct variety of learning. It involves the learning of a sequence of highly coordinated responses that are systematically related to one another: each response or component response is integrally related.

Investigations of motor learning can be traced back at least to studies of learning curves for apprentice telegraph operators developing their skill (Bryan and Harter, 1897). Such learning is often called motor-skill learning or sensorimotor learning. The latter term reflects the fact that sensory systems such as seeing and hearing play important roles both in directing the motor pattern and in providing feedback, including knowledge of results. It is clear also that there are verbal and other cognitive aspects of motor learning. For example, a baseball pitcher not only executes a predetermined

novel forms of violence has frequently been followed by waves of similar crimes.

Because the study of observational learning is still in its infancy, the limits on this variety of learning have not yet been fully established in the laboratory. Certainly one limit is the complexity of the behavior observed. We obviously do not learn to play the violin merely by watching and hearing a great violinist.

Illustration of Bandura's experiment on learning aggression by imitation, involving use of "Bobo" clown doll. In the top row an adult model exhibits four different ways to hurt the doll. The next two rows show a boy and a girl duplicating the model's efforts.

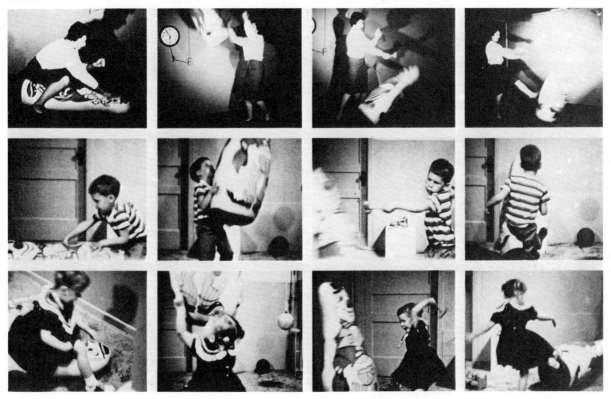

movement sequence involving the entire body, but also must make decisions: the pitcher must decide where to pitch the ball—low and over the outside corner of home plate, for example. Similarly, the batter intentionally gets set for a particular type of pitch—say, a fast ball or curve—although the cognitive plan may or may not facilitate hitting the ball.

One important characteristic of motor learning is that it appears to be an ongoing process (Schmidt, 1975). This contrasts with other varieties of learning, such as conditioning and rote memorization, where the limitations on improvement are fairly restricted. In those varieties, performance usually reaches a peak level within relatively few trials.

Let us examine two examples of continuous improvement in motor learning. E. Crossman (1959) provides data in which factory workers, using a simple tool called a jig to make cigars, showed improvement over a period of seven years in the time required to make each cigar. Although the gains were greatest in the early days of this period, some improvements were still taking place seven years later, after the workers had produced 10 million cigars. The second illustration concerns the ability of a baseball outfielder to run after and catch

Baseball outfielder catching fly ball. This is an extremely complex sensorimotor skill that continues to improve over years of practice.

a fly ball. This skill, which may seem routine to the uninitiated, is in fact an exceedingly complex sensorimotor skill that continues to improve over many years of practice. The expression "getting a good jump on the ball" lies at the heart of this skill. Although running speed obviously contributes to what the outfielder can accomplish, it is the skill in abstracting the trajectory that constitutes the ability of a good outfielder. The development of this skill begins in the young ballplayer and may not reach its upper limit even after several years of professional experience. It may well be that the main constraint on further improvement occurs when the process of aging limits what the body is physically capable of doing.

There are at least two ways to conceptualize the stages in motor learning. One way involves tasks or situations that consist of a series of levels. A particularly good example is the skill of typing. The first stage in acquiring this skill requires learning finger control and the location of the keys. This stage usually shows rapid improvement in terms of both speed and accuracy, although the beginning typist may feel that initial progress seems slow. The next stages involve moving from letter to word habits and from word to phrase habits. During each stage, initial improvement in performance tends to be followed by a plateau showing little improvement until the learner moves on to the next higher stage. Similar patterns of improvements followed by plateaus characterize learning to play musical instruments such as the piano.

A second way to analyze the stages of motor learning was provided by Paul Fitts and Michael Posner (1967). Their analysis is focused on the stages the learner passes through in terms of the way the learner performs.

In the first stage, termed the *cognitive stage*, the learner needs to know what the elements of the task are and what is expected in terms of performance. During this stage, learners draw upon reasoning abilities and past experiences to employ cognitive strategies that are subsequently modified as they gain experience with the task.

The *associative stage* enters in as the prior cognitive activities begin to drop out. Major errors are greatly reduced during this stage as the learner refines the responses to be made. Whereas the cognitive stage places initial emphasis on what responses to perform and in what order, the associative stage emphasizes how best to coordinate and integrate those responses.

The third stage, or *autonomous stage*, of motor learning refers to extremely advanced levels of performance. Errors are greatly reduced, and the performer seems to become more automatic in performing the task. At this stage less attention is required to perform the task, and more attention can be devoted to other activities at the same time.

These stages are illustrated in the process of learning to drive a car. At first, a certain amount of instruction is usually required. Following this the learner begins to drive, but it is usually necessary to devote full attention to the various components of this sensorimotor task. These demands may be so great that directions being given by the driving instructor are not even heard. After considerable practice, however, simultaneous activities such as carrying on a conversation and driving can be accomplished quite easily. Nonetheless, when the driver is faced with a novel situation, such as negotiating an unfamiliar highway, more attention may be required for successful and safe driving.

The level to which a motor skill can become automatic is demonstrated by a story about the author of this chapter. He frequently was so deep in thought that he often arrived at his office without even recalling that he had driven from home. The route was five miles long and involved making a series of turns, monitoring stop lights, and crossing a major thoroughfare and a busy railroad track. Yet upon arrival at the office he had no awareness of having performed these functions. Obviously, such a high level of automaticity is impressive, although it is certainly not to be recommended behind the wheel.

Once a skill becomes automatic, we can say that a *motor program* has been acquired. The learner has established a sequence of highly coordinated movements that are integrated in time and characterized by a rhythmic structure of their own. There are several types of evidence that point to the existence of motor programs. One consideration is the speed of certain highly skilled movements. For example, the fingers of one pianist were clocked at 16 movements per second (Lashley, 1951). Because this is apparently faster than the fingers could be controlled by sensory feedback, only a motor program could account for the speed.

The notion that highly integrated motor programs are acquired during advanced stages of motor learning is also supported by other observations. One is the ability to perform two tasks at the same time. Ulric Neisser (1976) cites cases of skilled pianists who can read prose while sight-reading music and professional typists who can type from copy while reciting nursery rhymes from memory. Perhaps the most persuasive evidence for motor programs derives from the extent to which well-learned skills can be performed despite years of nonuse. Examples we are all familiar with include bicycle riding, swimming, and even typing. To be sure, it may take some time and practice to regain the fine details of these skills, but—unlike other examples of human learning—motor skills are incredibly resistant to forgetting. It is as though the basic elements of these skills had become so highly integrated that they were retained as an intact unitary skill.

We have discussed a number of ways in which varieties of learning occur. All these varieties include relatively permanent behavior changes that result from prior experience. In the following chapter we will examine the vital role of memory and its structure in producing learning.

SUMMARY

1. Learning can be broadly described as a relatively permanent change of behavior that results from prior experience. Learning is inferred from performance, but it is not the same thing. Motivation is usually necessary for learning to be manifest in performance. Also, certain changes in performance do not reflect learning because either they are temporary or they are due to innate factors. The difference between learning and performance can also be described in terms, respectively, of capability and action.

2. Imprinting is the process by which certain young animals learn to follow their mothers. Imprinting is most pronounced in young birds that are able to walk or swim immediately after birth. Ethologists, scientists who study animals in their natural environments, have found that, in the absence of the mother, ducklings and chicks will imprint on almost any prominent moving object. Imprinting points to the importance of innate factors in some forms of learning.

3. Pavlov's experiments in classical conditioning demonstrated the stimulus-response relationship in some basic forms of learning. Pavlov observed

that dogs salivated (unconditioned response) at the presentation of food (unconditioned stimulus). The dogs then learned to salivate (conditioned response) in response to a previously neutral stimulus (conditioned stimulus), a bell.

4. Time relationships between the conditioned stimulus and unconditioned stimulus are important in classical conditioning. A short time between the conditioned stimulus and the unconditioned stimulus is often optimal for conditioning. Pavlov also demonstrated extinction, or weakening of a conditioned response, and the phenomena of stimulus generalization and discrimination.

5. E. L. Thorndike identified another variety of learning—learning by trial and error—that has become known as instrumental learning. B. F. Skinner took research in instrumental learning a step further and called it operant conditioning. Operant conditioning takes place when a learned, or operant, behavior occurs. The stimulus event—such as presentation of food—that increases the probability of the response occurring before this event is called reinforcement.

6. Primary reinforcers are those that meet biological needs, like food and water; secondary reinforcers, like praise and money, are learned and are more likely to be effective in human learning.

7. An operant response is generally conditioned by reinforcing every occurrence of the response—a schedule known as continuous reinforcement. After conditioning, the response can be maintained by a schedule of partial reinforcement, under which it is only occasionally reinforced. Partial reinforcement schedules include those that are fixed in ratio or interval and those that are variable in ratio or interval. Partial reinforcement usually produces greater resistance to extinction than does continuous reinforcement.

8. The training of novel behavior or sequences of actions—ones not normally performed by the organism—is called behavior shaping. Behavior shaping is typically accomplished by breaking up the desired sequence of action into small steps with rewards in a method known as successive approximations. Successful behavior shaping is contingent upon the effectiveness of the rewards. Another type of shaping, autoshaping, has been identified—in which a learned response results even when there is no contingency between the response and reinforcement.

9. Avoidance learning involves a combination of classical and instrumental conditioning: a classically conditioned fear response serves as the stimulus for an instrumental avoidance response. The predictability hypothesis states that in classical conditioning the conditioned stimulus must serve as a reliable basis for predicting the occurrence of the unconditioned stimulus.

10. Punishment is pain or annoyance administered in an attempt to eliminate a particular behavior; negative reinforcement, by contrast, results when a response leads to removal of a negative reinforcer, which serves the same purpose as would a positive reinforcer. Punishment seems less effective in learning situations than reinforcers that increase the probability of desired behavior.

11. Cognitive factors—perception and knowledge—influence various conditioning phenomena and are most likely to arise in conditioning situations when memory structures, established through prior experience, determine the way new experiences are interpreted. Insight experiments have demonstrated an important role for insight in problem-solving tasks: solutions achieved through insight can be applied to new problems.

12. A concept refers to the properties or relationships, both abstract and concrete, that are common to a class of objects or ideas. Concept learning, which orders our experience and perceptions, enables us to grasp the important similarities between things and to ignore irrelevant details. Concepts are learned in a variety of ways, not all of them yet understood.

13. Motor learning involves the learning of a sequence of highly coordinated responses that are systematically related to one another: each response or component response is integrally related. Sensorimotor learning involves the sensory systems such as seeing and hearing both in directing the motor pattern and in providing feedback, including knowledge of results. Motor learning, in contrast to other varieties of learning such as conditioning and rote memorization, appears to be an ongoing process.

14. Once a skill, such as typing, becomes automatic, we can say that a motor program has been acquired. The learner has established a sequence of highly coordinated movements that are integrated in time and characterized by a rhythmic structure of their own.

Chapter 8
Memory and Cognition

ognition is a complex set of processes that pertain to the acquisition of knowledge and its use. In the preceding chapter we saw how several aspects of cognition relate to learning. Aspects of cognition are also very much involved in such diverse phenomena as attention, perception, problem solving, judgment, decision making, and thinking. Memory is also part of cognition and, in a very fundamental sense, memory is the basic building block upon which all of human cognition is based.

An intimate relationship exists between learning and memory. You will recall that learning is defined as a relatively permanent behavior change as a result of experience. It is the brain's memory capability that allows most learning to take place. *Memory* is the brain's ability to recreate or reproduce past experience and thoughts, and we use that ability to change our behavior—to learn. Not only is learning inferred through performance measures based on memory of prior experiences, but, as we have also seen, what is learned in a particular situation (for example, learned helplessness) is often influenced by the presence or absence of memories of previous events. Similar relationships exist between memory and other cognitive processes. For example, when driving a car we must remember what to attend to and what can be ignored. When we see a friend approach, the act of perceiving that friend is intricately involved with memory. Many forms of cognition involve creative aspects, but all of our cognitive processes are closely tied to the contents of memory. In fact, the close interrelationships among our cognitive processes are such that it is impossible to discuss any one of them without at least implicit reference to other aspects of cognition.

Perhaps the most important reason for studying human memory is that memory is the repository of our knowledge of the world, including facts, beliefs,

attitudes, and so on. It is for this reason that much of what you will encounter in other chapters involves human memory to a large degree.

Stages of Memory

In developing theoretical models of the stages and processes involved in memory, psychologists have found that many of the information-processing concepts formulated for communications, engineering, and computer science can be applied to human beings. The information-processing approach analyzes memory in stages and examines the processes that take place at each stage. In this vein, we shall look at three stages of memory: sensory memory, short-term memory, and long-term memory (see Figure 8.1). Although these stages of memory can be distinguished both in terms of the ways they are studied and the processes being examined, they need not be considered as separate isolated stages in any very fundamental sense. Rather, the distinction among these stages is offered for convenience in discussing various phenomena of memory.

Sensory Memory

While the phenomenon of *sensory memory*—the momentary lingering of sensory information after a stimulus has been removed—was discovered in the last century, it is only since 1960 that any substantial amount of research dealing with the sensory effects of stimuli has been reported.

Visual Stimuli A typical experiment on sensory visual memory might involve the simultaneous exposure of nine different letters of the alphabet arranged in three rows of three letters each (Sperling, 1960). The letters are exposed to observers for a very

FIGURE 8.1 Illustration of the three stages of memory: sensory, short-term, and long-term memory.

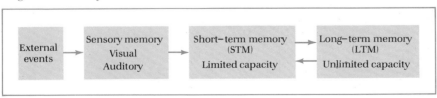

brief period of time, say 50 milliseconds. Because it requires approximately 200 milliseconds (1/5 of a second) to begin a directed eye movement, the observers do not have time to scan the array of letters, although they do see them all. Now the observers are asked to report all of the letters they have seen. Although the observers report having "seen" all of the letters, they can report only about four or five letters correctly. However, if the observers are asked to report only a single row of these letters, they can do so without error. Because the observers have no way of knowing which row is to be reported until the letters disappear, this observation suggests that all, or at least most, of the letters were available for recall. Why then should the observers fail to report all letters correctly using the full-report procedure?

George Sperling and others have provided at least a tentative answer to this question (Sperling, 1960; Baddeley, 1976). When the cue, in this case a signal tone, used to indicate which row of letters to report occurs after only a brief delay following letter presentation, accuracy of reporting declines (see Figure 8.2). In fact, if the cue is presented as little as one second later, the observers' performance, in terms of percent correct, is no better than obtained in full report. Sperling attributes these findings to a visual memory trace, or the persisting aftereffects of stimuli, called the *icon*, or *iconic trace* (Sperling, 1960), which has a relatively large storage capacity

but a duration of not more than one second. Thus, when using the full-report procedure, the trace or icon continues to decay while the observers are reporting the letters. By the time four or five letters have been reported, the icon is so faint that it is no longer possible to distinguish and report any more letters. However, the icon is present long enough to report all of the letters in any particular row.

It is not clear how iconic memory is related to retention over time spans ranging from seconds to years, but *eidetic imagery*, or what is commonly referred to as photographic memory, is an interesting example of its extension over long periods of time. Some individuals are able to describe in great clarity and detail an image, such as an intricate drawing, to which they have been exposed. This type of memory differs from the short-term effects of stimuli already discussed. Eidetic imagery is characterized by extreme vividness of detail in recall. It is quite rare (more children than adults have the capability); eidetic imagers report "seeing" the image in front of their eyes (Haber, 1969). Some researchers have speculated that eidetic imagers have a primitive, preverbal form of memory, which fades in most adults as linguistic skills strengthen (Richardson, 1969).

Auditory Stimuli Apart from the visual system, sensory memory has been clearly established only for audition. Ulric Neisser (1967) refers to this auditory trace as *echoic memory*, and it should be noted that its main characteristics are similar to those of iconic memory—that is, both refer to the persisting effects of sensory stimuli without regard to the nature of the observer's or listener's response. The capacity of the iconic trace is probably greater than that of the echoic trace because the spatial nature of the visual system permits simultaneous processing of several items at the same time. In contrast, the auditory system is designed to process information serially, one item at a time. However, at least under some conditions, there is evidence to suggest that the duration of the echoic trace may be somewhat longer (up to 2 seconds) than is found for the visual trace (Darwin, Turvey, and Crowder, 1972).

As an example of echoic memory, recall the feeling that someone just said something to you and of going back to "listen" to it. Perhaps what was said was in the form of a question. You may even have

FIGURE 8.2 Sperling's study of sensory memory, the number and percentage of correct letters recalled over a l-second interval declined the longer the delay between the presentation of the letters and the cue (signal tone) indicating which row of letters was to be reported.

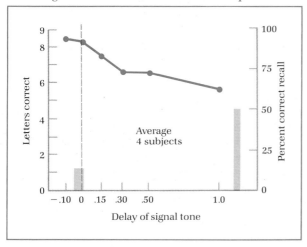

responded with "What?" before going back to listen to what was said and stored in echoic memory. You may be able to process the question and answer it before the original speaker has repeated the question.

Short-Term Memory

Sensory memory, at best, plays only a small role in most everyday activities, simply because we are seldom exposed to events of such brief duration. In contrast, *short-term memory (STM)* is used by all of us constantly. A common illustration involves looking up a telephone number, holding it in short-term memory until the number has been dialed, and noting a few minutes later that we may have no recollection of the number we dialed. Several exposures to an arbitrary sequence of items such as telephone numbers are usually required before they become part of our relatively permanent long-term memory.

Short-term memory has been assigned numerous labels including primary memory, working memory, what we are currently "paying attention to," and even consciousness. These various labels have been introduced to emphasize theoretical distinctions, which will be considered shortly, and to focus on the way we use short-term memory as well as on the contents of short-term memory.

Capacity Limitations   One reason for our interest in short-term memory stems from the fact that human beings can deal with only a limited amount of information at any given moment. For example, when you go to a grocery store you cannot usually remember a long list of things to purchase unless you write it down.

In his classic studies of memory, Hermann Ebbinghaus (1885/1964) memorized hundreds of lists of nonsense syllables on which he later tested himself for retention. Nonsense syllables are three-letter sequences, usually containing a vowel between two consonants, which have no meaning or inherent associations. Ebbinghaus chose nonsense syllables because he thought meaningful words already contained too many associations. He reported that the number of nonsense syllables he could recall following a single presentation was about seven. This observation suggested a fixed capacity for short-term memory or what has been called the *span of immediate memory*. Over half a century later, this notion was systematically developed in a paper by George A. Miller (1956). In reviewing the results of numerous studies, Miller proposed that the limit of the human short-term memory span was on the order of seven units plus or minus two units.

Studies of the memory span for arbitrarily related digits show that most people have a capacity within this range. However, Miller's proposal went beyond single units such as digits or letters arranged in arbitrary sequences. Instead, Miller introduced the psychological concept of a *chunk of information*. Chunks refer to memory units that result from recoding units or integrating together more elementary units. For example, the digits 1, 4, 9, and 2 could be recoded as 1492, the date of Columbus's discovery of America. Words also constitute chunks in which several letters become integrated into a single meaningful unit. Thus, a sequence of seven arbitrarily related but familiar words would be almost as easy to recall as a string of seven consonants, even though the seven words taken together contain many more than seven letters. In this case, the letters within each word have become integrated into a single chunk.

In general, *chunking* refers to the organization of material in such a way as to include more items of information per chunk. The analogy here is to a memory span consisting of seven bins, each of which may contain several items as long as the items within each bin are coherently related. However, chunks are not defined by the materials themselves. Instead, chunks are imposed on the materials by the individual and will vary from one person to another. For someone unfamiliar with American history, the digits 1, 4, 9, and 2 may not form a chunk. Similarly, words that are unfamiliar to us do not form single chunks of information but remain as strings of arbitrarily arranged letters.

Attention   Psychologists have been well aware of capacity limits in short-term memory for many years, but the question we wish to address here is whether attentional processes place even further constraints on what can enter into our memory. The issue is not whether our attentional abilities are limited, because we all know they are. Rather, the issue is whether attentional limitations are any different from those that characterize short-term memory.

The study of attention has a long history in psychology but current interest in this topic was stimulated by the work of E. Colin Cherry (1953). The topic that interested Cherry has been described as the "cocktail party phenomenon," and it refers to our ability to attend selectively to one conversation while ignoring others (see Chapter 4). The experimental task employed by Cherry is known as *shadowing:* two or more spoken messages are presented simultaneously to a listener whose task is to repeat one of the spoken messages aloud as it is heard, word for word. The repeated message is said to be shadowed, and the listener is instructed to stay as "close behind" the speaker's voice as possible. What is remembered of the message that is not shadowed is the main question of interest.

Cherry's findings indicate that subjects remember very little about the nonshadowed message. When speech is the nonshadowed message, the listeners always identify it as speech, but if the speech is changed from English to German or even to English speech played backwards, the listeners do not notice the change. They will notice a change in voice (a man's voice to a woman's voice) as well as a nonspeech signal such as a pure tone.

Although all of the words in the shadowed message are correctly repeated, the listeners remember very little of the content of that message. Apparently, the shadowing task of repeating the message is sufficiently demanding that little processing of meaning takes place.

Findings such as Cherry's have led to considerable research and theorizing over the past two decades. One of the most important theoretical approaches to attention is the *filter theory* proposed by Donald A. Broadbent (1958). He proposed the existence of a series of sensory channels over which information can be transmitted in parallel. What counts as a channel has not been well defined, but channels usually refer to different physical or spatial characteristics. For instance, a physical characteristic might refer to the difference between a male and a female voice, while a spatial character-

istic might refer to different locations from which auditory or visual messages might be transmitted.

While sensory information is transmitted in parallel, the basic element in Broadbent's theory is a selective filter that allows information only on a single channel to enter short-term memory while excluding or blocking out information on all other sensory channels. This means that some information never reaches short-term memory: it is not even perceived (see Figure 8.3). This theory helps account for results such as those reported by Cherry. The few characteristics of the nonshadowed message that are noticed by listeners can be explained on the basis of rapid filter switching to detect those physical characteristics such as voice quality that can be stored briefly in sensory, or echoic, memory. Note, however, that the physiological location of such a filter has not been identified, and therefore a physiological process description is lacking.

Since Broadbent's filter theory was introduced, the volume of research on attention has expanded enormously. The general pattern of this research has not been supportive of the operation of a selective filter. For instance, in a shadowing task, Neville Moray (1959) showed that information in the nonshadowed message was often noticed when it was preceded by the listener's own name. In another study, Anne Treisman (1964) had bilingual listeners shadow a message in English presented to one ear, while a foreign language translation of the message was presented to the other ear. About half of the listeners realized that the two messages had the same meaning. These results do not support the notion of a selective filter that allows information to be transmitted over a single channel while blocking out all information on other channels. The problem

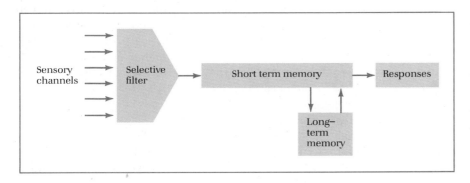

FIGURE 8.3 The basic element in Broadbent's filter theory is a selective filter that allows information only on a single channel to enter short-term memory while blocking out information on all other sensory channels.

for filter theory is that meaning is only supposed to be processed on the attended channel.

A number of questions remain about attention and short-term memory. Do we give any meaning to and perceive unattended information before rejecting it? Does material from secondary channels actually enter short-term memory, even briefly, before it is lost?

In recent years a series of studies quite convincingly indicated that selective attention to particular sensory channels takes place after initial registration (Shiffrin, Pisoni, and Castenada-Mendez, 1974). The stimuli presented to the listeners in these studies are often very simple—for example, single syllables. Listeners' prior knowledge of the channel on which a stimulus will appear (left or right ear) has no facilitory effect in terms of accuracy of response. The researchers interpreted these findings as an indication that the important capacity limitation is one involving short-term memory. They suggest that all incoming information is registered in short-term memory. However, because short-term memory has a fixed capacity, when the amount of information entering short-term memory exceeds this capacity, only some portion of the information can be processed further (rehearsed) and subsequently remembered. The remaining information is necessarily lost, even though it had been registered in short-term memory briefly.

In most shadowing experiments, the very act of shadowing occupies most of the capacity of short-term memory, and although information in the nonshadowed message may enter short-term memory and may be noticed at the time, it cannot be processed without interrupting the shadowing process. Therefore, it is not recalled when the retention test is administered. Support for this was reported by Donald Norman (1969), who found that when listeners are interrupted during shadowing and asked to report on the nonshadowed message, they can report the last few items even though there is no evidence of any lasting memory for the nonshadowed message overall.

Advocates of selective attention or filter theory could argue that the findings reported by Norman simply reflect the recall of items that had not yet faded from sensory memory. However, a fairly commonplace experience tends to favor Shiffrin's interpretation. Suppose you look up an unfamiliar telephone number that you intend to dial. While you are walking over to the telephone a friend, either intentionally or unintentionally, repeats aloud a series of numbers. You certainly perceive those numbers; they enter short-term memory. But if you are successful in maintaining the telephone number you looked up after dialing it, you will probably not remember the numbers your friend uttered. According to this view, attention does not restrict our ability to process and remember information in the sense of providing a capacity limitation. The capacity limitation is due to short-term memory, and attention refers to the act of processing information in short-term memory, which allows the information to be remembered subsequently.

Neisser (1976) proposed a similar view of attention, although it was stated in quite different terms. His view is that attention has no independent status apart from the perceptual process: attention is perception in that we choose what to look at, what to listen to, and so on. That is, we do not selectively block out inputs; rather, we simply do not pick them up.

Neisser offers several general criticisms of theories of selective attention based on either filtering or other capacity limitations. Among these is the failure to distinguish between the performance of skilled and unskilled observers on the secondary (nonattended) task. For example, he reports that after practicing for several hours on a number-detecting task while shadowing another message, performance on number detecting increased to 83 percent correct. In contrast, inexperienced listeners average only 4 percent correct in number detecting. The point here is that "dual attention" should be thought of as an acquired skill.

Neisser reports several other impressive demonstrations of such acquired skills including one mentioned in the previous chapter relating to skilled pianists who can shadow prose while sight-reading music at the piano. An important point to be emphasized in this context is that apparent limitations in performance may not reflect absolute capacity limitations. They may simply reflect lack of interest, practice, or skill. As Neisser points out, most theories of attention do not as yet provide for distinctions between the performance of adults and children; that is, they do not explain developmental changes in capacity.

Long-Term Memory

Long-term memory (LTM), because of its central role in all of our cognitive activities, is one of the most fascinating areas of psychological investigation. What is stored or represented in long-term memory quite obviously depends to a large extent on our previous experiences. At one level we can say that our experiences result in memory for a multitude of facts, concepts, skills, and beliefs (including attitudes, stereotypes, and so on) as well as programs and rules for guiding mental operations. That is, long-term memory represents the organized store of general information or knowledge we have about the world we live in, whether or not our knowledge is correct, as well as programs and rules for carrying out overt behaviors and mental action sequences (reasoning, decision making, thinking, and so so). This vast store includes knowledge of our language (which will be discussed in the following chapter), and plans for dealing with everyday, and, in some cases, not so everyday experiences. Thus long-term memory is not only the repository of our prior experiences, but it also includes information and beliefs derived from these experiences as well as plans for guiding what we shall do in the future.

How information is extracted from experience, how this information is subsequently represented in long-term memory, and how we can best remember the information are important issues, and we shall examine them shortly. However, several rather abstract contents of long-term memory that are often overlooked govern a substantial portion of our lives. These abstract contents of long-term memory include cognitive maps, schemata, motor programs, and generative processes.

Cognitive Maps   As a consequence of some of his studies in maze learning, Edward G. Tolman (see Chapter 7) began to question what it is rats learn when we say they have learned a maze. The earliest view was that the rats learned by doing, but subsequent studies indicated that this was not always the case—that the rats in fact acquired what Tolman called a *cognitive map*, which indicates what is where and what leads to what (Tolman, Ritchie, and Kalish, 1946; Tolman, 1948).

At least in terms of guiding our daily activities, *cognitive maps* constitute an important part of the human memory system. Cognitive maps, like other maps we are familiar with, have a distinctly spatial character. We all have cognitive maps of endless varieties, including those of the places where we live, work, and play. Once established, cognitive maps allow us to move about in the world in which we live without constant attention to everything around us. In fact, our cognitive maps are so efficient in guiding many daily activities that they are frequently taken for granted.

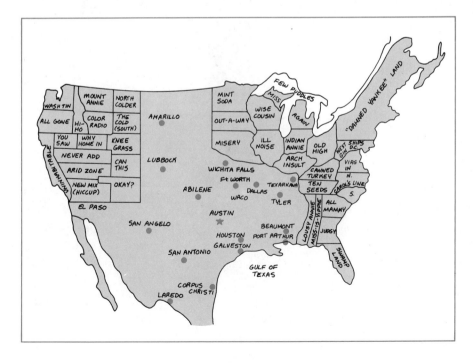

An example of a cognitive map is this tongue-in-cheek representation of a Texan's view of the United States.

Cognitive maps are typically represented in terms of landmarks, routes or paths, and boundaries. When we talk of cognitive maps, we are often referring to representations of cities, buildings, or even the arrangement of furniture in a room. The degree of detail represented in our cognitive maps depends to a large extent on both the frequency with which we experience particular spatially arranged situations, and our need to attend to the details that exist in those situations. Our cognitive maps not only assist our own activities but also allow us to assist others by giving directions or telling someone where to find, for example, a particular book in a room. Of course, cognitive maps also allow us to plan in advance which routes we will take when going somewhere, whether or not we actually make the trip.

At least for adults, cognitive maps seem to be acquired without a great deal of effort. Perhaps this is because as adults we know a great deal about the world and about the kinds of elements that go into the spatial nature of such maps. In addition, the elements represented in cognitive maps are highly concrete and easily imaged. Imagery, as we shall see later in this chapter, plays an extremely important role in memory.

Some cognitive maps, such as those used in telling someone how to get to where you live, are gradually developed through daily experiences. When you move to a new place, you gradually build up and elaborate upon your cognitive map of that place. Other cognitive maps, such as one of the continental United States, are more likely to be acquired by repeated exposure to actual maps.

The spatial information represented in cognitive maps is relational and relative in character. That is, the landmarks and routes represented in cognitive maps are located in relation to each other, although absolute distance and location may not be well preserved. If you mentally scan a cognitive map, it will take longer to travel between places that are far apart—New York to Los Angeles—than between places that are close together—Chicago to St. Louis, (Kosslyn, Ball, and Reiser, 1978; Richman, Mitchell, and Reznick, 1979). This does not necessarily indicate that you are scanning a mental picture, but it does mean that the spatial organization represented in memory does include knowledge of at least relative distance.

Schemata We can think of much of our general knowledge of the world as being represented in long-term memory in terms of *schemata*. Particular schemata can be loosely thought of as organized bodies of information. Much of what is stored in long-term memory, including beliefs, attitudes, and stereotypes, is organized in terms of schemata. Cognitive maps can be considered schemata in which the information represented in memory is highly spatial in character.

In the psychological literature, the notion of schemata is most closely linked to Sir Frederick Bartlett and his classic book *Remembering* (1932). Bartlett viewed schemata as the ways in which we organize our knowledge of the world based on our past experiences. These schemata are then used when we attempt to learn something new. Bartlett suggested that what is remembered about a new experience depends both on the character of the experience and our existing schemata at the time of the experience. He saw remembering as an active, constructive process that uses both what is retained from the new experience and our preexisting

The extent to which we enjoy and appreciate a sporting event is related to our schemata for that event. A general knowledge of the rules of the game as well as some of its subtleties contributes to our evaluation of both good and poor performances.

schemata. In this way existing schemata at any time may influence what we perceive, learn, and remember (Neisser, 1976).

Schemata play an important role in the educational process; for example, students may misunderstand what they read in a text because they interpret it in terms of one of their old schemata and not the schema that the author had in mind. Similar misunderstandings may occur in everyday interactions—even among friends.

Bartlett's work as well as much subsequent research focused on distortions or inaccuracies in remembering that result from conflicts between aspects of the to-be-remembered events and aspects of existing schemata. Numerous investigations have demonstrated that attitudes and prejudices can produce marked distortions in what is remembered about a particular story or event. Can you remember a situation in which you or someone you know misrecalled or misperceived an event because his or her attitude or prejudice at the time of the event did not "fit" with what actually happened?

Stereotypes often influence our memory from previous experiences. *Stereotypes* are mental sets we may have about the traits or physical characteristics of an entire group of people. Typical stereotypes include such notions as Cadillac owners are rich, the French are gourmets, Californians are suntanned. These descriptions do not apply to all people in the respective groups, but our long-term memories may cause us to see a group of Californians as being healthier looking than they are.

Stereotypes can also have a retroactive effect on memory. Suppose that after you have met someone, you are told that the person is Italian. If you have an existing stereotype of Italians (violent, prone to crime, dark or happy, musical, exuberant), you may reconstruct your memory of the person you have already met to fit your stereotype.

However, it is important to emphasize that existing schemata are modified by new experiences, with the result that distortions in remembering are minimized. Schemata are dynamic not static, and new learning experiences provide opportunities to modify or elaborate existing schemata. As you read this text there will be numerous opportunities for you to modify or elaborate many of your existing schemata including your conception of human memory.

Schemata are not only important in learning and memory, but they also play an important role in many other activities. We have schemata that guide our behavior in different social situations. The extent to which someone enjoys a sporting event or appreciates an outstanding performance by an individual player depends to a large degree on having a well-developed schema for that event. Well-developed schemata include general knowledge of the rules of the event as well as an appreciation of more subtle factors that allow you to evaluate both good and poor performances.

The effectiveness of well-developed schemata has been demonstrated in an experiment in constructive as opposed to simple reproductive memory (Bower, Clark, Winzenz, and Lesgold, 1969). Two groups of subjects were given twelve lists of ten unrelated words to memorize. The first group approached the task as one of rote memorization; the second group was instructed to develop simple stories including each word on the list. These procedures were followed for twelve 10-word lists. The memorization rates were dramatically different. Members of the first group could recall an average of 17 of the original words, while those who used the words in stories had an average recall of 100 of the original 120 words.

Motor Programs As we grow up all of us acquire a number of motor programs that guide daily activities. These *motor programs* allow us to carry out sequences of highly coordinated and integrated muscular movements that are related in a systematic fashion. Examples of behavior guided by such programs include our sensorimotor skills such as manipulating a pencil, discussed in the previous chapter, as well as seemingly more routine behaviors like walking, running, and speaking.

Motor programs are acquired through considerable practice, although the amount of practice required varies with the complexity of the skill. Overt instruction is not of much help in acquiring a motor program because these programs can only be grossly described. You can tell someone how to change a tire on a car and, assuming knowledge of the tools involved, he or she can change the tire. However, written or verbal instruction is not of much help in learning to run, speak, or swim.

While the variety of behaviors guided by motor programs differ widely, the programs themselves have certain common characteristics. Once estab-

A typical example of a motor program is driving a car. Although visual input is essential, once the motor program is well established a considerable amount of the visual information provided is not consciously processed.

lished, motor programs allow us to carry out complex sequences of movements without requiring a great deal of attention to the movements themselves. This is not to imply that sensory information is not important to the effective execution of a motor program. Visual input is essential when driving a car; once a motor program for driving a car is well established, however, much of the visual information provided may not be consciously processed.

Reading is another skill that psychologists and educators have long tried to understand. Many components go into good reading, and one of them functions like a motor program. All of us have experienced this aspect of reading, which is mind wandering. That is, at some point while reading a book, we may become preoccupied with something else. When this happens we sometimes stop reading altogether; at other times, we continue the superficial act of reading in the sense of carrying out the appropriate motor program, until we realize that we do not know what we have just "read." This experience is not unlike Cherry's (1953) shadowing task. The text being read becomes the unshadowed message, and what we are thinking about becomes the shadowed message. The words in the text enter short-term memory, but because the capacity of short-term memory is largely devoted to other thoughts, there is not sufficient capacity remaining to process the sense or meaning of the text message.

The phenomenon illustrated here, which might be called "mindless reading," has some parallels to driving a car over a very familiar route without remembering or being aware of having done so: in both cases the individual is preoccupied with other thoughts. The driver of the car no doubt notices appropriate places to turn, stops for stop signs, and executes the motor program accordingly. Because the route is familiar, and in the absence of anything unusual, very little short-term memory capacity is required, and the driver can successfully reach the destination. Unfortunately, in mindless reading the same happy conclusion does not result. The reader may process the meaning of the familiar individual words at some level that is sufficient to allow the motor program to continue. However, the goal of understanding what has just been read is not met.

Motor programs can also be characterized as being highly rhythmic in nature. That is, the particular elements or muscular movements are organized in time relative to one another—the timing of the elements in a sequence is relative and not absolute. We can run, swim, ride a bicycle, or speak at various speeds, and our motor programs are sufficiently flexible to guide the timing of each element relative to the other elements. It is tempting to speculate that this rhythmic character of motor programs plays a major role in their permanence in memory, even after many years of disuse.

Generative Processes Much of cognitive activity—thinking, reasoning, or remembering—involves generative processes. *Generative processes* can be viewed as mental programs that have a great deal in common with motor programs (Blumenthal, 1977) even though their consequences are quite different. That is, motor programs produce movements or actions whereas these mental programs produce conscious thoughts, mental images, and so on. Just as a motor program for an act such as speaking can only be described in a very gross and superficial manner, the mental programs we have termed generative processes can only be described in similarly superficial ways. In both cases the knowledge that underlies these programs is tacit or implicit knowledge; it is knowledge we acquire through practice, but not knowledge that is explicitly taught to us. As with motor programs, it is much easier to describe the consequences or products of generative processes than it is to describe the processes themselves.

The term generative process is intended to emphasize both the active nature of cognitive activity and the inventive character of the results of using these mental programs. An author writing fiction uses generative processes extensively by drawing upon other contents of memory, including concepts, schemata, and cognitive maps to invent the story. That is, the author uses explicit knowledge and beliefs that can be communicated to others, although the people, places, and events described in the story may be purely fictional.

Motor programs and generative processes also share the attribute of flexibility in terms of the contexts in which they can function. When a well-developed motor program for walking is established, an individual can walk on various surfaces at various speeds—can walk up hills or down them. When you have learned to speak, the motor program developed is not restricted to content; you can speak about anything you choose to speak about. Similarly, the generative processes that underlie thinking are not restricted to particular topics except insofar as other knowledge (concepts, schemata, and so on) is not available to think about. In other words, generative processes, like motor programs that require something to operate on—whether that be a surface to walk or run on—require concepts in memory to think about or remember.

Because generative processes represent tacit or implicit knowledge, it is not always easy to specify the domain over which they operate. Certainly, generative processes lie at the heart of cognitive activities such as thinking, reasoning, and remembering. However, some acts of remembering may not involve generative processes. For example, when you recall something acquired through rote memorization, such as the alphabet, your telephone number, or the order of the months of the year, generative processes need not be involved. Notice that in these instances what is learned and remembered is an arbitrary set of symbols or names of symbols that are arranged in an arbitrary order. Recalling the order of the symbols is not inventive and may not involve generative processes in any very basic way. Perhaps recall of materials of this sort can best be thought of as an instance of relatively "pure" memory independent of other cognitive activities.

Now that we have discussed some of the major classes of information in long-term memory it is appropriate to consider the way information gets into the brain for memory storage and use. While our discussion will focus on long-term memory it will be necessary to consider aspects of sensory memory and short-term memory as well.

Encoding, Storage, and Retrieval

Three basic questions arise in considering the way we store and use information in memory. First, what factors are involved in the way we extract information or encode information from our experiences? Second, how is the encoded information represented or stored in memory and how is it related to other information stored in memory? Finally, how do we successfully retrieve information from memory? Answers to these questions will be discussed in the following sections.

Encoding

In order to make use of any information, it must first get into memory. *Encoding* refers to the extraction of information from events we experience—under the conditions that the events are experienced. For instance, with the very brief exposures provided in studies of sensory memory, what is initially encoded appears to be the physical characteristics or features of the events such as shape, size, location, voice quality. The encoding of these features appears to be a relatively automatic pro-

241

TABLE 8.1 Confusion matrix for a short-term memory experiment using auditory stimulus presentation. The higher the number, the more often the two letters coming together at that point were confused.

STIMULUS LETTER

	B	C	P	T	V	F	M	N	S	X
B	—	171	75	84	168	2	11	10	2	2
C	32	—	35	42	20	4	4	5	2	5
P	162	350	—	505	91	11	31	23	5	5
T	143	232	281	—	50	14	12	11	8	5
V	122	61	34	22	—	1	8	11	1	0
F	6	4	2	4	3	—	13	8	336	238
M	10	14	2	3	4	22	—	334	21	9
N	13	21	6	9	20	32	512	—	38	14
S	2	18	2	7	3	488	23	11	—	391
X	1	6	2	2	1	245	2	1	184	—

Source: R. Conrad, "Acoustic Confusions in Immediate Memory," *British Journal of Psychology*, 1964, 55, pp. 75-83.

TABLE 8.2 Confusion matrix for a short-term memory experiment using visual stimulus presentation. Compare the similarity of the confusions in this condition with those of the auditory condition shown in Table 8.1.

STIMULUS LETTER

	B	C	P	T	V	F	M	N	S	X
B	—	18	62	5	83	12	9	3	2	0
C	13	—	27	18	55	15	3	12	35	7
P	102	18	—	24	40	15	8	8	7	7
T	30	46	79	—	38	18	14	14	8	10
V	56	32	30	14	—	21	15	11	11	5
F	6	8	14	5	31	—	12	13	131	16
M	12	6	8	5	20	16	—	146	15	5
N	11	7	5	1	19	28	167	—	24	5
S	7	21	11	2	9	37	4	12	—	16
X	3	7	2	2	11	30	10	11	59	—

Source: R. Conrad, "Acoustic Confusions in Immediate Memory," *British Journal of Psychology*, 1964, 55, pp. 75-83.

cess that is governed by the characteristics of our sensory systems (see Chapter 3). As noted previously, these features are lost very rapidly, unless they are quickly encoded into short-term memory. In studies in which the event was exposure to an array of letters of the alphabet, encoding into short-term memory involved naming the letters (Sperling, 1960). Of course, the letter names themselves had to be retrieved from long-term memory before encoding into short-term memory could be accomplished. Thus, even in this rather simple experiment, we see some of the complexities that arise in attempting to distinguish among various stages of memory.

Studies of sensory memory indicate that with very brief exposures, more information is encoded into sensory memory than can be subsequently encoded into short-term memory. Of course, under most everyday situations such brief exposures are rare. However, these studies also suggest that the encoded information is different in kind. Encoding into sensory memory involves the extraction of physical characteristics or features of the event. Encoding into short-term memory involves a deeper level of processing, such as the name of a particular shape, and typically requires some interaction with long-term memory where shape names are stored.

Acoustic Encoding A common process observed in encoding information into short-term memory is verbal rehearsal, or *naming*. This type of encoding

is often observed even in situations where the events are presented visually. For example, R. Conrad (1964) presented both visual and auditory sequences of six consonant letters to observers and then asked for immediate recall. The patterns of errors found with both modes of presentation were quite similar, and they suggested that encoding was auditory or acoustic in nature—that is, letters with similar-sounding names, such as *B* and *V*, were often confused with each other whether the mode of presentation was auditory or visual. Neither of these letters, however, was likely to be confused with the letter *X* (see Tables 8.1 and 8.2).

Conrad's findings indicate that with visual presentation of consonant letters the observers encode the name of the letter rather than the visual form presented. Given the nature of the observers' task, the outcome seems quite reasonable. The observers were only required to report which consonants they saw or heard. They were not required to notice any other aspect of the consonants such as where they occurred in the alphabet. The names of the consonants are names for shapes and, in our daily experiences, shapes can vary considerably and still have the same name. Letter shapes can be in capitalized form or in lowercase. They can also vary in size and tilt. What is usually important is the identity of the letter and not the particular instance of the shape presented. Thus, unless there is some reason for doing otherwise, the most natural thing to do when presented with a sequences of shapes, be they letters or other shapes, is to encode them acoustically by naming them.

Given the capacity limitations of short-term memory, acoustic encoding is not only a natural but a very efficient process. Encoding the names of five or six concepts allows us subsequently to retrieve more information about any one of them from long-term memory, if we need to do so. When we go to the grocery store to buy bread, butter, eggs, milk, and cheese, encoding these names allows us to retrieve more information later about each of them—what type of bread we want, what brand of butter, and so on. However, acoustic encoding is certainly not the only form of encoding observed in short-term memory. Other forms of encoding in short-term memory such as by visual form (imaging) or by meaning are utilized when the situation requires such encoding.

Recoding As we saw earlier in this chapter, encoding into short-term memory often requires the *recoding* or chunking of information. This process involves an interaction between long-term memory and short-term memory. For example, consider the following string of digits: $149-217-761-812$. This string of 12 digits is beyond the capacity of short-term memory. However, if we recode the string as $1492-1776-1812$ we have three meaningful chunks of information that easily fall within the capacity of short-term memory. This example also indicates the importance of attentional processing in encoding. In this example we must actively search through the digit string to find units that constitute meaningful chunks. To someone never exposed to American history, these units would not constitute meaningful chunks of information and would exceed the capacity of short-term memory.

Encoding Physically Sensible Factors As in the case of short-term memory, encoding in long-term memory is inferred from observing what we remember and what we fail to remember in a variety of situations. However, encoding in long-term memory as opposed to short-term memory is both more complex and more permanent. Physically sensible aspects of our experiences are often attended to, and encoded in, long-term memory, which allows us subsequently to remember familiar people, objects, and places. These encodings also allow us to remember familiar songs and voices as well as the way things taste, smell, or feel. This is not to say that any physically sensible aspect of

a particular experience will be automatically encoded. As noted previously, attentional processing is usually required for encoding to occur.

In addition to the directly sensory aspects of experiences we also encode their meanings. When we learn concept names, whether names of digits, letters, words, places, people, we encode how to pronounce those names and, most important, what the names mean.

Principle of Encoding Specificity A particularly important aspect of encoding is what Endel Tulving and his associates have called the *principle of encoding specificity* (Tulving and Pearlstone, 1966; Tolving and Osler, 1968). Broadly speaking, this principle refers to the interactions between prior knowledge and the context of new experiences. We have referred to this interaction a number of times previously and will do so again. The principle of encoding specificity can be illustrated in a very simple task.

Suppose you are shown a list of words to be remembered. Each word to be remembered is typed in capital letters and is presented with another word typed in lowercase letters. You are told the word typed in lowercase is not important to remember but that looking at it might help recall the word to be remembered. Now suppose you see pairs of words like *ground/COLD, train/BLACK,* and so on. After the list is presented you are given a cued recall task: a word is presented and you try to recall a word from the list of to-be-remembered words. If the cue presented is a word like *ground* or *train*, your recall of COLD and BLACK will be quite good. However, suppose cue words such as *hot* and *white* were presented. It turns out that these cues are quite ineffective in prompting recall of COLD or BLACK. However, if you were next presented words like *hot* or *white* and asked to report the first word that occurred to you, it is very likely that you would say *cold* and *black*. (Tulving and Thompson, 1973; Watkins and Tulving, 1975). What is surprising in those findings is that even though COLD and BLACK are produced, they are not recognized by subjects as having been members of the previously presented list.

The operation of the encoding specificity principle as illustrated above suggests that what is encoded and hence stored in long-term memory depends on the context in which the encoding takes place. Retrieval is facilitated by reinstating this context. On the other hand, presenting a cue that might be effective in a different situation does not facilitate retrieval in this situation.

Depth of Encoding Some psychologists have argued that the differences between short-term and long-term memory might be attributed to differences in the way information is processed rather than to separate memory systems. If information is processed shallowly, instatement into memory will be weak; if information is processed deeply, it is more likely to be remembered longer. This notion of *depth of encoding* implies a greater degree of semantic or cognitive analysis with a consequent improvement in memory. On several occasions we have mentioned the importance of attentional processing in encoding. A particularly good illustration comes from work on depth of encoding (Craik and Lockhart, 1972). For example, suppose a list of familiar words is read aloud to subjects in each of three conditions (see Table 8.3). One group, intentional learners, is simply asked to learn the words for subsequent recall. Two other groups, incidental learners, are asked either to rate each word on a scale ranging from pleasant to unpleasant or to indicate when each word is read aloud whether or not it contained the letter *E*. Notice that the incidental learners are not told that a recall test will follow. In a number of studies like this, incidental subjects who are required to attend to the meaning of each word as in pleasantness rating recall as many words as do the intentional learners. However, when subjects attend to superficial aspects of words as in *E*-checking, recall is much poorer (Jenkins, 1974; Hyde and Jenkins, 1969).

A series of studies reported by Fergus I. M. Craik and Tulving (1975) further supports the role of depth of encoding. In general these studies involved presenting words and asking various questions about the words. For instance, after presentation of a word, the subjects were asked if it appeared in uppercase or lowercase type, or they were asked if the word rhymes with another word, or if the word fit into a blank in a sentence (for example, "He met a _____ in the street"). As you might expect, both recall and recognition were shown to be an increasing function of depth with best recall and recognition for words followed by sentence questions, next best for words followed by rhyme questions, and poorest for words followed by case questions (did it appear in uppercase or lowercase?). With all three types recall was better for questions whose answers were "yes" rather than "no" (see Figure 8.4).

It should be noted that there is a relationship between these depth of encoding studies and the principle of encoding specificity, which was discussed previously: the particular question asked about each word specifies the aspect or feature of the word that is attended to and encoded. This is illustrated in a study that compared the rhyme and sentence conditions employed by Craik and Tulving using recognition tests exclusively (Morris, Bransford, and Franks, 1977). Their results replicated those of Craik and Tulving. However, when a second group of subjects was given a new recognition list and was asked to indicate which words rhymed with the words presented initially, performance was better for words initially followed by rhyme questions. While depth of processing generally leads to

FIGURE 8.4 In Craik and Tulving's recall studies, words that were followed by sentence questions were recalled better than words followed by rhyme questions or by case questions. With all methods the recall was better for words whose processing question was answered by "yes" rather than "no."

TABLE 8.3   Recall as a Function of Orienting Tasks

ORIENTING TASKS	AVERAGE NUMBER OF WORDS RECALLED
Pleasantness rating	16.3
E-Checking	9.4
Intentional instructions	16.1

Source: Adapted from T. S. Hyde and J. J. Jenkins, "Differential Effects of Incidental Tasks on the Organization of Recall of a List of Highly Associated Words," *Journal of Experimental Psychology*, 82(1969): 472–481.

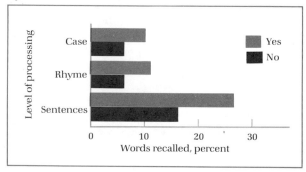

244

better memory, a match between the context at the time of encoding and the context at the time of retrieval is also an important factor in memory.

Storage

The preceding discussion clearly indicates that encoding and storage are intimately related. Our main emphasis in encoding was on either the processes of encoding—such as naming, imaging, and chunking—or the factors that influence encoding—such as the specific context or the depth of encoding. Note that in all of these instances, encoding was influenced by the existing contents of memory. In discussing *storage*, we will emphasize both the contents of long-term memory and the way these contents are represented and organized.

Episodic and Semantic Memory In terms of what is stored in long-term memory, Tulving (1972) distinguishes between episodic and semantic memory. *Episodic memory* involves storing spatial and temporal aspects of experiences that are of a highly autobiographical nature. That is, the experiences or events stored in episodic memory are unique to a given person, and the time at which these experiences occurred may be just as important as the experiences themselves. Tulving suggests that most psychological studies of memory have a strongly episodic character to them.

Semantic memory, according to Tulving, refers to our organized store of general knowledge including our knowledge of the world, rules that guide our mental operations, the solution of problems, and so on. Semantic memory is necessary for storing information in episodic memory in many instances. Remembering one's own wedding would represent episodic memory; the knowledge of what a wedding is would be held in semantic memory. In another example, learning a list of familiar words in an experiment involves an interaction between episodic memory and semantic memory. Remembering the time and place that the experiment took place may help us remember the words in the list from episodic memory, but the words are also stored in semantic memory where the time and place of original learning is not important.

Tulving's distinction between episodic and semantic memory is quite important. The most obvious reason is the notion that contents of memory can be organized in different ways, one highly personal and the other much less so. Of course, because what we experience and learn is determined

in part by what we know at the time, even semantic memory is personal in that sense. Both episodic and semantic memory are likely to be organized variously while retaining their distinctive functions.

Implicit in the issue of how knowledge and experience is represented in memory is the question of the organizational principles that characterize these representations. Organizational principles are typically inferred by studying retrieval from long-term memory. As you might expect, the task employed in a particular study has a major influence on the organization that is revealed. Nevertheless, studies indicate that human memory is highly complex and organized. The idea that different contents of long-term memory would be organized in different ways was implicit in our earlier discussion. Let us look next at some of those factors involved in the organization of memory.

Spatial Organization Cognitive maps appear to be organized in a spatial manner that reflects the nature of the learning experience. Spatial representation is also characteristic of our mental picture of concrete objects, which preserve much the same type of relative information that characterize cognitive maps. For example, your mental picture of a basketball may not include its absolute size, but it probably includes the fact that a basketball is substantially larger than a baseball.

Mental representations of objects like a basketball are highly particular, as are representations of particular objects like your favorite chair. However, we also have representations of a more general nature. These representations (such as a table) are also spatially organized, but they are not representations of a particular instance of the category (all tables). Such representations include our knowledge about kinds of objects, and they enable us to imagine things we know do not exist (for example, a cat larger than the Empire State Building).

Serial Organization Certain contents of memory are organized serially and in a specific sequential order. The best example of such serial organization is the letters of the alphabet. The English alphabet consists of 26 arbitrarily related symbols that have names. Because most of us only learn those names serially, beginning with *A* and ending with *Z*, our memory for them has that specific directional

245

character. Any normal adult can rapidly recite the alphabet from *A* to *Z* and use that sequential information to perform a variety of tasks that involve ordering the names of things alphabetically. However, it is very difficult to recite the alphabet in reverse order unless you have practiced that task a large number of times. Try reciting the alphabet backward and notice what you do.

Another example of serial organization is the order of months in the year or days in the week. Again there is a directional component to the organization in memory, although most people can recite the days in the week or months in the year backward with much less difficulty than the alphabet.

When we memorize materials by rote learning, or mechanical repetition, the materials are usually organized serially with a strong directional component. This is the case when we memorize prose such as Lincoln's Gettysburg Address in order to reproduce it in the correct order. In the case of prose, however, it is the order of the lines or phrases that is most difficult to memorize, not the individual letters or words. Notice also that understanding the meaning of a prose passage such as the Gettysburg Address is not a prerequisite of memorizing it by rote learning.

The kinds of organizational principles we have been discussing so far are fairly easy for most people to understand. This is not only because they are part of our common experience but also because they are externally imposed on the memory system. If your cognitive map for going somewhere is not a good one, you are likely to get lost or at least waste considerable time getting there. Similarly, the letters of the alphabet are organized in an externally imposed manner, and if we do not learn that order well, we could not readily perform alphabetizing tasks. Notice also that these organizational principles are applied to closely prescribed materials. There are, however, some organizational principles that appear to be less externally imposed on memory.

Associative Organization Several aspects of what is stored about words are revealed in a study by Roger Brown and David McNeill (1966). These investigators presented their subjects with dictionary definitions (but not the words themselves) of relatively uncommon words—for example, *nepotism* or *sampan*—and asked them to give the words corresponding to the definitions. The words of partic-

ular interest were those that the subjects reported as being on the "tip of the tongue" but that could not be produced. We all have experienced this phenomenon of being on the verge of being able to recall something that just will not come. When this "state" was signified, the subjects were asked a number of questions about the word such as initial letter, number of letters or syllables, words similar in sound and meaning. The overall results indicated that the subjects could answer these questions with considerable accuracy, even though they could not recall the words themselves.

The Brown and McNeill study suggests several important characteristics of storage in long-term memory. The questions answered suggest aspects or dimensions of storage. These include initial letter, syllable structure, sound pattern, and general meaning; that is, words may be stored in memory as a bundle of features loosely tied together. Evidence from studies of word association, which date back to the work of Sir Francis Galton (1883), support a number of these features as aspects of organization in memory.

The word association technique involves presenting a list of words and asking someone to report, for each word, the first word that comes to mind. Under these conditions of free association, the responses given typically reflect the general and most common meanings of the words presented. For instance, the word *table* usually leads to *chair*, *hot* leads to *cold*, *mother* leads to *father*. In each of these examples it is easy to see the aspects of general meaning reflected in the responses given to each stimulus word.

The free recall task has often been employed to investigate organizational factors in memory. This task involves presentation of a list of words, one at a time, which the subjects are then asked to recall in any order they choose. When the words in a list are common free associates or instances of semantic categories (bird names, items of clothing, or names of four-legged animals), the related words are likely to be closely clustered in recall even though they were spaced far apart when the list was presented (Jenkins and Russel, 1952; Bousfield, 1953)—that is, the free associates are likely to be recalled together as are the members of a particular semantic category (see Figure 8.5).

The clustering, or bringing up members of the same category together, of free associates suggests organization of general aspects of meaning, whereas clustering of category members involves more specific aspects of meaning. For example, free associates tend to come from the same grammatical class, although adults show this tendency much more than do young children. Nouns are names of things, and free associates to nouns are usually names of other things (*table-chair*). Verbs are names of actions, whereas adjectives are names of properties of things, and they are usually responded to with the names of other actions or properties (*run-walk, hot-cold*). In these cases rather general aspects of meaning are shared. In contrast, clustering of category members suggests organizational structures of things that share a number of more specific properties. Items of clothing share the characteristic of things we can wear.

Hierarchical Organization In recent years psychologists have become quite interested in examining the way in which semantic categories themselves are represented and organized in memory—an extremely important issue because it deals with the representation of knowledge. Some aspects of our semantic knowledge involve particular concepts: a canary is a bird. Other semantic aspects appear to involve making inferences about concepts: even if you have never seen a canary, you would probably say that it can fly because you know a canary is a bird and you know birds can fly. But do all birds fly?

One approach to investigating the structure of semantic categories suggests that much of human conceptual knowledge could be represented in memory in terms of hierarchically organized structures. Investigators (Bower, Clark, Winzenz, and Lesgold, 1969) have shown that hierarchically organized materials are learned and remembered better than randomly organized materials (see Figure 8.6). In addition, as we shall see in the next chapter, hierarchical organizations are thought to play an important role in language.

A. M. Collins and M. R. Quillan (1969) provide an example of one such hierarchically organized structure (see Figure 8.7). Note that the classes at each level are characterized by sets of properties that define the members of each class. In this example, the animal level is superordinate to all other levels. Thus, the bird class and fish class are subordinate to the animal class but are coordinate with each other. Similarly, the bottom classes are subordinates of classes above them but are coordinate with each other. Collins and Quillan assumed that each class is represented as a set of properties or features. They also assumed a principle of *cognitive economy* in the representation of these properties. For example, because most birds can fly, the property of flying is represented at the bird level and not at the level designating a particular class of birds (for example, canaries). Only when a property of a

FIGURE 8.5 Index of clustering in successive tenths of total items recalled. The dotted line indicates expected clustering if the items were recalled at random.

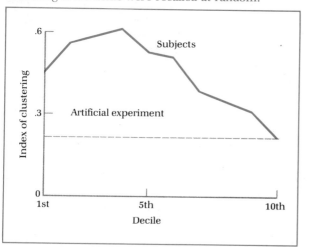

FIGURE 8.6 Mean number of words recalled out of 112 over several trials for subjects who studied organized versus random conceptual displays.

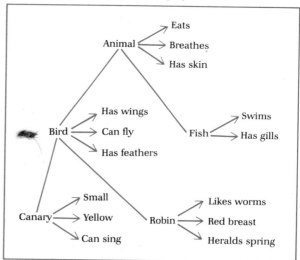

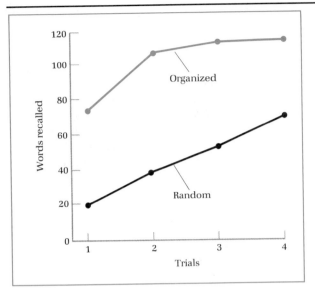

FIGURE 8.7 A simple hierarchy in semantic memory. The hierarchy consists of levels, properties of levels, and relationships among levels.

superordinate does not apply to a subordinate is that represented in the memory structure. Thus, "can't fly" is a property of the ostrich class. An important assumption of cognitive economy is that particular properties are not represented more than is necessary. This, in turn, requires making inferences about relationships among concepts. The concept of bird contains the information that they can fly but not that they eat. To discover that birds eat requires further search up the semantic hierarchy to the animal level.

Before testing their hypothesis about hierarchical representations, Collins and Quillian had to make some additional assumptions. The most basic were that it takes time to retrieve properties from a class (retrieving "can sing" from the canary class) and to move from one level to another searching the hierarchical structure. For example, if you were asked to verify a statement such as "a canary can fly," it would require moving from the canary level to the bird level to retrieve the property "can fly."

The basic experiment involved presenting statements such as "a canary can sing," "a canary can fly," and so on. When each statement was presented, the subject pressed one of two buttons to indicate that the statement was true or false. The measure of interest was reaction time to true statements because reaction time to false statements should, in general, be long. The results of this experiment indicated that not all aspects of our

knowledge are equally accessible. Thus, it takes longer to verify that "a canary is an animal" than "a canary is a bird," which in turn takes longer to verify than "a canary can sing." "A canary can sing" is verified most rapidly. The results also showed that inferences can be made even about things never actually experienced and that the time taken to make such inferences increases as the number of steps involved increases. Thus, it takes longer to verify that "a canary has skin" than it does to verify that "a canary can fly."

The work of Collins and Quillian certainly supports the notion of a hierarchical principle of organization in memory.

The classes or categories employed by Collins and Quillian were assumed to be organized according to a strictly logical hierarchy, with properties or features represented at the highest possible level in a particular hierarchy. There is reason, however, to question both of these assumptions. For example, if these assumptions were correct, it should take longer to verify the statement "a horse is an animal" than the statement "a horse is a mammal." As you might well expect, just the opposite outcome has been found (Rips, Shoben, and Smith, 1973). Observations such as this have led psychologists to question the strictly logical nature of hierarchies as well as the assumption that properties or features are only stored at the highest possible level in a given hierarchy.

Historically speaking, the treatment of conceptual knowledge in psychology has often involved the assumption that concepts are defined logically—that is, that concepts are clearly defined by a specific set of attributes or features and that all instances of a particular concept possess these defining features to an equal degree. Notice that in the Collins and Quillian model (see Figure 8.7) the properties represented at a particular level are considered to be equally representative of the concept.

Alternative Structures of Organization There is also evidence that organizations in memory may be quite flexible in that the same information may be organized in more than one way. For example, studies have shown that the same information is remembered equally well whether it is presented in a hierarchical organization or according to some other organizational principle (Broadbent, Cooper, and Broadbent, 1978). Thus, different people may organize the same information in different ways depending on their previous experiences. Because what we learn depends on complex interactions, it is not surprising that the way memory is structured or organized also reflects these interactions. The principle of encoding specificity also applies to organizational aspects of long-term memory; that is, organizations in long-term memory result from the interactions of prior knowledge and the context of new experience.

Alternative conceptions have been provided concerning the way concepts or categories might be organized without necessarily questioning the possibility of hierarchical relations among categories. Eleanor Rosch (1975) suggests that many natural categories or concepts are organized around prototypic features that are "most representative" of particular categories. For the category of "birds," her adult subjects rated robins and sparrows as being central to the concept and chickens and ducks less so; they were marginal to the prototype. They also verified statements such as "a robin is a bird" faster than statements such as "a turkey is a bird." Thus, Rosch sees category membership as being a matter of degree that depends on the features shared with the prototype. This requires that features or properties be represented at both the superordinate and subordinate levels. The importance of prototypes in Rosch's work is also supported by studies such as the Jeffrey Franks and John Bransford (1971) experiment we considered in the previous chapter. Recall that in their experiment subjects learned an abstract prototype that had never been presented to them.

Lance Rips, Edward Shoben, and Edward Smith (1973) also provide a model of conceptual knowledge that does not require strictly logical concepts. Their view is that concepts are represented in terms of both defining features and characteristic features. Defining features must be true of concepts. The concept "bird" might have defining features like "has a head," "has wings," "has feathers," and so on. Characteristic features for "bird" might include "can sing" and "can fly," because they are not defining features of all birds.

According to Rips and his colleagues, verifying statements such as "a canary is a bird" first involves comparing all features, both defining and characteristic. If the degree of feature overlap is high, responding should be rapid. However, if the characteristic features are not shared, as in "an ostrich is a bird," then a second comparison is made on the basis of the defining features alone, which causes verifying such statements to be slower.

We have now examined a number of organizational principles that characterize long-term memory. An important point to emphasize before concluding this section is that human memory is highly organized in one manner or another. It is also important to realize that the organizations described were presented in simple, single-word applications. Whole concepts are organized, drawn from, and shared among other items in memory just as single words are. All of memory is organized in some fashion, and these organizations are interrelated.

Retrieval

Much of what has already been discussed in this chapter deals with *retrieval* because what we know about human memory is often based on what we remember. In fact, some aspects of retrieval are at least implicit in encoding and storage.

Organizational Structures If someone asked you what letter of the alphabet followed the letter *B*, your answer would be prompt and correct. However, suppose you were asked what letter follows *J*. For most people this question is not as easy to answer and often requires retrieval of other information before the answer is given. You could begin by recalling that the alphabet begins with *A* and proceed through the alphabet until you arrive at the answer *K*. Most people do not have to start with *A*, however. They simply enter the serial organization at some well-known transition point, perhaps *G* followed by *H*, and proceed from there. The point of this example is that successful retrieval often requires recall of the organizational structure that is stored in memory before a specific piece of information can be provided. As more extreme examples of this point, what is the eleventh letter in the alphabet or what letter follows the letter *T*?

Retrieval of organizational structures previously stored in long-term memory may allow us to provide information that has not been stored explicitly. For example, suppose you were asked how many windows there are in your home or in the place where you currently live. Most of us have not bothered to store that sort of fact in memory. Nevertheless, we can usually answer such questions by retrieving a mental image of the place in question and simply counting the number of windows. In this case, the relevant organizational structure is the mental image or cognitive map we have of where we live.

In the preceding discussion of storage in long-term memory, we noted that the same information may be organized in more than one way. It also turns out that certain aspects of retrieval depend on which organizational structure we are using. This is nicely illustrated by some work by Steven Kosslyn (1975, 1976) and his co-workers. They asked subjects to verify the truth of statements such as "cat have claws" and "cats have heads." When the subjects were responding on the basis of their semantic knowledge of cats, the statement "cats have claws" was verified faster. A model such as that of Collins and Quillian would explain this finding by noting that "having claws" is a property of cats, whereas "having heads" is a property of all animals. However, when the subjects of this experiment were asked to form a mental image of a cat before the statements were presented, the statement "cats have heads" was verified faster. Apparently, when we use the organizational structure provided by a mental image of a cat, the head is more prominent than the claws.

The preceding example illustrates some important aspects of retrieval from long-term memory. It shows that organizational structures not only influence what we retrieve but guide our search as well. Related aspects of memory and retrieval can be illustrated by considering the following questions:

What is the telephone number of the White House?
What is the telephone number of the king of France?
What is the telephone number of your closest friend?

Your answer to the question about the White House probably would be "I don't know." Notice that the answer did not follow a lengthy search of all telephone numbers that you know. You might have wondered why anyone would ask you such a question, and you would probably agree that such a number does exist. When we know some piece of information is not stored in memory, we do not bother to search for it.

Your answer to the question about the king of France illustrates another aspect of retrieval and its relation to other cognitive activities. Again, the answer is "I don't know." But in this case you probably retrieved the fact that you could not know this number because there is no king of France. You may also have retrieved other related information

such as England has a queen, her name is Elizabeth, and she is the second queen of England to have that name. Retrieval of this last fact may even lead you to think about (retrieve?) at least some of what you know about the first Elizabeth.

The "Tip of the Tongue" Phenomenon The preceding example shows that even when a piece of information is not stored in memory and hence cannot be retrieval, it may still lead to the retrieval of other, related information. The retrieval of related information is a common experience as is the experience of searching for something in memory that cannot be retrieved at the moment. We saw this in our previous discussion of the Brown and McNeill (1966) "tip of the tongue" study. Even when subjects could not recall the words being probed for, they could recall features of those words such as the initial letter, number of letters or syllables, or words similar in meaning.

Retrieval of related aspects of an experience or event often facilitates retrieval of the experience or event itself. Have you ever had the experience of trying to remember the name of someone you met at a party and not being able to do so? The experience is often quite frustrating. You may be able to recall the names of other people present at the party, what they were doing, and why the party was given. Still the elusive name will not come to mind. Nevertheless, if you can retrieve enough aspects of the party, the name you are searching for may eventually be retrieved. At least the mental search should help you recognize the name when you hear it.

Context This example reinforces the importance of reinstating the context of encoding at the time of retrieval—what we referred to as the principle of encoding specificity. Recall that this principle states that what is encoded and subsequently stored in memory is to a large extent determined by the context at the time of encoding. Therefore, reinstating this context greatly facilitates retrieval, particularly in the case of our very personal episodic memories. This principle also helps us understand why cued recall and recognition are usually better than unaided recall (Tulving and Pearlstone, 1966; Tulving and Osler, 1968). In both of these cases more clues to the context of initial encoding are often provided (see Figure 8.8).

In some cases, cues presented at the time of retrieval often prove ineffective when we might think they should be effective. In one of our earlier examples, the word *cold* was presented in a list of words in the context of the word *ground*. *Ground* served as an effective cue for recalling that *cold* was a member of the list, while the semantically related word *hot* did not. Presentation of the cue word *hot* led to retrieval of the word *cold* but not to the fact that *cold* was a word in the list. This probably occurs because those features of the word *cold* having to do with *ground* were emphasized in episodic memory for the words on the list. Therefore, even though the cue word *hot* made the subjects think of the word *cold*, they did not recognize it as a list item. It is only when the same cues are presented during both learning and recall that they facilitate retrieval (Tulving and Thompson, 1973; Watkins and Tulving, 1975).

The importance of reinstating the encoding context at the time of retrieval appears to be quite general. Alan Baddeley (1976) discusses several studies pertaining to this issue. In one study, divers learned material either on land or under 10 feet of water, and retention was subsequently tested in one location or the other. Retention was much better when tested in the same environment in which original learning took place. If students are

tested in the same room where they were taught, they will score higher than if they are tested in a different location. A related phenomenon, called *state-dependent memory* (Baddeley, 1976) occurs when material learned in an altered physiological state—usually drug-induced—is recalled in the same state (see Chapter 5). For example, it has been shown that material learned under the influence of alcohol is best recalled under the influence of alcohol. There is clinical evidence of heavy drinkers who remember where they hid money while drunk only when they are again drunk (Goodwin, Powell, Bremer, Hoine and Stern, 1969).

Depth. Another concept that was considered earlier was depth of encoding or depth of processing. We noted that if subjects attend to relatively superficial aspects of words such as the letters they contain or the way they sound, retrieval is quite poor. However, if they attend to aspects such as the meaning or pleasantness of words, retrieval is much better. Thus, the more deeply material is processed at the time of encoding, the more likely it is to be subsequently retrieved.

We might summarize our discussion of encoding, storage, and retrieval in terms of some principles for better retrieval or good memory. At the time of initial encoding, organize the material you want to remember. Recall that some kinds of information may be organized in different ways, and the more ways it is organized, the more accessible it may be, depending on the retrieval context. In addition, multiple organizations often result in deeper levels of processing. As an illustration of such multiple organizations, recall that encoding specificity is a concept that is relevant to the encoding, storage, and retrieval of information, and not just to encoding alone. The principles of good memory are nicely illustrated in the following examination of mnemonics.

Mnemonics

The word *mnemonics* refers both to the centuries-old art of memory and to the devices, plans, or tricks that can be used as memory aids. Generally speaking, these aids are used to relate new material to some previously learned organizational scheme. As a result, the new material is both encoded and

FIGURE 8.8 Recall is often facilitated by cues. The first group does better on the second recall test because retrieval cues of category names have been presented. The second group does better than the first group on the first recall test because it benefits from the retrieval cues.

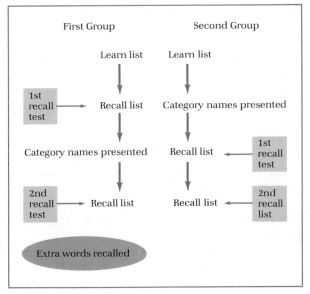

stored in an organized form and hence is easier to retrieve subsequently. Mnemonic aids can be useful in remembering many things. It is even helpful to invent a mnemonic for remembering how to spell the word *mnemonics.*

Almost any organizational scheme can be used as a basis for a mnemonic aid. However, the most commonly cited mnemonic aids involve the use of cognitive maps, images, or rhymes. Early Greek and Roman orators are reported to have used a combination of cognitive maps and images as mnemonic aids. For example, in preparing a speech the orators might mentally place the various topics at particular places along a well-known route or path. For example, topic C might be associated with the third house down the street. When it was time to give the speech, the orator would mentally travel along this route retrieving the topics to be talked about in the prescribed order. Because the places along the route were well known to the orator, retrieval of the order of topics would be facilitated. The task of encoding and storage of topics at particular places might have involved a great deal of effort, however.

In the discussion of motor programs we mentioned that the rhythmic nature of these programs could help explain why they are so resistant to forgetting. A similar reason could be given for the use of rhymes as mnemonic aids. Rhyme mnemonics can be quite effective if they are well constructed because mistakes in the order of recall destroy the rhyme.

A rhyme is commonly used to remember the number of days in each month of the year. "Thirty days hath September, April, June, and November, all the rest have thirty-one . . ." The rhyme establishes an organization that, once learned, is easy to remember. Of course, recalling the number of days in a particular month, say July, may be difficult without recalling the entire rhyme.

A combination of a rhyme and images is employed in the frequently cited pegword system. This system is based on words that rhyme with a sequence of numbers. Once the rhyme is established, the material to be memorized must be attached to the rhyme words. For example, one is a bun, two is a shoe, three is a tree, four is a door, five is a hive, six are sticks, seven is heaven, eight is a gate, nine is a line, and ten is a hen. The main feature of a numeric pegword list is that the list must only be learned once. Each new list of material is associated with the old pegwords. Now, if a new list of items is to be remembered, such as kite, duck, cow, ele-

phant, giraffe, lamp, desk, watch, coat, and cone, it is only necessary to think of an association between the new items and the pegwords. For example, you might imagine a kite inside inside a huge bun, a duck putting on a shoe, a cow in a tree, an elephant squeezing through a narrow door, and so on (see Figure 8.9). In the pegword system the rhyme is fairly easily learned. The hard part comes in encoding the features of the words to be imaged and the construction of the image itself. The pegword system works best when a strong visual image can be formed (Bower, 1972).

Well-constructed mnemonic aids are effective for several reasons. First, the material to be memorized is integrated into a well-known organization scheme that can be retrieved readily. Second, the process of integrating new material into the existing scheme involves an encoding context (one-bun, two-shoe) that is easily reinstated at the time of recall. Third, the integration of the new material with the encoding context is likely to involve fairly deep levels of processing—for example, remembering things monkeys commonly do when constructing an image of a monkey swinging in a tree. However, despite the effectiveness of good mnemonic aids, it should be emphasized that they are not always easy to use: you have to work hard at them.

Forgetting

Why do we forget? This question raises one of the intriguing issues in psychology. We seldom are concerned about why we remember (we just do), but we become very concerned about why we forget or fail to remember. And this concern becomes greater as we grow older. Although forgetting usually implies that something is lost from long-term memory, forgetting from short-term memory is relevant to the problem.

Forgetting from short-term memory is typically explained as being the result of displacement: new inputs displace old inputs in order to avoid capacity overload. This view of forgetting from short-term memory has been generally favored, at least since the work of Nancy Waugh and Donald Norman (1965). Prior to that time an alternative explanation held that forgetting from short-term memory would occur if material currently in short-term memory was not attended to, because the memory traces would decay over time.

To test these alternative explanations, Waugh and Norman devised an experiment using what is known as the probe technique. They presented subjects with several series of 16 digits. The last digit in each series was one that had appeared exactly once previously. This last digit is called the probe digit, and the subjects' task was to report the digit that followed the first appearance of the probe digit. Given a list such as 4, 9, 0, 4, 9, 8, 3, 5, 8, 2, 6, 3, 6, 2, 0, 5, the probe digit is 5, and the subject should recall the number 8.

The digits were presented verbally at either a fast (four per second) or slow (one per second) rate. For each list the probability of correct recall could be assessed as being due to either the number of digits or the amount of time occurring after the first presentation of the probe digit. Remember that the initial presentation of the probe digit had to be in short-term memory for the subjects to say what digit followed it. Thus, in the example above, eight digits follow the first presentation of the probe digit. With slow presentation eight seconds would elapse, and with fast presentation only two seconds would elapse. If the decay principle was correct, greater forgetting should be found with slow presentation than with fast presentation. However, if short-term memory operated according to displacement, presentation rate should make no difference. Of course, with displacement the number of digits following the first presentation of the probe digit should make a big difference.

The results of the Waugh and Norman experiment are summarized in Figure 8.10. The number of digits following initial presentation of the probe digit has a major effect. Presentation rate had no appreciable influence on recall. These findings strongly support the displacement principle as the major cause of forgetting from short-term memory. As the number of digits following the first presentation of the probe digit increases, the opportunity for displacement increases, and recall becomes increasingly poorer.

Before we discuss the reasons for forgetting from long-term memory, it is necessary to say something

FIGURE 8.9 A list of items can be remembered by forming an association between each item and a pegword.

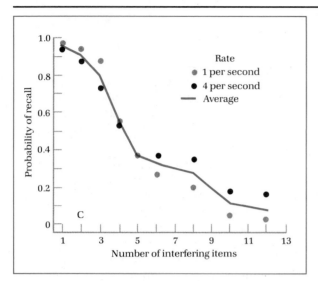

FIGURE 8.10 Probability of recall as a function of the number of digits following the digit to be recalled.

about the meaning of the word *forgetting*. When we forget something from short-term memory such as a recently looked-up telephone number, it is truly forgotten. If we need to dial the number again, we must look it up again. However, forgetting from long-term memory is much more complex. In fact, with long-term memory we can only be sure that we have failed to retrieve something; that is, we cannot be certain that a memory once in long-term memory has been truly forgotten, only that we cannot retrieve it. When we experience the "tip of the tongue" phenomenon in which some memory cannot be retrieved, we know it is still there. It is also fairly common to struggle to recall something, come to the conclusion that we must have forgotten it, and have the memory return at a later time.

We have considered several factors having to do with successful retrieval or good memory. Clearly the reverse of these factors will lead to memories that are easily forgotten or difficult to retrieve. Memory will be poor when materials to be learned are not well organized at the time of encoding and storage. Memory will also be poor when materials to be learned are not encoded at sufficiently deep levels or when the context at the time of encoding is quite different from that at the time of retrieval.

Proactive and retroactive interference are among the factors that make memories difficult to retrieve (see Figure 8.11). *Proactive interference* arises when material learned previously interferes with retrieval of recently learned material. *Retroactive interfer-*

ence is said to occur when the retrieval of previously learned material is interfered with by recently learned material. Notice that the terms *proaction* and *retroaction* refer to the temporal locus of interference. Thus, in proaction old memories operate forward in time to disrupt retrieval of newer memories, while in retroaction new memories operate backward in time to disrupt retrieval of older memories.

Either proactive or retroactive interference is particularly likely to occur when the same retrieval cue leads to different responses over time. Examples of such interference effects are commonly observed. A friend moves to a new home, and you have difficulty retrieving either the new address (proactive interference) or the old address (retroactive interference). A girlfriend you grew up with has been married for some time, and you have difficulty retrieving either her married name (proactive interference) or her maiden name (retroactive interference). In fact, proactive and retroactive interference effects are so common that the importance of these factors in explaining retrieval failures is often overlooked.

Another type of interference, which may be either proactive or retroactive in nature, is what is called mediated interference. *Mediated interference* is said to occur when some desired response is blocked by another response because both are linked to a common mediational concept. For example, suppose the office where you work has just purchased a photocopier; you know the name of the machine perfectly well, but you keep calling it a Xerox. In this case, the name Xerox is so strongly associated wth the photocopying industry that you have difficulty retrieving the name of the copier used in your office. A person named Schick might occasionally be introduced to others, not without embarrass-

FIGURE 8.11 Proactive interference arises when previously learned material interferes with the retrieval of recently learned material. Retroactive interference arises when the retrieval of previously learned material is interfered with by recently learned material.

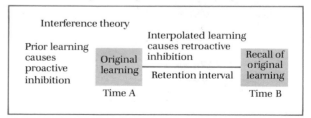

ment, as Mr. or Ms. Gillette. You can, no doubt, supply many similar examples.

Finally, emotional states can cause retrieval failure or forgetting. As any student knows, either through personal experience or that of an acquaintance, anxiety at the time of an exam can be a major source of retrieval failure. It is not that anxiety is unusual when taking exams, but when the anxiety level gets too high it often is accompanied by extraneous thoughts or worries that interfere with retrieval of the relevant information (Holmes, 1974).

Perhaps the most frequently cited theory of emotional factors in retrieval failure is Freud's (1914/1938) theory of repression. Because this topic will be treated extensively in a later chapter (see Chapter 12), it will only be outlined here. The basic theme of this theory is that certain childhood experiences as well as later experiences associated with them are so traumatic that the individual refuses to allow memories of them to enter consciousness. Repression is not a conscious process; it is unconscious, and the memories of these traumatic experiences are stored in the unconscious. Retrieval of such memories, according to Freud, occurs only when the emotion associated with them is reduced, usually through some form of therapy.

Short-Term Memory and Long-Term Memory: One Memory or Two?

As we have seen, there are a variety of reasons for distinguishing between short-term memory and long-term memory including the fact that short-term memory has a very limited capacity, while the capacity of long-term memory is enormous. Forgetting from short-term memory is largely due to displacement or overload, whereas quite different principles are used to explain forgetting from long-term memory. Another characteristic of short-term memory can be seen in our example of looking up a telephone number, dialing it, and noting that when the conversation is over the number is totally forgotten. The experience of briefly holding information in consciousness, after which it is no longer consciously available, is characteristic of short-term memory. In this example the telephone number can only be reinstated in short-term memory by looking it up again.

We do recall some well-known and frequently used telephone numbers. These telephone num-

bers are stored in long-term memory. However, soon after dialing one of these numbers, it is not consciously available either—unless we make the effort to reinstate it in short-term memory. We are aware of information present in short-term memory, and this does not depend on the information source. The information can enter from long-term memory or from an external source such as a telephone book. We consciously know what is currently in short-term memory and can report it immediately; in contrast, the contents of long-term memory are typically not available consciously, even though we do know quite a lot about what is stored in our long-term memory. For example, if asked whether or not you know the mailing address of a particular person, you might well answer affirmatively without recalling the address at all. You know that you know the address, but until the address is reinstated in short-term memory you may not be aware of it consciously or be able immediately to report it.

Frequently called numbers are stored in long-term memory and then transferred to short-term memory for current use.

One important focus of memory research is the process by which an item such as a telephone number is transferred from short-term memory to long-term storage. Researchers want to know, for example, what factors influence how strongly an item is registered in long-term memory. According to several widely held theories, the length of stay in short-term storage is one such factor. This notion states that an item's strength in the long-term store is directly related to the amount of time it has spent in short-term memory.

An experiment to test this notion was developed by Fergus M. Craik and Michael J. Watkins (1973). In designing their experiment, Craik and Watkins faced a twofold problem. First, they had to find a technique for measuring an item's length of stay in a subject's short-term memory; then they had to relate these findings to the probability that a subject could later recall the item, thus indicating its storage in long-term memory.

The subjects of their experiment were 54 introductory psychology students from a college in London. They were instructed to listen to a recorded series of 27 word lists, each containing 21 simple nouns. Their task was to report after each list the last word that began with a previously designated critical letter. For example, if the critical letter for a given list was T and the list ran STOVE, TABLE, GRAIN, HOUSE, RIFLE, TRAIN ..., the subject would first hold TABLE in his short-term memory and then replace it with TRAIN. This procedure continued until the end of the list, at which time the subject wrote down the last word beginning with T.

The words in a list were presented at regular intervals. Some lists were presented at a slow rate (one word every two seconds), some at a medium rate (one word every second) and others at a fast rate (one word every half second). This method provided the researchers with a means of measuring how long a given critical word was held in the subject's short-term memory.

After presentation of all the lists, the subjects were given a ten-minute test in which they were asked to write down all the words, both critical and noncritical, that they could recall from the lists. The test gave the researchers a measure of which critical words had actually registered in a subject's long-term memory. This enabled them to calculate the relationship between the time a critical word stayed in short-term memory and its registration in the long-term store.

The results in percentages of words recalled under each of the three variable conditions are shown in the table below. These three variable conditions are the nature of the critical word (whether it was "replaced" in short-term memory or "reported" as the last critical word in the list); the rate of presentation; and the i value (the number of intervening noncritical words appearing on the list between a critical word and its replacement or report).

The results indicate that recall on the test was best for words that had been presented at the slowest rate (one word every two seconds). However, for any given rate of presentation, recall of both reported words and replaced words was not influenced by the i value, their relative length of time in short-term memory. These findings suggest that the time available for processing each item and the way in which it is processed are critical for registration in the long-term store. Contrary to widely accepted theories, merely increasing the amount of time in the short-term store does not appear to influence long-term registration.

| Condition | Presentation rate | i VALUE | | | | | | | | | |
		0	1	2	3	4	5	6	8	12	Mean
Replaced	Slow	12	13	22	10	21	19	19	18	19	17
	Medium	10	15	22	12	14	19	09	12	11	14
	Fast	14	07	11	06	06	14	09	16	15	11
	Mean	12	12	19	10	14	17	13	15	15	14
Reported	Slow	19	20	20	20	31	39	22	26	28	25
	Medium	20	22	19	19	31	26	20	28	20	23
	Fast	26	15	22	26	20	31	19	11	20	21
	Mean	22	19	20	22	28	32	20	22	23	23

Another distinction between short-term memory and long-term memory derives from the study of patients suffering from bilateral damage to the temporal lobes as well as to the hippocampus. These patients perform normally on short-term memory tasks such as immediate memory span for digits or for randomly presented words and show unimpaired general intelligence. However, they are grossly defective when it comes to transferring new material from short-term memory to long-term memory, irrespective of practice. Such patients have little difficulty recalling events prior to the brain damage. Thus both long-term memory and short-term memory appear unimpaired, and although material in long-term memory can be recalled and reinstated in short-term memory, new material in short-term memory is not stored in long-term memory. We might note that a similar pattern of memory performance is found in certain cases of senility.

A particularly striking example of this memory pattern is found in a patient called H.M., as described by Brenda Milner (1970). The patient's condition resulted from brain surgery performed because of severe epileptic seizures. Generally speaking, H.M. showed normal memory for things learned prior to surgery. He had command of language and could maintain new experiences in short-term memory for short periods of time by verbal rehearsal. His problem was that new material either was not stored in long-term memory or could not be retrieved from long-term memory. For example, H.M. had difficulty remembering the surroundings of the house where he had lived for six years and in recalling the names of regular visitors if he met them on the street. During the years since surgery there has been little or no improvement in this situation (see Figure 8.12).

What are we to conclude about memory from cases such as that of H.M.? At one time it was generally believed that such a problem was one of being unable to store information in long-term memory because of some disruption of the consolidation process. This interpretation was consistent with the view, based on the differences between short-term memory and long-term memory noted previously, that short-term memory and long-term memory were separate memory systems. However, both of these views have been challenged in more recent years. While it is still useful to talk about short-term memory and long-term memory separately in order to emphasize different aspects

of memory, the existence of separate storage systems is questioned. Studies of patients such as H.M are also beginning to bring into question the dual-storage view. The results of tests, usually recognition tests but also motor or nonverbal learning tests, reveal some memory for recent events in such patients. These findings have led scientists to believe that failure of retrieval mechanisms is responsible for the observed deficits (Lindsay and Norman, 1977).

Memory and Thinking

At the beginning of this chapter we emphasized the extremely close relationship between memory and other cognitive activities. In the next chapter we will consider relationships among cognitive activities that are intimately related to language. Meanwhile, it is appropriate to conclude this chapter by illustrating some of the other relationships between memory and cognition.

FIGURE 8.12 In comparison to normal subjects H. M.'s recall ability varied as a function of time. In each trial subjects were presented with successive stimuli and were to say whether a stimulus was the same as the preceding one. The time interval between presentation of each stimulus and its recall was increased from 0 to 60 seconds. Normal subjects averaged 1 error per 12 trials. With 0 seconds delay, H. M. made only 1 error; with 60-seconds delay, he averaged close to 5 errors.

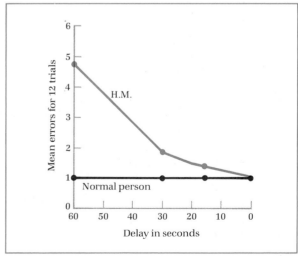

The term *thinking* refers to a variety of cognitive activities including problem solving, planning, decision making, judgment—even remembering. In carrying out these activities we rely on the contents of long-term memory to a large degree. These contents include specific information, our knowledge of the world, and various organized schemata. Consider, for example, a fairly commonplace activity such as "going out to dinner." Our schemata for this activity involves planning which restaurant to go to. Planning in turn involves making various decisions and judgments about what type of food we want to eat, how much we are willing to pay, what type of dress is appropriate, and so on. All of these decisions and judgments require remember-ing what we know about various restaurants including where they are located and how best to get to them (cognitive maps). If we drive a car to the restaurant and have a flat tire along the way, problem solving may also be required, and our success at solving this problem will depend on our schemata for "changing tires," including how to use the jack.

Retrieval of contents of long-term memory aids the cognitive activities involved in thinking, and they are constrained by failures of retrieval as well. Two examples illustrate these effects. First, suppose someone asked you where you were at 2 P.M. on the first Monday in March, two years ago. Unless that point in time was of particular significance for you,

FOCUS: In Search of the Engram

A fundamental assumption underlying memory re-search is that all learning somehow engraves a phys-ical imprint on the nervous system. Karl Lashley, the distinguished pioneer in the investigation of learn-ing's biological basis, labeled this presumed memory trace the *engram*—from the Greek for "that which is written in."

Lashley spent more than 30 years in search of the engram. His method was straightforward. He trained rats to negotiate a series of simple mazes, then surgically removed a portion of cerebral cortex from the brain of each animal. If the engram was stored in that particular portion of brain tissue, Lashley reasoned, then the rat would forget what it had learned about running the maze. The rat's loss of memory would be manifested in maze perform-ance: it would be slower in running the maze and would make more errors.

Lashley conducted hundreds of such experi-ments, cutting lesions in many different parts of the cortex. To his surprise, Lashley found that the ani-mal's performance in the maze was not affected specifically by damage to any single cortical area. Rather, the resulting deficits in maze performance seemed to be a function of the total amount of cor-tical tissue removed: the more tissue lost, the less the rat remembered. Near the end of his career, Lashley (1950) concluded with despair and irony: "I sometimes feel, in reviewing the evidence on the localization of the memory trace, that . . . learning is just not possible."

Lashley attempted to account for his frustrating results by proposing the principle of *mass action.* This principle suggested that the engram is actually everywhere, somehow distributed over the whole of the cortex rather than localized in a particular place. Critics, however, were quick to point to another pos-sible explanation for Lashley's experimental findings. The rat's learning of the maze is contingent upon several different parts of the sensory apparatus. The rat learns by seeing the maze, of course; but it also learns by feeling with its whiskers. These different types of engrams would be stored in different parts of the brain; hence destruction of one memory trace would still leave intact the other engram.

Although Lashley failed to localize the engram, his pioneering ideas and experimental techniques paved the way for contemporary researchers. For example, it was a suggestion by Lashley that inspired the famous split-brain experiments of Roger Sperry (see Chapter 2). One of the many interesting findings of the split-brain studies has permitted a reevalua-tion of the results of some of Lashley's experiments. Sperry's student, Ronald Myers (1961), provided evidence in cats that a visual memory may establish dual engrams—one in each hemisphere of the brain. It is now clear, from this and other findings, that Lashley's idea of mass action was most probably in error and that the principle of *multiple storage* can account for his findings. A single memory may somehow engrave more than one engram, and these multiple traces are stored in different parts of the brain.

Other researchers, by probing structures deep in the brain below the cortex, have succeeded in local-izing evidence of the engram. These experiments rely upon a modern technique not available in Lashley's time: microelectrodes that can monitor activity in a

it would be difficult to answer the question. However, by drawing on episodic memory and semantic memory, you could probably come up with a reasonable answer that was fairly likely to be correct. For example, if you were a student two years ago, you would know that Mondays are usually school days. You would also know that there are no national holidays in early March in the United States, so school was probably in session. Now if you also can remember what class, if any, was meeting at 2 P.M., you would be able to reconstruct a reasonably good answer.

As a second illustration, imagine entering a room in which two strings are hanging from the ceiling (Milner, 1970). You are told that your task is to tie the two strings together. The problem is that the strings are too far apart to reach both at the same time. Scattered about the room are a variety of objects including a pair of pliers. This is a classic problem used in the study of problem solving that most people find difficult to solve without some sort of hint such as the experimenter brushing against one string to start it swinging. However, if you happen to retrieve the concept of a pendulum from long-term memory the problem is readily solved. You simply tie the pliers to one string and set it swinging toward the other string. Now you can grasp both strings at the same time and tie them together (see Figure 8.13).

---

single nervous cell. Several such studies suggest that the structure known as the hippocampus, which is tucked up into the temporal lobe of the brain, may contain memory traces concerned with spatial representation of the visual world. In another part of the temporal lobe, Charles Gross and his colleagues discovered a nerve cell that fired when the monkey was presented with an image of a monkey's hand, a finding that implies the presence of the engram for a highly particular visual memory (Gross, Rocha-Miranda, and Bender, 1972).

The attempts to localize the engram seek to answer the question, *"Where* is it?" A second question asks, "Precisely *what* is it?" The physical form in which a memory is embodied has been the subject of considerable speculation. Most theories focus on two different possible mechanisms. One idea is that learning causes some sort of structural change at the synaptic gap separating nerve cells; for example, new and very short nerve fibers may sprout here, strengthening neural connections that presumably constitute the engram. The other idea centers on chemical alterations within the nerve cells. This view has been given impetus by the recent advances in genetics showing the enormous amount of information that can be precisely coded by large nucleotide molecules such as deoxyribonucleic acid (DNA) and ribonucleic acid (RNA). Engrams, it is suggested, may similarly be stored in protein molecules within nerve cells. A number of interesting experiments have attempted to test this notion—researchers have even tried to show that engrams can be transferred from one worm to another through cannibalism—but the results have been widely criticized as inconsistent or inconclusive. All of the theories about the physical or chemical nature of the engram remain largely speculative.

Perhaps the most promising current investigation of memory's biological basis focuses on habituation, which is the gradual decrease in behavioral response to a repeated stimulus. People living near train tracks, for example, at first may be bothered by the noise of the trains passing during the night. After a period of time, however, they get used to the sound and sleep through the night. Eric Kandel (1976) has painstakingly investigated habituation in the sea slug, *aplysia* (see Chapter 2 Research: "Studying Behavior at the Cellular Level"). Habituation occurs in *aplysia* when the gills are touched repeatedly. When first touched, the creature withdraws its gills vigorously, but repeated touching causes a gradual diminution of this reflex response. Kandel found that successive stimulation of the sensory neuron apparently caused a reduction in the amount of the chemical neurotransmitter released by that neuron into the synaptic gap. This reduction in transmitter provides a biological explanation for the diminution, or habituation, of the gill-withdrawal response.

Kandel's work, together with other research, appears to have pinpointed the fundamental mechanism for habituation not only in *aplysia* but also in many vertebrates. Although this mechanism may be far more elementary than the engram that Lashley set out to find many years ago, its discovery marks a significant step forward. The brain sciences typically make their greatest progress by mastering the study of such simple systems.

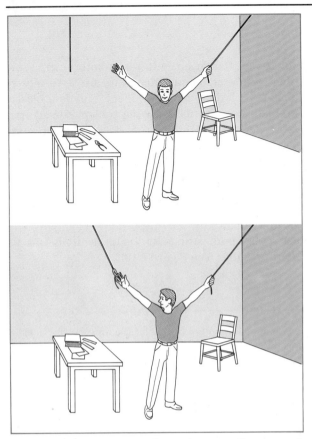

FIGURE 8.13 This is perhaps the most famous task used in laboratory studies of problem solving. The subject is required to figure out a way of tying two strings together, even though the two strings are too far apart to be held at the same time. A variety of objects are available for use in solving the problem, including a chair, tissue paper, a pair of pliers, and some paper clips. The solution involves tying the pliers to one of the strings and setting it in motion like a pendulum so that it can be reached while the subject is holding onto the other string.

The difficulty of the two-string problem lies in the failure to retrieve the concept of a pendulum from long-term memory. This retrieval failure occurs because most people placed in this situation fixate on the most conventional uses of the objects in the room including the pliers. This tendency is quite common in studies of problem solving and has been termed *functional fixedness.* However, functional fixedness is also an example of the principle of encoding specificity. The problem here is that an object, the pliers, is not a good retrieval cue for the concept of a pendulum.

Apart from retrieval failures, human memory also constrains the cognitive activities involved in thinking because of the limited capacity of short-term memory. Two illustrations of this constraint will illuminate the point. Suppose you are asked to place the months of the year in alphabetical order. You would have no difficulty recalling the names of the months, although for most of us the names are not stored in alphabetical order. You also know the alphabet quite well. With paper and pencil, the task is an easy one. However, try to perform this task without any external aids, and see how difficult it is to do. The difficulty is not due to any failure to retrieve information from long-term memory; rather, the capacity of short-term memory is overloaded by "keeping track" of the names while reordering them at the same time.

As a second illustration, try to multiply the number 23 by 67 in your head. Here again the problem is easy with paper and pencil, but doing it mentally, without external aids, is fairly difficult. The numbers 23 and 67 must be retained in short-term memory along with the numbers subsequently computed. Furthermore, short-term memory capacity is also taken up by applying the computational rules used to solve the problem. Both of the preceding examples illustrate the difficulty of thinking about anything that is complex in the sense of holding many components in short-term memory.

By no means is all thinking constrained by the limited capacity of short-term memory. Much of what is meant by thinking goes on beyond our conscious awareness, and only the products or results of those mental processes ever enter consciousness (Mandler, 1975). We referred to these mental processes as generative processes to reflect the inventive nature of their products. That is, generative processes serve to lead to new ideas. Such processes are thought to play an important role in language, as we shall see in the next chapter.

The nature of generative processes and the role that they play in thinking is not well understood at present and probably will not be for some time to come. However, several different approaches to the study of such processes are currently being attempted. As noted, the study of language is closely related to the study of generative processes. Another approach is illustrated by attempts to characterize organizational principles in memory as, for example, in the work of Collins and Quillian. Here the attempt is to discover how information is represented and organized in memory so that we can make inferences about how that information might be used in thinking.

Still a third approach is computer simulation of mental operations. Computers are being programmed so that they perform tasks in ways similar to the ways humans perform those tasks. To the extent that the simulation is a good one, it may be possible to infer characteristics of human mental operations from the nature of the computer program. Alan Newell and Herbert Simon (1972) have developed a general purpose program called the *General Problem Solver*, which does a reasonably good job of solving certain mathematical problems and of playing chess. While this approach is interesting in a number of ways, it is questionable whether it will lead to any major clarifications of human mental operations.

SUMMARY

1. Cognition is a complex set of processes that pertain to the acquisition of knowledge and its use. Memory is part of cognition and the basic building block upon which cognition is based. Learning and memory are closely interrelated.

2. For purposes of discussion, memory is classified into three types: sensory memory, short-term memory, and long-term memory. However, these varieties of memory are not necessarily separate and isolated stages. Sensory memory refers to the very brief span prior to perceptual processing. Visual memory trace, or iconic trace, has a relatively large storage capacity but a duration of not more than one second.

3. Short-term memory is longer in duration than sensory memory and has a limit of seven plus or minus two units of information, or chunks. Several theories of attention have been proposed. It is likely that attention does not restrict our ability to process and remember information in the sense of providing a capacity limitation. Capacity limitation is due to short-term memory, and attention refers to the act of processing information in short-term memory. A similar view states that attention has no independent status apart from the perceptual process.

4. Long-term memory is not only the repository of our prior experiences but also includes information and beliefs derived from these experiences as well as plans for guiding what we shall do in the future. Several abstract contents of long-term memory govern a substantial portion of our lives: cognitive maps, schemata, motor-programs, and generative processes.

5. Encoding refers to the extraction of information from events we experience—under the conditions that the events are experienced. This information is transformed into codes that memory can accept and store. More information is encoded into sensory memory than can be subsequently encoded into short-term memory. Encoding into short-term memory involves a deeper level of processing and typically requires some interaction with long-term memory. Short-term memory is usually encoded acoustically, but can also be encoded by visual form or meaning. An important aspect of encoding is the principle of encoding specificity, which refers to the interactions between prior knowledge and the context of new experiences.

6. Storage refers both to the contents of long-term memory and the way these contents are represented and organized. Episodic memory involves storing spatial and temporal aspects of experiences that are of a highly autobiographical nature. Semantic memory refers to our organized store of general knowledge. Memory is variously and complexly organized, and different contents may be organized in different ways, including spatial organization, serial organization, associative organization, and most important, hierarchical organization.

7. Retrieval of information from memory often requires recall of the organizational structure that is stored in memory before a specific piece of information can be provided. Organizational structures not only influence what we retrieve, but they also guide our search of long-term memory.

8. It is not unusual to have a piece of information stored in long-term memory but not be able to recall it at a given moment. One example of this is known as the "tip of the tongue" phenomenon.

9. The principle of encoding specificity also applies to retrieval; that is, reinstating the encoding context greatly facilitates retrieval, particularly in the case of personal, episodic memories. If words or concepts have been encoded by meaning (depth of encoding), they will be more easily retrieved than if superficially encoded.

10. Mnemonics refers both to the art of memory and to the devices, plans, or tricks that can be used

mory aids. Generally speaking, mnemonic
late new material to some previously learned
organizational scheme, such as a rhyme.

11. Forgetting from short-term memory is typically
explained as a result of displacement; new inputs
displace old inputs in order to avoid capacity overload. Forgetting from long-term memory is much
more complex. In fact, we can only be sure that we
have failed to retrieve something; we cannot be
certain that a memory once in long-term memory
has been truly forgotten. Among the factors that
make memories difficult to retrieve are proactive
and retroactive interference. Intense emotional
states, such as anxiety, can also cause retrieval failure or forgetting.

12. Regardless of the source, long-term memory or
an external source, information must enter short-
term memory for it to be consciously available. The
contents of long-term memory are typically not
consciously available.

13. Thinking refers to a variety of cognitive activities including problem solving, planning, decision
making, judgment, and even remembering. We rely
on the contents of long-term memory—specific information, our knowledge of the world, various
organized schemata—to accomplish the acts of
thinking. Constraints are placed on some forms of
thinking by the limited capacity of short-term
memory.

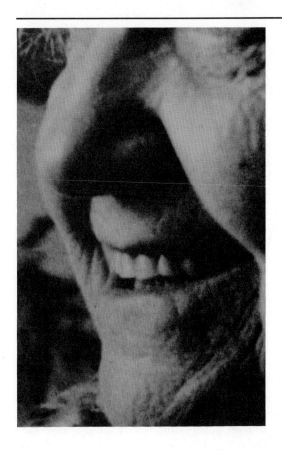

Chapter 9

Language

Our language constitutes what is perhaps the most striking difference between humans and all other species. In no other species do we find such a complex vehicle for communication as the languages used by humans. The speed and ease with which human children acquire and learn language invites our curiosity and study. Language provides very good examples for examining the motor programs and generative processes that are found in human behavior. Once a natural language has been acquired, the motor programs for speech production rarely require any particular attention to the complex sequences of motor movements involved. When we have decided what to talk about, the muscle groups that control the shape of our mouth as well as movements of the lips and tongue seem to take over automatically to produce the desired sequence of speech sounds with little or no conscious effort on our part.

In addition, the generative processes involved in natural language are revealed by a very important facet of language—*creativity*. Setting aside clichés, direct quotations, and customary greetings, many utterances we produce or hear are novel—ones we have never produced or heard before. In addition, we can continue to produce and understand novel utterances without limit so long as the vocabulary contained in those utterances is not unknown to us. The creativity found in natural language exemplifies the inventiveness of generative processes.

Another reason for treating language separately is its central importance in human cognitive activities. Language, spoken or written, serves as the medium through which most knowledge is communicated. We use language constantly in our daily activities for a variety of social, intellectual, and personal purposes. Thus, language serves as an important medium for observing the results of cognitive activities in human beings.

There are obvious parallels between spoken and written language. For example, when you read a sentence such as "The car has a flat tire," the same meaning is conveyed to you as when you hear someone utter that sentence. Despite the parallels, however, the main emphasis in this chapter will be on spoken language. Spoken language is much older than written language, and it is the form of language that we all learn first because formal training is required to learn written language. In addition, there are good reasons for believing that the processes involved in writing and reading do not totally mirror those involved in speaking and listening. Written and spoken language clearly differ in terms of the sensory-perceptual systems involved (visual versus auditory) as well as in terms of the motor systems involved in production (fingers and hands versus mouth, tongue, and lips).

Components of Spoken Language

Spoken language is typically divided into three components. The first component is the sound patterns that are found in all natural languages. The study of these sound patterns is called *phonology*. The second component is the grammatical structure or *syntax* of language. In English, as in any other natural language, it is this structure that determines whether or not a particular string of words ordered in a particular way constitutes an acceptable utterance. Most important, language is a vehicle for conveying the meaning of utterances, and the study of this component of language is called *semantics*. We will first explore phonology, syntax, and semantics and then see how each is used and acquired. Although these three components of language are clearly interrelated, it will be convenient in our discussion to treat them more or less separately.

Speech Production and Perception

To begin with, in any form of langauge production (speaking or writing) a complex set of skills is involved. These skills include translating mental representations ("ideas in the head") into sequential patterns that can then be translated into the sound of the language in question. For speech to be fluent, many of these skills must be highly automatic. For instance, during fluent speech, speakers mainly devote attention to the ideas they wish to express. Little conscious attention is paid to the particular form of the utterances (sentence types) or to the translation of meaning into sound.

The Sounds of Speech
Phonologists have developed a complex system for describing the speech sounds that occur in language. These sounds are called *phonemes*, and they correspond roughly to the letters of the written alphabet. There are more

phonemes in all languages combined than are found in any one particular language because some sounds that occur in one language do not occur in others. For example, in English there are different sounds for /r/ and /l/, but in Japanese this distinction does not exist. (It is conventional to put symbols for phonemes between slashes).

A phoneme is typically defined as the smallest unit of sound that makes a difference to the meaning of a larger sound unit such as a word. Consider the English word *tap*, for example. This word consists of three phonemes, and changing the middle one, the vowel, to /i/ changes the word to *tip*. Similarly, changing the initial consonant phoneme to /p/ gives us *pap*, whereas changing the final consonant to /b/ gives us *tab*.

For several decades it has been possible to represent the pattern of sound energy that occurs in speech in a visual form. An example of such a representation, which is called a *speech spectrogram*, is given in Figure 9.1. Three aspects of the speech signal are represented in a spectrogram. The vertical dimension represents the frequency of the sound in terms of cycles per second or hertz (Hz). Notice that the sound frequency is quite complex, with sound energy occurring at several different frequencies. The horizontal dimension represents elapsed time from the beginning to the end of an utterance in thousandths of a second or milliseconds. The amplitude of the sound is represented by the degree of darkening, with the darkest parts of the spectrogram reflecting the greatest sound energy. Notice that the darkest aspects of the spectrogram occur at several different frequency levels and that in many cases a "dark bar" changes rapidly across several frequency levels.

It is almost impossible to look at a particular spectrogram and determine which utterance might have produced it. There are striking contrasts between the visual representation of spoken language revealed in the spectrogram and the visual representation of the same message appearing in print. In the spectrogram there do not appear to be gaps between letters or words, as we see in the printed page of a book. It is even difficult to identify segments of the spectrogram that recur, although in terms of the phonemes involved in a particular message we know that some sounds must be recurring. Notice that the double "ee" in Figure 9.1 looks somewhat different in the word *speech* than it does in the word *see*.

Although spectrograms are difficult to read, they have made it possible for speech scientists to make important advances in the understanding of speech production and perception. These advances have been accomplished by creating imitation or synthetic spectrograms, developed partly through trial and error, that contain the essential elements required for particular patterns of speech sounds. These synthetic spectrograms can be converted into sound just as a phonograph needle can convert the grooves impressed on a record into sound. Sometimes very simple synthetic spectrograms are sufficient to generate an identifiable speech sound—one that would look very different and much more complex if you saw a spectrogram of the same sound produced by a human voice.

The human vocal apparatus produces a great deal of information that is not always required in order to identify a particular word or syllable: thus, these synthetic spectrograms are less complex. Much of the information produced by the human voice helps us determine such things as the age,

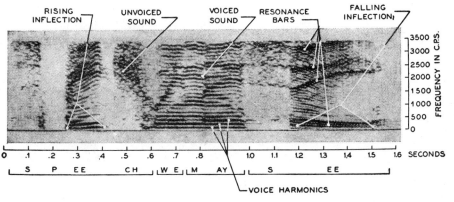

FIGURE 9.1 Typical speech spectrogram of the words "speech we may see."

sex, emotional state, and identity of the speaker. As a result, not all of the information represented in a spectrogram of natural speech is essential for identifying which words were said.

An illustration of the simplest elements that are sufficient to be heard as intelligible speech is shown in Figure 9.2. The figure shows patterns that will produce the identifiable syllables *di, du, gi,* and *gu.* Notice that the lowest bar for each syllable shows a rapidly rising transition across frequencies before it levels off and remains in a steady state. However, the second bars all differ to a noticeable degree. What these differences among the patterns indicate is that what will be heard as a particular consonant-vowel combination depends both on the consonant and on the vowel. That is, the vowel provides the context for the consonant, and the consonant provides the context for the vowel. The speech signal that leads to perception of particular syllables varies, depending on the contexts provided by the individual phonemes. Therefore speech is said to be characterized by *context-conditioned variation* (Liberman, Cooper, Shankweiler, and Studdert-Kennedy, 1967).

The importance of context-conditioned variation can be illustrated by comparing written and spoken language. In written language, as in this text, the symbols that represent letters of the alphabet are always the same. The symbols for the consonant letters just mentioned are d, D, g, G. Of course, different typefaces could be introduced, but there is little actual variation in the symbols used to represent a particular letter in written language.

When spectrographs were first developed, researchers thought that the same would be true for speech elements or phonemes in spoken language. They thought that some fixed acoustic signal, some particular sound or sound pattern, would always represent a particular phoneme. However, as we have just seen, this is not the case. The sound pattern that represents a given phoneme in a word depends on the other phonemes present in that word.

An important consequence of context-conditioned variation is that you cannot pull the consonant and vowel apart and have two separate speech sounds remaining. For example, there is no way to modify the synthetic spectrograms shown in Figure 9.2 and hear only the consonant: information about both the consonant and the vowel is being transmitted at the same time. In other words, speech production involves *parallel transmission* of the phonemic elements, a factor not important in written language (Liberman, Cooper, Shankweiler, and Studdert-Kennedy, 1967).

Another illustration of parallel transmission is shown in Figure 9.3. The synthetic spectrogram shown here, when converted to sound, would be heard as the single-syllable word *bag* (Liberman, 1970). The segments of the spectrogram associated with each phoneme indicate when information about that phoneme is being transmitted. Notice

FIGURE 9.3 Parallel transmission of phonetic segments after encoding by the rules of speech to the level of sound. Here the single-syllable word *bag* is represented.

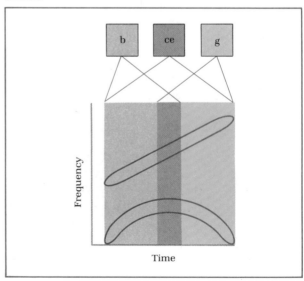

FIGURE 9.2 Spectrographic patterns that produce the syllables *di, du, gi,* and *gu.*

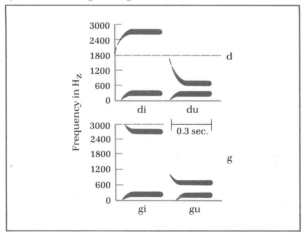

that vowel information is continuously present, whereas information about the consonants is present through approximately the first two-thirds or last two-thirds of the speech signal depending on the consonant. In other words, a change in the vowel (*bag* to *big*) would effect a change in the entire pattern, and changing a consonant (*bag* to *gag*) would effect a change in about two-thirds of the pattern.

Consider the relationship between the spoken and written forms of an English word such as *dog*. For present purposes let us ignore the meaning of the word because the relationship between the sound or spelling of a particular word and its meaning is essentially arbitrary. The same class of objects is signified by different sounds and spellings in different languages. Now we all know how to pronounce and spell *dog*. However, if the spelling of the word *dog* truly captured the pronunciation, it would be pronounced "dee-oh-gee." Suppose now we try to pronounce the word by grouping the letters into adjacent pairs. We would then have "do-og," which if said rapidly results in a better approximation to the word *dog*, even though it is still not correct. The word *dog* is properly produced

and perceived only when the interrelated, context-dependent sound information is combined into a single package. Another simple illustration of this packaging during production can be seen by pronouncing two similarly spelled words *sue* and *see* while paying close attention to what your mouth is doing. Notice that even as you begin the initial consonant your mouth is changing shape in anticipation of the following vowel. Changes in mouth shape produce changes in sound. As another example, say the syllables *ba*, *da*, and *ga*, and pay attention to the movements of your tongue.

The Speech Code When we write or print in English we produce one letter at a time: we produce an alphabetic sequence consisting of individual letters. However, when we speak, information about more than one phoneme is usually conveyed at any given point. The parallel transmission of phonemes means that we can perceive speech at the rate of 15 or more phonemes per second. Such a rate would not be possible if each phoneme had to be perceived individually in an alphabetic-like order. Alphabetic sound sequences are thus much less efficient than human speech. This is well illustrated by studies of Morse code (see Figure 9.4) and by attempts to build reading machines for the blind (see Figure 9.5). All of these systems are based on

FIGURE 9.4 International Morse code symbols for the 26 letters of the English alphabet.

Letter of the alphabet	Morse code	Letter of the alphabet	Morse code
A	•—	N	—•
B	—•••	O	———
C	—•—•	P	•——•
D	—••	Q	——•—
E	•	R	•—•
F	••—•	S	•••
G	——•	T	—
H	••••	U	••—
I	••	V	•••—
J	•———	W	•——
K	—•—	X	—••—
L	•—••	Y	—•——
M	——	Z	——••

FIGURE 9.5 Professor Paul Hegstad, legally blind for more than 18 months, demonstrates the use of an electronic device that translates written characters into tones that can be "read" by blind individuals.

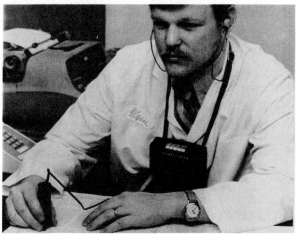

letter-by-letter transmission, and none of them are much better than one-tenth as efficient as human speech in terms of either sending or receiving (Liberman, Cooper, Shankweiler, and Studdert-Kennedy, 1967).

Because of the efficient packaging of speech sounds at the level of phonemes, speech has been characterized as a code rather than an alphabet. However, the efficient packaging is not the only reason that the term *speech code* has been used. Speech perception also does not seem to depend on any particular part of the frequency range. For example, filtering out all frequencies above 1,900 Hz (about the middle of the frequency range for speech) does not impair the perception of speech. Filtering out the frequencies below 1,900 Hz does not impair perception either. What does appear to be critical is the pattern of frequencies within whatever part of the frequency range that passes through the filter. Thus, to the extent that we can compare the phonemes of our spoken language to the letters of our written language, speech is best described as a code, and written language is best described as an alphabet.

The differences between spoken and written language are of critical importance in understanding the complexity of natural language. Computers can be programmed to process printed materials, but computers have not yet been programmed to process any substantial amount of spoken language. The difficulty lies in the unending variation of sound patterns found in spoken language. Not only do the sound patterns that represent phonemes vary depending on context, but entire syllables may also change depending on the syllables near them. Humans have an impressive ability to produce and perceive such complex patterns of sound. Furthermore, humans perceive these patterns even though almost everyone's voice produces some difference in sound pattern.

Grammar and Syntax

While phonemes make up the sound elements of language, they alone do not convey meaning. They must be combined into meaningful utterances. The smallest combinations of speech sounds that have meaning in a given language are called *morphemes*. They include words that can stand alone, such as *big, small, car, odd*; prefixes, such as *un-, anti-, pre-*; and suffixes, such as *-ed, -er, -ly*. Many of the words in the English language are made up of combinations of morphemes. The word *unquestionable*, for

example, is made up of the prefix *un-* meaning "not," the root word *question*, and the suffix *-able* meaning "capable of being."

Most authorities agree that to know a natural language, such as English, is to know a set of rules for generating and understanding the sentences of that language. These rules govern the grammatical structure or word-order relationships that characterize sentences of a natural language. For example, in English, "John hit the ball" is acceptable, whereas "Hit John ball the" is not. All natural languages involve structure, even though the grammatical rules may differ from one language to another. These rules, called *syntactic rules*, serve as the means of translating morphemes into meaningful phrases and sentences.

The knowledge represented by syntactic rules constitutes implicit or tacit knowledge; for the most part, these rules were not explicitly taught to us, nor can we explicitly teach them to someone else. The notion that language use is governed by a tacit set of rules may seem strange, but this assumption appears to be required to account for the creativity that is characteristic of natural language. As we noted earlier, most utterances we produce and understand are ones we have never produced or heard before. Furthermore, we can continue to generate such novel utterances almost without limit.

A simple example serves to illustrate one aspect of the creativity that characterizes natural language. Suppose you said that your favorite number is the number seven. You could, of course, have picked any other number. Now because there are an infinite number of numbers, there also are an infinite number of possible utterances concerning a favorite number. A sentence of potentially infinite length can be seen in the following example: "When she got up she put on her clothes, then she fed her cats, then she had breakfast, then she met her friends, then she went to school, then she came home, then she had lunch, then...." The creativity found in natural languages is certainly not limited to these simple examples. However, these examples do serve as an illustration of the way our implicit knowledge of syntactic rules allows us both to produce and to understand an infinite number of utterances.

Despite the fairly obvious creativity revealed in natural language, the importance of this creativity was only recognized in a scientific way comparatively recently (Chomsky, 1957). In part, this was because many utterances do not contain new words, and we might conclude that the supply of sentences must also be limited. The creativity that characterizes natural language may also escape notice because it implies that we are capable, in principle, of doing things that in fact we cannot do. Because our life span is finite, we cannot generate an infinite number of sentences or a sentence of infinite length. Not many years ago the notion that human beings could have the knowledge or competence required for an act that could never be manifest in performance would have been quickly rejected by psychologists. The distinguished linguist Noam Chomsky (1957) has drawn the distinction between *linguistic competence* and *linguistic performance.*

We have already illustrated one facet of the competence-performance distinction that arises because of our finite life span. A second facet of this distinction has a close parallel in arithmetic. The rules of arithmetic, unlike the rules of language, are explicitly taught to us. And once those rules are learned, there is no limit to the number of problems that can be solved using those rules, beyond the limit imposed by our finite life span. There is, however, a restriction that influences arithmetic performance as opposed to arithmetic competence. Suppose you were asked to multiply two six-digit numbers. Without paper and pencil or a calculator, you probably could not provide the solution even though you clearly have the competence to do so. The constraint in this case is due to the limited capacity of our short-term memory, as we saw in Chapter 8.

The limited capacity of short-term memory also influences language use. This sentence, "The man the dog bit died," is an example of what linguists call an *embedded construction* because one sentence, "The dog bit the man," is embedded within another sentence, "The man died." This embedded construction is easily understood even though the related elements, *the man* and *died*, become separated as a result of the embedding. However, embedding cannot occur repeatedly and still result in a comprehensible sentence because of the load placed on short-term memory. For example, consider this sentence: "The pen the author the editor liked used was new." Given paper and pencil and enough time, you would discover that "the pen was new," "the editor liked the author," and "the author used the pen." The point is that because of short-term memory constraints, the competence we may have for understanding certain sentence constructions may not be realized in performance.

Grammars as Theories   The set of syntactic rules that describes any particular language constitutes the *grammar* of that language. Linguists attempt to write grammars for each natural language, although the set of rules that applies to English or any other natural language is far from being fully worked out. Some syntactic rules are unique to a particular language or set of related languages, while others may be common to most if not all languages. Rules common to all languages are called *linguistic universals.*

According to Chomsky (1957), the grammars that linguists write are best considered as *theories of linguistic competence;* that is, they are theories about the implicit knowledge that language users have. As such, these grammars must be capable of generating *all* and *only* the grammatical sentences found in a given language: they must account for the notion of infinitely many sentences and sentences of infinite length. As theories of competence as opposed to performance, they ignore human limitations such as finite life span and a limited capacity short-term memory. While grammars must be capable of generating infinitely many sentences, they must do so with a finite number of syntactic rules. And because languages are mastered over a relatively short period of time, there must be some limit on the number of rules contained in a grammar.

Primary sources of data used by linguists in writing grammars are the linguistic skills manifested by language users. Careful observation of linguistic performance thus aids the linguist in writing theories of linguistic competence. For example, one fairly common observation in linguistic performance is when the meaning a speaker intends to convey is not the same as the meaning actually conveyed to a listener. Unfortunately, this happens all too often in human communication, be it in the classroom, in the home, or elsewhere.

Consider the sentences given below, each of which is ambiguous in terms of its meaning:

(1) The sailors like the port.
(2) Flying planes can be dangerous.
(3) The shooting of the hunters was dreadful.

Sentence (1) illustrates *lexical ambiguity* because the word *port* can refer to either a type of wine or a harbor. Such ambiguities are not particularly interesting because we are all aware that many English words have more than one meaning. However, the ambiguities revealed in sentences (2) and (3) are interesting. Sentence (2) can mean that either the act of flying planes is dangerous or the planes themselves are dangerous. Similarly, sentence (3) can refer to hunters being shot or to hunters being very poor at shooting. The fact that we can detect such ambiguities, not whether we usually notice them or not, is what is important here. This observation led linguists to distinguish between surface structure and deep structure. The *surface structure* refers to the form of the sentence we actually hear. The *deep structure* refers to the meaning of the sentence intended by the speaker. As sentences (2) and (3) illustrate, a single surface structure may have more than one deep structure, and it is the deep structure that determines the meaning of the sentence.

Just as one surface structure may result from more than one deep structure, the same deep structure can lead to more than one surface structure. Look at sentences (4) and (5) below. We all know that these two sentences mean exactly the same thing—that is, they have different surface structures based on the same deep structure:

(4) Mary sold the car.
(5) The car was sold by Mary.

Let us consider one more example of our linguistic skill before turning to a discussion of the form of syntactic rules. Sentences (6) and (7) below are identical except for the words *eager* and *easy*. Yet speakers of English know that they are quite different in meaning.

(6) John is eager to please.
(7) John is easy to please.

Sentence (6), in which *John* is the logical subject, means that John is eager to please someone. However, sentence (7), where John is the logical object, means that it is easy for someone to please John. Observations such as these have led linguists to propose particular types of grammatical rules for natural language.

Phrase Structure and Transformational Rules
Contemporary approaches to the development of grammars usually begin with a *constituent analysis* of the sentence. The sentence serves as the basic unit of analysis and is broken down into its various components or constituents. The objective of con-

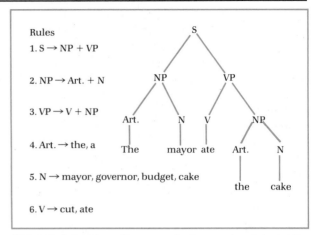

FIGURE 9.6 Tree diagram of phrase structure rules and the way they are used to generate the sentence "The mayor ate the cake."

stituent analysis is to identify the *phrase structure rules* that characterize a particular language.

An illustration of phrase structure rules and of the way they are used to generate a sentence is given in Figure 9.6. The diagram shown in the figure is called a tree diagram. The various levels shown in a tree diagram, going from top to bottom, represent the application of phrase structure rules in order to generate a particular sentence ("the mayor ate the cake"). The symbol (S), at the top, stands for sentence, and the arrow means that whatever appears to the left is rewritten or translated into whatever appears on the right.

Notice that only a single element is rewritten at each step. By using rule 1 we translate S into NP + VP, which is equivalent to subject plus predicate. Rule 2 translates the NP as Article (Art.) plus Noun (N), and rule 3 rewrites VP into Verb (V) plus NP. Applying the remaining rules gives us the surface structure of this sentence.

FIGURE 9.7 Constituent analysis of the sentence "They are flying planes," in which the main verb is *are*.

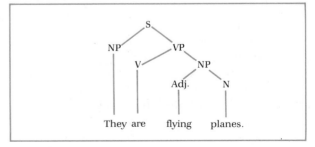

Quite obviously this illustration of using phrase structure rules is simplified: it does, however, show how a sentence can be generated according to these rules. In fact, even with the limited vocabulary provided in this illustration, several sentences can be generated. Thus, either the mayor or the governor or a mayor or a governor can "eat the cake" or "cut the budget." Clearly these rules are not sufficient by themselves because they also allow ungrammatical strings such as "The cake cut the budget."

Figures 9.7 and 9.8 illustrate the way constituent analysis can be applied to reveal the ambiguity of a sentence. In both cases the sentence (S) breaks down into a noun phrase (NP) and a verb phrase (VP), and the NP is translated into the pronoun *they*. However, in Figure 9.7 the main verb is *are*, which indicates that the pronoun refers to the planes. In Figure 9.8, *are* is an auxiliary verb, and the main verb is *flying*. Therefore, the pronoun refers to whomever is doing the flying.

Another type of phrase structure rule that is not shown in Figure 9.6 is of considerable importance. This rule is called a *recursive rule* because the symbol on the left also occurs on the right. For example, a rule such as S → NP + (S) + VP would allow embedding of one sentence within another, as we saw in "the man the dog bit died." Of course, additional rules would be needed to delete the duplicate reference to "the man" when "the dog bit the man" is embedded within "the man died." In this example the parentheses around the (S) on the right are used to indicate that the embedding is optional rather than required.

What are called *transformational rules* play an important role in theories of linguistic competence. Sentences (8) and (9) shown below have the same

meaning, but it is both awkward and difficult to capture this fact with phrase structure rules alone.

(8) John kissed Mary.
(9) Mary was kissed by John.

To show that sentences (8) and (9) have the same meaning, linguists have turned to the use of transformational rules, which allow the deep structures generated by phrase structure rules to be modified before the surface structure form emerges. These transformational rules can be exceedingly complicated and are beyond the scope of our present coverage. However, they allow for various modifications in deep structure, such as rearrangement and addition of elements shown in going from sentence (8) to (9) as well as deletion of elements required when embedding the sentence "the dog bit the man" within the sentence "the man died" to produce "the man the dog bit died." We do not say "the man—the dog bit the man—died."

With any reasonable vocabulary size, even a small number of these phrase structure and transformation rules will allow a large number of sentences to be generated. More important, when these rules are used in a theory of linguistic competence, they form the basis for explaining how words are grouped into phrases, how phrases are labeled in the surface structure (as NPs or VPs), and how meaningful relations may exist among words that do not occur together in the surface structure. In other words, these rules provide a way of understanding how the linguistic skills manifested by language users might come about. The use of these rules is not the only way to understand linguistic competence, however, as we shall see in subsequent sections.

Semantics and Syntax

When phrase structure and transformational rules were introduced, research suggested that these syntactic rules might play an important role in both sentence production and comprehension and even in memory for sentences as well. The basic idea was that a speaker would produce an utterance by unconsciously taking deep structures, which represent the meaning of a sentence, and applying the appropriate transformational rules to achieve the surface structure form. Of course, because the rules represent implicit knowledge, generation of a sentence would not involve a conscious application of

FIGURE 9.8 Constituent analysis of the sentence "They are flying planes," in which *are* is an auxiliary verb, and *flying* is the main verb.

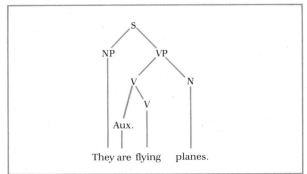

the rules. The reverse of the production process would thus explain comprehension of a sentence by a listener. In other words, the surface structure form would be "detransformed" in order to recover the deep structure and, hence, the meaning of the utterance.

Although this theory is almost impossible to evaluate in the case of sentence production, a variety of experiments suggests that at least some aspects of the theory may characterize sentence comprehension. For example, it takes longer to comprehend the meaning of a sentence involving several transformational rules than one involving only one or two transformational rules (Miller, 1962). Thus, a simple declarative sentence such as "The boy hit the girl" should be understood more quickly than the passive question "Has the girl been hit by the boy?" because the latter sentence involves both a passive transformational rule and a question transformational rule.

This theory can still be considered as providing a plausible explanation for sentence production and initial comprehension of sentences. However, the explanation of what is subsequently stored in memory no longer holds. The notion was that if comprehension involved detransforming a surface structure to recover a deep structure, then sentence memory should involve recollection of both the deep structure and the transformational rules that were involved. However, research on comprehension and memory led to alternative conceptions of what is retained in memory.

In 1967, Jacqueline Sachs reported an important study that has a direct bearing on this issue. She had subjects listen to short stories and then tested their memory for a critical sentence. The story was constructed in such a way that the critical sentence could reasonably occur at several different places, thus providing several retention intervals. Depending on where the critical sentence occurred, the retention intervals were approximately 0 seconds, 27 seconds, or 46 seconds. Consider the three sentences below:

(10) He sent a letter about it to Galileo, the great Italian scientist.
(11) Galileo, the great Italian scientist, sent him a letter about it.
(12) A letter about it was sent to Galileo, the great Italian scientist.

Suppose sentence (10) actually appeared in the passage. Sentence (11) involves a change in mean-ing, while sentence (12) preserves the meaning but changes the syntactic form. After the entire story was heard, the subjects were shown sentences like those given above and were asked whether or not they had heard the exact sentence.

When the test sentence immediately followed the critical sentence, the subjects were likely to detect change. That is, with zero delay both semantic and syntactic changes were detected. However, at other delay intervals, detection of semantic changes was close to 90 percent, while detection of syntactic changes dropped to nearly chance levels. These findings led Sachs to propose a cognitive-processing model in which the original form of the sentence is retained only briefly. As soon as the meaning of the sentence has been captured, the syntactic form is forgotten. In other words, what is usually important in memory for language is the "gist" of what was said and not the particular syntactic form used.

John Bransford and Jeffrey Franks (1971) reported that memory for a particular sentence depends more on the meaning of the content than it does on the syntactic form. They took sentences composed of four basic elements for their experimental materials. For example, the sentence, "The rock rolled down the mountain and crushed the tiny hut at the edge of the woods" contains the elements "the rock rolled down the mountain," "the rock crushed the hut," "the hut was tiny," and "the hut was at the edge of the woods." These four elements were presented to subjects either singly or in combinations such as "tiny hut was at the edge of the woods."

In the learning phase of the experiment, twenty-four sentences consisting of one, two, or three elements were presented to the subjects. Each sentence presented was derived in the manner just described from one of several four-element sentences. However, the four-element sentences were not presented. The memory test phase consisted of reading a number of sentences to the subjects and asking them to indicate which ones they had heard in the learning phase. The sentences presented in the memory test consisted of some of those previously presented (old) and some not presented previously (new). The new sentences included the four-element sentences from which both the old and new sentences were derived and some mixed sentences composed of elements taken from otherwise unrelated four-element sentences. For example, if one four-element sentence was about "The rock rolling down the mountain," and another was about "Ants eating jelly in the kitchen," a mixed sentence might be the one in (13).

> (13) The rock rolled down the mountain and crushed the ants eating in the kitchen.

The subjects were most likely to call a sentence "old" if it contained all four elements, even though no four-element sentences had been presented previously. In addition, three-element sentences, whether they were old or new, were more likely to be called old than two-element sentences. One-element sentences were least likely to be called old. The mixed sentences, however, were not confused with previously presented sentences: they were called new consistently.

The results (see Figure 9.9) of the Bransford and Franks study point strongly to contextual factors in abstracting the meaning of linguistic materials. The subjects were able to integrate the four basic elements from each four-element sentence into a single whole, despite the fact that sentences containing all four elements had not been presented. Once this mental integration had taken place, the subjects stored the entire four-element unit in memory and responded to each test sentence in terms of how closely it approximated the four-element unit.

Since the pioneering work reported by Sachs (1967) and Bransford and Franks (1971), evidence has accumulated supporting the importance of semantic as opposed to syntactic factors in the processing of linguistic materials. Much of this evidence relates to the role of context, and we shall examine some of it later in this chapter. For the moment, it is sufficient to point out that memory storage for linguistic material seems to rely on the type of semantic organization discussed in Chapter 8, even though initial comprehension may also depend to an important degree on syntactic structures.

Language Use

We do not give much conscious thought to the way we use language; we talk and we listen without being aware of the complex interrelated actions of our brains and speech programs. Further, we attend to content in speaking and hearing without much awareness of the form of our communication. Nevertheless, highly developed skills are at work in our use of language.

Subjective experience tells us that when we are speaking we are generally aware of the thoughts we are attempting to express but often are not aware of the particular grammatical constructions (sentence types) that we are using. Rarely do we attend to the particular lexical units we will utter more than two or three words in advance. In fact, James G. Martin (1971) has shown that during spontaneous speech, speakers pause more frequently before high information content words (nouns, verbs) than before low information function words (articles, prepositions, conjunctions). This observation suggests that, at least in some cases, word selection does not take place until the word needs to be produced by the speaker.

For a further example of automaticity in speech production, suppose you have memorized a prose passage or poem very thoroughly. Subsequent recitation of this passage requires very little thought or attention. In fact, you probably could recite the passage with little or no error while thinking at the same time about entirely unrelated ideas.

This observation should come as no surprise because the generative processes involved in sentence production are thought to be guided by tacit knowledge in the form of syntactic rules. Because this knowledge is implicit, and because the rules operate hierarchically, there is little reason to believe we should be consciously aware of their use in generating utterances. Much the same can be said

FIGURE 9.9 In a memory test, Bransford and Franks found that the degree of confidence that a sentence had been seen before depends on the number of familiar elements in that sentence. The greater the number of familiar elements the higher the rate of recall. Results of this kind support the importance of content as opposed to syntactic factors in memory.

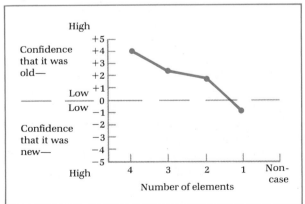

about the phonological rules used to translate words and phrases into perceivable speech sounds during fluent speech. For the fluent speaker these production rules constitute a motor program that can run with little or no attentional control. For instance, it is quite common for parents to read stories to young children and have little recollection of what they have read.

The automaticity that characterizes so much of human speech does not imply that speech occurs without error. Sometimes errors are observed and corrected by the speaker; at other times they pass unnoticed. Speech errors are observed at many levels ranging from phonological to syntactic to semantic. At the phonological level, errors may involve interchange of syllables (butterpillar and catterfly) or interchange of individual phonemes (the nipper is zarrow). According to Merrill Garrett (1975), interchanges of this sort typically occur within a single phrase. For instance, Garrett reports the following error pattern: "Children interfere with your nife lite" (night life). This example also illustrates a general characteristic of phonological errors, namely, that interchanges tend to occur among words that are similar in sound. An amusing illustration of such an interchange was observed when someone inquiring about a furnished apartment asked if it came with "rapes and drugs" instead of "drapes and rugs."

Speech errors of a syntactic or semantic nature are difficult, if not impossible, to disentangle. Purely syntactic errors presumably result from failure to apply syntactic rules correctly for translating mental representations into sentences. However, particular examples of such errors are often difficult to classify. An example cited by Donald Foss and David Hakes (1978) is: "Every time I put one of these buttons off, another one comes on." Here the interchange of the words *on* and *off* could result from either a syntactic or semantic error.

Both syntactic and semantic errors occur when a speaker's attention is overloaded or distracted. For instance, when our thoughts "come too fast," the organized activity characteristic of fluent speech often fails. Similar disruptions of ongoing speech occur when our attention is diverted because of some distraction.

A particularly extreme illustration of failure of cognitive control can be found in schizophrenic speech. This form of speech, which is illustrated in Chapter 14, has often been characterized as "word salad": individual words or, more commonly, phrases, are perfectly intact, but sequences of phrases do not form any coherent pattern. The schizophrenic speaker seems unable to control attention, and there is a fragmentation of experience, thought, and memories (Blumenthal, 1977).

Language Acquisition

Given the complexity that appears to characterize most aspects of natural language, it is rather remarkable that children learn language with such apparent ease. Indeed, available evidence suggests that children learn language with little or no systematic training.

Children acquire the sounds of speech quite readily. When these sounds are combined to produce words, children use these first words very efficiently. Children often use extra-linguistic context to expand the syntax of the message. In this way single words can be used in a variety of contexts to produce different messages.

Gradually children add new rules, although the form of these rules is usually simpler than the adult form. Children also appear to develop strategies for encoding and decoding messages. These strategies grow in complexity as they develop. The content of what children talk about is directly related to their level of cognitive development. What is interesting about language development is that it appears to be unrelated to efforts to teach language. Even though adults adjust their language when talking to children, there is little evidence that children attempt to imitate others. Children do appear to formulate broad rules and strategies for understanding and producing utterances. Despite the fact that individual children do vary, the formulation of these rules and strategies is quite regular both between children and across languages (Palermo, 1978).

Although the apparent ease with which children learn language is well known to all of us, the specific details of language development are not well established. Apart from the complexity of language, there are other reasons for this lack of knowledge. Most evidence concerning language development is necessarily observational or clinical in nature, particularly in the case of young children and infants. Such evidence is subject to misinterpretation by adult observers who tend to interpret children's speech in terms of adult language classifications. Adequate experimental evidence on language acquisition is difficult to get because young children and infants have severely limited attention spans.

Acquisition of Language Production

One general characteristic of language acquisition is that comprehension precedes production. This relationship between comprehension and production holds for all aspects of language including speech sounds, syntactic structures, and semantic interpretations or meaning. For example, infants as young as one month of age can distinguish between speech sounds such as /ba/ and /ga/ long before they can produce those sounds. Infants also can distinguish speech sounds from nonspeech sounds at very early ages (Molfese, 1972). The differential sensitivity of the left and right hemispheres of the brain to speech versus nonspeech sounds is present as early as the first week after birth (Palermo, 1978). Thus, it appears that the infant knows which sounds are speech sounds and which are not, essentially from birth.

On the production side, among the first characteristics of speech to be noted in the babbling of infants appears to be the intonation contour or rhythmic structure of utterances. Infants produce sound sequences that have recognizable intonation contours such as those characterizing questions or declarative statements (Lenneberg, 1967). It is likely that further development of the motor system is required before the fine movements needed for production of phonemes take place.

Once children do begin to produce phonemes with any appreciable frequency, vowel sounds occur most often. In fact, equality in the frequency of consonant and vowel sounds does not occur until around 30 months of age. After that, the relative frequency of consonant sounds increases dramatically as the children begin to produce words, phrases, and more complex utterances.

At one time it was thought that infants babbled all speech sounds but retained only those that occured in their own language. However, that does not appear to be the case. During babbling, speech sounds are produced according to a very definite pattern that appears to be comparable across most, if not all, languages. Interestingly, the most common speech sounds produced in the first year of life, involving front vowels and back consonants, are among the last speech sounds to be included in word production. During the second year of life, when most children are producing recognizable speech, the most common speech sounds involve the consonants produced at the front of the mouth and the vowels produced in the back of the mouth. Thus, children speaking English say *tut* before *cut*, German children say *topf* before *kopf*, and Japanese-speaking children say *ta* before *ka* (Jakobson, 1968; McNeill, 1970).

The fact that comprehension precedes production, particularly between 1½ and 3 years of age, suggests that language acquisition is not dependent on motor coordination. Of course there are matura-

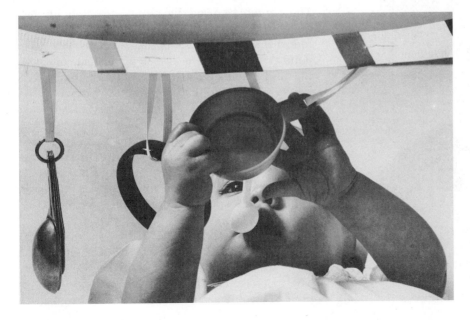

When infants babble, they produce sound sequences that have recognizable intonation contours.

tional factors in phoneme and word production. Also, speech development is quite different from the development of other motor activities. Although speech develops with no particular training, most other motor skills, such as piano playing, require years of intensive training. In fact, speech (like walking) seems to have a basic maturational basis.

When children begin to utter meaningful speech, the majority of utterances consist of single words. This stage of development has been termed *holophrastic speech*. The utterances consist mainly of nouns and adjectives, with verbs appearing later in development. Students of language acquisition consider the holophrastic stage to be one in which single words are used to express relatively complex ideas. For example, the utterance "milk" may signify that the child "wants more milk" or that the child "sees a milk bottle" or even that "some milk has been spilled." In effect, an apparently simple word such as *milk* acts as a comment on some extralinguistic context that serves as the topic for that comment. However, quite different topics or situations may elicit the same comment with quite different messages intended by the infant.

Although it is interesting to speculate about the structures represented by holophrastic speech, it is only when words are combined that speech becomes visibly grammatical. This period usually occurs around 18 months of age. Studying the acquisition of grammatical structures in young children is often a rather tedious task. Typical investigations involve recording utterances of children for several months and then attempting to determine the grammatical rules that characterize these utterances.

Acquisition of Grammatical Structure

When children first combine words, considerable evidence exists to indicate that they are using some kind of a system to construct utterances: even at this early stage, children do not combine words or order words at random. The task facing investigators of language acquisition is to unravel the system used to construct the utterances and to determine how that system is acquired.

Imitation and Grammatical Development Before turning to imitation per se, we should consider what is available for children to imitate. That is, what language do they hear? Adults speak to children quite differently than they do to other adults. The sentences used by adults are well formed, but they are much shorter and simpler than those found in conversations between adults. With very young children, adults also slow their rate of speaking, and they use a great deal of repetition. In fact, adults seem to adjust the complexity of what they say to a child. As a child's mastery of language increases, the complexity of what an adult says increases. This appears to be the case irrespective of who the adults are (parents or others) or the language being spoken. Furthermore, there is not much difference between the speech of mother to child and the speech of one child to another child (Slobin, 1975).

Although our knowledge of the way adults speak to children is quite extensive, we do not know a great deal about the way children use adult speech. The language environment that adults provide for children would seem ideal for learning language by

The most common speech sounds produced during the first year of life involve front vowels and back consonants. However, during the second year of life, when most children are producing recognizable speech, back vowels and front consonants predominate.

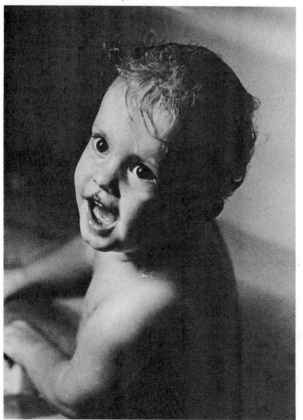

imitation. However, the question of what is learned by imitation is difficult to answer.

There is little doubt that imitation plays a role in language acquisition. Children learn the language they are exposed to, and they acquire the vocabulary that they hear. However, children also produce utterances, such as "all gone shoe" or "higher the swing," that they have never heard an adult say. Notice that the latter expression reflects the child's use of a rule. The reasoning process seems to go as follows: *high* means up, and *low* means down; therefore, if you can say "lower the swing," you should be able to say "higher the swing" as well.

Imitation and rule learning can both be seen even in the use of single words. When English-speaking children first use the past tense form of irregular verbs, they generally use them correctly and say "came," "went," "did," and so on. These verbs are common in adult speech, and it would not be surprising to find that children imitate them. However, regular verbs that use *-ed* to form the past

tense are more numerous overall. Once children learn the rule for forming the past tense of these regular verbs, they generalize it to all verbs and say things like "comed," "goed," or "doed" (Ervin-Tripp, 1964). In this case the child switches from a previously correct and supposedly reinforced form of the verb to an incorrect form that has never been heard in adult speech.

Beyond the level of single words, it is not clear what the child imitates. There is little evidence to indicate that the child imitates the syntactic form of adult speech, and adults do not seem to pay much attention to the syntactic form of child speech (Brown and Hanlon, 1970). For example, parents may accept utterances such as "He a girl" or "Her curl my hair" but reject "The animal farmhouse" because the building that the child is talking about is a lighthouse. Apparently most corrections

Adults speak to children in a different way than they do to other adults. They tend to speak more slowly and to use shorter and simpler sentences.

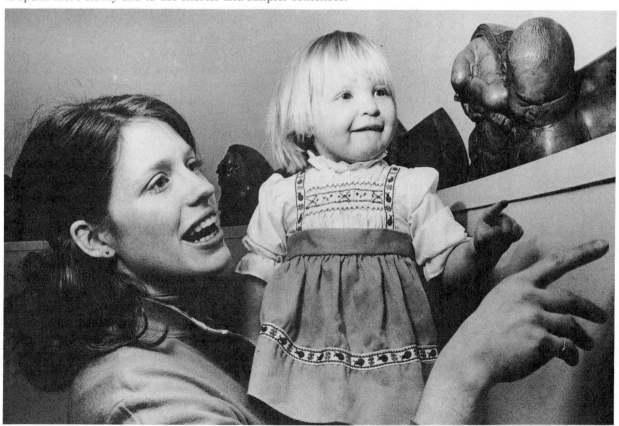

of children's speech by parents occur on nonsyntactic grounds.

Syntax Early attempts to characterize the utterances of young children focused on the syntactic structure of these utterances; investigators attempted to specify classes of words used by children and then to develop rules to combine words (Braine, 1963; McNeill, 1970). The emphasis in this approach was on a set of rules for combining words and not on the meaning of the utterances. An example of this approach was David McNeill's (1970) effort to characterize the speech of a 28-month-old child, Adam.

McNeill was able to classify Adam's vocabulary into three categories: nouns (N), verbs (V), and pivots (P). The pivot class was heterogeneous in terms of classifications used for adult speech. McNeill then proposed three syntactic rules to describe Adam's utterances. The rules are given below and, as you will notice, they are similar to the phrase structure rules discussed previously. The use of parentheses indicates an optional element that may appear in an utterance but is not required:

$$S \rightarrow NP \text{ and/or } VP$$
$$NP \rightarrow (P) N \text{ or } NN$$
$$VP \rightarrow (V) NP$$

Examples of utterances permitted by these rules include "ball," "that ball," "Adam ball," "Adam want ball," and "Adam mommy pencil." McNeill reports that these three rules described all of Adam's two- and three-word utterances. Even expressions such as "come eat pablum," which we might expect the child to imitate, do not appear in Adam's speech.

While McNeill's report is impressive, a major problem arises with all attempts to characterize these early utterances on the basis of syntactic rules alone. The problem arises from the fact that when a given expression is used by a child on more than one occasion it should always have the same meaning. However, as the following example shows, this is not always true of the utterances of young children. Lois Bloom (1970) reported that one child she studied used the expression "mommy sock" in two quite different contexts. In one case the expression was used when the child picked up her mother's sock; the other instance occurred when the mother was putting a sock on the child. Clearly the child was using the same words and word order to express quite different grammatical relationships. As with one-word utterances, it is necessary to consider the context of an utterance as well as the utterance itself in interpreting the child's speech.

Acquisition of Semantic Structure

Since Bloom's work, a number of investigations have dealt with the same issues. These studies indicate that early utterances of young children represent attempts to express grammatical relations that are quite different from those proposed by McNeill (1970) and others. These grammatical relations are called *case relations*, and they emphasize the semantic structure of the utterance, not just the syntactic form (Fillmore, 1968).

A sentence like "John hit the ball" illustrates both the agentive case and the objective case. The agentive case is expressed by indicating that a noun (John) is the agent or instigator of the action; the objective case is expressed when the role or state of a noun (the ball) depends on the meaning of the verb. In an utterance expressing the locative case, such as "The book was on the shelf," a noun (the shelf) indicates the location of a state or action. For a young child the expression "John ball" might reflect both the agentive and objective cases with the verb omitted.

Much of the early speech of young children can be characterized in terms of a relatively small number of case relations, perhaps six or eight (Bowerman, 1973). Even one-word utterances have been successfully analyzed in terms of case relations identified by context (Greenfield and Smith, 1976). In a cross-cultural study, Martin Braine (1976) looked at two-word combinations in the speech of English, Samoan, Finnish, Hebrew, and Swedish children. All the children expressed the three case relations illustrated above (agentive, objective, and locative), and while other case relations were observed, not all children used them all. As you might expect, different children tend to talk about different things. In one study, children tended to fall into one of two general categories: one group talked mainly about themselves and other people; the other group talked about objects around them (Nelson, 1973).

The emphasis on semantic considerations expressed in case relations is also congruent with the view that children use nonlinguistic information, such as prior knowledge of the world, in understanding language and in learning language (Macnamara, 1972). For instance, look at the four sentences shown below.

(14) Give the book to me.

(15) Give me the book.

(16) John hit Bill.

(17) Bill hit John.

Notice that in (14) and (15) the order of the words "me" and "book" are reversed, but the sentences have the same meaning. However, in (16) and (17) the change in word order results in a semantic change as well. A child's ability to interpret correctly such changes is based on the knowledge that books can be given to people but people cannot be given to books. Thus, a child uses this nonlinguistic information to decide what semantic information was intended.

Semantic considerations in language acquisition raise an important issue concerning the relationship between language development and cognitive development. Although the evidence is somewhat sketchy, it appears that the earliest semantic relations expressed in children's speech have parallels in children's cognitive functioning as described by Jean Piaget (see Chapter 6). During the sensorimotor period, for example, utterances about possession, location, recurrence, and other semantic relations are occurring (Brown, 1973). However, children do not use time-related linguistic structure (past, present, and future tense) before they have developed an adequate concept of time (Clark, 1971).

Language Comprehension

As we have seen, the process of language comprehension involves those cognitive activities normally associated with thinking. The work of Sachs (1967) as well as Bransford and Franks (1971) indicates that language perceivers do more than store verbatim copies of the materials to which they are exposed. Both investigations suggest an active process of abstraction in which the essential meaning of an utterance but not its formal syntactic structure is represented in memory. A considerable body of evidence now exists to suggest that language comprehension involves fairly complex interactions among (1) various components of the materials presented, (2) the implications or possible implications of those materials, and (3) the relationship between the materials presented and an individual's general knowledge of the world. Among the factors that influence these interactions are inference, general knowledge, and prior context, and schemata.

Inference When we are exposed to language, written or spoken, we commonly draw conclusions about what we were exposed to that go beyond a literal interpretation. If you were presented with a sentence such as the one discussed earlier in this chapter and at a later time you were asked whether the man died because of the dog's bite, you might very well say yes.

(21) The man the dog bit died.

This is an example of drawing an inference from a sentence that goes beyond the literal meaning of that sentence. Sentence (21), you will recall, is constructed by embedding one sentence (The dog bit the man) within another sentence (The man died): there is no necessary implication that the dog's bite caused the man's death. The speaker could have uttered the sentence in that manner to simply identify which man was being discussed.

Bransford, Richard Barclay, and Franks, (1972) studied inferences being drawn from sentences by presenting subjects with sentences like (22) and (23) below.

(22) Three turtles rested *on* a log and a fish swam under *it*.

(23) Three turtles rested *beside* a log and a fish swam under *it*.

After exposure to a number of sentences like (22) or (23) the subjects were given a recognition test that included sentences they had seen previously as well as others they had not seen. Among the new sentences were ones like (24) and (25).

(24) Three turtles rested *on* a log and a fish swam under *them*.

(25) Three turtles rested *beside* a log and a fish swam under *them*.

Subjects presented with a sentence like (22) falsely concluded that they had also seen sentence (24), whereas subjects shown sentence (23) rarely made the mistake of thinking they had previously seen sentence (25) as well. What we see here is a situation in which individuals often cannot discriminate between a sentence they have seen before and a sentence that can be logically inferred from the previously seen sentence.

A related example of inference that does not depend on strict logic was reported by Walter

Kintsch (1976). Kintsch and his associates had subjects read short paragraphs such as those shown in (26) and (27).

(26) A carelessly discarded burning cigarette started a fire. The fire destroyed many acres of virgin forest.

(27) A burning cigarette was carelessly discarded. The fire destroyed many acres of virgin forest.

On a subsequent retention test they were asked to indicate whether statements such as (28) were true or false.

(28) A discarded cigarette started a fire.

Notice that in (26) there is an explicit connection between the discarded cigarette and the fire. However, in (27) this relationship is only implicit. Nevertheless, subjects exposed to either (26) or (27) almost always indicated that (28) was true.

General Knowledge and Prior Context The examples of inference mentioned above constitute a subclass of the effects of context on language comprehension. In those examples the context consists of the subjects' general knowledge about the concepts involved. For example, if the turtles rested *on* a log and a fish swam under it (the log), then the fish swam under them (the turtles) as well. The example of inference reported by Kintsch is less straightforward, but it depends on knowing that a fire was started, that a burning cigarette was discarded, and that something started the fire. From this the subjects inferred that the fire was started by the cigarette. The following examples also illustrate the effects of knowledge and prior context. Read the short paragraph given in (29) below.

(29) With hocked gems financing him, our hero bravely defied all scornful laughter that tried to prevent his scheme. Your eyes deceive you, he had said, an egg not a table correctly typifies this unexplored planet. Now three sturdy sisters sought proof, forging along sometimes through calm vastness, yet more often over turbulent peaks and valleys. Days became weeks as many doubters spread fearful rumors about the edge. At last, from nowhere, welcome winged creatures appeared, signifying momentous success.

No doubt you had some difficulty making sense out of this passage. However, if you read the passage again and know that its title is "Christopher Columbus Discovering America," it will make a great deal of sense. The results of a study in which subjects were presented with just such passages, either with or without the title, indicated that subsequent recall of the passage was much better when the title had been presented (Dooling and Lachman, 1971).

This is an example of the role that memory or prior knowledge can play in language comprehension. The title activates the memories that allow the passage to be understood. While this illustration is quite extreme, it makes the point that language comprehension always involves some kind of interaction between the message being transmitted and what the listener already knows. Just as learning depends on contextual factors so does comprehension of language. As another illustration of the effects of context, read paragraph (30) below.

(30) If the balloons popped, the sound wouldn't be able to carry since everything would be too far away from the correct floor. A closed window would also prevent the sound from carrying, since most buildings tend to be well insulated. Since the whole operation depends on a steady flow of electricity, a break in the middle of the wire would also cause problems. Of course, the fellow could shout, but the human voice is not loud enough to carry that far. An additional problem is that a string could break on the instrument. Then there could be no accompaniment to the message. It is clear that the best situation would involve less distance. Then there would be fewer potential problems. With face-to-face contact, the least number of things could go wrong.

Again, you probably found this passage confusing. Now look at the picture in Figure 9.10, and then read the paragraph again. With the picture as context, the paragraph makes sense. Bransford and Marcia Johnson (1972) showed that with the appropriate context, subjects rated the paragraph as being more intelligible and recalled it better than without the picture context.

Both of the preceding examples illustrate important aspects of the use of language in communication. When attempting to communicate we all make assumptions about our audience: we assume certain general knowledge on the part of our audience; we make assumptions about the prior experiences of the person with whom we are communicating. The assumptions change as the audience changes. Different assumptions are made when talking to parents, friends, classmates, and teachers. Writers

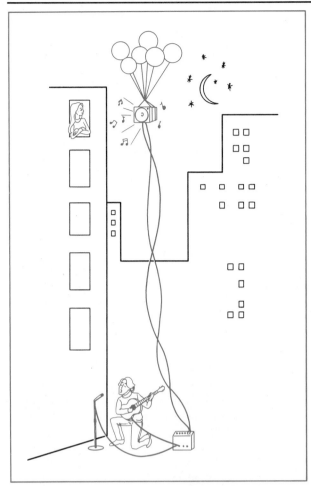

FIGURE 9.10 After you have studied this drawing of an "electronic serenade," go back and reread paragraph (30) and see whether the passage is easier to comprehend now that you have the relevant knowledge for understanding.

make assumptions about the background experiences of the readers of their books. If our assumptions about prior context are correct, we are much more likely to communicate what we intend than if our assumptions are incorrect.

Schemata and Comprehension Among the assumptions we make about individuals with whom we are communicating are the presence and nature of certain schemata we expect our audience to possess. In Chapter 8 schemata were loosely defined as organized bodies of information including beliefs and attitudes. The nature and organization of this information plays a major role in memory and in language comprehension as well. For example, if you tell about going to a certain restaurant and

eating a good steak, you probably do not have to include any reference to ordering a steak. Unless the listeners lack a schema for "going to a restaurant," they will infer that you ordered the steak. However, this inference would not occur if your context was eating at a friend's home. The schema for "eating at a friend's home" does not usually include the notion of "ordering something."

In recent years psychologists have become quite interested in the role of very abstract schemata in processing language. Possible schemata that might be used in writing or comprehending stories are often called "story grammars." A schema might consist of a hierarchy of basic episodes for a story. At the top of the hierarchy the schema might include sections such as introduction, complication, and resolution. In the introduction the main characters are introduced. Various episodes in the introduction provide the setting for the main characters as well as background events relevant to the story. The basic ideas presented in the introduction are, therefore, organized under that part of our story schema. When we attempt to remember or paraphrase the story, these ideas or episodes are organized together.

The sections labeled "complication" and "resolution" contain those episodes describing the complications that occur in the life of the main character and, subsequently, the ways in which these complications are resolved. The basic assumption is that the reader will fill in the empty slots in the schema as the story unfolds. Our story schema is what allows us to comprehend and to organize a story we are reading; it also serves as a basis for deciding what counts as a good story. For instance, a story that does not develop in a way that is appropriate to our story schema is not likely to be appreciated by the reader or to be recalled very well (Rumelhart, 1975; Kintsch, 1977).

Different schema are required to comprehend different types of writing. Our story schema is fine for stories but not for reading scientific research reports. Schemata based on knowledge of the conventions of scientific writing will be necessary.

Abstract schemata are also subject to modification through experience—a child's story schema is likely to be quite different from that of an adult. Also the nature of schemata is likely to be different in different cultures.

The Relationship Between Language and Thought

Human beings have demonstrably greater intellectual capacities than members of other species. To a large extent this superiority results from humans' capacity for thinking. Humans also have a unique system for communication—language—that serves as the primary vehicle for expressing thought. Therefore it is not surprising that psychologists are interested in the relation between language and thought as well as the extent to which these aspects of cognition are uniquely human.

Various hypotheses concerning the relationship between language and thought have arisen in the history of psychology. One of the earliest views, proposed by John B. Watson (1913), was that language and thought were the same thing. According to Watson, thinking involved the same motor activities used in speaking: when we "think out loud," it is called speech; when we "speak covertly," it is called thinking. Too much contradictory evidence exists to take Watson's position seriously any more. This evidence derives from the complex thought processes displayed by animals, nonspeaking humans, and humans who lose speech as a result of injury (Glucksberg and Danks, 1975). In addition, if thinking and speaking were the same activity, we would not correct ourselves while speaking by saying, "I didn't mean to say that."

The anthropologist-linguist Benjamin Lee Whorf (1956) proposed a sweeping, two-pronged hypothesis concerning language and thought. Whorf proposed first that all higher levels of thinking are dependent on language or that language determines thought (*linguistic determinism*). Because languages differ in many ways, Whorf also believed that speakers of different languages perceive

RESEARCH: Speech Perception and the Split Brain

The remarkable way in which human biology is specialized for the expression and comprehension of language has been demonstrated in the split-brain experiments of Roger Sperry. These experiments, which were discussed in detail in Chapter 2, involved the psychological testing of subjects in whom the principal connections between the two cerebral hemispheres had been surgically cut for the relief of severe epilepsy. From these tests and from other research it became dramatically clear that, in all of us who are righthanded and in most of us who are lefthanded, the left hemisphere is dominant for language.

Sperry's split-brain work focused on information received via two sensory systems, vision and touch. The anatomy of these two systems made it possible to restrict the input to one or the other hemisphere. For example, the left visual field makes nerve connections only with the right hemisphere; thus the split-brain patient cannot name or describe objects because they are "seen" only by the mute right hemisphere. Similarly, the left hand makes connections only with the mute right hemisphere, and the split-brain patient cannot name objects touched by that hand.

The perception of speech presents a different anatomical situation. Each ear is represented bilaterally in the brain; that is, it makes connections with both hemispheres. Either hemisphere thus can perceive speech through either ear. What happens, however, when different sounds are presented to the two ears simultaneously?

To find the answer to this question, Sperry joined with two researchers at McGill University, Brenda Milner and L. Taylor (Milner, Taylor, and Sperry, 1968). The principal subjects were seven patients, five male and two female, who had undergone split-brain surgery. The method was the dichotic-listening procedure. In this procedure, the subject wears stereophonic earphones that are connected to a dual-channel tape recorder. Sounds such as spoken digits (numbers one through nine) can be presented to either ear or to both simultaneously.

The subjects were given two different tasks. In the monaural task, six digits were presented to one ear and the subject was asked to report all of the numbers he or she heard. In the dichotic task, different digits were presented simultaneously to both ears, and the subject was aked to report which numbers he or she heard.

The result of monaural test showed roughly equal accuracy for each ear. The split-brain patients correctly reported 87 percent of the numbers presented to the left ear and 90 percent of the numbers presented to the right ear. (Because only the left hemisphere has the power of speech, only the connections to it from each ear were responsible for these reports.)

In sharp contrast were the results of the dichotic

and experience the world differently (*linguistic relativism*).

In short, his view was that the language we speak determines the way we perceive the world and hence the nature of thought. Whorf's views were based in part on a number of differences that he observed among languages used in various American Indian cultures. For instance, he noted that Eskimos have many words for *snow*, whereas most English speakers have only one. However, having only one name for snow does not mean that English speakers cannot perceive differences in varieties of snow. Any experienced skier, for example, is quite sensitive to a number of different types of snow.

In New Guinea there is a group of people called the Dani whose color names differ markedly from English. They use two names, *mili* (dark) and *mola* (light), to refer to all the colors of the spectrum. Comparing Dani speakers with English speakers should provide strong support of Whorf's hypothesis. Yet the Dani were found to represent colors in memory in the same way as English speakers do (Heider and Oliver, 1972).

Eric Lenneberg (Lenneberg and Roberts, 1956) has criticized Whorf's arguments. He believes that differences in language prove only that languages differ and that no conclusions can be drawn without separate measures of the thought patterns themselves. In addition, studies indicate the existence of language universals (Berlin and Kay, 1969). Even in the area of color names, languages do not label colors in totally unrelated ways. Although boundaries between color areas vary in languages, the focal areas recur in languages that are historically unrelated.

test. When presented with different sounds simultaneously, the patients were able to report very few of the digits from the left ear. In fact, five of the seven subjects had scores scarcely above zero for the left ear and, indeed, complained that they could hear nothing in that ear.

For purposes of comparison with these results, the researchers also tested two other groups of subjects. One group consisted of normal control subjects—student nurses and laboratory technicians. The other group was composed of 30 patients who had undergone a different sort of surgery for the relief of epilepsy: removal of the temporal lobe—and hence, the auditory cortex—from the left hemisphere (10 patients) or from the right hemisphere (20 patients).

The striking right-ear superiority on the dichotic-listening task among the split-brain patients is illustrated in the graph. The graph shows the mean number of digits correctly reported for each ear.

As can be seen, normal subjects demonstrated only a slight but significant superiority on the right ear. Subjects whose right temporal lobe had been removed showed an accentuation of the right-ear superiority found in normal subjects, while the ear difference in the split-brain patients is far more apparent.

What explains this pronounced ear difference in the split-brain patients? Milner, Taylor, and Sperry point out that the ability of the patients to report input to the left ear during the monaural test indicates effective use of the connection to the "vocal" left hemisphere. But in the presence of a competing sound from the right ear to the left hemisphere, input from the left ear to the left hemisphere is suppressed. Messages arriving over the connections from the opposite ear somehow take precedence over those from the near ear.

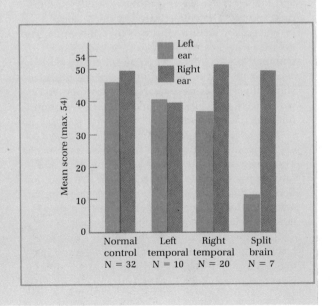

Although Whorf's linguistic relativity hypothesis was too sweeping, numerous situations exist in which language influences perception and memory as well as thought. For instance, subjects were presented with ambiguous figures, such as those shown in Figure 9.11, along with a suggested word label. The two circles connected by a straight line were said to resemble either eyeglasses or a dumbbell. In subsequent retention tests, drawings of the figures tended to be biased toward the particular verbal description that was provided at the time of original presentation (Carmichael, Hogan, and Walter, 1932).

A study that demonstrates a different way that language may influence thinking was reported by Elizabeth Loftus and John Palmer (1974). In this study subjects were shown a film of a traffic accident and then were questioned about the events they had seen. One question concerned the speed of the cars. Subjects who were asked how fast the

FOCUS: Language in Chimps

The use of natural language by human beings represents a unique system of communication. In no other species do we find a natural communication system that has the complexity and potential for creativity that characterizes human language. We have also seen that language plays a major role in human thinking and cognition. In fact, language plays such an important role for humans that it has often been argued that the cognitive processes required for language are uniquely human, that no other species is capable of mastering a skill as complex as human language. This claim is not without critics, and in recent years it has been challenged by several investigators working on communication systems with chimpanzees.

The earliest attempts to teach human language to chimps involved raising chimps in the homes of the investigators so as to increase the similarity to a human environment. Both of these efforts (Kellogg and Kellogg, 1933; Hayes and Hayes, 1951) were distinct failures. The chimp raised by the Kelloggs never produced any distinctly human speech sounds. The Hayeses were somewhat more successful. Their chimp, Viki, was finally able to produce the words, *papa*, *mama*, and *cup*. In addition she could understand other words to some degree. However, Viki's words were not clearly articulated and were often not understood by strangers.

These early failures to teach human language to chimps could have occurred for at least two reasons. The reason most often given is that the vocal apparatus of the chimp is not adequate for the production of human speech. The second reason given for failures to teach language to chimps is that they lack the necessary cognitive abilities.

Recently several attempts have been made to teach chimps communication systems that do not depend on the use of speech. The most widely publicized of these efforts is work with the chimp Washoe (Gardner and Gardner, 1971). The approach was to attempt to teach American Sign Language (ASL) to Washoe. The procedure involved the behavior shaping and instrumental conditioning techniques described in Chapter 7. With these procedures, Washoe learned a fairly large vocabulary of signs and combinations of signs, and when she was 5 years old she could understand several hundred signs and could use more than 130 in various combinations.

David Premack (1971) reported that his chimp, Sarah, was taught to communicate using a variety of plastic forms that varied in size, shape, and color (see Figure). The forms represented words that could be combined in various ways to produce sentences. Both Washoe and Sarah demonstrated an ability to

Washoe learning the sign for *toothbrush*.

cars were going before they "hit each other" judged the speed as slower than subjects asked how fast they were going before they "smashed into each other." Just the difference between the words "hit" and "smashed" resulted in an appreciable difference in judged speed of the cars.

A week later the same subjects were again asked questions about the film. One question asked about the presence of broken glass—something not shown in the film. Nevertheless, subjects questioned the previous week with the word "smashed" reported having seen broken glass more often than those questioned with the word "hit." Here we see how subsequent linguistic experience can influence what we remember about a prior, nonlinguistic perception. We also see a demonstration of the way the wording of questions may influence eyewitness testimony.

produce simple sentences, many of which were novel. Sarah, for example, acquired a vocabulary of more than 60 nouns, 20 verbs, and 30 other words that could be combined to produce a variety of sentences. A chimp named Lana was taught to communicate by typing on a keyboard console. The keys of the console represented about 100 words that Lana used to type messages (Rumbaugh, 1977). Finally, a gorilla named Koko was taught sign language (Patterson, 1978). Koko had a vocabulary of almost 400 signs and could combine them for longer utterances.

Although the accomplishments achieved by Washoe, Sarah, Lana, and Koko represent the most advanced communication systems taught to apes to date, there is still controversy over whether they can be said to use language in the human sense of the word. Some researchers believe that the achievements of these apes indicate that they do have some capacity for understanding syntax. Other researchers question whether the linguistic creativity of apes is limited to the ability to make word substitutions using restricted sentences—for example, "Sarah eat apple" to "Sarah wash apple" (Premack, 1976). It appears as though the level of syntactic and semantic complexity displayed by the animals is at best that displayed by a 2-year-old child and does not progress beyond that. This is an impressive observation (Terrace, Petitto, Sanders, and Bever, 1979), but by age 3 the human child is displaying a considerably more complex language than the chimps have achieved.

Although it appears that nonhuman primates have the potential to create grammatical sentences, no satisfactory evidence exists that they can, in fact, acquire syntax. There is no question that the linguistic abilities of nonhuman primates are probably greater than those of any other nonhuman animal, but whether there are limits to their ability to communicate symbolically, according to the rules of what we call language, remains to be seen.

Assuming chimps are not capable of acquiring a human-language-like communication system, what is suggested about the animals' cognitive capacities? It is tempting to think that chimps are lacking in certain cognitive characteristics, but it is virtually impossible to point out what these characteristics might be. Chimps demonstrate a wide range of cognitive structures in perceptual and motor tasks. Remember also that language acquisition in children bears little relationship to intelligence. As John Limber (1977) points out, it is no easier to identify the cognitive characteristics that are lacking in chimps than it is to identify those present in humans.

A few of the chimp, Sarah's "words" as she arranged them to form a complex sentence.

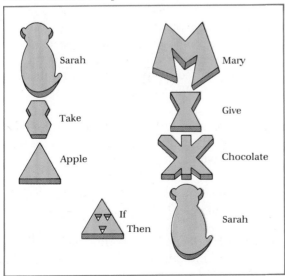

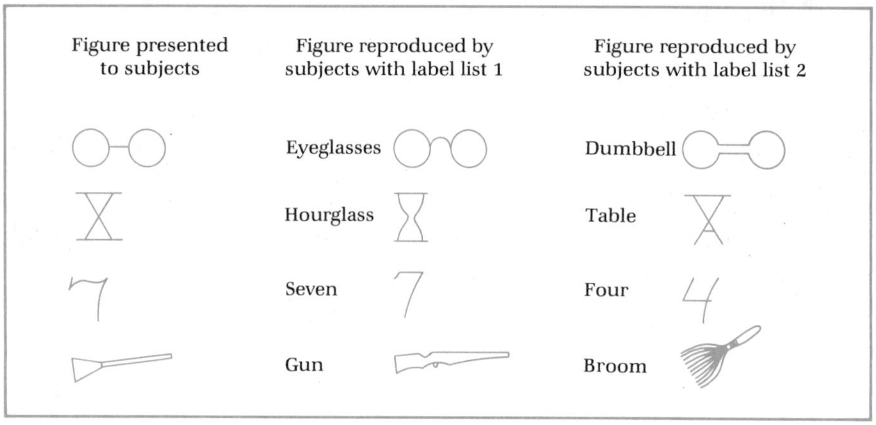

Figure presented to subjects	Figure reproduced by subjects with label list 1	Figure reproduced by subjects with label list 2
⊂–◯	Eyeglasses	Dumbbell
✕	Hourglass	Table
7	Seven	Four
➤—	Gun	Broom

FIGURE 9.11 Effects of verbal labels on memory for ambiguous figures. Subjects were presented with an ambiguous figure, as in column 1, along with a suggested label from either column 2 or column 3. In subsequent retention tests, descriptions of the figures were biased toward the description originally given.

A large amount of literature addresses the influence of language on perception, memory, and thought. We saw examples of this influence in our discussion of inference and the effects of context. Language is used to express concepts and relations as well as our thoughts about a variety of other things. However, language or speech, be it overt or covert, is but one way of thinking. In fact, most of the illustrations presented here concerning the influence of language on thought have also been demonstrated in nonlanguage situations. Let us consider one illustration of thinking in a situation that does not require the use of language.

James J. Jenkins, Jerry Wald, and John Pittenger (1978) report an interesting demonstration of inference in a visual perception task. These investigators took a series of still pictures of a woman making tea. The scene involved activities such as heating water, making the tea, and pouring the tea. Subjects were shown some of the pictures and then, in a subsequent recognition task, they were shown a much larger set of pictures and were asked to indicate which ones they had seen before.

The pictures presented in the recognition test included some of those seen before as well as others from the scene that had not been shown before. These pictures had all been taken from the same camera location, and the subjects could not tell which ones had been seen previously. However, other pictures of the scene were also included from a different camera location. These pictures were the only ones that the subjects could discriminate as not having been presented earlier. The subjects seemed to have integrated the events pictured with their schemata for making tea and then could no longer discriminate what they had seen from what they had "filled in."

It should not surprise us to see that language and thought are closely related. In humans, language serves as the basic tool for communication. Therefore, when we label our experiences with words and phrases, our language will influence how we remember and think about those experiences. However, when we do not use language to label our experiences, the relationship between language and perception, memory, or thinking will be greatly reduced.

SUMMARY

1. Natural language and the creativity of its generative processes constitute the most striking differences between humans and other species. Language is central to human cognition and to human communication. There are obvious parallels in spoken and written language, but they differ in terms of the sensory-perceptual systems involved (auditory versus visual) as well as in the motor systems involved in production (mouth, tongue, and lips versus fingers and hands).

2. For purposes of analysis and study, spoken language is broken down into three components: (1) phonology, the study of sound patterns, (2) syntax, the grammatical structure of language, and (3) semantics, the study of the meanings of utterances.

3. A phoneme is the smallest unit of sound that makes a difference to the meaning of a larger unit such as a word. Our perception of particular syllables varies depending on the contexts provided by individual phonemes of the syllables. Therefore, speech is said to be characterized by *context-conditioned variation*. Scientists study speech produc-

tion and context-conditioned variations through the use of speech spectrographs.

4. Written language is an alphabetic sequence of individual letters; in spoken language, however, information about more than one phoneme is usually conveyed at any given point. Because of the efficient packaging of speech sounds at the level of phonemes, speech has been characterized as a code rather than as an alphabet.

5. Phonemes are combined to make up morphemes, which are the smallest groups of speech sounds that have meaning. Morphemes are then combined to produce words and sentences. To know a natural language is to know a set of rules for generating and understanding the sentences of that language. These syntactic rules govern the grammatical structure or word-order relationships of the sentences of that language. The knowledge represented by syntactic rules is implicit or tacit knowledge that cannot be explicitly taught.

6. The set of syntactic rules that describes any particular language constitutes the grammar of that language. Rules common to all languages are called linguistic universals. Grammars written by linguists are best considered as theories of linguistic competence about the implicit knowledge that language users have. They are theories of competence as opposed to performance because they ignore human limitations such as finite life span and a limited-capacity short-term memory.

7. The surface structure of a sentence refers to the form of the sentence we actually hear. The deep structure refers to the meaning of the sentence intended by the speaker.

8. Grammars are usually developed through a constituent analysis of the components of the sentence. Sentences can be generated through sets of phrase structure rules, including a recursive rule. Linguists have also developed transformational rules, which allow the deep structures generated by phrase structure rules to be modified before the surface structure form emerges.

9. As soon as we capture the meaning of a sentence, we seem to forget the syntactic form of that sentence. What is important for memory of language is the "gist" of what was said—that is, its semantic organization is retained.

10. Children learn language with ease and with little systematic training. Comprehension precedes production in language acquisition, a relationship that holds for speech sounds, syntactic structures, and semantic interpretations. Language acquisition does not appear to depend on motor coordination, although maturation is necessary for phoneme and word production. Most children begin meaningful speech by uttering single words, a developmental stage called holophrastic speech. Most children begin to combine words into identifiable grammatical structures at around 18 months of age.

11. The generative processes involved in sentence production are thought to be guided by tacit knowledge in the form of syntactic rules. Because this knowledge is implicit, and because the rules operate hierarchically, we are not consciously aware of their use in generating utterances.

12. Early utterances of young children represent attempts to express grammatical relations that are called case relations. Case relations emphasize the semantic structure of the utterance and not just the syntactic form. Children also use nonlinguistic information, such as prior knowledge of the world, in understanding and learning language. Although imitation certainly plays a role in language learning, beyond the level of single words it is not clear what children imitate.

13. Language comprehension involves those cognitive activities normally associated with thinking. Evidence suggests that language comprehension involves fairly complex interactions among (1) various components of the materials presented, (2) the implications or possible implications of those materials, and (3) the relationship between the materials presented and an individual's general knowledge of the world. Inference, general knowledge and prior context, and schemata, are among the factors that affect these interactions.

14. Various hypotheses concerning the relationship between language and thought have been proposed. John B. Watson believed that thinking and speaking were the same thing. Benjamin Whorf held the view that the language we speak determines the way we perceive the world and hence the nature of thought. Whorf's hypothesis seems to have been too sweeping. Language or speech, overt or covert, is but one way of thinking.

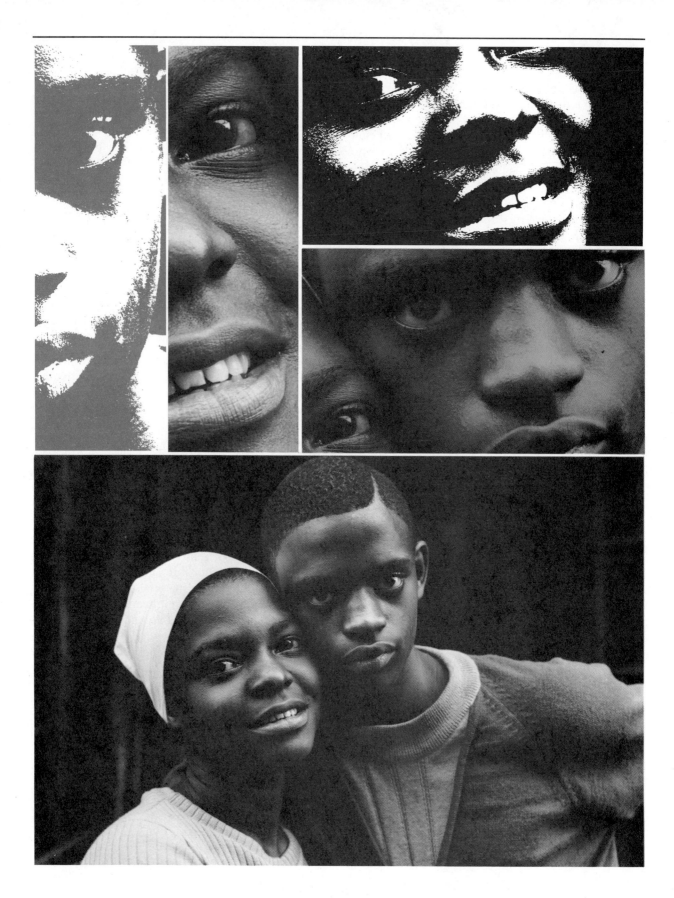

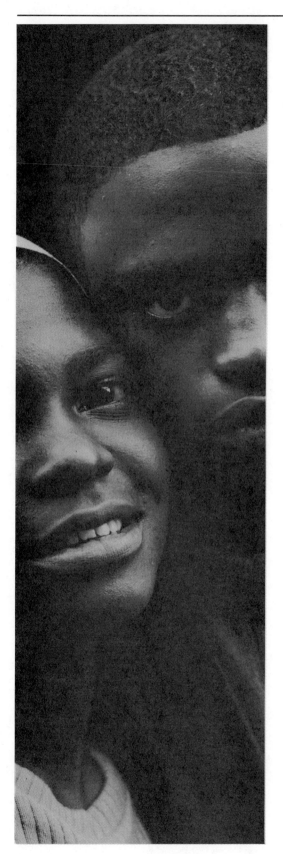

Part Four
Motives and Emotions

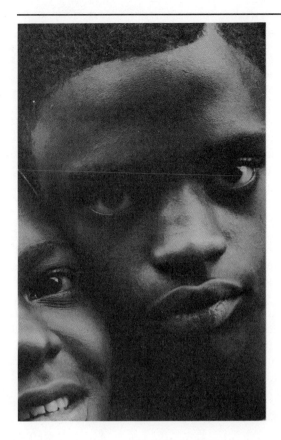

Chapter 10
Motivation and Emotion

Animal and human behavior is often organized so that specific goals can be obtained—food, water, a mate, good grades, a new car, and so on. In this chapter we will consider a number of the *needs*—physical states involving lacks or deficits—or *motives* that appear to impel certain goal-seeking behaviors. We will also consider the role of the emotions that are often closely associated with motivated behavior and the achievement of goals.

The concept of *motivation* has an interesting and rather tortuous history. For many years, psychologists attempted to explain motivation in terms of a single all-embracing theoretical construct. In the late nineteenth and early twentieth centuries, the pioneer psychologists William McDougall (1921) and William James (1890) ascribed motivation to *instincts*—innate patterns of behavior. They listed dozens of such instincts, ranging from hunting and fighting to acquisitiveness, curiosity, and jealousy. To James, instincts resembled reflexes in that they were called forth by specific sensory stimuli and elicited a specific type of behavior. However, unlike reflexes, which are localized to a specific organ or set of muscles, the instinct was presumed to direct all of the creature's behavior to a specific goal. A major problem with the instinctual view is that it lends itself to circular reasoning: people fight because they have fighting instincts. How do we know they have fighting instincts? Because they fight.

The instinctual view of motivation was largely superseded during the 1920s and 1930s by the concept of hypothetical states called *drives*. These hypothetical internal states are produced by a small number of primary biological needs such as water or food. If, for example, the organism is deprived of water, the need for water energizes an internal drive state that motivates and organizes behavior until that need is satisfied. For learning theorists such as Clark L. Hull (1943), the reduction of drive became a crucial concept. *Drive reduction* was considered the essential form of reinforcement and was thought to be necessary for learning to occur. According to this view, all drives and, therefore, all behavior, was motivated by eliminating or satisfying biological needs. The interpretation of all motivation in terms of a few primary biological needs now seems vastly oversimplified.

Today, neither instincts nor drives can be considered adequate as an all-embracing conceptual approach to the study of motivation. Most modern researchers take a more restricted view of motivation, investigating the problems of motivation one at a time instead of attempting to answer all questions at once through the formulation of a single, all-encompassing theory. This has led to the development of several distinctly different approaches to the study of motivation. In the first part of this chapter we will discuss three of these approaches: the evolutionary approach, the physiological approach, and the social-learning approach. In the second part of the chapter we will look at the emotions and their involvement in motivation. In the final part of the chapter we will see how all of these approaches can be put together in the case of one particularly important example of goal-directed behavior—aggression. In the next chapter we will continue our discussion of motivation and emotion by focusing on the biological and social aspects of sexual behavior.

Motivation and Evolution

When we study motivation we are often studying the ways in which animals behave to obtain the things they need to survive and reproduce. Motivated behavior plays a critical role in satisfying the needs of the organism. Therefore, we should expect the process of evolution to have affected motivated behavior, at least in the case of biological motives such as hunger, thirst, and sex. At this point, let us briefly review the main points of the theory of evolution.

Evolution

There are two parts to the evolutionary process that interact with one another. The first is the *generation of variation* through a number of mechanisms among the members of a species. At least some of this variation will usually be the result of genetic differences among the animals. These differences will be carried in the genes, the basic units of heredity that transmit traits from one generation to the next. Genetically based characteristics produce the similarities in parents and offspring. For example, if the members of a species varied in size and this variation in size had a genetic basis, then the offspring of parents who were relatively large would themselves tend to be relatively large.

The second part is called *natural selection.* If the trait in which the animals vary is related to survival, some of the animals will be better equipped to survive than others, and these animals would leave more offspring. This differential reproduction, caused by natural selection, will lead to change in the population over time. As the animals that are best equipped continue generation after generation to be more successful, succeeding generations become more and more like the best-adapted animals of previous generations.

For example, suppose that a group of animals varied in their tendency to eat when they needed food and that these differences were genetic. Some of them ate too little, some about the right amount, and some ate more than they needed. Obviously, many of those who ate too little would starve or be too weak to escape from predators and would leave few offspring. The genes responsible for eating too little would sooner or later disappear as possessors of these genes became less and less numerous. It is equally true though perhaps less obvious, that the animals that ate too much would also leave few offspring. Too much food might make the animals fat and slow them down so that they could not escape predators. After a period of such natural selection, all the animals should tend to eat about the optimal amount of food.

Several important implications can be drawn from this example. First, because the goals of motivated behavior are often biologically critical to the survival and/or reproduction of the organism, we should expect many motivational systems to be finely tuned to the needs of the organism. Second, evolution does not require the animal to "know" what it needs in any sort of subjective way. As long as an animal behaves appropriately, for whatever reason, it will leave offspring. Third, note that, strictly speaking, it is not survival that counts, but the leaving of offspring. An animal that engaged in no mate-seeking or sexual behavior, conserving time and energy for obtaining food and avoiding predators, might survive for a long time. But its genes would not be represented in the next generation.

Adaptive Behavior: Survival

This discussion of evolution and behavior clearly implies that behavior should often be adaptive, contributing directly to the number of offspring. How can the adaptive nature of that behavior be demonstrated? This question has been of special concern to ethologists, zoologists who study behavior—usually in the field under natural conditions. The ethologist most responsible for developing techniques for the study of the adaptive significance of behavior has been Niko Tinbergen, one of three ethologists to win the Nobel Prize in 1963.

Tinbergen and his students used the naturalistic experiment in which variation is created by the experimenter who then observes the effects of the variation on reproductive success. For example, when young birds hatch they leave pieces of eggshell scattered in the area of the nest. This is particularly obvious in the case of ground-nesting birds such as the black-headed gull. The parents of black-headed gull chicks fastidiously clean up these eggshell pieces by eating them or, more often, carrying them away from the nest. Is there any adaptive significance to this behavior?

One possibility is that the eggshell removal reduces predation on the nest. The outside of the shells are covered with splotches of brown, green, and khaki: they are nicely camouflaged. But the insides of the shells are white, and eggshell pieces are very conspicuous. A simple experiment was performed (Tinbergen, 1963). Artificial nests, each with a single egg in it, were placed near a gull colony. Some of these nests had eggshell pieces nearby; some did not. Predation on the nests with eggshells was much higher than on the nests without eggshells. This directly demonstrated that eggshell removal reduces predation on the nest and therefore increases the number of young that survive.

Another approach to the problem of empirically demonstrating the adaptiveness of behavior is to measure selective pressure directly. If the behavior in question varies among the members of a species, it may be possible to measure directly the success of the animals in terms of numbers of young produced as a function of the behavior. For example, black-headed gulls, like many birds, nest in large colonies. They appear highly motivated to nest in the center of the colony and will struggle over these nest sites in the center, even though there are plenty of apparently satisfactory nest sites at the edges of the colony. There is some advantage to nesting in the center of the colony. It has been found that nests at the edge of the colony suffered much higher rates of predation than nests in the center of the colony (Patterson, 1965). Those gulls who more successfully compete to nest in the center will raise more young.

Optimization of Adaptive Behavior

Natural selection would serve to increase the proportion of animals whose goal-oriented behavior is optimized. Another approach to the study of the adapativeness of behavior, called *optimization theory*, has been developed during the past few years. The optimization approach is based on the assumption that the behavior of animals is organized to achieve some biologically significant goal. A mathematical or graphical model of the situation in which the behavior occurs is then constructed and used to figure out the best strategy possible for obtaining the goal. Then experiments are conducted to see whether the behavior of the animal approaches the best—or optimal—solution.

Optimization theory has been applied to the study of foraging behavior. A foraging animal is an animal looking for food; the behavioral goal is unambiguous. Presumably, the behavior of the foraging animal should be organized for efficiency. This would minimize the amount of time required to obtain the needed food, leaving more time for other necessary activities such as finding a mate or caring for young. Therefore, optimal foraging models are constructed to discern the best possible strategy to follow when faced with a particular foraging problem. Experiments then determine the extent to which the behavior of the animals matches the results of the model building.

Optimal foraging models involve complex mathematical detail, but the basic logic can be seen through an example. A flycatcher is a bird that forages by sitting on a branch watching insects fly by and choosing certain insects to catch. Different types of insects fly by, some large and some small, some easy to catch and some hard to catch. Is there any rule the bird uses to determine which insects are worth chasing and which are not? The optimal foraging model developed originally by Robert MacArthur and Eric Pianka (1966) yields such a rule. They have shown mathematically that the bird should use a rule that depends on the abundance of the best types of insects. If the largest, easiest-to-capture insects are common, the bird should chase only these and ignore prey of less value. If the best types of prey are relatively rare, the bird should be less selective, taking all prey types.

Suppose there were only two types of insects,

each requiring about 10 seconds to capture and eat, but the better type is twice as large, with double the dietary value of the lesser-valued type. If a small insect flies by the flycatcher, it will take 10 seconds to capture and eat, and the bird will miss any large insects that happen by. If the larger insects are very common, the flycatcher is better off ignoring small ones and waiting for the large ones. But if large ones are rare, then a large insect is unlikely to come around during the 10 seconds spent on a small insect, and the small insect is worth chasing. The flycatcher should be selective when large insects are plentiful but should go after all insects when the large ones are relatively rare. And it should make no difference how common the small insects are.

This model suggests what the behavior of the bird should be if the foraging behavior is organized to maximize efficiency in terms of the amount of food eaten per minute. Several experiments have observed foraging birds to behave as predicted by the model. For example, John Goss-Custard (1981) watched red shanks feeding on a mud flat in southern England. There were several different sizes of prey available to them. On days when large prey were abundant, the birds ate almost all large prey; when the large prey were less common, the red shanks broadened their diet to include smaller prey. Thus the optimization approach to foraging behavior seems to help us understand and predict what animals will do.

Physiological Bases of Motivated Behavior

As we saw in the previous section, motivated behavior is often organized in ways that ensure the survival and reproductive success of the organism. Some motives function to fulfill needs that are particularly necessary for survival. In these cases we should expect to find the organism particularly well equipped to meet these needs efficiently. In the case of motives such as hunger and thirst, physiological factors are particularly crucial to survival, and neural mechanisms are involved in the regulation of these motivated behaviors.

Neural Control Mechanisms

Although many parts of the nervous system are involved in the control of motivated behavior, the hypothalamus and the endocrine system have particular importance.

The Hypothalamus The hypothalamus straddles the midline of the brain, extending from just below the thalamus to the base of the brain. Not much larger than the tip of a little finger and constituting less than 1 percent of the brain's entire weight, the hypothalamus is so vital to motivation that it has been called "the brain within the brain." It is one of the principal brain structures regulating hunger and thirst, body temperature, and sexual behavior. Through its connections to the autonomic nervous system, which controls glands and smooth muscles such as blood vessels and the heart, the hypothalamus also influences a great variety of emotional responses (see Figure 10.1). Many emotions, such as fear or anger, are accompanied by physiological arousal. Heart rate speeds up; blood is diverted from internal organs to the muscles carrying increased amounts of glucose or blood sugar. This process—the "fight or flight" response by which

FIGURE 10.1 Diagram of the hypothalamus and its connections to the autonomic nervous system.

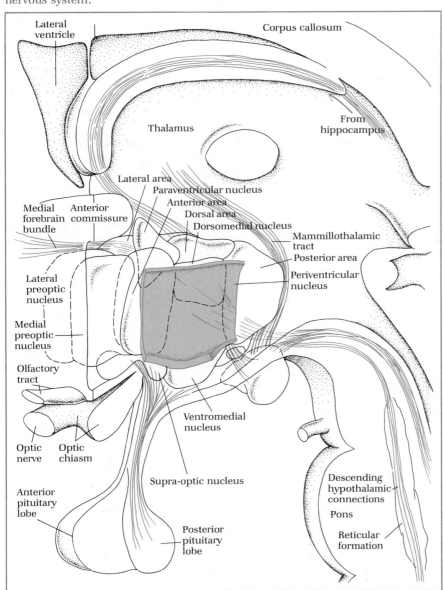

the body prepares for some kind of action—is regulated by the autonomic nervous system under the control of the hypothalamus.

The Endocrine System A principal means of hypothalamic control of motivation is exerted through its connections to the body's endocrine system. The endocrine system, which works in parallel with the nervous system, consists of various ductless glands such as the adrenals and the pancreas that discharge vitally important substances called hormones directly into the bloodstream. (Other glands—for example, sweat glands—have ducts that carry their secretions to the body surface.) Several dozen hormones have been identified. The name *hormone* stems from the Greek meaning "to excite to action," and hormones excite an extraordinary variety of activity.

Originally hormones were thought to regulate only physiological functions. For example, the first hormone to be identified, secretin, is secreted by the pancreas and helps regulate digestion. Thyroxin, which is secreted by the thyroid gland, controls the basic rate of metabolism. It became clear, however, that hormones are powerful regulators of behavior as well, and their secretion can be strongly influenced by environmental events. The adrenal glands just above the kidneys secrete two hormones, adrenalin and noradrenalin, that are associated with emotions such as fear and anger. They help increase blood pressure, heart rate, and respiration to arouse the body for action. This hormonal mechanism thus works in parallel with the autonomic nervous system during physiological arousal. As we will see in the next chapter, hormones released by the gonads—the testes in the males, the ovaries in females—not only help control the development of sexual characteristics but also greatly influence sexual behavior.

The Guiding Principle: Homeostasis A fundamental principle for understanding the neural control of motivation is the concept called *homeostasis.* The word (from the Greek for "maintaining stability") was coined early in this century by the American physiologist Walter B. Cannon (1929) to describe an organism's tendency to maintain its internal environment at a constant level.

Years before Cannon, French physiologist Claude Bernard (1865/1957) had correctly concluded that the principal regulator of this homeostatic harmony is the nervous system. The brain—and, in large part, the hypothalamus—mediates the complex interplay of physiology and behavior in motivation. Part of the time the hypothalamus operates automatically in the regulation of homeostasis, but it also is subject to conscious control. This joint physiological and behavioral control of homeostasis is illustrated in the functioning of body temperature.

Humans and other mammals maintain a nearly constant body temperature. In humans the temperature is about 98.6 degrees Fahrenheit. A number of automatic physiological mechanisms contribute to this homeostatic control. When external heat threatens homeostasis, the peripheral blood vessels dilate and carry more blood to the surface of the body, cause the face to become flushed, and assist in cooling the body surface. The body's heat loss is speeded up by perspiration, which absorbs energy as sweat evaporates. When it is too cold, the peripheral blood vessels constrict, limiting the amount of heat loss; we also may begin to shiver—a rapid alteration in the contraction of the muscles that creates heat.

These physiological mechanisms are under the command of the hypothalamus, largely through its control of the autonomic nervous system. The hypothalamus senses temperature extremes through the neural pathways that arise from temperature-sensitive nerve endings in the skin. Another source of information is the hypothalamus's own thermostat—heat-sensitive cells that monitor the temperature of the blood circulating through it.

Obviously there is also behavioral control of temperature regulation. When it is too cold, we wear coats or throw another log on the fire or turn up the furnace. Information about external temperature reaches the brain from the skin's nerve endings and motivates us to action. There is also evidence, however, that the hypothalamus itself can initiate behavioral responses. When a small heating probe is inserted into the hypothalamus of a rat, the animal will press a lever in order to receive a blast of cool air. This occurs even when the rat is in a cool environment (Corbit, 1970).

Thirst

The mechanisms that govern thirst and water intake provide a precise and classic model of the role of homeostasis in biological motivation. At one time it was believed that thirst could be accounted for simply by dehydration in the mouth—the familiar feeling of dryness that often precedes our desire to drink. But the dry-mouth theory failed on several counts. For example, even when sensory nerve connections arising from the lips, tongue, and mouth are severed, thirst and drinking are not significantly affected. In addition, merely moistening the mouth or throat has no lasting effect on thirst.

Modern research has demonstrated that two different systems control our intake of water. The osmotic and hypovolemic systems comprise intricate mechanisms that link the state of body fluids, nerve cells in the hypothalamus, and the secretion of hormones.

Osmotic Thirst One system of thirst, *osmotic thirst*, depends upon the flow of fluids through the thin membrane that encloses each cell of the body. These fluids are of two basic types: the intracellular fluid contained within the cells and the extracellular fluid, which is made up of the liquid portion of the blood and of the interstitial fluid that surrounds and bathes body cells. The cell membrane is freely permeable to water but does not permit free passage to certain substances dissolved in the bloodstream and in the interstitial fluid, mainly sodium. As extracellular fluid is lost from the body in urine and sweat, the concentration of sodium outside the cells increases. Because of *osmosis*—the tendency of fluids to equalize concentrations of solutes on both sides of a semipermeable membrane—the water inside the cell passes out through the membrane. This osmotic process leaves the cell dehydrated and shrunken.

How does cellular dehydration tell us that we are thirsty? In its anterior portion the hypothalamus contains nerve cells that appear to be specialized to detect such cellular loss of water. Studies have shown that some cells in this region of the hypothalamus fire nerve impulses in response to changes in the osmotic pressure of blood (Cross and Green, 1959; Fitzsimons, 1971). These cells, called *osmoreceptors*, apparently are uniquely sensitive to the minute changes in volume that are associated with cellular dehydration.

The osmoreceptors, through brain mechanisms that are not yet fully understood, tell us to drink fluids. At the same time, they set in motion another homeostatic means of regulating body fluids. They signal the pituitary gland to increase production of a chemical vitally important in the conservation of body fluids—antidiuretic hormone or ADH (see Figure 10.2). ADH, traveling through the bloodstream, acts on the kidneys where urine is formed.

Ordinarily, when plenty of water is available to the body, a large volume of urine is produced and excreted by the kidneys. But in times of water scarcity the presence of ADH causes the kidneys to reabsorb into the bloodstream much of the water that is ordinarily lost in urine.

One consequence of osmotic thirst is the high concentration of chemical waste products in the urine. For this reason, when we are thirsty or in the morning after a long period without drinking, our urine is a darker color than usual. Like the brain signals that tell us we are thirsty, this highly concentrated urine is a sign of the homeostatic process brought on by cellular dehydration or osmotic thirst.

Hypovolemic Thirst Cellular dehydration is a sufficient biological motivation for thirst but is not a

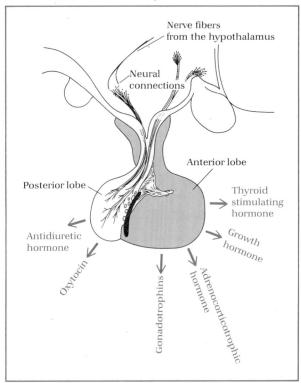

FIGURE 10.2 The pituitary gland and its major hormones. One of the important hormones is ADH (the antidiuretic hormone), which in times of water scarcity causes the kidneys to reabsorb into the bloodstream much of the water ordinarily lost in urine.

necessary one. There seems to be a second system regulating water intake. A hint of the nature of this mechanism long has been noted by surgeons who report that a sudden and dramatic loss of blood, such as might occur during hemorrhaging from a battlefield wound, produces immediate thirst. Laboratory experiments with animals have established that the loss of blood—and thus of extracellular fluid—results in low-volume or *hypovolemic thirst* (Russell, Adbelaal, and Mogenson, 1975).

Hypovolemic thirst constitutes a complex chain of events that is also not yet fully understood. When the volume of extracellular fluid is lowered, the kidneys release a chemical called renin, a substance long known to increase blood pressure. Renin acts as an enzyme to produce a blood hormone called angiotensin I, which in turn leads to the production of another hormone in the blood, angiotensin II. This latter hormone acts to conserve fluid by constricting the peripheral blood vessels, helping maintain normal blood pressure despite the loss of blood. In addition, angiotensin II affects certain nerve cells in the hypothalamus that signal thirst. When it is injected intravenously or directly into the hypothalamus of rats, it causes even a water-satiated animal to drink (Fitzsimons, 1972).

In summary there appear to be two different mechanisms of thirst—osmotic, which involves cellular dehydration, and hypovolemic, which depends upon a lowering of the volume of extracellular fluid. Research indicates that the two systems operate independently (Corbit, 1968).

Hunger

To some extent the homeostatic mechanisms within our bodies provide for lack of food. Sugar is stored in the liver and then released in times of deprivation. But when that supply is depleted, the motivation for food becomes so powerful that people will lie, connive, and even kill to get it. Hunger provides a good example of the control of motivated behavior by physiological factors and has been extensively investigated.

Feeding and Satiety Centers   Among stimuli that lead to the sensation of hunger are the familiar hunger pangs—contractions of the stomach. Cannon demonstrated the significance of stomach contractions when he had volunteer subjects swallow a recording balloon which was filled with air once in the stomach (see Figure 10.3). Stomach contractions, as measured by the balloon, correlated with the subjects' own reports of their hunger sensations (Cannon, 1911; Cannon and Washburn, 1912).

But stomach contractions cannot account for all hunger. People whose stomachs have been surgi-

FIGURE 10.3   To study the relationship between stomach contractions and hunger pangs, the subject swallowed a balloon, which was then filled with air. The record of stomach contractions, indicated by fluctuations in the top line, corresponds to that of hunger pangs, indicated by the horizontal straight lines. The subject produced these horizontal lines by pressing a key whenever he experienced hunger pangs.

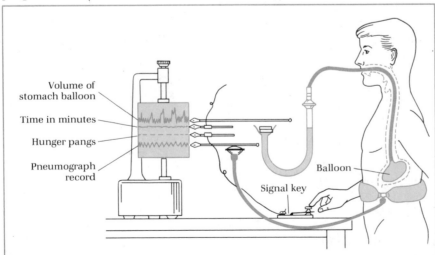

cally removed still report feeling hungry. In the 1940s, researchers began to study the role of the brain in eating behavior. One group found that brain lesions in certain areas of the hypothalamus could produce dramatic changes in feeding (Hetherington and Ranson, 1942). Lesions in the ventromedial hypothalamus (VMH) spurred animals to overeat intensely—a state known as *hyperphagia.* In some cases they actually burgeoned to three to four times their normal body weight. Ranson's work suggested that the VMH serves as a kind of *satiety center,* which, when functioning normally, tells us we have had enough to eat (see Figure 10.4).

This finding was paralleled by another related discovery: lesions placed in the lateral hypothalamus (LH) had the reverse effect (Epstein, 1971). Animals with such lesions were rendered unwilling or unable to eat—a state known as *aphagia.* These studies led to the theory that the LH is a *feeding center* that signals the need to eat.

A plausible and pleasantly simple picture of neural mechanisms involved in the control of feeding behavior thus arose. Eating was thought to be initiated and controlled by a set of neurons in the lateral hypothalamus, the feeding center. This feeding center was thought to be under inhibitory control from neurons in the ventromedial hypothalamus, the satiety center. As a consequence, lesions in the feeding center would be expected to impair normal eating in proportion to the severity of the damage; lesions in the satiety center would be expected to remove an inhibitory "brake" on the feeding center and produce overeating.

The Set-Point Theory In recent years the simple picture of feeding and satiety centers in the hypothalamus has been questioned. Richard Keesey and his colleagues argue that the hypothalamic centers play a different role in feeding: he believes they constitute the neural equivalent of a set point for body weight (Keesey and Powley, 1975). Like a thermostat in a home heating system, they sense body weight, turning on eating behavior when

FIGURE 10.4 Rats with damage to the ventromedial hypothalamus often overeat and become greatly overweight. The rat on the right has suffered damage to this region; the rat on the left is normal.

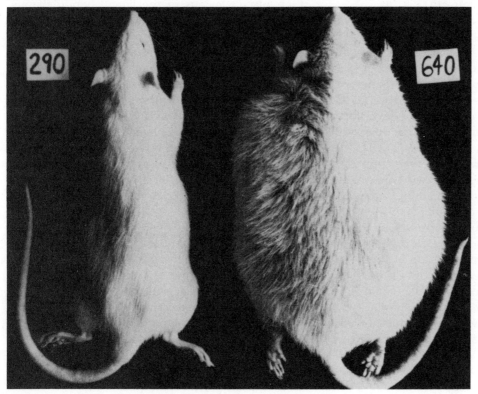

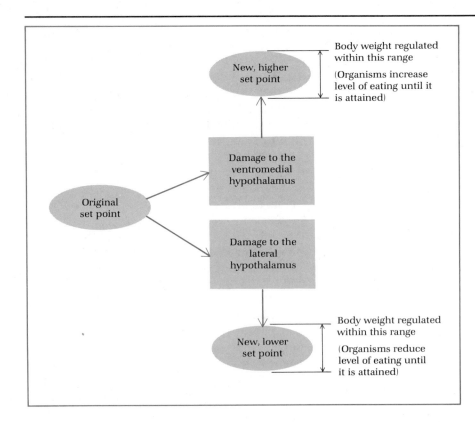

New, higher
set point

Body weight regulated
within this range

(Organisms increase
level of eating until it
is attained)

Damage to the
ventromedial
hypothalamus

Original
set point

Damage to the
lateral
hypothalamus

New, lower
set point

Body weight regulated
within this range

(Organisms reduce
level of eating until
it is attained)

FIGURE 10.5 According to one theory, damage to the ventromedial or lateral hypothalamus changes the "set point" around which body weight is regulated. Consequently, organisms increase or decrease their eating until the new "set point" is attained.

weight becomes too low and stopping it when weight is too high (see Figure 10.5).

Keesey's *set-point theory* depends, in part, on the interpretation of experiments that preceded his own work. For example, aphagic rats were produced by placing lesions in the LH feeding center (Teitelbaum and Epstein, 1962). Then the animals were nursed by tube feedings and with special diets. With careful nursing the rats eventually recovered and began to feed again on their own. This was interpreted in terms of the feeding center perspective. Damage to the feeding center stopped the rats from eating; recovery of feeding behavior was thought to be a result of the remaining undamaged cells taking over control of eating.

Keesey had a different interpretation. He suggested that instead of disrupting the feeding center, the lesions actually had lowered the set point of the rats, thus turning off feeding. The rats eventually began eating again when their weight had dropped below the new set points. Feeding behavior turned on the way a furnace switches on when the thermostat senses that the temperature is too low.

In support of his idea, Keesey conducted a cleverly designed experiment (Keesey and Powley, 1975). He deprived rats of food for several days to drop their weight below a presumed set point and then placed lesions in the lateral hypothalamus. According to the feeding center perspective, these rats should have stopped eating after the surgery. In fact, they began eating normally after recovering from the anesthetic. Some of the rats—deprived of food longer than others—even began overeating. Keesey found that the lesioned rats kept eating until they reached their set point, at which time feeding behavior diminished. This set point, however, apparently had been lowered by the lesions in the LH. The weight of these rats leveled off at a point lower than that of a control group of rats, which had not received brain lesions.

Other observations help support Keesey's set-point theory. If people of normal weight stop eating for any length of time, they lose weight, of course. But when they are allowed to eat freely, they rapidly return to precisely the same weight at which they started. The converse is also true. People who volunteered to eat an excessive amount of food—up to 8,000 calories a day—predictably gained weight. But given free choice, they quickly lost it, returning to almost precisely their original level.

The set-point theory helps explain the remarkable constancy with which most people maintain their body weight over a long period of time. It has been estimated that merely an extra pat of butter each morning would increase one's weight by 10 pounds in one year and 100 pounds in 10 years. Experimental animals have been shown to eat the right amount of food to maintain constancy of body weight even when caloric content is greatly varied. For example, if the animal's food is adulterated with nonnutrients such as mineral oil or water, the animal adjusts the amount it eats so that the caloric intake is roughly constant over an extended period of time (Kennedy, 1950). Moreover, after they are force-fed a very rich diet by tube to make them grossly obese, rats consume far less food than control animals when they are allowed to eat freely. They continue to eat less until their weight roughly equals that of the control animals (Hoebel and Teitelbaum, 1966).

Evidence for the set-point theory is less persuasive where the ventromedial hypothalamus is concerned. Perhaps lesions in the VMH produce a higher set point just as lesions in the lateral hypothalamus appear to lower it. But this interpretation is not consistent with all of the experimental evidence. For example, animals with VMH lesions are very sensitive to changes in the taste of food. They reject food that has been adulterated with quinine to make it bitter, although a normal rat does not (Miller, Bailey, and Stevenson, 1950). This rejection cannot be explained by the simple notion of a higher set point for body weight.

Assuming that Keesey is essentially right in his formulation of the set-point theory, how does the hypothalamus know that body weight is exceeding it or falling below it? Presumably, some sort of mechanism monitors either body weight or a correlate such as the extent of fat stores in the body. One possible correlate is the level of insulin, a hormone, secreted by the pancreas, that is involved in regulation of blood sugar.

Pursuing the insulin approach, Stephen Woods (Woods and Porte, 1976) ascertained that the level of insulin in the blood and cerebrospinal fluid is correlated with the relative weight of an individual. Obese animals, whatever the reason for their obesity, have a higher level of insulin than nonobese animals. Similarly, underweight animals, such as those with lesions in the lateral hypothalamus, show a lower level of insulin. Woods' research has focused on the cerebrospinal fluid where the levels of insulin are not subject to the dramatic short-term fluctuations that occur in the blood. He found that direct injection of insulin into the cerebrospinal fluid of monkeys markedly reduces the rate and amount of food they consume. He suggests that the concentration of insulin in the cerebrospinal fluid may signal the brain as to the amount of fat stores. The insulin signal may be "read" in the hypothalamus by specialized neurons that have insulin receptors on their membranes.

Obesity   *Obesity* is one of the most common health problems in the United States. According to one study, 32 percent of males and 46 percent of females described themselves as being overweight; most of them had actively attempted at some point to lose weight.

Obesity is one of the most common health problems in the United States. When people consume more energy than they use, the excess is stored as fat.

In most cases of obesity, the excess weight is due to excess amounts of fat tissue. The human digestive system is remarkably efficient at extracting available energy from the food we eat, but if we consume more energy than we use, we store the excess as fat, in special cells known as *adipocytes*. A logical question is whether obese people have more adipocytes or whether they simply store more fat in the same number of cells. Direct counts of the number of adipocytes in obese people and in people of normal weight indicate that most overweight people have more adipocytes (Knittle and Hirsch, 1968). Unfortunately, research suggests that the number of fat cells is fixed early in life, probably in the first two years (Lytle, 1977). According to one point of view, the number is partly determined through heredity and partly by eating habits in infancy (Knittle, 1975). Some researchers believe that adipocytes signal hunger when the cells are not full. This leads to a rather pessimistic view of the possibility of controlling obesity. Because obese people who reduce their weight still have the same number of fat cells, each adipocyte now contains less than the normal amount of fat. If these depleted cells signal hunger, then the obese person must either go chronically hungry or remain fat (Knittle, 1975). Unfilled adipocytes would be one possible intermediary in the biological basis of obesity. But any upward alteration of the set point for weight by any mechanism would produce obesity. Obese people would feel chronically hungry unless they reach their weight level (Nisbett, 1972).

Other researchers, while granting that such internal causes may mean that obesity is normal for some people, theorize that much overweight stems from a heightened responsiveness to cues in the external environment. Work with human subjects done by Stanley Schachter and Judith Rodin (1974) has shown that fat people tend to be more sensitive to environmental cues such as the time of day, social situation, and even the look and taste of food. For example, as indicated in Figure 10.6, if obese subjects are erroneously informed that it is time for dinner, they eat more than subjects of normal weight do (Schachter and Gross, 1968). In addition, although obese subjects drink more of a good-tasting milk shake than do nonobese subjects, they drink less when the milk shake is laced with bitter-tasting quinine. This resembles the finickiness of rats with VMH lesions, who also overeat but reject food made bitter with quinine.

A Balanced Diet Not only is it important to eat the right amount of food, it is also important that the food make up a balanced diet. Many organisms, including human children, instinctively put together a proper diet from a menu that includes many foods, each containing one or a few necessary substances (Davis, 1928). This ability is partially due to innate preferences, or *specific hungers* for some essential things such as salt (Stricker and Wilson, 1970). If rats are given two bottles to drink from, one containing pure water and the other containing salt water, the rats will prefer the saltwater solution as long as it is not too salty. If the need for salt is increased, the salt preference will become stronger. For instance, if a rat loses its adrenal glands, its need for salt is dramatically increased: without large amounts of salt, it will die. A rat without adrenals given access to strong salt solutions will drink them eagerly. Similarly, people with Addison's disease, which is due to a malfunction of the adrenal glands, will eat large amounts of salt.

The ability to select a balanced diet is also partially due to learning. Animals that have been fed on a deficient diet develop an aversion to that diet, so they will prefer any new diet when it is first introduced. If the new diet is a complete one, they will stay with it, ignoring the old diet and correcting the deficiency. This phenomenon has been investigated by Paul Rozin and his associates (Rodgers

FIGURE 10.6 Eating behavior differs according to perceived time for normal and obese subjects. In this experiment the actual time for all groups was 5:35 p.m. Obese subjects consumed more when they believed it was close to dinner time, whereas normal subjects eat less.

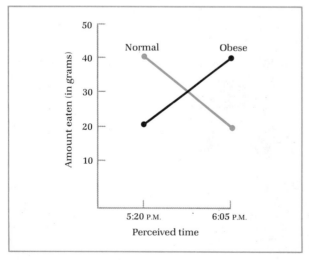

and Rozin, 1966). In this experiment, rats were first fed a diet that was deficient in thiamine. When a new diet was introduced, and the rats had a choice between the two diets, all of the rats initially switched to the new diet. For some of the rats this new diet was complete, and they stayed with it until a new aversion developed. For the rest of the rats the new diet was as deficient as the old one. After a few days these rats abandoned the new diet and returned to the old.

So far, we have seen that the behavior of organisms is partially motivated by the evolutionary processes that produced them and that biological factors are vital in basic drives such as hunger and thirst. In addition, social motivations play important roles in the behavior of both animals and humans.

Social Bases of Motivated Behavior

Humans are social as well as biological beings. Hunger and thirst satisfy basic bodily needs, but other things move us. Many of these, like the need to affiliate with others or the need to achieve, are social in nature. These are called *social motives* because they are acquired or expressed largely through interactions with others.

A sharp distinction is sometimes drawn between biological and social motives. While the satisfaction of a biological motive is obviously and immediately necessary for survival, the satisfaction of a social motive appears less necessary. But this distinction may be misleading. The satisfaction of social motives may be critical not only for psychological well-being but also for biological success in evolutionary terms. The general goals of social motives include such things as recognition, affection, companionship, and power that may affect success in the long run. The study of the evolutionary significance of social behavior is the focus of a relatively new field, sociobiology.

The Adaptive Nature of Social Behavior: Sociobiology

Sociobiology attempts to study social behavior in terms of its adaptive value, with a particular emphasis on the optimization theory approach. As we saw earlier, models are constructed based on the assumption that animals maximize their foraging efficiency. Sociobiological models are constructed on the assumption that animals behave in ways to maximize their contribution to the next generation, measured in terms of the number of their genes represented in the next generation. This usually means maximizing the number of offspring successfully raised, but it can be more complicated when animals are related to each other.

Sociobiology is a relatively young discipline, dating from the 1970s. It is already quite clear that the sociobiological perspective provides an extremely valuable way of looking at the social behavior of animals. And it will probably prove helpful, in the long run, in understanding human behavior. We will look at two examples of sociobiological research with animals to get the general flavor of the approach and then discuss the applicability of sociobiology to our own species.

The Choice of a Mate   How animals select their mates is an issue of concern to sociobiologists. Mate choice can be a critical matter: the selection of an inappropriate mate may lead to relatively few healthy offspring. Furthermore, animal mating systems are enormously variable. For example, some birds are *monogamous* (one male paired with one female), some *polygamous* (one male paired with two or more females), and a rare few are *polyandrous* (more than one male paired with each female see Chapter 11). Can this variety in mating systems be interpreted in terms of maximizing the number of offspring?

One research effort that attempts to answer this question is an extensive field study of the lark bunting by Wanda Pleszczynska (1978). Lark buntings are fairly common birds in the midwestern United States during the spring and summer. They spend their winters in warmer climates, from Texas down into Mexico; in spring they migrate north to their breeding areas. The males arrive first on the breeding grounds—open grassland. They set up territories and begin to sing, advertising their presence both to other males and to females. The females begin to arrive about a week after the males do, and their arrival is staggered over a nine-day period. Some of the males obtain two females (polygamy) who both nest on his territory; others obtain only one female (monogamy); the rest are unable to obtain females. This pattern is due to systematic choices by the arriving females among the available males and territories.

The dynamics of this social system can only be understood after several facts are put together. First, the territories of the males vary widely in quality as nest sites. This is primarily determined by the amount of overhead cover present. Cover is important because it prevents the detection of the nest by predators and filters sunlight reaching the nest that can overheat the young birds. Second, during the nine-day interval in which females are arriving, there are three stages. During the early stage, arriving females pick males with the best territories. During the middle stage, some females choose unmated males with good territories, while other females choose already mated males with excellent territories. Finally, during the late stage, females choose among the remaining unmated males, selecting those with the best territories.

The critical stage is the middle one, wherein some females choose already mated males, while others choose unmated males. Essentially, females arriving during this period are faced with a choice. They can choose unmated males with good territories and be the primary mate, or they can choose an already mated male with an excellent territory and be a secondary mate (secondary mates receive less help from the male than do primary mates). If the differences in territory quality are large enough, a decision to be a secondary mate on an excellent territory may produce more surviving offspring than a decision to be a primary mate on a poorer territory.

These data support three ideas suggested by the sociobiological approach: (1) Females actively select mates (or at least territories) in which the number of young they can successfully raise is increased. Females arriving first select males who have the best territories in which the number of young successfully raised per nest is highest. (2) Monogamy or polygamy depends upon which strategy offers the best chance of having many surviving young. When faced with an unmated male with a relatively poor territory or a mated male with a good territory, the female attempts to maximize the number of young she will be able to raise successfully. (3) There is clear evolutionary pressure on the males to obtain the best possible territory; a male who obtains a poor territory is less likely to attract a mate. And without a mate, no offspring are produced.

Altruistic Behavior and Kin Selection Other research also shows that animals tend to pick the best mates or best territories available. The sociobiological view suggests that the territorial, mating, and sexual behavior of many animals is organized around the adaptive goal of maximizing the number of offspring. But there are also examples of behavior that appear to violate this principle. The alarm sounding of many small, group-living animals when a predator approaches is one common, apparent exception.

Belding's ground squirrel is a small mammal that forms breeding colonies containing many burrows high in the Rocky Mountains. When a predator such as a hawk or a fox appears, the first squirrel to see it will sometimes give an alarm call. When they hear the call, the other squirrels in the vicinity usually stop what they are doing and either scan the environment for the predator or simply dive into their burrows. Because these animals do not always give the alarm call, it cannot be some simple innate response to the predators. But why give the alarm call at all? It would seem more adaptive for the animal just to dive for its burrow without calling attention to itself. This appears to be an example of *altruistic behavior*—behavior that helps others at some cost to the altruist. In sociobiological terms, altruistic behavior should not exist: animals that expose themselves to risk with no benefit to themselves should tend to leave few offspring.

However, sociobiology does offer some possible explanations for the evolution of altruistic behavior. Most important, close relatives have genes in common: full siblings share half their genes, aunts and nieces share one-quarter, and cousins share one-eighth. This is the basis for the concept of kin selection. If an animal acts in a manner that slightly reduces its own chances of surviving and reproducing but increases the prospects of some of its relatives, it could be increasing the number of its genes in the next generation because it shares genes with the children of its relatives.

The *kin selection hypothesis* predicts that helping behavior should be most common among closely related animals. Studies testing this idea are particularly difficult to carry out. Individual animals must be identifiable, either through natural markings or by marking of the animals by experimenters. In addition, studies must continue over several generations, so that kin relationships will be known. In spite of these difficulties, such experiments have been carried out, and the results of these studies are most often consistent with the kin selection hypothesis.

One of the best studies of the kin selection explanation for selective alarm calls is Paul Sherman's (1977) study of the Belding's ground squirrel. Individual squirrels were marked with blotches of colored dye so they could be recognized, and the group was observed over several generations. Within this colony, young males left the area before they were one year of age, and all of the adult males present had been born elsewhere. Thus, the adult males were not related to the females or young (except their own) in the area. Females, in contrast, tended to stay in the colony into which they were born, and many of them had relatives living in the immediate vicinity of their burrows. On the average, females are more related to animals in the area than are males. As one would expect from kin selection, females were more likely to give the alarm call after sighting a predator than were males. This could be a simple sex difference attributable to some factor other than relatedness. But Sherman also observed that some of the females had relatives living in the area (sisters, mothers, and descendants), whereas others did not. The females with relatives were much more likely to give alarm calls than were females without relatives.

Belding's ground squirrels take a risk by alarm calling—weasels and coyotes regularly stalked alarm callers and sometimes killed them. But this risk was probably offset by the gain to the relatives of the alarm callers. Other examples of cooperation among close kin exist in animals ranging from insects to birds to lions to primates. Kin relationships, with their genetic implications, appear to be basic to animal social behavior and organization.

Sociobiology, Motivation, and the Human Species

Can the sociobiological perspective be applied to human behavior? This problematic question has given rise to heated debate among psychologists, anthropologists, and zoologists. Sociobiological explanations of various aspects of human behavior are easy to postulate. Is nepotism (favoritism shown to a relative) due to kin selection? Does extended human courtship function to provide opportunities for the evaluation of prospective mates? In polygamous human societies, those men who have multiple wives were usually the richest. Is the parallel to the lark bunting more than coincidence?

At present, this is speculation, albeit very interesting speculation. In order to translate this speculation into something more substantial, research is needed—research that will be difficult to carry out. Furthermore, it must be remembered that the adaptive significance of behavior is most apparent in the environment in which the species evolved. The environment we live in has changed faster in the last several thousand years than the ability of evolution to produce behavioral changes; sociobiology, then, may prove more useful in understanding the social systems of primitive human societies than of modern civilization.

Human Social Motives

Sociobiology suggests that the roots of human sociality are to be found in our biological heritage. But this does not mean that the social needs and behavior of humans are genetically predetermined in some narrow, inflexible way. Rather, human social needs are heavily influenced by experience; learning and social experience are crucial shapers of human social motivation. In this section we will look at two important human social motives: the need for affiliation and the need to achieve.

The Need for Affiliation

One of the most important of the social motives, *affiliation*, is summed up in the familiar statement— people need people. We need others for many reasons: to mediate rewards for us, to help us attain our goals, to help us learn things, to define social reality for us, to establish and validate our beliefs and values.

Our tendency to associate with others is so powerful that some psychologists have proposed that the need to affiliate is not only a social motive but also an innate biological need. As evidence they point to the prolonged dependency of human children on parents and other caregivers. Of all animals, humans have the longest period of need for protection and of learning to cope with the environment: a biological need for affiliation would thus have great survival value for individuals and for the human species.

Although the need for affiliation may indeed have a strong biological component, biology alone cannot explain our tendency to seek out others after we are adults and are able to survive physically quite well on our own. As our early needs are satisfied by others, social interaction becomes a

305

learned source of reward and comfort. We learn that being with others is a necessary and enriching experience, and this social motive impels us throughout our lives.

Anxiety and Affiliation   The factors that influence the need to affiliate have been studied extensively by Stanley Schachter. In *The Psychology of Affiliation* (1959), Schachter examined these factors and, in particular, the role of anxiety. Schachter's focus on anxiety stemmed in part from his study of case histories of individuals who had to endure long periods of time alone. For example, shipwrecked sailors and members of certain monastic religious orders often report experiencing bouts of severe anxiety during their loneliness.

Schachter reasoned that if being alone produced anxiety, anxiety might produce a desire to affiliate with others. To test this hypothesis, he conducted an experiment to measure the possible relationship between anxiety and affiliation. To disguise the real purpose of the experiment, he told subjects that the aim was to test the effects of electric shock. Subjects were assigned to one of two conditions. In the high-anxiety condition, subjects were shown an ominous-looking complex of electrical gadgetry and were told that they would be given painful shocks. In the low-anxiety condition, the subjects were told the shocks would be extremely mild—scarcely more than a tickle. Then, in order to measure the effect of affiliation, the experimenter told the subjects that it would take a while to get the apparatus ready and that they could wait either in a room alone or in a room with others. Their decisions on how they would wait supported Schachter's hypothesis: 63 percent of the subjects in the high-anxiety condition chose to affiliate—wait in a room with others—but only 33 percent of the low-anxiety subjects made that choice.

In further research, Schachter tried to determine what sort of people anxious subjects would seek out. He varied the experiment so that there were two conditions of high anxiety. In one condition, anxious subjects were given the choice of waiting alone or waiting with others who were participating in the same shock experiment. In this condition, 60 percent of the subjects chose to wait with others. In the other condition, anxious subjects had the choice of waiting alone or of being with people who were ostensibly waiting in a room for a meeting with another professor. Interestingly, none of these subjects chose to wait with others. The anxiety-aroused desire to affiliate was directed only toward those who were presumably awaiting painful shocks

Sharing a common anxiety often results in a need for, and tendency toward, affiliation.

and thus in the same boat. As Schachter put it, "Misery doesn't love just any kind of company; it loves only miserable company."

Schachter explained this phenomenon in terms of the *theory of social comparison*, which holds that, in ambiguous situations, we tend to look to other people for help in determining appropriate behavior. Although the subjects were undeniably anxious, the situation was so strange that they needed cues from others to help clarify their own feelings about it. Only those who were in the same state of anxiety—waiting to be shocked—would be useful in this process of social comparison.

The Effect of Birth Order Having established a relationship between anxiety and affiliation, Schachter wondered why there were individual differences in the need for others even among anxious people. One possibility quickly suggested itself: early experience. Perhaps people who had learned as children to rely heavily on others to allay their anxieties might develop the strongest need to affiliate when anxious. All children rely to some extent on others for relief from anxieties, of course, but Schachter reasoned that children without siblings are most likely to have their needs and anxieties taken care of by parents. Children without siblings would include those who were first in the order of birth and, hence, for a while were the only children in the family. Parents tend to be very solicitous with

firstborn children. They respond to the slightest crying or hurt. By the time subsequent children arrive, however, they have come to realize that children are not all that fragile; they let children cry longer and do not fret over every fall or bruise. In any case, the proliferation of children means that parents simply do not have as much time to devote to any one child.

By this reasoning, first-borns ought to develop a stronger motive than later-borns to affiliate as a way of allaying anxiety. When Schachter reviewed his experimental data on anxiety and affiliation, he found support for this notion: only first-borns showed a great increase in the desire to be with others under high anxiety. In fact, he found that affiliative tendencies were precisely related to ordinal birth order. First-borns showed greater affiliative tendencies when anxious than did second-borns, who in turn showed greater desire to affiliate than did third-borns, and so on (see Figure 10.7).

These findings imply that first-borns seek social means to cope with anxiety while later-borns are more likely to try avenues that are nonsocial. Such an implication, Schachter speculated, might apply in many real-life situations. People who are tense and anxious can attempt to cope with those emotions in many ways. One common way is through

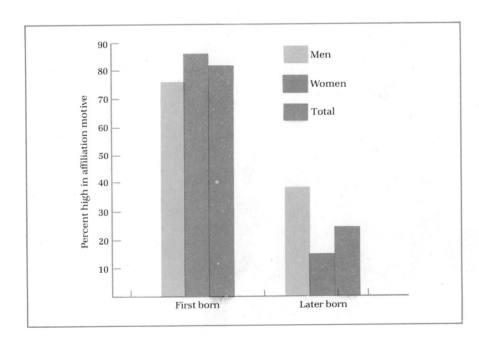

FIGURE 10.7 A number of studies have shown the affiliation motive to be higher among first-born children than among their younger brothers and sisters, especially in the case of women.

alcoholism—a distinctly nonsocial means. Another is through psychotherapy, which requires a form of dependency on another person. Schachter found support for these hypotheses. His analysis showed that later-borns were much more likely to become alcoholics than were first-borns. And first-borns were more likely to go into therapy and stick to it than were later-borns (although there was no difference in the extent to which the two groups suffered from psychological disturbance).

The Need for Achievement

Our society, and Americans in particular, put a high premium on *achievement*. From Little League baseball to Olympic competition, from third-grade spelling bees to the race for Nobel Prizes, doing well is highly valued by the participants and by those around them. Achievement often brings status and profit, of course, but even in the absence of external rewards, it makes us feel good.

David McClelland has found that individuals differ greatly in their need for achievement. An individual's level of need for achievement appears to be a stable and enduring characteristic that affects behavior in a variety of situations (McClelland, Atkinson, Clark, and Lowell, 1953). In addition, McClelland found that the need to achieve not only affects individual behavior, but also has a profound influence on economic and technological growth in a society (McClelland, 1961). Cultures and civilizations grow and prosper only when a significant number of people have a high level of achievement motivation; otherwise, the society will decline. To demonstrate this, McClelland analyzed the art, literature, and music of various cultures throughout history. These indicators showed high achievement themes, he found, just before a culture reached its zenith. But in the periods just prior to the decline of great civilizations, such as those of ancient Rome and Athens, the indicators showed a low need for achievement.

Measuring Achievement Need McClelland's principal tool for measuring the need for achievement in individuals is the Thematic Apperception Test (TAT). The TAT, which is also used in measuring personality (see Chapter 12), is called a projective test because subjects are presented with an ambiguous situation and then asked to tell a story about it, presumably projecting onto the situation their own inner feelings and needs. A typical TAT for measuring achievement motivation might consist of a picture of a man sitting at a large desk and staring out the window. The subject is then asked to tell what led to this situation and what will happen in the future. In response to this picture, a person with a high need for achievement presumably will project that motive onto the situation. For

As indicated by these three winners of the 200-meter men's freestyle event at the 1979 Pan American Games, achievement is highly valued in our society.

example, the subject might suggest that the man is trying to get ahead on his job and has come to work on a Sunday morning; he is developing a new product for his company that will win him a promotion. On the other hand, the subject with a low need to achieve might conclude that it is Friday afternoon and the man is daydreaming about how relaxing the weekend will be; in fact, he will leave work early to be with his family.

High Need versus Low Need   Through his work with the TAT and through experiments, McClelland has pinpointed a number of differences between high-need achievers and those with a low need to achieve. High-need achievers, for example, are motivated to succeed; low-need achievers are motivated to avoid failure. In choosing a task, a high-need achiever will typically pick one of intermediate difficulty—tough enough to create a challenge but not impossible. The low-need achiever typically picks either a task so easy that failure is impossible or a task so difficult that failure is to be expected and thus is unlikely to be condemned; in either case the possibility of true failure is avoided. This difference was demonstrated in a kindergarten class where children were asked to play a game in which they could choose the distance from which they attempted to throw rings over a stake. Children with a high need to achieve, as measured by the TAT,

stood at medium distances—far enough to create a challenge but close enough to make success possible. The low-need achievers stood either right next to the stake or so far away that they could not possibly succeed, but would not be condemned for their failure (see Figure 10.8).

Response to Failure   High-need achievers become upset when they fail and are motivated to work even harder; low-need achievers expect to fail and tend to give up when it happens. Success has the opposite effect: high-need achievers expect success and ease up after they achieve it; low-need achievers are so excited by success because it's unexpected that they are spurred to greater effort (Weiner, 1970).

Parental Influences   Research indicates that parents who reward self-control and independence tend to have children with high achievement motivation (Teevan and McGhee, 1972). Such parents set high standards for their children but allow them to work at their own level and to make their own mistakes. By contrast, parents of low-need achievers typically set impossibly high goals for their children and make extreme demands. In addition, parents of high-need achievers encourage good performance but don't berate their children when they fail. If a child comes home from school with four As and one B on a report card, the parents focus on the As; parents of a potential low-need achiever tend to ask, "Why the B?" Parents of high-need achievers respond to mediocre grades with warmth and suggestions for reasonable goals and ways to reach them. Parents of low-need achievers might say, "You're dumb and lazy—you'll never amount to anything," and punish the child. When a child is having trouble with a math problem, the parent of a potential high-need achiever will suggest the general procedure and let the child work out the particular solution; a low-need achiever's parent will solve the problem and then hand the child the answer.

That needs for affiliation and achievement exist within all of us, to varying degrees, is undeniable. And although biological bases for at least the affiliation need have been proposed, a great deal more is known about the psychological bases of these needs and how they come about.

FIGURE 10.8   People judged to be high achievers tend to set more rigorous goals for themselves and to expect more in return for their efforts. In this study involving a ring-toss game, high achievers set consistently larger monetary rewards than did low achievers when asked to recommend suitable prizes for success at each distance.

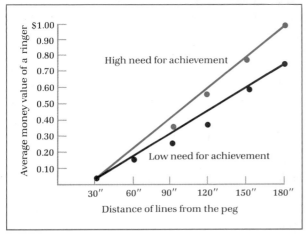

Closely related to motivation are emotions, which can activate and direct behavior in much the same way as physiological, social, and psychological motivations do. Emotions also accompany motivated behavior: love often goes with sex, anger with aggression, and so on. Although almost everyone feels emotions, they are difficult to define.

Emotions

Emotions such as rage, fear, love, hate, and joy are closely linked to motivation. Often they result from the fulfillment or frustration of biological or social motives. In addition, emotions themselves often serve as motivators of our behavior, moving us to actions that facts alone might never elicit.

What precisely constitutes an *emotion?* It usually consists of both a mental, or cognitive, component and a physiological response. Theories of emotions typically focus on the relationship between these two components.

The James-Lange Theory

The earliest modern theory of emotions was proposed shortly before the beginning of the twentieth century by the American psychologist and philosopher William James (1890) and the Danish physiologist Karl Lange. Both researchers, though working independently, concentrated on physiological reactions—increased heartbeat, for example—that accompany strong emotions. Intuitively, most people believe that these physiological reactions are a response to the emotion. James and Lange said just the opposite: they argued that emotions are perceptions of physiological reactions that precede and cause the specific emotion. People realize they are afraid because their hearts pound rapidly. As James (1890) put it, "We are afraid because we run; we do not run because we are afraid."

The James-Lange theory suggests that each of our many emotions is produced by a distinct physiological state. This seems unlikely. In many cases the physiological differences that do exist between different emotional states are very subtle (Ax, 1953).

Cannon (1927) attacked the James-Lange theory on two grounds. First, the physiological changes associated with emotional states occur too slowly to produce an emotional reaction. If a gun is pointed at you, you feel fear immediately—too quickly to result from physiological reactions. Second, the physiological changes that accompany emotions come about in other situations in which they do not produce emotions. Heavy exercise often produces many of the same physiological changes that accompany fear—increased heart rate, breathing rate, blood pressure, and so on—without causing a fear reaction. Cannon argued that the thalamus plays a central role in emotion (Cannon, 1927). His idea was elaborated on by Philip Bard, and the theory, known as the *Cannon-Bard Theory* (Cannon, 1929), places the source of the emotions in the thalamus, which, he believed, sent impulses to the sympathetic nervous system (producing the physiological changes) and at the same time to the cerebral cortex (producing the feeling of emotion). Although the importance of the thalamus to emotion has not been substantiated, there can be no doubt that physiological factors play an important role in emotional experience.

Physiological Bases of Emotion

Physiological changes accompany most emotional experiences. Blood pressure, heart rate, and respiration may change; the pupils of the eyes may dilate; the body may break out in a sweat. These bodily reactions are controlled largely by the autonomic nervous system, which in turn controls the glands and smooth muscles of the heart, the blood vessels, and the gastrointestinal tract.

Other evidence for physiological bases of emotion has been provided by studies using electrical stimulation of the brain. Electrical stimulation of certain parts of the brain can produce what appear to be full-fledged fear or rage responses in rats and cats. A most intriguing discovery was made accidentally by James Olds and Peter Milner (1954). Olds was studying the effects of physiological arousal on learning. Other physiologists had recently found an area just behind the hypothalamus that is involved in maintaining wakefulness. Olds, attempting to insert an electrode in this area of a rat brain, missed his intended target and placed it in the hypothalamus. Unaware of the misplacement of the electrode, Olds began to give the rat brief bursts of electrical stimulation. The rat, with the electrode attached to wires strung from its head, was free to roam a tabletop enclosure. To the researcher's astonishment, the rat kept returning to the corner where the stimulation occurred. The rat, reported Olds, seemed to be "coming back for more."

Olds suspected that, for some reason, the rat liked the feeling elicited by the stimulation. To test this possibility, he arranged an experiment in which the animal could control the stimulation of its own brain. He put the rat in a Skinner box set up so that when the animal pushed a lever, it received a burst of electrical stimulation in the brain (see Figure 10.9).

The results of this and other experiments that followed were clear and dramatic. Rats would stage veritable orgies of self-stimulation. Certain centers in the hypothalamus proved to be the most powerful motivators. Rats would pump the lever up to 5,000 times an hour. Some would press it as many as 2,000 times an hour for 24 consecutive hours, collapse from exhaustion, and then return to the lever for still more self-stimulation. To reach the lever, rats would even cross an electrified grid, enduring painful shocks of strengths much higher than those that will stop a hungry animal from reaching a reward of food. Given a choice between pressing a lever to obtain food and pushing one for self-stimulation, some rats eventually gave up all interest in food and devoted full time to their electric reward; but for the intervention of the experimenter, they would have starved to death (Spies, 1965). These areas that elicited repeated self-stimulation were labeled *reward centers* by Olds,

FIGURE 10.9 The presence of "pleasure centers" in the brain was discovered by James Olds. Using the apparatus shown, Olds studied the effects of electrical stimulation of the brain. Each time the rat pressed the lever, it received a weak pulse of electricity through a tiny electrode implanted in its brain.

but they soon became popularly known as "pleasure centers."

At about the same time that Olds was carrying out his early experiments on the reward centers, a group of researchers at Yale University were experimentally stimulating neural centers in the nearby midbrain (Delgado, Roberts, and Miller, 1954). Under this stimulation, cats reacted as if in great pain. When they were presented with food and the current was switched on, they immediately stopped eating and would not return to the food. They would even perform difficult tasks in order to avoid stimulation in these so-called punishment or *aversive centers*.

How are these fascinating phenomena related to the emotions we experience upon satisfying a motive? The answer is not clear, although it must be assumed that these experiences are somehow represented in the brain. For example, the feeling of pleasure that comes from drinking a glass of cold water on a hot day must result from a change in the activity of nerve cells. It is also possible that electrical stimulation artificially activates the same circuits that are involved in normal mechanisms of pleasure or pain. The location of the reward centers—near hypothalamic areas that help regulate eating, drinking, and sexual behavior—is suggestive. At the very least, these experiments show that events in the brain are related to feelings of pleasure and pain.

Cognitive Aspects of Emotion

Recent research and theory have placed considerable emphasis on the cognitive determinants of emotion.

Two-factor Theory of Emotions The clearest example of this approach is Schachter and Jerome Singer's (1962) *two-factor theory of emotions*. Schachter and Singer contend that the physiological arousal accompanying emotions is simply a general state. The exact nature of the emotion depends upon how the person interprets the cause and meaning of the physiological arousal. As we are aroused, we put a cognitive label on the arousal: we call it joy, rage, frustration, and so on—depending on how we interpret the feeling.

Schachter and Singer's two-factor theory indicates that an emotion consists of both arousal and cognition. If neither arousal nor the cognitive label is present, then there will be no emotion.

On what basis does a person determine the content of the cognitive label? The two-factor theory states that, in the absence of a ready explanation for arousal, we seek cues from the environment—signals from the situation itself or from other people in the situation to tell us what we are feeling. If we don't know whether to laugh or cry, we look to the situation—is it a party or a funeral?—and to the emotions others seem to be experiencing.

To test their theory, Schachter and Singer needed a basic experiment that would combine the two elements of arousal and environmental cues. They needed also to disguise the real purpose of the experiment. Their solution was a project ostensibly aimed at measuring the effects of injections of a vitamin supplement which they called "suproxin." In reality, suproxin was epinephrine, a drug that induces arousal by acting on the autonomic nervous system, much as the naturally occurring hormone adrenalin does.

Some subjects knew they would experience symptoms of arousal; they were told the suproxin would produce side effects such as increased heart rate, hand trembling, and flushed face—the normal effects of epinephrine. Thus informed, they presumably would not have to look to the environment to interpret their physiological state as a particular emotion. Other subjects were also injected with suproxin but were not told about any physiological symptoms. According to the Schachter-Singer theory, these subjects would look to situational cues in order to interpret their feelings of physiological arousal.

After the injection, the subjects were taken one at a time to a waiting room. There, each subject joined another "subject"—actually a confederate of the experimenters. The confederate then attempted to manipulate the unwitting subject's emotions by behaving in one of two ways: he acted either euphoric or angry. In the euphoric condition, the confederate began to act in a silly and bizarre manner: he played basketball by flipping wads of paper

FIGURE 10.10 Bar diagrams of behavior in the euphoria (A) and anger conditions (B) of the Schachter and Singer experiment using "suproxin." The subjects who were not informed of the probable effects of suproxin as well as those who were misinformed were more active in the euphoria condition. The uninformed showed more anger in the anger condition (the misinformed were not tested in the anger condition). The subjects who were informed about the drug's effects were less active in the euphoria condition and showed no anger in the anger condition. The control subjects were more active than the informed subjects but less active than the uninformed or misinformed ones in the euphoria condition. In the anger condition they showed more anger than the informed subjects but much less than the uninformed subjects.

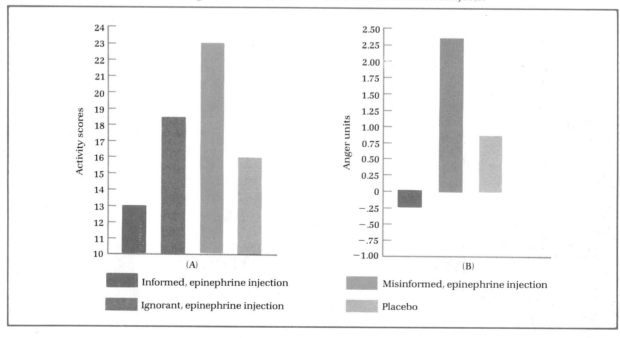

at a wastebasket, he folded paper airplanes and sent them flying around the room, he found a hula hoop behind a bookshelf and twirled it around his hips. In the anger condition, the confederate displayed annoyance and rage at a questionnaire that he and the subject were asked to fill out. Although it began innocently enough, the questionnaire gradually became very personal and insulting; the final item asked bluntly, "With how many men has your mother had extramarital relationships?" and then gave the respondent the choice of several numbers, none of which was zero. As the confederate proceeded through the questions, he displayed more and more annoyance, crossing out items and finally ripping up the entire questionnaire.

After all of this had taken place, the experimenters attempted to assess the mood of their subjects. They asked them to complete a questionnaire aimed at eliciting facts about mood. The results supported the two-factor theory. The subjects who had not been informed about the physiological symptoms reported more intense emotion than did the subjects who had been told that the suproxin would have side effects and thus had a ready explanation for their arousal. Moreover, in the anger condition, the uninformed subjects reported greater feelings of anger than did the informed subjects; in the euphoric condition they reported stronger feelings of happiness. In short, when subjects had no explanation for their feelings of arousal, they took their cues from the behavior of the confederate. If he seemed euphoric, they experienced the emotion of happiness; if he seemed angry, they were angry. The physiological state produced by the epinephrine injections produced increased happiness or increased anger, depending on the setting. This experiment demonstrates the influence of cognitive factors in the interpretation of our internal states (see Figure 10.10).

Transfer of Excitation   Imagine that you've just run a morning workout of three or four miles. Your heart is beating faster and you are feeling other signs of physiological arousal. Both factors in the Schachter-Singer theory of emotion are present: arousal, plus your cognition of the situation "I've just finished a hard workout."

Let's further imagine that after you've stopped to catch your breath, you drive to the grocery store. On your way there, another car suddenly runs through a stop sign and cuts you off. Your reaction most likely would be anger at the other driver. But would the fact that you had just exercised a few minutes ago lead you to be even angrier than would be normal in this situation? According to research by Dolf Zillman, the answer is yes (Zillman, 1971; Zillman, Katcher, and Milavsky, 1972). Working from the two-factor theory of emotion, Zillman has shown that arousal—whether caused by anger, physical exercise, or erotic stimulation—does not dissipate rapidly. Physiological excitation remains for a period of time even though we may not be aware of it. Zillman calls this the phase of residual excitation.

The residual excitation from exercise, when added to the arousal of anger, leads to an especially high level of arousal. As you experience this high level of arousal, you attempt to interpret it in terms of immediate situational cues—your anger at the other driver. Thus, the effect is to transfer to the emotion of anger the residual excitation from physical exercise. According to Zillman, this *transfer of excitation* will make you more angry, more willing to pick a fight with the other driver, than normally would be the case.

The enhancement of subsequent emotions by the transfer of residual excitation has been demonstrated by Zillman and his colleagues in a number of experiments. One study, for example, created physiological arousal through physical exercise and then assessed whether this excitation was transferred to the level of sexual arousal. (Cantor, Zillman, and Bryant, 1975). About five minutes after riding a stationary bicycle, and while they were in the phase of residual excitation, subjects were shown an erotic movie. Reports by these subjects of their feelings of sexual arousal were compared with those of subjects who either had not exercised first or who had watched the film immediately after or a long time after the exercise. The subjects in residual excitation reported being more sexually aroused by the film than did the other subjects.

The physiological and the cognitive aspects of emotions thus conjoin in varying ways, both to respond to, and to produce, the wide gamut of human feelings. One particular behavior that exemplifies this well is aggression: if the cognitive factor is anger or frustration, and it is accompanied by arousal, a strong emotion that might produce aggressive behavior is likely to result. Aggression has such powerful portents, in history and in the contemporary world, that it deserves a closer look.

313

Aggression

One of the most fascinating and most important of all the behaviors that come under the scrutiny of psychologists who study motivation and emotion is aggression. Aggression is as commonplace as two neighbors quarreling and as immediate as daily newspaper headlines about assault, terrorism, and murder. In its most serious potential form, nuclear warfare, it threatens the very existence of humankind. In the course of this chapter, we have discussed several different approaches to motivation—sociobiological, physiological, and social. In this section, we will examine aggression in light of those three views.

The Sociobiological Approach

Konrad Lorenz, an ethologist who won a Nobel Prize in 1973, has proposed a theory of aggression that is based on studies of animal behavior. In his book *On Aggression* (1967), Lorenz argued that in many species, fighting within the species is adaptive, fulfilling functions that enable the species as a whole to survive. For example, only the strongest win mates and reproduce, thus improving the species as a whole. In addition, because the losers may flee, Lorenz pointed out that the species will spread over a wider area, preventing overcrowding and insuring an adequate food supply.

Lorenz further postulated that because indiscriminate killing would not be adaptive, animals

RESEARCH: The Costs of Pleasure, the Benefits of Pain

How strange would appear to be this thing that men call pleasure! And how curiously it is related to what is thought to be its opposite, pain! The two will never be found *together* in a man, and yet if you seek the one and obtain it, you are almost bound always to get the other as well. . . . Wherever the one is found, the other follows up behind.
—Plato, *Phaedo*

People as diverse as drug addicts and marathon runners would probably agree with Plato's ancient wisdom. The addict achieves the sudden rush of euphoria at the cost of the subsequent pain of withdrawal; the distance runner undergoes the pain of great physical exertion at the benefit of high exhilaration at the end of the race.

The reciprocal relationships between pleasure and pain are the focus of an important new theory of motivation formulated by Richard Solomon of the University of Pennsylvania. Solomon (1980) calls his theory the opponent-process theory of acquired motivation. He believes that most acquired motives— such as love, social attachments, and even thrill seeking—as well as the needs for achievement, power, and affiliation, obey the same laws as various addictions. In his view, each of these motives is in fact a kind of addiction. Each addiction, whether to heroin, for example, or to social attachments, eventually produces a state opposite to that initially experienced: pleasure gives way to pain; pain turns to pleasure.

Solomon describes three phenomena that characterize the addictive type of acquired motive: (1) affective or emotional contrast, (2) habituation or tolerance, and (3) withdrawal or abstinence syndromes. These characteristics can be seen in the parallel emotional dynamics of two apparently contrasting types of acquired motivation—heroin addiction and thrill seeking. The first few doses of an opiate produce a state of euphoria. After the drug wears off, the user experiences the craving of withdrawal. If doses are repeated frequently, however, the tolerance to the drug builds up. The euphoria diminishes and gives way to the much more intense emotional and physiological pain of withdrawal. The positive reinforcement of pleasure loses power; the negative reinforcement of pain gains power.

By contrast, the acquisition of a thrill-seeking motive typically begins with negative or aversive reinforcement. In a study of parachute jumping, Seymour Epstein (1967) found that novices experienced a great deal of terror during their first few jumps. A few minutes after landing safely, however, they became highly elated. Over many jumps, tolerance to the terror of free-fall built up. Epstein found that some experienced jumpers actually became severely distressed when bad weather grounded them. It was as if they were addicted to the sport and were experiencing withdrawal symptoms. Here, the negative reinforcement of the danger of jumping loses power, and the positive reinforcement gains it. Although the heroin user begins with pleasure and the parachutist with terror, the result is the same—the craving that characterizes an acquired motive.

Solomon's theory assumes that the brain is somehow organized "to oppose and suppress many types of emotional arousals, whether they are pleasurable or aversive, whether they have been generated by positive

have evolved instinctive inhibitions against unrestrained aggression. These inhibitions are expressed in ritual behaviors that prevent fighting from resulting in death. For example, a defeated wolf turns and offers its throat to the victor, a gesture that ends their battle. The evolution of such inhibitors of aggression would be most developed in animals that have dangerous physical weapons like sharp teeth and claws. Lorenz suggested that over most of our evolutionary history, humans did not have such weapons. Therefore, humans did not evolve many effective inhibitors of aggression. When we began to manufacture weapons like knives, arrows, and rifles, the lack of such inhibitors became a lethal threat. We now had the weapons to kill with but

not the ritualized gestures to stop the aggression. This argument makes some sense, but we probably do have inhibitors that are effective at close range although not at a distance. It is easier to imagine killing someone with a rifle or a bomb than with a knife.

A critical and controversial part of Lorenz's arguments concerned the nature of an aggressive drive. Lorenz maintained that the aggressive drive was a *deprivation drive.* Deprivation drives are drives that, like hunger or thirst, get stronger and stronger as time passes without the satisfaction of the drive.

or by negative reinforcers." He postulates two processes at work in acquired motivation. The primary process is set in motion by a positive or negative reinforcer such as heroin or parachute jumping. It eventually arouses an opponent process, which functions to oppose and suppress the emotional state generated by the primary process.

How can Solomon's fascinating theory be tested? One line of experiments deals with the growth of social attachment in young ducklings. Social attachment in young birds is acquired through the process of imprinting. As we saw in Chapter 7, imprinting occurs when the newly hatched bird is first exposed to the movements of its mother or another object. If the imprinting stimulus is suddenly removed, however, the hatchling starts searching for the lost object and emits high-pitched cries, or distress calls. These distress calls are symptoms of withdrawal of the pleasurable stimulus and can be used as an index of the degree of social attachment, much in the way that drug withdrawal symptoms can be used to measure dependence on heroin.

Howard Hoffman and his colleagues (Hoffman, Eiserer, Ratner, and Pickering, 1974) exposed duck hatchlings to an imprinting stimulus for one-minute intervals that were alternated with one-minute periods in which the stimulus was removed. According to Solomon's theory, the opponent process—grief at the withdrawal of the mother surrogate—should be strengthened by use. As the figure indicates, that is precisely what happened in Hoffman's experiment. The opponent process, as measured by the intensity of distress calling, gradually increased.

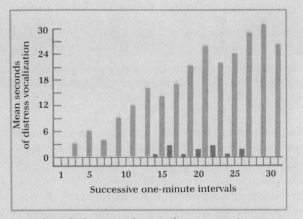

In an imprinting experiment, the opponent process, as indicated by the intensity of distress calling, increased as the number of trials, in which one-minute presentations were alternated with one-minute absences of the mother surrogate, increased.

Although Solomon's opponent-process theory still requires a great deal of testing before it can be widely accepted, the findings thus far may have important implications for the treatment of drug addiction. For example, the size and frequency of stimulus dosages appear to be crucial to the acquisition of an addictive type of motive. Solomon also suggests that there are implications for our understanding of psychosomatic disorders. He points out that we ordinarily think of physiological stress in terms of aversive events, but his theory "implies that often-repeated pleasures are just as fertile a source of physiological stress."

315

Konrad Lorenz proposed that fighting within a species is adaptive. Because only the strongest win mates and reproduce, the species as a whole is improved.

Lorenz pointed out that as a drive gets stronger, less stimulation is needed to set off behavior associated with the drive. Thus, if aggression is based on a deprivation drive, aggressive behavior is virtually inevitable. However, there is no evidence, convincing or even semiconvincing, that aggression is based on a deprivation drive. Lorenz's assertion is rejected by most ethologists and psychologists.

In general terms, Lorenz viewed aggression as a relatively inflexible, innate mode of behavior. His theory thus has problems accounting for the wide variations in aggression that exist throughout human societies. Lorenz's views are often treated as though they were typical of the evolutionary approach to aggression. But this is not so. From the sociobiological point of view, Lorenz's position is flawed. Although Lorenz emphasized the value of aggressive behavior for the species as a whole, sociobiology emphasizes its value for the individual's gene pool. From the sociobiological perspective, an animal should fight when the potential benefits of doing so outweigh the potential costs, and not otherwise. Benefits might include access to food, nesting sites, or potential mates. Costs might include the expenditure of time and energy, and the risk of injury or death.

Informal observation supports the notion that costs and benefits determine aggression. Animals are most likely to fight over important resources when these are in short supply. For example, suppose you placed a bird feeder outside your kitchen window and kept it well stocked with birdseed all year round. During the winter, when other food is scarce, many birds would use the feeder, squabbling and fighting over the food. But during the summer, when other food is plentiful, birds coming to the feeder would not be very likely to fight.

This approach to aggression has been supported by several naturalistic studies. Frank Gill and Larry Wolf (1975) studied the territorial behavior of African sunbirds, which feed on the nectar of flowers. On some days these birds set up territories from which they aggressively chase other sunbirds. On other days, they do not set up such territories; instead they feed over a wide area without chasing other birds. Could this difference in behavior be due to the kind of cost-benefit relationship suggested by sociobiology? To answer this question

Gill and Wolf studied this behavior intensively. They found that whether or not the birds were territorial depended upon the number of flowers available each day. For instance, if there were very few flowers the birds were not aggressive. When there are only a few flowers, a territory has to be very large in order to contain enough food for the bird. But a large territory is very difficult to maintain. Thus the aggressive territorial behavior of the sunbirds was correlated with the relative costs and benefits of the behavior.

The sociobiological approach suggests that aggression is much more flexible than Lorenz's instinctive approach suggests. Aggression is simply another type of behavior that can serve an adaptive function under the right circumstances. Note that there is nothing in this view that says that aggression is either good or bad. It is just another behavioral alternative shown by animals under some conditions.

Physiological Mechanisms and Aggression

During the evening of July 31, 1966, Charles Whitman killed his wife and his mother. The next morning he climbed to the top of the library on the University of Texas campus with a high-powered rifle, barricaded himself in, and began to shoot at anything that moved. Before he was finally gunned down, Whitman shot 38 people, killing 14 of them. He left behind a note that said he had been experiencing overwhelming violent impulses, which he was afraid would overcome him. He asked that after his death an autopsy be carried out to see if there was any visible physical disorder. The autopsy revealed a tumor about the size of a walnut in the temporal lobe near the amygdala.

It is tempting to conclude that Whitman's tumor caused his aggressive behavior. But even if the tumor did contribute to what happened, and this seems likely, the relationship between the tumor and the violence was not simple. For one thing, Whitman did not simply fly into a rage; he planned his attack over several days. And the murder of his wife was similarly premeditated. Before killing her he wrote, "It was after much thought that I decided to kill my wife Kathy..." (Sweet, Ervin, and Mark, 1969).

Occurrences like the case of Charles Whitman suggest that violent behavior might be controllable through surgery. But in fact such attempts have rarely produced clear-cut effects. Often there are undesirable side effects or the desired effect is not obtained (Valenstein, 1973). These mixed results may reflect our ignorance of brain functioning. It likely reflects the complexity of the brain, where single centers of behavior are rarely physically separate.

But there is no question that neural mechanisms do play a crucial role in aggression. Much of the relevant evidence comes from animal studies: scientists have known for almost a century that damage to certain parts of the brain—the amygdala, hippocampus, and hypothalamus—affect aggressive behavior. In early studies on monkeys this damage was observed to decrease aggressiveness (Kluver and Bucy, 1937, 1938, 1939). More recent studies have found that damage to some parts of these structures may increase aggressiveness, whereas damage to other parts may decrease aggressiveness (Smith, King, and Hoebel, 1970).

The most impressive evidence for the role of neural mechanisms in aggression comes from studies using electrical stimulation of the brain. Electrical stimulation of various areas of the brain in many species elicits aggressive behavior, which often appears completely natural. In fact, these experiments have helped establish a distinction made on purely behavioral grounds: the distinction between predatory attack and within-species aggression. Aggression is usually defined as an attack on a member of one's own species. Predatory attacks on other species appear quite different from within-species aggression. A lion killing an antelope or a zebra shows little emotion. But when fighting with another lion, the animals display considerable emotion. Research using electrical stimulation of the brain shows that these two types of behavior have different neural substrates.

Many experiments have discovered that stimulation of different areas of the brain elicit two different kinds of attack behavior—affective attack and quiet-biting attack. John Flynn and his associates (Flynn, Vanegas, Foote, and Edwards, 1970) have done extensive research on the neural bases of rat-killing by cats (it may seem strange, but laboratory cats do not spontaneously attack rats). When the medial hypothalamus is stimulated, affective attack is usually dramatically elicited: the cat behaves furiously; it arches its back; it erects the fur on its back and neck; it bares its teeth. The cat viciously attacks the rat with the claws, the attack often accompanied by growls or screams. Compared to this, the quiet-biting attack elicited by stimulation of the lateral hypothalamus is quite tame. When stimulated, the cat begins to search and when it sees the rat it pounces on it. In affective attack, the cat's behavior resembles that of a fight with another cat; quiet-biting attack, on the other hand, resembles normal hunting behavior.

The physiological approach to the study of aggressions reveals several important facts. First, neural mechanisms are associated with aggressive behavior. In fact, the electrical stimulation research with animals suggests that aggressive behavior is integrated into the nervous system. Second, there are different types of aggressive behavior organized within the brain. Third, there is no single center for aggression within the brain: several different areas seem to be involved, including the hypothalamus, hippocampus, and amygdala. Finally, nothing in this information means that aggression, since it has neural bases, is inevitable. A normal cat, with the affective attack circuits in its brain, would never show such attack if it never encountered a situation that called for that behavior. Sociobiology and physiology cannot account for all aggression. Social and environmental factors are also important, and it is to these we now turn.

Psychosocial Approaches to Aggression

While the sociobiological and physiological approaches emphasize the adaptive and the neural aspects of aggression, psychological theories emphasize environmental and social influences. Psychologists seek to understand aggression by asking questions such as "How do people learn to be aggressive? What kinds of situations prompt us to be aggressive? What role does anger play?" In this section we will look at two influential psychological theories: one emphasizes emotional causes of aggression; the other examines the role of learning in aggression.

The Frustration-Aggression Hypothesis In 1939, a team of five social scientists (Dollard, Doob, Miller, Mowrer, and Sears) theorized that frustration was the primary factor in aggression. "Aggression is always a consequence of frustration," they wrote, and "frustration always leads to some form of aggression."

Typically, frustration results when people are prevented from reaching goals or from engaging in desired activities. John Dollard and his associates

reasoned that the frustrated person wants to aggress against the frustrating individual. Because this is not always possible, the frustrated person displaces aggression by directing it against another target. For example, the person's boss may refuse to give the employee a day off, but because the boss is not a suitable target, the person may aggress against less powerful targets—a family member or a fellow worker.

The *frustration-aggression hypothesis* has been criticized for a number of reasons but perhaps most logically for its unbending absolutism. People often are frustrated without subsequently engaging in aggression; aggression also occurs without the precedent of frustration. Insults, for example, often lead to aggression without necessarily causing frustration. Moreover, the hypothesis fails to take into account a major form of aggression, *instrumental aggression*, which is aimed at obtaining a reward—robbing a bank, for example—and may not stem directly from either frustration or anger.

Catharsis An important corollary of the frustration-aggression hypothesis is *catharsis*. According to Dollard and his associates, realized aggression serves as a purgative: it reduces future tendencies to aggress and makes it relatively unlikely that the person will soon aggress again. This is reminiscent of Lorenz's idea of aggressive drive. The notion of catharsis is an ancient one, dating back at least as far as Aristotle, and over the centuries it has taken several forms. One long-standing theory holds that the mere act of fantasizing aggression or of watching another person aggress is cathartic. In this view, watching a boxing match or a football game has a cathartic value. It also has been suggested that verbalizing aggressive feelings enables us to "let off steam" and somehow reduces the possibility of more violent aggression. In fact, experimental evidence suggests that all of these notions about how to prevent aggression—fantasizing, watching, verbalizing aggression—are wrong. Indeed, these behaviors appear to increase the tendency to engage in aggression.

The cathartic effect has been established experimentally only when the frustrated or angered person is given an opportunity to harm the antagonist physically. In a study by Anthony Doob and Lorraine Wood (1972), subjects were angered by a confederate of the experimenters. In various conditions of the experiments, subjects were then either given opportunity to aggress against the confederate, or not given opportunity to harm the confederate. Afterward, subjects were allowed to administer ostensibly painful shocks to the confederate. Shock intensity chosen by subjects served as the aggression measure. The least intense shock was administered by those subjects who had previously aggressed against the confederate. In this condition, presumably, the aggressive feelings of the subjects had been drained away through catharsis. On the other hand, the act of watching the confederate as he was harmed by the experimenter did not reduce later aggression: mere observation did not have cathartic value. Catharsis appears to occur only if one is frustrated and angered and then directly aggresses against the source of frustration.

Cues for Aggression A modified version of the frustration-aggression hypothesis has been proposed by Leonard Berkowitz (1965). According to Berkowitz, frustration, insult, or attack produce anger or a readiness to aggress. Whether this anger actually prompts aggression depends upon the cues or stimuli present in the immediate situation.

There is a long-standing theory that merely watching others aggress, as in a boxing match, is cathartic.

Berkowitz placed a great deal of emphasis upon cues that have been associated with aggression in the past. An obvious example of such a cue is a gun. In one experiment, Berkowitz aroused his subjects with mild electric shocks. He then exposed half of his subjects to innocuous cues such as badminton rackets and shuttlecocks that were arrayed on a table. The other half were seated at a table containing cues that presumably would elicit aggression—a shotgun and a revolver. When all of the subjects were given the chance to retaliate against the experimenter by delivering electric shocks, those who had seen the guns demonstrated more aggression. Berkowitz concluded that the mere sight of a gun increases the tendency to commit aggression. "The finger pulls the trigger," Berkowitz wrote of guns, "but the trigger may also be pulling the finger."

Whereas Berkowitz's experiment has obvious implications for a society where guns are easily accessible, another experiment suggests that aggression-eliciting cues can be much more subtle than a shotgun or revolver. Berkowitz and Russell Geen (1966) found that even a name can increase aggressive tendencies. Some subjects were shown a movie containing a great deal of violence. Afterward, they and other subjects were given the opportunity to shock an experimenter's confederate who had angered them. The most intense shocks were delivered by subjects who were led to believe that the confederate's first name was the same as that of an actor in the movie. Thus, according to Berkowitz, even an innocuous-sounding name, if previously associated with aggression, can elicit aggression from people who previously have been insulted, frustrated or angered.

Lessons in Aggression The social learning theory of Albert Bandura (1973) emphasizes the idea that aggression, like many other behaviors, is learned and that the learning occurs through two principal mechanisms. One mechanism is direct reinforcement. Children are often rewarded for acting aggressively, winning praise from peers and sometimes from parents. A second mechanism in the learning of aggression is modeling, or observation. By watching others who serve as models, children learn new ways of aggression and appropriate targets for that aggression. Observational learning is at issue in the continuing debate over the effects on

319

children of the violence portrayed on television (see Focus).

As we saw in Chapter 7, Bandura's best-known work has focused on observational learning, most notably in the classic Bobo doll experiments. Although these experiments cast light on the vicarious acquisition of many behaviors, they are particularly relevant to the learning of aggression.

In these studies, children of nursery school age observed an adult model aggressing against a large inflatable clown called a Bobo doll (Bandura, Ross, and Ross, 1961). The model sat on the clown, punched it in the nose, hit it over the head with a toy mallet, kicked it around the room—all the while yelling "Sock him in the nose," "Sockeroo," "He sure is a tough fella." After observing this incident, the children were allowed to play freely in a room containing a number of toys including a "Bobo" doll. The children's behavior was carefully observed, and it was quite evident that the children were imitating the model's actions. The children's actions tended to match the aggressive behavior of the model, and the children also made some of the very same comments. Since the specific actions performed by the model were ones that were seldom performed by children in a control group who had

---

FOCUS: Effects of TV Violence

For more than a decade, a highly significant focus of psychological research has been the effect of television violence on young children. Many American children spend more time watching TV than they spend in school, and what they see consists to a great extent of conflict, mayhem, and murder. According to George Gerbner (1972), 80 percent of TV dramas depict some form of violence. Other researchers have found that violence tends to be portrayed on TV as the most common way of achieving one's goals (Larsen, Gray, and Fortis, 1968). It has been estimated that, by age 16, the average TV-watching child will have witnessed no fewer than 13,000 murders (Walters and Malamud, 1975).

How does all this TV violence affect young children? One effect that has been convincingly documented in the laboratory is the physiological response of young TV viewers to real-life aggression. In one experiment (Thomas, Horton, Lippincott, and Drabman, 1977), researchers took physiological measures while young children watched either an aggressive TV show ("S.W.A.T.") or a championship volleyball game, which was equally exciting but nonaggressive. The physiological measures indicated both shows were roughly equal in the extent to which they aroused the viewers. Shortly after watching the TV show, and while they were still attached to the physiological monitoring apparatus, the children were exposed to a videotape of a real-life incident in which preschoolers engaged in a series of aggressive actions. (The children believed that they were viewing the preschool playground through a camera.) The children who had watched "S.W.A.T." were much less aroused by the preschoolers' fight than were the children who had seen the film of the volleyball game.

This apparent willingness to be more tolerant of real-life violence after watching the TV variety was also demonstrated by Ronald Drabman and Margaret Thomas (1974). In their experiments, children who had viewed a violent TV show were less likely to intervene in a fight between other children than were young subjects who had seen a nonviolent show. Thus, faced by real-life aggression, children are less aroused and more willing to accept a fight than to break it up.

Does exposure to TV violence actually increase the likelihood that a child will engage in aggressive behavior? Two lines of psychological research discussed in our present chapter bear on this question; both suggest ways in which the tendency to aggress might be encouraged by watching TV violence. The social learning theory of Bandura, with its emphasis on observational learning, indicates that TV aggression provides a model for children to imitate. Such modeling has been demonstrated many times in the laboratory with children who view aggression either firsthand or in a filmed version. In addition, the research of Berkowitz on aggression cues as potential triggers of violence is similarly relevant. Through TV violence, many stimuli and cues can become associated with aggression and thus take on aggression-eliciting properties. Although the laboratory evidence strongly suggests the potential for engaging in aggression immediately after exposure to TV violence, psychologists are seeking answers to further questions. Does exposure to TV violence make it more likely that a child will be aggressive later in life? Do all those TV-land murders lead a child to internalize and value aggression as a means of coping with life?

Probably the most impressive work bearing on these questions was a long-term study (Eron, Lefko-

not observed the model, the findings suggest that the children learned from the model. That is, they acquired new forms of physical and verbal aggressions.

In variations of his basic Bobo doll experiments, Bandura (1965) went on to investigate the effects of reward or punishment of the model. After the model had been aggressive, an adult walked into the room and said either of two things to the model. In the reward condition, the model was told that he had been a "strong champion" and that he deserved a treat, including a large glass of soda and an assortment of candies. In the punishment condition,

the adult reprimanded the model—"Hey there, you big bully. You quit picking on that clown"—and threatened to give the model a "hard spanking." After observing either of these two scenes, the children were sent to the free-play room.

Interestingly, there was a vast difference between the behavior of those children who had seen the model rewarded and the behavior of those who had seen the model punished. The former group imitated the model's behavior; the latter did not.

witz, Huesmann, and Walder, 1972) of a sample of several hundred boys living in a rural district of New York State. The researchers compiled data on a number of factors, including the boys' TV-watching habits and their tendency to be involved in real-life aggression. They found that those boys who preferred TV violence also tended to be aggressive. This finding was not necessarily significant; it may be, for example, that boys who are aggressive happen to like TV violence.

What is important, however, is that Eron and his colleagues were able to study many of the boys again 10 years later when they were about 19. When the boys were again scored for aggressive behavior, a highly significant fact came to light: how much TV violence a boy had watched 10 years previously in the third grade turned out to be an accurate indicator of how aggressively he behaved at age 19. To rule out the possibility that aggressive boys prefer TV violence while young and simply continue to be aggressive later in life, Eron's group employed a variety of sophisticated statistical analyses. These analyses strongly implied that exposure to TV violence does increase aggressive behavior later in life (see figure).

This research tentatively answered some questions but raised others. For example, Eron and his colleagues also studied a large sample of girls and found that preference for TV violence in the third grade did not relate to aggression 10 years later. One possibility for this negative finding is that at the time the girls were in the third grade only a few aggressive female characters were featured on TV. Now that TV gives greater prominence to violent women, a similar study might now find that girls too are adversely affected. Though further research is needed, the work to date does suggest that TV violence may

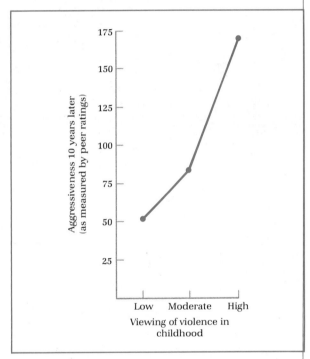

In a study of the relationship between childhood viewing of violence on television and adult aggressiveness, preference for viewing violent programs by 9-year-old boys was positively correlated with aggressive behavior at age 19.

be increasing our children's tolerance for aggression and enhancing the likelihood that they themselves will behave aggressively.

According to Albert Bandura, aggressive behavior is learned through direct reinforcement in the form of praise by parents and peers and through modeling, or observation.

Despite this difference at the level of freely performed behavior, however, it was quite clear that all the children had learned the model's aggressive behavior. When the children were specifically asked to show the experimenter what the model had done and said, the children in the two conditions imitated the model's aggressive behavior equally well. Thus, all the children had acquired the behavior, but only those who saw the model rewarded chose to perform the behavior. Apparently, the children had learned not only how to aggress toward the Bobo doll but also, through observation of reward or punishment, whether it was appropriate to engage in aggression.

Summing Up Aggression   One of the reasons that psychology is a complex area of inquiry is that the phenomena that psychologists study need to be analyzed and understood at several different levels simultaneously. And it is often difficult to put multilevel analyses together into a single scheme. Such

is the case with aggression. We have approached aggression from an evolutionary perspective, from a physiological point of view, and from a social point of view. What is the sum of those views?

We do not really know enough about aggression at present to put together a detailed picture, but an outline is beginning to emerge. As you recall, the epigenetic approach discussed in Chapter 6 viewed the development of behavior as due to the interaction of genetic and environmental influences on the organism. The information we have reviewed on aggression shows that both factors almost certainly have a bearing on human aggression also. The biological bases of aggression are clear in both the sociobiological and physiological research we have reviewed. Aggression can be adaptive, at least under some circumstances, and therefore can be affected by natural selection. The neural basis of aggressive behavior demonstrates that aggressive behavior is wired into the brain, at least in lower animals and quite possibly in humans. On the other hand, the research of Bandura, Berkowitz, Doob, and others, shows that experience and the environment also affect aggressive behavior. Aggression in humans is probably a moderately canalized behavior, with some genetic basis. But how, when, and if a particular person will be aggressive at a given moment depends heavily on previous experience and the environmental situation. In terms of social policy, it may well be possible to control aggression because aggression is dependent on environmental factors. But this may not be easy, because aggression also apparently has biological roots.

SUMMARY

1. Early psychologists ascribed motivation to instincts—innate patterns of behavior. The view was superseded by the concept of hypothetical states called drives—internal states that organisms sought to reduce. Today, instincts and drives do not seem adequate as all-embracing concepts for the investigation of motivation; instead, modern researchers investigate motives one at a time through various approaches. Among those approaches are the evolutionary approach, the physiological approach, and the social-learning approach.

2. The evolutionary emphasis holds that because the goals of motivated behavior are often biologically critical to survival and/or reproduction, evolution has finely tuned motivational systems to serve those goals. Strictly speaking, it is not survival that counts, but the leaving of offspring. Behavior is thus adaptive, contributing to the continuance of the species. Optimization theory assumes that animal behavior is organized to achieve biologically significant goals.

3. Physiological factors such as hunger and thirst are critical for survival, and neural mechanisms are involved in the regulation of these behaviors. The hypothalamus is a primary regulator of hunger, thirst, body temperature, and sexual behavior, and a determiner of a variety of emotional responses. The endocrine system, which works in parallel with the nervous system, causes the secretion of hormones into the bloodstream; the hormonal mechanisms are also powerful regulators of behavior. An organism's tendency to maintain its internal environment at a constant level is called homeostasis. The hypothalamus operates automatically in the maintenance of homeostasis but is also subject to conscious control.

4. Two different systems control our thirst and intake of liquids. In the osmotic system, osmoreceptors sense cellular dehydration and prompt thirst. They also signal the pituitary gland to release an antidiuretic hormone (ADH) into the blood causing the kidneys to reabsorb water. The hypovolemic system senses lowered volumes of extracellular fluid and causes the kidneys to release renin, which acts as an enzyme to produce angiotensin I, which in turn leads to the production of angiotensin II. Angiotensin II affects certain nerve cells in the hypothalamus and elsewhere that then signals thirst. Research indicates that osmotic and hypovolemic thirst operate independently.

5. Homeostatic mechanisms in the brain help regulate hunger and food intake. One view is that the ventromedial hypothalamus is a satiety center that tells us when we have had enough to eat; the lateral hypothalamus is a feeding center that triggers hunger. Set-point theory holds that the hypothalamic centers play a different role, acting like thermostats to turn eating behavior on and off to maintain proper body weight. Obese people have a higher than normal number of adipocytes, cells that store excess fat. Obese people also have heightened sensitivity to environmental cues about food. The ability to select a balanced diet is partially due to innate preferences for certain essential foods and partially due to learning.

6. Humans have social motives as well as biological needs. Sociobiology studies the interconnection of social and biological motivation. The sociobiological perspective has proved valuable in understanding the social behavior of animals and may prove equally illuminating in the long run in understanding human social behavior. Sociobiological research with human behavior is difficult to carry out and is still in its infancy.

7. Although human sociality may have some biological roots, learning and experience are crucial shapers of human social motivation. Among the strongest social motivators are our needs to affiliate and interact with others and our drives for achievement, which vary widely among individuals.

8. An emotion usually consists of both a mental, or cognitive, component and a physiological response. William James and Karl Lange believed that emotions are preceptions of physiological reactions that

precede and cause the specific emotion. Although physiological factors play an important role in emotional experience, it is unlikely that each of our many emotions is produced by a distinct physiological state.

9. Physiological changes in functions such as heart rate and blood pressure accompany most strong emotional experiences. Experiments with animals suggest the existence of pain and pleasure centers in the brain. The two-factor theory of emotions contends that the physiological arousal accompanying emotions is a general state, and we must put a cognitive label on the arousal for it to be an emotion. We seek cues from the situation or the environment to tell us what we are feeling. Experiments with the drug epinephrine, which induces physiological arousal, have pointed up the influence of cognitive factors in the interpretation of our internal states.

10. Aggression is one of the strongest, most fascinating, and potentially dangerous behaviors. Sociobiology suggests that aggressive behavior in animals should take place when its potential benefits—access to food, for example—outweigh its costs. Neural mechanisms involving the hypothalamus, the hippocampus, and the amygdala play a role in aggressive behavior, as animal research has shown. Psychosocial approaches to aggression emphasize emotional causes such as frustration, the need for catharsis, and the role of learning. Experiments have shown that children exposed to aggressive behavior will imitate it or condone it if the behavior is presented in a favorable light.

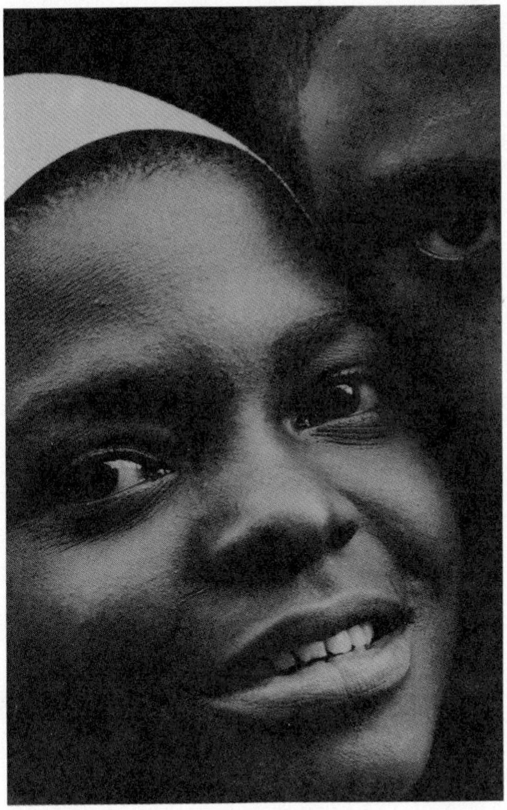

Chapter 11
Sexual Behavior

Pioneers in Human Sex Research
Freud: Psychosexual Development
Kinsey: Asking about Sex
Masters and Johnson: Into the Laboratory

Variations in Sexual Behavior
Interspecies Variance
Intercultural Variance
Cross-Cultural Variance and Similarities
Intracultural Variance
Individual Variance: The Life Cycle

The Role of Hormones in Sexual Behavior
Mechanisms of Hormonal Production
Effects of Hormones in Females
Effects of Hormones in Males
Effects of Hormones within the Brain

Sex Differences and Sexual Differentiation
The "Reversed Adam" Principle
The Influence of Learning in Sexual Differentiation
Androgen and Environment
Sex Differences and Similarities in Humans
Homosexuality
Transsexualism

Sex-Role Development
Biological Factors
Social and Cultural Factors
The Importance of Context

The Biosocial Complex

Research: Female Sexuality and the Menstrual Cycle

Focus: The Nature of Orgasm

Summary

When James Joyce's remarkable novel *Ulysses* was temporarily banned by the United States government half a century ago, it was not only the book's frank language that concerned the censors. They were also worried about the fact that Joyce's characters always seemed to be thinking about sex. His new stream-of-conciousness technique brimmed with erotic daydreams such as Molly Bloom's famous inner solilioquy that ends the novel: "...and then I asked him with my eyes to ask again yes and then he asked me would I yes to say yes my mountain flower and first I put my arms around him yes and drew him down to me so he could feel my breasts all perfume yes and his heart was going like mad and yes I said yes I will Yes." Even the United States federal judge who handed down the landmark decision lifting the ban on *Ulysses* felt compelled to rationalize "the recurrent emergence of the theme of sex in the minds of his characters" by pointing out that Joyce's "locale was Celtic and his season Spring."

Today, as a result of the sexual revolution of the past three decades, most of us are willing to acknowledge that a mental preoccupation with sex is not the sole province of the Irish in the springtime. We spend a considerable amount of time thinking, daydreaming, and nightdreaming about sex—a subject that not long ago was generally taboo.

This should not surprise us, given the enormous importance of sexual intercourse and related behaviors. To begin with, sexual behavior is obviously essential to the propagation of the species: any society that tried doing without it would not survive for long. Second, it is the source of much human pleasure and a medium for the expression of love and tenderness. Finally, as Sigmund Freud so forcefully suggested many years ago, sex sometimes plays an important role in seemingly unrelated areas of human behavior such as personality and even mental disorders.

For the student of psychology, sex is of additional interest. The study of sexual behavior offers a fascinating mode for the study of interactions between "mental" and "physical" mechanisms. In many ways, sexual behavior is a microcosm of human behavior in general, stemming from a complex interaction among biological, cognitive, experiential, and sociocultural determinants of how we think, feel, and act.

Although the importance of the evolutionary origins of human sexual behavior is conceded by most scientists, these factors are given the most emphasis by the new branch of science known as sociobiology (see Chapter 10). The sociobiologists tend to interpret sexual and other behaviors in terms of their evolutionary survival value (Daly and Wilson, 1978).

Sociobiology postulates, for example, that men want to have many sexual partners but women place greater emphasis on selectivity in the choice of mates. These and other apparent sex differences, say the sociobiologists, stem from differences in the parental investment of the two sexes. The male has large supplies of spermatozoa to expend and does not have to bear the child or, in many cases, help rear it. Thus he invests little in each offspring. The female has a much larger investment: pregnancy, lactation, and years of child care, along with the fact that she produces only one ovum per month. Sociobiologists conclude that much of sexual behavior is controlled by innate, genetically evolved mechanisms. Genes of males who inseminate many females and of females who select their mates carefully will be conserved by natural selection.

The evidence in support of sociobiology comes from the study of lower animal species. Its interpretations are highly speculative when applied to human beings. Such extreme claims about the genetic origins of human sexual behavior obviously must be measured against the tremendous importance of sociocultural factors.

Whether specific sexual behaviors spring from biological or environmental causes is a central issue in this chapter. We will thus focus frequently on the anatomy and physiology of sex. One section, for example, is devoted to the role of hormones in sexual behavior. The reasons for this emphasis are threefold. First, of all human behaviors, sex is the most subject to hormonal control. Second, a formidable body of experimental data exists, primarily animal research, that precisely shows the roles of the nervous and endocrine systems and that can be examined in human applications. Third, relatively little experimental research on the nonbiological aspects of sex has been performed, partly because of the taboos surrounding the subject until recent years and partly because of the obvious difficulties, even today, of studying human sex in the psychologist's laboratory.

Throughout the chapter, however, biological data will be evaluated in light of environmental factors that not only greatly influence sexual behavior but also appear to affect and modify our biology. At the end of the chapter, we will put the importance of both biological and the social determinants into perspective.

Pioneers in Human Sex Research

The scientific study of human sexuality is so new that its history covers less than a century. Three major figures dominate that short history—Sigmund Freud, Alfred Kinsey, and William Masters. Each of these pioneers made a different kind of basic contribution to our present concepts of sexuality by using radically different methods of research.

Freud, a Viennese psychiatrist, depended upon the revelations of his patients as he explored the unconscious through his therapeutic system of psychoanalysis. Kinsey, a zoologist, used the survey-questionnaire method to collect data on people's sex lives. Masters and Virginia Johnson, a gynecologist and a psychologist, respectively, studied sexuality by a very direct means—observation of the sexual responses of volunteers in the St. Louis laboratory.

Freud: Psychosexual Development

Sexuality is central to Freud's formulation of psychoanalytic theory. Psychoanalytic theory, as we see elsewhere in the book, attempts to account for the development of normal personality (see Chapter 12) and of psychopathology, or abnormal behavior (see Chapter 14). Freud believed that inner conflicts could be traced to infancy and early childhood, to what he termed the *psychosexual stages* of development.

Freud's major treatise on sex, *Three Essays on the Theory of Sexuality*, first was published in 1905. The book was not much more than 100 pages long, only 1,000 copies were printed, and it took more than four years to sell them. Nonetheless, this book, with its emphasis on infantile sexuality, had a profound impact.

To stunned Victorians, it appeared that Freud had "discovered" infantile sexuality. In fact, knowledge of childhood sexuality had been widespread until it began to be suppressed during the nineteenth century. The suppression of childhood sexuality was symbolized by the war on masturbation,

Representation of the Victorian concept of sexuality.

which was alleged to cause insanity and various physical ailments. From 1856 to 1919, no fewer than 49 United States patents were granted for devices aimed at stopping masturbation. Some physicians advocated clitoridectomy, the removal of the clitoris, the most sensitive of the female genital structures. In Europe, physicians even recommended the use of a device to prevent little boys from having erections while sleeping: it consisted of a series of metal rings equipped with spikes that quickly awakened the culprit if his penis became erect.

Freud broadened the concept of sexuality by naming not only the genital region as an erogeneous zone but also the mouth and anus. He then went on to describe the stages of psychosexual development in which the focus of sexual "energy," which he called *libido* (from the Latin meaning lust) shifts successively in infancy and early childhood from *oral* (first year) to *anal* (second year) to *phallic*. A period of *latency* follows the phallic stage and is, in turn followed in early adolescence by the *genital* stage, during which young people begin to direct their sexual interests toward others (see Chapter 12).

Boys in the phallic stage (ages 3—5) focus on the penis and the fear of its removal. Freud misnamed this *castration anxiety* (castration means removal of the testes, not the penis). In girls, the phallic phase is characterized by attention to the clitoris and by anxiety at lacking a penis. Freud termed this *penis envy*. He contended that a healthy maturity depends on the successful resolution of the problems of the psychosexual stages, especially the phallic phase.

While Freud's influence upon the intellectual and cultural course of the twentieth century has been profound, the scientific validity of his specific concepts and conclusions has been seriously questioned. This is true not only of sexuality but also of his theories about personality and psychopathology. Freud's work is not generally amenable to experimental verification: concepts such as the castration complex and penis envy resist testing by the conventional methods of modern science. As a result, many of his concepts of psychosexuality have been either partially or totally rejected by most modern sex researchers.

As we shall see, modern researchers have taken a narrower, more manageable approach that is amenable to testing and verification. They owe, however, an immeasurable debt to Freud who laid the intellectual foundation for subsequent study of human sexuality.

Kinsey: Asking about Sex

The second important pioneer in human sexual research was Alfred Kinsey. Until 1937, Kinsey, an Indiana University zoologist, had spent most of his career collecting and classifying gall wasps. When he was asked to teach a new course in sex and marriage, he went to the library to research the subject and concluded that science knew more about the sex lives of wasps than of humans.

Kinsey's approach to sex research differed markedly from that of Freud. Whereas Freud based his theories essentially on knowledge derived from a comparative handful of subjects—that is, his patients in psychoanalysis—Kinsey and his associates traveled the United States for 15 years, asking thousands of people to tell them about their sex lives. They asked, for example, how often respondents had intercourse and how often they masturbated. It is the most comprehensive study of sexual behavior ever undertaken: altogether, more than 5,000 males and an equal number of females were interviewed.

The results were published in *Sexual Behavior in the Human Male* (Kinsey, Pomeroy, and Martin, 1948) and in *Sexual Behavior in the Human Female* (Kinsey, Pomeroy, Martin, and Gebhard, 1953). Both works were popularly known as "The Kinsey Report," and these accounts of how Americans actually behave both shocked and fascinated people. Despite the absence of photographs, they became best-sellers.

Kinsey's findings revealed the large disparity between what the public thought of as acceptable sexual conduct and actual sexual behavior. He noted high incidences of behavior generally regarded as unacceptable such as premarital and extramarital sexual intercourse, homosexuality, masturbation, and sexual fantasizing. For example, more than half of the married women interviewed reported that they had engaged in coitus (intercourse) before marriage: this compared shockingly with data from the nineteenth century (cited in Kinsey, Pomeroy, Martin, and Gebhard, 1953), which reported that only 14 percent of brides were not virgins.

Kinsey also was able to report fascinating variations in behavior among different groups. For example, male college graduates tended to engage increasingly in extramarital sex as they grew older, whereas such behavior tended to decrease with age among less-educated males. College-educated women masturbated more frequently than less-educated women but had less premarital intercourse. Kinsey also found that masturbation was the most common means of experiencing orgasm for single women and the most reliable predictor of orgasm after they married. This finding was prophetic of current sex therapies that use masturbation in the treatment of *anorgasmia,* the inability to experience orgasm.

Scientists have criticized Kinsey's work because the sample of people interviewed was not representative of the United States population. The males were all white and did not represent an adequate geographical distribution. Nonetheless, his dryly fascinating statistics constituted a milestone in research. They provided a basis on which scientists and lay people alike could assess what was truly "normal" in American sexual behavior.

Masters and Johnson: Into the Laboratory

The first large-scale study of the physiological aspects of the human sexual response was begun in 1954 at Washington University in St. Louis by William Masters and his associate Virginia Johnson. Masters and Johnson brought human sex into the research laboratory. With instruments that monitored heart rate, blood pressure, and other physiological variables, they studied male and female orgasms resulting from masturbation or coitus.

It was not the first time scientists had attempted to measure the physiology of sex. One ill-fated study was carried out in the 1920s by the behavioral psychologist John B. Watson, whose early work in learning is discussed in Chapter 7. Watson recorded his own responses and those of a female assistant until his wife, who had refused to join him in the experiment, found out about the assistant, sued for divorce, and confiscated his data. Watson's career at Johns Hopkins University was damaged, and he eventually married his assistant and went into advertising.

The Masters and Johnson project also ran into difficulties in the beginning. Their laboratory had to be moved off campus and was supported by funds from private foundations rather than the federal government. During the early days, many of the best-known medical journals refused to publish their findings.

Masters and Johnson first used prostitutes as experimental subjects. Later, members of the academic community were used as subjects. There were 694 volunteers, men and women aged 18 to 89. The majority of the volunteers were married

couples. What the volunteers had in common was the ability to produce orgasms in the laboratory despite the presence of technicians, cameras, and elaborate monitoring equipment. In total they produced some 10,000 orgasms—2,500 male and 7,500 female. The orgasms were produced not only through coitus and self-stimulation but also through the use of an ingenious copulation machine. The machine consisted of a camera and a penislike probe, which was controlled by the female subject. The probe permitted the camera to record physiological events within the vagina.

In 1966 the results of the unprecedented investigation were published in the best-selling book *Human Sexual Response.* Most of the physiological events observed by Masters and Johnson can be subsumed under two principal headings: *vasocongestion*—increased blood flow to an area—and *myotonia*—increased muscle tone and contractions.

For both males and females, vasocongestion is seen primarily in the pelvic and genital areas but is also present in the abdomen, chest, neck, and face, where it causes the so-called sexual flush. Vasocongestion results in penile erections in the male and clitoral erections in the female and erections of nipples in both sexes, although in men there is no enlargement of the areola surrounding the nipple. Another consequence of vasocongestion is vaginal "lubrication," the appearance of a clear fluid that exudes from the walls of the vagina. Previously, it had been thought that the fluid was secreted by specific glands.

Like vasocongestion, myotonia also occurs in many areas of the body in both sexes. However, contractions of specific muscle groups are most dramatically pronounced during orgasm, when the muscles of the pelvic floor are affected. A series of rhythmic contractions in the muscles affecting the penis and the vagina occur during orgasm at about one-second intervals. Anal and other muscles in the region contract in synchrony with the genital muscles.

Masters and Johnson found that the physiology of human sexual response was basically the same for all subjects, both male and female, regardless of whether it was produced by coitus or masturbation. They somewhat arbitrarily subdivided the progression of events into four phases (see Figure 11.1):

1. *Excitement.* In the male, erection of the penis and perhaps of the nipples; in the female, erection of the nipples, swelling of the breasts, and lubrication of the vaginal lining.
2. *Plateau.* In the male, testes (reproductive glands located in the scrotum) swell to one and a half times normal; in the female, tissues around the outer third of the vaginal barrel swell and reduce the diameter of the vaginal opening (compared to the excitement phase), and the clitoris retracts under the hood that covers it.
3. *Orgasmic.* In the male, rhythmic contractions in the penis followed by ejaculation of the semen; in the female, rhythmic contractions of the outer third of the vagina and of the uterus; in both sexes, increase in respiration, heartbeat, and blood pressure.
4. *Resolution.* In both sexes, return of organs and tissues to normal conditions, which occurs more rapidly in the male than in the female. Men and women differ in their capacity to be rearoused after orgasm: men generally experience an intervening period after orgasm during which they are not capable of sexual arousal. (see Focus).

The findings of Masters and Johnson contradicted some of the myth and folklore surrounding sexual response in women. For example, they showed that the size of the penis had little to do with female sexual pleasure. Also, they found no physiological difference between female orgasms resulting from direct clitoral stimulation and those resulting from vaginal stimulation (which causes indirect stimulation of the clitoris). Freud and others (mostly male) had contended that there are two types of orgasm—one produced by vaginal stimulation and the other by clitoral stimulation—and that vaginal orgasms were somehow superior.

Critics have faulted the Masters and Johnson study for widely varying reasons. Some observers charged that it constituted little more than a new kind of voyeurism under the veil of science; sex, they said, should be left to the bedroom. Others pointed out the volunteers were not representative of the general population because they were better educated and were selected for their ability to produce orgasm on demand. Still others charged that the laboratory approach, by reducing sex to its mechanics, depersonalized this most intimate of behaviors. The most important criticism was that Masters and Johnson had frequently violated

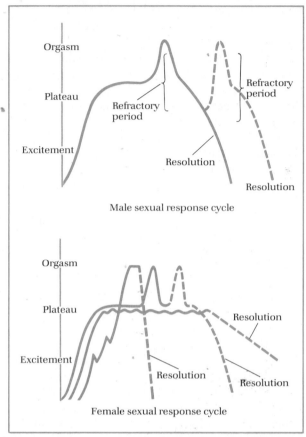

FIGURE 11.1 Diagrams of the typical sexual response patterns in males and females. As the graphs show, the sexual arousal of both males and females steadily increases until at a certain phase (plateau) it begins to level off. The orgasm is a brief and sudden surge of total arousal. The male begins to return to his original level of arousal immediately after orgasm; the female may peak twice or more before the onset of the resolution phase.

common scientific procedure by failing to support their conclusions with sufficiently detailed information on experimental methods and results.

The major impact of the study was to usher in an era of concern and preoccupation with physiological responses in sex as opposed to the previous emphasis on psychological aspects that originated with Freud. Building on their laboratory research, Masters and Johnson went on to develop a novel approach to sexual therapy derived from the methods of both behavioral modification (see Chapter 15) and conventional counseling. The new programs have helped men who suffer from premature ejaculation or impotence and women who are anorgasmic. Masters and Johnson's clinical observations were published in 1970 in *Human Sexual Inadequacy*.

Variations in Sexual Behavior

One of the most striking aspects of human sexual behavior is its wide variety. In recent decades the published work of Kinsey and other researchers has made evident what people had privately suspected for centuries: our sex lives differ in innumerable ways. These variations include who mates with whom, when, how, how frequently, and for how long.

In this section we will look at these differing patterns as they are manifested at four different levels: (1) among species, (2) among human cultures, (3) within a single culture, and (4) within the life cycle of the individual. This discussion begins with an examination of sexual behavior as a whole, in animals as well as in humans, then focuses on variations in smaller and more homogeneous groups, and ends with the individual.

Interspecies Variance

Animal behavior demonstrates that biology is an important determinant of different patterns of sexual behavior. Central to such a consideration is one overriding fact: although sexual behavior serves many purposes in humans and other higher species, it evolved principally to serve the aim of reproduction. In fact, we can understand much of the variety of sexual behavior evident in different species of animals in terms of biological evolution. Each species has evolved a so-called *reproductive strategy* that meets the particular needs of the species in relation to its environment. These strategies, which differ from species to species, shape many aspects of behavior ranging from the duration of copulation to the extent of the father's participation in rearing the young.

In humans and some other animals, the reproductive strategy usually dictates sexual *monogamy*—that is, the practice of having only one mate at a time. The human young mature slowly and are defenseless during a prolonged period of development. Furthermore, at least in all primitive societies, the human mother is heavily involved in child care and needs the protection and assistance of the father in obtaining food. On the other hand, most small mammals, including rodents, which are used most often in experimental psychology, are promis-

cuous, as are some large mammals like the African buffalo. Songbirds are monogamous for a breeding season; geese and swans for a lifetime. In many species, *polygyny*, in which one male is bonded with a number of females, is the rule. *Polyandry*, in which one female is bonded with a number of males, rarely occurs. One well-studied instance of polyandry exists in a tropical bird, the American jacona. The female maintains a harem of two to four males and deposits a clutch of eggs with each. She trusts the males first to incubate and then to care for the newborn chicks. In humans, polygynous marriages have been permitted in a majority of societies, including the Mormons, but polyandry has scarcely ever been allowed.

A second aspect of reproductive strategy can be seen in the evolution of genital anatomy. For example, among animals that are heavily preyed upon, evolutionary survival suggests rapid mating and the anatomy to make it possible. In many male hoofed animals, a hard fibroelastic penis provides for quick erection, with the organ shooting out like an arrow from a bow. The acme of such rapid performance occurs in the gerenuk antelope of eastern Africa, which can mate while literally on the run across the predator-infested plains. In contrast, mating tends to be a rather lengthy affair among carnivorous mammals, which have evolved a fleshy, slowly erecting penis. For example, in the dog, the penis swells within the female to form a

Several types of birds, including geese, are monogamous for a lifetime.

kind of ball and socket joint that keeps the mating pair linked for a quarter or even a half hour of semen transfer.

Perhaps the most astonishing mating behavior, however, is that of the praying mantis. During copulation, the female has the unique habit of devouring her male partner's head. This cannibalism does have a salutory effect on reproduction of the species. Literally losing his head, the male also loses centers in his primitive brain that ordinarily inhibit sexual drive. Though headless, he lives for several hours and, with inhibitions gone, copulates much more vigorously, increasing the transfer of sperm.

Among our closest animal relatives—the three species of great apes—reproductive strategies differ markedly (Nadler, 1977). Orangutans tend to be antisocial, ranging alone over wide territories. Sexual behavior reflects this antisocial tendency. Because encounters between males and females are limited, it is important to maximize the opportunities for mating. Thus, sexual encounters often resemble a wrestling match, with the sexually dominant male forcing the female to the ground, if she is not in heat (hormonally prepared for mating).

Gorillas, on the other hand, are highly social animals, and mating is controlled by the female. Mating tends to be strictly limited to the period when the female is "in heat" or *estrus*. During this period of receptivity, the female may aggressively back her mate into a corner.

The third species of great ape, the chimpanzee, occupies a position somewhere between the gorilla and orangutan in terms of when mating occurs and which sex dominates the encounter. In each species, sexual behavior is adapted to conditions of social living (see Table 11-1).

By comparing the great apes and humans we can discern the parallels between the evolution of reproductive behavior and the evolution of reproductive anatomy (Short, 1978). For example, coitus occurs less frequently among humans than among chimpanzees. Likewise, the human testis is smaller, relative to body weight, than the chimpanzee testis. This correlation makes evolutionary sense because if men ejaculate more often than every two or three days, the volume of the semen and the density of the sperm decline, reducing the potential for reproduction.

Other evolutionary adaptations are consistent with the human maximization of sexual pleasure. The erect human penis is larger, relative to body weight, than that of any monkey or ape and is usually conspicuous when flaccid. Similarly, the human female breast is bigger and more prominent outside of pregnancy or lactation than that of any of the apes or primates. This plays a role in visual attraction between the sexes. Along with female orgasm, which does not occur in any subprimate species so far as is known, this attraction is believed to strengthen the development of a lasting *pair bond* between the two partners in a monogamous relationship. These pair bonds are important for the prolonged care of the slow-maturing human infant. However, the most important sexual factor cementing male-female bonding in humans is likely to be maintenance of sexual receptivity in women throughout the menstrual cycle.

Intercultural Variance

The variations in patterns of sexual behavior found in different human societies are nearly as striking as those that occur among the different animal species. We are not always aware of these differences because our culture, like that of all societies, has its own value systems that label as deviant all behaviors that appear to fall outside of "normal" boundaries. Such behaviors are usually classified as

TABLE 11.1 **Socio-sexual relationships of the great apes. Number 1 indicates the highest rank per category, number 3 the lowest rank, and number 2 intermediate.**

	CHIMPANZEE	GORILLA	ORANGUTAN
Male sexual dominance	2	3	1
Cyclicity in sexual behavior	2	1	3
Female proceptivity	2	1	3
Consort accessibility	2	1	3

Source: R. Nadler, "Sexual Behavior of the Chimpanzee in Relation to the Gorilla and Orangutan," in *Progress in Ape Research*, ed., G. H. Bourne (New York, Academic Press, 1977).

pathological and then eliminated from consideration, except as they require suppression or "cure." By turning to the data of anthropologists, however, we can see how differing value systems shape vastly different norms of sexual behavior.

The Trobrianders The pioneer of modern anthropological studies of sex was Bronislaw Malinowski. For several years during World War I, Malinowski lived among the people of the Trobriand Islands in the South Pacific. His fascinating observations were published in 1929 in his classic study, *The Sexual Life of Savages in Northwestern Melanesia.*

The children of the Trobrianders were allowed a great deal of freedom. They roamed the village freely, forming what Malinowski called a "children's republic," in which they could engage in sexual games without parental restraints. This freedom of sexual play extended also to young unmarried adults, who were free to have premarital intercourse. Females were expected to experience orgasm and men encouraged to control ejaculation so as to maintain prolonged coitus.

Some of the apparent permissiveness no doubt stemmed from the Trobrianders' ignorance about the relationship between sex and having babies. They believed that pregnancy occurred because the baby was placed on the hair of the prospective mother by a special spirit and then carried to the womb by the mother's blood. The belief that the blood helped nourish the baby explained to the Trobrianders why the pregnant woman no longer menstruated.

For all of their apparent lack of constraints, the Trobrianders nonetheless put several important limits on sexual behavior. Incestuous relationships between brother and sister were so sternly forbidden that adult siblings were prohibited even from being together except in the presence of others. Adultery was also severely condemned, but as Malinowski observed, "The rules are as often and as easily broken, circumvented, and condoned as in our society."

Definite rules of propriety also governed the sexual techniques of the Trobrianders. They despised two important practices of Western society—namely, prolonged mouth-to-mouth kissing and the so-called missionary position (face-to-face copulation with the man prone over the woman). Trobrianders typically copulated with the woman on her back and the man squatting between her

legs. Partners often scratched fiercely at each other and proudly wore the resulting scars as insignia of their pleasure.

The East Bay Society A contrast to Trobiander sexual mores was found in the East Bay Society, a culture located on an island near the Trobriands. William Davenport (1965), who studied the East Bay Society, reported that the people had a positive attitude toward sex, but it differed from the Trobrianders in many respects, perhaps because, unlike the Trobrianders, they knew how babies are conceived. From the time boys and girls walked, they were separated socially, and any physical contact between them was a punishable offense after age five. Similarly, premarital sex between young men and women was forbidden, although masturbation was encouraged among both sexes and homosexuality among young men. Even after marriage, homosexual relationships between men and preadolescent boys were accepted.

Marital intercourse was reported to occur typically twice a day—in the morning, in the garden; in the evening, in the home. Unlike the Trobrianders, the East Bay people favored the missionary position. Following prolonged foreplay, the woman was expected to have an orgasm, although males were said to ejaculate in 30 seconds or less.

By comparing the studies from these two Melanesian peoples—the Trobriand Islanders and the East Bay Society—we can see readily how two cultures, which otherwise had much in common, differed radically in sexual behavior. These differences stemmed from differing social rules that governed not only the kinds of sexual acts that were permissible and with whom, but also at what age and even at what time of day.

A Tale of Two Tribes The power of environmental circumstances to influence differing patterns of sexual behavior was shown in a recent study by Ernestine Friedl (1975). Friedl studied two neighboring tribes in New Guinea: one lived in the highlands, the other in nearby lowlands. The highland tribe had such negative attitudes toward sexual intercourse that it was not permitted in gardens for fear it would stunt plant growth. Coitus was believed to weaken men; contact with the menstrual blood of women was thought to be harmful. There

Studies have shown that different social rules govern various aspects of sexual behavior among different groups. Among the Papua of New Guinea, for example, women are tattooed, but they may only be tattoed from the waist up before marriage, while after marriage, the lower part of the body is tattooed from a design chosen by the husband.

was much general antagonism between men and women, who lived in segregated quarters.

The lowland tribe studied by Friedl regarded sexual intercourse as pleasurable and even a source of revitalization for men. In contrast to the highlanders, these people wanted to perform coitus in gardens because it was thought beneficial to plant growth.

Friedl concluded that the striking differences in sexual attitudes between these neighboring societies probably resulted from a basic dichotomy in their immediate environments. The highland people lived in an area with scarce resources of land; they feared that any increase in their population would threaten food supplies. Conflict between the sexes and avoidance of intercourse were effective means of holding down the birthrate. The lowland people, by contrast, inhabited an uncrowded area that needed cultivation. A positive attitude toward relations between the sexes raised the birthrate and provided more farmers to cultivate the land.

Population control has also figured in the sexual norms of other societies. For example, on New Britain Island, men assiduously avoid sex to control population; they even worry about being raped by women (Reuben, 1971). Examples of sexual norms that increase birthrates can be found in organized religion. Roman Catholic prohibition of contraception (when effective) and the Orthodox Jewish avoidance of sexual relations during menstruation

and the week after (and thus increased activity during the more fertile part of the menstrual cycle) both increase fertility rates among their adherents.

Cross-Cultural Variance and Similarities

The anthropological studies cited make abundantly clear how widely sexual behavior varies among cultures. This is not to suggest, however, that commonalities of sexual attitudes and practices do not exist that transcend cultural barriers. The best single source of such data is the classic cross-cultural review carried out by Clellan Ford, an anthropologist, and Frank Beach, a psychologist. Ford and Beach painstakingly reviewed data from 191 different human societies, many of them preliterate and with only one Western society included, the United States. Their findings were published in 1951 in *Patterns of Sexual Behavior*.

Although the data Ford and Beach reviewed are now quite old, and many of the societies have undergone profound changes, their findings help illuminate the question of which behaviors tend to be widespread. We will briefly describe two of their findings:

- Masturbation exists in almost all the human societies studied (and indeed, among nonhuman primates and other mammalian species). While techniques of self-stimulation vary little in different cultures, the range in attitudes toward masturbation is great—from encouragement as in the East Bay Society, to benign scorn as in the Trobriand Islands, to complete rejection as in the United States not long ago.

• Male homosexuality in some form was accepted or encouraged in 64 percent of the 76 societies on which Ford and Beach were able to obtain information. (Lesbianism was considerably less frequent or at least more carefully concealed.) Attitudes toward male homosexuality ranged from prohibition as in some Bedouin tribes where it was penalized by death, to total acceptance as in ancient Greek society where, during the Classical period, sexual relations between men and boys were regarded as a higher expression of love than heterosexual coitus.

Other findings included the following: face-to-face copulation is extremely widespread, as is stimulation of the female breast; frequency of coitus is higher in other societies than is the norm in the industrial West (up to 10 times a night among the Chagga tribesmen of Tanzania); manual stimulation of the partner's genitals is universal and considerably more common than oral-genital activity.

Intracultural Variance

Within a single culture, there are many variations from that society's general norms of sexual behavior. Variations such as homosexuality are discussed elsewhere in this chapter. A different sort of variance—namely, changes in overall sexual behavior in our own society over a period of time—is of great interest to psychologists.

During the past few decades, the changes in our cultural norms regarding sex have been so profound that we refer to them collectively as the sexual revolution. The most noticeable change has been the remarkable opening of channels of communication about explicit sexual matters. Books and movies that not long ago were prohibited by legal statutes are readily available and make James Joyce's *Ulysses* seem tame by comparison. Contraceptive devices that used to be kept under the druggist's counter are now displayed next to the colognes; *Consumer Reports* recently devoted a long article to its ratings of the best condoms. People once modestly spoke of "limbs" instead of legs; now many people appear on television game shows and discuss the frequency of their sexual intercourse.

This change in attitudes about a subject that was once taboo has been accompanied by changes in actual behavior. Evidence points to real changes in the occurrence of certain sexual activities. Perhaps the most dramatic change is the incidence of premarital intercourse, especially among females (see Figure 11.2). About 30 years ago, Kinsey reported that among college-educated respondents 27 percent of females and 49 percent of males said they had engaged in premarital intercourse by the age of 21 (Kinsey, Pomeroy, Martin, and Gebhard, 1953; Kinsey, Pomeroy, and Martin, 1948). A comprehensive survey of American sexual behavior (Hunt, 1974) taken during the early 1970s showed a much higher incidence of premarital intercourse among the college students interviewed—depending on the group surveyed, 43 to 56 percent for females and 58 to 82 percent for males. It is interesting to note that this latter survey was sponsored by the Playboy Foundation, a benevolence of the magazine that both encouraged and symbolized the sexual revolution.

Changes in cultural norms have resulted in what is often called the "sexual revolution," as exemplified by this display of public nudity.

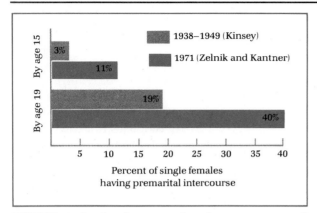

FIGURE 11.2 Graph comparing the percentage of single females having had premarital intercourse, in 1949 and in 1971. The percentage of 19-year-olds in this category doubled, while the percentage of 15-year-olds more than tripled.

An even more dramatic increase in premarital intercourse, one that occurred over a single decade, from 1965 to 1975, is shown in Table 11.2. This study compares the incidence of such behavior among students at one American university located in the southeastern United States (King, Balswick, and Robinson, 1977). In ten years, the number of females reporting that they had engaged in coitus before marriage almost doubled.

Apart from the increased availability of effective birth control and abortion, the increased willingness of female college students to participate in coitus before marriage presumably reflects two interrelated phenomena. One is the decline of the old double standard of sexual morality that permitted certain behavior for men but not for women; the other is the rise of modern feminism. Significantly, surveys indicate that, in addition to premarital coitus, other forms of sexual behavior such as masturbation are also increasing among women (King, Balswick, and Robinson, 1977).

TABLE 11.2 Incidence of Premarital Intercourse in College Students at a Southern University. (groups of 115–275 subjects each)

	FEMALE	MALE
1965	28.7%	65.1%
1970	37.3%	65.0%
1975	57.1%	73.9%

Source: K. King, J. O. Balswick, and I. E. Robinson, "The Continuing Premarital Revolution Among College Females," *Journal of Marriage and Family*, 39 (1977), 455.

Like the cross-cultural variations discussed previously, these examples of changes in a society's norms of sexual behavior over time reflect the importance of cultural attitudes. Next, we will narrow our focus to the cultural standards and the biological factors that influence individual, as opposed to societal, sexual behaviors.

Individual Variance: The Life Cycle

Our consideration of variance in sexual behavior has progressively narrowed to more homogeneous groups—from all beings including animals, to cross-cultural comparisons among humans, to a single culture. Now we will look at the individual human in order to identify varying sexual patterns as they are manifested over the entire life cycle.

Contrary to general belief, people seek sexual stimulation and gratification virtually from the cradle to the grave. Some of the quantitative and qualitative changes in the expression of sexual behavior during four broad phases of the life cycle—early childhood, prepuberty, puberty and beyond, and the declining years—concern us next.

Early Childhood Episodes of spontaneous sexual arousal are found in both sexes during the first year of life. These endure from a few seconds to several minutes and may occur a number of times a day. As we saw earlier, Freud was castigated for calling attention to infant sexuality, but its existence has been long known to observant parents and more recently has been documented by scientific scrutiny.

Investigators believe that stimulation of the infant genitals takes place during periods of restless behavior involving stretching and bending of the legs. Boys show erections on these occasions, and it is thought that orgasm (although not ejaculation) sometimes follows. Moreover, pelvic thrusting motions are seen in infants from eight to ten months of age. During the first two years of life, there appears to be no difference between boys and girls in their sexual behavior. After that, however, boys are reported to masturbate more frequently than girls (Langfeldt, 1979).

Prepuberty Despite Freud's suggestion that there is a period of sexual latency from about age 5 until puberty, youngsters continue to be sexually active during this period. Such activity was found by the anthropologist Malinowski (1929) in his study of the Trobriand Islanders and has been described much more recently by a number of observers. For example, one researcher noticed an increased frequency of male masturbation after age 7; in fact, the boys taught each other techniques of self-stimulation (Langfeldt, 1979). It is likely that Freud, in assuming a latency period, was misled by the effects of social sanctions in turn-of-the-century Vienna. Even in most modern societies, manifestations of sexuality in children are proscribed by the parents and consequently hidden by the child.

Puberty and Beyond Puberty has traditionally been considered a period of great sexual awakening. Certainly, at this stage, which begins at about 14 years of age in the male and 12 in the female, profound sexual changes take place as both sexes become capable of reproduction. Amazing as it may seem, however, there is a lack of systematic data correlating sexual behavior with these physiological changes. Such data might help clarify the ap-

Behavioral puberty is generally defined in terms of an increased sexual drive, which is most often manifest through the development of a largely heterosexual orientation.

parent contradiction between the concept of puberty as a time of sexual awakening and the evidence that there appears to be continuous sexual interest and activity from early childhood. For the moment, we must define behavioral puberty in terms of an increase in desire for sexual activity often accompanied by increased frequency of sexual outlet through masturbation and, most notably, through the development of a largely heterosexual social orientation. This is the time when the first manifestations of "falling in love" occur. This phenomenon, like other radically changed aspects of behavior during puberty, is often attributed by parents to "hormones." Later in this chapter we will take up the question of whether sexual behavioral changes can be reasonably related to changes in hormonal functioning. In any case, from early puberty, sexual capacity and activity generally is thought to build to a peak, which occurs at 15 to 18 years of age in the male but not until the late thirties or early forties in the female.

The Declining Years After reaching a peak, sexual capacity and activity tend to decline. According to a longitudinal study of several hundred aging individuals started at Duke University in 1957 (Verwoerdt, Pfeiffer, and Wang, 1969), both men and women showed a pattern of declining sexual activity and interest with age, but about one half of the subjects surviving into their eighties and nineties reported "mild or moderate" sexual interest. The patterns differ between the sexes, however. In men there is a growing discrepancy between interest and capacity, with the former being maintained or even increased (25 percent of subjects) with age in the face of increasing *impotence*—the inability to perform coitus, generally because of failure of erection. In aging women, declining sexual activity in our society is often associated with lack of sexual opportunities due to lack of partners or of partners' interest or capacity to have intercourse.

Some of the effects of aging in men were observed by Masters and Johnson (1966) during the course of their laboratory studies. They found that male orgasm appears to be the aspect of sexual behavior most vulnerable to aging, possibly due to weakening of the penile muscles. In young men at their sexual peak, erection follows instantly upon stimulation, semen spurts from 12 to 24 centimeters

337

during ejaculation, the penis takes about half an hour to return to its normal flaccid state, and sexual arousability is recovered soon (sometimes in less than a minute) after ejaculation. By contrast, men over 50 are slower to reach full erection, semen tends to seep out rather than spurt during ejaculation, the penis returns rapidly to its flaccid state, and the intervening refractory period before renewed sexual arousability may extend to 12 or even 24 hours.

It is also clear, however, that aging men can avoid absolute impotence through the maintenance of good health and the avoidance of serious psychological problems such as severe depression. As they grow older, men often insist that quantity of sexual experience is replaced by quality. Havelock Ellis, the English psychologist whose early writings on sex helped pave the way for Freud and the modern investigators of sex, became capable of sexual fulfillment through coitus only when he had reached his early fifties (Brecher, 1969).

The effect of aging on female sexuality is more complex and less well understood. Women may show increases, decreases, or lack of changes in their sexuality. What makes the difference is not precisely known. As we will see in the following section, *menopause*, the permanent cessation of menstruation that occurs during the late forties or early fifties as a result of fairly abrupt cessation of ovarian function, is marked by a sharp decrease in sex hormones. This deficiency can lead to dryness in the vagina and thinning of its walls, sometimes causing pain during coitus. But psychological factors also can play a role in changing sexuality. In some women the end of childbearing years may result in a sense of loss and in depression, which can lead to lack of interest in sex. In others, it may bring liberation from sexual inhibitions related to the fear of conception. But even if women are interested, the lower survival rate of males and the societal constraints on having relations with younger men or on having extramarital relations may mean that they will be sexually unfulfilled.

The Role of Hormones in Sexual Behavior

The biological study of sexual behavior focuses principally upon the role of *hormones*, the chemical messengers that are manufactured by the various endocrine glands and released into the bloodstream. The brain is vital to hormonal functioning, and the study of relationships among hormones, brain, and behavior is known as psychoneuroendocrinology.

Each of us produces both male and female sex hormones that exert a profound influence on the anatomy and physiology of our sexual systems and largely govern the differentiation of male and female anatomy and physiology. At puberty, a large increase in the production of sex hormones is responsible for the sudden blooming of the physical and sexual characteristics. These include maturation of such primary characteristics as the male penis and testes and of the female clitoris and ovaries. They also include such secondary characteristics as the deepening of the male voice and the growth of facial hair and, in the female, enlargement of the breasts and broadening of the hips. Of great importance is the fact that beginning at puberty, hormones regulate the female reproductive cycle.

Beyond these well-established endocrine principles, the role of hormones in sexual behavior is less clear. Do so-called raging hormones cause premenstrual mood swings? Do male hormones cause an increase in aggressiveness and "machismo?" Does homosexuality result from hormonal action?

There is a reasonable possibility that the answer to the above questions is "yes." A large percentage of the intelligent lay public and, indeed, of the medical profession shares such beliefs. The fact is, however, that none of the answers has been reliably established by experimental evidence. The answers are speculative or based on inadequate data, clinical impressions, or unverified extrapolation from animal research. Human sexual behavior is so profoundly affected by experience and sociocultural factors that it is often difficult to separate out the part played by hormones. In the following section we will evaluate the existing evidence and discuss the physiological and anatomical effects of hormones on sexual behavior.

Mechanisms of Hormonal Production

The production of hormones related to sex involves a complex interaction between brain and body. Hormonal production can be viewed as essentially a three-stage process (see Figure 11.3):

1. The hypothalamus, a tiny structure at the base of the brain (see Chapter 2), sends chemical signals via blood vessels that connect it to the so-called master gland, the pituitary.

2. The pituitary responds by manufacturing and releasing into the bloodstream two protein hormones, the *luteinizing hormone* (LH) and the *follicle-stimulating hormone* (FSH), both of which are essential for release of spermatozoa and eggs from the *gonads*—that is, the testes and ovaries. These hormones are called *gonadotropins*.

3. Gonadotropins, in turn, stimulate the production of sex hormones in the gonads. These gonadal hormones are called steroids, a class of hormones that also includes cortisone from the adrenal cortex. The main steroids produced by the male testes are *androgens,* the most important of which is *testosterone.* The primary steroids produced in the female's ovaries are estradiol (an *estrogen*) and *progesterone.*

Keep in mind that gonadotropin production is part of a process involving the brain and the pituitary gland. This process is a closed loop, and spe-

cialized cells in the brain and/or pituitary serve as a kind of thermostat. This "gonadostat" monitors the sex hormones circulating in the bloodstream; when they reach certain levels, it switches off production of the pituitary hormones, LH and FSH, that stimulate manufacture of the sex hormones. Contraceptive pills contain synthetic sexual steroids—artificial analogs of the natural female sex hormones, estrogen and progesterone. They prevent ovulation by signaling the pituitary to stop producing LH and FSH and have other antifertility effects such as preventing implantation of the fertilized egg in the womb.

Effects of Hormones in Females
The most pronounced effect of the steroid sex hormones in females is regulation of reproduction,

FIGURE 11.3 Hormonal production is a three-stage process in males and females. (A) Summary of hormonal control of the testicular function. The hypothalamus sends chemical signals to the pituitary, which responds by producing FSH and LH, which stimulate the release of spermatozoa and testosterone. When the amount of testosterone reaches a certain level, the hypothalamus and pituitary stop production of FSH and LH. (B) Summary of hormonal control of ovum development and estrogen secretion, which follows the same pattern as the male.

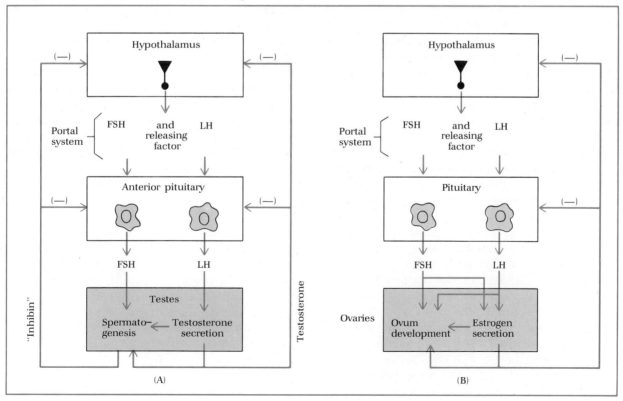

including the production of eggs (ova), the menstrual cycle, and pregnancy. The length of the reproductive cycle varies widely among mammals—from 4 days in the rat to 36 days in the chimpanzee. This cycle is essentially a fluctuation from a state in which the female is physiologically prepared to receive sperm to a state in which she is prepared to receive the fertilized ovum. Thus, in the 28-day human cycle, it takes two weeks to make the egg available for fertilization, while during the next two weeks the reproductive tract is prepared for implantation and growth of the fertilized ovum. These effects are mediated by changes in the production of female steroid hormones, which are controlled in turn by the gonadotropins.

In most mammals the gonadal hormones exert a profound influence on mating behavior. Because they are produced in greatest amount around the time of ovulation, mating is generally limited to that short period around the time of ovulation, a limitation that increases the probability that copulation will result in conception.

One result of the action of sex hormones is to make the female a receptive partner in mating. (Rape among animals is almost unknown.) In addition, the hormones may stimulate the female to initiate the sexual encounter by showing the male such stimuli as swollen or highly colored "sexual skin." This is known as *attractivity*. She also shows soliciting behavior or *proceptivity*, ranging from seductive hops, darts, and ear wiggles in the rat to the more brazen presentation of the rump in monkeys (Beach, 1976). If the source of these hormones—namely, the ovaries—is removed in a variety of subprimate species, all sexual behavior is suppressed. The behavior can be restored, however, with doses of estrogen and progesterone.

The principal mechanism by which hormones exert such a direct influence on sexual behavior in many female mammals was first proposed by Frank Beach in 1948. Beach suggested that hormones somehow affect nervous activity within the brain. Some years later two English investigators, Geoffrey Harris and Richard Michael, demonstrated this effect on a specific area of the brain. Harris and Michael (1964) worked with female cats whose ovaries had been removed, thus depriving them of sex hormones and, consequently, any interest in mating. They attached a tiny bit of estrogen to the end of a wire and inserted it into different parts of the cat's brain. When this hormonal implant was placed in a certain area of the hypothalamus, the cat soon became receptive to the male, and normal mating behavior occurred. More recently, other researchers (Barfield and Chen, 1978) have used smaller implants in rats to localize definitively hormone-responsive "sex centers."

Thus, in most mammals, there is an extraordinary coordination between the reproductive physiology and behavioral mechanisms. The brain signals the release of pituitary hormones, which control the ovarian production of sex hormones, which in turn act on the brain to influence behavior (as well as to "switch off" the pituitary and break the cycle).

In primates, however, this lock-step control of sexual behavior by ovarian hormones is not as strong as it is in other mammals. Although removal of the ovaries and treatment with sex hormones often have appeared to influence the behavior of female monkeys, the results may depend largely on a variety of social interactions that do not play important roles in subprimates. Interestingly, the male monkey's peak in sexual initiatives often coincides with ovulation in the female cycle. This suggests that the ovarian hormones of the female, peaking at ovulation, somehow produce maximal attractivity for the male. Another possibility is that the ovarian hormones stimulate subtle behavioral cues in the female that excite the male, although the female may be receptive to him even without midcycle hormones.

In humans the role of female hormones in sexual behavior becomes severely limited. Unlike any other species, the human female can continue an apparently normal sex life after surgical removal of her ovaries or the cessation of their function at menopause. It is true that a variety of studies have reported peaks of female sexual behavior occurring at various phases of the menstrual cycle. Because sex hormones also show considerable changes during these phases (see Figure 11.4), this suggests a hormonal role in women's sexuality. But such reports have also been explained in terms other than hormonal: for example, abstinence during menstruation or the conscious or subconscious desire to avoid or engage in coitus around the time of ovulation (Udry and Morris, 1977).

Similarly, there have been interesting observations about the possible link between female sex hormones and other behaviors. Many women report mood swings during the final days before menstruation (Dalton, 1977). In addition, one correlational study of female convicts found they had a much greater likelihood of committing a violent crime during this period. Indeed, in France, women accused of crimes committed in the final days before menstruation are permitted a legal defense called "temporary impairment of sanity." Such observations have not been verified by experimental methods.

What is surprising, however, is that sexual behavior in women may be significantly influenced by androgens, the hormones that are vital to male sexuality. Androgens are produced both in the ovaries and in the adrenal glands. Clinicians have long believed that administering androgens to women can stimulate their sexual desire by affecting the brain or perhaps by increasing sensitivity and even growth in the clitoris. Moreover, it has been shown that blood levels of naturally occurring androgen often increase at the midpoint of the reproductive cycle (Judd and Yen, 1973). Whether androgens normally play a role in female sexual behavior or if they have an effect only when large doses are administered awaits further research.

We have seen that hormones can affect female sexual behavior most dramatically in subprimate mammals. But such influence is not a one-way street. Data from animal experiments, and some

from human research, indicate that behavior itself, along with environmental and social factors, affects production of sex hormones.

This evidence derives partly from observations of the apparent effects of emotional stress on menstrual cycles in human females. For example, gynecologists report that some college women experience irregular menstrual cycles under the stress of the school year but have regular cycles when they are relaxing at home during the summer (Matsumoto, Tamada, and Konuma, 1979). During World War II, many women in German concentration camps ceased menstruating altogether (Bass, 1947).

These apparent effects on hormonal functioning are still speculative, but the influence of social and environmental factors is well established in many animals. Cats and rabbits ovulate in response to copulation or even the mere presence of the male because sexual stimulation triggers release of LH. Female laboratory mice, when brought together in the same cage, cease their normal reproductive cycles. A newly pregnant female mouse will abort in the presence of a male other than the father.

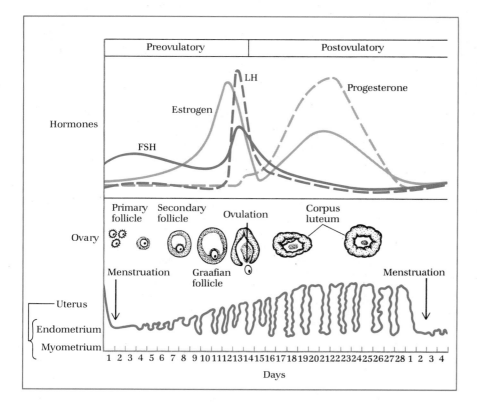

FIGURE 11.4 The menstrual cycle when fertilization does not occur. The events that take place within the pituitary, ovary, and uterus are precisely synchronized.

The importance of a scientist's methodology, which often seems less interesting than his or her results, is dramatically illustrated in the study of one highly significant aspect of sexual behavior: the suspected relationship between a woman's sexual desire and the phases of her menstrual cycle. In lower mammals, mating is limited to a brief period around the midpoint of the female's menstrual cycle, coinciding with ovulation, which is triggered by peak levels of the sex hormones. In humans, obviously mating can occur at any time during the female cycle.

Nonetheless, important questions remain. Do changes in hormonal levels, as reflected in the various phases of the menstrual cycle, influence sexual responsiveness in the human female? Are women, as is widely believed, truly emancipated from hormonal control of their sexual behavior? These questions have more than academic interest, if only because of the widespread use of oral contraceptives, which profoundly influence hormonal levels. If cyclic hormonal changes do, in fact, affect female sexual behavior, then oral contraceptives can be expected to influence the responsiveness of women who use them.

Early attempts to answer these questions employed a simple methodology. Women were asked to describe their frequency of coitus in relationship to the phases of their menstrual cycles. Interestingly, most of these studies showed a peak in sexual activity not at midcycle but just before or just after menstruation. The problem with such studies was that the results did not necessarily reflect hormonal changes. For example, many women abstain from intercourse during menstruation. Thus, intercourse may well increase just before and after this period of abstention because of other factors such as the anticipation of abstention or the accumulation of desire after it.

Later studies produced opposite results, indicating a strong correlation between midcycle hormonal peaks and peaks in frequency of coitus or orgasm. But these studies, too, had methodological problems. Udry and Morris (1968) paid working-class black women to report to the laboratory each day and record their sexual behavior for the past 24 hours. This was an improvement on unreliable retrospective methods in which women might be asked to record their sexual activities during previous weeks or months. But the study was severely criticized for failing to solve the problem of how to summate results from cycles of different lengths—and hence of how to determine midcycle ovulation. In fact, Udry and Morris (1977) later demonstrated that completely different conclusions could result from different methods of pooling and calculating data.

Regardless of results, all of the studies suffered from two critical shortcomings in methodology. One shortcoming was the implicit assumption that the frequency with which a woman participates in coitus depends upon her own feelings as opposed to the demands of her male partner. To remedy this problem, one study focused on female-initiated behavior, whether heterosexual or masturbatory (Adams, Gold, and Burt 1978). However, their findings—a midcycle peak of behavior coinciding with a midcycle peak of a particular sex hormone—illustrated the other shortcoming in such studies: they failed to measure the actual hormonal levels of their subjects directly. Without these measurements, it is clearly impossible to reliably assess possible relationships between changes in sexual behavior throughout the menstrual cycle and the fluctuating hormone levels, which are postulated to cause these changes.

In recent years, an accurate methodology for measuring hormonal levels by labeling the hormones with a radioactive substance has come into general use. This advance has made possible two new studies, still unpublished, which confirm the early reports that sexual behavior reached a peak at times other than the midcycle surge of hormones. John Bancroft, a psychiatrist at the University of Edinburgh, and Diana Sanders found peaks of sexual interest just before menstruation and peaks of sexual activity just after the end of menstruation (Bancroft, 1981). An American investigator, Patricia Schreiner-Engel, has taken a different approach, using an instrument to record vaginal blood flow as a measure of sexual arousal. She found that maximal increases in sexual responsiveness and fantasizing when listening to an erotic tape recording occurred four to seven days before and just after menstruation. Her study, in particular, appears to have overcome the earlier problems of methodology. She was also able to correlate a behavioral event, sexual arousal, which is not dependent upon the actions of a partner, with actual measurements of hormonal concentrations in the blood (1981).

These effects on female reproductive function are caused by the presence of chemical substances called *pheromones* in the urine of male and female mice. Such pheromones act chemically upon the glands of other mice to influence the production of their sex hormones.

A different kind of effect in animals is produced by the *signaling pheromones* (also known as sex attractants). These chemical messengers are excreted through urine or through the vagina and activate sexual behaviors in the male, reaching the nervous system through the sense of smell. Signaling pheromones have been identified in many invertebrate animal species, particularly insects.

Although pheromones have been chemically isolated in many animals, their possible existence in human females has been debated for many years. A study carried out by Martha McClintock (1971) provides evidence of the effect of social stimuli and perhaps of pheromones on menstrual cycles. She found that roommates or close friends living together in a college dormitory tended to have their menstrual periods at the same time. Moreover, shorter cycles were found among those women "who spent more time" with males.

McLintock's hypothesis was that pheromones produced both by the females and the males were responsible for these apparent influences on hormonal functioning. In a more recent study she has shown that the reproductive cycles of female rats living in isolated cages tend toward synchrony when air is circulated between the cages (McClintock, 1979).

There is some evidence that women experience an increased acuity in the sense of smell at midcycle, the time of ovulation. For example, adult women can perceive a synthetic compound with a musklike odor that cannot usually be detected by males or by young girls before puberty (Le Magnen, 1952). This perceptual ability reaches its peak at midcycle. Interestingly, musk, which is a common component of perfumes, is derived from a sex gland of the male Tibetan musk deer, where it is believed to perform a pheromonal function.

Effects of Hormones in Males

In contrast to females, where fluctuations in hormonal levels dictate the reproductive cycle, sex hormones in the male are produced at a fairly constant rate. Also in contrast to females, the key role of male sex hormones in mediating behavior is clearly established, from lower mammals to humans.

Classically, the first step in demonstrating the effects of a hormone is to remove the gland that produces the hormone and then observe the subsequent changes in behavior. The male sex hormones, androgens, including testosterone, are produced by the testes; removal of the testes—castration—has been a frequently used surgical technique throughout history.

Men were castrated to provide "safe" companions for ladies in ancient Rome and to furnish eunuchs for the harems of Arab sheiks. In fact, the very word *eunuch* comes from the Greek for "guardian of the bed." The medieval Roman Catholic Church made use of a physiological fact that is now well known: castration before puberty eliminates the glandular source of testosterone that causes the adolescent voice to deepen. The "castrati" choirboys of Italy were men who kept their high-pitched voices because their testes had been excised before puberty. The Russian sect, Skoptsi, practiced castration to ensure male abstinence. Not surprisingly, this sect has died out.

Castration invariably produces a decrease and, frequently, a total disappearance of sexual behavior in males, although the effects may take several years to be manifested (Bermant and Davidson, 1974). After sexual behavior disappears, it can be restored by administering testosterone (Davidson, Camargo, and Smith, 1979). The rapid effects of administering testosterone to men without functioning testes can be seen in Figure 11.5.

The importance of androgens to male sexual behavior is so obvious that the question arises: can differences in male sex drive and activity be related to differences in androgen levels? The answer was given in a recent study of 101 young adult men whose reported sexual activities were correlated with the level of testosterone in their blood (Brown, Monti, and Corriveau, 1978). No positive relationship was found between high sexual activity and high testosterone level. The probable explanation for this is that the normal range of testosterone levels exceeds that necessary to maintain sexual behavior. Nature apparently has provided a considerable excess of androgen (in rats, up to tenfold) over the amount necessary for normal sexual functioning. This is a kind of evolutionary safety factor to ensure survival of the species.

In late middle age, the decline in blood levels of testosterone is occasionally quite precipitous. In such cases, symptoms are similar to those found in female menopause including hot flashes. Men with these symptoms are sometimes said to be undergoing the *male climacteric.* They show a rapid loss

343

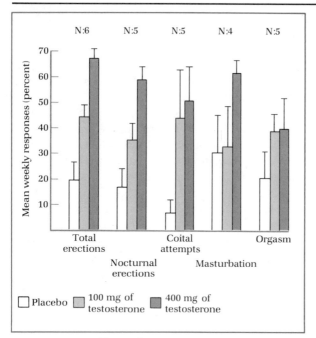

FIGURE 11.5 Effects of testosterone treatments on the sexual activity of men without functioning testes including mean frequencies of diurnal and nocturnal erections, coitus (including unsuccessful attempts), masturbation, and orgasms. All responses were normalized by expressing them as a percentage of the maximum weekly performance of that subject during the course of the cycle.

of sexual drive and potency, indicating a clear relationship to the loss of male sex hormones. In contrast, as we previously noted, women often maintain or actually increase sexual behavior after menopause despite their sharp decline in female sex hormones.

Stressful events in a man's life can profoundly affect sex hormone level. Both physical trauma such as surgery and psychological stress have been shown to reduce the amount of testosterone in the blood (Davidson, Smith, and Levine, 1978). Although studies are lacking, it is a fair assumption that such environmental-biological interactions can result in impotence.

Effects of Hormones within the Brain

The mechanisms by which male hormones affect sexual behavior have been the subject of much research in recent years. The prevailing hypothesis is that these hormones influence the action of nerve cells in the brain, especially in the hypothalamus, which, as we saw earlier, appears to be the site where female sex hormones affect behavior. Many investigators believe that hormones somehow influence the action of neurotransmitters—the chemical messengers between brain cells (see Chapter 2). One widely held theory suggests that, at least in rats and some other animals, male hormones first must be converted in the brain to the female hormone estrogen before having an effect on male sexual behavior (Luttge, 1979).

The evidence that male hormones exert a direct influence on the brain comes principally from animal research. For example, a male rat that has become inactive following castration will resume the whole complex of mating behavior when solid testosterone is implanted in a specific area of the hypothalamus (Davidson, 1966). Sexual behavior can be eliminated in rats, cats, dogs, and rhesus monkeys by destroying this same area in the hypothalamus. Injections of testosterone into the bloodstream of these animals does not restore normal sexual behavior (Hart, in press).

These experiments pinpoint at least one area of the brain as being specifically involved in controlling mating behavior in experimental animals. Other parts of the brain also have been implicated in sexual behavior. For example, when areas in the limbic system, which sends afferent nerves to the hypothalamus, are disrupted by a form of epilepsy in humans or by surgical lesions in experimental animals, increases or decreases in sexual behavior are reported. An example of "hypersexuality" in such an experiment involved a male cat with surgical lesions in the limbic system. The cat attempted to mate with a teddy bear and kept up his copulatory movements until he was put to sleep.

Increases in sexual behavior in female animals also have been observed from lesions in another area of the limbic system, the septum. One researcher, Robert Heath, has even implanted electrodes in the septum of a few human patients. Heath (1972) reported that electrical stimulation of the septum resulted in sexual arousal and generally pleasurable sensations. Questions have been raised, however, about both the results and the ethics of this research.

Sex Differences and Sexual Differentiation

In recent years, the roles of the two sexes have begun to change radically in our society. These changes apply to practically all branches of human behavior, including sexual behavior.

At various places in this chapter we have described several differences between males and females in sexual behavior—for example, in the physiology of arousal and the incidence of premarital intercourse. To what extent are these factors determined by learning, culture, and other environmental factors? To what extent are they determined by the biological factors of anatomy and physiology?

The answers to these questions appear to be the easiest to obtain in the realm of animal research. Among subprimate species and among certain primates, biological determination predominates in sexual behavior and in many other sexually differentiated behaviors such as aggression, parenting, and emotions.

The "Reversed Adam" Principle

The Old Testament makes no bones about sexual differentiation: man came first, and from his rib was formed woman. In fact, however, the model of sexual differentiation provided by animal research is just the opposite. Anatomically and physiologically, the basic pattern is female. If the embryo is genetically destined to be a male, that is, if the father's fertilizing sperm carried a Y chromosome, masculinity is imposed by the presence of the male hormone androgen, which triggers development of internal and external male sexual structures. This androgen is provided at a critical stage in early development by the testes, which develop under the influence of the XY combination of sex chromosomes. Without androgen at the proper time, the developing animal remains female. (Androgen, in fact, takes its name from the Greek meaning "producer of males.") This principle of masculine superimposition on a basic female pattern may be called the *reversed Adam principle.*

Animal Studies Compelling and powerful in its simplicity and apparent universality, the reversed Adam principle derives from several decades of animal research. This research shows that the reversed Adam principle is responsible for sexual differentiation at the level of sexual anatomy, physiology, and behavior. Alfred Jost and associates (Jost, Jones, and Scott, 1969) established that androgen produced by the testes of the rabbit fetus was responsible for male anatomical differentiation, that is, development of the external genitalia and of the internal reproductive structures. Charles Barraclough (1966) demonstrated the drastic physiological effect of testosterone on newborn female rats: a single injection of the male hormone masculinized the physiology of their reproductive system so that they never cycled or ovulated in adulthood.

One of the key experiments in establishing the behavioral effects of the reversed Adam principle was carried out by Geofrey Harris and Seymour Levine (1965). Newborn male rats were castrated, depriving them of the male sex hormone produced by the testes, and an ovary was transplanted into the eye in front of the lens, where it could be observed. Although the external genitalia of these young rats were not feminized, they developed a female cycle of hormone production and ovulated. When males castrated at birth were given female sex hormones in adulthood, they displayed female patterns of sexual receptivity. These effects, it was found, could be prevented by a single injection of testosterone at the time of castration. Moreover, when newborn female rats were given testosterone, they grew up sterile and showed male mating and other behavior.

These findings were extended to monkeys by investigators Robert Goy and Charles Phoenix (Goy, 1970). Pregnant monkeys given testosterone produced female offspring with masculine genitalia: the clitoris, for example, grew to resemble a small penis. These females also displayed patterns of play typical of male monkeys: they were more assertive and engaged in rough games. They also displayed masculine sexual behavior such as the male pattern of mounting. Furthermore, there was a delay in the onset of puberty. Interestingly, however, when these females reached adolescence, there was little disruption of the typical female reproductive functions.

In summary, androgen is the key to sexual differentiation, especially in subprimate mammals. In its absence, the basic female pattern continues to develop. The female sex hormones produced by the ovaries have no known role in sexual differentiation. Research suggests that androgen brings about differentiation by laying down new patterns of neural activity in the hypothalamus, somehow changing the brain's future responsiveness to the gonadal hormones and to environmental stimuli. Actual changes in the growth pattern of certain neurons in the hypothalamic area, caused by sex hormone treatment at birth, have been demonstrated in rats (Harlan, Gordon, and Gorski, 1979).

Human Studies Obviously, the findings about the reversed Adam principle cannot be extended to humans through direct experimentation. One possibility, however, is to study females who have been exposed in the womb to abnormal amounts of male hormones. For example, the genetic disorder known as *adrenogenital syndrome* produces a tumor or excessive growth in the adrenal glands that results in the production (commencing before birth) of large amounts of androgen. Other girls have had prenatal exposure to hormones with androgenic (masculinizing) actions that were given to their pregnant mothers to prevent spontaneous abortion. The degree of masculinization can vary from slight enlargement of the clitoris to its metamorphosis into a penis with fusion of the vagina and growth of a scrotum—albeit empty, because internal structures are feminine.

John Money and Anke Ehrhardt (1972) conducted long-term follow-up studies on such girls, most of whom had their anomalous genitals corrected by early surgery and lifelong hormone treatments. They found that prenatal exposure to male hormones resulted in unusually "tomboyish" behavior while growing up. This included a predilection for masculine dress and toys and a tendency, which had been observed previously in the female monkeys given testosterone before birth, to engage in masculine forms of rough-and-tumble play. There were, however, two important differences from the observations in most of the animal experiments described earlier: the reproductive cycles of the girls were not disrupted (in the monkeys, onset of menstruation was delayed), and they exhibited no deviance in later sexual behavior.

In humans, then, as well as in animals, the reversed Adam principle appears to be at work, although it is apparently less profound in its effects. Male hormones act on the brain at critical periods in early development to bring about masculinization of reproductive anatomy and some aspects of behavior. In the human females studied, however, there was no clear change in sexual behavior nor in their feeling of gender identity: they regarded themselves as normal females.

The Influence of Learning in Sexual Differentiation

What explains the lesser effects of early androgen in humans? Money and Ehrhardt (1972) point to the importance of the social environment in establishing gender identity, sex roles, and behavior appropriate to the sex of the individual. That environment was shaped in such a way as to teach the androgen-exposed girls that they were indeed girls. They were given girls' names, usually treated early with plastic surgery and hormones to erase the masculinization of their genitals, and raised as girls.

Even more dramatic evidence of the vital role of social learning in sexual differentiation comes from work by these and other investigators. Money reports, for example, on a pair of identical male twins. One of the twins had his penis removed shortly after birth because of damage during circumcision. He was reared as a girl and, at last report, had responded to this role by developing feminine play and dress behavior. The twin brother, meanwhile, was reared as a boy and shows normal male behavior (Money and Ehrhardt, 1972).

The most famous study of the effects of early social learning on sexual behavior was carried out by Harry Harlow (Harlow, 1965). Rhesus monkeys were raised in isolation without any contact with their mothers or peers during the first six months to one year of life. When they matured, these monkeys did not engage in normal sexual behavior. When placed with other monkeys, they were aggressive, showed symptoms typical of depression in humans such as withdrawal and inactivity, and failed to engage in appropriate mounting and copulatory activity.

Androgen and Environment

A fascinating recent observation apparently involved both hormonal and socio-environmental factors. In the early 1970s, endocrinologists (Imperato-McGinley, Peterson, Gautier, and Sturla, 1979) discovered a number of boys in a village in the Dominican Republic with an enzyme defect that prevented utilization of testosterone by their tissues. Because of this defect, they were born with female genital anatomy and accordingly reared as girls.

When these children reached puberty, however, their tissues began to respond to naturally occurring testosterone, and they became masculine in anatomy, hence the name by which they were known locally—*guevedoces*, or "penis at 12." Apparently because of the accepting attitude of the community, they were able to make a satisfactory transition in gender from female to male. A few cases of these recently have been discovered in the United States, including one individual who made a successful gender transition at puberty. These late gender transitions contradict current psychiatric thinking (Hampson and Hampson, 1960), which insists that gender reassignment cannot be attempted after about two years of age without risking dire psychological consequences.

While social factors were clearly at work in the successful gender adaptations made by the boys both before and after puberty, biological factors were also important. Julienne Imperato-McGinley and her colleagues (1979) interpret it as strongly supporting the reversed Adam principle. They concluded that the boys were able to develop into normal adult males only because their brains were exposed to male sex hormones while they were still in the womb. That conclusion could be verified only by examining the susceptibility of the human brain to such hormonal influences, an examination that is not yet possible.

Sex Differences and Similarities in Humans

We have seen a sharp contrast in sexual differentiation between rats, for example, and human beings. In rats, the development of sexual behavior can be shifted between masculine and feminine simply by altering the level of male hormone at an early stage; in humans, some behaviors, but apparently not sexual behavior, are affected by such changes.

This contrast should not be surprising if we look closely at the apparent differences between males and females in sexual behavior. As science delves more deeply into male and female sexual behavior in humans, it becomes apparent that the similarities exceed the differences. This is evident if we reconsider, in the light of recent findings, two sex differences noted by Kinsey in his pioneering studies nearly three decades ago.

One difference noted by Kinsey was in masturbation. He reported that only 58 percent of female respondents engaged in self-stimulation while 92 percent of the male respondents did. This wide disparity has narrowed considerably in more recent surveys (Schmidt and Sigusch, 1973). Moreover, anthropological data suggest that such differences are likely to be culturally determined rather than dictated by biology.

A second difference reported by Kinsey was the apparent lower propensity of women to be aroused by erotic material presented in visual form—pictures of nudes, genitalia, or sexual behavior. This finding would seem to be borne out by everyday observation; the people who buy sexually explicit books and attend stag movies are predominantly male. However, recent studies have recorded physiological responses in young men and women to erotic pictures and have found no significant differences between the sexes (Schmidt and Sigusch, 1973). People either have changed in their responses to visual erotica or, more likely, Kinsey's data collection procedure was at fault in this case. Nevertheless, more research is needed on this question.

A third apparent sex difference—the differing nature of the orgasm—may also be less significant than formerly thought. For example, it has been recently suggested that men as well as women are capable of multiple orgasm (Robbins and Jensen, 1976); a new hypothesis raises the possibility that similar neural mechanisms may underlie orgasm in both sexes (see Focus).

Homosexuality

Differences in sexual behavior obviously also exist among the members of one sex. One dramatic example is homosexuality. The study of *homosexuality* is fraught with difficulties and ambiguities. Even the word *homosexual* is often used ambiguously. It usually is applied to men who prefer sex with other men, but it also applies to women who prefer sex with other women (*lesbians*). Nor is it clear precisely what constitutes homosexuality. Kinsey (1948, 1953) found that one half of his male respondents and 28 percent of female respondents reported having had at least one homosexual experience (see Figure 11.6). Yet only 4 percent of males and 2 percent of females said they were exclusively homosexual. The classification of homosexual behavior as pathological is a cultural determination. The American Psychiatric Association no longer classifies it as a mental or emotional disorder, although many states still outlaw consensual sodomy. By contrast, in the East Bay Society studied by Davenport (1965), a male's refusal to engage in anal intercourse at a male friend's request was considered a serious breach of etiquette.

Many studies have attempted to find a relationship between hormonal imbalance and homosexual behavior. Data collected in the United States, Britain, and Czechoslovakia, for example, show that about one third of the female homosexuals studied had higher than normal levels of the male hormone androgen. Studies of testosterone levels in male

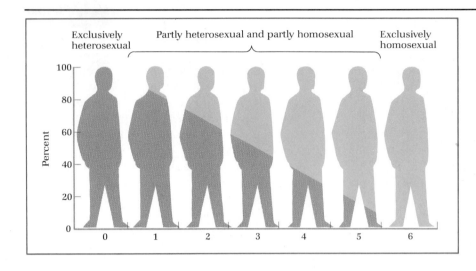

Exclusively heterosexual · Partly heterosexual and partly homosexual · Exclusively homosexual

0 1 2 3 4 5 6

FIGURE 11.6 Alfred Kinsey's research established that homosexuality and heterosexuality are not mutually exclusive categories. Elements of both are found in most people in varying degrees. Kinsey's seven-point homosexual rating scale provides a way of measuring the balance in particular individuals. The scale runs from one extreme of exclusively heterosexual acts or feelings through the other extreme of exclusively homosexual acts or feelings.

homosexuals have found differing levels of testosterone; some were above normal, some normal, and others below normal, indicating the lack of a relationship between testosterone levels and homosexuality in males. Administering hormones to hormone-deficient homosexuals may increase their sexual drive—as it does in heterosexuals—but does not alter their preferences for the same sex (Green, 1979).

In West Germany a few years ago, brain surgery was even carried out on criminal sex offenders who happened to be homosexual in an attempt to reduce homosexual behavior: lesions were placed in an area of the hypothalamus that controls sexual behavior in some animals (Roeder, 1966). Aside from the ethical considerations against this practice, there is no consistent evidence that homosexuality has a neuro-anatomical basis, let alone one that could be "cured" by brain surgery. Yet, it is possible, although not yet demonstrated scientifically, that hormonal factors acting upon the brain of the fetus may somehow predispose humans to homosexuality. If so, social factors might later elicit such predisposed behavior.

Psychological explanations for homosexuality focus on the role of early experience. The psychoanalytic view, first advanced by Freud, centers on certain unresolved conflicts in the young child. The child becomes sexually oriented to the parent of the same sex and for various reasons fails to outgrow this attachment. According to this view, male

Male homosexual couple displaying affection at demonstration.

homosexuals harbor unconscious fears of women; female homosexuals have unconscious fears of men.

Increasingly, some researchers look to early learning experiences as the dominant factor in shaping homosexuality. Through the processes of conditioning and reinforcement that we described in Chapter 7, children develop a preference for others of the same sex. Current longitudinal studies are investigating the possible relationship of feminine ("sissy") behavior in boys to future homosexuality. One study found that two thirds of male and female homosexuals described themselves as having experienced cross-gender ("sissy" or "tomboy") behavior as children (Saghir and Robins, 1973). The learning approach has gained credibility, in part, because of the recent success of conditioning techniques in changing sex preferences. In this therapy, individuals may be punished by mildly painful electric shocks when they become sexually aroused by visual images of homosexual behavior and rewarded for arousal in response to heterosexual images (Bancroft, 1974). Finally it should be emphasized that most homosexuals are not candidates for this or any other "treatment" for their sex preferences, which need not be regarded as pathological.

Transsexualism

Transsexualism is commonly confused with homosexuality. Although transsexuals often are homosexual in sex preference, the chief distinguishing characteristic is a strong feeling of gender identity with the opposite sex. A male transsexual, for example, typically reports that he feels like "a woman in a man's body."

The attempts to explain transsexualism generally tend to coincide with the biological and psychological explanations of homosexuality. Gunter Dörner and his associates (Döner, Rhode, Stahl, Krell, and Masius, 1975) have speculated that some instances of male-to-female transsexualism may re-

"Before" and "after" photographs of James Morris, who became Jan Morris after a sex-change operation.

sult from androgen deficiency in the prenatal brain. Such an instance, it is postulated, might occur after the formation of the external genitals but before the brain has fully developed mechanisms that influence male and female behavior. Conversely, prenatal androgen excess could, in this view, account for female-to-male transsexualism.

Robert Stoller (1968) suggests that male transsexuals have mothers who are overprotective, confused, and unhappy about their own gender identity as females and maintain intimate physical closeness with the child for an unusually long period. Richard Green (1979) points out that many transsexual males were treated like girls by their mothers, who dressed them in feminine clothes; these males also preferred the company of girls as playmates during childhood. Green suggests that the causes of male transsexualism are probably complex, resulting from an interaction between prenatal androgen deficiency and an early socialization process in which feminine behavior is reinforced.

Several thousand transsexuals have undergone so-called sex-change surgery to make their outward appearance conform with their inward gender feelings. In males, hormone treatments (estrogen) help enlarge the breasts and reduce beard growth; in women, androgenic hormones can increase beard growth and muscle development and deepen the voice. Plastic surgery for males removes the testes and penis and creates an artificial vagina; for women, it reduces breast tissue, removes the ovaries and uterus, and creates an artificial penis.

Emotional adjustment after such surgery apparently varies widely. Many patients, such as Renee Richards, who became a woman tennis star after a sex-change operation, report successful adjustment. Recently, however, Johns Hopkins University, which pioneered in the surgery, announced it would no longer perform the operations, contending that surgery was no more successful than psychotherapy in helping transsexuals cope with their feelings. Most authorities dispute this view.

Sex-Role Development

The prolonged period of dependency required by the human infant places special demands upon the caregiving environment. One of these demands is a division of labor within the family: one parent typically takes on the role of provider/protector, while the other nurtures the young (La Barre, 1954). In principle, these respective roles can be assumed by any member of the family or indeed by any non-family surrogate. In practice, however, biological considerations have tended to dictate the pattern. The female, with her biological responsibilities for childbearing, has been the most likely candidate for nurturer. The male, with his greater strength, has been the most likely candidate for provider/protector. This pattern seems to have characterized most human societies (D'Andrade, 1966).

Today, however, in many modern industrialized societies, this pattern is changing. It is under assault both philosophically and in terms of everyday reality: in the United States, for example, a large number of mothers with young children have jobs outside the home. This means that in many families the roles of provider/protector and nurturer have to be shared.

The new questions about women's roles—and consequently about men's roles—have placed increased importance on this area of research. Much of the research on sex-role differences has focused on personality and behavioral traits that are as-

Traditional roles in the household are changing. With more and more mothers working outside the home, fathers are increasingly assuming greater responsibilities for nurturing their children.

sumed to accompany the traditional allocation of male and female roles. It seeks to answer such questions as: are boys more aggressive than girls? Are young girls smarter? Are boys more active?

A highly significant milestone in this research came in 1974 with the publication of *The Psychology of Sex Differences* by Eleanor Emmons Maccoby and Carol Nagy Jacklin. This work represents the authors' review of more than 2,000 books and research articles dealing with sex-role differences. The authors' findings expose many of the myths inherent in sex-role stereotypes but also help establish several essential differences. For example, as parents long have observed, boys *are* more aggressive physically and verbally, beginning at about age two.

A summary of sex differences, however, does not necessarily shed light on the sources of these differences. Are boys and girls different because of biological factors? Or do cultural and social factors predominately shape such differences?

Biological Factors

Many experiments with monkeys show that even when placed in isolation from adults, infant monkeys show sex differences in behavior. For example, when Harry and Margaret Harlow (1965) raised monkeys alone in cages but allowed them to play with other infants the same age in a large room once a day, sex differences in play behavior were observed. Rough-and-tumble play in which the monkeys wrestle, roll, and sham bite each other is much more common in males than in females. This suggests that, at least for monkeys, some sex differences are innate. Many of these differences may be mediated by the effects of sex hormones as Money and Ehrhardt (1972) found in their studies of female children who were exposed to male hormones while still in the mother's uterus.

Certain biological factors in traditional sex roles are obvious—the mother's obvious connection to childbearing, and the father's greater strength (although modern technology has reduced the significance of the latter). Other factors suggesting a built-in specialization of sex roles have eluded investigators. For example, if females are biologically destined to play the role of nurturer, we might expect them to be inherently more responsive to signals from infants. Although some research has found greater responsiveness among adolescent and older females, the measures seem limited to behavior displayed toward others. When more private situations are used for measurement, such as in the home, the differences in responsiveness diminish or disappear. This suggests that the causes are social rather than biological. Thus, it is not clear that the basis for a marked differentiation of family roles related to sex is necessarily biological.

Social and Cultural Factors

Most psychologists account for the development of sex differences in terms of social and cultural factors that are assimilated through learning. The child is constantly surrounded by influences that present and reinforce social expectations and values. These factors appear to be learned in two ways: through rewards and punishment and through the imitation of models.

A number of different agents within the society—parents, teachers, peers, media—lay down patterns of reinforcement that directly shape the child's behavior. These rewards and punishments not only tell the child what to do but also what not to do (Hetherington and Parke, 1979). For boys, what not to do is to behave like girls (Emmerich, 1959). Boys are often condemned by society for playing with dolls, failing to be sufficiently aggressive, or otherwise acting like "sissies." By contrast, there is a greater tolerance for a wide range of behaviors among girls, especially in their early years (Fagot, 1977).

These patterns of reinforcement from parents and other socializing agents seem to be matched by the results of studies that investigate the course of sex-role identification. Boys show earlier and more consistent patterns of making sex-stereotyped choices than do girls. This finding occurs generally in two types of methodology: observational studies in which children are given a free choice of toys to play with, and tests in which they are asked whether they want to grow up to be a mother or a father. Similar results have been found in studies of school and peer influences. In school, for example, boys are more closely monitored in terms of sex-appropriate activities than are girls (Fagot and Patterson, 1969).

Generally speaking, girls seem to have an easier time in school. Traits usually attributed to boys—aggressiveness, for example—are not likely to be valued in the traditional school setting. Girls tend

Reinforcement of sex-role behavior in school is exemplified by use of dollhouse as a plaything for a little girl.

to like school more in the early grades, and boys report that they feel less well liked by the teachers. Indeed, recent research (Collins, Henker, and Whalen, 1980) indicates that boys are more likely than girls to be identified as being hyperactive or otherwise a problem in class.

However, another study (Dweck and Goetz, 1977) suggests that teacher evaluations tend to reinforce feelings of intellectual inferiority in girls. Negative evaluations by teachers of girls were based on the intellectual content of the girls' performances. By contrast, negative teacher evaluations of boys were related to the form of the work—"sloppy," for example—rather than to its intellectual content. Positive evaluations for boys, however, were based on intellectual content.

The pattern of feedback girls receive when they have difficulty on a mental task makes it likely that they will attribute their failure to a lack of ability. Because boys do not have to cope with negative evaluations of their intellectual ability, and girls do, it is easy to understand how girls can begin to believe that boys possess a superior intellect.

A second means by which children can learn their sex-role characteristics is through exposure to models in the family, in school, and from newspapers, books, and television. The tendency of children to imitate models through so-called ob-

servational learning or modeling has been well established, although precisely how the child selects which aspects of the model to emulate is less clear.

A number of studies have sought to establish the transmission of parental characteristics to sons and daughters through modeling. Several studies have shown that the quality of nurturance in the parent of the same sex is related to the corresponding masculinity or femininity of their children (Bronson, 1959). Interestingly, warmth on the part of either parent increases femininity in girls, but in boys only paternal warmth has this effect (Hetherington, 1967). Moreover, families where the father has a central role in decision making tend to produce boys who are highly masculine. Where the father is more passive and the mother dominates decision making, the boys are more feminized.

How can researchers be certain that imitation of models rather than learning through reinforcement is responsible for the development of sex-role characteristics? One possible test is through the study of a phenomenon that is on the increase in the United States—single-parent families. Eileen Hetherington (1966) has studied the relationship between masculinity in boys and the absence of the father. Her findings indicate that if the separation from the father occurs before the boy is six years old, he is more likely to show feminine characteristics.

The Importance of Context

Sex-role development is subject to so much social stereotyping that it must be approached with great caution. Psychologists tend to limit their studies to the manner in which children either conform or do not conform to various expected behavioral patterns such as masculinity or femininity. We seem to seek broad categorizations of children based upon their performance on a selected test, a standard observational setting, or various self-reports and behavioral rating systems. At the same time, however, we have come increasingly to understand that the treatment of certain behavioral characteristics as if they were enduring traits is probably an oversimplification.

Indeed, a great deal of evidence suggests that context—the particular setting and the social demands inherent in that setting—may contribute more to a given behavior than do apparently stable personality traits. Even the most aggressive person is nonaggressive in some situations; the most passive and dependent person is quite independent in some contexts.

What is more, it seems almost anachronistic to look for stable, ideal types of male and female sex roles in a time of such rapid social change. High rates of divorce along with the increasing entry of women into the labor force are altering traditional roles within the family. Closer attention will have to be paid to the behavioral tendencies in children that are fostered by such changes. We may have to begin to look at the development of sexual identities in the context of cognitive and political changes that serve to alter people's horizons and their ways of thinking about the world. These changes may actually outstrip the child-rearing practices of parents and institutions such as the schools. Future theories of sex-role development will have to make room for these changes.

A recent theory of sex-role development reflecting this view (Kohlberg, 1966) suggests that the child's sense of gender identity precedes rather than follows social influences such as reinforcement and modeling. The child begins by understanding that he or she is a boy or a girl and then tends to organize subsequent learning in terms of that understanding—"I am a boy; I'll learn about boy things." In the new world where a diversity of characteristics define women and men, such a child might naturally acquire sophisticated understandings of this diversity. As the child's exposure to models of diversity increases, so, too, would the child's differentiated understanding of what it means to be a woman or a man.

Dressed in a police officer's uniform, this child is imitating or modeling the role of police officer.

The Biosocial Complex

Sexual behavior is culturally determined; sexual behavior is biologically determined. Throughout this chapter we have seen examples of both kinds of effects. In experimental situations it is often possible to demonstrate specifically biological or specifically sociocultural causes for sexual phenomena. But in real-life situations the two types of determinants are typically so intertwined that it is often extremely difficult, and frequently impossible, to separate one from the other. It makes sense then to sum up the determinants of sexual behavior in terms of a *biosocial complex.*

This chapter has tended to emphasize the first part of that complex—the "bio"—because of the wealth of carefully controlled experimental data available, especially from animal studies. At the same time, we should be on guard against hasty conclusions about biological determinants. Consider, for example, the clear-cut anatomical and physiological events of puberty. These occur earlier in the female than in the male, and yet the arousal of sexuality in the two sexes often follows a different pattern, which may be largely culturally deter-

mined. Sexual arousal in the young female may be inhibited by cultural factors—her anticipation of future domesticity and childbearing, for example, or by a double standard that encourages sexuality in young males but not in females. Here, biological processes, sociocultural expectations, and individual cognitive factors are involved in a mutually interactive system in which each component influences the other.

At the same time, the importance of biology should not be underestimated. This is especially true when anatomical and/or hormonal differences seem to determine behavior (as in untreated androgenital syndrome or in males with inadequate

FOCUS: The Nature of Orgasm

Only in recent years has science begun to explore one of the most intense, gratifying, and least-understood human experiences—orgasm. The word itself is derived from the Greek *orgasmos*, which means "to swell," "to be lustful." Physiologically, orgasm is typified by an explosive release of built-up neuromuscular tensions; psychologically, it can be characterized by a great variety of feelings, ranging from mild relief to something approaching a mystical experience.

Interestingly, there appears to be no direct evidence that the subjective experience of orgasm differs consistently between males and females. Ellen Vance and Nathaniel Wagner (1976) asked a group of men and women to submit written descriptions of their orgasms. These descriptions were then given to a panel of qualified "judges" who lacked any overt clues as to the gender of each writer. The judges were unable to identify which descriptions came from men and which came from women.

Several important differences between the physiological responses of males and females during orgasm are apparent. The most obvious is that male orgasm typically is accompanied by ejaculation of seminal fluid. This must be preceded by emission of semen into the urethra from the testes and semen-producing glands by the contraction of involuntary muscles. Another difference is the occurrence of uterine contractions in the female, which has not yet been studied systematically. Masters and Johnson (1966) have established the capacity of the female, but not the male, to show multiple orgasms. Many females can go from one orgasm to another without pausing for the intervening refractory period characteristic of males and during which the male is

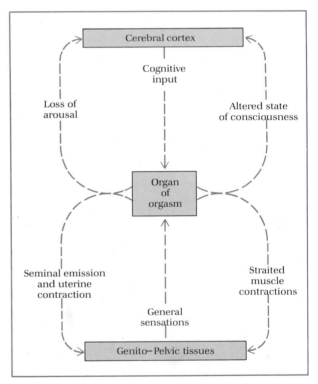

The bipolar hypothesis of orgasmic psychophysiology in men and women.

not capable of sexual arousal.

This picture of apparent differences has been complicated by a recent report from California of men who seem capable of multiple orgasms, presumably after self-training (Robbins and Jensen,

testosterone production by their testes). Yet the cognitive evaluation of these differences may exert a crucial influence on sexual behavior rather than, or in addition to, the biology itself.

We can view biological factors less as determinants of sexual behavior than as constraints that often can be overcome if the environmental influence or the individual's will is strong enough. Thus, some people can fantasize to orgasm, and paraplegics often learn to enjoy sex despite the loss of genital sensation. Seldom must we regard biological factors as preordaining sexual behavior; they are always open to influence by cognitive, sociocultural, and learning factors.

SUMMARY

1. Three major figures dominate the short history research into human sexual behavior: Sigmund Freud, Alfred Kinsey, and William Masters. Freud based his theories on his observations of his patients in psychoanalysis. He formulated five stages of infantile psychosexual development in which the libido shifts successively from the oral, to the anal, and to the phallic stages. These stages are followed by a period of latency which is followed in

---

1976). As in the female, the series of orgasms may continue to ten or more without a refractory period, which is characterized by loss of erection and sexual arousal. Each orgasm shows characteristic contractions of the pelvic regions, including the penile muscles, but complete ejaculation of semen is found only during the final orgasm in the series. In other words, they can experience continued orgasms so long as seminal emission is prevented from occurring.

One explanation for multiple orgasms in men can be found in a new hypothesis proposed by Julian Davidson (1980). This theory, termed the *bipolar hypothesis*, suggests that male orgasm is linked to two different neural mechanisms (see Figure 11.7). One neural mechanism fires "upward" to activate the altered state of consciousness that is the essence of the orgasmic experience. The other "pole" of this mechanism fires "downward" to produce the strong pelvic (skeletal or striated) muscle contractions. The second neural mechanism Davidson hypothesizes also has two components: one is responsible for complete seminal emission via the smooth muscles controlled by the sympathetic nervous system, and the other causes the brain to activate the loss of sexual arousal after emission. Thus according to this theory, it is the seminal emission that brings on the refractory period after a single male orgasm.

Davidson also has suggested that the bipolar hypothesis might be extended to female orgasm. He notes first that females lack seminal emission and have the greater capacity for multiple orgasm. Then he points out a direct analogy between seminal emission and uterine contractions. The contraction of the uterus is controlled by the same nerve that

triggers seminal emission in the male. It is therefore possible that the nature of the uterine contractions may distinguish multiple and single orgasms (orgasms followed by a refractory period) in women.

If so, the bipolar hypothesis might also help clarify an issue first raised by Freud, who postulated two types of female orgasm, clitoral and vaginal. According to Freud (1905), vaginal orgasms were more satisfying and more "mature" than orgasms produced by stimulation of the clitoris, and this view became an important part of the psychoanalytic perspective on female sexuality. Kinsey (1953) questioned this. He asked five gynecologists to test the sensitivity to touch of various areas of the external and internal genitalia. Although all of the women responded with great sensitivity to touching the clitoris, the vaginal wall and cervix were largely insensitive to tactile stimulation. In fact, the vaginal wall and cervix have so few nerve endings that surgery is sometimes possible there without anesthesia.

Masters and Johnson (1966) in their laboratory studies could find no physiological evidence for the existence of both clitoral and vaginal orgasms. They pointed out that the thrusts of the penis during intercourse provide indirect stimulation to the clitoris; hence, perhaps all female orgasms are clitoral.

Nevertheless, many women seem to prefer one or the other mode of stimulation to orgasm. Davidson speculates that deep penile thrusting may induce uterine contractions, activating the same neural mechanism that causes seminal emission and loss of arousal in men. This could result in a more satisfying orgasm that at least temporarily terminates arousal, in a way similar to the refractory period after male orgasm.

early adolescence by the genital stage. Kinsey and his associates used the survey-questionnaire method to ask thousands of Americans about their sex lives. Masters and his associate, Virginia Johnson, based their findings on laboratory observation of the physiology of sexual behavior.

2. One of the most striking aspects of sexual behavior, both human and animal, is its wide variety; however, most sexual behaviors evolved principally to serve the aim of reproduction of the species. Reproductive strategy in humans and many other animals usually dictates sexual monogamy, although the small mammals on which most research is done are generally promiscuous. In many species, polygyny (one male mating with several females) is the rule; polyandry (one female mating with a number of males) occurs rarely. The evolution of genital anatomy seems also to have followed reproductive strategy. Humans exhibit evolutionary adaptations consistent with the maximization of sexual pleasure.

3. The value systems of different cultures shape vastly different norms of sexual behavior. The classic studies by Bronislaw Malinowski of the people of the Trobriand Islands and by William Davenport of the East Bay Society demonstrated striking differences in sexual norms between neighboring cultures, as did the studies by Friedl of neighboring tribes in New Guinea.

4. Within a single culture, many variations from a general norm of sexual behavior exist. Within our own society, the sexual revolution of the last few decades has produced profound changes in our cultural norms regarding sex: the increase in premarital intercourse, particularly among females, is the most dramatic of those changes.

5. People seek sexual stimulation from the cradle to the grave. Four broad phases of individual life cycles of sexual behavior have been described: early childhood, prepuberty, puberty and beyond, and the declining years. Episodes of spontaneous sexual arousal are found in both sexes during the first year of life; many older people are sexually active well into their eighties.

6. The biological study of sexual behavior focuses primarily on hormones, chemicals that are manufactured by the endocrine glands and released into the bloodstream. The increase in the production of sex hormones at the onset of puberty is responsible for the emergence of primary and secondary sexual characteristics.

7. The production of sexual hormones is essentially a three-stage process:

a. The hypothalamus sends chemical signals via blood vessels that connect it to the so-called master gland, the pituitary.

b. The pituitary responds by manufacturing and releasing into the bloodstream two protein hormones, the luteinizing hormone (LH) and follicle-stimulating hormone (FSH), both of which are responsible for release of spermatozoa and eggs from the testes and ovaries (gonads). These two hormones are collectively called gonadotropins.

c. Gonadotropins also stimulate the production of sex hormones in the gonads. These gonadal hormones are called steroids, a class of hormones that also includes cortisone from the adrenal cortex. The main steroids produced by the male's testes are androgens, the most important of which is testosterone. The primary steroids produced in the female's ovaries are estrogens and progesterone. Small amounts of male sex hormones are produced in the female ovaries, and small amounts of female sex hormones in the male testes.

8. The steroid sex hormones in females are produced in cyclically varying amounts and are responsible for regulation of many aspects of its regulation of reproduction, including the production of eggs (ova), menstruation, and the fertility cycle. In most mammals the female gonadal (ovarian) hormones influence mating behavior by stimulating (and in some situations inhibiting) attractivity, receptivity, and proceptivity. In humans, however, the role of female hormones in sexual behavior seems to be minor, at least as indicated from the limited studies to date.

9. Sex hormones in the male are produced at a fairly constant rate, consistent with the noncyclic nature of male reproductive function, which they are instrumental in regulating. Their role in mediating sexual behavior is clearly established.

10. Current research suggests that male sex hormones influence the action of nerve cells in the brain, especially in the hypothalamus, which controls masculine sex behavior. This evidence comes principally from animal research.

11. The roles of the two sexes have begun to change radically in our society with profound implications for sexual behavior. Among subprimate species, and

among certain primates, biological determination predominates in sexual behavior. Learning, culture, and environment seem to play a much larger role in determining human sexual behavior. Animal research has demonstrated what may be called the reversed Adam principle: the superimposition of masculine anatomy, physiology, and behavior on a basic female pattern. Research indicates that this mechanism obtains in humans for the development of sexual anatomy but much less profoundly for behavior than in animals. As science delves more deeply into male and female sexual behavior in humans, it becomes apparent that the similarities exceed the differences.

12. Homosexuals are men and women who prefer sexual partners of their own sex. At this point, research has not established a hormonal or genetic disposition toward homosexuality; psychological explanations for homosexuality focus on the role of early experience. In recent years a majority of psy-chiatrists have come to believe that homosexuality is not a pathological condition; rather, they view it as an alternate preference.

13. Transsexuals have strong feelings of gender identity with the opposite sex. A male transsexual, for example, typically reports that he feels like "a woman in a man's body." Current research does not show consistent biological explanations for transsexualism; psychologists focus on early learning as its basis.

14. Sexual behavior is both biologically and culturally determined. The two types of determinants are typically so intertwined that it is difficult, and sometimes impossible, to separate one from the other. The determinants of sexual behavior may be summed up as a biosocial complex.

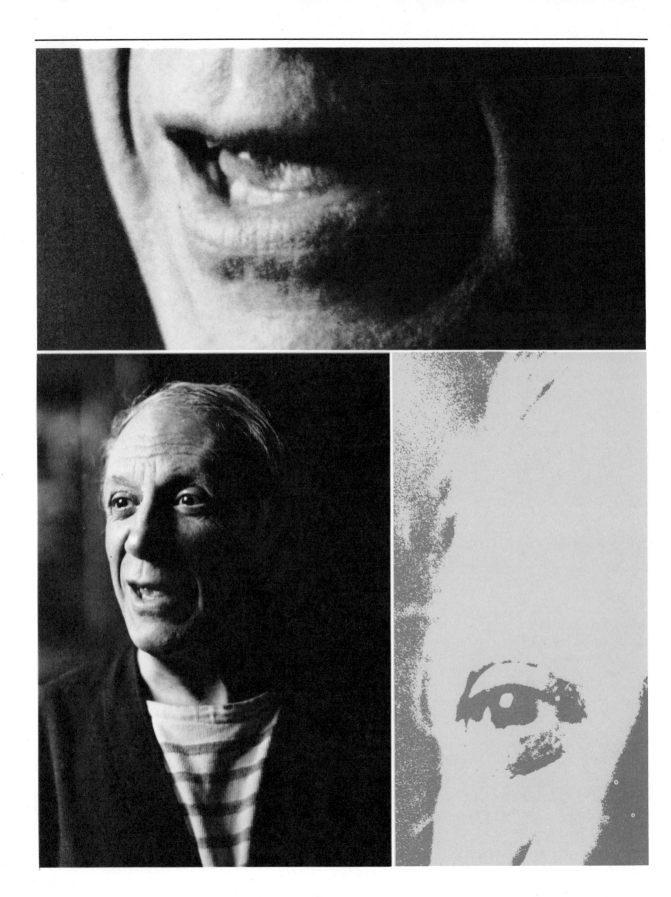

Part Five
Personality and Intelligence

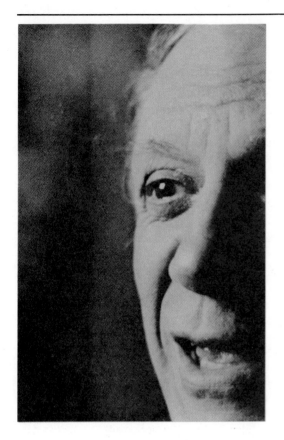

Chapter 12
Personality and Its Assessment

Assume you have taken a test that purports to assess your personality. After a few days, the examiner sends you the following report: "You tend to be critical of yourself and have a strong need to have other people like you. Although you tend to be pretty well controlled on the outside, you frequently feel insecure inside. At times your sexual adjustment has been a problem for you. You like a certain amount of change in your life and become unhappy when you are hemmed in by restrictions and limitations. Sometimes you feel sociable and outgoing. At other times you tend to be very reserved and inward-looking."

If you feel this description sums up your personality, you are not alone. In experiments in which students were given an assessment report with statements like these, most of the students said the assessment fit them quite well—even though each student was given an identical report (Snyder and Larson, 1972).

This is an illustration of what psychologist Paul Meehl (1966) called the "Barnum effect" in personality description. The great circus showman, P. T. Barnum, believed that entrepreneurial success required the provision of a little something for everybody. The personality description has a little something for everyone because it is composed of statements that are true about almost everyone.

Astrologers, fortune-tellers, and others who purport to analyze personality and predict behavior have long known the power of the Barnum effect. They construct a series of general statements and make the client feel the description is prepared especially for him or her.

Any truly scientific theory of personality must avoid the easy temptations of the Barnum effect. A theory of personality must distinguish what makes each of us unique and explain why we behave as we do. This is an enormous task, one that encompasses all branches of psychology. Consider the breadth of the definition of *personality:* the characteristic way in which a person thinks and behaves as he or she adapts to the environment. This includes visible behavior patterns as well as less apparent but relatively enduring characteristics such as values, motives, attitudes, abilities, and self-image.

Accurately characterizing people and predicting their behavior is difficult; even the origin of the word *personality* suggests its elusive quality. Its

The root of *personality* is the Greek word *persona,* meaning "mask." In early Greek drama the actors wore masks that represented the characters being portrayed.

root is *persona*, from the Greek word meaning "mask." Greek actors wore stylized masks to represent the characters they were playing.

None of us is what he or she appears to be at first sight, and even our most intimate friends have great difficulty in discerning the whole of our personality. This is dramatically evident in the lives of many great women and men whose abilities were long hidden from their own families. Charles Darwin, who developed the theory of evolution by natural selection, is a classic example of a late bloomer. "You care for nothing but shooting, dogs and rat-catching," his father once told him, "and you will be a disgrace to yourself and your family (Good, 1974)."

Although scientists have developed a number of theories of personality and many methods for assessing it, none is so all-encompassing that it can predict or explain the genius of a Darwin—or the uniqueness of any one of us. Nonetheless, personality theories have furthered our understanding of individual behavior and have had profound practical consequences, influencing how we raise children, why we are hired, and even how we use everyday language.

In this chapter we will examine the most influential theories of personality. These theories, in their assumptions about behavior and its development, fall into four general categories: psychodynamic, dispositional, phenomenological, and social learning theories. Each of the four perspectives we will consider reflects a distinguishably different way of viewing the complexity of personality. For each of these approaches we will describe the relevant theories and techniques for assessing personality. We will also consider in each category an example of research aimed at testing the theories and then discuss key issues.

Personality theorists are concerned with questions of consistency. They want to know why it is that a particular individual seems to behave in strikingly similar ways in a variety of different situations or on different occasions. In addition, personality theorists are interested in uniqueness. They want to know why is it that each individual's patterns of behavior and styles of interaction seem distinctive and singular. Why do two people in highly standardized situations behave in strikingly different ways? Much of what we will discuss in this chapter addresses the broad questions of how individual behavior is influenced by situational factors and by unique personality characteristics or past experiences. As we shall see, each of the approaches we discuss has different answers to these questions and frames then in different ways.

Psychodynamic Theories

One of the first comprehensive approaches to personality and its development was formulated by Sigmund Freud. His insistence that behavior is determined by the interplay of events and conflicts within the inner life of the individual is central to his approach and to that of other dynamic theories.

A crucial aspect of Freud's approach was his emphasis on psychological processes that are not ordinarily available to a person's consciousness. Freud saw evidence of such processes in his practice as a psychiatrist. Patients under hypnosis, for example, were able to recall traumatic events of childhood that normally eluded their conscious memories (Freud, 1916/1961, 1916/1963).

From these observations and from his later experiences with patients in psychoanalysis, Freud postulated three different provinces of mental activity (Freud, 1900/1953, 1933/ 1965):

Conscious mental activity includes all those thoughts and feelings that are being experienced at the moment. Although easily accessible, this activity represents only a small fraction of mental life.

Preconscious mental activity refers to all those thoughts and feelings that are outside immediate awareness but easily available—for example, a telephone number that can be summoned at will.

Unconscious mental activity is a vast reservoir of childhood and current memories, wishes and impulses, fears and hopes that lie beyond awareness. They are kept there, Freud believed, by a censoring process that protects the person from unacceptable wishes or threatening impulses. Although the unconscious could not be directly examined, its presence could be inferred from dreams, through hypnosis, and in the free association process of psychoanalysis. Of these three types of mental activity, Freud was convinced that the unconscious played the dominant role in shaping personality.

A second aspect of Freud's theory that is important for our understanding of personality from a dynamic viewpoint is his view of development. Freud believed that the degree to which the child was able to gratify—or was frustrated in gratifying—

its biological needs was crucial in shaping the child's behavior in the world of people and relationships.

Stages of Personality Development

Freud was one of the first investigators to insist that the early years were decisive in the formation of personality. Certain motives, aims, or drives may be arrested, or fixated, early in childhood because of overindulgence or deprivation, said Freud, and these *fixations* remain in the unconscious, shaping bevavior throughout life.

Freud discerned four distinct stages of development: *oral*, *anal*, *phallic*, and *genital* as shown in Table 12.1 (Freud, 1905/1962). As these names imply, Freud placed a great deal of emphasis on biological forces in the early shaping of personality. To Freud, not only the genitals but also the mouth and anus were erogenous (sensitive to sexual stimulation). The pleasure derived from each of the erogenous zones is related to one general source—the *libido* or energy of the sexual instincts. In each stage the libido focuses on the pleasure-giving zone that characterizes that stage. A person's experiences at each stage leave an imprint that influences future development.

Oral Stage   During the first year or two of life, Freud argued, the primary erogenous zone is the mouth. Children gratify their hunger through sucking and then through biting. A child who becomes fixated at this stage—perhaps through early weaning—may later develop an *oral personality*, which may be characterized by oral aggression expressed through verbal hostility and feelings of deprivation or even gullibility.

Anal Stage   During the second and third year, the anus becomes a focus of discomfort or erotic pleasure. If the parents are strict and harsh in their methods of imposing toilet training, the child may hold back the feces. Fixation during this stage may later result in a *retentive personality*, which is characterized by overconcern with cleanliness or saving. On the other hand, a child praised for performance on the toilet may later become productive and creative in adult life, perhaps even as a writer or artist.

Phallic Stage   During the fourth and fifth years, the child's erotic interests shift to the genital organs. Sexual feelings are directed toward the parent of the opposite sex. The boy wishes to possess his mother and displace his father, a condition Freud called the *Oedipus complex*, after the legendary Greek king who murdered his father and married his mother. The boy associates sensations from his genital organs with his affection for his mother and fears his father will remove the offending organ. Freud called this fear *castration anxiety* and said it leads the boy to repress his lust for his mother and to identify with his father. According to Freud, the Oedipus complex takes a different form for girls—a form sometimes referred to as the *Electra complex*, after the princess in a Greek play who helped bring about the death of her mother. She blames her mother for the fact that she lacks a prominent exterior sex organ and desires her father because he has such an organ. Freud called these feelings *penis envy*. He said that problems arising during the phallic stage—for example, if the mother rejects her son's love, or the father disappoints his daughter by

TABLE 12.1   Stages of Psychosexual Activity in the Psychoanalytic Perspective

STAGE OF PSYCHOSEXUAL DEVELOPMENT	EROGENOUS ZONE	PROTOTYPICAL ACTIVITY	LATER PERSONALITY
Oral Stage (0–2 years)	Mouth	Sucking; incorporation; biting	Oral-incorporative; "sucker"; aggressive; oral sadistic
Anal Stage (2–3 years)	Anal sphincter	Urge for elimination; strict toilet training rewarded	Anal-retentive or expulsive; productive; creative
Phallic (4–5 years)	Genital organs	Masturbation; autoerotic activity; castration fear; penis envy	Oedipus complex; Electra complex; later relations with men *and* women
Genital (puberty-adulthood)	Genital organs	Sexual desire; sexual relations	Socialization; genuine friendships; stable, mature, long-term relationships; vocational choice

Source: Richard Price, *Abnormal Behavior*, 2nd ed. (New York: Holt, Rinehart and Winston, 1978).

leaving home—can result in permanent damage to the child's sense of self and sexual identity.

Genital Stage   After a period of five or six years of latency, the child enters a final active stage of psychosexual development. During adolescence, the self-oriented erotic concerns of the first three stages of development are directed outward onto other persons, usually of the opposite sex. The child becomes concerned with vocational choice, socialization, and peer relationships.

As we have seen, most stages of development carry potential crises for the child. Successful resolution of each crisis, Freud believed, was necessary for the child to arrive at a reasonably healthy personality in adulthood. Furthermore, how each stage is resolved was important for the shaping of the adult character or personality of the individual.

The Ego Psychologists

Many of the scientists who gravitated to Freud and his revolutionary view of personality later broke with him over theoretical issues. Usually, the differences revolved around Freud's belief that sex and other biological drives were the primary forces in shaping personality.

In the United States, influential theorists such as Karen Horney, Erich Fromm, and Erik Erikson were called *ego psychologists* because they felt the conscious ego was more important in shaping personality than were the instinctual drives of the id. Although the neo-Freudians retained many of the basic assumptions of Freud's dynamic theory, with its emphasis on unconscious processes and a fixed sequence of personality development, they were also greatly influenced by the American social sciences. Cultural and social factors, they suggested, played a far greater role than had been granted by the biological determinism of Freud.

Fromm insisted that differences in the social environments markedly affect personality development. He suggested, for example, that a capitalistic society produces different personality types than would a "humanistic, communitarian socialism (Fromm, 1947)." Horney rejected much of Freud's thinking about women. Many years before the modern women's liberation movement, she detected male chauvinism in some of Freud's teachings. She pointed out, for example, that the idea of penis envy may not be built into women biologically but only reflects the favored position of men in most cultures (Horney, 1939).

Erikson, a Viennese who spent most of his life in the United States, proposed a life cycle of personality development, comprising eight distinct sequential stages that differs substantially from the Freudian view (see Chapter 6). Unlike Freud's theory of psychosexual development, which focuses on early life events, Erikson's stages extend into adolescence, young adulthood, parenthood, and aging. In addition, each of the stages is characterized by personal or interpersonal crises that are more psychosocial than biological in nature (Erikson, 1963, 1968).

The most familiar of the developmental conflicts postulated by Erikson is the *identity crisis* of adolescence (Erikson, 1963). At puberty, the youth must face both the sudden bloom of sexuality and the need to adopt the roles to be played in adult society. Erikson summed up this identity crisis by citing the teenager Biff in Arthur Miller's play *Death of a Salesman*: "I just can't take hold, Mom," says Biff. "I can't take hold of some kind of a life." For all the emphasis on social processes, however, Erikson and the other ego psychologists still retain Freud's essential focus on the internal dynamics of personality development.

Jung's Analytical Approach

Carl Jung, a Swiss psychiatrist, was one of Freud's earliest disciples, but Jung soon broke away to develop his own version of Freud's dynamic theory of personality (Jung, 1916/1969, 1963). Jung called his new approach *analytical psychology*. It differed from the Freudian view on several important issues. Jung thought sexual forces and the Freudian concern with the early development of personality and the understanding of past childhood traumas were far less significant in shaping personality. Jung stressed the present conflicts and problems of his patients during therapy and believed that what he called *individuation*—psychological maturation—was a lifelong process (Jung, 1939/1969, 1916/1969).

Perhaps the most significant difference, however, was Jung's identification of an additional construct. He believed that all of us possess not only a *personal unconscious*—similar to the Freudian repository of forgotten or suppressed memories—but also share in the *collective unconscious*. He defined this as "the all-controlling deposit of ancestral experi-

365

ence from untold millions of years, the echo of prehistoric world events in which each century adds an infinitesimally small amount of variation and differentiation." These ancient memories take the form of *archetypes*, master patterns of images that are transmitted from generation to generation. Examples of archetypes include such concepts as Mother, a Supreme Being, the Hero, and a sense of wholeness. Symbolic manifestations of these same archetypes, Jung said, can be found in all human cultures—in religion, in mythology, and even in a person's own dreams (Jung, 1917/1966).

The interpretation of dreams was seen by both Jung and Freud as a source of data for understanding personality. But while Freud considered dreams a form of wish fulfillment, Jung perceived them as an unconscious effort to resolve personality problems. By bringing the forces of the personal unconscious and the collective unconscious into harmony with the conscious self, Jung believed, an individual can achieve psychological integration.

Psychodynamic Approaches to Assessment

Given their emphasis on the unconscious, dynamic theorists must necessarily penetrate that domain if they are to assess an individual's personality. One method used by Freud and his followers is *free association* (Freud, 1913/1958). In this process, which typically takes place during psychoanalysis, the person is instructed to give his or her thoughts complete freedom and to report all the daydreams, feelings, and images that flash through the mind no matter how incoherent or meaningless they might seem. These fragments are believed to provide a glimpse into the unconscious elements of personality.

A second major method espoused by Freud, Jung, and others is *dream interpretation*. Freud called dreams "the royal road to the unconscious (1900/1953)." He believed dreams had two primary psychological functions: they fulfilled wishes and they served as safety valves to release unconscious tensions. In both functions, he suggested, dreams give form to desires and impulses that would be unacceptable to the dreamer's conscious awareness.

Freud made a distinction between two different levels of dream content (1925/1961). He referred to the *manifest content*, which is what we remember about our dreams. *Latent content*, on the other hand, is the underlying psychic material that led to the manifest content. For example, a woman may

dream of kissing her husband; this is the manifest content. However, the latent content may, in fact, involve the repressed desire to kiss her father.

Often the latent content of dreams is cloaked in symbols—objects or ideas that stand for something else. In dynamic theory, symbols usually substitute for unconscious desires that are threatening to the ego or superego. Thus, the appearance of children in a dream may be interpreted as symbols for the genital organs. Dream interpretation typically involves a description of the dream followed by the subject's free associations about the content.

The assessment of personality through free association and dream interpretation is a lengthy process that depends largely on the intuition of the clinician.

Another major method of assessment used by dynamic theorists, *projective tests*, aims at preserving clinical judgments while providing a more standardized and objective means of glimpsing the unconscious. These tests require the person to respond to a series of deliberately ambiguous stimuli;

Photographic montage representing a typical dream situation. According to Freud, dreams serve to fulfill wishes and to act as safety valves for the release unconscious tensions.

they are called projective because it is assumed that in interpreting the stimuli, the person will project hidden aspects of personality onto them.

The most familiar projective technique, the *Rorschach Test*, was developed in 1921 by the Swiss psychiatrist Hermann Rorschach. As a boy Rorschach dabbled so much in ink sketches that he was nicknamed Kleck—Swiss-German for inkblot. Appropriately, his test consists of a series of inkblots on ten separate cards (see Figure 12.1 and Plate 15). Subjects look at the inkblots one at a time and tell the examiner what they see there—bugs, bats, humans, clouds, or whatever else they see. As in dream interpretation, the examiner looks for symbolic relationships to particular personality characteristics. If the subject sees masks among the

inkblots, for example, this might be interpreted as revealing a preoccupation with the outward appearance of things. The examiner may also take into account other factors such as whether the subject responds to the entire inkblot or to only a part of it and whether the subject seems cooperative or defensive in response.

Evaluation of the Psychodynamic Approach

No approach to personality has so profoundly affected the modern view of human nature as Freud's dynamic perspective. His descriptions of unconscious motives and of early childhood development have penetrated every aspect of modern life from child-rearing practices to film and literature. Even the phrases associated with Freudian theory—unconscious, ego, Oedipus complex, Freudian slip, free association—are embedded in the fabric of everyday conversation.

The undeniable impact notwithstanding, close evaluation of Freud's personality theory raises a number of perplexing issues. We will briefly examine one such issue—the status of the psychodynamic view as a scientific theory.

The dynamic view as a scientific theory has received criticism from contemporary theorists. One line of criticism focuses on the fact that the bulk of support for psychoanalytic theory derives from clinical evidence. Such evidence is subject to bias by the clinician. It does not tell us whether the childhood traumas reported by the patient actually occurred. It makes no provision for establishing that the reported childhood traumas actually led to the personality characteristics in question. And it makes no attempt to assess whether reported changes in the patient's behavior might not have occurred over time without psychoanalytic therapy.

Ernest Nagel (1959) has evaluated psychoanalysis as a scientific theory in terms of three criteria and found it lacking. He cites its inability to produce "if-then" statments that predict explicit consequences following from the theory, its failure to define clearly such concepts as the Oedipus complex, and its vague formulations that permit manipulation to fit the evidence at hand.

Another way of stating Nagel's criticism is that dynamic theory contains assertions that are true in every conceivable case—and hence by definition

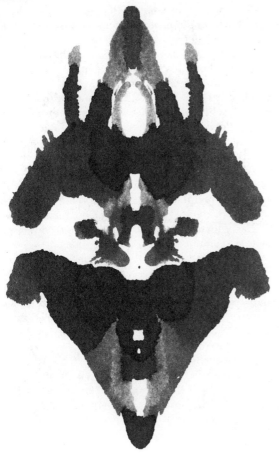

FIGURE 12.1 The Rorschach test uses inkblots of the type illustrated for assessing personality. Typical responses might be to see animals or human beings in the pattern.

The interpretation of projective tests designed to measure personality is subject to a number of problems. Not the least of these is the preconceptions that the clinician may bring to the task of assessing test results. Loren J. and Jean Chapman (1967) have demonstrated how laypeople as well as experienced clinicians can fall into the trap of using "common sense" in the interpretation of projective test results. For example, in assessing the results of the Draw-a-Person test, clinicians and laypeople may believe that men who are concerned about their manliness will draw pictures of broad-shouldered, muscular physiques or they may believe that people who are particularly suspicious will emphasize the eyes in their drawings. The Chapmans found that these beliefs occurred even though such correlations did not actually exist in the clinical materials developed for their experiment.

This tendency of observers to find "illusory correlations" between preconceived projective-test indicators and personality traits was further investigated by the Chapmans (1969) in a series of studies based on interpretation of the widely used Rorschach Test. The personality trait chosen for the experiments was male homosexuality. Research has shown that, although clinicians commonly report a number of indicators of male homosexuality in their assessment of Rorschach results, only two indicators are valid signs of it. One sign is the client's description of a particular inkblot card as a "human or animal—contorted, monstrous, or threatening." The second sign is the description of another card as a "human or humanized animal."

In the first stage of these new experiments, the Chapmans sent questionnaires to a number of practicing clinicians asking them what signs of male homosexuality they had observed in their Rorschach results. Of the clinicians queried, 32 indicated they had seen the Rorschach results of a number of men with homosexual problems. Of these 32, only two listed either of the signs that research has shown to be valid. Most of the clinicians listed at least one of five signs, such as "human or animal anal content" or "feminine clothing," that research has found to be invalid.

These invalid signs are ones that appear to have a popular "commonsense" association with male homosexuality. That this is so was confirmed by the Chapmans when they asked a group of undergraduate students to rate these signs, along with the two valid signs and a number of other filler items, for the strength of their associative connection to homosexuality.

The second phase of the Chapmans' experiments was designed to determine whether laypeople would make the same errors of diagnosis as those evidenced in the survey of clinicians. A total of 693 students in introductory psychology served as the subjects in three different experiments.

In one of these experiments, subjects were shown 30 Rorschach cards, each of which contained the purported response of a fictitious patient, along with two symptoms of this patient's emotional problems. The fictitious patient's responses were rigged so that they fell into five different categories: an invalid sign such as "feminine clothing," two valid signs of male homosexuality, and two filler categories—geographic features and food. The purported symptoms included two of the following: "He has sexual feelings toward other men." "He believes other people are plotting against him." "He feels sad and depressed much of the time." "He has strong feelings of inferiority." The responses and symptoms were deliberately paired in such a way that there was no valid relationship between them.

The subjects, after viewing each of the Rorschach cards for one minute, were given a questionnaire listing the four symptoms and asking if the subject had noticed "any general kind of thing that was seen most often by men with this problem." If so, they were to list that "kind of thing" and an example.

The results confirmed the prediction of the researchers: subjects reported that they had observed the five invalid signs as accompanying homosexual problems more than any other category of Rorschach response. By contrast, the valid signs of male homosexuality were not reported as correlates any more often than were the two filler categories. In short, these laypeople demonstrated the same errors of diagnosis as had the clinicians, even though the perceived relationships did not actually exist in the Rorschach materials. They were illusory correlates based on "commonsense" preconceptions.

Another experiment in the Chapmans' series is of particular interest. The researchers used essentially the same procedure that we have described but eliminated the five invalid signs of male homosexuality. In this instance, the subjects nearly doubled their accuracy in reporting valid correlates. The results of this experiment suggest to the Chapmans that preconceptions—the illusory correlates of male homosexuality—can "blind the observer to the presence of valid correlates of the symptom." This appears to be true whether the observer is a layperson or a highly experienced clinician.

cannot be disproved or proved. Bert Kaplan (1964) singles out one such idea from Freudian theory—the assertion that boys are sexually attracted to their mothers. If boys express this attraction, it fits the theory. "If on the contrary," observes Kaplan, "they behave as though their mothers were detestable, this conduct only indicates a reaction against their own forbidden desires, and again the claims holds good; so it is true no matter what."

Many broad formulations of personality share this difficulty. Sweeping theories that attempt to capture universal truths about human personality are extremely difficult to test empirically, and the dynamic view is no exception.

Dispositional Theories

A second major approach to understanding personality assumes that people have prevailing internal tendencies to behave in certain predictable ways. All of us, without quite realizing that we are dispositional theorists, tend to make that same assumption in our everyday judgments about people. We are constantly categorizing people in terms of a few characteristics that seem to typify them: "She has a pleasant disposition," or "He's the moody type." And having classified people, we tend to expect their future behavior to fit into that category.

Dispositional theories are of several kinds. One attempts to relate a person's physical or character type to his or her behavior. This view is familiar in the common assumption that a fat person, for example, is likely to be jolly. A second dispositional approach proposes to discover certain traits, such as aggressiveness, as the principal factors in personality. Finally, a third dispositional approach assumes that an understanding of individual needs, such as the need for love or respect, and their patterning will provide us with the clearest understanding of underlying personality dispositions.

Typological Theories

The possibility of a link between physical makeup and personality has long fascinated scientists. Nearly 2,500 years ago, the Greek physician Hippocrates suggested that biochemistry shaped personality. He proposed four basic human temperaments corresponding to four body humours, or fluids: happy or sanguine (blood), hot tempered or choleric (yellow bile), sad or melancholic (black bile), and sluggish or phlegmatic (phlegm).

Much later, in the nineteenth century, scientists investigated associations between behavior and measurable physical characteristics. The founder of phrenology, Franz Josef Gall, thought bumps on an individual's skull were clues to personality (Gall and Spurzheim, 1810-1819). It remained, however, for William Sheldon to undertake the first systematic study of personality and physical types.

Sheldon's Somatotypical Approach In the 1940s, Sheldon conducted an extensive study in which 4,000 male college students were photographed from the front, side, and rear. (Sheldon, 1942, 1954). After examining the photographs, Sheldon concluded that there were three basic kinds of body structure and physique, which he called *somatotypes* (see Figure 12.2). His three somatotypes were *endomorph* (soft and round), *mesomorph* (sturdy and muscular), and *ectomorph* (thin and fragile).

Then, by studying other male subjects through interviews and observation, Sheldon developed his Scale of Temperament, which consisted of patterns of personality traits that seemed to characterize his subjects. Finally, in an attempt to find correlations between his somatotypes and temperament, he studied 200 male volunteers over a five-year period.

Sheldon reported striking correlations and, interestingly, they tended to confirm popular wisdom about such matters. The soft and round endomorphs were pleasure-loving, sociable, and relaxed (riscerotonic). Sturdy and muscular mesomorphs were outgoing, assertive, and dominating (somatotonic). Thin and fragile ectomorphs were inhibited, intense, and inward-looking (cerebrotonic).

Sheldon's somatotyping scheme did not purport to find pure endomorphs, mesomorphs, or ectomorphs. Instead, the person was somatotyped by assigning three numbers, each ranging from 1 to 7, that represented the relative strength of each basic type. A muscular person might be rated 1-7-1, thus nearing the somatotype of a pure mesomorph. A person of average physique could be somatotyped 4-4-4.

Although subsequent correlational studies have found some support for Sheldon's somatotypes (Brouwer, 1957; Hammond, 1957), the causes or mechanisms of the purported link between personality and physique have never clearly been

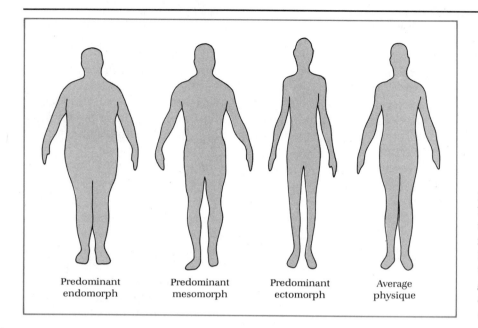

FIGURE 12.2 Sheldon's three basic somatotypes include the entomorph (soft and round), the mesomorph (sturdy and muscular), and the ectomorph (thin and fragile). The average physique is also shown for purposes of comparison.

Predominant endomorph | Predominant mesomorph | Predominant ectomorph | Average physique

established. Sheldon, who was the son of an animal breeder, believed the causes were genetic in origin. Indeed, he thought evidence of this genetic blueprint could be seen in the development of the human embryo and took his three somatotypes—endomorph, mesomorph, and ectomorph—from the names of three distinct layers of cells that develop respectively into the digestive system and internal organs (endomorph), bone and muscle (mesomorph), and the central nervous system (ectomorph). As these physical systems developed, Sheldon said, one became dominant, along with its associated personality type.

Obesity and Personality Experimental evidence in support of the various typological theories is rare. In the case of Sheldon's somatotypes, for example, most of the follow-up studies have been correlational in nature. One notable example is the comparison of nearly 500 pairs of boys, one delinquent and the other nondelinquent, which indicated a clear relationship with somatotype differences (Glueck and Glueck, 1950, 1956). The findings from this study show a much higher percentage of muscular mesomorphs and much lower percentage of thin ectomorphs among the delinquents than chance would dictate. This does not mean that most mesomorphs become delinquent, the more plausible interpretation is that a muscular body lends itself to a physical orientation that might manifest itself in aggressive, even antisocial, behavior.

Such correlational studies, like Sheldon's original work with somatotypes, tell us little about the processes that might link physique and personality. However, one fascinating line of experimental research exists that suggests some possible clues. This research, initially concerned with patterns of eating, was done by Stanley Schachter.

Schachter had no particular interest in furthering Sheldon's theory, but he was intrigued by the relationship between physiological and psychological states in emotionality. This interest attracted him to the results of an experiment that suggested that fat people tended to report hunger even in the absence of a normal physiological indicator of hunger—stomach contraction (Stunkard and Koch, 1964). The obese subjects said they were hungry, as Schachter (1971) later described it, no matter what the state of their stomachs.

Intrigued by this evidence of a link between a person's physique and behavior, Schachter conducted his own experiment, carefully varying the body types of the subjects and their state of physiological hunger (Schachter, Goldman, and Gordon, 1968). Some of the subjects were first fed roast beef sandwiches; others were not. Then, under the guise of a taste preference experiment, all the subjects were encouraged to try five kinds of crackers. Schachter found that, as might be expected, persons of normal weight ate considerably more crackers when their stomachs were empty than when they were full. But among the obese subjects, having eaten roast beef sandwiches first did not seem to reduce the number of crackers consumed. In fact, the obese subjects actually ate slightly more crackers after their stomachs had already been filled.

From this and other experiments, Schachter concluded that external cues, such as sight, smell and taste of food, rather than the state of the gut controlled the eating of fat people. He also began to suspect that fat people may also be more responsive to external stimuli in other kinds of behavior than are persons of normal weight.

To test this broader hypothesis, one of Schachter's students, Judith Rodin (1970), asked obese and normal subjects to perform a simple proofreading task. The environments varied according to the amount of distraction provided by tape recordings. As predicted by Schachter, the fat subjects were more prone to distraction and more responsive to external stimuli. However, in the absence of the distracting tapes, obese subjects were able to concentrate on their task even better than the normal subjects.

Whether such broad psychological dispositions can be linked to somatotype through further research remains to be seen. Of course, physical appearance can also affect the way in which others react to us and how we behave and feel about ourselves in social situations. Unraveling the relationship between physical type and personality will require disentangling a number of such factors.

Eysenck's Typological Approach to Personality

Another typological approach to personality is reflected in the extensive research and theory of H. J. Eysenck. Eysenck's approach is based on his belief, supported by elaborate research and sophisticated statistical methololudy, that there is a small number, perhaps no more than two or three, of underlying personality dimensions along which all people differ.

For a number of years, Eysenck (1967, 1975) has argued that one of the most important of these dimensions is that of *introversion* and *extraversion*. As the name implies, extraverts are, on the average, more sociable, active, lively, and excitable than introverts, who tend to be quieter, more reserved, and less sociable.

A second major personality dimension suggested by Eysenck is stability and instability. In general, this dimension reflects the degree to which a person is calm and even-tempered as opposed to being

moody and changeable. Figure 12.3 shows how Eysenck arranges these two dimensions to form four quadrants. These quadrants reflect a combination of introversion, extraversion, stability, and instability. Thus, in Eysenck's system, one may be a stable introvert or extravert or an unstable introvert or extravert.

In some of his research, Eysenck has suggested that a third factor, "psychoticism" may be an underlying third personality dimension reflecting insensitivity, oddness, hostility, and a lack of caring for others. Like many other dispositional theorists, Eysenck is concerned primarily with discovering a theoretical structure that provides for the arrangement of personality dimensions or traits so that any particular individual can be described using the terms of the system.

Trait Theories

As we suggested earlier, personality theorists are frequently concerned with developing theories of personality that help explain both the uniqueness of each individual and the fact that a person's be-

FIGURE 12.3 Eysenck's arrangement of the dimensions of personality is depicted by four quadrants that represent a combination of stability, instability, introversion, and extraversion.

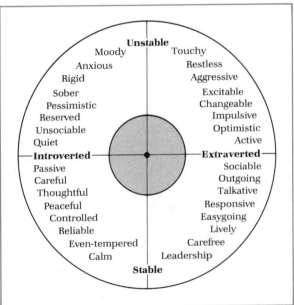

havior appears consistent across different occasions and situations. In some ways, this is the commonsense meaning of the term *personality*. In trying to understand and explain personal uniqueness and consistency, psychologists have used a variety of different theoretical strategies. One of the best known strategies has been to argue that individuals have traits that help explain the uniqueness and consistency that we observe in behavior.

Allport: Traits as the Basic Units of Personality

One of the most influential trait psychologists is Gordon Allport, who developed and clarified a classical trait approach to describing and understanding personality (1937, 1961, 1966). Searching for distinctive styles of expressive behavior and personality traits, he has conducted intensive studies of single individuals and studies of groups of people.

Allport's concept of trait begins in much the same way as our everyday language usage of the term. For Allport, a trait is a characteristic that summarizes a consistent pattern of behavior that we can observe in an individual. Thus, we may say that a person is "aggressive" if we notice that in a variety of situations he or she behaves in forceful and brusque ways and if on the various occasions when we meet the person we notice that he or she leaves us with the same impression of aggressiveness.

However, Allport went further than simply arguing for the existence of traits. He suggested that we could differentiate between traits of different kinds and that it would be theoretically useful to do so. For example, he argued that traits may vary with respect to how generally they pervade the whole personality: *cardinal traits* should be extremely strong characteristics that shape the whole personality, whereas *central traits* would be important but not pervasive. Finally, *secondary traits* would reflect very narrow patterns of behavior or habits and be of less theoretical importance.

In addition to arguing that personality traits could vary in their generality, Allport also distinguished between what he called *adaptive traits*, which are necessary to carry out a particular task situation, and *expressive traits*, which are particular styles of behavior. In fact, Allport and Phillip Vernon conducted a study, which they summarized in a book entitled *Studies in Expressive Movement* (1933). The interesting thing about this study is that Allport believed that the uniqueness of individuals and their consistency over time could be captured only if many tests and measures were administered to large numbers of people on a number of different occasions. The unique expressive style of individuals would be reflected in the way in which these test results correlated with each other. In their study they used 300 different performance measures, including tasks of drawing and counting, rhythmic tapping, and physical strength. Allport and Vernon administered them to 25 men in a series of research sessions. Allport believed that if he was right about the unique expressive styles of individuals, then certain test results should correlate with each other reflecting distinctive personality traits such as speed or vigor.

While some tests revealed substantial correlations if repeated in the same session or if repeated for the same individual on two occasions, the correlations for different tests presumably measuring the same trait were not as high as Allport had hoped. Nevertheless, the study was intended to show that there were patterns of expressive styles reflected in the behavior of individuals and that these patterns could be observed over occasions.

Allport believed that personality traits vary according to whether they are common to most people or whether they are unique to a particular individual. He believed that some traits are common; that is, that they can be observed in most people to a greater or lesser degree. Thus, for example, one might discover that the trait of submissiveness would be relatively normally distributed in the population, with some people demonstrating a great deal of dominance and others considerably less so. Indeed, many psychologists have developed tests that they believe measure traits existing in varying quantities in the population. This approach, which involves studying many people with a relatively limited number of measures or tests to discover whether there is substantial individual variation in a characteristic, is called *nomothetic research*.

However, perhaps more than most personality theorists, Allport was fascinated by the unique characteristics of individuals. He believed that some personality traits are unique to particular individuals and can best be understood by studying a single individual intensively over a long period of time. This type of study, *idiographic research*, is illustrated by one of Allport's best-known studies summarized in his book *Letters from Jenny* (1965). This intensive case study was based on the letters written by Jenny Masterson between the ages of 58 and 70, which trace her personal relationships with her son and the rest of her family in great detail. Allport believed that much could be learned about her unique characteristics by studying these letters both in terms of their content and style. His strategy was to ask a large number of judges to read the letter and then to have the judges assign nearly 200 descriptive adjectives to Jenny based on their overall impressions of her personality. In addition, a content analysis of the frequency with which Jenny used various words was done to provide still another strategy for observing unique traits that Jenny might display. From these two research strategies a variety of characteristics emerged that seemed important in describing Jenny's personality. They included traits of aggressiveness, possessiveness, sentimentality, and a certain self-centered and self-pitying quality as well as strong indications of drama and intensity. Through careful study of the stylistic and personal documents of a single person's life, Allport attempted to understand the uniqueness of a single personality.

Although Allport was interested in studying the unique characteristics of particular individuals, he believed all personality traits existed in the context of a hierarchical structure. His concept of the structure of personality depended greatly on thinking of it as organized at the most basic level in terms of very small units of behavior along with physiological units such as "neural cells." Figure 12.4 shows how Allport believed these smaller units could then be combined into increasingly larger units, which he called conditioned reflexive habits; then at a somewhat broader level, personal traits; and finally overarching "selves." Selves were broad patterns of personal traits that emerged in different ways in

different people in different situations. Thus, at a party we may show one "self," whereas at work we may show another. Nevertheless, all of these selves at the broadest level are organized into the total personality of the individual shown at the top of the figure.

Allport's dispositional theory of personality is particularly important to us because it is such a classic example of how the concept of trait has been used creatively to account for both the uniqueness and the consistency of personality.

Cattell: The Search for Source and Surface Traits Another important trait theorist is Raymond Cattell (1950, 1952, 1957), who also believed that traits are the fundamental components of personality. Indeed, Cattell claimed that it is possible to understand the underlying structure of personality by discovering which traits are fundamental in behavior and which are less important. He believed that fundamental traits, which he called *source traits*, are the roots of overt behavior and identified 16 of them (see Figure 12.5). He described *surface traits*, as clusters of overt behavior that seem to go together. Thus, nervous traits, such as trembling or stammering, may be surface traits that result from some more general source trait such as timidity or apprehensiveness.

Unlike Allport, who relied heavily on his own theoretical intuition and observational skills in deciding which traits are central and which are less so, Cattell believed that the structure of personality

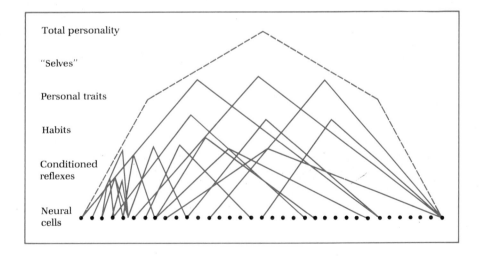

Total personality

"Selves"

Personal traits

Habits

Conditioned reflexes

Neural cells

FIGURE 12.4 Allport's concept of the structure of a total personality is based on a hierarchical structure. An individual's neural cells give rise to the formation of conditioned reflexes, which combine into habits. In turn, many habits combine to form personal traits. Combinations of traits make up the various "selves" we present to others. The entire integrated structure is known as the total personality.

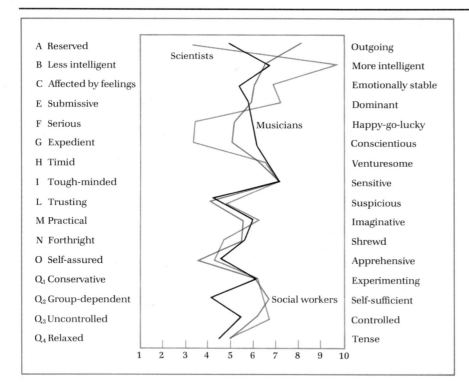

A	Reserved	Outgoing
B	Less intelligent	More intelligent
C	Affected by feelings	Emotionally stable
E	Submissive	Dominant
F	Serious	Happy-go-lucky
G	Expedient	Conscientious
H	Timid	Venturesome
I	Tough-minded	Sensitive
L	Trusting	Suspicious
M	Practical	Imaginative
N	Forthright	Shrewd
O	Self-assured	Apprehensive
Q_1	Conservative	Experimenting
Q_2	Group-dependent	Self-sufficient
Q_3	Uncontrolled	Controlled
Q_4	Relaxed	Tense

FIGURE 12.5 Cattell's personality traits are listed to the left and right of the graph. These traits, which are paired and describe the ends of the scale that make up the dimension, are personality factors obtained by factor analysis of many ratings. The profiles show the average scores on the 16 traits exhibited by groups of scientists, social workers, and musicians.

can be discovered through the empirical means of *factor analysis*—a statistical strategy for extracting common factors or sources of variance that summarize test results from large numbers of people. Thus, a factor analyst may give 500 people a battery of tests with as many as 300 separate measures and then attempt to summarize either the characteristics of the people or the characteristics of the tests by correlating the results of each test to discover common sources of variance or "factors" in the test. Cattell believed that by conducting such studies repeatedly using different types of measures and different groups of people, common factors of personality ultimately would emerge.

On the face of it, this strategy seems to be logical. However, there are some real limitations on the use of factor analysis. One of them relates to deciding how many factors are to be used to summarize the data. In principle, as many factors as there are measures could be used, but by doing so the summarizing power of factor analysis would be lost, and the amount of variance accounted for by many of the factors would be extremely small. Similarly, many of the factors extracted may not reappear on subsequent tests using different measures and different individuals. This problem raises some questions about the degree to which some of the factors

Cattell has described are replicable. Indeed, replicability is both a common demand of good scientific evidence and one that Cattell acknowledges is crucial in supporting his approach to describing the structure.

Need Approaches

A third major approach to the understanding of personality through an examination of dispositions is one that emphasizes the concept of *need*. Unquestionably the major theorist in this area was Henry A. Murray. Murray inferred the existence of needs in people's behavior from the observation of various behavioral sequences (1938). For example, a sequence involving a person's being presented with a difficult problem, experiencing tension as a result, mastering the problem, and finally exhibiting pride may reveal a need for achievement (Bavelas, 1978). Repeated observation of such sequences, particularly when they involve a variety of different behaviors or circumstances, led Murray to suggest that distinctive needs exist for particular people. Table 12-2 lists 20 representative needs that Murray felt were present to some degree in all people.

Murray's approach to understanding personality in terms of needs requires some way for the researcher to take into account the social environment as well as the individual. Murray's approach, although oriented to the individual, relies heavily on the idea that needs are best understood in the context of the situations that may elicit them. As a consequence, Murray developed a second concept, which he called *press*, to describe the characteristics of situations that initiate or direct behavior. Thus, a situation may have a press of danger for achievement or affiliation or perhaps order.

Murray further distinguished between two kinds of press: *alpha press* and *beta press*. Alpha press reflects aspects of a situation that are objectively perceived, objectively exist, and are compelling to the individual such as the objectively dangerous aspects posed by the situation of a car speeding directly toward you. Beta press characterizes those aspects of a situation that are perceived to be present by the individual and thus influence his or her behavior such as seeing a classroom as a "threatening" place.

In developing his needs theory of personality, Murray (1938) was particularly interested in examining sequences or patterns of behavior that reflect the underlying needs that he assumed were so important to an understanding of the overall

TABLE 12-2.   Twenty Human Needs Identified by Henry Murray

NEED	BRIEF DEFINITION
N Abasement	To submit passively to external force. To accept injury, blame, criticism, punishment. To admit inferiority, error, wrongdoing, or defeat.
N Achievement	To accomplish something difficult. To master, manipulate, or organize physical objects, human beings, or ideas as rapidly and as independently as possible. To surpass others and excel oneself.
N Affiliation	To draw near and enjoyably cooperate or reciprocate with an allied other. To adhere and remain loyal to a friend.
N Aggression	To overcome opposition forcefully. To revenge an injury. To attack, injure, or kill another.
N Autonomy	To get free, shake off restraint, break out of confinement. To resist coercion and restriction. To be independent and free to act according to impulse.
N Counteraction	To master or make up for a failure by restriving. To overcome weaknesses, to repress fear. To efface a dishonor by action. To search for obstacles and difficulties to overcome.
N Defendance	To defend the self against assault, criticism, and blame. To conceal or justify a misdeed, failure, or humiliation.
N Deference	To admire and support a superior. To praise, honor, or eulogize. To conform to custom.
N Dominance	To control one's human environment. To influence or direct the behavior of others by suggestion, seduction, persuasion, or command. To dissuade, restrain, prohibit.
N Exhibition	To excite, amaze, fascinate, entertain, shock, intrigue, amuse, or entice others.
N Harmavoidance	To avoid pain, physical injury, illness, and death.
N Infavoidance	To avoid humiliation. To leave embarrassing situations or avoiding conditions that may lead to belittlement. To refrain from action because of the fear of failure.
N Nurturance	To give sympathy to and gratify the needs of a helpless other. To feed, help, support, console, protect, comfort, nurse, heal.
N Order	To put things in order. To achieve cleanliness, arrangement, organization, balance, neatness, tidiness, and precision.
N Play	To act for "fun" without further purpose. To like to laugh and make a joke of everything. To seek enjoyable relaxation of stress.
N Rejection	To exclude, abandon, expel, or remain indifferent to an inferior other.
N Sentience	To seek and enjoy sensuous impressions.
N Sex	To form and further an erotic relationship. To have sexual intercourse.
N Succorance	To be nursed, supported, sustained, surrounded, protected, loved, advised, guided, indulged, forgiven, consoled. To always have a supporter.
N Understanding	To ask or answer general questions. To be interested in theory. To speculate, formulate abstractly, analyze, and generalize.

Source: Workers at the Harvard Psychological Clinic, *Explorations in Personality: a Clinical and Experimental Study of Fifty Men of College Age*, Henry A. Murray (ed.) (New York: Oxford University Press, 1938, 1966).

workings of the personality. Murray believed that in many cases it is possible to infer needs simply from examining overt behavior. By examining a pattern of behavior—such as the length of time that people engage in a task, their persistence in the face of difficult problems in accomplishing the task, and their apparent engagement in the task—a high need for achievement might be inferred. However, such a *manifest need*—a need observed in overt behavior—is not the only type that interested Murray. He also believed that each individual could be understood in terms of *latent needs*— needs reflected in fantasy, imagination, and thoughts and wishes about the world rather than in overt behavior.

As a strategy for measuring these latent needs, Murray developed the *Thematic Apperception Test (TAT)*, which consists of a set of 20 pictures showing either one person or several people standing in relation to each other (Murray 1951, 1962). An example of a TAT picture is shown in Figure 12.6. Murray and his colleagues assumed that when asked to tell a story about the TAT pictures, people would "project" their latent needs into the story as they do when they explain what they see in the inkblots of the Rorschach Test.

A subject tells a story about each of the 20 cards, and the stories are recorded. Then the stories are scored according to a standard for a variety of different needs, including achievement, recognition, order, dominance, autonomy, and affiliation. The themes that come out in these stories can also be scored to indicate what sorts of presses the pictures elicit from the subjects—that is, how he or she sees the press of each situation depicted in the pictures.

In recent years a number of Murray's colleagues and students have used the TAT in the context of studying a variety of different motives and needs (Atkinson, 1958; McClelland, Atkinson, Clark, and Lowell, 1953).

Issues in the Dispositional Approach to Personality

Many psychologists feel that dispositional theories are no longer as important in the study of personality as they once were. Dispositional theories are better at describing personality than explaining the development of enduring behavior patterns. Type and trait theories capture something important about the ways in which people differ from one another.

For example, it is easy to find exceptions to Sheldon's somatotype scheme: the most renowned artist of our time, Pablo Picasso, was no frail ectomorph but a bull-necked mesomorph. On the other hand, it is equally easy to imagine how physique might influence temperament: it affects others' perceptions of us and hence our perceptions of ourselves.

The major drawback of the dispositional approach relates to its failure to take into account the role of the specific situation in behavior. The

FIGURE 12.6 Typical example of a picture used in Murray's Thematic Apperception Test to measure latent needs. The subject is asked to tell a story about each of 20 such pictures. These stories are then scored against standards for a variety of different needs such as achievement, recognition, dominance, and affiliation.

most influential attack on dispositional theories, mounted by Walter Mischel (1968), hinged on this failure.

Mischel focused on two important assumptions that underlie not only dispositional theories but also the dynamic approach of Freud and others. Both perspectives assume, in their theories and in their methods of assessment, that individual behavior is stable over time and general across situations. In other words, if a person is judged to be assertive, that person will be consistently assertive regardless of the particular circumstances.

In an extensive evaluation of evidence from assessment methods favored by both the dynamic and dispositional perspectives, Mischel found little support for either basic assumption. When tests are repeated, he said, measures of traits tend to change, and the traits themselves fail to serve as reliable predictors of how a person will behave as situations change. Mischel (1977) has proposed that it is not possible to locate personality dispositions either in the actor or the person perceiving the actor. Instead, we must examine the continuous interaction between the observed and the observer to understand personality.

Mischel believes that we can take both dispositional (or personality) variables and situations into account by developing what he calls *cognitive learning person variables.* Such variables include the individual's competencies to construct or to generate a wide variety of behaviors under various conditions. Furthermore, such person variables include the individual's (1) ability to categorize and encode various social situations, (2) expectancies about the outcomes of those situations, and (3) self-regulatory systems and plans. Each of these major classes of variables, from Mischel's point of view, represents important person variables that are characteristics of the individual. Each will lead individuals to behave differently in different situations. Although Mischel has less to say about the characteristics of situations that bring out these differences among individuals, he does suggest that ambiguously structured situations are more likely to bring out individual differences than are highly structured situations (Price and Bouffard, 1974).

Learning Theories

While dispositional theories of personality focus on internal properties of the individual, learning theories focus outward on the environment. From the learning perspective, stable patterns of behavior are not evidence of traits or dispositions but are the consequence of repeated experiences with various stimulus situations. There are several learning approaches to the understanding of personality.

Skinner: Operant Approaches

One personality theory based on learning owes much to B. F. Skinner (1938, 1953, 1971, 1974). In effect, Skinner (1953) argues that there is no such thing as personality: there are only operant behaviors that are strengthened or weakened as a consequence of reinforcement. These behaviors are predictable and primarily controlled by measurable external stimuli. Behaviors that are positively reinforced tend to be repeated; those that are negatively reinforced tend not to be repeated. Skinner (and many other learning theorists) says the key to understanding personality is to examine the stimulus conditions under which the behaviors have developed in the past and are maintained in the present.

Skinner's ideas about personality have been dramatized in a novel called *Walden Two* (1948), in which he creates a utopian community based on his principles of operant conditioning. The founder of this community argues that people's behavior can be predicted and controlled like chemical reactions in a test tube. The idea of an inner self, he asserts, is myth and superstition.

The operant learning emphasis on environmental and situational influences on personality inevitably requires different methods of assessment than those favored by other approaches. Because behavior is said to speak for itself, the aim is to observe behavior carefully in its natural setting and to describe accurately the situational factors that appear to influence it—an assessment called *functional analysis.* With this technique, psychologists not only observe and describe the conditions they suspect are shaping a particular behavior pattern, but they may also attempt to change the behavior. They may induce a modification of stimulus conditions and then observe whether or not this produces a predicted change in behavior. In this way, researchers can determine whether or not the stimuli that are apparently controlling the behavior are actually doing so.

A classic example of this method is the case of Ann (Allen, Hart, Buell, Harris, and Wolf, 1964). Ann was a bright four-year-old who came from an up-per-middle-class home. After six weeks in nursery school, however, she seemed increasingly with-drawn and isolated from the other children, al-though she was clearly succeeding in winning the warm attention of teachers and other adults in the school.

Functional analysis of Ann's behavior began with a five-day observation period in the nursery school. Two observers each spent half of the morning re-cording at 10-second intervals what Ann was doing in relation to the other children and to the adults. The data collected during this five-day period showed that Ann spent about 50 percent of the time alone, 40 percent interacting with adults, and only about 10 percent interacting with the other children. The authors of the study concluded that Ann's isolate behavior was being maintained and probably strengthened inadvertently by adult social reinforcement.

It is interesting to note how this description of behavior differs from that of other personality theo-rists. Behavior that a trait theorist might describe as

FIGURE 12.7 This graphic presentation of the use of functional analysis in "case of Ann," shows that Ann's interaction with other children increased dramatically during periods when such behavior was reinforced by approval and attention from adults.

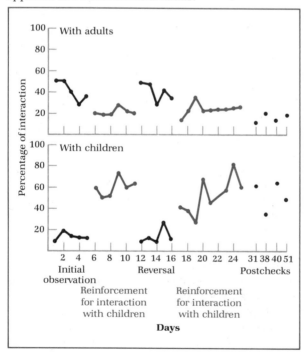

resulting from an internal disposition toward shy-ness with other children or that a dynamic theorist might interpret in terms of intrapsychic events is seen solely in terms of a particular stimulus condi-tion—the situational presence of adult reinforce-ment. Note also the functions served by the five-day observation period. It establishes the solitary nature of Ann's behavior along with a hypothesis about the cause of that behavior. Moreover, it lays down a baseline of data against which to compare peer interaction after the investigators introduce a change in stimulus conditions. The change in stimulus conditions introduced was quite simple: the adults in the nursery school were instructed to stop giving Ann attention during her periods of withdrawal and during her attempts at interaction with them. They were told to give Ann attention only when she played with other children. Adult reinforcement in the form of attention thus became contingent on a change in her behavior—playing with her peers more often.

Now, whenever Ann started to interact with other children, even if that interaction was nothing more than standing or playing near another child, an adult quickly paid attention to her. For example, an adult would approach Ann and the others and say, "You three girls have a cozy house. Here are some more cups, Ann, for your tea party." And whenever Ann left the group, the adults im-mediately stopped paying attention to her.

Two observers continued to record Ann's social interaction every 10 seconds, and the change was immediately evident. On the very first day of the new arrangement, Ann spent nearly 60 percent of her time with other children—a sixfold increase over the five-day baseline. During one four-day period the researchers instructed the adults to re-vert to their former procedure—rewarding Ann with their attention for interacting with the adults but not the children—and Ann's interaction with children suddenly dropped dramatically. This drop helped confirm the researchers' hypothesis that the change in stimulus conditions was re-sponsible for the change in Ann's behavior. Periodic checks after the 25-day study ended indicated that Ann's increased interaction with her peers re-mained fairly stable—presumably because the teachers continued to reinforce it. A graph display-ing the entire analysis is shown in Figure 12.7.

This study lends some empirical support to the operant approach to understanding personality. Rather than interpreting Ann's behavior in terms of a trait, "shyness," the operant learning approach views the behavior as controlled, and controllable, by changing the reinforcement in the external stimulus environment.

Bandura: Social Learning through Observation

Broader learning theories of personality than Skinner's have been offered by several investigators. The most prominent of these is the *social learning approach* developed by Albert Bandura. Although behaviorally oriented, Bandura (1971) rejects the concept of a one-way process involving the environment as the influencer of behavior and shaper of personality. Instead, his aim is to describe the two-way interaction between the individual and the environment: "Behavior partly creates the environment and the resultant environment in turn, influences the behavior. In this two-way casual process the environment is just as influenceable as the behavior it controls (Bandura, 1971).

Bandura's approach differs from the Skinnerian perspective in several important respects. It is based on human learning research rather than on animal conditioning. Furthermore, it stresses the importance of cognitive and social factors as opposed to simple classical or operant conditioning. As we saw in Chapter 7, Bandura has shown that considerable learning takes place vicariously— through observational learning, or modeling. We watch the behavior of others—models—and take note of the consequences of their actions, observing whether they are positively or negatively reinforced. These models may be parents, peers, or even performers on television.

In Bandura's social learning theory, the concept of reinforcement takes on a broader meaning. It may be direct—an external reinforcement experienced firsthand, or it may be vicarious—experienced through the observation of a model who is reinforced. In addition, reinforcement may be self-administered—the compliment, banana split, or other reward we give to ourselves for behaving in a certain way. "If actions were determined solely by external rewards and punishments," Bandura (1971) has written, "people would behave like weathervanes, constantly shifting in radically different directions to conform to the whims of others."

Thus, for Bandura, behavior depends on the special characteristics of the situation, the person's cognitive appraisal of the situation—the individual's awareness and expectations—and the history of reinforcements (direct, vicarious, or self-administered) in similar circumstances.

Unlike dynamic and dispositional theories, the social learning approach lends itself readily to testing by the experimental method. Because the primary emphasis is on external conditions rather than on internal structures or processes, the researcher can control and vary the stimuli that are said to shape behavior.

To test Bandura's social learning approach, Bandura himself and Mischel (1965) conducted an experiment that demonstrates the acquisition of behavioral characteristics through the observation of models. The characteristic in question involved self-control—in this instance, the willingness to delay gratification. Typically, the delay of gratification means postponing an immediate reward in favor of a potentially more valuable delayed reward. For example, a student decides to forgo dropping out of school to get a job in order to graduate and presumably to obtain a better job in the future.

To determine whether children can acquire this sort of self-control merely by observing, Bandura and Mischel worked with a group of fourth- and fifth-grade students. First, they classified the children according to whether they preferred high delay of reward or low delay of reward, by giving them a series of 14 choices between a small immediate reward (a small candy bar right away) and a larger postponed reward (a bigger candy bar a week later).

To test whether these initial preferences could be changed by observation of an appropriate adult model who made choices between immediate and postponed rewards, Bandura and Mischel exposed the children in the high-delay-of-reward group to a model who consistently opted for the immediate-reward choice and the children in the low-delay-of-reward group to a model who consistently selected the postponed reward. In some conditions the model was actually present, and in others written (symbolic) materials provided the modeling roles. The adult models, in making the choice, sometimes commented on the reasons for their choice. For example, in choosing a plastic chess set that was available immediately over a more expensive wooden set that would not be obtainable for two weeks, the model explained: "Chess figures are chess figures. I can get much use out of the plastic ones right away (Bandura and Mischel, 1965)."

The children were then given a delay-of-reward test. As predicted, the experiment produced marked changes in the children's willingness to delay gratification (see Figure 12.8). These changes remained moderately stable when the children were tested about a month later.

Issues in the Learning Approach to Personality

After the elusive and sometimes metaphorical formulations of the dynamic and dispositional theories, the apparent straightforwardness of the learning approach to personality has an immediate appeal. Unlike most other approaches to personality, the learning perspective purports to explain both the variation of personality over time and its consistency in given situations. In its methods of assessment and of experimental research, learning theory provides a sense of clear-cut cause and effect. If the stimulus condition that is believed to be determining a particular behavior is pinpointed, and the stimulus changed, then predictably the behavior will change.

This is an oversimplified view, of course. Implicit in the learning perspective are a number of issues. One is the widely held belief that Skinner's approach, in particular, reduces human beings to mere stimulus-response machines. Bandura's social learning approach is less susceptible to this criticism because it emphasizes internal processes, such as awareness and expectation, in individual responses to external stimuli.

On a more specific level, Janet Bavelas (1978) pointed out weaknesses in both Skinner's and Bandura's theories. Skinner, Bavelas points out, often confuses the concepts of the cause of behavior with those of behavioral control: "... it is wrong for any theory to conclude that whatever changes a behavior also illuminates the original cause of the behavior. For example, this author's vision is improved by wearing glasses. Does this mean that poor vision is caused by being born without eyeglasses? ... evidence that demonstrates that *operant* conditioning is *sufficient* to cause changes in behavior does not in addition demonstrate that operant conditioning is *necessary* to cause the behavior."

Evaluating Bandura's social learning theory and its emphasis on acquiring behavior through modeling, Bavelas identifies five shortcomings. First, as Bandura himself has acknowledged, mere exposure is not always sufficient to produce observational learning; in addition it is not yet possible to predict that, in a given situation, observational learning will actually occur. Second, the evidence is confusing as to how much children actually learn in modeling experiments. Third, there is also confusion as to what precisely constitutes a model in observational learning. Bandura has used verbal instructions—whether spoken by the model or simply in print—as a kind of model. Fourth, the Bandura theory fails to make clear what happens when there is a conflict between external reinforcement and self-reinforcement: which takes

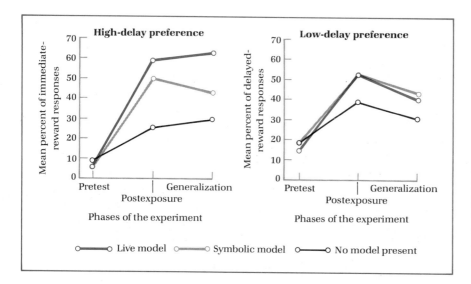

FIGURE 12.8 The results of Bandura and Mischel's social learning experiment indicate that children may acquire behavioral characteristics through the observation of models. The percentage of immediate-reward choices by children who initially preferred high-delay increased after exposure to immediate-reward models as did the percentage of delayed-reward choices by children who initially preferred low-delay after exposure to delay-reward models.

precedence, an individual's anticipation of good feelings or the promise of a concrete reward? Finally, although Bandura acknowledges the influence of cognitive factors in social learning, he does not elaborate on how these factors might operate.

Phenomenological Theories

Phenomenological theories of personality take a very different view of the person: they focus on the conscious experience of the individual rather than on overt behavior, as in the behavioral approach, or on traits or types, as in the dispositional approach. Most other theories of personality view people from the outside, while phemenological theories attempt to enter into the person's own psychological experience in order to understand personality (Bavelas, 1978). Furthermore, like the later psychodynamic approaches to personality, the phenomenological approach is concerned primarily with conscious rather than unconscious experience.

Phenomenological theories are sometimes called "self theories" primarily because they are concerned with how one experiences one's own self. Carl Rogers is interested in the experience of the self and how this experience affects an individual's adjustment; Abraham Maslow, another theorist in this tradition, focuses primarily on how the self develops; George Kelly, although oriented to the individual phenomenology or experience of the self, is more concerned with how people develop categories for interpreting and evaluating their own experience.

Rogers: The Concept of Self-Actualization

Central to Rogers' view of personality, as to several of the humanistic theories, is the concept of *self-actualization*. This process has been described by Rogers (1961) as "the directional trend which is evident in all organic and human life—the urge to expand, extend, develop, mature—the tendency to express and actuate all the capacities of the organism."

Rogers (1959) believes the tendency toward self-actualization is innate as indicated by the goal-directed behaviors of infants—reaching, sucking, touching—which are their attempts to actualize themselves in terms of reality as each infant perceives it. As children engage in the actualizing process, they begin to symbolize—that is, to view their own behavior as a separate entity. Eventually their self-experience develops into a *self-concept*, the perceptual object that each child may experience as "me" or "I." This self-concept may change as a result of experiences with others and of reactions of others to the child. Thus, from the reality the child experiences evolves not only a sense of the outside world but also a sense of the self—the "I" or "me" of experience. The field of experience or *phenomenal field* contains a self as well as a view of others such as parents, teachers, and friends.

As the child's self-concept develops, the child also develops a need for positive regard on the part of others, a need Rogers considers so pervasive as to be universal. It is usually satisfied by children reciprocally: in satisfying others people's needs for positive regard, they also satisfy their own need. Sometimes this need becomes so compelling that children may seek the positive regard of others instead of seeking actualizing experiences. When this happens, Rogers suggests that *conditions of worth* develop. These conditions of worth are behaviors and experiences that a person perceives as being valued by others rather than as being valued intrinsically. For example, when a person strives for athletic achievement or excellence in school primarily because it will raise his or her value in the eyes of others rather than for the inherent pleasure that comes from mastering new skills, conditions of worth have been established as opposed to self-actualization.

When people begin to do things primarily because they are praised by others, the sense of self may become distorted and primarily shaped by others' approval. A gap can then develop between a person's actual experiences and his or her self-concept. Rogers call this gap *incongruence*. He also says that incongruence can develop between an individual's self-concept and ideal self—the vision of what a person would like to be. In either case, the result of incongruence is likely to be anxiety and psychological maladjustment.

Rogers' view of personality primarily focuses on the individual's own experience, not on the person as seen by others or on the person as a bundle of traits, a set of behavior patterns, or a fixated developmental drive. In particular, how individuals view their own selves and their experiences is central to Rogers' theory of personality.

Most of the research on Rogers' theory has occurred in the course of psychotherapy, and effective therapy has been seen as a confirmation of Rogers' ideas. Among the attempts to verify aspects of the theory experimentally, the work most consistently cited by Rogers was the research carried out by B. Chodorkoff (1954). Chodorkoff sought to test different hypotheses derived from Rogers' self-theory, the most important of which states that if a person has a self-concept that agrees with other people's view of him or her, then there is congruency between self and experience and no need to distort perceptions or experiences.

In testing this, Chodorkoff sought to measure three characteristics of 30 male undergraduate students: (1) the degree to which their self-description is congruent with the description of them by others; (2) the degree to which threatening experiences are denied in awareness; and (3) the degree to which the individual is psychologically adjusted. Chodorkoff asked his subjects to attend three testing sessions. These sessions covered a variety of personality tests: a biographical inventory based on multiple-choice questions, the Rorschach inkblot test, a word association test, the Thematic Apperception Test, and finally a perceptual-defense test in which the subjects were confronted with words deemed to be most threatening and least threatening from the previous word association test. After these three sessions, the subjects were given a self-descriptive Q-sort test, which allowed them to identify adjectives that characterized their view of their "real" selves as they saw themselves and their "ideal" selves as they would like to be.

Chodorkoff and other judges scored each of the tests in terms of his three postulated characteristics—accuracy of self-description, perceptual defense, and psychological adjustment—and the results confirmed the hypothesis derived from Roger's theory: students who were able to describe themselves accurately were also better adjusted and showed less perceptual defense. These findings have been criticized because of overlap (1) among the tests used to evaluate adjustment, and (2) the judges doing the ratings. However, more carefully designed studies of the type carried out by Chodorkoff could provide some evidence in support of Rogers' propositions.

Maslow: The Hierarchy of Needs

Unlike Rogers, who derived his ideas about self-actualization from his practice of psychotherapy, Maslow (1962, 1963) studied friends as well as the lives of public figures whom he considered unusu-ally creative—Abraham Lincoln and Albert Einstein, for example. From this study, Maslow compiled a list of characteristics of self-actualizers. Among these characteristics are an efficient perception of reality, autonomy, and an openness to mystical experiences.

Maslow also postulated a *hierarchy of needs* (see Figure 12.9). The basic physiological needs such as hunger and thirst are at the bottom of the hierarchy. Then come the needs for safety, and love and esteem. Self-actualization is the highest need of all. Maslow contended that the gratification of all the needs is necessary to psychological well-being but that needs lower in the hierarchy must be satisfied before those above them can be satisfied.

One of Maslow's concepts that has entered into our general language is the *peak experience*. As defined by Maslow, the peak experience is a moment of self-actualization, a transcendent ecstasy in which perceptions are greatly sharpened. A peak experience resembles some of the altered states of consciousness discussed in Chapter 5 and may occur in relation to music, religion, or other transcendent experiences.

Maslow was most interested in the positive, growth-oriented aspects of personality. Like other phenomenologically oriented theorists, he was concerned not so much with externally observed traits as with the experience of the fully functioning person.

FIGURE 12.9 Maslow's hierarchy of needs ranges from the basic physiological needs, including hunger and thirst, to self-actualization needs, the highest needs.

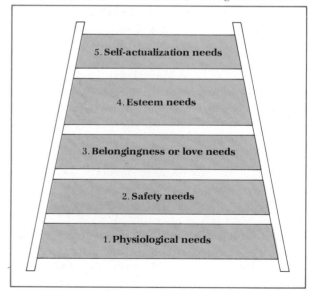

5. Self-actualization needs
4. Esteem needs
3. Belongingness or love needs
2. Safety needs
1. Physiological needs

Kelly: The Personal Construct Theory of Personality

Still another phenomenological approach to the understanding of personality has been developed by George Kelly (1955). While Rogers' approach to personality focuses on the person's self-concept, Kelly begins with the basic notion that the way the individual conceptually organizes his or her social world—the way the individual personally interprets and categorizes events and the behavior of others—is the essence of personality. The way people view other people and events is, according to Kelly, strikingly personal and individual. Kelly was always fascinated by the notion that people, no matter how much they seem to be living in the same public world, actually inhabit strikingly different personal worlds.

The key concept in Kelly's theory, that of *personal construct*, is essentially the idea that each of us has certain basic concepts or ideas that we use to understand the world. We see others as friendly or hostile; we describe situations as cooperative or competitive. It is these individual views that each of us holds that both help us understand and predict the behavior of others and affect the way we behave in interpersonal situations. In essence, Kelly believes that personality consists of the organized system of ideas and assumptions that each of us holds about various other individuals in our world and the various roles that they may occupy.

Kelly's theory is essentially phenomenological in its orientation; it is interested in how each individual experiences the surrounding world. In particular, Kelly believed that the concepts or constructs that we use shape our experience of the world and our expectations about others in it. In addition, Kelly's theory relates to individual differences and the study of individuals' constructs rather than to developing generalizations about constructs or traits.

Kelly has developed a widely known personality test to identify and measure the personal constructs of each person as he defined them in his theory. This *Role Construct Repertory Test* is designed to elicit from respondents their own constructs about other people and roles, particularly roles that are presumably very important to them, including the self, mother, spouse, pal, rejecting person, or attractive person (Kelly, 1955).

Kelly's strategy in eliciting the individual's personal constructs about each of these ideas is to ask respondents to think of at least three individuals or "figures" who occupy each of these roles. Then the respondent is asked to identify the ways in which two of these people are alike and are different from the third. The idea here is to identify the two ends of the personal constructs that best characterize a particular role. For example, a respondent might think of two fathers who are seen as "accepting" and different from a third father who is viewed as being "hostile." Thus, the two poles of the respondent's personal construct become "accepting" at the one end and "cold" at the other.

Once these personal constructs have been established, the respondent is asked to fill out a grid form of the kind seen in Figure 12.10 by applying each of the constructs that have been elicited to each of the figures listed. This procedure should produce a grid in which important personal constructs in the respondent's life are used to rate important roles, resulting in a completely personalized perception of the respondent's own social role. Both the personal constructs obtained and the roles to which they are applied refer only to that particular respondent.

Results from the role repertory test have been used in a variety of ways. In particular they have been used as a basis for counselors and psychotherapists to understand the personal phenomenological worlds of their clients. A counselor may learn a great deal about the roles that are important to people, the ways in which they see their social worlds, their expectations about their relationships, and their own personal views of themselves.

Issues in the Phenomenological Approach to Personality

Unquestionably, some of the strengths of the phenomenological approach are also its greatest weaknesses. This approach is distinctive in placing great importance on an appreciation of the subjective inner life of the person as a way of understanding personality. But, like any other perspective on the nature of human behavior, the emphasis on the phenomenological field of the individual neglects other important aspects of behavior. These theories have almost no behavioral content and are limited almost exclusively to subjective experience. Consequently, their ability to predict behavior or to link internal subjective phenomena to external behavior in the social world is severely limited.

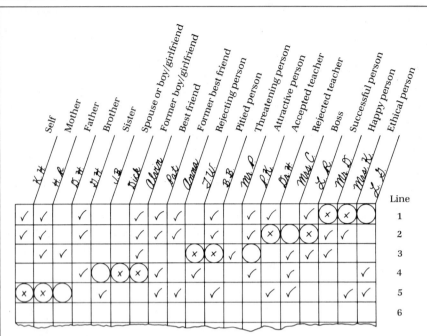

1. Think of the people you know who fit the roles given across the top of the grid. Write in the first name or initials of these people.

2. Beginning with line 1, consider the three people indicated by circles.
   a. Put an "X" in the circles of the two who are, in some important way, similar to each other and different from the third person.
   b. Under "similar," on the same line, write a word or phrase that says how they are alike.
   c. Under "contrast," write how the third person is different.
   d. Look over the other people on your grid and check everyone else who is also similar. Leave blank those who are like the contrast person.
   e. Repeat this process for each line. Try not to repeat the ways in which people are alike or different but think of new ones for each line.

Similar	Contrast
understanding	cold
forgiving	rigid about rules
uneducated	good taste
very political	apathetic
female	male

FIGURE 12.10 The grid form of Kelly's Role Construct Repertory Test is designed to elicit respondents' own constructs concerning other people and roles.

Some of the phenomenological theories have been criticized as naively romantic (Liebert and Spiegler, 1974; Millon, 1967). This is truer of Maslow's perspective than it is of Kelly's.

As appealing as these theoretical approaches are in attempting to appreciate the inner psychological life of each individual, the research emerging from both Rogers' self-theory and Kelly's role-repertory orientation has been criticized because of its excessive reliance on self-report. In particular, Bavelas (1978) has noted that the reliability of individual role-constructs reported for the same people at different periods of time is relatively poor. Thus, the question of whether these personal constructs are indeed stable over time, as Kelly suggests they are, is not yet settled. Similarly, much of the research stimulated by Rogers' theory has relied on methods that have also been criticized because they depend so exclusively on the respondents' reports about their experiences and behaviors.

Reliance on self-report can also be problematic because these studies assume that respondents are aware of and able to report about significant aspects of their behaviors. It is just as plausible to assume that much of the important behavior that a personality theorist may wish to study is not directly accessible to a respondent's awareness but must either be observed by others or inferred from other aspects of overt behavior.

Metatheories of Personality

The four perspectives we have discussed may appear to be so disparate as to make it very difficult to arrive at a coherent view of personality. These differences also concern many psychologists who are looking for ways to synthesize a single all-encompassing view of personality and behavior from the conflicting evidence.

Any attempt at synthesis must examine the theories for similarities as well as differences. If the root assumptions of the four personality perspectives are examined, two basic approaches or *metatheories*—theories behind the theories—emerge (Bavelas, 1978).

These two metatheories are essential individual or social in their underlying assumptions. The individual metatheory, embracing the dynamic, dispositional, and phenomenological perspectives,

---

FOCUS: Sex Stereotypes in Psychological Assessment

The various methods of personality assessment tend to assume that the assessor brings to the process an unbiased judgment, free of preconceptions about the individual in question. However, clinicians are confronted not with an abstract list of behaviors but with a living, breathing person who is the product of a lifetime of socialization in differing roles shaped by biological, ethnic, and cultural factors.

Given this human context, can the assessor truly be expected to bring a bias-free judgment to the assessment of personality? For example, might clinicians have preconceptions bases solely on the gender of the subject? According to a study by Inge Broverman and her colleagues (Broverman, Broverman, and Clarkson, 1970), the answer may well be yes.

These investigators asked 79 clinically trained mental health workers to respond to a questionnaire. The task was to choose the adjectives that best characterized a male, a female, and a mature, healthy adult. The adjectives were bipolar choices such as "strong-weak."

Broverman and her colleagues found that there was a great deal of agreement about the attributes characterizing healthy men, healthy women, and healthy adults whose sex was unspecified. This is not surprising because most of us can readily call up images that conform to conventional sex role stereotypes in our society. For example, if a person were described as independent, objective, active, logical, worldly, direct, adventurous, and self-confident, a typical reaction would be to say the person was a male. Similarly, if the person were described as being emotional, having sensitive feelings, disliking math and science, and being easily influenced, most people would likely say it was a female.

What was particularly interesting about the Broverman findings was that clinicians have different concepts of mental health for men and for women. These concepts parallel our sex role stereotypes. Their judgments about the mental health of a man vary with their perceptions of how closely he conforms to the male sex role stereotype. Women who conform to the female sex role stereotype also are judged to be healthier than women who do not.

The authors suggest that these findings show a powerful negative assessment of women. A healthy woman is defined by the clinicians as more submissive, more dependent, less adventurous, more easily influenced, and less objective than men. This constellation of characteristics, the authors note, is an unusual way to describe a mature healthy individual.

Moreover, Broverman and her co-workers also found that the mental health professionals' conception of an "adult healthy individual" more closely resembled the male stereotype than it did the female stereotype. This evident bias in favor of stereotypical male characteristics held regardless of the professional's own gender.

The authors feel that this bias reflects the general acceptance by mental health professionals of an "adjustment" notion of health. This notion assumes that people who conform to sex role stereotypes are better adjusted than people who do not conform to these roles.

views personality as a set of internal dispositions or intrapsychic mechanisms that differ from one person to another and help determine behavior. The social metatheory, including the various social learning theories, sees personality as a set of principles by which an individual interacts with the social environment. Bavelas (1978) has closely examined these two metatheories and described the five essential ways in which they actually differ and the ways in which they only appear to differ.

1. *Internal versus External Orientation.* Individual theories, while not denying that the environment plays a role in personality development, look for the basic determinants of personality—in the unconscious, in traits and types, or in the self-concept. Social theories emphasize conditions outside the individual—stimuli, reinforcers, models.

2. *Individual versus Situational Differences.* Individual theories suggest that individual differences arise out of early childhood experiences, while social theories assume that environmental forces continue to act on individuals throughout life so that people continue to change and to differentiate from one another as a result of situational differences.

3. *Stability versus Change.* Individual theories predict relative stability of personality once internal dynamics or structures have developed, while social theories assert that behavior will change as situations change.

4. *Cross-Situational Consistency versus Situational Specificity.* Individual theories see personality differences as not only stable but also general—that is, manifest in any relevant situation. By contrast, social theories look for situational changes that can evoke completely different behaviors—through the influence of modeling, for example.

5. *Correlational versus Experimental Research.* Individual theories must rely on correlational methods of research, which assess already existing differences in responses. Social theories frequently require the investigator to engage in experimental research, arranging different situations where responses can be measured.

Although these differences between the individual and social metatheories are compelling, Bavelas (1978) goes on to describe ways in which the two approaches often appear to differ but in fact do not. She calls these pseudo-differences.

One pseudo-difference is methodological rigor. Because the advocate of individual theories uses correlational methods, Bavelas points out, it does not necessarily follow that he or she is "more humanistic, more intuitive, or more fuzzy or free-ranging thinkers. Nor is the experimental psychologist (in this case the social personality theorist) automatically more precise, surer of cause-effect relations, less interested in individual human beings, or inclined to mistake rats and statistics for people."

A second pseudo-difference often attributed to the metatheories involves the importance of the individual. Individual theories are often said to respect human uniqueness, while social theories are said to favor an anonymous, deterministic version of human nature. In fact, with the notable exception of Skinner's learning theory, both approaches assume individual variations in behavior. The differences are a matter of emphasis.

"The error that leads to such propaganda on both sides," Bavelas (1978) concludes, "is in believing that one's theoretical position is a complete and final statement on human nature. None of the theories we have encountered encompasses all of human nature; all are tentative bets on where the major causal factors of some behaviors lie."

SUMMARY

1. Personality is the characteristic way in which a person thinks and behaves as she or he adapts to the environment. Any theory of personality must explain why we behave in the ways we do and what makes each of us unique. Personality theories fall into four general categories: psychodynamic, dispositional, social learning, and phenomenological theories.

2. Freud's psychoanalytic theory insisted that behavior is determined by the interplay of events and psychological processes that are not normally available to a person's consciousness. Freud placed a great deal of emphasis on sexual energy and motives in the early shaping of personality. He proposed four distinct stages of development: oral, anal, phallic, and genital. Each stage of development carries potential crises, and Freud believed that successful resolution of each crisis was necessary for a child to arrive at a healthy personality in childhood.

3. Neo-Freudians, the "ego psychologists," such as Karen Horney, Erich Fromm, and Erik Erikson, re-

tained many of the basic assumptions of Freud's dynamic theory but felt that the conscious ego was more important in shaping personality than the instinctual drives of the unconscious. Carl Jung's analytical psychology proposed that the archetypes of the collective unconscious affect our personality development in a lifelong process of psychological maturation called *individuation.*

4. Dynamic theorists assess individual personality through the techniques of free association, dream interpretation, and projective tests in which subjects respond to deliberately ambiguous stimuli. Psychodynamic theories have been criticized for their inability to produce explicit "if-then" statements to predict consequences following from the theories, failure to define clearly such concepts as the Oedipus complex, and broad formulations that can be manipulated to fit the evidence at hand.

5. Dispositional theories assume that people have prevailing internal tendencies to behave in predictable ways. Dispositional theories may be broken down into their emphases on types, on traits, and on individual needs. William Sheldon proposed personality patterns based on three basic body structure, or somatypes: endomorph (soft and round), mesomorph (sturdy and muscular), and ectomorph (thin and fragile). Sheldon believed that as these physical systems developed, one became dominant, along with an associated personality type.

H. J. Eysenck proposed the existence of a small number of underlying dimensions of personality along which all people differ—introversion and extroversion, stability and instability, for example.

6. Gorden Allport proposed that individuals have traits that help explain the uniqueness and consistency that we observe in behavior. Allport argued that traits vary in their effect on the whole personality: cardinal traits are strong characteristics that shape the whole personality; central traits are important but not pervasive; secondary traits reflect very narrow patterns of behavior. Some traits can be observed in most people to a greater or lesser degree, whereas some traits are unique to particular individuals.

Raymond Cattell identified fundamental traits, which he called source traits, as underlying and fundamental roots of overt behavior. Surface traits were clusters of overt behavior that seemed to go together but have more than one source trait as their determinants. Cattell also believed that the structure of personality can be discovered through the empirical means of factor analysis.

Henry A. Murray proposed a theory of personality based on observable sequences of needs and the idea that individuals have distinctive needs. Murray also proposed a concept he called "press" to describe the characteristics of situations that initiate or direct behavior. Murray and his colleagues developed the Thematic Apperception Test (TAT), in which subjects are believed to project their needs onto stories they make up about pictures provided by the test.

7. Dispositional theories have been criticized because they are better at describing personality than in explaining the development of enduring behavior patterns. In addition, dispositional theories tend to slight the importance of the role of specific situations in accounting for behavior.

8. B. F. Skinner argues, in effect, that there is no such thing as personality: there are only operant behaviors that are strengthened or weakened as a consequence of reward and punishment. These behaviors are predictable and primarily controlled by measurable external influences, or stimuli. Operant learning emphasizes environmental and situational influences and must be assessed differently than other personality theories. Since behavior is said to speak for itself, it must be carefully observed in its natural setting, and the situational factors that appear to influence it must be accurately described—an assessment approach called functional analysis.

9. Albert Bandura's social learning approach to personality stresses the importance of cognitive and social factors and of observational learning, or modeling. In Bandura's theory, reinforcement may be experienced directly or vicariously, and it may be self-administered. For Bandura, behavior depends upon situational characteristics, a person's cognitive appraisal of the situation, and the history of reinforcement.

10. In its methods of assessment and experimental research, learning theory has a sense of clear-cut cause and effect. However, it is important to avoid confusing the concepts of the cause of behavior with those of behavioral control. Bandura's theory has been questioned because mere exposure is not always sufficient to produce observational learning,

and it is not always possible to predict that, in a given situation, observational learning will actually occur.

11. Phenomenological approaches focus on the conscious experience of the individual and attempt to enter into the person's own psychological experience in order to understand personality.

Carl Rogers believes in an innate tendency toward self-actualization and that self-experience develops into a self-concept. How individuals experience and view themselves and their experiences is crucial to Roger's theory.

Abraham Maslow postulated a hierarchy of needs with basic physiological needs at the bottom and self-actualization at the top. Maslow also proposed the peak experience, a transcendent moment of self-actualization in which perceptions are greatly sharpened.

George Kelly proposed that the way one conceptually organizes one's social world, and the way in which one personally interprets and categorizes events and the behavior of others, is the essence of one's personality. Kelly suggested that each of us develops a personal construct, a set of concepts and ideas that we use in order to understand ourselves and the world around us.

12. Phenomenological theories have little behavioral content. Consequently, their ability to predict behavior or to link internal subjective phenomena to external behavior in the social and interpersonal world is severely limited. These theories are also limited by their reliance on self-reports.

13. Bavelas has proposed that the four major approaches to personality fall into two overriding metatheories—social and individual. The social metatheory sees personality as a set of principles by which an individual interacts with the social environment. The individual metatheory embraces the dynamic, dispositional, and phenomenological views and sees personality as a set of internal dispositions or intrapsychic mechanisms that differ from one person to another and help determine behavior.

Chapter 13
Intelligence

Consider these items from the news:

- A California businessman announced the creation of The Repository for Germinal Choice, a storage bank from which the sperm of Nobel Prize winners could be used for artificially inseminating women of exceptionally high IQs in order to produce offspring of unusual intelligence.
- The National Education Association, with a membership of 1.8 million teachers, called for the abolition of all standarized intelligence aptitude and achievement tests, labeling them "at best wasteful, and, at worst, destructive."
- In Virginia, it was revealed, more than 4,000 men and women deemed mentally unfit had previously been legally sterilized by the state in order to prevent the birth of "misfits" and to raise "the average intelligence of the people."

As these news items suggest, in our culture intelligence is one of the most highly valued of human characteristics—and one of the most controversial. Few areas of psychological investigation have such volatile implications for society at large. Intelligence and the methods by which it is measured create social and political policy, shape our schools, and even influence some people's choice of mates.

What is intelligence? Most of us typically use the word in the dictionary sense of general knowledge-ability or capacity for reasoning and understanding. Psychologists have learned a great deal about measuring intelligence but do not always agree about precisely what it is they are measuring. About 60 years ago several leading researchers were asked by the *Journal of Educational Psychology* to define the concept of intelligence. The ensuing disagreement prompted Edwin Boring, the eminent historian of psychology, to conclude wryly that intelligence is merely "the capacity to do well in an intelligence test (Rice, 1979)."

It would be a mistake, however, to treat intelligence and the efforts to measure it in a cavalier way. For both scientific and social reasons the study of intelligence and its measurement is central to psychology. We are just now beginning to understand the nature of intellectual abilities that produce effective problem solving. While individual differences in problem solving have been studied for years, it is only recently that scientists have taken this phenomenon into the laboratory in order to study some of the underlying components of intellectual ability and to answer additional questions about individual differences in intellectual ability.

Because intellectual ability is so highly valued in our culture, differences in intelligence as they are measured by various tests of intellectual promise form an important basis for social decisions regarding opportunities and responsibilities in our society. Because we live in a highly technological society that is growing more complex each year, intellectual ability may become an even more socially valued characteristic in the future. Because social opportunity, social environment, and genetic background play important roles in intelligence, environmental conditions that reduce the opportunity to develop intellectual ability are of great social concern. Thus, for both social and scientific reasons, the study of intelligence and its measurement have become important areas of study in modern psychology.

Theories of Intelligence

Psychologists who have developed theories about the nature of intelligence have taken one of two approaches. One approach, favored historically and underlying most forms of testing, was to view intelligence as a psychological structure, something that could be broken down into parts and then analyzed. The other approach, which has gained favor in recent years, looks at intelligence as a way of processing information.

Structural Theories

Theories of the structure of intelligence have been for the most part based on a technique called *factor analysis*, a statistical method that defines the common components or dimensions underlying multiple tests or measures. The aim is to find common factors that underlie performances on separate mental tests; for example, a vocabulary test and a reading comprehension examination may be analyzed for the intercorrelations among the test scores of a sample of respondents.

Spearman's "g" Factor The pioneer in the application of factor analysis to intelligence was an English psychologist, Charles Spearman. His theory grew out of the simple observation that people who did well on one kind of mental test also did well on others; their scores tended to be positively correlated. In 1904 he posited the "universal Unity of the Intellect" and suggested that this unity was based on what he called general *mental facility* or simply *g factor*. In addition to this general factor, Spearman believed that performance on any particular intellectual task requires a *specific mental capability*, or *s*. While excellence on a given test would depend on the operation of both *g* and *s*, overall excellence is based on the *g* factor, or general intelligence (Spearman, 1927).

Spearman's notion of the *g* factor fit well with the concept of standardized IQ tests, which came into widespread use in the 1920s and which purported to measure general intelligence. These tests greatly influenced education, particularly in England where the *g* factor became part of the underlying rationale for assigning British schoolchildren to separate schools at the early age of 11. Interestingly, no correlations at all have been found between an individual's scores on a number of the tests. This would suggest, contrary to Spearman's original theory of a unitary *g* factor, that intelligence does consist of many different components.

Thurstone's Primary Mental Abilities During the 1930s, L. L. Thurstone developed a different theory of the structure of intelligence (Thurstone, 1938). Applying factor analysis to the same type of data used by Spearman, he concluded that intelligence was not a single entity but composed instead of seven components. He called these *primary mental abilities (PMAs)* and labeled them numerical ability, reasoning, verbal fluency, spatial relations, perception, memory, and verbal comprehension.

The operation of one or more of these PMAs, Thurstone said, could account for a subject's performance on a given test item. He believed that different people displayed different patterns of mental ability, and he developed special tests to measure these different abilities (see Figure 13.1). On the basis of his factor analysis, he was able to prepare a profile of any test subject, showing the strength of each ability, from which reasonable predictions could be made about the subject's suitability for a given career.

Guilford's Theory of the Structure of the Intellect The concept that intelligence comprises a number of different components was greatly ex-

panded by J. P. Guilford, who postulated that no fewer than 120 separate factors, or mental abilities, exist. Guilford's interesting three-dimensional structure of intellect is depicted graphically in Figure 13-2 (Guilford, 1967). The three dimensions are contents (what the individual knows), operations (the processing of what is known), and products (the end results). Each dimension is subdivided into components, the interaction of which results in Guilford's 120 factors—4 content factors × 5 operation factors × 6 product factors equals 120.

Information Processing Theory

In contrast to the structural theories of intelligence, the information processing approach, as the name suggests, views intelligence as a process. This theory attempts to break down the reasoning operation into distinct steps and then to explain how they are organized.

Robert J. Sternberg, a leading exponent of the information processing approach, has studied how people solve problems of the type found on IQ tests (Sternberg, 1977). Sternberg suggests that, during reasoning, information processing occurs on two different levels. One level consists of the sequential steps—components—that a person proceeds through in solving a complex mental problem. The other level consists of metacomponents—the processes that organize the components that a person goes through in deciding how to solve the problem.

As an illustration of this two-level process, Sternberg (1977) cites the following example:

> Suppose that you want to convert Grecian drachmas to dollars, and you know that a drachma is worth about three cents. You need to know how many dollars you can get for 500 drachmas. Metacomponents are used to figure out how to solve the problem: The sum three cents has to be converted into its dollar equivalent, and then multiplied by 500. Components are used to actually obtain the solution: .03 × 500 equals $15.

Components Much of Sternberg's research focused on the processes involved in solving analogies, an ability considered highly indicative of general intelligence. In a typical experiment, the subject sits at a computer terminal, where the problem is presented in parts on the viewing screen, and responds one step at a time by pushing buttons.

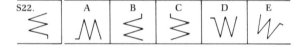
FIGURE 13.1 The sample items shown in this test correspond to Thurstone's primary mental abilities.

Through such methods, Sternberg measured the speed of each step in the problem-solving process. Analogy solving, Sternberg believes, has six sequential components: encoding, inferring, mapping, applying, justifying, and responding.

Consider, for example, his componential analysis of an analogy typical of those found in IQ tests.

WASHINGTON is to ONE as LINCOLN is to: a. FIVE, b. TEN, c. FIFTEEN, d. FIFTY.

First, the person must encode the various terms of the analogy, identifying attributes that may be relevant to a solution. Both Washington and Lincoln were presidents of the United States, for example; both are portrayed on pieces of currency.

Next, the subject infers a relationship between the first two terms of the analogy, Washington and one; Washington's portrait appears on the $1 bill.

Then, the person maps this inference to the second half of the analogy, Lincoln and five. Lincoln also appears on currency.

The subject applies the relationship inferred to each of the possible answers and then attempts to justify an answer option as preferable to the others even if it does not seem ideal. Finally, the subject responds with the answer deemed best.

Metacomponents Behind this analysis are the metacomponents, the higher-order decision processes. These processes help us decide what components to use in problem solving and what strategies to use to combine the components. Sternberg believes that metacomponents are more important to intelligence than are components. "IQ tests," he says, "may work as well as they do not only because they measure the speed and accuracy with which we solve various kinds of problems, but because they measure the speed and accuracy with which we go about deciding how to solve these problems (Sternberg, 1977)."

Surprisingly, Sternberg has found that people with high IQs may actually spend more time on a particular component than do people with low IQs (Sternberg and Dettermann, 1979). For example, in Sternberg's studies, higher-IQ people tend to take longer to encode the information presented by a problem. The time spent on this component, he suggests, pays off later in the problem-solving process, enabling them to carry out later steps more efficiently and more rapidly.

Sternberg's two-level theory may have important implications for improving individual reasoning

FIGURE 13.2 According to Guilford's structure of the intellect, each cell of this three-dimensional block represents a unique intellectual ability.

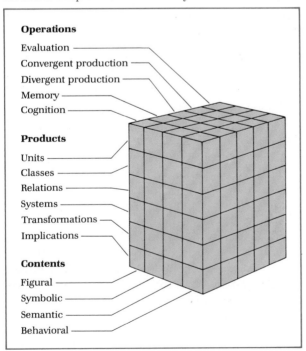

Operations

Evaluation
Convergent production
Divergent production
Memory
Cognition

Products

Units
Classes
Relations
Systems
Transformations
Implications

Contents

Figural
Symbolic
Semantic
Behavioral

ability. On the componental level, people can be helped to pinpoint the particular steps where they are having trouble solving problems. On the meta-componental level, people can be taught to think about how they are approaching the problem instead of the particular strategies for solving it.

Whether intelligence is a structure or a process, standards must exist for examining and judging it. It is to the methods of measurement designed by psychologists to test intelligence that we next turn.

Measurement of Intelligence

In recent decades practically every American schoolchild has been subjected to a test of intelligence. The social significance of intelligence tests is enormous. In the United States as well as in many other highly developed nations they lie at the heart of selection processes and are influential in determining the life course of many people. Typically, test scores determine who goes to college and who gets special education training; they often determine whether a child is placed in fast, average, or slow tracks in school (with all that implies in terms of teacher expectations and the child's own self-esteem); in the military they select who will serve in the front-line infantry and who will operate electronic equipment in the rear echelons.

The tests are also the subjects of several continuing controversies concerning their fairness to various cultural groups, what it is they actually predict, and to what uses they should be put. We will look first at the tests themselves and then present a framework for evaluating intelligence tests and the charges leveled against them.

The Binet Scales

The first practical measure of intelligence, and in its modern form still widely used, was developed by the French psychologist Alfred Binet. His study of children's mental abilities began when he noticed that his two daughters Madeleine and Alice walked differently and wondered whether they might also think differently. He and his coworker, Theophile Simon, set about devising a way to test their intellectual performance (Binet and Simon, 1916). Binet's method was based on the simple observation that the intellectual performance of a child increases with age. By testing children of various ages, he

An intelligence test is being administered to a schoolchild.

could discover the intellectual milestones that marked each age.

In 1905, at the request of the Paris school authorities who wanted a means of identifying children who were slow learners, Binet prepared the forerunner of the modern intelligence test. Binet's test consisted of 30 questions corresponding in difficulty to the varying abilities of children between the ages of 3 and 13. The questions ranged from simple tasks, such as asking children to identify their eyes, nose, and mouth, to more complex activities, such as constructing a sentence around certain words. The questions were arranged so that a three-year-old would be expected to answer only the easiest ones correctly, while older children would be expected to answer progressively more difficult ones. By analyzing the results of experimental tests previously given to children of different ages, Binet standardized his test; that is, he established a standard of performance for each age group. Thus, the standard achieved by a child taking Binet's test constituted that child's mental age.

The Stanford-Binet

Binet's test soon crossed the Atlantic and, in the hands of Lewis Terman of Stanford University, took a revised form. The revision, known as the *Stanford-Binet Test* and published in 1916, replaced Binet's test items with ones considered more suitable for American children and was standardized on a sample of 1,400 children aged 3 to 16 (Terman, 1916). Terman's revision incorporated an idea suggested by William Stern (1914), a German psychologist, for representing the relationship between mental and chronological age. Mental age as shown on the Stanford-Binet was divided by chronological age and the resulting number multiplied by 100. The result was the child's *intelligence quotient* or *IQ*. Thus, if a child of six successfully completed all items expected of a nine-year-old, he or she was said to have a highly superior IQ of 150 (that is, 9/6 × 100).

The new test was enthusiastically welcomed in America, and while Binet's original intention was to use it to identify slow students who needed remedial instruction, the Stanford-Binet often became the primary means of selecting the intellectually superior. Despite Binet's warning against regarding the test results as fixed for life, it often was used to make long-term predictions about the intellectual abilities of young children.

Today the most popular of the IQ tests is the Stanford-Binet revision of 1960, which is considered appropriate for children from 3 to 18. The questions sample a wide variety of abilities, including memory, vocabulary, motor skills, comprehension, and reasoning. Typical test items for various levels are shown in Table 13.1.

The IQ determined by the modern Stanford-Binet no longer reflects the original formula of dividing mental age by chronological age and multiplying by 100. The problem with that simple formula was that the rate of growth in mental age typically slows down during the adolescent and adult years. The old formula has been replaced by the *deviation IQ,* which reflects test performance relative to others of the same chronological age.

The Wechsler Scales

During the 1930s many clinicians criticized the Stanford-Binet because of its emphasis on verbal abilities and its built-in limitations for use on adults. One such clinician, David Wechsler, set about constructing an intelligence test aimed at overcoming both of these failings.

Wechsler's first test, published in 1939, was intended for people 17 and older. Unlike the Stanford-Binet, it made no attempt to measure mental age; instead the Wechsler IQ reflected a comparison of points earned on the test with those achieved by test takers of the same age. Perhaps the most significant departure from the Stanford-Binet, however, was Wechsler's increased emphasis on nonverbal abilities. His test was subdivided into 11 groups, or subtests, each arranged in terms of increasing difficulty. There were six verbal subtests (information, comprehension, arithmetic, similarities, digit span, and vocabulary) along with five performance subtests (digit, symbol, picture completion, block design, and picture arrangement and object assembly), examples of which are shown in Figure 13.3. This structure of subtests also was adapted for use in schools as the *Wechsler Intelligence Scale for Children (WISC)* (Wechsler, 1949).

The test was revised in 1955 as the *Wechsler Adult Intelligence Scale (WAIS),* and today it is the most popular means of measuring adult intelligence (Wechsler, 1955, 1958). Typical items from the WAIS subtests are shown in Table 13.2. The popularity of the Wechsler scales stems from its subtests that enable clinicians to infer patterns of abilities; such inferences can be useful, for example, in assessing the possibility of localized brain damage.

New Approaches

Dissatisfaction with the Stanford-Binet and Wechsler tests has led researchers to formulate new approaches to the measurement of intelligence. Among the most intriguing new methods are the learning potential approach and neurometrics.

TABLE 13.1 Items of the Type Included in the 1960 Edition of the Stanford-Binet

Age 2:	Place geometric shapes into corresponding openings; identify body parts; stack blocks; identify common objects.
Age 4:	Name objects from memory; complete analogies (e.g., fire is hot; ice is _____); identify objects of similar shape; answer simple questions (e.g., "Why do we have schools?").
Age 6:	Define simple words; explain differences (e.g., between a fish and a horse); identify missing parts of a picture; count out objects.
Age 8:	Answer questions about a simple story; identify absurdities (e.g., in statements like "John had to walk on crutches because he hurt his arm"); explain similarities and differences among objects; tell how to handle certain situations (e.g., finding a stray puppy).
Age 10:	Define more difficult words; give explanations (e.g., about why people should be quiet in a library); list as many words as possible; repeat 6-digit numbers.
Age 12:	Identify more difficult verbal and pictured absurdities; repeat 5-digit numbers in reverse order; define abstract words (e.g., "sorrow"); fill in missing word in a sentence.
Age 14:	Solve reasoning problems; identify relationships among points of the compass; find similarities in apparently opposite concepts (e.g., "high" and "low"); predict the number of holes which will appear when folded paper is cut and then opened.
Superior Adult I:	Supply several missing words for incomplete sentences; repeat 6-digit numbers in reverse order; create a sentence using several unrelated words (e.g., "forest," "businesslike," and "dismayed"); describe similarities between concepts (e.g., "teaching" and "business").

Source: Douglas A. Bernstein and Michael T. Nietzel, *Introduction to Clinical Psychology* (New York: McGraw-Hill, 1980), p. 187.

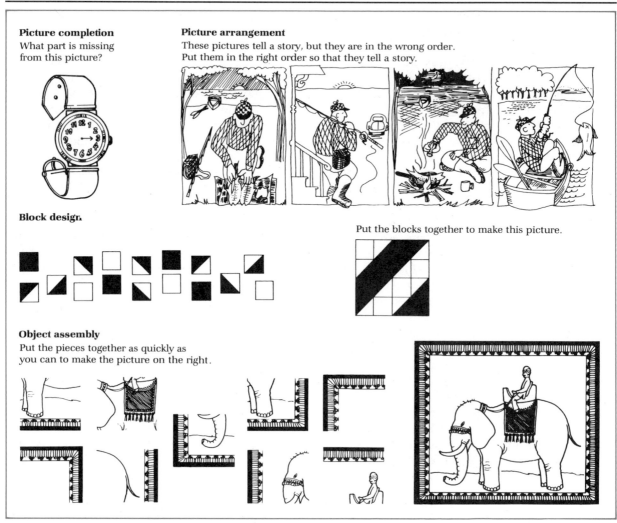

Picture completion
What part is missing from this picture?

Picture arrangement
These pictures tell a story, but they are in the wrong order.
Put them in the right order so that they tell a story.

Block design

Put the blocks together to make this picture.

Object assembly
Put the pieces together as quickly as you can to make the picture on the right.

FIGURE 13.3 These items are similar to those appearing in the performance portion of the Wechsler Adult Intelligence Scale.

Learning Potential All tests that purport to measure intelligence succeed to some degree in measuring a child's potential for learning. In recent years, a new approach to testing has focused on the particularities of learning potential. These methods attempt to measure the difference between the scores children are capable of achieving without any help and what they can achieve with coaching. The measure, in short, reflects how much coaching the child needs to answer a given question correctly.

Learning potential tests owe much to the work of the Russian developmental psychologist L. S. Vygotsky (1978). Vygotsky calls the gap between children's present capabilities and their future potential the *zone of proximal development*. To measure the zone of proximal development, Vygotsky constructed techniques for grading the amount of coaching, or number of prompts, needed before a child can answer a given question correctly. These techniques are particularly useful for distinguishing between children with learning disabilities and those who are mentally retarded. The learning-disabled child is much more likely to profit from adult coaching—and thus have more potential for intellectual growth—than is the mentally retarded child.

In the West, the best-known researcher of learning potential is Reuven Feuerstein, an Israeli clinical psychologist. Feuerstein's method employs a test-teach-test technique called the *Learning Potential Assessment Device* (Feuerstein, 1980). First, the child is given one of several standardized tests. Among these tests, shown in Figure 13.4, are:

- Raven's Progressive Matrices, which requires completion of like matrices in which all but one square has already been filled in according to a certain pattern (Raven, 1941).
- Organization of Dots Test, in which the child draws lines between dots that define shapes.
- Stencil Design Test, which requires identification of stencils used in a design constructed by superimposing two or more stencils.

After completing all the tests, the child is taught the principles and skills involved in the tests. Then, a final test is administered, presenting increasingly difficult tasks. A measure of the child's learning potential emerges from this test.

Neurometrics   The new branch of testing known as *neurometrics* seeks to assess mental processes by more direct means. The focus is on reactions within the brain and the body rather than on such responses as verbal answers. Still in the experimental stage, neurometric tests were developed to examine children whose age or handicaps prevented use of traditional tests.

One method makes use of a neurophysiological technique that measures *evoked potential*. The child's brain is monitored by an electroencephalograph, or EEG, which registers neural electrical activity in response to stimuli such as sounds or a flashing light. The brain's responses to sudden changes in the stimuli, the evoked potential, is isolated from other electrical brain activity by computer analysis. These computerized brain diagnoses have shown a correlation with IQ scores from traditional tests.

Evaluating the Tests

Recent controversies surrounding the measurement of intelligence have made it clear that not everyone agrees about the value of intelligence tests for making important social decisions. How do we judge, for example, whether tests measure what they claim to measure? Can we evaluate evidence and decide whether a test of intellectual ability actually predicts school performance? Should administrators use test scores to decide who should be admitted to universities? We will look at

TABLE 13.2   Items of the Type Included in the Weschler Adult Intelligence Scale (WAIS)

Information:	What is the shape of an orange?
	What does bread come from?
	What did Shakespeare do?
	What is the capital of France?
	What is the Malleus Malleficarum?
Comprehension:	Why do we eat food?
	What should you do with a wallet found in the street?
	Why do foreign cars cost more than domestic cars?
	What does "the squeaky wheel gets the grease" mean?
Arithmetic:	If you have four apples and give two away, how many do you have left?
	How long will it take a person to walk 20 miles at 3 miles per hour?
	If four people can finish a job in 6 days, how many people would it take to do the job in 2 days?
Similarities:	Identify similar aspects of pairs like: hammer-screwdriver, portrait-short story, dog-flower.
Digit span:	Repeat in forward and reverse order: 2- to 9-digit numbers.
Vocabulary:	Define: chair, dime, lunch, paragraph, valley, asylum, modal, cutaneous.
Picture completion:	Find missing objects in inreasingly complex pictures.
Block design:	Arrange blocks to match increasingly complex standard patterns.
Picture arrangement:	Place increasing number of pictures together to make increasingly complex stories.
Object assembly:	Arrange parts of puzzles to form recognizable objects (e.g., dog, flower, person).

Source: Douglas A. Bernstein and Michael T. Nietzel, *Introduction to Clinical Psychology* (New York: McGraw-Hill, 1980), p. 189.

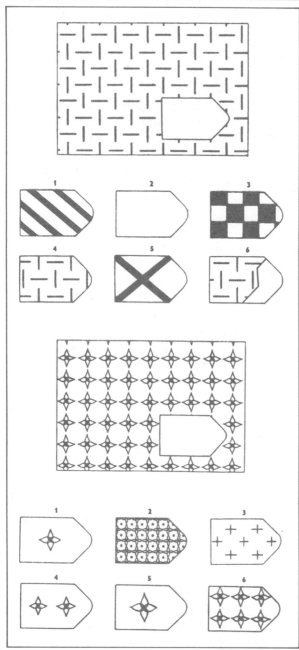

FIGURE 13.4 Sample items from the Raven Progressive Matrices Test, which requires completion of matrices by choosing from a group of possible patterns. In the top matrix, 4 completes the pattern; in the bottom one, 6 completes the pattern.

the principal criticisms of measures of intellectual ability in terms of three criteria for evaluating tests of all types: reliability, validity, and standardization.

Reliability   The *reliability* of a test can be shown if it measures the same thing consistently from occa-

sion to occasion, if it is administered by different testers and gets the same results, or if two comparable forms of the test produce a similar result. In order to have confidence in a test score, we must be able to examine evidence of reliability and be convinced that the test produces consistent scores for the same person.

We can measure reliability in a number of different ways. The same person can be given the same test on two different occasions, and we can then assess how similar the scores are. This is assessing the test-retest reliability of the test. Another way to assess reliability is to divide the test into two equal parts and to assess whether or not the scores are similar on the two parts (split-half) for the same individual. Still another measure of reliability is to produce two tests that are parallel or comparable in form and examine the similarity of scores. Traditional tests such as the Stanford-Binet or the Wechsler scales have proved to be highly reliable. Test-retest or parallel forms of reliability correlations tend to be 0.9 or higher. Because correlations provide a measure of the degree to which the ranking of people on one measure is similar to their ranking on another basis, a correlation of 0.9 or higher suggests a high degree of consistency in measurement. It is important to note, however, that reliability reflects nothing about what the test says it measures; it only reflects the fact that whatever the test measures is being measured consistently.

Standardization   Test results usually refer to the distribution of scores among a group of respondents. In order to know whether a person's score is "high" or "low," psychologists compare it to the scores of others in the same age group who have taken the test. The meaning or usefulness of the test result, of course, depends on how similar the individual being tested is to the *standardization group* on which the test has been standardized. For example, if the test score of a person who is just learning English is compared with a standardization group of people who are all native English speakers, then the respondent's verbal ability may be underestimated because of the lack of comparability between the subject and the standardization.

When Lewis Terman adapted Binet's original scale for use in the United States, he standardized the test on a sample consisting of only native-born white Americans. Clearly many respondents from other groups may be disadvantaged by being compared only to this group. It was only in 1972 that the Stanford-Binet was standardized in order to reflect the diversity of the U.S. population. A 2,100-child sample representing a broad range of socio-economic, geographical, racial, and cultural groups was used in that standardization. Similarly, the Wechsler Adult Intelligence Scale was originally standardized on a white New York sample but now has been standardized on adequate comparison groups. Today most of the individually adminis-tered intelligence tests are regarded as being ade-quately standardized. If, however, the meaning of a score reflecting intellectual ability is being evalu-ated, it is important to know whether the respon-dent's score is being compared with a comparable standardization sample.

Validity Another criterion that helps us to eval-uate tests has to do with whether they measure what they are intended to measure. Researchers have several ways of determining the *validity* of a test. If, for example, a test had been designed to measure memory ability, the score that a subject obtains on the test can be compared with some other measure of memory, the *criterion measure*. If the relationship between the two measures is high, then a tester may conclude that the test is a rea-sonable measure of memory ability.

However, most tests of intellectual ability are designed for predictive purposes. That is, the intel-ligence test score is expected to predict outcomes such as later school achievements. This sort of validity is called *predictive validity* and is another important way in which to evaluate intelligence tests and other tests of intellectual ability. If a test is intended to predict school achievement, then it would be reasonable to examine the relationship between scores on the test and subsequent grades in school. If the relationship or correlation is high, then it is reasonable to conclude that the test is a valid predictor of scholastic achievement.

Generally, tests of intelligence have been quite effective in predicting how a child will fare in school. The correlations between IQ scores and academic grades is approximately 0.6, which while far from perfect is still relatively high. Of course, tests of intellectual ability designed to predict school achievement may do so relatively well with-out necessarily predicting other measures of achievement such as success in later life—a fact that suggests the limitations of the relationship be-tween intelligence (or at least performances on tests) and worldly success.

Criticisms of Tests

The controversy over the value of intelligence tests has had some important ramifications in recent years. The National Education Association has for-mally called for the abolition of intelligence tests in the schools; in many school systems, such as New York City and Los Angeles, IQ tests actually have been abolished in the lower grades. Industry also has largely abandoned their use, in part because of a U.S. Supreme Court ruling in 1971—*Griggs* v. *The Duke Power Company*—in which the Court ruled that an electric utility worker in North Carolina had been deprived of his civil rights when he was denied promotion because of poor performance on an IQ test. Tests are proper to use, the Court said, only when they are used to predict specific job skills rather than overall intelligence.

Why is intelligence testing so controversial? We will examine three of the principal criticisms.

Achievement versus Aptitude It is important to distinguish between two types of tests: aptitude tests and achievement tests. The most important distinction has to do with the purposes to which they are put. In general, *aptitude tests* are designed to predict later performance, which has not yet been achieved. Thus, a test of aptitude for learning languages might be composed of various measures of abilities that are thought to be important in the learning of languages. Such a test might be com-posed of measures of memory ability, concentra-tion, and verbal fluency. Intelligence tests have been historically thought of as general tests of aptitude, particularly scholastic ability.

Achievement tests, on the other hand, are tests designed to measure the degree to which a particu-lar skill or body of knowledge has already been mastered. For example, written and performance tests of driving ability necessary to obtain a driver's license are achievement tests. Similarly, classroom tests, such as a final exam in introductory psychol-ogy, reflect the mastery and understanding of the material and are another specific type of achieve-ment test.

A number of critics have argued that traditional intelligence tests reflect achievement as well as aptitude characteristics (Stalnaker, 1965). Most questions in intelligence tests require previous knowledge of language or the basics of arithmetic, for example. This criticism is true in the sense that intelligence test scores reflect what individuals have already learned as well as their aptitudes or learning potentials.

Cultural Bias The issue of *cultural bias* represents a second major criticism of intelligence tests. Generations of blacks, Hispanics, and other minorities have been tested with questions that were standardized on a white, middle-class group.

Allegations of cultural bias focus on two aspects of discrimination. First, intelligence tests typically have required knowledge or perceptions that may be culture-specific: only a decade ago, for example, one test asked its subjects to fill in the word that best completed this sentence: "How the _____ roses flush up in the cheeks." The possible answers were red, pretty, yellow. The right answer was red, but, as *Testing Digest* pointed out recently, "only if the cheek in question is white (*Time*, 1979)."

The second form of discrimination is the language in which the test is written. Formal English puts at a disadvantage the sizable number of minority group members for whom English is a second language—Hispanics, for example, and even blacks who are exposed daily to black English.

Faced with such criticisms, test designers have attempted to eliminate the most obvious instances of cultural bias. In addition, there have been attempts to devise tests that are either culture-free or culture-specific—aimed at measuring special skills of minority groups. Culture-specific tests emphasize factors, such as minority languages, which may not play major roles in the larger culture.

Other approaches to the problem of cultural bias attempt to augment traditional tests with additional measures that take into account special traits or problems of minorities. Jane Mercer has developed an interlocking battery of measures for children from ages 5 to 11 called *System of Multicultural Pluralistic Assessment (SOMPA)* (Mercer and Lewis, 1977). The child is given the Wechsler scale but is also assessed for a number of other factors. For example, the examiner interviews the parent and prepares a sociocultural inventory of the family's background and an adaptive-behavior inventory of the child's performance in nonacademic activities. A thorough medical examination searches for problems, such as impairment of motor skills, that might affect the child's performance on the test and in school. The result is an *adjusted IQ* that is typically higher than the traditional IQ. In practical terms,

this means children with a Wechsler IQ of 68, which would make them eligible for a class for the mentally retarded, might be shown to be capable of progressing in a regular class. SOMPA already has been adopted by the states of California and Louisiana for determining student placement in special-education programs.

The Pigeonhole Effect A third major criticism of intelligence testing is that it fails to take into account varying rates of intellectual growth and risks locking young children into categories prematurely. This *pigeonhole effect* can stigmatize some youngsters unfairly by sidetracking them into classes for slow learners. It was concern over this issue that led the British to abandon their long-established "11 plus" system during the 1960s. Under this system an examination intended to measure intelligence and achievement was administered to all children around the eleventh birthday—hence the name 11 plus. The results determined whether children would be eligible for state grammar schools, which prepared them for university admission—and, therefore, the prospect of better jobs—or whether they would be sent instead to trade schools.

The possible effects of pigeonholing American children under fast or slow labels has been demonstrated in an experiment by Robert Rosenthal and Lenore Jacobson (1966). The experiment was conducted in an elementary school where children were tracked in classes according to the results of an IQ test taken at the beginning of the year. In 18 classes, teachers were given the names of children who purportedly had been identified by the IQ test as intellectual bloomers who would likely show marked improvement in their academic performance during the year. These children represented 25 percent of the pupils in the 18 classes. The story about their being specially marked for improvement was a ruse: they had not been chosen by the test at all but rather by random selection. By the end of the year, however, these randomly chosen "bloomers" had indeed bloomed. Their grades had improved and so had their IQs. Nearly half of the test population—47 percent—showed an increase of more than 20 points on the end-of-the-year IQ test; only 19 percent of the nonlabeled pupils showed similar improvement.

What can explain these startling results? One possibility is that the teachers expected more from the pupils labeled as bloomers and spent more time with them. Another possibility is that the teachers' expectations influenced their perception of the children's performance and thus the grades they awarded; the better grades, in turn, encouraged the children to work harder. A third possibility is that the teachers' expectations were somehow communicated to the children who, believing themselves more capable than before, proceeded to be more capable.

Although some studies have qualified the original results obtained by Rosenthal and Jacobson, the effects of pigeonholing the children seem fairly clear: the intellectual performance of those students labeled as bloomers tended to improve more than the performance of those who were not so labeled.

While a number of researchers are working on devising accurate measures of intelligence, others are looking into the factors that determine the level of individual intelligence.

Determinants of Intelligence

Why is one person more intelligent than another? The answers proposed by psychologists are even more controversial than the various theories as to what intelligence is and the methods of measuring it. As in many of the other debates that arise from the study of human behavior, the controversy over the determinants of intelligence revolves around the two polarities of nature and nurture. Is intelligence essentially an inherited characteristic that is determined by our individual genetic makeup? Or is it largely the product of environmental influences such as education, child-rearing practices, social class, and culture?

Hereditary Influences on Intelligence

The case for inheritance of intelligence rests on evidence amassed from the pursuit of a simple proposition: if the primary influence on intelligence is genetic, then two individuals who have a close genetic relationship should have similar IQs. Such an approach depends on statistical correlations, because research in human genetics is not sufficiently advanced to explain the precise relationships between genetic endowment and complex behaviors or abilities such as intelligence.

Statistical correlations tend to bear out the proposed link between genetic relationship and IQ (Erlenmeyer-Kimling and Jarvik, 1963). Figure 13.5, which is based on data from 52 different studies, shows how correlations of IQ increase with increasingly closer genetic relationships. The categories of genetic relationship progress from one extreme, individuals who are totally unrelated, to the other

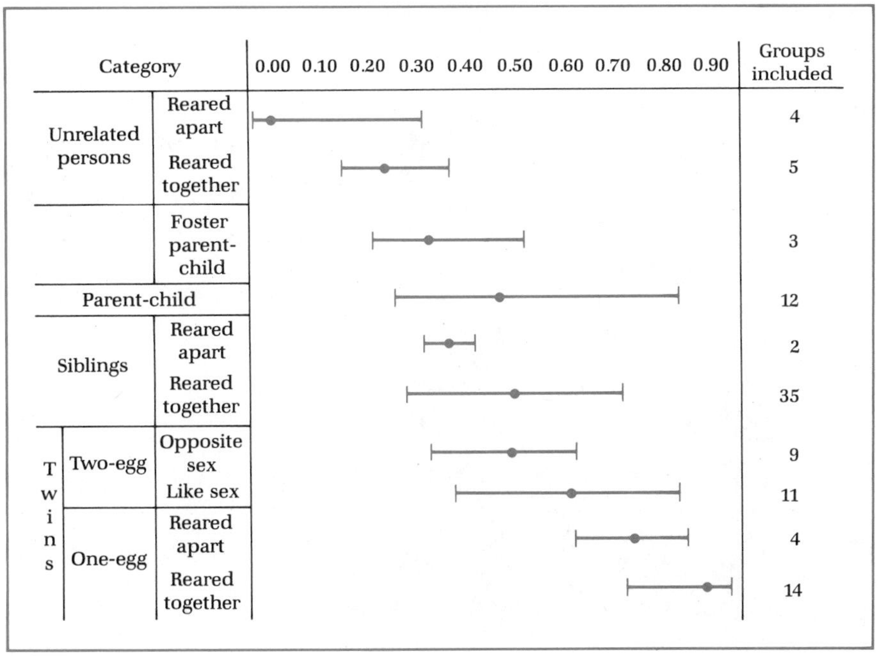

FIGURE 13.5 Correlation coefficients for IQ test scores from 52 studies. Medians are shown by dots intersecting the horizontal lines, which represent the ranges. The relationship categories progress from totally unrelated persons reared apart to identical twins reared together.

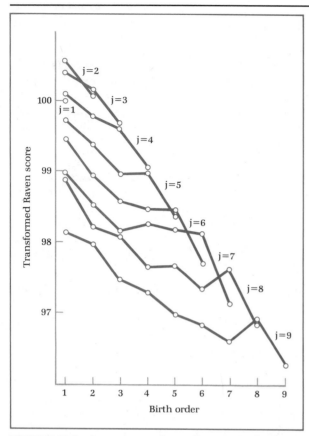

FIGURE 13.6 Average transformed scores on the Raven test are shown as a function of birth order and family size (j indicates family size) with the score of the only child set at 100. The findings indicate that the larger the family, the lower the relative score. There also appears to be a systematic relationship between birth order and test scores.

extreme, identical twins, who are identical genetically. The systematic increase in correlation between IQs that is shown here strongly suggests a genetic influence on intelligence.

One problem with interpreting the possible cause of such correlations is obvious: closer genetic relationships also typically involve environmental similarities. Brothers, for example, not only draw from similar gene pools provided by their parents, but they also are exposed to similar environmental influences—class, culture, education, child-rearing practices.

The best method researchers can use to isolate the effects of heredity from those of environment is to study twins. Fraternal twins, who are said to be dizygotic because they originate in two separate eggs, are no more genetically alike than are other siblings. Thus, differences in intelligence between dizygotic twins are assumed to be determined by both genetic and environmental factors. Identical, or monozygotic, twins have identical genetic makeups because they originate in the same egg. As Figure 13.6 shows, the correlation of intelligence is usually much higher among monozygotic twins than among dizygotic twins.

Twin studies of unusual interest are those that compare identical twins who were raised together with twins who were separated soon after birth and raised apart.

Studies of monozygotic twins raised apart tend to indicate such astonishing similarities and behaviors, despite differences in environment, that they

Fraternal, or two-egg, twins may be of the same sex or of different sexes. They are generally more comparable in characteristics to ordinary siblings than to identical, or one-egg twins, who are always of the same sex.

buttress the argument for genetic influences. An important new study by Thomas Bouchard (Holden, 1980) which is still in progress, has provided preliminary but impressive evidence for such similarities (see *Focus*). Bouchard and his colleagues are measuring a number of personality characteristics in addition to intelligence. In their studies to date, however, intelligence has shown the highest correlation of all the measurements—a tentative finding but one that speaks powerfully for the heritability of intelligence.

At the same time, comparisons of monozygotic twins raised apart also provide evidence for the influence of environmental factors. Any differences between such twins are assumed to be environmentally based because the two individuals are genetically identical. Such differences are demonstrated by the higher correlation of intelligence for identical twins raised together, as shown in Figure 13.7.

Environmental Influences on Intelligence

Studies of twins examine the relationship between intellectual variation and genetic variation. If there is a positive correlation between genetic similarity and similarity in intelligence test scores, we assume that intelligence and genetic background are related to one another. The impact of environmental factors on intelligence cannot be as easily compared as genetic makeup among individuals.

Scientists must either create or discover differences in the environments of individuals that may be related to differences in intellectual performance. If researchers can show that contrasting environments produce differences in intellectual attainment, then a case can be made for social, cultural, and environmental factors as well as genetic background in the development of intelligent behavior.

Family Environment: Birth Order and Intellectual Attainment The impact of the family environment on intellectual behavior and on intelligence is unquestionably important. Language development, problem-solving skills, and other critical intellectual abilities are first learned in the family context, not only from parents but also from siblings.

Lillian Belmont and Francis Marolla (1973) studied the results of intelligence tests given to nearly 400,000 19-year-old men in the Netherlands. This sample consisted of practically all males born in that country from 1944 to 1947. Belmont and Morolla found that firstborn males scored higher on the test than did later-borns within the same family. Moreover, IQ scores declined in relation to the ordinal position of birth within the family: second-borns scored higher than third-borns, who scored higher than fourth-borns, and so on. Similar conclusions have been drawn from a study of 800,000 U.S. students—both male and female—who applied for National Merit Scholarships.

This phenomenon is usually explained in terms of the amount of time and concern parents devote to their children. They are simply likely to lavish more attention on the firstborn. As the number of children increases, parents have less time and energy available to devote to any single offspring.

Another study of 400,000 19-year-olds reflects the impact of family environment on intelligence (Zajonc and Markus, 1975). Figure 13.6 shows the overall results of this study, which indicate several things. First, the IQs of children from larger families are somewhat lower than the IQs of children from smaller families. This difference is regular and systematic: the larger the family, the lower the relative IQ score. Second, there is a systematic relationship between birth order and intelligence, with individuals born earlier in the family showing some advantage in intellectual attainment over those born later.

In addition, the figures for the last child in the sequence show a decline in IQ level that is even larger than that for preceding children. It appears as if being a last child, particularly in larger families, produces a unique disadvantage of its own. Furthermore, the IQs for only children are systematically lower than for firstborn children with either one or two siblings. By way of explanation Robert Zajonc suggests that the family can be thought of as a group that provides intellectual resources to its members; this is the intellectual environment that affects intelligence. Zajonc concludes that increased family size is uniformly detrimental to intellectual development. He also believes that spacing between siblings is critical: larger spacing tends to benefit younger children, while it is detrimental to older siblings. Zajonc explains the comparatively lower IQs of last children and only children by the fact that neither has an opportunity to be a "teacher" to younger siblings. The opportunity to be a teacher to others tends to stimulate intellectual growth, whereas a lack of this opportunity will produce a somewhat lower level of intelligence.

All of the differences observed by Zajonc are small in the absolute sense but are extremely regular. The fact that Zajonc and his colleagues were able to obtain birth order and intelligence test data on such a large sample means that even small differences associated with family size and birth order will be observable in the average values for various groups. On the other hand, numerous other factors also affect performance on intelligence tests, and family size and birth order are simply another set of contributors to performance. Thus, family size and birth order are part of a larger puzzle involved in understanding the role of environmental factors and genetic background in the development of intellectual ability.

Social Class and Ethnic Group Differences   In our society there are extremely large variations in the opportunities available to black versus white and wealthy versus less economically advantaged children. The degree to which ethnic or racial differences on the one hand and social class differences on the other affect intelligence or intellectual achievement is a subject of continuing debate. The issue is complex and researchers cannot easily disentangle the effects of class on IQ. For example, does restricted opportunity in lower socioeconomic

RESEARCH: A Classic Study of Environmental Influence

Researchers who want to investigate the effects of early childhood environment on human intelligence must overcome formidable obstacles. Because the presumed environmental effects occur over a long period of time, it obviously would be impractical to conduct experiments in the laboratory. Moreover, ethical considerations ordinarily constrain researchers from manipulating the real-life environment of a child.

In the classic study by Harold M. Skeels (1966), however, these obstacles were overcome because of the researcher's adroitness in seizing on a serendipitous "experiment in nature." Skeels' study began by chance during the 1930s when he was serving as a psychologist for the state of Iowa. Among his duties was the psychological testing of young children in an orphanage. One day he examined two baby girls who had been legally committed to the orphanage not long after birth because their feebleminded mothers had neglected them. The girls were emaciated and pitifully inactive, spending their days in the orphanage rocking and whining. Skeels found that, although there was no evidence of physiological or organic defects, the girls showed developmental levels of children less than half their ages: the 16-month-old had a level of seven months; the 13-month-old had a level of six months. In those days, intelligence was generally regarded by psychologists as a genetically determined characteristic that was relatively fixed at birth. The two little girls were given up as unadoptable and, two months later, they were transferred to the Glenwood State School, an institution for the mentally retarded.

Six months after the transfer, Skeels visited Glenwood. He scarcely recognized the two little girls. They were alert, smiling, and active. Skeels tested them again and found to his astonishment that they were now approaching normal mental development for their age. Subsequent tests when the girls were about three years of age confirmed their progress.

What could explain the remarkable changes in their behavior and mental development? Skeels concluded that the change in environment had to be responsible. The orphanage where the girls spent their early months was understaffed and overcrowded. Much of the time, the young children were confined to large cribs with very little chance for human interaction. At Glenwood, by contrast, the two little girls had a home-like environment, rich in affection and interesting experiences. They lived in a ward with women ranging in age from 18 to 50 years (mental age from 5 to 9) who, in effect, "adopted" them. They also received a lot of affection and attention from attendants and nurses who bought them toys and picture books and took them out for auto rides and shopping excursions.

Skeels thereupon decided to undertake a bold experiment. He prevailed on the administrators of the orphanage to transfer 10 more children to the Glenwood State School, pointing out that the children all seemed destined for mental retardation in any case. His experimental group consisted of 13 children—the two little girls who had transferred earlier, a third girl who had been transferred at about the same time, and the ten new transfers. All were under three years of age, and all were certified as "seriously retarded by tests and observation before transfer was made." Their average age was 19.4 months; their IQ scores ranged from 35 to 89 with a mean of 64.3.

groups produce lower levels of intellectual attainment or do individuals with lower levels of intellectual ability "drift" to the lower socioeconomic strata of society?

A recent study attempted to map some of the effects of race and social class on the intellectual and personality characteristics of young children (Yando, Seitz, and Zigler, 1979). The investigators studied 304 eight-year-old children from the Boston area. They carefully selected children representing higher and lower socioeconomic status as well as black and white children from both higher and lower status families. They were interested in what differences would remain after the variation in IQ was taken out of other measures. They studied a number of different characteristics including creativity, self-confidence, autonomy, curiosity, tolerance for frustration, dependency, and self-image. A number of fascinating results were obtained. For example, when social class effects were controlled in this study, few race differences were found. On the other hand, differences that appeared to be a consequence of social class were substantial. Less advantaged children appeared to be creative problem solvers who were willing to take risks and persevere in the face of frustration. Advantaged upper-class children, on the other hand, tended to be

---

The progress of this experimental group at Glenwood was measured against that of a comparison group of 12 children who remained at the orphanage. The comparison group was slightly younger, with a mean age of 16.6 months, and considerably brighter, with a mean IQ of 86.7.

The contrasts between the two different environments—the drab, sterile orphanage and the lively, stimulating mental institution—became even more marked as the children grew older. At the orphanage, children over two years old lived in cottages where one matron, aided by three or four untrained girls, had charge of 30 to 35 boys or girls. The cottages were so crowded that the children had to be tightly regimented. At age six, the children attended the orphanage elementary school. Later, they were sent to public junior high school where there were few opportunities for individual attention and where the children quickly fell behind in their work.

Meanwhile, at Glenwood, the transfers from the orphanage were "adopted" by adults—attendants as well as the mentally retarded residents. Each child thus was afforded the opportunity for an intense one-to-one emotional relationship with an older person. The children could play outdoors often on tricycles, swings, and other equipment. And when they attended school at Glenwood, the matron in charge made it a regular practice to single out children in need of special attention, allowing them to spend stimulating time each day visiting her office.

After several months, Skeels tested the children in the experimental and comparison groups. The 13 children in the enriched environment at Glenwood showed an average gain in IQ of 27.5 points; 3 children gained over 45 points. In contrast, the 12 children in the deprived environment at the orphanage showed a decline in average IQ of 26.2 points.

Even more impressive were the results of the follow-up study conducted by Skeels 21 years later. All 13 children in the Glenwood experimental group—11 of whom had been placed for adoption—were self-supporting; in the comparison group, four were still wards of institutions and one had died in a state institution during adolescence. The median education level in the experimental group was the twelfth grade; in the comparison group less than the third grade. In the experimental group, subjects held jobs ranging from professional and business occupations to domestic service. Comparison group members who were not institutionalized tended to have low-level jobs.

Perhaps the most striking contrast occurred in the next generation. The experimental group had 28 offspring with IQs ranging from 86 to 125, with a mean of 104; in no instance was there any evidence of mental retardation. The comparison group had five children. Four, the offspring of one male subject, were of average intelligence. But the other second-generation child showed marked mental retardation with indications of probable brain damage.

Skeels' study had one methodological shortcoming: there was no way in which he could completely rule out possible innate differences in his subjects. Nonetheless, it provides extremely persuasive evidence—in the short run and over a period of more than two decades—for early environment as a powerful force in the shaping of intelligence.

better at solving more conventional problems but also were overly concerned and anxious about failure.

One of the most important aspects of this study is the fact that the investigators designed it to allow assessment of differences that are a consequence of race and class where intelligence has been controlled. These differences, when they emerge, could be important factors that affect children's intellectual achievement as well as their achievement in other life domains.

A very different study illuminates the question of race differences and intelligence. This study capitalized on the "natural experiment" associated with adoption (Scarr and Weinberg, 1978). The researchers studied IQs of black children who had been adopted early in life by upper-middle-class white families with more than average educational attainment and income; they found that the average IQ of these adopted black children was 106, much higher than the national average of comparable children who had not been adopted. In addition, the investigators examined a number of different variables that presumably reflect differences in intellectual environment, and these variables also correlated with differences in IQ. Thus, the impact of environmental differences on intellectual attainment of black children is considerable. This study throws doubt on the claim of Arthur Jensen (1969) who has argued that variation in IQ among blacks reflects genetic differences in intellectual potential.

The Heredity versus Environment Controversy

Any attempt to sort out the evidence in the heredity versus environment debate over the determinants of intelligence faces a major hurdle. A great deal of educational and social policy—tracking of students, for example, and efforts to ameliorate poverty and upgrade slum schools—hinges on interpretation of the evidence, which often tends to be shaded by preexisting biases. These biases, in turn, sometimes lead to an exaggeration of the evidence and unwarranted conclusions. Several issues have clouded the debate in recent years.

The Jensen Controversy Too often the debate is obfuscated by the uses to which data and theories are put. A prime example is the work of Arthur Jensen, who in 1969 published a monograph alleging that about 80 percent of differences in IQ are attributable to differences in genetic background. This assertion was controversial, but Jensen went on to set off a much greater controversy. Jensen noted that the IQ scores of American blacks average more than 15 points below those of whites and that compensatory educational programs had done little to change that fact. In short, Jensen implied that the disparity between black and white IQs had relatively little to do with poverty, racial discrimination, inferior slum schools, or even cultural bias in testing.

Critics assailed Jensen on a number of counts:

- His conclusion lent itself to racist purposes and could be used to justify all manner of discrimination, including racial segregation in schools and the neglect of compensatory education.
- The IQ tests, on which Jensen built his theory, were culturally biased against blacks and hence invalid.
- IQ tests are based on the notion that IQ is a measurable and unalterable "thing"—a highly questionable assumption.
- The disparity in IQ scores between blacks and whites can be explained in terms of environmental factors such as nutrition, child-rearing practices, and poor schools (see Figure 13.7).
- Heritability of intelligence may account for differences in IQ within a group, but this does not justify the comparison across cultural or racial boundaries.

In order to understand this last criticism more clearly, it is necessary to consider the concept of heritability in more detail because this concept, often misunderstood, fuels the debate.

The Concept of Heritability The concept of *heritability* is a measure of relative variation. It indicates how much of the variation in a particular trait for a particular population is due to genetic as opposed to environmental factors. Thus, the first thing to recognize about the concept of heritability is that it depends on both environmental and genetic variation for a particular population. Measures of heritability in characteristics such as intelligence are applied to a specific group under a specific set of circumstances.

Herrnstein (1973) uses the example of skin color to illustrate the meaning of heritability. He points out that in the United States, which has a substantial mix of racial groups, the heritability of skin color is high. On the other hand, in a small and isolated Norwegian town, Scandinavians with generations of pale-skinned ancestors display little variation in skin color, and any variation observed is more likely to be due to environmental factors. Thus, in the Scandinavian town the heritability should be low—that is, any variation in skin color is likely to be caused by environmental factors such as exposure to the sun.

When the race and IQ controversy stimulated by Jensen is considered, several factors must be carefully looked at. First, the estimates of heritability for intelligence are based on white populations; no adequate measures of heritability of intelligence for the black population is available. Furthermore, it is clear that the environmental circumstances for black people in the United States are dramatically different, on the average, than those of white people. Therefore, the heritability estimates for whites may tell us little or nothing about the heritability of IQ among blacks in the United States. Estimates of the heritability of intelligence are specific to particular populations under particular circumstances, and variations in environmental factors, such as blocked opportunity or deprived environment, may strongly affect heritability estimates.

FIGURE 13.7 Multiple environmental factors can affect intellectual ability. Among populations in poverty, many of these factors may combine to produce a poor learning environment.

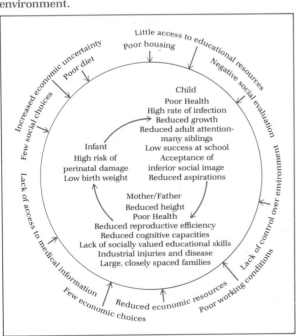

However, there is an important corollary to this notion, as Herrnstein notes. If an environmental factor that would affect IQ were found—a diet or a particular type of educational program—and were provided to the American people, such an environmental factor would raise the average IQ of the American public and, at the same time, would actually increase the heritability of IQ. Equalizing circumstances would mean that less and less variation in IQ would be due to environmental factors, and more and more would be due to genetic background. Thus, improving environmental circumstances may have the paradoxical effect of actually raising the degree to which intelligence runs in families.

Herrnstein offers the following syllogism, which draws out some of the social implications of these observations. He says "(1) if differences in mental abilities are inherited, and (2) if success requires those abilities, and (3) if earnings and prestige depend on success, (4) then social standing (which reflects earnings and prestige) will be based to some extent on inherited differences among people (Herrnstein, 1973)."

Herrnstein goes on to offer several corollaries of this syllogism. We have already discussed the first of these: the argument that as the environment becomes more favorable for intellectual development, the more certainly will differences in intelligence be inherited. In addition, as the social barriers to upward mobility are removed in our society, more and more of the barriers to upward mobility will be based on innate differences. He argues further that our society's technological advances will require intellectual ability to an increasing degree, and he suggests that "as technology advances, the tendency to be unemployed may run in the genes of a family about as certainly as bad teeth do now (Herrnstein, 1973)."

None of this should be seen as a justification for social discrimination based on group membership. Genetics may affect potential intellectual attainment of individuals, but environment, just as surely, determines the degree to which people fulfill their potential.

The Question of Modifiability The evidence is substantial that genetic background helps determine intelligence, perhaps establishing upper and lower limits. At the same time, evidence is also substantial that life experiences help dictate where an individual's intelligence will fall within this assumed range laid down by nature. Therefore, it may be fruitful to look for those factors that may enable people to attain greater intellectual achievement as has been done with other conditions that clearly are genetic in origin and yet subject to environmental modification.

One such condition is phenylketonuria (PKU), a disorder caused by the pairing of two defective recessive genes. Infants with PKU are unable to metabolize a certain amino acid. This deficiency interferes with the development of myelin, the white sheathing of nerve cells necessary for rapid transmission of electric impulses (see Chapter 2), and can lead to irreversible brain damage and profound mental retardation. Many children with PLU never learn to walk or talk; more than half have IQs of less than 20. However, PKU can be detected in the postnatal blood test required by state laws. If the test is positive, a special diet low in the problem protein can allow normal brain development to occur. Thus, in the case of PKU, an environmental influence—a special diet—can modify or eliminate the behavioral effects of a genetically dictated condition.

The PKU example suggests one way of clarifying the debate over the determinants of intelligence. Even if intelligence has a genetic component, every effort should be made to provide the "special diet" of environmental influences that can help every individual attain full intellectual growth.

Changes in Intellectual Ability over the Life Span

We have already seen that the intelligence quotient is adjusted for an individual's chronological age. Thus, individuals actually are being compared to people of their own age when IQ is used as a measure of intellectual ability. A pertinent question is whether or not a person's IQ—that is, an individual's relative standing compared with people of a similar age—changes over time. In general, intelligence quotients remain relatively stable for most people, particularly after age seven.

Before age seven, tests of intelligence, particularly those given to infants, are not good predictors of future intellectual performance. One reason is that tests given to children early in life depend heavily on visual and motor ability, whereas tests given

later in life depend much more heavily on verbal ability; results from one type of test of intellectual ability do not necessarily predict results in another domain. In addition, infant tests seem to be poor predictors of future performance because of the great plasticity of the behavior of infants.

Even though relative standing in IQ remains stable for most people over the life span, *intellectual ability*—that is, the ability to master a variety of tasks requiring memory, perception, reasoning, and other abilities—has a growth curve of its own. Figure 13.8 shows data that indicates that intellectual growth occurs very rapidly over the first 20 or so years of life and then levels out (Bayley, 1970).

Toward middle and old age, intellectual abilities begin to change again, but to say that intellectual ability simply declines in old age is much too simple. Some abilities remain relatively intact for most people even fairly late in life. Verbal ability, deductive reasoning ability, and general information retention remain constant well into later life (Blum, Jarvik, and Clark, 1970). Other abilities, however, do appear to decline in old age, particularly those requiring speed of response and short-term memory (Schaie and Strother; 1968; Craik; 1977). Again, there are wide individual differences in the

FIGURE 13.8 The scores in this theoretical growth curve of intelligence are based on age-appropriate tests, including Bayley infant scales, Stanford-Binet, and Wechsler Adult Scales. The curve shows rapid growth through childhood, with a leveling off at about age 20.

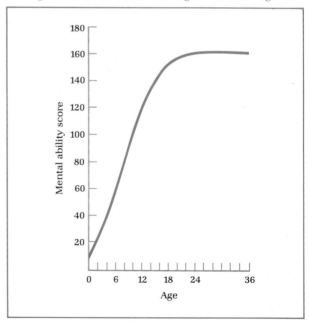

size and rate of these changes: some people retain most of their intellectual vigor well into later life, whereas others lose it rather early. Changes in health and the degree to which an individual is intellectually challenged in daily life have a good deal to do with how rapidly intellectual abilities decline over time (De Carlo, 1971; Spirduso, 1973).

Extremes of Intelligence

In the wide spectrum of intelligence, the majority of us are clustered around the middle. For example, on the Stanford-Binet scale, the IQs of 46 percent of all Americans fall in the range between 90 and 109 (see Table 13.3). At either end of the spectrum are extremes that are of particular interest to the psychologist. About 3 percent of the population, approximately 7 million Americans, have IQs below 68 and are considered mentally retarded; about 1 percent of Americans have IQs above 140 and are considered mentally gifted.

Mental Retardation

"What is retardation? It's hard to say, I guess it's having problems thinking." This straightforward definition was offered by a 26-year-old man, who at the age of 15 had been placed in a state institution for the retarded. His case, which was studied extensively, points up some of the difficulties in distinguishing between the intellectually normal and subnormal (Bogdan and Taylor, 1976).

Most formal definitions of mental retardation take into account not only subnormal IQ but also two other variables: the degree of social adaptation and the age at which intellectual problems are first manifested. The problems of retardation develop early in life, well before the eighteenth year. Thus

TABLE 13.3 Percentages of Population in Various Stanford-Binet IQ Ranges

IQ	PERCENTAGE IN GROUPS	CHARACTERIZATION
Above 139	1	Very superior
120–139	11	Superior
110–119	18	High average
90–109	46	Average
80–89	15	Low average
70–79	6	Borderline
Below 70	3	Mentally retarded
	100	

the current manual of the American Association on Mental Deficiency (AAMD), an organization of professionals concerned with the problem, states that *mental retardation* "... refers to significantly subaverage general intellectual functioning existing concurrently with deficits in adaptive behavior ..." (Robinson and Robinson, 1976).

Levels of Retardation The current AAMD manual recognizes four levels of mental deficiency. Significantly, the former category of borderline retardation has been dropped in response to criticism that people with IQs as high as 83 on the Stanford-Binet can adapt to conventional classrooms and should not be stigmatized. The following descriptions summarize key characteristics of each of the four levels of retardation recognized by the AAMD (Robinson and Robinson, 1976).

1. *Mild Retardation.* IQ 52 to 67 on the Stanford-Binet. This group comprises about 90 percent of the mentally retarded. Children in this group are eligible for classes for the educable mentally retarded and are expected to attain a sixth-grade level of academic performance. Adults usually can work in unskilled jobs.
2. *Moderate Retardation.* IQ 36 to 51. This group comprises about 6 percent of the mentally retarded. Children are eligible for classes for trainable retardates that emphasize self-care rather than academic skills. Few adults hold jobs but instead depend on their families or are institutionalized.
3. *Severe Retardation.* IQ 20 to 35. This group comprises about 3 percent of the retarded. Children require prolonged training just to learn to speak and take care of basic needs. Adults can usually communicate on a rudimentary level.
4. *Profound Retardation.* IQ below 20. This group comprises about 1 percent of the retarded. These individuals require total supervision, and it is assumed that they can learn little except possibly to walk, utter a few phrases, and feed themselves.

Not everyone of subnormal intelligence fits neatly into the four categories of mental retardation. A special and unusually interesting case in point is the *idiot savant*, a retardate who shows superior functioning in one narrow area of mental activity.

409

Idiot savants have displayed extraordinary talents in music, mathematical calculation, and rote memory.

One of the best-documented case histories of an idiot savant is the study of L. (Scheerer, Rothman, and Goldstein, 1945). The investigators studied L., who had an IQ of 50 on the Stanford-Binet, which classified him as moderately retarded, from his eleventh through sixteenth years. Yet L. had several remarkable abilities. He could quickly spell forward or backward practically any word pronounced to him, although he did not necessarily know its meaning. He could play a number of melodies by ear on the piano but seemed to have no idea of what he was doing. He could add up to a dozen two-digit numbers as fast as they were recited to him but was unable to learn to add larger numbers. He could name the day of the week for any date between 1880 and 1950 but had no sense of chronology.

What explains such special talents in people who otherwise function on an intellectual level so far below normal? M. Scheerer and his colleagues suggested that L.'s low IQ score reflected his deficiency in the ability to reason abstractly, and this lack may have forced him to cope with the world by channeling his energy into feats of rote memory.

Determinants of Retardation A number of factors are involved in the causes of mental retardation depending in part on the severity of the deficiency. The more serious forms of retardation—moderate, severe, and profound—can typically be traced to organic factors such as chromosomal abnormalities or brain trauma. In mild retardation cultural-familial factors are believed to play the major role.

Organic causes of retardation can be grouped into three categories—genetic, infectious, and traumatic. The most prevalent genetic cause is Down's syndrome (formerly known as mongolism), which accounts for at least 10 percent of the cases of moderate to severe retardation. In addition to low IQ—typically under 50—Down's syndrome victims have a number of physical abnormalities, including eyes that are slanted upward and outward, flat face and nose, and stunted growth. With proper encouragement and instruction, however, they can perform housework and simple carpentry and seem to thrive better in a loving home than in an institution. The cause of Down's syndrome is a chromosomal abnormality: victims have 47 chromosomes instead of 46, the extra one apparently resulting from a defective separation of pair 21 in the mother's egg cell before ovulation. For reasons that are still not clearly understood, about two thirds of all children with Down's syndrome are born to women over the age of 40.

Infectious diseases can cause retardation before or after birth. The fetus is particularly vulnerable during the first month of pregnancy, when its nervous system is developing at a rapid rate. If a mother is infected by rubella, or German measles, during this period, there is a 50 percent chance her child will suffer both mental and physical abnormalities. Young children born normal can suffer impairment of the brain, and hence mental retardation, if they are infected by encephalitis, an inflammation of the brain, or by mengitis, an inflammation of the brain's protective membranes.

Traumatic causes of retardation also can affect the brain before or after birth. These causes range from incompatibility between the blood of the mother and the fetus (leading to oxygen deprivation in the fetal brain), to excessive exposure to X rays in utero, to head injuries, and to ingestion by the child of poisonous metals such as lead (from automobile emissions or lead-based paints) and mercury (from industrial wastes consumed by fish).

A child with Down's syndrome which is the result of a chromosomal abnormality, usually displays symptoms that include such physical abnormalities as stunted growth and mild to severe retardation.

Another nonorganic factor believed to be widespread in the development of mental retardation is malnutrition. An estimated 300 million preschool children throughout the world have inadequate diets. Malnutrition is thought to be particularly harmful during the period of the brain's most rapid growth—in utero and in the first few months after birth. The evidence for the effects of malnutrition comes from a variety of sources. Much of its rests on animal studies demonstrating that the total number of neurons in the brain is permanently reduced if the creature suffers from malnutrition during periods of cell division (Davison and Dobbing, 1966). In addition, a study of human children at autopsy showed that children who had died from malnutrition had fewer than normal brain cells (Winick, Rosso, and Waterlow, 1970).

People whose retardation can be traced to organic causes are fairly evenly distributed throughout all socioeconomic, ethnic, and racial groups. Generally, those whose mental retardation is organic in origin fall into the categories below an IQ of 51—moderate, severe, and profound retardation. The greatest proportion of the mentally retarded, however, have an IQ above 51 and thus are considered only mildly retarded. Most of them show no indications of brain pathology, but typically are members of families in which the levels of intelligence and of socioeconomic status are low. These cultural-familial factors, many researchers believe, are responsible for mild retardation. Such home environments may not provide the early intellectual stimulation and encouragement thought necessary for normal mental growth. Children from such homes may also attend deficient schools.

The evidence for the cultural-familial view is correlational. Various studies have shown high correlations between mild retardation and homes of low socioeconomic levels where one or more parents or siblings have a subnormal IQ (Zigler, 1967). It may be that other environmental characteristics of poverty such as malnutrition—before and after birth—also contribute heavily to mild retardation. In any case, whether the causes are organic or cultural-familial or both, the majority of retarded children can achieve higher levels of intellectual functioning with appropriate training.

The Intellectually Gifted

The intellectually gifted sometimes face problems similar to those encountered by the mentally retarded. Like the mentally retarded, extremely bright children have been subject to popular bias and misunderstanding. Not too long ago, folk wisdom had it that "early ripe, early rot" and suggested that precocious children were prone to insanity and other severe problems. Such dire prophecies have not been borne out; nonetheless studies in recent years have shown that extremely bright children, like subnormal ones, may often need special education. They may become bored in conventional schools. Some studies indicate that gifted students account for up to 20 percent of all high school dropouts (Hershey, 1976).

Concern about the gifted has resulted in several innovative educational programs. Several states now mandate special education programs for gifted students in public schools. These special programs usually consist of enrichment classes that meet once or twice a week, accelerated classes that cover traditional academic material faster than usual, or independent research projects or internships (Rice, 1980).

Understanding of intellectually gifted children has benefited enormously from a long-term study launched in 1921 by Terman, who developed the Stanford-Binet IQ test. Terman and his coworkers selected 1,528 California schoolchildren—857 boys and 671 girls—with IQs of 135 or higher for their study (Terman and Oden, 1947). Most of these subjects were between the ages of 8 and 12. For more than half a century since then, Terman and, after his death, other Stanford University researchers, have kept track of this highly gifted group through periodic interviews and questionnaires—most recently in 1977 (Sears, 1977).

The data from the study have long since achieved Terman's original aim: to disprove the myth that exceptional intelligence is a handicap. For contemporary researchers, the results provide illumination, if not definitive answers, to a number of questions. What is the relationship between intelligence and later achievement? Does intelligence alone guarantee extraordinary accomplishment? Is there a correlation between IQ and creativity?

The group did extremely well in school, and the majority excelled in their careers. All but 11 finished high school, two thirds graduated from college, 97 received doctorates, 57 got medical degrees, and 92 earned law degrees. Careers ranged from letter carrier to brigadier general; there were a number of

411

scientists and some corporation heads. Among the group was a leading writer of science fiction and an Academy Award–winning film director. In 1955, the group had an average income of $33,000, more than four times the national average of $8,000.

At the same time, however, the group produced no towering geniuses, no Nobel Prize winners, "no Einsteins." Similarly, there is an absence of exceptional people in the creative arts—no poets, no great musicians, no painters. This suggests that although intelligence and creativity may overlap, they are not the same.

One important finding was that these bright people tended to produce bright offspring. The average IQ of their children was 133, although the range extended from a high of 200 to below 68, the upper limit of mental retardation. The high average cannot be attributed only to genetic factors, however, because the offspring typically were surrounded by environmental influences, such as the stimulation of high-IQ parents, that are known to be associated with above-normal intelligence.

Of particular interest in the Terman study is a comparison of career success among men within

FOCUS: Identical Twins: "Living Laboratories"

When identical twins James Arthur Springer and James Edward Lewis were reunited for the first time after being separated shortly after birth 39 years previously, they were astonished to discover a remarkable string of similarities and seeming coincidences. The apparent coincidences concerning names were the most obvious: each had been given the same first name by his adoptive parents, each had been married first to a woman named Linda and then to one named Betty, each had named a son either James Alan or James Allan, and each once had a dog named Toy. But Springer and Lewis also discovered other similarities: both liked to work with wood; both had served as auxiliary sheriff's deputies;

Identical twins James Arthur Springer and James Edward Lewis were reunited in 1979 after having been separated shortly after birth 39 years earlier. Although they were raised apart, there turned out to be a remarkable number of similarities between them.

both had vacationed at the same Florida resort, both smoked the same brand of cigarettes, drank the same beer, and drove the same model of automobile.

The reunion of the "Jim twins," as they came to be known, occurred in February 1979. About a month later, they became the first subjects in a new study by researchers at the University of Minnesota, of identical twins raised apart. Identical twins, because they develop from the division of a single fertilized egg, or monozygote, and thus have the same genes, have long been regarded as "living laboratories" for the study of the effects of heritability and environment on intelligence, mental illness, and many other aspects of behavior (Chen, 1979). Identical twins are rare enough (they occur about 3.5 times in every 1,000 live births), but ones who were separated early in life and reared apart are even rarer. The fact that they have been raised in differing environments can provide a measure of the importance of genetic factors in behavior.

The Minnesota project, headed by psychologist Thomas Bouchard, promises to be the most comprehensive study ever undertaken of twins raised apart (Holden, 1980). Subjects undergo an intensive six-day battery of tests, interviews, and examinations by psychologists, psychiatrists, and medical doctors. In addition to the Wechsler Adult Intelligence Scale, they are given tests for various mental abilities, such as memory and vocabulary, and no fewer than three different comprehensive psychological inventories. Thus far, more than a dozen sets of twins raised apart have been tested, and the publicity received by the project has helped generate leads to perhaps 20 other pairs.

Although Bouchard and his colleagues emphasize that their data have yet to be analyzed and that any conclusions are still highly tentative, even the raw

the group (Sears and Barbee, 1978). The criteria for job success included income, status as generally judged by society, and the respondent's self-assessment of whether he "had made use of his superior intelligence in his life work, both in his choice of vocation and in the attainment of a position of importance and responsibility in an area calling for a high degree of intellectual ability." By these criteria, the 100 most successful men were designated as the "A group," which included many university professors, lawyers, research scientists, physicians, and business executives. The 100 least successful men were designated as the "C group," which included only five professionals and mostly clerks, salesmen, and small businessmen.

The A group had originally scored only six points higher in IQ than had the C group, a difference so slight that it scarcely could account for the significant disparities in career success. An assessment of the backgrounds of the two groups, however, revealed several more important differences. For

data are fascinating. For example, many of the twins reported very similar medical histories. Springer and Lewis each described the onset at age 18 of a type of headache known as mixed headache syndrome—a tension headache that turns into a migraine—which had previously been thought to have no genetic basis. Electroencephalogram patterns for many of the twin pairs also tended to be similar. One pair of female twins shared the same phobias—fears of heights, bodies of water, and closed-in places.

Even more striking were the test results and researchers' observations on personality characteristics. In body language, their manner of speaking, the way they gesture, Springer and Lewis "were like bookends," Bouchard said. ". . . the genetic effect pervades the entire structure of personality (Jackson, 1980)." Although some similarities might conceivably be attributable to environment—the Jim twins were both raised in small-town Ohio working-class families—others had growing-up experiences radically different from those of their twin. For example, one set of twins were separated at age six months in Trinidad after their parents' divorce. One was raised there as a Jew by his Jewish father and later joined a kibbutz in Israel at age 17; the other was raised a Catholic by his grandmother in Germany and became involved in the Hitler Youth Movement. Although differences in attitude persist, they have a similar temperament and even similar idiosyncrasies—absentmindedness, the habit of storing rubber bands on their wrists, and a strange penchant for sneezing loudly in public to gain attention.

How might observable similarities in personality be explained in terms of genetic similarity? Bouchard speculates that the genetic background might create certain predispositions that are associated with certain patterns of behavior. Body language, for example, may be a function of predispositions in the anatomy and physiology of the muscles; color preferences may be more soothing to eyes with particular organic characteristics.

On many of the psychological tests, the twin pairs scored so similarly to each other that they approximated the results obtained when one person takes the same test twice. Interestingly, the highest correlation was on the IQ test. In the few instances in which there was a marked difference in measured intelligence, the twin with the greater education had the higher score. These findings suggest that IQ has a high degree of heritability.

Bouchard suspects that identical twins reared apart may actually turn out to be more alike than those raised in the same environment. He speculates that in order to establish their own individuality, twins raised together sometimes exaggerate their differences. One twin, for example, might avoid pursuing an interest in music if the other twin is taking piano lessons. This interpretation is in marked contrast to the more usual speculation that identical twins may share more similarities in the family environment than fraternal twins because their similarity in appearance and manner elicits more similar responses from others.

It may be several years before the Minnesota project is completed and all of the data analyzed. Even then, it cannot be expected to furnish any definitive answers to the nature-nurture debate because the sample of subjects is so small. If the preliminary findings are any indication, however, it will provide further evidence for both perspectives: while the striking similarities in the behavior of identical twins raised apart may bolster the case for genetic determination, differences that are found will reflect and clarify the role of the environment.

example, the *A*s came from families in which the members were better educated and more stable. But the key difference appeared to lie in the need to achieve. Ratings by parents and teachers beginning when the subjects were still in elementary school showed that the one dimension that clearly distinguished *A*s from *C*s was "prudence and forethought, willpower, perseverance, and desire to excel." This theme was repeated in later ratings by parents, wives, and even the men themselves. *A*s often singled out "persistence in working toward a goal" as the key factor in their success; *C*s saw "lack of persistence" as responsible for their own lesser achievement.

Members of the *A* group also seemed happier than members of the *C* group. They were less concerned about making money (while making more). They were more likely to be satisfied with their careers and had more accurately predicted their vocation. They were less likely to report having personal problems such as overuse of alcohol. They were less likely to be divorced.

The Terman study thus appears to bear out other surveys suggesting that intelligence is only one factor in the achievement of a successful career. Other factors include family background, years of schooling completed, and early personality characteristics such as studiousness. But among those of virtually equal IQs, the most important factor seems to be a special need to achieve.

Intelligence in Perspective

Although intelligence is so highly valued in our society, its measurement so assiduously pursued, and its determinants so significant in the study of human behavior, it is important to keep intelligence and IQ scores in perspective for several reasons:

* Research increasingly suggests that intelligence is not a static, unalterable thing but a dynamic and still poorly understood process.
* While IQ scores are generally good at predicting academic performance, there appears to be less correlation with achievement in later life. It may be that motivation and interpersonal skills, such as sensitivity to others, which is sometimes called social intelligence, contribute more to successful performance in life than does a high IQ.
* No IQ test yet devised can measure all of the other dimensions, including common sense, intellectual independence, wit, and openness to experience, that are usually considered attributes of an intelligent person.
* Although intelligence and creativity obviously overlap, they are not the same; creative genius and even creativity in everyday life often require characteristics and processes that are seldom revealed in an IQ test.
* Finally, there is no evidence that a high IQ confers on its bearer two of the conditions that are prized even more than intelligence—wisdom and happiness.

SUMMARY

1. The earliest theories of the nature of intelligence viewed it as a psychological structure that could be broken down into parts and analyzed. Charles Spearman proposed a "universal Unity of the intellect" which he labeled the "*g*" factor, or general mental facility. L. L. Thurstone divided intelligence into seven primary mental abilities: numerical ability, reasoning, verbal fluency, spatial relations, perception, memory, and verbal comprehension. J. P. Guilford postulated a three-dimensional structure of intellect composed of contents, operations, and products. More recently, researchers have proposed an information processing view of intelligence. Robert J. Sternberg has proposed two levels in this approach: one level consists of the sequential steps—components—that a person proceeds through in solving a complex mental problem. The other level consists of metacomponents—the processes that organize the problem-solving components.

2. The first practical measure of intelligence was developed by the French psychologist, Alfred Binet. Binet established a level of performance for each age group; the results achieved by a child on the test constituted that child's mental age.

3. Lewis Terman of Stanford University revised the Binet test for American use. Mental age as shown on the Stanford-Binet was divided by chronological age and the resulting number was multiplied by 100, yielding an intelligence quotient, IQ. Modern versions of the Stanford-Binet test yield a deviation IQ, which reflects test performance relative to others of the same chronological age.

4. Two other intelligence tests in use today are the Wechsler Adult Intelligence Scale (WAIS) for people 17 and older and the Wechsler Intelligence Scale for Children (WISC). The Wechsler scales test non-verbal as well as verbal abilities.

5. New measurements of intelligence include learning potential testing, which reflects how much coaching a child needs to answer a question correctly, and neurometrics, which focuses on measurement of reactions within the brain and body rather than on verbal responses.

6. All intelligence tests are judged by the criteria of reliability, validity, and standardization. If a test is reliable, test scores will be consistent over time; if it is valid, the test measures what it is intended to measure; if the test has been adequately standardized, one's scores are measured against those of a similar group of people.

7. Intelligence tests have historically been designed as aptitude tests, which predict later performance. Achievement tests, on the other hand, are designed to measure the degree to which a particular skill or body of knowledge has already been mastered.

8. Intelligence tests have been criticized because traditionally they have tested achievement as well as aptitude, because they have been culturally biased (improperly standardized), and because of the pigeonhole effect—that is, the failure to take varying rates of intellectual growth into account.

9. The controversy over the determinants of intelligence is linked to the nature-nurture debate; that is, whether intelligence is determined by our individual genetic makeups or whether it is the product of environmental influences such as education, family life, social class, and culture. Studies correlating the IQs of people with varying genetic relationships show a definite role for heredity in intelligence. The concept of heritability, however, is a measure of relative variation that attempts to tell us how much of the variation in a particular trait for a particular population is due to genetic factors or to environmental factors at any given time. Most likely, heredity is responsible for the possible range of a

person's intelligence; environment determines how well the hereditary potential is realized.

10. Intelligence quotients for most people remain relatively stable, particularly after age 7; however, the ability to master a variety of intellectual tasks has a growth curve of its own, and peaks around age 40. The decline of intellectual abilities in later years varies widely among individuals.

11. In the wide spectrum of intelligence, most people fall around the middle of the scale. About 3 percent of the American population have IQs below 68 and are considered mentally retarded; about 1 percent have IQs above 140 and are considered mentally gifted.

12. Mental retardation has been classified as mild (IQ 52 to 67 on the Stanford-Binet); moderate (IQ 36 to 51); severe (IQ 20 to 35); and profound (IQ below 20). In mild retardation, cultural-familial factors are believed to play the major role. The more serious forms of retardation—moderate, severe, and profound—are generally caused by organic factors such as chromosomal abnormalities or brain trauma. Organic causes of retardation are grouped into three categories—genetic, infectious, and traumatic. Malnutrition is also believed to play a role in retardation.

13. Data from research, such as the long-term Terman study, disprove the old myth that exceptional intelligence is a handicap. In general, people with superior intellects do well in school, excel in their careers, are happier than those with low IQs, and have bright offspring. There does not, interestingly enough, appear to be a high correlation between intelligence and creativity.

415

Part Six
Abnormal Behavior: Patterns and Treatment

Chapter 14
Abnormal Behavior

A middle-aged accountant finds it increasingly difficult to get to work on time because of the elaborate grooming he feels is necessary before he is ready for work. His preparations often start at 3 or 4 o'clock in the morning, with slow and meticulous washing, shaving, and dressing. Often he is unable to leave his apartment before 4 o'clock in the afternoon because he has not yet finished preparing himself for the day.

- William F., having just lost his job, decides to open a local automobile dealership. He has taken out loans from four different banks to do so, using his house as a collateral in each case. Despite his recent job loss he seems full of enthusiasm and excitement. On his first day as an auto dealer he decides to open a nationwide network of car dealerships.
- Operating under considerable stress as the newly appointed feature editor of a large city newspaper, Janet S. has been working long and irregular hours to meet deadlines and to improve the quality of her section. A burning feeling in the pit of her stomach bothers her, but she ignores it until a routine physical examination reveals she is suffering from a severe peptic ulcer.

These examples of psychological distress reflect the range of human behavioral problems that are the subject of this chapter. Every year approximately 7 million Americans receive treatment for some form of psychological distress in public or private mental health facilities. The social and emotional costs of psychological disturbance are enormous, both in terms of personal distress and the loss of creativity and productivity to society at large. There is no single definition of *abnormal behavior*, but most definitions fall into one or more categories.

One definition of abnormal behavior focuses on behavior that is disturbing to other people. This definition suggests that an individual's behavior is literally "away from the norm" because it violates the values and expectations of others. It is important to note that this particular definition of abnormal behavior depends heavily on the cultural norms and rules of the local setting. What is seen as abnormal in central Africa may be highly appropriate in Wisconsin or Delaware.

A second definition of abnormal behavior suggests that *subjective distress* be the criterion because most forms of abnormal behavior involve at least some degree of subjective distress, including feelings of sadness, fear, or loss of control. As one of our examples above suggests, however, not all forms of abnormal behavior necessarily involve distress. Indeed, a person with some forms of mood disorder may feel temporarily elated.

A third definition emphasizes the psychological handicaps that interfere with or diminish an individual's ability to cope with the demands and stresses of life. Some severe forms of abnormal behavior—schizophrenia, for example—can be extremely disabling. Other forms of abnormal behavior may exist in an individual's life with no serious debilitation.

As these three definitions of abnormal behavior indicate, it is very difficult to establish a sharp dividing line between what may be considered normal and abnormal behavior. Rather, behavior seems to range along a normal distribution with most people clustering around the central point or average, and the rest spreading out toward the two extremes. From time to time, most people shift somewhat along the continuum. For example, some major change in a person's life, such as a hurtful divorce or a serious business failure, may temporarily result in severe depression or excessive drinking, until the person gets over the experience and begins to cope better with the problem.

In fact, although patients in mental hospitals and clinics are often depicted as engaging in all types of weird behavior—spending their time ranting and raving, crouching in corners, or posing as God—most hospitalized people are usually aware of what is going on around them, and only a small percentage exhibit behavior that might be called bizarre. The behavior of most mental patients is usually indistinguishable from that of "normal" people.

The criteria for defining abnormal behavior help us to understand the multidimensional nature of behavior disorders, but they tell us little about potential determinants of abnormal behavior. Various theories have been offered to account for the causes of abnormality, and we shall examine several. One group of investigators searches for the causes of abnormal behavior in the social environment. A second group of investigators focuses on individual biology and searches for the causes of abnormal behavior in genetic, physiological, or biochemical makeup. Still other theoretical approaches concentrate on the psychological makeup of the person—human needs and conflicts and their ultimate translation into maladaptive behavior.

We will examine the historical evolution of these three approaches to understanding abnormal behavior and consider modern theories that have evolved from them. We will also examine different types of abnormal behavior, concentrating primarily on psychological disorders associated with stress and anxiety, with mood disorders, and with major problems of perception and thought, such as schizophrenia.

Abnormal Behavior: Past and Present

The study of abnormal behavior, perhaps more than any other area of psychology, requires understanding of history. From the earliest times, humans have sought to explain and cure abnormal behavior. Greek myths are particularly rich in accounts of irrational actions. Ajax, apparently suffering from the delusion that some sheep were his enemies, killed them and then committed suicide in remorse. The Greeks believed that the gods were capable of making people mad. The Bible, too, tells of ancient Hebrews afflicted by their God. The patriarch Job, stripped of his health, wealth, and family as a test of his faith, echoes millions who have suffered deep depression when he cries out to Jehovah: "Why didst thou bring me forth from the womb?"

Among some early peoples, madness was attributed to possession by evil spirits, and treatments were often extreme. Like all attempts to deal with human problems, however, they must be seen in the cultural, religious, and social context of the times. As recently as the Middle Ages, people who behaved abnormally were burned at the stake. Even the three major ways of examining abnormal behavior that emerged in the modern era—the environmental, organic, and psychological viewpoints—must be viewed against the background of their beginning.

Environmental Approaches to Abnormal Behavior

The first theoretical approach focused on the social environment as the major cause—and potential cure—of abnormal behavior. The roots of this tradition can be traced to the emerging humanism of the Renaissance and the social and political awareness stimulated by the French and American revolutions.

In Europe especially, the environmental approach took the form of revulsion against the treatment of the insane. Along with such "undesirables" as criminals and debtors, the insane were relegated to filthy and appalling prisons—as were lepers a couple of centuries earlier. Some insane people were forced aboard ships and sent from port to

In early days, people exhibiting abnormal behavior were often considered witches possessed by evil spirits. One sure-fire, though drastic, way of dealing with these individuals was to burn them at the stake.

port, where for an admission fee the public could view the "ship of fools." Reformers in France and England, convinced that a more benign environment could alleviate madness, established mental hospitals where inmates could be treated with at least some kindness and concern.

In America social and environmental factors also attracted the attention of reformers, but treatment here took a different form. Americans did not begin institutionalizing severely disturbed people until about 1820. Impetus to do so came from the widespread conviction that the rapid social change of the Jacksonian era was to blame for insanity and other deviant behavior. Social mobility, inflation, politics—all were seen as root causes.

Scientists and physicians set out to create in the asylum an environment that would reduce tensions and stresses. David Rothman (1971) sums up the asylum solution in this way: "Create a different kind of environment, which methodically corrected

Aberrant behavior exhibited by a "husband liberationist," who employs an unusual means to advertise his point of view.

the deficiencies of the community, and a cure for insanity was at hand."

The asylum program came to be known as a "moral treatment," and its heart was disciplined routine. To ensure the peace and serenity believed essential for curing the insane, asylums were placed in rural areas. The daily schedule and the physical environment were both carefully arranged and ordered. Such institutions, it was believed, provided models of what society itself should be like.

Two perspectives on the nature and causes of abnormal behavior emerged from earlier concerns with the social environment. The first, the *social perspective* argues that it is how others view deviant behavior and how they react to odd or puzzling behavior that is crucial. Thus, the social perspective is more concerned with perceptions of abnormal behavior than with the behavior itself. Advocates of the social perspective argue that understanding abnormal behavior hinges on the audience or observer. Madness, in a sense, is in the eye of the beholder.

The second view is the modern *learning perspective.* We have examined this view briefly before, particularly in considering learning theory approaches to understanding personality in Chapter 12. An early champion of the learning approach to understanding behavior was John B. Watson. In his 1913 article, "Psychology as the Behaviorist Views It," Watson championed the idea that conditioning was responsible for much of our social behavior. From the learning perspective, behavior—normal and abnormal—represents responses to stimuli and events in the environment. More specifically, the contingency between behavior and stimuli in the environment is critical. Both the social and learning perspectives bear closer examination.

The Social Perspective Many advocates of the social perspective—for example Erving Goffman (1961) and Thomas Scheff (1966)—were trained in sociology. They emphasize that "abnormal" people were labeled as such because they violate certain norms, or socially agreed-upon rules of behavior. If no other likely explanation for puzzling behavior exists, it may be viewed as mental illness. Furthermore, this label tends to alter the behavior of others toward the persons in question. They are cast in the role of "mental patients," and we tend to see their behaviors as consistent with the label of mental illness. People so labeled, seeing changes in attitudes of others, may in turn act in even more puzzling ways. The social perspective, sees this process of interactions as producing a deviation amplifying system that finally leads to hospitalization. Once a person is hospitalized, deviation is further amplified.

This new role—that of "mental patient"— is illustrated in a study conducted by D. L. Rosenhan (1973). To find out whether the sane could be distinguished from the insane, Rosenhan contrived an elaborate hoax. He enlisted the aid of eight friends and collaborators—three psychologists, a pediatrician, a painter, and a homemaker—and asked them to become patients in mental hospitals.

For the examining physicians, these pseudopatients falsified their names and occupations and reported one imaginary symptom. They said they heard voices that, though unclear, sounded empty or hollow or made thumping sounds. Each was promptly admitted to the hospital, even though such a symptom had never been recorded in the literature as an indicator of severe psychological disorder. Moreover, all but one were diagnosed as suffering from schizophrenia.

This experiment confirmed Rosenhan's suspicion that it may not always be possible to distinguish the sane from the insane. What happened to the pseudopatients after they were admitted to the hospital is also fascinating. All but one were now cast in the role of schizophrenic and treated as such, even though they all acted perfectly normally and "sane" throughout the experiment, and it took an average of 19 days for them to be discharged. As Rosenhan points out, the sources of aberration in behavior now could be attributed to the individual rather than the surrounding environment.

For example, when the pseudopatients exhibited perfectly normal behavior, such as asking the psychiatrists when they would be eligible for privileges, they were treated as disturbed people. "Good morning, Dave" was the nonreply of one doctor. "How are you today?" The doctor then moved away without waiting for a response. It is easy to see how, in such circumstances, people cast into the roles of mental patient eventually accept their roles, question their own stability and, most significantly, begin to behave in accord with the role.

Much of what we regard as abnormal behavior actually is a kind of social role. A new and controversial view holds that our perceptions of, and actions toward, people labeled as mentally ill contribute to mental problems—a perspective that will reemerge throughout this discussion.

The Learning Perspective One of the newest and fastest-growing approaches to the study of abnormal behavior seeks to understand it through the principles of learning. According to this viewpoint, abnormal behavior is learned and maintained—and can be eliminated—largely through processes of conditioning.

Two of these processes, classical conditioning and instrumental (or operant) conditioning, were discussed at length in Chapter 7. Recall that classical conditioning was first described by Ivan Pavlov. Using his methods, followers succeeded in classically conditioning laboratory animals to show that they exhibited various forms of abnormal behavior, which some scientists labeled "experimental neuroses." We also saw in Chapter 7 how the American psychologist John Watson conditioned abnormal behavior in a human being. By pairing a white rat with a frightening noise, Watson taught 11-month-old Albert to be afraid not only of white rats but also of other white furry objects (Watson and Rayner, 1920).

The second process used to explain how abnormal behavior is learned and maintained, instrumental conditioning, was developed by psychologists Edward Thorndike (1932) and B. F. Skinner (1938). Recall that, in this form of conditioning, positive or negative reinforcements greatly affect the likelihood that it will occur again.

An example of the learning of abnormal behavior through instrumental conditioning has been provided by using the technique of behavior shaping, the contingent use of reinforcements to elicit gradually a particular pattern of behavior (Haughton and Ayllon, 1965). The subject of the study was a 54-year-old mental patient. The aim was to show that it was possible to shape her behavior so that she would do things that would appear senseless or peculiar—in this case to stand upright holding a broom.

The experiment began by depriving the woman of cigarettes. Next, whenever the patient was given a broom to hold, a staff member would approach, hand her a cigarette, and leave without explanation. As might be predicted, the woman began spending much of her time standing upright and holding the broom. Having succeeded in shaping this particular behavior, the investigators called in two psychiatrists. Without explaining how the patient had acquired the broom-holding behavior, they asked the psychiatrists to interpret her behavior. The psychiatrists saw it as a "magical act" in which the broom might represent either a "phallic symbol" or the "scepter of an omnipotent queen."

Leaving aside the problematical ethics of this experiment, it raises several important questions. For example, because it is possible to produce such abnormal behavior in an artificial situation, are the same learning mechanisms responsible for abnormal behavior in natural settings?

The idea that the social environment is the source of stimuli and reinforcements for abnormal behavior—as well as normal behavior—is at the heart of the learning perspective. Thus, the two perspectives complemented each other. In considering various forms of abnormal behavior, particularly disorders of stress and depression, we will encounter learning formulations that explain the development of psychological disorders.

Psychological Approaches to Abnormal Behavior

The second approach to the study of abnormal behavior—the psychological approach—emerged at the beginning of the twentieth century, but stemmed in part from the ideas of Anton Mesmer, a physician and mystic who worked in Austria more than 100 years earlier. As the word "mesmerize" suggests, Mesmer was the father of hypnosis. Mesmer believed that physical disease as well as some forms of irrational behavior resulted from an imbalance of magnetic fluids in the human body. In 1779 he opened a clinic in Paris where he set out to cure ailments by "animal magnetism"—a mysterious force that he thought emanated from his hands and affected the magnetic fluids.

Although Mesmer was attacked as a fraud, he did manage to relieve a variety of disorders, including hysterical paralysis and psychosomatic ailments. His use of hypnotic suggestion helped to promote the psychological approach to human behavior. Mesmer's work fostered the idea that thinking could be both conscious and unconscious and suggested that one person could help another person remedy irrational behavior (Mesmer and Bloch, 1980).

The Dynamic Perspective Others took up the use of hypnotic suggestion, but it was a young Viennese physician, Sigmund Freud, who formulated a uniquely psychological view of abnormal

behavior. At first, Freud worked with another Viennese physician, Josef Breuer, who had developed a treatment that he called the "cathartic method," in which repressed emotional tension could be released (Freud, 1905/1953; Freud and Breuer, 1895/1966). Breuer hypnotized his patients, who were then encouraged to discuss their concerns while under hypnosis.

Freud was struck by the fact that much of what patients said under hypnosis was not ordinarily accessible to them. He called such thoughts "unconscious" and theorized that they were significant determinants of the patients' behavior, even though the patients were not ordinarily aware of them (Freud, 1905/1953; Freud and Breuer, 1895/1966).

It is important to grasp how Freud's point of view related to the Victorian era in which it developed. Freud believed that irrational behavior resulted largely from internal conflicts between sexual or aggressive impulses and the demands of conscience and reality. This should not be surprising because the Victorian era emphasized tight control over personal impulses. The times were so proper that housewives draped curtains over the legs of their pianos so as not to offend the moral sensibilities of guests. No wonder that Freud's patients revealed conflicts between natural sexual impulses and the prevailing prudish social standards. These conflicts, the products of Victorian morality, thus became central, in the Freudian view, as the sources of abnormal behavior.

Because it has been a major source of ideas in abnormal psychology, we will examine the dynamic perspective more closely, confining ourselves primarily to concepts intended to explain abnormal behavior. As we saw in Chapter 12, much of the rest of the dynamic point of view focuses on personality development.

To Freud, behavior resulted from the dynamic interplay among three major mental structures, which he called the id, the ego, and the superego. Of course, these terms represented domains of thought and motivation rather than actual structures (Freud, 1933).

The *id* represented the primitive biological drives of the organism. "A caldron of seething excitement," according to Freud (1933), the id had a single aim: to release its biological energy in either aggressive or erotic ways. Its self-seeking mechanisms are thus governed by the *pleasure principle*.

The *ego* was seen by Freud as a kind of executive judging the feasibility and appropriateness of our actions. While the id operates by the pleasure principle, the ego operates by the *reality principle.* It assesses the realism of engaging in aggressive or sexual acts demanded by the id.

The *superego* greatly resembles the familiar notion of "conscience." It controls and judges our actions as we plan or fantasize them and as we carry them out. The standards of the supergo are laid down during the childhood socialization process of learning that certain acts and impulses are "good" and others "bad."

It is inevitable that these three mental structures come into conflict. This conflict, said Freud, determines much of our behavior. A common example would be the conflict between the sexual demands of the id and the moral strictures of the superego. Such a conflict, if not readily resolved, produces tension and anxiety. To reduce the tension and anxiety, the ego brings into play a whole range of automatic and unconscious responses called *defense mechanisms.* The most important of these defense mechanisms is *repression.* In repression, unpleasant thoughts or dangerous impulses are barred from conscious awareness. For example, impulses arising from the id may signal to a married woman that another man is highly attractive. Since these reactions conflict with her superego—her moral notions about marital fidelity—she represses them into her unconscious. Freud found clues to repression in dreams and in memory lapses about certain names or events.

In addition to repression, Freud described a number of other defense mechanisms. They include:

- *Projection*—the attribution of personally unacceptable impulses to others. The married woman mentioned above might project her own sexual impulses onto other women by accusing them of having "dirty thoughts."
- *Reaction formation*—the expression of conscious attitudes that are the opposite of an internal wish or impulse. It often takes the form of an intense reaction to a seemingly commonplace circumstance. The woman's violent reaction to adulterous relationships, for example, might indicate a repressed attraction to men other than her husband.
- *Displacement*—the shifting of an impulse directed at one person onto a substitute person or object deemed more acceptable. The woman directs her attentions to her brother, for example, instead of expressing her attraction to the other man.

Although defense mechanisms may seem irrational at first glance, they have an internal logic of their own. All of us have experienced them, but only when they begin to interfere with our functioning do they become a source of concern. In that event, understanding defense mechanisms may provide clues about the underlying conflict from which one suffers.

The idea that conflicting impulses can produce anxiety and that abnormal behavior may actually be a defense mechanism against that anxiety is at the center of the psychodynamic perspective on abnormal behavior. Later in the chapter the psychodynamic view will be discussed again in relationship to anxiety disorders.

Organic Approaches to Abnormal Behavior

A third approach to looking at abnormal behavior—the organic and medical viewpoint—focused on physiology. The nineteenth century ushered in a new age of technology and with it the conviction that science could solve problems of human behavior.

Medical science was beginning to understand the origins of many infectious diseases. Louis Pasteur had demonstrated that disease could be produced by bacteria, and there was a growing belief that microorganisms caused virtually everything that went wrong with people—even madness. This belief was strengthened by the observation that three of the most common diseases of the time—syphilis, tuberculosis, and typhus—sometimes produced irrational behavior in victims. The brain disease associated with syphilis is called general paresis and, the century-long chronicle of the discovery and successful treatment of this disease gave medical science enhanced credibility as an authority in the study of abnormal behavior.

At the same time, *neurology*—the study of the brain and nervous system—was becoming an important medical specialty. Physicians like Paul Broca (1861/1960), who discovered the speech area of the brain, were localizing specific behavioral functions in the brain.

Progress in neurology and in the general treatment of disease gave birth to a new specialized branch of medicine, *psychiatry.* Early psychiatry's approach to abnormal behavior was typified by the thinking of Emil Kraepelin. Kraepelin catego-

425

rized and classified such behavior in great detail so that it could be described in terms of diseases associated with symptoms (Kraepelin, 1896). Thus he helped transform the study of abnormal behavior—once the province of witch doctors—into a medical discipline.

The idea that abnormal behavior is a form of illness or disease is reflected in the terms frequently used to describe it. We speak of *mental illness;* we treat people who act peculiarly in *mental hospitals;* we give them *therapy;* we regard them as *patients.* The examination of a person's behavior in order to determine the disorder is *diagnosis.* A statement concerning the likely course and outcome of the disorder is a *prognosis.*

Thus, a tradition of dealing with some forms of abnormal behavior as medical illnesses is reflected in our language, institutions, and ways of thinking. But this tradition is irrelevant to the question of the origins of abnormal behavior. Are they organic, as the disease perspective suggests?

Evidence that some forms of abnormal behavior are at least partly organic in origin is accumulating rapidly. The *diathesis-stress* model seems to explain the origins of some mood disorders as well as some severe disorders of perception and thought. In general, this model suggests that some people may possess higher levels of vulnerability to stress and that this vulnerability is at least partly determined by genetic factors. Thus, when confronted by stressful events—the loss of a job or a loved one—people so predisposed are more likely to develop a behavior disorder than are people who are not so predisposed.

Scientists look for evidence to support this viewpoint in two areas. First, they may attempt to demonstrate that people who develop behavior disorders are more genetically similar to each other than to those who do not develop the disorders. If this can be demonstrated, then the case for genetic origins of behavior disorders is strengthened. Second, because any genetic disorder must express itself through biochemical pathways before manifesting itself as abnormal behavior, scientists may look for biochemical differences between normal and disturbed populations. Again, evidence that abnormal behavior is due to a disease process would be far from unequivocal, but it would strengthen the case.

Indeed, some forms of behavior disorders have been shown to have organic or biochemical origins. For example, some severe vitamin deficiency diseases, if untreated, result in disturbances of perception and behavior. As we shall see, genetic and biological factors are emerging as important determinants of some forms of abnormal behavior.

Diagnosis and Classification of Abnormal Behavior

Classification has always been an important part of a developing science. The periodic table in chemistry, for example, has been revised as new elements

TABLE 14.1   Major Diagnostic Headings in DSM III

DISORDERS USUALLY FIRST EVIDENT IN INFANCY, CHILDHOOD OR ADOLESCENCE	AFFECTIVE DISORDERS
Mental retardation	ANXIETY DISORDERS
Attention deficit disorder	SOMATOFORM DISORDERS
Conduct disorder	DISSOCIATIVE DISORDERS (OR HYSTERICAL NEUROSES, DISSOCIATIVE TYPE)
Anxiety disorders of childhood or adolescence	PSYCHOSEXUAL DISORDERS
Other disorders of infancy, childhood or adolescence	Gender identity disorders
Eating disorders	Paraphilias
Stereotyped movement disorders	Psychosexual dysfunctions
Other disorders with physical manifestations	FACITIOUS DISORDERS
Pervasive developmental disorders	DISORDERS OF IMPULSE CONROL NOT ELSEWHERE CLASSIFIED
ORGANIC MENTAL DISORDERS	ADJUSTMENT DISORDERS
Senile and presenile dementias	PSYCHOLOGICAL FACTORS AFFECTING PHYSICAL CONDITION
Substance-induced dementias	CONDITIONS NOT ATTRIBUTABLE TO A MENTAL DISORDER THAT ARE A FOCUS OF ATTENTION OR TREATMENT
SUBSTANCE USE DISORDERS	
SCHIZOPHRENIC DISORDERS	
PARANOID DISORDERS	
PSYCHOTIC DISORDERS NOT ELSEWHERE CLASSIFIED	

Source: *Diagnostic and Statistical Manual of Mental Disorders,* 3rd ed. (Washington, D.C.: American Psychiatric Association, 1980), pp. 15-19.

have been discovered. Much of our understanding of evolutionary theory would not be possible without reliable classification of various species of animals and plants. Psychologists studying abnormal behavior are still in the early stages of developing a classification system.

Classification systems are more than just pigeonholes and are intended to do more than to place labels on individuals. Roger Blashfield and Juris Draguns (1976) suggest that classification systems have a number of functions in all fields of scientific work. They serve as a base for communication among investigators, provide keys to the scientific literature, make shorthand descriptions of phenomena possible, and enable predictions about behavior based on assignment in the classification system. Finally, the concepts used in a classification system provide a basic building block for scientific theory. For example, the term *schizophrenia* is a summary statement about a pattern of behavior that scientists currently believe involves social withdrawal and severe disorganization of perception, thought, and emotion. As scientific classification systems for the study of abnormal behavior develop further, broad concepts, such as schizophrenia, will probably give way to finer discriminations that will better serve scientists.

Currently the *Diagnostic and Statistical Manual of Mental Disorders* published by the American Psychiatric Association (DSM III) is in its third edition (1980). This latest version of the diagnostic system represents an attempt to provide reliable descriptions of patterns of abnormal behavior. In developing it, the framers attempted to include common disorders as well as the more unusual and severe forms of abnormal behavior (see Table 14.1).

Critics of DSM III have been concerned that this inclusive strategy increases the danger of labeling and stigmatizing people who have relatively mild difficulties as "abnormal." As we saw in discussing the social perspective on abnormal behavior, there is some evidence that such labeling can have negative effects for the individual.

DSM III attempts not only to identify the major pattern of abnormal behaviors under consideration but also to classify individuals on other dimensions, including patterns of personality disorders, associated medical disorders, occurences of severe recent stresses, and recent levels of functioning of the individual (see Table 14.2).

Some concern remains about the usefulness of this latest diagnostic classification system (Schacht and Nathan, 1977). For example, questions exist about the degree to which it is possible to assess accurately some of the dimensions in this system. Fair assessments of individuals from different ethnic groups are also of concern. Continuing research on this diagnostic classification system should help in determining whether these are real problems and, if so, how they might be remedied.

Any classification system can be misused. Naming or classifying an object is not the same as understanding it, but as we noted, classification is a first, if tentative, step in scientific understanding.

Perhaps the most critical issue is the question of how such a newly developed diagnostic and classification system will actually be used in practice. If it is used extensively to make decisions about the treatment of individuals before it has been rigorously tested, then abuses are possible. If, on the

TABLE 14.2   Multiaxial Classification System of DSM III

AXES OF DSM III		EXAMPLE
Axis I	Formal psychiatric syndrome	296.80 Atypical depressive disorder
Axis II	Personality disorders (adults) and specific developmental disorders (children)	301.81 Narcissistic personality disorder
Axis III	Nonmental medical disorders	Diabetes, hypertension
Axix IV	Severity of psychosocial stressors one year preceding disorder (range: 1–7)	Psychosocial stressors: 5, severe (business failure)
Axis V	Highest level of adaptive behavior one year preceding disorder (range: 1–7)	Highest adaptive behavior past year: 3, good

Source: Adapted from T. Schacht and P. E. Nathan, "But Is It Good for Psychologists? Approval and Status of DSM III," *American Psychologist*, December 1977, p. 1017.

other hand, it is treated tentatively as a research instrument, potential benefits are great.

A major classification in DSMIII is anxiety disorders. The pace and stress of modern lifestyles seem likely to be the root causes of such disorders. However, as we shall see in our next section, which focuses on disorders of anxiety and stress, some evidence for a "biological preparedness" for such disorders is emerging.

Disorders of Anxiety and Stress

Most of us have experienced both the subjective feelings and physical symptoms of *anxiety* and *stress.* Shortness of breath, perspiration, hand tremor, and "butterflies" of anxiety may increase before exams or at other stressful times, but for most of us these symptoms are transient and manageable. However, for some, intense anxiety and stress are almost continuous experiences.

In the past these disorders were classified as "neurotic" or "psychosomatic." More recently, researchers have focused on specific forms of anxiety and stress disorders and have attempted to understand each as a unique form of human adaptation. We will do much the same thing in our consideration of phobias and psychophysiological disorders as examples of maladaptive reactions to stress and anxiety.

Anxiety: Phobias

Ethel H., a married woman of 26, suffered her first acute anxiety attack two years before she began therapy. She was arriving alone by plane from England after visiting her parents there. As she entered the high-ceilinged terminal—no one met her—she felt suddenly terrified in the huge, empty space. She began "shaking like a leaf"; she could not get her bags through customs without constant help; she had the impulse to tell everyone around who she was in case she went mad. A porter, sensing her anxiety, expressed open concern and this comforted her. She managed the rest of the trip by train without mishap, but reached home exhausted and unnerved, certain that something awful was happening to her (Cameron, 1963).

"Ethel H." suffers from a disorder known as *agoraphobia*—the irrational fear of wide-open places such as halls, fields, parks, and beaches. Phobias are among the most common the anxiety disorders. The most familiar are *acrophobia* (fear of high places), *claustrophobia* (fear of enclosed places), and *zoophobia* (fear of certain animals such as dogs, horses, and snakes). But there have been notable instances of less familiar phobias. The composer Frederic Chopin had an intense fear of being buried alive, and the German philosopher Arthur Schopenhauer was so afraid of razors that he singed his beard with a flame rather than shave it (Kisker, 1964).

Unlike generalized anxiety, phobias focus on a specific object or situation—one that presents no real danger to the individual. In the presence of that object or situation, the person may sweat profusely, shake, experience shortness of breath, or attempt to hide. By some estimates, perhaps 8 percent of the population suffers from phobias of varying types and intensity (Agras, Sylvestar, and Oliveau, 1969).

Relatively few individuals are suited for the type of work shown. Most of us, to a greater or lesser degree, suffer from some form of acrophobia (fear of high places).

Phobias are even more prevalent in children than in adults. Between the ages of 2 and 4, for example, fear of animals is fairly common. Between 4 and 6, fears of the dark and of imaginary creatures are more prevalent (see Figure 14.1).

But these fears usually decline with the approach of adulthood. As Isaac Marks (1977) notes, "Fears and rituals appear in children for little or no apparent reason and disappear just as mysteriously." What then accounts for the persistence into adulthood of certain fears among people?

The Psychodynamic View One of Freud's most famous case histories, published in 1909, described an instance of zoophobia—fear of animals (Freud 1909/1956). A five-year-old boy, whom Freud called "little Hans," was so afraid of being bitten by a horse that he refused to go into the street.

The clearest modern exposition of the dynamic view on the development of phobias is offered by Norman Cameron (1963). Cameron lists four basic stages in the development of phobias. First, the person experiences a threatening impulse, typically of an aggressive or sexual nature; in the case of little Hans, Freud theorized that the boy had an unacceptable sexual desire for his mother and hate for his father. Second, the person cannot repress these impulses—that is, keep them from intruding into conscious awareness. Third, intruding impulses crystallize in the shape of fearful fantasies; for little

Hans, they took the form of fear of being harmed by his father. Fourth and finally, the fear is displaced onto another object that can be avoided; this occurred in little Hans when the horse-drawn carriage in which he and his mother were riding was involved in an accident.

Thus, according to the psychodynamic view, phobias result when forbidden impulses and the fear associated with them become transformed and externalized. Moreover, Cameron believes that the feared object and the actual fear are frequently linked by a symbolic relationship. The fear of heights—acrophobia—may symbolize the fear of falling in the esteem of others. The fear of closed places—claustrophobia—may symbolize the fear of being left alone with one's own dangerous impulses and fantasies.

The Learning View Learning theorists have questioned the interpretations of psychodynamic theorists. They argue that phobias can be accounted for by the mechanisms of classical conditioning. They do not regard phobias as being indicative of some type of underlying disorder but see them as resulting from a purely coincidental pairing of an intense emotional state with the phobic stimulus. In the view of learning theorists, "any neutral

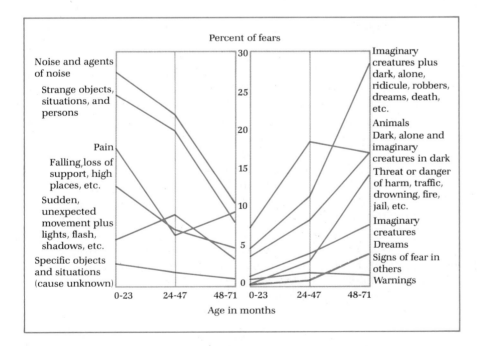

FIGURE 14.1 Relative frequencies of various fear responses among children.

stimulus, simple or complex, that happens to make an impact on an individual at about the time that a fear reaction is evoked acquires the ability to evoke fear subsequently" (Wolpe and Rachman, 1960). They see the horse phobia of little Hans as merely a matter of classical conditioning: the fear evoked by the accident was paired with the horse and hence conditioned to that previously neutral stimulus. In the terminology of classical conditioning, the accident was the unconditioned stimulus, horses were the conditioned stimulus, and fear the conditioned response. This explanation of phobias is similar to that invoked in little Albert, which we have discussed previously. Albert, you will recall, acquired a conditioned fear of white rats and other white furry things after he was frightened by a loud noise while playing with a white rat.

The Biological View A third view of phobias does not rule out the learning perspective but suggests that certain fears may have a biological basis. This reasoning begins by looking at the objects or situations that are the foci of phobias. Phobias involving naturally occurring phenomena such as heights, snakes, or open spaces are relatively common; on the other hand, phobias involving manufactured objects, such as filing cabinets or plastic cups, are practically nonexistent. From the standpoint of evolution, fears of heights, snakes, or even open spaces make a great deal of sense—they have obvious survival value. Biological theorists describe them as *prepotent targets* for phobias.

Evidence in support of the idea of *biological preparedness* in the learning of phobias comes from a number of recent studies. For example, researchers found that skin-conductance measures of anxiety in response to pictures of snakes and spiders took longer to extinguish than did responses to pictures of nonprepotent targets such as houses (Ohman, Eriksson, Fredericksson, Hugdahl, and Oloffson, 1974).

Even more striking is this clinical example: "A four-year-old girl was playing in the park. Thinking she saw a snake, she ran into her parent's car and jumped inside, slamming the door behind her. The girl's hand was caught by the closing door, resulting in severe pain and several visits to the doctor. Before this, she may have been afraid of snakes, but was not phobic. After this experience, a phobia developed, *not of cars or car doors, but of snakes.* The snake phobia persisted into adulthood (Marks, 1977)."

In examining phobias we have considered three distinctively different views of the development of the disorder. The psychodynamic view sees phobias as fears associated with forbidden impulses; the learning perspective argues for a classical conditioning exploration; the biological preparedness approach suggests that the organism may be biologically predisposed to become fearful of stimuli more easily than others.

Stress: Psychophysiological Disorders

John R., 33, suffered from severe asthma attacks from age 16. The first attack occurred at a summer camp where he had been sent while his parents were traveling in Europe. The attack was so bad that his parents had to cut short their trip and return home. Another severe attack occurred while he was a freshman at a college away from home; it was decided that he should attend college in the city where his parents lived. Following his marriage, the attacks increased in frequency and severity. The usual medical diagnostic and treatment procedures did little to relieve his symptoms. Finally, he was referred to psychological treatment. During treatment, he came to understand how his asthma symptoms had become an effective way of protecting himself against separation from his family, especially from an overprotective mother. As he adjusted his emotional attitudes toward his wife and his mother, the asthma symptoms gradually disappeared (Kisker, 1964).

John R.'s asthma serves to remind us again of the artificiality of distinctions between mind and body. His asthmatic symptoms reflect the intimate relationship between psychological and physiological processes. His emotional state brought on actual physical distress.

The range of psychophysiological disorders is wide and may include headache, bronchial asthma, arthritis, hypertension, sexual dysfunctions, insomnia, hay fever, peptic ulcer, or colitis. Even the angina pains associated with heart attacks sometimes have emotional components. Most standard medical textbooks suggest that 50 to 80 percent of all diseases have significant psychological aspects (Pelletier, 1977).

The precise role of the emotions in disease is not always easy to pinpoint. It is likely that all diseases or organic disorders may have some psychological component. For example, after a period of prolonged stress, we tend to be more susceptible to the common cold; stress seems to affect substantially our resistance to infectious diseases. Hypertension may be directly related to stress or it may be the result of hereditary or dietary factors: most commonly, a combination of all three factors is involved. However, disorders that are sometimes psychosomatic in nature are not always so. Many people with asthma, for example, suffer from allergies to specific chemical substances in the air.

Psychophysiological disorders are usually characterized by (1) physical symptoms, (2) emotional causes, (3) a single-organ system that is controlled by the autonomic nervous system such as the circulatory system, (4) physiological changes that are the same as those associated with normally occurring emotional states but are more intense and last longer, and (5) a lack of awareness of the emotional state and a resulting attribution of the disorder to organic causes.

Headaches To understand better the relationship between emotional factors and physical symptoms, let us consider closely one of the most familiar and common of psychosomatic disorders—the headache. Practically everyone has had a severe headache at one time or another, and an estimated 20 percent of Americans suffer from some form of chronic headache.

All headaches involve a disturbance of blood flow within and around the brain. Blood vessels expanding or shrinking stimulate highly sensitive nerve endings within the blood vessels themselves. Recall that nerve endings within the brain itself are insensitive to pain. Several types of headaches apparently lack a psychological component. The common "hangover," for example, is a consequence of chemicals produced during the digestion of alcohol; these chemicals bring about a dilation of cranial blood vessels. Similarly, some foods contain chemicals, such as the common seasoning monosodium glutamate, that enlarge blood vessels.

Nearly half of all headaches are a result of muscle tension. Feelings of frustration, anger, or anxiety often are accompanied by muscle tension in the face, forehead, or neck. Extreme tension increases the demand for oxygen in muscles, and when the blood flow cannot keep up with the oxygen demand, the blood vessels in the head expand, causing pain.

Another type of headache, migraine, is associated with other symptoms, including nausea, blurred vision, extreme sensitivity to light and sound, and visual images of flashing lights.

Migraine headaches typically occur in two phases. In the first phase, a reduced flow of blood to the brain causes malfunctions in the nerve cells. There is no pain but, depending on which area of the brain is affected, sufferers may see various visual images or slur their speech. In the second phase, blood rushes into those areas of the brain that were deprived during the first phase. This produces a rapid expansion of arteries in the scalp and severe pain that may last for a day or more.

In looking at the causes of tension and migraine headaches, one investigator has concluded that nonspecific stress is a major triggering event (Bakal, 1975). He notes that sufferers of migraine headaches tend to attribute their headaches to emotional causes. Indeed, headaches often are related to the stress brought on by a variety of changes in our lives such as vacations, school examinations, and increased responsibilities. Evidence also exists for a hereditary basis for migraine headaches.

The Disregulation Theory Explanations for headaches and other psychophysiological disorders come from several different perspectives. Genetic factors, learning, stress—all almost certainly play a role. But none of these approaches tells the entire story.

G. E. Schwartz (1977) offers a framework for understanding these disorders that takes all of these factors into account and provides a single explanation. His hypothesis is known as the *disregulation theory* because our internal regulation system is disrupted during the development of psychophysiology disorders.

To understand the disregulation theory, it is necessary to recall certain processes and concepts from Chapter 1. One concept is homeotasis, the process by which the organism, for purposes of survival, constantly adapts to its internal and external environments, keeping such variables as heartbeat and body temperature within certain limits. Homeotasis is maintained principally through the autonomic nervous system (ANS). The autonomic nervus system, via its internal nerve receptors, carries messages about the state of the body to the brain and then, in turn, carries orders from the brain to the heart, lungs, and other internal organs.

Remember, too, that much of this feedback process takes place outside conscious awareness. For example, if you voluntarily hold your breath, carbon dioxide builds up in the bloodstream, stimulating chemical receptors that send messages to respiratory control centers in the brain stem. These brain centers automatically activate the respiratory system, causing a breath. We are consciously aware of only the end result of this complex process—taking a breath.

According to Schwartz, all psychophysiological disorders—whether hypertension, hives, migraine headaches, or ulcers—result from a state of disregulation in this system. He identifies four stages in the feedback process and suggests that disregulation—and hence psychophysiological disorders—can occur at any one of these stages or from all of them in combination (see Figure 14.2).

1. *Stage One.* The brain receives negative feedback from some organ system. For example, a person undergoing stress may experience stomach pain associated with hyperacidity. But because the stress is unavoidable—perhaps the person is involved in a divorce or a job change—the negative feedback must be ignored.

2. *Stage Two.* The central nervous system itself may be involved. For genetic reasons, or perhaps because of patterns laid down by prior experience, the brain may respond inappropriately to stimuli in the external environment. This may cause it to ignore the corrective feedback or to use that feedback in ways that place unreasonable demands on the affected organ. Thus, disregulation at this stage might be the result of prior experience, making it consistent with both the learning and the psychodynamic perspective, or of genetic factors, making it consistent with the organic perspective.

3. *Stage Three.* An organ, such as the stomach, may react inappropriately to nerve signals from the brain. It may overreact, thus upsetting the brain's regulation of the organ.

4. *Stage Four.* The feedback emanating from the organ may be inappropriate. The brain may thus fail to receive the information needed for control of the organ.

Conceptually, the disregulation theory represents an advance in our consideration of physical ailments that result from emotional causes. Instead of isolating one particular determinant and ignoring others, it shows how all of the potential factors—learning, genetics, and stress—might be involved in the development of psychophysiological disorders.

We have specifically examined phobias and psychophysiological disorders in light of their basis in anxiety and stress. Psychological processes, learning factors, a biological predisposition may interact to produce these—and other—disorders.

Personality Disorders

Many abnormal behaviors are characterized by sudden disruptions or changes in patterns. After the loss of a loved one a person may fall into a deep depression, or a traumatic event may trigger a phobic reaction. One set of disorders, however, does not happen suddenly; the patterns of behavior appear to be deeply ingrained and are manifested primarily as exaggerations: these are referred to as personality disorders. Everyone has probably known people who act strangely but whose behavior hardly seems pathological. Everyone, too, has probably known people who are so neat and meticulous that, in this regard at least, they seem out of the ordinary. In the extreme, such patterns may make it difficult for people to cope effectively in the world because their behavior may negatively affect others and, therefore, disrupt personal relationships. Table 14.3 shows descriptions of *personality disorders* as they are listed in DSMIII.

It is important to note that these extreme patterns of personality disorders need not necessarily disrupt an individual's life adjustment. Indeed, for

FIGURE 14.2 Representation of Schwartz's disregulation theory. The four stages of disregulation are illustrated.

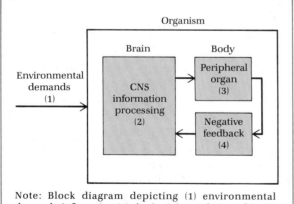

Note: Block diagram depicting (1) environmental demands influencing (2) the brain's regulation of its (3) peripheral organs, and (4) negative feedback from the peripheral organ back to the brain. Disregulation can be initiated at each of these stages.

an accountant, extreme orderliness, as it is reflected in the compulsive personality, may be a distinct advantage. Similarly, a certain amount of suspiciousness in a police detective may be an asset rather than a liability.

In a recent study of compulsive personalities, researchers visited the homes of subjects and found that the home environments bore the stamp of the subjects' individual personalities (Rachman and Hodgson, 1980).

> Telltale signs of compulsive cleaners are easily spotted. One encounters endless boxes of tissue paper; rolls of paper toweling; bottles of disinfectant; hordes of soap bars, washing powders of all sizes, makes, and varieties; innumerable pairs of rubber gloves, and all the other signs of the dedicated cleaner. Quite commonly the lavatory is the most

carefully tended room in the house and is overstocked with extra rolls of toilet tissue.

> The homes of compulsive checkers are less obviously different. Here the distinguishing features are escessive tidiness and orderliness. Each piece of furniture has its designated place; the pictures hang straight; and attempts by others to rearrange things quickly produce alarm. Checklists are placed at strategic points, and the common habit of making lists is elevated to a fine art (Rachman and Hodgson, 1980).

Depression and Mania

Compulsive cleaners and checkers may be regarded simply as mildly eccentric. The behavior of those

---

TABLE 14.3   The DSM III Classification of Personality Disorders

ECCENTRIC CLUSTER	FEARFUL CLUSTER	ERRATIC CLUSTER
Paranoid personality: A pervasive and long-standing suspiciousness and mistrust of people in general. Individuals with this disorder are hypersensitive and easily slighted. They continually scan the environment for clues that validate their original prejudicial ideas, attitudes, or biases. Often their emotional experience is restricted.	**Avoidant personality:** Hypersensitivity to rejection, unwillingness to enter into relationships unless given an unusually strong guarantee of uncritical acceptance. Social withdrawal, yet a desire for affection and acceptance.	**Histrionic personality:** Behavior that is overly reactive, intensely expressed, and perceived by others as shallow, superficial, or insincere. Often associated with disturbed interpersonal relationships.
Introverted personality: A defect in the capacity to form social relationships; introversion and bland or constricted affect.	**Compulsive personality:** Restricted ability to express warm and tender emotions, preoccupation with matters of rules, order, organization, efficiency, and detail. Excess devotion to work and productivity to the exclusion of pleasure. Compulsive personalities are often indecisive.	**Narcissistic personality:** Grandiose sense of self-importance or uniqueness, preoccupation with fantasies of unlimited success, exhibitionistic needs for constant attention and admiration.
Schizotypal personality: Various oddities of thinking, perception, communication, and behavior. Peculiarities in communication with concepts expressed unclearly or oddly.	**Passive-aggressive personality:** Resistance to demand for adequate activity or performance in both occupational and social areas of functioning. Resistance is not expressed directly. As a consequence, pervasive or long-standing social or occupational ineffectiveness often result.	**Antisocial personality:** History of continuous and chronic antisocial behavior in which the rights of others are violated. Onset before age 15, failure to sustain good job performance, lying, stealing, fighting, truancy in childhood.
		Borderline personality: Instability in various areas of life including interpersonal relationships, behavior, mood, and self-image. Interpersonal relationships are often tense and unstable with marked shifts of attitude over time.

Source: *Diagnostic and Statistical Manual of Mental Disorders*, 3rd ed. (Washington, D.C.: American Psychiatric Association, 1980).

afflicted by depression, however, is truly disturbing and affects their ability to function in the world.

Imagine, for a moment that you are a clinical psychologist interviewing someone who has just come to you for help. The young man sitting across from you finds it hard to talk about what is bothering him. At first his conversation was animated, but now as he continues to talk his voice flattens into a monotone. His face loses its expression and becomes mask-like, suggesting the despair below the surface.

As the hour goes on, you begin to get a picture of his life. He maintains a pleasant, active facade only at great personal cost. Even the simplest activities, like dressing or driving to work, have become enormous acts of will. He reports difficulty sleeping, and, unaccountably, he wakes before dawn each day. Frequently at night this man withdraws into his apartment, refusing to answer the telephone. He lies listlessly for hours in front of the television set. Lately, he reports, he has begun to think about suicide.

As you listen to him you are ftruck by several things. His mood is obviously downcast and occasionally tears well up in his eyes. His thinking seems pessimistic and he frequently talks about himself in a disparaging way. The stains on his suit and his rumpled appearance suggest that he no longer cares as much as he once did about his appearance. The bagginess of his suit also suggests that he has lost a fair amount of weight recently. His world is gray and bleak, not very promising.

As you sit there, listening, you begin to notice your own mood. The world seems less exciting to you, too, now, and you feel somewhat depressed. As time goes on you begin to feel some mild irritation with this person. His apparent inability to "shake off" his feeling of sadness and his lack of response to your encouragements are frustrating and vaguely annoying.

You have just interviewed a person suffering from the typical symptoms of a moderately severe depression. Depression has been called the "common cold" of psychological disorders, and over a quarter of a million Americans are hospitalized for this disorder each year. The chances are about one in five that each of us will suffer at least one severe depression during our lifetime. Students, musicians, laborers, physicists, clerks, psychiatrists, and housewives all are subject to depression. Lincoln and Hemingway, F. Scott Fitzgerald and Sylvia Plath all suffered from severe depression (Price and Lynn, 1981).

Depression is part of a cluster of disorders of mood and affect that are among the most important forms of abnormal behavior. In addition to depression, mood disturbances involving intense episodes of elation called *manic episodes* as well as alternating swings between elation and depression called *bipolar affective disorders* are classified by DSMIII as primary disturbances of mood.

Although it might seem that positive or elated moods would not be a problem to the person experiencing them, manic episodes can become extremely severe, as the following account by a 45-year-old housewife suggests:

When I start going into a high, I no longer feel like an ordinary housewife. Instead I feel organized and accomplished and I begin to feel I am my most creative self. I can write poetry easily. I can compose melodies without effort. I can paint. My mind feels facile and absorbs everything. I have countless ideas about improving the conditions of mentally retarded children, of how a hospital for these children should be run, what they should have around them to keep them happy and calm and unafraid. I see myself as being able to accomplish a great deal for the good of people. I have countless ideas about how the environment problem could inspire a crusade for the health and betterment of everyone. I feel able to accomplish a great deal for the good of my family and others. I feel pleasure, a sense of euphoria or elation. I want it to last forever. I don't seem to need much sleep. I've lost weight and feel healthy and I like myself. I've just bought six new dresses, in fact, and they look quite good on me.

I feel sexy and men stare at me. Maybe I'll have an affair, or perhaps several. I feel capable of speaking and doing good in politics. I would like to help people with problems similar to mine so they won't feel hopeless.

It's wonderful when you feel like this. . . . The feeling of exhilaration—the high mood—makes me feel light and full of the joy of living. However, when I go beyond this stage, I become manic, and the creativeness becomes so magnified I begin to see things in my mind that aren't real. For instance, one night I created an entire movie, complete with cast, that I still think would be terrific. I saw the people as clearly as if watching them in real life. I also experienced complete terror, as if it were actually happening, when I knew that an assassination scene was about to take place. I cowered under the covers and became a complete shaking wreck. As you know, I went into a manic psychosis at that point. My screams awakened my husband, who tried to reassure me that we were in our bedroom and everything was the same. There was nothing to be afraid of. Nevertheless, I was admitted to the hospital the next day (Fieve, 1975).

These examples illustrate some of the clinical characteristics of depression and elation. To get an even more detailed picture of the range of clinical behavior typically observed in mood disturbances see Table 14.4. The bipolar type of mood disorder is relatively rare, yet its dramatic mood swings make it the best-known type of mood disturbance. Joseph Mendels (1970) notes cases in which people have alternated between manic and depressive episodes every 24 hours for months. Such observations suggest that manic-depressive disorders may be affected by the body's biological rhythms.

Because so many people suffer from depression at some time in their lives, research into its causes is an important area of study for psychologists. Although various explanations have been offered, no single one can account for this disorder.

Separation, Loss, and Change Depression is often associated with stressful life events such as the death of a family member, the loss of a job, serious illness, or divorce (see Table 14.5). Not surprisingly, such stress often precipitates depression. Depression apparently can occur in reaction to success as well as to trauma. The second man to walk on the

TABLE 14.4 Mood Scale Used to Monitor Treatment Progress

(To be filled out in Metabolic Unit twice daily, before breakfast and before retiring, by both nurses (0-100) and patients (20-80). Also adaptable to lithium clinic outpatients.)

100 Medical emergency. Wildly manic and psychotic; can't stop talking; incoherent, overactive, belligerent, c. elated. Not sleeping at all. At times delusional; hallucinating. May be either violent or paranoid.

90 Extreme elation so that patient can't rate self; in need of more medication and control. Completely uncooperative.

80 Severe elation. Should be admitted, or if in hospital usually wants to sign out of ward. Sleeping very little; hostile when crossed, loss of control. Needs medication.

70 Moderate elation. Overactivity and talkativeness; irritable and annoyed. Needs only four to six hours' sleep. Socially inappropriate; wants to control. Outpatient treatment has been advised by doctors.

60 Mildly elated mood and many ideas for new projects; occasionally mildly obtrusive. If creative, the energy is highly useful. Hyperperceptive. Feels wonderful, on top of the world. Increased sexual drive, wants to spend money and travel. Treatment may be contraindicated or not needed.

50 Mood is within normal range (45-55).

40 Mildly depressed mood, but noticeable lack of energy; chronic lack of optimism and pleasure. Feels slowed down. Treatment may not be desired, although it may be indicated. Decreased interest in sex. Decreased motivation.

30 Moderate depression. Loss of energy; disinterested in others; early weight, sleep, and appetite disturbance; able to function with effort but wants to stay in bed during day; doesn't want to go to work; feels life is not worthwhile. Little sexual interest. Outpatient treatment advised by doctors.

20 Severe depression. Takes care of daily routine but needs prodding and reminding; loss or gain of weight; sleep disorder is serious. Volunteers suicidal feelings; very withdrawn, may be paranoid.

10 Extreme depression. Actively suicidal, totally withdrawn or extremely agitated. Difficulty rating self on mood scale.

0 Medical emergency. Unable to eat or take medication; can't follow ward routine; delusional, suicidal. Stuporous. Stares into space, very little response on questioning. May require tube feeding.

Nurses' and psychiatrists' rating scale

Patient's self-rating scale

Inpatient

Outpatient treatment

Inpatient

Source: R. R. Fieve, *Moodswing* (New York: Bantam, 1976), p. 187.

TABLE 14.5 A Scale of Stress Produced by Various Events

EXPERIENCE	STRESS UNITS
Death of spouse	100
Divorce	73
Separation	65
Jail term	63
Death of close family member	63
Getting married	50
Being fired	47
Reconciliation in marriage	45
Retiring	45
Getting pregnant	40
Sex problems	39
New member in family	39
Change in finances	38
Death of close friend	37
Change to new kind of work	36
Change in work responsibilities	29
Trouble with in-laws	29
An outstanding achievement	28
Wife starts job or stops	26
Begin or end school	26
Trouble with boss	23
Change in work conditions	20
Move to new residence	20
Changing schools	20
Changing social activities	18
Vacation	13
Christmas holidays	12
Minor law violation	11

Source: Adapted from T. H. Holmes & R. H. Rahe, "The Social Readjustment Rating Scale," *Journal of Psychosocial Research*, 1967, 11, pp. 213-218.

moon, Colonel Edwin E. Aldrin, Jr., has written in his autobiography, *Return to Earth*, of the public adulation that attended his space flight—and of the progressive loss of his own confidence and self-esteem (Aldrin and Warga, 1973). Aldrin experienced crying spells after some speaking engagements and even developed physiological symptoms, including neck pains and numbed fingers. Aldrin recovered after undergoing psychotherapy and receiving antidepressant medication.

Both the dynamic and the learning perspectives emphasize the role of prior experiences. Research in this area has focused on the relationship between depression and losses (or other severe stresses) during early childhood. The psychodynamic hypothesis holds that losses or stresses

might sensitize the person to depression in later life. For example, a child who lost a parent at an early age might find these early feelings of despair reactivated later when another relative dies.

There seems to be little question that separation from the mother can have an immediate and profound effect on offspring. Early emotional deprivation among humans has been studied most notably by Renee Spitz (1946, 1946), who observed the reactions of infants separated from their mothers between the ages of 6 and 12 months. These children typically displayed what has been called *anaclitic depression*. They cried continuously and showed apprehension, withdrawal, stupor, inability to sleep, weight loss, and retarded growth and development.

Perhaps the most famous research on separation, however, was that carried out by Harry and Margaret Harlow (1966) using rhesus monkeys. Working with monkeys instead of humans gave the researchers the opportunity to control closely a number of variables, including the length and type of separation and the age at which it occurred. The Harlows and their colleagues found that, once the mother-infant bond had been established, separation of the infants produced clinical effects in the infants very similar to the anaclitic depression reported by Spitz in human babies (Spitz, 1946, 1946). Moreover, separation of the young monkeys from peers of the same age also yielded reactions that resembled despair and depression (see Figure 14.3).

Research by the Harlow group suggests that separation not only causes immediate symptoms of depression in young rhesus monkeys but also seems to predispose them to later abnormal behavior (Harlow and Harlow, 1969). Monkeys separated from one another at three to four years of age show more abnormal behavior if they have been separated from their mothers during infancy. Separation thus seems to be important in depression both as a precipitating and as a predisposing factor.

Learned Helplessness The learning perspective views depression as a state in which the person is not being reinforced for behaviors. Lacking reinforcement, the person shows fewer and fewer behaviors—or, in the terminology of learning, a low rate of response. For the causes of these symptoms, the learning theorists look to the individual's prior experiences.

In recent years, many such theorists have come to believe that depressed people suffer from a sense of helplessness that they have learned. This hypothesis grows out of the experiments by Martin Seligman and his colleagues that were described in Chapter 7 (Seligman, Maier, and Geer, 1968; Seligman, Maier, and Solomon, 1971; Seligman, 1975). Recall that when dogs are first subjected to a series of inescapable shocks they are unable later to learn a simple escape behavior such as jumping over a shuttle-box partition to avoid shock. Seligman refers to this as *learned helplessness* because the unavoidable shocks administered to the dogs apparently have taught them that they are helpless to avoid further shocks.

To Seligman and his colleagues there is a striking analogy between the apparent learned helplessness of the dogs and the behavior of depressed humans. After closely examining the clinical literature on depression in light of his own research on animal helplessness, Seligman (1975) has described six types of parallel symptoms shown in Table 14.6. Seligman argues that the relationship between learned helplessness and clinical depression extends beyond these behavioral parallels. He believes that the feeling of helplessness is central to depression.

Seligman points out that the kinds of events precipitating depression—the death of a loved one, failure at work, physical disease—tend also to un-

dermine the sense of control over an individual's own life. Moreover, many of the therapies aimed at overcoming depression can be viewed as attempts to overcome helplessness. He suggests that people who are particularly resistant to depression are those whose prior experiences have allowed them to control effectively sources of reinforcement. They see the future positively and believe that they can control their own fates no matter what losses and failures they may encounter.

As plausible as Seligman's theory of learned helplessness seems, it has been criticized on a number of grounds. The cognitive complexity of humans means that learned helplessness depends on factors to which failure experiences are attributed (Miller and Norman, 1979). Furthermore, the specific research results from which Seligman has drawn his analysis of depression have been reinterpreted from a biochemical point of view (Weiss, Glazer, and Pohorecky, 1976).

Organic Determinants of Mood Disorders Although the experiments conducted by Weiss and his colleagues are persuasive in reinterpreting the

FIGURE 14.3 Studies by the Harlows and their colleagues demonstrated that young monkeys reared alone exhibited reactions resembling despair and depression.

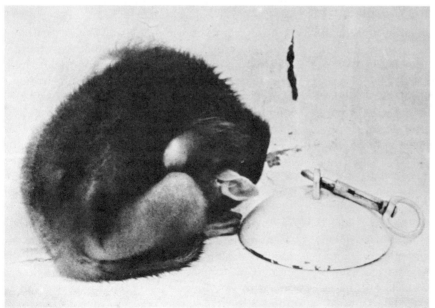

TABLE 14.6   Parallels between Learned Helplessness and Depression

LEARNED HELPLESSNESS		DEPRESSION
Symptoms	Passivity	Passivity
	Difficulty learning that responses produce relief	Negative cognitive set
	Dissipates in time	Time course
	Lack of aggression	Introjected hostility
	Weight loss, appetite loss, social and sexual deficits	Weight loss, appetite loss, social and sexual deficits
	Norepinephrine depletion and cholinergic activity	Norepinephrine depletion and cholinergic activity
	Ulcers and stress	Ulcers (?) and stress
		Feelings of helplessness
Cause	Learning that responding and reinforcement are independent	Belief that responding is useless
Cure	Directive therapy: forced exposure to responses that produce reinforcement	Recovery of belief that responding produces reinforcement
	Electroconvulsive shock	Electroconvulsive shock
	Time	Time
	Anticholinergics; norepinephrine stimulants (?)	Norepinephrine stimulants; anticholinergics (?)
Prevention	Immunization by mastery over reinforcement	(?)

Source: From M. E. P. Seligman, *Helplessness: On Depression, Development and Death* (San Francisco: Freeman) 1975, p. 106.

Seligman research with animals, they do not by themselves provide a broader base of evidence for assessing the degree to which genetic and physiological factors are important determinants of mood disorders.

Many scientists suspect that a family of neurotransmitters called catecholamines, including norepinephrine, dopamine, and epinephrine, play a key role in depression. It has been suggested that a depletion of norepinephrine in the brain results in depressed behavior (Schildkraut and Ketty, 1967).

The evidence for this catecholamine hypothesis stems from several sources. One line of evidence indicated that drugs that increase the level of norepinephrine in the brain tend to produce overactivity in laboratory animals. Another line of evidence comes from the effects of drugs used in the treatment of depression. These drugs, called monoamine oxidase inhibitors (MAO inhibitors), are effective apparently because they maintain the level of norepinephrine in the brain. MAO inhibitors block the action of an enzyme, MAO, which breaks down neurotransmitters such as norepinephrine. Hence, scientists reason, depression may be associated with—and perhaps caused by—the lack of sufficient levels of norepinephrine or other catecholamines.

Evidence for genetic causes of some mood disorders have also been found. A study of bipolar effective disorders (violent mood alternation), found that when the disorder occurs in twins, both members of the pair are far more likely to be affected if they are monozygotic, rather than dizygotic, twins (Rosenthal, 1970). This finding suggests a genetic component in the disorder.

Another line of evidence involves the treatment of mood disorders. A new and effective pharmacological treatment, using lithium carbonate, indicates that the biochemistry of the brain is involved in some mood disorders (Fieve, 1975). Lithium carbonate apparently reduces the brain's level of norepinephrine, the neurotransmitter that also has been implicated in depression. Interestingly, the element lithium is contained in mineral water, which probably explains why ancient Greek and Roman physicians prescribed mineral water for their manic-depressive patients, even though they could not have identified the chemical itself.

Thus mood disorders, like many other disorders, may be based in psychological trauma, may be learned, and may have biochemical or genetic origins. Strong evidence for organic causes of some mood disorders has emerged in recent years.

Schizophrenia: A Major Disorder of Perception and Thought

Small tasks become incredibly intricate and complex. It started with pruning the fruit trees. One saw cut would take forever. I was completely absorbed in the sawdust floating gently to the ground, the feel of the saw in my hand, the incredible patterns in the bark, the muscles in my arm pulling back and then pushing forward. Everything was slowing down and I would never finish sawing the limb. Then, by some miracle that branch would be done and I'd have to rest, completely blown out. The same thing kept happening over and over. Then I found myself being unable to stick with any one tree. I'd take a branch here, a couple there. It seemed I had been working for hours and hours but the sun hadn't moved at all. I began to wonder if I was hurting the trees and found myself apologizing. Each tree began to take on personality. I began to wonder if any of them liked me (Vonnegut, 1975).

Schizophrenia is a bewildering, terrifying experience, and seldom has it been described with such insight and poignant good humor as young Mark Vonnegut did in his book, *The Eden Express.* In the brief excerpt above, which concerns his first episode of the disorder, Vonnegut describes several of the classic symptoms of schizophrenia: impairment of thought processes, distortion of perception, and delusion.

Schizophrenia is no respecter of race, religion, intelligence, economic status, or geographic boundaries. About 1 percent of the people in the United States will be diagnosed as schizophrenic at some point in their lives, but it is a worldwide disorder. A recent survey sponsored by the World Health Organization suggests a 1 percent incidence of schizophrenia in all of the countries studied: Nigeria, Colombia, Denmark, the Soviet Union, and India, as well as the United States (Tsuang, 1976).

Schizophrenia is one of the most troubling of the *functional psychoses.* Unlike *organic psychoses*, which occur as the consequence of a specific disease, such as syphilis, or from brain damage, schiz-

Young schizophrenic patient in the hospital. About half the patients in U.S. mental institutions suffer from some form of schizophrenia.

439

ophrenia and other functional psychoses have no known single cause. Schizophrenics make up about half the patients in U.S. mental institutions; many more continue to live in society but must return to institutions periodically for treatment. Roughly one third of schizophrenics improve, about a third get worse, and the remaining third stay the same throughout their lives. Peak incidence occurs between the ages of 25 and 35 (Price and Lynn, 1981).

Despite thousands of scientific studies, schizophrenia remains one of the great puzzles confronting abnormal psychology. Perhaps more than any other area of abnormal psychology, schizophrenia is beset by questions and controversies, two of which are key to understanding the issues regarding it.

1. Is schizophrenia a single unitary disorder? Some scientists say yes. Others believe it is a group of similar-appearing disorders with different underlying causes. Still others argue that schizophrenia is merely a label for describing a range of behavior that we do not understand.
2. What are the causes of schizophrenia? Scientists are divided on this question, with one group insisting that the disorder is inherited and the other group insisting that it is a result of prior experience.

Clinical Descriptions

The word *schizophrenia* was coined by the Swiss psychiatrist Eugen Bleuler (1911/1950) from the Greek words *schizen* ("to split") and *phren* ("mind").

RESEARCH: "Helplessness"—Learned or Biochemical?

Scientific experiments serve two important functions: to test existing theories and to provide the raw material for new ones. Sometimes, however, the findings of such experiments are subject to more than one interpretation. They may, for example, fit plausibly into two quite different theoretical approaches to human behavior.

A dramatic illustration of this occurred in the late 1960s when Martin Seligman and his colleagues observed the intriguing phenomenon that they labeled learned helplessness.

Seligman (1975) drew an analogy between the behavior of the dogs and that of depressed humans. ". . . the depressed patient," he argued, "believes or has learned that he cannot control those elements of his life that relieve suffering, bring gratification, or provide nurture—in short, he believes that he is helpless."

Seligman's conclusions were of particular interest to another group of researchers. Like Seligman, Jay Weiss and his colleagues (Weiss, Glazer, and Pohorecky, 1976) were investigating the impact on behavior of stressful events such as unavoidable shocks, but from a different theoretical perspective. The focus of their work was the biochemistry of the brain, particularly certain neurotransmitters thought to play an important role in human depression. Weiss did not question the results of the Seligman experiments, but he did question Seligman's explanation of those results as learned helplessness.

Weiss and his associates suspected that the behavior of the dogs, far from being attributable to learning, could be explained in terms of biochemistry. They already had found in animal experiments that stress causes depletion of a particular neurotransmitter in the brain called norepinephrine. And as they studied the data from Seligman's work they were struck by the fact that dogs tested 48 hours after being subjected to inescapable shock had no trouble jumping the shuttle-box partition. The helplessness thus appeared to be temporary—not characteristic of learned responses but just what they would expect if the norepinephrine had been depleted and then gradually returned to normal levels. Because norepinephrine was believed to be essential to active behavior, Weiss formulated an alternative hypothesis: unavoidable shock, instead of teaching the dogs they were helpless, simply lowered the levels of norepinephrine in the brain; this depletion, in turn, reduced the ability of the animals to produce the movements necessary to jump over the shuttle-box barrier.

Here then was a classic confrontation of two theoretical perspectives—learning versus biological—over how to interpret the uncontested results of an important experiment.

To test their alternative hypothesis, Weiss and his associates devised a series of experiments that have been praised for their logic and elegant simplicity. Let us look briefly at the major findings and how they were arrived at.

1. Depletion of norepinephrine produces behaviors that look like learned helplessness. Weiss required laboratory rats to swim for 3½ minutes in cold water—an experience known to result in decreased

Although Bleuler's intention was to emphasize a "splitting off" of the person's thoughts and emotions from external reality, schizophrenia is sometimes confused in popular literature with the "split" or multiple personality. Multiple personality, however, is a rare form of disassociative disorder in which an individual behaves like one person one moment and like another the next.

Bleuler suggested the following key characteristics of the disorder as a result of observing his schizophrenic patients:

- *Autism* is the tendency to withdraw from involvement in the external world and to become preoccupied with private fantasies. In autistic fantasies, perceptions frequently become distorted.

- *Associative disturbance* (also called "loose associations" or "thought disorder") often takes the form of language that wanders and skips from topic to topic in a vague, disjointed way. A graphic example of this can be seen in the reply of a man who was asked whether he felt that people imitated him.

> Yes . . . I don't quite gather. I know one right and one left use both hands, but I can't follow the system that's working. The idea is meant in a kind way, but it's not the way I understand life. It seems to be people taking sides, as I understand it. . . . To say things are all wrong means right in turn, but I don't

norepinephrine. When these rats were later placed in a shuttle box, they showed behavior similar to the learned helplessness of Seligman's dogs; they were unable to jump the partition to avoid shock. To ensure that the cold water rather than the experience of swimming produced their behavior, Weiss exposed a control group to a similar swim in warm water. These rats had no trouble avoiding shock by jumping the partition in the shuttle box.

2. Norepinephrine depletion inhibits motor activity. To test his belief that norepinephrine depletion resulted in the lack of vigorous motor activity by Seligman's dogs, Weiss devised an experiment that would allow animals to avoid shock without having to leap a barrier. When his animals were exposed to inescapable shock and then given an opportunity to avoid shock by using a small movement, they were able to do so. Thus, they were not helpless when the motor activity required was small.

3. Animals recover from helplessness by adaptation. Weiss found that animals exposed to inescapable shock daily over a period of two weeks did not show helpless behavior in the shuttle-box situation. This conforms to the biochemist's expectation that the brain adapts to repeated experiences, showing norepinephrine depletion only at first. It also runs contrary to the learning theorist's expectation that repeated trials of inescapable shock would strengthen the helplessness rather than weaken it. Moreover, Weiss obtained direct measures of norepinephrine levels in his test animals. Although one session of inescapable shock produced deple-

tion, repeated sessions did not. Adaptation apparently was occurring in the brain chemistry of the animals exposed to repeated sessions.

4. Pharmacological experiments support Weiss's interpretation. When drugs known to deplete levels of norepinephrine were injected into laboratory animals, the symptoms of learned helplessness resulted. By the same token, drugs that prevent depletion of norepinephrine levels served to prevent the animals from helplessness when they were exposed to inescapable shock; they could jump the barrier.

This chain of findings, each link fitting neatly into the next, provides persuasive evidence for Weiss's refutation of the learned helplessness interpretation. Weiss is careful to point out that the refutation applies only to the results of the original Seligman experiments. His findings do not necessarily rule out the existence of learned helplessness. It may indeed play a role, as Seligman suggests, in human depression, although apparently not in the behavior of the dogs in his original experiments.

The Weiss experiments also have illuminated the connection between psychosocial and biochemical factors in a particular instance of abnormal behavior. A stressful event—inescapable shock—leads to biochemical changes in the brain that, in turn, lead to a disturbance in behavior. This is a promising model for the understanding of disturbed behavior in general and may point the way to clarification of the precise determinants of human depression.

appreciate it that way (Mayer-Gross, Slater, and Roth, 1969.)

- *Ambivalence* was Bleuler's way of describing the frequent juxtaposition of opposing emotions or impulses. For example, schizophrenics frequently report that they simultaneously experience love and hate for the same person.
- *Affective disturbance* refers to inappropriate emotional responses. Situations or stimuli that elicit joy or sadness in most of us may bring little response. Conversely, some schizophrenics may burst into laughter when told a friend or relative has died.
- *Delusions* are strongly held beliefs not shared by others in our culture.
- *Hallucinations* are sensations not experienced by others—seeing, hearing, or smelling things that do not actually exist but are perceived as being real (Feinberg, 1962).

Bleuler had a singular aptness for describing precisely the behavior he observed among his schizophrenic patients, and his descriptions remain useful when dealing with this disorder today.

Schizophrenics Describe Schizophrenia

Some valuable insights into schizophrenia also come from descriptions provided by those who experienced it at first hand (Chapman, 1966). James Chapman interviewed patients and asked them to describe their experiences as clearly as possible. Based on these interviews, he reported that the first signs of an oncoming schizophrenic episode are often frightening changes in perception. "Last week I was with a girl," said one patient, "and she seemed to get bigger and bigger, like a monster coming nearer and nearer. The situations become threatening and I shrink back."

After such perceptual distortions, patients seem to have extreme difficulty in controlling their thoughts. "I can't keep thoughts out," says a patient. "It comes on automatically. It happens at most peculiar times—not just when I'm talking, but when I'm listening as well. I lose control at conversation, then I sweat and shake all over. . . . I can hear what they were saying all right, it's remembering what they have said the next second that is difficult. It just goes out of my mind. I'm concentrating so much on little things I have difficulty in finding an answer at the time." Such reports show that schizophrenics have trouble focusing their attention on external events.

Thus, clinical descriptions of schizophrenia clearly suggest that it involves severe disturbances of perception and thought. But what are the causes of the disorder?

Determinants of Schizophrenia

Most scientists would probably agree, in a general way, that both biology and experience play some role in the development of schizophrenia. But as one researcher notes, "After paying homage to the concept of genotype-environment interaction, most investigators, unwittingly or by choice, slip back into more comfortable modes of thought and place their etiological bets on one or the other side (Kessler, 1969)."

Consider the following evidence concerning the transmission of schizophrenia. It is well established that a child with one schizophrenic parent has a risk of developing the disorder 10 times greater than someone selected at random from the general population. Moreover, a child with two such parents has a risk 40 times greater.

Biologically oriented researchers view this as evidence of an inherited genetic defect. From the same set of facts, researchers, whose perspective is social and environmental see schizophrenia as learned through constant exposure to the parent.

Biological Factors The search for possible biological determinants of schizophrenia has proceeded simultaneously along two principal lines. Along one, researchers look for underlying genetic factors; along the other, scientists who for the most part are already convinced of the importance of genetic factors seek specific solutions to schizophrenia in the biochemistry of the brain.

The strategy in genetic research is to study families where schizophrenia is prevalent. As we have already noted, however, the results of such family studies, which show much greater risk among children of schizophrenic parents, are subject to conflicting interpretations. Consequently, in an attempt to rule out the experience of living in a schizophrenic family as a possible cause, genetic researchers have narrowed their focus by studying twins.

To understand the strategy behind these studies, remember that there are two genetic types of twins. Identical twins are monozygotic—they develop from the same egg and therefore are genetically identical. Fraternal twins, by contrast, are dizygotic—they develop from separate eggs and are no more genetically similar than other siblings. By comparing incidence of schizophrenia in identical and fraternal twins, researchers can help separate the possible effects of environment from those of heredity. If there is an important hereditary factor in schizophrenia, it follows that both members of a pair of identical twins ought to be more likely to develop the disorder than would both members of a pair of fraternal twins.

Over the past half century, a number of such twin studies have been conducted (Rosenthal, 1970). The results, with one or two exceptions, tend to buttress the arguments of the genetic perspective. Both members of identical twin pairs tend to develop schizophrenia more often than do fraternal twins.

Heredity is not unequivocally established as a determinant, however. Many of the early twin studies have been strongly criticized even by other genetic researchers. For example, researchers point to the high variances in results from study to study, which probably were a consequence of differences in sampling and diagnostic methods. Moreover, at the time of the early studies, techniques used for determining whether twins were identical or fraternal were subject to error. Newer studies, based on modern techniques for distinguishing the types of twins, tend to produce lower, less-convincing concordance rates among identical twins.

As a result of such criticisms, researchers have switched to a different strategy for separating possible genetic and environmental factors. They study children who were born to schizophrenic parents but were put up for adoption early in life. If heredity is a factor in schizophrenia, such children ought to be more likely to develop the disorder than would

other adopted children who were born to non-schizophrenic parents.

For his study of adoption, David Rosenthal (1970) took advantage of the fact that some countries, such as Denmark, maintain highly detailed birth records. These records made it possible for the researchers to begin their study with a list of all the children in Denmark who had been adopted over a 23-year period and later became schizophrenic. The results support the genetic hypothesis (see Table 14.7). Adopted children born to a parent suffering from either schizophrenia or a manic-depressive disorder were more likely to develop schizophrenia symptoms than were adopted children whose biological parents had no history of psychological disorder.

Further support for the genetic perspective comes from a cross-fostering study in which three groups of adopted children were compared (Wender, Rosenthal, Kety, Schulsinger, and Weiner, 1973, 1974). Children in the first group were born to a schizophrenic parent but had been raised by normal parents who had never received any kind of psychiatric diagnosis. Children in the second group were born to normal biological parents and raised by normal parents. Children in the third group were born to normal biological parents and raised by parents of whom one was schizophrenic.

Extensive interviews and tests were conducted with each child, and then trained interviewers were asked to describe each child. These descriptions were then sorted by another group of judges who did not know which groups were being described.

TABLE 14.7   Schizophrenic-spectrum Disorders in Adoptees Who Had a Biological Schizophrenic or Manic-depressive Parent, or Both Biological Parents without Psychiatric History

DIAGNOSIS OF ADOPTEE	ONE PARENT SCHIZOPHRENIC OR MANIC-DEPRESSIVE (n = 39)	PARENTS WITHOUT PSYCHIATRIC HISTORY (n = 47)
Schizophrenia		
Hospitalized	1	0
Never hospitalized	2	0
Borderline schizophrenia	7	1
Near or probable borderline	0	2
Schizoid or paranoid	3	4
Not in schizophrenic spectrum	26	40

Source: D. Rosenthal, *Genetic Theory and Abnormal Behavior* (New York: McGraw-Hill, 1970).

The results strongly suggest a genetic component in schizophrenia.

Even if there is a genetic component to schizophrenia as evidence suggests, investigators are still interested in the form it might take in the physiological functioning of the person who develops the disorder. The search for answers has focused on two aspects of human biochemistry—the metabolism of the schizophrenic and the chemistry of the brain.

The history of the search for a metabolic mechanism has been discouraging. Researchers have so assiduously sought a biochemical "X-factor" unique to schizophrenics that there have been many premature reports of such a discovery (Kety, 1967). A dramatic instance of this was the report in the late 1950s of a "pink spot" in the blood and urine of schizophrenics (Hoffer, Osmond, and Smythies, 1954). This report, like many others, turned out to

be a blind alley (see Focus). Nonetheless, researchers continue to seek the elusive factor.

The newer—and more promising—biochemical approach, however, involves investigations into the chemistry of the brain. Instead of looking for some factor unique to schizophrenia, researchers try to understand the chemical functioning of the brain. They then build theories based on how chemical imbalances or malfunctions might lead to schizophrenic behavior.

The focus of their attention is the brain's neurotransmitters. As we saw earlier, several of these chemicals, which transmit electric impulses from one nerve cell to the next, have been implicated in the development of depression. About a dozen neurotransmitters have been positively identified and, as we pointed out in Chapter 2, interference with their functioning by drugs or disease can dramatically affect behavior.

One particular neurotransmitter, dopamine, is the target of perhaps the most promising line of research into biochemical determinants of schizophrenia. Dopamine is know to be involved in the fine control of certain muscle movements; too little of it apparently leads to Parkinson's disease. Now, according to the so called *dopamine hypothesis*, too much of it may cause symptoms of schizophrenia (see Figure 14.4).

The evidence for the dopamine hypothesis is indirect (Snyder, 1976). First, excess amounts of 1-dopa, a dopaminelike drug that is given to sufferers of Parkinson's disease, tend to create the symptoms of schizophrenia. Second, major tranquilizers such as the phenothiazines, which are used in the treatment of schizophrenia, have the effect of interfering with the action of dopamine: they inhibit the transmission of nerve impulses by blocking the nerve cell receptor sites where dopamine normally acts. Finally, the amphetamines, which are known to stimulate the central nervous system, appear to "soup up" the transmission of nerve impulses by blocking the normal reuptake of dopamine. Because the dopamine is not taken up again in nerve endings, large amounts of it are left in the synaptic gaps between nerve cells, thus magnifying its effect. Moreover, amphetamines tend to worsen the symptoms of schizophrenia.

Thus it appears that too much dopamine may somehow be responsible for the symptoms of schizophrenia. Several possibilities might account for the excess of dopamine (Keith, Gunderson, Reifman, Buchsbaum, and Mosher, 1976). The nerve

FIGURE 14.4 Representation of the hypothesis that the neurotransmitter dopamine is a biochemical determinant of schizophrenia.

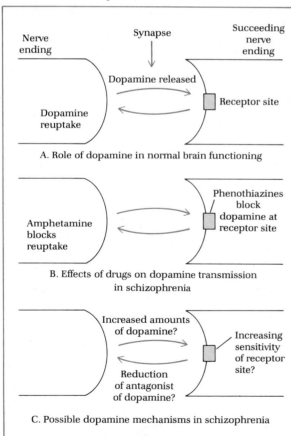

A. Role of dopamine in normal brain functioning

B. Effects of drugs on dopamine transmission in schizophrenia

C. Possible dopamine mechanisms in schizophrenia

endings could be producing too much for some reason or some hypothetical chemical that normally reduces the amount of dopamine in the synaptic cleft might not be present in sufficient quantities. Whatever the mechanism, the question of how an excess of dopamine might produce schizophrenia still remains.

It is interesting to note that, even if the dopamine hypothesis is correct, it would not necessarily prove that schizophrenia is inherited. Some evidence suggests that the experience of learning may bring about biochemical changes in the brain (Rose, 1973). If so, a case could then plausibly be made that the imbalance of dopamine results from experience rather than genetics.

Environmental Factors   The quest for environmental determinants of schizophrenia takes several forms. It looks at the role played by society at large, for example, but its most important focus is the family itself.

Support for the family approach can be found in at least three factors. First, to most psychologists, the family is seen as the focal point of learning. Second, the studies of twins discussed earlier, while suggesting a strong genetic component, cannot fully explain the incidence of schizophrenia. Third, it is a common observation among clinicians that the themes, preoccupations, fears, delusions, and hallucinations of their schizophrenic patients tend to center on the patient's family. In fact, the clinical literature persuades many psychologists that schizophrenic behavior can be understood only in the context of the family.

How does the family contribute to the development of the disorder? Different theorists have set fourth different hypotheses based on clinical experience. Here are six such hypotheses.

1. *Attachment.* Schizophrenia reflects disruptions in attachment between child and parent (Will, 1970). The formation of basic trust is disrupted, resulting in later fear of loss and separation, withdrawal, panic, odd symbolic communication, and lack of ego development.
2. *Double Bind.* Certain forms of communication between parent and child may elicit schizophrenic behavior (Bateson, Jackson, Haley, and Weakland, 1956). The parent, or "binder," communicates in paradoxical ways that demand contradictory responses—for example, "Don't be so obedient." The child copes with such con-

tradictions in ways that appear schizophrenic, withdrawing or looking for hidden meanings in all communications.
3. *Marital Schism and Skew.* The parents are in open conflict, and each attempts to recruit the child to his or her side. In other instances, there is a "marital skew" in which one parent dominates and shows overtly pathological behavior (Lidz, Fleck, and Cornelison, 1965).
4. *Mystification.* The apparent schizophrenia observed in some children may actually be a rational means of coping with parents who act in inconsistent and mystifying ways (Laing and Esterson, 1971).
5. *Schizophrenogenic Mother.* Mothers can be so overprotective, smothering, insensitive, rejecting, seductive, and controlling that they elicit schizophrenic behavior in their children (Arieti, 1959).
6. *Social Learning.* Differential reinforcement by the family may be a key factor in learning schizophrenic behavior. Normal behavior is extinguished because it is ignored; bizarre behavior is reinforced through attention (Ullmann and Krasner, 1975).

Although all of these hypotheses seem quite plausible, they are extremely difficult to test. The clinical experience that yields such theories does not provide an adequate arena for testing them. We cannot determine whether attachment, for example, is a cause of the schizophrenic behavior or simply a response to it. Attachment may actually be a response to the stress of having a severely disturbed person in the family.

Furthermore, unusual behavior does not appear to be unique to families that produce schizophrenic children. A recent review could not find consistent evidence that conflict or either a positive or a negative emotion were uniquely characteristic of such families (Jacob, 1975).

Interestingly, however, the review did find evidence that there are more communication difficulties in schizophrenic families (Jacob, 1975). Similarly, Lyman Wynne (1970) has found what he calls "communication deviancy" in the parents of schizophrenics. Although Wynne emphasizes a family environmental interpretation of this phenomenon, it could also be explained in terms of genetics. The parents with this trait might be show-

FOCUS: The Model Psychosis Hypothesis

For the past quarter century, scientists have been intrigued by certain apparent similarities between the subjective states induced by psychedelic drugs and those reported by schizophrenics. Those who experiment with drugs such as mescaline and LSD often report experiencing hallucinations and loss of self-identity resembling the symptoms of schizophrenia. In fact, another name for psychedelic drugs, psychotomimetic, literally means "capable of producing states that mimic psychotic states." Some investigators thus have hypothesized that drugs produce a kind of "model psychosis," which can help them better understand the nature of schizophrenia.

One research strategy suggested by this hypothesis is that the physiology of schizophrenics may produce some toxic substance resembling a psychedelic drug. For example, in 1962, two British scientists, noted a chemical similarity between mescaline and adrenalin, the hormone that prepares the body for action during stress (Hoffer, Osmond, and Smythies, 1962). They speculated that perhaps adrenalin is metabolized by some people into a mescalinelike substance, which then produces schizophrenic behavior.

Soon afterward, Abram Hoffer reported a breakthrough that appeared to confirm the Osmond-Smythies speculation (Hoffer, Osmond, and Smythies, 1962). Hoffer said he had found a derivative of adrenalin called adrenochrome in samples of blood and urine taken from schizophrenics. This pink-colored chemical results when oxygen combines with adrenalin. Hoffer thus had reason to believe that the pink-spot substance, which he thought was adrenochrome, might be the long-sought X-factor in schizophrenia—the biological cause. To test this possibility, he administered the substance to normal subjects. He reported that they experienced effects similar to those of people who took LSD.

Hoffer's report stirred great excitement. But when scientists all over the world attempted to repeat his experiments, they could not find adrenochrome in the blood of either schizophrenics or normal subjects. The general conclusion was that Hoffer's exciting results stemmed from poorly controlled laboratory procedures. The pink spots had appeared because the laboratory samples from schizophrenics had been allowed to remain in the open air for longer than those from nonschizophrenics. As for the reported psychedelic effects of the blood samples administered to normal subjects, it was quite likely the result of the placebo effect. Hoffer and his colleagues might have been so eager to demonstrate their theory that they unwittingly suggested the expected effects to their subjects, who obliged with reports of symptoms of disorientation that resembled those of schizophrenia.

A second research strategy for investigating the psychedelic experience as a "model psychosis" has focused on the apparent similarities of behavior between schizophrenics and people under the influence of psychedelic drugs. On closer examination, similarities as well as important differences emerge. For example, Leo Hollister (1962) conducted a simple but carefully controlled experiment. He asked a group of mental health professionals to listen to tape-recorded interviews. Some of the interviews were with normal subjects who were under the influence of LSD; the other interviews were with schizophrenics. The professionals had no difficulty distinguishing between the two groups. Hollister also reports a clear distinction in the disturbances experienced by the two groups. LSD seemed to affect perception primarily, whereas schizophrenia affected thought processes. Another investigator found differences in the types of hallucinations (Feinberg, 1962). Schizophrenic hallucinations tend to involve hearing voices, whereas psychedelic aberrations are primarily visual, involving alterations of color, size, shape, movement, and number.

Although these findings and the failure to pinpoint an X-factor in the metabolism of schizophrenics led many scientists to reject the model psychosis approach, others still feel it may yet shed light on schizophrenia. Researchers have found evidence of similarities to psychedelic breakdown (Bowers and Freedman, 1966). Another investigator suggests it is possible that the prolonged experience of altered perceptions in schizophrenia may produce still other changes that mask essential similarities in the two states (Snyder, 1975).

---

ing "communication deviancy" simply because they possess schizophrenic genes.

To avoid such ambiguous findings, researchers have attempted to examine the family over a long period of time. Ideally, a longitudinal study that looks at the same families over a period of time would have the advantage of examining the family environment before schizophrenic behavior appears in a child. This is usually impractical, however, because the researcher cannot know what families to study. One solution is the follow-up study, which examines clinical records of children made before they developed schizophrenia and then follows them up.

One follow-up study looked at children who had been seen early in life at a child guidance center and had later become schizophrenic (Waring and Ricks, 1965). The clinical records revealed some interesting information. For example, severely disturbed chronic schizophrenics were much more likely to have been raised in one of the following two kinds of family environments: (1) emotional divorce—an environment marked by much hostility and distrust between parents; or (2) symbolic union—an environment in which one spouse is dominating and overcontrolling, while the other is passive and accepting.

In addition, in a third kind of environment, called *family sacrifice*, the child is openly rejected and frequently forced to leave the home. Children from this type of family fared better than those in the first two kinds of environment. This third group had the highest proportion of schizophrenics who were able to be released from hospital settings after treatment and returned to the community.

This study suggests that the severity of schizophrenic behavior may be significantly affected by the family environment.

The Vulnerability Model of Schizophrenia

There is little doubt that schizophrenia is at least partly hereditary. How it is transmitted genetically is not yet clear, although the most promising new evidence suggests that the neurotransmitters of the brain—particularly dopamine—play an important role in the development of the disorder.

At the same time, it is clear that social and environmental factors, especially the family, are important. The social environment can affect the potential schizophrenic in two ways: it is the source of stresses, and it is the teacher of various abilities and skills that shape the way a person copes with those stresses.

Thus, there appear to be several determinants of schizophrenia, all of them intertwined in ways that are difficult to separate. Several models have been proposed in an attempt to incorporate all these factors in a coherent fashion. One such attempt is the *vulnerability model* (Zubin and Spring, 1977).

This model's basic premise is that each of us is endowed with some degree of vulnerability to schizophrenia (see Figure 14.5). The degree of vulnerability is determined by some combination of both biological and environmental factors. Whether this vulnerability will express itself in an episode of schizophrenia depends on the impact of any of a number of challenging life events. Among these events are bereavement, marriage, divorce, and unemployment. Moreover, the actual impact of a given event may differ depending on the person's vulnerability. For example, most of us are able to cope adequately with a death in the family, but for others who are more vulnerable, that loss may precipitate a schizophrenic episode. The model thus brings together genetic and environmental factors, including stress, and accounts for the episodic nature of schizophrenia.

Like all useful formulations, the vulnerability model raises as many questions as it answers. But it provides a model that can be applied not only to schizophrenia but also to other disorders, thus suggesting a way of incorporating evidence from conflicting perspectives into a more coherent picture of how severe disturbance in behavior may develop.

FIGURE 14.5 The vulnerability model of causation in schizophrenia is based on the premise that the degree of vulnerability to schizophrenia in each of us is determined by some combination of biological and environmental factors.

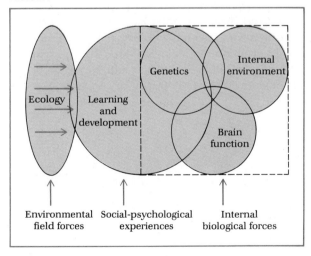

SUMMARY

1. Most definitions of abnormal psychology focus on (1) behavior that is disturbing to others, (2) subjective distress, or (3) psychological handicaps that prevent normal coping with the demands and stress of life. Theories to account for the causes of abnormal behavior fell into three general groups. Those concerned with the social environment focus on the social perspective, which considers abnormal behavior as a violation of social norms, and the learning perspective, examines the contingency between behavior and stimuli in the environment. Biological theories search for behavior determinants in genetics, physiology, and biochemistry. Psychological theories, particularly those with a psychodynamic orientation, concentrate on inner conflicts that produce anxiety and, in turn, defense mechanisms.

2. The third and current edition of the *Diagnostic and Statistical Manual* of the American Psychiatric Association (DSMIII) represents an attempt to provide reliable descriptions of patterns of abnormal behavior. While this classification system can be a valuable tool, advancing scientific knowledge about abnormal behavior, some psychologists voice concerns about labeling and stigmatizing people with mild difficulties and about the accuracy of a system that classifies behavior on the basis of several dimensions.

3. Phobias and psychophysiological disorders are examples of maladaptive reactions to stress and anxiety. Phobic reactions focus on specific objects or situations, but ones that present no actual danger to the individual. According to the psychoanalytic view, phobias result when forbidden impulses and associated fear become transformed and externalized. Learning theorists argue that phobias can be accounted for by the mechanisms of classical conditioning. Biological theorists suggest the existence of biological preparedness, an inherited disposition to become fearful of certain stimuli.

4. The precise role of emotions in disease is not always easy to identify, although it is likely that all diseases or organic disorders may have some psychological component. The disregulation theory proposes a framework for examining the genetic factors, learning, and stress that may interact to provoke physiological disorders such as some headaches. This theory proposes that internal regulation systems are disrupted during the development of such disorders.

5. Personality disorders appear to be deeply ingrained and appear primarily as behavioral exaggerations. Some traits—compulsive neatness, for example—are not considered disorders until they become extreme, making it difficult for individuals concerned to cope effectively in their social worlds.

6. Disorders of mood and affect are among the most important forms of abnormal behavior. They include depression, manic episodes (intense periods of elation), and biopolar affective disorders (alternating states of elation and depression). Both the dynamic and learning perspectives emphasize the role of prior experiences as causes of these disorders. Biological research suggests some possible genetic and biochemical factors in such disorders as helplessness and in biopolar affective disorders.

7. Schizophrenia is one of the major disorders of perception and thought. It is a functional psychosis with no known single cause; delusions and hallucinations are common symptoms. Most scientists agree that some combination of biological and environmental factors works to produce schizophrenia. Strong evidence exists for a genetic, inherited component; recent research suggests some biochemical basis; environmental theories focus on the role of the family. The vulnerability model proposes that each of us has some vulnerability to schizophrenia. The degree of vulnerability is determined by some combination of biological and environmental factors.

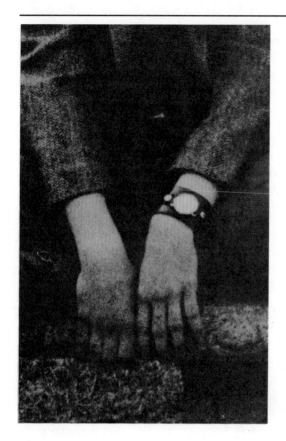

Chapter 15
Behavior Change

We all engage in attempts to change our own behavior and that of others every day. We may attempt to change our patterns of eating, to improve our own memory, or to persuade others to change their beliefs. Throughout this text, in fact, we have examined psychological principles that are often used for the purposes of changing behavior.

In Chapter 14 we saw that most cultures have developed methods for offering help to people experiencing psychological disturbances and to change the behavior in question. More than most, our own society has invested resources in the development of effective methods of behavior change to help those who are experiencing intense personal distress or who are particularly disturbing to others.

Although psychological research in the area of behavior change is still in its early stages, knowledge is increasing rapidly. Techniques available for treatment of depression, schizophrenia, and other forms of psychopathology were sadly limited until this century. For many centuries people with behavioral disturbances were believed to be possessed by demons, and because treatment related to the presumed cause of the behavior, therapy consisted principally of trying to get rid of the demons. People were flogged, burned at the stake, and even had holes drilled in their skulls—a procedure called trepanning—to let out the evil spirits. Even after the first mental asylum, Bethlehem Hospital, was founded in London in 1547, patients were chained and subjected to gawking tourists at a penny a look. Bethlehem was so noisy and chaotic, in fact, that *bedlam*, a word derived from the hospital's name, came into the language. As recently as the early 1800s in the United States, mental patients were sometimes treated by trying to break their will: one method was to place the patient in a coffinlike box with air holes and then submerge the box in water until the bubbles of air stopped rising, after which an attempt was made to revive the occupant.

Today, of course, behavior change methods are more benevolent and are provided in most cases by someone with professional training. The professionals who treat disordered behavior are classified principally according to their educational background:

- *Psychiatrists* are physicians who usually have spent a postgraduate residency training in psychotherapy and specialize in diagnosis and treatment of abnormal behavior.
- *Psychoanalysts* are practitioners, usually but not always physicians, who have received specialized training at a psychoanalytic institute in the methods of therapy first developed by Sigmund Freud.
- *Clinical psychologists* hold Ph.D.s in psychology and have had extensive training in research, psychological testing, and therapy techniques.
- *Counseling psychologists* have graduate training similar to that of clinical psychologists but typically with less emphasis on research.
- *Psychiatric social workers* hold master's degrees in social work and have special training in treatment procedures with emphasis on the home and community.

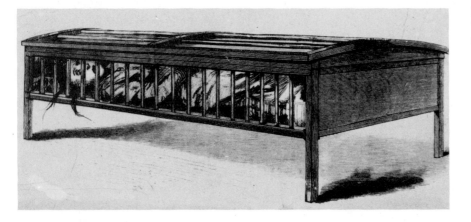

Insane patient confined in a "crib," a device used in institutions as late as the 1880s.

A debate is currently raging over a new degree—the Psy.D. or doctor of psychology degree—which is offered by seven of the 158 doctoral programs accredited by the American Psychological Association. The Psy.D. requires broader clinical experience in preparation for a career of service, while the Ph.D. emphasizes original research leading to a disseration that contributes to knowledge of psychology. Champions of the new degree believe that it reflects the division of the field of psychology between research scientists and an ever-increasing number of private practitioners who help clients build coping skills; they assert that it gives the latter group a new identity before the public. Supporters of the traditional Ph.D. maintain that unproven credentials would destroy the respectability that psychology has earned.

Mental health professionals administer two major categories of treatment—the psychotherapies and the biological therapies—which are sometimes used together.

Psychotherapies

Psychotherapy has been defined as "an interpersonal process designed to bring about modifications of feelings, cognitions, attitudes, and behavior which have proven troublesome to the person seeking help from a trained professional" (Strupp, 1978). There are many forms of psychotherapy. Freud, who started it all in Vienna nearly a century ago with his formulation of psychoanalysis, would surely be astonished at the remarkable range of therapies available today. Psychotherapists now treat children, entire families, drug addicts, alcoholics, prison inmates, the very old, and the terminally ill. They work with psychotics who were once thought to be unreachable and with clients who are simply seeking expanded personal awareness and more meaningful ways of living. Between these two extremes are those who seek help because of feelings of helplessness or social isolation, a sense of failure or lack of worth. Many feel excluded from the mainstream of life or blocked from living up to their potential.

There are four major classes of psychotherapy—psychodynamic, humanistic, behavioral, and group. In theory, these therapies differ markedly from one another; in practice, however, the theoretical lines between the types are blurred, and increasingly, psychotherapists describe themselves as eclectic. They select techniques from the various theoretical perspectives and tailor them to the problems of the particular patient. In fact, it is not uncommon for a psychotherapist to combine one of the psychologically oriented therapies with the use of drug treatment, one of the types of biological therapies.

Psychodynamic Therapy

Freud's original formulation of psychoanalysis (1904/1959) has been changed and adapted by later practitioners including Carl Jung, Karen Horney, and others. Whatever the dimensions of their dissent from Freudian doctrine, however, all of the psychodynamic schools have retained an emphasis on intrapsychic dynamics.

Psychoanalysis This approach to therapy begins with the first Freudian principle: the goal of *psychoanalysis* is to make conscious the images, fantasies, and wishes of the patient's unconscious (Freud, 1904/1959). This is achieved in large part through the development of a therapeutic relationship between patient and therapist and is aimed at providing insight into emotional problems.

Freud recognized that his technique would not work for everyone. He described the ideal patient in psychoanalysis as being younger than 50, fairly well educated, of good character, sufficiently motivated to seek therapy willingly, and neither psychotic, confused, nor deeply depressed. Freud also envisioned the ideal psychoanalyst—a person of irreproachable character who "must have overcome in his own mind that mixture of lewdness and prudery with which ... many people consider sexual problems (Freud, 1904/1959)." This latter requirement was important, of course, because Freud believed that repression of sexual impulses is basic to most emotional disturbances.

Techniques Psychoanalytic treatment is a slow and gradual process; typically a patient will spend several hours a week for several years in psychoanalysis. Freud developed a set of procedures for psychoanalytic treatment that are basically still followed by modern psychodynamic therapists. Techniques may vary in nuance but seldom in essence.

- *Free Association.* Freud's fundamental rule of psychoanalysis is free association. In order to

451

lower defenses the analyst instructs the patient to say freely whatever comes to mind and to avoid censoring the material no matter how silly, embarrassing, or illogical it may seem. To facilitate free association, the patient typically lies in a relaxed position on a couch. The analyst, to avoid distracting the patient, sits out of sight, maintaining an attitude of—as Freud put it—"evenly hovering attention (Freud, 1904/1959)."

As the patient pours out whatever enters the mind, long-repressed wishes and impulses begin to well up. The analyst notes the possible connections between this formerly unconscious material and the patient's everyday problems as expressed during the therapy. From these data the analyst forms hypotheses regarding the origin and nature of the patient's difficulties. These hypotheses are articulated by the analyst and, eventually, the patient begins self-discovery of the implications of materials elicited during the free-association process.

Patient "free associating" on couch in analyst's office during therapy session.

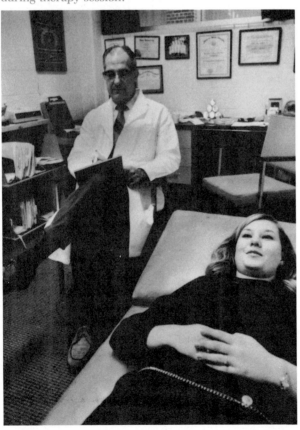

- *Dream Analysis.* Closely related to free association and its interpretation is a second procedure—*dream analysis.* As was discussed in Chapter 5, Freud viewed dreams as symbolic representations of hidden conflicts that were reawakened by the previous day's activities. The psychoanalyst looks at dream content on two levels: the *manifest* or surface, *content*, and the *latent*, or hidden, *content.* For example, an ogre in a dream would be the manifest content, but the analyst may interpret its latent, or true meaning, as representing the patient's secretly hated and feared father. According to Freudian theory, this process of *dream censorship*—the masking of real meanings—occurs because the meaning would be unacceptable to the patient's conscious standards of morality.

  The analyst views the dream in the context of the particular patient's personality, relating it to the patient's conscious experiences and to the latent symbolic significance. Above all, the analyst will be guided by the patient's own comments about various aspects of the dream during free association. Freud maintained that, if clearly understood, dreams contain "the psychology of the neurosis in a nutshell (Freud, 1897/1953)."

- *Resistance.* Through free association and dream analysis patients become aware of previously unconscious aspects of their personalities. At this point, patients often show signs of *resistance:* they may miss therapy appointments, remain silent when asked to free-associate, or report that they have no dreams to relate.

  According to psychoanalytic theory, resistance has the effect of protecting the patients' neurosis; unconsciously, they want to avoid the anxiety evoked by facing previously repressed impulses. To overcome resistance, the analyst attempts the following: (1) making patients aware that they are unconsciously resisting therapy, (2) pointing out to patients precisely how they are resisting the elimination of repressions, and (3) clarifying to patients just what it is they are avoiding (Reich, 1949).

- *Interpretation.* The process by which the analyst tries to overcome resistance is called interpretation. Typically, interpretation takes the form of a statement aimed at helping patients see the unconscious basis of a symptom that has been masked by resistance—for example: "Having these repeated accidents perhaps assured you of getting the attention you felt you could not get otherwise." Or interpretation may direct the patient's attention to a repressed impulse—for example: "Could it be that your present shyness is a defense against the aggressiveness your mother punished when you were little?"

Analysts offer interpretation only when they have developed a reasonably clear picture of the dynamics of the patient's personality and the biographical roots of difficulties. Timing of interpretation is critical: if offered too soon, anxiety and resistance may be aroused; if timed correctly, a flow of new associations may be elicited leading to significant progress in the therapy.

- *Transference.* As analysis progresses, patients may begin to express intense and unrealistic feelings and expectations toward the analyst. They may feel that the analyst is indifferent to them, for example, or that the analyst is attempting to manipulate them. If early ungratified strivings for love have been reactivated, they may begin to act seductively toward the analyst, bring presents, and spend hours rehearsing what they will say in the next therapy session. This process, through which the analyst becomes the focus of emotions once directed at parents or other significant people in the patients' childhoods, is called transference.

When transference occurs, the analyst points out to patients that their behavior is inappropriate and actually a form of resistance to getting better. This may trigger negative transference—focusing on the therapist of feelings of frustration and violent anger that were once directed at disapproving parental figures. Ruth Munroe (1955), cites the case of a patient who actually pulled a gun on his analyst: "I admire the *sang-froid* of the analyst who looked in a gun . . . and said calmly, 'This is what I meant about your murderous feelings toward your father (laugh). Do you see it now?' According to the analyst, the patient laughed also, albeit a bit hysterically, and lay down on the couch—in such a position that the analyst could now unobtrusively wipe the sweat off his brow."

Munroe's dramatic example illustrates how the analyst's skillful use of interpretation can transform transference into a therapeutic instrument. By emotionally reliving painful aspects of childhood, patients in transference give the analyst a clear view of the unconscious determinants of their behaviors. And with the help of the analyst's interpretation, patients come to understand better the irrational expectations and demands that they bring not only to the analyst but also to people in everyday life.

On the other hand, transference can fail if analysts themselves have not resolved the conflicts in their own unconscious. When analysts respond to the hostile or seductive transference of patients with unconscious emotional reactions of their own, *countertransference* is said to occur. To prevent countertransference, analysts themselves must undergo thorough analysis before they attempt to treat patients.

- *Working through.* Difficulties often occur even when analysis appears to be on the way to successful completion. New experiences in a patient's life may threaten the recent and fragile adjustment, and neurotic responses may reappear. In the continuing therapy, resistance may once again become a factor, and, as Karl Menninger (1958) put it, "It often appears as if the patient had never heard the analyst's previous interpretation." Interpretations must be repeated and related again to the patient's past and present. In successful therapy, however, the healthy part of a patient's personality has been activated and ultimately works to integrate the insights so painfully achieved.

Psychoanalysis was not only Freud's method of treatment but also his primary mode of research. He developed the methods of interpretation and the analysis of transference, which are used in treatment, as ways of gaining insight into psychological conflict. The fact that treatment and research are so tightly intertwined makes psychoanalysis extremely difficult to evaluate.

Humanistic Therapy

Humanistic therapy developed in part as a reaction against the psychoanalytic view. Whereas psychoanalysis emphasizes the primitive sexual and aggressive impulses of the id and their management by the ego, humanism takes an optimistic view that stresses the human potential for growth. Clients, or patients, are regarded as having the freedom and capacity to choose their own goals in life. They are seen as integrated wholes rather than as conflict-ridden combinations of id, ego, and superego impulses.

453

Client-Centered Therapy The most prominent example of the humanistic approach is the *client-centered therapy* of Carl Rogers (1957, 1959). Rogers believes that all humans have an innate tendency toward self-actualization (Chapter 12) and, given the opportunity, will find their own paths toward self-development. Patients themselves set the goals of therapy, and the therapist refrains from giving advice or specific prescriptions for change, unlike the directive interpretation offered in psychoanalysis. With nondirective therapy the therapist neither defines patients' problems nor tells patients how to solve them.

The Rogerian approach emphasizes the critical importance of the relationship between therapist and client. Rogers' vision of the ideal therapist is expressed in the form of ten difficult questions therapists must ask themselves (Rogers, 1961).

1. Can I *be* in some way which will be perceived by the other person as trustworthy, as dependable or consistent in some deep sense ...?
2. Can I be expressive enough as a person that what I am will be communicated unambiguously ...?
3. Can I let myself experience positive attitudes towards this other person—attitudes of warmth, caring, liking interest, respect ...?
4. Can I be strong enough as a person to be separate from the other ...?
5. Am I secure enough within myself to permit him his separateness ...?
6. Can I let myself enter fully into the world of his feelings and personal meanings and see these as he does ...?
7. Can I be acceptant of each facet of this other person which he presents to me? Can I perceive him as he is? Can I communicate this attitude? Or can I only receive him conditionally, acceptant of some aspects of his feelings and silently or openly disapproving of other aspects?
8. Can I act with sufficient sensitivity in the relationship that my behavior will not be perceived as a threat ...?
9. Can I free him from the threat of external evaluation ...?
10. Can I meet this other individual as a person who is in the process of *becoming* or will I be bound by his past and by my past ...?

Rogers also has cited six conditions that the therapist-client relationship must fulfill in order to be successful (Rogers, 1957):

1. Client and therapist must be fully aware of each other.
2. The client must be a state of incongruence—that is, not freely and genuinely himself or herself—and thus feeling vulnerable or anxious.
3. The therapist must be congruent—an authentic person who wears no mask and plays no role.
4. The therapist must express unconditional positive regard, listening with a nonjudgmental attitude that permits clients to be themselves without threat of sanctions.
5. The therapist must relate to clients with complete empathy, sensing "the client's world as if it were your own, but without ever losing the 'as if' quality."
6. The client must feel, at least to some degree, the therapist's acceptance and understanding.

Techniques Unlike psychoanalysts, Rogerian therapists make no attempt to trace the early roots of difficulties. The focus is on the client's present functioning, and therapy is concluded in a relatively brief period. Rogers (1957) defines therapy as the "releasing of an already existent capacity in a potentially competent individual, not the expert manipulation of a more or less passive personality." To this end, he advocates three principal techniques of therapeutic procedure:

- *Reflection of feelings.* The therapist accepts the client's feelings and communicates understanding by restating them in words that mirror their essence. For example:

  Client: I was small and envied people who were large. I was—well, I took beatings by boys and I couldn't strike back.
  Therapist: You've had plenty of experience in being the underdog.

- *Clarification of feelings.* When the client becomes confused in trying to express feelings, it is up to the therapist to help clarify them so that the client can express them clearly. For example:

  Therapist: And so, little by little, you have come to hold back things that previously you would have communicated to your wife? Is that It?

- *Expression of therapist's feelings.* Rogers has recently concluded that, in order truly to be genuine, therapists should reveal their own reactions when it seems appropriate (Meador and Rogers, 1979).

  Client: I think I'm beyond help.
  Therapist: Huh? Feel as though you're beyond help? I know. You feel just completely hopeless

about yourself. I can understand that. I don't feel hopeless, but I realize you do.

Through these techniques, the therapist helps clients to see inconsistencies between their self-concepts and their behaviors and to accept feelings that previously had been denied. These insights facilitate a reorganization of the self on a more realistic level. With this restructuring comes behavior that is more adaptive, less anxious, and more effective (Rogers, 1961).

Behavior Therapy

Psychodynamic and humanistic therapies are both based on the assumption that disordered behavior can be changed through insight into its internal causes. *Behavior therapy*, as its name suggests, focuses on the behavior itself rather than on subjective determinants. What a psychoanalyst would call the symptom of an underlying problem is, in the eyes of a behavior therapist, actually the problem. Behavior therapists assume that emotional disturbances are learned reactions to coping with various stresses. In therapy, they put into practice the principles of learning—and unlearning—developed in the laboratory by experimental psychologists.

Another notable departure in behavior therapy relates to the role of the therapist. Unlike psychoanalysts and humanistic therapists, many practitioners of behavior therapy minimize the importance of the relationship between therapist and patient and emphasize instead impersonal techniques of treatment (Parloff, Waskow, and Wolper, 1978). In fact, some therapists take the extreme position that the therapist is essentially a "social reinforcement machine (Krasner, 1962)."

There are five major behavioral approaches to treatment. Two of them—counterconditioning and operant techniques—are derived respectively from the principles of classical and operant conditioning. The third, modeling, originated in Albert Bandura's theory of observational learning. The fourth, cognitive restructuring, reflects the increasing interest of behaviorists in the processes of cognition. And finally, self-control procedures require individuals themselves to rearrange environmental contingencies in order to reduce undesirable behaviors and increase or strengthen desirable behaviors.

Counterconditioning The aim of *counterconditioning* is to break the connection between a given stimulus and response that has been classically conditioned. Remember, for example, the story of

Little Albert who was conditioned, through the use of a frightening noise, to fear white rats. A connection was established between the conditioned stimulus (white rat) and Little Albert's response (fear). A few years after this experiment, Mary Cover Jones (1925) demonstrated that such fears could be counterconditioned by substituting a new response to the stimulus. In this instance, the old response was a little boy's fear of rabbits. She eliminated this by feeding the boy in the presence of a rabbit, gradually moving him closer to the animal on successive occasions. The new response—positive feelings associated with eating—"crowded out" the old response—fear.

Three basic techniques are employed in counterconditioning—systematic desensitization, implosive therapy, and aversion therapy. Each uses entirely different methods.

- *Systematic Desensitization.* The counterconditioning technique developed by Joseph Wolpe (1958), systematic desensitization, is based on the medical procedure of giving increasing doses of allergens to hay fever sufferers. In systematic desensitization, patients are taught a new response, deep muscle relaxation, and then gradually conditioned to substitute the new response for fear as they mentally visualize increasing "doses" of anxiety-provoking situations.

  Suppose, for example, you have a terrible fear of flying. After you have learned a series of exercises that help you relax the entire body, the therapist asks you to draw up a list of all the situations that trigger your fear of flying—for example, the decision to buy a plane ticket, the drive to the airport, boarding the plane, the takeoff. You and the therapist rank these situations in an *anxiety hierarchy*, from the least to the most fear-evoking. The therapist then tells you to relax in a reclining chair and imagine the least fearful situation. When you are able to do this without muscular tension, you then contemplate the next situation in the hierarchy. This process may continue for ten separate sessions or more, until you can imagine the entire hierarchy of anxieties without feeling fear. In addition, the therapist may assign "homework" between sessions—actually placing yourself in the progressively frightening situations.

455

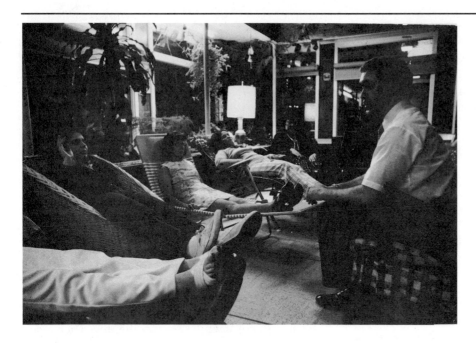

Patients at a systematic desensitization session are taught a new response, deep muscle relaxation, and then are conditioned to substitute that response for fear as they imagine anxiety-provoking situations.

Does the effect of learning to relax while merely imagining the stressful situations carry over into real life? Studies have shown that it generally does, resulting in reduction of anxiety in situations imagined during therapy (Wolpe, 1958; Goldfried and Davison, 1976). Success has been reported with a wide range of complaints, including phobias, psychosomatic disorders, and depression brought on by external stresses.

- *Implosive Therapy.* A second type of counterconditioning, *implosive therapy*, differs radically from systematic desensitization. Instead of fighting fear by gradually increasing the patient's tolerance for anxiety as in desensitization, implosive therapy fights fear by attempting to create a massive dose of it. At the outset, patients are instructed to visualize themselves in the most frightening circumstances imaginable—for example, trapped on a tiny island, with no means of escape, surrounded by hideous beasts. The aim is to create an inward explosion, or implosion, of anxiety. By repeatedly confronting this implosive panic the patient gradually becomes accustomed to it, and eventually anxiety is extinguished (Stampfl and Levis, 1967).

Implosive therapy is controversial and has been attacked as cruel and inhumane. The technique offends behaviorists because its theoretical underpinnings encompass not only classical conditioning but also certain tenets of psychoanalytic theory. The conditioned stimuli for fears, implosive therapists assert, originate in infantile aggression and sexuality, and these fears must be confronted.

Support for implosive therapy comes from both clinical experience and laboratory research with animals. Animal fear of a stimulus that has previously been paired with shock can sometimes be rapidly extinguished if the animal is prevented from escaping shock. Clinical data indicate that implosion is about as effective as desensitization in reducing a variety of phobias (Gelder, Bancroft, Gath, Johnston, Mathews, and Shaw, 1973).

- *Aversion Therapy.* Another controversial technique of counterconditioning is aversion therapy. In desensitization the goal is to substitute a positive response, relaxation, for anxiety; in the aversion approach, by contrast, the aim is to substitute negative feelings for positive ones by conditioning aversion to stimuli that are considered inappropriately attractive. To reduce the attraction of cigarette smoking, for example, the therapist might give the client repeated electric shocks whenever pictures of cigarettes are presented. Thus, an anxiety response would be substituted for the good feelings a heavy smoker might ordinarily associate with cigarettes.

A second kind of aversion therapy, called *covert sensitization*, relies on the power of the imagination (Lazarus, 1958). Clients are asked to imagine the aversive effects of an undesirable behavior such as heavy drinking. A treatment program for alcoholics has been developed using covert sensitization (Cautela, 1966). It includes the following instructions from the therapist:

> As you are approaching the bar you have a funny feeling in the pit of your stomach. Your stomach feels all queasy and nauseous. Some liquid comes up your throat and it is very sour. You try to swallow it back down, but as you do this, food particles start coming up your throat to your mouth. . . . As the bartender is pouring the beer, puke comes up into your mouth.

Although aversive therapy has helped clients control such habits as overeating, heavy drinking, and cigarette smoking, it has been criticized for both ethical and scientific reasons. Critics question the wisdom of inflicting pain and discomfort on people; they also question how long people will react anxiously to a stimulus such as cigarettes once they are no longer being shocked.

The most controversial use of aversion therapy has been an attempt to change the sexual orientation of male homosexuals (Feldman and MacCulloch, 1971). Clients were presented with pictures of males and given electric shocks while they viewed the picture; then a picture of an attractive female was presented without the electric shock. Using this procedure, the researchers reported that more than half of 43 male homosexual patients were judged to have become significantly more oriented toward heterosexual activities. It should be noted, however, that homosexual feelings and behavior were not completely eliminated. Also, those who sought treatment did not accept their homosexuality and were desirous of change. The procedure has been strongly criticized by gay liberation organizations who contend that it contributes to the general impression of homosexuality as a form of aberrant behavior.

Operant Techniques   The second major theoretical approach to behavior therapy stems largely from the research in operant conditioning by B. F. Skinner. *Operant techniques* are based on the use of positive and negative reinforcement to shape, or modify, the behavior of patients. For example, the process of shaping—rewarding each stage in a series of gradual approximations—has been employed to change the behavior of psychotics.

The most notable successes of operant therapy have been attained with children. By working with parents and teachers, operant therapists have been able to change reinforcement practices and eliminate a wide range of childhood problems, including aggression, bed-wetting, and asthmatic attacks. For example, in the instance of an overdemanding child, the operant therapist might make a *functional analysis* in the home, carefully noting the correlation between child's demands and the parents' unwitting reinforcement policies. Then a strategy would be developed in which the parents would reinforce, through their attention and other rewards, the child's nondemanding actions.

Detailed operant techniques have been developed to teach normal speech to severely disturbed children (Lovass, 1977). Many of the children did not speak at all or were only able to vocalize simple vowels. The program begins by teaching the child a few recognizable words. Then it proceeds to teaching the child to label events and objects, then to verbalize relationships between events, and, finally, to develop spontaneous conversation skills. Reinforcement is used throughout the process. The following example shows how a child in the third month of language training begins to develop discriminations in the context of a conversation (Lovass, 1977). During the conversation the child received an M&M candy after each correct response.

E:	Ricky, what's your name?
Ricky:	Ricky.
E:	That's right.
Ricky:	How are you feeling?
E:	No. Ask me what I asked you. Ricky! Say what's your name?
Ricky:	Ricky.
E:	No. Say, what's . . .
Ricky:	What's (pauses) . . .
E:	Your . . .
Ricky:	Your (pauses) . . .
E:	Say, name.
Ricky:	Name.
E:	Now, say it all together.
Ricky:	What's your name?
E:	Joan. Good boy, Ricky. That's good. That's good. Come here, Ricky. Stand up, Ricky. Ricky, how are you feeling?
Ricky:	I am feeling fine.
E:	That's good. Ricky, come here. Ricky, come. Now you ask me.
Ricky:	How are you feeling?

E: I am feeling fine. That's good. That's good.

Ricky: Lie down, please. Lie down. (Preceding this hour Ricky had been taught how to order E to stand up, lie down, smile, etc.)

E: Ricky, how old are you?

Ricky: I'm 7 years old.

E: That's right. Ask me, Ricky.

Ricky: Ask me.

E: No. That's not what I asked you. Ask me how old I am. Say, how . . .

Ricky: Are you feeling?

E: No. That's not what I asked you either. I asked you how old you are. Now, you ask me. Say, how . . .

Ricky: Old . . .

E: Say, are you.

Ricky: Are you.

E: That's right. Now say it all together. Say, how old are you?

Ricky: I am 7 years old. How old are you?

E: I am 21 years old. That's very good. That's good.

Operant techniques are also widely used in the so-called *token economy*—a system for changing behavior in an institutionalized setting. Ted Ayllon and Nathan Azrin (1968) set aside an entire ward of a mental hospital and instituted what they called a token economy. As reinforcement for activities such as making beds, brushing teeth, and combing hair, severely disturbed patients were given plastic tokens that could be exchanged for special privileges, including a private room or extra visits to the canteen. The token economy succeeded in bringing about a number of changes in overt behavior and has since been introduced at mental hospitals, prisons, and other institutions throughout the United States.

An example of a residential token economy is Achievement Place, a home-style facility for 12- to 16-year-old boys who have been referred to the courts for getting into trouble with the law (Fixsen, Phillips, and Wolf, 1972). The program is aimed at reducing antisocial behavior and increasing interpersonal skills as well as improving self-care and academic achievement. Target behaviors are identified, and a token system is developed in which the boys in the Achievement Place home receive points every time they complete the task or behave appropriately. They then can exchange their points for privileges or things they desire such as use of the telephone, tools, radios, record players, snacks, visits home, or allowances. Each resident of Achievement Place records the points he has earned on an index card, and at the end of the day the points can be exchanged for privileges to be used on the following day, if a stipulated number of points has been accumulated. Thus far, Achievement Place has been quite successful; for example, its graduates have had fewer contacts with the police and committed fewer acts that resulted in contact with the courts than children who received more traditional institutional treatment or had been placed on probation.

Token economy techniques also have been applied to the education of retarded children with encouraging results. In a six-week program at a school for retarded children, specially designed teaching materials were used, and performance was rewarded with tokens that could be exchanged for soft drinks, extra time watching television, and other privileges (Ayllon and Kelly, 1972). At the end of the program, tests showed that the IQ of the subjects had increased by an average of almost four points. Meanwhile, the average IQ of children in the control group not participating in the program had actually declined nearly three points.

A problem of operant therapy used in institutional settings is that of generalizing to real-life situations (Kazdin, 1979). If it is the reinforcement contingencies of real-life environments that are assumed to have produced the problems in the first place—as many behavior therapists assume—what happens when the client returns there? To make new behavior patterns more persistent, operant therapists have tried several approaches. One is to move patients away from a continuous schedule of reinforcement to an intermittent schedule so that reinforcement occurs regularly but infrequently. Another strategy is to encourage clients to reinforce themselves for the desired behavior. The staff of Achievement Place, for example, has dealt with the problem by phasing out the point system as quickly as possible and shifting to a merit system so that the boys do not come to rely on the token economy program.

Modeling The third major theoretical approach to behavior therapy employs the concept of *modeling,* or observational learning, formulated by Albert Bandura. In treatment through modeling, the patient unlearns anxiety about a given stimulus by watching the therapist perform a behavior and then imitating that behavior (Bandura, 1971).

Bandura's most celebrated demonstration of modeling therapy was an experiment with people who had an intense fear of snakes (Bandura, 1971).

Although, strictly speaking, these people were not patients (they were subjects who had answered a newspaper ad seeking individuals with a fear of snakes), their fear amounted to a phobia. Some of them so dreaded the possibility of encountering snakes that they had to forgo pleasures such as hiking and gardening. Bandura first tested their fear by confronting his subjects with a four-foot king snake. Then he divided the subjects into four groups and compared three different methods of treatment. One group underwent systematic desensitization, substituting a relaxed response while progressively imagining increasingly anxiety-provoking situations involving snakes. The second group, after learning muscle relaxation procedures, watched a movie on snake handling. The third group watched a live model, the therapist, play with a large king snake; then, in a series of stages, the members of this group were encouraged to approach the snake and imitate all the maneuvers the therapist had performed with the snake. The fourth group was the control group; members received no treatment at all.

The test to determine the effectiveness of the various treatments was dramatically direct: subjects had to sit in a chair for 30 seconds while a snake crawled over their bodies. Although only a few members of the other treatment groups passed the test, everyone in the modeling therapy group suc-

ceeded. Later, Bandura used modeling therapy to reduce snake phobia in members of the other groups.

Modeling also has been successful with childhood phobias such as fear of dogs or fear of dentists. In addition, something very much like modeling is evident in the procedure called *behavioral rehearsal* in which the therapist demonstrates how to handle an interpersonal problem in a better way and the patient then imitates the therapist, continually rehearsing this new behavior (Lazarus, 1971). Modeling also has been combined with other behavioral therapies, including operant approaches, in the effective treatment of schizophrenic patients (Bellack, Herser, and Turner, 1976).

Cognitive Restructuring Another general approach in behavior therapy, *cognitive restructuring*, differs from the other methods in its emphasis on manipulation, or restructuring, of the cognitive processes. Until recent years, as we have seen previously, the behavioral perspective in psychology had focused on overt behavior, which could be measured objectively, and largely neglected the subjective processes of reasoning and thinking.

One important method of cognitive restructuring

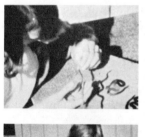

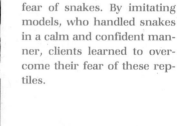

Bandura demonstrated the use of modeling therapy with clients who had an intense fear of snakes. By imitating models, who handled snakes in a calm and confident manner, clients learned to overcome their fear of these reptiles.

is the *rational-emotive therapy* of Albert Ellis (1976, 1977), which was long ignored by most behavior theoreticians. Ellis traced many emotional problems to internal sentences that people repeat to themselves. For example, depressed people may say to themselves, "What a worthless person I am." Or anxious people may create internal problems by adopting unrealistic expectations such as those embodied in the internal sentence, "I must win the love of everyone." External events are then interpreted in terms of these assumptions.

Although cognitive behavior therapists may differ in the details of the specific procedures they employ, they agree that changing maladaptive thought patterns is central to the therapeutic effort (Price and Lynn, 1981). Cognitive behavioral methods have been used with success in treating test anxiety, lack of dating skills, chronic anger, and schizophrenia.

Cognitive behavior therapists believe that it is unnecessary to assume that hidden motivations or unconscious processes are modifying behavior. The cognitive behavior therapist's direct focus on conscious thought patterns and their modification is what most distinguishes cognitive restructuring from other techniques of behavior modification and psychotherapy.

Self-control Procedures   One of the more recent developments in behavior therapy is the use of *self-control procedures*. With the therapist operating as a consultant, clients set up their own goals—for example, losing weight or stopping smoking—and provide their own reinforcements.

Clients utilize operant-oriented steps in their programs: (1) Desirable behavior is positively reinforced; negative behavior is not reinforced. (2) Reinforcement is contingent—that is, it is gained only if the desired behavior takes place. (3) Environments are controlled by the clients themselves to increase the possibilities of performing the targeted behaviors (Watson and Tharp, 1972).

Weight-control through behavior change is perhaps the most prevalent goal of self-control programs. By rearranging environmental cues that stimulate eating, clients attempt to increase the chances for performing the desired behavior of moderate eating. After a certain number of days of eating controlled-amount meals slowly, consciously, and in a particular setting, they reward themselves for changes in behavior with some type of reinforcement such as buying a new article of clothing.

In some ways, the techniques of self-control procedures resemble those of token economies, but they are not institutionalized programs, and clients administer their own reinforcements. Therapists serve as advisers and intervene only when needed.

Group Therapy

The therapies discussed so far typically occur on a one-to-one basis between therapist and patient or client. There are several potential advantages, however, if a therapist can treat more than one patient at a time. In recent years, *group therapy* consisting of a therapist and up to a dozen patients has become highly popular in the United States. The following advantages are cited by proponents of group therapy:

- Therapists can use time more efficiently, see more patients, and presumably charge lower fees.
- Patients who have difficulty relating to other people can experience effective interaction first-hand.
- Patients are subjected to social pressures from others to change.
- Patients may be comforted by the knowledge that others have similar problems.
- Patients can learn vicariously—by watching the behavior of others—to solve their own problems.

Practically every theoretical approach or method of therapy used with individuals has also been applied in group settings. Behavioral methods are used in groups essentially as a time-saving device; these groups usually retain much of the therapist-to-patient relationship found in individual therapy. By contrast, the four types of group therapy we will examine—psychodrama, sensitivity training, encounter groups, and family therapy—all emphasize interaction among group members.

Psychodrama   One of the pioneers of group therapy was J. L. Moreno, who had an abiding interest in the theater and in 1921 founded an improvisional drama company. Out of this experience grew Moreno's inspiration for a type of group therapy that he called *psychodrama* (Moreno and Kipper, 1965).

In psychodrama the members of a therapeutic group act out their feelings as if they were actors in a play, improvising their lines. Often the psychodrama centers on the problems of one patient, with the others playing the roles of principal figures in the patient's life. Moreno believed that such role playing revealed the patients' deepest emotions and enabled them to change more effectively than by merely attempting to verbalize their feelings. In a special method of role playing, the *mirroring technique,* one member of the group portrays another member, giving that individual the opportunity to see himself or herself as others do. The director of the psychodrama is the therapist. Often the drama actually takes place on a stage in front of an audience. Moreno believed that members of the audience might be helped with their own problems if they saw them portrayed on the stage.

Sensitivity Training The *sensitivity training* group —often called the *T-group* (*T* for training)—originated in 1947 at the National Training Laboratories in Bethel, Maine (Buchanan, 1964). It began as a method to make business executives more sensitive in their relationships with others but has since burgeoned into an educational movement aimed at helping people who, although functioning well, want to improve interpersonal interactions.

Members of a T-group are encouraged to drop their guard, to speak frankly, and to listen attentively. The emphasis is on the process of interaction among the participants and the problems that arise during it. As the interaction develops, participants are encouraged to examine their reactions to the others and to analyze their own true feelings and perceptions.

The role of the leader, or trainer, differs from that of a one-to-one therapist: the trainer is a full member of the group (Aronson, 1972). Other members are free to comment on the trainer's feelings and reactions. Trainers are not supposed to impose their will or ideas on the other participants, although they sometimes intervene if one of the members is being subjected to undue coercion by the rest of the group.

Encounter Groups While the *encounter group* movement developed from separate origins— Rogers (1970) traces it to his program of training counselors at the University of Chicago after World War II—its techniques are often difficult to distinguish from those used in T-groups. Rogers' groups tend to follow the tenets of his client-centered therapy with the group leader, or facilitator, working to clarify the feelings of group members.

Encounter groups are widely employed in public institutions, especially juvenile correctional centers. They are best known, however, from their association with centers of the human potential movement

In T-groups, people are taught to be more sensitive in their relationships with others.

In encounter groups, participants attempt to become more open with one another.

such as Esalen. One form of encounter group is the *marathon*, a weekend-long session in which participants seldom sleep—the supposition being that fatigue will help participants drop their social masks and become more open with one another.

Critics of both T-groups and encounter groups contend that the group experience teaches members only how to participate in such groups. They assert that the insights and skills learned in these groups are difficult to transfer to real life, where complete openness and candor are seldom considered virtues (Houts and Serber, 1972). Some research suggests that participants view themselves more favorably after a group experience but, surprisingly, are not necessarily less prejudiced or more open-minded (Lieberman, Yalom, and Miles, 1973). There is also the danger that, if an individual's faults are pointed out but not fully dealt with by the group, problems may be aggravated rather than solved. A participant may leave feeling worse than before taking part in the therapy (Lieberman, Yalom, and Miles, 1973). For these reasons T-groups and encounter groups are not recommended for those with moderate to severe emotional problems.

Family Therapy Many investigators believe that the family is instrumental in producing and maintaining disordered behavior, especially in children. Underlying this belief is the view, known as a *systems approach*, that the dynamics of family interaction may be responsible for the symptoms of the individual; the individual, in other words, is part of a larger, disordered system. Therefore, some therapists involve several members of the family in the treatment process.

Family therapists, by talking with all the members of the family, attempt to pinpoint disordered interactions. For example, take the case of Laura, a 14-year-old girl who refused to eat and had to be hospitalized because of excessive weight loss (Aponte and Hoffman, 1973). In the following excerpt from the first therapy session, the therapist asks Laura what happens when she refuses to eat:

Therapist: (To Laura.) When you get annoyed, how do you express your annoyance? What do you say to Dad? Say it now, the way you said it them.

Laura: (To father.) No, I don't want any food. (Pause.)

Therapist: What do you do then? (Pause.) Dad, what do you do then, when she says that?

Father: I naturally insist.

Therapist: You insist. Insist now. I want to know how it works.

Father: (Overlapping.) Well, this is more present than recent. This is not . . .

Therapist: OK, yeah, OK. Make believe that it's happening.

Father: OK (To Laura.) I'm going downstairs, Laura. Do you want something.

Laura: No.

Father: Nothing at all, no snitch, something, a piece of fruit?

Laura: Nothing. I don't want anything.

Father: A little ice cream?

Laura: No.

Father: OK.

Therapist: (To Laura.) Do the same thing with Mom. How does it go? (To Mother.) It goes also with you similar?

Laura: Uh . . .

Therapist: (Indicating that Laura should continue.) OK.

Father: (To Laura.) Try it at the dinner table with Connie. I think that might be better because (to Mother) you don't go down as often as I do. (Laughter.)

Thus, the therapist focuses on Laura's problem as a struggle with her parents rather than as a symbol of an inner conflict, as in the psychodynamic approach. The therapist calls the attention of the family to such disordered interactions and suggests ways that such interactions can be modified. Family members are helped to express their desires and feelings directly and clearly to one another. The therapist may even have them rehearse such interactions. Often, family therapy sessions are videotaped and then rerun so that parents and children can see for themselves the nuances of their behavior toward one another.

Evaluating Psychotherapy

The effectiveness of psychotherapy is extremely difficult to measure because it is subject to so many variables—patient, therapist, and the nature of the disorder. Subjective reports by therapists or patients may be valuable but scarcely qualify as dispassionate evidence of effectiveness. Therapists have vested interests in proving the value of their efforts. The patients' own assessments may be influenced by what has been called the hello-good-bye effect: when they say "hello" to the therapist, there is a tendency to exaggerate their problems to make clear they really need help; when they say "good-bye" at the end of therapy, there is a tendency to exaggerate how much better they feel in order to show appreciation to the therapist and to convince themselves that the time and money were well spent.

Nonetheless, a number of attempts have been made to evaluate psychotherapy. Such studies typically ask two questions:

1. Does psychotherapy work?
2. Which method among the many approaches to psychotherapy works best?

Does Psychotherapy Work? Given the enormous amounts of money, energy, and hope expended each year on psychotherapy, the question may seem superfluous. In fact, however, psychotherapy as a means of behavior change has long been subject to scientific skepticism.

The most forceful attack on the effectiveness of psychotherapy was mounted in 1952 by the British psychologist Hans J. Eysenck (Eysenck, 1952, 1965). Eysenk surveyed studies of several thousand people who either underwent psychotherapy or were not treated; psychoanalytic techniques were used

Family therapy involves discussion of problems with all the members of a family in an effort to uncover and resolve conflicts.

on the majority of those who had been treated. As a result of this survey, Eysenck concluded that about 75 percent of neurotics got better within two years whether or not they received therapy. Eysenck's conclusions were disputed on several grounds: he focused on changes in behavior and ignored personality changes, and he also ignored the fact that many in the nontreated category actually were receiving help from their physicians. In attacking Eysenck's findings, one investigator used newer studies to conclude that although about 30 percent of neurotics improve spontaneously without treatment, about 65 percent improve in therapy (Bergin, 1971).

It remained, however, for Mary L. Smith and Gene V. Glass (1977) to provide the most persuasive evidence yet that psychotherapy does, in fact, work. The scope of the Smith and Glass study was unprecedented. They analyzed 375 previously published studies that compared the effects of therapy with untreated control groups. Smith and Glass

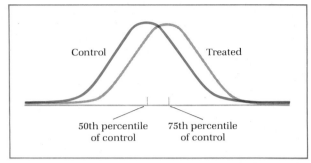

FIGURE 15.1   The results of the Smith and Glass study of the effectiveness of psychotherapy indicated that the average person receiving therapy was better off than 75 percent of the control group.

included a wide range of techniques of individual therapy but excluded studies of group therapies and peer counseling. Altogether, the studies reviewed represented about 25,000 people who had undergone therapy and 25,000 people who had

RESEARCH: A Way to Find Out Whether Psychotherapy Works

One of the major problems in evaluating the effectiveness of psychotherapy is that the research in this field is extremely fragmented. It consists of large numbers of relatively small studies dealing with diverse treatment methods and employing different measures of effectiveness. All of these data, observe Mary L. Smith and Gene V. Glass, are "atomized and sprayed across a vast landscape of journals, books, and reports." The impressive achievement of Smith and Glass (1977) has been to search out all of these fragments of data, subject them to complex statistical analysis, and then provide tentative answers to two vital questions: Does psychotherapy work? Which type of therapy works best?

In their "meta-analysis," Smith and Glass carried out an exhaustive search of the literature that turned up no less than 1,000 different evaluations of psychotherapy. Of these, 375 studies were selected for complete statistical analysis. One criterion for inclusion in the analysis was that a study had to compare at least one therapy treatment group to an untreated group or to a different therapy group. The following definition of psychotherapy was used in the selection process:

Psychotherapy is taken to mean the informed and planful application of techniques derived from established psychological principles, by persons qualified through training and experience to understand these

principles and to apply these techniques with the intention of assisting individuals to modify such personal characteristics as feelings, values, attitudes, and behaviors which are judged by the therapist to be maladaptive or maladjustive (Meltzoff and Kornreich, 1970).

By this definition, the following were excluded from the analysis: drug therapies, hypnotherapy, bibliotherapy, occupational therapy, milieu therapy, peer counseling, sensitivity training, marathon encounter groups, consciousness-raising groups, and psychodrama.

After selecting the studies, Smith and Glass classified the different types of outcomes assessed in the studies. There were ten categories, including such measures as fear and anxiety reduction, self-esteem, and achievement in school or on the job. Altogether, the 375 studies yielded 833 outcomes. (Some studies had more than one outcome because they measured the effect of therapy at more than one time or on more than one type of effect.) All of these outcomes measures were more or less related to "well-being" and thus are generally comparable.

Through statistical measurement, Smith and Glass then determined the magnitude of effect for each therapy outcome. (Magnitude of effect, or effect size, was the mean difference between the treated and

served as part of a control group. The studies measured differences in areas such as self-esteem, anxiety, achievement in work and school, and physiological stress. Smith and Glass measured the magnitude of effect of each study by comparing the average change produced in treatment with that in the control group. They concluded that the average person receiving therapy was better off than 75 percent of those not receiving therapy (see Figure 15.1).

Which Psychotherapy Method Works Best?
Proponents of the various therapies have long debated the purported advantages of their own method and the shortcomings of other techniques. The psychodynamic approach is often challenged as too costly and too intellectual. Behavior therapies are accused of being mechanistic and of dealing with symptoms rather than root causes.

For the most convincing study of which therapy works best, we must look again to the ambitious analysis by Smith and Glass. In addition to their assessment of the effectiveness of psychotherapy in general, these investigators compared a number of individual therapeutic techniques. They then conducted a series of careful analyses. Their conclusions, while not likely to stop the debate over which therapy works best, is enlightening: there appears to be little or no difference in effectiveness among therapies.

As Smith and Glass put it: "Despite volumes devoted to the theoretical differences among different schools of psychotherapy, the results of research demonstrate negligible differences in the effects produced by different therapy types. Unconditional judgments of superiority of one or another type of psychotherapy and all that these claims imply about treatment and training policy are unjustified.

control subjects divided by the standard deviation of the control group.)

The 833 effect-size measures represented about 25,000 subjects in the treatment groups and a similar number in the control groups. On the average, the therapy clients were 22 years of age, and received an average of 17 hours of therapy from therapists with an average of about 3½ years of experience. The effects of their treatment were measured on an average of a little less than four months after therapy.

How effective was their treatment? According to Smith and Glass, the average client receiving therapy was better off than 75 percent of the untreated members of the control groups. That finding was arrived at by lumping all of the 833 effect sizes together.

In order to compare the effectiveness of the general types of treatment, Smith and Glass asked 25 clinicians and counselors to classify the ten methods of therapy evaluated in the various studies. Two "superclasses" of therapy were perceived: behavioral therapies, including implosion, systematic desensitization, and behavior modification, and nonbehavioral therapies, including psychoanalytic therapy, Rogerian therapy, and eclectic therapy, among others.

Smith and Glass then selected 120 effect-size measures in which a behavioral therapy and a nonbehavioral therapy had been compared simultaneously with an untreated control group. Thus, for these studies, the two superclasses were equated for such important variables as nature of the clients' problems, duration of therapy, and experience of the therapists. In this analysis, Smith and Glass found that the behavioral and nonbehavioral therapies were about equally effective.

In further analyses, the researchers were able to manipulate statistically several of the variables. Consider, for example, a prototypical subject of high intelligence, 20 years of age, being treated for a simple phobia by a therapist with two years' experience, and being evaluated immediately after therapy. Smith and Glass found that two behavioral therapies—systematic desensitization and behavioral modification—showed effects superior to psychodynamic therapy. This finding suggests that some therapies may be more effective than others for a particular type of person with a particular disorder. Overall, however, Smith and Glass reported that they could find only negligible differences in the effects produced by different therapy types.

In view of the continuing controversy over the effectiveness of psychotherapy and of competing types of therapy, the Smith and Glass meta-analysis is a highly significant contribution. It demonstrates a new strategy for summarizing research in a way that allows psychologists and mental health policymakers alike to draw overall conclusions.

Scholars and clinicians are in the rather embarrassing position of knowing less than has been proven, because knowledge atomized and sprayed across a vast landscape of journals, books and reports, has not been accessible (Smith and Glass, 1977)."

After a survey of patients, another group of researchers concluded that the relationship between patient and therapist plays a major role in the success of any type of therapy: "Psychotherapy was seen by our respondents as an intensely personal experience. Most important, the therapist's warmth, his respect and interest, and his perceived competence and activity emerged as important ingredients in the amount of change reported by the patients (Strupp, Fox, and Lessler, 1969)."

Although there is no convincing evidence that a particular type of therapy is clearly superior in all cases, researchers have suggested that there are certain common factors that provide the vehicles for effective change in psychotherapy (Murray and Jacobson, 1978):

1. Clients expect to be helped. Clients' expectations that they will be able to perform new behaviors successfully may be a powerful ingredient for change in both the insight- and behavior-oriented psychotherapies.
2. Changing maladaptive beliefs about the world may facilitate behavior change. The psychodynamic therapist's permissive attitude may encourage the client to rethink views about sexual behavior, for example. The rational emotive therapist's focus on "irrational thinking" may not only lead to changes in beliefs but also to behavioral change. Behavioral techniques, such as systematic desensitization, may change the client's beliefs about the phobic object or situation, and modeling and operant procedures may inform the client about real-world reinforcement contingencies.
3. Clients may come to alter their beliefs about themselves as a consequence of acceptance by the therapist. In the case of behavior therapy, the expectation on the part of therapists that they can positively change socially undesirable behavior often has a positive effect on clients' attitudes.
4. Clients develop skills in social living. In the case of many of the insight and behavior therapies, the therapist may provide an effective model for skillful social interaction. In the case of other therapies, such as client-centered therapy, feedback on the appropriateness or acceptability of certain feelings and thoughts may also promote the development of social competencies.

Thus it may be that the psychological methods of behavior change that we have reviewed share more in common than is at first evident. Even though hundreds of studies of the effectiveness of psychotherapy are now available, large-scale efforts to examine systematically the relative effectiveness of different therapeutic approaches for different types of problems, using commonly agreed-upon standards for success, are only now beginning. Studies of the kind conducted by Smith and Glass— as valuable as they are—only highlight the need for large-scale research to determine more definitively the relative effectiveness of different therapeutic approaches.

Biological Therapies

The psychotherapies attempt to bring about changes in behavior through manipulation of psychological processes such as learning and insight; the biological therapies seek the same goal through manipulation of the brain's physiological and chemical processes. The primary biological therapies consist of two highly controversial approaches to behavior change—electroconvulsive therapy and psychosurgery—as well as psychoactive drug treatment, a method that has proved to be dramatically effective in helping alleviate the symptoms of many people with emotional disturbances.

It is interesting to note that whereas psychotherapies tend to derive from theoretical formulations about behavior, biological therapies were discovered largely by happenstance. However, the effectiveness of drug therapy has led to promising new theories about the chemical mechanisms by which the brain mediates behavior.

Electroconvulsive Therapy
During the 1930s several European investigators began the experimental treatment of schizophrenia by inducing convulsions through the injection of various chemicals. They believed, erroneously, that schizophrenia and epilepsy were mutually exclusive disorders and that by inducing convulsions the schizophrenic could be cured. In 1939, the Italian psychiatrist Ugo Cerletti, who was interested in epilepsy, stumbled on a more effective way of in-

ducing seizures. On a visit to a slaughterhouse he saw animals being rendered unconscious by electric shocks to the head. Soon afterward, Cerletti tried the technique on a schizophrenic patient—and *electroconvulsive therapy*, or *shock treatment*, was born.

Today shock treatment is used principally in cases of severe depression that fail to respond to other therapies. After being injected with an anesthetic, the patient is given a muscle relaxant and strapped down onto a bed to prevent bone fractures and bruises during the convulsions. Electrodes are placed on each side of the patient's forehead and, for about two seconds, a current is sent through the brain to produce a convulsion much like that of a *grand mal* epileptic seizure. Typically, the patient receives ten treatments over a period of about three weeks.

Electroconvulsive therapy, or shock treatment, is effective in relieving symptoms of many severely depressed individuals, but how or why it works remains a mystery.

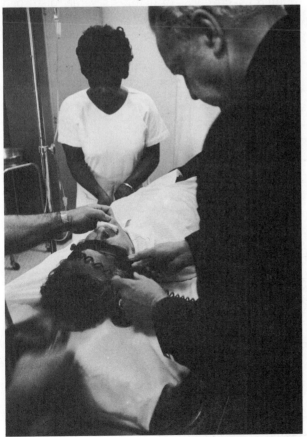

After a shock treatment, the patient often is confused and cannot remember the shock itself or events that occurred just before and after the convulsion. Impairment of long-term memory also has been reported in some cases. Ernest Hemingway, who underwent shock treatment for severe depression, asserted that it had ruined his writing career by erasing his store of long-term memories (*Time*, 1979). A new method of treatment, which causes convulsions only in one side of the brain (usually the nondominant hemisphere), apparently produces less confusion and memory loss.

A number of researchers (Greenblatt, Grosser, and Wechsler, 1964) have confirmed the effectiveness of shock treatment in relieving the symptoms of severely depressed patients, but no one knows how or why it works. The brain researcher Steven Rose (1975) has likened shock treatment to "attempting to mend a faulty radio by kicking it." More than 50 different explanations for its effectiveness have been offered, ranging from a modification of brain chemical levels to the old notion that shock punishes the unconscious, enabling patients to expiate the guilt said to be at the core of depression. The prospect of shock treatment terrifies many patients, a view held by the public at large and reinforced by the brutal shock scenes in the movie *One Flew over the Cuckoo's Nest*.

Psychosurgery

Like shock treatment, surgery performed to alter mental or emotional functioning and behavior—*psychosurgery*—is highly controversial, although apparently much less effective. History records a number of early instances of surgery aimed at controlling behavior, including the practice of castration, which eliminates the source of male sex hormones. Modern psychosurgery was launched in 1935 by Antonio de Egas Moniz, a Portuguese diplomat and psychiatrist. Moniz was impressed by a report by Carlyle Jacobsen, a Yale researcher who had removed a portion of the prefrontal lobe region from the brains of two chimpanzees, Becky and Lucy. The surgery eliminated the quarrelsome tendencies of the chimps who now "acted as though they had joined the happiness cult . . . and placed their burdens on the Lord (Bailey, 1975)."

Despite the fact that little was then known—or is now—about the functions of this part of the brain,

Moniz persuaded a colleague to perform a *prefrontal lobotomy* on a psychotic patient. The patient was calmer after the surgery, and soon lobotomies were being performed in the United States and elsewhere for all types of emotional disturbances. For his work, Moniz shared a Nobel Prize in 1949, although by then he was retired and partially paralyzed—the result of a bullet in the spine, which was fired by one of his lobotomized patients.

During the 1950s it became clear that the reports of dramatic improvements in lobotomized patients were premature, and the procedure fell out of favor. Although the surgery had a calming effect, it also often brought unintended side results, including stupor, impaired intellect, and epileptic seizures. Newer techniques have made lobotomies more precise, destroying much less brain tissue and resulting in fewer undesirable side effects. Nonetheless, this surgery is generally considered a last resort, suitable only for patients with long-term severe disturbances, such as obsessive compulsive disorders, that do not respond to other therapies.

An even more controversial type of psychosurgery, *amygdalectomy*, involves destruction of centers deep in the brain that some researchers believe are responsible for violence and aggression. It has been suggested, for example, that malfunctions in the amygdala, a structure of the brain's limbic system, may trigger violent behavior (Mark and Ervin, 1970). Researchers implanted electrodes in the amygdala and then switched on an electric current in an attempt to locate the "aggression centers." If the patient reported a feeling of rage, these centers were then destroyed with a larger burst of current (Mark, Sweet, and Ervin, 1972).

Elliot S. Valenstein (1973), in an extensive critique of psychosurgery, has evaluated the cases of ten patients who underwent amygdalectomies. He found little evidence for optimism. Patients' violent episodes were not eliminated in all cases, and there were indications of undesirable side effects—including an instance of voracious appetite—presumably caused by damage to neighboring neural tissue. Aside from the ethical questions raised by psychosurgery, this latter consideration—damage to other neural tissue—is a decisive one for many investigators. So closely entwined are the myriad circuits of the brain that, given the present inadequacy of knowledge, it seems impossible to tamper with certain neural centers without affecting others.

Drug Treatment

Freud, who recognized that his talking cure was of limited effectiveness in helping severely disturbed patients, predicted: "The future may teach us how to exercise a direct influence by particular chemical substances (Clark, 1979)."

Beginning in the 1950s, this prediction came true with the development of psychoactive drugs. These

Effect group	Chemical group	Generic name	Trade name
Minor tranquilizers	propanediols	meprobamate	Miltown, Equanil
	benzodiazepines	chlordiazepoxide diazepam	Librium Valium
Major tranquilizers (antipsychotics)	phenothiazines	chlorpromazine trifluoperazine thioridazine	Thorazine Stelazine Mellaril
	butyrophenones	haloperidol	Haldol
	thioxanthenes	chlorprothixene	Taractan
Stimulants	amphetamines	dextroamphetamine	Dexedrine
	piperidyls	methylphenidate	Ritalin
Antidepressants	tricyclics	imipramine amitriptyline doxepin	Tofranil Elavil Sinequan
	monoamine oxidase inhibitors	phenelzine tranylcypromine	Nardil Parnate

FIGURE 15.2 A number of psychoactive drugs categorized by their effects on behavior.

drugs, while falling far short of providing permanent cures for disordered behavior, have had an extraordinarily dramatic impact on some types of mental illness. By relieving many of the worst symptoms of schizophrenia and depression, they have helped make possible a reduction in the population of mental hospitals, enabling patients to return to the community.

The psychoactive drugs used in treatment are classified into four categories—major tranquilizers for psychotic symptoms, minor tranquilizers for anxiety, antidepressants, and stimulants (see Figure 15.2). None of these drugs is a panacea: practically all of them can produce undesirable side effects, and some are physically addictive. When a patient stops taking the medication, symptoms usually return. Nonetheless, they have helped millions of people to overcome personal crises or simply to function in everyday life. They also have made it possible for many who previously could not be reached by psychotherapy to benefit from psychological as well as biological treatment.

Major Tranquilizers The *major tranquilizers* are use to alleviate extreme symptoms of agitation and hyperactivity (Davis, 1975). For many centuries, people of Africa and India relied on a botanical remedy, the snakeroot plant, or *Rauwolfia sepentina*, for a variety of ailments including hysteria. This use of the drug was not known in the West until 1952, when Swiss chemists, who had experimented with *Rauwolfia* in treating high blood pressure, discovered the plant had a calming effect and extracted from it the first major tranquilizer, reserpine.

At about the same time, another series of events led to the synthesis of chlorpromazine, an even more effective tranquilizer. Chlorpromazine belongs to a remarkably useful class of compounds called the phenothiazines. The nucleus of these compounds was first synthesized in 1880 as a treatment for parasitic worm infections in animals. It was later used in the antihistamines, which were prescribed for a variety of conditions, including the common cold, allergies, and lowered blood pressure. The use of antihistamines during surgery to reduce shock led to the discovery of the chemical's calming effect. Soon after, chlorpromazine was synthesized, and it quickly became the treatment of choice for schizophrenia: in the decade after its introduction, it was given to an estimated 50 million patients around the world (May, 1968).

The effectiveness of chlorpromazine and the other phenothiazines in reducing the incidence of hallucinations and delusions and in enabling schizophrenics to leave mental hospitals has been established in a number of studies (May, 1968; MacDonald and Tobias, 1976).

The phenothiazines do, however, have some serious shortcomings. Not all schizophrenics are helped by the drugs. Moreover, often those who are helped are released from mental hospitals only to be readmitted later. This revolving-door pattern of admission, discharge, and readmission stems in part from disagreeable side effects, such as blurred vision, that lead patients to stop taking the medication when they are on their own. More serious side effects involve the motor systems. Patients may display symptoms such as rigidity of the facial muscles similar to that experienced in Parkinson's disease (Parkes, 1976). From 10 to 15 percent of patients treated with phenothiazines for a long period of time develop a neurological disorder called tardive dyskinesia (Jus, Pineau, Lachance, Pelchat, Jus, Pires, and Villeneuve, 1976), which is characterized by lip-smacking and chin-wagging motions. Tardive dyskinesia causes some patients such acute embarrassment that they avoid all contact with people (Widroe and Heisler, 1976).

These effects on the motor systems were among the first clues to the neural chemistry now believed to underlie the action of the drugs. The major tranquilizers interfere with the workings of dopamine, one of the neurotransmitters that carries electric impulses between nerve cells. Dopamine is known to be active in neural systems mediating both emotions and voluntary movement. By mixing radioactively labeled drugs with brain tissue, Solomon Snyder (1975) has shown that the drugs attach to nerve cell receptor sites normally occupied by dopamine. When the major tranquilizers attach to the dopamine receptors, they apparently block the action of dopamine, thereby blocking transmission of nerve impulses in these pathways. Snyder's research and the work of others strongly implies that the hallucinations and delusions of schizophrenia are linked to an excess of dopamine.

Minor Tranquilizers The *minor tranquilizers* are antianxiety drugs that reduce excitability and cause drowsiness and are usually prescribed for patients who suffer anxiety or psychophysiological disorders. The first of the minor tranquilizers, Miltown, a propanediol, was introduced in the early 1950s, about the same time that the major tranquilizers came on the market. Later came the benzodiazepines (Librium, Valium), which are now among the most widely prescribed drugs in the world (Ray, 1978).

Recent brain research suggests that, like the major tranquilizers, Valium and the other minor tranquilizers exert their effects by occupying neural receptor sites in the brain (Schmeck, 1979). An earlier discovery by Candace Pert and Solomon Snyder (1973)—of receptors to which opiates, such as morphine, would bind—led to the successful isolation of endogenous painkillers in the brain (see Chapter 2). With this in mind, researchers now believe that the receptors to which Valium attaches are normally occupied by some naturally occurring chemical. This postulated chemical might be an endogenous tranquilizer, the brain's own means of controlling anxiety.

Like the other psychoactive drugs, the minor tranquilizers are a mixed blessing. Some of them can be addictive if taken regularly for a long period. A further danger is that many people resort to these pills instead of attempting to deal with everyday stress on their own.

Antidepressants   Whereas tranquilizers serve to calm arousal, *antidepressants* act to elevate mood and hence are sometimes called energizers. The first antidepressant, iproniazid, which belongs to a class of drugs called monoamine oxidase (MAO) inhibitors, originally was synthesized for treatment of tuberculosis patients. When researchers noticed in the late 1950s that iproniazid lifted the spirits of TB patients, it was given to people suffering from depression. The MAO inhibitors are highly toxic and can cause harm to the liver, brain, and cardiovascular system. They also interact dangerously—sometimes lethally—with other chemicals and with foods and beverages containing tyramine (beer, certain cheeses, pickled herring). The MAO inhibitors generally have been supplanted by another class of antidepressants, the tricyclics, which were first tried as a treatment for schizophrenia because they have a molecular structure similar to that of the phenothiazine tranquilizers.

Like other psychoactive drugs, the antidepressants are thought to act on the brain by interfering with the neurotransmitters. The tricyclics, it is believed, increase the level of the transmitter norepinephrine by preventing the reuptake of that transmitter by the nerve cell after the firing of electric impulses (Baldessarini, 1977).

Another drug, lithium carbonate, has been reported effective in managing the wide mood swings of manic-depressives by reducing the frequency of both manic and depressive episodes. How lithium accomplishes these two contrary actions—elevating mood and reducing arousal—has not been established. Lithium is highly toxic and can be fatal if its level in the bloodstream becomes too high (Branchey, Charles, and Simpson, 1976).

Stimulants   The most familiar of the *stimulants* used in treatment are the amphetamines, which were developed in the early 1930s as medication for asthma. Soldiers during World War II took Dexedrine and other amphetamines to fight fatigue. Frequently called "pep pills" or "uppers," they have been widely abused for their euphoric effects. The amphetamines stimulate the central nervous system, increasing the available supply of the neurotransmitter dopamine; in excessive doses they produce symptoms resembling those of schizophrenia. This observation by Snyder (1975) provided further evidence for the hypothesis that schizophrenia is related to an excess of dopamine.

In recent years, the amphetamines and a piperidyl derivative, Ritalin, have been prescribed for hyperactive children. Although this use has been criticized, it has proved to be effective in managing hyperactivity (Gittelman-Klein, Klein, Katz, Saraf, and Pollack, 1976). This may seem strange because a stimulant would be expected to stimulate not calm, but these drugs have a pronounced effect on the attention of hyperactive children, making them less subject to distraction and thus exerting a calming influence (Conners, 1972).

We can identify a number of landmarks in the history of treatment of disordered behavior. One such noteworthy event occurred in 1792 when the reformer Philippe Pinel took over the Paris mental hospital Bicetre and unchained the patients, leading to an era of concern with humane treatment (Pinel, 1801/1962). A second landmark dates roughly from the turn of this century and Freud's formulation of mental illness as psychological in nature and psychoanalysis as a method of treatment. A third landmark came in the 1950s with the use of psychoactive drugs to treat certain disorders. A more recent landmark had its beginnings in the early 1960s and is known as the community mental health movement, which arose in part from opportunities and challenges provided by the introduction of the new drug therapies. These treatments, by allowing a large reduction in the population of mental institutions, brought into focus the role of the community in both the treatment and the prevention of mental illness.

Community Mental Health

The passage of the Community Mental Health Center Act of 1963 resulted in the creation of community mental health centers to provide care for the large numbers of patients being released from institutions and to bring low-cost psychological help to the general public, especially the poor. The centers typically provide short-term hospitalization, outpatient treatment, 24-hour emergency service, and community programs aimed at the prevention of psychological distress.

The community mental health movement primarily focuses on five new perspectives in helping: the trend toward community living, the emphasis on crisis intervention, the investigation of new methods of prevention, the increasing concern about legal and ethical issues, and the new role of the nonprofessional.

Community Living

The national trend toward deinstitutionalization has shifted much of the burden of looking after the mentally ill from hospitals to the community, a change that has brought about some problems. The community is seldom ready to receive mental patients; the patients themselves, although their symptoms are temporarily under control, are seldom prepared to function on their own after spending many years in a hospital. Too often, there is a lack of follow-up therapy. Many former hospital patients live alone, often in slum conditions, and roam the streets aimlessly. Nearly 40,000 poor, chronic mental patients have been "dumped" in New York City alone—many in cheap residential hotels where they receive little or no care, subsist on public assistance, and rarely see a social worker (Koenig, 1978). One result of this situation is the previously mentioned revolving-door phenomenon, where as many as one-half of all patients released from mental hospitals return within a year. Some critics argue that "decarceration" actually is not a reform but simply a less expensive way than mental hospitals of handling the mentally ill (Scull, 1977).

In 1792, after assuming control of Bicetre, the Paris mental hospital, Philippe Pinel unchained the patients thus ushering in a period of more humane treatment.

If there is a dark side to community living for the mentally ill, there also is a bright side. In many communities, there are halfway houses and other means of easing the transition from hospital living. Two demonstration projects exemplify how formerly hospitalized patients can be supported effectively in the community.

One highly persuasive project was carried out by George Fairweather and his colleagues (Fairweather, 1964; Fairweather, Sanders, Cressler, and Maynard, 1969). Fairweather began by teaching hospitalized patients skills in group decision making and problem solving. He moved his experimental group from the hospital to a house in the community that Fairweather later labeled a "lodge." The patients received training as gardeners and janitors, were placed in jobs and encouraged to become self-sufficient and self-governing at the lodge. The results were dramatic. Over a 40-month period the members of the lodge spent more than 80 percent of their time in the community and only 20 percent back at the hospital. Meanwhile, a control group, consisting of patients given similar hospital treatment but discharged individually into the community without benefit of the lodge, spent only 20 percent of the time in the community and 80 percent in the hospital.

Another kind of support system was provided by Training in Community Living, a program conducted by the Mendota Mental Health Institute in Madison, Wisconsin (Marx, Test, and Stein, 1973; Fields, 1978). Patients moving from the hospital into the community were helped by a staff that included a psychiatrist, a psychologist, nurses, an occupational therapist, and a number of aides and trainees. Before the patients left the hospital, staff members trained them in job and social skills. The staff also found them places to live and jobs and generally paved the way for the transition by talking with the police and other agencies in the community. Staff members went grocery shopping with patients and taught them how to cook and to do laundry. It was the staff's responsibility to keep tabs on each patient's progress and problems, and the members met regularly to discuss each patient.

The results of the first Training in Community Living project illustrate both the potential benefits and the perils of deinstitutionalization. After five months, the supported patients proved to be far more successful in the community than a comparable control group that did not receive special help. However, once the support program was with-drawn, many patients returned to the hospital. Without support, they could not cope in the community. A second study provided support for 14 months. On practically all measures, these patients fared better than did the unsupported control groups. They spent little time in institutions, were better adjusted to their homes, and experienced greater satisfaction in their jobs and social relationships. Interestingly, the cost was about the same for supported community living as for hospitalization of the patients.

Such projects demonstrate the potential of community living. They suggest what could be achieved on a much larger scale if sufficient resources and commitment were mobilized.

Crisis Intervention

An important aim of community mental health programs is to provide a variety of immediate services for people caught up in emotional crises. Such crises may include threats of suicide, severe drug reactions, serious family conflicts, and other behavioral emergencies. *Crisis intervention* in these situations seeks to alleviate the precipitating stress and to mobilize the person's own capabilities for coping—without requiring expensive hospitalization. Special facilities for crisis intervention take several forms:

Walk-in clinics, usually part of a community mental health center and staffed by professionals, offer round-the-clock service without an appointment. A person may receive brief psychotherapy, consisting of several sessions over a short period of time, and may also receive medication such as tranquilizers or antidepressants. A variant of the walk-in clinic is the so-called free clinic, the first of which was established during the early 1960s in the Haight-Ashbury district of San Francisco to provide medical, psychological, and social services to the young people who had congregated there. Free clinics are usually staffed by volunteers, including trained professionals. However, it is typically the presence of knowledgeable and sympathetic non-professionals, such as former drug addicts with a great deal of experience on the street, that makes the free clinic appealing to many clients who might be wary of more traditional treatment facilities.

Hotlines are telephone emergency service centers that enable people with personal problems to talk to a trained and sympathetic listener. Although many hotlines offer conversation, advice, and referral for a variety of problems, others specialize in a particular problem such as drugs, rape, or suicide. A notable example is the suicide prevention movement launched around the turn of the century by the National Save-A-Life League, which established a 24-hour telephone answering service for suicidal people in New York City. Volunteers are trained to evaluate the caller's potential for suicide, convey a sense of empathy, give reassurance, and get the caller's name and phone number so the case can be followed up.

Family-crisis help is provided in several United States cities by police who have been specially trained to intervene in domestic emergencies. Such programs were originated in New York City by researchers who noted that half of the calls for assistance to an urban police department may involve family crises or other complaints of a personal or interpersonal nature (Bard and Berkowitz, 1967; Bard, 1970). These crises range from juvenile delinquency to intrafamily violence. In a precinct on the upper west side of Manhattan, 18 police volunteers were selected and given an intensive 160-hour training program in crisis intervention. Then, for two years, these men served, one pair to a shift, as the Family Crisis Intervention Unit. Among the positive findings reported were a decrease in the

Crisis intervention centers provide "hotlines" which make trained presonnel available on a round-the-clock basis to offer conversation, advice, and referral services for a large variety of problems.

number of assaults within families and the fact that none of the specially trained police sustained injuries in handling family disturbances (Bard, 1970).

Prevention

Another key characteristic of the community mental health movement is the focus on preventing disordered behavior before it occurs. The hope is to emulate modern medicine and public health, which have scored their greatest triumphs over disease and suffering through programs of prevention— vaccination programs, for example, and water purification.

Three basic strategies for the prevention of mental illness have been identified (Bloom, 1977):

1. Community-wide efforts include those programs, such as newspaper or television campaigns, that educate people in more effective parenting skills or that alert the public about child abuse. An analogy to public health would be community-wide programs to purify water and prevent typhoid fever.
2. Milestone programs expose people to help at specified intervals in their lives, much as couples are given a blood test before marriage or preschool children are immunized against certain diseases. At milestones such as the first year of marriage, the birth of the first child, and enrollment in school, people could be given training to help reduce the stresses of these critical life stages.
3. High-risk programs focus on those people who are deemed particularly vulnerable to specific disorders because of genetic makeup (children of schizophrenics), unusual personal experiences (a child whose parent dies), or extreme environmental stresses (survivors of disasters such as earthquakes or plane crashes).

A number of suggested prevention programs on the milestone and high-risk types are shown in Table 15.1.

Although widespread prevention of mental illness remains a goal rather than a reality, the results of several studies demonstrate great potential. Research has shown that the emotional hazards associated with medical treatment in young children can be prevented (Cassell, 1965). Working with

TABLE 15.1   Suggestions for Possible Primary Prevention Programs Applicable to Various Institutions and Agencies

INSTITUTIONS AND AGENCIES	NORMAL EMOTIONAL HAZARD	POSSIBILITIES FOR PREVENTIVE ACTION
1. Family	Loss of father through death, divorce, or desertion	Reinforcement of child-care services for working mothers
	Loss of mother	Reinforcement of foster-home services
	Adolescence	Increase in staff and professionalization of high school counselors, deans, and vice-principals
	Birth of sibling	Pediatric or well-baby clinic counseling
	Death	Management of grief—religious or community agency worker
2. Public health	Phenylketonuria (a form of mental retardation)	Detection and diet
	Childhood illnesses	Vaccination, immunization
	Stress caused by children—economic, housing, etc.	Reinforcement of well-baby clinic through mental health consultation to staff
	Pregnancy	Adequate prenatal care for mothers of lower socioeconomic status
3. School	Birth of sibling	Recognition of event by school and appropriate intervention
	School entrance of child	Screening vulnerable children
	Intellectual retardation	Special classes and assistance
	Teacher concern and anxiety about a child's behavior	Consultation by mental health specialists
	School failure	Early identification and prevention through appropriate school program
4. Religion	Marriage	Counseling by clergy
5. Job or profession	Promotion or demotion	Opportunity to define role through services of a mental health counselor
6. Recreation	Appropriate and rewarding use of leisure time	Active community and city recreational programs
7. Housing	Lack of space, need for privacy	Working with architects and housing developers

From "Primary Prevention of Mental and Emotional Disorders: A Conceptual Framework and Action Possibilities," by E. M. Bower, *American Journal of Orthopsychiatry*, October 1963, **33**(5), 832-848.

children between the ages of 3 and 11 who were about to undergo cardiac catheterization—a diagnostic procedure in which a tube is first inserted into a vein and then fed through into the heart—the researcher rehearsed everything that would happen in the operating room with each child, using a puppet as the stand-in for the young patient. Then the child was asked to play the role of the doctor while the therapist acted out the role of the frightened child, asking for reassurance from the "doctor." Later, in the operating room, the chil-

dren who underwent this anticipatory coping showed much less emotional upset than did a control group who did not receive such guidance.

George Spivak and Myrna Shure (1974) reasoned that training in solving social and cognitive problems would help children cope with interpersonal problems and reduce their vulnerability to stress. They provided four-year-olds with an intensive ten-week training program, teaching the abilities to sense problems, identify feelings, and look for alternative solutions. When these children were followed up a year later, they had retained their coping skills.

The Rights of Patients

Increased community responsibility for the treatment of mental patients has generated a new concern for the constitutional rights of mental patients. This reflects both the changing attitudes of the public at large toward the mentally ill and recent court decisions to safeguard the rights of patients.

Until about two decades ago the courts largely deferred to the expertise of mental health professionals in deciding what was best for hospitalized patients. Since then, however, the courts have taken a more direct hand, intervening on behalf of constitutional rights. The most notable decision, handed down by the United States Supreme Court in 1979, relates to the involuntary commitment of patients to mental institutions. The court ruled that patients who do not represent a danger to society must either be treated by the institution or released. This decision was aimed at eliminating the so-called warehousing of the mentally ill—locking up patients while failing to treat them. Other decisions have safeguarded the right of institutionalized patients to refuse treatment, requiring carefully defined procedures for obtaining the patient's informed consent before certain therapeutic techniques can be used. Among these techniques are psychosurgery, shock treatment, and aversion therapy. The courts also have limited effectively the types of reinforcers that can be used in behavioral techniques employing the token economy. For example, neither privacy nor meals can be offered as reinforcers because the patient has a legal right to these amenities without having to earn them. The result of such decisions is that the professional's judgment of what is best for the patient must now be weighed against the court's interpretation of the patient's rights.

The patient's right to refuse treatment can create a number of ethical dilemmas with which the mental health professional must cope (Price and Lynn, 1981). For example, consider the case of an extremely disturbed schizophrenic patient who reports hearing voices that are commanding suicide. Should this patient be given antipsychotic drug treatments, even if the patient refuses them believes that they will be harmful? The dilemma is a real one.

Because such dilemmas are encountered almost daily by many mental health professionals, particularly those dealing with people experiencing severe disturbances in behavior, a number of legal and ethical guidelines have been established to help mental health professionals decide when they can or should provide treatment over a patient's objections. One important guideline is whether the patients are judged by mental health professionals to be dangerous to themselves or others.

Guidelines are also being developed to establish procedures for informing patients about the kind of treatment they will receive and the likely outcome of the treatment. Before patients are asked whether they will accept treatment, psychiatrists are required to give patients information about the benefits and risks of the proposed treatments, alternative treatments, and the likely outcomes if the treatments are refused. Furthermore, if patients are unable to understand the information, psychiatrists are required to inform a responsible guardian or relative.

The Role of the Nonprofessional

The community mental health movement, by decentralizing treatment and attempting to reach out to a broader segment of the general public, requires large numbers of workers. This demand not only far outstrips the number of mental health professionals now available but also exceeds the foreseeable prospects for training psychiatrists, clinical psychologists, and social workers. To meet the demand, professionals increasingly are turning to nonprofessionals.

The potential role of the nonprofessional in community mental health was first heralded in an important book titled *Americans View Their Mental Health* (Gurin, Veroff, and Feld, 1960). The authors pointed out that largely untapped human resources for helping already were available in the community. Through sympathetic day-to-day contacts with friends and neighbors, hundreds of thousands of Americans provide a kind of psychotherapy for those who lack the inclination or financial wherewithal to seek out professional help. These home-grown therapists—without psychiatric training or degrees but capable of warmth and caring—include religious leaders, homemakers, college students, bartenders, hairdressers, and others.

In recent years, many such people have been enlisted by the community mental health move-

475

ment, enabling the professionals who train them to multiply many times over the impact of their own knowledge and skills. These laypeople have been put to work as volunteers or paid staff in myriad programs, ranging from college peer counseling to crisis intervention services. After a comparatively brief training period, they qualify as paraprofessionals who can take their places alongside the fully trained professionals. In addition to recruiting lay helpers into the mainstream of mental health care, professionals have taken a new interest in the unconventional therapies practiced by indigenous folk healers (see Focus).

Despite the widespread use of paraprofessionals in community mental health, there persists (at least among professionals) the assumption that professional clinicians are more effective psychotherapists than those without extensive training. This assumption has been called sharply into question in a study by Joseph A. Durlak (1979). Durlak examined 42 studies that compared the effectiveness of professionals and paraprofessionals in treating a number of different types of clients. Paraprofessionals were defined as mental health workers who had received no formal postgraduate clinical training in professional programs of psychiatry, social work, and psychiatric nursing. Durlak found that "paraprofessionals achieve clinical outcomes equal to or significantly better than those obtained by profes-

FOCUS: Therapy through Folk Healing

All of the methods of treatment described in this chapter are rooted in the assumptions of Western culture. For example, biological therapies, such as drug treatments, reflect the direct cause-and-effect tenets of scientific materialism. Psychoanalysis, with its emphasis on intellect and verbal expression, still reflects the upper-middle-class values of Freud's turn-of-the-century Vienna.

Other societies have developed different means of treatment that are rooted in their own cultural assumptions. Western psychologists refer to these therapies as folk healing. In recent years, with the rise of the community mental health movement and the expanding importance of the nonprofessional, psychologists have taken a new interest in folk healing. Interestingly, researchers have noted several parallels between various forms of folk healing and the psychodynamic therapies of Freud and others (Fields, 1976). Here we will look briefly at two varieties of folk healing practiced by subcultures in the United States—Puerto Rican *espiritismo* and the treatment procedures of Navajo medicine men.

Espiritismo, or spiritism, flourishes in Puerto Rican communities in urban areas of the United States, such as New York City's South Bronx. It is based on the belief that everyone is imbued with benevolent and malevolent spirits. The healer, or *espiritista*, is thought to have the ability to get rid of evil spirits that inflict suffering and psychological disturbances and to get in touch with the good spirits. Although such beliefs may sound alien to Western science, Vivian Garrison, an anthropologist who has studied *espiritismo*, points out that healers often interpret the spirits symbolically, rather than literally, as "representatives of current or recurrent problems." In this sense, says Garrison, spiritism is not so far removed from Western psychodynamic theory. "Just as there is no empirical reality which corresponds to the concept of an id, an ego, or a superego, the spirits are concepts which can be understood as behavioral manifestations (Fields, 1976)."

A wide variety of problems are treated in storefront *centros*, or healing centers, including nervous disorders and marriage and family crises. When a person first comes to the *centro* for help, the *espiritista* often conducts a kind of initial psychiatric interview, spending considerable time learning the background and problems of the person. From this consultation, the healer attempts to identify the particular *causas*, or spirits, responsible for the person's suffering. The *causas* are then treated at seances attended by the patient and a number of others, including several healers and perhaps members of the family. All who are present are encouraged to use their spiritual faculties and to communicate their visions about the patient. The seance resembles psychodrama, complete with an eerie candlelit setting and elaborate ritualistic props and with the healers entering trancelike states and acting out the roles of the malevolent spirits.

Garrison and other anthropologists who have studied the *espiritistas* suggest that they are at least as effective as—and in some cases more effective than—traditional mental health services in helping members of the Puerto Rican community.

Like the *espiritistas*, the Navajo medicine men—sometimes also known as singers—draw on the folkways of their own people. Traditional Navajo philosophy emphasizes the unity of all experience. Sickness—of body or mind—is considered a state of

sionals." In addition, Durlak classified the studies under review by the particular purpose or method of therapy: individual or group psychotherapy or counseling; academic counseling; crisis intervention; specific target programs for problems such as sleep difficulties, stuttering, overweight, and smoking; and other more general interventions. In general, paraprofessionals were even more effective relative to professionals when they were working with highly specific target problems such as sleep difficulties and stuttering.

How can we explain such surprising findings? One possibility is that the general enthusiasm of paraprofessionals and the basis for their selection made them more effective helpers. A second possibility is that the paraprofessionals were shown to be effective for the particular target problem and the techniques used before they were employed. If so, the superiority of paraprofessionals may be true only for well-defined problems where highly specific treatment methods are applicable.

In any case, Durlak's findings have forced professionals to reexamine the question of how much training is actually needed for various helping roles. If his findings are verified by additional careful re-

---

fragmentation. Healing involves becoming whole again and in harmony with friends, family, and nature. The Navajo makes no distinction between healing and worship, and the ceremonies conducted by medicine men involve both. Robert Fulton, a Navajo healer, has said: "Each man must have a prayer; he must dream of something and believe in something which is more than himself (Fields, 1976)."

Like psychotherapists, medicine men train for many years. In recognition of this, the National Institute of Mental Health has funded a training program that combines apprenticeship to established medicine men with teaching in Western principles of medicine. Apprentices must learn the songs, prayers, and stories of the ancient healing ceremonies by heart because, by Navajo tradition, they cannot be written down.

Healing rituals typically are elaborate and lengthy, sometimes lasting for a week or more. Planning them requires a number of meetings between the medicine man and the patient's family—consultations that, in themselves, represent a kind of family group therapy. The healing ceremonies bring together family and friends in a *hogan*, the simple Navajo eight-sided earthen dwelling. A number of different ceremonies can be conducted depending on the symptoms of the patient. They usually involve ritual objects from the natural world such as juniper branches, bird feathers, and dyes from berries and barks. These objects are used in reenactment of old Navajo religious stories that describe a problem similar to that afflicting the patient. Through the old songs and chants the medicine man takes on the role of the supernatural being who

A Navajo medicine man uses feathers to perform his ancient rites for therapeutic purposes.

cured the patient in the ancient story. The emphasis on ancient myths is reminiscent of the teachings of Freud's former disciple Carl Jung, who postulated that archetypal symbols, revealed in dreams, art, and literature, were a vital part of the therapeutic process (Jung, 1964).

Navajo healing rituals often are effective in relieving depression, grief, and anxiety. This should not be surprising in light of the fact that such ceremonies have the effect of bringing patients closer to their families and their society. As Fields (1976) has observed, "The Navajos have been pulled between two cultures ... often with tragic results. The medicine man, as he offers tales of noble adventures, sparks a renewed pride in Indian tradition. The ceremonies provide a structure to develop, support, and affirm this cultural pride and identity."

search, it may be that the pool of helpers can be greatly increased at relatively little cost, expanding the available services and further accelerating the diffusion of responsibility for mental health from the professional to the community itself.

SUMMARY

1. The professionals who treat disordered behavior are classified principally according to their educational backgrounds. Psychiatrists are physicians who have spent a postgraduate residency training in psychotherapy. Psychoanalysts, usually physicians, have received specialized training at a psychoanalytic institute. Clinical psychologists hold Ph.D.'s in psychology, and have had extensive training in research, psychological testing, and therapeutic techniques. Counseling psychologists have graduate training similar to that of clinical psychologists, but typically with less emphasis on research. Psychiatric social workers hold master's degrees in social work and have special training in treatment procedures that emphasize the home and community.

2. The treatment of mental disorders through psychological means is a simplified definition of psychotherapy. A number of offshoots have arisen from Freud's original formulation of psychoanalysis, but all of the psychodynamic schools retain an emphasis on intrapsychic dynamics. The processes of classical psychotherapy include free association, by which repressed thoughts and feelings are brought to awareness. Analysts interpret these associations to help patients understand the roots of some of their problems. As they face previously unconscious aspects of their personalities, patients may begin to resist self-confrontation. They may also transfer to the analyst feelings about other important people in their lives; when transference occurs, the analyst points out to the patient that the behavior is inappropriate and actually a form of resistance to getting better. Successful analysis is often a lengthy and intense process, requiring working through neurotic responses and fragile adjustments several times over.

3. Humanistic therapies take an optimistic view of the human potential for growth. In Carl Rogers' client-centered approach, the clients themselves set the goals of the therapy and the topics to be discussed. The humanistic therapist takes a positive attitude toward clients and believes that they have an innate tendency toward self-actualization.

4. Behavior therapy focuses on behavior itself rather than on subjective determinants. Among the major behavioral approaches to treatment are counterconditioning and operant techniques—derived respectively from the principles of classical and operant conditioning; modeling of appropriate behaviors stems from Bandura's theory of observational learning; cognitive restructuring is based on altering maladaptive thought patterns; and self-control techniques are based on control of environmental techniques by the patients themselves.

5. Practically every approach and method of treatment used with individuals has also been applied to *group therapy*. Four types of group therapy that emphasize interaction among group members—as opposed to the therapist-client relationship—are psychodrama, sensitivity training, encounter groups, and family therapy.

6. Measuring the effectiveness and "success" of psychotherapy is difficult because of the many variables involved—patient, therapist, setting, goals, spontaneous remission, and so on. Research—most notably a major review by Smith and Glass (1971)—indicates that psychotherapy does help most patients and that different approaches to therapy do not differ greatly in effectiveness.

7. Biological therapies include electroconvulsive therapy (electroshock), psychosurgery, and drug treatment. Of these, drug therapy has been the most effective. The psychoactive drugs used in treatment are classified as major and minor tranquilizers, antidepressants, and stimulants. Tranquilizers such as chlorpromazine have been effective in the treatment of schizophrenia; antidepressants such as the tricyclics have served as successful mood elevators for depressed patients.

8. The role of the community in treating and preventing mental illness has grown enormously in the past 20 years as a result of the patients released from hospitals after drug therapy and by the enactment of the Community Mental Health Centers Act of 1963. Among the successful efforts have been community living programs for former mental patients, various forms of crisis intervention, and prevention programs. In recent years, the courts have moved to safeguard the rights of the mentally ill. Finally, the emergence of paraprofessionals in the community health movement has enabled highly trained practitioners to stretch their training in new and effective ways.

Part Seven
Social Influence and Interaction

Chapter 16
Social Influence

By proposing a simple experiment we can illustrate, quite simply, social influence. Suppose that the students in your psychology class are asked to play a trick on the instructor, who for some reason tends to lecture primarily from the right side of the room. The students respond to the lecture with interested looks, well-timed nods, and smiles whenever the lecturer speaks from the left side of the room. When the instructor goes back to the right, they feign boredom and give little response. The hypothesis of our experiment is that the instructor will be visibly influenced by the contrasting behaviors of the class. In a class where this experiment was tried (Whaley and Malott, 1969), the instructor was so affected that he spent much more time lecturing from the left side of the room—the side on which his words had been rewarded.

In this chapter we will discuss such instances of *social influence*—the ways in which an individual's actions affect the behavior, attitudes, or judgments of another. As in the experiment above, the effects of social influence usually reflect simple one-way processes; the social world is not, however, always one way. The instructor's response to the looks of the students, for example, might in turn further affect the level of student interest and of class attendance. In turn, this would then affect the instructor's behavior. Thus, the effects of the instructor on students and vice versa are mutual and reciprocal. This two-way process is known as *social interaction* and will be discussed in the next chapter.

Social Psychology Focuses on People

The study of both social influence and social interaction is the province of social psychology. Social psychology examines how people, as opposed to impersonal stimuli such as word lists or drug levels, affect other people. It thus differs from other branches of psychology in a number of ways:

* People are clearly our most important stimuli. We are basically social animals, and people can arouse us, anger us, or delight or depress us more than anything else.
* People often change as we perceive or judge them: nonsocial objects, on the other hand, maintain a certain degree of object constancy. We can judge the length of a line, kiss a silver dollar, or kick a football without changing these objects. Judging a student's performance, kissing a date, or kicking a potential mugger are obviously different matters. People change in significant ways as we do things to them.
* Unlike objects, people typically react to our actions. Rather than passively accepting our behavior, people respond to us. We may not hesitate to kick a broken candy machine when it frustrates us, but we are likely to stop short of aggression if a person frustrates us because we know the person might kick back.
* Social judgments frequently have less basis in reality than our judgments of nonsocial objects do. We can measure the accuracy of our judgments about the length of a line (2 inches) or the weight of a rock (3 pounds). But how can we check the accuracy of our judgments about, for example, the honesty and aims of other people?
* Social psychologists focus on how people in general respond to given situations. Other branches of psychology, such as personality and development, focus primarily on how an individual or a type of individual behaves in different situations.
* Social psychology emphasizes the world as it is perceived. Whether we interpret another's remark as witty, mean, thoughtless, sarcastic, or friendly, influences our subsequent behavior toward that person. Such perceptions are often biased and distorted to fit our needs and wishes as was shown in a study by Albert Hastorf and Hadley Cantril (1954). Dartmouth and Princeton students were asked to watch a film showing an especially rough and dirty football game between the two schools and to state their perceptions of the game. Not surprisingly, the perceptions of the two groups differed sharply. Each group noted many more infractions by the other team and typically interpreted questionable calls by referees in their own team's favor. Obviously, such differing perceptions affect behavior both during and after a football game.

To recap, the most important stimuli in our environments are people—who change as we perceive them. Our behavior is affected by the reactions of others to our actions. Our social judgments are not readily quantifiable. Social psychology focuses on how people, in general, perceive and respond to situations. We shall next examine the various stimuli that can affect those perceptions and responses.

Behavior and Stimuli

Stimuli affect our behavior in three basic ways:

1. *Arousal.* When our arousal level is affected by a loud clap of thunder, a day without food, or an injection of adrenalin, our behavior is influenced.
2. *Reinforcement.* Whether a flower smells good and "rewards" us or causes a skin rash and "punishes" us will affect our behavior toward that type of flower in the future.
3. *Information.* A red light tells us to step on the brakes: control of behavior is exerted by the stimulus of the signal—a source of information.

Other people are social stimuli, and they affect our behavior through these processes of arousal, reward and punishment, and information. A closer look at these three types of influence will help us to understand a wide variety of social behavior.

Arousal: The Mere Presence of Others

The behavior of others can arouse us in many ways. As we saw in Chapter 10, people can anger us and cause us to behave aggressively. Members of the opposite sex can arouse us by the manner in which they dress. But can the mere presence of others increase our arousal level and thus affect our behavior?

Much anecdotal evidence from everyday life suggests that it can. A well-rehearsed speech suddenly falls apart when the speaker faces an audience and experiences stage fright. Tired joggers quickly perk up when they happen upon a group of other joggers. In these simple social situations, the other people are not offering rewards or conveying information: they are merely present.

Scientific investigation of the effects of an audience dates back nearly a century. In 1904, a German researcher conducted experiments concerned with muscular effort and fatigue (Meumann). He noted that his subjects were able to exert far more muscle effort on the days when he watched as compared to the days on which no one watched.

More recently, Bruce Bergum and Donald Lehr (1963) reported increases in performance on a quite

different task when others watched. Subjects were placed in a booth where they observed a circle of red lamps lighting rapidly in sequence. They were asked to press a button whenever a light failed to blink on in proper sequence. Half of the subjects performed the task while alone in the booth; the other half had an observer with them. Subjects performed the task for 2 hours and 15 minutes. Figure 16.1 divides this period into five 27-minute segments and shows the average percentage of correct detections for each interval for both accompanied and solitary students. As the figure shows, the performance of both groups diminished over time because of boredom and fatigue. More important, the accuracy of subjects with a passive audience—albeit an audience of one—was consistently better than those who were alone. Behavior is thus affected by even a passive audience.

Behavior is also affected when one performs a task in the presence of others who are also engaged in a similar task—a situation called *coaction*. Many years ago, Floyd Allport (1920) administered various tests to subjects. On some occasions they worked alone in cubicles. At other times they worked while

FIGURE 16.1 Accuracy on a monitoring task performed alone and under supervision. It can be seen that the scores were consistently higher when the task was performed in the presence of an observer.

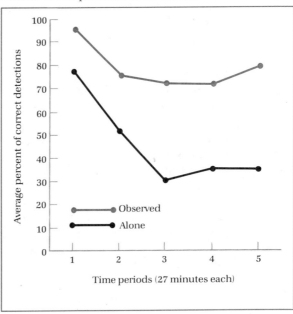

seated around a table (a coaction condition). Performance rates for simple tasks such as vowel cancellation and multiplication were much higher in the coaction situation.

Researchers have also observed increases in performance in coaction situations in several different species of animals. Chickens deprived of food and then allowed to eat until full will still eat half as much when placed in the presence of another chicken that is eating (Bayer, 1929). Ants digging nests in groups of two or three dig more quickly and more sand per ant than ants working alone (Chen, 1937).

Such results led psychologists to assume that the presence of others always increased or facilitated performance, a phenomenon known as *social facilitation*. This assumption, however, was contradicted by the results of several experiments. For example, human subjects who were instructed to learn lists of nonsense syllables performed better when alone (Pessin, 1933). Similarly, research shows that both humans (Husband, 1931) and cockroaches (Gates and Allee, 1933) learn complex mazes more quickly when alone than when fellow creatures are present. In other words, an audience sometimes facilitates performance; at other times the presence of others impairs performance.

Zajonc's Arousal Theory This apparent contradiction has been explained by Robert Zajonc (1965) in terms of arousal. The presence of others energizes us and increases our drive level. An increase in drive strengthens the dominant response of the organism—that is, the response most likely to occur. At the same time, an increase in drive weakens responses that already are weak. In a simple or well-learned task, familiarity with what is required exists or the task has been practiced several times. Thus the strongest and most likely response is the one that is appropriate and correct. In a complex and difficult task, on the other hand, the strongest response is likely to be the wrong one. Consider the task of backing a car into a tight parking space. For an experienced driver this is a well-learned behavior, and the "most natural" and most probable responses will get the car into the space. However, for a novice driver, the most likely responses are incorrect, and parking will be difficult. Because a passive or coacting audience strengthens the most likely response, an audience will improve the parking performance of the experienced driver but interfere with the performance of the novice driver. In the

same way, an audience will improve performance on simple and well-learned tasks, such as weight pulling or eating, but impair performance on difficult tasks, such as list learning or negotiation of complex mazes. In Allport's coaction study, performance of tasks such as solving logic problems was worse with an audience, while simple tasks such as vowel cancellation improved in a coaction situation.

Zajonc's arousal theory has been supported by subsequent research. For example, although humans and cockroaches do worse on complex mazes in the presence of an audience, the presence of others facilitates performance when the maze is simple (Zajonc, Heingartner, and Herman, 1969). Recent studies have also reported that the presence of others enhances the dominant response and thus affects performance of relevant behaviors such as laughter in children (Chapman, 1973), game-playing behavior (Grush, 1978), and competitive swimming (Sorrentino and Sheppard, 1978).

If the presence of others acts as a source of

Recent studies have indicated that game-playing performance is enhanced by the presence of others.

arousal, we might expect that other, nonsocial factors that increase drive should have similar effects. That is, any source of arousal should enhance the dominant response and lead to better performance on simple tasks but result in diminished performance on complex tasks. This has been confirmed by other studies. Kenneth Spence, Janet Taylor, and Ronnie Ketchel (1956) found that high-anxiety people perform better on easy tasks and worse on complex tasks than low-anxiety people. In addition, George Mandler and Seymour Sarason (1952) reported that students suffering from test anxiety showed improved performance on easy tests but impaired performance on hard tests. Further, in a task where subjects had to recognize sets of words flashed on a screen, those who had been motivated by the offer of money more often guessed words that were strongest in their response hierarchy than did subjects not offered money. The offer of money enhanced the dominant response (Zajonc and Nieuwenhuyse, 1964). Interestingly, a similar experiment showed that the presence of others had similar effects (Zajonc and Sales, 1966). Subjects who guessed in the presence of others had their dominant responses strengthened when compared with subjects who guessed while alone.

Cottrell's Theory   One modification of Zajonc's original theory was made by Nickolas Cottrell (1968). *Cottrell's theory* suggested that it was not just the presence of an audience that aroused a person and enhanced the dominant response, but the presence of an audience capable of evaluating and rating the subject. In his own work (Cottrell, Wack, Sekerak, and Rittle, 1968) he found that, in word recognition tasks, blindfolding an audience did not lead to an increase in subjects' guessing the dominant response. Likewise, other investigators reported enhanced choice of dominant response words only when an expert audience was used (Henchy and Glass, 1968).

Arousal, then, does strengthen the dominant response—the one most likely to occur—but weakens responses that are already weak. The presence of others will most likely increase the dominant response if the audience, or observer, is capable of evaluating the subject's performance.

Social Reinforcement: Reward

Arousal through their presence is only one of the ways in which others influence our behavior. An even more prevalent means of social influence is *reinforcement.* People serve as real or potential sources of both reward and punishment. Others dramatically affect us through bribes, kisses and hugs, cash bonuses, good grades, praise, and other rewards. They also control our behavior through the use of threats, spanking, guilt, social rejection, and other punishments.

People may provide *primary reinforcers* that satisfy such basic physiological needs as food, water, or shelter; more important, however, they administer *secondary reinforcers* that are not inherently rewarding but that an individual has learned to associate with positive outcomes. Money, for example, serves no direct biological need, but it is associated with primary reinforcers that do satisfy primary needs since it can buy food, drink, and comfort. Some secondary reinforcers such as approval, love, and attention are by their very nature social: they cannot be obtained from the nonsocial environment.

Verbal Reinforcement   One of the most effective social rewards is praise. One experiment indicated that even a simple statement such as "good" or "mm hmm" could affect verbal behavior (Greenspoon, 1955). He asked subjects to utter words at random (as they thought of them) for 50 minutes. Some subjects were reinforced by an "mm hmm" or a "good" for every singular noun they generated, while others were reinforced only for plural nouns. For both groups, the *verbal reinforcement* significantly increased the generation rate for the type of word that was rewarded. Richard Centers (1963) studied the control of everyday conversation through the use of simple social reinforcers. While supposedly waiting for an experiment, subjects sat in the lobby of a psychology laboratory. A confederate of the experimenter (who acted like a subject) joined the real subjects and initiated conversation. Through the use of head nods, "mm hmms," and smiles, the confederate was able to influence the total verbalization of subjects, the number of statements they made conveying information, and the number of statements of opinion.

Can such verbal reinforcement also affect underlying attitudes and beliefs? Chester Insko (1965) sought to answer that question in an experiment involving students in an introductory psychology course at the University of Hawaii. Students were interviewed by telephone about their feelings toward a proposed springtime festival. Half of the students were reinforced with a "good" or "mm hmm" whenever they expressed feelings of support of the festival. The other half were verbally reinforced for statements opposing the festival. One week later during their psychology class, all subjects were given a general opinion survey. One item in the survey concerned opinions about a springtime festival. The answers of those who previously had been verbally reinforced for profestival statements showed more favorable attitudes toward the festival than did the answers of those who had not received the reinforcements. The verbal reinforcement during the telephone interview had evidently affected their opinions.

Verbal reinforcers often are used by parents as they socialize with their children. Parents, however, typically give so much attention and affection to their children that these reinforcers may lose their effectiveness. Indeed, a few kind words from a stranger may prove far more effective. Researchers observed preschool children playing a game that involved dropping marbles into various holes and found that verbal reinforcers from adult strangers ("that's good" or "you're terrific at this game") had a far greater influence on the children's responses than did similar reinforcers from parents (Stevenson, Keen, and Knights, 1963).

As the above findings suggest, the effect of verbal reinforcers is often dependent upon the particular situation. Jacob Gewirtz and Donald Baer (1958) reasoned that, just as an organism responds more powerfully to food reinforcement when it is hungry, people who recently have been deprived of social approval and attention will be far more responsive to verbal reinforcement. In their experiment, nursery school children dropped marbles into a box through two holes. Each child played the game twice, once after social interaction with others and again after spending 20 minutes alone with no social contact. The experimenter used the verbal reinforcers "good" and "mm hmm" in an attempt to influence which hole the children dropped the marbles through. As predicted, the children were far more responsive to the verbal reinforcement after the social deprivation period. Interestingly, this effect was even more pronounced in children whom their teacher previously had rated as high in seeking approval.

Social reinforcement takes forms other than verbal reinforcement, of course. Approval can be expressed subtly without a word being spoken—through a smile, nod of the head, or even increased eye contact. The unconscious use of social reinforcers may shape many significant behaviors. Since we are most likely to reinforce in subtle ways behaviors in others that we expect and desire, we are likely to bring about those behaviors. Clinical psychologists who expect their clients to improve may subtly reinforce their healthy-sounding verbalizations without really improving their mental health. One area where subtle social reinforcement is likely to have a significant effect is political polling. There are often differences noted in polls taken by the two major political parties in the United States. Democrats typically report that their polls indicate strong support for Democratic candidates, while Republican polls show just the opposite. Even if the same questions are used in different polls, we might conjecture as to why the results of the polls would differ. It is likely that the Democratic and Republican interviewers subtly reinforce their respondents—through a smile or nod of the head—for answers that support their own party. This subtle reinforcement may not only affect the expressed opinion of the respondents but also influence their subsequent behavior in the election booth.

Interpersonal Attraction Psychologists are concerned with the various factors that determine why people like certain other people and show definite preferences in their choices of others as friends, roommates, or lovers. The area of study concerned with the question of why people like or dislike others is called *interpersonal attraction*. Both the actual and potential rewards that others might supply, underlie most theories of interpersonal attraction.

1. *Propinquity.* One of the simplest facts about interpersonal attraction is that people generally come to like those who happen to live or work physically close to them—*propinquity*. Friendships typically develop between people who live in adjacent apartments or who are assigned seats that are close to each other in a classroom. Obviously it is difficult for friendships to develop between people who rarely see each other. On the other hand, neighbors are likely to engage in friendly hellos, to seek help from each other, and to borrow needed items from each other. It is through these kinds of interactions that friendships develop.

Leon Festinger, Stanley Schachter, and Kurt Back (1950) studied friendship patterns among residents of a housing complex. The closer the residents lived to each other in terms of sheer physical distance, the more likely they were to be close friends (see Figure 16.2 on the next page). In addition, residents who lived in strategic locations that would put them in contact with many residents (at the bottom of a stairway or in the middle of an inner court) were most popular.

Theodore Newcomb (1961) acquired an entire dormitory at the University of Michigan and recruited students to live there free if they filled out questionnaires at various times throughout the year. A major determinant of liking in this study was how close the students lived to one another. Students who happened to be assigned as roommates became friends—even if their initial attitudes were incompatible. Other research confirms the effects of physical closeness on attraction. People who are physically close to each other during work are likely to become friends (Kipnis, 1957), and marriages are more likely among people who happen to live near each other (Bossard, 1932).

2. *Familiarity.* One reason why propinquity might lead to attraction is that we tend to see frequently and to become familiar with those who live nearby. Zajonc (1968) has proposed that the frequency with which we are exposed to people or objects is a major determinant of our liking. Mere continued exposure to a person's face (even in the absence of interaction) is sufficient condition for liking that person. In one study demonstrating this effect, subjects went from room to room in the laboratory to taste either pleasant or noxious drinks. As they went from room to room, they found themselves in the company of other subjects. According to plan, some of these subjects were encountered frequently during the experiment, whereas others were encountered infrequently. At the end of the experiment, subjects were asked how much they liked each of the other subjects. Those who had been encountered more frequently were liked better—even if the encounters took place while tasting noxious drinks (Saegert, Swap, and Zajonc, 1973)! More will be said about the relationship between frequency of exposure and attraction later in the chapter, when theories of attitude change are discussed.

3. *Similarity-attraction.* Perhaps the most frequently cited theory of interpersonal attraction is the *similarity-attraction theory* offered by Donn Byrne (1969). In essence, Byrne's theory recalls the adage, "Birds of a feather flock together." People seem to like others of the same "feather." Attraction by similarity seems to apply on almost any dimension, ranging from personality traits, attitudes, and political views, to less important aspects such as city of birth, physical characteristics, and athletic

As the factor of propinquity suggests, friendships often develop among people who live close to one another as this neighborhood barbecue indicates.

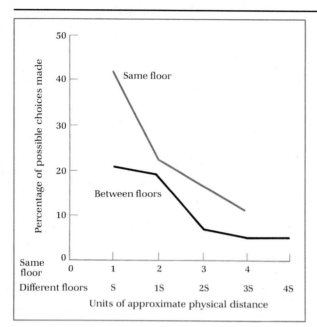

FIGURE 16.2 The relationship between proximity and liking. "Units of approximate distance" represent how many doors apart people live; for example, 2S means 2 doors and a stairway apart. It can be seen that the closer together people live, the more likely it is that they will become friends.

ability. Examples of attraction by similarity abound in everyday life: computer dating services depend upon it by matching people in terms of their similar attitudes and characteristics.

To investigate the role of similarity in interpersonal attraction, Byrne has carried out an extensive research program. In his standard experiment (Byrne, 1961), subjects first fill out a questionnaire in which they describe many of their attitudes toward current issues. Later, they are shown answers purportedly given by other people to the same questionnaire and asked to judge the likability of those people. The other people do not exist, of course. Their answers are fabricated by the experimenter who can manipulate them to be either very similar to those of the subject or very different. The more similar the attitudes expressed by the subject and the bogus "other person," the greater the liking expressed by the subject. Other work (Byrne, Ervin, and Lamberth, 1970) found that couples who were matched on similarity before a computer date liked each other more than couples who were not so matched. They even stood closer during a postdate interview with the experimenter.

Interpersonal attraction has been shown to re-

flect similarities not only in attitudes but also in abilities such as intelligence and athletic prowess and even physical similarity. For example, married couples are more similar in height (Berscheid and Walster, 1969) and attractiveness (Murstein, 1972) than would be expected by chance. A study of the 1971 New York mayoral election found that people who preferred the taller candidate were significantly taller than those who preferred the shorter candidate (Berkowitz, Nebel, and Reitman, 1971).

Among the most impressive studies of similarity in interpersonal attraction was the previously mentioned large-scale naturalistic study carried out by Newcomb (1961) in the dormitories of the University of Michigan. Recall that Newcomb discovered that physical closeness was a major determinant of attraction. In addition, he measured the initial attitudes of all residents and found that initial similarity of attitudes was also an important determinant of whether or not students liked each other later in the semester.

Why does similarity lead to attraction? The most likely reason is that people who are similar to us are rewarding in several different ways. Interaction with someone who shares similar interests and attitudes is likely to be smooth, effortless, and interesting to both persons. Similar people find it easier to share pleasant experiences and to find conversational topics of mutual interest. Beyond such obvious rewards, similarity of beliefs and attitudes offers another kind of reinforcement. Similar others help us confirm our own beliefs, reduce uncertainty, and validate our own way of viewing reality.

4. *Complementarity.* Despite the evidence given above, similarity can interfere with liking in some situations. The adage "opposites attract" has some support from psychological research. Two people who talk a lot may find each other irritating—a dominating woman and a dominating man cannot both control the relationship. On the other hand, a good talker and a good listener are likely to get along well; a dominating wife and a submissive husband (or vice versa) may have a smooth relationship. The meshing of people's different needs in such a way that each is satisfied is called *complementarity.* Television's *Odd Couple* was a dramatic demonstration of complementarity. Oscar Madison could be as sloppy as he liked while Felix Unger could express his obsession with neatness by cleaning up after his roommate. In a complementary relationship; each person rewards the

490

other by allowing and encouraging expression of important needs and desires. Some research supports the role of complementarity in attraction. James Palmer and Byrne (1970) reported that submissive subjects preferred dominant others, and Clyde Hendrick and Steven Brown (1971) found that introverted subjects preferred extroverts.

5. *Balance.* Fritz Heider (1958), in formulating his *balance theory* of interpersonal attraction, pointed out the tendency of people to seek consistency among their *own* thoughts, feelings, and actions. When inconsistency arises, people try to reduce the conflict by changing their attitudes and beliefs and thus restore the more rewarding state of affairs—consistency or balance. According to Heider, a relationship is balanced if two people either like or dislike each other. If one person likes the other but is disliked in return, the relationship is imbalanced. Thus, balance theory proposes that *reciprocity* is an important factor in interpersonal attraction. We will come to like those who like us and dislike those who dislike us. Zajonc and Eugene Burnstein (1965) showed that reciprocity is an important bias in interpersonal relationships. In three-person relationships, there is balance if the people who like each other share their likes and dislikes of other people. Tybalt and Montague, for example, share their dislike for Romeo and share their liking for Juliet (see Figure 16.3). Similarly, people who dislike each other are likely to disagree in their feelings about others.

Balanced relationships, said Heider, make people feel comfortable. But imbalanced relationships feel wrong and will motivate people to restore balance by changing their pattern of likes and dislikes. For example, if you learn that someone you dislike is a good friend of your best friend, you can resolve the inconsistency and restore balance in two different ways. You can start liking the person you disliked, or you can stop liking—or at least think less of—your best friend.

6. *Gain-loss.* Suppose someone who previously disliked you starts to like you? How will you react to that person? Sometimes the approval of someone who in the past has disliked you is even more rewarding than the approval of an old friend. Eliot Aronson and Darwyn Linder (1965) have called this the *gain-loss theory* of interpersonal attraction. This theory says that we like someone better if the other person first dislikes us and then likes us than if the person had liked us all along. To test their theory, Aronson and Linder staged an experiment in which

subjects interacted with an accomplice, or confederate, of the researchers in several meetings. After each meeting, the subjects heard the confederate's opinion of them. The subjects were grouped in four experimental conditions (see Figure 16.4 on the next page). In the consistent positive condition, all evaluations by the confederate were positive. In the consistent negative, all evaluations were negative. In the gain condition, the confederate began by giving negative evaluations but then became positive. In the loss condition, evaluations started as positive but then became negative.

As predicted by gain-loss theory, subjects in the gain condition liked the confederate most; subjects in the loss condition liked the confederate least. The gain of approval from someone who previously disliked you is somehow more rewarding than

FIGURE 16.3 Demonstration of Zajonc and Burnstein's balance theory of relationships as represented in the Reagan administration.

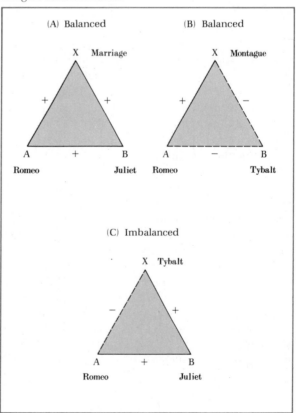

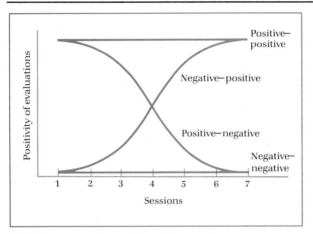

FIGURE 16.4 The gain-loss theory of interpersonal attraction. Evidently the gain of approval from someone who had disliked you previously is more rewarding than the constant approval of someone who has liked you all along. (Positive and negative feedback were systematically varied over seven sessions.)

constant approval. Perhaps the initial dislike upsets you, and you feel a rewarding relief when the dislike changes. In addition, you are likely to view the person who changes from disliking to liking you as a more discerning and credible source—one who does not like just anyone but who is highly selective.

7. *Just-world.* It is reasonable to assume that we might feel sorry for, or even like, victims of accidents or bad fortune. But the set of beliefs and feelings that Melvin Lerner has called the *just-world hypothesis* suggests just the opposite. This hypothesis refers to our tendency to believe that the world is fair, orderly, and just: people get the rewards and punishments they deserve and deserve what they get. When bad things happen to good people, it surprises and upsets us. Hence we rationalize that victims must deserve their fate.

An experiment demonstrates the just-world hypothesis at work (Lerner and Simmons, 1966). Subjects watched participants in a memory task learn series of words. These participants were actually confederates of the experimenters, and they intentionally made a number of errors. The experiment was rigged so that it appeared to the subjects that some of the participants received electric shocks for each error while other participants received no shock. Afterward, the subjects were asked to evaluate the participants. The subjects showed more dislike for those who had appeared to receive shocks. They apparently decided that, in a just

world, innocent victims would not receive such punishment. Hence there must have been something wrong with the victims.

Similar dislike or derogation of victims often has been evidenced in the real world. In 1970, after four students where shot to death by the National Guard during an antiwar protest at Kent State University in Ohio, there was a tendency among Americans to suggest that the victims "got what was coming to them." In one public opinion poll, 60 percent of those questioned blamed the victims themselves, even though two of them were bystanders not even involved in the demonstration.

Social Reinforcement: Punishment

Just as other people can influence our behavior by serving as sources of reward, they also can influence us by serving as sources of punishment. We

National Guard on campus at Kent State University during antiwar protest in 1970. As an example of the "just-world" hypothesis, many people thought that the students who were shot by the National Guard "got what was coming to them."

often go along with other people simply to avoid punishment—social rejection or banishment to positions of low status, for example. We do not want to be thought of as different or deviant from group norms.

Deviance *Deviance* describes behavior that departs in a marked and noticeable way from accepted group norms. The consequences of being considered deviant were powerfully demonstrated in a classic experiment carried out by Schachter (1951). The subjects of the experiment were organized into a series of "discussion clubs." Concealed in each group were three of Schachter's confederates, who pretended to be subjects. As the group began to discuss the prescribed topic, one of the confederates took a position similar to that of the group. A second confederate took a position deviant from the group and remained steadfast in this dissenting opinion. The third confederate began by taking a deviant position but eventually came to side with the group, pretending to be convinced by the group's arguments.

At the end of the discussion, when it came time to assign jobs, the groups punished the deviant by assigning him the jobs that no one wanted. Furthermore, on a measure that asked the subjects to consider how much they liked each of the others, the deviant was clearly disliked. Interestingly, the confederate who began as deviant but eventually agreed with the group was not punished. This person was liked just as much as the confederates who had agreed with the group right from the beginning.

The Schachter study demonstrates the harsh manner in which people are often treated for differing with the opinions of others. But deviance is not simply a matter of failing to listen to the wisdom of the group. The mere appearance of being different can lead to group rejection, even if the apparent deviance is meaningless. Jonathan Freedman and Anthony Doob (1968) asked groups of five or six subjects to take a written personality test. Then each subject was shown score sheets that purportedly contained the distribution of test results for all members of the group. In fact, these results had been fabricated by the experimenters and so rigged that one person was shown to have scored differently from all the others. This person was the deviant, although it was never made clear precisely how the score differed from the other scores in the group, not even whether it was more favorable or less favorable than the other scores. This manipula-

tion was successful; the deviants felt different, and the rest of the group considered them so. The group was then asked to select a member for a learning experiment that would purportedly require the subject to receive occasional electric shocks. Not surprisingly, the groups selected the deviants. In an interesting variation of this experiment, Freedman and Doob arranged the situation so that the "learner" was to receive money rather than shocks; in this condition the group avoided selecting the deviant for the experiment.

The punishment of deviance and our fear of such rejection help explain much of our general social behavior. We are constantly in situations where we must comply with certain group or societal norms. We comply in part because we tend to believe in the norms and see their value. But we also comply because we fear that we might be punished by others if we do not.

Deindividuation The crucial role of punishment in influencing our behavior, which we have seen in our consideration of deviance, also is dramatically evident when the fear of punishment is temporarily absent. Such a situation can result in mob behavior. During power blackouts, it is not uncommon to find roving gangs of residents looting local stores. In the old South, lynchings of blacks by white mobs occurred with sickening frequency. Victory celebrations after football games sometimes erupt into vandalism.

Common to all these instances of mob behavior is what researchers call a state of *deindividuation*—the submerging of the individual into the group. When individuals perform criminal acts alone, they can normally expect to be punished for their behavior. However, when they are part of a group in which all or most of the members are acting in the same way, individuals are relatively free of such concerns. Because the group provides a protective cloak of anonymity, individuals feel less responsible for their actions and hence less accountable to others.

Although the mere fact of membership in a mob tends to make people feel faceless, deindividuation is greatly enhanced when distinctive personal characteristics such as name or face are literally obscured. In typical laboratory investigations of deindividuation, subjects are made to feel identifi-

Local residents looting a store during a power blackout. Researchers refer to this type of behavior as deindividuation, the submerging of the individual into the group.

able by wearing name tags and by frequent use of their names or to feel anonymous by being required to wear lab coats or even hoods and by never having their names mentioned (Zimbardo, 1969; Singer, Brush, and Lublin, 1965). The subjects who are made to feel anonymous are much more willing to engage in antisocial behavior; for example, they might use much more obscenity during a group discussion or deliver higher levels of what they thought were electric shocks to another person.

Examples of deindividuation can be found in daily newspaper headlines. Members of terrorist groups such as the Ku Klux Klan wear hoods not only to hide their identity from the police but also to submerge their identity into the group. According to some reports, the murderers of three civil rights workers in Mississippi in 1964 passed the gun from hand to hand so that each would feel equally responsible and none would feel individually guilty.

But we need look no further for the experience of deindividuation than our own feelings of anonymity when as children we dressed up for Halloween. Behind our costumes and masks we felt unidentifiable and thus more likely to engage in mildly antisocial behavior such as soaping windows. A

clever study of children's behavior was carried out during this naturally occurring state of deindividuation at Halloween (Diener, Fraser, Beaman, and Kelem, 1976). The researchers arranged to observe trick-or-treaters at a number of different homes. As the Halloweener approached the home, a hidden observer recorded one important variable—that is, whether the child was alone or in a group. At the door, the children were greeted by an experimenter who made appropriate approving comments about the costumes and set up a second variable of the study: half of the time, the children were asked their names and addresses; the other half of the time the children were allowed to remain anonymous. The experimenter next pointed to a table, told each trick-or-treater to take one piece of candy from the bowl, and then left the room. The children were being watched, however, by a hidden observer, who noted whether the children helped themselves to an extra piece of candy or to money from a bowl of pennies and nickels on the table.

Both anonymity and group membership affected the behavior of the children. The children were more likely to steal if their anonymity had been protected or if they had arrived in a group. As can be seen in the accompanying table, stealing was

494

most prevalent among those children who were most deindividuated—anonymous and in a group. More than half of these children helped themselves to an extra piece of candy or to money from the bowl of pennies.

| Anonymity | PERCENTAGE OF CHILDREN IN EACH CONDITION WHO STOLE | |
	Alone	Group
Nonanonymous	7.5%	20.8%
Anonymous	21.4%	57.2%

Social reinforcement with its positive and negative rewards does have an amply documented effect on many of our behaviors. Social reinforcers, in addition to arousal, are stimuli that affect the way we act. In the next section we shall examine the ways in which other people serve as stimuli to our behavior by acting as sources of information.

Information: Social Comparison

In addition to serving as sources of arousal and of reinforcement, other people influence our behavior in a third major way—by serving as useful sources of information. We observe the behavior of other people in a given situation, and their behavior gives us information about how to act in that situation. Much of a child's learning is acquired through the observation of others. This same process influences adults, especially in ambiguous circumstances where what constitutes appropriate behavior may not be clear.

People are constantly making *social comparisons*, looking to others as a guide for their own interpretations of what is appropriate in a given situation. Cigarette smokers will frequently look around the room to see if anyone else is smoking before they decide to light up. Similarly, when we want to applaud a speaker or a musical performance, we turn to others to see if they are ready to applaud: they serve as models.

A theory of social comparison relevant to such situations was proposed in 1954 by Festinger. The basic tenet of the theory is that whenever we are uncertain about the validity of our own opinions or judgments, we turn to others for information. Their responses serve as guides for us in determining what our own interpretation or response ought to be.

Here is a typical example of the social comparison process at work on campus. In an exam where grades are assigned on a curve, you learn that your score was 42 out of a possible 65 points. How well did you do? You do not know how to interpret this score. It could be that everyone in the class did poorly and your score is actually in the top quarter of the class distribution—or it could be that everyone did well and your score is actually one of the lowest in the class. Typically, you will want to know immediately what other people's scores were. By comparing your score to theirs, you arrive at an interpretation of how well you did on the test.

Affiliation   One of the first experimental investigations of social comparison was conducted by Schachter (1959). Because people must at least get together in order to engage in the social comparison process, Schachter focused on *affiliation*—that is, the desire to associate and interact with others. He hypothesized that fear would lead to affiliation, inasmuch as fearful individuals want to affiliate so that others can give them information that will help them evaluate how appropriate their feelings of fear are.

To test this hypothesis, Schachter ran an experiment in which subjects were told they would receive electric shocks. Half of the subjects were told the shocks would be very severe. The experimenter, an ominous-looking man dressed in a lab coat and supposedly named "Dr. Gregor Zilstein," warned them: "Now I feel I must be completely honest with you and tell you exactly what you are in for. These shocks will hurt. They will be painful ... but, of course, they will do no permanent damage." For the other half of the subjects, the experimenter described the shocks quite differently: "Do not let the word 'shock' trouble you; I am sure that you will enjoy the experiment ... I assure you that what you will feel will not in any way be painful. It will resemble more a tickle or a tingle than anything unpleasant." After hearing one of these two descriptions, subjects were given a choice of how they could spend their time while the shock apparatus was supposedly being put in order: they could wait with other people or wait alone. The subjects in the high-fear condition—those who were anticipating severe shocks—showed a stronger desire to wait with others than did those in the low-fear condition.

495

In other words, high fear led to a need for information from others and thus affiliation.

Further research by Schachter (1959) suggests that in high-fear situations people do not want to affiliate with simply anyone. They prefer to affiliate with other subjects who are participating in the experiment and expecting to be shocked—that is, people with information about the subject at hand. This affiliation enables them to undergo the social comparison process, obtaining information from others around them about how to interpret the severity of the shock situation. Additional research (Gerard, 1963; Wrightsman, 1960) indicates that affiliation in the fear situation is due to a desire for social comparison along with a desire for reassurance and the reduction of fear.

Other experiments by Schachter have shown that during a state of physiological arousal subjects tend to interpret their own emotions in terms of social comparison. They variously report feelings of happiness or anger, for example, depending upon informational cues supplied by others.

Bystander Intervention One of the most dramatic situations where the behavior of other people serves as an important source of information is the apparent emergency. You are walking down the street and see an old woman sprawled on a patch of ice. Has she fallen and hurt herself? Is she merely drunk? Perhaps she is only shaken up and will easily get back on her feet unaided. Or she may have broken a bone and is in a true emergency situation. Are others standing by? What are they doing? The situation is obviously ambiguous. How you define it, what informational cues you take from other people, may be the determining factors in whether you intervene and offer help.

The factors that determine whether or not bystanders intervene in such situations have been investigated by Bibb Latané and John Darley. Their original interest was prompted by an extraordinary and tragic instance of nonintervention by bystanders that occurred in 1964 in New York City. Shortly after 3 A.M. a young woman named Kitty Genovese, who was returning from work, was attacked by a man in front of her apartment building. The man stabbed her, but she struggled free, crying out in terror and screaming for help. Then the man attacked her again and stabbed her to death. Kitty Genovese's death struggle lasted more than 30 minutes. During this period, reporters from the *New York Times* later learned, at least 38 residents

An instance of "bystander intervention." How a given situation is defined and what informational cues one takes from others may determine whether one offers assistance or not.

of the building heard her scream and came to the windows. Yet not one of those people came to her aid or telephoned the police.

The incident received a great deal of publicity. It was interpreted in the press in terms of apathy and indifference, of people having "lost concern for our fellow man." Such explanations focused on the personalities of the bystanders who had failed to help: something was lacking in their character. However, Latané and Darley (1970) sought a different explanation. They attempted to determine precisely what situational variables and social psychological processes lead people in general to respond—or not—to an emergency.

Latané and Darley began by proposing a "decision tree" analysis (see Figure 16-5) showing that responding to an emergency requires more than personal altruism: it involves a sequence of appropriate decisions. First and most obvious, an individual must notice the incident. Second, that individual must resolve any apparent ambiguity and interpret the event as an emergency. Third, that person must assume some responsibility, must "make it his or her business" to intervene. Finally, the individual must know the appropriate form of assistance and then render it. Only if the bystander makes the appropriate decision at each point in the sequence will he or she intervene, and these decisions typically must be made in a matter of seconds.

In their experiments on *bystander intervention*, Latané and Darley isolated particular decision points and then examined the variables affecting that decision and the subject's response. In one experiment (Darley and Latané, 1968), the emergency was so obvious that it had to be noticed and interpreted as an emergency; thus the subject was at the third point on the decision tree—deciding whether to assume responsibility. Ostensibly, the experiment involved a discussion about adjustment to college life, with the subjects placed in individual booths connected by an intercom system. In fact, only one subject participated at a time; the other subjects were actually tape recordings prepared by the experimenters. During the discussion, one of the voices loudly announced the onset of an epileptic seizure: "I er um I think I need help er if if could er er somebody er er er er give me a little er give me a little help … I'm gonna die er er I'm gonna die er help er help er er seizure er." The voice choked, then lapsed into silence.

How did the subjects respond to this obvious emergency? It all depended on how many people the subject thought were tuned into the emergency on the intercom. The experimeters, by use of the appropriate number of tape recorders, manipulated this variable. Some subjects thought that the group consisted of only two people (subject and victim); others thought it consisted of three people (subject, victim, and one additional discussant) or six people (four additional discussants). The measure of helping was whether the subject stepped out of the booth and sought some help for the victim. Helping, as it turned out, was a direct function of the size of the group. The greater the number of other people the subject thought had heard the victim's plea for help, the less likely the subject was to respond. Eighty-five percent of the subjects who thought they were alone with the victim responded before the victim's taped voice ran out. Of those who believed that the group consisted of three, 62 percent responded. And of those who believed the group consisted of six, only 31 percent offered help.

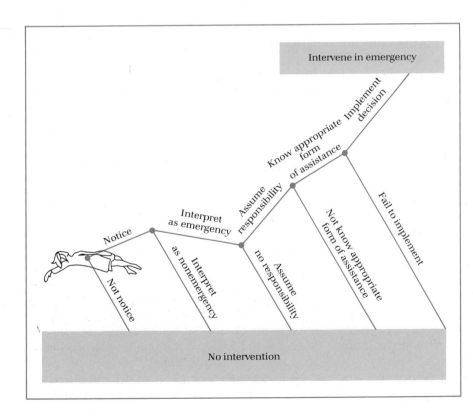

FIGURE 16.5 Latané and Darley's "decision tree" analysis demonstrates that intervention in an emergency involves a sequence of appropriate decisions.

Latané and Darley concluded that a *diffusion of responsibility* had occurred in the larger groups: knowing that others were present meant that the subject was not solely responsible for the victim's welfare. Thus, one variable that determines whether a bystander will intervene is the number of bystanders believed to be present. The larger the number of others present, the less responsibility the individual is likely to assume. (Bystanders in the Kitty Genovese case lived in a large apartment building. Listening from behind their windows, they must have assumed there were many others present.)

Another experiment by Latané and Darley (1968) focused on an earlier point in their decision-tree analysis—defining the event as an emergency. They created an ambiguous event and then examined variables that influenced how the event was defined. The setting for the experiment was a small waiting room where subjects sat filling out a questionnaire. Suddenly, a stream of smoke poured into the room through a wall vent. Some subjects were alone when this happened: 75 percent of these subjects stepped out of the room and reported the emergency. Other subjects were with two other people, actually accomplices of the experimenters who had been instructed to react passively and display no emotional reaction to the smoke. Of these subjects, only 10 percent reported the smoke. Faced with the apparent ambiguity of the situation, they went through the social comparison process to reduce their own uncertainties: they observed the passivity of the two others in the waiting room and defined the event as a nonemergency.

In a final condition of the experiment, three subjects were in the waiting room. All of them were naive; that is none was a confederate of the experimenter. Reporting of the emergency was also relatively low in this condition. In only 38 percent of these groups did even one person report the smoke. Latané and Darley concluded that in the groups of three a state of *pluralistic ignorance* apparently had developed. They pointed out that, since our culture does not encourage display of emotions, each of the three subjects was probably attempting to appear calm. When these subjects made social comparisons, they saw everyone else acting undisturbed by the smoke. Hence they defined the event as a nonemergency. Later interviews with the subjects who had not responded to the emergency elicited an astonishing variety of interpretations of what the smoke was. These interpretations ranged from air-conditioning vapors to smog (introduced, it was thought, to simulate an urban environment) to a "truth gas" designed to make the subject reply honestly to the questionnaire.

Further research on the state of pluralistic ignorance that can develop among bystanders in an emergency was conducted by Latané and Judith Rodin (1969). This experiment showed subjects who were alone were far more likely to help a woman in distress (a woman experimenter who collapsed to the floor in apparent pain) than were subjects in pairs. Interestingly, however, when the pairs consisted of friends instead of strangers, helping behavior increased. Pluralistic ignorance was less likely to occur among friends who have less need to hide their emotional reactions from one another. These reactions provided information cues that enabled each person to decide that an emergency was indeed in progress.

Conformity

The underlying feature of social comparison and affiliation as well as diffusion of responsibility are the comforts the individual has in knowing that others all essentially believe the same thing. In all of these situations the individual changes judgments or behavior as a result of exposure to the ideas and judgments of a group. In other words, the individual conforms.

Public Compliance versus Private Acceptance

Sometimes *conformity* consists solely of a kind of public compliance. Other times it goes far deeper and results in private acceptance. The distinction between two of the types of social influence—reinforcement and information—helps to differentiate between public compliance and private acceptance. The two processes operate in very different ways and with differing effects. The most important distinction is that reinforcement in the form of punishment brings about public compliance but not private acceptance. There is no change in private internalized beliefs. Once the person who has offered rewards or threatened punishment is no longer watching, behavior reverts to what it was prior to the attempt at social control. By contrast, social control achieved through the use of others as sources of information leads not only to public compliance but also to changes of internalized attitudes and beliefs. These changes persist even after the source of information is no longer present and watching.

Sherif: The Autokinetic Effect The first systematic work in the study of conformity was carried out by Muzafer Sherif (1937). To demonstrate conformity, Sherif took advantage of a well-known optical illusion, the *autokinetic effect.* If an individual is placed in a totally dark room with no frame of reference and then a single point of light is introduced, the light appears to move erratically. This effect is caused by random movements of the person's own eyes (see Chapter 3). (During World War II, two versions of this effect proved so distracting to American pilots flying in formation at night that blinking lights were introduced to eliminate the problem.)

Sherif asked his subjects to make judgments as to how far the light seemed to be moving. Different subjects tended to develop different, though stable, ranges for their estimates. Some estimates were in the ¼-inch to 2-inch range, for example, while others ranged from 5 to 7 inches. However, when several people with differing individual ranges were brought together, the group quickly established its own range, which was an average of the individual ranges. After only a few trials, Sherif found that he could easily get subjects to change their estimates by placing accomplices in the room with the subjects. This proved true even when the purported judgments of the accomplices varied widely from the subjects' individual range. Sherif thus demonstrated a clear instance of conformity: subjects' judgments changed when faced with the differing judgments of one or more others.

Asch: The Length of Lines Solomon Asch (1951) approached conformity in a different way. He felt that Sherif's research had misrepresented people as blind conformists. He believed that the subjects had conformed only because of the built-in ambiguity of the autokinetic effect. He reasoned that with a clear object of perception, subjects in groups would show much less conformity in judgment.

To test his ideas, Asch devised a set of simple and elegant experiments. His subjects were shown a pair of white cards (see Figure 16.6). On one card was a single black vertical line. On the other card were three vertical lines of differing lengths. The subject's task was to judge which of those three lines exactly matched the standard line on the other card. It was an easy task because two of the

lines were appreciably longer or shorter than the standard line. When subjects made their judgments alone, without group pressure, they almost never made an error.

In a group judgment situation, the subject's estimates were made after each of five other group members gave their judgments. The elegant twist in Asch's setup was that all of the members of the group, except for one real subject, were his accomplices. On the first couple of trials, the confederates behaved normally. Like the subject, they gave the correct answer when shown each pair of cards. Beginning with the third trial and on several later trials, however, the confederates all gave a prearranged incorrect answer, selecting lines that were obviously much too long or much too short. What would happen when the subject's senses indicated one thing and the group indicated something else? Would the subject stick to the perceptual evidence or conform to group opinion, no matter how obviously wrong?

Asch reported that subjects conformed to the group's incorrect judgment on more than one third of the trials. Indeed, more than 80 percent of all subjects conformed on at least one trial (see Figure 16.7). Thus, Asch had proved himself wrong: indeed, subjects did conform even when there was virtually unmistakable perceptual evidence upon which to base their judgments.

Information versus Reinforcement: Two Different Processes

Subjects in both the Sherif and Asch experiments conformed—but for different reasons. In the Sherif

FIGURE 16.6 Cards used in Asch's conformity experiments. After viewing card *A*, the subject is asked to pick the line from card *B* that matches card *A*.

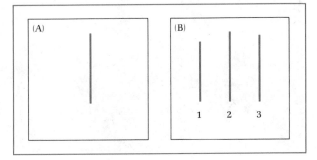

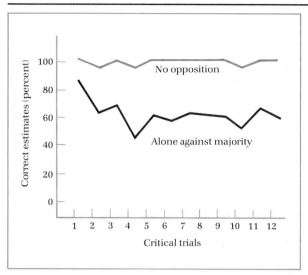

FIGURE 16.7 Asch's experiments clearly demonstrate conformity to group judgment. When the group told the truth (correct identification), the subject also answered correctly, as shown by the "No opposition" curve. However, when the group deliberately gave incorrect answers, the subject often conformed to the group's incorrect judgment, as shown in the "Alone against majority" curve.

procedure the autokinetic situation was so ambiguous that subjects were impelled to look to the judgments of others. The others served as useful sources of information: the subjects were under informational social influence.

On the other hand, the subjects in the Asch experiments needed no informational cues. The relative lengths of the lines were not ambiguous and were easily judged when the subjects were alone. The subjects were under a different social influence, that of reinforcement. They conformed because of the rewards and punishments that could be administered by others. Conforming gave them the rewarding feeling of going along with the group, of acceptance by others. By conforming they avoided the possibility of rejection by group members. Remember from our earlier discussion of the deviance experiments how harshly groups treat deviance. Under reinforcement influence, people tend to conform to the standards of their group whether it be a fraternity, football team, or a board of directors, even when they feel the group might be wrong.

As we noted at the beginning of this section, reinforcement influence leads to public compliance but not internal change. This was clear when Asch's subjects were removed from the group situation and asked to make individual judgments. They immediately reverted to their earlier, correct judgments: their conformity to the group had involved public compliance not internal change. On the other hand, for the Sherif subjects, the informational impact of the group judgments left a mark. They continued to conform to the group judgments even in the absence of the others: there had been internalized change.

The difference in process between the two conformity experiments is also demonstrated by the differing effects of anonymity. Asch's subjects made

People tend to conform to the standards of their group, such as a board of directors, even when they feel that the group might be wrong.

their judgments in a face-to-face setting. When the subjects make their judgments anonymously (that is, when they are placed in private rooms where they can hear the judgments of others but no one is seen or identified by name), conformity drops off dramatically (Deutsch and Gerard, 1955). No such effect would be expected in the Sherif procedure. In fact, his subjects did make their judgments anonymously: subjects were in a dark room and could not identify each other. When we accept information from others as evidence of reality, we use the information regardless of whether we are in public or alone.

Factors Affecting Conformity

In addition to anonymity, several other factors can affect conformity as it develops through informational and reinforcement social influence.

Ambiguity When the subject is under informational influence, uncertainty about the correct judgment leads the individual to look to others for information. Ambiguity thus has a major effect on conformity. Any increase in ambiguity should increase conformity, whereas decreases in ambiguity decrease conformity. Asch (1951), in a variation on his initial experiment, demonstrated this effect quite clearly. He found that as the lengths of the three test lines were made more similar, increasing the difficulty or ambiguity of the task, conformity also increased markedly.

Self-Confidence Another factor affecting conformity through informational influence is the confidence of subjects in their own ability to make accurate judgments. Conformity decreases in the group situation when subjects are first told they are very accurate in individual judgments. Conversely, conformity increases when subjects are told they are terrible at the task (Samelson, 1957). Varying the perceived competence of the confederates in the group also affects the confidence and the resulting conformity of the subject (Mausner, 1954). If, for example, the confederate in the Sherif procedure were introduced as a graduate student in visual perception, conformity would increase. It would decrease if the confederate were presented as a high school student with bad eyes.

Group Goals One factor affecting conformity through the power of the group to reward or punish is the salience of the group's goals. For example, using the Asch procedure, Morton Deutsch and Harold Gerard (1955) introduced an attractive group goal. Subjects were told that each member of the five groups making the fewest total errors would receive a pair of tickets to a play. This goal induced a mutual dependence among the group members. The fact that each member cared more about the performance of others led to a large increase in conformity.

Allies A second factor affecting the reinforcing power of the group—and hence conformity—is the presence of allies. When Asch (1951) provided the subject with a confederate who always gave the right answer no matter what the other accomplices did, conformity was drastically reduced. Two possibilities account for this effect: (1) having at least one ally reduces the likelihood of rejection by the group, and (2) if rejection does occur, one can at least share the deviant state with a friend and partner.

Cohesiveness Finally, the cohesiveness of the group—that is, the attraction that members have for the group and for each other—influences conformity through reinforcement. Leonard Berkowitz (1954) established groups that were either high or low in cohesiveness. He did this by telling the groups that they had been preselected and had been put together because of their congeniality and the scientific prediction that they would like each other (high cohesiveness) or that it had been impossible to arrange a congenial group (low cohesiveness). The task of each group was to produce checkerboards made of cardboard. Although subjects worked alone in separate rooms, they could communicate with other members of their group by writing notes. The experimenter manipulated the conditions by intercepting the notes written by the subjects and substituting his own. In one condition, the notes requested the subjects to work hard and raise productivity. In the other condition, subjects were urged to slow down and not work so hard. Which groups conformed more significantly to the apparent wishes of other members? Relative to those in the low-cohesiveness groups, subjects in high-cohesiveness groups greatly increased productivity when asked to do so and greatly decreased productivity when asked to do that. The greater the cohesiveness of a group, the greater the tendency was for individual members to accept influence from others in the group.

Degree of conformity is influenced by many different factors. Reinforcement in the form of punishment brings about public compliance but not private acceptance, and information brings about both public compliance and changes in internalized attitudes and beliefs. Anonymity, ambiguity, self-confidence, the importance of group goals, the presence of allies, and the cohesiveness of the group all have important effects on conformity.

In addition to affecting how we define events, other people are also instrumental in helping us to define ourselves.

Learning About Ourselves

We already have discussed several examples of social influence in which others help us to define events. In bystander intervention, for example, the behavior of others helps us to decide whether an emergency is actually in progress. In conformity, the social comparison process provides information that influences our judgments about exterior phenomena. Social psychology also studies how others help us learn about ourselves and, indeed, help us define ourselves.

Clearly, social comparison is one way we define our own opinions, abilities, judgments, and emotions. Take a simple example of athletic ability. If you want to know how good you are at tennis, you compare your performance on the court with the performance of others. Let us consider several other ways in which others help define us.

How Others Treat Us

We can learn about ourselves by looking at how others treat us (Mead, 1934). Their treatment presumably reflects their evaluation of us, which in turn shapes our evaluations of ourselves.

This process is demonstrated clearly in an experiment by Robert Kraut (1973). The experimenter, posing as a door-to-door canvasser, approached residents of a middle-class neighborhood and asked them to donate money to a charitable agency. Half of those who donated money received an explicit label from the experimenter: "You are a generous person. I wish more of the people I met were as charitable as you." The other half who donated money were not labeled in any way. Similarly, half of those who did not donate received no label and the other half were directly labeled as uncharitable: "Let me give you one of our health leaflets anyway. We've been giving them to everyone, even people like you who are uncharitable and don't normally give to these causes."

Thus, half of the donors and half of the nondonors received explicit information about the canvasser's evaluation of them. How did these evaluations affect the subjects? A week to two weeks later, the same subjects were approached by a second experimenter, who was posing as a canvasser for another charitable agency. Those donors who previously had been labeled as charitable gave more money to this campaign than did donors who had not been labeled. Similarly, those who had not donated the first time, and who had been labeled as uncharitable, gave less than did the nondonors who had not been labeled. In sum, the evaluation by the first canvasser had apparently affected the subject's own self-image and hence the likelihood that the person would or would not donate to other agencies.

Self-Perception

Another way in which we can learn about ourselves is by observing our own behavior. For example, you walk home from a party, glance at your watch and, amazed at how late it is, remark to yourself, "Gee, I must have had a good time. Look how late I stayed." Or you eat a surprisingly large amount of food at dinner and exclaim, "I must have been hungrier than I thought."

Daryl Bem (1972) proposed a *theory of self-perception* to account for such phenomena: "Individuals come to know their own attitudes, emotions and other internal states partially by inferring them from observations of their own overt behavior and/or the circumstances in which this behavior occurs."

Observing One's Own Behavior Self-perception processes have been demonstrated in another door-to-door canvassing experiment (Freedman and Fraser, 1966). The experimenter, posing as a canvasser, approached a number of homeowners and asked them to sign a petition promoting safe driving. It was a small request, and almost everyone who was asked complied. Later, these same subjects were approached by a second canvasser who asked them to comply with a more demanding request: they were asked to place on their front lawns a large, unattractive sign that said, "Drive

Carefully." To provide a control group, the experimenter made the same request of some homeowners who had not been approached with the small initial request. Those people who had complied with the first request were more likely to agree to the larger request than were the control group subjects. In the process of complying with the first request, the subjects observed themselves as being "concerned citizens." This self-perception made them more willing to go along with the more demanding request.

This phenomenon has links to the conventional wisdom of door-to-door salespeople who claim that if they can merely "get their foot in the door" (that is, get the homeowner to comply with the small request of letting them in the house), they can subsequently make their sale.

How the self-perception process can lead to inferences about one's internal state is shown in a fascinating study by Stuart Valins (1966). Here, male subjects observed what they believed to be their own physiological reactions to external stimuli. They were rigged up with electrodes that supposedly measured heart rate. Then they were shown several centerfold photographs of nudes from *Playboy* magazine. As they viewed the pictures, the subjects were permitted to listen to what was purported to be their "amplified heartbeat." Actually, the sound was simulated by the experimenter and arranged so that the "heartbeat" increased when the subject was viewing certain of the nudes. Later, the subjects were asked to rate the attractiveness of each nude and asked which of the photos they would like to take home as a reward for participating in the experiment. The subjects liked best the photos that supposedly had stimulated increases in their heart rate. By observing their own physiological behavior, albeit bogus, they inferred how they must have felt toward each photo.

Overjustification: Too Much Reward In self-perception we learn something about ourselves because of behavior that we attributed to internal forces. We also can learn about ourselves when we attribute the behavior to some strong external force. Suppose someone asks you to read ten books and promises you a reward for doing so. If you agree to the request, chances are that you will attribute your compliance to the promise of reward. But what if you would have read those books anyway without the offer of reward? Research indicates that you would still attribute your compliance to the reward

and, as a result, grow to like the activity less. If it took a reward to get you to perform the activity, then you must not like it.

This phenomenon is called *overjustification* because the reward provides too large an external justification for performing a behavior. Overjustification was convincingly demonstrated in an experiment by Mark Lepper, David Greene, and Richard Nisbett (1973). The experimenter observed children in a nursery school and selected as subjects those who played with felt pens a great deal during free-play period. Thus, all the subjects already had an intrinsic interest in playing with felt pens. Each of the children was asked to draw a picture with some felt pens. There were three different conditions. In the "Expected Reward" condition, the children were told that as a reward for drawing the picture, they would be given a "Good Player Award," an attractive certificate with colored ribbons. In the "No Reward" condition, the children heard nothing of a reward. In the "Unexpected Reward" condition, the children were given a "Good Player Award" after drawing the picture, but the reward was unexpected: it had not been mentioned beforehand.

Several days later the experimenter observed these same children in the nursery school and recorded the amount of time each spent with the felt pens during the free-play period. The children in the "Expected Reward" condition played with the felt pens significantly less than did the children who had heard nothing of a reward or received the reward unexpectedly. The researchers concluded that agreeing to draw the picture in order to earn a reward undermined the child's intrinsic interest in working with the felt markers. In effect, these children, by attributing their behavior to the external reward, learned that they were not really all that interested in the activity itself.

The experimental findings are an example of how rewards can sometimes produce atypical effects. To understand the negative effects of reward, it is necessary to understand the difference between extrinsic rewards and intrinsic rewards. Extrinsic rewards, such as trophies, prize money, applause of an audience, and praise, are those received as a result of performing an action. Intrinsic rewards, on the other hand, derive from the process of carrying out an action. For example, children are intrinsically motivated to learn; they find learning and discovery rewarding in their own right (Deci, 1975). We saw earlier that rewards usually increase the likelihood of one's performing the rewarded behavior. But here, at least in the condition where the reward was expected and the activity served as a means of obtaining the reward, just the opposite occurred. Apparently, if one is already intrinsically interested in the activity, the perception that one is performing the activity in order to obtain a reward can undermine that intrinsic interest. We can even sometimes learn about what it is that we do not like by observing that it seems to take a strong external force to get us to perform the behavior.

Intentional Social Influence

Most of the examples of social influence we have discussed thus far represent *unintentional social influence.* They are instances where others arouse us, reinforce us, or serve as sources of information inadvertently. But other people often clearly intend to influence us. Police give orders they clearly expect us to obey. Advertisers try to persuade us to buy their products. Politicians attempt to talk us into voting for them. We will examine next some instances of such *intentional social influence.*

Obedience to Authority

The most obvious and perhaps the most effective form of intentional social influence is a directive issued by an authority figure. Millions of people have died in wars because of the willingness to obey orders blindly and to kill others. This process of blind obedience to authority has been explored by Stanley Milgram (1963) in a research program widely publicized because of its relevance to events in Nazi Germany. For example, Adolph Eichmann, a Nazi official during World War II, justified his role in the deaths of hundreds of thousands of Jews by saying he was simply obeying orders.

Working at Yale University in the early 1960s, Milgram created an ingenious experimental design to measure obedience. He used the cover story that the purpose of the experiment was to investigate "the effects of punishment on learning." Subjects were told that they would serve as the teachers. They asked the learner—ostensibly another subject—a series of questions involving word pairs and then punished any mistakes with an electric shock. The shock apparatus contained a number of levers with the voltage level indicated above each lever. The voltages ranged in 15-volt increments from 15

volts to 450 volts, with the lower range labeled "Slight Shock" and the upper range labeled "Danger: Severe Shock." The highest level bore the label *XXX.* Subjects were told that each time the learner erred or failed to respond they should increase the shock level by 15 volts.

The learner was strapped into a chair in the next room with electrodes connected to the wrists. The learner was a fake, of course, an accomplice of the experimenter, and received no electric shocks. It had been prearranged for the learner to make many errors and to respond to the supposed escalation of shocks in a predescribed manner. At 90 volts, the learner began to cry out in pain; at 150 volts, the learner asked to be let out of the experiment. At 180 volts, the learner banged on the wall, and at 285 volts, screamed in agony. At 330 volts and thereafter, through the 450-volt limit, there was only ominous silence.

The authority in this setting was the researcher, who sat next to the subject. In a white lab coat, the experimenter, in effect, personified the authority of "science." Subjects were not physically coerced into administering shocks. If the subjects hesitated in raising the shock level, the experimenter prodded them to proceed with instructions such as, "The experiment requires that you continue."

How would you respond in this situation? Before he conducted the experiments, Milgram suspected that only a few of his subjects would be willing to obey all the way to the 450-volt limit. As it turned out, nearly two thirds of Milgram's subjects—teachers, salespeople, laborers, clerks—obeyed the experimenter all the way and delivered the maximum shock of 450 volts (see Figure 16.8). To Milgram, the lesson of the study was that "ordinary people, simply doing their jobs, and without any particular hostility on their parts, can become agents in a terrible destructive process." (Milgram, 1974).

In further research, Milgram (1974) attempted to examine what variables affect the level of obedience to an authority figure. One variable was the "psychological distance" between subject and learner. The closer the subject was to the learner, the lower the obedience level. Subjects obeyed most when they could neither see nor hear the learner's reactions to the shocks; they obeyed least when the subject was required actually to hold the learner's hand on a shock plate in order to deliver the punishment.

A second variable was the "psychological dis-

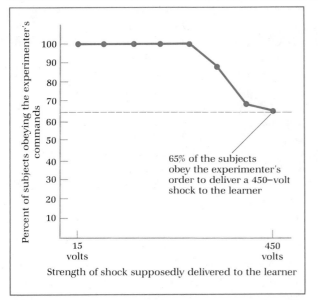

65% of the subjects obey the experimenter's order to deliver a 450–volt shock to the learner

FIGURE 16.8 The process of blind obedience to authority was demonstrated by Stanley Milgram. As shown, a high percentage of the subjects obeyed the experimenter's commands that they deliver electric shocks to another person. Fully 65 percent continued to obey all the way to the 450-volt shock.

tance" between the subject and the authority figure. The greater the distance from the experimenter, the less the obedience level. Obedience was least when the experimenter delivered instructions to the subject via a tape recorder and was never actually seen by the subject. Interestingly, in the absence of the experimenter, several subjects disobeyed orders by using only the lowest level of shock: they were willing to undermine the experiment but not create an open break with authority.

Many critics in and out of the scientific community have raised questions about the ethics of Milgram's experiment. In fact, when Milgram's book, *Obedience to Authority*, was published in 1974, the *New York Times* Sunday reviewer was so incensed at the method used in the research that he virtually ignored the findings. The principal criticism was that the subjects were led under false pretenses into behavior likely to burden them with guilt. In reply, Milgram has pointed out that immediately after the experiment each subject was informed of the true purpose and given emotional support, whether the subject had obeyed or disobeyed. A follow-up questionnaire administered some time later found that only 1.3 percent of the subjects expressed regret at having participated in the experiment, whereas 83.7 percent were glad.

Furthermore, a university psychiatrist interviewed 40 of the subjects and reported no evidence of emotional harm. In fact, many of these subjects said their participation in the experiment had been an enriching and instructive experience.

Persuasion: Changing Attitudes by Changing Perceptions

Another major form of intentional social influence is *persuasion*. Unlike orders from an authority figure, which aim directly at our behavior, persuasion aims only indirectly at changing our behavior. Persuasion aims first at changing our attitudes; attitude change, it is hoped, will lead to behavior change. Advertisers trust that, by persuading us of the worth of their products and thus changing our attitudes, we will be led to purchase those wares.

An *attitude* represents a categorization of an object along an evaluative dimension. The object can be an actual physical object, another person, or some issue, and the attitude represents one's degree of favorability. Social psychologists typically measure attitudes by having subjects judge objects on scales that range from "good" to "bad" or "agree" to "disagree."

It is obvious that we all have attitudes. Just think about how often you have been asked questions of this sort: "How was the movie?" "Do you like Joe?" "Do you want to see marijuana legalized?" An important issue that arises is why we form attitudes and what use they are to us. The most common answer is one that centers upon the "knowledge function" that attitudes serve (Katz, 1960; Smith, Bruner, and White, 1956). Attitudes help us to categorize the complex social environments in which we live. They are functional in the sense that they serve to simplify our environment. "Objects" are classified as "good" or "bad," and hence the behavior of these "objects" and additional qualities that they might possess are more easily predicted.

How are attitudes formed? They can be formed in any number of different ways, some of which we have already discussed. Attitudes can be formed through social comparison processes, through the informational social influence that all groups of which we are members can have upon us, and through self-perception processes. Socialization, in particular socialization by parents, undoubtedly exerts an influence upon attitude formation. For example, children tend to adopt the same political party affiliation selected by their parents.

Attitudes also form through classical conditioning processes (see Chapter 7). Objects continuously associated with bad events take on negative value; those associated with positive events become valued positively. For example, Mark Zanna, Charles Kiesler, and Paul Pilkonis (1970) demonstrated that words that signaled shock onset for a subject came to be viewed more negatively than words that signaled shock offset. Such a process is clearly not unfamiliar to commercial advertisers, who frequently attempt to associate a catchy jingle or a pleasant musical score with their product.

Attitudes also are formed by the familiarity of the object to the individual. Zajonc (1968) has demonstrated that frequency of exposure encourages positive attitudes toward the object. He found, for example, that students subsequently liked other students depicted in yearbook photographs to which they had been exposed frequently more than they liked those whose photographs they had seen less frequently. This hypothesis that familiarity, or frequency of exposure, shapes attitudes was given a clever test by Theodore Mita, Marshall Dermer, and Jeffrey Knight (1977). The experiment hinged on the fact that individuals typically see the mirror image of their faces while friends see the true image. Photographs of the subjects were reproduced in two ways: one showed the subject's true image and the other the subject's mirror image. Given a choice, the subjects preferred the mirror-image photo—the only image to which they had been exposed previously. However, friends of the subjects tended to select the true-image photo—the image to which they had been exposed previously.

The principle by which frequency of exposure, and thus familiarity, produces favorable attitudes is often used by commercial advertisers. Advertisers introducing a new product are likely to blitz television and various print media with their name and visual image in hopes that familiarity will breed increased sales.

Attitude change through persuasion depends to a great extent on the communicator, the source of the persuasive message. What characteristics of the communicator tend to promote attitude change? Credibility is one characteristic.

Credibility of the Communicator To test the effects of credibility, researchers exposed two groups of subjects to the same persuasive message concerning the practicality of building nuclear submarines (Hovland and Weiss, 1952). In one condition, the message was attributed to the eminent physicist, J. Robert Oppenheimer. In the other condition, it was attributed to the official Russian Communist party newspaper *Pravda*. The more credible source, Oppenheimer, produced more attitude change. Communicator credibility, additional research has shown, consists of two important components: expertise and trustworthiness. Oppenheimer, the physicist, was perceived as more expert in the field of atomic energy than was *Pravda*. He also was perceived as more trustworthy—that is, less likely to be making statements for purposes of propaganda than would *Pravda*.

The use of experts as communicators is common in television commercials. Who can better extol the virtues of a particular tennis racquet than a professional tennis player, for example? Trustworthiness is a more subtle component of credibility. Is the communicator sincere? Does she or he have ulterior motives? Another study demonstrated how the perceived trustworthiness of an individual varies depending upon his or her message (Walters, Aronson, and Abrahams, 1966). A fictitious Mafia extortionist, Joe "The Shoulder" Napolitano, said to be currently in prison, argued that courts were too strict in sentencing criminals. Joe's trustworthiness was clearly in doubt: he obviously had an ulterior motive in advocating less stringent sentencing procedures. In this condition, Joe produced no attitude change. The result was different, however, when Joe argued that the courts were too lenient with criminals. He was taking a position in opposition to his own self-interest and the subjects perceived him as being sincere and trustworthy. In this case he produced a great deal of attitude change.

Television advertising often manipulates the perceived trustworthiness of the communicators to enhance their persuasiveness. For example, commercials sometimes make use of a hidden-camera ploy to create the impression that the communicator has nothing to gain by endorsing the product. Similarly, in political advertising, the camera eavesdrops upon candidates in situations where they appear to be talking privately, and hence candidly, to a friend.

Attractiveness of the Communicator. Attractiveness is a second important characteristic of effective communicators. A number of experiments have demonstrated that the more attractive the communicator, the greater the change in attitudes. Television advertising's most frequently used ploy is probably the attractive and sexy celebrity who endorses a given product.

There is an important difference between attractiveness and the other communicator characteristic we have discussed—credibility. Changing attitudes through credibility is the more rational process in which the expertise and trustworthiness of the communicator are judged. Attitude change through attractiveness stems from a desire to be similar to those we admire.

The distinction between credibility and attractiveness is nicely illustrated in a recent experiment by Ross Norman (1976). The subjects, all females, read a message that advocated sleeping less than the typical eight hours a night. For half of the subjects, this assertion was supported by some plausible arguments; for the other half, there were no arguments in support of the message. In addition, half of the subjects were led to believe that the author of the message was highly credible—a 43-year-old professor of physiological psychology who had recently coauthored a book on sleep. These subjects were shown a picture of an unattractive, middle-aged man. The other subjects were led to believe that the author was not an expert but a highly attractive 20-year-old male undergraduate who was athletic and musical and recently was elected to the student government council. These subjects were shown a picture of a smiling, physically attractive young man.

Which characteristic proved to be more important, credibility or attractiveness? The attractive communicator produced attitude change in favor of less sleep regardless of whether or not he presented arguments to support his assertion. The other communicator was effective in producing attitude change only when he presented arguments to support his assertion.

Dissonance: Changing Attitudes by Changing Behavior

Intentional social influence can take yet another form. As we have seen, persuasion aims at changing a person's behavior by first changing attitudes. But it is also possible for a person to change your attitude by first getting you to perform a behavior that is inconsistent with that attitude.

This phenomenon is explained by Festinger's *theory of cognitive dissonance* (1957). Like balance theory, Festinger's theory assumes that people prefer consistency. Dissonance theory and research emphasize consistency between people's attitudes and their behavior. The theory proposes that when individuals behave in a manner inconsistent with their attitudes they experience *dissonance*, an unpleasant state of tension. Individuals can reduce the state of dissonance in either of two ways. One is to reduce the number of inconsistent cognitions—for example, by changing the relevant attitude. The other is to increase the number of consistent cognitions—for example, by concluding that they were "forced" to perform the behavior.

In one of the earliest experimental tests of the theory of cognitive dissonance, Festinger and J. Merrill Carlsmith (1959) had subjects perform a very dull and boring task: the subjects had to place a large number of spools on pegs on a board, turn each spool a quarter turn, take the spool off the pegs and then put them back on. As you can imagine, subjects' attitudes toward this task were highly negative. The subjects were then induced to tell a female "subject," who was actually an accomplice of the experimenter, that this boring task she would be performing was really interesting and enjoyable. Some of the subjects were offered $20 to tell this falsehood; others were offered only $1. Almost all of the subjects agreed to walk into the waiting room and persuade the subject-accomplice that the boring experiment would be fun.

Obviously, there is a discrepancy here between attitudes and behavior. Although the task was boring, subjects tried to convince another person it was fun. Why? To the subjects who received $20, the reason was clear: they wanted the money. The larger payment provided an important external justification consistent with the counterattitudinal behavior. There was no dissonance, and the subjects experienced no need to change their attitudes. But for the subjects who received only $1, there was much less external justification and more dissonance. How could subjects reduce the dissonance? They could do so by changing their attitude toward the task. This is exactly what happened. When the subjects were asked to evaluate the experiment, the subjects who were paid only $1 rated the tedious task as more fun and enjoyable than did either the subjects who were paid $20 to lie or the subjects in

When we commit ourselves to a decision such as buying a car, choosing a college, or even making a small wager on a horse, we sometimes experience initial second thoughts about the decision. By choosing Alternative X, we have given up all the positive qualities of the other alternative—the sleek lines of Car Y, for example. In addition, we call to mind some of the negative aspects of the chosen alternative X. Because these misgivings are inconsistent with our behavior of selecting a particular option, we experience cognitive dissonance, an unpleasant state of tension.

According to Festinger's theory of cognitive dissonance, one way in which we reduce this postdecisional conflict is by changing our thinking so as to increase the attractiveness of the choice to which we are already committed. A number of investigations of this theoretical proposition have been conducted in the laboratory, but Robert Knox and James Inkster (1968) wanted to test postdecisional dissonance as it occurs in real-life behavior in a natural setting. The setting they selected was the racetrack; the behavior was that of $2 bettors.

Knox and Inkster reasoned that $2 bettors have to make decisions about which horse they think will win the race, then commit themselves to that choice by going to the parimutuel window and placing their bets. If Festinger's theory is correct, once a person has placed a bet, postdecisional dissonance should arise and attempts should be made to reduce this dissonance by increasing the attractiveness of the chosen horse. In short, the bettor ought to feel more confident that the chosen horse will win after placing the bet than before placing it.

To test this experimental hypothesis, the two researchers interviewed 141 bettors at the Exhibition Park racetrack in Vancouver, British Columbia. Of these subjects, 69 were interviewed less than 30 seconds *before* making a $2 bet to win; 72 were interviewed a few seconds *after* making a $2 bet to win. In the interview, each subject was asked to rate on a 7-point scale his or her horse's chances of winning the race. "Never mind now what the tote board or professional handicappers say," each subject was instructed. "What chance do *you* think your horse has?" The rating scale shown to the subject ranged from 1 (slight chance to win) through 7 (excellent chance to win).

The results of these interviews appeared to confirm the researchers' hypothesis. The median rating given by the subjects in the prebet group was 3.48—only a little above a "fair" chance of winning. In the postbet group, by contrast, the subjects gave a median rating of 4.81; they rated the chances of their horse winning as close to "good." The table below shows the number of subjects in each group who believed that their chances of winning were above or below the overall median.

	PREBET GROUP	POSTBET GROUP
Above the median	25	45
Below the median	44	27

Though the results accorded with their predictions from dissonance theory, Knox and Inkster realized that the results might conceivably have been attributable to another factor. A substantial number of their postbet subjects might simply have made last-minute switches from relative long shots to favorites. If so, this could account for the greater confidence expressed by the postbet group. However, the researchers talked with a number of bettors on other days at the racetrack and found virtually no evidence to support this "switch-to-favorites" explanation. Moreover, in a second experiment at another racetrack, in which Knox and Inkster were able to replicate their general findings from the first experiment, none of the postbet subjects indicated that he or she had switched to the favorite just before placing the bet in question.

Thus the results of experiments at two different racetracks provided support for Festinger's notion of postdecisional reduction of dissonance. Bettors tended to feel more confident about their horse after committing their money than before. And this reduction in dissonance occurred very rapidly, no more than 30 seconds after the bet.

The authors summed up the overall effect observed in their research by citing the reaction of one subject in their first experiment. This subject had been interviewed by one researcher before he placed his bet. After making his bet, he approached the other experimenter and said: "Are you working with that other fellow there? Well, I just told him that my horse had a fair chance of winning. Will you have him change that to a good chance? No, by God, make that an excellent chance." The belief that his horse had an excellent chance to win obviously made the bettor feel better. "In the human race," the authors concluded, "dissonance had won again."

a control group who were not required to lie about the task. Since the external justification—the $1 payment—was too low to justify the counterattitudinal behavior, the subjects simply changed their attitudes to make them consistent with behavior.

Cognitive dissonance theory also suggests another way in which behavior influences attitudes. This is the notion of *effort justification;* that is, people like what they have chosen to suffer for. This notion was demonstrated in an interesting experiment by Aronson and Judson Mills (1959). College women were invited to join a group that supposedly was discussing various aspects of sex. Before the students could join, however, they had to undergo a screening process. For some of the subjects, this screening involved nothing more than reading aloud a number of ordinary but sexually related words. In the severe initiation condition, however, the subjects had to read aloud some rather embarrassing material: a list of obscene words and two very explicit descriptions of sexual activity. Dissonance is created in this condition. The cognitions—that one does not like to be embarrased but nonetheless has engaged in embarrassing behavior—are discrepant. A third group did not have to undergo any screening process. Then all the subjects in all three conditions listened to what was ostensibly a discussion by the group they were joining. Actually what they heard was a tape-recorded discussion of "secondary sex behavior in lower animals" that was intended to be very dull. Afterward, the subjects were asked to rate the club and the discussion. Those who underwent little or no effort to get into the group rated the discussion as it actually was—dull and boring. But the subjects who underwent the severe initiation procedure rated the discussion and the club quite high. In short, the greater the effort expended in order to join the group, the more attractive the group seemed. By convincing themselves that the club was worthwhile, subjects justified the effort and reduced dissonance: they came to like what they had "suffered" for.

One interesting implication of this effort justification effect concerns the marketing of new products. Dissonance theory suggests that, whenever we purchase a product, we feel a need to justify our expenditure of effort, that is, our expenditure of money. The more we pay for the product, the more we should come to like it. New products, however, are often introduced at a low price or with a coupon-discount offer. Purchases are then likely to be justified by the low price rather than the attractiveness of the product.

A study of the relation between dissonance theory and the actual marketing of new products was conducted by Doob and his colleagues (Doob, Carlsmith, Freedman, Landauer, and Toms, 1969). They arranged for the introduction of a number of products such as mouthwash and toothpaste at a number of different stores. In half the stores, the product was introduced at its regular price; in others, it was sold at a discount. Predictably, more sales occurred at the "discount stores" than at the "regular-price stores." After awhile, however, the discount offer was ended and all stores began to sell the product at the standard price. Now the sales trend was reversed. Over the next 20 weeks, the stores where it had not been discounted in the beginning sold more of the product than the stores that had initially offered the discount (see Figure 16.9). Thus, in the long run, introducing the product at its regular price produced more sales than introducing the product at a discount. According to dissonance

FIGURE 16.9 Demonstration of dissonance theory. Introducing a product (in this case, mouthwash) at its regular price and maintaining that price, as shown by the dashed line, is more effective in the long run than introducing it at a discount price and then raising it to the regular price, as shown by the solid line.

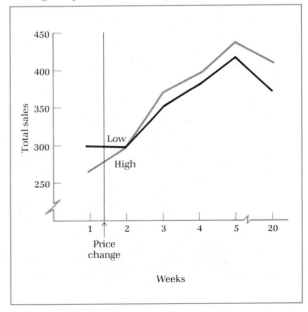

theory, the greater "effort" expenditure involved in paying more for the product led those people who initially purchased the product at the regular price to persuade themselves of the product's value, and, hence, to purchase the product on a regular, long-term basis. Their behavior— buying at the regular price—had affected their attitudes toward the product, and this new attitude in turn had influenced later behavior.

Brainwashing: Extreme Social Influence

An extreme form of intentional social influence is the process widely known as *brainwashing*. The term first was used during the late 1940s to describe the attempts of Chinese Communists to change the political thinking of the Nationalist Chinese and, during the Korean War, of American and other Western prisoners of war. More recently, it has been applied to the political conversion of the young heiress, Patricia Hearst, after she was kidnapped by the Symbionese Liberation Army (SLA) in 1974. The young revolutionaries of the SLA considered her "a prisoner of war." During her captivity, she underwent marked changes. About the time she was released by the SLA, Patty Hearst renounced her former life and identity and announced that she had changed her name to Tania and joined her captors. She took part in a bank robbery, helped other SLA members escape from another robbery, and eluded arrest for nearly two years. When finally captured, she listed her occupation as "urban guerrilla." Then, over the next year, another transformation

FOCUS: The Process of Religious Conversion

One of the most fascinating social phenomena of the past decade has been the conversion of large numbers of Americans, especially young people, to fringe religious cults. For example, during this period about 10,000 young Americans have abandoned their past social ties and identities to become followers of the Unification Church of the Reverend Sun Myung Moon.

The most dramatic instance of religious conversion involved the members of the People's Temple, a California cult that emigrated to the jungles of Guyana. There, in November 1978, members of the cult dutifully lined up and, upon the orders of their

In 1978 at Jonestown Guyana, the members of the People's Temple followed the orders of their leader, Jim Jones, and committed mass suicide.

leader, Jim Jones, took cups of a soft drink spiked with cyanide poison. Parents squirted the poison into the mouths of infants and children, then drank some themselves. Nearly 800 people, including 200 children, died in this bizarre and shocking mass suicide.

The tragic drama at Jonestown suggests that some occult trauma must be at work in converting people into true believers willing to give up their money, their past identities, and even their lives. We can easily conjure up visions of converts to the People's Temple or to the Unification Church, being kidnapped, drugged, and tortured. But, in fact, evidence suggests otherwise. People become true believers through many of the same processes of social influence that affect the behavior of us all. For example, conversion to the Unification Church usually begins with a low-key exercise in friendly persuasion—an invitation to dinner. This pleasant meal is followed by a further invitation to spend a weekend on a quiet and lovely farm.

The potential convert is confronted with a cohesive group of happy, attractive, young people who appear to be supportive, open, and friendly. This is especially persuasive to potential converts who are uncertain about their own identities and are experiencing anxiety. (Recruiters often station themselves in campus libraries during exam time, a period of great student stress.) If the person has been religious in the past, the cult will likely be particularly attractive.

Another key factor is the isolation of the potential

occurred, and Patty seemed to revert to her prekid-napping identity as an unaffected young woman.

How can we account for the dramatic changes in attitudes and behavior Patty Hearst underwent during captivity? As was true in the case of the Communist Chinese prisoner-of-war camps, our first impulse is to assume that brainwashing consists of coercive techniques of mind control and body abuse such as drug use, hypnosis, torture, and sexual abuse. However, several analyses (Szasz, 1976; Schein, Schneier, and Barker, 1961) have questioned whether the techniques involved in brainwashing are actually so radical or extreme. In fact, other commentators (Zimbardo, Ebbesen, and Maslach, 1977; Lifton, 1963) view brainwashing in terms of traditional methods of intentional social influence

such as simple persuasion. (Many of these same methods are involved in the process of religious conversion; see Focus.) They suggest several factors that determine the effectiveness of brainwashing, including victim vulnerability, milieu control, the cohesiveness and attractiveness of the captors, and the ability to come to a confession.

- *Victim Vulnerability.* Patty Hearst lacked a strongly held and well-thought-out set of political beliefs and was thus vulnerable to the dogmatic ideology of her captors. In addition, her wealth made her susceptible to guilt about the poor and

---

convert so that all other sources of social influence are removed. The weekend on the Moonie farm ensures there will be no social contact with noncultists. Similarly, the People's Temple moved from San Francisco to remote Guyana to isolate members. The absence of radio, television, and newspapers contributes to a situation in which the only sources of social influence, and hence of information and reinforcement, are the cult members. Moreover, the cults tend to emphasize the here and now, dismissing concerns with the past or the future, and thus further strengthening isolation.

The Reverend Sun Myung Moon (standing at left) plays matchmaker at a mass engagement ceremony in 1981. During a two-day period, more than 840 couples were engaged in this manner. Many of the couples had never met each other before.

Attachment to the group is another important aspect of the conversion process. Passivity and dependency are encouraged, providing a psychological readiness for obedience to the dictates of the group. Cult members are the principal sources of social reinforcement. They freely offer smiles, compliments, and hugs. They profess sadness (though not anger) at the potential convert's "misdirected" thoughts, producing guilt and shame. As the individual identity is submerged into the group, a state of deindividuation develops. The "I" is lost in the "we." Cultists are referred to as "brother" or "sister" rather than by name, increasing the loss of personal identity.

Finally, the success of a cult, and of concomitant conversion, depends on the influence of a powerful and charismatic leader. The members of the cult and the potential convert come to believe that this leader is all-knowing and capable of solving the problems of the members and, indeed, of society. Typically, leaders such as Jim Jones and Sun Myung Moon are flamboyant in their behavior and spellbinding as speakers, filling their oratory with allegory and mysticism.

Once a person actually converts to membership in a cult, commitment gradually intensifies. Members come to perceive the world through the filter of the cult's language and ideas and to view everything in terms of what it means to the cult. Most of the sense of individual identity is lost. Now, any suggestion or perception by the cult leader is accepted without question. Violence and even mass suicide thus can become acceptable behaviors.

oppressed people whom the SLA professed to speak for.

- *Milieu Control.* Like most effect agents of brainwashing, the SLA had total control over the victim's environment. They controlled all sources of information and all reward and punishment. Patty Hearst was exposed daily to the SLA philosophy and rhetoric, but she had no contact with past friends or family and little access to outside information sources such as newspapers and television. The SLA bombarded her with brief, oversimplified, catch phrases that, through their ritual repetition, became familiar to the young woman and hence easy to accept.

- *The Captors.* The members of an effective brainwashing group must be cohesive, committed, and attractive. SLA members appeared strong and attractive and brooked no signs of disbelief or dissension. Thus they quickly became important sources of approval and identification for Patty Hearst.

- *Confession.* An important aspect of brainwashing involves confession of wrongdoing and renunciation of the past. This is all the more effective if the victim retains the illusion of free choice. Patty Hearst believed that her decision to remain with the SLA was made of her own free will. This is consistent with the theory of cognitive dissonance. Joining the SLA obviously created dissonance—in effect, "SLA is a bad organization; I'm not bad." Dissonance could be reduced in either of two ways: if she had been forced to join by threat of severe punishment or if she changed her attitude toward the SLA. In the absence of severe threat, she changed her attitude. This provided internal justification for her behavior and made her such a committed convert that she was willing to become a bank robber.

William McGuire (1964) has suggested that individuals can be made immune to propaganda by being exposed to arguments opponents might use against the ideas they hold. McGuire argues that in much the same way that people can be inoculated against disease with a weakened form of the infectious material to stimulate their biological defense mechanisms prior to exposure to more virulent forms, so, too, can people be inoculated against propaganda by being exposed to weakened forms of the opposition's arguments before they experience the main attack.

To test his idea, McGuire presented college stu-dents with four cultural truisms relating to various health measures, including brushing one's teeth after every meal is desirable, having a physical examination once a year is wise, and eating vegetables every day promotes good health. In the first session, one of the truisms was accompanied by supportive information—for example, that brushing one's teeth after every meal improves one's appearance and destroys decay-causing bacteria. Another truism was accompanied by the equivalent of inoculation, or a weak counterargument and its refutation—for example, some people say that brushing one's teeth too often injures the gums, but dental evidence indicates that brushing actually stimulates and improves the gums. The remaining truisms were controls and were neither attacked nor supported.

Two days later, the subjects were exposed to strong attacks against three of the truisms—the one that had received supportive information, the one that had received inoculation, and one of the control truisms. Analysis of the subjects' attitudes revealed that the undefended truism was highly vulnerable to attack. In contrast, the truism accompanied by supportive information was less vulnerable to attack. But of greatest interest was the fact the the the truism accompanied by inoculation was the least vulnerable to attack. Apparently, the ability to resist propaganda is strengthened when people experience an earlier weak attack. The attack enables them to prepare arguments to support their position, construct counterarguments, and otherwise bolster their defenses.

Although most of the social influences we encounter are considered unintentional, there are some instances when intentional social influence is brought to bear including obedience to directives issued by people in authority and persuasion aimed at changing attitudes, the success of which is influenced by the credibility of the communication and attractiveness of the communicator. Attitudes can also be changed by creating dissonance—a state of tension resulting from a situation in which people behave in a manner that does not coincide with their attitudes. People in this state often change the relevant attitudes in order to create consistency again. Taken to its extreme, intentional social influence becomes brainwashing. Very few people ever experience brainwashing. However, almost everyone falls prey to some of the less extreme forms of intentional social influence on a daily basis.

SUMMARY

1. Social influence is usually a simple, one-way process, in which an individual's actions affect the behavior and attitudes of another. Mutual and reciprocal actions and reactions constitute social interaction.

2. Social psychology examines the most important stimuli in our environments—people, who change as we perceive them. Our behavior is affected by the reactions of others to our actions. Social psychology studies general, as opposed to individual, responses and perceptions. Social perceptions and judgments are not readily quantified.

3. Our behavior is affected by social stimuli through the process of arousal, reward and punishment, and information. The presence of others energizes us and increases our drive level: it arouses us. An increase in drive strengthens the dominant response (the one most likely to occur) of the organism; an increase in drive weakens responses that are already weak. By increasing the dominant response, arousal leads us to better performance on simple and well-learned tasks, but results in diminished performance on hard and complex tasks. The presence of others will most likely increase the dominant response if the audience, or observer, is capable of rating the subject's performance.

4. People serve as real or potential sources of reinforcement—reward or punishment. People may provide primary reinforcers that satisfy basic physiological needs; or they may serve as secondary reinforcers, providing stimuli that are not inherently rewarding but that we have learned to associate with positive outcomes. Reinforcement from others can be verbal and nonverbal.

5. Seven major factors have been found to determine why we like some people and dislike others.

1. Propinquity. Physical closeness increases interpersonal attraction.
2. Familiarity. Frequency of exposure increases interpersonal attraction.
3. Similarity-attraction. Interpersonal attraction reflects similarities in attitudes, abilities, and in physical likeness.
4. Complementarity. In a complementary relationship, each person rewards the other by allowing and encouraging expression of important needs and desires.
5. Balance. Balance theory proposes that reciprocity is an important factor in interpersonal attraction; we will come to like those who like us and dislike those who dislike us.
6. Gain-loss. This theory says that we like someone better if the other person first disliked us and then likes us, than if the person had liked us all along. Gain of approval is more rewarding than constant approval.
7. Just-world. We tend to believe that the world is fair; people get the rewards and punishments they deserve. When bad things happen to good people, it surprises and upsets us. Hence we rationalize that victims must deserve their fate.

6. People influence our behavior not only by serving as sources of reward but also by acting as sources of punishment. Deviance, behavior that departs from accepted group norms, is often "punished" by others through rejection and relegation to undesirable social position. Our behavior is also dramatically affected when the fear of punishment is temporarily absent in a state of deindividuation. Individuals will perform, as members of groups, acts that they will not perform alone because the fear of punishment is removed or lessened.

7. Other people also influence our behavior by serving as useful sources of information: we observe their behavior in a given situation, and their behavior gives us clues as to how we should act in that situation. By observing others we are engaging in social comparison. People are subject to affiliation, the desire to associate and interact with others so that they may engage in the social comparison process. Studies in bystander intervention, how we act to help others in emergencies, have provided striking evidence of our dependency on clues from the behavior of others.

8. Individuals change their behavior and judgments as a result of exposure to the ideas and judgments of a group, in other words, individuals conform. Conformity may result solely in public compliance; other times it goes far deeper and results in private acceptance. Reinforcement in the form of punishment usually results in public compliance but not private acceptance. Social control achieved through the use of others as sources of information, by contrast, leads not only to public compliance but also to changes of internalized attitudes and beliefs. Conformity drops when people have anonymity. In addition to anonymity, con-

513

formity is affected by the ambiguity of situations, by self-confidence, by group goals, by the presence of allies, and by group cohesiveness.

9. Other people help us to learn about ourselves and to define ourselves; we can learn about ourselves by analyzing how others treat us. The process of self-perception—observing our own behavior—is another avenue of self-knowledge.

10. Social influence can be unintentional and inadvertent, or it can be intentional. The most obvious forms of intentional social influence are directives issued by authority figures whom we obey. Another form of intentional social influence is persuasion which aims first at changing our attitudes; attitude change will normally lead to behavior change. Attitude change through persuasion depends to a great extent on the credibility of the communicator, the source of the persuasive message, and on the attractiveness of the communicator.

11. Another form of intentional social influence is explained by Leon Festinger's theory of cognitive dissonance, which proposes that when individuals behave in a manner inconsistent with their attitudes, they experience dissonance, an unpleasant state of tension. The state of dissonance can be reduced by reducing the number of inconsistent cognitions, by changing the relevant attitudes. Dissonance can also be reduced by increasing the number of consistent cognitions, by concluding that behavior has been forced.

12. The most extreme form of intentional social influence is the process known as brainwashing. The effectiveness of brainwashing is determined by victim vulnerability, milieu control, the cohesiveness and attractiveness of the captors, and the subject's ability to come to a confession.

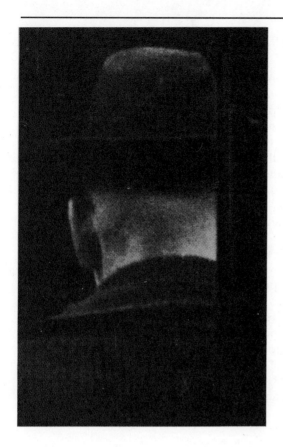

Chapter 17
Social Interaction

All of us who survive the often difficult relationships between parent and child, wife and husband, employer and employee, friend and friend, understand intuitively the distinction between social influence and social interaction. Social influence, as we saw in the previous chapter, is essentially a one-way process. For example, the socialization of children for many years was treated as an instance of social influence. These early conceptions emphasized the effects that parental attitudes and behavior had on the development of children. Among the main issues were the age of weaning, severity of toilet training, and the types of punishment administered.

It is clear now, of course, that this approach ignored the many effects that children, in turn, exert on their parents. Parents who must awaken for the 3 A.M. feeding or spend time driving children to Little League practice, ballet class, and swimming lessons are fully aware of how their behavior is shaped by children. Children can influence the intellectual and cultural tastes of their parents—the books they read, the music they like, the movies they see.

Child socialization is a prime example of the two-way process called *social interaction*. In this chapter we will be concerned with the mutual and reciprocal effects that people have on each other as they interact. This field of investigation covers an enormous range, from the study of two-person, or *dyadic*, relationships such as socialization and friendship, to the consideration of cooperation and conflict between groups and even nations. We will look first at a general theory of social interaction. Next, we will discuss the critical importance of social perception, that is, how we view other people and interpret their behavior. Then we will consider group interactions from two points of view—behavior within the group and behavior between two groups. Finally, we will focus on a different kind of social interaction—namely, the environmental effects people exert on one another through noise and crowding.

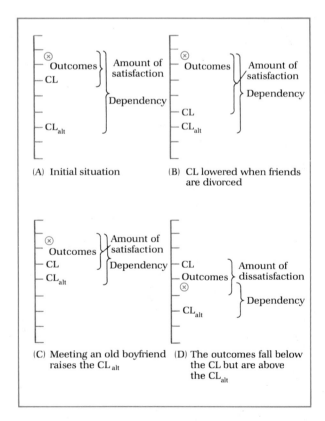

(A) Initial situation

(B) CL lowered when friends are divorced

(C) Meeting an old boyfriend raises the CL_{alt}

(D) The outcomes fall below the CL but are above the CL_{alt}

Variations in a wife's comparison level (CL) and comparison level for alternatives (CL_{ALT}), and the outcomes in four marriage situations. (A) Initial situation. The outcomes experienced in the relationship with her husband are above the CL and the CL_{ALT} and provide the wife with a moderate amount of satisfaction. (B) When the wife hears about the divorce of friends, her CL is lowered, and the amount of satisfaction she has with her own marriage is increased. (C) Meeting an old boyfriend raises the CL_{ALT}, but the outcomes she experiences in her own marriage are still above the CL and the CL_{ALT}. If these outcomes should decrease, they could easily fall below the raised CL_{ALT}, and the wife would then end her marriage. (D) The husband had changed his behavior, and the wife's outcomes fall below the CL, but they are still above the CL_{ALT}. The wife will be dissatisfied but will stay in the relationship. Should the outcomes fall below the CL_{ALT} the wife will leave her husband. These are only sample situations. The CL, the CL_{ALT}, and the outcomes can all vary in relationship to one another. Both the amount of satisfaction or dissatisfaction and the maintenance of the marriage will depend on the relative positions of these variables.

Social Relationships: Thibaut and Kelley's Theory of Social Interaction

The basic form of social interaction is a relationship between two people. No matter what the nature of the relationship—husband and wife, teacher and student, boss and employee, storekeeper and customer—each person exerts influence on the other. Of course, the amount of influence differs in different types of relationships: husband and wife influence each other more than do storekeeper and customer. And although the traffic of influence may be two-way, it may flow more heavily in one direction; the boss, for example, typically has a greater effect on the employee than does the employee on the boss.

In order to understand how two people affect each other in this basic form of social interaction, let us consider a general theory that attempts to account for the formation, maintenance, and breakup of relationships. The theory was first developed in the field of economics and later applied to social relationships by John Thibaut and Harold Kelley (1959).

Rewards and Costs

The *Thibaut and Kelley theory of social interaction* postulates that relationships depend largely upon each participant's analysis of the rewards and costs. This analysis occurs (usually unconsciously) whenever two people interact, and it shapes the responses of each person. Even in the simplest social situation, many responses are available. A person alone on an elevator with another person, for example, may intentionally look away or may make eye contact to get the other's attention and start to discuss the weather, the world situation, or the slowness of the elevator. The other person may respond in turn by ignoring the eye contact or by mumbling a brief reply or by joining or expanding the conversation.

According to Thibaut and Kelley, the choice of each response depends on an analysis of the potential costs (for example, embarrassment, boredom, or loss of esteem) and rewards (for example, pleasure, money, or affection) of that response. Each person tries to adopt the response and induce in the other the response that will yield the best outcome—that is, the greatest rewards at the least cost. In this view then, as people interact they are constantly computing the reward-cost ratio in order to determine the overall satisfaction of the relationship. Unless both participants compute the profit as greater than the costs, the interaction is likely to stop. The two people in the elevator might smile, nod their heads, and go their separate ways, moving on to relationships with greater potential for profit.

The Comparison Level

Suppose that the two people on the elevator do begin a social relationship. What determines their feelings of satisfaction in the relationship? According to Thibaut and Kelley, satisfaction depends in part on one's expectations, or *comparison level* (CL). The comparison level for any interaction is the level of outcome you expect or feel you deserve. It depends on past experiences, what you have seen others get out of relationships, and your general level of optimism. Some people have high expectations in relationships, feeling they deserve more rewards than costs. They will not be happy on a date unless it is a special evening. Others are more pessimistic and expect costs to be relatively high: on a date they are satisfied with a moderately pleasant evening.

Thus happiness in a relationship is not determined by the absolute level of outcome but by the outcome relative to comparison level. Whenever the outcome is above a person's comparison level, that person will be satisfied and happy in the relationship. But when outcomes fall below the comparison level, unhappiness and dissatisfaction result.

Considering the Alternatives

Whereas the comparison level helps determine the general level of satisfaction, the make-or-break factor depends on the alternative relationships available. The outcome level from such alternatives—that is, what people feel they could get in another relationship—is called the *comparison level for alternatives* (CL_{ALT}). According to Thibaut and Kelley, any time the outcome of the present relationship falls below the comparison level for alternatives, the person will break up the relationship.

The comparison level for alternatives is clearly an extremely important aspect of any two-person relationship because it determines one's level of power and dependency. The availability of an alternative almost as good as the present relationship reduces dependency and increases power. On the other hand, if the potential rewards from the next best available alternative are low, dependency on the present relationship is increased. Consider, for example, a marriage where the wife likes the relationship but has alternatives with very good reward potential—a new career she has thought about pursuing or other men who are interested in her. Let us assume that the husband, by contrast, has no possible alternatives that even come near the rewards he gets from the marriage. In such a relationship, the wife holds the power, and the husband is very dependent. She can hurt him, and he will stay on. But anything he does to make her slightly unhappy might force the rewards of the relationship below those of her alternatives and cause her to break up the relationship.

Limitations of the Theory

This view of people as constant calculators of rewards and costs presents a highly selfish model of human nature. As such, the Thibaut and Kelley theory is hard put to explain behavior such as pure altruism (helping others in need), which seems to occur without any explicit rewards. Another limitation of the theory is its inability to specify all the responses available in a social interaction and the rewards and costs associated with them. It is seldom easy to predict what might be rewarding or costly for each person. Not only is one person's reward another person's cost, a given individual's perception of what is rewarding often changes relative to situation and mood. A closer examination of these all-important perceptions is in order.

Social Perception

How we interact with other people depends to a great extent upon how we perceive them and how we interpret their behavior. These perceptions of people—what we *think* they are like—will influence how we respond to them. If you think the woman next door is hostile, you are unlikely to want to interact with her. In terms of interaction then, the true nature of that neighbor is less important than your *social perception* of her. In this section we will take up two different processes that are important in social perception: (1) how we arrive at an overall impression of another person, and (2) how we interpret the causes of another person's behavior.

Impression Formation

Suppose you learn the following facts about your psychology instructor: she once went out of her way to help a lost little boy find his way home; she was a Phi Beta Kappa in college, is a fan of the Boston Celtics basketball team, and dislikes fast-food restaurants; she once fasted for three days just to see whether she could do it. As you learn these individual facts, you organize the information, integrate it, and arrive at your own general summary picture of what she is like—bright and helpful, but nutty. This is the essence of *impression formation*—the process by which we form global impressions of people based on specific facts we have learned. We can identify three important general features of impression formation: impressions are usually thought to be structured, stable, and constructive.

Structure: Categorizing People and Groups When we exclude human beings, we have convenient categories for classifying things: animals, vegetables, and minerals; furniture, appliances, and artwork. Having categories for things with shared, identifiable attributes helps us to simplify a complex world. In this same way we create structure in the process of perceiving people, categorizing what they are like. One familiar set of categories, originally described by the Swiss psychologist Carl Jung (1939), consists of introverts and extraverts (see Chapter 12). Introverts are passive, withdrawn, cautious, and reflective; extraverts are outgoing, sociable, active, impulsive, and fond of parties (Eysenck and Eysenck, 1967).

Although few people fit neatly into the introvert versus extravert dichotomy, this kind of general categorizing provides an important framework in impression formation. In fact, Nancy Cantor and Walter Mischel (1977) have shown that people learn and remember information about others more proficiently if they can code particular facts about them into *trait categories* such as introvert and extravert. In their study they presented subjects with selected adjectives to describe four characters: an extravert, an introvert, and two characters that fit no particular personality type. Tests showed that subjects could recognize more facts and recall more characteristics and behaviors of characters who fit the pure introvert or extravert personality types. Thus personality traits serve as categories around which we organize information about people. Of course, as Chapter 8 shows, organized information is more easily recalled than unorganized information.

Trait categories enable us not only to organize information about others but also to suggest other traits the people might possess. We have implicit theories about what trait categories are associated with what other traits; generous people, for example, are assumed also to be intelligent, honest, and considerate. Researchers have tried to develop a picture of what traits go with what other traits according to our implicit theory (Rosenberg, Nelson, and Vivekananthan, 1968). They asked subjects to describe people they knew by selecting personality traits from a list. By seeing which traits often occurred together in descriptions of people and

which did not, they were able to identify the important dimensions in personality impressions and the traits that clustered together. Figure 17.1 shows that the two important dimensions in personality impression are social (from good to bad) and intellectual (from good to bad). That is, we tend to think of people mainly in terms of their social and intellectual qualities. The position of each trait in the figure shows the dimension to which it is relevant. For example, "scientific" and "determined" cluster together as "good-intellectual" traits. "Unsociable" and "humorless" are "bad-social" traits. The further

FIGURE 17.1 Two-dimensional configuration of 60 traits showing best-fitting axes of properties of social desirability and intellectual desirability. The farther apart two traits are in the diagram, the less likely they are to be perceived as occurring in a person's character.

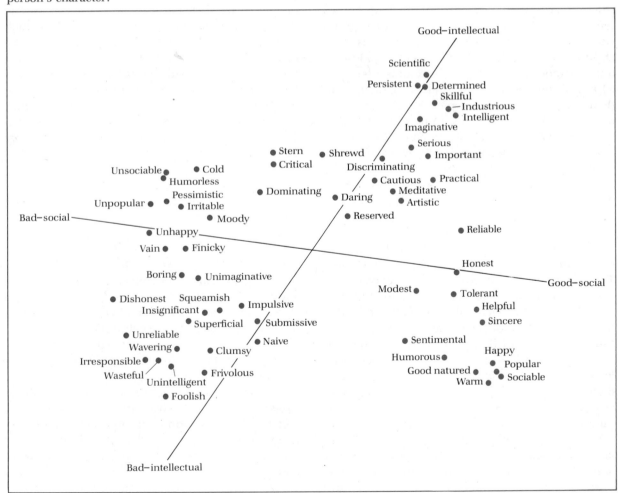

apart two traits are in the picture, the less likely they are to be perceived as occurring together in a person's character. Thus, "happy" and "popular" are very likely to be judged as occurring together in a person's character; "irresponsible" and "imaginative" are very unlikely to be judged as occurring together.

Just as we make assumptions about what traits go together, we also have implicit theories about what kinds of traits are associated with various groups of people. We simplify and structure the complex world of other people by seeing them as members of groups and perceiving each group as having special and identifiable characteristics. These general pictures of large groups of people are called *group stereotypes.*

We can all call to mind such general pictures, or stereotypes, of a great variety of groups—races, nationalities, the sexes, occupational groups such as police, politicians, and college professors, even students grouped by college. Studies have shown that college students are consistent in their group stereotypes of students from other colleges (Fink and Cantril, 1939). Undergraduates of Yale, Princeton, Dartmouth, and Harvard were presented with 50 adjectives (for instance, brilliant, athletic, studious) and were asked to pick the five that best described a Harvard student, a Yale student, and so on. There was considerable agreement as to the nature of the students at each college. For example, in their choices of 5 out of 50 adjectives to describe a Harvard student, all subjects from Dartmouth used a total of only 10 different adjectives. Different sets of adjectives were consistently used to describe students from Yale or Princeton.

Agreement about ethnic stereotypes has also been demonstrated in both early and recent studies. The first empirical study of ethnic stereotypes was conducted in 1933 (Katz and Braly). One hundred Princeton students were asked to list the traits that they considered most characteristic of 10 groups: Negroes, Jews, Irish, Turks, Germans, Italians, Americans, Chinese, Japanese, and English. Subjects showed very high agreement on the assignment of traits. For example, Negroes were characterized as "superstitious" by 84 percent of the sample and as "lazy" by 75 percent; Germans were seen as "scientifically minded" by 78 percent. Most agreement was seen in the stereotypes of Negroes, and least stereotyping was done in the ratings of Turks. It is interesting that these were the two most disliked groups. Thus, degree of stereotyping seems to bear no relationship to prejudice toward a group. Nearly 40 years later, a similar study at Princeton replicated the early results in showing consistent stereotyping of the various ethnic groups (Darley, Lewis, and Glucksberg, 1972).

Among the most widely held group stereotypes are those associated with the sexes. In our society, women are generally perceived as less creative, logical, aggressive, and proficient at quantitative tasks than men, and as more timid, dependent, and submissive than men. Most of these characteristics are merely stereotypes and have no basis in actual sex differences (see Chapter 11).

Another common stereotype relates to physical appearance. Although most of us would say it is illogical to evaluate another person solely on the basis of physical appearance, most of us do exactly that. Karen Dion, Ellen Berscheid, and Elaine Walster (1972) demonstrated that attractive people are perceived quite differently from unattractive people. They showed subjects a series of photographs of people and asked the subjects for their impressions. Some of the people in the photographs were very attractive; others were unattractive. The subjects, with no information other than the photographs, tended to judge the people in terms of the "beautiful is good" stereotype: they rated the attractive people as brighter, kinder, happier, and as having rosier futures—with more money and better marriages.

Later in this chapter we will consider the effects of such stereotyping on social interaction. For now, keep in mind the existence of group stereotypes and their role in structuring our impressions of other people.

Stability: Sticking with Our Impressions   A second general feature of impression formation, in addition to structure, is that impressions tend to be stable. Early in a relationship, we seek permanent qualities in others. Once we find them, we are hesitant to change our perceptions. These impressions endure even though we may learn facts that seem to contradict them.

What explains the enduring quality of impressions? Once we have structured a meaningful picture of another person or group of people, we normally interpret any new information in the light of this impression. Thus if someone we perceive as considerate and friendly aims a negative remark at us, we interpret it as a joke. But the same remark by someone perceived as inconsiderate and unfriendly, is seen as hostile. Remember from the previous chapter the study of spectator perception at a Dartmouth-Princeton football game (Hastorf and Cantril, 1954). Students from each college interpreted the many infractions committed on the playing field in the light of their existing impressions: players from their own college were rule-abiding athletes, and those from the rival college were not.

One way to maintain a stable stereotype of any group is to interpret the behavior of any group member as fitting that stereotype. This often occurs when racial stereotypes are involved. In one study (Duncan, 1976), white subjects viewed a group situation in which an ambiguous shove was given by one actor to another. This act was perceived as far more violent when performed by a black actor than by a white actor. Such interpretations allow subjects to maintain stable stereotypes of blacks as an aggressive group.

Constructiveness: Inferring Other Qualities In addition to structure and stability, there is a third general feature of impression formation: the process is constructive. Once we have categorized a person, we build on this general picture. We believe that all kinds of characteristics that seem to be

consistent with our general picture are true. If we perceive a politician as a "liberal," we infer a host of characteristics consistent with this category: for example, most liberals have ordinarily been in favor of national health insurance and more funding for welfare programs. Any particular liberal may or may not really hold these positions: what is fascinating is how we make the assumptions even in the absence of relevant information.

This tendency to build on our existing impression was demonstrated in a laboratory study by Cantor and Mischel (1977). They presented subjects with characteristics of a hypothetical person that were consistent with those of an extravert. When the subjects tried to identify elements in the specific information they had been given, they mistakenly chose many characteristics that, though consistent with extraversion, they had not been given. Significantly, they did not mistakenly choose characteristics associated with introversion. They simply built on general impressions of an extravert. Opposite effects were seen when subjects were presented with a typical introverted character. Then, they mistakenly recognized traits consistent with the introverted personality type. Thus, once

Although it seems illogical to evaluate others solely on the basis of physical appearance, most of us do just that. Such stereotyping greatly affects social interactions.

we can categorize or "pigeonhole" a person, we tend to believe they have all the qualities and characteristics consistent with that category.

Major Determinants in Impression Formation

The process of impression formation naturally relies on information about the other person, but some facts are perceived as more important than others. We give special importance to when information is received, emphasize certain facts and disregard others, and interpret the facts in terms of their context. These three determinants in impression formation have been labeled *primacy-recency*, *central traits*, and *context*.

Primacy-Recency   When you get to know another student, you are apt to learn a number of facts about the person—their college major, hometown, ambitions for the future, food preferences. Which information has a greater effect on your overall impression? The earliest information you get— college major (primacy)—or the more recent information—food preferences (recency)?

Research indicates that the old advice "make a good first impression" is sound counsel. Abraham Luchins (1957) presented subjects with descriptions of people that contained the same facts but varied the order in which the information was presented. In one case, the first half of the description portrayed the target person as friendly, while the last half pictured an unfriendly character. In the other test condition, the order of presentation was reversed. In the friendly-unfriendly order, 78 percent of the subjects rated the target person as friendly. When the order was unfriendly-friendly, 87 percent rated the imaginary person as unfriendly. Thus, even when the total information presented was exactly the same, the first impression almost always won out.

The primacy effect also has been established for impressions of a person's ability. Edward Jones and his associates (Jones, Rock, Shaver, Goethals, and Ward, 1968) had subjects watch a student attempting to solve a number of difficult problems. The "student," actually a confederate of the experimenter, solved 15 of the 30 problems correctly. In one case, the 15 correct answers were given very early in the series. In the other condition, the successes came mainly toward the end. Subjects were asked to indicate how intelligent they felt this student was. The "student" who solved more problems early was seen as smarter than the "student" who solved the same number of problems but had arrived at correct answers later in the test.

Why should there be a primacy effect in the way we perceive others? To begin with, there is a greater need for information when we first meet someone. We want to form a stable picture quickly, and thus we pay more attention to early information. Another reason for the primacy effect is related to the general proposal made earlier, that impressions have stability. Once we form an initial impression based on early information, later facts, even if contradictory to the initial impression, tend to be interpreted in light of the first impression. They might be seen as circumstantial deviations from the person's true characteristics or even be ignored. In the Jones experiment the first impression of the "student" who quickly solved 15 problems was one of intelligence. Subsequent failure to solve problems was attributed to the difficulty of the problems or to the student's being bored and not trying hard.

Central Traits   Aside from the primacy effect, certain facts carry a special weight in the overall impression. Solomon Asch (1946) demonstrated this by focusing on the possibility that certain central traits might play a key role. Subjects were asked to form an impression of a person described as intelligent, skillful, industrious, warm, determined, practical, and cautious. Almost all subjects felt that such a person was generous, happy, and good-natured. Then Asch changed one word in the list of traits: he left out *warm* and substituted *cold*. Now the impressions were quite different: only a small percentage perceived this person as generous, happy, or good-natured, although they did see the person as more important. When Asch tried alternating other traits such as polite versus blunt, there was little difference in overall impressions. Asch concluded that the warm-cold dimension was a central one around which general impressions of people were formed.

Context   We learn facts about people in the context of other information; this context has an effect on how we interpret the traits in question. Say, for example, we learn that a person is highly charitable but is also very wealthy. This context shades our interpretation of the person's charitable impulses and thus affects our overall impression.

Context is particularly important in interpreting the meaning of a trait such as aggressiveness. In the context of traits like intelligence and kindness, aggressiveness might imply that the person is a hard worker or a go-getter. In the context of dumbness and meanness, it might imply hostility.

Asch (1948) demonstrated just how markedly context can change the meaning of information. He had his subjects read the following statement: "I hold it that a little rebellion, now and then, is a good thing and necessary in the political world as storms are in the physical." When subjects were told that the author of the statement was Thomas Jefferson, they perceived the word *rebellion* in the context of known Jeffersonian traits and interpreted it as meaning agitation and civil disobedience. But when the statement was attributed to Lenin, subjects interpreted rebellion in terms of their perception of Lenin as a revolutionary communist and saw it as meaning full-scale revolution. Thus, the context of the information we receive about a person is an important determinant of our overall impression.

The Attribution Process

As we have seen, impression formation is an important part of social perception. A second significant process, closely linked to impression formation, is attribution—that is, the inferences we make about the *causes* of other people's behavior. How we perceive *why* people behave the way they do will greatly affect our interaction with them. *Attribution theory* deals with the underlying principles by which we decide the causes of another person's actions.

Attribution theory has implications for many areas of social policy. In education, for example, urban ghetto schools are a pressing issue. Why do children in such schools often fail? Is it because of the lack of individual ability or motivation? Is it because of racial discrimination, difficulties at home, or inadequate teaching? How society attributes the causes of failure will obviously determine its approaches to changing this behavior.

Dispositional versus Situational Attribution The perceived causes of other people's behavior can be classified into two general categories. If we think that a person acts in a certain way because of something internal in that person—for example, attitudes, personality traits, and mood—we attribute the behavior to *dispositional reasons.* If, on the other hand, the particular behavior seems to stem from external causes such as an offer of money or a threatened punishment, we attribute it to *situational reasons.*

Our perceptions of what a person is really like usually depend upon dispositional attributions. For example, if a person who has been offered $1,000 to sign a petition in favor of saving the world's whales signs the petition, it tells us nothing about the person's attitude toward whales. The reasons for signing are obviously situational; we assume that practically anyone would sign such a petition in return for $1,000. On the other hand, if a person freely chooses to sign the petition in the absence of external influences, we attribute the behavior to dispositional causes. We infer that the person actually wants the whales to be saved. In the absence of obvious rewards or punishments, behavior is assumed to reflect dispositional factors such as attitudes and traits. This fact helps explain the presumed effectiveness of "hidden-camera" commercials on television. If we are led to believe that a person has endorsed a product without being paid for it—indeed, without even knowing the camera is recording the endorsement—we are more likely to believe that the person really likes the product.

Key Factors in Attribution Kelley (1967) has proposed that people attribute the causes of behavior by using three key factors—*distinctiveness*, *consensus*, and *consistency*—as well as by some additional basic principles. Kelley points out that we all behave much like scientists in seeking these three factors and in collecting evidence and arriving at logical conclusions.

1. *Distinctiveness.* Suppose we see Harvey crying at the movie and try to figure out why. Are the reasons dispositional: is he softhearted, emotional, easily moved to tears? Or are they situational: is the movie a real tearjerker or does Harvey have something in his eye? As we consider this question, a first useful piece of information is whether or not Harvey typically cries at movies. Here we are assessing the distinctiveness of Harvey's behavior. If he almost never cries at movies, his behavior is distinctive; thus we are likly to attribute the cause to situational reasons—the movie itself. But if the crying is nondistinctive (he cries even during cartoons),

we would conclude that the cause was dispositional and had something to do with Harvey's personality.

2. *Consensus.* A second factor in attributing Harvey's behavior would be information about how other people reacted to the same movie. If practically everyone came out of the movie with handkerchief in hand, there was obviously a high consensus that the movie was a tearjerker; thus Harvey's crying could reasonably be attributed to the situation. By the same token, if no one else cried, indicating low consensus, we would learn something about Harvey.

When people act much like everyone else, we learn little about them. Jones, Keith Davis, and Kenneth Gergen (1961) had subjects listen to tape recordings of people applying for a job as an astronaut. The experimenters described this job as requiring someone very introverted. Some subjects heard a job applicant behave in the expected introverted way—the right way to get the job. Others heard an applicant behave in a very extraverted manner. Subjects were then asked to give their impressions of what the applicant was really like. Those who had heard the introverted applicant were not confident in their attributions: the applicant had acted like anyone looking for the job would act. Consensus was high. The behavior was due to

situational forces; hence little could be learned about the person. Those who heard the applicant behave in an extraverted way assumed that few others would have acted in this way (perceived low consensus). These subjects thus believed that the behavior reflected the dispositions of the actor and were confident that the applicant was outgoing and extraverted (see Figure 17-2).

3. *Consistency.* A final factor in determining the cause of Harvey's crying is the consistency of his behavior when he sees this particular movie. If this is the only time Harvey cried at this movie, that is, if there is low consistency, we assume that the cause is situationally specific to this occasion (Harvey was in a very sad mood or had something in his eye). If Harvey always cries at this movie, that is, if there is high consistency, the reason he is crying could be either dispositional (something general about Harvey's personality), or situational (the movie is a real tearjerker).

4. *Principles in attribution.* In addition to these three factors, Kelley (1972) also has identified interesting principles that people use in attributing causality to behavior. One is the *discounting principle*, that is, we discount dispositional factors when situational causes are evident. Assume you are watching a child playing with a new puzzle. In the absence of plausible external causes, you will attribute the child's behavior to a dispositional reason: she likes to play with this puzzle. But if there is a plausible external reason—for example, the child's mother has told her if she does not play with the puzzle she will have to help with the dishes—you are likely to discount the dispositional possibility. Thus, when several possible causes for a behavior exist simultaneously, the perceived role of any one of them is discounted. Behavior is discounted as an indicator of dispositions when plausible external reasons exist.

The *augmentation principle*, by contrast, points to instances where the role of the dispositional cause is augmented, or increased. For example, if the child played with the new puzzle even though her mother had threatened her with a spanking for this behavior, we would infer intense dispositional causality: the child must really like the puzzle. The findings of the study cited earlier by Jones, Davis, and Gergen (1961) support the role of the augmentation principle. When subjects listened to job applicants who had pressing external reasons for acting introverted (it was a condition for getting the job), but who nonetheless behaved like extraverts,

FIGURE 17.2 Perception of an outgoing personality versus an introverted personality. In this study the job of astronaut was described as requiring an introverted personality. Applicants whose behavior countered this requirement were seen as very outgoing. Those whose behavior matched this requirement were perceived as falling at the midpoint of the scale.

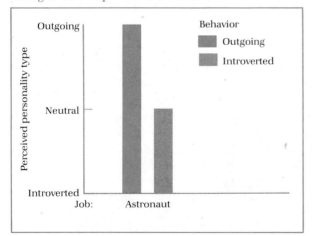

the subjects decided the applicants must really be extraverts. The perceived role of this disposition was augmented since the behavior emerged in the face of an external barrier. In a similar way, we tend to give a high credibility rating to politicians who take a position in the face of opposition from their audience. We judge them as really believing what they say (Mills and Jellison, 1967).

Biases in the Attribution Process   As we have described it thus far, attribution appears to be a relatively rational and logical process of assessing the causes of behavior. By attending to implicit rules and principles, we are able to infer the attitudes and traits of another person. In fact, however, we are not always as rational as attribution theory implies. In practice, certain biases creep into the process.

Foremost among these biases is the tendency to attribute the behavior of another person to dispositional reasons. We assume people act in a certain way because they *are* that way. This tendency is nicely illustrated in the results of an experiment conducted by Jones and Victor Harris (1967). The task of the college student subjects was to read a speech about Fidel Castro and then to assess the attitude of the speechwriter, who was ostensibly a member of the university debate team. Half of the subjects read a speech that was favorable to Castro; the other half read a speech that was highly critical of the Cuban leader. Moreover, half of the subjects who read the pro-Castro speech and half who read the anti-Castro version were informed that the debater had freely chosen that position. The other half in each condition were told that the debater had no choice in the matter; the position for or against Castro had been assigned by the debate coach.

The logic of the attribution process ought to enable us to predict the results easily. But such predictions would be only half right. In the conditions in which the debater ostensibly had freely chosen the position taken in the speech, the subjects were quite logical. They saw the speech as reflecting the debater's true attitude toward Castro. They attributed strong pro-Castro attitudes to the author of the speech that was favorable to Castro, and anti-Castro attitudes to the author of the speech critical of him.

However, logic went awry in the conditions where the debater supposedly was assigned the position, pro or anti, and thus had no choice. Al-though the behavior logically should have been attributed to situational causes (the debater had no choice), the subjects attributed it to dispositional reasons. They judged the debater who was assigned the pro-Castro speech to be more favorable to Castro than was the debater who was assigned the anti-Castro speech.

Thus, when we observe someone else's behavior, we tend to overemphasize the power of dispositional forces. But what happens when we are actors rather than observers? If you were the purported debater in the Jones and Harris experiment, would writing a pro-Castro speech that you had been assigned make you decide that you were in favor of Castro? Probably not. Chances are, you would perceive your own behavior—writing the speech—as a response to situational pressures, namely that you were assigned the task. As Jones and Richard Nisbett (1971) have pointed out, there tends to be an important difference between actors and observers in the attribution of causality. As actors we see our own behavior largely in terms of situational forces; as observers we perceive the behavior of others as stemming largely from their own dispositions.

This *actor-observer difference* has been documented in a number of studies, including a simple writing exercise conducted by Nisbett and his associates (Nisbett, Caputo, Legant, and Maracek, 1973). Male college students were asked to write paragraphs on several topics: why they liked their girlfriends and why they had selected their college majors; why their best male friend liked his girl-friend and why he had chosen his college major. The subjects, in explaining their own behavior, emphasized external reasons: the girl was attractive and had a nice sense of humor, their college major offered inviting career opportunities, and so on. But in explaining the behavior of their best friends, the subjects cited dispositional reasons that emphasized the friend's own personal qualities: he likes a certain kind of girl, and he is very logical and hence suited for a major and a career in computer programming.

In an even more direct test of the actor-observer difference, the same researchers presented subjects with a list of pairs of opposite traits such as quiet-talkative and cautious-bold. The subjects were asked to rate themselves or an acquaintance on each trait pair. They were also given the option of noting that a given trait "depends on the situation." The results showed that subjects selected this situational option much more frequently when rating themselves than when judging acquaintances. In the picture that emerged, their acquaintances possessed definite personality traits, but the subjects themselves merely responded to the demands of the situation.

Our tendency to attribute dispositional causes to other people's behavior may seem illogical, but it serves a function. Assigning personality traits and other characteristics to another person leads us to believe that we "know" the person. Such knowledge, whether objectively warranted or not, enables us to make predictions about how that person will behave (especially toward us) in the future. This feeling that we can predict whut will happen gives us a sense of control over our interaction with the person.

This desire for control is not unlike that found in another kind of interaction, gambling. In gambling we attempt to control chance. People pursue all sorts of strategies aimed at controlling the outcome: at the craps table, for example, they talk to the dice, blow on them, roll them softly for low numbers or hard for high numbers, and even try intensely to visualize the desired outcome. All of these rituals are perceived by gamblers as ways of changing the odds in their favor, or of transforming what is clearly a chance event into a controllable one.

The *illusion of control* in gambling has been studied by Ellen Langer (1975), who found that people tend to infer a power over chance outcomes that in fact does not exist. Langer concluded that when people believed they had some control over a chance outcome they felt relatively likely to win. For example, subjects who were given the opportunity to select a lottery ticket felt more confident they would win than did those who were simply handed one by the ticket vendor.

In light of this powerful tendency to infer the ability to control what are obviously chance events, it is no wonder that we assume we "know" others and thus can predict their behaviors. Attributing dispositional traits gives us at least the illusion of control in social interaction. As we will see later in this chapter, this same desire for control tends to influence our peception of people who are members of groups that we have stereotyped, leading us to feel that we already "know" a lot about such people.

The illusion of control is a common phenomenon among those who gamble. This powerful tendency to believe we can control what are obviously chance events extends to the illusion of control in many social situations.

Links Between Social Perception and Social Interaction

The two processes of social perception—impression formation and attribution of traits—serve as guides in our behavior toward others. By acting in terms of our perceptions of another person, we forge another link in the complex chain connecting social perception and social interaction. Suppose that you have formed the impression that someone is hostile and attribute their hostility to dispositional traits. This perception is apt to affect your behavior toward that person; you are likely to behave coldly, if not with outright hostility. Social perception can influence social interaction even when the perception is false.

The Self-Fulfilling Prophecy Let us assume that your perception of another as hostile is erroneous. You attributed the hostility to dispositional reasons when in fact it had a situational cause; for example, you observed that person after she or he had just flunked an exam. Nonetheless, the next time you meet you act on your perception and behave in a cold and aloof manner. How will the other person

react to this behavior? She or he is likely to respond in kind—with coldness and hostility. In short, your original perception, though erroneous, has become true.

Such an instance, in which the perceiver causes another person to behave in a manner that confirms the perceiver's expectations, is called a *self-fulfilling prophecy.*

Sociologist Robert Merton (1957), who first proposed this concept, has characterized the self-fulfilling prophecy in the following way: ". . . definitions of a situation (prophecies or predictions) become an integral part of the situation and thus affect subsequent developments. . . . The self-fulfilling prophecy is, in the beginning, a *false* definition of the situation evoking a new behavior which makes the originally false conception come *true.* The specious validity of the self-fulfilling prophecy perpetuates a reign of error. For the prophet will cite the actual course of the events as proof that he was right from the beginning."

The self-fulfilling prophecy, by perpetuating "a reign of error," has obvious implications for the study of stereotypes. The stereotypes we hold about various groups can bias the social interaction process in such a way that members of those groups will often conform to the expected stereotypical behavior. Thus false stereotypes are confirmed and the reign of error perpetuated.

A recent experiment (Snyder, Tanke, and Berscheid, 1977) convincingly demonstrated the self-perpetuating, self-fulfilling nature of false stereotypes. The aim was to test the effects of the physical attractiveness stereotype described earlier in this chapter—the assumption that says, in effect, "beautiful is good."

The subjects were male and female college students. A male and female were taken into separate laboratories and told that they would engage in a "get-acquainted" telephone conversation. The male was then given a photograph, which was purportedly a just-snapped Polaroid of the woman with whom he was to talk. The photograph, in fact, was a phony, the manipulation prearranged by the researchers. It showed either a beautiful woman or an unattractive one and was thus intended to generate the stereotypes associated with physical attractiveness.

After the males were shown the photo, they filled out a questionnaire that asked how they thought their telephone partner would behave. Males

shown the attractive photo indicated that they expected her to be more sociable, poised, and humorous than did the males who were shown the unattractive picture. These expectations affected the behavior of the men once they got on the telephone. Judges listened to the males during the phone conversation and rated their behavior. The judges were unaware of the nature of the photograph the male subject had seen, and thus their ratings were unbiased by any knowledge of "whom" the male was talking to. (This procedure is referred to as keeping the judge "blind to experimental conditions.") The judges' ratings displayed an interesting effect. Those males who thought they were talking with an attractive woman were judged more sociable, interesting, outgoing, humorous, and animated than the males who thought they were talking with an unattractive woman.

These results should not surprise us in view of our earlier discussion on how stereotypes influence social perception and behavior. What is more striking is the behavior of the women during the phone conversation. They responded in the same way that they were treated by the males. According to the judges who listened to the females during the phone conversation, those speaking with males who thought they were attractive were more animated and sociable than the women talking with males who thought them unattractive.

Lest we forget, the males' impressions had been based upon bogus photographs; the females in the two experimental conditions were actually about equal in physical attractiveness. Even though the males' expectations about the warmth and sociability of their partner had no basis in reality whatsoever, those expectations had a pronounced effect on social interaction. They affected how the males behaved on the telephone; this in turn affected how the females behaved. The false male stereotypes of physical attractiveness started a chain of events culminating in the self-fulfilling prophecy: the females who were expected to be sociable became sociable.

The self-fulfilling prophecy is responsible for the maintenance of many of our false stereotypes including those that relate to race and sex roles. For example, the stereotype that blacks are not competent for certain occupations may lead a white inter-

The stereotype that blacks are incompetent for certain occupations could lead a white interviewer to behave in such a way that the applicant might get nervous and thus create a negative impression. Consequently, the interviewer's false stereotype would become self-fulfilling.

viewer to behave in such a way that any job applicant—black or white—would become nervous and botch the interview. Because the applicant performs poorly during the interview, the person is judged unfit for the job, and the interviewer's false stereotype is confirmed (Word, Zanna, and Cooper, 1974). Similarly, stereotypes about female behavior can become reality through biased social interaction (Zanna and Pack, 1975). For example, imagine a male employer who never challenges a female employee with difficult assignments. As a result, the woman does not receive the kind of training and experience she needs. If and when she is finally asked to work on a difficult task, she is likely to fail because of lack of training. Such failure confirms original beliefs about her lack of "male-type" competence.

Biased Perceptions Stereotypes also can be maintained through a second process. In the self-fulfilling prophecy, the behavior of the other person actually conforms to the perceiver's expectations. It is also possible for the perceiver only to *think* that the expected behavior is confirmed. In such instances, the perceiver's expectations are, in effect, self-confirming.

What explains *biased perceptions?* We saw earlier that our impression formation tends to be constructive and stable; that is, we build upon and

embellish the impression that we have already. Two perceivers may interpret another person's behavior differently because they are building on differing impressions.

An experiment by Kelley (1950) makes essentially this point. A guest instructor was introduced to classes of students. Half the students received a biographical note describing the instructor as "a rather cold person, industrious, critical, practical, and determined." The other students received a description that differed from this only in that it substituted the word *warm* for the word *cold.* After the guest instructor had finished leading the day's discussion, the students were asked to complete an evaluation form. Those students who had been informed that the instructor was warm consistently gave a higher rating than those who had been told that the instructor was a cold person. The students interpreted the teacher's behavior in such a way that their expectations, whether of warmth or coldness, were confirmed.

Similarly, our stereotypes may guide our perceptions so as to make it likely that we perceive just what we expected. Consider the following imaginary but highly plausible dialogue presented by Gordon Allport in his book *The Nature of Prejudice:*

Mr. X: The trouble with the Jews is that they only take care of their own group.

Mr. Y: But the record of the Community Chest campaign shows that they give more generously, in proportion to their numbers, to the general charities of the community, than do non-Jews.

Mr. X: That shows they are always trying to buy favor and intrude into Christian affairs. They think of nothing but money; that is why there are so many Jewish bankers.

Mr. Y: But a recent study shows that the percentage of Jews in the banking business is negligible, far smaller than the percentage of non-Jews.

Mr. X: That's just it; they don't go in for respectable business; they are only in the movie business or run night clubs. (Allport, 1954)

In this dialogue we see how contrary evidence can be misconstrued to appear to be consistent with the original negative stereotype. Each apparently favorable trait is twisted so as to confirm Mr. X's expectations. Other false stereotypes are maintained by similar biases in perception. Blacks thought to be "lazy" are said by racists to be "uppity" when they behave aggressively. Women said to be "passive" are then often viewed by male chauvinists as "pushy" when they perform competently in a professional occupation. No matter the nature of the behavior, it is construed so as to confirm expectations.

What is interesting in such examples from real life is that the same behavior can be interpreted in diametrically opposite ways depending upon our stereotypes. In the laboratory such bias was clearly demonstrated by Dion (1972), who presented adults with a description of misbehavior on the part of a 7-year-old child said to have thrown stones at a dog. The adults were also provided with a photo purportedly showing the child. Half were shown a photo of a physically attractive child; half saw a picture of a physically unattractive child. Although all of the adults were given precisely the same description of the child's misbehavior, they interpreted it according to the stereotypes of physical attractiveness ("beautiful is good"). Those who thought the child was attractive perceived the wrongdoing to be less severe and less likely to occur in the future than did those who saw the unattractive picture.

At one time or another we all can fall into the twin traps of perceiving others in a biased manner and behaving in ways that will create self-fulfilling prophecies. Such outcomes of social interaction can occur not only in one-to-one relationships but also in group interactions.

Group Interactions

Much of our social interaction occurs in groups. We all belong to many groups—ranging from large aggregations such as political parties or college student bodies, to smaller, more intimate groups, such as families or circles of friends. In the following discussion, we will look first at interaction within groups, and then turn to relations between groups.

Intragroup Behavior

When we are in groups, we often behave differently than when we act alone or as individuals. In the preceding chapter we saw several examples of the profound effect of groups on individual behavior: the mere presence of others affects our performance on tasks; the operations of norms in a group can lead to conformity by its members and, through a process of deindividuation, members sometimes abandon their own personal sense of identity to the group. In addition, there are two other important ways in which behavior within the group can differ from that of the individual acting alone.

A considerable amount of our social interaction occurs within groups. The presence of others affects our behavior in many ways, including possible conformity to group norms and abandonment of our own personal sense of identity to the group.

529

The Risky Shift One fascinating line of research in group behavior has focused on the kinds of decisions that are made by groups as opposed to those made by individuals. Among the questions investigators have explored is whether groups tend to make decisions that are more conservative or riskier than those made by individuals.

Let us examine this question by considering a dilemma often used in the study of individual and group decision making. Mr. F needs help in making an important decision:

> Mr. F is currently a college senior eager to pursue graduate study in chemistry leading to the doctor of philosophy degree. He has been accepted by both University X and University Y. University X has a worldwide reputation for excellence in chemistry. While a degree from University X would signify outstanding training in this field, the standards are so very rigorous that only a fraction of the degree candidates actually receive the degree. University Y, on the other hand, has a less notable reputation in chemistry but almost everyone admitted is awarded the doctor of philosophy degree. As a result, the degree from University Y is much less prestigious than the corresponding degree from University X.

Suppose that you are asked to advise Mr. F in this matter. It is your job to determine the lowest

RESEARCH: The Effects of Sex-Role Stereotypes

Women behave differently from men. As we saw in Chapter 11 in our discussion of sex-role development, many studies have found a number of apparent differences in the behavior of the two sexes. For example, women appear to conform to social norms more than do men and to perform less well on certain intellectual tasks such as a mathematical aptitude test.

There is disagreement as to the reasons for these apparent sex differences. One school of thought asserts that they stem from basic biological differences such as hormonal functioning. Others postulate personality differences that develop because of the differing ways in which socialization affects the two sexes.

In recent years, however, many social psychologists have focused on the role of interpersonal dynamics and, in particular, the effects of sex-role stereotypes. Stereotypes create expectations about how people will behave, and it may be that men and women behave differently because of society's expectations. A particular behavioral difference thus might be the result not of biological or personality differences, but of the self-fulfilling prophecy: a woman performs less proficiently on a mathematical aptitude test, for example, because she is living up (or down) to society's expectations. Sex-role stereotypes may be particularly forceful when they are held by someone of the opposite sex who is attractive to the person.

An experiment designed to test this notion was conducted by Mark Zanna and Susan Pack (1975) at Princeton University. Their subjects were 80 female Princeton undergraduates. Their aim was to affect the attitudes and behavior of these women by manipulating two factors: the sex-role stereotypes held by hypothetical male partners and the desirability or attractiveness of those partners.

Before the experiment, each subject was asked to complete a battery of questionnaires about herself. The intent was to obtain initial data about how the subject viewed herself on 11 items related to sex-role stereotypes (for example, aggressiveness, tenderness, and concern about personal appearance). Each item required responses on a six-point rating scale in such a manner that a higher number indicated agreement with a traditional female stereotypic trait.

About three weeks later, each subject returned to the laboratory for an experiment ostensibly concerned with the process by which people form impressions of one another. Each subject was given a set of questionnaires and told that they had been filled out by a young man whom she would get to meet later in the experiment. The male didn't exist, of course. Information about each hypothetical male partner had been manipulated by the researchers so that he seemed either highly desirable (tall, unattached, Princeton senior, has car, enjoys sports) or not very desirable (short, has a girlfriend, freshman at another university, does not particularly enjoy sports). Next, the subject was shown a questionnaire purporting to indicate her male partner's image of the ideal woman. This information indicated that the partner held either the traditional stereotype (for example, "the ideal woman would be very emotional," "very passive") or an untraditional, more liberated stereotype (exact opposite of the above).

Each subject then completed a set of questionnaires on her own background and attitudes. Although these questionnaires were supposedly to be shown to the male partner, they actually were intended to elicit a self-description on the same 11 items concerning sex-role traits and behavior that had

possible chance of success at University X—the more difficult but potentially more rewarding course of action—that you would be willing to accept before advising him to go there. The risk of the decision about which university to attend hinges upon the level of the odds you are willing to accept; the lower the chance, the riskier the decision.

At the same time you are making your recommendation, five other people are individually going through the same decision-making process. You all arrive at individual decisions. Then the six of you are brought together and asked to discuss the dilemma and arrive at a unanimous decision. In which direction of risk do you think the group will go? Compared with the average individual decision,

will the group's advice be riskier, more conservative, or about the same?

Common sense would seem to dictate that groups would be more conservative than individuals. Psychologists long assumed that groups were cautious and moderate, anathema to the extreme risk taker who would quickly be pulled into line. Research shows otherwise. Group decisions on problems like the one facing Mr. F turn out to be far riskier than the average individual decision. This tendency of the group to shift in the direction of risk has been called the *risky shift*. It has been

been contained in the questionnaires administered three weeks previously. The researchers wanted to measure how much a subject's answers had changed in response to the sex-role attitudes and attractiveness of her male partner.

Finally, the researchers administered an anagrams test—four-letter groupings that had to be transposed into words. Unlike the previous tests, this task was designed to provide a measure of actual behavior as opposed to attitudes.

The results of the experiment supported the notion that sex-role behavior is often shaped by the expectations of attractive others. Subjects who expected to meet a highly desirable male tended to live up to his expectations in her portrayal of her own attitudes. When the desirable male favored untraditional women, subjects described themselves as more untraditional; when he favored traditional qualities, subjects endorsed traditional traits. No such effects were observed when the male was undesirable. The table below shows the mean changes in subjects' self-

descriptions in terms of the sex-role stereotypic traits.

In addition, on the anagrams test, subjects anticipating a meeting with a desirable male holding untraditional expectations of women outperformed subjects who anticipated a meeting with a desirable male holding the traditional stereotype. Poor performance, of course, fulfills the traditional sex-role stereotype. Again, there were no such differences when the partner was unattractive. This result is particularly important because it indicates an actual change in behavior as opposed to attitudes. The mean scores in the anagram test are shown in the table below.

	Partner's Stereotypic View of Women	
Partner's Desirability	Untraditional	Traditional
High desirability	44.25	37.40
Low desirability	41.50	40.35

NOTE: *N* equals 20 per condition. Scores range from a possible low of zero to a possible high of 50.

	Partner's Stereotypic View of Women	
Partner's Desirability	Untraditional	Traditional
High desirability	5.05	−2.35
Low desirability	.60	.60

NOTE: *N* equals 20 per condition. Positive scores indicate changes in self-presentation in the untraditional direction; negative scores, in the traditional direction.

Although this experiment dealt with the effects of stereotypes on female behavior, Zanna and Pack believe that men who are highly motivated to impress a woman will also behave in ways that live up to her expectations. The authors conclude that "Some apparent sex differences in behavior may be just that: only apparent and easily changeable; but only if traditional stereotypes are induced to change."

demonstrated in a variety of situations involving decisions of many types (Wallach and Kogan, 1965; Stoner, 1961).

In one such study, Michael Wallach, Walter Kogan, and Daryl Bem (1964) asked subjects individually to choose among a set of problems to try to solve in order to earn money. They could choose easier problems where correct solutions paid a minimum, or difficult problems where there was low probability of success but high payoffs. The harder the problems chosen the more risky, since there is a good chance of failing but some chance of earning a lot. After individuals made decisions, they were put into groups to come to a unanimous decision about the level of problems that each would then solve. Group decisions were significantly riskier. That is, groups were more likely to decide that members should attempt difficult, high-payoff problems.

Such findings of riskier decisions by groups have important implications in a world where increasingly crucial political, economic, and military decisions are made by groups rather than by individuals.

Why do groups make riskier decisions than do individuals? There are at least two reasons: *diffusion of responsibility* and *cultural values*.

1. *Diffusion of responsibility.* Acting as a member of a group lessens one's own feeling of responsibility about the outcome by diffusing it among the other members. As an individual decision maker, you might feel full of responsibility if Mr. F enrolled at University X on your personal recommendation and then flunked out; hence you would tend toward conservatism in your advice. Group decision makers, by contrast, can always point their fingers at one another and assert, quite rightly, that the decision was not theirs alone.

2. *Cultural values.* A second factor that helps account for the risky shift is that risk itself tends to be a general cultural value in our society, where "nothing ventured, nothing gained" is a popular maxim. The cultural value explanation implies that individuals making decisions alone try to take risks; however, a person acting alone may not realize just how far others are willing to go in level of risk (Brown, 1965). Once in a group a member can see that his or her own decision was really not that risky, and, in an attempt to achieve the cultural value of risk, that person is willing to go along with the other riskier members. Moreover, since risk is valued in the culture, most of the arguments brought up during group discussion will favor the risky alternative, pushing participants to become more daring in their decisions (Vinokur, Trope, and Burnstein, 1975).

If the cultural value explanation has validity, it also ought to apply in special situations where risk is not valued by the society. Where conservatism is valued (for example, making a decision about whether or not to perform life-threatening surgery) we would logically expect the group to make choices that are more conservative than those made by individuals acting alone. In fact, studies (Stoner, 1968; Rabow, Fowler, Bradford, Hofeller, and Shibuya, 1966) show that such group-induced conservative shifts do occur. Questions involving a dangerous operation, a potentially serious illness, or family savings all led to conservative shifts during group decision making. Thus, although both individuals and groups try to make decisions in keeping with cultural values, group decisions typically shift further in the direction of those values than do individual choices.

The Roles People Play Another factor that helps differentiate behavior within the group is the existence of various roles that members are expected to play. All groups—families, fraternities, or professional football teams—have a number of different positions. The pro football team, for example, has an owner, a coach, an equipment manager, a number of cheerleaders, and, of course, a number of playing positions such as tight end. Each position has a set of prescribed and expected behaviors; these behaviors are what psychologists call *roles*. The role of tight end is essentially the same on any pro team. He is expected to learn the plays, listen to the quarterback in the huddle, block for the running backs, and catch passes. He is not expected to know how to fix a broken shoulder pad or to call the plays. The tight end who departs from his role during duty hours, say, by playing practical jokes on the halfbacks instead of practicing pass patterns, will not last long in his particular group, the pro football team. Groups expect all members to fulfill their particular roles. Whatever one's behavior outside the group, continued membership in the group usually hinges upon meeting the expectations associated with the role. It may be all right for our tight end to play jokes all he wants at home or in the off-season; when he is a member of the team, however, he had better behave like a tight end.

The powerful behavioral effects of playing a role

have been demonstrated both in field studies and in elaborate laboratory experiments. In a field study the impact of various job roles on the attitudes of workers employed by a home appliance manufacturer was examined (Lieberman, 1950). All 2,354 workers filled out an initial questionnaire designed to reveal various personal attitudes including how they felt about management and about their labor union. Nine months later, they filled out a similar questionnaire. During the intervening period, 23 workers had been promoted to foremen and 35 had been elected union stewards. The new questionnaire showed that these workers took on new attitudes to fit the expectations of their new roles. Those promoted to foremen became much more favorable to management; those elected stewards became more pro-union. A short time later, economic recession caused a cutback in the work force, resulting in the demotion of eight of the recently promoted foremen, who returned to their old roles as workers. In addition, several of the new union stewards did not seek reelection and they, too, returned to the worker role. As these foremen and stewards reverted to the worker role, their attitudes also reverted to those typical of the factory worker.

Laboratory explorations of role expectations have sometimes produced startling changes in behavior. We saw in the previous chapter how the subjects in the Stanley Milgram (1963) obedience experiments—normal, ordinary people—were willing to administer what they thought were dangerously high levels of electric shocks to another person even when that person was apparently screaming in pain. The discrepancy between their normal behavior and how they acted in the experiment can be understood in terms of roles. As subjects in an experiment, they had temporarily joined a group—"science"—and their role was to follow the instructions of the researcher (whose own role was clearly defined by the white lab coat that was worn).

Whereas the Milgram study necessarily involved deceiving subjects about the real purpose of the experiment, an equally dramatic demonstration of role expectations required no such subterfuge. Philip Zimbardo (1975) set up an experimental mock prison in a basement at Stanford University. The subjects, 18 young male volunteers recruited through a newspaper ad, were told quite truthfully that the purpose of the experiment was to study the effects of imprisonment. They were paid $15 per day and randomly assigned to play roles as prisoners or guards. To simulate real conditions,

the prisoners were picked up at their homes in a police car, fingerprinted, deloused, and locked in a cell. They wore smocks with stenciled numbers and, to simulate prison haircuts, pulled nylon stockings over their heads. The guards wore uniforms of khaki shirts and pants and, to prevent eye contact with the prisoners, silver sunglasses that were opaque from the outside. They were given billy clubs and told to maintain order but not to resort to physical violence.

Both prisoners and guards played their roles so convincingly that soon it was impossible for observers to distinguish acting from reality. The guards became authoritarian, tough, even brutal. They harassed prisoners by denying them toilet privileges and by calling them out of their cells in the middle of the night to do pushups; when prisoners tried to rebel, the guards sprayed them with streams of foam from fire extinguishers. After their brief attempt at rebellion, the prisoners became servile and passive; in the first few days five prisoners developed symptoms of emotional disturbance, including depression, uncontrollable crying, and fits of rage, and had to be dismissed. So powerful were the effects of role playing that the experiment, which was scheduled to run two weeks, had to be terminated after six days.

Group interaction thus has strong effects on our behavior. The cultural values of groups and the roles molded into us by groups influence our decision making (rightly or not) and our general behavior.

Intergroup Relations

Just as individuals can interact, so too can groups that range in size from a family or teenage gang to nations. Interactions between groups parallel, in many ways, the processes in interpersonal relations that we discussed earlier in this chapter. Like two individuals, two groups can enjoy a relationship that leads to their mutual satisfaction; one group can be more powerful than the other or can be dependent on the other; two groups can be in a state of conflict with each other. Similarly, as in interpersonal interaction, the ways in which one group perceives the other group influences relationships between them. Groups, too, are prone to the self-fulfilling prophecy, creating through their treatment of other groups the very characteristics

Conflict between groups is often the result of negative ways in which each group perceives the other. One a group forms an impression of another group, that impression tends to persist even in the face of contrary evidence.

they had mistakenly perceived in the first place. And, once a group forms an impression of another group, that impression tends to persist even in the face of contrary evidence, biasing perceptions of the other group's subsequent behavior.

At the same time, two important differences between interpersonal and intergroup interactions have particular impact on intergroup conflict, tending to render it unusually severe and persistent. First, no individual is absolutely essential to the group. The group and its conflict with another group can survive the loss of individuals; family feuds, for example, have been known to persist through several generations. Second, intergroup conflict increases group cohesiveness against the common enemy, reinforcing biased perceptions and increasing the likelihood of continuing hostility.

The Dynamics of Conflict Perhaps the most ambitious study of intergroup dynamics ever un-

dertaken was the classic research program carried out by Muzafer Sherif and his associates (Sherif and Sherif, 1953). Beginning in 1949, Sherif set up a series of bogus summer camps for 11- and 12-year-old boys. Because it was then widely believed that conflict between groups stemmed largely from racial or religious differences, Sherif purposely selected the boys for the homogeneity of their background; all were from stable, white, middle-class, Protestant homes. The boys were unaware that they were the subjects in an experiment because the behavioral manipulations were carried out under the guise of everyday camp activity. The camp staff consisted of Sherif's accomplices; Sherif himself watched the proceedings in the persona of "Mr. Mussee," the camp caretaker. Sherif set out to create groups, to generate hostility among them, and finally to reduce group conflict.

Sherif's most detailed study was conducted in the summer of 1954 and is known as the "Robbers Cave" experiment because of the camp's location near a landmark of that name in rural Oklahoma (Sherif, Harvey, White, Hood, and Sherif, 1961). In the first phase of the experiment, the researchers set about aligning the boys, who were previously unacquainted, into two distinct and cohesive groups. They segregated the boys into two separate residential groups in areas sufficiently far apart to eliminate most incidental contact between the two. Then they began to build cohesion within each subcamp by staging activities such as cookouts and overnight hikes that required the boys to cooperate closely with one another. Soon friendship patterns developed. The groups became such closely knit units that they even coined group names. One group was the "Rattlers"; the other was the "Eagles."

In the second phase of the experiment, Sherif and his associates deliberately attempted to create conflict between the Rattlers and the Eagles. Their method was to pit the two groups against each other in highly competitive tournaments. The two groups competed for attractive prizes in touch football, tug-of-war, and a number of other games. Since only one of two groups could win any given game, the atmosphere of highly charged competition soon gave way to intergroup hostility. The groups traded insults and engaged in food fights. They staged raids on the enemy cabins, vandalizing the possessions of the other group. They even began stockpiling apples to use as ammunition.

Biased preceptions of the opposing group were obviously quite prevalent during this stage of the research. Members overestimated the quality of their own group performance and underestimated the quality of the opposing group. For example, Sherif had the two groups of boys compete in a bean collection contest. Later, the beans collected by each boy were displayed, and campers were asked to estimate the number of beans that each boy had gathered. These estimates were strongly biased. The boys judged the collections of other members of their own group to be larger than the collections of members of the other group. Similar findings have resulted from other group evaluations of performance by opposing groups. (Hinkle and Schopler, 1979). Thus, as often occurs in interpersonal perception, evaluations of the behavior of the opposing group were distorted to be consistent with the hostility toward that group.

In the final phase of the experiment, the researchers sought to diminish the hostility and end the conflict. Several methods were tried without success. Camp counselors lectured on the necessity for friendly camp relations; pleasant social contacts such as mingling at movies were encouraged, but these contacts only heightened tensions. Interestingly, Sherif and his associates had succeeded in reducing tension between two groups at a previous summer camp but only by employing a stratagem often used by shaky national governments— the threat of a common enemy. When competitions were arranged with a team from a neighboring town, the two camp groups formed an all-star team and worked together. Such solutions are only temporary, however, and threaten an escalation of hostilities—the entire camp against an outside enemy.

For the Robbers Cave experiment, the researchers introduced a new approach. They had the two groups work together toward *superordinate goals*, tasks that appeal to both groups but lie beyond the resources of a single group. The reasoning behind this approach was described by Sherif: ". . . just as competition generates friction, working in a common endeavor should promote harmony."

In real life, superordinate goals often grow out of the necessities of a compelling emergency that calls for unusual human cooperation—for example, a flood, a catastrophic fire, or an earthquake. The Robbers Cave researchers created their own emergencies. When the camp's water supply was disrupted, the two groups worked together to find the cause—faucets the researchers had plugged up and a valve they had turned off. When a food truck "mysteriously" stalled, both groups literally pulled together—on the same rope they had used before in a fierce tug-of-war competition—to get the truck into the camp. The latter was a particularly clear example of a superordinate task because neither group could have pulled the truck without help from the other. Slowly, as the two groups had to cooperate on these and other staff-arranged tasks, the bickering and hostility decreased. Friendships formed across group boundaries. The two groups began cooperating even in the absence of superordinate goals, and the tendency to perceive the other group in a biased and unfavorable manner virtually disappeared. Indeed, at the conclusion of the camp, all the boys voted to go home on the same bus; en route home the Rattlers bought refreshments for all with the money they had won in one of the competitions with their former foes, the Eagles.

The Importance of Success In the Robbers Cave experiment the researchers were careful to arrange tasks so that the groups would be successful in attaining their superordinate goals. Success in such cooperative ventures is essential if intergroup hostility is to be reduced. This was illustrated in recent laboratory research by Stephen Worchel, Virginia Andreoli, and Robert Folger (1977). In a number of sessions, they created two competitive groups of college students and then had the groups cooperate on a series of superordinate tasks. In half of the sessions the two groups were told that their joint venture had been successful enough to win the monetary reward that had been offered. In the other half of the sessions the groups were told that their cooperative efforts had been unsuccessful, and therefore they would not receive the reward.

The results of a subsequent questionnaire administered to the subjects illuminate the importance of success in reducing intergroup conflict. Conflict fostered by competition was reduced only when working together led to success. When the joint efforts failed, there was no reduction in hostility; in fact, there was a slight increase in hostility. Worchel and his associates point out that when a cooperative endeavor between two conflicting groups fails, each group uses the other as a scapegoat, blaming the other for not pulling its own weight.

As we have seen, individuals, members of groups, and groups themselves, interact, perceive, and influence each other in many ways—positively and negatively, logically and illogically, safely and dangerously. Individuals and groups are subject to yet another force. Much of that force is created by people, but it is distinct from them individually: it is the environment.

Interaction with the Environment

A further kind of social interaction, namely, the interaction between the individual and the social and physical aspects of the environment, is the

There has been much recent concern about the psychological effects of crowding, which is becoming an increasingly common problem in view of the world's rapid population growth and the tendency toward greater urbanization.

province of a relatively new branch of social psychology known as environmental psychology. Interaction with the environment is social because it typically entails mutual and reciprocal effects caused by people. For example, the two areas of investigation that we will discuss—crowding and noise—are created by people, and these environmental influences, in turn, exert psychological effects on individuals.

Crowding

Concern about the psychological effects of crowding stems from two closely entwined facts about world population. First, the earth's population is growing so rapidly that it is expected to double within the next 35 years. Second, world population is becoming increasingly urbanized, with more and more people being packed into less and less space; in urban areas such as New York's Manhattan Island, population density has now reached levels of up to 70,000 people per square mile.

Animals: A "Behavioral Sink"   One approach to the study of high population density has been to pack laboratory animals together in small spaces and to investigate the effects on their behavior. The best-known study of animal crowding was conducted by John Calhoun (1962), who formed a colony of 32 rats in a limited space and allowed the population to expand rapidly (see Figure 17.3). Although Calhoun ensured that ample food and water were available to serve the growing population, the rats' behavior became alarmingly pathological as density increased. Females were often unable to carry pregnancy to full term or to survive the delivery of their litters. The females who survived made poor mothers; at one point the infant mortality rate reached 96 percent. Sexual behavior changed; young rats of either sex were mounted by male rats. Aggression was common, and there were even instances of cannibalism. Some rats were hyperactive, constantly dashing about their cages; others isolated themselves in their nests and emerged only to eat when the other rats slept. So staggering were the effects of the increased population density that Calhoun coined the term *behavioral sink* to refer to the negative behavior displayed.

Humans: Density versus Crowding   The dramatic findings in animal experiments have fueled interest in, and helped lead to, a number of studies on human crowding. Typically, the early research involved examining the correlation between population density in an urban area and various indices of social pathology such as mental illness and crime. The studies have been conducted in a number of cities, including Chicago (Galle, Gove, and McPherson, 1972; Winsborough, 1965) and New York (Freedman, Heshka, and Levy, 1975). Usually the city is divided into districts by the researchers who then examine the potential relationship between density and, for example, crime rates in a given district.

Do those districts high in population density also have high crime rates? The answer is yes, but . . . The important *but* is that the districts with the highest density and highest crime also are the poorest areas of the city. Thus it is quite possible that poverty may be the cause of both the high density and the high crime. In fact, when income is taken into account, there appears to be no correlation at all between density and crime; high-density, high-income areas did not have higher crime rates than low-density, high-income areas.

This sort of evidence has caused researchers to reconsider the issue of human crowding and to draw some important distinctions. Instead of looking for a strict cause-and-effect relationship between density and negative social behavior, they have begun to investigate the particular conditions under which density and negative behavior might be linked. They also now draw a distinction between density and crowding. *Density* denotes the actual state of physical conditions—that is, how may people per square foot occupy a room or a square mile in a city. *Crowding* refers to a psychological state—that is, the discomfort associated with having more people around than one would prefer.

Viewed in these terms, density affects our behavior only as it produces the psychological state of crowding. It is clear that density alone does not always produce crowding. People often pack into a football stadium or rock concert arena without feeling crowded. In fact, football games and rock concerts are probably less exciting and less enjoyable when the house is only half full.

Excessive Stimulation   What are the conditions under which density produces the state of crowding? J. A. Desor (1972) has suggested that density is

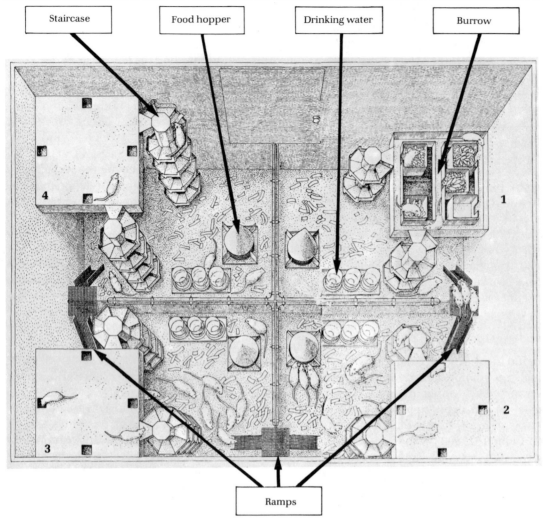

Ramps

FIGURE 17.3 One technique for studying the effects of extreme crowding. In John Calhoun's "rat city," the conical objects are food hoppers and the winding staircases lead to burrows (the burrow in pen 1 is shown with its top removed). Originally there were 32 rats, but the population was allowed to expand rapidly. Although there was always ample food and water available, overcrowded conditions resulted in hostility, high infant mortality rate, aberrant sexual behavior, and even cannibalism.

associated with crowding only to the extent that the situation results in *excessive stimulation*—the "overloading" of our cognitive capacities. At a football game, for example, density may be extremely high, but we are not paying attention to everyone in the stadium; we are not overstimulated by the people around us. Hence we do not feel crowded.

In order to test her excessive stimulation hypothesis, Desor staged a series of clever experiments. She built dollhouse-like rooms to scale and then had subjects place stick figures that represented people in the rooms. Subjects were instructed to put "as many people as you can without overcrowding them" into a room. In one ex-

periment, Desor set up two rooms that were exactly alike in shape but different in size: one room had twice as much square footage as the other. In the smaller room, subjects placed an average of 18.9 "people." But in the larger room they placed only 34.1 people—less than twice the number placed in the smaller room. This result supports the earlier point that density alone does not determine crowding. If it did, the subjects would have put in the larger room precisely twice the number of people as in the smaller room.

In further experiments, Desor examined more directly the relationship between excessive stimulation and the feeling of crowding. One method was to manipulate various architectural features that influence the level of stimulation. For example, when she divided a room with a partition, subjects placed many more people in this room than they did in an identical room without the partition. A partition has the effect of reducing stimulation from people on the other side of the room; thus it takes more people to make you feel crowded. Another architectural feature, the number of doors, also proved to be a factor. The more doors leading into a room, the fewer stick people the subjects placed in the room. Open doors open up the possibility of more stimulation and, with it, an increase in the feeling of being crowded.

Recent work by other researchers has tended to confirm Desor's proposition that stimulation is critical to the perception of crowding. For example, Jack Heller, Bradford Groff, and Sheldon Solomon (1977) created four different experimental conditions in terms of density and stimulation. To vary density they placed groups of six to eight subjects in either a small room or a large room. To vary stimulation they had some of the subjects perform a task at a private little table so that the subjects could effectively ignore the other people in the room (low stimulation); other subjects had to walk around the room to collect materials necessary to perform the task, forcing them to pay a great deal of attention to the other people and thus to become highly stimulated.

The results highlighted the role of stimulation. In the low-stimulation condition, the density of the room had no effect upon performance. In the high-stimulation condition, density became important; many more performance errors occurred in the high-density condition than in the low-density condition. In short, it appears that high density produces a feeling of crowding and the ill effects from it only when there is also excessive stimulation.

One way to avoid crowding in high-density situations is to reduce the stimulation that impinges on us. This stratagem was demonstrated by Andrew Baum and Carl Greenberg (1975) in an experiment that varied the expectations of subjects about the number of people who were to arrive in a room. Some of the subjects thought there eventually would be four people in the room; this was the low-density condition. Other subjects thought there would eventually be ten people; this was the high-density condition. The subjects who expected ten people reacted very differently from those who expected four. For example, as shown in Table 17.1,

TABLE 17.1 Number of Subjects Assuming Each Seat Position

EXPECTED GROUP SIZE	SEAT POSITION		
	Corner	Wall	Middle
4 persons	5	11	23
10 persons	31	8	1

Source: A. Baum and C. I. Greenberg, "Waiting for a Crowd: The Behavioral and Perceptual Effects of Anticipated Crowding," *Journal of Personality and Social Psychology* 32 (1975): 671-679.

these subjects tended to avoid the middle of the room and sit in a corner of the room or against the wall—positions from which they could better control the amount of stimulation received. (The division of the room into its various components is displayed in Figure 17.4.) Furthermore, they spent less time gazing at the face of the next person to walk into the room than did those who were expecting only four people.

Although such stratagems apparently enable people to cope with high density by reducing stimulation, there may be costs involved in such adaptations. We will return to this issue following our discussion of the environmental effects of noise.

Noise

An important environmental characteristic of urban areas usually associated with population density is the noise level. City dwellers tend to get used

FIGURE 17.4 Classification of seat position of experimental room. When people expected the arrival of a small group, they tended to place themselves near the center of the room. However, when they were told a large group was expected, the corners and walls were overwhelmingly chosen.

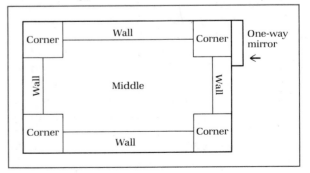

Protesters against noise pollution, which is an important environmental characteristic of urban areas. Short-term and long-term exposure to noise can have both physiological and psychological effects on individuals.

to it, but anyone who goes from the country into a densely packed urban area like San Francisco is immediately struck not only by the presence of all those people but also by the presence of all that noise. The staccato thump of jackhammers, the banging of garbage cans against sanitation trucks, the roar of airplanes overhead and subways below, the blare of taxi horns, and the shouts of people all contribute to the disconcerting din.

Short-Term Effects The classic studies of the effects of exposure to high levels of noise were carried out by David Glass and Jerome Singer (1972). Glass and Singer exposed subjects to 23 minutes of very loud bursts of noise over headphone sets and tested them during this exposure. Almost as soon as the noise began, there were immediate and marked effects on both the physiology and behavior of subjects. Physiological changes included increased heart rate and other signs of heightened arousal. Behavioral change was measured by testing the subjects' performance on various arithmetic and word problems. Those exposed to noise tended to make more errors than did those in the control group, who were not exposed to noise.

These particular effects proved to be short-lived, however. As the exposure to noise continued, subjects quickly adapted to it. Within a few minutes after the noise began, heart rate and other physiological measures returned to normal; performance on the arithmetic and word tasks equalled that of the no-noise control group.

Although this finding is a powerful demonstration of the ability of the human organism to adapt to stress, it does not tell the whole story. Glass and Singer also tested for aftereffects of adaptation to noise. After the noise was turned off, subjects had to perform a variety of cognitive tasks. One of these tasks was proofreading a typed manuscript to identify and correct errors. Those subjects who had earlier been exposed to noise did rather poorly, missing more of the typographical errors than did the subjects who had not been exposed to noise.

Even these findings, however, were subject to subtle variations. Glass and Singer showed, for example, that these aftereffects occurred only when the noise had been unpredictable in nature. Bursts of noise that occurred predictably—say, at regularly spaced intervals—produced little or no aftereffect. Predictability apparently enables individuals to prepare themselves for each burst of noise. This, in turn, may give them a feeling of some control over the noise and hence lessen the aftereffect.

The feeling of control also appeared to be at work in other experiments by Glass and Singer. Subjects were exposed to unpredictable noise but given control over the noise—a button that would stop it. After the researchers terminated the noise, subjects who had the control button available showed no aftereffect when tested at proofreading and other tasks. Interestingly, the subjects did not actually press the button: just the feeling that they had control over the noise was enough.

These findings again illustrate the importance of perceptions of control. Recall the earlier discussion of the illusion of control and the role that it plays in social perception and interaction. The desire for control appears to act as a basic human motive that underlies many social psychological processes, including person perception, attitude formation, gambling fallacies, and, as we have just seen, the effects of noise upon performance.

Long-Term Effects The Glass and Singer experiments had built-in limitations because they were able to measure only short-term effects during and after short-term exposure. What about long-term effects of exposure to noise over long periods of time? A group of researchers hypothesized that prolonged exposure to noise may produce in people a "filtering mechanism" that makes them less attentive to sounds (Cohen, Glass, and Singer, 1973). An ideal natural laboratory for testing this hypothesis was found in a 32-story apartment building that was literally built over a heavily traveled expressway in New York City. Noise levels were particularly high on the lower floors of this building because they were closer to the highway. Measurements showed, for example, that the noise level on the eighth floor was twice as high as that on the thirty-second floor.

The subjects in this investigation were elementary school children who had lived in the building for at least four years. One important test was the measurement of their auditory discrimination. Each child was presented with two spoken words that sounded similar—gear-beer, for example, or coke-cope—and then asked whether they detected a difference between the two words. Children who lived on the lower, noisier floors were much poorer at this task than those who lived on the upper floors. Because auditory discrimination is related to

reading ability, the investigators also gave each child a standardized reading test. Again, children from the noisier floors scored significantly lower than the children from the quieter floors—the lower the floor the lower the score (see Figure 17.5).

Prolonged exposure to noise thus appeared to adversely affect such important skills as hearing and reading. The children on the lower floors of the building apparently adapted to the highway noise, the authors suggest, by developing a filtering mechanism. But this ability to filter out sounds made them less sensitive to auditory cues and thus impaired their reading ability. In short, they adapted but had to pay a price.

Aftereffects of Crowding

The findings about the aftereffects of noise—decreased performance after adaptation—have inspired parallel research in crowding. As we saw in

FIGURE 17.5 Reading and auditory skills of children are shown as a function of noise levels in their apartment building. Children living on the lower, noisier floors scored significantly lower on auditory discrimination and reading tests than did children living on higher floors.

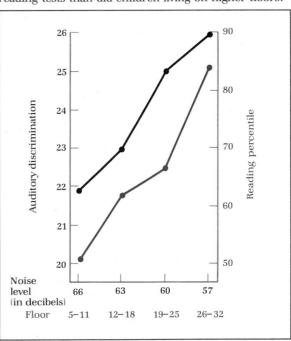

our earlier discussion of crowding, people sometimes adapt to high-density situations by controlling the amount of stimulation they receive—for example, by sitting against the wall or by paying less attention to the people in the room. Does such adaptation result in negative aftereffects as it does when people cope with exposure to noise?

To find out, Drury Sherrod (1974) adopted several of the techniques used in the Glass and Singer noise experiments. He placed groups of eight subjects in either a large room (150 square feet) or a small one (37 square feet). While in these rooms, the subjects were asked to perform various irrelevant tasks. Then, much as Glass and Singer turned off the noise in their experiments, Sherrod "turned off" the crowding by escorting the subjects into a much more spacious room. There, the subjects performed a task designed to measure their tolerance to frustration; they worked on a series of difficult paper-and-pencil puzzles, some of which were not solvable. The measure of frustration tolerance was the length of time in which subjects persisted in trying to find a solution to the unsolvable puzzles. Subjects who earlier had been in the smaller, more

---

FOCUS: Proxemics: The Space We Call Our Own

A concept closely related to both interpersonal interaction and crowding is personal space—the physical distance that we maintain during interaction with others. The study of personal space is known as *proxemics*, a word coined by the anthropologist Edward T. Hall (1966). Hall and others have suggested that personal space constitutes a kind of portable psychological bubble that envelops us. Whenever personal space is intruded upon, we become uncomfortable or even angry.

Some of the aspects of personal space have been demonstrated in a series of field studies by Robert Sommer (1969). In one study, Sommer had a female confederate approach female students who were seated alone at tables in the library. When the confederate sat down at the table several chairs away from the unwitting subject, there was an apparent invasion of personal space. Subjects would variously turn away, draw in their arm or head, mark off personal boundaries on the table with a book or purse, or even get up and walk away.

Most of the time we avoid infringing upon the personal space of others. A clear instance of this was shown by Eric Knowles and his associates (Knowles, Kreuser, Hyde, and Schuchart, 1976) in a clever field study. Knowles set up his study in a 10-foot-wide corridor in which there was a shallow alcove containing a bench. He had confederates sit on the bench and then observed the behavior of passersby. Even though the bench did not protrude into the corridor, people passing made a slight detour in order to give the bench sitters a wide berth. Interestingly, when there were two bench sitters, passersby made a wider detour than when only one person occupied the bench.

The physical dimensions of personal space vary widely, depending upon a number of factors. Among these factors are the relationship between two persons, the setting, personal characteristics, and even ethnic and nationality differences. Lovers, for example, obviously stand closer together than do strangers; coworkers are likely to huddle at a cocktail party although they are at arm's length in the office. Hall has classified distances maintained during interpersonal encounters into four zones, the boundaries of which depend upon the nature of the interaction:

* The intimate zone ranges from touching to about 18 inches. This distance is used by mothers and children, by lovers, and by—quite literally—close friends.
* The personal zone extends from 18 inches to 4 feet. This zone is ordinarily used for conversation by casual friends and acquaintances.
* The social zone is from 4 to 12 feet. Most formal and business contacts take place in this zone; it is close enough for clear seeing and hearing but sufficiently distant to preclude truly personal interaction.
* The public zone ranges beyond 12 feet and typically describes the space between listeners and a teacher or public speaker.

The actual dimensions of these zones tend to change with ethnic and cultural differences. For example, Hall and others have noted that Europeans typically carry on conversations at a closer range than do North Americans or the English and that Arabs and South Americans tend to converse almost toe to toe. These differences in the dimensions of our personal bubble of space can lead to misunderstandings and awkward social scenes. Jonathan

densely packed room displayed less tolerance to frustration than did those who had been in the larger, less densely packed room.

In addition to these two conditions of the experiment (large room and small room) Sherrod set up a third condition that gave subjects control over their situation. Subjects in this condition were placed in a dense environment, the small room, but given the freedom to leave it if they became uncomfortable. This condition paralleled that used in the Glass and Singer experiments where subjects were given a button to press if they wanted to turn off the noise. Interestingly, the results were also similar. Although subjects in this condition did not actually leave the small room, the mere availability of the option increased their sense of control over the situation. And the feelings of control, in turn, led to a decrease in the negative aftereffects on the frustration tolerance test. The frustration tolerance of these subjects ranked in the middle in the results of the three conditions; they were more tolerant to

Edward T. Hall and others have suggested that personal space represents a "psychological bubble" with which we surround ourselves. The dimensions of these zones tend to change with ethnic and cultural differences. English and North Americans, for example, tend to carry on conversations at a further range (left) than Europeans or South Americans (right).

Freedman, in his book *Crowding and Behavior* (1975), has vividly described the kind of minuet that can result when unspoken cultural concepts of personal space come into conflict:

> When someone from England meets someone from Mexico, for example, they might execute a complex little dance. The Mexican stands a little closer than the Englishman would like, while the Englishman stands a little farther away than the Mexican considers appropriate. Naturally they cannot both have their way, so they shift back and forth. The Englishman backs up slightly to adjust the distance, the Mexican moves forward to readjust it, the Englishman moves some more, and so on. Eventually, the Englishman may find himself backed into a corner while the Mexican finds that he has been chasing the other all around the room. They both feel misused. The Englishman thinks the Mexican is pushy, aggressive, overly enthusiastic, and familiar. The Mexican thinks the Englishman is cold, distant, unfriendly, and defensive. Yet all that has happened is that they were both trying to stand a comfortable and appropriate (for them) distance apart.

frustration than those subjects who had been in the small room without the option to leave, but less tolerant than those who had been in the large room.

The results of Sherrod's research, the Glass and Singer work on noise, and many other experiments make clear the remarkable adaptability of people in their interactions with the urban environment. But they also suggest that in the long run such adaptation is purchased at a price. These costs include decreased performance at certain tasks and even the tendency to become more easily frustrated (Sherrod and Downs, 1974)

SUMMARY

1. Social interactions are mutual, reciprocal, two-way processes, be they two-person (or dyadic) relationships or interactions within or between groups. Another kind of social interaction can be found in the environmental effects people exert on one another through factors like noise and crowding. Social interactions are often affected by our physical environments.

2. Thibaut and Kelley's theory of social interaction proposes that relationships depend largely upon each participant's analysis of the rewards and costs: each person tries to adopt the response that will yield the greatest rewards at the least cost. Satisfaction in a relationship depends in part on one's expectations, or comparison level. The comparison level for any interaction is the level of outcome you expect or feel you deserve. Thus, satisfaction in a relationship is not determined by the absolute level of outcome, but by the outcome relative to the comparison level. The comparison level for alternatives is the expected outcome from alternate relationships. According to Thibaut and Kelley, any time the outcome of the present relationship falls below the comparison level for alternatives, the person will break up the relationship. This theory of social interaction presents a highly selfish model of human nature and does not explain behavior such as pure altruism.

3. How we interact with people depends to a great extent upon how we perceive them and how we interpret their behavior. Impression formation is the process by which we form global impressions of people based on specific facts we have learned. Impressions are usually structured, stable, and constructive. We create structure in the process of perceiving people by categorizing what they are like. A tool of categorization is the attribution of traits, which we assign, rightly or wrongly, to individuals and to groups. Our impressions of others tend to be stable and to endure, even though we may learn facts that contradict them. In addition to structure and stability, the process of impression formation is constructive: once we have categorized a person or group, we build on the general picture.

4. There are three determinants in impression formation: primacy-recency, central traits, and context. Primacy-recency refers to the old saying that first impressions are lasting; we tend to rely more on our first impressions about others than on our latest information. Certain facts (is a person "warm" or "cold"?) are considered central traits, and we base a large part of our overall impression of others on these traits. We also learn facts about people in the context of other information; this context has an effect on how we interpret the traits in question.

5. Closely linked to impression formation is attribution, the inferences we make about the causes of other people's behavior. The perceived cause of other people's behavior can be classified into two general categories. If we think that a person acts in a certain way because of something internal in that person, we attribute the behavior to disposition. If we believe that a behavior stems from external causes, we attribute it to situation. Our perceptions of others usually depend upon dispositional attributions. We normally look for three key factors in attributing the causes of behavior: distinctiveness, consensus, and consistency. When situational causes are evident, we will frequently discount disposition (the discounting principle); conversely, there are instances when the dispositional cause is augmented, or increased (the augmentation principle), as we attribute causality to behavior.

6. In practice, certain biases creep into the attribution process. Foremost among these biases is our tendency to attribute the behaviors of others to disposition: we assume that people act in certain ways because they are that way. Another bias comes into play when we are actors rather than observers. As actors we tend to see our own behavior as situationally motivated; as observers we perceive the behavior of others as stemming largely from their own dispositions. In addition, we tend to attribute the behavior of others to dispositional causes because that leads us to believe that we "know" those people, can predict their behaviors, and thus have a sense of control over our interaction with them.

7. The two processes of social perception—impression formation and attribution of traits—serve as guides in our behavior toward others. But social perception càn influence social interaction even when the perception is false. In the self-fulfilling prophecy the perceiver causes another person to behave in a manner that confirms the perceiver's expectations. In addition, when we have biased perceptions it is possible for us only to *think* that expected behaviors have been confirmed.

8. While a number of the principles of social interaction apply both to individuals and groups, there are some notable differences in collective behaviors. One example is the risky shift, wherein research has shown that groups faced with difficult or controversial questions are more likely to decide upon or recommend more daring courses of action than would members of the group acting alone. This can be explained by (1) a diffusion of responsibility—responsibility for outcomes is diffused among group members—and (2) cultural value—risk itself has a general cultural value in our society, and groups seem to be more affected by this value than are individuals acting alone. Group behavior is also differentiated from individual behavior by the fact that all groups have behavioral expectations of its members that must be met for continued group membership; that is, groups assign us roles to play.

9. Interactions between groups parallel in many ways the processes in interpersonal relations. At the same time, two important differences between interpersonal and intergroup interactions have particular impact on intergroup conflict: (1) no individual is absolutely essential to the group, and (2) intergroup conflict increases group cohesiveness, often reinforcing biased perceptions.

10. In a classic study (the "Robbers Cave" experiment), Muzafer Sherif and his associates explored the dynamics of group conflict by creating two groups, generating hostility between them, and attempting to reduce the resulting conflict. Two factors were important in reducing conflict between the groups: (1) the introduction of superordinate goals, tasks that appealed to both groups but lay beyond the resources of a single group, and (2) ensuring success in the cooperative ventures.

11. A further kind of social interaction, that between the individual and the social and physical aspects of the environment is the province of a relatively new branch of social psychology known as environmental psychology. Interaction with the environment is social because it typically entails mutual and reciprocal effects caused by people. Two major areas of investigation for environmental psychology are crowding and noise.

12. Early research into the problems of densely populated urban areas showed a high correlation between population density and high crime rates; however, because districts with the highest density and the highest crime are also the poorest areas of the cities, it is quite possible that poverty may be the cause of both the density and the crime. Thus, instead of looking for a strict cause-and-effect relationship between density and negative social behavior, recent researchers have begun to investigate the particular conditions under which density and negative behavior might be linked. These researchers also now draw a distinction between density and crowding. Density denotes the actual state of physical conditions, that is, how many people per square foot occupy a room or square mile in a city; crowding refers to a psychological state: the discomfort associated with having more people around than one would prefer. Density produces crowding only to the extent that the situation results in excessive stimulation—the "overloading" of our cognitive capacities.

13. Another important environmental characteristic of urban areas is noise level. Studies have shown short-term negative effects of noise on human task ability; the same studies have also demonstrated a high degree of adaptability to noise by the same subjects. Long-term effects of noise may adversely affect important skills such as hearing and reading ability. Studies have also shown that our adaptability to noise and crowding may be purchased at the price of decreased performance at certain tasks and the tendency to become more easily frustrated.

Appendix:
Statistical Methods

Statistical methods are essential to psychological researchers in the communication and interpretation of research findings. An understanding of basic statistics is also important to users of research findings for the proper analysis and evaluation of those findings. Statistical methods are used to describe and summarize the results of research (*descriptive statistics*), as well as to make inferences about the meaning of research findings (*inferential statistics*).

For example, if 100 students in basic psychology take a midterm examination consisting of 100 questions and the average score is 70, that average score is a descriptive statistic—a fact. If the professor hypothesizes that the average score for all students in the college would also be 70, that would be drawing an inference—and a highly suspect inference at that.

Some Uses of Numbers

Statistical methods are applied to numbers that refer to various characteristics of individuals, events, objects, and processes; however, not all of the ways numbers are used have the same meaning. For example, a particular basketball player has a uniform with a number on it. This basketball player's height is represented by a number as is his or her body temperature. Even preference for a food, such as hot dogs, can be assigned a number. Yet, from a mathematical point of view, each of these numbers has a different meaning. Let us briefly consider how these uses of numbers differ.

When numbers are used to identify members of a basketball team, for example, the numbers are usually assigned to each player in an arbitrary fashion. The only restriction is that each player has a different number; thus the numbers assigned have no mathematical meaning. The numbers assigned do not represent a player's skill or any other characteristic of the player. When numbers are assigned merely as labels for purposes of identification, we refer to this as the *nominal use of numbers*.

A more mathematically meaningful assignment of numbers is found in the *ordinal use of numbers*. Such a use of numbers might arise in a rank order of color preferences. The color most preferred would be assigned the rank of 1, the next the rank of 2, and so on. Unlike the nominal use of numbers,

the ordinal use implies an underlying scale or dimension. In this example, the underlying dimension is color preference; the numbers assigned to various colors indicate locations along this dimension. However, the assigned numbers are only meaningful relative to each other. For example, the ranks 1, 2, and 3 might be assigned to three colors that were quite close together in terms of preference, or to three colors that differed greatly in terms of preference. The assigned ranks tell us the order of these colors and that they were the three most preferred of those ranked. But they do not provide any information about the degree of preference in absolute terms. If your favorite color was not among those being ranked, some other color would be assigned a rank of 1.

The number assigned to a person's body temperature, or more generally any use of either the Fahrenheit or Celsius scales of temperature, involves the *interval use of numbers;* the unit distance between all adjacent pairs of numbers is the same. For example, the change in body temperature from 98° to 99° is the same as the change from 100° to 101°. Similarly, in measuring air temperature in Fahrenheit, the difference in heat going from 50° to 60° is the same as the difference from 80° to 90°. The interval use of numbers allows us to locate points along a dimension and to determine how far apart they are in terms of scale units. However, the interval use of numbers only gives us relative information about any two numbers because the zero point does not indicate a total absence of what is being measured. As a consequence, an air temperature of 20° Fahrenheit cannot be said to be twice as warm of one of 10°. Such a comparison is only meaningful mathematically when the zero point is absolute, rather than being arbitrarily placed as it is in the Fahrenheit and Celsius scales.

When numbers are assigned in such a way that the scale units are equal and the zero point is absolute (indicating a total absence of what is being measured), we have an example of the *ratio use of numbers*. Examples of the ratio use of numbers include height, weight, and elapsed time. In each of these instances every assigned number is located along a dimension in an absolute sense. Therefore, it is possible to say that one person took twice as long as another to solve a problem, or that a growing child's weight had doubled in the past five years. In other words the ratio use of numbers allows us to perform all arithmetic operations (addition, subtracting, multiplication, and division) in a mathematically meaningful fashion.

Measurement Categories

Numbers are assigned and used to measure and categorize. Behavioral scientists employ three types of categorization and measurement: (1) unordered categorization, (2) ordered categorization, and (3) ordered categorization based on the natural number system. All categorization refers in some way to measurement, and these measurements are referred to as measurement scales.

- A *nominal scale* of measurement represents unordered classification. Classifying people as Texans, New Yorkers, and Alaskans is an example of a nominal scale: no meaningful descriptions are used or judgments made.
- An *ordinal scale* names the order or the rank in which the subject at hand falls. Ranking members of the basketball team by the number of quarters played in a season would represent an ordinal scale: Smith (1)—32 quarters; Jones (2)—29 quarters, and so on.
- The Fahrenheit and Celsius scales represent *interval scales*. They differ from ordinal scales in that difference in adjacent categories is the same in the number scale. The difference between 5°C and 6°C is the same as the difference between other adjacent categories—10°C and 11°C.
- A *ratio scale* differs from an interval scale in that the zero point is absolute. A weight system—ounces and pounds, for example—has an absolute zero point at which there is no weight.

Descriptive Statistics

Data, the plural of datum, refer to uncategorized and uncompared information: a group of test scores, for example, is data that have not been meaningfully processed. When researchers deal with large numbers of individuals, there is a need for making large amounts of data usable.

The main purpose of descriptive statistics is to answer the need for condensing and summarizing data. For example, suppose you wanted to describe the academic ability of the freshman class at a particular college as indicated by its performance on a scholastic aptitude test (SAT). The data, consisting of SAT scores for every student, might involve several hundred or several thousand scores. Out of this massive collection of scores, you will want to make some summary statements about the academic ability of the freshman class—for example, which score is most representative of the class as a whole. Statistics that provide such summary statements are called measures of central tendency. That is, these statistics provide ways of best representing the scores for an entire group of individuals.

Measures of Central Tendency

Central tendency is measured by the *mode* (the score that occurs most frequently), the *median* (the middle score in a distribution), and the *mean* (the arithmetic average).

The most widely used measure of central tendency is the *arithmetic mean*, or *average*. The mean of a set of scores is the number obtained by adding up all of the scores and dividing by the number of scores. Table A.1 provides an illustration of this procedure for two groups of students. It is typical to use the letter X to stand for any score for an individual. Then the symbol ΣX (the Greek letter sigma, "Σ," stands for "the sum of") indicates the

TABLE A.1 Scores on a Biology Exam for Two Groups of 10 Students

SECTION 1	SECTION 2
41	90
35	76
34	34
32	32
32	32
Median 31.5	Median 31.5
31	31
30	30
29	29
28	28
28	28

The mean ($\overline{X}$) is the sum of the scores (ΣX) divided by the number of scores (N).

SECTION 1	SECTION 2
$\overline{X} = \dfrac{\Sigma X}{N}$	$\overline{X} = \dfrac{\Sigma X}{N}$
$32 = \dfrac{320}{10}$	$41 = \dfrac{410}{10}$
Mean = 32.0	Mean = 41.0

result of adding up all of the individual scores. The letter N designates the number of scores added up. X is the symbol for the mean or average score. The bar over the X is thus used to indicate that it is the mean and not the score of an individual.

Although the arithmetic mean is the most widely used measure of central tendency, it is not always the value that is most characteristic of the scores as a whole. Because the computation of the mean takes into account the actual magnitude of each score, the mean is influenced considerably by extreme or atypical scores. When this is the case, the *median* is often used as the measure of central tendency. The median is the middlemost value in a distribution of scores. Determination of the median only considers whether a score is in the upper half or the lower half and not its absolute magnitude. To obtain the value for the median the scores are arranged in order of magnitude, as shown in Table A.1. The median is the value that divides the distribution of scores in half. If the total number of scores is even, as in Table A.1, the median is the value halfway between the two middle scores. When the number of scores is odd, the median value is the same as the middlemost score. For example, if a score of 27 was added to the scores for either Section 1 or Section 2 in Table A.1, the median value would then be 31. In all instances the number of scores above the median value must be the same as the number of scores below the median value.

The data shown in Table A.1 indicate that the means for the two sections differ substantially, although the medians are the same. This arises be-cause the two highest scores in Section 2 are extreme or atypical scores. In the case of Table A.1 the median is the better measure of central tendency because it is closer to the majority of the scores of the entire group than is the mean. Notice, for example, that the mean for Section 2 (41 as opposed to the median of 31.5) is larger than eight of the ten scores.

A third measure of central tendency is the *mode*. The mode is a relatively crude index, easy to calculate, and its value is equal to the score that occurs most often. To determine the mode you arrange the scores into a *frequency distribution*, such as Table A.2, and examine the column of frequencies to see which score occurred most often. The value of that score (43) is the mode.

Frequency Distributions and Central Tendency

A frequency distribution is a technique for showing the way in which the frequency of actually obtained scores is distributed over the range of possible score values. A frequency distribution may appear either in tabular form, as shown in Table A.2, or in graphic form, as shown in Figure A.1. In both cases the number of times each score occurred can be determined. A frequency distribution table is more convenient for computational purposes, such as determining a measure of central tendency, whereas a graphic presentation is superior for communicating the shape of a distribution.

Frequency distributions may take on any shape imaginable. For practical purposes, however, most frequency distributions that psychologists deal with are found within the range of shapes shown in Figure A.2. Notice that the top panel shows a *symmetrical distribution*, in which the value of the

TABLE A.2 Frequency Table for Introductory Psychology Exam Scores of 118 Students (55 Possible Points)

SCORE (X)	FREQUENCY OF EACH SCORE (F)
49	1
48	2
47	5
46	8
45	13
44	18
43	24
42	18
41	13
40	8
39	5
38	2
37	1

FIGURE A.1 Frequency polygon for the data presented in Table A.2

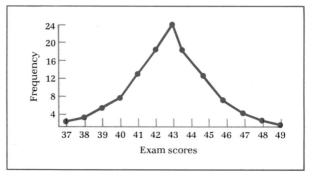

mean and median are the same. The distribution is symmetrical because the upper and lower halves (above and below 50) are mirror images of each other.

The distributions shown in the lower two panels of Figure A.2 are called *skewed* or *asymmetrical.* All skewed distributions have a longer "tail" on one end than on the other end. When the tail extends to the higher-score values, the distribution is said to be *positively skewed;* when the tail extends to the lower score values, the distribution is said to be *negatively skewed.* Notice also that in both of these distributions there is a particular relationship between the measures of central tendency. By definition, the mode is always the score occurring most often, or the score corresponding to the peak of the distribution. By comparison, the mean and median are toward the tail of the distribution, with the

FIGURE A.2 One symmetrical and two skewed distributions showing the relative locations of measures of central tendency.

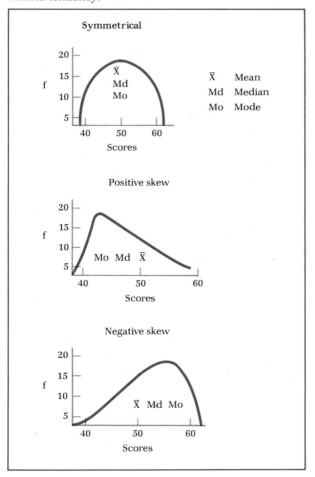

mean being furthest from the mode. Thus, in a positively skewed distribution the mean will be a larger score value than the median; in a negatively skewed distribution, the median will be a larger score value than the mean. This relationship exists because, as we noted previously, the extreme scores in the tail have more influence on the value of the mean than they do on the value of the median.

Measures of Variability

The most basic reason for using statistical methods is the existence of variation or individual differences. People differ from one another in height, weight, intelligence, attitudes, and most things of interest to psychologists. A crude but easily calculated measure of variability is the *range*. The range is obtained from a frequency distribution by subtracting the lowest obtained score from the highest obtained score. For example, the range of scores on the biology exam represented in the first section of Table A.1 is 13 ($41 - 28 = 13$); the range in Section 2 is 62 ($90 - 28$). The range of Section 2 is exaggerated by the two abnormally high scores. Because the range is based on only the two extreme scores, it tells us little about where each score lies. In addition, if either the highest or lowest obtained score is very extreme (as in Section 2), the range provides an exaggerated impression of the extent of individual differences.

The most commonly used measures of variability are the *variance* and *standard deviation*. The calculation of the variance and standard deviation is illustrated in Table A.3. Notice that the first step is to compute the mean for each distribution. In this example the means are the same (40) for the two distributions.

The next step is to calculate a *deviation score* $(X - \overline{X})$ corresponding to each obtained score. The deviation scores indicate how far from the mean of a particular distribution each obtained score is located. In Distribution A of Table A.3, the highest and lowest scores (42 and 38), deviate from the mean (40) by only 2 points each. For any given distribution the sum of the deviation scores will always be zero. This is because the mean is calculated to be the arithmetic balancing point of the distribution.

The next step is to square each deviation score

TABLE A.3 Illustration of the Calculation of the Variance and Standard Deviation for Two Distribution of Scores

Distribution A			Distribution B		
X	$X - \overline{X}$	$(X - \overline{X})^2$	X	$X - \overline{X}$	$(X - \overline{X})^2$
42	+2	4	56	+16	256
42	+2	4	52	+12	144
41	+1	1	48	+ 8	64
41	+1	1	44	+ 4	16
40	0	0	40	0	0
40	0	0	40	0	0
39	−1	1	36	− 4	16
39	−1	1	32	− 8	64
38	−2	4	28	−12	144
38	−2	4	24	−16	256

$\Sigma X = 400$ $\Sigma(X - \overline{X})^2 = 20$ $\Sigma X = 400$ $\Sigma(X - \overline{X})^2 = 960$
$N = 10$ $N = 10$ $N = 10$ $N = 10$
$\overline{X} = 40$ $\sigma^2 = 2.0$ $\overline{X} = 40$ $\sigma^2 = 96.0$
$\sigma = 1.414$ $\sigma = 9.798$

in order to generate a variability measure that increases as the spread of a distribution increases. Then we add up these squared deviation scores and divide by the number of squared deviation scores (N). This calculation gives us the variance (σ^2), which can be defined in words as the average squared deviation score or the mean of the squared deviation scores.

$$\text{Variance} = \sigma^2 = \frac{(X - \overline{X})^2}{N}$$

The standard deviation is simply the square root of the variance. In other words, it is defined as the square root of the mean squared deviation score. Thus

$$\text{Standard deviation} = \sigma = \sqrt{\frac{(X - \overline{X})^2}{N}}$$

The symbol used to represent the variance and the standard deviation is the lowercase Greek letter sigma (σ). Either the variance or standard deviation can be used to indicate variability. In either case, the larger the value the greater the variability because in wider distributions the scores are farther away on the average from the mean. Thus, the average squared distance is greater. For example, in Table A.3, greater variability is found for Distribution B than Distribution A with either measure. The variance and standard deviation could not be

represented by a value below zero, and a value of zero would only arise when there was no variability among individuals.

Variability and the Normal Distribution

The *normal distribution* is one of many possible distributions that are symmetrical in shape. The normal distribution is particularly useful to students of statistical methods. A representation of a normal distribution is shown in Figure A.3 As a symmetrical distribution, the two halves are mirror images of each another—that is, if you folded the distribution at the mean, the shape of both halves would be the same. The normal distribution is bell-shaped, with most scores occurring near the mean value. As you move away from the mean in either direction, the frequency of occurrence of the score values decreases. How are the properties of the normal distribution of use to us?

Suppose a student took a psychology exam consisting of 100 multiple-choice questions. Further suppose that the scores obtained on the exam were normally distributed and that our hypothetical student received a score of 80 correct answers. Is 80 a good score? This question cannot be answered on the basis of the information given.

Next, suppose that the mean score on the exam was 75. Now you would know that the student scored in the upper half of the class because 80 is above the mean. Remember that the mean and median values are the same in a normal distribution. Because half of the scores are found below the median, a score of 80 is in the upper half of the

FIGURE A.3 Graphic illustration of the shape of the normal distribution.

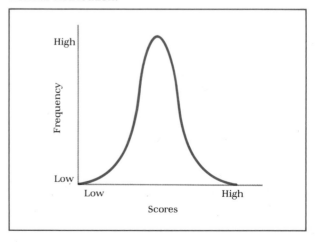

class; however, we still do not know how good a score of 80 is. Unless we know the standard deviation of the scores, we do not know how far a score of 80 is above the mean. Given this additional information we can compute the student's *standard score*. For example, given that the standard deviation is 5, we can see that a score of 80 is 5 points above the mean score of 75 or one standard deviation above the mean. This calculation is shown below, where the standard score is obtained by dividing the student's deviation score by the standard deviation of the distribution.

$$\text{Standard score} = \frac{X - \overline{X}}{\sigma} = \frac{80 - 75}{5} = \frac{+5}{5} = +1.0$$

Standard scores, or z scores, can be computed for distributions of any shape, but in the normal distribution there is a particular relationship between standard scores and areas of the distributions. This relationship is illustrated in Figure A.4. (Note that standard scores are often called z scores when the distribution is normal in shape.)

Figure A.4 shows the percentage of obtained scores occurring between the various z score values. In the normal distribution almost all scores fall within six standard deviation units. Approximately 34 percent of the scores are found between the mean (z score = 0) and one standard deviation above the mean (z score = +1). Since the distribution is symmetrical, the same percentage of scores are found between the z scores of 0 and −1. If you add up the percentages shown in Figure A.4, you will see that more than 99 percent of the scores fall

within three standard deviation units above and below the mean. This will always be the case whenever a distribution is normal in shape.

Now we can precisely evaluate the score of 80. We know that half or 50 percent of the scores are located below the mean, and that 34 percent are located between the mean and a z score of +1. Therefore, 84 percent of the scores are below an obtained score of 80. In other words, this student's percentile rank is 84. Like a z score, a percentile score is a transformed score: it is the percentage of raw scores that are less than or equal to that particular raw score. Only 16 percent of the scores were better than or equal to our student's score.

The advantage of using standard scores when the distribution of scores is normal is that once we know the mean and standard deviation we can answer a variety of questions about the distribution. For example, IQ as measured by intelligence tests is normally distributed with a mean of 100 and a standard deviation of 15. Given this information we can draw a graph like that shown in Figure A.4 in order to answer such questions as the following:

1. How many people have IQ's between 85 and 115?
   Answer: Approximately 68 percent.
2. How many people have IQ's over 115?
   Answer: 16 percent.
3. How many people are below average in IQ?
   Answer: 50 percent.

These and other questions can be answered about any set of scores that are distributed normally once the mean and standard deviation are known.

Correlation and Regression

Correlation is one of the most useful statistical methods used by psychologists. It describes the relationship between two sets of score values, which can be related in a variety of ways. The numerical index of the degree of relationship between two sets of scores is called the *coefficient of correlation*. The value of the correlation coefficient may range from −1.00 to +1.00.

It is important to realize that the sign (plus or minus) only refers to the direction of the relationship and not to the degree of relationship. For example, if high scores from one set tend to go with

FIGURE A.4 Illustration of the relationship between the normal distribution and z scores.

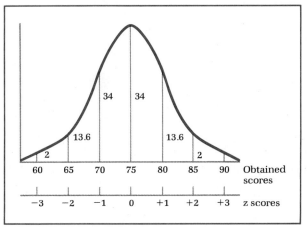

high scores from the other set while the low scores similarly go together, the relationship is said to be a *positive* (+) or *direct correlation*. If you correlated height and weight for a group of people, the resulting correlation would be a positive value: people with large scores on height tend to have large scores on weight, and vice versa. On the other hand, a *negative* (−) or *inverse correlation* exists when high scores from one set go with low scores from the other set, and vice versa. For example, as elementary school children grow older—say age 7 to age 12—they make fewer spelling errors on standardized achievement tests. There is an inverse relationship between age and the number of errors.

The relationships described by the correlation coefficient can be illustrated graphically by means of the "scatter plot" as shown in Figure A.5. Notice in the figure that the score sets are labeled X and Y. Dots are placed in the scatter plot to represent each subject's X and Y scores. It is conventional to use the letter X to designate scores on the abscissa or X axis (the horizontal axis) of the scatter plot,

and Y to designate scores on the ordinate or Y axis (the vertical axis).

Panel (a) illustrates a perfect positive correlation. Each dot in the plot represents two scores, one on X and one on Y, for the same individual. Panel (a) thus indicates for any two individuals that the one with the higher score on X also has the higher score on Y. The relationship between the two sets of scores is linear because all of the dots, or data points, fall on a straight line going from lower left to upper right. Now look at Panel (d), where a perfect negative correlation is shown. Everything said about Panel (a) applies to Panel (d) except that the data points go from upper left to lower right. In both panels the degree of relationship is the same (1.00); only the sign indicating direction of relationship differs. Positive relationships are also referred to as direct relationships; negative relationships are also referred to as inverse relationships.

Panels (b) and (e) also indicate equally strong correlations, with (b) showing a positive relationship and (e) showing a negative relationship. How-

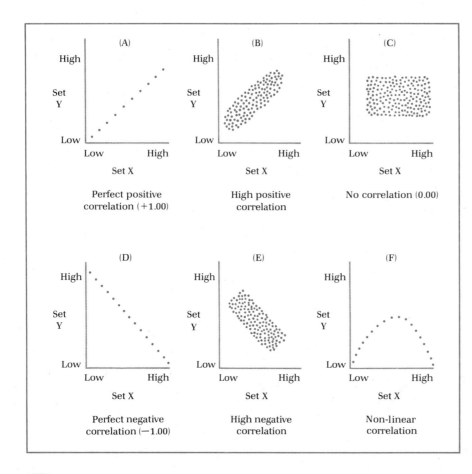

FIGURE A.5 Scatter plots illustrating several degrees of correlation between two sets of scores.

ever, the correlation is no longer perfect. In Panel (b), for example, you can readily find a pair of dots indicating that one individual has a higher score on X but a lower score on Y. Yet from the scatter plot you can also see a distinct trend for high scores on X to go with high scores on Y and for low scores on X and Y to go together; similarly in Panel (e), there is a distinctly negative or inverse relationship between X and Y, although the trend is not perfect.

Panel (c) illustrates an absence of relationship between X and Y. Notice that the range of Y values for low scores on X is the same as the range of Y values that go with high scores on X. In other words, knowing the way an individual scores on X does not tell us anything about the way that individual would score on Y. We shall return to this aspect of correlation shortly. Panel (f) is included in Figure A.5 to illustrate a strong, in fact perfect, relationship between X and Y, but one that is not linear.

The coefficient of correlation is used to describe the relationship between two sets of scores. However, to understand better the meaning of a correlation coefficient it is necessary to show how it can be used to make predictions. This is illustrated in the hypothetical and partial scatter plot shown in Figure A.6. Suppose you wanted to predict a certain person's score on Y. If all you knew were the values on Y that were obtained, all you could say is that the score would be somewhere between 30 and 90, the most extreme scores on Y. However, if you also knew this person's score on X was, say 60, then you could narrow your prediction about the Y score to a value between 50 and 70, the range of Y scores that go with X equal to 60. A similar narrowing of

FIGURE A.6 Illustration of the use of a regression line in predicting scores on Y from scores on X.

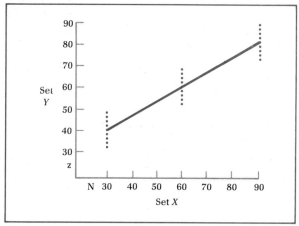

the range of Y scores also occurs for X scores equal to either 30 or 90.

The most commonly used correlation method is the *Pearson product-moment correlation*, which is based on the index designated r. As we have already seen, r increases from 0.00 to plus or minus 1.00 as the degree of relationship between the two sets of scores increases. However, the important point to note here is that r^2 and not r itself is the appropriate index of the degree of relationship that exists between the sets of scores. What r^2 measures is the proportion of Y variation that is accounted for by X variation. Let us now return to Figure A.6 to get an idea of what this statement means.

In using correlational methods for predicting performance we begin by considering the extent of variation or individual differences in one set of scores, say, in the absence of any other information. In Figure A.6 the range of Y scores is from 30 to 90. However, suppose the relationship between X and Y is that shown in the figure. The straight line running from lower left to upper right is the line that best "fits" the data points, and it is called the *regression line*. In our illustration the regression line connects the average or mean Y score for each separate value of X. Thus, the average Y score is 40 for an X of 30. For X equal to 60, the average Y is 60, and for X equal to 90, the average Y is 80.

Now if you knew that a particular person's X score is 60, your best prediction on Y would be the average Y score of 60. That is, the predicted Y score is the average Y score obtained by everyone having an X score of 60. Notice that errors in prediction will still occur, but the magnitude of the errors will be considerably reduced compared to a situation in which no knowledge of the relationship between X and Y is provided. If you know that X is 60, you no longer will be concerned about Y values below 50 or above 70 in making predictions. If you know that X is 90, the variations in Y below 70 will not be of concern. In other words, for any value of X, two-thirds of the total range of Y scores will be eliminated from concern in making predictions about Y scores. Thus, in making any single prediction about a Y score on the basis of a given value of X, we can say that two-thirds of the variations in Y have been accounted for by knowledge of X. For X and Y in general, we can say that two-thirds of the individual differences in Y scores are accounted for by knowl-

TABLE A.4 Illustration of the Relation Between r (the Correlation Coefficient) and r^2 (the Proportion of Y Variation Accounted for by X)

r	r^2
1.00	1.00
.90	.81
.80	.64
.70	.49
.60	.36
.50	.25
.40	.16
.30	.09
.20	.04
.10	.01
.00	.00

edge of the individual differences in X scores. Since this proportion (two-thirds or 0.67) equals r^2, we know that r equals 0.82. Table A.4 shows the relationship between r and r^2 for several values of r.

Notice that a correlation of 1.00 means that all of the Y variation is explained by knowledge of X. Look back at Panels (a) and (d) of Figure A.5 for an illustration. In both panels if you knew a person's score on X, you would also know the corresponding Y score. However, below values of 1.00 the relationship between r and the degree of actual relationship between scores on X and Y is not very similar. For example, an r value of 0.50 indicates that only one-fourth, or 25 percent, of the variation in Y scores is accounted for by X. Thus, it is the square of the correlation coefficient that is the best indicator of the degree of relationship described.

Two additional points need to be made before we conclude our discussion of correlation. One is that in order to correlate two sets of scores meaningfully, each pair of scores must come from the same source. You can correlate individual characteristics of people (height, weight, IQ, and so on) with one another because everyone can be described in terms of these characteristics. But you could not meaningfully correlate the heights of one group of people with the weights of another group because the pairing of a given height and a given weight would be arbitrary.

Although the correlation coefficient is an index of relationship between two sets of scores, it is not an index of a causal relationship. That is, the fact of correlation does not mean that the two sets of scores are causally related. For example, suppose you identify a group of children between the ages of 4 and 12 and correlate their mental ages with the length of their big toes. You would find the correlation to be quite high, perhaps +0.80. Recall that the notion of mental age is such that at age 4 a child with an IQ of 100 would have a mental age of 4, and that the mental age would increase one year for every year of chronological age. Thus the high correlation does not indicate a causal relationship or indicate that the brain is in the big toe. Instead it describes the fact that between the ages of 4 and 12 big toes increase in length and intellectual functioning improves.

Inferential Statistics

The methods of inferential statistics are of considerable importance in psychology but are properly reserved for more advanced textbooks. However, on the basis of our rather brief treatment of descriptive statistics it is possible to introduce some of the questions that inferential statistics are designed to answer. We can also introduce a few concepts that are basic to the use of inferential statistics.

Few factual claims made by psychologists are based on studies of everyone belonging to a defined population. Most such claims are based on studies of a subset or sample of the population. The mean of the sample and the variation or individual differences observed in the sample provide a basis for making estimates about the population as a whole. Populations can be defined in a number of ways. For instance, if you wanted to know the average IQ of plumbers, then the population would consist of all plumbers.

The concepts of a sample and a population are vital to inferential statistics. A *population* might be all 18-year-old female college students in the United States. If you wanted to know how many of those young women had used marijuana, you would find it impossible to interview all of them. You could, instead, interview a sample of 18-year-old female college students, say 2,000 of them. You would infer from your findings that the experience of the women in your sample would be similar to the experience of the population as a whole.

However a population is defined, it is important that a sample chosen for the purpose of estimation of characteristics of the population be representative of the population. This is typically done by taking a *random sample* of the population. Sampling randomly means that every member of the defined population has an equal chance of being included in the sample. Sampling randomly does not ensure correct estimation, but it does avoid any obvious sample bias. If you wanted to estimate the intelligence (IQ) of all Americans, you would not sample only from people living in Chicago. You would need samples from other urban areas, smaller towns, and from rural areas.

All the descriptive statistics discussed previously, including the measures of central tendency and variability as well as the correlation coefficient, can be used for purposes of estimation. Other questions that arise in the case of estimation include those concerning the accuracy of estimates and the degree to which estimates for one population differ from estimates for another population. The following hypothetical example that arises in inferential statistics can be used to illustrate these issues.

Suppose you were wondering whether the students enrolled in College A were more intelligent than those enrolled in College B. To answer this question you select a random sample of the students at the two schools and give each sample an intelligence test. You find that the mean IQ for students from College A was 120, and from College B it was 115. Would you be justified in concluding that College A students were more intelligent? Let us consider some factors that might influence your answer.

Figure A.7 shows three pairs of population distributions that could give rise to the results given above. The top panel illustrates two nonoverlapping populations of IQ. The middle and bottom panels show two levels of overlap for the populations. In the middle panel the populations overlap somewhat, and in the bottom panel the overlap is complete. Even restricting ourselves to just these three possibilities, the question of interest is which pair of population distributions gave rise to our sample results.

Let us first consider the sample means of 120 for College A and 115 for College B. These sample means can be considered as estimates of the corresponding populations, although it should be clear that sample means can and do differ from the means of populations from which the samples are drawn. Notice, however, that the sample means in this case do not help us in answering our basic question. As you can see in Figure A.7 the respective population means are 115 for College B and 120 for College A in both the top and middle panels. In the bottom panel, where the distributions totally overlap, the mean between 115 and 120 could easily

result from small errors in estimation due to unintentional sample bias. How then would we decide whether or not the students at College A were more intelligent?

Look again at Figure A.7 but this time consider the extent of individual differences in the three pairs of population distributions. In the top panel the range of IQs in both populations is about 5 points, in the middle panel it is about 10 points, and in the bottom panel it is about 20 points for both populations. Now if the extent of individual differences in our sample, as indexed by the variance and standard deviation, was quite small, we

FIGURE A.7 Illustration of possible relationship between IQs of students at two colleges (populations).

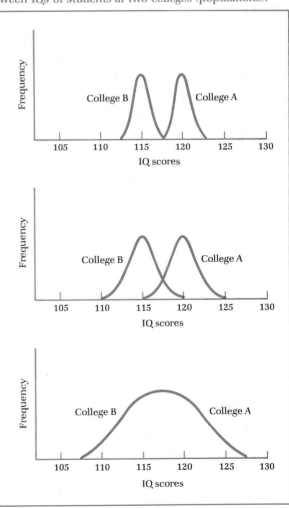

would conclude that the top panel probably best represents the true populations. This conclusion would be particularly well justified if all IQs in the sample for College B were between 112 and 117, and all those in the College A sample were between 117 and 122. On the other hand, if the variances and standard deviations were large, with both samples including some IQ values such as 110 and 125, we would conclude that the lower panel best represents the true populations.

It should be apparent that the conclusions discussed above could only be reached if the samples for College A and B truly represented their respective populations. Obviously, it would be possible in the case of the bottom panel to select samples with small variances and standard deviations. For instance, the College B sample could contain IQs mainly clustered around 115, while the College A sample IQs were clustered around 120. If that were to happen we might easily make an incorrect inference concerning the true populations. However, incorrect inferences would be more likely to arise if the middle panel represented the true populations, because even fairly small errors in sample represen-

tativeness could result in incorrectly choosing the populations in the top and bottom panels. Notice that sample bias in samples selected from the populations shown in the middle panel of Figure A.7 need not be terribly large for those samples to look like samples chosen from the populations shown in the top or bottom panels. In contrast, the sample bias in samples chosen from the bottom panel would have to be considerable before those samples would lead us incorrectly to infer that the top panel best represented the true populations.

Notice that in reaching any of the conclusions just mentioned, the major factors were the amount of variation or individual differences in the populations and the representativeness of the samples. As the variation increased, the overlap among the populations increased and the opportunity for error in estimating the population means increased. That is, the more variation that exists in a population, the greater the opportunity for a sample drawn from that population to provide a poor estimate of the population mean. Thus, in applying the techniques of inferential statistics there is always some risk of making incorrect inferences.

Glossary

Designations in parentheses following definitions indicate the primary chapter(s) in which the term is discussed.

abnormal behavior Abnormal behavior is commonly defined in one of three ways: (1) as behavior that is disturbing to others, (2) as behavior that is characterized by subjective distress, or (3) as behavior characterized by impairing psychological handicaps. (*14*)

absolute threshold Minimum level of intensity at which we can perceive a sensation. (*3*)

accommodation Process in which muscles within the eye change the shape, or curvature, of the lens and hence the focus as objects approach or recede. (*3*)

achievement Social motive that causes us to strive for bigger and better accomplishments. (*10*)

achievement tests Tests designed to measure the degree to which a particular skill or body of knowledge has already been mastered. (*13*)

acrophobia Fear of high places. (*14*)

action potential In reference to electrical activity in the neuron, a sudden change of voltage across the axon membrane. (*2*)

actor-observer difference As actors we see our own behavior largely in terms of situational forces; as observers we perceive the behavior of others as stemming largely from their own dispositions. (*17*)

acuity Maximal visual sharpness. (*3*)

adaptive traits According to Allport, personality traits that are necessary in order to carry out a particular task situation; see also *expressive traits*. (*12*)

adequate stimulus The stimulus to which a sense organ normally responds; adequate stimulus for the eye is the range of electromagnetic radiation called light. (*3*)

addiction Drug dependence that may be psychological, physiological, or both. (*5*)

additive mixture A mixture of wave lengths of light; mixing two or more wave lengths will add up to a new color; see also *subtractive mixture*. (*3*)

adipocytes Special cells in which the body stores fat. (*10*)

adjusted IQ A measure that results from the System of Multicultural Pluralistic Assessment; typically yields a higher IQ than traditional measures. (*13*)

aerial perspective One of the monocular cues for perceiving depth in which outlines of distant objects appear blurred and fuzzy. (*4*)

affective disturbance Inappropriate emotional responses; a symptom of schizophrenia. (*14*)

afferent nerves Fibers that carry sensations of warmth, cold, touch, pain, and body awareness from the receptors, or sense organs, to the spinal cord and then to the brain. (*2*)

affiliation Social motive that impels us to associate with others; some psychologists believe affiliation need has some biological as well as social basis. (*10*)

alcoholism Addiction to the depressant drug alcohol. (*5*)

alloplastic view Literally, "change outside of self"; this approach to development stresses the ability of the organism to alter nature and thus affect canalization. (*6*)

all-or-none law In reference to nerve conduction, describes the fact that once a neuron fires, increases in the stimulus do not increase the action potential. (*2*)

alpha press According to Murray, those aspects of a situation that are objectively perceived, objectively exist, and are compelling to the individual; see also *beta press* and *press*. (*12*)

alpha waves EEG pattern produced by a subject who is awake but relaxed; characterized by relatively slow synchronous rhythms (neurons firing in an orderly pattern) with a frequency of about 10 waves per second. (*5*)

altered states of consciousness States of consciousness variously typified by such characteristics as lack of self-awareness, hallucination, altered time perception, and loss of contact with present reality. (*5*)

alternate states Term designating all forms of consciousness; implies that normal waking consciousness and altered states cannot be clearly differentiated. (*5*)

altruistic behavior Behavior that helps others at some cost to the individual. (*10*)

amacrine cells Unipolar nerve cells that are without axons; found in the inner nuclear layer of the retina and in other organs; see also *bipolar cells* and *horizontal cells*. (*3*)

ambivalence Behavior characterized by the frequent juxtaposition of opposing emotions or impulses; a symptom of schizophrenia. (*14*)

amplitude One of the physical properties of sound that measures intensity or loudness of a sound wave; see also *frequency* and *phase*. (*3*)

amygdala Almond-shaped structure of the limbic system that functions in the arousal and control of emotional and motivational behavior and apparently as a receptive center for reinforcing stimuli such as pain, food, and so on. (*2*)

amygdalectomy Through electrodes planted in the amygdala, the destruction of certain "aggression centers"; there is little evidence of success in those amygdalectomies that have been performed. (*15*)

anaclitic depression Reaction of some infants when separated from their mothers; characterized by continuous crying, apprehension, withdrawal, weight loss, and retarded growth and development. (*14*)

analgesia Loss of pain without loss of consciousness. (*5*)

analgesics Pain-blocking drugs that do not produce a

loss of consciousness when used at the site of the source of pain. (5)

anal stage According to Freud, the second stage of psychosexual development during which sexual energy of the libido is anally directed; see also *genital stage*, *oral stage*, and *phallic stage*. (11, 12)

analytical psychology The theories of Jung; characterized by less emphasis on early psychosexual development than Freud; focus on present conflicts and problems and on the concepts of the collective unconscious and archetypes. (12)

andrenogenital syndrome Genetic disorder of the female that produces a tumor or excessive growth in the adrenal glands resulting in the production (commencing before birth) of large amounts of androgen (a male sex hormone). (11)

androgens Main steroids (gonadal hormones) produced by the male testes. (11)

anesthetics Agents that produce insensitivity to pain. (5)

anomalous trichomats People with a type of color blindness caused by a condition in which the pigment in the middle- or long-wavelength cones is present but has a different maximal sensitivity than the pigment in the cones of the normal eye. (3)

anorgasmia Inability to experience orgasm. (11)

antidepressants Drugs that act to elevate mood. (18)

anxiety State of uneasiness or apprehension, which is related to fear but less object-specific than fear. (14)

anxiety hierarchy A list of situations to which a person responds with anxiety ranked in order from the least to the most fear evoking; used by behavior therapists in systematic desensitization. (15)

aphagia State of being unwilling or unable to eat; lesions in the lateral hypothalamus have produced aphagia in laboratory animals. (10)

aphasia Loss or impairment of the ability to use language, usually resulting from brain damage. (5)

aptitude tests In general, tests that are designed to predict later performance that has not yet been achieved. (13)

aqueous humor Watery fluid that fills the bulge at the front of the eyes. (3)

arachnoid The middle layer between the dura and the pia mater, of the three meninges surrounding the central nervous system. (2)

archetypes According to Jung, the master patterns of images that are transmitted from generation to generation; examples include such concepts as Mother, a Supreme Being, the Hero, and a sense of wholeness; see also *personal unconscious*. (12)

archival study Study that attempts to find historical data that sheds light on a particular kind of behavior. (1)

arithmetic mean The most widely used measure of central tendency that is obtained by adding up all of the scores and dividing by the number of scores; see also *median* and *mode*. (App.)

assimilation Process through which individuals take in and incorporate information from their environment in light of their current understandings of the world. (6)

association areas Regions of the cerebral cortex whose functions are not completely understood but that are presumed to integrate or associate information arriving at the precisely mapped cortical centers for sensation and movement; also called silent areas. (2)

associative disturbance Behavior that takes the form of vague and disjointed language; a symptom of schizophrenia; also called loose associations or thought disorder. (14)

associative stage The second stage in motor learning in which cognitive activities begin to drop out and coordination and integration of responses is learned; see also *autonomous stage*, *cognitive stage*, and *motor learning*. (7)

asymmetrical distribution See *skewed distribution*. (App.)

attachment Special bond formed between infant and care-giver. (6)

attitude Disposition that makes a person categorize objects, people, or issues along an evaluative dimension. (16)

attractivity Initiation of the sexual encounter by the female of the species by showing the male such stimuli as swollen or highly colored "sexual skin." (11)

attribution theory Deals with the underlying principles by which we decide the causes of another person's actions; attribution refers to the inferences we make about the causes of other people's behavior. (17)

audition The act of hearing; requires both rhythmical variations in the pressure of a medium near us and the reception of these variations by the ear. (3)

auditory canal The visible opening of the ear; a hollow tube that concentrates sound waves. (3)

auditory masking Drowning out of one sound by another not simply because of tone intensity but because of similarities in frequency of the two tones. (4)

augmentation principle The practice of increasing or adding to dispositional causes in attributing causality to behavior; see also *discounting principle*. (17)

autism The tendency to withdraw from involvement in the external world and to become preoccupied with private fantasies; a symptom of schizophrenia. (14)

autokinetic effect If an individual is placed in a totally dark room with no frame of reference and then a single, stable point of light is introduced, the light appears to move erratically. (16)

automatic writing Act of writing understandably without awareness of what is being written; a result of posthypnotic suggestion. (5)

autonomic nervous system One of the two parts of the peripheral nervous system that controls the functioning of the internal organs such as arteries, heart, stomach, and sweat glands; see also *somatic nervous system*. (2)

autonomous stage   Third stage of motor learning in which the performer seems to become more automatic in performing the task; see also *associative stage*, *cognitive stage*, and *motor learning*. (7)

autoshaping   Development of a learned response under circumstances in which there is no contingency between the response and the delivery of reinforcement. (7)

average   See *arithmetic mean*. (*App.*)

aversive centers   Areas in the midbrain near the hypothalamus that seem to produce pain or discomfort in laboratory animals when those areas are electrically stimulated. (10)

aversion therapy   Type of counterconditioning, behavior therapy that aims at substituting negative feelings for positive ones by conditioning aversion to stimuli that are considered inappropriately attractive; see also *implosive therapy* and *systematic desensitization*. (15)

avoidance learning   Conditioning to a cue so that in anticipation of punishment the animal learns to avoid the punishing stimulus. (7)

axon   One of a neuron's three essential parts—a single long appendage jutting out from the soma on the side opposite the dendrites; see also *dendrite* and *soma*. (2)

axon hillock   A gentle swelling at the point on the nerve cell body from which the axon originates. (2)

balance theory   Theory of interpersonal attraction based on the tendency of people to seek consistency among their own thoughts, feelings, and actions. (16)

barbiturate   Sedative-hypnotic drug that induces general anesthesia when used in large doses. (5)

basilar membrane   A delicate fibrous membrane located within the coils at the base of the cochlea of the inner ear. (3)

behavioral rehearsal   A procedure similar to modeling in which the therapist demonstrates how to handle an interpersonal problem in a better way, and the patient then imitates the therapist, continually rehearsing the new behavior. (15)

behavioral sink   Term coined by Calhoun to refer to the negative behavior displayed by laboratory animals in an overcrowded situation. (17)

behaviorism   School that views psychology as the study of behavior that is observable and measurable and the ways in which stimulus-response relationships are formed. (1)

behavior shaping   The training of novel behavior or sequences of actions by breaking up the desired action into small steps and then reinforcing the proper response to each step until the desired behavior is learned. See also *successive approximation*. (7)

behavior therapy   Therapy that focuses on behavior itself rather than on subjective determinants; see also *cognitive restructuring*, *counterconditioning*, *modeling*, *operant techniques*, and *self-control procedures*. (15)

beta press   According to Murray, those aspects of a situation that are perceived to be present by the individual and thus influence his or her behavior; see also *alpha press* and *press*. (12)

beta waves   EEG patterns produced by subjects who are alert, mentally active, and attending to external stimuli; characterized by more rapid waves of smaller amplitude (height) and less synchrony than alpha waves. (5)

biased perception   A situation in which the perceiver of another person's behavior only thinks that expected behavior is confirmed, even when the other person's behavior does not actually conform to the perceiver's expectations. (17)

bilateral symmetry   Arrangement by which structures of the body and brain are paired or divided into similar halves. (2)

binaural   Refers to our two-eared system of audition. (3)

binocular cues   Cues for visual depth perception that require the use of both eyes. (4)

biofeedback   Process by which subjects can observe their own physiological processes that do not ordinarily reach awareness such as brain waves and blood pressure, so that they can attempt consciously to control them. (5)

biological clock   Internal time-keeping mechanisms that control an individual's circadian rhythm, or daily round of sleep and waking; see also *circadian rhythm*. (5)

biological preparedness   Theory suggesting that an organism may be biologically predisposed to become fearful of certain stimuli more easily than others. (14)

biosocial complex   The sum of the cultural and biological determinants of sexual behavior. (11)

bipolar affective disorders   Part of a cluster of disorders of mood and affect characterized by alternating swings between elation and depression. (14)

bipolar cells   Cells of the inner nuclear layer of the retina that organize information coming from the rods and cones and transmit it to the ganglion cells; see also *horizontal cells* and *amacrine cells*. (3)

brain stem   Stalklike portion of the brain rising from the spinal cord into the skull. (2)

brainwashing   Extreme form of intentional social influence. (16)

brain waves   Wavy patterns shown by an electroencephalograph that represent fluctuations or oscillations in voltage, which in turn reflect the sum of many nerve cells firing in the cerebral cortex. (5)

brightness   The psychological aspect of color that refers to the physical intensity of color; see also *hue* and *saturation*. (3)

brightness constancy Tendency to perceive an object's brightness as stable over a wide range of illumination; see also *color constancy, perceptual constancy, shape constancy,* and *size constancy.* (4)

bystander intervention Refers to the decisions people must make about whether to step in and help in an emergency. (16)

calcarine fissure Fissure in the occipital lobe at the back end of the cortex; involved in the human visual system. (2)

canalization Development of systems in which genetic influence is relatively strong and environmental influence is relatively weak. (6)

Cannon-Bard theory Theory that physiological arousal alone does not cause emotion but is produced simultaneously with the subjective experience of emotion. (10)

cardinal traits According to Allport, extremely strong characteristics that shape the total personality; see also *central traits* and *secondary traits.* (12)

case history Technique used in clinical psychology; a compilation of a kind of psychological biography of the client. (1)

case relations Grammatical relations that emphasize the semantic structure of utterances, not just the syntactic form. (9)

castration anxiety Freud's term for the fear of removal of the penis experienced by males during the phallic stage. (11)

catharsis Relief of emotional tension by reestablishing the association between the present emotion and the past causal event. (10)

cell body See *soma.* (2)

center-off The process in which certain of the eye's ganglion cells increase their firing rate when light falls in the peripheral area surrounding the center of the receptive field; see also *center-on.* (3)

center-on The process by which certain of the eye's ganglion cells decrease their firing rate when light falls in the peripheral area surrounding the center of the receptive field; see also *center-off.* (3)

center-surround The concentric organization of the receptive field of the eye's ganglion cells. (3)

central fissure Major fissure of the cerebral cortex cutting laterally across the surface separating the frontal lobe from the parietal lobe; also called the fissure of Rolando. (2)

central nervous system Made up of the brain and spinal cord that together regulate and control the activity of the entire body; see also *peripheral nervous system.* (2)

central traits According to Allport, characteristics that are important but not pervasive in shaping personality;

see also *cardinal traits* and *secondary traits.* Facts or perceptions that carry special weight in impression formation. (17)

cerebellum Large structure attached to the rear of the brain at the level of the pons; helps maintain the body's equilibrium and coordinate muscles during fine movements. (2)

cerebral cortex Fissured, grayish surface that covers much of the brain's exterior; controls the more complex functions of the organism. (2)

cerebral dominance Specialization of one or the other of the brain's hemispheres for certain tasks or abilities. (2)

cerebral hemispheres The two large connected bodies that make up the cerebrum; see also *cerebrum.* (2)

cerebrospinal fluid Fluid in the thin layer of space between the arachnoid and the pia mater of the brain; supplements the brain's arterial circulatory system by supplying nutrients and removing waste matter; also serves as a buoyant shock absorber. (2)

cerebrum The two massive connected bodies that arch above and around the brain stem and its connected structures; see also *cerebral hemispheres.* (2)

choroid The dark-pigmented lining, rich in blood vessels, that forms the middle layer of the eye and serves to keep out all light except for that which enters through the pupil. (3)

chromosomes Microscopic, rodlike units of the male sperm and the female ovum that contain the genes. (6)

chunking Organization of material in such a way as to include more items of information per unit; see also *chunks of information.* (8)

chunks of information Memory units that result from recoding or integrating more elementary units. (8)

circadian rhythm Biological cycle that governs an individual's daily round of sleep and waking; see also *biological clock.* (5)

classical conditioning A form of conditioning attributed to Pavlov in which a neutral stimulus, the conditioned stimulus (CS), is paired with an unconditioned stimulus (US), to produce a conditioned response (CR) similar to the unconditioned response (UR); primarily restricted to the acquisition of involuntary associations. (7)

claustrophobia Fear of enclosed places. (14)

client-centered therapy Humanistic therapy developed by Rogers, in which patients themselves set the goals, and therapists refrain from giving advice. (15)

clinical psychologist A practitioner who holds a PhD in psychology and has had extensive training in research, psychological testing, and therapy techniques. (15)

closure Perceptual tendency to fill in the gaps in an otherwise continuous pattern. (4)

cochlea Principal structure of the inner ear; essentially a long, rolled-up bony tube filled with fluids that contains the basilar membrane, which stimulates the auditory receptors. (*3*)

coaction Situation in which a person performs a task in the presence of others who are also engaged in a similar task. (*16*)

cochlear partition Structure running the coiled-up length of the cochlea of the inner ear; on its bottom side is the basilar membrane. (*3*)

cocktail party effect The ability to track a specific person's voice in a crowded, noisy room. (*4*)

coefficient of correlation Numerical index of the degree of relationship between two sets of scores; value of the correlation coefficient may range from −1.00 to +1.00. (*App.*)

cognitive development Processes of intellectual growth and the stages at which they come into play. (*6*)

cognitive economy Principle at work in hierarchically organized memory structures; only when a property of a superordinate does not apply to a subordinate is that represented in the memory structure. (*8*)

cognitive learning person variables Variables that include the individual's competencies to construct or to generate a wide variety of behaviors under various conditions. (*12*)

cognitive map Representation in memory of what is where in terms of landmarks, routes or paths, and boundaries. (*8*)

cognitive restructuring Approach in behavior therapy that emphasizes manipulation, or restructuring, of cognitive processes. (*15*)

cognitive stage The first stage of motor learning in which learners draw on reasoning abilities and past experiences in order to learn the elements and skills of a new task; see also *associative stage, autonomous stage,* and *motor learning.* (*7*)

collective unconscious What Jung defined as "the all-controlling deposit of ancestral experience from untold millions of years, the echo of prehistoric world events in which each century adds an infinitesimally small amount of variation and differentiation"; these ancient memories take the form of archetypes. (*12*)

color blindness A hereditary visual disability generally characterized by some abnormality of the cones of the retina or their pigmentation. (*3*)

color constancy Tendency to perceive the colors of an object as constant whether in bright or dim light; see also *brightness constancy, perceptual constancy, shape constancy,* and *size constancy.* (*4*)

color spindle A mechanism that visually represents the relationship among hue, brightness, and saturation of color. (*3*)

commissures Several bands of nerve fibers that connect the cerebral hemispheres. (*2*)

comparison level Level of outcome you expect or feel you deserve in any interaction; determines the degree of satisfaction attained in a relationship; see also *comparison level for alternatives.* (*17*)

comparison level for alternatives The make-or-break factor in a relationship that depends on the alternative relationships available; if the comparison level of the present relationship falls below the comparison level for the alternatives, the relationship will break up; see also *comparison level.* (*17*)

complementarity Meshing of people's different needs in such a way that each is satisfied. (*16*)

complex cells One of three types of feature detector cells in the visual cortex that are sensitive to a line or edge at a given orientation but also respond to an edge or line at any place in their receptive field; see also *feature detectors, hypercomplex cells,* and *simple cells.* (*4*)

concentrative meditation Meditation in which alteration of consciousness is sought through detachment from both the external environment and internal thought processes. (*5*)

concept Properties or relationships common to a class of objects or ideas. (*7*)

concept learning A way of ordering experience and perceptions of the world in order to grasp the important similarities between things while ignoring the irrelevant details. (*7*)

concrete operational period In Piaget's theory, the period from about age 7 to age 11 during which children display a logical organization of thought and can perform mental operations of actions that previously had to be carried out in actuality. (*6*)

conditioned response (CR) In classical conditioning, a response elicited by some initially neutral stimulus, the conditioned stimulus (CS), as a result of pairing between that conditioned stimulus and an unconditioned stimulus (US); similar but usually not identical to the original unconditioned response; see also *classical conditioning.* (*7*)

conditioned stimulus (CS) In classical conditioning, the neutral stimulus that comes to elicit the desired response through pairing with the unconditioned stimulus; see also *classical conditioning.* (*7*)

conditions of worth According to Rogers, behaviors and experiences that a person perceives others as valuing rather than as being intrinsically valued. (*12*)

cones Light-sensitive receptor cells of the retina that convert light into neural signals; they function principally in bright illumination and detect true colors as well as black and white; see also *rods.* (*3*)

conformity Situation in which an individual changes judgments or behavior as a result of exposure to the ideas and judgments of a group. (*16*)

conscious mental activity Freud's term for all those thoughts and feelings that are being experienced at the moment, which represent only a small fraction of mental life; see also *preconscious mental activity* and *unconscious mental activity*. (*12*)

consonance Occurs when the frequencies of two tones are sufficiently different to be heard as distinct sounds; see also *dissonance*. (*3*)

constituent analysis Breaking a sentence down into its various components in order to identify the phrase structure rules that characterize a particular language. (*9*)

context A determinant in impression formation; we learn facts about people in the context, or light, of other information. (*17*)

context-conditioned variation The characteristic of the speech signal that causes perception of particular syllables to vary, depending on the contexts provided by the individual phonemes. (*9*)

continuity Perceptual tendency to see elements in interesting patterns as being grouped together. (*4*)

continuous reinforcement In operant conditioning, the schedule of reinforcement in which an operant response is reinforced at every occurrence of the response. (*7*)

control group In experiments, a group of subjects that do not receive the conditions being studied; group used as a source of comparison to be certain the experimental group is being affected by the independent variable and not other factors. (*1*)

convergence A cue for binocular vision that results from the angle formed by the convergence of the two eyes as they pivot inward to focus on a single object. (*4*)

cornea Transparent, tissuelike coating of the front of the eye. (*3*)

corollary discharge In vision, an hypothetical neural event in which perceptual mechanisms somehow compensate for the movement of our own eyes. (*4*)

corpus callosum Largest of the bands of nerve fibers that join the cerebral hemispheres. (*2*)

correlation Describes the relationship between two sets of score values; see also *negative correlation* and *positive correlation*. (*App.*)

correlational research Methods for analyzing relationships between variables through observation, queries, or data gathering. (*1*)

Cottrell's theory Modification of Zajonc's theory to suggest that it is not just the presence of an audience that arouses a person and enhances the dominant response but the presence of an audience capable of evaluating and rating the subject. (*16*)

counseling psychologist A practitioner who has graduate training similar to that of a clinical psychologist but typically with less emphasis on research. (*15*)

counterconditioning Approach in behavior therapy that aims to break the connection between a given stimulus and a classically conditioned response; see also *aversion therapy*, *implosive therapy*, and *systematic desensitization*. (*15*)

countertransference In a therapy situation, the condition that occurs when analysts respond to the hostile or seductive transference of patients with unconscious emotional reactions of their own. (*15*)

covert desensitization A technique in aversion therapy in which clients are asked to imagine the aversive effects of an undesirable behavior, such as heavy drinking, in order to stop the behavior. (*15*)

cranial nerves A set of motor and sensory nerves (effectors and receptors) serving the muscles and sense organs of the head. (*2*)

creativity In natural language, the ability exemplified by the inventiveness of generative processes. (*9*)

crisis intervention A service of community mental health programs that provides immediate help to people who are experiencing serious emotional crises by attempting to alleviate the precipitating stress and to mobilize the person's own capabilities for coping. (*15*)

criterion measure In test validation, the measure to which subject's score on a test can be compared. (*17*)

critical period Period of maximum sensitivity for learning or acquiring certain skills or behaviors. (*6, 7*)

cross tolerance In drug use, the situation that occurs when tolerance to one drug renders other drugs less effective; see also *tolerance*. (*5*)

crowding The psychological state characterized by discomfort associated with having more people around than one would prefer; see also *density*. (*17*)

cultural bias Issue raised as a criticism of intelligence tests for being culture-specific and favoring native speakers of the testing language. (*13*)

data Uncategorized and uncompared information; the plural of datum. (*App.*)

decibel Unit for measuring the relative intensity of sound. (*3*)

deep hypnosis State in which subjects may no longer respond to the suggestions of the hypnotist but experience, on their own, ego loss, a sense of timelessness and bliss, and other feelings removed from normal consciousness. (*5*)

deep structure The meaning of a sentence intended by the speaker; see also *surface structure*. (*9*)

defense mechanisms A range of automatic and unconscious responses brought into play by the ego in order to reduce the tension and anxiety brought on by the conflict between the id and the superego. (*14*)

deindividuation Submerging of the individual into the group; common to mob behavior. (*16*)

delayed conditioning Learning that takes place when the conditioned stimulus begins several seconds before the unconditioned stimulus and continues to the onset of the unconditioned stimulus; (*7*)

delta waves EEG patterns that appear as the descent into deep sleep progresses. (*5*)

delusions   Strongly held beliefs not shared by others in a culture; a symptom of schizophrenia. (*14*)

dendrite   One of a neuron's three essential parts—a projection that receives impulses from other neurons and conducts them to the cell body and axon; see also *axon* and *soma*. (*2*)

density   The actual state of crowded physical conditions; see also *crowding*. (*17*)

dependent variable   In psychological research, the response being measured; under the hypothesis being tested, it is presumed to be dependent on the independent variable. (*1*)

depressant   Any drug that has a depressing effect on central nervous system activity. (*5*)

depression   Part of a cluster of disorders of mood and affect; characterized by feelings of dejection and melancholy. (*14*)

deprivation drive   Theory proposed by Lorenz, that the drive toward aggression is a deprivation drive, that is, an unsatisfied drive. (*10*)

depth of encoding   Theory that the differences between short-term and long-term memory are due to how shallowly or how deeply information is processed. (*8*)

descriptive statistics   Use of statistical methods to describe and summarize the results of research. (*App.*)

determinants of intelligence   The combination of hereditary and environmental factors that determine intelligence. (*13*)

deuteranopia   A type of color blindness caused by an absence of green-catching middle-wavelength cones. (*3*)

development   Branch of psychology concerned with the scientific study of changes that occur in individual growth, thinking and learning, and social behavior over time. (*6*)

deviance   Behavior that departs in a marked and noticeable way from accepted group norms. (*16*)

deviation IQ   The IQ determined by the 1960 Stanford-Binet test, which reflects performance relative to others of the same chronological age. (*13*)

deviation score   A number that indicates how far from the mean of a particular distribution each obtained score is located. (*App.*)

diasthesis stress model   An explanation for the origins of some forms of abnormal behavior, which suggests that some people may possess higher levels of vulnerability to stress and that this vulnerability is at least partly determined by genetic factors. (*14*)

difference threshold   The smallest difference between two stimuli that can be reliably perceived. (*3*)

direct correlation   See *positive correlation*. (*App.*)

direct reinforcement   In Bandura's social learning theory, an external reward experienced at firsthand; see also *vicarious reinforcement*. (*12*)

directional vision   The visual ability to determine accurately the direction of a stimulus. (*4*)

discounting principle   The practice of discounting dispositional factors when situational causes are evident in attributing causality to behavior; see also *augmentation principle*. (*17*)

discrimination   The process of learning to respond to certain stimuli and not to others. (*7*)

discriminative stimulus   In operant conditioning, a specific stimulus that comes to control a response. (*7*)

disparity   In visual depth perception, the subtle difference resulting from the slightly different point of view of each eye. (*4*)

displacement   A defense mechanism—the shifting of an impulse directed at one person onto a substitute person or object deemed more acceptable. (*14*)

dispositional reasons   One of the categories in the attribution process by which people make judgments about the causes of other people's behavior based on the belief that something internal in the other person is responsible for the behavior; see also *situational reasons*. (*17*)

disregulation theory   Theory proposed to explain psychophysiological disorders, based on disruption of the internal regulatory system. (*14*)

dissociation   Postulated process whereby certain mental processes split off from normal consciousness and function independently, which helps explain what occurs during hypnosis; see also *hidden observer*. (*5*)

dissonance   Occurs when two tones sounded together produce a third tone, based on the difference in their frequencies, that does not harmonize with the fundamental tones sounded thus producing a "rough" or "harsh" sound; see also *consonance*. (*3*)

dopamine hypothesis   Theory that dopamine, a neurotransmitter known to be involved in the fine control of certain muscle movements, may, when present in excess, cause symptoms of schizophrenia. (*14*)

dorsal root ganglia   A group of cells containing sensory cell bodies situated just outside the spinal cord. (*3*)

double-blind technique   Safeguard in drug experiments when neither the experimenter nor the subject knows which group is getting the drug and which is getting the inert substance or placebo. (*1*)

dream analysis   See *dream interpretation*. (*15*)

dream censorship   According to Freudian theory, a masking of the real meaning of dreams (latent content) because the meaning would be unacceptable to the patient's conscious standards of morality. (*15*)

dream interpretation   Method employed by Freud, Jung, and others to explore the unconscious; closely related to free association; patients report their

567

dreams, which are analyzed by the psychoanalyst for manifest and latent content; see also *manifest content* and *latent content*. (*12*)

drive-reduction theory A theory, that claims that all behavior is motivated by the need to eliminate or satisfy a biological drive. (*10*)

drives Hypothetical internal states produced by a small number of primary biological needs such as water or food. (*10*)

dura mater Heavy and leathery membrane that forms the outermost layer of the three meninges surrounding the central nervous system. (*2*)

dyad A two-person relationship—the smallest social unit. (*17*)

eardrum A taut membrane in the ear that vibrates rhythmically with the cycle of pressure and rarefaction from sound waves. (*3*)

echoic memory An auditory memory trace, or the persisting aftereffects of stimuli, of very short duration similar to the visual, or iconic trace. (*8*)

ectomorph One of Sheldon's somatotypes—describes those whose physiques are thin and fragile; see also *endomorph* and *mesomorph*. (*12*)

EEG Acronym for electroencephalograph. (*5*)

effectors Muscles and glands. (*2*)

efferent nerves Nerve fibers that carry messages from the brain, down the spinal cord, to the effectors, or muscles and glands. (*2*)

effort justification Notion that people like what they have chosen to suffer for. (*16*)

ego psychologists Psychologists, including Horney, Fromm, and Erikson, who followed Freud but departed from strict psychoanalytical thought in believing that the conscious ego was more important in shaping personality than the instinctual drives of the id. (*12*)

eidetic imagery A relatively rare form of memory characterized by extreme vividness of detail in recall; commonly referred to as photographic memory. (*8*)

Electra complex According to Freud, a conflict that arises among females during the phallic stage when they blame the mother for their own lack of a prominant exterior sex organ; see also *Oedipus complex*. (*12*)

electroconvulsive therapy A form of biological treatment principally used in cases of severe depression in which a brief electric current is sent through the brain to produce a convulsive seizure; also called shock treatment. (*15*)

electroencephalograph (EEG) Instrument that records gross electrical activity in the brain. (*5*)

electromagnetic spectrum Entire range of wavelengths or frequencies of electromagnetic radiation. (*3*)

embedded construction A sentence within which another sentence is enclosed or "embedded". (*9*)

emotion Any strong feeling consisting of both a mental, or cognitive, and a physiological component. (*10*)

encoding Extraction of information from events we experience under the conditions that the events are experienced. (*8*)

encounter group A form of group therapy, group members are encouraged to relate intimately with one another and to express themselves more fully than in ordinary interpersonal interactions. (*15*)

endomorph One of Sheldon's somatotypes—describes those whose physiques tend to softness and roundness; see also *ectomorph* and *mesomorph*. (*12*)

ensemble code A theory of visual perception that proposes that the firing of various combinations of the same set of nerve cells should signify different perceptions. (*4*)

epigenetic landscape One model for portraying the relationship between genetically determined and paced factors and the interaction between the developing organism and its environment; depicts the biological control of development in terms of constraints of varying strengths. (*6*)

episodic memory Memory of spatial and temporal aspects of experiences that are of a highly autobiographical nature; see also *semantic memory*. (*8*)

escape learning Form of learning in which an acquired response removes an organism from a painful stimulus; reinforcement consists of the reduction or cessation of an aversive stimulus. (*7*)

estrogen One of the primary steroids (gonadal hormones) produced in the female's ovaries. (*11*)

estrus In mammalian mammals, period in which the female of the species is sexually receptive (in heat). (*11*)

ethologists Scientists who study animals in their natural environments. (*7*)

evoked potential The brain's responses to sudden changes in stimuli, as measured by an electroencephalograph, that have been found to correlate with IQ scores from traditional tests; a technique used in neurometrics; see also *neurometrics*. (*13*)

excessive stimulation The "overloading" of our cognitive capacities. (*17*)

excitatory neurotransmitter Neurotransmitter serves to encourage the firing of a nerve impulse; see also *inhibitory neurotransmitter* and *neurotransmitter*. (*2*)

expressive traits Particular styles of behavior as defined by Allport in his trait theory of personality; see also *adaptive traits*. (*12*)

extinction Weakening of a conditioned response by continuous presentation of the conditioned stimulus without the unconditioned stimulus. (*7*)

extraversion One of the major dimensions of personality proposed by Eysenck; extraverts are more sociable, lively, and excitable than introverts; see also *introversion*. (*12*)

factor analysis Statistical method that defines the common components or dimensions underlying various tests or measures. In order to find commonalities that run through all or some of the tests. (*13*)

familiarity Factor in interpersonal attraction—we tend to see frequently and become familiar with people who live nearby; see also *propinquity*. (*16*)

family therapy Form of therapy that involves several members of the family in the treatment process; based on the belief that the dynamics of family interaction may be responsible for the symptoms of an individual; see also *group therapy*. (*15*)

feature detectors Nerve cells of the visual cortex that respond to specific linear features of shape or orientation in their receptive fields; see also *complex cells; hypercomplex cells,* and *simple cells.* (*4*)

Fechner's law The assertion that the relationship between stimulus intensity and the strength of sensation is a logarithmic one in which a constant ratio of stimulus produces a constant difference in sensation. (*3*)

feeding center Term used to describe the role of the lateral hypothalamus as an appetite activator that signals the need to eat; see also *satiety center*. (*10*)

figure-ground relationship The differentiation of the visual field into a part (the figure) that stands out from the remainder (the ground). (*4*)

fine motor skills Small body movements, such as drawing, that are difficult for very young children to master; see also *gross motor skills*. (*6*)

fissure of Rolando See *central fissure*. (*2*)

fissure of Sylvius See *lateral fissure*. (*2*)

fissures Folds and grooves in the gray matter of nerve cells that make up the brain's cerebral cortex. (*2*)

fixations According to Freud, those motives, aims, or drives that may be frozen, or fixated, early in childhood, remaining in the unconscious and shaping behavior throughout life. (*12*)

fixed-interval (FI) schedule Schedule of reinforcement in which reinforcement depends on a lapse of a specified amount of time instead of the organism's behavior; see also *fixed-ratio schedule, variable-interval schedule,* and *variable-ratio schedule*. (*7*)

fixed-ratio (FR) schedule Schedule of reinforcement in which reinforcement is given only after a specific number of responses have been made; see also *fixed-interval schedule, variable-interval schedule,* and *variable-ratio schedule*. (*7*)

follicle-stimulating hormone (FSH) One of the two protein hormones, called gonadotropins, that is manufactured and released into the bloodstream by the pituitary gland and that is essential for release of spermatozoa from the testes and eggs from the ovaries; see also *luteinizing hormone*. (*11*)

formal operational period In Piaget's theory, the fourth and final stage of cognitive development during which young people extend the ability to reason logically to abstract matters. (*6*)

fovea Area in the center of the retina containing cones and no rods; daylight vision is most acute in the fovea. (*3*)

free association A method for delving into the unconscious used in psychoanalysis in which clients are instructed to give their thoughts complete freedom and to report all the daydreams, feelings, and images that flash through their minds no matter how incoherent or meaningless they might seem. (*12*)

frequency One of the physical properties of sound that measures the number of sound waves per second noted in units called hertzes (Hz); see also *amplitude* and *phase*. (*3*)

frequency distribution A technique for showing, either in tabular or in graphic form, the way in which the frequency of actually obtained scores is distributed over the range of possible score values. (*App.*)

frequency theory Theory of how the ear codes pitch, which proposes that the pitch we hear is determined by the frequency of the firing of nerve impulses in the auditory nerve fibers; see also *place theory*. (*3*)

frontal lobe A lobe in each cerebral hemisphere of the brain that contains the motor cortex, which helps control voluntary movements. (*2*)

frustration-aggression hypothesis Theory that aggression is always a consequence of frustration which results from people being prevented from reaching goals or engaging in desired activities. (*10*)

functional analysis One of the techniques used in operant therapy with children in which the therapist visits the home to observe the child's behavior and the parents' unwitting reinforcement policies, notes correlations, and then devises a strategy to help parents reinforce desired behaviors. (*15*)

functional fixedness The inability to recognize the various possible uses of an object beyond its conventional uses. (*8*)

functionalism Early school of psychological thought that was concerned with the use of the mind rather than its contents. (*1*)

functional psychoses Psychoses, such as schizophrenia, for which there is no known single cause and which are not the consequence of disease or brain damage; see also *organic psychoses*. (*14*)

funiculi A butterfly-shaped gray mass in the spinal cord made up of nerve cell bodies surrounded by white nerve fibers of afferent and efferent nerves. (*2*)

g factor See *mental facility*. (*13*)

gain-loss theory Theory of interpersonal attraction

that holds that we like someone better if the other person first dislikes us and then likes us, than if the person had liked us all along. (*16*)

ganglia Groups of nerve cells that, along with fiber tracts lying outside of the central nervous system, make up the peripheral nervous system. (*2*)

ganglion cells Third layer of the retina; fibers of which bundle together to form the optic nerve. (*3*)

general anesthesia Loss of sensation accompanied by loss of consciousness. (*5*)

generation of variation A part of the evolutionary process that ascribes variations among members of a species to a number of mechanisms, one of which is genetic differences; see also *natural selection.* (*10*)

generative processes Mental programs for cognitive activities, such as thinking reasoning, or remembering, that are similar to motor progams. (*8*)

generator potential Depolarization of a receptor cell in response to a stimulus. (*3*)

genes The basic units of hereditary transmission that contain the complex nucleic acid known as DNA, which provides the primary hereditary information and controls. (*6*)

genital stage According to Freud, the period of early adolescence, in which the self-oriented erotic concerns of the first three stages of development are directed outward onto other persons, usually of the opposite sex; see also *anal stage, oral stage,* and *phallic stage.* (*11, 12*)

genotype Characteristics that an individual has inherited and will transmit to his or her descendants whether or not the individual manifests those characteristics; see also *phenotype.* (*6*)

Gestalt psychology German school of psychology that emphasizes the wholeness and organization of mental experience. (*1*)

glia See *neuroglia.* (*2*)

gonadotropins Two types of protein hormones—the luteinizing hormone and the follicle-stimulating hormone—both of which are essential for release of spermatozoa and eggs from the gonads and are manufactured and released by the pituitary gland. (*11*)

gonads Reproductive organs—the ovaries of the female and the testes of the male. (*11*)

grammar The set of syntactic rules that describes any particular language. (*9*)

grandmother cell A hypothetical visual processing mechanism that postulates the existence of specific cells that are the neural equivalents of specific perceptions and that would be able to recognize all the features that add up to a particular pattern, such as your grandmother and only fires at optimal frequency when it recognizes that specific pattern. (*4*)

gross motor skills Large body movements, such as running and jumping, that improve dramatically between the ages of two and six; see also *fine motor skills.* (*6*)

group stereotypes The categorizing of other people by seeing them as members of groups and perceiving each group as having special and identifying characteristics. (*17*)

group therapy A form of therapy, using many techniques including psychodrama, sensitivity training groups, encounter groups, and family therapy, in which a therapist works with a group of up to a dozen patients at one time to help them work together in solving problems; see also *encounter groups, family therapy, psychodrama,* and *sensitivity training groups.* (*15*)

growth spurt A rapid period of physical growth that is the first readily observable sign of the onset of puberty. (*6*)

hallucinations Sensations not experienced by others— seeing, hearing, or smelling things that do not actually exist but are perceived as being real; a symptom of schizophrenia. (*14*)

hallucinogens Agents or substances that induce hallucinations or dreams. (*5*)

heritability A concept that relates to the measurement of the degree to which the variation in a particular trait for a particular population is due to genetic factors as opposed to other factors, presumably environmental; measures of heritability in characteristics such as intelligence are applied to specific groups under specific sets of circumstances. (*13*)

hertz (Hz) Unit employed to measure the frequency of sound waves; one hertz denotes one cycle per second. (*3*)

hidden observer Term used by Hilgard to describe the concealed level of awareness operating during hypnosis; see also *dissociation.* (*5*)

hierarchy of needs A concept, postulated by Maslow to explain personality development as occurring in a positive growth-oriented experience that proceeds in a progression in which the lower needs in the hierarchy must be satisfied before those above can be satisfied. (*12*)

higher-order conditioning Type of classical conditioning in which a new stimulus comes to elicit the conditioned response as a result of being paired wth an effective conditioned stimulus, which serves as the unconditioned stimulus in the new conditioning situation. (*7*)

hippocampus Seahorse-shaped structure in the limbic system that is involved in learning, memory, and motivation. (*2*)

holophrastic speech Children's first meaningful utterances, which consist of single words—mainly nouns and adjectives. (*9*)

homeostasis Term describing an organism's tendency to maintain its internal environment at a constant level. (*12*)

homosexuality Sexual preference for members of the same sex. *(11)*

homunculus The little man that can be drawn by mapping the organization of the motor cortex, the neighboring points of which faithfully represent neighboring regions of the body. *(2)*

horizontal cells Cells of the inner nuclear layer of the retina that organize information coming from the rods and cones and transmit it to the ganglion cells; see also *bipolar cells* and *amacrine cells.* *(3)*

hormones Chemicals manufactured by the various endocrine glands and released into the bloodstream that play a major role in bodily function and behavior particularly sexual behavior. *(11)*

hue The psychological attribute of color that is usually referred to as color itself; see also *brightness* and *saturation.* *(3)*

humanistic therapy A form of therapy that is based on treating patients as integrated wholes rather than as conflict-ridden combinations of id, ego, and superego impulses and that takes an optimistic view of the human potential for growth. *(15)*

hypercomplex cells One of the three types of feature detector cells in the visual cortex, one class of which responds to a line anywhere in the visual field but only if the edge has a specific length as well as orientation; see also *complex cells, feature detectors,* and *simple cells.*

hyperphagia A disorder characterized by excessive appetite, seemingly without satiation. *(10)*

hyperpolarization Increase in the voltage outside of a nerve membrane caused by some neurotransmitters and resulting in a lessening of the likelihood that a nerve impulse will be set off. *(2)*

hypnagogic state Drowsy interval between waking and sleeping, characterized by an EEG pattern of theta waves and by brief, hallucinatory, dreamlike experiences that resemble vivid still photographs. *(5)*

hypnosis A temporary trancelike state of consciousness characterized by high suggestibility, easy access to mental imagery and imagination, decline of the conscious planning function, and reduction in reality testing. *(5)*

hypothalamus A small structure located at the top of the brain stem that governs the autonomic nervous system and the pituitary gland, and hence is involved in the regulation of body temperature, appetite, thirst, and sexual activities. *(2)*

hypothesis Tentative theory or supposition adopted provisionally to account for certain facts and to guide in the investigation of other facts. *(1)*

hypovolemic thirst One of two systems of thirst that results from loss of blood and thus of extracellular fluid; see also *osmotic thirst.* *(10)*

icon A visual memory trace, or the persisting aftereffects of stimuli, that has a relatively large storage capacity but a duration of not more than one second; also called iconic trace. *(8)*

iconic trace See *icon.* *(8)*

identity One of two categories of visual skills characterized by the ability to distinguish classes of objects, for example, a triangle from a circle; see also *unity.* *(4)*

identity crisis The conflict facing adolescents as they attempt to assimilate their own blooming sexuality and adopt the roles they will play in adult society. *(12)*

idiographic research The long-term study of personality traits unique to a single individual. *(12)*

idiot savant A retardate who shows superior functioning in one narrow area of mental activity. *(13)*

illusion of control The sense of control over interactions with other people that results from attributing dispositional causes to other people's behavior, which enables us to feel that we know them and thus can predict their actions in the future. *(17)*

implosive therapy Type of counterconditioning, a form of behavior therapy that creates a massive dose of fear in order to cause an inward explosion or implosion of anxiety and eventually to extinguish that anxiety; see also *aversion therapy* and *systematic desensitization.* *(15)*

impotence Inability to perform coitus, generally because of failure of erection. *(11)*

impression formation Process by which we form global impressions of people based on specific facts we have learned. *(17)*

imprinting Process by which organisms acquire a learned attachment at a particular period in life. *(7)*

incongruence Gap between one's actual experiences and one's self-concept that occurs when people begin to do things primarily to obtain praise from others, and the sense of self, especially one's ideal sense of self, becomes distorted and primarily shaped by others' approval. *(12)*

incus Tiny bone of the middle ear that connects the malleus and the stapes. *(3)*

independent variable In an experimental situation, the condition manipulated by the researcher. *(1)*

individuation Jung's term for the lifelong process of psychological maturation. *(12)*

inferential statistics Use of statistical methods to make inferences about the meaning of research findings. *(App.)*

inhibitory neurotransmitter Neurotransmitter that serves to retard or discourage the firing of a nerve impulse; see also *excitatory neurotransmitter* and *neurotransmitter.* *(2)*

inner ear That portion of the ear immediately past the oval window in which the mechanical energy of sound waves is converted into electrical energy; see also *middle ear* and *outer ear.* *(3)*

inner nuclear layer   Second layer of the retina that is made up of horizontal, bipolar, and amacrine cells. (3)

insight   A novel (unpracticed) solution to a task or problem that appears suddenly. (7)

instincts   Innate patterns of behavior. (10)

instrumental aggression   Aggression that is aimed at obtaining a reward—robbing a bank, for example. (10)

instrumental conditioning   Type of learning that uses reinforcers to change the frequency of a behavior; usually applied to situations in which the experimenter must initiate each trial that a subject experiences; see also *operant conditioning*. (7)

intellectual ability   Ability to master a variety of tasks requiring memory, reasoning, perception, and other abilities. (13)

intelligence quotient (IQ)   Measure of intelligence obtained by dividing the mental age as shown on the 1916 Stanford-Binet test by chronological age and multiplying the resulting number by 100. (13)

intentional social influence   Instances in which others purposefully arouse us, reinforce us, or serve as sources of information. (16)

interpersonal attraction   Area of study concerned with the question of why people like or dislike others. (16)

interposition   See *overlap*. (4)

interpretation   In psychodynamic therapy, the process by which the analyst tries to overcome resistance, usually by making a statement aimed at helping patients see the unconscious basis of a symptom that has been masked by resistance; see also *resistance*. (15)

interval scale   Type of measurement scale in which the difference in adjacent categories is the same in the number scale, examples include Farenheit and Celsius scales; see also *nominal scale*, *ordinal scale*, and *ratio scale*. (App.)

interval use of numbers   The assignment of numbers in which the unit distance between all adjacent pairs of numbers is the same; used to locate points along a dimension and to determine how far apart they are in terms of scale units; see also *nominal use of numbers*, *ordinal use of numbers*, and *ratio use of numbers*. (App.)

introversion   One of the major dimensions of personality proposed by Eysenck; introverts are quieter, more reserved, and less sociable than extraverts; see also *extraversion*. (12)

inverse correlation   See *negative correlation*. (App.)

ions   Electrically charged molecules that, in the transmission of nerve impulses, move across the membrane of an axon. (2)

IQ   See *intelligence quotient*. (13)

iris   Part of the eye surrounding the pupil that gives the eye color and serves as a diaphragm for regulating the size of the pupil and thereby the amount of light entering the eye. (3)

just noticeable difference (jnd)   A quantitative method of determining the smallest perceptable difference between stimuli. (3)

just-world hypothesis   Refers to the tendency to believe that the world is orderly, fair, and just and that people get the rewards and punishments they deserve. (16)

kappa-effect   Phenomenon in which the perception of experienced time and space is influenced by the manipulation of distance; see also *tau-effect*. (4)

kinesthesis   A general term for sensory information generated by receptor cells in the muscles, tendons, and joints that informs us of our skeletal movement. (3)

kin selection hypothesis   Predicts that helping behavior should be most common among closely related animals. (10)

latency period   According to Freud, the period that follows the phallic stage of psychosexual development. (11)

latent content   The underlying psychic material of dreams that leads to the manifest content, or specifics, of dreams; see also *manifest content*. (12)

latent learning   Learning that occurs without any apparent reinforcement and that is not manifest in behavior until reinforcement is introduced. (7)

latent needs   According to Murray, the needs of individuals that are reflected in fantasy, imagination, and thoughts and wishes about the world rather than in overt behavior; see also *manifest needs*. (12)

lateral fissure   Major fissure of the cerebral cortex that demarcates each hemisphere into lobes; also called the fissure of Sylvius. (2)

lateral geniculate body   Subdivision of the thalamus, the cells of which are involved in the transmission, or regulation of transmission, of visual information from the eye to the cerebral cortex. (2)

lateral inhibition   The tendency of adjacent neural elements in the visual system to inhibit each other that results in emphasizing contours or edges in what we see and in enhancing contrasts between different levels of illumination. (3)

law of effect   Thorndike's theory that in trial and error learning, the connections between a stimulus and a response are strengthened if reinforcement follows the response and weakened if the response is not followed by reinforcement. (7)

law of specific nerve energies   The principle that only one kind of sensation is transmitted over a given nerve fiber. (3)

learned helplessness   A condition created by exposure to inescapable aversive stimuli that retards or prevents learning in new situations in which escape or avoidance is possible. (7)

learning A relatively permanent change of behavior that results from prior experience. (7)

learning perspective Idea that conditioning is responsible for behavior—that normal and abnormal behavior represent responses to stimuli and events in the environment; see also *social perspective*. (14)

Learning Potential Assessment Device A test-teach-test technique for measuring a child's learning potential. (13)

learning potential tests Tests that measure the gap between children's present capabilities and their future potential; see also *zone of proximal development*. (13)

lens Transparent structure in the eye that changes shape to focus the optic array on the retina at the back of the eye. (3)

lexical ambiguity The characteristic of language that allows the assignment of different meanings to the same word. (9)

libido According to Freud, the general source of sexual instincts, residing in the id. (12)

limbic system Ringlike structure located at the top of the brain stem that includes the *amygdala*, the *hippocampus*, and the *septal region* and is involved, along with the hypothalamus, in intense emotions such as anger, fear, and pleasure. (2)

linear perspective One of the monocular cues for perceiving depth in which parallel lines seem to converge at a distant spot known as the vanishing point. (4)

linguistic competence Implicit knowledge that language uses have of the syntactic rules that allow them both to produce and to understand an infinite number of utterances; see also *linguistic performance*. (9)

linguistic determinism Theory that all higher levels of thinking are dependent on language or that language determines thought; see also *linguistic relativism*. (9)

linguistic performance Constraints on language users, including a finite life span and the limits of short-term memory, that limit the capacity for generating an infinite number of utterances; see also *linguistic competence*. (9)

linguistic relativism Theory that speakers of different languages perceive and experience the world differently; see also *linguistic determinism*. (9)

linguistic universals Syntactic rules common to all languages. (9)

lobes Distinct regions in each hemisphere of the cerebral cortex. (2)

local anesthetics Pain-blocking drugs used at the site of the source of pain to produce analgesia. (5)

localization Theory that many aspects of behavior can be traced to specific regions of the brain. (2)

longitudinal studies Research in which the behavior of the same subjects is investigated over a long period of time. (1)

long-term memory (LTM) Organized store of general information or knowledge about the world as well as programs and rules for carrying out overt behaviors and mental action sequences; see also *sensory memory* and *short-term memory*. (8)

luteinizing hormone (LH) One of two protein hormones called gonadotropins, that is manufactured and released into the bloodstream by the pituitary gland and that is essential for release of spermatozoa and eggs from the gonads—the testes and ovaries; these hormones are called gonadotropins; see also *follicle-stimulating hormone*. (11)

Mach bands A device used to demonstrate the phenomenon of lateral inhibition in which an observer perceives a narrow bright band on the lighter side of the boundary between two areas of markedly different light intensities and a narrow darker band on the other side even though the light intensity is unchanged. (3)

major hemisphere Obsolete label applied to the brain's left hemisphere at a time when the right hemisphere was thought to have only a limited role in brain functioning; see also *minor hemisphere*. (2)

major tranquilizers Drugs, such as chlorpromazine and the other phenothiazines, used to alleviate extreme symptoms of agitation and hyperactivity; see also *minor tranquilizers*. (15)

male climacteric Term used to describe symptoms experienced by men in late middle age that are similar to those found in female menopause and that are related to loss of testosterone. (11)

malleus Tiny bone of the middle ear that is attached to the eardrum at one end and the incus at the other. (3)

manic episodes One of the disorders of mood and affect characterized by intense episodes of elation. (14)

manifest content Remembered content of a dream, including the characters and their actions; see also *latent content*. (12)

manifest needs According to Murray, the needs of individuals that may be observed in overt behavior; see also *latent needs*. (12)

mean See *arithmetic mean*. (App.)

meninges Membranes lying directly under the skull, surrounding the central nervous system; see also *arachnoid*, *dura mater*, and *pia mater*. (2)

median The measure of central tendency that represents the middlemost value in a distribution of scores; see also *mean* and *mode*. (App.)

mediated interference One of the factors that makes memories difficult to retrieve, which occurs when some desired response from memory is blocked by another response because both responses are linked to a common mediational concept. (8)

medulla The lowest part of the brain stem that contains all ascending and descending tracts interconnecting the brain and the spinal cord. (2)

memory The brain's ability to recreate or reproduce past experience and thoughts. (8)

menopause The permanent cessation of menstruation that occurs in women during their late forties or early fifties and is marked by a sharp decrease in sex hormones. (11)

mental facility Term used by Spearman to refer to the unity of the intellect or general intelligence; also called the g factor; see also *specific mental capability*. (13)

mental retardation According to the current manual of the American Association on Mental Deficiency (AAMD), "significantly subaverage general intellectual functioning existing concurrently with deficits in adaptive behavior." (13)

mesomorph One of Sheldon's somatotypes—describes those whose physiques are primarily sturdy and muscular; see also *ectomorph* and *endomorph*. (12)

method of contrast Procedure in classical conditioning used to produce discrimination among similar stimuli by continuously presenting the unconditioned stimulus only after a particular conditioned stimulus and not after other, similar stimuli. (7)

midbrain The part of the brain that contains a large number of nerve fibers, which connect structures above and below it. (2)

middle ear That portion of the ear that contains three tiny bones called ossicles, which amplify the vibrations of the eardrum and pass them along to the inner ear; see also *inner ear* and *outer ear*. (3)

mild retardation One of the levels of retardation characterized by IQ scores of 52 to 67 on the Stanford-Binet—children are eligible for classes for the educable mentally retarded, and adults can usually work in unskilled jobs; see also *moderate retardation, profound retardation*, and *severe retardation*. (13)

mind-body problem Complex issue relating to how the mind affects the behavior of the body and how the body affects the behavior of the mind. (5)

mindfulness meditation Form of meditation in which the meditator focuses on both internal and external stimuli in order to observe thoughts and impressions with complete detachment. (5)

minor hemisphere Obsolete label applied to the brain's right hemisphere at a time when the left hemisphere was thought to have a major role in brain functioning; see also *major hemisphere*. (2)

minor tranquilizers Drugs, such as the benzodiazepines (Librium, Valium), that are usually prescribed for patients who suffer anxiety or psychosomatic disorders; see also *major tranquilizers*. (15)

mirroring technique One form of psychodrama in which one member of the group plays another member, giving that individual the opportunity to see himself or herself as others do; see also *psychodrama*. (15)

mnemonics Devices, plans, and tricks that facilitate memory. (8)

mode The measure of central tendency that represents the score that occurs most often in a distribution of scores; see also *mean* and *median*. (*App.*)

modeling Approach in behavior therapy formulated by Bandura in which the patient unlearns anxiety about a given stimulus by watching the therapist perform a behavior and then imitating it. (15)

moderate retardation One of the levels of retardation characterized by IQ scores of 36 to 51 on the Stanford-Binet—children are eligible for classes for trainable retardates that emphasize self-care, and few adults hold jobs; see also *mild retardation, profound retardation*, and *severe retardation*. (13)

monochromats People who suffer from an extreme and rare form of color blindness, characterized by very poor visual acuity and extreme sensitivity to even moderate levels of light. (3)

monocular cues Cues for visual depth perception that require the use of only one eye. (4)

monogamy The practice of having only one mate at a time, which is common among human beings and many other animals. (11)

moral development Growth of the ability to distinguish between right and wrong. (6)

morpheme The smallest combination of speech sounds that have meaning. (9)

motion parallax One of the monocular cues for perceiving depth, which relates to the difference in the apparent rate of movement of objects at different distances and depends on the observer's position (when the head moves, close objects appear to move faster than far objects). (4)

motivation Those forces or influences that provide incentives for behavior. (10)

motive An inferred process (desire, need, drive, or emotion) within people that consciously or unconsciously propels them toward specific goals. (10)

motor cortex The part of the cerebral cortex that controls body movements. (2)

motor learning Distinct variety of learning that involves the learning of a sequence of highly coordinated responses that are systematically related to one another and integrally related. (7)

motor program The result of motor learning that occurs once a skill becomes automatic, and the learner has established a sequence of highly coordinated movements that are integrated in time and characterized by a rhythmic structure of their own. (7)

muscle spindles Specialized receptors located within voluntary muscles that contain sensory nerve endings, which signal to the spinal cord and the brain when a muscle is stretched. (3)

myelin Sheath of fatty white substance that insulates the axons of many neurons and prevents the free passage of sodium and potassium ions across each adjacent patch of membrane during an action potential. (2)

myotonia Increased muscle tone and contractions that are part of the physiology of human sexual responses; see also *vasocongestion*. (11)

naming Verbal rehearsal process used in encoding information into short-term memory. (8)

nanometer Unit measurement of the wavelengths of light, equivalent to one billionth of a meter. (3)

narcolepsy Disorder characterized by uncontrollable seizures of sleep during waking hours. (5)

narcotic analgesics Drugs, such as the opium derivatives morphine and heroin, that ease pain while inducing significant elevation of mood. (5)

natural selection A part of the evolutionary process in which animals that are better equipped to survive leave more offspring; see also *generation of variation*. (10)

nature-nurture controversy Debate over which factor is more influential in development, nature—factors based on the genetic endowment of the organism—or nurture—factors based on the previous experience of the organism. (6)

needs Physical states involving lacks or deficits such as hunger and thirst. (10)

negative afterimage Phenomenon in which a visual stimulus persists (briefly), but in a reversed state; chromatic and black-and-white effects are reversed; see also *positive afterimage*. (3)

negative correlation Relationship between two variables in which a high rank on one goes with a low rank on the other; see also *positive correlation*. (App.)

negative reinforcement Results when a response leads to removal of an aversive stimulus or negative reinforcer and, therefore, increases the probability that the desired behavior will be performed. (7)

negatively skewed distribution Distribution of scores in which extreme scores appear at the lower end; see also *positively skewed distribution*. (App.)

neonate A newborn infant. (6)

nerve impulse An electrically measured stimulus that travels down the axon of the neuron usually in a direction away from the cell body and is the nervous system's basic means of communication. (2)

nerves Bundles of axons from separate cell bodies traveling together. (2)

nervous system All of the nerve cells in the body and all of their supporting cells. (2)

neuroglia Myelin-producing cells of the central nervous system; also called the glia; see also *phagocytes Schwann cells*. (2)

neurology The study of the brain and the nervous system. (14)

neurometrics New branch of intelligence testing that focuses on reactions within the brain and the body rather than on such responses as verbal answers. (13)

neuron doctrine Fundamental principle of neuroanatomy, which states that the nervous system is made up of cells called neurons, and they interact by making contact with one another. (2)

neurons Cells that make up the nervous system. (2)

neurotransmitter Chemical released by the synaptic vesicles of a neuron through which electrical activity in one neuron is communicated to the next nerve cell in the pathway; see also *excitatory neurotransmitter* and *inhibitory neurotransmitter*. (2)

nodes of Ranvier Gaps, or nodes, at which the axon of a myelinated neuron is bare of protective myelin; the only places in a myelinated axon at which an action potential can occur. (2)

nominal scale A measurement scale representing unordered classification of information; see also *interval scale*, *ordinal scale*, and *ratio scale*. (App.)

nominal use of numbers The assignment of numbers merely as labels for purposes of identification; see also *interval use of numbers*, *ordinal use of numbers*, and *ratio use of numbers*. (App.)

nomothetic research Testing of many people with a limited battery of measures to discover whether there is substantial individual variation in a characteristic. (12)

normal distribution Bell-shaped distribution of scores with most scores occurring near the mean value and with both halves having the same shape. (App.)

normal waking consciousness State of consciousness in which an individual maintains maximum alertness to the external environment. (5)

obesity Condition of being overweight. (10, 12)

object permanence Term used by Piaget to refer to a child's realization that an object continues to exist even if it is hidden from view. (6)

observational method Research technique in which psychologists observe the behavior of subjects in a systematic, objective, and precise manner. (1)

occipital lobe Lobe in each cerebral hemisphere of the brain that contains the visual cortex, which processes the sensations of light. (2)

Oedipus complex According to Freud, a conflict that arises among males during the phallic stage when they wish to possess the mother and displace the father; see also *Electra complex*. (12)

olfactory bulbs Structures vital to the sense of smell that receive sensory information from receptors in the nasal cavity and are connected to the olfactory cortex of the brain. (3)

operant behavior Any behavior that operates on or has an effect on the environment. (7)

operant conditioning Type of learning in which the subject has to operate on the environment in order to produce a particular consequence such as obtaining food; usually applied to situations in which a subject is freely able to respond; see also *instrumental conditioning*. (7)

operant level Frequency of an operant response, such as bar pressing, prior to conditioning or any reinforcement training. (7)

operant techniques Approach in behavior therapy that uses positive and negative reinforcement to shape, or modify, behavior. (15)

opponent process theory Mechanism in the retina and visual pathways through which cells appear to code opposing colors by increasing or decreasing their rate of firing. (3)

opposing colors Certain pairs of colors (blue and yellow and red and green) that when combined cancel each other out and appear gray. (3)

optic chiasma Point behind the eyes where the bundled fibers of the two optic nerves meet and cross over before reaching the brain. (3)

optimization theory An approach to the study of the adaptiveness of behavior, which proposes that the behavior of animals is organized to achieve some biologically significant goal. (10)

oral personality According to Freud's psychodynamic theory of personality development, the type of personality that results when a child becomes fixated in the oral stage; often characterized by oral aggression expressed through verbal hostility and feelings of deprivation or even gullibility; see also *retentive personality*. (12)

oral stage According to Freud, the first stage of psychosexual development during which sexual energy of the libido is orally focused; see also *anal stage*, *genital stage*, and *phallic stage*. (11, 12)

ordinal scale A measurement scale that orders or ranks information; see also *interval scale*, *nominal scale*, and *ratio scale*. (App.)

ordinal use of numbers Assignment of numbers on the basis of a rank order or preference; see also *interval use of numbers*, *nominal use of numbers*, and *ratio use of numbers*. (App.)

organic psychoses Psychoses that occur as the consequence of a specific disease, such as syphilis, or from brain damage and that are characterized by definable changes in the central nervous system; see also *functional psychoses*. (14)

organ of Corti The actual receptor for hearing, located in the inner ear attached to the basilar membrane and consisting of thousands of receptor cells with project fine, hairlike fibers, the bending of which converts the mechanical energy of sound waves into electrical energy. (3)

orienting reflex In classical conditioning, an initial response including turning and looking attentive, to a new stimulus. (7)

osmoreceptors Cells in the anterior portion of the hypothalamus that are apparently uniquely sensitive to the minute changes in volume that are associated with cellular dehydration and that stimulate drinking as well as signal the pituitary gland to increase production of antidiuretic hormone. (10)

osmosis Tendency of fluids to equalize concentrations of solutes on both sides of a semipermeable membrane. (10)

osmotic thirst One of two systems of thirst that results from cell dehydration due to osmosis; see also *hypovolemic thirst*. (10)

oval window Membrane that transmits vibrations from the middle ear to the inner ear. (3)

overjustification Phenomenon in which a reward provides too large an external justification for performing a behavior. (16)

overlap One of the monocular cues for perceiving depth, also called interposition, in which things appear nearer that partially obscure other things behind them. (4)

pacing genes Genes that set the pace for emerging systems of development, such as motor coordination, that are characterized by the gradual appearance of different behaviors at different ages. (6)

pair bond Joining of two partners in a monogamous relationship. (11)

papillae Dark red spots on the tongue that contain the primary sensory organs for detecting taste. (3)

parallel transmission An aspect of speech; information about the consonant and the vowel is transmitted at the same time. (9)

parasympathetic nervous system One of two parts of the autonomic nervous system, which tends to conserve bodily resources; see also *sympathetic nervous system*. (2)

parietal lobe Lobe in each cerebral hemisphere of the brain that monitors such sensations as pressure on the skin, heat and cold, and awareness of the location of the body's limbs. (2)

parietal lobe syndrome Neurological disorder that affects half of the parietal lobe and, depending on which half, causes lack of awareness of the opposite side of the body. (2)

partial reinforcement Maintenance of a conditioned operant response by a schedule of occasional as opposed to continuous reinforcement; see also *partial reinforcement effect*. (7)

partial reinforcement effect The result of any form of partial reinforcement, which produces greater resistance to extinction and which produces the response for a longer period of time and more often without reward than continuous reinforcement; see also *partial reinforcement*. (7)

Pavlovian conditioning Another term for classical conditioning, after the first student of the topic, Ivan Petrovich Pavlov. (7)

peak experiences Term used by Abraham Maslow to describe various mysterious states of consciousness generally characterized by a sense of unity with others and the outside world, a feeling of bliss, a sense of sacredness, difficulty in describing the experience, an enhanced sense of reality, transcendence of time and space, and reconciliation of contradictory propositions. (5)

Pearson product-moment correlation The most commonly used correlation method based on the index designated *r.* (*App.*)

penis envy Freud's term for the anxiety at lacking a penis experienced by females during the phallic stage. (11)

perception Transformation of the evidence of the senses into mental representations; see also *sensation.* (4)

perceptual adaptation Ability to compensate for an artificially displaced visual field. (4)

perceptual constancy The tendency to perceive objects as having certain stable properties, such as shape, size, brightness, and color, despite variations in physical stimuli; see also *brightness constancy, color constancy, shape constancy,* and *size constancy.* (4)

performance Observable responses or behavior in a given task; learning is inferred from performance, but it is not the same as performance. (7)

peripheral nervous system Transmits information back and forth between the various organs of the body and the central nervous system; see also *central nervous system.* (2)

personality The characteristic way in which a person thinks and behaves as he or she adapts to the environment, including visible behavior patterns as well as such less apparent characteristics as values, motives, attitudes, abilities, and self-image. (12)

personality disorders Patterns of behavior that appear to be deeply ingrained and are manifested primarily as exaggerations—for example, excessive neatness. (14)

personal unconscious According to Jung, a repository of forgotten or suppressed memories that every person has, which take the form of archetypes. (12)

persuasion Form of intentional social influence that aims only indirectly at changing behavior. (16)

phagocytes Glial cells that eat up the debris left by an injury to the brain; see also *neuroglia.* (2)

phallic stage According to Freud, the third stage of psychosexual development during which the child's erotic interests shift to the genital organs, and sexual feelings are directed toward the parent of the opposite sex; see also *anal stage, genital stage,* and *oral stage.* (12)

phase Relates to the precise timing of a sound wave. (3)

phasic events One of two classes of physiological events that occur during REM sleep, characterized by rapid eye movements and increases in various phenomena controlled by the autonomic nervous system such as pulse, respiration and blood pressure; see also *tonic events.* (5)

phenomenal field One of the steps in the process Rogers calls self-actualization when the child's field of experience contains a self as well as a view of others such as parents, teachers, and friends. (12) ·

phenomenological theories Theories of personality that focus on the conscious experience of the individual rather than on overt behavior or on traits or types. (12)

phenotype Characteristics that are exhibited by the individual organism, such as eye color, that express the individual's genetic makeup; see also *genotype.* (6)

pheromones Chemical substances secreted by many animals that influence the production of sex hormones in other members of the same species. (11)

phi phenomenon An illusion of apparent movement that results when two stationary light sources are alternately illuminated about 1/20 of a second apart, and the light appears to move across the space from one to the other; the basis for motion pictures. (4)

phobias Intense, neurotic, and irrational fears of certain objects or situations; among the most common of the anxiety disorders. (14)

phonemes The smallest units of sound that make a difference to the meaning of a larger sound unit such as a word. (9)

phonology Study of the sound patterns found in all natural languages. (9)

phosphene A flash of light that occurs when pressure on the eye activates cells in the retina. (4)

phrase structure rules The rules by which sentences are generated and structured in a particular language. (9)

phrenology Pseudoscience based on reading the bumps of the skull in order to understand character and mental ability. (2)

physical development Changes in an individual's physiological functioning over time reflecting the process of physical maturation. (6)

pia mater Innermost of the three meninges surrounding the central nervous system. (2)

pigment epithelium A single cell lining between the rods and cones of the retina and the choroid that absorbs stray light, serves as a metabolic channel for nourishment of the receptors, and plays a role in the continuous renewal of the light-sensitive outer segments of the rods. (3)

pigeonhole effect The premature categorizing of young children that may result from intelligence testing that fails to take into account varying rates of intellectual growth. (13)

pineal Small gland attached to the top of the brain stem, which although not composed of nerve cells, serves as a regulator of body chemistry and thus influences behavior. (2)

pitch The apparent highness or lowness of a note, determined by the frequency of a sound wave. (3)

pituitary Small gland attached to the base of the brain just in front of the brain stem, which secretes hormones that influence a wide range of functions, from body growth to human reproduction. (2)

place theory Theory of how the ear codes pitch, which suggests that the pitch we hear depends on the place on the basilar membrane that is stimulated by the sound waves; see also *frequency theory.* (3)

plasticity The brain's capacity for modification through experience. (4)

pleasure principle According to Freud, the governing mechanism of the id, which seeks to release its biological energy in either aggressive or erotic ways; see also *reality principle.* (4)

pluralistic ignorance A situation that occurs when individuals in a group do not know that there are others in the group who share their feelings. (16)

polarization The slightly uneven distribution of electrically charged ions across the membrane of a nerve cell axon that causes the inside of the cell to be negative and the outside of the cell to be positive. (2)

polyandry Mating system of one female paired with more than one male. (10, 11)

polygamy Mating system of one male paired with two or more females. (10)

polygyny Practice found in a number of species in which one male is bonded with a number of females at the same time. (11)

polygentic determinism Refers to developing systems that are under the control of a number of genes. (6)

pons Arching band of nerve fibers just above the medulla at the base of the brain that controls such largely automatic functions as heart rate and respiration. (2)

Ponzo illusion The illusion of depth or distance created in two-dimensional drawing when what the viewer interprets as being parallel lines are drawn as converging lines. (4)

population Any group of individuals (persons, other organisms, objects, or items of data) making up the total of all possible cases from which samples may be taken for measurement. (*App.*)

positive afterimage Phenomenon in which the perception of a visual stimulus persists in its original chromatic or black-and-white configuration; see also *negative afterimage.* (3)

positive correlation Relationship between two variables in which a high rank on one goes with a high rank on the other or in which a low rank on one goes with a low rank on the other; see also *negative correlation.* (*App.*)

positively skewed distribution Distribution of scores in which extreme scores appear at the higher end; see also *negatively skewed distribution.* (*App.*)

posthypnotic amnesia A condition, achieved through posthypnotic suggestion, in which subjects under hypnosis forget everything that happened during hypnosis until they are signaled to remember. (5)

posthypnotic suggestion A suggestion made to a person under hypnosis that he or she will feel or act in a prescribed way when no longer hypnotized. (5)

postsynaptic element The dendrite of a neuron. (2)

preconscious mental activity Freud's term for all those thoughts and feelings that are outside immediate awareness but easily available; see also *conscious mental activity* and *unconscious mental activity.* (12)

predictability hypothesis Hypothesis that classical conditioning will not occur unless the conditioned stimulus serves as a reliable basis for predicting the occurrence of the unconditioned stimulus. (7)

predictive validity Measure of a test's validity based on the correlation between test scores and some criteria of behavior the test predicted such as between scores on a scholastic aptitude test and subsequent grades in school. (13)

prefrontal lobotomy A form of psychosurgery, in which a portion of the prefrontal lobe region of the brain is removed, that is used only as a last resort. (15)

preoperational period In Piaget's theory, the period from about age two to age seven during which children begin to deal with the world symbolically, such as recognizing that one thing can stand for another. (6)

prepotent targets Certain objects, organisms, and situations that hold some possible and actual threat to people and, therefore, from a biological viewpoint, are likely to become the foci of phobias. (14)

press According to Murray, the characteristics of situations that initiate or direct behavior; see also *alpha press* and *beta press.* (12)

presynaptic element The axon of a neuron. (2)

preterminal fibers Fine branches at the end of the axons of some nerve cells. (2)

primacy-recency A determinant in impression formation, which holds that first impressions tend to outweigh more recent ones even if the latter seem to contradict the former. (17)

primary mental abilities (PMAs) Seven components of intelligence proposed by Thurstone: numerical ability, reasoning, verbal fluency, spatial relations, perception, memory, and verbal comprehension. (13)

primary process According to Freud, a primitive, irrational, childlike type of thinking that is often manifested in dreams. (5)

primary reinforcers Those stimuli that satisfy basic physiological needs such as food, water, or shelter; see also *secondary reinforcers*. (7, 16)

principle of encoding specificity A factor in memory that relates to the interactions between prior knowledge and the context of new experiences and suggests that what is encoded and stored in long-term memory depends on the context in which the encoding takes place and that retrieval is facilitated by reinstating the same context. (8)

proactive interference One factor that makes memories difficult to retrieve, which occurs when material learned previously interferes with retrieval of recently learned material; see also *retroactive interference*. (8)

proceptivity Sexually soliciting behavior by the female of the species. (11)

profound retardation One of the levels of retardation, characterized by IQ scores of below 20 on the Stanford-Binet—individuals require total supervision and it is assumed that they can learn little except possibly to walk, utter a few phrases, and feed themselves; see also *mild retardation*, *moderate retardation*, and *severe retardation*. (13)

progesterone One of the primary steroids (gonadal hormones) produced in the female's ovaries. (11)

projection A defense mechanism—the attribution of personally unacceptable impulses to others. (14)

projective tests Personality tests in which subjects reveal or "project" themselves through imaginative association with a stimulus; see also *Rorschach Test, Thematic Apperception Test*. (12)

propinquity Factor in interpersonal attraction—we generally come to like people who happen to live or work close to us; see also *familiarity*. (16)

protanopia A type of color blindness caused by the absence of red-sensitive long-wavelength cones. (3)

protensity Perceived passage of time as contrasted with the duration of time. (4)

proximity Perceptual tendency to see elements that are physically close to one another as belonging together. (4)

pyramidal tract One of the major motor pathways in the nervous systems that projects from the cerebral cortex to the spinal cord. (2)

psychedelics Drugs that typically modify the normal perceptual environment by greatly intensifying the sensory intensity of characteristics such as color and texture. (5)

psychoactive drugs Chemical substances that affect mood, thought, and behavior. (5)

psychiatric social worker A practitioner who holds a master's degree in social work and who has special training in treatment procedures with emphasis on the home and community. (15)

psychiatry The branch of medicine concerned with mental health and mental illness. (14)

psychiatrist A physician who usually has spent a post-graduate residency training in psychotherapy and specializes in diagnosis and treatment of abnormal behavior. (15)

psychoanalysis A form of psychotherapy, based on Freud's principle of making conscious the images, fantasies, and wishes of the patient's unconscious. (15)

psychoanalyst A practitioner, usually but not always a physician, who has received specialized training at a psychoanalytic institute in the methods of therapy first developed by Sigmund Freud. (15)

psychodrama A form of group therapy in which members act out their feelings as if they were performers in a play, improvising their lines; see also *mirroring technique*. (15)

psychodynamic approach School of psychology based on the work of Sigmund Freud that looks beyond conscious awareness to unconscious desires and impulses. (1)

psychometrics Branch of psychology concerned with testing of abilities, interests, traits, attitudes, and behavioral tendencies. (1)

psychophysics Branch of psychology concerned with the measurement of relationships between the physical attributes of stimuli and the resulting sensations. (3)

psychophysiological disorders A variety of body reactions that are assumed to be closely related to psychological phenomena—for example, stress. (14)

psychosexual stages According to Freud, the stages of development, each of which centers on a specific pleasurable area of the body and presents the opportunity for fixation, that all human beings pass through in early life. (11)

psychosocial development A lifelong process of social development that Erikson divided into eight different stages that all interrelate. (6)

psychosurgery A form of biological treatment that uses surgery to alter mental or emotional functioning and behavior; see also *prefrontal lobotomy*. (15)

psychotherapy An interpersonal process designed to bring about modifications of feelings, cognitions, attitudes, and behavior that are troublesome to the person seeking help from a trained professional. (15)

puberty Period of physical growth that ends childhood and brings the young person to adult size, shape, and sexual potential. (6)

Pulfrich effect An illusion, which illustrates the role of disparity as a cue for depth perception, that is caused by placing a filter over one eye to alter slightly the brain's processing of the speed of a moving stimulus. (4)

punishment Pain or annoyance administered in an attempt to eliminate a particular behavior. (7)

pupil Structure that regulates the amount of light entering the eye by constriction and dilation. (3)

pyramidal cell One of the two principal types of nerve cells of the cerebral cortex, so named because of the pyramidal shape of its cell body; see also *stellate cell*. (2)

quanta Tiny particles of energy that make up light. (3)

random assignment Assigning of subjects to various experimental conditions by methods of chance, in order to neutralize the variables that are not being manipulated in the experiment. (1)

random dot stereogram A tool for the study of the mechanism of stereoscopic vision, which consists of a pair of patterns of computer-generated randomly positioned dots. (4)

random sample Unbiased sample of a population that is taken to be representative of the population as a whole. (1)

range A measure of variability, calculated from a frequency distribution by subtracting the lowest obtained score from the highest obtained score. (*App.*)

rapid-eye-movement (REM) sleep Stage of sleep characterized by eye muscle activity, a high state of brain activity similar to waking, and, frequently, dreaming. (5)

rational-emotive therapy A method of cognitive restructuring developed by Ellis that traces emotional problems to the sentences people repeat to themselves and attempts to get people to change these maladaptive thought patterns. (15)

ratio scale Measurement scale in which the zero point is absolute such as for weight; see also *interval scale*, *nominal scale*, and *ordinal scale*. (*App.*)

ratio use of numbers The assignment of numbers in such a way that the scale units are equal and the zero point is an absolute; see also *interval use of numbers*, *nominal use of numbers*, and *ordinal use of numbers*. (*App.*)

reaction formation A defense mechanism—the expression of conscious attitudes that are the opposite of an internal wish or impulse. (14)

reality principle According to Freud, the governing mechanism of the ego, which assesses the realism of engaging in aggressive or sexual acts prompted by the id; see also *pleasure principle*. (14)

receiver operating characteristic (ROC) curve A graph of the results of a signal detection test that indicates a subject's percentage of correct versus incorrect responses in identifying the presence of a given stimulus, which is used by psychophysicists to obtain a clear picture of how well a given stimulus can be detected; see also *signal detection theory*. (3)

receptive field The region of the visual field that can affect the response of a given cell in the retina—either to excite or inhibit it. (3)

receptors Peripheral endings of sensory neurons that receive stimuli. (2)

receptor sites Sites on the postsynaptic dendrite membrane of a neuron to which neurotransmitters bind. (2)

reciprocity Factor in interpersonal attraction—we will come to like those who like us and dislike those who dislike us. (16)

recoding Process of encoding information into short-term memory by reorganizing it into more meaningful units; see also *chunking*. (8)

recursive rule A phrase structure rule in which an element on the left of a diagram also occurs on the right. (9)

redundancy A duplication of functions by built-in backup mechanisms of the brain. (2)

regression line In statistics, a procedure for predicting a person's score on one variable when the person's score on another variable is not known but when the relationship between the two variables is provided. (*App.*)

refractory period A resting period during which a neuron is inexcitable and cannot fire. (2)

reinforcement The use of stimuli to increase the likelihood of responses occurring before their presentation. (7, 16)

relative size A monocular cue to visual depth perception—we assume that smaller-appearing objects are more distant. (4)

reliability One criterion for evaluating psychological tests—can be shown if a test measures the same thing consistently from occasion to occasion, when administered by different testers, or when two comparable forms of the test produce similar results; see also *standardization* and *validity*. (13)

repression The most important of the defense mechanisms—unpleasant thoughts or dangerous impulses are barred from conscious awareness. (14)

replication The ability of other researchers to perform an experiment in the same manner and obtain the same results as the initial researcher. (1)

resistance The reaction of many patients in analysis when they become aware of previously unconscious aspects of their personalities, characterized by missing therapy appointments, refusing to free associate, and reporting they have no dreams to relate. (15)

resting potential An electric potential difference—or voltage—between the inside and outside of the axon of a neuron. (2)

retentive personality According to Freud, a personality type that results from being fixated in the anal stage and is characterized by over-concern with cleanliness or saving. (12)

reticular formation Interior of the midbrain extending from the brain stem upward to higher portions of the brain that plays an important role in arousal and awareness. (2)

reticular theory Nineteenth-century theory that the nerve cells were physically connected to one another. (*2*)

retina Photosensitive surface at the back of the eye that contains the visual receptor cells. (*3*)

retrieval Process of recalling information from memory, which often requires recall of an organizational structure before a specific piece of information can be provided. (*8*)

retroactive interference One factor that makes memories difficult to retrieve, which occurs when material learned recently interferes with the retrieval of previously learned material; see also *proactive interference*. (*8*)

reward centers Areas in the hypothalamus that seem to induce pleasure in laboratory animals when those areas are electrically stimulated. (*10*)

reproductive strategy Strategy evolved by each species that meets the particular reproductive needs of the species in relation to its environment. (*11*)

reversed Adam principle Model of sexual differentiation based on the principle of masculine superimposition on a basic female pattern. (*11*)

rhodopsin Pigment that absorbs light in the rods of the retina. (*3*)

risky shift The tendency of group decisions to shift in the direction of risk, away from more cautious individual decisions. (*17*)

ROC curve see *receiver operating characteristic curve*. (*3*)

rods Light-sensitive receptor cells of the retina that convert light into neural signals and that function principally in dim illumination and detect no true colors—only black, white, and shades of gray; see also *cones*. (*3*)

Role Construct Repertory Test Test designed by Kelly to elicit from respondents their own constructs about other people and roles such as self, mother, spouse, pal, rejecting person, or attractive person. (*12*)

roles The set of prescribed and expected behaviors attached to each position in a group. (*17*)

Rorschach test Projective technique for personality assessment in which subjects look at a series of inkblots on separate cards and tell the examiner what they see; see also *projective tests*. (*12*)

s factor See *specific mental capability*. (*13*)

saccule One of two saclike organs of the inner ear that help control posture; see also *utricle*. (*3*)

satiety center Term used to describe the role of the ventromedial hypothalamus as an appetite control that signals that we have had enough to eat; see also *feeding center*. (*10*)

saltatory conduction Transmission of a nerve impulse along myelinated axons. (*2*)

saturation The psychological aspect of color that refers to a hue's vividness, richness, and purity; see also *brightness* and *hue*. (*3*)

schemes Intellectual structures or organizations proposed by Piaget that underlie the processes of assimilation and accommodation in cognitive development. (*6*)

schemata In long-term memory, organized bodies of information representing our general knowledge of the world. (*8*)

schizophrenia A functional psychotic disorder, characterized by a split between aspects of personality functioning, especially between emotion and behavior. (*14*)

Schwann cells A group of supportive, myelin-producing cells found throughout the brain and nervous system; see also *phagocyte* and *Schwann cells*. (*2*)

sclera The outermost layer, or white, of the eye, that is the major structural element of the eye, providing its firm outer framework. (*3*)

scotomas Blind spots in the visual field of each eye, caused by the lack of rods and cones where the optic nerves exit from the eye near the fovea. (*3*)

secondary reinforcers Those stimuli that an individual has learned to associate with positive outcomes such as approval, love, attention, and money; see also *primary reinforcers*. (*7, 16*)

secondary traits According to Allport, characteristics that reflect very narrow patterns of behavior or habits and are of less importance in shaping personality than cardinal traits and central traits; see also *cardinal traits* and *central traits*. (*12*)

sedatives Barbiturates taken in small doses that impair consciousness in the process of suppressing pain. (*5*)

self-actualization According to Rogers, the central concept of personality development, based on the idea that all organisms tend to strive toward expressing all their capacities. (*12*)

self-administered reinforcement In Bandura's social learning theory, the reinforcements we give to ourselves for behaving in certain ways. (*12*)

self-concept According to Rogers, the perceptual object, developed through self-experience, that each child may experience as "me" or "I." (*12*)

self-control procedures Approach in behavior therapy in which clients set up their own goals and provide their own reinforcements with the therapist operating as a consultant. (*15*)

self-fulfilling prophecy An instance in which the perceiver causes another person to behave in a manner that confirms the perceiver's expectations. (*17*)

semantic generalization The type of generalization that is based on a meaningful relationship as opposed to a physical relationship between a conditioned stimulus (flashing blue light) and a test stimulus (spoken word "blue"). (7)

semantic memory Organized store of general knowledge, including knowledge of the world, rules that guide mental operations, the solution of problems, and so on; see also *episodic memory*. (8)

semantics Study of the meaning of utterances. (9)

semicircular canals A set of structures in the inner ear that serve to detect changes in the angular movement of the head. (3)

senescence Period during which people grow old, that begins at different ages for different people. (6)

sensation The process by which we receive and code stimuli such as a spot of light or a musical tone; see also *perception*. (3)

sensitivity training group A form of group therapy aimed at helping people who, though functioning well, want to improve interpersonal interactions, which is often called a *T group* (T for training). (15)

sensorimotor period In Piaget's theory, the first two years of life during which children explore the relationship between sensory processes and their own bodily movements. (6)

sensory memory Momentary lingering of sensory information after a stimulus has been removed; see also *long-term memory* and *short-term memory*. (8)

sensory thresholds Levels at which a stimulus or changes in a stimulus can be detected. (3)

septal region Wall-like region in the limbic system of the brain, located between the amygdala and the hypothalamus, that when operated on produces aggressive behavior in animals and when electrically stimulated seems to produce a pleasurable emotion in rats. (2)

set In reference to the use of psychedelics, one of the two psychological factors that affect the nature of the resulting alterations of consciousness—the mental condition of the individual before ingestion; see also *setting*. (5)

set-point theory In terms of hunger, theory that the hypothalamic centers act like a thermostat by sensing body weight and turning on eating behavior when weight goes too low and turning off eating behavior when weight goes too high. (10)

setting In reference to the use of psychedelics, one of the two psychological factors that affect the nature of the resulting alterations of consciousness—describes the external conditions around the individual taking the drug; see also *set*. (5)

severe retardation One of the levels of retardation, characterized by IQ scores between 20 and 35 on the Stanford-Binet—children require prolonged training just to learn to speak and take care of basic needs, and adults can usually communicate on a rudimentary level; see also *mild retardation, moderate retardation*, and *profound retardation*. (13)

shadowing In the study of attention, occurs when two or more messages are presented at the same time to a listener, whose task is to repeat one of the spoken messages aloud word for word as it is heard. (8)

shape constancy Tendency to perceive the shape of objects as constant despite rotation or differences in the point from which we view them; see also *brightness constancy, color constancy, perceptual constancy*, and *size constancy*. (4)

shock treatment See *electroconvulsive therapy*. (15)

short-term memory (STM) Memory of brief duration—example, remembering a telephone number only until it is dialed—also called primary memory, working memory, what we are currently "paying attention to," and even consciousness; see also *long-term memory* and *sensory memory*. (8)

signal detection theory Method of determining how well a given stimulus can be detected, by presenting a stimulus at different intensities over a large number of trials and plotting the number of correct responses versus incorrect responses; see also *receiver operating characteristic*. (3)

signaling pheromones Chemicals, also called sex attractants, excreted through urine or through the vagina that activate sexual behaviors in male animals, reaching the nervous system through the sense of smell. (11)

silent areas See *association areas*. (2)

similarity Perceptual tendency to see similar elements (proximity being equal) as being grouped together. (4)

similarity-attraction theory Theory of interpersonal attraction that holds that people tend to like others who are similar to themselves on almost any dimension. (16)

simple cells One of three types of feature detection cells in the visual cortex that respond best to a linear shape or edge at a particular orientation and place in their receptive field; see also *complex cells, feature detectors*, and *hypercomplex cells*. (4)

simultaneous conditioning In classical conditioning, when the conditioned stimulus is presented at exactly the same time as the unconditioned stimulus. (7)

situational reasons One of the categories in the attribution process by which people make judgments about the causes of other people's behavior based on the belief that something external to the other person is responsible for the behavior; see also *dispositional reasons*. (17)

size constancy Tendency to perceive the size of objects as constant despite its distance from the viewer; see also *brightness constancy, color constancy, perceptual constancy*, and *shape constancy*. (4)

skewed distribution Distribution, also called asymmetrical distribution, in which there are more values on one end than on the other end; see also *symmetrical distribution*. (App.)

sleep spindles   Short periods of rhythmical responses, with an EEG frequency of 13 to 15 cycles per second, that appear as light sleep begins to deepen. (*5*)

social comparison   Looking to others as a guide for an individual's own interpretation of what is appropriate behavior in a given situation. (*16*)

social facilitation   Phenomenon in which the presence of others increases or facilitates an individual's performance of a task. (*16*)

social influence   Ways in which an individual's actions affect the behavior, attitudes, or judgments of another. (*16*)

social interaction   Mutual reciprocal effects that people have on each other as they interact. (*16, 17*)

socialization   Process of social interaction through which the young acquire the social skills and knowledge needed to function as a member of the culture. (*6*)

social learning approach   Learning theory of personality developed by Bandura that aims at describing the two-way interaction between the individual and the environment. (*12*)

social motives   Needs that are acquired or expressed largely through interactions with others. (*10*)

social perception   The ways in which we perceive others and interpret their behavior. (*17*)

social perspective   Idea that it is how others view deviant behavior and how they react to odd or puzzling behavior that defines that behavior's abnormality; see also *learning perspective*. (*14*)

sociobiology   The study of social behavior in terms of its adaptive value, with a particular emphasis on the optimization theory approach. (*10*)

soma   One of a neuron's three essential parts—the cell body that uses oxygen and glucose and other material from the blood to manufacture protein and other materials necessary for the neuron's survival and functioning; see also *axon* and *dendrite*. (*2*)

somatic nervous system   One of the two parts of the peripheral nervous system that controls movement and receives sensory information; see also *autonomic nervous system*. (*2*)

somatic sensory cortex   Portion of the parietal lobe devoted to skin sensations. (*3*)

somatotypes   Three basic types of body structure and physique identified by Sheldon; see also *ectomorph*, *endomorph*, and *mesomorph*. (*12*)

somesthesis   Sensations arising from the skin—touch, warmth, cold, and pain. (*3*)

SOMPA   See *System of Multicultural Pluralistic Assessment*. (*13*)

source traits   According to Cattell, fundamental traits that are the roots of overt behavior; see also *surface traits*. (*12*)

specific mental capability   Term used by Spearman to refer to performance of any specific intellectual task; also called the *s* factor; see also *mental facility*. (*13*)

speech code   A term applied to speech because of the efficient packaging of speech sounds at the level of phonemes and the lack of dependency on any particular frequency for speech perception. (*9*)

speech spectrogram   Visual representation of the patterns of sound energy, including frequency, time, and amplitude. (*9*)

spontaneous recovery   Partial recovery of a conditioned response following extinction. (*7*)

stabilized image   Phenomenon in which a stimulus image fades and disappears if the image falls constantly on the same receptors. (*3*)

standard deviation   A measure of the variability or scatter of a frequency distribution that is obtained by calculating the square root of the variance; see also *variance*. (*App.*)

standardization   One criterion for evaluating psychological tests—developing a set of scores for a particular test, which reflect the diversity of the overall population who will take the test, against which any individual's score can be evaluated; see also *reliability* and *validity*. (*17*)

standardization group   Group on which a test has been standardized, which should be representative of the overall population who will take the test. (*13*)

standard score   A score for each value in any distribution that expresses the deviation from the mean in standard deviation units. (*App.*)

Stanford-Binet Test   Revision of Binet's original intelligence test for use with American children, which was first published in 1916 and revised in 1960. (*13*)

stapes   The third and last bone in the ossicular chain of the middle ear that couples directly with the oval window. (*3*)

state-dependent learning   Learning that is profoundly affected by the learner's internal physiological state, which must be replicated for recall to occur. (*5*)

state-dependent memory   Phenomenon in which material learned in an altered physiological state (usually drug-induced) can only be recalled when the person is in the same state. (*8*)

states of consciousness   Sets of structural conditions that are distinct from the actual content of consciousness—the major features that influence the ways in which we experience ourselves or the world as opposed to the experience itself. (*5*)

stellate cell   One of two principal types of nerve cells of the cerebral cortex, so named because the radial pattern of its dendrite branches gives it a starlike appearance; see also *pyramidal cell*. (*2*)

stereoscopic vision   The slight disparity between the images recorded by each eye that results in the perception of depth. (*4*)

stereotypes   Existing mental sets people may have

about the traits or physical characteristics of an entire group of people. (8)

Stevens' Power Law Law formulated by Stevens that the magnitude of a sensation is equal to the physical magnitude of the stimulus producing the sensation raised to a certain power, which varies depending on the sensation that is being measured. (3)

stimulants Amphetamines and other drugs that stimulate the central nervous system increasing the available supply of the neurotransmitter dopamine. (15)

stimulus generalization Phenomenon in which a conditioned response can be evoked by stimuli that are similar to but not the same as the original conditioned stimulus. (7)

storage Refers both to the contents of long-term memory and the way in which these contents are represented and organized. (8)

strabismus Condition commonly referred to as "crossed eyes," which is caused by an extraocular muscle imbalance. (4)

stress State of psychological and physiological tension that is caused by threatening demands from the environment. (14)

structuralism Early school of psychological thought that sought to understand the structure of the mind through analysis of the basic elements of mental experience: sensations, images, and feelings. (1)

subjective distress Feelings of sadness, fear, or loss of control that accompanies most forms of abnormal behavior. (14)

subtractive mixture A mixture of pigments, which absorb or subtract some wavelengths and reflect remaining wavelengths to produce a unique hue; see also *additive mixture*. (3)

successive approximations Behavior shaping accomplished by breaking down the desired sequence of actions into small steps and then reinforcing the organism as it approaches closer and closer to the desired response at each step. (7)

superordinate goals Tasks that appeal to more than one group but lie beyond the resources of any single group and, therefore, require that the groups work together toward accomplishing them. (17)

surface structure The form of the sentence we actually hear; see also *deep structure*. (9)

surface traits According to Cattell clusters of overt behavior that seem to go together; see also *source traits*. (12)

survey Research technique in which the opinions, attitudes, and experiences of large numbers of people can be assessed through the use of written questionnaires or interviews. (1)

sustained receptors Receptors that will maintain their generator potential and keep firing impulses as long as the stimulus is present; see also *transient receptors*. (3)

symmetrical distribution Distribution in which the value of the mean and median are the same and both halves are mirror images; see also *skewed distribution*. (App.)

sympathetic nervous system One of two parts of the autonomic nervous system, that tends to mobilize resources of the body for emergencies; see also *parasympathetic nervous system*. (2)

synapse The contact between the axon of one neuron and the cell body or dendrite of another neuron. (2)

synaptic cleft Very thin gap between the membranes of the presynaptic element (the axon) and the postsynaptic element (the dendrite). (2)

syntactic rules The means of translating the sounds of speech into meaningful phrases and sentences. (9)

synaptic vesicles Assemblage of tiny spheres in a knob on the tip of an axon, each of which is surrounded by a membrane and very likely contains a neurotransmitter. (2)

syntax The grammatical structure of language. (9)

systematic desensitization Type of counterconditioning behavior therapy in which patients are taught a new response, muscle relaxation, and then gradually conditioned to substitute the new response for fear as they visualize increasing "doses" of anxiety-provoking situations; see also *aversion therapy* and *implosive therapy*. (15)

System of Multicultural Pluralistic Assessment (SOMPA) Battery of intelligence measures for children from 5 to 11 that produces an adjusted IQ that is typically higher than the traditional IQ. (13)

TAT See *Thematic Apperception Test*. (12)

tau-effect Phenomenon in which the perception of space is influenced by time; see also *kappa-effect*. (4)

temporal conditioning Type of classical conditioning in which the subject is conditioned to give the conditioned response at certain time intervals, and time itself becomes the conditioned stimulus. (7)

temporal lobe Lobe in each cerebral hemisphere of the brain that contains areas concerned with hearing, visual recognition, and the understanding of language. (2)

testosterone Most important of the androgens (steroids, or gonadal hormones) produced in the male testes. (13)

texture One of the monocular cues for perceiving depth, in which the grain of most surfaces appears to change gradually from coarse to fine as distance increases. (4)

T-group See *sensitivity training group*. (15)

thalamus Complex structure located at the top of the brain stem through which nerve fibers carry all sensory impressions except smell. (2)

Thematic Apperception Test (TAT) Projective test for personality assessment that consists of a set of 20 pictures showing either one person or several people standing in relation to each other, about which subjects tell stories. (*12*)

theories of linguistic competence According to Chomsky, the grammars that linguists write, which must be capable of generating all and only the grammatical sentences found in a given language. (*9*)

theory A systematic explanation that consists of a group of unified hypotheses. (*1*)

theory of cognitive dissonance Festinger's theory that proposes that when individuals behave in a manner inconsistent with their attitudes they experience dissonance, an unpleasant state of tension, which can be relieved either by reducing the number of inconsistent cognitions or by increasing the number of consistent cognitions. (*16*)

theory of self-perception Bem's theory that people learn about themselves by observing their own behavior. (*16*)

theory of social comparison Theory which holds that, in ambiguous situations, we tend to look to other people for help in determining appropriate behavior. (*10*)

theta waves EEG patterns of from 4 to 6 cycles per second produced during the drowsy interval between waking and sleeping known as the hypnagogic state. (*5*)

Thibaut and Kelley theory Postulates that relationships depend largely on each participant's analysis of the rewards and costs, which occurs (usually unconsciously) whenever two people interact and shapes the responses of each person. (*17*)

thinking A variety of cognitive activities including problem solving, planning, decision making, judgment, and even remembering. (*8*)

threshold The level of excitation necessary to trigger an action potential in a neuron. (*2*)

timbre A measure of a sound's purity. (*3*)

token economy An operant technique used for changing behavior in institutionalized settings in which severely disturbed patients are given plastic tokens as reinforcement for activities such as making beds and combing hair that can be exchanged for special privileges. (*15*)

tolerance Level at which users need to increase the dose of a drug in order to achieve the same effect previously experienced from a smaller dose. (*5*)

tonic events One of two classes of physiological events that occur during REM sleep, characterized by penile erection in men and probably increased blood supply to the vagina in women and a decrease in muscle activity in both men and women; see also *phasic events*. (*5*)

tonotopical organization Organization of the brain's auditory structures, in which neighboring cells respond best to similar frequencies, and these frequencies change progressively from one place to another. (*3*)

trace conditioning Learning that takes place when the conditioned stimulus is presented briefly, then removed, followed after a relatively brief interval, by the presentation of the unconditioned stimulus. (*7*)

trait categories Personality classifications, such as introvert and extravert, around which information about people is organized. (*17*)

transcendental meditation Variant of concentrative meditation in which the meditator makes no active attempt to control mental experiences but focuses on a mantra, thereby resisting indirectly the intrusion of thoughts. (*5*)

transfer of excitation The transfer of residual excitation from one state or activity (such as physical exercise) to another state (the emotion of anger). (*10*)

transference A frequent occurrence in analysis in which the analyst becomes the focus of emotions once directed at parents or other significant people in the patient's childhood. (*15*)

transformational rules Rules that allow the deep structures generated by phrase structure rules to be modified before the surface structure form emerges. (*9*)

transient receptors Receptors that fire when a stimulus is first applied but quickly return to their normal state, the resting potential, even if the stimulus is maintained; see also *sustained receptors*. (*3*)

transsexualism Strong feelings of gender identity with the opposite sex. (*11*)

trial-and-error learning Type of learning in which the subject begins a task with activity that is apparently random until the correct response is made by chance and reinforced. (*7*)

trichromatic theory Theory that there are only three types of color receptors for visions. (*3*)

two-factor theory of emotions Theory that emotions consist of both arousal and cognition and if neither exists there will be no emotions. (*10*)

unconditioned response (**UR**) Response that automatically occurs, without training, whenever the unconditioned stimulus is presented; see also *classical conditioning*. (*7*)

unconditioned stimulus (**US**) Stimulus that automatically elicits, without any training, the desired response; see *classical conditioning*. (*7*)

unconscious mental activity Freud's term for the reservoir of childhood and current memories, wishes, impulses, fears, and hopes that lie beyond awareness, which he believed play the dominant role in shaping personality; see also *conscious mental activity* and *preconscious mental activity*. (*12*)

unintentional social influence Instances where others

585

inadvertently arouse us, reinforce us, or serve as sources of information. (*16*)

unity One of two categories of visual skills characterized by the ability to detect the presence of an object, that is, to separate an object from its background; see also *identity*. (*4*)

utricle One of two saclike organs of the inner ear that help control posture; see also *saccule*. (*3*)

validity One criterion for evaluating psychological tests —can be shown if a test measures what it was intended to measure; see also *reliability* and *standardization*. (*13*)

variable-interval (VI) schedule Schedule of reinforcement in which reinforcement is given after variable time intervals; see also *fixed-interval schedule, fixed-ratio schedule*, and *variable-ratio schedule*. (*7*)

variable-ratio (VR) schedule Schedule of reinforcement in which reinforcement is given after a varying number of responses; see also *fixed-interval schedule, fixed-ratio schedule*, and *variable-interval schedule*. (*7*)

variance The average squared deviation score or the mean of the squared deviation scores; see also *deviation score*. (*App.*)

vasocongestion Increased blood flow to an area of the body, which results in penile erections in the male and clitoral erections in the female; see also *myotonia*. (*11*)

verbal reinforcement Form of social reinforcement in which words or sounds are employed to indicate approval or disapproval of an action or response. (*16*)

vermis Central, unpaired region that separates the two hemispheres of the cerebellum. (*2*)

vestibulo-ocular reflex Reflex originating in the three semicircular canals of the inner ear that serves the function of stabilizing the body and eyes in space. (*4*)

vicarious learning In Bandura's social learning theory, learning by observing others, or modeling. (*12*)

vicarious reinforcement In Bandura's social learning theory, reinforcement that is experienced through observation of a model who is rewarded; see also *direct reinforcement*. (*12*)

visible spectrum Narrow range of the electromagnetic spectrum that the human eye can see. (*3*)

visual acuity The visual ability to resolve fine detail. (*4*)

visual capture Tendency of vision to dominate the other senses. (*4*)

visual cliff A laboratory apparatus designed for testing depth perception in infants. (*4*)

vitreous humor Transparent jellylike substance that fills most of the interior of the eye. (*3*)

vulnerability model Model of the determinants of schizophrenia based on the premise that everyone is endowed with some degree of vulnerability to schizophrenia, which is determined by some combination of biological and environmental factors. (*14*)

WAIS See *Wechsler Adult Intelligence Scale*. (*13*)

wavelength The difference between the crest of one light wave and the crest of the next light wave—determines color. (*3*)

Weber's law The principle that the size of the difference threshold is proportional to the intensity of a standard stimulus. (*3*)

Wechsler Adult Intelligence Scale (WAIS) The most popular means of measuring adult intelligence through a series of subtests designed to measure verbal and performance abilities. (*13*)

Wechsler Intelligence Scale for Children (WISC) Adaptation of the Wechsler Adult Intelligence Scale for use in schools. (*13*)

WISC See *Wechsler Intelligence Scale for Children*. (*13*)

working through In psychoanalysis, the process of reeducation by having patients face the same conflicts repeatedly until they can face life independently and master the conflicts of everyday life. (*15*)

Zajonc's arousal theory Theory that the arousal produced by the presence of others strengthens the dominant response of the organism, which is, a simple or well-learned task is likely to be appropriate or correct, whereas in a complex and difficult task, it is likely to be wrong. (*16*)

zone of proximal development The gap between childrens' present capabilities and their future potential. (*13*)

zoophobia Fear of certain animals. (*14*)

References

Abrahams, D., see Walters, Aronson, & Abrahams (1966).

Adams, D. B., Gold, A. R., & Burt, A. D. Rise in female-initiated sexual activity at ovulation and its suppression by oral contraceptives. *New England Journal of Medicine*, 1978, *299*, 1145–1150.

Adbelaal, A. E., see Russell, Adbelaal, & Morgenson (1975).

Agras, S., Sylvester, D., & Oliveau, D. *The epidemiology of common fears and phobias.* Unpublished manuscript, 1969.

Ainsworth, M. D. S. *Infancy in Uganda.* Baltimore, Md.: Johns Hopkins Press, 1967.

Ainsworth, M. D. S., Bell., S. M., & Stayton, D. J. Individual differences in strange situation behavior of one-year-olds. In H. R. Schaffer (Ed.), *The origins of human social relations.* London: Academic Press, 1971.

Ainsworth, M. D. S., see Blehar, Lieberman, & Ainsworth (1977).

Alcock, J. The evolution of the use of tools by feeding animals. *Evolution*, 1972, *26*, 464–474.

Aldrin, E., & Warga, W. *Return to earth.* New York: Random House, 1973.

Allee, W. C., see Gates, & Allee (1933).

Allen, K. E., Hart, B., Buell, J. S., Harris, F. R., & Wolf, M. M. Effects of social reinforcement on isolate behavior of a nursery school child. *Child Development*, 1964, *35*, 511–518.

Allport, F. H. The influence of the group upon association and thought. *Journal of Experimental Psychology*, 1920, *3*, 159–182.

Allport, G. W. *Personality: A psychological interpretation.* New York: Holt, 1937.

Allport, G. W. *The nature of prejudice.* Reading, Mass.: Addison-Wesley, 1954.

Allport, G. W. *Pattern and growth in personality.* New York: Holt, Rinehart and Winston, 1961.

Allport, G. W. *Letters from Jenny.* New York: Harcourt, 1965.

Allport, G. W. Traits revisited. *American Psychologist*, 1966, *21*, 1–10.

Allport, G. W., & Vernon, P. E. *Studies in expressive movement.* New York: Macmillan, 1933.

American Psychiatric Association. *Diagnostic and statistical manual of mental disorders* (DSM III) (3rd ed.). Washington D.C.: American Psychiatric Association, 1980.

Amoore, J. E. *Molecular basis of odor.* Springfield, Ill.: Charles C Thomas, 1970.

Amoore, J. E. Olfaction. In L. Beidler (Ed.), *Handbook of sensory physiology: Vol. 4. Chemical senses: Pt. 1.* Berlin, Heidelberg, and New York: Springer, 1971.

Andreoli, V. A., see Worchel, Andreoli, & Folger (1977).

Apgar, V. A proposal for a new method evaluation in the newborn infant. *Current Research in Anesthesia and Analgesia*, 1953, *32*, 260.

Aponte, H., & Hoffman, L. The open door: A structural approach to a family with an anorectic child. *Family Process*, 1973, *12*, 1–44.

Arend, R. A., see Matas, Arend, & Sroufe (1978).

Arieti, S. Manic-depressive psychosis. In S. Arieti (Ed.), *American handbook of psychiatry.* New York: Basic Books, 1959.

Aronson, E. *The social animal.* San Francisco: Freeman, 1972.

Aronson, E., & Linder, D. Gain and loss of esteem as determinants of interpersonal attractiveness. *Journal of Experimental Social Psychology*, 1965, *1*, 156–172.

Aronson, E., & Mills, J. The effect of severity of initiation on liking for a group. *Journal of Abnormal and Social Psychology*, 1959, *59*, 177–181.

Aronson, E., see Walters, Aronson, & Abrahams (1966).

Asch, S. E. The doctrine of suggestion, prestige, and imitation in social psychology. *Psychological Review*, 1948, *55*, 250–276.

Asch, S. E. Forming impressions of personalities. *Journal of Abnormal and Social Psychology*, 1946, *41*, 258–290.

Asch, S. E. Effects of group pressure upon the modification and distortion of judgment. In H. Guptzkow (Ed.), *Groups, leadership, and men.* Pittsburgh, Pa.: Carnegie, 1951.

Aserinsky, E., & Kleitman, N. Regularly occurring periods of eye motility and concomitant phenomena during sleep. *Science*, 1953, *118*, 273–274.

Atkinson, J., Braddick, O., & Braddick, F. Acuity and contrast sensitivity of infant vision. *Nature*, 1974, *247*, 403–404.

Atkinson, J. W. (Ed.). *Motives in fantasy, action, and society.* Princeton, N.J.: Van Nostrand, 1958.

Atkinson, J. W., see McClelland, Atkinson, Clark, & Lowell (1953).

Atkinson, R. C., & Raugh, M. R. An application of the mnenomic keyword method to the acquisition of a Russian vocabulary. *Journal of Experimental Psychology: Human Learning and Memory*, 1975, *104*, 126–133.

Ax, A. F. The physiological differentiation between fear and anger in humans. *Psychosomatic Medicine*, 1953, *14*, 433–442.

Ayllon, T., & Azrin, N. H. *The token economy: A motivational system for therapy and rehabilitation.* New York: Appleton-Century-Crofts, 1968.

Ayllon, T., & Kelly, K. Effects of reinforcement on standardized test performance. *Journal of Applied Behavior Analysis*, 1972, *4*, 477–484.

Ayllon, T., see Haughton, & Ayllon (1965).

Azrin, N. H., see Ayllon, & Azrin (1968).

Back, K., see Festinger, Schachter, & Back (1950).

Baddeley, A. D. Time-estimation at reduced body temperature. *American Journal of Psychology*, 1966, *79*, 475–479.

Baddeley, A. D. *The psychology of memory.* New York: Basic Books, 1976.

589

Baer, D. M., see Gewirtz, & Baer (1958).

Bailey, C. J., see Miller, Bailey, & Stevenson (1950).

Bailey, R. H. *The role of the brain.* New York: Time-Life Books, 1975.

Bakal, D. Headache: A biopsychological perspective. *Psychological Bulletin*, 1975, *82*, 369–382.

Baldessarini, R. J. *Chemotherapy in psychiatry.* Cambridge, Mass.: Harvard University Press, 1977.

Ball, T. M., see Kosslyn, Ball, & Reiser (1978).

Balswick, J. O., see King, Balswick, & Robinson (1977).

Baltes, P. B., & Schaie, K. W. Aging and the IQ: The myth of the twilight years. *Psychology Today*, March 1974, *7*, 35–40.

Bancroft, J. *Deviant sexual behavior: Modification and assessment.* Oxford: Clarendon Press, 1974.

Bancroft, J. Hormones and human sexual behavior. *British Medical Bulletin*, 1981, *37*, 153–158.

Bancroft, J. H. J., see Gelder, Bancroft, Gath, Johnston, Mathews, & Shaw (1973).

Bandura, A. Influence of models' reinforcement contingencies on the acquisition of imitative responses. *Journal of Personality and Social Psychology*, 1965, *1*, 589–595.

Bandura, A. Psychotherapy based on modeling principles. In A. E. Bergin & S. L. Garfield (Eds.), *Handbook of psychotherapy and behavior change.* New York: Wiley, 1971.

Bandura, A. *Social learning theory.* Morristown, N.J.: General Learning Press, 1971.

Bandura, A. *Aggression: A social learning analysis.* New York: Holt, Rinehart, and Winston, 1973.

Bandura, A. Social learning analysis of aggression. In E. Ribes-Inesta (Ed.), *Analysis of delinquency and aggression.* Hillsdale, N.J.: Erlbaum, 1976.

Bandura, A., Blanchard, E. B., & Ritter, B. The relative efficacy of desensitization and modeling approaches for inducing behavioral, affective, and attitudinal changes. *Journal of Personality and Social Psychology*, 1963, *13*, 173–199.

Bindura, A., & Mischel, W. Modification of self-imposed delay on reward through exposure to live and symbolic models. *Journal of Personality and Social Psychology*, 1965, *2*, 698–705.

Bandura, A., Ross, D., & Ross, S. A. Transmission of aggression through imitation of aggressive models. *Journal of Abnormal and Social Psychology*, 1961, *63*, 575–582.

Bandura, A., Ross, D., & Ross, S. A. Imitation of film-mediated aggressive models. *Journal of Abnormal and Social Psychology*, 1963, *66*, 3–11.

Barbee, N. H., see Sears, & Barbee (1978).

Barber, T. X. *LSD, marijuana, yoga and hypnosis.* Chicago: Aldine, 1970.

Barclay, J. R., see Bransford, Barclay, & Franks (1972).

Bard, M. *Training police as specialists in family crisis intervention.* Washington D.C.: U.S. Government Printing Office, 1970.

Bard, M., & Berkowitz, B. Training police as specialists in family crisis intervention: A community psychology action program. *Community Mental Health Journal*, 1967, *3*, 315–317.

Barfield, R. J., & Chen, J. Activation of estrous behavior in ovariectomized rats by intracerebral implants of estradiol benzoate. *Endocrinology*, 1978, *101*, 1716–1725.

Barker, C. H., see Schein, Schneier, & Barker (1961).

Barraclough, C. A. Hormones and development: Modifications in the CNS regulation of reproduction after exposure of prepuberal rats to steroid. *Recent Progress in Hormone Research*, 1966, *22*, 503–539.

Barrett, J. E. Learning theories: Operant paradigm. In G. U. Balis, L. Wurmser, E. McDaniel, & R. G. Grenell (Eds.), *The behavioral and social sciences and the practice of medicine; the psychiatric foundations of medicine* (Vol. 2). Boston: Butterworth Publishers, Inc., 1978.

Bartlett, F. C. *Remembering.* Cambridge, England: Cambridge University Press, 1932.

Bass, F. L'aménorrhée au camp de concentration de Térézin. *Gynáecologia*, 1947, *123*, 211.

Bateson, G., Jackson, D. D., Haley, J., & Weakland, J. Toward a theory of schizophrenia. *Behavioral Science*, 1956, *1*, 251–264.

Baum, A., & Greensberg, C. I. Waiting for a crowd: The behavioral and perceptual effects of anticipated crowding. *Journal of personality and Social Psychology*, 1975, *32*, 671–679.

Bavelas, J. B. *Personality: Current theory and research.* Monterey, Calif.: Brooks/Cole, 1978.

Bayer, E. Beiträge zur Zweikomponententheorie des Hungers. *Zeitschrift für Psychologie*, 1929, *112*, 1–54.

Bayley, N. Development of mental abilities. In Mussen, P. (Ed.), *Carmichael's manual of child psychology.* New York: Wiley, 1970.

Beach, F. A. *Hormones and behavior.* New York: Hoeber, 1948.

Beach, F. A. Sexual attractivity, proceptivity and receptivity in female mammals. *Hormones and Behavior*, 1976, *7*, 105–138.

Beach, F. A., see Ford, & Beach (1951).

Beaman, A. L., see Diener, Fraser, Beaman, & Kelem (1976).

Beard, R. J. The menopause. *British Journal of Hospital Medicine*, 1975, *12*, 631–637.

Békésy, G. von. *Experiments in hearing.* New York: McGraw-Hill, 1960.

Bell, S. M., see Ainsworth, Bell, & Stayton (1971).

Bellack, A. S., Hersen, M., & Turner, S. M. Generalization effects of social skills training in chronic schizophrenics: An experimental analysis. *Behaviour Research and Therapy*, 1976, *14*, 391–398.

Belmont, L., & Marolla, F. A. Birth order, family size, and intelligence. *Science*, 1973, *182*, 1096–1101.

Bem, D. J. Self-perception theory. In L. Berkowitz (Ed.), *Advances in experimental social psychology* (Vol. 6). New York: Academic Press, 1972.

Bem, D. J., see Wallach, Kogan, & Bem (1964).

Bender, D. B., see Gross, Rocha-Miranda, & Bender (1972).

Benson, H. *The relaxation response.* New York: Morrow, 1975.

Berger, H. Über das elektroenkephalogramm des menschen. *Archiv Für Psychiatrie und Nervenkrankheiten,* 1929, *87,* 527–570.

Bergin, A. E. The evaluation of the therapeutic outcomes. In A. E. Bergin & S. L. Garfield (Eds.), *Handbook of psychotherapy and behavior change: An empirical analysis.* New York: Wiley, 1971.

Bergum, B. O., & Lehr, D. J. Effects of authoritarianism on vigilance performance. *Journal of Applied Psychology,* 1963, *47,* 75–77.

Berkowitz, B., see Bard, & Berkowitz (1967).

Berkowitz, L. Group standards, cohesiveness, and productivity. *Human Relations,* 1954, *7,* 509–519.

Berkowitz, L. The concept of aggressive drive: Some additional considerations. In L. Berkowitz (Ed.), *Advances in experimental social psychology* (Vol. 2). New York: Academic Press, 1965.

Berkowitz, L., & Geen, R. G. Film violence and the cue properties of available targets. *Journal of Personality and Social Psychology,* 1966, *3,* 525–530.

Berkowitz, W. R., Nebel, J. C., & Reitman, J. W. Height and interpersonal attraction: The 1969 mayoral election in New York City. *Proceedings of the 79th Annual Convention of the American Psychological Association,* 1971, *6,* 281–282.

Berlin, B., & Kay, P. *Basic color terms: Their universality and evolution.* Berkeley and Los Angeles: University of California Press, 1969.

Berlucchi, G., see Rizzollatti, Umilta, & Berlucchi (1971).

Bermant, G., & Davidson, J. M. *Biological bases of sexual behavior.* New York: Harper & Row, 1974.

Bernard, C. *An introduction to the study of experimental medicine* (H. C. Greene, Trans.). New York: Dover, 1957. (Originally published, 1865.)

Berscheid, E., & Walster, E. H. *Interpersonal attraction.* Reading, Mass.: Addison Wesley, 1969.

Berscheid, E., see Dion, Berscheid, & Walster (1972).

Berscheid, E., see Snyder, Tanke, & Berscheid (1977).

Bever, T. G., see Terrace, Petitto, Sanders, & Bever (1979).

Beverley, L., see Regan, Beverley, & Cynader (1979).

Bexton, W. H., Heron, W., & Scott, T. H. Effects of decreased variation in the sensory environment. *Canadian Journal of Psychology,* 1954, *8,* 70–76.

Binet, A., & Simon, T. *The development of intelligence in children.* (E. S. Kite Trans.) Baltimore, Md.: Williams & Wilkins, 1916.

Birren, J. E., see Welford, & Birren (1965).

Bischof, L. J. *Adult psychology* (2nd ed.). New York: Harper & Row, 1976.

Blanchard, E. B., see Bandura, Blanchard, & Ritter (1969).

Blashfield, R. K., & Draguns, J. G. Evaluative criteria for psychiatric classification. *Journal of Abnormal Psyology,* 1976, *85,* 140–150.

Blehar, M. C., Lieberman, A. F., & Ainsworth, M. D. S. Early face-to-face interaction and its relation to later infant-mother attachment. *Child Development,* 1977, *48,* 182–194.

Bleuler, E. *Domentia praecox, or the group of schizophrenias* (J. Zinkin, Trans.). New York: International Universities Press, 1950. (Originally published, 1911.)

Blewett, D., see Chwelos, Blewett, Smith, & Hoffer (1959).

Bloch, G., see Mesmer, & Bloch (1980).

Bloom, B. *Community mental health.* Monterey, Calif.: Brooks-Cole, 1977.

Bloom, L. *Language development: Form and function in emerging grammars.* Cambridge, Mass.: MIT Press, 1970.

Blough, D. Dark adaptation in the pigeon. *Journal of Comparative and Physiological Psychology,* 1956, *49,* 425–430.

Blough, D. S. Experiments in animal psychophysics. *Scientific American,* 1961, *205,* 113–122.

Blum, J. E., Jarvik, L. F., & Clark, E. T. Rate of change on selective tests of intelligence: A twenty-year longitudinal study. *Journal of Gerontology,* 1970, *25,* 171–176.

Blumenthal, A. L. *The process of cognition.* Englewood Cliffs, N.J.: Prentice-Hall, 1977.

Bogdan, R., & Taylor, S. The judged, not the judges: An insider's view of mental retardation. *American Psyologist,* 1976, *31,* 47–52.

Bogen, J. E. The other side of the brain: An appositional mind. *Bulletin of The Los Angeles Neurological Societies,* 1969, *34,* 135–162.

Boring, E., see Herrnstein, & Boring (1966).

Borton, R., see Teller, Morse, Borton, & Regal (1974).

Bossard, J.H.S. Residential propinquity as a factor in mate selection. *American Journal of Sociology,* 1932, *38,* 219–224.

Botwinick, J. *Cognitive processes in maturity and old age.* New York: Springer, 1967.

Bouffard, D. L., see Price, & Bouffard (1974).

Bousfield, W. A. The occurrence of clustering in the recall of randomly arranged associates. *Journal of General Psychology.* 1953, *49,* 229–240.

Bower, G. H. Mental imagery and associative learning. In L. Gregg (Ed.), *Cognition in learning and memory.* New York: Wiley, 1972.

Bower, G. H., Clark, M., Winzenz D., & Lesgold, A. Hierarchical retrieval schemes in recall of categorized word lists. *Journal of Verbal Learning and Verbal Behavior,* 1969, *8,* 323–343.

Bowerman, M. Structural relationships in children's utterances: Syntactic or semantic? In T. E. Moore (Ed.), *Cognitive development and the acquisition of language.* New York: Academic Press, 1973.

Bowers, M. B., Jr., & Freedman, D. X. Psychedelic experiences in acute psychosis. *Archives of General Psychiatry*, 1966, *15*, 240–248.

Bowlby, J. Separation anxiety. *International Journal of Psychoanalysis*, 1960, *41*, 89–113.

Bowlby, J. *Attachment*. In *Attachment and loss* (Vol. 1). New York: Basic Books, 1969.

Braddick, F., see Atkinson, Braddick, & Braddick (1974).

Braddick, O., see Atkinson, Braddick, & Braddick (1974).

Bradford, D. L., see Rabow, Fowler, Bradford, Hofeller, & Shibuya (1966).

Brady, K., see Katz, & Brady (1933).

Braine, M. D. S. On learning the grammatical order of words. *Psychological Review*, 1963, *70*, 323–348.

Braine, M. D. S. Children's first word combinations. *Monographs of the Society for Research in Child Development*, 1976, *41*(Serial No. 164).

Branchey, M. H., Charles, J., & Simpson, G. M. Extrapyramidal side effects in lithium maintenance therapy. *American Journal of Psychiatry*, 1976, *133*, 444–445.

Bransford, J. D., Barclay, J. R., & Franks, J. J. Sentence memory: A constructive versus interpretive approach. *Cognitive Psychology*, 1972, *3*, 193–209.

Bransford, J. D., & Franks, J. J. The abstraction of linguistic ideas. *Cognitive Psychology*, 1971, *2*, 331–350.

Bransford, J. D., & Johnson, M. K. Contextual prerequisites for understanding: Some investigations of comprehension and recall. *Journal of Verbal Learning and Verbal Behavior*, 1972, *11*, 717–726.

Bransford, J. D., see Franks, & Bransford (1971).

Bransford, J. D., see Morris, Bransford, & Franks (1977).

Brazelton, T. B. *Neonatal behavioral assessment scale*. Philadelphia, Pa.: International Ideas, 1974.

Brazelton, T. B., Koslowski, B., & Main, M. The origins of reciprocity: The early mother-infant interaction. In M. Lewis & L. A. Rosenbaum (Eds.), *The effect of the infant on its caregiver*. New York: Wiley, 1974.

Brecher, E. M. *The sex researchers*. Boston: Little, Brown, 1969.

Breland, K., & Breland, M. The misbehavior of organisms. *American psychologist*, 1961, *16*, 681–684.

Breland, K., & Breland, M. *Animal behavior*. New York: Macmillan, 1966.

Breland, M., see Breland, & Breland (1961).

Breland, M., see Breland, & Breland (1966).

Bremer, D., see Goodwin, Powell, Bremer, Hoine, & Stern (1969).

Breuer, J., see Freud, & Breurer (1966).

Broadbent, D. E. *Perception and communication*. London: Pergamon Press, 1959.

Broadbent, D. E., Cooper, P. J., & Broadbent, M.H.P. A comparison of hierarchical and matrix retrieval schemes in recall. *Journal of Experimental Psychology: Human Learning and Memory*, 1978, *4*, 476–497.

Broadbent, M. H. P., see Broadbent, Cooper, & Broadbent (1978).

Broca, P. Remarques dur la siége de la faculté du langage articulé; suivies d'une observation d'aphémie (perte de lar parole). In G. von Bonin (Trans.), *Some papers on the cerebral cortex*. Springfield, Ill.: Charles C Thomas, 1960. (Originally published, 1861.)

Bromley, D. B. *The psychology of human aging* (2nd ed.). Baltimore, Md.: Penguin Books, 1979.

Bronson, F. H., see Whitten, Bronson, & Greenstein (1968).

Bronson, W. C. Dimension of ego and infantile identification. *Journal of Personality*, 1959, *27*, 532–545.

Brouwer, D. Somatotypes and psychosomatic diseases. *Journal of Psychosomatic Research*, 1957, *2*, 23–34.

Broverman, D. M., see Broverman, Broverman, & Clarkson (1970).

Broverman, I. K., Broverman, D. M., & Clarkson, F. E. Sex role stereotypes and clinical judgments of mental health. *Journal of Consulting and Clinical Psychology*, 1970, *34*, 1–7.

Brown, B. *New mind, new body*. New York: Harper & Row, 1974.

Brown, R. *Social Psychology*. New York: Free Press, 1965.

Brown, R., & Hanlon, C. Derivational complexity and order of acquisition in child speech. In J. R. Hayes (Ed.), *Cognition and the development of language*. New York: Wiley, 1970.

Brown, R. W. Development of the first language in the human species. *American Psychologist*, 1973, *28*, 97–106.

Brown, R. W., & McNeill, D. The "tip of the tongue" phenomenon. *Journal of Verbal Learning and Verbal Behavior*, 1966, *5*, 325–337.

Brown, S. R., see Hendrick, & Brown (1971).

Brown, W. A., Monti, P. M., & Corriveau, D. P. Serum testosterone and sexual activity and interest in men. *Archives of Sexual Behavior*, 1978, *7*, 97–103.

Bruce, H. M. An exteroreceptive block to pregnancy in the mouse. *Nature*, 1959, *184*, 105.

Bruner, J. S. On cognitive growth: II. In J. S. Bruner, R. R. Olver, & P. M. Greenfield, *Studies in cognitive growth*. New York: Wiley, 1966.

Bruner, J. S., Olver, R. R., & Greenfield, P. M. *Studies in cognitive growth*. New York: Wiley, 1966.

Bruner, J. S., see Smith, Bruner, & White (1956).

Brush, C., see Singer, Brush, & Lublin (1965).

Bryan, W. L., & Harter, N. Studies in the physiology and psychology of telegraphic language. *Psychological Review*, 1897, *4*, 27–53.

Bryant, J., see Cantor, Zillmann, & Bryant (1975).

Buchanan, P. C. Innovative organizations: A study in organizational development. In *Applying behavioral science research in industry*. New York: Industrial Relations Counselor, 1964.

Buchsbaum, S., see Keith, Gunderson, Reifman, Buchsbaum, & Mosher (1976).

Bucke, R. M. *Cosmic consciousness*. New York: Causeway Books, 1900.

Bucy, P. C., see Kluver, & Bucy (1937).

Bucy, P. C., see Kluver, & Bucy (1938).

Bucy, P. C., see Kluver, & Bucy (1939).

Buell, J. S., see Allen, Hart, Buell, Harris, & Wolf (1964).

Bullock, T. H., & Cowles, R. B. Physiology of an infrared receptor—the facial pit of pit vipers. *Science*, 1952, *115*, 541–543.

Burnstein, E., see Zajonc, & Burnstein (1965).

Burnstein, E., see Vinokur, Trope, & Burnstein (1975).

Burt, A. D., see Adams, Gold, & Burt (1978).

Butler, R. N. *Why survive? Being old in America.* New York: Harper & Row, 1975.

Byrne, D. Interpersonal attraction and attitude similarity. *Journal of Abnormal and Social Psychology*, 1961, *62*, 713–715.

Byrne, D. Attitudes and attraction. In L. Berkowitz (Ed.), *Advances in experimental social psychology* (Vol. 4). New York: Academic Press, 1969.

Byrne, D., Ervin, C. R., & Lamberth, J. Continuity between the experimental study of attraction and real-life computer dating. *Journal of Personality and Social Psychology*, 1970, *16*, 157–165.

Byrne, D., see Palmer, & Byrne (1970).

Calhoun, J. B. Population density and social pathology. *Scientific American*, 1962, *206*, 139–148.

Callenbach, E., see Leefeldt, & Callenbach (1979).

Camargo, C. A., see Davidson, Camargo, & Smith (1979).

Cameron, N. *Personality development and psychopathology: A dynamic approach.* Boston: Houghton Mifflin, 1963.

Cann, M. A. *An investigation of a component of parental behavior in humans.* Unpublished master's thesis, University of Chicago, 1953.

Cannon, W. B. *The mechanical factors of digestion.* London: Arnold, 1911.

Cannon, W. B. The James-Lange theory of emotions: A critical examination and an alternative theory. *American Journal of Psychology*, 1927, *39*, 106–124.

Cannon, W. B. *Bodily changes in pain, hunger, fear, and rage* (2nd ed.). New York: Appleton-Century-Crofts, 1929.

Cannon, W. B., & Washburn, A. L. An explanation of hunger. *American Journal of Physiology*, 1912, *29*, 441–454.

Cantor, J. R., Zillmann, D., & Bryant, J. Enhancement of experienced sexual arousal in response to erotic stimuli through misattribution of unrelated residual excitation. *Journal of Personality and Social Psychology*, 1975, *32*, 69–75.

Cantor, N., & Mischel, W. Traits as prototypes: Effects on recognition memory. *Journal of Personality and Social Psychology*, 1977, *35*, 38–48.

Cantril, H., see Fink, & Cantril (1939).

Cantril, H., see Hastorf, & Cantril (1954).

Carlsmith, J. M., see Festinger, & Carlsmith (1959).

Carlsmith, J. M., see Doob, Carlsmith, Freedman, Landauer, & Toms (1969).

Carlsson, A. The occurrence, distribution and physiological role of catecholamines in the nervous system. *Pharmacology Review*, 1959, *11*, 490.

Carlton, P. N., see Weisman, Hamilton, & Carlton (1972).

Carmichael, L. The onset and early development of behavior. In P. H. Mussen (Ed.), *Carmichael's manual of child psychology* (3rd ed.) (Vol. 1). New York: Wiley, 1970.

Carmichael, L., Hogan, H. P., & Walter, A. A. An experimental study of the effect of language on the reproduction of visually perceived forms. *Journal of Experimental Psychology*, 1932, *15*, 73–86.

Carpenter, G. Mother's face and the newborn. In R. Lewin (Ed.), *Child alive.* London: Temple Smith, 1975.

Caputo, C., see Nisbett, Caputo, Legant, & Marecek (1973).

Cassell, S. Effect of brief puppet therapy upon the emotional responses of children undergoing cardiac catheterization. *Journal of Counsulting Psychology*, 1965, *29*, 1–8.

Castenada-Mendez, K., see Shiffrin, Pisoni, & Castenada-Mendez (1974).

Cattell, R. B. *Personality: A systematic, theoretical, and factual study.* New York: McGraw-Hill, 1950.

Cattell, R. B. *Factor analysis: An introduction and manual for psychologist and social scientist.* New York: Harper, 1952.

Cattell, R. B. *Personality and motivation: Structure and measurement.* New York: World Book Co., 1957.

Cautela, J. R. Treatment of compulsive behavior by covert sensitization. *Psychological Record*, 1966, *16*, 33–41.

Centers, R. A. Laboratory adaptation of the controversial procedure for the conditioning of verbal operants. *Journal of Abnormal and Social Psychology*, 1963, *67*, 334–379.

Chapman, A. J. Social facilitation of laughter in children. *Journal of Experimental Social Psychology*, 1973, *9*, 529–541.

Chapman, J. The early symptoms of schizophrenia. *British Journal of Psychiatry*, 1966, *112*, 225–251.

Chapman, J. P., see Chapman, & Chapman (1967).

Chapman, J. P., see Chapman, & Chapman (1969).

Chapman, L. J., & Chapman, J. P. Genesis of popular but erroneous psychodiagnostic observations. *Journal of Abnormal Psychology*, 1967, *72*, 193–204.

Chapman, L. J., & Chapman, J. P. Illusory correlation as an obstacle to the use of valid psychodiagnostic signs. *Journal of Abnormal Psychology*, 1969, *74*, 271–280.

Charles, J., see Branchey, Charles, & Simpson (1976).

Chen, E. Twins reared apart: A living lab. *The New York Times Magazine*, December 9, 1979, pp. 112–126.

Chen, J., see Barfield & Chen (1978).

Chen, S. C. Social molification of the activity of ants in nest-building. *Physiological Zoology*, 1937, *10*, 420–436.

Cherry, E. C. Some experiments on the recognition of speech with one and two ears. *Journal of the Acoustical of Society of Ameica*, 1953, *25*, 975–979.

Chodorkoff, B. Self-perception, perceptual defense, and adjustment. *Journal of Abnormal and Social Psychology*, 1954, *49*, 508–512.

Chomsky, N. *Syntactic Structures*. The Hague: Mouton, 1957.

Chow, K. L. Effects of partial extirpations of the posterior association cortex on visually mediated behavior in monkeys. *Comparative Psychological Monographs*, 1951, *20*, 187-217.

Chung, D., see Li & Chung (1976).

Chwelos, N., Blewett, D. B., Smith, C. M., & Hoffer, A. Use of d-LSD in the treatment of alcoholism. *Quarterly Journal of Studies on Alcohol*, 1959, *20*, 577–590.

Clark, E. T., see Blum, Jarvik, & Clark (1970).

Clark, E. V. On the acquisition of the meaning of before and after. *Journal of Verbal Learning and Verbal Behavior*, 1971, *10*, 266–275.

Clark, M. Drugs and psychiatry: A new era. *Newsweek*, November 12, 1979, p. 98.

Clark, M., see Bower, Clark, Winzenz & Lesgold (1969).

Clark, R. A., see McClelland, Atkinson, Clark, & Lowell (1953).

Clarkson, F. E., see Broverman, Broverman, & Clarkson (1970).

Cohen, J., Hansel, C. E. M., & Sylvester, J. D. Interdependence of temporal and auditory judgments. *Nature*, 1954, *174*, 642.

Cohen, S., Glass, D. C., & Singer, J. E. Apartment noise, auditory discrimination, and reading ability in children. *Journal of Experimental Social Psychology*, 1973, *9*, 407–422.

Collins, A. M., & Quillian, M. R. Retrieval time from semantic memory. *Journal of Verbal Learning and Verbal Behavior*, 1969, *8*, 240–247.

Collins, B., Henker, B., & Whalen, C. Ecological and pharmacological influences on behaviors in the hyperkinetic behavioral syndrome. In S. Salzinger, J. Antrobus, & J. Glick (Eds.), *The Ecosystem of the 'sick' kid*. New York: Academic Press, 1980.

Comeback for shock therapy? *Time*, November 19, 1979, p. 76.

Conners, C. K. Pharmacotherapy of psycholpathology in children. In H. C. Quay & J. S. Werry (Eds.), *Psychopathological disorders of childhood*. New York: Wiley, 1972.

Conrad, R. Acoustic confusions in immediate memory. *British Journal of Psychology*, 1964, *55*, 75–83.

Cooper, F. S., see Liberman, Cooper, Shankweiler, & Studdert-Kennedy (1967).

Cooper, J., see Word, Zanna, & Cooper (1974).

Cooper, P. J., see Broadbent, Cooper, & Broadbent (1978).

Corbit, J. D. Cellular dehydration and hypovolaemia are additive in producing thirst. *Nature*, 1968, *218*, 886–887.

Corbit, J. D. Behavioral regulation of body temperature. In J. D. Hardy, A. P. Gagge & J. A. Stolwijk (Eds.), *Physiological and behavioral temperature regulation*. Springfield, Ill.: C. C. Thomas, 1970.

Corby, J. C., Roth, W. T., Zarcone, V. P. Jr., & Kopell, B. S. Psychophysiological correlates of the practice of tantric yoga meditation. *Archieves of General Psychiatry*, 1978, *35*, 571–577.

Cornelison, A., see Lidz, Fleck, & Cornelison (1965).

Cornsweet, J. C., see Riggs, Ratliff, Cornsweet, & Cornsweet (1953).

Cornsweet, T., see Riggs, Ratliff, Cornsweet, & Cornsweet (1953).

Cornsweet, T. N. *Visual perception*. New York: Academic Press, 1970.

Corriveau, D. P., see Brown, Monti, & Corriveau (1978).

Cottrell, N. B. Performance in the presence of other human beings: mere presence, audience, and affiliation effects. In E. C. Simmel, R. A. Hoppe & G. A. Milton (Eds.), *Social facilitation and imitative behavior*. Boston: Allyn and Bacon, 1968.

Cottrell, N. B., Wack, D. L., Sekerak, G. J., & Rittle, R. H. The social facilitation of dominant responses by the presence of an audience and the mere presence of others. *Journal of Personality and Social Psychology*, 1968, *9*, 251–256.

Cotzias, G. C., Papasilou, P. S., & Gellene, R. Modification of parkinsonism-chronic treatment with L-Dopa. *New England Journal of Medicine*, 1969, *280*, 337.

Cowles, R. B., see Bullock, & Cowles (1952).

Craik, F. I. M. Age differences in human memory. In J. E. Birren & K. W. Schaie (Eds.), *Handbook of the psychology of aging*. New York: Van Nostrand, 1977.

Craik, F. I. M., & Lockhart, R. S. Levels of processing: A framework for memory research. *Journal of Verbal Learning and Verbal Behavior*, 1972, *11*, 671–684.

Craik, F. I. M., & Tulving, E. Depth of processing and the retention of words of episodic memory. *Journal of Experimental Psychology*, 1975, *104*, 268–294.

Craik, F. I. M., & Watkins, M. J. The role of rehearsal in short-term memory. *Journal of Verbal Learning and Verbal Behavior*, 1973, *12*, 599–607.

Cressler, D. L., see Fairweather, Sanders, Cressler, & Maynard (1969).

Cross, B. A., & Green, J. D. Activity of single neurons in the hypothalamus: Effect of osmotic and other stimuli. *Journal of Physiology*, 1959, *17*, 347–392.

Crossman, E. R. F. W. A theory of the acquisition of speed-skill. *Ergogomics*, 1959, *2*, 153–166.

Crowder, R. G., see Darwin, Turvey, & Crowder (1972).

Cruz-Coke, R., & Varela, A. Inheritance of alcoholism: Its association with color-blindness. *Lancet*, 1966, *2*, 1282–1284.

Csikszentmihalyi, M. Play and intrinsic rewards. *Journal of Humanistic Psychology*, 1975, *15*, 41.

Curtiss, S., see Fromkin, Krashen, Curtiss, Rigler, & Rigler (1972/1973).

594

Cynader, H., see Regan, Beverley, & Cynader (1979).

Dale, H. H. Acetylcholine as a chemical transmitter of the effects of nerve impulses. *Journal of Mt. Sinai Hospital*, 1938, *4*, 401–415.

Dalton, K. *The premenstrual syndrome and progesterone therapy.* London: Heinemann, 1977.

Daly, M., & Wilson, M. *Sex, evolution and behavior.* North Scituate, Mass.: Duxbury Press, 1978.

D'Andrade, R. Cross-cultural studies of sex differences in behavior. In E. E. Maccoby (Ed.), *The development of sex differences.* Stanford, Calif.: Stanford University Press, 1966.

Danks, J. H., see Glucksberg, & Danks (1975).

Darley, J. M., & Latané, B. Bystander intervention in emergencies: Diffusion of responsibility. *Journal of Personality and Social Psychology*, 1968, *8*, 377–383.

Darley, J. M., Lewis, L. D., & Glucksberg, S. *Stereotype persistence and change among college students: One more time.* Unpublished manuscript, Princeton University, 1972.

Darley, J. M., see Latané, & Darley (1968).

Darley, J. M., see Latané, & Darley (1970).

Darwin, C. J., Turvey, M. T., & Crowder, R. G. An auditory analogue of the Sperling partial report procedure: Evidence for brief auditory storage. *Cognitive Psychology*, 1972, *3*, 255–267.

Davenport, W. Sexual patterns and their regulation in a society of the Southwest Pacific. In F. A. Beach (Ed.), *Sex and behavior.* New York: Wiley, 1965.

Davidson, J. M. Activation of the male rat's sexual behavior by intracerebral implantation of androgen. *Endocrinology*, 1966, *79*, 783–794.

Davidson, J. M. The physiology of meditation and mystical states of consciousness. *Perspectives in Biology and Medicine*, 1976, *19*, 345–379.

Davidson, J. M. The psychobiology of sexual experience. In J. M. Davidson & R. J. Davidson (Eds.), *The psychobiology of consciousness.* New York: Plenum Press, 1980.

Davidson, J. M., Camargo, C. A., & Smith, E. R. Effects of androgen on sexual behavior in hypogonadal men. *Journal of Clinical Endocrinology and Metabolism*, 1979, *48*, 955–958.

Davidson, J. M., Smith, E. R., & Levine, S. Testosterone, In H. Ursin, E. Baade, & S. Levine (Eds.), *Psychobiology of stresses: A study of coping men.* New York: Academic Press, in press. (Article originally published, 1978.)

Davidson, J. M., see Bermant, & Davidson (1974).

Davila, G. H., see Roche, & Davila (1972).

Davis, C. M. Self-selection of diet by newly weaned infants. *American Journal of Disease of Children*, 1928, *36*, 651–679.

Davis, J. M. Overview: Maintenance therapy in psychiatry: 1. Schizophrenia. *American Journal of Psychiatry*, 1975, *132*, 1237–1245.

Davis, K. E., see Jones, Davis, & Gergen (1961).

Davison, A. N., & Dobbing, J. Myelination as a vulnerable period in brain development. *British Medical Bulletin*, 1966, *22*, 40–44.

Davison, G. C., see Goldfried, & Davison (1976).

De Carlo, T. J. *Recreational participation patterns and successful aging: A twin study.* Unpublished doctoral dissertation, Columbia University, 1971.

Deci, E. L. *Intrinsic motivation.* New York: Plenum Press, 1975.

Delgado, J., Roberts, W., & Miller, N. Learning motivated by electrical stimulation of the brain. *American Journal of Physiology*, 1954, *179*, 587–593.

Dement, W. C. The effect of dream deprivation. *Science*, 1960, *131*, 1705–1707.

Dement, W. C. *Some must watch while some must sleep.* Stanford, Calif.: Stanford University Press, 1972.

Dement, W. C., & Wolpert, E. The relation of eye movements, bodily motility, and external stimuli to dream content. *Journal of Experimental Psychology*, 1958, *53*, 543–553.

Dennis, W. Creative productivity between the ages of twenty and eighty years. In B. Neugarten (Ed.), *Middle age and aging.* Chicago: University of Chicago Press, 1968.

Dermer, M., see Mita, Dermer, & Knight (1977).

DesCartes, R. 1662 *Traité do l'homme.* Haldane, E. S., & Ross, G. R. T. (Trans.), Cambridge, England: Cambridge University Press, 1911.

Desor, J. A. Toward a psychological theory of crowding. *Journal of Personality and Social Psychology*, 1972, *21*, 79–83.

Dettermanm, D. K., see Sternberg & Determanm, (Eds.), (1979).

Deutsch, M., & Gerard, H. B. A study of normative and informational social influences upon individual judgment. *Journal of Abnormal and Social Psychology*, 1955, *51*, 629–631.

DeValois, R. L., Smith, C. J., Karoly, A. J., & Kitai, S. T. Electrical responses of primate visual system: I. Different layers of macaque lateral geniculate nucleus. *Journal of Comparative and Physiological Psychology*, 1958, *51*, 662–668.

Diamond, I., & Neff, W. D. Ablation of temporal cortex and discrimination of auditory patterns. *Journal of Neurophysiology*, 1957, *20*, 300–315.

Dickinson, G. E. Adolescent sex information sources: 1964–1974. *Adolescence*, 1978, *13*, 653–658.

Diener, E., Fraser, S. C., Beaman, A. L., & Kelem, R. T. Effects of deindividuation variables on stealing among halloween trick-or-treaters. *Journal of Personality and Social Psychology*, 1976, *33*, 178–183.

Dion, K. K. Physical attractiveness and evaluation of children's transgressions. *Journal of Personality and Social Psychology*, 1972, *24*, 207–213.

595

Dion, K. K., Berscheid, E., & Walster, E. What is beautiful is good. *Journal of Personality and Social Psychology,* 1972, *24,* 285–290.

Ditchburn, R. W. *Eye movements and visual perception.* Oxford: Clarendon Press, 1973.

Dobbing, J., see Davison, & Dobbing (1966).

Dollard, J., Doob, L., Miller, N., Mowrer, O., & Sears, R. *Frustration and aggression.* New Haven: Yale University Press, 1939.

Doob, A. N., Carlsmith, J. M., Freedman, J. L., Landauer, T. K., & Toms, S. Effect of initial selling price on subsequent sales. *Journal of Personality and Social Psychology,* 1969, *11,* 345–350.

Doob, A. N., & Wood, L. E. Catharsis and aggression: Effects of annoyance and retaliation on aggressive behavior. *Journal of Personality and Social Psychology,* 1972, *22,* 156–162.

Doob, A. N., see Freedman, & Doob (1968).

Doob, L., see Dollard, Doob, Miller, Mowrer, & Sears (1939).

Dooling, D. J., & Lachman, R. Effects of comprehension on retention of prose. *Journal of Experimental Psychology,* 1971, *88,* 216–222.

Dörner, G. E., Rhode, W., Stahl, F., Krell, L., & Masius, W. A neuroendocrine predisposition for homosexuality in men. *Archives of Sexual Behavior,* 1975, *4,* 1–8.

Downs, R., see Sherrod, & Downs (1974).

Drabman, R. S., & Thomas, M. H. Does media violence increase children's tolerance to real-life aggression? *Developmental Psychology,* 1974, *10,* 418–421.

Drabman, R. S., see Thomas, Horton, Lippincott, & Drabman (1977).

Dragoin, W. B., see Wilcoxin, Dragoin, & Kral (1971).

Draguns, J. G., see Blashfield, & Draguns (1976).

Duncan, B. L. Differential social perception and attribution of intergroup violence: Testing the lower limits of stereotyping of blacks. *Journal of Personality and Social Psychology,* 1976, *34,* 590–598.

Dweck, C. S. & Goetz, F. E. Attributions and learned helplessness. In J. H. Harvey, W. Ickes, & R. F. Kidd (Eds.), *New directions in attribution research.* (Vol. 2) Hillsdale, N.J.: Lawrence Erlbaum, 1977.

Durlak, J. A. Comparative effectiveness of paraprofessional and professional helpers. *Psychological Bulletin,* 1979, *56,* 80–92.

Ebbesen, E. B., see Zimbardo, Ebbesen, & Maslach (1977).

Ebbinghaus, H. *Memory* (H. A. Ruger & C. E. Bussenius, Trans.). New York: Dover, 1964. (Originally published, 1885).

Eccles, J. C. *The physiology of synapses.* Berlin: Springer, 1964.

Eckerman, C. O., see Rheingold, & Eckerman (1973).

Edson, L. *How we learn.* New York: Time-Life Books, 1975.

Edwards, S., see Flynn, Vanegas, Foote, & Edwards (1970).

Ehrhardt, A. A., see Money, & Ehrhardt (1972).

Eighmy, B., see Miles, & Eighmy (1980).

Eiserer, L. A., see Hoffman, Eiserer, Ratner, & Pickering (1974).

Ellis, A. Rational emotive therapy. In V. Binder, A. Binder & B. Rimland (Eds.), *Modern therapies.* Englewood Cliffs, N.J.: Prentice-Hall, 1976.

Ellis, A. The basic clinical theory of rational-emotive therapy. In A. Ellis & R. Grieger (Eds.), *Handbook of rational-emotive therapy.* New York: Springer, 1977.

Emmerich, W. Parental identification in young children. *Genetic Psychology Monographs,* 1959, *60,* 257–308.

Emerson, P. E., see Schaffer, & Emerson (1964).

Emerson, R. C., see Stevens, Emerson, Gerstein, Kallos, Neufeld, Nichols, & Rosenquist (1976).

Enright, J. T. Stereopsis, visual latency, and three-dimensional moving pictures. *American Scientist,* 1970, *58,* 536–545.

Epstein, A. N. The lateral hypothalamic syndrome and its implication for the physiological psychology of hunger and thirst. In E. Stellar & J. M. Sprague (Eds.), *Progress in physiological psychology* (Vol. 4). New York: Academic Press, 1971.

Epstein, A. W., see Teitelbaum, & Epstein (1962).

Epstein, S. M. Toward a unified theory of anxiety. In B. A. Maher (Ed.), *Progress in experimental personality research* (Vol. 4). New York: Academic Press, 1967.

Erikson, E. H. *Childhood and society.* New York: Norton 1950.

Erikson, E. H. *Childhood and society* (2nd rev. ed.). New York: Norton, 1963.

Erikson, E. H. *Identity, youth and crisis.* New York: Norton, 1968.

Erickson, E. H. *Ghandi's truth.* New York: Norton, 1969.

Erikson, E. H. *Life history and the historical moment.* New York: Norton, 1975.

Eriksson, A., see Ohman, Eriksson, Fredriksson, Hugdahl, & Oloffson (1974).

Erlenmeyer-Kimling, L., & Jarvik, L. F. Genetics and intelligence: A review. *Science,* 1963, *142,* 1477–1479.

Eron, L. D., Lefkowitz, M. M., Huesmann, L. R., & Walder, L. Q. Does television violence cause aggression? *American Psychologist,* 1972, *27,* 253–263.

Ervin, C. R., see Byrne, Ervin, & Lamberth (1970).

Ervin, F., see Sweet, Ervin, & Mark (1969).

Ervin, F. R., see Mark, & Ervin (1970).

Ervin, F. R., see Mark, Sweet, & Ervin (1972).

Ervin-Tripp, S. Limitation and structural change in children's language. In E. H. Lenneberg (Ed.), *New directions in the study of language.* Cambridge, Mass.: MIT Press, 1964.

Esterson, A., see Laing, & Esterson (1971).

Estes, W. K. An experimental study of punishment. *Psychological Monographs,* 1944, *57,* (Whole No. 263).

Eveleth, P. B., & Tanner, J. M. *Worldwide variation in human growth.* Cambridge, England: Cambridge University Press, 1976.

Eysenck, H. J. The effects of psychotherapy: An evaluation. *Journal of Consulting Psychology*, 1952, *16*, 319–324.

Eysenck, H. J. *Fact and fiction in psychology*. Baltimore: Penguin, 1965.

Eysenck, H. J. *The biological basis of personality*. Springfield, Ill.: C. C. Thomas, 1967.

Eysenck, H. J. *The inequality of man*. San Diego: Edits Publishers, 1975.

Eysenck, H. J., & Eysenck, S. B. G. *Personality structure and measurement*. London: Routledge & Kegan-Paul, 1967.

Eysenck, S. B. G., see Eysenck, & Eysenck (1967).

Fadiman, J., see Harman, McKim, Mogar, Fadiman, & Stolaroff (1966).

Fagot, B. I. Consequences of moderate cross-gender behavior in pre-school children. *Child Development*, 1977, *48*, 902–907.

Fagot, B. I. & Patterson, C. R. An in vivo analysis of reinforcing contingencies for sex role behaviors in the preschool child. *Developmental Psychology*, 1969, *1*, 563–568.

Fairweather, G. W. (Ed.). *Social psychology in treating mental illness: An experimental approach*. New York: Wiley, 1964.

Fairweather, G. W., Sanders, D. H., Cressler, D. L., & Maynard. H. *Community life for the mentally ill: An alternative to institutional care*. Chicago: Aldine, 1969.

Falk, J. L. Theoretical review: The nature and determinants of adjunctive behavior. *Physiology and Behavior*, 1971, *6*, 577–588.

Fantz, R. L. The origin of form perception. *Scientific American*, 1961, *204*, 66–72.

Fantz, R. L. Visual perception and experience in infancy: Issues and approaches. In *Early experience and visual information processing in perceptual and reading disorders*. New York: National Academy of Science, 1970.

Fechner, G. T. *Elements of psychophysics* (H. E. Adler, Trans.). New York: Holt, Rinehart and Winston, 1966. (Originally published, 1860).

Feinberg, I. A comparison of the visual hallucinations in schizophrenia and those induced by mescaline and LSD-25. In L. J. West (Ed.), *Hallucinations*. New York: Grune & Stratton, 1962.

Feld, S., see Gurin, Veroff, & Feld (1960).

Feldman, M. P., & MacCulloch, M. J. *Homosexual behavior: Therapy and assessment*. Oxford, England: Pergamon Press, 1971.

Ferrier, D. *Functions of the brain*. London: Smith Elder & Co., 1876.

Festinger, L. A theory of social comparison processes. *Human Relations*, 1954, *7*, 117–140.

Festinger, L. *A theory of cognitive dissonance*. Stanford, Calif.: Stanford University Press, 1957.

Festinger, L., & Carlsmith, J. M. Cognitive consequences of forced compliance. *Journal of Abnormal and Social Psychology*, 1959, *58*, 202–210.

Festinger, L., Schachter, S., & Back, K. *Social pressures in informal groups*. New York: Harper, 1950.

Feuerstein, R. *Instrumental enrichment: An intervention program for cognitive modifiability*. Baltimore, Md.: University Park Press, 1980.

Filliozat, A. M., see Hindley, Filliozat, Klakenberg, Nocolet-Meisten, & Sand (1966).

Fields, S. Folk healing for the wounded spirit. *Innovations*, 1976, *3*, 3–18.

Fields, S. Support and succor for the "walking wounded." *Innovations*, 1978, *5*(1), 2–15.

Fieve, R. R. *Moodswing: The third revolution in psychiatry*. New York: Bantam, 1975.

Fillmore, C. J. The case for case. In E. Bach & R. T. Harms (Eds.), *Universals in linguistic theory*. New York: Holt, Rinehart and Winston, 1968.

Fink, K., & Cantril, H. The collegiate stereotype as frame of reference. *Journal of Abnormal and Social Psychology*, 1939, *32*, 352–356.

Fisher, C., Gross, J., & Zuch, J. Cycle of penile erection synchronous with dreaming. *Archives of General Psychiatry*, 1965, *12*, 29–45.

Fisher, R. The biological fabric of time. *Interdisciplinary Perspectives of Time: Annals of the New York Academy of Sciences*, 1967, *138*, 451–465.

Fitts, P. M., & Posner, M. I. *Human performance*. Belmont, Calif.: Brooks-Cole, 1967.

Fitzsimons, J. T. The physiology of thirst: A review of the extraneural aspects of the mechanisms of drinking. In E. Stellar & J. M. Sprague (Eds.), *Progress in physiological psychology*. New York: Academic Press, 1971.

Fitzsimons, J. T. Thirst. *Physiological Reviews*, 1972, *52*, 468–561.

Fixsen, D. L., Phillips, E. L., Phillips, E. A., & Wolf, M. M. *The teaching-family model of group home treatment*. Paper presented at the meeting of the American Psychological Association, Honolulu, Hawaii, September 1972.

Flavell, J. H. Metacognitive development. In J. M. Scandura & C. J. Brainerd (Eds.), *Structural-process theories of complex human behavior*. Leyden: Sijthoff, 1978.

Fleck, S., see Lidz, Fleck, & Cornelison (1965).

Fleischer, S., see Foulkes, & Fleischer (1975).

Flynn, J., Vanegas, H., Foote, W., & Edwards, S. Neural mechanisms involved in a cat's attack on a rat. In R. F. Whalen, M. Thompson, M. Verzeano, & N. Weinberger (Eds.), *The neural control of behavior*. New York: Academic Press, 1970.

Foerster, O. Beiträge zur Pathophysiologie der Sehsphäre. *Journal für Psychologie und Neurologie*, 1929, *39*, 463–485.

Folger, R., see Worchel, Andreoli, & Folger (1977).

Foote, W., see Flynn, Vanegas, Foote, & Edwards (1970).

Ford, C. S., & Beach, F. A. *Patterns of sexual behavior*. New York: Harper, 1951.

Fortris, J. G., see Larsen, Gray, & Fortris (1968).

Foss, D. J., & Hakes, D. T. *Psycholinguistics*. Englewood Cliffs, N.J.: Prentice-Hall, 1978.

Fothergill, L. A., see Hughes, Smith, Kosterlitz, Fothergill, Morgan, & Morris (1975).

Foulkes, D., & Fleischer, S. Mental activity in relaxed wakefulness. *Journal of Abnormal Psychology*, 1975, *84*, 66.

Fowler, F. J., see Rabow, Fowler, Bradford, Hoefeller, & Shibuya (1966).

Fox, R. E., see Strupp, Fox, & Lessler (1969).

Fraisse, P. *The psychology of time*. New York: Harper & Row, 1963.

Franks, J. J., & Bransford, J. D. Abstraction of visual patterns. *Journal of Experimental Psychology*, 1971, *90*, 65–74.

Franks, J. J., see Bransford, Barclay, & Franks (1972).

Franks, J. J., see Bransford, & Franks (1971).

Franks, J. J., see Morris, Brandsford, & Franks (1977).

Fraser, S. C., see Diener, Fraser, Beaman, & Kelem (1976).

Fraser, S. C., see Freedman, & Fraser (1966).

Fredriksson, N., see Ohman, Eriksson, Fredriksson, Hugdahl, & Oloffson (1974).

Freedman, D. X., see Bowers, Jr., & Freedman (1966).

Freedman, J. L. *Crowding and behavior*. New York: Viking Press, 1975.

Freedman, J. L., & Doob, A. N. *Deviancy: The psychology of being different*. New York: Academic Press, 1968.

Freedman, J. L., & Fraser, S. C. Compliance without pressure: The foot-in-the-door technique. *Journal of Personality and Social Psychology*, 1966, *4*, 195–202.

Freedman, J. L., Heshka, S., & Levy, A. Population density and pathology: Is there a relationship? *Journal of Experimental Social Psychology*, 1975, *11*, 539–552.

Freedman, J. L., see Doob, Carlsmith, Freedman, Landauer, & Toms (1969).

Freud, S. *Three essays on the theory of sexuality*. London: Hogarth Press, 1905.

Freud, S. *New introductory lectures on psychoanalysis*. New York: Norton, 1933.

Freud, S. Psychopathology of everyday life. In A. A. Birell (Ed.), *The writings of Sigmund Freud*. New York: Modern Library, 1914/1938.

Freud, S. Fragment of an analysis of a case of hysteria. In J. Strachey (Ed. & trans.), *The standard edition of the complete psychological works of Sigmund Freud* (Vol. 7). London: Hogarth Press, 1953. (Originally published, 1905.)

Freud, S. The interpretation of dreams. In J. Strachey (Ed. and trans.), *The standard edition of the complete psychological works of Sigmund Freud* (Vols. 4 & 5). London: Hogarth Press, 1953. (Originally published, 1900.)

Freud, S. A letter to Fleiss, 1897. In E. Jones (Ed.), *The life and works of Sigmund Freud* (Vol. 1). New York: Basic Books, 1953.

Freud, S. Analysis of a phobia in a five-year-old boy, 1909. *In Collected works of Sigmund Freud* (Vol. 10). London: Hogarth Press, 1956.

Freud, S. On beginning the treatment. In J. Strachey (Trans.), *The standard edition of the complete psychological works of Sigmund Freud* (Vol. 12). London: Hogarth Press, 1958. (Originally published, 1913.)

Freud, S. On psychotherapy. In E. Jones (Ed.), *Sigmund Freud collected papers* (Vol. 1). New York: Basic Books, Hogarth Press, Ltd., 1959. (Originally published, 1904.)

Freud, S. Introductory lectures on psychoanalysis. In J. Strachey (Trans.), *The standard edition of the complete psychological works of Sigmund Freud* (Vol. 15). London: Hogarth Press, 1961. (Originally published, 1916.)

Freud, S. Some additional notes on dream-interpretation as a whole. In J. Strachey (Trans.), *The standard edition of the complete psychological works of Sigmund Freud* (Vol. 19). London: Hogarth Press, 1961. (Originally published, 1925.)

Freud, S. The interpretation of dreams. In J. Strachey (Ed. and trans.), *The standard edition of the complete psychological works of Sigmund Freud* (Vol. 4 & 5). London: Hogarth Press, 1962. (Originally published, 1900.)

Freud, S. *Three essays on the theory of sexuality* (J. Strachey, Trans.). New York: Avon Books, 1962. (Originally published, 1905.)

Freud, S. Introductory lectures on psychoanalysis. In J. Strachey (Trans.), *The standard edition of the complete psychological works of Sigmund Freud* (Vol. 16). London: Hogarth Press, 1963. (Originally published, 1916.)

Freud, S. *New introductory lectures on psychoanalysis* (J. Strachey, Trans.). New York: Norton, 1965. (Originally published, 1933.)

Freud, S., & Breuer, J. *Studies on hysteria* (J. Strachey, Trans.). New York: Avon Books, 1966. (Originally published, 1895.)

Friedl, E. *Women and Men*. New York: Holt, Rinehart and Winston, 1975.

Fritsch, G. T., & Hitzig, E. Über die elektrische Erregbarkeit des Grosshirns. In G. Von Bonin (Trans.), *Some papers on the cerebral cortex*. Springfield, Ill.: Charles C Thomas, 1960. (Originally published, 1870.)

Fromkin, V., Krashen, S., Curtiss, S., Rigler, S., & Rigler, M. The development of language in Genie: A case of language acquisition beyond the "critical period." *Brain and Language*, 1972/1973, *1*, 81–107.

Fromm, E. *Man for himself: An inquiry into the psychology of ethics*. New York: Rinehart, 1947.

Galin, D. The two modes of consciousness and the two halves of the brain. In P. Lee, R. E. Ornstein, C. T. Tart, A. Deikman, & D. Galin (Eds.), *Symposium on Consciousness*. New York: Viking Press, 1976.

Gall, F. J., & Spurzheim, J. C. *Anatomie et physiologie du systéme nerveux en général et du cerveau en particulier* (4 vols. and Atlas). Paris: Schoell, 1810–1819.

Galle, O. R., Gove, W. R., & McPherson, J. M. Population density and pathology: What are the relations for man? *Science*, 1972, *176*, 23–30.

Galton, F. *Inquiries into human faculty and its development.* London: Macmillan, 1883.

Garcia, J., see McGowan, Hankins, & Garcia (1972).

Garcia, J., see Revusky, & Garcia (1970).

Gardner, B. T., & Gardner, R. A. Two-way communication with an infant chimpanzee. In A. M. Schrier & F. Stollnitz (Eds.), *Behavior of nonhuman primates* (Vol. 4). New York: Academic Press, 1971.

Gardner, R. A., see Gardner, & Gardner (1971).

Garrett, M. F. The analysis of sentence production. In G. H. Bower (ed.), *The psychology of learning and motivation* (Vol. 9). New York: Academic Press, 1975.

Gates, M. F., & Allee, W. C. Conditioned behavior of isolated and grouped cockroaches on a simple maze. *Journal of Comparative Psychology*, 1933, *15*, 331–358.

Gath, D. H., see Gelder, Brancroft, Gath Johnston, Mathews, & Shaw (1973).

Gautier, T., see Imperato-McGinley, Peterson, Gautier, & Sturla (1979).

Gazzaniga, M. S. The split brain in man. *Scientific American*, 1967, *217*, 24–29.

Gazzaniga, M. S. *The bisected brain.* New York: Appleton-Century-Crofts, 1970.

Gebhard, P. H., see Kinsey, Pomeroy, Martin, & Gebhard (1953).

Geen, R. G., see Berkowitz, & Geen (1966).

Geer, J., see Seligman, Maier, & Geer (1968).

Gelb, T. K. Die "Farbenkonstauz" der Schdinge. *Handbuch der Hormalen und Pathologischen Physiologie*, 1929, *12*, 594–678.

Gelder, M. G., Bancroft, J. H. J., Gath, D. H., Johnston, D. W., Mathews, A. M., & Shaw, P. M. Specific and non-specific factors in behavior therapy. *British Journal of Psychiatry*, 1973, *123*, 445–462.

Gellene, R., see Cotzias, Papasilou, & Gellene (1969).

Gerard, H. B. Emotional uncertainty and social comparison. *Journal of Abnormal and Social Psychology*, 1963, *66*, 568–573.

Gerard, H. B., see Deutsch, & Gerard (1955).

Gerbner, G. Violence in television drama: Trends and symbolic functions. In G. Comstock, A. Rubenstein, & J. Murrary (Eds.), *Television and social behavior* (Vol. 1). Washington D. C.: Government Printing Office, 1972.

Gergen, K. J., see Jones, Davis, & Gergen (1961).

Gerstein, G. L., see Stevens, Emerson, Gerstein, Kallos, Neufeld, Nichols, & Rosenquist (1976).

Getting testy: A rebellion gathers steam. *Time*, November 26, 1979.

Gewirtz, J. L., & Baer, D. M. The effect of brief social deprivation on behavior for a social reinforcer. *Journal of Abnormal and Social Psychology*, 1958, *56*, 49–56.

Gibson, E. J., & Walk, R. D. The "visual cliff." *Scientific American*, 1960, *202*, 64–71.

Gibson, J. J. Adaptation, after-effect, and contrast in the perception of curved lines. *Journal of Experimental Psychology*, 1933, *16*, 1–31.

Gibson, J. J. *The perception of the visual world.* Boston: Houghton Mifflin, 1950.

Gill, F. B., & Wolf, L. L. Economics of feeding territoriality in the golden-winged sunbird. *Ecology*, 1975, *56*, 333–345.

Gittelman-Klein, R., Klein, D. F., Katz, S., Saraf, K., & Pollack, E. Comparative effects of methylphenidate and thiordazine in hyperkinetic children. *Archives of General Psychiatry*, 1976, *33*, 1217–1231.

Glass, D. C., & Singer, J. E. *Urban stress: Experiments on noise and social stressors.* New York: Academic Press, 1972.

Glass, D. C., see Cohen, Glass, & Singer (1973).

Glass, D. C., see Henchy, & Glass (1968).

Glass, G. V., see Smith, & Glass (1977).

Glazer, H. I., see Weiss, Glazer, & Pohorecky (1976).

Glucksberg, S., & Danks, J. H. *Experimental psycholinguistics.* Hillsdale, N.J.: Lawrence Erlbaum, 1975.

Glucksberg, S., see Darley, Lewis, & Glucksberg (1972).

Glueck, E., see Glueck, & Glueck (1956).

Glueck, E., see Glueck, & Glueck (1950).

Glueck, S., & Glueck, E. *Unraveling juvenile delinquency.* New York: Commonwealth Fund, 1950.

Glueck, S., & Glueck, E. *Physique and delinquency.* New York: Harper, 1956.

Goethals, C. R., see Jones, Rock, Shaver, Goethals, & Ward (1968).

Goetz, F. E. See Dweck, & Goetz (1977).

Goffman, E. *Asylums: Essays on the social situation of mental patients and other inmates.* Garden City, N.J.: Anchor, 1961.

Gogel, W. C. The metric of visual space. In W. Epstein (Ed.), *Stability and constancy in visual perception.* New York: Wiley, 1977.

Gold, A. R., see Adams, Gold, & Burt (1978).

Goldiamond, I., see Isaacs, Thomas, & Goldiamond (1960).

Goldfried, M. R., & Davison, G. C. *Clinical behavior therapy.* New York: Holt, Rinehart and Winston, 1976.

Goldman, R., see Schachter, Goldman, & Gordon (1968).

Goldstein, K., see Scheerer, Rothman, & Goldstein (1945).

Goleman, D. *Varieties of meditative experience.* New York: Dutton Press, 1977.

Golgi, C. Recherches sur l'histologie des centres nerveux. *Archives Italiennes de Biologie*, 1883, *3*, 285–317.

Gonshor, A., & Melvill Jones, G. Extreme vestibulo-ocular adaptation induced by prolonged optical reversal in vision. *Journal of Physiology*, 1976, *256*, 381–414.

Good, P. *The individual.* New York: Time-Life Books, 1974.

Goodwin, D. W., Powell, B., Bremer, D., Hoine, H., & Stern, J. Alcohol and recall: State dependent effects in man. *Science*, 1969, *163*, 1358.

Goodwin, G. M., McCloskey, D. I., & Mathews, P. B. C. The contribution of muscle afferents to kinesthesia shown by vibration induced illusions of movement and by the effects of paralysing joint afferents. *Brain*, 1972, *95*, 705–748.

Gordon, A., see Schachter, Goldman, & Gordon (1968).

Gordon, J. H., see Harlan, Gordon, & Gorski (1979).

Gore, R. In search of the mind's eye. *Life*, October 22, 1971, pp. 56–64.

Gorski, R. A., see Harlan, Gordon, & Gorski (1979).

Goss-Custard, J. D. Feeding behavior of redshank, *Tringa totanus*, and optimal foraging theory. In A. C. Kamil & T. D. Sargent (Eds.), *Foraging behavior: Ecological, ethological and psychological approaches.* New York: Garland Publishing Co., 1981.

Gove, W. R., see Galle, Gove, & McPherson (1972).

Goy, R. W. Experimental control of psychosexuality. *Philosophical Transactions of the Royal Society, (B).*, 1970, *259*, 149–162.

Graham, C. H., see Hartline, & Graham (1932).

Gray, L. N., see Larsen, Gray, & Fortris (1968).

Green, D. M., & Swets, J. A. *Signal detection theory and psychophysics.* New York: Wiley, 1966.

Green, J. D., see Cross, & Green (1959).

Green, R. Biological influences on sexual identity. In A. Katchadourian (Ed.), *Human Sexuality—a comparative and developmental perspective.* Berkeley: University of California Press, 1979.

Greenberg, C. I., see Baum, & Greenberg (1975).

Greenblatt, M., Grosser, G. H., & Wechsler, H. Differential responses of hospitalized depressed patients to somatic therapy. *American Journal of Psychiatry*, 1964, *120*, 935–943.

Greene, D., see Lepper, Greene, & Nisbett (1973).

Greenfield, P. M. On culture and conservation. In J. S. Bruner, R. R. Olver, & P. M. Greenfield, *Studies in cognitive growth.* New York: Wiley, 1966.

Greenfield, P. M., & Smith, J. H. *The structure of communication in early language development.* New York: Academic Press, 1976.

Greenfield, P. M., see Bruner, Olver, & Greenfield (1966).

Greenspoon, J. The reinforcing effects of two spoken sounds on the frequency of two responses. *American Journal of Psychology*, 1955, *68*, 409–416.

Greenstein, J. A., see Whitten, Bronson, & Greenstein (1968).

Gregory, R. L. *Eye and brain* (2nd ed.). New York: World University Library, 1973.

Gregory, R. L. *Eye and brain: The psychology of seeing* (3rd ed.). London: Weidenfeld and Nicolson, 1977.

Griffin, D. R. *Listening in the dark.* New Haven: Yale University Press, 1958.

Grinspoon, L. *Marijuana reconsidered.* Cambridge, Mass.: Harvard University Press, 1977.

Groff, B. D., see Heller, Groff, & Solomon (1977).

Gross, C., Rocha-Miranda, C. E., & Bender, D. B. Visual properties of neurons in inferotemporal cortex of the macaque. *Journal of Neurophysiology*, 1972, *35*, 96—111.

Gross, J., see Fisher, Gross, & Zuch (1965).

Gross, L. P., see Schachter, & Gross (1968).

Grosser, G. H., see Greenblatt, Grosser, & Wechsler (1964).

Grush, J. E. Audiences can inhibit or facilitate competitive behavior. *Personality and Social Psychology Bulletin*, 1978, *4*, 119—122.

Gudhea, D., see Kiester, Jr., & Gudhea (1974).

Guilford, J. P. *The nature of human intelligence.* New York: McGraw-Hill. 1967.

Gunderson, J. G., see Keith, Gunderson, Reifman, Buchsbaum, & Mosher (1976).

Gurin, G., Veroff, J., & Feld, S. *Americans view their mental health.* New York: Basic Books, 1960.

Haber, R. N. Eidetic images. *Scientific American*, 1969, *22*, 36—44.

Hakes, D. T., see Foss, & Hakes (1978).

Haley, J., see Bateson, Jackson, Haley, & Weakland (1956).

Hall, C., & Van de Castle, R. L. *The content analysis of dreams.* New York: Appleton-Century-Crofts, 1966.

Hall, E. T. *The hidden dimension.* Garden City, N.Y.: Doubleday, 1966.

Hamilton, L. W., see Weisman, Hamilton, & Carlton (1972).

Hammond, W. H. The constancy of physical types as determined by factorial analysis. *Human Biology*, 1957, *29*, 40—61.

Hampson, J. G., see Hampson, & Hampson (1960).

Hampson, J. L., & Hampson, J. G. The ontogenesis of sexual behavior in man. In W. C. Young (Ed.), *Sex and internal secretions* (3rd ed.) (Vol. 2). Baltimore: Williams & Wilkins, 1900.

Hankins, W. G., see McGowan, Hankins, & Garcia (1972).

Hanlon, C., see Brown, & Hanlon (1970).

Hansel, C. E. M. *ESP and parapsychology: A critical evaluation.* Buffalo, N.Y.: Prometheus Books, 1979.

Hansel, C. E. M., see Cohen, Hansel, & Sylvester (1954).

Harlan, R. E., Gordon, J. H., & Gorski, R. A. Sexual differentiation of the brain: Implications for neuroscience. In D. M. Schneider (Ed.), *Reviews of neuroscience* (Vol. 4). New York: Raven Press, 1979.

Harlow, H. F. Sexual behavior in the rhesus monkey. In F. A. Beach (Ed.), *Sex and behavior.* New York: Wiley, 1965.

Harlow, H. F., & Harlow, M. K. The affectional systems. In A. M. Schrier, H. F. Harlow, & F. Stollnitz (Eds.), *Behavior of nonhuman primates* (Vol. 2.). New York: Academic Press, 1965.

Harlow, H. F., & Harlow, M. K. Learning to love. *American Scientist.* 1966, *54*, 244—272.

Harlow, H. F., & Harlow, M. K. Effects of various mother-infant relationships on rhesus monkey behaviors. In B. M. Foss (Ed.), *Determinants of infant behavior: IV.* London: Methuen, 1969.

Harlow, M. K., see Harlow, & Harlow (1965).

Harlow, M. K., see Harlow, & Harlow (1966).

Harlow, M. K., see Harlow, & Harlow (1969).

Harman, W., McKim, R., Mogar, R., Fadiman, J., & Stolaroff, M. Psychedelic agents in creative problem-solving: A pilot study. *Psychological Reports*, 1966, *19*, 211—227.

Harris, C. S. Perceptual adaptation to inverted, reversed, and displaced vision. *Psychology Review*, 1965, *72*, 419—444.

Harris, F. R., see Allen, Hart, Buell, Harris, & Wolf (1964).

Harris, G. W., & Levine, S. Sexual differentiation of the brain and its experimental control. *Journal of Physiology*, 1965, *181*, 379—400.

Harris, G. W., and Michael, R. P. The activation of sexual behavior by hypothalamic implants of estrogen. *Journal of Physiology*, 1964, *171*, 275—301.

Harris, V. A., see Jones, & Harris (1967).

Hart, B., see Allen, Hart, Buell, Harris, & Wolf (1964).

Hart, B. Neural bases of sexual behavior: A comparative analysis. In R. W. Goy & D. W. Pfaff (Eds.), *Handbook of behavioral neurobiology*. New York: Plenum Press, in press.

Harter, N., see Bryan, & Harter (1897).

Hartline, H. K., & Graham, C. H. Nerve impulses from single receptors in the eye. *Journal of Cellular and Comparative Physiology*. 1932, *1*, 277—295.

Hartmann, E. L. *Functions of sleep*. New Haven: Yale University Press, 1973.

Harvey, O., see Sherif, Harvey, White, Hood, & Sherif (1961).

Hastorf, A., & Cantril, H. They saw a game: A case study. *Journal of Abnormal and Social Psychology*, 1954, *49*, 129—134.

Haughton, E., & Ayllon, T. Production and elimination of symptomatic behavior. In L. Ullmann & L. Krasner (Eds.), *Case studies in behavior modification*. New York: Holt, Rinehart and Winston, 1965.

Hawkins, J. E., Jr., see Stebbins, Miller, Johnsson, & Hawkins, Jr. (1969).

Hayes, C., see Hayes, & Hayes (1951).

Hayes, K. J., & Hayes, C. Intellectual development of a home-raised chimpanzee. *Proceedings of the American Philosophical Society*, 1951, *95*, 105—109.

Heath, R. G. Pleasure and brain activity in man. *Journal of Nervous and Mental Disease*, 1972, *154*, 3—18.

Hebb, D. O. *The organization of behavior*. New York: Wiley, 1949.

Hecht, S., Shalaer, S., & Pirenne, M. H. Energy, quanta, and vision. *Journal of General Physiology*. 1942, *25*, 819—840.

Heider, E. R., & Oliver, D. The structure of the color space in naming and memory for two languages. *Cognitive Psychology*, 1972, *3*, 337—354.

Heider, F. *The psychology of interpersonal relations*. New York: Wiley, 1958.

Heingartner, A., see Zajonc, Heingartner, & Herman (1969).

Heisler, S., see Widroe, & Heisler (1976).

Heller, J. F., Groff, B. D., & Solomon, S. H. Toward an understanding of crowding: The role of physical interaction. *Journal of Personality and Social Psychology*, 1977, *35*, 183—190.

Helmholtz, H. L. F. von. *On the sensations of tone* (A. J. Ellis, Trans.). London: Longmans, Green, 1875.

Helmholtz, H. L. F. von. *Helmholtz' treatise on physiological optics* (Vol. 2), (J. P. C. Southall, Trans.) Rochester, N.Y.: Optical Society of America, 1924. (Originally published, 1896.)

Helmholtz, H. L. F. von. *Helmholtz' treatise on physiological optics* (J. P. C. Southall Ed. and trans.). New York: Dover, 1962. (Originally published, 1910.)

Helms, D. B., see Turner, & Helms (1979).

Helson, H., & King, S. M. The tau-effect: An example of psychological relativity. *Journal of Experimental Psychology*, 1931, *14*, 202—218.

Henchy, J., & Glass, D. C. Evaluation apprehension and the social facilitation of dominant and subordinate responses. *Journal of Personality and Social Psychology*, 1968, *10*, 446—454.

Hendrick, C., & Brown, S. R. Introversion, extraversion, and interpersonal attraction. *Journal of Personality and Social Psychology*, 1971, *20*, 31—36.

Henker, B., see Collins, Henker, & Whalen (1980).

Henning, H. *Das Geruch*. Leipzig: Barth, 1916.

Hering, E. *Zur Lehre vom Lichtsinne*. Wien: Gerhold's Sohn, 1878.

Herman, E. M., see Zajonc, Heingartner, & Herman (1969).

Heron, W., see Bexton, Heron, & Scott (1954).

Herrnstein, R., & Boring, E. *A source book in the history of psychology*. Cambridge, Mass.: Harvard University Press, 1966.

Herrnstein, R. J. *I.Q. in the meritocracy*. Boston: Atlantic-Little, Brown, 1973.

Hersen, M., see Bellack, Hersen, & Turner (1976).

Hershey, M. *Characteristics of gifted children*. Gifted Association Conference. Kansas City, Mo., 1976.

Heshka, S., see Freedman, Heshka, & Levy (1975).

Hess, E. H. The conditions limiting critical age of imprinting. *Journal of Comparative and Physiological Psychology*, 1959, *52*, 515—518.

Hess, E. H., & Polt, J. M. Pupil size as related to interest value of visual stimuli. *Science*, 1960, *132*, 349—350.

Hetherington, A. W., & Ranson, S. W. The spontaneous activity and food intake of rats with hypothalamic lesions. *American Journal of Physiology*, 1942, *136*, 609—617.

Hetherington, E. M. Effects of paternal absence on sex-typed behaviors in Negro and White pre-adolescent males. *Journal of Personality and Social Psychology*, 1966, *2*, 188—194.

Hetherington, E. M. The effects of familial variables on

sex-typing, on parent-child similarity and on imitation in children. In J. P. Hill (Ed.) *Minnesota Symposium on Child Psychology (Vol. 1)* Minneapolis: University of Minnesota Press, 1967.

Hetherington, E. M., & Morris, W. N. The family and primary groups. In W. H. Holtzman (Ed.), *Introductory psychology in depth: Developmental topics.* New York: Harper & Row, 1978.

Hetherington, E. M., & Parke, R. D. Child Psychology: *A Contemporary Viewpoint.* (2nd ed.) New York: McGraw-Hill, 1979.

Hilgard, E. *Divided consciousness.* New York: Wiley, 1977.

Hindley, C. B., Filliozat, A. M., Klakenberg, G., Nocolet-Meister, D., & Sand, E. A. Difference in age of walking in five European longitudinal samples. *Human Biology*, 1966, *38*, 364—379.

Hinkle, S., & Schopler, J. Ethnocentrism in the evaluation of group products. In W. G. Austin & S. Worchel (Eds.), *The social psychology of intergroup relations.* Monterey, Calif.: Brooks/Cole, 1979.

Hirai, T., see Kasematsu, & Hirai (1966).

Hirsch, H., & Spinelli, N. Visual experience modifies distribution of horizontally and vertically oriented receptive fields in cats. *Science*, 1970, *168*, 869—871.

Hirsch, J., see Knittle, & Hirsch (1968).

Hitai, S. T., see DeValois, Smith, Karoly, & Hitai (1959).

Hitzig, E., see Fritsch, & Hitzig (1960).

Hoagland, H. The physiological control of judgments of duration: Evidence for a chemical clock. *Journal of General Psychology*, 1933, *9*, 267—287.

Hoagland, H. *Pacemakers in relation to aspects of behavior.* New York: Macmillan, 1935.

Hodgkin, A. L., & Huxley, A. F. A quantitative description of membrane current and its application to conduction and excitation in nerve. *Journal of Physiology*, 1952, *117*, 500—544.

Hodgson, R. J., see Rachman, & Hodgson (1980).

Hoebel, B. C., & Teitelbaum, P. Weight regulation in normal and hypothalamic rats. *Journal of Comparative and Physiological Psychology*, 1966, *61*, 189—193.

Hoebel, B. C., see Smith, King, & Hoebel (1970).

Hofeller, M. A., see Rabow, Fowler, Bradford, Hofeller, & Shibuya (1966).

Hoffer, A., Osmond, H., & Smythies, J. R. Schizophrenia: A new approach. *Journal of Mental Science*, 1954, *100*, 29—45.

Hoffer, A., see Chwelos, Blewett, Smith, & Hoffer (1959).

Hoffman, H. S., Eiserer, L. A., Ratner, A. M., & Pickering, V. L. Development of distress vocalization during withdrawal of an imprinting stimulus. *Journal of Comparative and Physiological Psychology*, 1974, *86*, 563—568.

Hoffman, L., see Aponte, & Hoffman (1973).

Hoffman, M. L. Parental discipline and moral internalization: An information processing analysis. In E. T. Higgins, D. Ruble & W. Hastings (Eds.), *New directions in social-cognitive development.* New York: Cambridge University Press, in press.

Hogan, H. P., see Carmichael, Hogan, & Walter (1932).

Hoine, H., see Goodwin, Powell, Bremer, Hoine, & Stern (1969).

Holden, C. Identical twins reared apart. *Science*, 1980, *207*, 1323—1328.

Hollister, L. E. Drug induced psychoses and schizophrenic reaction: A critical comparison. *Annals of the New York Academy of Sciences*, 1962, *96*, 80—88.

Holmes, D. S. Investigations of repression: Differential recall of material experimentally or naturally associated with ego threat. *Psychological Bulletin*, 1974, *81*, 632—653.

Honzik, C. H., see Tolman, & Honzik (1930).

Hood, W., see Sherif, Harvey, White, Hood, & Sherif (1961).

Horney, K. *New ways in psychoanalysis.* New York: Norton, 1939.

Horton, R. W., see Thomas, Horton, Lippincott, & Drabman (1977).

Houts, P. S., & Serber, M. (Eds.) *After the turn-on, what? Learning perspectives on humanistic groups.* Champaign, Ill.: Research Press, 1972.

Hovland, C. I., & Sears, R. R. Minor studies in aggression: VI. Correlation of lynchings with economic indices. *Journal of Personality*, 1940, *9*, 301—310.

Hovland, C. I., & Weiss, N. The influence of source credibility on communication effectiveness. *Public Opinion Quarterly*, 1952, *15*, 635—650.

Hubel, D. H., & Wiesel, T. N. Receptive fields, binocular interaction and functional architecture in the cat's visual cortex. *Journal of Physiology*, 1962, *160*, 106—154.

Hubel, D. H., & Wiesel, T. N. Binocular interaction in striate cortex of kittens reared with artificial squint. *Journal of Neurophysiology*, 1965, *28*, 1041—1059.

Huesmann, L. R., see Eron, Lefkowitz, Huesmann, & Walder (1972).

Hugdahl, K., see Ohman, Eriksson, Fredriksson, Hugdahl, & Oloffson (1974).

Hughes, J., Smith, T. W., Kosterlitz, H. W., Fothergill, L. A. Morgan, B. A., & Morris, H. R. Identification of two related pentapeptides from the brain with potent opiate agonist activity. *Nature*, 1975, *258*, 577—579.

Hull, C. *Principles of behavior.* New York: Appleton-Century-Crofts, 1943.

Hull, C. *Essentials of behavior.* New Haven: Yale University Press, 1951.

Hull, C. *A behavior system: An introduction to behavior theory concerning the individual organism.* New Haven: Yale University Press, 1952.

Hulse, S. H. Patterned reinforcement. In G. H. Bower (Ed.), *The psychology of learning and motivation* (Vol. 7). New York: Academic Press, 1973.

Hunt, M. *Sexual behavior in the 1970's.* Chicago: Playboy Press, 1974.

Husband, R. W. Analysis of methods in human male learning. *Journal of Genetic Psychology*, 1931, *39*, 258—277.

Huxley, A. F., see Hodgkin, & Huxley (1952).

Hyde, M., see Knowles, Kreuser, Hyde, & Schuchart (1976).

Hyde, T. S., & Jenkins, J. J. Differential effects of incidental tasks on the organization of recall of highly associated words. *Journal of Experimental Psychology*, 1969, 82, 472—481.

Imperato-McGinley, J., Peterson, R. E., Gautier, T., & Sturla, E. Androgens and the evolution of male gender identity in male pseudohermaphrodites with 5α reductase deficiency. *New England Journal of Medicine*, 1979, 300, 1233.

Inkster, J. A., see Knox, & Inkster (1968).

Insko, C. Verbal reinforcement of attitude. *Journal of Personality and Social Psychology*, 1965, 2, 261—623.

Isaacs, W., Thomas, J., & Goldiamond, I. Application of operant conditioning to reinstate verbal behavior in psychotics. *Journal of Speech and Hearing Disorders*, 1960, 25, 8—12.

Itard, J. *The wild boy of Aveyron* (G. Humphrey & M. Hunphrey, Trans.). New York: Appleton-Century-Crofts, 1932.

Ittelson, W. H. *The Ames demonstrations in perception.* Princeton, N.J.: Princeton University Press, 1952.

Jacklin, C. N., see Maccoby, & Jacklin (1974).

Jackson, D. D. Reunion of identical twins named Jim, raised apart for 39 years, reveals astonishing similarities. *Smithsonian*, October 1980, pp. 48—56.

Jackson, D. D., see Bateson, Jackson, Haley, & Weakland (1956).

Jacob, T. Family interaction is disturbed and normal families: A methodological and substantive review. *Psychological Bulletin*, 1975, 82, 33—65.

Jacobson, L., see Rosenthal, & Jacobson (1966).

Jacobson, L. I., see Murray, & Jacobson (1978).

Jakobson, R. *Child language, aphasis, and general sound laws* (A. Keiler, Trans.). The Hague: Mouton, 1968.

James, W. *Principles of psychology* (Vols. 1 & 2). New York: Holt, 1890.

James, W. *The varieties of religious experience.* New York: Modern Library, 1900.

Jarvik, L. F., see Blum, Jarvik, & Clark (1970).

Jarvik, L. F., see Erlenmeyer-Kimling, & Jarvik (1963).

Jellison, J. M., see Mills, & Jellison (1967).

Jenkins, H. M. Resistance to extinction when partial reinforcement is followed by regular reinforcement. *Journal of Experimental Psychology*, 1962, 64, 441—450.

Jenkins, H. M. Effects of the stimulus reinforcer relation on selected and unselected responses. In R. A. Hinde & J. Stevenson-Hinde (Eds.), *Constraints on learning: Limitations and predispostions.* London: Academic Press, 1973.

Jenkins, J. J. Remember that old theory of memory? Well, forget it! *American Psychologist*, 1974, 29, 785—795.

Jenkins, J. J., & Russell, W. A. Associative clustering during recall. *Journal of Abnormal and Social Psychology*, 1952, 47, 818—821.

Jenkins, J. J., Wald, J., & Pittenger, J. B. Apprehending pictorial events: An instance of psychological cohesion. In C. W. Savage (Ed.), *Perception and cognition: Issues in the foundations of psychology.* Minneapolis: University of Minnesota Press, 1978.

Jenkins, J. J., see Hyde, & Jenkins (1969).

Jensen, A. R. How much can we boost I.Q. and scholastic achievement? *Harvard Educational Review*, 1969, 39, 1—123.

Jensen, J. D., see Robbins, & Jensen (1976).

Johnson, M. K., see Bransford, & Johnson (1972).

Johnson, V. E., see Masters, & Johnson (1966).

Johnson, V. E., see Masters, & Johnson (1970).

Johnsson, L. G., see Stebbins, Miller, Johnsson, & Hawkins, Jr. (1969).

Johnston, D. W., see Gelder, Brancroft, Gath, Johnston, Mathews, & Shaw (1973).

Jones, E. E., Davis, K. E., & Gergen, K. J. Role playing variations and their informational value for person perception. *Journal of Abnormal and Social Psychology*, 1961, 63, 302—310.

Jones, E. E., & Harris, V. A. The attribution of attitudes. *Journal of Experimental Social Psychology*, 1967, 3, 1—24.

Jones, E. E., & Nisbett, R. E. *The actor and the observer: Divergent perceptions of the causes of behavior.* Morristown, N. J.: General Learning Press, 1971.

Jones, E. E., Rock, L., Shaver, K. G., Goethals, C. R., & Ward, L. M. Pattern of performance and ability attribution: An unexpected primary effect. *Journal of Personality and Social Psychology*, 1968, 9, 317—340.

Jones, H. W., see Jost, Jones, & Scott (1969).

Jones, M. C. A laboratory study of fear: The case of Peter. *Pedagogical Seminary*, 1925, 31, 308—315.

Jost, A., Jones, H. W., & Scott, W. W. (Eds.). *Hermaphroditism, genital anomalies and related endocrine disorders* (2nd ed.). Baltimore: Williams & Wilkins, 1969.

Judd, H. L., & Yen, S. S. C. Serum androstenedione and testosterone levels during the menstrual cycle. *Journal of Clinical Endocrinology and Metabolism*, 1973, 36, 475—481.

Julesz, B. *Foundations of cyclopean perception.* Chicago: University of Chicago Press, 1971.

Jung, C. G. The concept of the collective unconscious. In H. Read, M. Fordham, & G. Adler (Eds.), *Collected works of C. G. Jung* (Vol. 9), (Pt. 1). Boston: Routledge & Kegan-Paul, 1936.

Jung, C. G. *The integration of the personality.* New York: Farrar and Rinehart, 1939.

Jung, C. G. *The collected works of Carl G. Jung* (20 vols.) (G. Adler, M. Fordham, & H. Read, Eds.; And, R. F. C. Hull,

Trans.). Princeton, N.J.: Princeton University Press, 1954—1979.

Jung, C. G. *Memories, dreams, reflections*. New York: Pantheon, 1963.

Jung, C. G. Approaching the unconscious. In C. G. Jung (Ed.), *Man and his symbols*. London: Aldus Books, 1964.

Jung, C. G. Two essays on analytical psychology. In *The collected works of C. G. Jung* (Vol. 7). Princeton, N.J.: Princeton University Press, 1966. (Originally published, 1917.)

Jung, C. G. General aspects of dream psychology. In *The collected works of C. G. Jung* (Vol. 8). Princeton, N.J.: Princeton University Press, 1969. (Originally published, 1916.)

Jung, C. G. Conscious, unconscious and individuation. In *The collected works of C. G. Jung* (Vol. 9). Princeton, N.J.: Princeton University Press, 1969. (Originally published, 1939.)

Jus, A., Pineau, R., Lachance, R., Pelchat, G., Jus, K., Pires, P., & Villeneuve, R. Epidemiology of tardive dyskinesia, Part I, *Diseases of the Nervous System*, 1976, *37*, 210—214.

Jus, K., see Jus, Pineau, Lachance, Pelchat, Jus, Pires, & Villeneuve (1976).

Kagan, J. The concept of identification. *Psychological Review*, 1958, *65*, 296—305.

Kalish, D., see Tolman, Ritchie, & Kalish (1946).

Kallos, T., see Stevens, Emerson, Gerstein, Kallos, Neufeld, Nichols, & Rosenquist (1976).

Kamiya, J. Operant control of EEG alpha rhythm and some of its reported effects on consciousness. In C. Tart (Ed.), *Altered states of consciousness*. New York: Wiley, 1969.

Kandel, D. Inter and intragenerational influences on adolescent marijuana use. *Journal of Social Issues*, 1974 , *30*(2), 107—135.

Kandel, E. Nerve cells and behavior. *Scientific American*, 1970, *223*, 57—70.

Kandel, E. *Cellular basis of behavior*. San Francisco: Freeman, 1976.

Kandel, E. Small systems of neurons. *Scientific American*, 1979, *241*, 66—76.

Kaplan, B. *The conduct of inquiry: Methodology for behavioral science*. San Francisco: Chandler, 1964.

Karoly, A. J., see De Valois, Smith, Karoly, & Hitai (1959).

Kart, C. S. Some biological aspects of aging. In C. S. Kart & B. B. Manard (Eds.), *Aging in America: Readings in social gerontology*. New York: Alfred Publishing Company, 1976.

Kasematsu, A., & Hirai, T. An electroencephalographic study on the zen meditation. *Folia Psychiatrica et Neurologica*, 1966, *20*, 315—336.

Katchedourian, H. *The biology of adolescence*. San Francisco: W. H. Freeman and Co., 1977.

Katcher, A. H., see Zillmann, Katcher, & Milavsky (1972).

Katz, D. The functional approach to the study of attitudes. *Public Opinion Quarterly*, 1960, *24*, 163—204.

Katz, D., & Braly, K. Racial stereotypes in one hundred college students. *Journal of Abnormal and Social Psychology*, 1933, *28*, 280—290.

Katz, S., see Gittleman-Klein, Klein, Katz, Saraf, & Pollack (1976).

Kay, P., see Berlin, & Kay (1969).

Kazdin, A. E. Fictions, factions, and functions of behavior therapy. *Behavior Therapy*, 1979, *10*, 629—654.

Keen, R., see Stevenson, Keen, & Knights (1963).

Keesey, R. E., & Powley, T. L. Hypothalamic regulation of body weight. *American Scientist*, 1975, *63*, 558—565.

Keith, S. J., Gunderson, J. G., Reifman, A., Buchsbaum, S., & Mosher, L. R. Special report: Schizophrenia, 1976. *Schizophrenia Bulletin*, 1976, *2*, 510—565.

Kelem, R. T., see Diener, Fraser, Beaman, & Kalem (1976).

Kelley, H. H. The warm-cold variable in first impressions of persons. *Journal of Personality*, 1950, *18*, 431—439.

Kelley, H. H. Attribution theory in social psychology. In D. Levine (Ed.), *Nebraska Symposium on Motivation* (Vol. 15). Lincoln: University of Nebraska Press, 1967.

Kelley, H. H. Attribution in social interaction. In E. E. Jones, D. E. Kanouse, H. H. Kelley, R. E. Nisbett, S. Valins, & B. Weiner (Eds.), *Attribution: Perceiving the causes of behavior*. Morristown, N.J.: General Learning Press, 1972.

Kelley, H. H., see Thibaut, & Kelley (1959).

Kellogg, L. A., see Kellogg, & Kellogg (1933).

Kellogg, W. N., & Kellogg, L. A. *The ape and the child*. New York: McGraw-Hill, 1933.

Kelly, G. A. *The psychology of personal constructs* (Vols. 1 & 2). New York: Norton, 1955.

Kelly, K., see Ayllon, & Kelly (1972).

Kennedy, G. C. The hypothalamic control of food intake in rats. *Proceedings of the Royal Society of London: B*, 1950, *137*, 535—548.

Kessler, S. The etiological question in mental illness. *Science*, September 26, 1969, pp. 1341—1342.

Ketchel, R., see Spence, Taylor, & Ketchel (1956).

Kety, S. S. Current biochemical approaches to schizophrenia. *New England Journal of Medicine*, 1967, *276*, 325—331.

Kety, S. S., see Schildkraut, & Kety (1967).

Kety, S. S., see Wender, Rosenthal, Kety, Schulsinger, & Weiner (1973).

Kety, S. S., see Wender, Rosenthal, Kety, Schulsinger, & Weiner (1974).

Kiesler, C. A., see Zanna, Kiesler, & Pilkonis (1970).

Kiester, E., Jr., & Gudhea, D. Albert Bandura: A very modern model. *Human Behavior*, September 1974, p. 31.

Kimble, G. A. (Ed.). *Hilgard and Marguis' conditioning and learning* (2nd ed.). Englewood Cliffs, N.J.: Prentice-Hall, 1961.

King, K., Balswick, J. O., & Robinson, I. E. The continuing

premarital revolution among college females. *Journal of Marriage and Family*, 1977, *39*, 455.

King, M. B., see Smith, King, & Hoebel (1970).

King, S. M., see Helson, & King (1931).

Kinsey, A. C., Pomeroy, W. B., & Martin, C. E. Sexual behavior in the human male. Philadelphia: Saunders, 1948.

Kinsey, A. C., Pomeroy, W. B., Martin, C. E., & Gebhard, P. H. *Sexual behavior in the human female*. Philadelphia: Saunders, 1953.

Kintsch, W. Memory for prose. In C. N. Cofer (Ed.), *The structure of human memory*. San Francisco: Freeman, 1976.

Kintsch, W. *Memory and cognition*. New York: Wiley, 1977.

Kipnis, P. S. Interaction between members of a bomber crew as a determinant of sociometric choice. *Human Relations*, 1957, *10*, 253—270.

Kipper, D. A., see Moreno, & Kipper (1968).

Kisker, G. W. *The disorganized personality*. McGraw-Hill, 1964.

Klakenberg, C., see Hindley, Filliozat, Klakenberg, Nocolet-Meister, & Sand (1966).

Klein, D. F., see Gittleman-Klein, Klein, Katz, Saraf, & Pollack (1976).

Kleitman, N., see Aserinsky, & Kleitman (1953).

Kluver, H., & Bucy, P. C. "Psychic blindness" and other symptoms following bilateral temporal lobectomy in rhesus monkeys. *American Journal of Physiology*, 1937, *119*, 352—353.

Kluver, H., & Bucy, P. C. An analysis of certain effects of bilateral temporal lobectomy in the rhesus monkey, with special reference to "physic blindness." *Journal of Psychology*, 1938, *5*, 33—54.

Kluver, H., & Bucy, P. C. Preliminary analysis of functions of the temporal lobes in monkeys. *Archives of Neurology and Psychiatry*, 1939, *42*, 979—1000.

Knight, J., see Mita, Dermer, & Knight (1977).

Knights, R. M., see Stevenson, Keen, & Knights (1963).

Knittle, J. L. Early influences on development of adipose tissue. In G. A. Bray (Ed.), *Obesity in perspective*. Washington, D.C.: U.S. Government Printing Office, 1975.

Knittle, J. L., & Hirsch, J. Effect of early nutrition on the development of rat epididymal fat pads: Cellularity and metabolism. *Journal of Clinical Investigation*, 1968, *47*, 2091.

Knowles, E. S., Kreuser, S. H., Hyde, M., & Schuchart, G. E. Group size and the extension of social space boundaries. *Journal of Personality and Social Psychology*, 1976, *33*, 647—654.

Knox, R. E., & Inkster, J. A. Postdecision dissonance at post time. *Journal of Personality and Social Psychology*, 1968, *8*, 319—323.

Knudsen, E. L., & Konishi, M. Space and frequency are represented separately in auditory midbrain of the owl. *Journal of Neurophysiology*, 1978, *41*, 810—884.

Koch, C., see Stunkard, & Koch (1964).

Koenig, P. The problem that can't be tranquilized. *New York Times Magazine*, May 21, 1978, pp. 14—16.

Kohlberg, L. A. A Cognitive-Developmental analysis of children's sex-role concepts and attitudes. In E. E. Maccoby (Ed.) *The development of sex differences*. Stanford, Calif.: Stanford University Press, 1966.

Kogan, W., see Wallach, & Kogan (1965).

Kogan, W., see Wallach, Kogan, & Bem (1964).

Kohlberg, L. The development of children's orientations toward a moral order: I. Sequence in the development of moral thought. *Vita Humana*, 1963, *6*, 11—33.

Köhler, W. *The mentality of apes* (E. Winter, Trans.). New York: Harcourt, Brace and World, 1925.

Kolodner, R. M., see Kolodny, Masters, Kolodner, & Toro (1974).

Kolodny, R. C., Masters, W. H., Kolodner, R. M., & Toro, G. Depression of plasma testosterone levels after chronic intensive marijuana use. *New England Journal of Medicine*, 1974, *290*, 872.

Konishi, M., see Knudsen, & Konishi (1978).

Konuma, S., see Matsumoto, Tamada, & Konuma (1979).

Kopell, B. S., see Corby, Roth, Zalcone, Jr., & Kopell (1978).

Kornreich, M., see Meltzoff, & Kornreich (1970).

Koslowski, B., see Brazelton, Koslowski, & Main (1974).

Kosslyn, S. M. Information representation in visual images. *Cognitive Psychology*, 1975, *7*, 341—370.

Kosslyn, S. M. Can imagery be distinguished from other forms of internal representation? Evidence from studies of information retrieval time. *Memory and Cognition*, 1976, *4*, 291—297.

Kosslyn, S. M., Ball, T. M., & Reiser, B. J. Visual images preserve metric spatial information: Evidence from studies of image scanning. *Journal of Experimental Psychology: Human Perception and Performance*, 1978, *4*, 47—60.

Kosterlitz, H. W., see Hughes, Smith, Kosterlitz, Fothergill, Morgan, & Morris (1975).

Kraepelin, E. *Lehrbuch der psychiatrie* (5th ed.). Leipzig: Barth, 1896.

Kral, P. A., see Wilcoxin, Dragoin, & Kral (1971).

Krashen, S., see Fromkin, Krashen, Curtiss, Rigler, & Rigler (1972/1973).

Krasner, L. The therapist as a social reinforcement machine. In H. H. Strupp & L. Luborsky (Eds.), *Research in psychotherapy* (Vol. 2). Washington D.C.: American Psychological Association, 1962.

Krasner, L., see Ullmann, & Krasner (1975).

Kraut, R. E. Effects of social labeling on giving to charity. *Journal of Experimental Social Psychology*, 1973, *9*, 551—562.

Krell, L., see Dörner, Rhode, Stahl, Krell, & Masius (1975).

Kreuser, S. H., see Knowles, Kreuser, Hyde, & Schuchart (1976).

Kripke, D. F., & Sonnenschein, D. *A 90 minute daydream cycle.* Paper presented at the meeting of the Association for the Psychophysiologic Study of Sleep, San Diego, 1973.

Kuffler, S. W. Discharge patterns and functional organization of mammalian retina. *Journal of Neurophysiology,* 1953, *16,* 37—68.

La Barre, W. *The human animal.* Chicago: University of Chicago Press, 1954.

Lachance, R., see Jus, Pineau, Lachance, Pelchat, Jus, Pires, & Villeneuve (1976).

Lachman, R., see Dooling, & Lachman (1971).

Laing, R. D., & Esterson, A. *Sanity, madness, and the family.* New York: Basic Books, 1971.

Lamberth, J., see Byrne, Ervin, & Lamberth (1970).

Landauer, T. K., see Doob, Carlsmith, Freedman, Landauer, & Toms (1969).

Langer, E. J. The illusion of control. *Journal of Personality and Social Psychology,* 1975, *32,* 311—328.

Langer, E. J., & Rodin, J. The effects of choice and enhanced personal responsibility for the aged: A field experiment in an institutional setting. *Journal of Personality and Social Psychology,* 1976, *34,* 191—198.

Langer, E. J., & Roth, J. Heads I win, tails, it's chance: The illusion of control as a function of the sequence of outcomes in a purely chance task. *Journal of Personality and Social Psychology,* 1975, *32,* 951—955.

Langfeldt, T. Child sexuality and problems. In J. M. Sampson (Ed.), *Childhood and sexuality.* Montreal: Etudes Bivantes, 1979.

Larson, G. R., see Snyder, & Larson (1972).

Larsen, O. N., Gray, L. N., & Fortris, J. G. *Achieving goals through violence on television.* In O. N. Larsen (Ed.), *Violence and the mass media.* New York: Harper & Row, 1968.

Lashley, K. S. Physiological mechanisms and animal behavior. In *Symposium of the Society for Experimental Biology* (Vol. IV). New York: Academic Press, 1950.

Lashley, K. S. The problem of serial order in behavior. In L. A. Jefress (Ed.), *Cerebral mechanisms in behavior.* New York: Wiley, 1951.

Latané, B., & Darley, J. M. Group inhibition of bystander interventions in emergencies. *Journal of Personality and Social Psychology,* 1968, *10,* 215—221.

Latané, B., & Darley, J. M. *The unresponsive bystander: Why doesn't he help?* New York: Appleton-Century-Crofts, 1970.

Latané, B., & Rodin, J. A lady in distress: Inhibiting effects of friends and strangers on bystander intervention. *Journal of Experimental Social Psychology,* 1969, *5,* 189—202.

Latané, B., see Darley, & Latané (1968).

Lazarus, A. A. New methods of psychotherapy: A case study. *South African Medical Journal,* 1958, *33,* 660.

Lazarus, A. A. *Behavior therapy and beyond.* New York: McGraw-Hill, 1971.

Lazarus, A. A., see Wolpe, & Lazarus (1969).

Leefeldt, C., & Callenbach, E. *The art of friendship.* New York: Pantheon, 1979.

Lefkowitz, M. M., see Eron, Lefkowitz, Huesmann, & Walder (1972).

Legant, P., see Nisbett, Caputo, Legant, & Mareck (1973).

Lehman, H. C. *Age and achievement.* Princeton, N.J.: Princeton University Press, 1953.

Lehr, D. J., see Bergum, & Lehr (1963).

LeMagnen, J. Les phenomenes olfactosexuels chez le rat blanc. *Archives Scientifiques Physiologiques,* 1952, *6,* 295—332.

Lenneberg, E. H. *Biological foundations of language.* New York: Wiley, 1967.

Lenneberg, E. H., & Roberts, J. M. The language of experiences: A study in methodology. *International Journal of American Linguistics,* 1956, Memoir *13.*

Lepper, M. R., Greene, D., & Nisbett, R. E. Undermining children's intrinsic interest with extrinsic reward: A test of "overjustification" hypothesis. *Journal of Personality and Social Psychology,* 1973, *5,* 189—202.

Lerner, M. J., & Simmons, C. Observer's reaction to the innocent victim: Compassion or rejection. *Journal of Personality and Social Psychology,* 1966, *4,* 203—210.

Lesgold, A., see Bower, Clark, Winzenz, & Lesgold (1969).

Lessler, K., see Strupp, Fox, & Lessler (1969).

Levine, S., see Davidson, Smith, & Levine (1978).

Levine, S., see Harris, & Levine (1965).

Levinson, B. W. States of awareness during general anesthesia. In J. Lassner (Ed.) *Hypnosis and psychosomatic medicine,* New York: Springer, 1967.

Levis, D. J., see Stampfl, & Levis (1967).

Levitt, F., see Van Sluyters, & Levitt (1980).

Levy, A., see Freedman, Heshka, & Levy (1975).

Levy, J. Autokinetic illusion: A systematic review of theories, measures, and independent variables. *Psychological Bulletin,* 1972, *78,* 457—474.

Lewis, J., see Mercer, & Lewis (1977).

Lewis, L. D., see Darley, Lewis, & Glucksberg (1972).

Li, C. H., & Chung, D. Isolation and structure of an untriakontapeptide with opiate activity from camel pituitary. *Proceedings of the National Academy of Science, U.S.A.,* 1976, *73,* 1145—1148.

Liberman, A. M. The grammars of speech and language. *Cognitive Psychology,* 1970, *1,* 301—323.

Liberman, A. M., Cooper, F. S., Shankweiler, D., & Studdert-Kennedy, M. Perception of the speech code. *Psychological Review,* 1967, *74,* 431—461.

Lidz, T., Fleck, S., & Cornelison, A. *Schizophrenia and the family.* New York: International Universities Press, 1965.

Lieberman, A. Preschoolers' competence with a peer: Relations with attachment and peer experience. *Child Development,* 1977, *48,* 1277—1287.

Lieberman, A. F., see Blehar, Lieberman, & Ainsworth (1977).

Lieberman, M. A., Yalom, I. D., & Miles, M. B. *Encounter groups: First facts.* New York: Basic Books, 1973.

Lieberman, S. The effects of changes in roles on the attitudes of role occupants. *Human Relations*, 1950, *9*, 385—403.

Liebert, R. M., & Spiegler, M. D. *Personality: Strategies for the study of man* (Rev. ed.). Homewood, Ill.: Dorsey Press, 1974.

Lifton, R. J. *Thought reform and the psychology of totalism: A study of brainwashing in China.* New York: Norton, 1963.

Lilly, J. C. *The deep self.* New York: Lippincott, 1977.

Limber, J. Language in child and chimp? *American Psychologist*, 1977, *32*, 280—295.

Linder, D., see Aronson, & Linder (1965).

Lindsay, P. H., & Norman, D. A. *Human information processing* (2nd ed.). New York: Academic Press, 1977.

Link, R. The literary digest poll: Appearances can be deceiving. *Public Opinion*, February—March 1980, p. 55.

Lippincott, E. C., see Thomas, Horton, Lippincott, & Drabman (1977).

Lipscomb, D. M. Ear damage from exposure to rock and roll music. *Archives of Otolaryngology*, 1969, *90*, 543—555.

Lockhart, R. S., see Craik, & Lockhart (1972).

Loewi, O. Über humorale Übertragbarkeit der Herznervenwirkung. *Pflügers Archiv für die Gesamte Physiologie des Menschen und der Tiere*, 1921, *189*, 239—242.

Loewi, O. The Ferrier lecture: On problems connected with the principle of humoral transmission of nerve impulses. *Proceedings of the Royal Society of London: Series B, Biological Sciences*, 1935, *118B*, 299—316.

Loftus, E. F., & Palmer, J. C. Reconstruction of automobile destruction: An example of the interaction between language and memory. *Journal of Verbal Learning and Verbal Behavior*, 1974, *13*, 585—589.

Loh, H., see Wei, & Loh (1976).

Lorenz, K. *On aggression.* New York: Bantam, 1967.

Lorenz, K. Z. The companion in the bird's world. *Auk*, 1937, *54*, 245—273.

Lorenz, K. Z., & Tinbergen, N. Taxis und Instinkthandlung in der Eirollbewegung der Graugans. In C. H. Schiller (Ed.), *Instinctive behavior.* New York: International Universities Press, 1957. (Originally published, 1938.)

Lowell, E. L., see McClelland, Atkinson, Clark, & Lowell (1953).

Lovass, I. O. *The autistic child.* New York: Irvington Publishers, 1977.

Lublin, S. D., see Singer, Brush, & Lublin (1965).

Luce, G. G., & Segal, J. *Sleep.* New York: Coward, McCann & Geoghegan, 1966.

Luchins, A. Primacy-recency in impression formation. In C. I. Hovland (Ed.), *The order of presentation in persuasion.* New Haven, Conn.: Yale University Press, 1957.

Luttge, W. G. Endocrine control of mammalian sexual behavior: An analysis of the potential role of testosterone metabolites. In C. Beyer (Ed.), *Endocrine control of sexual behavior,* New York: Raven Press, 1979.

Lynn, S. J., see Price, & Lynn (1981).

Lytle, L. Control of eating behavior. In R. J. Wurtman & J. J. Wurtman (Eds.), *Nutrition and the brain.* New York: Raven Press, 1977.

MacArthur, R. H., & Pianka, E. R. On optimal use of a patchy environment. *American Naturalist*, 1966, *100*, 603—609.

Maccoby, E. E., & Jacklin, C. N. *The psychology of sex differences.* Stanford, Calif.: Stanford University Press, 1974.

MacCulloch, M. J., see Feldman, & MacCulloch (1971).

MacDonald, M. L. & Tobias, L. L. Withdrawal causes relapse? Our response. *Psychological Bulletin*, 1976, *83*, 448—451.

MacKinnon, G. E., see Matin, & MacKinnon (1964).

Macnamara, J. Cognitive basis of language in infants. *Psychological Review*, 1972, *79*, 1—13.

MacNichol, E. F., Jr., see Svaetichin, & MacNichol, Jr. (1958).

MacNichol, E. F., Jr., see Wagner, MacNichol, Jr., & Wolbarsht (1960).

Maier, S. F., Seligman, M. E. P., & Solomon, R. L. Pavlovian fear conditioning and learned helplessness: Effects on escape and avoidance behavior of (a) the CS-US contingency and (b) the independence of the US and voluntary responding. In B. A. Campbell & R. M. Church (Eds.), *Punishment and aversive behavior.* New York: Appleton-Century-Crofts, 1969.

Maier, S. F., see Seligman, Maier, & Geer (1968).

Maier, S. F., see Seligman, Maier, & Solomon (1971).

Main, M., see Brazelton, Koslowski, & Main (1974).

Malamud, P., see Waters, & Malamud (1975).

Malinowski, B. *Sexual life of savages in Northwestern Melanesia.* New York: Harcourt, 1929.

Malott, R. W., see Whaley, & Malott (1969).

Mandell, A. J. Towards a psychobiology of transcendence. In J. M. Davidson & R. J. Davidson (Eds.), *Psychobiology of consciousness.* New York: Plenum Press, 1980.

Mandler, G. *Mind and emotion.* New York: Wiley, 1975.

Mandler, G., & Sarason, S. B. A study of anxiety and learning. *Journal of Abnormal and Social Psychology*, 1952, *47*, 166—173.

Marecek, J., see Nisbett, Caputo, Legant, & Marecek (1973).

Mark, V. H., & Ervin, F. R. *Violence and the brain.* New York: Harper & Row, 1970.

Mark, V. H., Sweet, W. H., & Ervin, F. R. The effect of amygdalectomy on violent behavior patients with temporal lobe epilepsy. In E. Hitchcock, L. Laitinen, & K. Vaernet (Eds.), *Psychosurgery.* Springfield, Ill.: Charles C Thomas, 1972.

Mark, V. H., see Sweet, Ervin, & Mark (1969).

Marks, I. M. Phobias and obsessions. In J. Maser, & M. Seligman (Eds.), *Experimental psychopathology*. New York: Wiley, 1977.

Markus, G. B., see Zajonc, & Markus (1975).

Marler, P. A comparative approach to vocal learning: Song development in white-crowned sparrows. *Journal of Comparative and Physiological Psychology*, 1970, *71*, 1—25.

Marolla, F. A., see Belmont, & Marolla (1973).

Marquis, D. P. Learning in the neonate: The modification of behavior under three feeding schedules. *Journal of Experimental Psychology*, 1941, *29*, 263—282.

Martin, C. E., see Kinsey, Pomeroy, & Martin (1948).

Martin, C. E., see Kinsey, Pomeroy, Martin, & Gebhard (1953).

Martin, J. G. Some acoustic and grammatical features of spontaneous speech. In D. L. Horton, & J. J. Jenkins (Eds.), *The perception of language*. Columbus, Ohio: Charles E. Merrill, 1971.

Marx, A. J., Test, M. A., & Stein, L. I. Extrahospital management of severe mental illness. *Archives of General Psychiatry*, 1973, *29*, 505—511.

Masius, W., see Dörner, Rhodes, Stahl, Krell, & Masium (1975).

Maslach, C., see Zimbardo, Ebbesen, & Maslach (1977).

Maslow, A. H. *Toward a psychology of being*. Princeton, N.J.: Van Nostrand, 1962.

Maslow, A. H. Self-actualizing people. In G. B. Levitas (Ed.), *The world of psychology* (Vol. 2). New York: Braziller, 1963.

Maslow, A. H. *Farther reaches of human nature*. New York: Viking Press, 1971.

Masters, W. H., & Johnson, V. E. *The human sexual response*. Boston: Little, Brown, 1966.

Masters, W. H., & Johnson, V. E. *Human sexual inadequacy*. Boston: Little, Brown, 1970.

Masters, W. H., see Kolodny, Masters, Kolodner, & Toro (1974).

Matas, L., Arend, R. A., & Sroufe, L. A. Continuity of adaptation in the second year: The relationship between quality of attachment and later competencies. *Child Development*, 1978, *49*, 547—556.

Mathews, A. M., see Gelder, Brancroft, Gath, Johnston, Mathews, & Shaw (1973).

Mathews, P. B. C., see Goodwin, McCloskey, & Mathews (1972).

Matin, L., & MacKinnon, G. E. Autokinetic movement: Selective manipulation of directional components by image stabilization. *Science*, 1964, *143*, 147—148.

Matsumoto, S., Tamada, T., & Konuma, S. Endocrinological analysis of environmental menstrual disorders. *International Journal of Fertility*, 1979, *24*, 233—239.

Mausner, B. Prestige and social interaction: The effect of one's partner's success in a relevant task on the interaction of observed pairs. *Journal of Abnormal and Social Psychology*, 1954, *49*, 557—560.

Maxwell, J. C. Experiments on colour as perceived by the eye, with remarks on colour blindness. *Transactions of the Royal Society of Edinburgh*, 1855, *21*, 275—298.

May, P. R. A. *Treatment of schizophrenia: A comparative study of five treatment methods*. New York: Science House, 1968.

Mayer-Cross, W., Slater, E., & Roth, M. *Clinical psychiatry*. Baltimore, Md.: Williams & Wilkins, 1969.

Maynard H., see Fairweather, Sanders, Cressler, & Maynard (1969).

McClearn, G. Genetic influences on behavior and development. In P. Mussen (Ed.), *Carmichael's manual of child psychology*. New York: Wiley, 1970.

McClearn, G., & Rodgers, D. Differences in alcohol preference among inbred strains of mice. *Quarterly Journal on the Study of Alcohol*, 1959, *20*, 691—695.

McClelland, D. C. *The achieving society*. New York: Van Nostrand, 1961.

McClelland, D. C., Atkinson, J. W., Clark, R. A., & Lowell, E. L. *The achievement motive*. New York: Appleton-Century-Crofts, 1953.

McClintock, M. K. Menstrual synchrony and suppression. *Nature*, 1971, *229*, 244—245.

McClintock, M. K. Estrous synchrony and its mediation by airborne chemical communication. *Hormones and Behavior*, 1979, *10*, 264.

McCloskey, D. I., see Goodwin, McCloskey, & Mathews (1972).

McDougall, W. *An introduction to social psychology* (14th ed.). Boston: J.W. Luce, 1921.

McGhee, P. E., see Teevan, & McGhee (1972).

McGowan, B. K., Hankins, W. G., & Garcia, J. Limbric lesions and control of the internal and external environment. *Behavioral Biology*, 1972, *7*, 841—852.

McGuire, W. J. Introducing resistance to persuasion. In L. Berkowitz (Ed.), *Advances in experimental social psychology* (Vol. 1). New York: Academic Press, 1964.

McKim, R., see Harman, McKim, Mogar, Fadiman, & Stolaroff (1966).

McNeill, D. *The acquisition of language: The study of developmental psycholinguistics*. New York: Harper & Row, 1970.

McNeill, D., see Brown, & McNeill (1966).

McPherson, J. M., see Galle, Gove, & McPherson (1972).

Mead, G. H. *Mind, self, and society*. Chicago: University of Chicago Press, 1934.

Meador, B. D., & Rogers, C. R. Person centered therapy. In J. R. Corsini (Ed.), *Current psychotherapies*, Itasca, Ill.: Peacock, 1979.

Medawar, P. *Advice to a young scientist*. New York: Harper & Row, 1979.

Meehl, P. E. Some ruminations on the validation of clinical procedures. In E. Megargee (Ed.), *Research in clinical assessment*. New York: Harper & Row, 1966.

Meltzoff, J., & Kornreich, M. *Research in psychotherapy*. New York: Atherton, 1970.

Melvill Jones, G., see Gonshor, & Melvill Jones (1976).

Mendels, J. *Concepts of depression.* New York: Wiley, 1970.

Menninger, K. *Theory of psychoanalytic technique.* New York: Basic Books, 1958.

Mercer, J. R., & Lewis, J. *System of multicultural pluralistic assessment.* New York: Psychological Corporation, 1977.

Meredith, H. V. Research between 1960 and 1970 on the standing height of young children in different parts of the world. In H. W. Rease & L. P. Lipsitt (Eds.), *Advances in child development and behavior* (Vol. 12). New York: Academic Press, 1978.

Merton, R. K. *Social theory and social structure.* New York: Free Press, 1957.

Mesmer, F. A., & Bloch, G. *Mesmerism.* Los Altos, Calif.: Kaufmann, 1980.

Meumann, E. Haus-und Schularbeit: Experimente an Kindern der Volksschule. *Die Deutsche Schule,* 1904, *8,* 278—303; 337—359; 416—431.

Michael, R. P., see Harris, & Michael (1964).

Milavsky, B., see Zillmann, Katcher, & Milavsky (1972).

Miles, F., & Eighmy, B. Long term adaptive changes in primate vestibulo-ocular reflex: I. Behavioral observation. *Journal of Neurophysiology,* 1980, *43,* 1406—1425.

Miles, M. B., see Lieberman, Yalom, & Miles (1973).

Milgram, S. Behavioral study of obedience. *Journal of Abnormal and Social Psychology,* 1963, *67,* 371—378.

Milgram, S. *Obedience to authority.* New York: Harper & Row, 1974.

Miller, G. A. The magical number seven, plus or minus two: Some limits on our capacity for processing information. *Psychological Review,* 1956, *63,* 81—97.

Miller, G. A. Some psychological studies of grammar. *American Psychologist,* 1962, *17,* 748—762.

Miller, H. A., see Weingartner, Miller, & Murphy (1979).

Miller, I. W., & Norman, W. H. Learned helplessness in humans: A review and attribution theory model. *Psychology Bulletin,* 1979, *86,* 93—118.

Miller, J. M., see Stebbins, Miller, Johnsson, & Hawkins, Jr. (1969).

Miller, N., see Delgado, Roberts, & Miller (1954).

Miller, N., see Dollard, Doob, Miller, Mowrer, & Sears (1939).

Miller, N. E. Learning of visceral and glandular responses. *Science,* 1969, *163,* 434—435.

Miller, N. E. Biofeedback and visceral learning. *Annual Review of Psychology,* 1978, *29,* 375—404.

Miller, N. E., Bailey, C. J., & Stevenson, J. A. F. "Decreased hunger" but increased food intake resulting from hypothalamic lesions. *Science,* 1950, *112,* 256—259.

Millon, T. (Ed.). *Theories of psychopathology.* Philadelphia: Saunders, 1967.

Mills, J., & Jellison, J. M. Effect on opinion change of how desirable the communication is to the audience the communicator addressed. *Journal of Personality and Social Psychology,* 1967, *6,* 98—101.

Mills, J., see Aronson, & Mills (1959).

Milner, B. Memory and the medial temporal regions of the brain. In K. H. Prilram & D. E. Broadbent (Eds.), *Biology of memory.* New York: Academic Press, 1970.

Milner, B., Taylor, L., & Sperry, R. W. Lateralized suppression of dichotically presented digits after commissural section in man. *Science,* 1968, *161,* 184—185.

Milner, P., see Olds, & Milner (1954).

Mischel, W. *Personality and assessment.* New York: Wiley, 1968.

Mischel, W. The interaction of person and situation. In D. Magnusson & N. S. Endler (Eds.), *Personality at the crossroads: Current issues in interactional psychology.* Hillsdale, N.J.: Lawrence Erlbaum, 1977.

Mischel, W., see Bandura, & Mischel (1965).

Mischel, W., see Cantor, & Mischel (1977).

Mishkin, M., & Pribram, K. H. Visual discrimination performance following partial ablations of the temporal lobe: I. Ventral vs. lateral. *Journal of Comparative and Physiological Psychology,* 1954, *47,* 14—20.

Mita, T. H., Dermer, M., & Knight, J. Reversed facial images and the mere exposure hypothesis. *Journal of Personality and Social Psychology,* 1977, *35,* 597—601.

Mitchell, D. B., see Richman, Mitchell, & Reznick (1979).

Mittelstadt, H., see von Holst, & Mittelstadt (1950).

Mogar, R., see Harman, McKim, Mogar, Fadiman, & Stolaroff (1966).

Molfese, D. L. *Cerebral asymmetry in infants, children and adults: Auditory evoked responses to speech and noise stimuli.* Unpublished doctoral dissertation, Pennsylvania State University, 1972.

Money, J., & Ehrhardt, A. A. *Man and woman, boy and girl.* Baltimore: Johns Hopkins University Press, 1972.

Monti, P. M., see Brown, Monti, & Corriveau (1978).

Moody, R. *Life after life.* New York: Mockingbird Books, 1976.

Moray, N. Attention in dichotic listening: Affective cues and the influence of instructions. *Quarterly Journal of Experimental Psychology,* 1959, *11,* 56—60.

Moreno, J. L., & Kipper, D. A. Group psychodrama and community-centered counseling. In G. M. Gazda (Ed.), *Basic approaches to group psychotherapy and group counseling.* Springfield, Ill.: Charles C Thomas, 1968.

Morgan, B. A., see Hughes, Smith, Kosterlitz, Fothergill, Morgan, & Morris (1975).

Morgenson, G. J., see Russell, Adbelaal, & Morgenson (1975).

Morris, C. D., Bransford, J. D., & Franks, J. J. Levels of processing versus transfer appropriate processing. *Journal of Verbal Learning and Verbal Behavior,* 1977, *16,* 519—533.

Morris, H. R., see Hughes, Smith, Kosterlitz, Fothergill, Morgan, & Morris (1975).

Morris, N. M., see Udry, & Morris (1968).

Morris, N. M., see Udry, & Morris (1977).

Morris, W. N., see Hetherington, & Morris (1978).

Morse, R., see Teller, Morse, Borton, & Regal (1974).

Mosher, L. R., see Keith, Gunderson, Reifman, Buchsbaum, & Mosher (1976).

Mowrer, O., see Dollard, Doob, Miller, Mowrer, & Sears (1939).

Müller, J. *Handbuch der Physiologie des Menschen Coblentz, Holsher I* (W. Baly, Trans.). London: Taylor & Walton, 1838. (Originally published, 1833.)

Müller, J. *Handbuch der Physiologie des Menschen Goblentz, Holsher II* (W. Baly, Trans.). London: Taylor & Walton, 1940. (Originally published, 1842.)

Müller, J. The specific energies of nerves. In W. Dennis (Ed.), *Readings in the history of psychology*. New York: Appleton-Century-Crofts, 1948. (Article originally published, 1838.)

Munroe, R. *Schools of psychoanalytic thought*. New York: Dryden, 1955.

Murphy, D. L., see Weingartner, Miller, & Murphy (1979).

Murray, E. J., & Jacobson, L. I. Cognition and learning in traditional and behavioral therapy. In S. L. Garfield & A. E. Bergin (Eds.), *Handbook of psychotherapy and behavior change* (2nd ed.). New York: Wiley, 1978.

Murray, H. A. *Explorations in personality: A clinical and experimental study of fifty men of college age*. New York: Oxford University Press, 1938.

Murray, H. A. Uses of the Thematic Apperception Test. *American Journal of Psychiatry*, 1951, *107*, 577—581.

Murray, H. A. *Explorations in personality*. New York: Science Editions, 1962.

Murstein, B. I. Physical attractiveness and marital choice. *Journal of Social Psychology*, 1972, *22*, 8—12.

Myers, R. E. Interocular transfer of pattern discrimination in cats following section of crossed optic fibers. *Journal of Comparative and Physiological Psychology*, 1955, *48*, 470—473.

Myers, R. E. Function of corpus callosum in interocular transfer. *Brain*, 1956, *79*, 358—363.

Myers, R. E. *Brain mechanisms and learning*. Springfield, Ill.: Charles C Thomas, 1961.

Nadler, R. Sexual behavior of the chimpanzee in relation to the gorilla and orangutan. In G. H. Bourne (Ed.), *Progress in ape research*. New York: Academic Press, 1977.

Nagel, E. Methodological issues in psychoanalytic theory. In S. Hook (Ed.), *Psychoanalysis, scientific method, and philosophy*. New York: Viking Press, 1959.

Nathan, P. E., see Schact, & Nathan (1977).

Nebel, J. C., see Berkowitz, Nebel, & Reitman (1971).

Neff, W. D., see Diamond, & Neff (1957).

Neisser, U. *Cognitive psychology*. New York: Appleton-Century-Crofts, 1967.

Neisser, U. *Cognition and reality*. San Francisco: W. H. Freeman, 1976.

Nelson, C., see Rosenberg, Nelson, & Vivekananthan (1968).

Nelson, K. Structure and strategy in learning to talk. *Monographs of the Society for Research in Child Development*, 1973, *38*(Nos. 1—2).

Neufeld, G., see Stevens, Emerson, Gerstein, Kallos, Neufeld, Nichols, & Rosenquist (1976).

Neugarten, B. The rise of the young old. *The New York Times*, January 18, 1975.

Newcomb, T. M. *The acquaintance process*. New York: Holt, Rinehart and Winston, 1961.

Newell, A., & Simon, H. A. *Human problem solving*. Englewood Cliffs, N.J.: Prentice-Hall, 1972.

Newton, I. *Opticks*. London: William Innys, 1704.

Nichols, C., see Stevens, Emerson, Gerstein, Kallos, Neufeld, Nichols, & Rosenquist (1976).

Nieuwenhuyse, B., see Zajonc, & Nieuwenhuyse (1964).

Nisbett, R. E. Hunger, obesity, and the ventromedial hypothalamus. *Psychological Review*, 1972, *79*, 433—453.

Nisbett, R. E., Caputo, C., Legant, P., & Marecek, J. Behavior as seen by the actor and as seen by the observer. *Journal of Personality and Social Psychology*, 1973, *27*, 154—164.

Nisbett, R. E., see Jones, & Nisbett (1971).

Nisbett, R. E., see Lepper, Greene, & Nisbett (1973).

Noble, G. K., & Schmidt, A. Structure and function of the facial and labial pits of snakes. *Proceedings of the American Philosophical Society*, 1937, *77*, 263—288.

Nocolet-Meister, D., see Hindley, Filliozat, Klakenberg, Nocolet-Meister, & Sand (1966).

Norman, D. A. Memory while shadowing. *Quarterly Journal of Experimental Psychology*, 1969, *21*, 85—93.

Norman, D. A., see Lindsay, & Norman (1977).

Norman, D. A., see Waugh, & Norman (1965).

Norman, R. When what is said is important: A comparison of expert and attractive sources. *Journal of Experimental Social Psychology*, 1976, *12*, 294—300.

Norman, W. H., see Miller, & Norman (1979).

Norton, T., see Wagner, Thomas, & Norton (1967).

Oden, M. H., see Terman, & Oden (1947).

Ogle, K. N. The optical space sense. In H. Davson (Ed.), *The eye*. New York: Academic Press, 1962.

Ohman, A., Eriksson, A., Fredriksson, N., Hugdahl, K., & Oloffson, C. Habituation of the electrodermal at orienting reaction to potentially phobic and supposedly neutral stimuli in normal human subjects. *Biological Psychology*, 1974, *2*, 85—92.

Olds, J., & Milner, P. Positive reinforcement produced by electrical stimulation of the septal area and other regions of the rat brain. *Journal of Comparative and Physiological Psychology*, 1954, *47*, 419—427.

Olds, S. W. Menopause: Something to look forward to? *Today's Health*, May 1970, p. 48.

Oliveau, D., see Agras, Sylvester, & Oliveau (1969).

Oliver, D., see Heider, & Oliver (1972).

Oloffson, C., see Ohman, Eriksson, Fredriksson, Hugdahl, & Oloffson (1974).

Olver, R. R., see Bruner, Olver, & Greenfield (1966).

Ornstein, R. *The psychology of consciousness.* San Francisco: W.H. Freeman, 1972.

Ornstein, R. E. *On the experience of time.* Baltimore, Md.: Penguin Books, 1969.

Osler, S., see Tulving, & Osler (1968).

Osmond, H., see Hoffer, Osmond, & Smythies (1954).

Overton, D. A. Experimental methods for the study of state-dependent learning. *Federation Proceedings,* 1974, *33,* 1800—1813.

Owens, W. A. Age and mental abilities: A second adult follow-up. *Journal of Educational Psychology,* 1966, *57*(6), 311—325.

Pack, S. J., see Zanna, & Pack (1975).

Pahnke, W. M., & Richards, W. A. Implication of LSD and experimental mysticism. *Journal of Religion and Health,* 1966, *5,* 175—208.

Palermo, D. S. *Psychology of language.* Dallas: Scott Foresman, 1978.

Palmer, J., & Byrne, D. Attraction toward dominant and submissive strangers: Similarity versus complementarity. *Journal of Experimental Research in Psychology,* 1970, *4,* 108—115.

Palmer, J. C., see Loftus, & Palmer (1974).

Papasilou, P. S., see Cotzias, Papavasilou, & Gellene (1969).

Parke, R. D., see Hetherington, & Parke (1979).

Parkes, J. D. Clinical aspects of tardive dyskinesia. In H. F. Bradford and C. D. Marsden (Eds.), *Biochemistry and Neurology.* New York: Academic Press, 1976.

Parloff, M. B., Waskow, E., & Wolper, B. E. Research on therapist variables in relation to process and outcome. In S. Garfield & A. Bergin (Eds.), *Handbook of psychotherapy and behavior change.* New York: Wiley, 1978.

Patterson, C. R., see Fagot, & Patterson (1969).

Patterson, F. G. The gestures of a gorilla: Language acquisition in another pongid. *Brain and Language,* 1978, *5,* 72—97.

Patterson, I. J. Timing and spacing of broods in the black-headed gull *Larus ridibundis. Ibis,* 1965, *107,* 433—459.

Pavlov, I. P. *Conditioned reflexes* (G. V. Anrep, Trans.). New York: Oxford University Press, 1927.

Pearlstone, Z., see Tulving, & Pearlstone (1966).

Peck, R. C. Psychological developments in the second half of life. In B. L. Neugarten (Ed.), *Middle age and the aging.* Chicago: University of Chicago Press, 1968.

Pelchat, G., see Jus, Pineau, Lachance, Pelchat, Jus, Pires, & Villeneuve (1976).

Pelletier, K. R. *Mind as healer, mind as slayer.* New York: Dell, 1977.

Penfield, W., & Roberts, L. *Speech and brain mechanisms.* Princeton, N.J.: Princeton University Press, 1959.

Pert, C. B., & Snyder, S. H. Opiate receptor: Demonstration in nervous tissue. *Science,* 1973, *179,* 1011—1014.

Pessin, J. The comparative effects of social and mechanical stimulation of memorizing. *American Journal of Psychology,* 1933, *45,* 263—270.

Peterson, R. E., see Imperato-McGinley, Peterson, Gautier, & Sterla (1979).

Petitto, L. A., see Terrace, Petitto, Sanders, & Bever (1979).

Pfeiffer, E., see Verwoerdt, Pfeiffer, & Wang (1969).

Phillips, E. A., see Fixsen, Phillips, Phillips, & Wolf (1972).

Phillips, E. L., see Fixsen, Phillips, Phillips, & Wolf (1972).

Piaget, J. *The language and thought of the child.* New York: Harcourt, Brace, 1959. (Originally published, 1926.)

Piaget, J. The stages of the intellectual development of the child. *Bulletin of the Menninger Clinic,* 1962, *26,* 120—145.

Piaget, J. Piaget's theory. In P. Mussen (Ed.), *Carmichael's manual of child psychology.* New York: Wiley, 1970.

Piaget, J. *The origins of intelligence in children.* New York: Norton, 1974. (Originally published, 1963.)

Piaget, J. *The grasp of consciousness.* Cambridge, Mass.: Harvard University Press, 1976.

Pianka, E. R., see MacArthur, & Pianka (1966).

Pickering, V. L., see Hoffman, Eiserer, Ratner, & Pickering (1974).

Pilkonis, P. A., see Zanna, Kiesler, & Pilkonis (1970).

Pineau, R., see Jus, Pineau, Lachance, Pelchat, Jus, Pires, & Villeneuve (1976).

Pinel, P. *A treatise on insanity,* D. D. Davis (Trans.). New York: Hafner, 1962. (Originally published in 1801.)

Pirenne, M. H., see Hecht, Shalaer, & Pirenne (1942).

Pires, P., see Jus, Pineau, Lachance, Pelchat, Jus, Pires, & Villeneuve (1976).

Pisoni, D. B., see Shiffrin, Pisoni, & Castenada-Mendez (1974).

Pittenger, J. B., see Jenkins, Wald, & Pittenger (1978).

Pleszczynska, W. Microgeographic prediction of polygyny in lark bunting. *Science,* 1978, *201,* 935—937.

Pohorecky, L. A., see Weiss, Glazer, & Pohorecky (1976).

Pollack, E., see Gittleman-Klein, Klein, Katz, Saraf, & Pollack (1976).

Polt, J. M., see Hess, & Polt (1960).

Pomeroy, W. B., see Kinsey, Pomeroy, & Martin (1948).

Pomeroy, W. B., see Kinsey, Pomeroy, Martin, & Gebhard (1953).

Pope, K. S., & Singer, J. L. The waking stream of consciousness. In J. M. Davidson & R. J. Davidson (Eds.), *Psychobiology of consciousness.* New York: Plenum Press, 1980.

Porte, D., see Woods, & Porte (1976).

Posner, M. I., see Fitts, & Posner (1967).

Post, R. M., see Reus, Weingartner, & Post (1979).

Powell, B., see Goodwin, Powell, Bremer, Hoine, & Stern (1969).

Powley, T. L., see Keesey, & Powley (1975).

Premack, D. On the assessment of language competence in the chimpanzee. In A. M. Schrier & F. Stollnitz (Eds.), *Behavior of nonhuman primates* (Vol. 4). New York: Academic Press, 1971.

Premack, D. Language and intelligence in ape and man. *American Scientist*, 1976, *64*, 674—683.

Pribram, K. H., see Mishkin, & Pribram (1954).

Price, R. H., & Bouffard, D. L. Behavioral appropriateness and situational constraint as dimensions of social behavior. *Journal of Personality and Social Psychology*, 1974, *30*, 579—586.

Price, R. N., & Lynn, S. J. *Abnormal behavior in the human context*. Homewood, Ill.: Dorsey Press, 1981.

Quillian, M. R., see Collins, & Quillian (1969).

Rabow, J., Fowler, F. J., Bradford, D. L., Hofeller, M. A., & Shibuya, Y. The role of social norms and leadership in risk taking. *Sociometry*, 1966, *29*, 16—27.

Rachman, S. J., & Hodgson, R. J. *Obsessions and compulsions*. Englewood Cliffs, N.J.: Prentice-Hall, 1980.

Rachman, S. J., see Wolpe, & Rachman (1960).

Ramon y Cajal, S. *Histologie du systéme nerveux de l'homme et des vértebrès* (2 vols.), (L. Azoulay, Trans.). Paris: Maloine, 1909—1911.

Ramon y Cajal, S. *Recollections of my life*. (E. H. Craigie & J. Cano, Trans.). Philadelphia: American Philosophical Society, 1937.

Ranson, S. W., see Hetherington, & Ranson (1942).

Ranvier, L. A. Contributions a l'histologie et á la physiologie des nerfs periphériques. *Comptes Rendus Hebdomaoaires des Seances de L'Academie des Sciences, Paris*, 1871, *73*, 1168—1171.

Ratliff, F. *Mach bands: Quantitative studies on neural networks in the retina*. San Francisco: Holden-Day, 1965.

Ratliff, F., & Riggs, L. A. Involuntary motions of the eye during monocular fixation. *Journal of Experimental Psychology*, 1950, *40*, 687—701.

Ratliff, F., see Riggs, Ratliff, Cornsweet, & Cornsweet (1953).

Ratner, A. M., see Hoffman, Eiserer, Ratner, & Pickering (1974).

Raven, J. C. Standardization of progressive matrices. *British Journal of Medical Psychology*, 1941, *19*, 137—150.

Raugh, M. R., see Atkinson, & Raugh (1975).

Ray, O. *Drugs, society, and human behavior*. (2nd ed.) St. Louis, Mo.: Mosby, 1978.

Rayner, R., see Watson, & Rayner (1920).

Reed, G. *Psychology of anomalous experience*. Boston: Houghton Mifflin, 1972.

Regal, D., see Teller, Morse, Borton, & Regal (1974).

Regan, D., Beverley, K., & Cynader, H. The visual perception of motion in depth. *Scientific American*, 1979, *24*, 136—151.

Reich, W. *Character analysis*. New York: Orgone Institute Press, 1949.

Reifman, A., see Keith, Gunderson, Reifman, Buchsbaum, & Mosher (1976).

Riegel, K. F., & Riegel, R. M. Development, drop, and death. *Developmental Psychology*, 1972, *6*(2), 306—319.

Riegel, R. M., see Riegel, & Riegel (1972).

Reiser, B. J., see Kosslyn, Ball, & Reiser (1978).

Reitman, J. W., see Berkowitz, Nebel, & Reitman (1971).

Rescorla, R. A., & Solomon, R. L. Two-process learning theory: Relations between Pavlovian conditioning and instrumental learning. *Psychological Review*, 1967, *74*, 151—182.

Reuben, D. *Everything you always wanted to know about sex but were afraid to ask*. New York: Bantam, 1971.

Reus, V. I., Weingartner, H., & Post, R. M. Clinical implications of state-dependent learning. *American Journal of Psychiatry*, 1979, *136*, 927—931.

Revusky, S. H., & Garcia, J. Learned associations over long delays. In G. H. Bower & J. T. Spence (Eds.), *The psychology of learning and motivation: IV*. New York: Academic Press, 1970.

Reznick, J. S., see Richman, Mitchell, & Reznick (1979).

Rheingold, H. L., & Eckerman, C. O. The fear of strangers hypothesis: A critical review. In H. Reese (Ed.), *Advances in child development and behavior* (Vol. 8). New York: Academic Press, 1973.

Rhine, J. B. *Extra-sensory perception*. Boston: Bruce Humphries, 1935.

Rhode, W., see Dörner, Rhode, Stahl, Krell, & Masius (1975).

Rice, B. Brave new world of intelligence testing. *Psychology Today*, September 1979, p. 27.

Rice, B. Going for the gifted gold. *Psychology Today*, 1980, *13*, p. 55.

Richards, W. A., see Pahnke, & Richards (1966).

Richardson, A. *Mental imagery*. New York: Springer, 1969.

Richman, C. L., Mitchell, D. B., & Reznick, J. S. Mental travel: Some reservations. *Journal of Experimental Psychology: Human Perception and Performance*, 1979, *5*, 13—18.

Ricks, D., see Waring, & Ricks (1965).

Riesen, A. Arrested vision. *Scientific American*, 1950, *183*, 16—19.

Riggs, L. A., Ratliff, F., Cornsweet, J. C., & Cornsweet, T. The disappearance of visual test objects. *Journal of the Optical Society of America*, 1953, *43*, 495—501.

Riggs, L. A., see Ratliff, & Riggs (1950).

Rigler, M., see Fromkin, Krashen, Curtiss, Rigler, & Rigler (1972/1973).

Rigler, S., see Fromkin, Krashen, Curtiss, Rigler, & Rigler (1972/1973).

Ring, K. *Life at death*. New York: Coward, McCann & Geoghegan, 1980.

Rips, L. J., Shoben, E. J., & Smith, E. E. Semantic distance and the verification of semantic relations. *Journal of Verbal Learning and Verbal Behavior*, 1973, *12*, 1—20.

Ritchie, B. F., see Tolman, Ritchie, & Kalish (1946).

Ritter, B., see Bandura, Blanchard, & Ritter (1969).

Rittle, R. H., see Cottrell, Wack, Sekerak, & Rittle (1968).

Rizzollatti, G., Umilta, C., & Berlucchi, G. Opposite superiorities of the right and left hemispheres in discriminative reaction time to physiognomical and alphabetical material. *Brain*, 1971, *94*, 431—442.

Robbins, M. B., & Jensen, J. D. Multiple orgasms in males. In R. Gemme & C. C. Wheeler (Eds.), *Progress in sexology*. New York: Plenum Press, 1976.

Roberts, J. M., see Lenneberg, & Roberts (1956).

Roberts, L., see Penfield, & Roberts (1959).

Roberts, W., see Delgado, Roberts, & Miller (1954).

Robins, E., see Saghir, & Robins (1973).

Robinson, H. B., see Robinson, & Robinson (1976).

Robinson, I. E., see King, Balswick, & Robinson (1977).

Robinson, N. M., & Robinson, H. B. *The mentally retarded child* (2nd ed.). New York: McGraw-Hill, 1976.

Rocha-Miranda, C. E., see Gross, Rocha-Miranda, & Bender (1972).

Roche, A. F., & Davila, G. H. Late adolescent growth in stature. *Pediatrics*, 1972, *50*(6), 874—880.

Rock, I., & Victor, J. Vision and touch: An experimentally created conflict between the two senses. *Science*, 1964, *143*, 594—596.

Rock, L., see Jones, Rock, Shaver, Goethals, & Ward (1968).

Rockstein, M., & Sussman, M. *Biology of aging*. Belmont, Calif.: Wadsworth, 1979.

Rodgers, D., see McClearn, & Rodgers (1959).

Rodgers, W., & Rozin, P. Novel food preferences in thiamine-deficient rats. *Journal of Comparative and Physiological Psychology*. 1966, *61*, 1—4.

Rodin, J. *Effects of distraction on the performance of obese and normal subjects*. Unpublished doctoral dissertation, Columbia University, 1970.

Rodin, J., see Langer, & Rodin (1976).

Rodin, J., see Latané, & Rodin (1969).

Rodin, J., see Schachter, & Rodin (1974).

Roeder, F. D. Stereotaxic lesion of the tuber cinereum in sexual deviation. *Confinia Neurologica*, 1966, *27*, 162—163.

Rogers, C. R. *Counseling and psychotherapy*. Boston: Houghton Mifflin, 1942.

Rogers, C. R. The necessary and sufficient conditions of therapeutic personality change. *Journal of Consulting Psychology*, 1957, *21*, 95—103.

Rogers, C. R. A theory of therapy, personality, and interpersonal relationships as developed in client-centered framework. In S. Koch (Ed.) *Psychology: A study of a science (Vol. III) formulation of the person in the social context*. New York: McGraw-Hill, 1959.

Rogers, C. R. *On becoming a person*. Boston: Houghton Mifflin, 1961.

Rogers, C. R. *On encounter groups*. New York: Harper & Row, 1970.

Rogers, C. R., see Meador, & Rogers (1979).

Rosch, E. H. Cognitive representations of semantic categories. *Journal of Experimental Psychology*, 1975, *104*, 192—233.

Rose, S. *The conscious brain*. New York: Knopf, 1975.

Rosenhan, D. L. On being sane in insane places. *Science*, 1973, *179*, 250—258.

Rosenquist, A. C., see Stevens, Emerson, Gerstein, Kallos, Neufeld, Nichols, & Rosenquist (1976).

Rosenthal, D. *Genetic theory and abnormal behavior*. New York: McGraw-Hill, 1960.

Rosenthal, D., see Wender, Rosenthal, Kety, Schulsinger, & Weiner (1973).

Rosenthal, D., see Wender, Rosenthal, Kety, Schulsinger, & Weiner (1974).

Rosenthal, R., & Jacobson, L. Teachers expectancies: Determinants of pupils I.Q. gain. *Psychological Reports*, 1966, *19*, 115—118.

Rosenberg, S., Nelson, C., & Vivekananthan, P. S. A multidimensional approach to the structure of personality impression. *Journal of Personality and Social Psychology*, 1968, *9*, 283—294.

Ross, D., see Bandura, Ross, & Ross (1961).

Ross, D., see Bandura, Ross, & Ross (1963).

Ross, S. A., see Bandura, Ross, & Ross (1963).

Rosso, P., see Winick, Rosso, & Waterlow (1970).

Roth, J., see Langer, & Roth (1975).

Roth, M., see Mayer-Gross, Slater, & Roth (1969).

Roth, W. T., see Corby, Roth, Zarcone, Jr., & Kopell (1978).

Rothman, D. *The discovery of the asylum*. New York: Little, Brown, 1971.

Rothman, E., see Scheerer, Rothman, & Goldstein (1945).

Rozin, P., see Rodgers, & Rozin (1966).

Rubin, E. Figure and ground. In D. C. Beardslee & M. Wertheimer (Eds.), *Readings in perception*. New York: D. Von Nostrand, 1958. (Article originally published, 1915.)

Rumbaugh, D. M. (Ed.). *Language learning by a chimpanzee: The Lana project*. New York: Academic Press, 1977.

Rumelhart, D. E. Notes on a schema for stories: In D. G. Bobrow & A. M. Collins (Eds.), *Representations and understanding: Studies in cognitive science*. New York: Academic Press, 1975.

Russell, P. J., Adbelaal, A. E., & Mogenson, G. J. Graded levels of hemorrhage, thirst, and Angiotensin II in the rat. *Physiology and Behavior*, 1975, *15*, 117—119.

Russell, W. A., see Jenkins, & Russell (1952).

Sachs, J. S. Recognition memory for syntactic and semantic aspects of connected discourse. *Perception and Psychophysics*, 1967, *2*, 437—442.

Sackett, G. P. Monkeys reared in isolation with pictures as visual input: Evidence for an Innate Releasing Mechanism. *Science*, 1966, *154*, 1468—1473.

Saegert, S., Swap, W., & Zajonc, R. B. Exposure, context, and interpersonal attraction. *Journal of Personality and Social Psychology*, 1973, *25*, 234—252.

Sagan, C. *The dragons of Eden*. New York: Random House, 1977.

Saghir, M. T., & Robins, E. *Male and female homosexuality*. Baltimore: Williams and Wilkins, 1973.

Sales, S. M., see Zajonc, & Sales (1966).

Samelson, F. Conforming behavior under two conditions of conflict in the cognitive field. *Journal of Abnormal and Social Psychology*, 1957, *55*, 181—187.

Sand, E. A., see Hindley, Filliozat, Klakenberg, Nocolet-Meister, & Sand (1966).

Sanders, D. H., see Fairweather, Sanders, Cressler, & Maynard (1969).

Sanders, R. J., see Terrace, Petitto, Sanders, & Bever (1979).

Sankar, D.V.S. *LSD—A total study.* Westbury, N.Y.: PJD Publications, 1975.

Saraf, K., see Gittleman-Klein, Klein, Katz, Saraf, Pollack (1976).

Sarason, S. B., see Mandler, & Sarason (1952).

Scarr, S., & Weinberg, R. A. The influence of "family background" on intellectual attainment. *American Sociological Review*, 1978, *43*, 674—692.

Schachter, S. Deviation, rejection and communication. *Journal of Abnormal and Social Psychology*, 1951, *46*, 190—207.

Schachter, S. *The psychology of affiliation.* Stanford, Calif.: Stanford University Press, 1959.

Schachter, S. Some extraordinary facts about obese humans and rats. *American Psychologist*, 1971, *26*, 129—144.

Schachter, S., Goldman, R., & Gordon, A. Effects of fear, food deprivation, and obesity on eating. *Journal of Personality and Social Psychology*, 1968, *10*, 91—97.

Schachter, S., & Gross, L. P. Manipulated time and eating behavior. *Journal of Personality and Social Psychology*, 1968, *10*, 98—106.

Schachter, S., & Rodin, J. *Obese humans and rats.* Washington D.C.: Erlbaum/Halsted, 1974.

Schachter, S., & Singer, J. E. Cognitive, social, and physiological determinants of emotional state. *Psychological Review*, 1962, *69*, 379—399.

Schachter, S., see Festinger, Schachter, & Back (1950).

Schact, T., & Nathan, P. E. But is it good for psychologists? Appraisal and status of DSM III. *American Psychologist*, 1977, *32*, 1017—1025.

Schaie, K., & Strother, C. A cross-sequential study of age changes in cognitive behavior. *Psychological Bulletin*, 1968, *70*, 671—80.

Schaie, K. W., see Baltes, & Schaie (1974).

Scheerer, M., Rothman, E., & Goldstein, K. A case of "idiot savant": An experimental study of personality organization. *Psychological Monographs*, 1945, *58* (whole No. 269).

Scheff, T. J. *Being mentally ill: A sociological theory.* Chicago: Aldine, 1966.

Schein, E. H., Schneier, I., & Barker, C. H. *Coercive persuasion.* New York: Norton, 1961.

Schiavi, R. C., see Schreiner-Engel, Schiavi, Smith, & White (1981).

Schiffman, H. R. *Sensation and perception: An integrated approach.* New York: Wiley, 1976.

Schiffman, S. S. Physiochemical correlates of olfactory quality. *Science*, 1974, *185*, 112—117.

Schildkraut, J. J., & Kety, S. S. Biogenic amines and emotion. *Science*, 1967, *156*, 21—30.

Schlodtmann, W. Ein Beitrag zur Lehre von der Optischen Localisation bei Blindgeborenen. *Archiv für Opthalmologie*, 1902, *54*, 256—267.

Schmeck, H. M., Jr. Trend in growth of children lags. *The New York Times*, June 10, 1976, p. 13.

Schmeck, H. M., Jr. Researcher's tracking brain's own tranquilizers. *The New York Times*, April 10, 1979, p. C1.

Schmidt, A., see Noble, & Schmidt (1937).

Schmidt, G., & Sigusch, V. Woman's sexual arousal. In J. Zubin & J. Money (Eds.), *Contemporary sexual behavior: Critical issues in the 1970's.* Baltimore: Johns Hopkins University Press, 1973.

Schmidt, R. A. A schema theory of discrete motor skill learning. *Psychological Review*, 1975, *82*, 225—260.

Schneier, I., see Schein, Schneier, & Barker (1961).

Schopler, J., see Hinkle, & Schopler (1979).

Schreiner-Engel, P., Schiavi, R. C., Smith, H., & White, D. Sexual arousability and the menstrual cycle. *Journal of Psychosomatic Medicine*, 1981, *43*, 199—214.

Schuchart, G. E., see Knowles, Kreuser, Hyde, & Schuchart (1976).

Schulsinger, F., see Wender, Rosenthal, Kety, Schulsinger, & Weiner (1973).

Schulsinger, F., see Wender, Rosenthal, Kety, Schulsinger, & Weiner (1974).

Schultes, R. E. The utilization of hallucinogens in primitive societies: Use, misuse or abuse? In W. Keup (Ed.), *Drug abuse: Current concepts and research.* Springfield, Ill.: C C Thomas, 1972.

Schwann, T. *Mikroskopische Untersuchungen über die Übereinstimmung in der Struktur und dem Wachstum der Thiere und Pflanzen.* Berlin: Reimer, 1839.

Schwartz B. *Psychology of learning and behavior.* New York: Norton, 1978.

Schwartz, G. E. Psychosomatic disorders and biofeedback: A psychobiological model of disregulation. In J. D. Maser & M. E. P. Seligman (Eds.), *Psychopathology: Experimental models.* San Francisco: Freeman, 1977.

Scott, T. H., see Bexton, Heron, & Scott (1954).

Scott, W. W., see Jost, Jones, & Scott (1969).

Scull, A. T. Community treatment and the deviant: A radical view. In *Decarceration.* Englewood Cliffs, N.J.: Prentice-Hall, 1977.

Sears, P. S., & Barbee, N. H. Career and life satisfaction among Terman's gifted women. In *The gifted and the creative: 50-year perspective.* Johns Hopkins University Press, 1978.

Sears, R., see Dollard, Doob, Miller, Mowrer, & Sears (1939).

Sears, R. R. Sources of life satisfaction of the Terman-gifted men. *American Psychologist*, 1977, *32*, 119—128.

Sears, R. R., see Hovland, & Sears (1940).

Segal, J., see Luce, & Segal (1966).

Seitz, V., see Yando, Seitz, & Zigler (1979).

Sekerak, G. J., see Cottrell, Wack, Sekerak, & Rittle (1968).

Seligman, M. E. P. *Helplessness: On depression, development and death.* San Francisco: Freeman, 1975.

Seligman, M. E. P., Maier, S. F., & Geer, J. The alleviation of learned helplessness in the dog. *Journal of Abnormal and Social Psychology*, 1968, 73, 256—262.

Seligman, M. E. P., Maier, S. F., & Solomon, R. L. Unpredictable and uncontrollable aversive events. In R. F. Brusch (Ed.), *Aversive conditioning and learning.* New York: Academic Press, 1971.

Seligman, M. E. P., see Maier, Seligman, & Solomon (1969).

Serber, M., see Houts, & Serber (1972).

Schaffer, H. R., & Emerson, P. E. The development of social attachments in infancy. *Monographs of the Society for Research in Child Development*, 1964, 29(3, Serial No. 94).

Shalaer, S., see Hecht, Shalaer, & Pirenne (1942).

Shankweiler, D., see Liberman, Cooper, Shankweiler, & Studdert-Kennedy (1967).

Shattuck, R. *The forbidden experiment.* New York: Farrar Straus Giroux, 1980.

Shaver, K. G., see Jones, Rock, Shaver, Goethals, & Ward (1968).

Shaw, P. M., see Gelder, Brancroft, Gath, Johnston, Mathews, & Shaw (1973).

Sheldon, W. H. *The varieties of temperament: A psychology of constitutional differences.* New York: Harper, 1942.

Sheldon, W. H. *Atlas of men: A guide for somatotyping the adult male at all ages.* New York: Harper, 1954.

Sheppard, B. H., see Sorrentino, & Sheppard (1978).

Sherif, C., see Sherif, Harvey, White, Hood, & Sherif (1961).

Sherif, C., see Sherif, & Sherif (1953).

Sherif, M. An experimental approach to the study of attitudes. *Sociometry*, 1937, 1, 90—98.

Sherif, M., Harvey, O., White, B., Hood, W., & Sherif, C. *Intergroup conflict and cooperation: The robbers' cave experiment.* Norman, Okla.: University Book Exchange, 1961.

Sherif, M., & Sherif, C. *Groups in harmony and tension.* New York: Harper & Row, 1953.

Sherman, P. W. Nepotism and the evolution of alarm calls. *Science*, 1977, 197, 1246—1253.

Sherrington, C. *The integrative action of the nervous system.* New Haven: Yale University Press, 1906.

Sherrod, D. R. Crowding, perceived control, and behavioral aftereffects. *Journal of Applied Social Psychology*, 1974, 4, 171—186.

Sherrod, D. R., & Downs, R. Environmental determinants of altruism: The effects of stimulus overload and perceived control on helping. *Journal of Experimental Social Psychology*, 1974, 10, 468—479.

Shibuya, Y., see Rabow, Fowler, Bradford, Hofeller, & Shibuya (1966).

Shiffrin, R. M., Pisoni, D. B., & Castenada-Mendez, K. Is attention shared between the ears? *Cognitive Psychology*, 1974, 6, 190—215.

Shoben, E. J., see Rips, Shoben, & Smith (1973).

Shor, R. E. The frequency of naturally occurring "hypnotic like" experiences in normal college population. *International Journal of Clinical and Experimental Hypnosis*, 1960, 8, 151—163.

Short, R. V. Sexual-Selection and its component parts, somatic and genital selection, as illustrated by man and the great apes. *Advances in the Study of Behavior*, 1978, 9, 131.

Shure, M. B., see Spivack, & Shure (1974).

Sigusch, V., see Schmidt, & Sigusch (1973).

Simmelhag, V. L., see Staddon, & Simmelhag (1971).

Simmons, C., see Lerner, & Simmons (1966).

Simon, H. A., see Newell, & Simon (1972).

Simon, T., see Binet, & Simon (1916).

Simpson, G. M., see Branchey, Charles, & Simpson (1976).

Singer, J. E., Brush, C., & Lublin, S. D. Some aspects of deindividuation: Identification and conformity. *Journal of Experimental Social Psychology*, 1965, 1, 356—378.

Singer, J. E., see Cohen, Glass, & Singer (1973).

Singer, J. E., see Glass, & Singer (1972).

Singer, J. L., see Pope, & Singer (1980).

Singer, J. E., see Schachter, & Singer (1962).

Skeels, H. M. Adult status of children with contrasting early life experiences. *Monographs of the Society for Research and Child Development*, 1966, (Vo. 31).

Skinner, B. F. *The behavior of organisms.* New York: Appleton-Century-Crofts, 1938.

Skinner, B. F. Superstition in the pigeon. *Journal of Experimental Psychology*, 1948, 38, 168—172.

Skinner, B. F. *Walden two.* New York: Macmillan, 1948.

Skinner, B. F. *Science and human behavior.* New York: Macmillan, 1953.

Skinner, B. F. A case history in scientific method. *American Psychologist*, 1956, 11, 221—233.

Skinner, B. F. *Beyond freedom and dignity.* New York: Knopf, 1971.

Skinner's utopia: Panacea, or path to hell? *Time.* September 20, 1971, pp. 47—53.

Skinner, B. F. *About behaviorism.* New York: Knopf, 1974.

Slater, E., see Mayer-Gross, Slater, & Roth (1969).

Slobin, D. I. On the nature of talk to children. In E. H. Lenneberg & E. Lenneberg (Eds.), *Foundations of language development: A multidisciplinary approach* (Vol. 1). New York: Academic Press, 1975.

Smart, R. G. *LSD in treatment of alcoholism.* Toronto: University of Toronto Press, 1967.

Smith, C. J., see De Valois, Smith, Karoly, & Hitai (1959).

Smith, C. M., see Chwelos, Blewett, Smith, & Hoffer (1959).

Smith, D. E., King, M. B., & Hoebel, B. C. Lateral hypothalamic control of killing: Evidence for a cholinoceptive mechanism. *Science*, 1970, 167, 900—901.

Smith, E. E., see Rips, Shoben, & Smith (1973).

Smith, E. R., see Davidson, Smith, & Levine (1978).

615

Smith, E. R., see Davidson, Camargo, & Smith (1979).

Smith, H., see Schreiner-Engel, Schiavi, Smith, & White (1981).

Smith, J. H., see Greenfield, & Smith (1976).

Smith, M. B., Bruner, J. S., & White, R. W. *Opinions and personality.* New York: Wiley, 1956.

Smith, M. L., & Glass, G. V. Meta-analysis of psychotherapy outcome studies. *American Psychologist,* 1977, *32,* 752—760.

Smith, T. W., see Hughes, Smith, Kosterlitz, Fothergill, Morgan, & Morris (1975).

Smythies, J. R., see Hoffer, Osmond, & Smythies (1954).

Snyder, C. R., & Larson, G. R. A further look at student acceptance of general personality interpretations. *Journal of Consulting and Clinical Psychology,* 1972, *38,* 384—388.

Snyder, M., Tanke, E. D., & Berscheid, E. Social perception and interpersonal behavior: On the self-fulfilling nature of social stereotypes. *Journal of Personality and Social Psychology,* 1977, *35,* 656—666.

Snyder, S. Opiate receptors and internal opiates. *Scientific American,* March 1977, pp. 44—56.

Snyder, S. H. *Madness and the brain.* New York: McGraw-Hill, 1975.

Snyder, S. H. The dopamine hypothesis of schizophrenia. *American Journal of Psychiatry,* 1976, *133,* 197—202.

Snyder, S. H., see Pert, & Snyder (1973).

Solomon, R. I. The opponent-process theory of acquired motivation. *American Psychologist,* 1980, *691,* 691—712.

Solomon, R. L., see Rescorla, & Solomon (1967).

Solomon, R. L., see Maier, Seligman, & Solomon (1969).

Solomon, R. L., see Seligman, Maier, & Solomon (1971).

Solomon, S. H., see Heller, Groff, & Solomon (1977).

Sommer, R. *Personal Space.* Englewood Cliffs, N.J.: Prentice-Hall, 1969.

Sonnenschein, D., see Kripke, & Sonnenschein (1973).

Sorensen, C. *Adolescent sexuality in contemporary America.* New York: World Publishing Co., 1973.

Sorrentino, R. M., & Sheppard, B. H. Effects of affiliation-related motives on swimmers in individual versus group competition: A field experiment. *Journal of Personality and Social Psychology,* 1978, *36,* 704—714.

Spear, N. E. *Organizational aspects of memory in temporal lobatomy patients.* Unpublished doctoral dissertation, University of Maryland, 1972.

Spearman, C. *The abilities of man.* London: Macmillan, 1927.

Spence, K. W., Taylor, J., & Ketchel, R. Anxiety (drive) level and degree of competition in paired associates learning. *Journal of Experimental Psychology,* 1956, *53,* 306—310.

Sperling, G. A. The information available in brief visual presentations. *Psychological Monographs,* 1960, 74(Whole No. 498).

Sperry, R. W. The great cerebral commissure. *Scientific American,* 1964, *210,* 42—52.

Sperry, R. W. Cerebral organization and behavior. *Science,* 1961, *133,* 1749.

Sperry R. W. In G. E. W. Wolstenholme & M. O'Conner (Eds.), *Growth of the nervous system.* London: Churchill, 1968.

Sperry, R. W. Lateral specialization in the surgically disconnected hemispheres. In F. O. Schmitt & F. G. Worden (Eds.), *The neurosciences third study program.* Cambridge, Mass.: MIT Press, 1974.

Sperry, R. W., see Milner, Taylor, & Sperry (1968).

Spiegler, M. D., see Liebert, & Spiegler (1974).

Spies, G. Food versus intracranial self-stimulation reinforcement in food deprived rats. *Journal of Comparative and Physiological Psychology,* 1965, *60,* 153—157.

Spinelli, N. see Hirsch, & Spinelli (1970).

Spirduso, W. W. Reaction and movement time as a function of age and physical activity level. *Journal of Gerontology,* 1973, *30,* 435—440.

Spitz, R. A. Anaclitic depression. *Psychoanalytic Studies of the Child,* 1946, 2, 313—342.

Spitz, R. A. Hospitalism: A follow-up report. *Psychoanalytic Studies of the Child,* 1946, 2, 113—117.

Spivack, G., & Shure, M. B. *Social adjustment of young children: A cognitive approach to solving real life problems.* San Francisco: Jossey-Bass, 1974.

Spring, B., see Zubin, & Spring (1977).

Spurzheim, J. C., see Gall, & Spurzheim (1810—1819).

Stace, W. T. *Philosophy of mysticism.* New York: Macmillan, 1960.

Staddon, J. E. R., & Simmelhag, V. L. The "superstition" experiment: A reexamination of its implications for the principles of adaptive behavior. *Psychological Review,* 1971, 78, 3—43.

Stahl, F., see Dörner, Rhode, Stahl, Krell, & Masius (1975).

Stalnaker, J. M. Psychological tests and public responsibility. *American Psychologist,* 1965, *20,* 131—135.

Stampfl, T. C., & Levis, D. J. Essentials of implosive therapy: A learning-therapy-based psychodynamic behavior therapy. *Journal of Abnormal Psychology,* 1967, 72, 496—503.

Stayton, D. J., see Ainsworth, Bell, & Stayton (1971).

Stebbins, W. C., Miller, J. M., Johnsson, L. G., & Hawkins, J. E., Jr. Ototoxic hearing loss and cochlear pathology in the monkey. *Annals of Otology, Rhinology, and Laryngology,* 1969, 78, 598—602.

Stein, L. I., see Marx, Test, & Stein (1973).

Stern, D. N. Mother and infant at play: The dyadic interaction involving facial, vocal and gaze behaviors. In M. Lewis & L. A. Rosenblum (Eds.), *The effect of the infant on its caretaker.* New York: Wiley, 1974.

Stern, J., see Goodwin, Powell, Bremer, Hoine, & Stern (1969).

Stern, W. *The psychological methods of testing intelligence.* G. W. Whipple (Trans.) Baltimore, Md.: Warwick & York, 1914.

Sternberg, R. J. *Intelligence, information processing and*

analogical reasoning: Componential analysis of human abilities. Hillsdale, N.J.: Lawrence Erlbaum, 1977.

Sternberg, R. J., & Dettermanm, D. K. (Eds.), *Human intelligence: Perspectives on its theory and measures.* Norwood, N.J.: Ablex, 1979.

Stevens, J. K., Emerson, R. C., Gerstein, G. L., Kallos, T., Neufeld, G., Nichols, C., & Rosenquist, A. C. Paralysis of the awake human: Visual perceptions. *Vision Research*, 1976, *16*, 93—98.

Stevens, S. S. On the psychophysical law. *Psychological Review*, 1957, *64*, 153—181.

Stevens, S. S. To honor Fechner and repeal his law. *Science*, 1961, *133*, 80—86.

Stevenson, H. W., Keen, R., & Knights, R. M. Parents and strangers as reinforcing agents for children's performance. *Journal of Abnormal and Social Psychology*, 1963, *67*, 183—186.

Stevenson, J. A. F., see Miller, Bailey, & Stevenson (1950).

Stewart, K. Dream theory in Malaya. In C. Tart (Ed.), *Altered states of consciousness.* New York: Wiley, 1969.

Stolaroff, M., see Harman, McKim, Mogar, Fadiman, & Stolaroff (1966).

Stoller, R. *Sex and gender.* New York: Science House, 1968.

Stoner, J. A. F. *A comparison of individual and group decisions involving risk.* Unpublished master's thesis, M.I.T., 1961.

Stoner, J. A. F. Risky and cautious shifts in group decisions: The influence of widely held values. *Journal of Experimental Social Psychology*, 1968, *4*, 442—459.

Stricker, E. M., & Wilson, N. E. Salt-seeking behavior in rats following acute sodium deficiency. *Journal of Comparative Physiology*, 1970, *72*, 416—420.

Strother, C., see Schaie, & Strother (1968).

Sroufe, L. A., & Waters, E. Attachment as an organizational construct. *Child Development*, 1977, *48*, 1184—1199.

Sroufe, L. A., see Matas, Arend, & Sroufe (1978).

Sroufe, L. A., see Waters, Wippman, & Sroufe (1979).

Strupp, H. H., Psychotherapy research and practice. In S. Garfield & A. Bergin (Eds.), *Handbook of psychotherapy and behavior change.* New York: Wiley, 1978.

Strupp, H. H., Fox, R. E., & Lessler, K. *Patients view their therapy.* Baltimore, Md.: Johns Hopkins Press, 1969.

Studdert-Kennedy, M., see Liberman, Cooper, Shankweiler, & Studdert-Kennedy (1967).

Stunkard, A., & Koch, C. The interpretation of gastric motility, I. Apparent bias in the reports of hunger by obese persons. *Archives of General Psychiatry*, 1964, *11*, 74—82.

Sturla, E., see Imperato-McGinley, Peterson, Gautier, & Sturla (1979).

Sussman, M., see Rockstein, & Sussman (1979).

Svaetichin, G., & MacNichol, E. F., Jr. Retinal mechanisms for chromatic and achromatic vision. *Annals of the New York Academy of Science*, 1958, *74*, 385—404.

Swap, W., see Saegert, Swap, & Zajonc (1973).

Sweet, W. H., Ervin, F., & Mark, V. H. The relationship of violent behavior to focal cerebral disease. In S. Garattini & S. Eigg (Eds.), *Aggressive behavior.* New York: Wiley, 1969.

Sweet, W. H., see Mark, Sweet, & Ervin (1972).

Swets, J. A., see Green, & Swets (1966).

Sylvester, D., see Agras, Sylvester, & Oliveau (1969).

Sylvester, J. D., see Cohen, Hansel, & Sylvester (1954).

Szasz, T. Patty Hearst's conversion: Some call it brainwashing. *The New Republic*, 1976, *174*, 10—12.

Tamada, T., see Matsumoto, Tamada, & Konuma (1979).

Tanke, E. D., see Snyder, Tanke, & Berscheid (1977).

Tanner, J. M. Physical growth. In P. H. Mussen (Ed.), *Carmichael's manual of child psychology* (Vol. 1) (3rd ed.). New York: Wiley, 1970.

Tanner, J. M. Sequence, tempo, and individual variation in the growth and development of boys and girls aged twelve to sixteen. *Daedalus*, 1971, *100*, 907—930.

Tanner, J. M., see Eveleth, & Tanner (1976).

Taylor, J., see Spence, Taylor, & Ketchel (1956).

Taylor, L., see Milner, Taylor, & Sperry (1968).

Taylor, S., see Borgdan, & Taylor (1976).

Teevan, R. C., & McGhee, P. E. Childhood development of fear of failure motivation. *Journal of Personality and Social Psychology*, 1972, *21*, 345—348.

Teitelbaum, P., & Epstein, A. Recovery of feeding and drinking after lateral hypothalamic lesions. *Psychological Review*, 1962, *69*, 74—90.

Teitelbaum, P., see Hoebel, & Teitelbaum (1966).

Teller, D. Y., Morse, R., Borton, R., & Regal, D. Visual acuity for vertical and diagonal gratings in human infants. *Vision Research*, 1974, *14*, 1433—1439.

Terman, L. M. *The measurement of intelligence.* Boston: Houghton Mifflin, 1916.

Terman, L. M., & Oden, N. H. *The gifted child grows up.* Stanford, Calif.: Stanford University Press, 1947.

Terrace, H. S., Petitto, L. A., Sanders, R. J., & Bever, T. G. Can an ape create a sentence? *Science*, 1979, *206*, 891—902.

Test, M. A., see Marx, Test, & Stein (1973).

Tharp, R. G., see Watson, & Tharp (1972).

Theios, J. The partial reinforcement effect sustained through blocks of continuous reinforcement. *Journal of Experimental Psychology*, 1962, *64*, 1—6.

Thibaut, J. W., & Kelley, H. H. *The social psychology of groups.* New York: Wiley, 1959.

Thomas, J., see Isaacs, Thomas, & Goldiamond (1960).

Thomas, M. H., Horton, R. W., Lippincott, E. C., & Drabman, R. S. Desensitization to portrayals of real-life aggression as a function of exposure to television violence. *Journal of Personality and Social Psychology*, 1977, *35*, 450—458.

Thomas, M. H., see Drabman, & Thomas (1974).

Thomas, S. E., see Wagner, Thomas, & Norton (1967).

Thompson, D. M., see Tulving, & Thompson (1973).

Thorndike, E. L. Animal intelligence: An experimental study of the associative processes in animals. *Psychological Review Monograph*, 1898, *2*(4, Whole No. 8).

Thorndike, E. L. *The psychology of learning*. New York: Teachers College, 1932.

Thurstone, L. L. Primary mental abilities. *Psychometric Monographs*. 1938, *1*, 1—121.

Tinbergen, N. The shell menace. *Natural History*, 1963, *72*, 28—35.

Tinbergen, N., see Lorenz, & Tinbergen (1957).

Tobias, L. L., see MacDonald, & Tobias (1976).

Tolman, E. C., & Hoznik, C. H. Introduction and removal of reward, and maze performance in rats. *University of California Publications in Psychology*, 1930, *4*, 257—275.

Tolman, E. C. *Purposive behavior in animals and men*. New York: The Century Co., 1932.

Tolman, E. C. Determinants of behavior at a choice point. *Psychological Review*, 1938, *45*, 1—41.

Tolman, E. C. Cognitive maps in rats and men. *Psychological Review*, 1948, *55*, 189—208.

Tolman, E. C., Ritchie, B. F., & Kalish, D. Studies in spatial learning. Part II: Place learning versus response learning. *Journal of Experimental Psychology*, 1946, *36*, 221—229.

Toms, S., see Doob, Carlsmith, Freedman, Landauer, & Toms (1969).

Toro, G., see Kolodny, Masters, Kolodner, & Toro (1974).

Treisman, A. M. Monitoring and storage of irrelevant messages in selective attention. *Journal of Verbal Learning and Verbal Behavior*, 1964, *3*, 449—459.

Troll, L. E. *Early and middle adulthood*. Monterey, Calif.: Brooks/Cole Publishing Co., 1975.

Trope, Y., see Vinokur, Trope, & Burnstein (1975).

Tsuang, M. Schizophrenia around the world. *Comparative Psychiatry*, 1976, *17*, 477—481.

Tulving, E. Episodic and semantic memory. In E. Tulving & W. Donaldson (Eds.), *Organization of memory*. New York: Academic Press, 1972.

Tulving, E., & Pearlstone, Z. Availability versus accessibility of information in memory for words. *Journal of Verbal Learning and Verbal Behavior*, 1966, *5*, 381—391.

Tulving, E., & Osler, S. Effectiveness of retrieval cues in memory for words. *Journal of Experimental Psychology*, 1968, *77*, 593—601.

Tulving, E., & Thompson, D. M. Encoding specificity and retrieval processes in episodic memory. *Psychological Review*, 1973, *80*, 352—373.

Tulving, E., see Craik, & Tulving (1975).

Tulving, E., see Watkins, & Tulving (1975).

Turiel, E. An experimental test of the sequentiality of developmental stages in the child's moral judgments. *Journal of Personality and Social Psychology*, 1966, *3*, 611—618.

Turner, J. S., & Helms, D. B. *Life span development*. Philadelphia: W. B. Saunders Company, 1979.

Turner, S. M., see Bellack, Hersen, & Turner (1976).

Turvey, M. T., see Darwin, Turvey, & Crowder (1972).

Udry, J. R., & Morris, N. M. Distribution of coitus in the menstrual cycle. *Nature*, 1968, *220*, 593—595.

Udry, J. R., & Morris, N. M. The distribution of events in the human menstrual cycle. *Journal of Reproduction and Fertility*, 1977, *51*, 419—425.

Ullmann, L. P., & Krasner, L. *A psychological approach to abnormal behavior* (2nd ed.). Englewood Cliffs, N.J.: Prentice-Hall, 1975.

Umilta, C., see Rizzollatti, Umilta, & Berlucchi (1971).

Valenstein, E. S. *Brain control*. New York: Wiley, 1973.

Valins, S. Cognitive effects of false heartrate feedback. *Journal of Personality and Social Psychology*, 1966, *4*, 400—408.

Vance, E. B., & Wagner, N. N. Written descriptions of orgasms: A study of sex differences. *Archives of Sexual Behavior*, 1976, *5*, 87—98.

Van de Castle, R. L., see Hall, & Van de Castle (1966).

Vanegas, H., see Flynn, Vanegas, Foote, & Edwards (1970).

Van Sluyters, R., & Levitt, F. Experimental strabismus in the kitten. *Journal of Neurophysiology*, 1980, *43*, 686—699.

Varela, A., see Cruz-Coke, & Varela (1966).

Vaughan, C. J. *The development and use of an operant technique to provide evidence for visual imagery in the rhesus monkey under "sensory deprivation."* Unpublished doctoral dissertation, University of Pittsburgh, 1963.

Vernon, P. E., see Allport, & Vernon (1933).

Veroff, J., see Gurin, Veroff, & Feld (1960).

Verwoerdt, A., Pfeiffer, E., & Wang, H. S. Sexual behavior in senescence. *Geriatrics*, 1969, *24*, 137—154.

Victor, J., see Rock, & Victor (1964).

Villeneuve, R., see Jus, Pineau, Lachance, Pelchat Jus, Pires, & Villeneuve (1976).

Vinokur, A., Trope, Y., & Burnstein, E. A decision-making analysis of persuasive argumentation and the choice-shift. *Journal of Experimental Social Psychology*, 1975, *11*, 127—148.

Vivekananthan, P. S., see Rosenberg, Nelson, & Vivekananthan (1968).

von Holst, E. Relations between the central nervous system and the peripheral organs. *British Journal of Animal Behavior*, 1954, *2*, 89—94.

von Holst, E., & Mittelstadt, H. Das reafferenz-princip. *Die Naturwissensdraften*, 1950, *20*, 464—467.

Vonnegut, M. *The Eden express*. New York: Praeger, 1975.

Vygotsky, L. S. *Mind in society*. Cambridge, Mass.: Harvard University Press, 1978.

Wack, D. L., see Cottrell, Wack, Sekerak, & Rittle (1968).

Waddington, C. H. *The strategy of the genes*. New York: Macmillan, 1957.

Wagner, A. R., Thomas, S. E., & Norton, T. Conditioning with electrical stimulation of motor cortex: Evidence of a possible source of motivation. *Journal of Comparative and Physiological Psychology*, 1967, *64*, 191—200.

Wagner, H. G., MacNichol, E. F., Jr., & Wolbarsht, M. L. The response properties of single ganglion cells in the goldfish retina. *Journal of General Physiology*, 1960, *43*, 45—62.

Wagner, N. N., see Vance, & Wagner (1976).

Wald, J., see Jenkins, Wald, & Pittenger (1978).

Walder, L. Q., see Eron, Lefkowitz, Huesmann, & Walder (1972).

Walk, R. D., see Gibson, & Walk (1960).

Wallach, M. A., & Kogan, N. The rules of information, discussion, and consensus in group risk taking. *Journal of Experimental Social Psychology*, 1965, *1*, 1—19.

Wallach, M. A., Kogan, N., & Bem, D. J. Diffusion of responsibility and level of risk taking in groups. *Journal of Abnormal and Social Psychology*, 1964, *68*, 263—274.

Walster, E. H., see Berscheid, & Walster (1969).

Walster, E., see Dion, Berscheid, & Walster (1972).

Walter, A. A., see Carmichael, Hogan, & Walter (1932).

Walters, E., Aronson, E., & Abrahams, D. On increasing the persuasiveness of a low prestige communicator. *Journal of Experimental Social Psychology*, 1966, *2*, 325—342.

Walters, E., Wippman, J., & Sroufe, L. A. Attachment, positive affect, and competence in the peer group: Two studies in construct validation. *Child Development*, 1979, *50*, 821—829.

Wang, H. S., see Verwoerdt, Pfeiffer, & Wang (1969).

Ward, L. M., see Jones, Rock, Shaver, Goethals, & Ward (1968).

Ward, R. H. *A drug taker's notes.* London: Gollancz, 1957.

Warga, W., see Aldrin, & Warga (1973).

Waring, M., & Ricks, D. Family patterns of children who become adult schizophrenics. *Journal of Nervous and Mental Disease*, 1965, *140*, 351—364.

Washburn, A. L., see Cannon, & Washburn (1912).

Waskow, E., see Parloff, Waskow, & Wolper (1978).

Waterlow, J., see Winick, Rosso, & Waterlow (1970).

Waters, E., see Sroufe, & Waters (1977).

Waters, H. F., & Malamud, P. Drop that gun, Captain Video. *Newsweek*, March 10, 1975, *85*(10), 81—82.

Watkins, M. J., & Tulving, E. Episodic memory: When recognition fails. *Journal of Experimental Psychology*, 1975, *104*, 5—36.

Watkins, M. J., see Craik, & Watkins (1973).

Watson, D. L., & Tharp, R. G. *Self-directed behavior: Self-modification for personal adjustment.* Monterey, Calif.: Brooks/Cole, 1972.

Watson, J. B. Psychology as the behaviorist views it. *Psychological Review*, 1913, *20*, 158—177.

Watson, J. B. *Behaviorism.* New York: Norton, 1925.

Watson, J. B., & Rayner, R. Conditioned emotional reactions. *Journal of Experimental Psychology*, 1920, *3*, 1—14.

Waugh, N. C., & Norman, D. A. Primary memory. *Psychological Review*, 1965, *72*, 89—104.

Weakland, J., see Bateson, Jackson, Haley, & Weakland (1956).

Weber, E. H. *The sense of touch.* New York: Academic Press, 1978.

Wechsler, D. *The Wechsler intelligence scale for children.* New York: Psychological Corporation, 1949.

Wechsler, D. *Wechsler adult intelligence scale manual.* New York: Psychological Corporation, 1955.

Wechsler, D. *The measurement and appraisal of adult intelligence.* Baltimore, Md.: Williams & Wilkins, 1958.

Wechsler, H., see Greenblatt, Grosser, & Wechsler (1964).

Wei, E., & Loh, H. Physical dependence on opiate-like peptides. *Science*, 1976, *193*, 1262.

Weil, A. *The natural mind.* Boston: Houghton Mifflin, 1973.

Weinberg, R. A., see Scarr, & Weinberg (1978).

Weiner, B. New conceptions in the study of achievement motivation. In B. A. Maher (Ed.), *Progress in experimental personality research* (Vol. 5). New York: Academic Press, 1970.

Weiner, J., see Wender, Rosenthal, Kety, Schulsinger, & Weiner (1973).

Weiner, J., see Wender, Rosenthal, Kety, Schulsinger, & Weiner (1974).

Weingartner, H., Miller, H. A., & Murphy, D. L. Mood state-dependent retrieval of verbal associations. *Journal of Abnormal Psychology*, 1979, *86*, 276—284.

Weingartner, H., see Reus, Weingartner, & Post (1979).

Weisman, R. N., Hamilton, L. W., & Carlton, P. L. Increased gustatory aversion following VMH lesions in rats. *Physiology and Behavior*, 1972, *9*, 801—804.

Weiss, J. M., Glazer, H. I., & Pohorecky, L. A. Coping behavior and neurochemical changes: An alternative explanation for the original "learned helplessness" experiments. In G. Serban & A. Kling (Eds.). *Relevance of the animal model to the human.* New York: Plenum Press, 1976.

Weiss, N., see Hovland, & Weiss (1952).

Welford, A. T. & Birren, J. E. (Eds.), *Behavior, aging, and the nervous system.* Springfield, Ill.: Charles C Thomas, 1965.

Wender, P. H., Rosenthal, D., Kety, S. S., Schulsinger, F., & Weiner, J. Social class and psychopathology in adoptees: A natural experimental method for separating the roles of genetic and experiential factors. *Archives of General Psychiatry*, 1973, *28*, 318—325.

Wender, P. H., Rosenthal, D., Kety, S. S., Schulsinger, F., & Weiner, J. Crossfostering: A research strategy for clarifying the role of genetic and experiential factors in the etiology of schizophrenia. *Archives of General Psychiatry*, 1974, *30*, 121—128.

Wertheimer, M. Experimentelle studien über das sehen von Bervegung. *Zeitschrift für Psychologie*, 1912, *61*, 161—265.

Whalen, C., see Collins, Henker, & Whalen (1980).

619

Whaley, D. L., & Malott, R. W. *Elementary principles of behavior*. Kalamazoo, Mich.: Behaviordelia, 1969.

Wheatstone, C. On some remarkable and hitherto unobserved phenomena of binocular vision. *London Royal Society: Philosophical Transactions of the Royal Society*, 1838, pp. 371—394.

White, B., see Sherif, Harvey, White, Hood, & Sherif (1961).

White, D., see Schreiner-Engel, Schiavi, Smith & White (1981).

White, R. W., see Smith, Bruner, & White (1956).

Whitten, W. K., Bronson, F. H., & Greenstein, J. A. Estrus-inducing pheromone of male mice: Transport by movement of air. *Science*, 1968, *161*, 584—585.

Whorf, B. L. *Language, thought and reality: Selected writings of Benjamin Lee Whorf* (J. B. Carroll, Ed.). New York: Wiley, 1956.

Widroe, H. J., & Heisler, S. Treatment of tardive dyskinesia. *Diseases of the Nervous System*, 1976, *37*, 162—164.

Wiesel, T. N., see Hubel, & Wiesel (1962).

Wiesel, T. N., see Hubel, & Wiesel (1965).

Wilcoxin, H. C., Dragoin, W. B., & Kral, P. A. Illness-induced aversions in rat and quail: Relative saliences of visual and gustatory cues. *Science*, 1971, *71*, 826—828.

Will, O. A. Analytic etiology: A primer. In J. O. Cole & L. E. Hollister (Eds.), *Schizophrenia*. New York: MEDCOM, 1970.

Wilson, M., see Daly, & Wilson (1978).

Wilson, N. E., see Stricker, & Wilson (1970).

Winick, N., Rosso, P., & Waterlow, J. Cellular growth of cerebrum, cerebelium, and brain stem in normal and marasmic children. *Experimental Neurology*, 1970, *26*, 393—400.

Winsborough, H. H. The social consequences of high population density. *Law and Contemporary Problems*, 1965, *30*, 120—126.

Winzenz, D., see Bower, Clark, Winzenz, & Lesgold (1969).

Wippman, J., see Waters, Wippman, & Sroufe (1979).

Wolbarsht, M. L., see Wagner, MacNichol, Jr., & Wolbarsht (1960).

Wolf, L. L., see Gill, & Wolf (1975).

Wolf, M. M., see Allen, Hart, Buell, Harris, & Wolf (1964).

Wolf, M. M., see Fixsen, Phillips, Phillips, & Wolf (1972).

Wolfe, J. B. Effectiveness of token-rewards for chimpanzees. *Comparative Psychology Monographs*, 1936, *12* (Whole No. 60).

Wollard, H. H. Observations on terminations of lutaneous nerves. *Brain*, 1935, *58*, 352.

Wolpe, J. *Psychotherapy by reciprocal inhibition*. Stanford, Calif.: Stanford University Press, 1958.

Wolpe, J., & Lazarus, A. A. *The practice of behavior therapy*. New York: Pergamon, 1969.

Wolpe, J., & Rachman, S. J. Psychoanalytic "evidence": A critique based on Freud's case of Little Hans. *Journal of Nervous and Mental Diseases*, 1960, *130*, 135—148.

Wolper, B. E., see Parloff, Waskow, & Wolper (1978).

Wolpert, E., see Dement, & Wolpert (1958).

Wood, L. E., see Doob, & Wood (1972).

Woodrow, H. Time perception. In S. S. Stevens (Ed.), *Handbook of experimental psychology*. New York: Wiley, 1951.

Woods, S. C., & Porte, D. Insulin and the set-point regulation of body weight. In D. Novin, W. Wyrwicka, & G. Bray (Eds.), *Hunger: Basic mechanisms and clinical implications*. New York: Raven Press, 1976.

Woodworth, R. S. *Experimental psychology*. New York: Holt, 1938.

Worchel, S., Andreoli, V. A., & Folger, R. Intergroup cooperation and intergroup attraction: The effect of previous interaction and outcome of combined effort. *Journal of Experimental Social Psychology*, 1977, *13*, 131—140.

Word, C. O., Zanna, M. P., & Cooper, J. The nonverbal mediation of self-fulfilling prophecies in interracial interaction. *Journal of Experimental Social Psychology*, 1974, *10*, 109—120.

Wrightsman, L. S. Effects of waiting with others on changes in level of felt anxiety. *Journal of Abnormal and Social Psychology*, 1960, *61*, 216—222.

Wynne, L. C. Communication disorders and the quest for relatedness in families of schizophrenics. *American Journal of Psychoanalysis*, 1970, *30*, 100—114.

Yalom, I. D., see Lieberman, Yalom, & Miles (1973).

Yando, R., Seitz, V., & Zigler, E. *Intellectual and personality characteristics of children: Social class and ethnic group differences*. Hillsdale, N.J.: Lawrence Erlbaum, 1979.

Yen, S. S. C., see Judd, & Yen (1973).

Young, T. On the theory of light and colours. *Philosophical Transactions of the Royal Society of London*, 1802, *92*, 20.

Zaehner, R. C. *Zen, drugs, and mysticism*. New York: Random House, 1972.

Zajonc, R. B. Social facilitation. *Science*, 1965, *149*, 269—274.

Zajonc, R. B. Attitudinal effects of mere exposure. *Journal of Personality and Social Psychology Monograph Supplement*, 1968, *9*, 1—27.

Zajonc, R. B., & Burnstein, E. Structural balance, reciprocity, and positivity as sources of cognitive bias. *Journal of Personality*, 1965, *33*, 570—583.

Zajonc, R. B., Heingartner, A., & Herman, E. M. Social enhancement and impairment of performance in the cockroach. *Journal of Personality and Social Psychology*, 1969, *13*, 83—92.

Zajonc, R. B., & Markus, G. B. Birth order and intellectual development. *Psychological Review*, 1975, *82*, 74—88.

Zajonc, R. B., & Nieuwenhuyse, B. Relationship between work frequency and recognition: Perceptual process or response bias. *Journal of Experimental Psychology*, 1964, *67*, 276—285.

Zajonc, R. B., & Sales, S. M. Social facilitation of dominant and subordinate responses. *Journal of Experimental Social Psychology*, 1966, 2, 160—168.

Zajonc, R. B., see Saegert, Swap, & Zajonc (1973).

Zanna, M. P., Kiesler, C. A., & Pilkonis, P. A. Positive and negative attitudinal affect established by classical conditioning. *Journal of Personality and Social Psychology*, 1970, 14, 321—328.

Zanna, M. P., & Pack, S. J. On the self-fulfilling nature of apparent sex differences in behavior. *Journal of Experimental Social Psychology*, 1975, 11, 583—591.

Zanna, M. P., see Word, Zanna, & Cooper (1974).

Zarcone, V. P. Jr., see Corby, Roth, Zarcone, Jr., & Kopell (1978).

Zener, K. The significance of behavior accompanying conditioned salivary secretion for theories of the conditioned response. *American Journal of Psychology*, 1937, 50, 384—403.

Zigler, E. Familial mental retardation: A continuing dilemma. *Science*, 1967, 155, 292—98.

Zigler, E., see Yando, Seitz, & Zigler (1979).

Zillmann, D. Excitation transfer in communication-mediated aggressive behavior. *Journal of Experimental Social Psychology*, 1971, 7, 419—434.

Zillmann, D., Katcher, A. H., & Milavsky, B. Excitation transfer from physical exercise to subsequent aggressive behavior. *Journal of Experimental Social Psychology*, 1972, 8, 247—259.

Zillmann, D., see Cantor, Zillmann, & Bryant (1975).

Zimbardo, P. G. The human choice: Individuation, reason, and order versus deindividuation, impulse, and chaos. In W. J. Arnold & K. Levine (Eds.), *Nebraska Symposium on Motivation* (Vol. 17). Lincoln: University of Nebraska Press, 1969.

Zimbardo, P. G. On transforming experimental research into advocacy for social change. In M. Deutsch & H. Hornstein (Eds.), *Applying social psychology: Implications for research, practice, and training*. Hillsdale, N.J.: Lawrence Erlbaum, 1975.

Zimbardo, P. G., Ebbesen, E. G., & Maslach, C. *Influencing attitudes and changing behavior* (2nd ed.). Reading, Mass.: Addison-Wesley, 1977.

Zubin, J., & Spring, B. Vulnerability: A new view of schizophrenia. *Journal of Abnormal Psychology*, 1977, pp. 103—126.

Zuch, J., see Fisher, Gross, & Zuch (1965).

Zucker, I. Behavior, and biologic rhythms. In D. Krieger, (Ed.), *Neuroendocrinology*. Sunderland, Mass.: Sinauer, 1980.

Credits

Part and Chapter Opening Photos

Part I and p. 1: Jeff Albertson, Stock, Boston.
Part II and pp. 31, 63, 97, 127: B. Brake, Photo Researchers.
Part III and pp. 165, 199, 231, 263: Elliott Erwitt, Magnum.
Part IV and pp. 291, 325: Bruce Davidson, Magnum.
Part V and pp. 361, 389: Robert Capa, Magnum.
Part VI and pp. 419, 449: Constantine Manos, Magnum.
Part VII and pp. 483, 515: Charles Harbutt, Magnum.

Chapter 1

Photo, p. 3, The Bettmann Archive.
Photo, p. 4, The Bettmann Archive.
Photo, p. 6 (left), The Bettmann Archive.
Photo, p. 6 (right), courtesy of Albert Bandura.
Photo, p. 7, courtesy of the California Institute of Technology.
Photo, p. 8, Robert M. Kraus.
Photo, p. 10, The Bettmann Archive.
Photo, p. 11, The Bettmann Archive.
Photo, p. 12, The Bettmann Archive.
Photo, p. 15, Van Bucher, Photo Researchers.
Photo, p. 16, Van Bucher, Photo Researchers.
Photo, p. 17, Myron Wood, Photo Researchers.
Photo, p. 18, R. Van Nostrand, National Audubon Society/ Photo Researchers.
Photo, p. 20, UPI.

Chapter 2

Drawing, p. 32, The Bettmann Archive.
Photo, p. 33, The Bettmann Archive.
Fig. 2.2, p. 34 (bottom), adapted from H. D. Patton, J. W. Sundsten, W. E. Crill and P. W. Swanson, *Introduction to Basic Neurology*. Philadelphia: W. B. Saunders Co., 1976, p. 35.
Fig. 2.3, p. 36, after W. Etkin, R. M. Devlin, T. G. Bouffard, *A Biology of Human Concern*. Copyright © 1972 by J. B. Lippincott Co. Reprinted by permission of Harper & Row Publishers, Inc.
Fig. 2.7, p. 40, The Bettmann Archive.
Fig. 2.8, p. 41, W. Penfield and T. Rasmussen, *The Cerebral Cortex of Man*. New York: Macmillan, 1950.
Fig. 2.9, p. 42, adapted from C. B. Noback and R. J. Demerest, *The Human Nervous System*. New York: McGraw-Hill, 1975.
Fig. 2.10, p. 43, redrawn from Fig. X-4 from Wilder Penfield and Lamar Roberts, *Speech and Brain Mechanisms*. Copyright © 1959 by Princeton University Press, p. 201.

Figs. 2.11 and 2.12, pp. 46 and 47, Michael S. Gazzaniga, "The Split Brain in Man." Copyright © 1967 by Scientific American, Inc. All rights reserved.
Photo, p. 48, D. A. Sholl, *The Organization of the Cerebral Cortex*. New York: Wiley, 1956, p. 13. Reprinted by permission of Menthuen & Co., Ltd.
Fig. 2.13, p. 49 (left), after C. F. Stevens, "The Neuron." *Scientific American*, September 1979, p. 56.
Fig. 2.14, p. 49 (right), C. F. Stevens, *Neurophysiology: A Primer*. New York: Wiley, 1966.
Figs. 2.15 and 2.16, page 50, C. F. Stevens, *Neurophysiology: A Primer*. New York: Wiley, 1966.
Fig. 2.17, p. 51, C. B. Noback and R. J. Demerest, *The Human Nervous System*. New York: McGraw-Hill, 1975. Used by permission of the publisher.
Fig. 2.18, p. 52, A. M. Schneider and B. Tarshis, *An Introduction to Physiological Psychology*. New York: Random House, 1975.
Fig. 2.19, p. 54, after C. F. Stevens, "The Neuron." *Scientific American*, September 1979, p. 57.
Photo, p. 58, The Bettmann Archive.

Chapter 3

Fig. 3.1, p. 66, D. Blough, "Dark Adaptation in the Pigeon." *Journal of Comparative Physiological Psychology*, Vol. 49, 1956, p. 425. Copyright © 1956 by the American Psychological Association. Reprinted by permission of the publisher and author.
Fig. 3.3, p. 69, F. A. Geldard, *The Human Senses*. New York: Wiley, 1972.
Fig. 3.4, p. 70, after George Wald, "Eye and Camera." *Scientific American*, August 1950.
Fig. 3.7, p. 71, A. M. Schneider and B. Tarshis, *An Introduction to Physiological Psychology*. New York: Random House, 1975.
Photo, p. 72, Omikron/Photo Researchers.
Fig. 3.8, p. 73, after F. W. Billmeyer and M. Saltzman, *Principles of Color Technology*. New York: Wiley, 1966.
Fig. 3.10, p. 75, G. Wald, "The Receptors of Human Color Vision." *Science*, Vol. 145, September 1964, pp. 1007-1016. Copyright © 1964 by the American Association for the Advancement of Science.
Fig. 3.12, p. 78, after L. A. Riggs, F. Ratliff, J. C. Cornsweet and T. N. Cornsweet, "The Disappearance of Visual Test Objects." *Journal of the Optical Society of America*, Vol. 43, 1953, pp. 495-501.
Fig. 3.15, p. 82, adapted from A. Chapanis, *Man-Machine Engineering*. Belmont, Calif.: Wadsworth, 1965 and A.

Chapanis, W. R. Garner, and C. T. Morgan, *Applied Experimental Psychology—Human Factors in Engineering Design*. New York: Wiley, 1949.

Fig. 3.18, p. 85, adapted from O. Stuhlman, Jr., *An Introduction to Biophysics*. New York: Wiley, 1943, Reprinted by permission of Mrs. William T. Couch.

Fig. 3.19, p. 86, adapted from E. Gardner, *Fundamentals of Neurology*. Philadelphia: Saunders, 1975.

Photo, p. 87, Judy Porter, Photo Researchers.

Fig. 3.20, p. 88, adapted from E. Gardner, *Fundamentals of Neurology*. Philadelphia: Saunders, 1975.

Fig. 3.22, p. 91, after W. Penfield and T. Rasmussen, *The Cerebral Cortex of Man*. New York: Macmillan, 1950. Copyright 1950 by Macmillan Publishing Co., Inc., renewed 1978 by Theodore Rasmussen. Reprinted by permission of Macmillan Publishing Co., Inc.

Fig. 3.23, p. 93, redrawn from A. M. Schneider and B. Tarshis, *An Introduction to Physiological Psychology*. New York: Random House, 1975.

Photo, p. 93, Ross Hutchins, Photo Researchers.

Chapter 4

Fig. 4.1 (c), p. 98, after J. J. Gibson, *The Perception of the Visual World*. Boston: Houghton Mifflin, 1950. Used by permission of Houghton Mifflin Co.

Fig. 4.2, p. 100, I. Rock and C. S. Harris, "Vision and Touch." Copyright © 1967 by Scientific American, Inc. All rights reserved.

Photo (top), p. 102, The Bettmann Archive.

Photo (bottom), p. 102, Baxter Venable.

Fig. 4.6, p. 104, adapted from J. E. Hochberg, *Perception*. Englewood Cliffs, N.J.: Prentice-Hall, 1964.

Photo, p. 107, The Bettmann Archive.

Photo (left), p. 108, Erich Hartmann, Magnum.

Photo (right), p. 108, The Bettmann Archive.

Photo (top), p. 109, The Bettmann Archive.

Photo (bottom), p. 109, Constantine Manos, Magnum.

Fig. 4.15, p. 110, Courtesy of William Vandivert and *Scientific American*.

Photo (bottom), p. 110, Sergio Larrain, Magnum.

Drawing, p. 111, The Bettmann Archive.

Fig. 4.18, p. 112, B. Julesz, *Foundations of Cyclopean Perception*. The University of Chicago Press, 1971. Reprinted by permission of The University of Chicago Press.

Fig. 4.19, p. 113, from *Eye and Brain* by R. L. Gregory. Copyright © 1973 by World University Library. Used with the permission of McGraw-Hill Book Company.

Drawing, p. 115, David Regan, Kenneth Beverley and Max Cynader, "The Visual Perception of Motion in Depth." Copyright © 1979 by Scientific American, Inc. All rights reserved.

Photo, p. 116, courtesy of David Linton and *Scientific American*.

Fig. 4.23, p. 124, after H. R. Schiffman, *Sensation and Perception*. New York: Wiley, 1976, p. 361.

Photo, p. 124, Gilles Peress, Magnum.

Fig. 4.24, p. 125, after H. R. Schiffman, *Sensation and Perception*. New York: Wiley, 1976, p. 360.

Chapter 5

Photo, p. 128, The Bettmann Archive.

Photo, p. 130, Courtesy of the Montreal Neurological Institute, Montreal, Canada.

Photo, p. 131, Bruce Roberts, Photo Researchers.

Fig. 5.1, p. 132, after R. A. Levitt, *Physiological Psychology*. Copyright © 1981 by Holt, Rinehart and Winston. Reprinted by permission of Holt, Rinehart and Winston.

Photo, p. 134, from *Psychology: Understanding Behavior*, second edition, by Robert A. Baron, Donn Byrne, and Barry H. Kantowitz. Copyright © 1977 by W. B. Saunders Co. Copyright © 1980 by Holt, Rinehart and Winston. Reprinted by permission of Holt, Rinehart and Winston.

Figs. 5.2 and 5.3, pp. 135-136, Theodore Spagna, from *Dreamstage Exhibit Catalog*, Copyright © 1977, by Allan Hobson and Hoffman-LaRoche Inc.

Fig. 5.4, p. 137, from E. Hartman, *The Biology of Dreaming*. Charles C Thomas. Courtesy of Charles C Thomas, Publisher, Springfield, Illinois.

Photo, p. 137, Christopher Springmann, Black Star.

Drawing, p. 139, The Bettmann Archive.

Photo (top), p. 141, UPI.

Photo (bottom), p. 141, Marilyn Silverstone, Magnum.

Photo, p. 142, courtesy of Dr. Bernard Brucker.

Photo, p. 143, Rene Burri, Magnum.

Photo, p. 144, Ray Ellis, Photo Researchers.

Fig. 5.5, p. 145, J. Allison, "Respiratory Changes During the Practice of the Technique of Transcendental Meditation." *Lancet*, No. 7651 (London, England, 1970) pp. 833-834.

Photo, p.147, LeClair Bissell, Nancy Palmer.

Photo, p. 151, Ernest Baxter, Black Star.

Fig. 5.6, p. 153, Frank Barron, Murray E. Jarvik and Sterling Bunnell, Jr., "The Hallucinogenic Drugs." Copyright © 1964 by Scientific American, Inc. All rights reserved.

Photo, p. 156, George E. Jones III, Photo Researchers.

Fig. 5.7, p. 158, James V. McConnell, *Understanding Human Behavior*. Copyright © 1980 by Holt, Rinehart and Winston. Used by permission of Holt, Rinehart and Winston.

Chapter 6

Fig. 6.4, p. 170, C. H. Waddington, *The Strategy of the Genes: A Discussion of Some Aspects of Theoretical Biology*. London: George Allen & Unwin, 1957, pp. 29, 36.

Photo, p. 173, Eve Arnold, Magnum.

624

Fig. 6.5, p. 174, from *Psychology: Understanding Behavior*, second edition, by Robert A. Baron, Donn Byrne, and Barry Kantowitz. Copyright © 1980 by Holt, Rinehart and Winston. Copyright © 1977 by W. B. Saunders Co. Reprinted by permission of Holt, Rinehart and Winston.

Photo, p. 183, Charles Harbutt, Magnum.

Photo, p. 185, courtesy of H. F. Harlow, University of Wisconsin Primate Lab.

Photo, p. 186, Richard Kalvar, Magnum.

Fig. 6.8, p. 187, H. R. Schaffer and P. E. Emerson, "The Development of Social Attachments in Infancy." *Monographs of the Society for Research in Child Development*, 1964, 29 (3). Copyright © 1964 by The Society for Research in Child Development, Inc. Reprinted by permission.

Fig. 6.9, p. 188, George Zimbel, Monkmeyer.

Photo, p. 189, Barbara Young, Photo Researchers.

Photo, p. 190, Suzanne Szasz, Photo Researchers.

Photo, p. 191, Barbara Young, Photo Researchers.

Photo, p. 192, Ron Benvenisti, Magnum.

Photo, p. 196, Charles Harbutt, Magnum.

Fig. 6.10, p. 197, from "Development of Moral Character and Moral Ideology" by Lawrence Kohlberg in *Review of Child Development Research Volume I* by Martin L. Hoffman and Lois Wladis Hoffman. Copyright © 1964 by Russell Sage Foundation. Used by permission of Russell Sage Foundation.

Chapter 7

Fig. 7.1, p. 201, E. H. Hess, "Imprinting." *Science*, Vol. 130, 1959, pp. 133-141. Copyright © 1959 by the American Association for the Advancement of Science.

Photo, p. 204, The Bettmann Archive.

Fig. 7.5, p. 205, after I. V. Pavlov, *Conditioned Reflex*. Oxford, 1927.

Fig. 7.9, p. 210, after E. L. Thorndike, *The Psychology of Learning*. New York: Columbia University Press, 1921.

Photo, p. 212, courtesy of Yerkes Regional Primate Research Center, Emory University.

Photo, p. 213, Inge Morath, Magnum.

Photo, p. 216, Jeanne White, National Audubon Society/ Photo Researchers.

Fig. 7.14, p. 220, adapted from I. V. Pavlov, *Conditioned Reflexes*. Oxford, 1927.

Fig. 7.16, p. 222, E. C. Tolman and C. H. Honzik, "Introduction and Removal of Reward and Maze Performance in Rats." *University of California Publications in Psychology*, Vol. 4, 1930. Published in 1930 by the University of California Press. Reprinted by permission of the University of California Press.

Photos, p. 227, A. Bandura, D. Ross and S. A. Ross, "Imitation of Film-Mediated Aggressive Models." *Journal of Abnormal and Social Psychology*, Vol. 66, 1963, pp. 3-11. Copyright © 1963 by the American Psychological Associ-

ation. Reprinted by permission of the publisher and authors.

Photo, p. 228, UPI.

Chapter 8

Fig. 8.2, p. 233, after G. Sperling, "The Information Available in Brief Visual Presentations." *Psychological Monographs*, 74, Whole No. 498, 1960. Copyright © by the American Psychological Association. Reprinted by permission of the publisher and author.

Fig. 8.3, p. 235, after D. Broadbent, *Perception and Communication*. Oxford, England: Pergamon Press, 1958.

Drawing, p. 237, Curt Teich & Company, Inc.

Photo, p. 238, Richard Kalvar, Magnum.

Photo, p. 240, UPI.

Fig. 8.4, p. 244, after F. I. M. Craik and E. Tulving, "Depth of Processing and the Retention of Words in Episodic Memory." *Journal of Experimental Psychology*, Vol. 104, 1975, pp. 268-294. Copyright © 1975 by the American Psychological Association. Reprinted by permission of the publisher and authors.

Fig. 8.5, p. 247, after W. A. Bousfield, "The Occurrence of Clustering in the Free Recall of Randomly Arranged Associates." *Journal of General Psychology*, Vol. 49, 1953, pp. 229-240. Reprinted by permission of The Journal Press and the author.

Fig. 8.6, p. 247, G. H. Bower, "Organizational Factors in Memory." *Cognitive Psychology*, Vol. 1, 1970.

Fig. 8.7, p. 248, adapted from A. M. Collins and M. R. Quillian, "Retrieval Time From Semantic Memory." *Journal of Verbal Learning and Verbal Behavior*, Vol. 8, 1969, pp. 240-247.

Fig. 8.8, p. 251, adapted from E. Tulving and Z. Pearlstone, "Availability Versus Accessibility of Information in Memory for Words." *Journal of Verbal Learning and Verbal Behavior*, Vol. 5, 1965, pp. 381-391.

Fig. 8.9, p. 253, from *Psychology: Understanding Behavior*, second edition, by Robert A. Baron, Donn Byrne, and Barry H. Kantowitz. Copyright © 1980 by Holt, Rinehart and Winston. Copyright © 1977 by W. B. Saunders Co. Reprinted by permission of Holt, Rinehart and Winston.

Fig. 8.10, p. 254, after N. C. Waugh and D. A. Norman, "Primary Memory." *Psychological Review*, Vol. 72, 1965, pp. 89-104. Copyright © 1965 by the American Psychological Association. Reprinted by permission of the publisher and the authors.

Photo, p. 255, Gilles Peress, Magnum.

Fig. 8.12, 257, B. Milner, "Amnesia Following Operation of Temporal Lobes." In C. W. N. Whitty and O. L. Zurwill, eds., *Amnesia*. London: Butterworth, 1966.

Fig. 8.13, p. 260, after W. J. McKeachie and C. L. Doyle,

Psychology. Reading, Mass.: Addison-Wesley, 1976. Reprinted with permission.

Chapter 9

Fig. 9.1, p. 265, R. K. Potter, G. A. Kopp, and H. C. Green, *Visible Speech*. Litton Educational Publishing, Inc., 1947. Copyright © 1947 by Bell Telephone Laboratories. Reprinted with permission.
Fig. 9.3, p. 266, A. M. Liberman, "The Grammars of Speech and Language." *Cognitive Psychology*, Vol. 1, 1970, pp. 301-323.
Fig. 9.4, p. 267, The Bettmann Archive.
Photo, p. 267, UPI.
Fig. 9.9, adapted from J. D. Bransford and J. J. Franks, "The Abstraction of Linguistic Ideas." *Cognitive Psychology*, Vol. 2, 1971.
Photo, p. 275, Burk Uzzle, Magnum.
Photo, p. 276, Burk Uzzle, Magnum.
Photo, p. 277, Abigail Heyman, Magnum.
Fig. 9.10, p. 281, J. D. Bransford and M. K. Johnson, "Considerations of Some Problems of Comprehension." In W. G. Chase, ed., *Visual Information Processing*. New York: Academic Press, 1973. Used with permission of the publisher and authors.
Fig. 9.11, p. 283, B. Milner, L. Taylor, and R. W. Sperry, "Lateralized Suppression of Dichotically Presented Digits After Commissural Section in Man." *Science*, July 12, 1968, pp. 184-186. Copyright © 1968 by the American Association for the Advancement of Science.
Photo, p. 284, Paul Fusco, Magnum.
Fig. 9.12, p. 285, after A. J. Premack and D. Premack, "Teaching Language to an Ape." *Scientific American*, October 1972, p. 97.
Fig. 9.13, p. 286, adapted from Carmichael, Hogan and Walter, 1932.

Chapter 10

Fig. 10.1, p. 295, Copyright © 1953, 1972 CIBA Pharmaceutical Company, Division of CIBA-GEIGY Corporation. With permission from *The CIBA Collection of Medical Illustrations* by Frank H. Netter, M.D. All rights reserved.
Fig. 10.2, p. 297, from *Psychology: Its Principles and Meanings*, third edition, by Lyle E. Bourne, Jr., and Bruce R. Ekstrand. Copyright © 1973 by the Dryden Press. Copyright © 1976, 1979 by Holt, Rinehart and Winston. Reprinted by permission of Holt, Rinehart and Winston.
Fig. 10.3, p. 298, after W. B. Cannon, "Hunger and Thirst." In C. Murchison, ed., *Handbook of General Experimental Psychology*. Worcester, Mass.: Clark University Press, 1934.
Photo, p. 299, courtesy of Dr. Devendra Singh.
Fig. 10.5, p. 300, from *Psychology: Understanding Behavior*, 2nd. edition, by Robert A. Baron, Donn Byrne, and Barry H. Kantowitz. Copyright © 1977 by W. B. Saunders Co. Reprinted by permission of Holt, Rinehart and Winston.
Photo, p. 301, Alex Webb, Magnum.
Fig. 10.6, p. 302, after S. Schachter and L. P. Gross, "Manipulated Time and Eating Behavior." In D. C. Glass, ed., *Neurophysiology and Emotion*. Copyright 1967 by Rockefeller University Press and The Russell Sage Foundation.
Photo, p. 306, UPI.
Fig. 10.7, p. 307, after W. N. Dember, "Birth Order and Need for Affiliation." *Journal of Abnormal and Social Psychology*, Vol. 68, 1964. Copyright 1964 by the American Psychological Association. Adapted by permission of the publisher and author.
Photo, p. 308, UPI.
Fig. 10.8, p. 309, from *The Achieving Society* by David C. McClelland. Copyright © 1961 by Litton Educational Publishing, Inc. Reprinted by permission of Wadsworth Publishing Co., Belmont, Calif.
Photo, p. 311, courtesy of Dr. James Olds.
Fig. 10.10, p. 312, from S. Schachter and J. Singer, "Cognitive Social and Physiological Determinants of Emotional State." *Psychological Review*, Vol. 69, 1962. Copyright 1962 by the American Psychological Association. Adapted by permission of the publisher and authors.
Fig. 10.11, p. 315, after H. S. Hoffman, L. A. Eiserer, A. M. Ratner and V. L. Pickering, "Development of Distress Vocalization During Withdrawal of an Imprinting Stimulus." *Journal of Comparative and Physiological Psychology*, Vol. 86, 1974. Copyright 1974 by the American Psychological Association. Reprinted by permission of the publisher and authors.
Photo, p. 316, Karl and Stephen Maslowski, National Audubon Society/Photo Researchers.
Photo, p. 319, UPI.
Fig. 10.12, p. 321, from L. Eron, L. Huesmann, M. Lefkowitz and L. Walder, "Does Television Violence Cause Aggression?" *American Psychologist*, Vol. 27, 1972. Copyright 1972 by the American Psychological Association. Reprinted by permission of the publisher and authors.
Photo, p. 322, Bill Stanton, Magnum.

Chapter 11

Drawing, p. 327, The Bettmann Archive.
Fig. 11.1, p. 330, William H. Masters and Virginia F. Johnson, *Human Sexual Response*. Boston: Little, Brown and Company, 1966.
Photo, p. 331, Russ Kinne, Photo Researchers.
Photo, p. 334, The Bettmann Archive.
Photo, p. 335, Charles Gatewood, Magnum.
Fig. 11.2, p. 336, adapted from M. Zelnik and J. F. Kantner, "Sexual and Contraceptive Practices Experience of Young Unmarried Women in the United States, 1976 and 1971." *Family Planning Perspectives*, Vol. 9, 1977, pp. 55-71. A. C. Kinsey, W. B. Pomeroy, C. E. Martin and P. H. Gebhard,

Sexual Behavior in the Human Female. Philadelphia: Saunders, 1953. Reprinted by permission of the Institute for Sex Research.

Photo, p. 337, Roger Malloch, Magnum.

Fig. 11.5, p. 344, J. M. Davidson, C. A. Camargo, E. R. Smith, "Effects of Androgen on Sexual Behavior in Hypogonodal Men." *Journal of Clinical Endocrinology and Metabolism,* Vol. 48, 1979, pp. 955-958. Reprinted with permission of The Endocrine Society.

Fig. 11.6, p. 348, after A. C. Kinsey, W. B. Pomeroy, C. E. Martin, *Sexual Behavior in the Human Male.* Philadelphia: Saunders, 1948. Reprinted by permission of the Institute for Sex Research.

Photo, p. 348, Ian Berry, Magnum.

Photos, p. 349, UPI.

Photo, p. 350, Bruce Roberts, Photo Researchers.

Photo, p. 352, Vivienne della Grotta, Photo Researchers.

Photo, p. 353, Rafael Macia, Photo Researchers.

Fig. 11.7, p. 354, J. M. Davidson, "The Psychobiology of Sexual Experience." In J. M. Davidson and R. J. Davidson, eds., *The Psychobiology of Consciousness.* New York: Plenum Press, 1980, p. 303.

Chapter 12

Photo, p. 362, The Bettmann Archive.

Photo, Nina Howell Starr, Photo Researchers.

Fig. 12.1, p. 367, from *Psychology: Its Principles and Meanings,* third edition, by Lyle E. Bourne, Jr., and Bruce R. Ekstrand. Copyright © 1973 by the Dryden Press. Copyright © 1976, 1979 by Holt, Rinehart and Winston. Reprinted by permission of Holt, Rinehart and Winston.

Fig. 12.2, p. 370, After Sheldon, 1942.

Fig. 12.3, p. 371, after H. J. Eysenck, "Principles and Methods of Personality: Description, Classification and Diagnosis." *British Journal of Psychology,* Vol. 55, 1964, pp. 284-294.

Fig. 12.4, p. 373, after G. W. Allport, *Personality: A Psychological Interpretation.* Copyright © 1961 by Holt, Rinehart and Winston. Reprinted by permission of Holt, Rinehart and Winston.

Fig. 12.5, p. 374, taken from the Handbook for the 16 PF © 1970, by the Institute for Personality and Ability Testing, Inc. Reproduced by permission.

Fig. 12.6, p. 376, reprinted by permission of the publishers from Henry Alexander Murray, *Thematic Apperception Test.* Harvard University Press, 1943. Copyright © 1943 by the President and Fellows of Harvard College. Copyright © 1971 by Henry A. Murray.

Fig. 12.7, p. 378, K. E. Allen, et. al., "Effects of Social Reinforcement on Isolate Behavior of a Nursery School Child." *Child Development,* Vol. 35, 1964, pp. 511-518. Copyright © 1964 by The Society For Research in Child Development, Inc.

Fig. 12.8, p. 380, A. Bandura and W. Mischel, "Modification of Self-imposed Delay of Reward Through Exposure to Live and Symbolic Models." *Journal of Personality and Social Psychology,* Vol. 2, 1965, pp. 698-705.

Fig. 12.10, p. 384, George A. Kelly, *The Psychology of Personal Constructs.* New York: W. W. Norton, 1955.

Chapter 13

Fig. 13.1, p. 392, L. L. Thurston and T. G. Thurstone, *SRA Primary Mental Ability Test.* Reprinted by permission of Science Research Associates.

Fig. 13.2, p. 393, J. P. Guilford, *The Nature of Human Intelligence.* New York: McGraw-Hill, 1967, p. 63.

Photo, p. 394, Ann Zane Shanks, Photo Researchers.

Fig. 13.3, p. 396, from *Psychology: Understanding Behavior,* second edition, by Robert A. Baron, Donn Byrne, and Barry H. Kantowitz. Copyright © 1980 by Holt, Rinehart and Winston. Copyright © 1977 by W. B. Saunders Co. Reprinted by permission of Holt, Rinehart and Winston.

Fig. 13.4, p. 398, J. C. Raven, "Standardization of Progressive Matrices." *British Journal of Medical Psychology,* Vol. 19, 1941, pp. 137-150.

Fig. 13.5, p. 401, L. Erlenmeyer-Kimling and L. F. Jarvik, "Genetics and Intelligence: A Review." *Science,* December 13, 1963. Copyright © 1963 by American Association for the Advancement of Science.

Fig. 13.6, p. 402, R. B. Zajonc and G. B. Markus, "Birth Order and Intellectual Development." *Psychological Review,* Vol. 82, 1975, pp. 74-88. Copyright © 1975 by the American Psychological Association.

Photo, p. 402, Erika Stone, Photo Researchers.

Fig. 13.7, p. 407, K. Richardson and D. Spears, *Race and Intelligence.* New York: Penguin Books, 1972, p. 187.

Fig. 13.8, p. 408, N. Bayley, "Development of Mental Abilities." In P. Mussen, ed., *Carmichael's Manual of Child Psychology.* New York: Wiley, 1970.

Photo, p. 410, Bruce Roberts, Photo Researchers.

Photo, p. 412, Wide World Photos.

Chapter 14

Drawing, p. 421, The Bettmann Archive.

Photo, p. 422, Jill Freedman, Magnum.

Photo, p. 428, Ernst Haas, Magnum.

Fig. 14.1, p. 429, Reprinted by permission of the publisher from Arthur T. Jersild and Frances G. Holmes, *Children's Fears.* New York: Teacher's College Press. Copyright © 1935. All rights reserved.

Fig. 14.2, p. 432, J. D. Maser and M. E. P. Seligman, eds., *Psychopathology: Experimental Models.* San Francisco: W. H. Freeman, 1977, p. 281.

Photo, p. 437, courtesy of H. F. Harlow, University of Wisconsin Primate Lab.

Photo, p. 439, Burk Uzzle, Magnum.
Fig. 14.4, p. 444, Price and Lynn, *Abnormal Behavior in the Human Context*. Homewood, Ill.: The Dorsey Press, 1981, p. 300.
Fig. 14.5, p. 447, J. Zubin and B. Spring, "Vulnerability: A New View of Schizophrenia." *Journal of Abnormal Psychology*, Vol. 86, 1977. Copyright © 1977 by the American Psychological Association. Reprinted by permission.

Chapter 15

Drawing, p. 450, The Bettmann Archive.
Photo, p. 452, Van Bucher, Photo Researchers.
Photo, p. 456, Van Bucher, Photo Researchers.
Photos, p. 459, courtesy of Dr. Albert Bandura.
Photo, p. 461, Ian Berry, Magnum.
Photo, p. 462, Bonnie Freer, Magnum.
Photo, p. 463, Hanna W. Schreiber, Photo Researchers.
Fig. 15.1, p. 464, after M. L. Smith and G. V. Glass, "Meta-analysis of Psychotherapy Outcome Studies." *American Psychologist*, Vol. 33, 1977, pp. 752-760. Copyright © 1977 by the American Psychological Association. Reprinted by permission.
Photo, p. 461, Paul Fusco, Magnum.
Painting, p. 471, The Bettmann Archive.
Photo, p. 473, Van Bucher, Photo Researchers.
Photo, p. 477, The Bettmann Archive.

Chapter 16

Fig. 16.1, p. 485, after R. B. Zajonc, *Social Psychology: An Experimental Approach*. Wadsworth, 1966, p. 12. Copyright © 1967 by Wadsworth Publishing Co., Inc. Adapted by permission of the publisher, Brooks/Cole Publishing Co., Monterey, Calif.
Photo, p. 486, Richard Kalvar, Magnum.
Photo, p. 489, Bill Owens, Magnum.
Fig. 16.2, p. 490, reprinted from *Social Pressures in Informal Groups* by Leon Festinger, Stanley Schachter, and Kurt Back with the permission of the publisher, Stanford University Press. Copyright © 1950 by Leon Festinger, Stanley Schachter, and Kurt Back. Copyright renewed 1978.
Fig. 16.3, p. 491, adapted from S. Worchel and J. Cooper, *Understanding Social Psychology*. Homewood, Ill.: The Dorsey Press, 1976.
Fig. 16.4, p. 492, E. Aronson and D. Linder, "Gain and Loss of Esteem as Determinants of Interpersonal Attractiveness." *Journal of Experimental and Social Psychology*, Vol. 1, 1965, pp. 156-171.
Photo, p. 492, UPI.
Photo, p. 494, UPI.
Photo, p. 496, Jill Freedman, Magnum.

Fig. 16.5, p. 497, B. Latané and J. M. Darley, *The Unresponsive Bystander: Why Doesn't He Help?* Copyright © 1970 by Prentice-Hall. Reprinted by permission of Prentice-Hall, Inc., Englewood Cliffs, N.J.
Fig. 16.6, p. 499, adapted from S. Asch, "Opinions and Social Pressure." *Scientific American*, 1955.
Fig. 16.7, p. 500, adapted from S. Asch, "Opinions and Social Pressures." *Scientific American*, 1955.
Photo, p. 500, Magnum.
Fig. 16.8, p. 505, from S. Milgram, "Behavior Study of Obedience." *Journal of Abnormal and Social Psychology*, Vol. 67, 1963, pp. 371-378. Copyright 1963 by the American Psychological Association. Adapted by permission of the publisher and author.
Fig. 16.9, p. 509, A. N. Doob, J. M. Carlsmith, J. L. Freedman, T. K. Landauer, and S. Toms, "Effect of Initial Selling Price on Subsequent Sales." *Journal of Personality and Social Psychology*, Vol. 11, 1969, pp. 345-350. Copyright 1969 by the American Psychological Association. Reprinted by permission of the publisher and authors.
Photo, p. 510, UPI.
Photo, p. 511, UPI.

Chapter 17

Drawing, p. 516, J. W. Thibaut and H. H. Kelley, *The Social Psychology of Groups*. New York: Wiley, 1959.
Fig. 17.1, p. 519, S. Rosenberg, C. Nelson, P. S. Vivekananthan, "A Multidimensional Approach to the Structure of Personality Impression." *Journal of Personality and Social Psychology*, Vol. 9, 1968, pp. 283-294. Copyright 1968 by the American Psychological Association. Reprinted by permission of the publisher and authors.
Photo, p. 521, Ray Ellis, Photo Researchers.
Fig. 17.2, p. 524, E. E. Jones, K. E. Davis, K. J. Gergen, "Role Playing Variations and Their Informational Value for Person Perception." *Journal of Abnormal and Social Psychology*, Vol. 63, 1961, pp. 302-310. Copyright 1961 by the American Psychological Association. Reprinted by permission of the publisher and authors.
Photo, p. 526, Fritz Henle, Photo Researchers.
Photo, p. 528, Burk Uzzle, Magnum.
Photo, p. 529, Cornell Capa, Magnum.
Photo, 534, Alex Webb, Magnum.
Photo, p. 536, Burk Uzzle, Magnum.
Fig. 17.3, p. 538, after J. B. Calhoun, "Population Density and Social Pathology." *Scientific American*, Vol. 206, 1962, pp. 139-148.
Fig. 17.4, p. 539, after Baum and Greenberg, 1975.
Photo, p. 540, Charles Gatewood, Magnum.
Fig. 17.5, p. 541, S. Cohen, D. C. Glass and J. E. Singer, "Apartment Noise, Auditory Discrimination and Reading Ability in Children." *Journal of Experimental Social Psychology*, Vol. 9, 1973, pp. 407-422.
Photo (left), p. 543, Martine Frank, Magnum.
Photo (right), p. 543, Alex Webb, Magnum.

Name Index

Feuerstein, R., 396
Fields, S., 476, 477
Fieve, R. R., 434, 435
Filliozat, A. M., 174
Fillmore, C. J., 278
Fink, K., 520
Fisher, C., 138
Fisher, R., 124
Fitts, P., 228
Fitzsimons, J. T., 297
Fixsen, D. L., 458
Flavell, J., 182, 183
Fleck, S., 445
Fleischer, S., 138
Flynn, J., 317
Foerster, O., 80
Folger, R., 536
Foote, W., 317
Ford, C., 334
Fortis, J. G., 320
Foss, D., 274
Fothergill, L. A., 59
Foulkes, D., 138
Fowler, F. J., 532
Fox, R. E., 466
Fraisse, P., 124
Franks, J., 223, 225, 244, 249, 272-273, 279
Franz, R., 117-118
Fraser, S. C., 494, 502
Frederiksson, N., 430
Freedman, J., 493, 502, 509, 537, 542-543
Freud, S., 8, 11, 12, 14, 16, 19, 137, 138, 140, 147, 150, 254, 326, 327, 330, 336, 338, 348, 355, 363-366, 367, 377, 424-425, 429, 450, 451-452, 468, 470, 476
Friedl, E., 333-334
Fritsch, G., 15, 40, 129
Fromkin, V., 195
Fromm, E., 14, 365

Galin, D., 132, 133
Gall, F. J., 40, 369
Galle, O. R., 537
Garcia, J., 208, 209
Gardner, B. T., 284
Gardner, R. A., 284
Garrett, M., 274
Garrison, V., 476
Gates, M. F., 486
Gath, D. H., 456
Gautier, T., 346
Gazzaniga, M., 45, 46
Gebhard, P. H., 328, 335
Geen, R., 319

Geer, J., 219, 437
Gelb, T. K., 103
Gelder, M. G., 456
Gellene, R., 57
Gemme, R., 332
Genovese, K., 496, 498
Gerard, H., 496, 501
Gerbner, G., 320
Gergen, K., 524
Gerstein, G. L., 116
Gewirtz, J., 488
Gibson, E., 118
Gibson, J., 109
Gill, F., 316-317
Gittelman-Klein, R., 470
Glass, D., 487, 540, 541, 542, 543
Glass, G. V., 464-466
Glazer, H. I., 437-440
Glucksberg, S., 282, 520
Glueck, E., 370
Glueck, S., 370
Goethals, C. R., 522
Goetz, F. E., 352
Goffman, E., 422
Gogel, W. C., 111
Gold, A. R., 342
Goldfried, M. R., 456
Goldiamond, I., 216
Goldman, R., 370
Goldstein, K., 410
Goleman, D., 143, 144
Golgi, C., 53
Gonshor, A., 120
Good, P., 363
Goodwin, D. W., 251
Goodwin, G. M., 92
Gordon, A., 370
Gordon, J. H., 345
Gore, R., 80, 98
Gorski, R. A., 345
Goss-Custard, J., 294
Gove, W. R., 537
Goy, R., 345
Graham, C. H., 77
Gray, L. N., 320
Green, D. M., 68
Green, J. D., 297
Green, R., 348, 350
Greenberg, C., 539
Greenblatt, M., 467
Greene, D., 503
Greenfield, P. M., 183, 278
Greenspoon, J., 487
Greenstein, J. A., 87
Gregory, R. L., 98, 111, 112
Griffin, D. R., 93
Grinspoon, L., 151

Groff, B., 539
Gross, C., 106, 259
Gross, J., 138
Grosser, G. H., 467
Grush, J. E., 486
Gudhea, D., 9
Gunderson, J. G., 444
Gurin, G., 475

Haber, R. N., 233
Hakes, D., 247
Haley, J., 445
Hall, C., 137, 138
Hall, E. T., 542, 543
Hamilton, L. W., 209
Hammond, W. H., 369
Hampson, J. G., 347
Hampson, J. L., 340
Hankins, W. G., 209
Hanlon, C., 277
Hansel, C. E. M., 123, 125
Harlan, R. E., 345
Harlow, H., 185, 189, 346, 351, 436
Harlow, M., 185, 189, 351, 436
Harman, W., 154
Harris, C., 100
Harris, F. R., 377
Harris, G., 340, 345
Harris, V., 525
Hart, B., 344, 377
Harter, M., 227
Hartline, H. K., 77
Hartmann, E., 140
Harvey, O., 535
Hastorf, A., 484, 521
Haughton, E., 423
Hawkins, J. E., Jr., 83
Hayes, C., 284
Hayes, K. J., 284
Hearst, P., 510
Heath, R., 344
Hebb, D. O., 116-117
Hecht, S., 90
Heider, E. R., 283
Heider, F., 491
Heingartner, A., 486
Heisler, S., 469
Heller, J., 539
Helmholtz, H. L. F. von, 74, 75, 84, 99
Helms, D. B., 176
Helson, H., 125
Henchy, J., 487
Hendrick, C., 491
Henker, B., 352

633

Subject Index

645